אוצר התורה

the tobias heller edition

ArtScroll Mesorah Series®

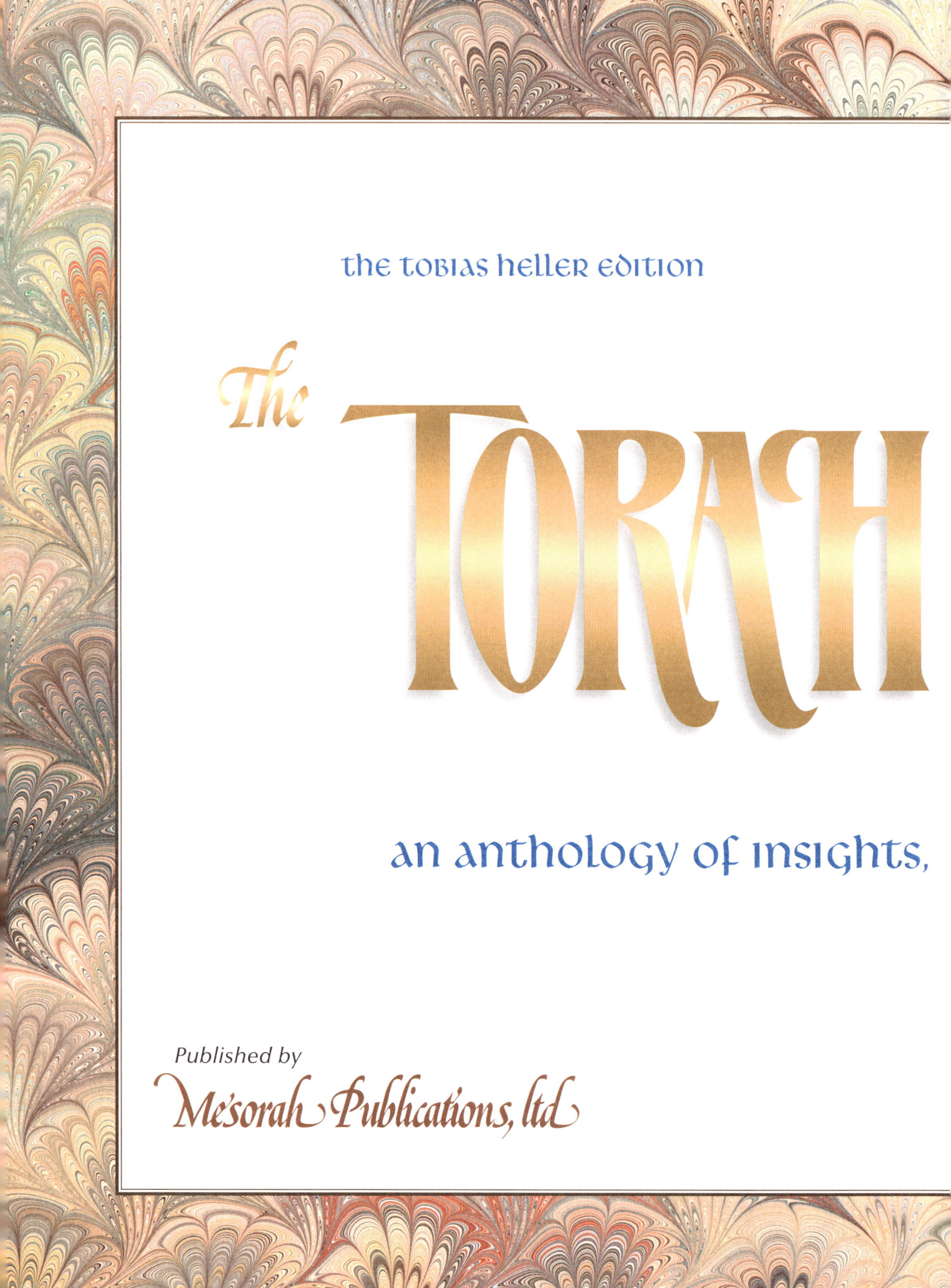

the tobias heller edition

The

TORAH

an anthology of insights,

Published by

Me'sorah Publications, ltd

אוצר התורה

TREASURY

commentary and anecdotes
on the weekly torah readings

by Rabbi Moshe M. Lieber
Edited under the direction of
Rabbi Nosson Scherman

"THE TORAH TREASURY"

An anthology of insights, commentary and anecdotes on the weekly Torah readings

© *Copyright 2002 by* Mesorah Publications, Ltd.
First edition – First impression: November, 2002
              Second impression: October, 2003
              Third impression: November 2003
              Fourth impression: May 2008
              Fifth impression: June 2013

Published by **MESORAH PUBLICATIONS, LTD.**
4401 Second Avenue / Brooklyn, N.Y 11232 / (718) 921-9000 / Fax: (718) 680-1875
e-mail: artscroll@mesorah.com

Distributed in Israel by SIFRIATI / A. GITLER
6 Hayarkon Street / Bnei Brak 51127

Distributed in Europe by LEHMANNS
Unit E, Viking Business Park, Rolling Mill Road / Jarrow, Tyne and Wear, NE32 3DP/ England

Distributed in Australia and New Zealand by GOLDS WORLD OF JUDAICA
3-13 William Street / Balaclava, Melbourne 3183 / Victoria Australia

Distributed in South Africa by KOLLEL BOOKSHOP
Northfield Centre / 17 Northfield Avenue / Glenhazel 2192, Johannesburg, South Africa

Printed in the United States of America by
Noble Book Press Corp.
Custom bound by Sefercraft, Inc. / 4401 Second Avenue / Brooklyn N.Y. 11232

ISBN 10: 1-57819-720-1
ISBN 13: 978-1-57819-720-0

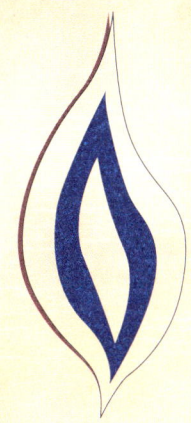

This volume is dedicated to the memory of
Tobias Heller ז״ל
טוביה בן מאיר לייב ז״ל
1902-1996 / 5662-5756
New York / Yerushalayim

Toby Heller's parents, Max and Rose,
emigrated to New York City from Kracow and Sanz, Poland, in the late 1880's.
They imbued him with a keen sense of obligation
to education and charitable causes.

Following in their footsteps, Tobias was involved in many Jewish projects
with an emphasis on Torah education for youth.
Toby Heller acquired his business acumen from his father
and became a successful building contractor and real estate developer.

He and his first wife, Anna (Becker), had an only son, Arthur,
but both Anna and their son tragically passed away in the 1940's.

He remarried and had two daughters, Rachel and Debbie,
who live in Yerushalayim.

When Toby died in Yerushalayim, at the age of 94, he was survived by:
Nathan and Rachel Bernstein and Moshe and Debbie Lifschitz,
a dozen "Sabra" grandchildren and two great-grandsons!

The Bernstein and Lifschitz Families

are proud to dedicate this contribution to Torah learning
in honor of their Father's blessed memory
and his legacy of devotion to religious Jewish education.

This book was published through the assistance of
**The Max and Rose Heller
and Anna Heller Foundation**

established by

Tobias Heller

Publisher's Preface

We are proud to present **The Torah Treasury** to the Jewish public. It is exactly what its title implies: a treasury of ideas, insights and anecdotes woven around the weekly Torah reading. King David says, לְכָל תִּכְלָה רָאִיתִי קֵץ רְחָבָה מִצְוָתְךָ מְאֹד, *To every goal I have seen an end, but Your commandment is exceedingly broad (Psalms* 119:96). The breadth of Torah and the myriad avenues into which its messages branch show how it speaks to every generation and every segment of *Klal Yisrael.* The Torah speaks to every Jew, whatever his level of knowledge, material circumstances, or host culture. The appeal of this anthology is that it was written by someone who is firmly rooted in the eternal *Mesorah* of our people and who knows what messages are most relevant to our people in this century.

There is a famous maxim among Chassidic masters that "A Jew must live with the times," and that those "times" are the weekly Torah readings, i.e., that the *parashah* of the week has something relevant to say to every Jew. Without doubt, many of those messages can be found in this volume; there is hardly a Sabbath table or a thoughtful hour at any time that cannot be enriched by this anthology. It contains nearly 2,000 selections, enough to satisfy every taste and need.

Rabbi Moshe M. Lieber is familiar to ArtScroll/Mesorah readers from his stellar volumes on Pirkei Avos and the Pesach Haggadah. Those anthologies are justly popular and we have no doubt that *The Torah Treasury* will join their ranks as one of the most useful, popular, and highly regarded works of its kind. A Torah scholar and a master of his craft, Rabbi Lieber has performed a service that will be appreciated by many thousands of families, who will find this volume an important contribution to their understanding of the Torah and its perspectives, and will add to the beauty of their Sabbath tables.

We applaud **The Max & Rose Heller and Anna Heller Foundation,** established by **Tobias Heller,** and **Mr. and Mrs. Nathan Bernstein,** whose support made this work possible, and who chose Rabbi Lieber to bring the concept to fruition. All his life, Toby Heller was dedicated to others and to the cause of Jewish education. *The Torah Treasury* is a worthy addition to the good works sponsored by him in his lifetime and that are now his memorial.

We express out appreciation to **Rabbi Moshe Wein** who helped facilitate this project.

We are grateful to the many people who collaborated in creating this volume: In addition to Rabbi Lieber's editor in Israel, **Reb Avrohom Biderman** (in addition to coordinating the production), **Rabbi Zev Meisels** and **Rabbi Yechezkel Sochaczewski** performed the final editing.

Shmuel Blitz, director of our Jerusalem office, who managed the flow of the work across the ocean, is a dear friend and an indispensable part of ArtScroll/Mesorah.

The striking page design is the work of our colleague **Rabbi Sheah Brander,** the graphics genius who has raised the level of Judaica publication to a new plateau.

Mrs. Faygie Weinbaum proofread and offered useful comments with her customary thoroughness, and **Mrs. Judi Dick's** comments further enhanced the work. The book was typeset and paginated by **Mrs. Chumie Lipschitz.**

Mrs. Esther Feuerstein, Mrs. Toby Goldzweig, Mrs. Ruchie Reifer, Mrs. Chaya Surie Posner and **Libby Zweig** meticulously typed and corrected the manuscript. **Mrs. Zissel Keller** and **Leah Seeve** helped coordinate and manage the flow of the voluminous material.

The beautiful graphics and cover design was done by **Reb Eli Kroen,** whose taste and skill win the plaudits and admiration of laymen and fellow craftsmen alike.

Most of all, we express our gratitude to Hashem for enabling us and our colleagues to bring His Torah to His people. May our work continue to help quench the Jewish people's thirst for the word of Hashem.

Rabbi Meir Zlotowitz / Rabbi Nosson Scherman

Kislev 5763
November 2002

Author's Preface

Torah is not merely a book of Divine laws or social conventions, it is a "user's guide" to Creation — and much, much more.

Man in general and every Jew in a unique way is imbued with a Godly soul, the *neshamah*. By activating one's *neshamah* one can catalyze his potential to live in the image of his Creator. There is no greater joy than achieving this goal. Torah, the Godly intelligence, is the tool He provides us with which to tap into the deep well of potential for holiness that lays within each of us.

In the words of *R' Tzadok HaKohen of Lublin* "The main thing God wanted to plant in this world is the soul of a Jew. The Torah is a commentary on the Jewish soul, allowing each of us to penetrate the depths of his own soul," (*Tzidkas HaTzaddik* 196).

This is but one facet of the words of *R' Shneur Zalman of Liadi,* who said, regarding the weekly Torah reading "One must live with the *parashah.*" Just as Torah was God's blueprint for Creation (see *Bereishis Rabbah* 1:1), so the weekly Torah reading is the vehicle through which He interacts with His world and particularly with His beloved People.

The Torah is like a diamond with multiple facets. The academic and halachic levels are two of them. Torah must be mined in order to realize its impact on the human condition and how it speaks to the soul.

R' Avraham of Slonim once met an itinerant *maggid* (preacher), who was always in search of new material. "Please tell me a nice Torah thought" requested the *maggid*. R' Avraham replied with a homiletical interpretation of a phrase from the Sabbath hymn *D'ror Yikra:* דְּרוֹשׁ נָוִי וְאוּלָמִי, *Seek My Temple and My Hall.* Reinterpreting the words homiletically, R' Avraham said, "If one's purpose in teaching Torah is merely to give a beautiful (נָוִי from נָאֶה) discourse (דְּרוֹשׁ as in דְּרָשָׁה), he might do better to remain silent (אוּלָמִי — from אִלֵּם which means *mute*).

My goal in writing this book is to mine the weekly Torah reading for ideas that can strengthen our commitment to spiritual growth and that provide the ability to arouse our souls, to turn God from an abstract idea into a living Reality, with Whom we yearn for an intense relationship.

As the *Nesivos Shalom* would often tell his students in a homiletic vein, יָקֵם סְעָרָה לִדְמָמָה, *Arouse a [soul] storm from the calm.* (*Psalms* 107:29). The Torah must arouse a soul-stirring storm to replace the calm of spiritual apathy.

If I succeed to any degree in introducing light into Jewish homes and in making the Sabbath table an uplifting experience, I will feel deeply rewarded.

According to the Midrash, the name Toviah (or Tobias) was one of Moses' seven names. Thus *Otzar HaTorah* (*The Torah Treasury*) might well be called *Otzar Toviah* (see *Targum Yonasan* to *Isaiah* 33:6).

In the vision of **Tobias Heller,** Jewish education and the dissemination of Torah knowledge were the key to linking young and old alike to our eternal treasure. How fitting that this work is dedicated to his sterling memory.

Among the many people to whom I owe a deep debt of gratitude, none occupy a more prominent place than **Nat** and **Rachel Bernstein** עמו״ש. Their vibrant commitment to spreading Torah and their vision of the centrality of *Eretz Yisrael* to Jewish life energized their decision to have the Heller Foundation underwrite this book as a living memorial to Rachel's father, Tobias Heller ז״ל. May they see much *Yiddisheh nachas* from themselves and their dear family as they continue to link their destiny with his vision.

Dr. Moshe and **Debbie Lifschitz,** עמו״ש, Rachel's sister and brother-in-law, are actively involved in Torah scholarship and serve as living role models for many young people. My warmest thanks to them.

R' Moshe Wein, עמו״ש, director of the Heller Foundation, was fired by his characteristic enthusiasm about this project from the outset. His unfailing graciousness and sincere friendship leave me eternally grateful.

My sincerest thanks and admiration go to **Dafna Breines,** whose outstanding editing and sensitive reading upgraded this work considerably. I am grateful, as well, to her husband for his significant contributions.

A small cadre of loyal comrades in Har Nof have helped me persevere by dint of their care, concern and authentic friendship. They have a powerful share in this book.

R' Meir Zlotowitz, R' Nosson Scherman and **R' Sheah Brander** שליט״א seem to never tire of taking the ArtScroll Revolution to yet undreamt of heights. The *zechus* to add my little part to their colossal efforts להגדיל תורה ולהאדירה is priceless.

R' Avraham Biderman, a rare breed of *talmid chacham* and friend is a blessing not only for *Klal Yisrael,* but also for everyone who is lucky enough to cross his path.

R' Eli Kroen, good-humored even when "the kitchen gets very hot" dedicates his considerable graphic talents to bring Torah literature to new levels of beauty.

I am grateful to **R' Tzvi Segal,** one of Jerusalems most talented *melamdim,* who graciously ferried material between Jerusalem and Beitar.

To the entire ArtScroll Family who always go the extra mile to present Torah in ways that grant it honor — Thank you.

To my wife **Batsheva** תחי׳, a seasoned מחנכת who has touched countless lives in ways that set off a ripple effect, both now and in generations to come, I humbly dedicate my work on this project. May we together merit that ייראו עינינו וישמח לבנו ותגל נפשנו בישועתך באמת, to בע״ה see our dear children Avraham, Aba Yehoshua, Toby, Chana Malya, Aharon, and Yisroel Shimon עמו״ש grow into תלמידי חכמים ויראי אלוקים, following in the footsteps of those who implanted in them the potential for גדלות אמיתית.

Last but not least, to the *Ribbono Shel Olam* Who grants me so much more than I deserve from His אוצר מתנת חנם, I can only say אין אנחנו מספיקים להודות לך.

Moshe M. Lieber

משה מרדכי ליעבער

בעיר אלוקינו הר קדשו

כסלו תשס״ג

Table of Contents

ספר בראשית

BEREISHIS/GENESIS

פרשת בראשית ⤷
Parashas Bereishis

Background

As the Torah is primarily the Creator's hand-book to Jewish life, it would seem appropriate for it to begin with the first mitzvah given to the Jewish people. Instead, the Torah opens by identifying God as the Creator and Master of the world, and it designates man as its central player. This firmly establishes the basic credo of faith in God as the sole Creator and His Torah as the binding guide to life.

בְּרֵאשִׁית בָּרָא אֱלֹקִים אֵת הַשָּׁמַיִם וְאֵת הָאָרֶץ
In the beginning of God's creating the heavens and the earth (1:1).

Rather than the familiar *In the beginning God created, Rashi* understands this phrase as setting a time frame: *In the beginning of God's creating the heavens and the earth . . . God said . . .* The implication is that God's creative act continues, for He renews His creation every day. Unlike a crafts-man whose finished product has no further need for the one who made it, the world cannot survive without God's constant involvement. As the *Baal Shem Tov* said, God's words *Let there be a firmament* (1:6) made the heavens solidify and achieve permanence. This, however, was not a one-time occurrence; it is God's constant utterance that keeps the heavens from collapsing. This is equally true of all of creation, and therefore we praise God in our prayers as the One Who *in His goodness renews daily, perpetually, the work of* Creation (*R' Simchah Bunim of P'shis'cha*).

Midrash HaNe'elam writes that the letters of the word בְּרֵאשִׁית can be rearranged to spell שִׁיר תָּאֵב, *desires song*. All of Creation is imbued with a burning desire to sing the praises of God, as it were. The very complexity of the universe is a "song" attesting to the glory of its Creator. In the words of *Psalms* (19:2), *The heavens declare the glory of God and the firmament tells of His handi-work.*

Man has the opportunity — and responsibility — to be the conductor of this cosmic symphony by using the world as an instrument to advance the greater glory of Heaven. In the words of *R' Moshe Chaim Luzzato,* "If man takes charge of him-self and cleaves to his Creator, using the world only as an aid to serving Him, he is elevated and he elevates the entire world with him; for it is a source of elevation and fulfillment for all crea-tures when they serve the ideal person who is sanctified with Divine sanctity" (*Mesillas Yesharim* Chapter I). When man utilizes this world to per-form the commandments for the sake of Heaven, he is in essence bringing the entire world closer to achieving its ultimate purpose — the service of God.

Chashavah L'Tovah offers a homiletical render-ing of this verse: *In the beginning* [of every day, one should ponder that] *God created the heavens and earth.* One who focuses on this belief will realize that *the earth is astonishingly empty,* meaning that our earthly concerns are devoid of the true mean-ing of life. When one recognizes that God is the Master Creator and that it is our duty to follow His will, he begins to realize how inconsequential his mundane concerns are.[1]

Rashi writes: The phrase *In the beginning* calls for homiletical interpretation. The word בראשית is a contraction of the words בִּשְׁבִיל רֵאשִׁית, because of the things that Scripture refers to as רֵאשִׁית, *a beginning.* As the Sages taught: God brought the world into existence for the sake of the Torah, which occupies the highest level in the hierarchy of values (see *Proverbs* 8:22), and on behalf of the nation of Israel which is of primary importance to Him. Everything that was and will be created, from the beginning of time until its end, came into being in order to serve the Jewish people which was destined to accept, study and fulfill the Torah.[2] As *Rambam (Introduction to Mishnah Commentary)* writes: "It is possible that a person will build a palace breathtaking in its splendor, which serves no other true purpose except to one day provide shade for a truly righteous man, thus saving him from death." The entire cosmos is that palace and the Jewish people are that righteous man who justify every last molecule of Creation.

A fascinating dialogue in the Talmud may be understood in this light.

When the Messiah comes, God will figuratively hold up a Torah scroll and announce that all those who occupied themselves with Torah should step forward to receive their well-deserved reward. The Romans will come forward and claim, "Master of the world, we built many places for public gatherings; we established many bathhouses and greatly increased the financial stability of the Land of Israel. All of this we did on behalf of the Jews so that they might study and practice the Torah." Hashem will reply, "Fools! Everything that you did,

---

1. **Acronym of Values.** According to the *Vilna Gaon,* the word בראשית is an acronym for the values that fill life with meaning:

The ב stands for בִּטָּחוֹן, rock-solid *trust* in God and firm belief that He is the very essence of kindness and goodness.

The ר alludes to רָצוֹן, *desire* to live according to His will. Not always do circumstances provide us with the optimal conditions to do so; nevertheless, one must always maintain the desire.

The א stands for אַהֲבָה, *love,* for love of God and man is the essence of the Torah way. וְאָהַבְתָּ אֵת ה' אֱלֹהֶיךָ, *You shall love Hashem your God (Deuteronomy* 6:5), and וְאָהַבְתָּ לְרֵעֲךָ כָּמוֹךָ, *you shall love your fellow as yourself* (*Leviticus* 19:18), are the bases for the *mitzvos* between man and God and between man and his fellow.

The ש symbolizes שְׁתִיקָה, *silence,* for it is the degree of control one exercises over his mouth that defines his spiritual level. As R' Shimon ben Gamliel says, "All my days I have been raised among the Sages and I found nothing better for oneself than silence" (*Avos* 1:17).

The י represents יִרְאָה, *reverence.* While love is vital to a relationship with God, one must be wary of overfamiliarity, which can breed irreverent contempt. One must therefore fear God no less than he loves Him. [The Torah likewise teaches us both to honor and revere parents.]

The ת stands for Torah. Only through the study and practice of Torah can one truly transform one's life into one with sanctity and meaning.

2. **Cosmic Locomotive.** Unfortunately, many people have disdain for those who dedicate themselves to Torah study, especially since they cannot afford to maintain high standards of living. *R' Shlomo Slovtitzky* offers a parable:

A wealthy minister was once traveling on a steamboat. The boat sped effortlessly through the ocean, heading for its destination. Fascinated, the minister asked his entourage, "Tell me, what makes this boat run?" They explained, "Below there is a room with a huge coal furnace. The heat creates steam that turns the motor, thus propelling the boat." The minister wanted to see it for himself. When he went below deck to the furnace room, he was shocked. The walls were pitch black and the workers' faces were encrusted with soot and grime. Aesthetically repulsed, he said, "It is beneath the honor of such an elegant cruiser that its motor room be so ugly and that those who work there are so filthy and smoke stained. I insist that the walls of this room be broken immediately and the workers be sent away." No amount of arguing could convince the minister that breaking down the furnace room would cause the boat to capsize, and all its passengers — including himself — to drown.

The world was created for the sake of the Jew who studies God's Torah. His efforts are the energy that "turn the motor" of existence and allow us to enjoy such a lovely world. Thus the Torah scholars, those noble souls who "blacken themselves" by forgoing the luxuries that others view as necessities, are truly carrying the rest of us through life. Rather than behaving like the foolish minister and demanding that they join us on the leisure deck, we would do well to appreciate that they are the motor that propels mankind.

you did for yourselves." This dialogue will repeat itself with all the nations of the world (*Avodah Zarah* 2b).

The audacity of the nations is hard to fathom. How, in a world of total truth, will they be able to lie so brazenly to God, claiming that all they did was on behalf of the Jews?

R' Yitzchak Zev Soloveitchik explained that the nations are not lying. God does not call them liars; He rebukes them as fools. While they had only their own self-interest in mind, what they did *really was* for the Jews.[3] Since God created the world בִּשְׁבִיל יִשְׂרָאֵל שֶׁנִּקְרְאוּ רֵאשִׁית וּבִשְׁבִיל הַתּוֹרָה שֶׁנִּקְרֵאת רֵאשִׁית, for Israel and the Torah, both of which are called *beginning*, i.e., the primary reasons for creation, the various nation's actions were inspired from Above to benefit the Jewish people. Nevertheless, since their motives were completely selfish, they deserve no reward.

וְרוּחַ אֱלֹקִים מְרַחֶפֶת עַל פְּנֵי הַמָּיִם
and the Divine Presence hovered upon the surface of the waters (ibid. 2).

The Midrash (*Bereishis Rabbah* 2:4) interprets רוּחַ אֱלֹהִים (literally *the spirit of God*) as the spirit of the Messiah. God created the world exactly as it is meant to be when the Messiah comes. The entire Messianic dream is nothing more and nothing less than the world that God originally envisioned and created. By sinning and moving away from the Divine Presence, Man brought spiritual diminution and ruination to God's world. Man must now endure a long and painful exile in order to return to his original state of spiritual purity and restore the world to that which it was meant to be.

After being purged of spiritual dross and infused with spiritual antibodies to resist spiritual impurity, the nation of Israel was charged with the mission of perfecting itself and hence the world. The spirit of the Messiah hovers over the world, and we are the only ones who can bring it down and make it a reality. It is the Jewish people who have the power to say "Let there be light" (*Maayana Shel Torah*).[4]

Water, the *Rambam* teaches, is a metaphor for Torah (*Hilchos Talmud Torah* 3:9). The spirit of God hovers over the water, i.e., Torah, and those righteous people who maintain a powerful link to the Torah are those who are truly imbued with the spirit of God. The Talmud (*Berachos* 3b) teaches that the wind would blow on the harp of King David causing it to play. This is an allusion to the ability of the spirit of God, which is encapsulated in Torah, to create the enchantingly great song of the Davidic Messiah (*Likutei Moharan*).[5]

---

3. **Made for Israel.** When the train tracks from St. Petersburg, Russia to Berlin were built, *R' Chaim Soloveitchik* commented, "This train line was built for the yeshivah students so that traveling to Volozhin be made easier. Everything in the world is for Torah and those who learn it."

His son, the *Brisker Rav,* continued with his father's perspective. "Over a period of decades, the cruel czars of Russia had the peasants lay the Trans-Siberian railway. Fantastic amounts of money and a great many lives were invested in order to run the railway through the most inhospitable parts of Siberia all the way to the port at Vladivostok which faces toward Japan and the Far East. At the time, the project seemed to make no sense and many wondered exactly why it was done. Only years later, when the students of the Mirrer Yeshivah escaped the European inferno and arrived in Shanghai, China by way of Siberia and the Trans-Siberian railway did the whole thing become clear. The railway, and all the funds and labor that went into it, were justified for it was for the sake of Torah and the Jews that God created the world and its history."

4. **Hovering over the Water.** The prophet describes the Messianic era as a time when the earth will be filled with knowledge and recognition of God, as the sea is filled with water (*Isaiah* 11:9). Hence the Torah, at the very outset, speaks of the spirit of Hashem (the Messiah) hovering over the water (*R' Moshe Sternbuch*).

5. **Overtones.** The relationship between homiletical teachings and the text often seems to be vague and even at odds with the plain meaning of the words. These overtones of meaning, however, are also a basic part of the Torah. Our verse alludes to this by teaching that *the Divine Presence hovered over the water*. Like the mother bird that hovers over her young with her wings barely touching them, so the lessons that our great men derived from the Torah hover over the text, simultaneously connected and unconnected (*R' Baruch of Medziboz*).

וַיֹּאמֶר אֱלֹקִים יְהִי אוֹר וַיְהִי אוֹר
God said, "Let there be light,"
and there was light (ibid. 3).

Rashi notes (verse 4) that God saw that the wicked were undeserving of the intense spiritual light He had created. He therefore separated that light from the rest of the universe and set it aside to be reserved for the righteous in the future. Where did He place that spiritual light?

According to the *Baal Shem Tov*, He placed it in the Torah. That intense spiritual vision — which allows us to view life with clarity and to differentiate between good and evil, right and wrong — can be found only in Torah. Just as the soul is invisible yet is certainly the most vibrant source of light in one's life, so the primordial light of Creation still exists, ready to be discovered by those who search for it in Torah. One who toils in Torah is granted the ability to live an enlightened life. One whose life is illuminated by Torah sees the light of God in every molecule of the cosmos (*Nesivos Shalom*).[6]

Why, asks *R' Eliyahu Eliezer Dessler,* would God bother creating something only to store it for thousands of years into the future?

The answer lies in the Talmudic description of a human embryo. "A candle is lit above his head, which allows him to see from one end of the world to the other. An angel teaches him the entire Torah, and just as he leaves the womb he forgets it all" (*Niddah* 30b). The same question arises: What is the purpose of learning the entire Torah if it is destined to be forgotten? The answer is that retrieval of pre-existing knowledge is easier than learning it from scratch. The Torah one learns in the womb is lodged deep in the subconscious, waiting for man to discover it. Thus the Godly light that grants the embryo the clarity of spiritual vision is a temporary exposure to the entire Torah. This clarity enables us to re-learn and re-live the experience through our own efforts. On a cosmic level, God exposed Creation to that intense spiritual light so that the Jewish people could then access it by studying and living according to the Torah.

R' Noach of Lechovitch homiletically sees the verse as the prayer of a Jew. A Jew turns to God and says, "Let there be light," meaning "Enlighten my life with Your light, dear God. How much longer can I continue to grope in spiritual darkness?" God responds to this genuine, heartfelt plea, "And there was light."

וַיַּבְדֵּל אֱלֹקִים בֵּין הָאוֹר וּבֵין הַחֹשֶׁךְ
and God separated between the
light and the darkness (ibid. 4).

Separation is critical if God's creations are to survive in their purest form. When reciting *Havdalah* at the end of the Sabbath, we delineate four types of separation. *Blessed are You . . . Who separates between holy and secular, between light and darkness, between Israel and the nations, between the seventh day and the six days of labor.*

In all these instances, man is called upon to draw a clear line of demarcation between the opposites. Just as the difference between day and night is

---

6. **Relighting from the Beginning.** *Meor V'Shemesh* explains the basis for *Rashi's* comment. Throughout the Creation narrative, the utterance of God is followed with the words וַיְהִי כֵן, *and it was so,* indicating that whatever God called into being emerged exactly as He commanded. Here the Torah simply says *there was light.* In this verse, however, the Torah does not say *and it was so,* implying that although there was light, it was not identical to the light God had initially created.

Ohr Gedalyahu (*Beha'aloscha*) notes that the Torah describes Aaron's kindling of the Menorah in the Tabernacle as וַיַּעַשׂ כֵּן אַהֲרֹן, *Aaron did so.* In the Tabernacle, from which the light of Torah was to permeate the nation, Aaron kindled the lamps with that original light that God had put away. When the Jews, in an act of repentance after the sin of the Golden Calf, built the Tabernacle, they illuminated it with the spiritual light of Creation which is found in Torah.

The Sages alluded to this when they taught, "One who seeks [Torah] wisdom should turn [slightly] to the south while praying, for the Menorah (the symbol of Torah) is in the south [side of the Tabernacle]" (*Bava Basra* 25b).

Even after the destruction of the Temple, we can still experience that original light in the lights of Chanukah. While the Greeks and their counterparts tried to extinguish the light of Torah by (God forbid) replacing it with secular culture, it was the light of Torah that triumphed. In our Chanukah lamps we see a glimmer of the light of Creation, which God suffused in the Torah.

obvious, so the differences between holy and secular or between Israel and the nations must never become blurred.

The difference between competing values is sometimes very subtle. In real life, people must be able to evaluate situations carefully and critically, and differentiate between what is good and what is bad. This is why, as *Yerushalmi* (*Berachos* 5:2) teaches, the *Havdalah* blessing recited after Shabbos in the *Maariv* prayer is inserted in the blessing of wisdom, because אִם אֵין דַּעַת, הַבְדָּלָה מִנַּיִן, *if there is no wisdom how can there be differentiation*?][7]

R' Joseph B. Soloveitchik writes:

"We are a distinctive faith community with a unique commitment, singular relationship to God and a specific way of life. We must never confuse our role as the bearers of a particular commitment and destiny with our role as members of the family of man.

"In the area of faith, religious law, doctrine, and ritual, Jews have throughout the ages been a community guided exclusively by distinctive concerns, ideals, and commitments. Our love of and dedication to God are personal and bespeak an intimate relationship which must not be debated with others, whose relationship to God has been molded by different historical events and in different terms. *Discussion will in no way enhance or hallow these emotions.*

"We are, therefore, opposed to any public debate, dialogue or symposium concerning the doctrinal, dogmatic or ritual aspects of our faith vis a vis "similar" aspects of another faith community. We believe in and are committed to our Maker in a specific manner and we will not question, defend,

---

7. **Unthinkable Employment.** The *Chafetz Chaim* related an incident that underscores the need for clarity in creating a separation between the profane or secular and the sanctified.

In Eastern Europe, traveling peddlers would come to a town with *tzitzis,* prayer books, *mezuzos, tefillin,* holy books and other religious articles. They would generally display their wares on a table near the furnace in the back of the synagogue during the services and wait for the customers to make their purchases after the prayers.

One such peddler came to a synagogue in Stavisk, Poland. *R' Chaim Leib Mishkovsky,* Rav of Stavisk, approached the table and was shocked to see, among the books offered for sale, *haskalah* literature of the most spiritually insidious kind. Without delay, R' Chaim Leib fulfilled the Torah command to "destroy evil from your midst" (*Deuteronomy* 13:6) by throwing the heretical books into the furnace. The peddler complained, "Rabbi, not only have you caused me a loss of three rubles, the value of the books; by burning them, you don't allow me to earn a living. Do you really think I can support my family from the few kopeks I make on a pair of *tzitzis* or a *mezuzah*? On the books you just threw into the furnace I am able to turn a handsome profit."

R' Chaim Leib said to him quietly, "I will pay you from my pocket for the books I burned; I will even pay the retail price. However, with regard to supporting your family, one may not make a living from selling books full of heresy. If you can't make a living from your present occupation, you must look for another one, and I will try to help you. Come to the synagogue tomorrow and remind me of what I told you now."

The next day, after the morning prayers, the peddler reminded the rav of his promise. The rav replied that he had begun his efforts to help. He had asked the sexton of the synagogue to ask the local parish priest to come by the rav's home. "I think," said R' Chaim Leib, "that with the priest's help I can get you a new position."

"How can the priest help?" asked the peddler.

"Simple," responded R' Chaim Leib. "Last week I met him and he told me that the man who rings the church bells every morning died. I will ask him to offer you the job. It is a respectable and decent-paying position."

The peddler was shocked and insulted. "Rabbi, do you think that in my old age I would sell my soul to serve as an assistant to the priest?"

The rav replied, "Listen to your own words. To ring bells to awaken non-Jews to go to church is unthinkable in your eyes, yet to sell heretical books that will entice young Jewish children to idolatry is permissible?!"

Once, R' Chaim Leib was asked to decide on the proper punishment for a Jewish bookbinder who bound a *Chumash Bereishis* together with a Russian novel.

"Rather than asking me this," said R' Chaim Leib, "ask me what to do with yeshivah students who dabble in *haskalah* literature and combine Torah and Talmudic passages with anti-Torah propaganda and poison in the same brain. The book can at least be cut apart, separating the Torah from the secular novel. But how are we to rectify the illicit mingling of sacred and profane in a young man's mind?!"

We must emulate God and separate between light and darkness.

offer apologies, analyze or rationalize our faith in dialogues centered about these "private" topics which express our personal relationship to the God of Israel" (*Treasury of Tradition*).

Sfas Emes sees these verses as instructions on how to maintain courage and focus in our service of God. One who endeavors to serve God and come close to Him is often beset by feelings of inadequacy and despair, and feels overwhelmed with the sense that his life has no clear direction. Even after he succeeds in making some spiritual progress, he experiences backsliding and feels that his life is a chaotic whirlpool of light and darkness, sanctity and impurity.

God teaches us that man is a microcosm sharing the qualities of the macrocosm. Initially the world (and life) is astonishingly empty, with no form or direction. Even after there is light, it is intermingled with darkness until one is able to separate the two so that light emerges in its purest form. The beginning of the spiritual trek is difficult and disappointing. Even after man has tasted some success, light and darkness still wrestle for control of his soul. Man must make "*havdalah*," clearly differentiating between these two ways of life.

Then man, like God, will recognize that the light is good.

וַיְהִי עֶרֶב וַיְהִי בֹקֶר יוֹם אֶחָד
And there was evening and there was morning, one day (ibid. 5).

Although day and night seem to be opposites, they are complementary parts of a whole. Therefore, the Torah calls them *one day* rather than "the first day," for they are parts of the day created by the One (*Kli Yakar*). R' Yisrael of Rizhin understood this in a metaphorical fashion:

No matter whether life is dark and foreboding and the sun of success seems to have set (*and it was evening*), or whether life shines its face upon you (*it was morning*), know that it is *one day.* Even that which seems like night is an expression of Divine kindness.

Imrei Shefer notes that it is from this verse that we derive the principle that the halachic day begins the night before. This sequence is symbolic of the Jews' destiny. The darkness and suffering we initially endure will eventually yield to a future brilliant with light. In contrast, the nations of the world (especially those who oppress us) seem to enjoy a great deal of power and success. In reality, however, their dominance will be shortlived, destined to be shattered in the End of Days. As our Sages teach, "The righteous initially suffer pain but their end is peace; the beginning of the wicked is serene, but their end is full of travail" (*Bereishis Rabbah* 66:4).[8]

וַיַּבְדֵּל בֵּין הַמַּיִם אֲשֶׁר מִתַּחַת לָרָקִיעַ וּבֵין הַמַּיִם אֲשֶׁר מֵעַל לָרָקִיעַ וַיְהִי כֵן
and [He] separated between the waters which were beneath the firmament and between the waters that were above the firmament and it was so (ibid. 7).

This is the only day of which the Torah does not report *it was good.* The Midrash (*Bereishis Rabbah* 4:6) explains: On this day strife was created, for the division of the waters symbolizes the breakup of relationships among people and the resulting divisiveness. R' Tuvyum said, "If divisiveness such as the dividing of the waters, which is ultimately for the benefit of the world, does not deserve to be described as 'it was good,' then strife, which leads only to divisiveness, certainly is not good."[9]

---

8. **From Pain to Pleasure.** This is further reflected in the contrast between the Jewish and non-Jewish days of rest. Jews begin the week with six days of toil and only then follow with Sabbath, the day of rest. Many non-Jews switch the order; they start the week with Sunday as a day of rest and then begin the grueling weekday schedule. For a Jew, life is an uphill, often painful struggle followed by eternal pleasure. For the non-Jew, life's temporary pleasures eventually yield to stress and pain (*Imrei Shefer*).

9. **Unbearable Strife.** During the Russian Revolution of 1917, a group of insurgents founded a new Burial Society in Radin, intending to depose the old, well-established group and its strict halachic standards. The town seemed to be on the verge of a raging, emotional conflagration. The next Sabbath, the *Chafetz Chaim* asked for permission to speak publicly in the synagogue and there he said, "Dear brothers! Even had I been given thousands of rubles I would not have agreed to come here to speak. I am an old man and my time is too valuable. Even for money I

Why then, asks *R' Yaakov of Husyatin,* does the Torah say *it was good* regarding the first and fourth days on which God separated light and darkness?

The essence of unity is a positive force in which different elements join together and harness their energy toward the achievement of positive goals. Unity should never be the cause for opposing forces to join together so that their uniqueness is obliterated. In such instances, such as the separation of light and darkness, separation rather than unity is appropriate.

When dividing water from water, however, strife and divisiveness are a negative force, all good intentions and results notwithstanding. The Torah therefore does not refer to the division between the upper and lower waters as *good.* Light and darkness are a different story; it is imperative that they remain separate with each one retaining its unique function.

וְהָיוּ לִמְאוֹרֹת בִּרְקִיעַ הַשָּׁמַיִם לְהָאִיר עַל הָאָרֶץ
and they shall serve as luminaries
in the firmament of the heaven to
shine upon the earth (ibid. 15).

In the previous verse, *Rashi* explains that the luminaries serve as omens; when an eclipse occurs, it is a bad omen for the world. When Jews follow the Torah, however, they are impervious to the influence of such forces. In addition, the cycles of the sun and moon affect the way in which the *beis din* establishes the calendar and hence the festivals.

Here, *Rashi* adds that the sun and moon also serve as our sources of light. Were one to ask a person of even average intelligence for God's primary reason in creating the sun, moon and stars, he would state the obvious: to provide light and warmth to the world so as to enable people to see, and to help trees and plants to grow. Any other benefits would be considered of secondary importance.

But the Torah views the cosmos not as an end in itself but rather as a means to be used in the service of Hashem and His Torah. Thus, the solar system exists primarily in order to assist Israel in its performance of commandments. The heavenly bodies were created not so much for light as to provide the means for proclaiming the months and the proper days to observe the festivals, the time for the daily prayers, and to indicate the conclusion of the Sabbath. Their purpose in providing light and warmth is a secondary one (*Chafetz Chaim*).[10]

Background

After creating the entire "backdrop" and properly setting the stage, on the sixth day God created the centerpiece of creation — Man.

נַעֲשֶׂה אָדָם בְּצַלְמֵנוּ כִּדְמוּתֵנוּ
Let us make Man in Our image,
after our likeness (ibid. 26).

Although no one helped God create Man, He told Moses to write *Let us,* in the plural, implying

---

don't sell my time. I feel, however, that I have no choice. I have lived here in Radin for over 50 years and I remember all the Jews who once prayed in this synagogue. Where are they all now? The only thing left of them are the tombstones over their graves. Many of you weren't even born then. Those of you who were are already old people. How wonderful it would be if everyone lived to a ripe old age, but sooner or later we will all come to the World of Truth, where we will have to make an honest reckoning.

"Strife is a terrible thing! Even if one has kept many *mitzvos,* strife can still cause his downfall. I am sure that when you realize how serious a sin strife is, you will seek to justify yourselves, claiming not to have realized how terribly divisive it can be. You will want to claim that in our town of Radin there was an old Jew by the name of Yisrael Meir (the *Chafetz Chaim's* name) whom people looked up to as a Torah scholar, and even he did not say a word about the entire affair. I therefore beg you; don't invoke my name. I have my own spiritual baggage and am afraid of my own chances of surviving Divine judgment. Please don't expect me to carry responsibility for others."

While talking, he began to shake and cry bitter tears. His words hit home and the new group disbanded.

10. **A Spot of Light.** Generally, the light source which illuminates a space is smaller than the space itself. The lamp in a room is obviously smaller than the actual room. Why, then, is the sun so many times larger than the earth?

R' Aharon of Sadigura suggests that the question is based on a misconception. The world was created on behalf of Israel. The sun, moon and stars pale into insignificance when compared to one Jew. Thus the entire solar system is like a small lamp which must cast light in a vast room.

that other forces were partners in creating man. This teaches that one should act humbly by consulting with others, even those who are less gifted or intelligent, before making major decisions. God used this phrase even though it could conceivably open the door for heretical ideas, such as a belief in more than one deity. But why run the risk of heresy simply in order to teach humility? Apparently, in God's scheme of things, the development of spiritual refinement and humility is so crucial that the risk is worthwhile. As the Sages taught, דֶּרֶךְ אֶרֶץ קָדְמָה לַתּוֹרָה, *character refinement is the prelude to Torah* [*Vayikra Rabbah* 9:3] (*R' Elazar M. Shach*).

R' Yaakov Moshe Charlop suggests that the risk is limited. Positive character development influences one's ideology and beliefs in a positive way, while character flaws leave a negative impact on one's beliefs. And, as *Rashi* states, those who want to err will do so in any case. *Rashi's* implication is clear: someone who approaches the Torah honestly will not err; someone who looks for an excuse to engage in heretical ideas, will err — because he *wants* to.

When God teaches us the importance of humility and seeking the counsel of others, the intensity of our beliefs can only be enhanced, not weakened.

Since man was created with an intrinsic sense of right and wrong, under normal circumstances he will maintain the proper attitudes and beliefs. Faith becomes warped when, as a result of deficient character traits and unchecked desires, we seek to reject our beliefs in order to justify (or at least self-justify) our unethical or immoral behavior. Thus God had no fear that objective people would be drawn into heresy as a result of the Torah's seeking to build character. Only those who desire to make the mistake will do so.[11]

The Midrash records a "dialogue" between the various character traits as to whether Man should be created. Kindness maintained that man's creation was justified by the acts of lovingkindness he would perform, while Truth opposed the creation because people would lie. Righteousness countered that man would act righteously and charitably, Peace argued that Man is essentially quarrelsome. What did God do? He cast Truth to the earth, thus allowing Kindness and Righteousness to form a majority opinion, overruling Peace.

If the idea was to create a majority, God could have just as well cast Peace to earth. Why did He cast off Truth and allow Peace to remain in heaven?

R' Yosef Chaim Sonnenfeld explained: Peace is a very subtle concept. If not coupled with Truth and Honesty, Peace can be viewed as a goal to be pursued at all cost — even at the sacrifice of sacred principles and values. The generation of the Dispersion (see *Genesis* 11:1-9) is a classic example of Peace and Unity employed as a means to reject the sovereignty of God.

Thus to cast Peace to earth without Truth to accompany and regulate it would have been dangerous. As harmful as Truth without Peace may be, it is not nearly as threatening as Peace without Truth.

An alternative perspective is offered by *R' Alexander Moshe Lapidus*. He explains that Truth had to be removed from the Heavenly debate, because every majority is rendered meaningless if it opposes the Truth. Had Truth remained in Heaven, even as a minority, it would have been impossible to create Man. Once Truth was cast away and removed from the debate, Kindness and Righteousness could overrule Peace, and Man could be created.[12]

---

11. **Answering Answers?** Some *maskilim* ("enlightened" Jewish secularists) came to *R' Chaim of Brisk.* "Rebbe, we have a few questions in matters of faith. Would you be kind enough to give us some answers?"

R' Chaim replied, "Were you to have questions I might try to provide answers. I, however, am afraid that you already have your own answers. For me to answer answers with answers is futile."

12. **Minority Rule.** A priest once asked *R' Yonasan Eibeschutz* why, since the Torah calls for following the majority opinion, we insist on following our religion rather than Catholicism which certainly enjoys a larger following than Judaism.

R' Yonasan replied: "We follow the majority only when we are unsure. In this case, we have not the slightest shadow of a doubt that the Torah way is the truth for a Jew. Why follow the majority when we know what is right?"

R' Elchanan Wasserman offers another answer to the priest's question. Majority rule is relevant only when all those offering opinions are not influenced by bribes. If, however, the judges have been bribed, their opinions must be discarded. The Sages teach that the verse *and [do] not explore after your heart* (*Numbers* 15:39) refers to

When God said *let us make Man,* whom was He talking to?

According to *Mei HaShiloach,* God was responding to all of Creation. All that He had created up to that point — whether inanimate, vegetative, or animal — suddenly realized that they would never achieve full self-realization if there was no man to harness their combined energies and provide them with a connection to God.

The inanimate earth puts its energy into vegetation, which in turn is consumed by the animals, who then serve Man as a source of sustenance. Hence, Man encompasses all the different levels of energy in Creation, and provides them with meaning through sincere service of God.

Creation itself demanded of God that He make a man who could elevate it and give it significance. God responded by asking every element to give of itself to be part of Man so that through him, Creation would achieve self-realization.[13]

R' Yisrael of Tchortkov, however, sees Man himself as the one God speaks to. God tells him, "I have provided you with all the potential you need to become great and truly human. Now, it is you who will have to take your raw potential and fashion it into Man. *Let us make Man.* Every day we will make Man as you will refashion and reshape yourself anew."[14]

After completing all of Creation in six days, God rested on the seventh. We, in *imitatio Dei,* are commanded to rest on the seventh day as well, by refraining from all creative labor so that we may figuratively step back and assess the real purpose of Creation. Our Sabbath rest constitutes testimony that God is the Creator and that he "rested," as it were, on the seventh day.

וַיְהִי עֶרֶב וַיְהִי בֹקֶר יוֹם הַשִּׁשִּׁי. וַיְכֻלּוּ הַשָּׁמַיִם

And there was evening and there was morning the sixth day. Thus the heavens were finished (1:31-2:1).

The Friday night *Kiddush* begins with the words יוֹם הַשִּׁשִּׁי, *the sixth day.* Many commentators question this practice since one is not allowed to recite only part of a Torah verse (*Megillah* 22a).

Arugas HaBosem suggests an explanation based on the Talmud (*Shabbos* 88a), which explains that the definite article ה of הַשִּׁשִּׁי signifies a *particular* sixth day, i.e., the sixth day of *Sivan* at Mount Sinai, when the Jewish people would choose whether to accept or reject the Torah. At the time of Creation, God said that the universe would survive only if Israel accepted the Torah. On that sixth day, all of Creation was figuratively in limbo, its fate contingent on what the Jews would do. It was only

heretical beliefs. At first glance, belief seems to be a product of the mind, not the heart. Why does the Torah link heresy to emotions? The answer is that finding the true belief is not *that* difficult, from an intellectual standpoint. If people are unable to believe, it is because belief comes with a price; it requires people to curb some desires and give up their sinful behavior. The heart, with its physical and emotional desires, is unwilling to pay that price. Those who fail to see the truth in Torah and belief in One God are blinded by a form of emotional graft. As "bribed judges" they cannot be deemed a majority opinion.

13. **Collective Effort.** The *Vilna Gaon* offers a variation on this based on the Talmud (*Eruvin* 100b) which states that even had the Torah not been given, we still could have derived many positive character traits from the mere observation of nature. For instance, modesty could be learned from cats, respect of private property from the ant, which does not take food from other ants, and so on. Thus God asked every part of nature to contribute its positive traits so that these would become an integral part of Man.

[*R' Yekele Orenstein* suggests that when God pondered the Torah's prohibition against theft, He created the ant. God looked into the Torah as the blueprint of the world and thus created.]

14. **Humanizing the Beast.** *R' Aharon Kotler* phrased it as follows: "My rebbi, the *Alter of Slabodka,* would often say: 'People often become *better* and [spiritually] more attractive but they don't become *different.* Man was created in the image of God so that he would be able to transform himself from the wild foal which he was at birth into an elevated human being.' "

The *Alter of Kelm* explained the verse וְעַיִר פֶּרֶא אָדָם יִוָּלֵד not merely as a statement of fact that *as a wild foal was man born (Job* 11:12) but rather as a challenge that *from a wild foal shall be born a human being.*

on *the* sixth day of Sivan, when the Jews accepted the Torah, that God truly finished heaven and earth for only then did Creation achieve a sense of permanence and purpose.

Why should the existence of heaven and earth be contingent on the Jews accepting the Torah? If the Jewish people made the wrong choice, then *they* should be punished; why must heaven and earth suffer?

According to *Zekan Aharon,* the destruction of heaven and earth would not be a punishment; rather, their end would be the natural result of the Jews' rejection of Torah. The universe was created as nothing but a backdrop for the ultimate purpose — that the Jewish people would live according to the Torah. Of what use is the stage if the performance is canceled?

Sfas Emes views this conditional cause and effect relationship not as a way of coercing Jews to accept the Torah, but rather as a means to subjugate all of nature to aid man in his service of God. Knowing that its very existence was conditioned on Israel's allegiance to the Torah, nature would not stand in the way, as it were. As the prophet writes: *For [now] the seed is of peace: The wine gives forth its fruit, the land gives forth its produce, and the heavens give forth their dew (Zechariah 8:12).*

וַיְכַל אֱלֹקִים בַּיּוֹם הַשְּׁבִיעִי מְלַאכְתּוֹ אֲשֶׁר עָשָׂה
By the seventh day God completed His work which He had done (ibid. 2).

This verse seems to imply that God finished His creative work on the seventh day yet the Torah teaches that God worked only six days and rested on the seventh (See *Exodus* 31:17).

The Midrash reconciles this apparent contradiction by stating that the only thing lacking from Creation was the true rest, which God created on the seventh day. Why is rest such an integral part of Creation?

R' Simchah Zissel of Kelm explains: Restlessness of the soul is the most debilitating of spiritual maladies. The feeling that one is simultaneously drawn in conflicting directions and lacks focus in life is a source of deep emotional pain and even despair. It is the root cause of much sin, since it brings in its wake emotional confusion and reckless impulsiveness. *Isaiah* (57:20) describes the wicked as the embodiment of this characteristic by saying, *"Their life is like the raging sea";* for they feel themselves tugged in all directions. From the obsessive pursuit of money, to the hedonistic cravings of the flesh, to the foolish race after "honor," all lead to frustration, disappointment, and pain.

Just as a directionless soul is the epitome of spiritual torment, so a restful soul at peace with itself is the ultimate in perfection.[15] A serene soul experiences a taste of the World to Come and realizes the purpose of Creation. This is the character of the Sabbath, a day of rest and sanctity. On the Sabbath we experience the sanctity of a soul in total synchronization with itself.

After God finished creating the entire world, He created the restfulness of the Sabbath, a time when man can enjoy life with all the disparate elements of his personality united and focused on his Creator.

Included in the rest of the Sabbath is the mitzvah of עֹנֶג שַׁבָּת, enjoyment of the physical pleasures of food, drink, and rest on the Sabbath. The Sages teach that one who is מְעַנֵּג אֶת הַשַּׁבָּת, *gives enjoyment to the Sabbath,* will merit a reward without [spiritual or physical] limitations (*Shabbos* 118a)[16]

Why is this such an integral part of Shabbos?

Beis HaLevi explains that there are two categories of *mitzvos.* Some *mitzvos* call for us to go against the grain of human nature in our attempts to control our baser instincts. Other *mitzvos* are intended not to suppress human nature but rather

---

15. **Dispersion of Heart.** *Chovos HaLevavos* cites the prayer of a righteous man who made the following request of God: הַמָּקוֹם יַצִּילֵנִי מִפִּזּוּר הַנֶּפֶשׁ, *May the Omnipresent rescue me from a scattering of the soul.* His intent was that God should prevent him from owning properties and possessions in too many locations, causing his mind and heart to be preoccupied and dispersed.

16. **Indulging the Sabbath.** Elder *chassidim* noted that the Sages do not speak of הַמְעַנֵּג עַצְמוֹ בְּשַׁבָּת, "one who provides *himself* with enjoyment on the Sabbath," but rather of one who gives enjoyment to the Sabbath. One's enjoyment of physical pleasures on the Sabbath should be an expression of honor to the Sabbath, not as an exercise in self-indulgence and gastronomic excess.

to edify it and infuse it with spiritual content and meaning. The Sabbath is *the* classic example of sanctifying pleasure and elevating physicality, so that they serve the spirit. Since the Sabbath and our observance of it are living testimony to God as the Creator of the world, it is appropriate that we, in God's image, build a physical world dedicated to the enhancement of His glory.

וַיְבָרֶךְ אֱלֹקִים אֶת יוֹם הַשְּׁבִיעִי וַיְקַדֵּשׁ אֹתוֹ

God blessed the seventh day and sanctified it (ibid. 3).

According to the *Zohar*, the Sabbath is the source of all physical and spiritual blessings. As the Midrash explains, "*The blessing of God grants wealth (Proverbs 10:22)* is a reference to the Sabbath."[17]

---

17. **Source of Blessing.** When the *Chafetz Chaim* was at a rabbinic convocation in St. Petersburg, many wealthy Jews approached him for a blessing. One of them offered a very sizable donation for the Chafetz Chaim's yeshivah, but the great rabbi did not want to take the money. He held the wealthy man's hand in his own and said to him, "Isn't it a shame that such a special hand that tries so hard to give *tzedakah* will undergo such terrible suffering only because it participates in desecrating the Shabbos?" He stared the man in the face, crying bitter tears as if begging him to stop desecrating the Sabbath. The man's heart began to melt from the warm pleading of the old sage and he told the Chafetz Chaim that he would begin observing the Sabbath the following week.

"This Shabbos I need to complete some important unfinished business; next week I will begin," he said.

The Chafetz Chaim took hold of the man's hand again and said, "Were the Shabbos to belong to me I might consider your offer. However, the Sabbath belongs to God. I cannot grant you permission for even one second of Shabbos desecration." Moved by the heartfelt words and tears of the Chafetz Chaim, this man became a full-fledged Sabbath observer and an upstanding, committed Jew.

Another incident involving the Chafetz Chaim sheds light on his perception of the Sabbath as a source of blessing.

A young man in the Lithuanian city of Zhetel bought a car and made a living driving people between the train station on the outskirts of town and the town itself. Slowly but surely he started working later on Friday and earlier after the Sabbath until he began to actually desecrate the Sabbath itself. All the protests of the town's rabbi and responsible laymen did not sway him. His father, a fine Torah-observant Jew, suffered terribly from a crippling disease and was unable to change his son's ways.

Once, *R' Zalman Sorotzkin,* Rav of Zhetel, was in Vilna, traveling on the same train as the Chafetz Chaim, who was heading back to Radin. When the train was in Zhetel for a half-hour stopover, R' Zalman noticed the sickly old father hobbling about with a cane. R' Zalman inquired about his health. "Are you feeling better? Where are you headed?" he asked. The man told him that he was taking the train to Radin to see the Chafetz Chaim." "I had a dream last night in which my grandmother appeared to me and told me, 'Don't waste your time in hospitals, doctors cannot help you. Travel to the Chafetz Chaim, let him bless you and all your ailments will be healed.' I came here to travel to Radin." R' Zalman happily informed him that there was no need to travel to Radin — the Chafetz Chaim was right there on the train. The sick old man saw it as a Heavenly sign. He entered the other railroad car where he found the Chafetz Chaim praying with a crowd of people swallowing up his every word. While the Chafetz Chaim was praying, R' Zalman sent *R' Hillel Ginsburg,* husband of the Chafetz Chaim's granddaughter, to tell him about the sick old man and his son's desecration of Shabbos.

By the time R' Hillel got back to his grandfather, it was too late; the old man was already speaking to the Chafetz Chaim. He told him the story of his sickness, his dream, and how his grandmother had told him to ask the Chafetz Chaim for a blessing.

The Chafetz Chaim was shaken by the story. "Who can grant you a blessing? Yisrael Meir (the Chafetz Chaim's name)? Do you think his blessing will really help? No! Do you know who holds the key to the blessings? The holy Shabbos! She was blessed by Hashem and is the source of all blessing. Why ask me for a blessing?" The Chafetz Chaim was pensive for a moment. "Why not? If you observe Shabbos properly and therefore receive *its* blessing, then Yisrael Meir will also give you *his* blessing. But if you think that Yisrael Meir's blessing can help you although you are not ready to really keep Shabbos, then you are making a big mistake. It is simply not in my power!"

After another pause, the Sage of Radin continued, "Do you think that if you yourself observe Shabbos, it is enough to receive its blessing? Look in the Torah; it is written that *you shall not do any work — you, your son, your daughter . . . (Exodus* 20:10). It is the only mitzvah about which the Torah speaks of one's children and a parent's obligation to see to it that they keep Shabbos. If you keep Shabbos but your son drives, or your daughter brushes her hair [with a hard brush], then you cannot receive the blessing of Shabbos and Yisrael Meir can't help you either."

The old man was sobbing heavily. When he promised to make sure that his children truly observe Shabbos, the Chafetz Chaim offered him a warm blessing.

In fact, the Sages teach that although man's material sustenance is determined on Rosh Hashanah, the money one spends on food for the Sabbath is not included in this calculation. Why is this so?

When Adam sinned, God placed severe limitations on mankind's ability to sustain itself: *Through suffering shall you eat of it* [the earth] . . . *Thorns and thistles shall sprout for you . . . By the sweat of your brow shall you eat bread* (*Genesis* 3:17-19). However, these limitations may be suspended under certain circumstances. For example, the Tabernacle and later the Temple were not affected by these curses. Hence, the Kohanim ate only a minuscule portion of the show bread [לֶחֶם הַפָּנִים], yet they were satiated (see *Yoma* 39a).

The Sabbath, in the dimension of time, is equivalent to the Temple, in the dimension of space. Just as physical curses did not affect the Temple, they do not affect the Sabbath. Thus, the money one spends on food for the Sabbath is not reckoned in the yearly budget set on Rosh Hashanah (*Simchas Aharon*).[18]

---

18. **Sinless Sabbath.** The Sabbath is a taste of the World to Come, when all of Creation will revert to the state it enjoyed before Adam and Eve sinned. Thus on the Sabbath we taste a world unlimited by the curses that followed their sin. Therefore, the food of Shabbos is not included in the decree issued on Rosh Hashanah.

The *Vilna Gaon* finds an allusion to this concept in the text of the Torah. Although Man's sin occurred chronologically before the Sabbath, it was not recorded in the Torah until afterwards. This teaches us that the sin left no mark on the Sabbath.

פרשת נח &
Parashas Noach

Background

Disappointed, as it were, that man had brought His world to an intolerable level of moral decadence, God decided to decimate His Creation almost entirely and to create the world anew. By saving Noah, his family and the number of animals necessary to replenish the earth, He created the nucleus for His new world.

אֵלֶּה תּוֹלְדֹת נֹחַ נֹחַ . . .
These are the offspring of Noah, Noah . . . (6:9)

Although the Torah seems to be introducing Noah's offspring, it in fact describes his righteousness before listing his children. The Midrash sees this verse as teaching that the main "offspring" of people are their righteous deeds and their spiritual accomplishments (*Rashi*).

R' Elazar Azkari (*Sefer HaChareidim*) elucidates the perspective expressed in the Midrash.

Certainly, one must expend endless energy and effort to ensure that his offspring develop into God-fearing servants of Hashem who maximize their spiritual potential and accomplish their Heavenly mission in life; however one must first ascertain that he himself is pleasing in the eyes of God. If he is comparable to a delightful tree with his actions its desirable fruit, then the Master of the Garden will see to it that he produces seedlings of equal quality.[1] The Torah therefore introduces Noah's offspring by noting that Noah himself was a righteous man who was able to produce children of his caliber.

According to *R' Yaakov Aaron of Aleksander* the Torah alludes to this idea with the words *these are the offspring of Noah, Noah . . .* Noah understood that one's primary offspring is oneself. He did not abandon his own growth in order to invest in his children; he understood that a great father sets an example that produces great children.[2]

---

1. **Do as I Do.** If we want our children to take Torah study seriously, then they must see us learning even at the expense of self-sacrifice. If we want our children to view the service of God as the primary agenda of life, then our actions have to send them that message. If we hope that our children will enjoy domestic bliss and harmony and will know how to show love and care for those around them, then we must, by our actions and words, be their role models. If we are to have any chance of inculcating our offspring with a passion for charity, then they must see us giving with a smile and with sensitivity to the human dignity of those to whom we give, even when it is difficult. The main offspring of the righteous are their good deeds which shape the minds and hearts of their descendants.

2. **Spiritual Self-Sufficiency.** *Beis HaLevi* expressed it succinctly when he said, "Although the Talmud teaches that a child grants merit to his father (*Sanhedrin* 104a), I always pray that I should not need that merit."

   R' Yitzchak Hutner once suggested to *R' Shlomo Freifeld* that he undertake to learn certain profound areas of Torah. When R' Shlomo claimed that doing so would force him to curtail his involvement with his students, R' Hutner replied, "When a mother eats well, it is good for her children."

צַדִּיק תָּמִים הָיָה בְּדֹרֹתָיו

[Noah was] a righteous man,
perfect in his generations (ibid.)

The phrase *in his generations* implies that Noah's righteousness was relative to the period in which he lived. Some Sages view this as praise of Noah; he was righteous even though he was surrounded by corruption, but if he had lived in the times of Abraham, the positive exposure would have propelled him to far-greater spiritual achievements. Others interpret it the opposite way: only in this corrupt generation was Noah considered righteous; in Abraham's times, he would not have been considered extraordinary in comparison with Abraham.

Mizrachi notes that the two approaches are not necessarily exclusive and in fact are complementary. Had Noah been a contemporary of Abraham, he would have achieved even more as a result of Abraham's powerful influence, but he would never have become an Abraham. Only in his own generation could his righteousness play such a significant role.[3]

The obvious question is why the Torah's words should be interpreted in a pejorative sense when they could just as well be understood positively.[4]

Beis Avraham suggests that it was Noah himself who was critical of his "righteousness."[5] "In a generation as corrupt as this, even I am considered a righteous man. Were I to be among the truly righteous, like Abraham, I would be recognized as the nobody I really am."

In a variation on this theme, *R' Yitzchak of Radzivil* views the critical interpretation of the verse as a paraphrase of Noah's self-criticism and his attempt to temper his feelings of arrogance. Given the moral climate of his generation, Noah felt somewhat smug about his greatness. However, one who is truly righteous does not take personal pride in his own spiritual superiority. Thus *Noah was* [aware that he was] *righteous* [because he functioned] *in his generations.*

He therefore rebuked himself by contemplating what his status would have been in the times of Abraham. "If I could have been born in a generation like Abraham's, I might have observed the humility he expressed when he said, '*I am but dust and ash*' (*Genesis* 18:27). Then I would realize that I am really nothing."

---

3. **Overcoming Adversity:** The *Chazon Ish* submits that the two interpretations reflect dual aspects of the same reality. One who functions in a society where spirituality is at best insignificant, if not scorned, is bound to be spiritually dragged down by his surroundings. As *Rambam* (*Hilchos Deios* 6:1) writes, "People's actions and character are deeply affected by the opinions, actions and spiritual level of their friends and acquaintances." Thus in an objective sense, Noah never became the great man he would have been had he lived in the generation of Abraham. The amount of emotional energy required to overcome his society's negative atmosphere was so great that he did not have enough left over to propel him to even higher levels of growth.

On the other hand, the spiritual level Noah *did* succeed in reaching was phenomenal, given the prevailing atmosphere. Growth, under such circumstances, even limited growth, is of inestimable value.

During the period between the world wars, when the spiritual level of Eastern Jewry was declining, the *Chafetz Chaim* often wrote that even small spiritual accomplishments were as significant as great gains in earlier centuries. In the 1920's and 30's, the obstacles to Jewish observance were very great; at such a time, even relatively minor growth required great inner strength.

4. **Rising Above.** The *Alter of Novardok* suggests that the negative interpretation of this verse does not reflect badly on Noah; rather, it defines the driving force behind his righteousness.

When Noah saw the subhuman level of decadence to which society had fallen, he made a herculean effort to distance himself from the prevailing spiritual climate. As a result, he evolved into a righteous person. Had he lived in Abraham's generation, nothing would have forced him to grow and he might have remained a complacent mediocrity. In such a generation he would have been an insignificant player.

Noah's strength of character and his willingness to be different stand as an example to us. When everything around us is corrupt, we must feel so repulsed that we are compelled to grow in righteousness.

5. **Rabbinic Positivist.** *Shem MiShmuel* notes that *Rashi* refers to those who interpret the phrase in a positive sense as "our Rabbis" while the negative explanation is introduced as "according to others." The Sages explained the verse in a positive vein while others (namely Noah himself) offered a far less flattering interpretation.

According to *R' Yisrael of Tchortkov*, those who view people in a positive light deserve the appellation "our Rabbis" since their perspective should be emulated. We should not adopt negativists as our mentors.

[It is noteworthy that *Rambam* describes an authentic Torah scholar as one who "judges all people favorably and always speaks the praises of others, never focusing on their flaws" (*Hilchos Deios* 5:7).]

תָּמִים הָיָה בְּדֹרֹתָיו אֶת הָאֱלֹהִים הִתְהַלֶּךְ נֹחַ

Perfect in his generations,
Noah walked with God (ibid.).

How often do we avoid virtuous company in order to compare ourselves to those on lower spiritual levels thus inflating our own egos?

Noah was perfect and humble in spite of the gaping chasm between his spiritual level and that of his generation. What kept him humble was the fact that *Noah walked with God,* always aware that compared to what he owed God and how far he was from Him, he fell terribly short of what he should be (*Noam Megadim*).[6]

What does it mean to "walk with God"?

R' Avraham of Slonim offers a parable: A merchant traveled to the great fair to purchase merchandise. On the way he passed through many towns and hamlets. Obviously, he did not have the slightest reason to be there, except that he had to pass through them to arrive at the fair. So too, Noah. He passed through his generations in an entirely incidental way. In reality, he was on his way to come close to God. *Noah walked with God.* [7]

וַתִּשָּׁחֵת הָאָרֶץ לִפְנֵי הָאֱלֹהִים וַתִּמָּלֵא הָאָרֶץ חָמָס

Now the earth had become corrupt before God; and the earth had become filled with robbery (ibid. 11).

Sin and immorality are not merely instances of misbehavior which brand the perpetrator as a wicked person. Sin creates an impurity that pervades all of existence, so that even the inanimate elements of one's surroundings are tainted.

Rashi (verse 12) notes that even the animals began to cohabit with other species. Since man sets the tone of the entire world, his manner of behavior affects his surroundings. When men begin practicing perversion, the very air is polluted with immorality. Thus the earth became corrupt as a result of the human model (*R' Elazar M. Shach*).

In spite of the pervasive nature of immorality and its effect on the surroundings, the people did not sense that anything was wrong. The spiritual cancer had eaten so deeply into the people that they failed to see the depths to which they had fallen. Immorality became a legitimate "alternative lifestyle." *The earth had become corrupt* but only *before God,* but not before man. Drowning in his own spiritual quagmire, man lost the sensitivity to realize how deficient his character had become.

At this stage, rebuke would not help, because people saw themselves as paragons of virtue and upstanding members of society (*R' Shlomo Ganzfried; Alter of Kelm*).

The *Maggid of Mezritch* homiletically relates the moral breakdown to a corrupt sense of priorities. The corruption came about when, in the minds of the populace, physical pleasure came before God and His spiritual agenda.[8]

---

6. **Penetrating Rebuke.** The *Baal HaTanya* once asked a preacher to offer him rebuke; this is what he told him: "Whatever I know, you also know; whatever you don't know, I don't know either. So what is the difference between us? Those things that you know and I don't. However, the gap between what you know and I don't is much smaller than the chasm between what God knows and you don't." The *Baal HaTanya* cried.

7. **Sifting for Jewels.** "Man! View the mundane activities of life as if you were sifting the sand in search of a precious jewel. Once you find the jewel you will discard the sand." Service of God is the jewel; all the rest is sand. Never confuse the goal with the means to achieve it (*Sefer HaChareidim*).

Chassidim of Lechovitch used to say that the body is much like a pair of boots one puts on when ready to walk across the muddy street in the middle of the winter. He wears them in order not to get dirty. The body, too, is here to assure that the soul not be soiled by being in places where it will be sullied by spiritual mud.

8. **Penultimate Safety Net.** Many of the interpersonal *mitzvos* are moral imperatives which theoretically would be followed by man regardless of his attitude toward *mitzvos* between man and God. For example, even if one does not observe Shabbos, one understands that it is wrong to steal. Nevertheless, if people do not possess a healthy dose of fear of Heaven, there are no guarantees with regard to *mitzvos* between man and man either.

A classic example of this phenomenon is found in Abraham's response to Abimelech, when asked why he was less then forthright about his relationship to Sarah. Abraham said that she was his sister because his life would have been in danger if it had been known that she was his wife. In response to Abimelech's complaint that he had been deceptive, Abraham answered, *"Because I said, 'There is but no fear of God in this place and they will slay me*

קֵץ כָּל בָּשָׂר בָּא לְפָנַי כִּי מָלְאָה הָאָרֶץ חָמָס מִפְּנֵיהֶם

The end of all flesh has come before Me,
for the earth is filled with robbery through them
(ibid. 13).

Rashi comments that the proverbial "straw that broke the camel's back" was robbery. Although society committed gross iniquities such as idolatry, murder, and immorality, it was robbery that sealed their fate. Why was robbery viewed as such a powerful source of indictment?[9]

The *Dubno Maggid* offers a stunning parable: A man made a banquet for his acquaintances and served the finest delicacies and drinks. Suddenly, he was shocked to see the guests grabbing food from one another's plates amid screaming, cursing, pushing, and coming to blows. The host pulled the table away from his guests and announced, "Now you have nothing left to fight about."

The world and its pleasures are the feast that God prepares for man; He provides generously so that there is enough for all. Robbery indicates that man is afraid that somebody else will take away from his share, and that the only way to protect himself is to take from others. At that point

Hashem said: "I will take the table away and you won't have anything to fight over." *The end of all flesh* was brought about by the unbridled invasion of private property.

Maharal views the tragic result of rampant theft in a different light. As long as the people's sins were limited to transgressions between man and God, they had not yet corrupted their basic human decency. The chasm between God and man was still bridgeable, since God has compassion and concern for humanity. But once the social infrastructure broke down, and blatant disregard for private property became the norm, the basic foundation of humanity had collapsed. Once that happened, God no longer maintained a caring concern for the world, and the end of all flesh had come before Him.[10]

Kli Yakar suggests a homiletic rendering of the verse which carries a powerful message. Were one to live with the reality that life and its material opportunities are only temporary, he would never steal from others. It is the illusion that we are here forever that tempts us to invest energy in accruing worldly goods even through illegal and unethical means. [As the *Zohar* teaches, "Man [foolishly]

---

because of my wife' " (*Genesis* 20:11). Without fear of God even murder is a possibility.

The beginning of the verse regarding the society in which Noah lived explains the end. *The earth had become corrupt before God,* without true fear of God, and this is why *the earth had become filled with robbery.* Only ethics designed by God and practiced out of reverence for Him can survive. Take Him out of the picture and a "no-holds-barred" atmosphere prevails (*R' Yehoshua of Kutna*).

9. **Microcosmic Sin.** In a certain sense, theft really encompasses aspects of all three cardinal sins (idolatry, murder, and immorality). One who truly believes in God knows that everything he has is because He wants him to have it. Therefore, in a subtle sense, one who robs his fellow is like an idolater, for he believes that he must take his destiny into his own hands.

One who forces others to give him their property, even if he pays for it, and then derives enjoyment from that property, is to a degree comparable to an adulterer, for obvious reasons. Theft is related to murder, for the theft of someone's property may impoverish him and harm him emotionally (see *S'machos* 2:11).

Thus theft was the sin that doomed the world (*Avnei Nezer*).

10. **Moral Hypocrisy.** *Divrei Shaul* invokes a parable from *R' Berachiah HaNakdan's Mishlei Shualim* to explain why theft was the final blow that doomed Noah's generation to destruction. A stork stuck its long beak into a lake and caught a fish. Before the stork could swallow it, the fish opened its mouth and began to beg for its life. "Please," the fish implored, "don't kill me. Don't destroy one of God's creatures." As the fish was opening its mouth to plead its case, a small fish was dislodged out of the captured fish.

The stork exclaimed "Fraud that you are! You devour your own brother fish, yet you want me to have mercy and spare you!"

Many horrible sins might have indicted the people of that generation, but in His mercy, God did not punish them. But once God saw how they cruelly and callously robbed one another, His mercy was no longer aroused. He has mercy on those who are merciful to others. Those who are cruel toward their fellow man can expect no compassion from Above. Theft did not cause them to be punished; it caused God to rescind His mercy. Therefore, theft sealed their fate.

believes that the whole world is his and will be his forever.]

"קֵץ כָּל בָּשָׂר, *the end of all flesh* — the angel of death — *has come before Me,"* says God. "He complains that mankind is steeped in a life of larceny because no one remembers him."

צֹהַר תַּעֲשֶׂה לַתֵּבָה
A window you shall make for the Ark (ibid. 16).

Some commentators say that this verse refers to a skylight or window while others understand it to mean a precious stone that would refract the outside light and illuminate the Ark within (*Rashi*).

The function of the window was not limited to letting in light; it was also meant for those inside to be able to see the cataclysmic destruction raging around them. By allowing the survivors to witness the Flood, God ensured that they felt the pain of the victims and did not become callous to human suffering (*R' Moshe Shatzkes*).[11]

Borrowing the Mishnaic idiom in which תֵּיבָה means *word, Sfas Emes* suggests homiletically that the "words" of one's prayers and Torah study save him from the deluge of crass materialism and hedonistic obsession that floods the world.[12]

The *Zohar* teaches that the name נֹחַ alludes to the Sabbath, which is a day of מְנוּחָה (spiritual rest). Just as Noah was the one who saved the world from being totally destroyed by the Flood, so the Sabbath saves a Jew from being overwhelmed by the mundane spirit that accompanies his weekday pursuits.

The Ark had a precious stone to light up the surrounding physical darkness. We, in turn, must make the Sabbath a day that casts its light on our entire earthly existence.[13], [14]

---

11. **Righteousness Link.** The *Chasam Sofer* links the question of whether the צֹהַר was a window or a precious stone to the debate of whether Noah was deemed righteous only in comparison with his generation or whether the Torah views him as an objectively great man regardless of his contemporaries. Noah was objectively righteous; he was entitled to view the destruction of the victims. God therefore instructed him to make a window which would simultaneously provide light and allow him to view the world's disintegration before his eyes.

According to those who see Noah's greatness as only relative to his society, it is improbable that God would allow him to see the destruction of those outside of the Ark. In this sense, he was similar to Lot's wife who was severely punished for looking back at the destruction of Sodom since she deserved the same fate. According to this view, the צֹהַר was not transparent — it was a precious stone.

12. **Idle Talk.** A somewhat simple fellow, who was rather arrogant to boot, read in a holy book that one who does not speak any idle talk for forty consecutive days will merit that the Holy Spirit will rest upon him. The man did so for forty days — but there was no Holy Spirit! Disappointed, he traveled to the *Baal Shem Tov* to ask him why his efforts were unrewarded.

The *Baal Shem Tov* asked him, "Did you pray during those forty days?" "Of course," the man replied. "Three times a day." "And did you recite the Psalms?" the *Baal Shem Tov* queried further. "Definitely," replied the "saint." "Well, there is your answer," said the *Baal Shem Tov*. "There you have the idle talk you thought you didn't speak."

Prayer is not merely reciting from page 2 to page 84 in the *siddur*. R' Chaim Kenig suggests that sometimes we think of prayer as mouthing the right words. A Jew must put his heart and soul into the words of his prayers, illuminating them with the very essence of his soul. Anything less is tantamount to idle talk.

13. **Seventh Day Haven.** The power of the Sabbath to serve as a haven from the mundane is alluded to by the *gematria* (numerical value) of this verse. *You shall make a* צֹהַר, a source of light for the תֵּבָה. The numerical value of צהר = 295 and that of תבה = 407. The combined value is 702, the same as the numerical value of Shabbos.

14. **Sanctified Ark.** R' Yitzchak Hutner said that yeshivah students in our times have a greater obligation than those of earlier times to sense the great privilege and joy of learning and living in a yeshivah. He explained:

If a doctor were to tell a patient that unless he eats delicacies reserved for royalty he will die of hunger, it would be clear to the patient that his condition is critical. Under normal circumstances, royal delicacies and hunger are polar extremes; remarkably, however, the Torah speaks in such extreme terms. We say every day in the second

וַאֲנִי הִנְנִי מֵבִיא אֶת הַמַּבּוּל
And as for me — Behold, I am about to bring the Flood waters (ibid. 17).

The prophet refers to the Deluge as *the waters of Noah* (*Isaiah* 54:9), implying that he was partially to blame for the Flood. According to the *Zohar*, Noah was, to a great degree, responsible for the Flood since, unlike Abraham, he did not actively seek to reform the people of his times by bringing them closer to God. Excessively humble, he did not believe that he could affect his surroundings and merely built the Ark, responding to any questions with the news that God was planning to bring a flood (*Shem MiShmuel*)

Alshich views this unwillingness to influence others as alluded to in God's call to Noah to build the Ark, as it is written *Make for yourself an Ark* (verse 14). God saw in Noah someone who could not actively rebuke his generation and was concerned only for his own family. Since he showed no interest in living with others and sharing their company, God put him into the Ark where he would live with animals.

The *Midrash HaNe'elam* elaborates: When Noah eventually left the Ark he looked around at a world destroyed and cried, "You Who are called a Merciful God, where is Your mercy? Why didn't You have mercy on Your creatures?" God replied,

"Foolish shepherd, *now* you say this!? When I told you *I am about to bring the Flood waters,* you didn't even think about the terrible fate of the world. You focused only on the fact that you were to be saved by entering the Ark." Although Noah was righteous, his humility paralyzed his ability to reach out to help save others.

וַיַּעַשׂ נֹחַ כְּכֹל אֲשֶׁר צִוָּה אֹתוֹ אֱלֹקִים כֵּן עָשָׂה
Noah did according to everything God commanded him, so he did (ibid. 22).

According to *Rashi,* this verse refers to God's command to build the Ark, while the later repetition of this phrase (7:5) speaks of the command to enter the Ark.

Maharsham views the verse as testimony to Noah's pure, unselfish intent in building the Ark. There are *mitzvos* from which one derives personal physical pleasure; eating matzah at the Seder is but one example of a mitzvah that provides physical enjoyment. When one performs such a mitzvah it is difficult to ascertain the purity of his motives, for he might be doing it for personal pleasure. Only when one fulfills a mitzvah from which he derives no personal gain may we assess his level of altruistic commitment. Thus the *mitzvos* which provide no physical enjoyment shed light on the level of one's

---

paragraph of the *Shema. Beware for yourself, lest your heart be seduced and you turn astray and serve gods of others . . .* (*Deuteronomy* 11:16). *Rashi* explains *you turn astray* as referring to laxity in Torah study. Torah study is equal to the royal delicacies of Hashem, yet if we refrain from them we will soon find ourselves serving other gods, the ultimate form of spiritual starvation. How is this possible? The answer lies in an axiom of spiritual physics. The soul abhors a vacuum. If the soul is emptied of Torah, it quickly becomes filled up with the worst forms of spiritual toxins (see *Rambam, Hilchos Isurei Biah* 22:21).

The Torah speaks twice of building: building the Ark and building the *Mishkan* (Tabernacle). We were commanded to erect a *Mishkan* (and later the Temple) during periods in which the surrounding atmosphere pulsated with an intense spirituality. It was in such times that God commanded us to erect a central establishment in which the Divine Presence could concentrate itself.

The Ark, on the other hand, was a means of survival in a world deluged by the unleashed forces of destruction.

Once, a yeshivah was exclusively a *Mishkan,* a spiritual epicenter in a society whose atmosphere was a living expression of Torah and Godliness.

Today we live in the times of a Flood. Outside there is a torrential downpour of immorality, heresy, and materialistic decadence. The only way to save oneself is to escape to the world of Torah and its communities. Today a yeshivah is both a *Mishkan* and an Ark.

The *Mishkan* is spiritually a luxury and a royal delicacy, while the Ark is a means for survival. Today's yeshivah students find themselves in a rare situation. If they do not partake of the royal delicacies of living in a *Mishkan,* they face the fate of one trapped in a deluge without an Ark.

Thus today's students have a unique reason to rejoice over the privilege of living and learning in a yeshivah.

fulfillment of the enjoyable *mitzvos*. [15]

Noah had a vested interest in the Ark's construction since it would serve as a refuge for him and his family; therefore his motives in building it may have been tainted. The Torah testifies that Noah did everything for the sake of Heaven — even the building of the Ark. He built the Ark just as he performed all the other tasks he was assigned — *according to everything God commanded him.*

Background

As the end approached and God was ready to unleash the torrential downpour of the Flood, He called on Noah to enter the Ark with his family and to gather the nucleus of animal life, from which the new world would be born.

כִּי אֹתְךָ רָאִיתִי צַדִּיק לְפָנַי בַּדּוֹר הַזֶּה

for it is you that I have seen to be righteous before Me in this generation (7:1).

Earlier the Torah describes Noah as "perfectly righteous" (see 6:9), yet here, when speaking directly to Noah, God addresses him simply as "righteous." The Sages derive from this that praise offered to others in their presence should be partial, but if they are not present, their praises may be given in full.[16]

Maharal (*Nesiv HaTochachah* Ch. 1) explains that to offer total praise smacks of flattery, a trait that the Sages scorned. On the other hand, one should speak *partial* praise when addressing a person, since this advances interpersonal love. When one hears that his friend views him in a positive light, he too develops positive feelings toward his friend.

כִּי לְיָמִים עוֹד שִׁבְעָה אָנֹכִי מַמְטִיר עַל הָאָרֶץ

For in seven more days I will send rain upon the earth (ibid. 4).

Rashi (citing *Sanhedrin* 108b) submits that the additional days were the seven days of mourning for Methuselah (Noah's righteous grandfather) . . . who had just passed away. God delayed the beginning of the Flood in his honor.

R' Elazar M. Shach explains, based on a comment of the *Vilna Gaon*, that Divine justice is so exact that God does not punish a person if innocent parties will suffer as a result. For example, only if one's family also deserves punishment will God punish a sinner, because otherwise the family will suffer unjustly.

God decided to punish humanity for its reprehensible moral breakdown, but He would not do so at the expense of Methuselah's honor. Only after Methuselah was properly mourned would God bring the Deluge.

Taam V'Daas sees here a lesson regarding man's potential to repent. We often are so obsessed by the pursuit of pleasure and livelihood that we fail to focus on the temporary nature of life. When, however, we hear of the death of a righteous person, we are frequently inspired to seek the truth and rectify our own lifestyle. It is for this reason that we eulogize the righteous; we hope that their lives will inspire us to change ours.

It was because of this potential for inspiration that God delayed the Flood. God hoped that the evil generation that had failed to repent even after hundred years of warnings about the impending Deluge might still be brought back from the brink of destruction during the mourning period of Methuselah. Perhaps his death and the inspiring

---

15. **Litmus Test.** Colloquially, the third Sabbath meal is called שָׁלֹשׁ סְעוּדוֹת (literally *three meals*) rather than סְעוּדָה שְׁלִישִׁית, *the third meal*. Why?

Since the first two meals are eaten at normal mealtimes when people are usually hungry, one might have them simply to satisfy his hunger. The third meal, eaten in late afternoon when one is still satiated from his midday meal, is clearly eaten in order to fulfill the mitzvah. Hence it is proof of the person's commitment to fulfill God's will, even when he stands to gain nothing. This indicates that all three meals were eaten for the sake of Heaven. Therefore, the third meal is referred to as "three meals."

16. **Prestige as Kindness.** [People are often wary of praising others, thinking in some distorted way that it might take away from their own prestige. The Sages therefore tell us that we should lavishly praise our fellow Jew in his absence. It is a shining example of kindness to add to another's prestige.]

story of his life could accomplish what nothing else had.[17]

וַיָּבֹא נֹחַ . . . מִפְּנֵי מֵי הַמַּבּוּל
Noah . . . went into the Ark because of the waters of the Flood (ibid. 7).

This verse implies that only in face of the rising waters did Noah and his family enter the Ark. In the words of *Rashi*, Noah was מִקְּטַנֵּי אֲמָנָה, *a man of diminished faith,* מַאֲמִין וְאֵינוֹ מַאֲמִין שֶׁיָּבֹא הַמַּבּוּל, *he believed and yet he didn't believe that the Flood would come to pass.*

How is it possible that Noah, whom the Torah describes as perfectly righteous, could suffer from flawed faith?

R' Simchah Zissel of Kelm offers a parable that explains the idea of various levels of faith and how one's faith can become diminished:

David asked Michael if Daniel is trustworthy. "Of course," replied Michael. "You can trust him without reservation." Michael really believes this to be so and will certainly be ready to extend a modest loan to Daniel should he request one. Nevertheless, if Daniel wanted to borrow a large amount of money, Michael might have second thoughts. "Is he *really* that reliable? Can I *really* trust him?"

This is what the Sages meant when they said מַאֲמִין וְאֵינוֹ מַאֲמִין, *he believed and yet he didn't believe.* Faith must be unlimited and unconditional. When we place our faith in Hashem on a limited basis we believe and yet we don't truly believe. Faith is authentic only when that which we believe is as real to us as that which we see with our eyes. Anything less is flawed faith.

This is the message of *R' Eliezer HaGadol*: "One who has bread for today yet asks, 'What will I eat tomorrow?' suffers from flawed faith" (*Sotah* 48b). Faith must grant such a clarity of vision that what we believe is no less a reality than what we see; the bread I have in my basket right now must be no more real to me than the bread I am sure Hashem will provide for me tomorrow. Thus, one who has bread today yet asks, "What will I eat tomorrow?" suffers from flawed faith.

Noah was a righteous and believing person. However, seeing the waters rise was more of a reality to him than his faithful belief in God's promise that He would bring the Deluge. He believed, yet he did not believe fully (*R' Yerucham Levovitz of Mir*).[18]

Oheiv Yisrael views this "flaw" in faith in a positive light. Faith has the power to create reality. One's powerful faith and trust in Hashem can cause his desires and hopes to become real. Therefore, while Noah truly believed that the Flood would happen, he was afraid of believing it too firmly, for fear that his faith might *cause* it to happen. Thus he found himself in a dilemma — he believed God's word, yet he didn't want to believe for fear of causing the Flood. Only when he saw the rising waters and realized that his "lack of faith" would not make a difference did he enter the Ark.[19]

---

17. **Setting Our Sights High.** [The death of great people and their biographies often elicit inappropriate responses. Comments such as, "An era is over; we will never have people like him again" or "This person was so great; I will never be able to be like him," may well induce despair and self-pity. To the contrary, let us view the great people who have passed on as a source of inspiration, teaching us how one can take charge of his life. Even if we will never achieve their greatness, we can use their examples in order to shape our own destiny.]

18. **Believing Is Greater than Seeing.** This almost blind reliance on faith, even more than on sensual perception, explains a statement of the Talmud. The Sages ask, "How do we know that Babylonia is to the north of *Eretz Yisrael*?" They answer that the prophecy "The evil will develop from the north" (*Jeremiah* 1:14) implies that the Babylonian kingdom would conquer the Land and destroy the Temple (*Bava Basra* 25b).

Any traveler from *Eretz Yisrael* knows that Babylonia lies to the north; why did the Sages need a verse to establish what anyone can see? The answer is that the Sages' belief in Torah was so powerful that to them, a verse in the Torah is more of a reality than sensual perception.

19. **Hoping Against Hope.** *R' Yitzchak of Vorki* alters the punctuation of *Rashi* to offer an enchanting homiletic interpretation. נֹחַ מִקְּטַנֵּי אֲמָנָה הָיָה מַאֲמִין, Noah believed in those of diminished faith, and hoped that they would repent before God unleashed the Flood. Therefore וְאֵינוֹ מַאֲמִין שֶׁיָּבֹא הַמַּבּוּל, he did not believe that the Deluge would come, certain that the people would repent at the eleventh hour.

וַיְהִי הַגֶּשֶׁם עַל הָאָרֶץ אַרְבָּעִים יוֹם וְאַרְבָּעִים לָיְלָה
*And the rain was on the earth
forty days and forty nights* (ibid. 12).

Why did Hashem destroy the world with water? Furthermore, what is the significance of forty days and nights?

Maharal (*Gur Aryeh* on *Deuteronomy* 25:3) explains that in spite of the Biblical injunction *forty* [lashes] *shall he strike him,* the Sages rule only thirty-nine lashes are necessary (see *Makkos* 22b).

The Midrash says that the forty lashes administered in punishment for certain sins correspond to the forty days during which an embryo is formed. In fact, however, the Sages explained the verse to mean that only thirty-nine lashes are given, not forty. When man sins, his corporeal being must be cleansed. According to *Maharal* the body of the embryo is formed during the first thirty-nine days, and the soul enters on the fortieth day. Since the entire person, body and soul, was involved in sin, the Torah speaks of forty lashes. However after thirty-nine lashes the body is cleansed, allowing the intrinsic purity of the soul to reassert itself, and once the body is pure, the soul needs no cleansing.

Forty is the time it takes to be formed or re-formed, born or born again. Thus the Flood took forty days, the amount of time necessary for a new world to be born and emerge. The destruction of the old world allowed a new world to come into being.

New life always emerges from water. Just as a newborn emerges from the amniotic fluid, so the prelude to Creation was a world of astonishing emptiness with darkness upon the surface of the deep and the Divine Presence hovering upon the surface of the waters (see *Genesis* 1:2). Out of this water emerged a world. Here, too, the new world created after the Flood emerged from forty days and forty nights of rainfall (*Simchas Aharon*).[20]

וַיִּשָּׁאֶר אַךְ נֹחַ
Only Noah survived (ibid. 23).

Although in previous verses the Torah constantly reiterates Noah's righteousness, here he is merely called "Noah." This might be understood in light of the Midrash which teaches that Noah sinned by not praying on behalf of the people of his times and by failing to influence them to repent.

One may never try complacently to be righteous yet ignore the spiritual depravity around him, thinking that by doing so he will remain untouched on his spiritual perch. If one does nothing to improve others, then he too will fall.

Once he remained alone, only Noah [without the great righteousness] survived (*R' Meir Shapiro*).

The Midrash relates that since Noah had to single-handedly tend to the needs of an Ark full of animals he became overwhelmed by the task. Once when he was late in bringing the lion its food, the lion hit his leg and injured him.

Why should Noah receive such a stern punishment for coming late to the lion that one time?[21]

R' Eliyahu Eliezer Dessler explains: The generation

---

20. **Born Anew.** This may shed light on the secret of the *mikveh* which according to the Talmud must contain a minimum of forty *se'ah* of rain water.

R' S. R. Hirsch teaches that all *tumah* (spiritual contamination) relates to death. Corpse-*tumah* is contracted when one comes in contact with death. *Niddah* is the *tumah* which occurs when a woman's potential for creating and sustaining life temporarily breaks down. Likewise, all the other forms of *tumah* have some connection to death.

When we confront death, we must withdraw from life, face our mortality and then renew our connection to life, for only our physical being is mortal, but our spiritual existence is eternal. This cycle of mortality-immortality is the nexus of the *tumah/taharah* flux.

When we immerse in the waters of the *mikveh* we enter the "universal solvent," symbolically leaving our mortal self submerged beneath the water. We reemerge invigorated, born anew, with a powerful sense of our link to purity and eternity.

Thus the *mikveh* contains forty *se'ah* of water (*Simchas Aharon*).

21. **The Last Lion.** *R' Avraham Kalmanowitz,* one of the greatest heroes of rescue efforts during the Holocaust, once raised this question at a gathering of the American Vaad Hatzalah, an organization that exerted valiant efforts to save Jews during and after World War II: Why was Noah punished severely merely for being late one time? He answered that the animals on Noah's Ark were the survivors of a world gone by, the last remnants of the pre-Deluge world. They therefore deserved to be treated with the greatest care and concern, out of a deep sense of responsibility. This is even

of the Flood was punished due to their disregard for personal property and the accompanying breakdown of normal interpersonal relationships. Therefore, the key to being saved from the Flood and rebuilding a functional world was *chessed* (interpersonal kindness). When Noah, his children and their mates took care of thousands of living creatures for an entire year, they planted through their supreme exercise in *chessed,* the seeds of a new world. In the words of King David: עוֹלָם חֶסֶד יִבָּנֶה, *The world will be built with kindness* (*Psalms* 89:3).

The *chessed* necessary to rebuild a world in ruins had to be flawless. Noah came late once and was immediately punished, for his tardiness was an outward manifestation of an internal blemish which effected his capacity for *chessed.*

לֹא אֹסִף לְקַלֵּל עוֹד אֶת הָאֲדָמָה בַּעֲבוּר הָאָדָם כִּי יֵצֶר לֵב הָאָדָם רַע מִנְּעֻרָיו
I will not continue to curse again the ground because of man, since the imagery of man's heart is evil from his youth (8:21).

Up to this point, man's free choice had such a cosmic effect that he could cause the destruction of the world. The sphere of influence of man's choice was now narrowed. The world would always exist, regardless of his actions. This is the first instance of a בְּרִית, *covenant,* which assured uncondi-

tional survival for all that were included in the covenant (see *Ramban* to *Genesis* 6:18).

The Torah states the reason: *Since the imagery of man's heart is evil from his youth.*

Ohr HaChaim employs a halachic analogy to explain the mitigating circumstances that temper man's guilt and thus the ripple effect of his misdeeds.

A bull trained to perform in the arena is not put to death if it gored and killed a human being, even in a nonsport setting. Since this is what it was trained to do, we do not view its goring as an indication of intrinsic perversion, but rather as a result of its training (see *Bava Kamma* 39a).

Here the Torah teaches that when man sins it is often the result of a built-in propensity to sin, rather than a conscious decision to do evil. The evil inclination trains us to sin; therefore, we are not entirely at fault. Sin is not a clear indication of moral and ethical decay; it may simply be inner coercion brought on by habituation.

Maasei Hashem adds: In a certain sense, God understands that man's sins are not a result of moral decay, nor because he is intrinsically evil.[22] Man is evil due to his youthful foolishness.

Just as humanity at large was young and foolish when the earlier generations sinned, so every person has inside himself a young fool who is controlled by the "old king," the evil inclination (See *Zohar* I:179).[23]

---

more so because Noah himself was a survivor, who understood the level of sensitivity required of him. It is not surprising, therefore, that he was punished for a slight oversight. "We too," R' Avraham concluded, "are survivors of a world we will never see again. It is especially incumbent upon us to bear the responsibility of expending superhuman effort in order to save our brothers and sisters and aid them in reconstructing their lives."

22. **Intrinsically Good.** *Rabbi Shlomo Freifeld* once told a young man who had led a tragic life and fought valiantly (though not always successfully) to keep his head spiritually above water, "Chaim, you are not a bad person. You're a good person with a big *yetzer hara* (evil inclination). When you mess up spiritually, don't think that it defines you as a bad person. You're a good person who did something wrong. Pick yourself up and start doing *mitzvos* and good things again. That's the real you."

R' Mordechai of Lechovitch said: "A Jew who is not ready, the moment after he did a terrible sin, to stand in front of Hashem and pour his heart out in prayer has yet to step over the threshold of *chassidus.*" He paused for a moment and continued, "No! No! He has yet to step over the threshold of *Yiddishkeit* (Judaism)."

23. **Misplaced Passions.** *R' Shlomo of Karlin* raised his eyes to Heaven and said, "Save me, O Hashem, from the evil inclination who is so much more powerful than I. He is an angel who needs neither to eat nor drink nor support a wife and a family, but I am a mere mortal. He fulfills his mission to entice me to sin with no one standing in his way. He has no evil inclination to stop him while I . . . "

The *Shpoler Zeide* put it this way. "Master of the world! What do You want from Your holy nation of Israel? Had You painted a portrait of the purgatory in front of their eyes and placed all of the illicit desires of this world in the famed *Mussar* work *Reishis Chochmah,* You would be entitled to have complaints to Your people as to why they are not afraid to sin. Now, however, that You did just the opposite, gross passions dance in front of their eyes, while the image of *Gehinnom* is buried someplace deep inside the *Reishis Chochmah.* How do you expect them not to sin?!"

פרשת לך לך ⋖
Parashas Lech Lecha

Background

The Torah now begins the story of Abraham and his descendants who would eventually become the nation charged with achieving God's goals in Creation. The first step in the birth of the nation was for Abraham to leave his birthplace behind and set out on a spiritual trek, spreading the word of God along the way.[1]

וַיֹּאמֶר ה׳ אֶל אַבְרָם לֶךְ לְךָ מֵאַרְצְךָ
Hashem said to Abram,
"Go for yourself from your land" (12:1).

Ramban wonders why the Torah describes the righteousness of Noah as a prelude to his being chosen by God for his historical role, yet says nothing of Abraham's spiritual greatness before speaking of God's choosing him.

Maharal sees this question as opening a window on the unique relationship between God and the Jewish people. Were the Torah to say that God chose Abraham because of his great deeds, one might infer that the closeness to God that he and his descendants enjoyed is contingent on their righteous behavior. Such a relationship is fragile by its very nature, as the *Mishnah* teaches, "Any love that depends on a specific cause, when that cause is gone, the love is gone" (*Avos* 5:19). Israel's relationship with God is based on its essence rather than its behavior. The covenant between God and Israel is inviolable, it cannot be nullified by

---

1. **Discovering God.** *Rambam* (*Hilchos Avodas Kochavim* 1:1-3) describes the evolution of idolatry in the world and Abraham's role in combating it.

Initially, people rationalized that since the sun, moon and stars are "aides" of God, they deserve to be praised and to be given recognition, just as one honors the ministers of a ruler. Eventually, people began to believe that the heavenly bodies are autonomous and that they affect human destiny; therefore one should revere and serve them. Certain charlatans went further and claimed that the heavenly bodies "spoke" to them and "revealed" the appropriate ways in which they should be served. Eventually the One God was forgotten and the masses knew only what they had been taught, namely, to serve idols. Only rare individuals such as Enoch, Methuselah, Noah, Shem and Eber still recognized the true Creator. This state of affairs continued until Abraham was born.

At the age of 3, he began to contemplate nature. Day and night he was obsessed by the question of how a planet could be in perpetual motion without a Mover. He had neither teacher nor instructor, and was surrounded by family and friends who served idols, but his heart drew him onward in his pursuit until he eventually perceived the path of truth and righteousness and came to the realization that there is One God. At the age of 40, when Abraham came to fully recognize God, he began to teach monotheism and engage in debates with his countrymen, seeking to prove it to them. He physically smashed their idols in an attempt to show them the futility of serving wood and stone and to impress upon them that Hashem is the only true God. When he succeeded in convincing people of God's existence, the ruler of the time, Nimrod, had him thrown into a burning furnace in order to silence him. God miraculously saved him and he left Ur Kasdim for Haran. Gradually, but surely, tens of thousands of people accepted his message and gathered around him as he made his way toward the land of Canaan. He implanted this cardinal doctrine in the hearts of his followers and passed it on to his descendants.

sin or inappropriate behavior.

Thus the Torah begins its account of God's choosing Abraham with no mention of his righteousness or the reasons for which he was chosen.

The Midrash compares Abraham's discovery of God to a person wandering through a thick, overgrown forest. Suddenly, at a distance, he sees a large, brilliantly lit palace. He says to himself, "Am I to believe that this palace has no owner?" Suddenly the owner calls out to him, "I am the owner of the palace." So too, Abraham contemplated nature, sure that it must have a Master. Suddenly God spoke to him: "I am the Owner of the palace."

This Midrash is the story of man. In times when the world seems topsy-turvy, with no recognizable guiding force (God forbid), and when God seems to have absented Himself from our lives, it seems as if the palace is on fire with no one in control. This is the perspective of our flesh and blood eyes.

Those, however, who are in search of God, suddenly sense Him peeking through the veil and calling out to them, "I am the Owner of the Palace" (*Nesivos Shalom*).[2]

לֶךְ לְךָ
Go for yourself (ibid.).

This phrase can be rendered as *Go to yourself.* God calls upon every Jew to discover his essential self and to make every effort to quantify it. We must tap into our own intrinsic potential and become ourselves; However, he does not expect us to be anyone other than ourselves. As *R' Zusia of Anipoli* said, "In Heaven they won't ask me why I didn't become the *Baal Shem Tov* because I'm not the *Baal Shem Tov*. But what will I answer when they ask me why I didn't become Zusia?" (*R' Avraham Chen*).[3]

R' Gedaliah Schorr interprets *Go to yourself* as an expression of the test involved in God's command. Generally, we merit Divine assistance in our efforts to serve God. When He tests us, however, He abandons us to our own abilities so that we must stand on our own merit. A verse about King Chizkiyahu bears this out: "God abandoned him to test him in order to know that which is in his heart" (*II Chronicles* 32:31). When man is tested, the only source of strength that remains with him is his fear of Heaven.[4]

Rashi explains לֶךְ לְךָ as *Go for yourself,* for your own benefit and your own good. But if God told him clearly that the move away from his land and birthplace was for Abraham's benefit, why is it reckoned among the ten tests that Abraham underwent (see *Avos* 5:3 and *Pirkei Avos Treasury* ad loc.)?

Panim Yafos and *Sfas Emes* explain:

To fulfill a Divine command for the sake of Heaven is not easy. However it is far more difficult for a person to do something solely for the sake of Heaven if he benefits directly from it. Here, even though God told him that the trek to the Holy Land would bring him personal benefit, Abraham did so exclusively in order to obey the word of Hashem.

2. **Inestimable Greatness.** A Jew once came to *Rabbi Shlomo of Lutzk* to share his spiritual woes. "I want desperately to cleave to Hashem and those who fear Him, yet my worldly preoccupations distract me. There are even times when I temporarily forget about Him. What shall I do?" R' Shlomo wondered aloud, "God's greatness is inestimable. The entire cosmos is but a mustard seed when compared to Him. How can so small a world block out so tremendous a God?"

3. **Land of Self-Discovery.** *Olelos Ephraim* expands on this theme. When God commanded Abraham to go to the Land of Israel, He said, *Go to yourself.* The Jewish soul can reach its full potential only in its natural habitat — the Land on which God sets His eyes from the beginning of the year to its end (see *Deuteronomy* 11:12). When a Jew goes to the Land of Israel he is really on the path to self-discovery.

4. **Parental Support.** When teaching a child to walk, the parent holds his hands, steadying him and insuring that he does not fall. In order to see if the child has learned to walk on his own the parent must let go, but a loving parent will do so only when she is sure that the child can successfully pass the test. Hashem is our parent. Until we learn to stand spiritually on our own two feet, He supports us, helping us succeed. At a certain point, He tests us by figuratively telling us, "Go to yourself" — now you must withstand spiritual tribulation according to the level of your own fear of Heaven. We must garner the courage to pass the test from our knowledge that, as a loving Father, God will never abandon us unless He is sure we are capable of passing the test.

His personal gain played no role in his decision to comply. *So Abram went as Hashem had spoken to him* (ibid. 4) bears this out. In spite of the promise of personal benefit, Abraham went only in obedience to Hashem's command.[5]

Additionally, the promise that withstanding this trial would be for his good might be understood in light of the following incident:

R' Nachum of Chernobyl devoted his entire being to the mitzvah of ransoming captives. He would go from door to door, raising the exorbitant sums necessary to free the unfortunate victims of anti-Semitic violence and extortion.

Once, when he was in Zhitomir, local ruffians besmirched his name before the municipal powers, who promptly jailed him. R' Nachum tried to understand why he was jailed while attempting to do a mitzvah. That night, he dreamt the following dream regarding the reason for which Abraham was commanded to leave his birthplace:

Since Abraham was the paragon of hospitality, he was constantly in search of new ideas about how to perform this mitzvah in a better way. Hashem therefore told him, "Go out in exile, and become a wandering guest. Then and only then, will you fully understand the discomfort of a wanderer. Thus the wandering is for *your* benefit, for it will help you fulfill the mitzvah in a more perfect way."

Likewise, R' Nachum dreamt, it is from Heaven that you find yourself imprisoned. Since you are so wholeheartedly involved in freeing captives, you should feel the bitterness of imprisonment on your own flesh. Then you will appreciate your *mitzvah* even more and do it with greater alacrity.

Thus the trial is for your own good.[6]

מֵאַרְצְךָ וּמִמּוֹלַדְתְּךָ וּמִבֵּית אָבִיךָ
From your land, from your relatives and from your father's house (ibid.)

Nesivos Shalom notes that the stages of disengagement are listed in reverse order of their chronological sequence. One first leaves his father's home, then his hometown and extended family and only afterwards his land. Why is the order reversed?

The answer is that the order indicates the stages of emotional disengagement that Hashem expected of Abraham. First Abraham had to distance himself from the spiritually contaminating influences of his land. Furthermore, he had to separate himself from the negative traits of the immediate surroundings of his native habitat. In an even more radical form of emotional and psychological severance, Abraham had to free himself from all vestiges of his father's home — the place which had the greatest impact on his values and personality.

Thus the Torah lists Abraham's challenges in ascending order of difficulty. The influence of one's country is certainly less than that of one's birthplace, while that of one's birthplace can in no way

---

5. **Selfless Reward.** A comment of *R' Chaim of Volozhin* might suggest a different approach. Antignos Ish Socho (*Avos* 1:3) teaches that one should serve Hashem not out of a desire to be rewarded but rather out of love, yet the Talmud (*Sotah* 14a) teaches that Moses longed to enter the Holy Land in order to receive reward for the *mitzvos* that can only be performed in the Land. How are we to reconcile these seemingly contradictory statements?

R' Chaim of Volozhin explains: God, as the ultimate Good, desires to bestow His goodness on others — but if favors are not earned, they are humiliating to the recipient. In order that people can legitimately deserve His goodness, God commands us to perform *mitzvos*. One who truly loves God seeks to meet His expectations in order that He be able to bestow His kindness, as He wishes. The true lover of God wants only to enable God to bestow goodness on others; for his part, it would be just as well if the reward went to someone else.

Since, however, most of us are not on that level, Antignos felt it necessary to warn us not to serve Hashem as a servant who seeks reward. Only Moses, totally dedicated to Hashem, could legitimately want to do *mitzvos* and receive reward — in order that His desire to bestow kindness be satisfied.

It is in this vein that we may understand the test of לֶךְ לְךָ. God told Abraham to leave his land, home and birthplace. Although this move was for Abraham's own benefit and good, he was expected to obey for no other reason than to provide Hashem with an opportunity to bestow reward. As the passage concludes, *So Abraham went as Hashem had spoken to him* — not for any selfish reason (*Simchas Aharon*).

6. **Good and Beneficial.** Not always is the good pleasurable; sometimes it is painful. Conversely, many things which we enjoy immensely are really detrimental. God told Abraham that leaving his homeland and going to the Land would be both to his benefit and to his good (*R' Henach of Aleksander*).

compete with the hold of the parental home. Only after extricating himself from all these influences could Abraham begin the process of becoming a great nation.[7]

וְהְיֵה בְּרָכָה
And you shall be a blessing (ibid. 2).

Rashi (citing *Pesachim* 117b) explains that this teaches that although we mention Abraham, Isaac and Jacob in the first blessing of *Shemoneh Esrei*, the last blessing concludes with the words "Shield of Abraham." According to *Rabbi Menachem Mendel of Kotzk,* this homiletically teaches us the key to our ultimate redemption. The Mishnah (*Avos* 1:2) teaches that the world's existence depends on Torah study, on the service of God and on kind deeds. Abraham was the epitome of kindness, constantly involved in caring for others, both physically and spiritually. Isaac, himself offered as a sacrifice, was a paradigm of Divine service while Jacob the "tent dweller" — i.e., the tent of Torah study — was the model of devotion to Torah study. Before the Messiah comes, Torah study and Divine service will be greatly diminished among Jews. The saving grace of the nation will be the love and care we will show to one another (see *Isaiah* 1:27). Thus the conclusion of the exile, the last step before the redemption, will be characterized by the unique trait of Abraham.[8]

HaDerash V'Halyun offers an alternative approach. *I will bless you* with wealth *and make your name great and you shall be a blessing* (Rashi). When people become rich and famous, they often forget their less fortunate family and friends. They begin to feel that helping others is beneath their dignity. Consequently, they may acquire many enemies as a result of their newfound fame and wealth.

God promised Abraham, therefore, that riches and fame would not bring him enemies; rather, *you shall be a blessing,* blessed by all who come in contact with you.

וְאֶת הַנֶּפֶשׁ אֲשֶׁר עָשׂוּ בְחָרָן
And the souls they made in Haran (ibid. 5).

The *souls* refer to those whom Abraham and Sarah had "converted" to faith in Hashem (*Rashi*). *Targum,* in this vein, translates it as the souls they indentured to Torah [and service of God].

After Abraham's death, these converts are never mentioned again. What happened to them?

R' Henach of Aleksander explains: After Abraham's death, those converts refused to become students of Isaac, for in their eyes, he was a far cry

---

7. **Three-Tiered Disengagement.** This three-tiered disengagement mirrors the three elements necessary to produce a proper setting for educational growth: ideal surroundings and a good educational climate, genetically inherited refined character and a healthy and appropriate home atmosphere create the necessary background for educational success (*Nesivei Chinuch*). [Thus the home and background of students impacts immeasurably on the educator's chances for success.]

8. **In Abraham's Spirit.** Between the two world wars, the spiritual state of the European Jewish community was at an all-time low. Mass defection by the youth from the *yeshivos,* as well as from commitment to Torah Judaism, was reaching epidemic proportions and a sense of despair overcame much of the Jewish leadership. In those dark days *R' Shimon Shkop, Rosh Yeshivah of Grodna,* offered a novel historical approach to the idea that we conclude the first blessing of *Shemoneh Esrei* with Abraham.

Abraham came from a home of idolaters, and only on his own did he come to belief in One God. Not so Isaac or Jacob, who were propelled to their spiritual achievements as a result of the merits and education of their parents and grandparents.

One would think that this process of earlier generations building on the accomplishments of their predecessors would last forever, but the Sages taught that this is not to be. "One might think that we would conclude (the first blessing of the *Amidah*) with all of the forefathers; therefore, the Torah teaches that we conclude with Abraham." Homiletically, this teaches us that in later generations we will again see young people who, in the spirit of Abraham, will find their way to God all alone, without the benefit of parental merit or education. Even when we see mass defections, let us not despair, for although the parents may be far from Torah and *mitzvos,* the children will awaken from spiritual slumber and return.

The amazing *Teshuvah* Revolution of modern times is vibrant evidence that Jewish history will conclude with Abraham's spirit of independent discovery of God.

from his father's greatness. Under Abraham's tutelage they learned the path of kindness, hospitality and charity; Isaac followed a totally different and unfamiliar path to which Abraham's "converts" were unable to acclimate themselves. In their eyes, after Abraham there could be no teacher or mentor. They therefore disappeared from history.[9]

וַיַּעְתֵּק מִשָּׁם הָהָרָה מִקֶּדֶם לְבֵית אֵל
וַיֵּט אָהֳלֹה בֵּית אֵל מִיָּם וְהָעַי מִקֶּדֶם

From there he relocated to the mountain east of Beth-El and pitched his tent, with Beth-El on the west and Ai on the east (ibid. 8).

Why does the Torah go into such detail in its description of where Abraham lived?

The *Chafetz Chaim* explains: King Solomon teaches a fundamental principle with regard to our involvement in Torah and *mitzvos*. "If you will seek it like silver and search for it like hidden treasure, then you will achieve fear of Heaven" (*Proverbs* 2:4-5).

Just as the proper location for a business is crucial to its success, so one must live in a place that is conducive to his spiritual growth. In spirit, even more than in real estate, everything depends on "location, location, location." The Torah teaches us the extreme care Abraham took in settling in a place that would allow him full opportunity to pursue his involvement in hospitality.[10]

This verse presents another difficulty. It defines the mountain where Abraham settled in relation to Beth-El, which is necessary since the mountain is an obscure, unknown location, while the city is defined and well known. Why, then, does the Torah continue by describing Beth-El as west of Abraham's tent as if Beth-El need be defined in terms of Abraham's whereabouts?

Rabbi Yehuda Leib Fein, speaking at the dedication ceremony of the new building of Yeshivas Kletzk in Poland, explained: "I was once traveling on a train when I heard one Jew ask another, 'Where is Lida located?' His friend replied, 'It is next to Radin.' I found the response strange since I remembered from my childhood that Lida is a rather large city while Radin is a mere village. Why should one describe Lida as near Radin?

"The answer is that since Radin is the home of the *Chafetz Chaim,* who is world renowned for his books and his phenomenal righteousness, it has become a household word in the Jewish world. While it is small geographically, it is a spiritual metropolis, a much greater city than Lida. Thus the Jew was right when he said that Lida is near Radin."

Before Abraham pitched his tent on the mountain, the insignificant mountain was described as near Beth-El. However, when Abraham lived on the mountain, it was a spiritual landmark, with Beth-El a comparatively insignificant city to the west of Abraham's mountain.[11]

---

9. **Realistic Greatness.** To expect our leaders to be as great as those of yesteryear is both futile and foolish. One may never say, "Today's leaders are not like those I remember." We must accept the leader God gives us, with faith that they are the most appropriate conduits through whom God intends to guide us. In the words of the Sages, "Jephtah in his day as Samuel in his day. You have only the judge in your days." Jephtah was a far cry from Samuel by all accounts. Nevertheless, he was the judge for his times.

Yesod HaAvodah writes: "One need not believe that his teacher is the greatest man of all time or even of his generation. One must truly believe, however, that his teacher is the conduit through which God communicates with him."

10. **The Business of Torah.** The comparison of Torah and *mitzvos* to business holds some interesting lessons for us. First, we must emulate a businessman who spares no effort in order to further his financial success. A businessman never says, "I made enough money today; I will take it easy now"; likewise, we must feel that we can never have enough of Torah. Secondly, just as a businessman always seeks the most profitable deal, so we should utilize our time to reap the maximum spiritual profit.

11. **Divine Map.** On maps, a prominent dot indicates a larger city, while a smaller one denotes a town. The size of the dot depends on the population and importance of the place; villages are so small that they do not even appear on the map.

The *Ponevezher Rav* used to say that in Heaven there is a different kind of map. On that map Paris and Moscow are marked by little dots, if at all. However, Mir, Ponevezh, Ger, Sochatchov, Satmar and Slabodka are capital cities. Radin, Gateshead and Dvinsk are metropolitan centers, while London, Peking, and Washington are mere specks on the map.

Background

Immediately after Abraham settled in the Land that God had shown him, he was tested by a famine which forced him to relocate to Egypt. Although this seemingly contradicted God's promise to bless him with multileveled success, his faith never wavered. Pharaoh took Sarai (Sarah) and was punished mightily, after which Abraham left Egypt with very great wealth.

וַיְהִי רָעָב בָּאָרֶץ . . . כִּי כָבֵד הָרָעָב בָּאָרֶץ

There was a famine in the Land . . .
for the famine was severe in the Land (ibid. 10).

The Torah begins by telling us that there was famine in the Land as a result of which Abraham went down to Egypt. Why does it repeat *for the famine was severe in the Land?*[12]

Furthermore, *Ramban* submits that Abraham sinned by leaving *Eretz Yisrael*. He should have relied on God to provide him with sustenance. Why did he in fact leave for Egypt?

Mikrah Meforash explains: *Eretz Yisrael* is the Land toward which God's eyes are constantly turned, for it is there that we merit His personal attention [see *Ramban* to *Leviticus* (18:25)]. Accordingly, when He brings a famine on the Land of Israel, it is a far more intense form of "hiding His

countenance" from us than when He causes a famine elsewhere. To remain in Israel during the famine is to bear the brunt of God's "hiding from us." Thus *the famine was severe in the Land,* for besides the lack of food, Abraham would have had to bear the punishment of experiencing God's hidden face. Abraham found the thought of remaining in God's palace under such conditions unbearable. He therefore went to Egypt.[13]

וַיְהִי כַּאֲשֶׁר הִקְרִיב לָבוֹא מִצְרָיְמָה . . .
הִנֵּה נָא יָדַעְתִּי כִּי אִשָּׁה יְפַת מַרְאֶה אָתְּ

And it occurred as he was about to enter Egypt . . .
"See now, I have known that you are a woman
of beautiful appearance" (ibid. 11).

Rashi notes that until this point, Abraham had never noticed how beautiful a woman Sarah was. This seems to contradict the dictum of the Sages that one is forbidden to marry a woman sight unseen (see *Kiddushin* 42a).

The proper way to view outward beauty is to see it as an expression of inner beauty. Due to the intrinsic *tznius* (modesty) of Abraham and Sarah, they never viewed her physical beauty as anything more than a reflection of her pristine inner being. Only upon coming in contact with the immoral atmosphere of Egypt did Abraham sense that there was an independent physical dimension to his wife's beauty.

---

12. **Limited Appetite.** The Midrash teaches that this was one of the ten great famines that will occur in human history. The last of the famines, which will occur before the coming of the Messiah, is described by the prophet as *neither a famine for bread nor a thirst for water but rather* [a famine] *to hear the word of Hashem (Amos 8:11).* The Sages teach that this famine will be the worst of all, which seems strange, since this last famine would seem to be a blessing. What could be better than a burning thirst for the word of Hashem?

R' Yosef Kahaneman (Ponevezher Rav) explained:

In times of famine, people are forced to subsist on a bare minimum of food and drink. Under such circumstances people are not particular about the quantity or quality of their food. People are so thirsty that they will drink even a few drops of dirty water in order to satiate their thirst, and they will struggle to obtain a crust of stale bread. Before *Mashiach* comes, the burning desire for spiritual food and drink will be so overwhelming that people will be satisfied with the slightest bit of Torah. The crying need for a spiritually uplifting experience will seduce people to accept bits of knowledge, even when they are denied the richness of Torah.

This will be the terrible tragedy of the last famine.

13. **Vote of No Confidence.** *Rambam (Hilchos Melachim* 5:9) writes that one may not leave *Eretz Yisrael . . .* unless there is a famine in the Land [and one cannot make a living]. Although it is permitted to leave for this reason it is not the way of the righteous to do so. Machlon and Chilion were great men, yet they were punished, forfeiting their lives for having left the Land of Israel due to terrible famine (see *Ruth* 1:1).

When there is no food in the royal palace, abandoning the king adds insult to injury. One must trust the king that at least in his palace he will provide for his children. A Jew in the Land of Israel is a royal child in his Father's palace. To leave when times are hard is an unacceptable vote of no confidence in Hashem *(Zekan Aharon).*

Of course Abraham knew that Sarah was a beautiful woman, but now, in the spiritually noxious atmosphere of Egypt, he perceived her beauty in external terms.[14]

וַיֵּלֶךְ לְמַסָּעָיו
He proceeded on his journeys (13:3).

The implication is that these *journeys* were part of a known itinerary. *Rashi* comments that on Abraham's way back from Egypt, he returned to the places where he had previously lodged in order to pay the bills he had incurred on the way. How did Abraham set off on his journey without money to pay for his lodgings? Furthermore, why were the innkeepers ready to extend him credit?

Chida explains that Abraham set off on his travels with a limited amount of money. Wherever he stayed, he asked the inkeeper to be considerate and charge him the poor man's rate. Nonetheless, after Abraham became wealthy in Egypt (see 13:2), he felt obligated to return to his considerate benefactors and pay the full rate since he considered the discount to be a bridge loan. *R' Yechezkel of Kuzmir* and *Chasam Sofer* offer a homiletical approach to the question. Wherever Abraham went, he proclaimed that the One God created all, and that, therefore, man is obligated to serve Him. Many were skeptical of his message and asked: If Abraham is such a righteous person, why does God force him to wander from place to place instead of allowing him serenity and peace of mind? On his travels to Egypt, Abraham had no satisfactory answer to the questions. Only on his way back was he able to answer the question. After word spread about the miraculous plagues that struck Pharaoh as a result of his taking Sarah, and after Abraham and Sarah returned with great wealth, he was able to show the cynics that God in reality was deeply involved in caring for him.

Thus Abraham settled his debts while on the way back.[15]

וְלֹא נָשָׂא אֹתָם הָאָרֶץ לָשֶׁבֶת יַחְדָּו כִּי הָיָה רְכוּשָׁם רָב
And the Land could not support them dwelling together, for their possessions were abundant (ibid. 6).

When Abraham and Lot returned to *Eretz Yisrael*, it became apparent that they could not coexist in the same area. *Eretz Yisrael* is a small Land with limited resources, but it has a supernatural ability to support all who want to live in it. The Talmud teaches that Israel is called "the Land of the deer," for just as the deer's hide has an elasticity that accommodates its bulk, so the Land of Israel figuratively expands to accommodate all who want to live there. When Lot and his shepherds made it clear that the Land was too small for them, Abraham realized that they lacked the spiritual qualities necessary to live there (*Zekan Aharon*).[16]

וַיְהִי רִיב בֵּין רֹעֵי מִקְנֵה אַבְרָם . . . וַיֹּאמֶר אַבְרָם אֶל לוֹט אַל נָא תְהִי מְרִיבָה בֵּינִי וּבֵינֶךָ
And there was quarreling between the herdsmen of Abram's livestock . . . So Abram said to Lot, "Please let there be no strife between me and you (ibid. 7-8).

The Torah describes the quarrels as a רִיב (in the masculine form), yet Abraham asks Lot to help

---

14. **Outside/Inside.** The message of *tznius* is that your internal being is the real you; that of all the parts of you, it is your innermost self by which you want to be defined. In order to convey this message you must know how and when to reveal yourself, your abilities and everything else in your internal make-up so that these things do not hide but rather express who you really are. [See *Outside/Inside A fresh look at tzniut* by *Gila Manolson* (*Targum/Feldheim* 1997).]

15. **Circuitous Existence.** The word הַקְפוֹתָיו, *his credit bills,* also means *his circuits.* We frequently wonder why God allows bad things to happen to us. In hindsight, however, we often realize that what seemed to be terrible was really a circuitous route by which He did us a great favor.

16. **Plenty of Room.** The Sages spoke of this expansive quality when they taught that "nor did any man say to his fellow, 'The space is insufficient for me to stay overnight in Jerusalem' " (*Avos* 5:7). The key to this phenomenon is alluded to earlier in that Mishnah. "The people stood crowded together [in the Temple courtyard] yet they [miraculously] prostrated in ample space." When one Jew yields to another, there is enough space for everyone. As the timeless maxim teaches us: מִי שֶׁאֵינוֹ תּוֹפֵס מָקוֹם בְּשׁוּם מָקוֹם, יֶשׁ לוֹ מָקוֹם בְּכָל מָקוֹם, *Whoever grabs no space anywhere has enough space everywhere.*

him assure that there be no מְרִיבָה (strife), framing the quarrel in the feminine form.

Shelah submits that Abraham was aware that arguments have a way of getting blown out of proportion. While there may be some "legitimate" grounds for the initial fight, it doesn't take long for petty quarrels to snowball into major arguments. Thus Abraham asked Lot that the initial fracas not "give birth" to escalating arguments, like a mother giving birth to children.[17]

Background

Lot was captured during the war between the four kings and the five, and Abraham went to war to rescue him. Although the victory was his, Abraham refused to benefit personally from the spoils of war.

וַיָּבֹא הַפָּלִיט
Then came the fugitive (14:13).

Rashi teaches that "the fugitive" refers to Og, king of Bashan, the giant who was either a fugitive from the flood or from the battle of Rephaim (see *Deuteronomy* 3:11). Og had an ulterior motive in informing Abraham that Lot had been captured; he hoped to incite Abraham to go to war where he would be killed, thus allowing Og to marry Sarah.

In spite of his nefarious motive, Og was rewarded for his act of kindness. When Moses was about to battle Og, God told him, "Do not fear him [Og]." Although Moses feared no mortal man, he was afraid that the merit of Og's telling Abraham about Lot's capture might protect him.

This thought is incredible. Six hundred thousand Jews with Moses at their head are afraid of the merit of Og for having once performed a good deed for worse than checkered motives. The good deed was not even done for Abraham's benefit, but rather for Lot's, and Og's motive was sinister. And yet Moses was wary.

How great, then, must the merit be of one who does a good deed for another Jew with the proper intent. Certainly such merit will live on for eternity (*R' Yosef Zundel of Salant*).[18]

וַיַּגֵּד לְאַבְרָם הָעִבְרִי
And he told Abram the Ivri (ibid.).

The Sages teach that Abraham was called "*Ivri*," literally, *on one side*, because the entire world was מֵעֵבֶר אֶחָד, on one side of a moral and spiritual divide, while he was מֵעֵבֶר הַשֵּׁנִי, on the opposite side. The defining character of Abraham and his children was their ability to be individualists, ready to pursue their own path of truth even if the masses were "marching to the beat of a different drummer."[19] Abraham the *Ivri* is ready to take on the entire world in his battle for recognition of the true God.

But, of all the places where Abraham is mentioned, why is the appellation *the Ivri* here? *R' Yoel*

---

17. **Disproportionate Strife.** Strife has a way of multiplying far beyond the proportions of its origin. *Rabbi Nisson Alpert* explained that the term שִׂנְאַת חִנָּם does not necessarily mean *hatred without cause,* as it is usually rendered, since animosity is often precipitated by very real and justifiable factors. Instead, שִׂנְאַת חִנָּם is the *extra* hatred caused by allowing the animosity to rankle and grow. When the parties discuss the point of contention in a constructive manner, the problem can often be resolved; if not, the anger only becomes intensified. The *extra* enmity exists for no good reason — it is חִנָּם, *without cause.*

18. **Spiritual Schizophrenia.** The schizophrenic character of man is reflected in the image of Og. One can place himself in danger to save someone — yet in his heart of hearts he wants to kill him.

One can run to *shul* with his *siddur* in hand, wearing his *tallis* and *tefillin,* and all the while he is thinking about how, when he gets to *shul,* he is going to figuratively kill a certain person by embarrassing him. This is one more manifestation of the fact that man is a synthesis of earth from the ground and a sublime Divine soul. All of life is a battle to tame the beast within (*R' Eliezer M. Shach*).

19. **Back to the World.** When *R' Gershon Henach of Radzin* was a child, his father once asked him, "What did you learn today in *cheder*?" The young child replied, "We learned that when the Jewish people stood at Mt. Sinai, *Israel encamped there, opposite the mountain.* I told the teacher that it means that they stood with their backs to the world."

of Satmar explains (based on *Rashi's* comment) that Og informed Abraham of Lot's capture in order to draw him into battle. He was confident that Abraham would be killed and he could make Sarah his queen. Why was Og so sure that Abraham would endanger himself in order to save his nephew?

The answer lies in the words *he told Abraham the Ivri*. Og knew that Abraham is an *Ivri*, unfazed by the odds. Even if he is on one side with the entire world against him, he is ready to endanger himself to do the right thing.

ham erred in returning the people since he thereby lost the opportunity to teach them the way of God. The Midrash softens the criticism, submitting that he returned only the older people, those set in their ways. When the king of Sodom asked for even the young children, Abraham replied by raising his hand, Heavenward symbolic of his life's goal of bringing the young and uninitiated to a vibrant faith in God. He saw that returning the young would be an act of spiritual treason towards his earthly mission.[20]

וַיֹּאמֶר מֶלֶךְ סְדֹם אֶל אַבְרָם תֶּן לִי הַנֶּפֶשׁ וְהָרְכֻשׁ קַח לָךְ
The king of Sodom said to Abram, "Give me the people and take the possessions for yourself" (ibid. 21).

Abraham not only agreed to return the prisoners, he also returned the spoils of war. Unlike the gifts which he took from Pharaoh (12:16), here he refused all spoils.

He did this not for the sake of the impression it would leave on others, but rather to reinforce his own faith that no one but God provides success. He lifted his hand to Hashem (see verse 22) as if to state that "it is not this warring hand that brought me this wealth, but rather Hashem"; therefore, he refused to take the spoils of war.

The Talmud (*Nedarim* 32a) maintains that Abra-

Background

God promised Abraham children who would inherit the Land under all circumstances. He also taught that the "mortgage" for the Land would be the Egyptian Exile.

וְהֶאֱמִן בַּה׳ וַיַּחְשְׁבֶהָ לּוֹ צְדָקָה
And he trusted in Hashem, and He reckoned it to him as righteousness (15:6).

The translation follows *Rashi's* opinion that God viewed Abraham's faith as an act of righteousness. *Ramban* disagrees, claiming that since Abraham was a prophet it is not remarkable that he believed in God's promise. He therefore renders *and* **he** *reckoned it to* **Him** *as righteousness* [and kindness], i.e., by unconditionally promising Abra-

---

20. **Priceless Souls.** The *Beis Yisrael of Ger* resurrected Polish Jewry after the Holocaust. Every Polish Jew, wherever in the world and whatever his degree of commitment to Torah and *mitzvos*, was a challenge he felt driven to conquer.

A Jew whose commitment had weakened drastically after suffering the horrors of the Holocaust moved to America where he found unusual financial success. For years he was riding the wave of financial prosperity when suddenly he was named in a lawsuit which threatened to leave him penniless.

Once a *chassid*, always a *chassid*; he felt an urge to travel to Jerusalem and ask the *Beis Yisrael* to pray on his behalf. He arrived at the rebbe's room, poured out his tale of woe and asked for the rebbe's blessing. The *Beis Yisrael* assured him that all would be well. The man then handed the rebbe an envelope with $10,000 in it. The *Beis Yisrael* took the envelope and put it under the tablecloth.

The Jew flew back to New York and began a grueling series of court appearances. All the evidence seemed stacked against him; yet, at the final hearing, the judge threw the case out on a technicality. Sure that the rebbe's blessing had helped him, the man returned to Jerusalem to personally thank the rebbe and present a sizable donation.

When he arrived and placed the new envelope on the table the rebbe lifted the tablecloth, pulled out the first, still unopened envelope, and handed it to the Jew with the words תֶּן לִי הַנֶּפֶשׁ וְהָרְכֻשׁ קַח לָךְ, "Give me the souls and take the possessions for yourself."

"Please keep your money, but send your children to Jerusalem to study here in our *yeshivos*."

The man's children came to learn and they and their children are staunch Gerrer *chassidim*.

ham children, God had, by Abraham's reckoning, practiced righteous kindness toward him.

HeChassid Yaavetz expands on the *Ramban's* approach. Abraham was fearful of what would happen to his children if they sinned. God told him that not only would they be like stars — numerous and brilliant — but they would always maintain their faith in God, for He promised to do all in His power to create conditions that would allow them to maintain their faith.[21] Abraham saw this promise as God's charitable and kind act.

According to the *Kozhnitzer Maggid*, Abraham believed in Hashem and viewed his ability to achieve faith as a Heavenly gift. *He trusted in Hashem,* and he *reckoned it* [the ability and sensitivity to believe] *to Him as* [charitable] *righteousness.*

R' Meir of Stavnitz notes that the Torah does not say וַיַּאֲמִן, *he believed,* but rather וְהֶאֱמִן, which implies that he got others to believe. Abraham planted faith in the hearts of all who crossed his path.[22]

A thinking Jew views whatever God gives him as charity. As *Ramban* explains (*Deuteronomy* 6:25): A servant indentured to his master must serve him under all circumstances, even if doing so entails no reward. If the master nevertheless decides to reward the servant, then he has performed an act of benevolence.

Furthermore, whatever we do for God does not grant us the right to anything since it all pales into insignificance when compared to what He does for us. As King David said: וּלְךָ אֲדֹנָי חָסֶד כִּי אַתָּה תְשַׁלֵּם לְאִישׁ כְּמַעֲשֵׂהוּ, *Yours, my Lord, is kindness, for You reward each man in accordance with his deeds* (*Psalms* 62:13)

Although He rewards us for our actions, it is really an undeserved kindness.

Thus Abraham, who made God known to the world, reckoned God's promise of a child not as recompense for services rendered but rather as pure charity (*Zekan Aharon*).[23]

---

21. **Charitable Monarch.** When a king promises to reward his subjects if they comply with his will, he practices justice and fairness. When he commits himself to create conditions which force them to remain loyal to him so that he may reward them, then he is following a charitable path.

22. **Reassuring Faith.** Accordingly, we might suggest a possible explanation of *Rashi's* approach. It was not Abraham's personal faith that was the charitable act but rather the faith he implanted in others. He brought the masses to merit and was rewarded accordingly.

R' Yaakov Rakovsky adds a different shade of interpretation. Abraham gave the world a priceless gift when he taught faith in a single God. "The righteous person lives by his faith" (*Habakkuk* 2:4), for faith lends meaning and purpose to life. If life is nothing more than reckless happenstance, then it offers no hope to man in times of distress. Abraham saved mankind from misery and despair and provided life with rhyme, reason and redeeming value. Hence Abraham caused others to believe, and God reckoned it as a shining example of true righteous charity.

23. **Humbly Undeserving.** *R' Elimelech of Lizhensk* was the epitome of humility. One day, while making a personal reckoning, he came to the conclusion that he had sinned so grievously and so often that the deepest of purgatories would be insufficient to cleanse him. He began to feel despondent, and feared deeply for his future.

Suddenly five of his greatest students entered his room: the *Chozeh of Lublin,* the *Oheiv Yisrael of Apta, R' Mendel of Rimanov,* the *Maggid of Kozhnitz* and *R' Moshe Leib of Sassov.* He was overjoyed to see them, and his despondency began to subside. "Praised is Hashem. Because of you I will be saved from purgatory. The Sages taught that it is improper that the teacher be relegated to purgatory while his students are in the Garden of Eden." He then became pensive. "But how will I merit a share in the World to Come?"

A moment later he began to think aloud, seeking to raise his flagging spirits, "Hashem is the most charitable of all. In terms of the World to Come, I am certainly the most impoverished of all creatures. Surely, then, He will give me a present from His storehouse for those who are not deserving of anything."

The *Oheiv Yisrael* turned to his friends and said, "The Rebbe speaks like Abraham our forefather. Hashem said to him *your reward is very great* (*Genesis* 15:1) yet in the Torah Hashem writes *and he [Abraham] reckoned it to Him as righteousness* (ibid. 6). Abraham thought that Hashem was giving him a great reward as charity."

פרשת וירא §⇦
Parashas Vayeira

Background

On the third day after Abraham circumcised himself, God caused an extraordinary heat wave so that no people were traveling that day. Abraham, the epitome of kindness and hospitality, sought opportunities to extend kindness to others even in his weakened condition. God therefore sent him three angels disguised as wayfarers, so that Abraham could show them hospitality.[1]

וַיֵּרָא אֵלָיו ה׳ בְּאֵלֹנֵי מַמְרֵא
*Hashem appeared to him
in the plains of Mamre (18:1).*

Rashi (based on *Tanchuma*) teaches that the appearance of God at this location was a reward to Mamre for having advised Abraham to obey God's command to circumcise himself.

Why did Abraham seek the advice of Eshkol, Anair, and Mamre as to whether he should fulfill the Divine command?

Maharal explains: One should never act impulsively in his service of God, unless he is afraid that his enthusiasm will wane. Abraham sought the counsel of his friends not for their approval but rather in order to emphasize that he did what he did as the result of a reasoned and rational decision. *Avnei Nezer* offers a different approach. Abraham's life mission was to influence others to believe in Hashem and to develop a relationship with Him, which required that he maintain a close relationship with others. Abraham was afraid that by making himself physically different from those around him, he would create an unbridgeable emotional distance between himself and those whom he sought to bring closer to God. He therefore solicited Mamre's advice so that he, too, could be part of this decision. In this way, Abraham could maintain a close relationship with Mamre, in spite of the tangible difference between them.

---

1. **No Excuses.** The Sages explain the verse וַיִּטַּע אֵשֶׁל, *He* [Abraham] *planted an eishel* (21:33), as an acrostic of the words אֲכִילָה, *eating;* שְׁתִיָּה, *drinking;* and לְוָיָה, *escorting,* the three basic courtesies a host should provide his guests, indicating that Abraham was constantly occupied with hospitality. Why then does the Torah highlight Abraham's hospitality with this episode of the angels who were sent to him by God, rather than through any of the countless times when Abraham entertained mortal men? *Kehilas Yitzchak* sees this as a lesson in the lengths to which one must go in fulfilling *mitzvos.* When presented with opportunities to help people who are experiencing hard times, we frequently ignore their pleas. There is always a reasonable excuse for why we can not help now. Sometimes we claim to be busy with other *mitzvos* or public projects, while other times we claim that the expense of supporting our own family does not permit involvement in the plight of others. "I really feel bad, but I can't help," we claim.

Abraham had all the reasons in the world not to entertain guests. A 99-year-old man who just underwent surgery (circumcision) has every reason to ignore potential guests on a swelteringly hot day. Yet he ran after them and welcomed them warmly, and then served them with alacrity, sensitive to their every need.

Thus the Torah uses this specific incident to teach us the extent to which we must exert ourselves in order to care for guests.

אִם נָא מָצָאתִי חֵן בְּעֵינֶיךָ אַל נָא תַעֲבֹר מֵעַל עַבְדֶּךָ

If I find favor in your eyes, please pass not away from Your servant (ibid. 3)

Abraham asked that God "wait" while he tended to his guests. The Talmud (*Shabbos* 127a) derives from this verse that hospitality to wayfarers is more meaningful than receiving the Divine Presence. How can this be? How is it possible that it is more meritorious to honor ordinary human beings than the One Who created them?

When one joyfully welcomes a close friend and extends him every courtesy, it is certainly an expression of love and respect for him. But when one warmly welcomes the friend's child and treats *him* with respect and kindness only because of his father, it is even more meaningful to his friend, for if not for the relationship with the father, why would one go out of his way for the child? Thus, welcoming the child can be understood as a great expression of love and respect for the father.

When we receive the Divine Presence, we honor our Father. But when we welcome His children, it is an even more powerful expression of our love and respect for Him (*Simchas Aharon*).[2]

R' Avraham Chaim Feuer suggests an alternative approach. There is no greater form of honor than emulation. When one receives the Divine Presence he meets God; when one welcomes guests he acts like God, Who visits the sick and welcomes guests.[3]

Background

In fulfillment of the prophetic message they received from the angels who visited them, Abraham and Sarah were blessed with a child.

וה' פָּקַד אֶת שָׂרָה

Hashem had remembered Sarah (21:1).

In the previous *parashah,* Abraham had prayed to God on behalf of Abimelech and his household, and they were relieved (*Genesis* 20:17). Here the Torah teaches that Hashem *had* remembered Sarah, implying that God had responded to Sarah

---

2. **Host's Manual.** According to the *Chafetz Chaim,* this incident might serve as a manual for how one should treat guests. Just as Abraham provided the angels with water to wash their feet, so we should offer guests the opportunity to wash up or even to shower if they wish to refresh themselves. Furthermore, he did not serve them food immediately; instead, he asked them to rest under the tree. We would do well to emulate this practice by first asking our guests to rest from the grueling trip and only then to sit down to a meal. Sometimes guests want to get back to their journey quickly, thus one should first offer a light repast and only then serve a proper meal. This, too, we learn from Abraham who initially told them *I will fetch a morsel of bread that you may sustain yourselves, then go on* (verse 5), and then he served them a full-fledged meal.

Finally, just like Abraham, we should personally serve our guests as it says *he stood over them beneath the tree and they ate* (verse 8).

3. **A Memorable Seder.** It was late on the eve of Pesach, after R' Yosef Chaim Sonnenfeld had already completed the search for *chametz,* when there was a knock at his door. He opened the door to admit four respected community leaders from Budapest. Despite the late hour, he received them warmly. In the ensuing conversation, the visitors expressed their desire to spend the Seder with R' Yosef Chaim, an experience they would consider priceless, and they insisted on paying for the added expense that he would incur. R' Yosef Chaim agreed to both proposals, which was somewhat surprising, since they had been assured that their insistence on paying would be futile. One of them placed a large sum of money on the table and the four left. They returned the following evening and in the words of one of them, "It was one of the most awesome experiences of my life to see the holy, glowing face of R' Yosef Chaim on the Seder night."

On the first night of Chol HaMoed, R' Yosef Chaim visited his guests at their hotel while they still *davening.* After they had finished, he engaged them in a conversation and then placed their payment for the Seder under the tablecloth. They were unable to do anything about this since they were still under *Yom Tov* restrictions, since they, as residents of the diaspora, were obligated to observe two days of *Yom Tov.* One of them mustered the courage to ask him to explain his conduct.

"It is really quite simple," replied R' Yosef Chaim. "Pesach is the festival of freedom. What kind of freedom is it for a person to feel that he is partaking of another person's meal? I therefore accepted your payment in order that you would feel comfortable in my home and also so that you would feel free to eat as much as you wanted. Now that you have enjoyed your *Yom Tov,* I can safely return your money" (*Guardian of Jerusalem,* ArtScroll).

and provided her with the means to have children even before healing Abimelech and his household. This is the source of our Sages' axiom that "If someone prays for mercy on behalf of another person and he himself needs that very same thing, he is answered first" (*Bava Kamma* 92a).[4]

According to *R' Yechezkel Levenstein,* this teaches that personal success is linked to one's concern for the community. By broadening our focus beyond our own personal concerns and bearing the pain and anguish of others, we turn our prayers from private into communal pleas. Since God never completely rejects the prayers of the community (*Berachos* 8a), we will be granted our own needs as well.

This is why all our prayers are expressed in the plural. We do not ask merely for ourselves; we ask for all our fellow Jews.[5]

Rashi (*Genesis* 25:19) teaches that the cynics of the generation claimed that Isaac was Abimelech's child. It was therefore in Abraham's best interest that the king remain sterile, thus refuting the malicious claim of the skeptics. Despite all this, however, Abraham prayed that God heal Abimelech. God is quick to answer one who puts aside his own interests and prays for another, even though it is to his benefit that his friend continue to suffer (*R' Simchah Bunim of P'shis'cha*).[6]

אֶת שֵׁם בְּנוֹ הַנּוֹלַד לוֹ . . . יִצְחָק
The name of the son who was born to him . . . Isaac (21:3).

It seems incongruous that Isaac, who was the epitome of strict justice and self-restraint, was given a name that suggests the happy laughter of his parents and all those who heard the good news of his birth. [The Hebrew יִצְחָק means *he will laugh.*]

Chidushei HaRim explains: The gravest of sins, such as idolatry, murder and sexual misconduct, are referred to as צְחוֹק, *mockery* (see *Rashi* to 21:9), because evil people laugh off even the most severe sins as insignificant. Likewise, the righteous mock the evil inclination. Those activities which others might consider great pleasures are nothing but mere foolishness in the eyes of those loyal to God.

Thus Isaac, the human embodiment of reverence for God, is symbolized by laughter. So devoted was he to the service of God that he could laugh at all of the temptations and distractions of the physical world.

---

4. **Full Empathy.** The great Chassidic Masters interpreted this to mean that if one prays for a friend with the feeling that his *personal* need is that God show mercy toward his friend, then God will respond to the petitioner's own need first. The most efficacious prayers are those in which one is more pained by another's predicament than by his own.

5. **Among My Nation.** In this light we may understand why this chapter was chosen as the Torah reading for the first day of Rosh Hashanah. On the Day of Judgment, we wish to be judged as members of the community, rather than as individuals.

According to the *Zohar* (1:69b), this was the intent of the Shunamite woman when she visited the prophet Elisha after the death of her young son. Not knowing why she had come, Elisha assumed that she might need him to intercede for her with the government, so he asked if she had a request of the king. She said, "I dwell among my people" (*II Kings* 4:13), meaning that she preferred to be considered not as an individual but rather as part of her nation. The *Zohar* interprets the incident as an allusion to a Jew's approach to the King, God Himself, for judgment on Rosh Hashanah. Rather than making personal requests of the King, we should pray as part of our people.

6. **My Customers?** *R' Moshe Mordechai Heschel,* the late *Kopitchnitzer Rebbe,* was a Jew who lived with this perspective. A young man trying to start out on his own in the diamond business asked friends and relatives to suggest potential customers. The typical response was, "Best wishes, but I can't give away my customers." Dejected, the man poured out his heart to R' Moshe, who had not yet become the rebbe, and earned his livelihood by dealing in diamonds. Without hesitation, R' Moshe gave the man his own list of buyers and sellers. The young man asked him, "Which ones should I try?" R' Moshe replied, "Any of them. All of them, if you have the time."

The young man said, "But R' Moshe, all of them?! I don't want to take away your business." R' Moshe smiled, *"Vos is far mir ungeshribben vest di mir nisht tzinemen.* Whatever was inscribed in Heaven as destined for me, you cannot take away. Our *parnassah* is in the hand of the *Ribbono Shel Olam* and He has enough for both of us."

יִצְחַק לִי
Will laugh for me (21:6)

The Midrash (*Bereishis Rabbah* 53:8) teaches that along with Sarah's miraculous conception, many other barren women conceived, sick people were healed, and the blind were able to see. Homiletically this means that as a result of the miraculous birth of Isaac to an old and infertile couple, a great number of people who were blind to the reality that God is intimately involved with mankind and its difficulties were granted the spiritual insight to achieve real faith (*Yalkut Eliezer*).

Background

God commanded Abraham to yield to Sarah and banish Ishmael, as he posed a serious danger to Isaac's spiritual growth. In spite of his personal misgivings over treating Hagar and Ishmael so harshly, Abraham followed the Divine command.

וַתֵּרֶא שָׂרָה אֶת בֶּן הָגָר הַמִּצְרִית . . . מְצַחֵק
Sarah saw the son of Hagar, the Egyptian . . . mocking (21:9).

As a result of Ishmael's mockery, Sarah asked that he be banished so that he not inherit from Abraham jointly with Isaac. Why was Ishmael's mockery sufficient cause to banish him? According to *Rashi*, the term מְצַחֵק, *mocking*, is a euphemism for the three cardinal sins of idolatry, immorality and murder. Fearful that Isaac might follow Ishmael's cynical and mocking example, Sarah insisted that the latter be sent away. In a second comment, *Rashi* says that Ishmael was engaging Isaac in "playful" sport, shooting arrows toward his little brother. His intention was to kill Isaac "accidentally," so that only he would be Abraham's heir. Sarah reacted immediately and decisively.

Damesek Eliezer and others offer a novel explanation: Sarah overheard Ishmael repeating the snide comment of the scoffers who claimed that Sarah had conceived from Abimelech (see *Rashi* to 25:19). Upon hearing this, Sarah became concerned that Ishmael might claim that he, and only he, was Abraham's legitimate heir. Therefore she said, "The son of that slavewoman shall not inherit with my son, with Isaac" (21:10).

וַתֹּאמֶר לְאַבְרָהָם גָּרֵשׁ הָאָמָה הַזֹּאת
And she said to Abraham, "Drive out this slavewoman" (21:10).

Had Ishmael continued to be educated together with Isaac, he undoubtedly would have been influenced positively, and his innate wildness might have been tempered; on the other hand, by living in close quarters with Ishmael, Isaac might have absorbed some of his half brother's unsavory character. Sarah came to the conclusion that the possible detrimental effect of Ishmael on Isaac could not be justified by the positive influence which Isaac might have on Ishmael. Agreeing with her, God sent a clear message that sometimes one must forego the opportunity to be a positive influence on others out of fear that, rather than changing them, one will become negatively influenced himself (*Chafetz Chaim*).[7]

R' Simchah Wasserman viewed the three maxims of the Men of the Great Assembly (*Avos* 1:1) as interlinked guidelines for those who seek to bring others closer to Torah: *Be deliberate in judgment,*

---

7. **Piping Hot.** The *Chafetz Chaim* illustrated this point with the following incident.

One day as the Chafetz Chaim was about to immerse himself in the *mikveh* (ritual bath), he asked R' Yidel the attendant if he had heated the water. R' Yidel replied, "Of course, Rebbe. Just a short while ago I emptied half of the hot-water tank into the *mikveh.*" The Chafetz Chaim went into the water and much to his chagrin, it was very cold. When he came out, he went over to the hot-water tank and stuck his hand inside. Sure enough, it was no more than lukewarm. He then commented to R' Yidel, "If the hot-water tank itself is lukewarm, then the frigid *mikveh* will be no more than cool."

Only people whose commitment to Torah and *mitzvos* is very "hot" can try to warm others to the cause. One with limited commitment runs the risk of being cooled off by those he tries to inspire.

develop many disciples and erect a fence around the Torah. Be deliberate in judgment teaches us to be slow to judge those who are less committed than we are. Doing so will help one to *develop many disciples;* however, one must *erect a fence* [for himself] *around the Torah* so that he remains untouched by the spiritually alien influence of his surroundings.

אַל יֵרַע בְּעֵינֶיךָ עַל הַנַּעַר וְעַל אֲמָתֶךָ
Be not distressed over the youth or your slavewoman (21:12).

Although personally sending away his own son ran counter to his very essence, Abraham was ready to entirely subordinate his nature in obedience of God. Not having been told *when* to evict Ishmael and Hagar, Abraham could have procrastinated. Nevertheless, he arose early with the same alacrity that he would later show at the *Akeidah* (see 22:3), and in an act of seeming cruelty sent the feverish youth away.

Greatness means doing what is right, not what is comfortable (*Zichron Meir*).

כֹּל אֲשֶׁר תֹּאמַר אֵלֶיךָ שָׂרָה שְׁמַע בְּקֹלָהּ
Whatever Sarah tells you, heed her voice (ibid.).

We often hear people speak, yet we do not listen carefully enough to understand what they mean to say. In other cases, we attribute less than perfect motives to those speaking, in order to hear what we want to.

God warned Abraham against this widespread malaise. "Do not think that Sarah is a jealous woman with a personal agenda of protecting her son's position. Whatever Sarah tells you, the *Shema* [שְׁמַע] is in her voice; her intentions in banishing Ishmael are purely so that Isaac not be impeded in accepting the yoke of Heaven (as symbolized by our daily recitation of *Shema Yisrael*)."

The true Jewish mother has no personal agenda. All her dreams and aspirations have but one purpose: to inculcate within her children the unswerving faith and spirit of self-sacrifice that a Jew seeks to achieve when he recites the *Shema* (*Tiferes Shlomo*).

Once her water supply had depleted, Hagar despaired of Ishmael's fate and cast him off beneath a tree. Suddenly God opened her eyes and in the middle of the desert she saw a well. She filled her flask and gave Ishmael water.

וַיִּכְלוּ הַמַּיִם מִן הַחֵמֶת וַתַּשְׁלֵךְ אֶת הַיֶּלֶד תַּחַת אַחַד הַשִּׂיחִם
When the water in the flask was consumed she cast off the boy beneath one of the trees (21:15).

Much of life's direction is related to our priorities. When we can afford to provide our children with a proper Jewish education, most of us are ready to do so. However, when resources are hard to come by, we must be ready to make great sacrifices in order to give our children a vibrant Jewish education. When contemplating budget cuts, our children's future as Jews must be seen as a nonnegotiable item.

R' Yehoshua of Kutna sees a homiletic allusion to this in the episode of Hagar and Ishmael. When the water in the flask was consumed and Hagar began to experience hard times, her reaction was to cast off the boy, an allusion to ignoring the educational needs of one's children when met with financial hardship.

וַיִּפְקַח אֱלֹקִים אֶת עֵינֶיהָ וַתֵּרֶא בְּאֵר מָיִם
Then God opened her eyes and she perceived a well of water (21:19).

The verse does not state that God created a new well or that He brought the well from somewhere else; therefore, we must conclude that it had stood there to begin with. The Midrash (*Bereishis Rabbah*) derives from this that all people are essentially blind until God opens their eyes. The well had been there all along — yet Hagar did not see it until God opened her eyes.

Chidushei HaRim sees this lesson in broader terms. All of man's needs, both physical and spiritual, are really within his grasp at all times. If one merits that God should open his eyes, he will see everything he needs to see in order to progress through life. One never truly lacks the solution to life's problems; he lacks the vision and foresight to perceive the obvious. As long as man suffers from spiritually impaired eyesight, all his efforts to escape the darkness are futile. Only with God's help is the obvious accessible.

This is especially so with regard to earning a livelihood. As the prophet teaches, "Man is like the fish of the sea" (Habakkuk 1:14). Large fish do not chase small fish from behind. This is a display of God's kindness, for if the large fish were to swallow the small fish from the back, the protruding fins of the prey would puncture the larger fish's throat and choke it. In His great mercy, God provides the large fish with its food in the opposite manner. A small fish swims head first toward the large one and painlessly enters its throat. As it continues into the large fish its fins fold in and it is engulfed smoothly inside.

How wondrous a phenomenon! The large fish will endlessly but futilely *chase* its prey, while God provides it with sustenance in an effortless fashion.

This is a simile to man, who expends all his energy and talent hunting for his daily bread. He fails to realize, however, that although he must go through the motions of earning his living, it is really God Who provides all his needs.[8]

וַתֵּלֶךְ וַתְּמַלֵּא אֶת הַחֵמֶת מַיִם
She went and filled the flask with water (ibid.).

After almost losing her own life and that of her child to thirst, Hagar witnessed a miracle as God provided water. She therefore filled the flask with water to prepare for the rest of the journey. This would seem to be an instance of legitimate foresight, but the Midrash (*Bereishis Rabbah* 53:14) views her act as indicative of weak faith.

R' Leib Chasman explained: Imagine someone traveling together with a kind-hearted king in the royal carriage. Certainly he need not worry what he will eat and drink while en route, for the king will obviously provide for him!

If in fact the man brings his own food, we must assume that either he is unaware of the king's reputation for kindness or that he doubts that the king will provide for him. Furthermore, the king should be admired for his patience and kindness in allowing the guest to remain in his carriage despite the implied personal insult.

Man is that passenger in the King's carriage! We all know that God can provide for us, but we are taught by our Sages not to rely on miracles (*Pesachim* 64b). One who *does* experience miracles yet immediately reverts to "trying to fend for himself," forgetting that God is not only the source of his success but has actually provided for him in a miraculous manner, shows a lack of faith that borders on an affront to God.

Hagar was an Egyptian princess who had abandoned her father's palace out of recognition that being a maidservant in the house of Abraham is worth more than all the honors of royalty. She of all people should have had faith that just as God had miraculously delivered

---

8. **From His Open Hand.** *R' Yisrael of Rizhin* offered the following parable: A poor man heard about a place where people said that after a month of backbreaking labor one could ask for his heart's desires. Left with no other way to support himself and his family, the ne'er-do-well decided to go there and take up the offer.

At the end of thirty days, the worn and weary man turned to his host and said, "Well, I've put in the thirty days of hard labor, now I would like to receive all my desires." The host laughed cynically. "This is not the place you are looking for; that place is located just up the block." Broken and downhearted, the poor man trudged over to the other house and knocked on the door. When someone answered, the poor man said, "Tell me — but please be honest — is this the place where one may ask for whatever he needs or wants once he has toiled for thirty days?" The man at the door replied "Toil? Work? Here everything is absolutely free. Just tell us what you need."

Man, the *Rizhiner* explained, must work either because God decreed, "By the sweat of your brow you shall eat bread" (*Genesis* 3:19), or as an atonement for his sins. Sustenance, however, comes from God's gracious hand. Hard work and a livelihood are distinctly separate, with barely a link between the two. Man can often toil at one business venture and see no results, while his success comes from another venture to which he devoted hardly any effort. This is the lesson of Hagar. She searched in vain. Once God opened her eyes, she saw the well that was there all along.

her once before, He could and would do so again.[9]

וַיְהִי אֱלֹקִים אֶת הַנַּעַר וַיִּגְדָּל
וַיֵּשֶׁב בַּמִּדְבָּר וַיְהִי רֹבֶה קַשָּׁת

*God was with the youth and he grew up,
he dwelt in the desert and became
an accomplished archer* (21:20).

When God hearkened to Ishmael's cries, He blessed him with success. Nevertheless, Ishmael developed into a nomadic bandit who robbed and plundered travelers. This teaches us, said *R' Yaakov Dovid of Amshinov*, not to assume that a successful person is necessarily a moral and ethical one. Success does not prove that one is pleasing to God. There can be many reasons for which God allows evil to flourish, at least temporarily. Just because one enjoys success does not mean that he is righteous.

Background

Abraham was put to the ultimate test of loyalty when God commanded him to sacrifice Isaac on the altar. His success in withstanding the trial serves as a merit for all of his descendants until the end of time.

In his introduction to the *Akeidah, Ramban* explains that trials are not like a test that a teacher administers to a student. That sort of test benefits the teacher by providing information as to the student's scholastic level, but God knows everything there is to know about the person being tested. When God tests someone, it is solely for the benefit of the individual. God already knows a person's potential and fine intentions, and a person is rewarded for his desire to do good. However, reward and punishment are reserved primarily for voluntary *performance* of deeds. Thus when God puts a great person to a test, it permits him to translate potential into reality, affording him the opportunity to achieve a higher spiritual level by overcoming obstacles in his service of God. When a person surmounts obstacles and passes the test, he can then be rewarded for the actual performance.

Many commentators note that the word נִסָּיוֹן, *trial,* is related to נֵס, *a banner,* that is raised up high. In this sense, the purpose of a trial is not to "test" a person in the usual sense of the word, namely to see what he will do, nor is it intended as a trap for the wicked. Rather, a trial is meant to "raise up" the righteous by lifting them to new spiritual heights. It is a well-known phenomenon that those who successfully survive the crucible

---

9. **Let Him Bear the Burden.** The *Chazon Ish* writes: "As for my livelihood, it comes by means of constant miracles."

An enigmatic incident in the Talmud (*Megillah* 18a) becomes clear based on this perspective. The Talmud states that the Sages did not know the meaning of the verse הַשְׁלֵךְ עַל ה' יְהָבְךָ וְהוּא יְכַלְכְּלֶךָ, "Cast upon Hashem your burden and He will sustain you" (*Psalms* 55:23). Once an Arab was traveling with Rabbah bar Chama who was carrying a load. The Arab said to him, "Take your *yahav* (burden) and throw it on my camel." It was only then that they understood the verse clearly.

Were the Sages actually unaware of the translation of the word יְהָבְךָ? Did they need the Arab to teach them a verse from *Psalms?* Obviously not. The lesson of the Arab was to what extent one should put his trust in God. Just as a person who puts his load on the camel no longer needs to worry about how he can bear its weight so, as it were, man can place all his worries aside as he allows God to carry the brunt of his sustenance. We foolishly believe that God needs our help in bearing the burden (*R' Aharon Luria*).

The *Dubno Maggid* offered the following parable, to illustrate how ludicrous is the common human perspective.

A fellow was walking along the road carrying a heavy load when a wagon pulled up alongside him. The wagon driver invited him to hop aboard. As they were traveling, the driver noticed that the passenger was holding his package while sitting on the wagon. When he asked for an explanation, the passenger said, "It is enough that you allow me to ride on your wagon. Why should I burden you with my package as well?" The driver laughed. "Foolish one! Just as my wagon carries you, it carries the package. Do you really think that you are helping it?"

God carries us, granting us life. He also carries our "packages," providing us with a livelihood. Are we foolish enough to think that with our efforts we "help" Him carry the burden?

In the words of the Sages, "He Who grants life grants livelihood" (see *Taanis* 8a).

of difficult experiences emerge as better people. No matter what the situation, someone who turns potential into practice under difficult circumstances gains wisdom and strength of character. Abraham was already a great man, but he became greater with each triumphant navigation of a new trial. This, then, is the purpose of a trial — not to show God what He already knows, but to raise His servants to new heights, just as a banner is lifted higher and higher on its mast. Furthermore, just as a banner is a signal that something significant lies beneath it, so trials bring to light man's hidden qualities, which had been unknown and unrevealed until then.[10]

The Midrash explains the angel's repetition of Abraham's name at the *Akeidah* (*Genesis* 22:11) with the phrase: אַבְרָהָם דִּלְעֵילָא אַבְרָהָם דִּלְתַתָּא, *Abraham above, Abraham below*. *Abraham above* is the Abraham that God imbued with almost superhuman potential; *Abraham below* is the fully developed person that emerged when he actualized all of that potential by prevailing in the ten trials. At the tenth and final trial, the last bit of innate potential imbued in the *Abraham of above* was realized and became synonymous with the flesh-and-blood *Abraham below*. Thus, the ten trials manifested the

greatness of God's love for Abraham, for they made clear the extent of the potential with which God had endowed him (*R' Gedaliah Schorr*).[11]

וְהָאֱלֹקִים נִסָּה אֶת אַבְרָהָם
And God tested Abraham (ibid.)

Abraham was the epitome of true humility. All his life he was the living example of a humble spirit (see *Avos* 5:22). This self-image finds expression in his words "though I am dust and ashes" (*Genesis* 18:27). Certain that he had never done anything out of the ordinary, Abraham hoped that at the very least his son Isaac would, through his own Divine service, bring the Heavenly plan to fruition and give God cause to rejoice. This hope and dream carried Abraham through life and gave him strength. In light of this, imagine Abraham's soul-rending turmoil as God asked him to snuff out the last shred of hope that his entire existence might be validated! Abraham rose to the challenge and was willing to obey — even if it meant abandoning his dream for Isaac.

Thus the *Akeidah* was a test to show that Abraham would set aside all his hopes and dreams in obedience to God (*Beis Avraham*).[12]

---

10. **Outer Limits.** *Sfas Emes* relates the word נִסָּיוֹן to נֵס, *miracle.* Just as a miracle is God's way of helping man by going beyond the "limitations" of nature, a trial of faith calls on man to supersede his own "natural" limitations for the sake of God.

11. **Untapped Resources.** We all are blessed with almost infinitely more potential than we realize. So much human ability remains dormant and unused, a true tragedy! Only when we are placed under stress are we forced to draw upon our untapped resources and talents.

The purposes of life's difficulties, the trials and tribulations that God imposes on people, is to enable them to actualize their emotional and spiritual powers.

The town of Dvinsk was blessed with two world-renowned geniuses who served its two congregations concurrently. The *Rogatchover Gaon, R' Yosef Rosen,* outlived his colleague the *Ohr Some'ach, R' Meir Simchah HaKohen,* and eulogized him with the following observation: "One trapped under a fallen beam in a burning building can find the strength to move the beam and escape the flames, even though under ordinary circumstances he would never be able to push the beam even an inch. When R' Meir Simchah learned, he always tapped into that strength."

Ordinary people, if they are worthy, are presented with trials which force them to find strengths they never realized they had. While we all pray daily that God not bring us "into the grip of challenge [and test]" this reflects our fear of failing the test and, as it were, "disappointing" God. However, in reality spiritual and emotional growth is spurred on only by overcoming life's difficulties. Without tests we might never become whom we really could be!

12. **It's Your Problem.** *R' Naftali Tzvi Yehudah Berlin,* the renowned *Netziv,* was *Rosh Yeshivah* (dean) of the Yeshivah of Volozhin for 37 years. In one of its frequent fits of anti-Semitism, the Czarist Russian government demanded the introduction of Russian language and other secular disciplines into the curriculum of the yeshivah. If the administration would not comply, the yeshivah would be closed down. Since Volozhin was the primary yeshivah of the generation, which had developed much of the rabbinic leadership of the time, many prominent rabbis suggested that the yeshivah should accede to the government's demands.

The *Netziv* called a meeting of some of his greatest colleagues, in order to decide the future of the yeshivah. The

"What exactly was the great test?" asked *R' Elchonon Wasserman.* "Many, many great and simple Jews throughout our history were ready to make the ultimate sacrifice for God; why was Abraham's test considered so severe and his loyalty so remarkable? Furthermore, why was it deemed a test for Abraham and not for Isaac?"

R' Elchonon explained: To make the ultimate sacrifice for God's Name is really the logical and informed choice. Why should one not exchange existence in a transitory world for the bliss of eternity in the next world? This was the obvious choice for Isaac, as well. Abraham, however, was different. He had no interest in personal reward; he sought only to serve God. When God promised him great reward, Abraham argued, "What can you give me, seeing that I go childless" (*Genesis* 15:2). He wanted children as a means to propagate of faith in God and allegiance to His teachings. He foresaw that none of his many disciples would remain completely true to those ideals; even his own nephew Lot had deserted them. Consequently, if he were to remain childless, all of God's blessings would be in vain. He therefore protested, "Of what value is the next world to me if Your Name will be forgotten in this world?"

The *Akeidah* was truly a test of Abraham's loyalty, for by sacrificing his only son, one whom God would not replace (see *S'fas Emes*), his entire life's work of introducing the world to monotheism and the Godly way would disappear with the slice of his knife.

Would Abraham do what God asked, even if it meant destroying his life's mission and "harming" the Divine cause? This was the underlying essence of the tenth and final trial.

R' Chaim of Volozhin views "spiritual genetics" as the key to understanding why Jewish self-sacrifice for the sake of God became the norm throughout history. All of Abraham's actions that the Torah records have monumental consequences for our national character, for it is a principle of Jewish spiritual history that the actions of our forefathers portend the future of their descendants [מַעֲשֵׂה אָבוֹת סִימָן לַבָּנִים]. Many of the attributes of the forefathers were transmitted to their offspring as part of a spiritual legacy. The Jewish people's eternal willingness to sacrifice their lives for the sake of God is rooted in Abraham's willingness to be thrown into the fiery furnace, and later in his readiness to slaughter Isaac. Thus, Abraham was the genetic prototype; self-sacrifice is in our blood thanks to him.[13]

---

august group decided that the yeshivah should close rather than compromise its standards. One of those who participated in the discussion, the *Beis HaLevi,* summed up, "The Talmud teaches that when the Temple was on the verge of destruction by the Romans, the young *Kohanim* threw its keys heavenward and proclaimed, 'Since we were unable to be proper caretakers of Your Temple, please God, let its keys be given to You' (*Taanis* 29a). Likewise, we were entrusted to guard the authentic tradition of Torah and not allow any foreign influences to corrupt its purity. Since we are unable to do so, we will give the keys back to God rather than tamper with Torah or compromise its integrity." The *Netziv,* whose laborious toil on behalf of the yeshivah was legendary, was willing to see his life's work disintegrate overnight, rather than compromise God's will.

13. **Uninformed Hero.** A lovely story about the *Kozhnitzer Maggid* may shed a slightly different perspective on the question.

A woman who had been childless for many years came to the *Kozhnitzer Maggid* to ask him to pray that she be blessed with a child. She poured out her heart and begged him to pray on her behalf. The *Kozhnitzer* placed his head on the table for a few moments and then looked up, "I'm sorry, but I see there is nothing I can do," he sadly told the woman. "Please, please," she pleaded, "you must do something!" Replied the Rebbe, "I cannot pray for you, but let me tell you a story.

"Many years ago, a woman in your predicament came to the *Baal Shem Tov.* She and her husband had prayed, recited *Psalms,* given charity — they tried whatever they could in order that God bless them with a child, but to no avail. When they heard that the *Baal Shem Tov* was coming to their town, they decided to go to him; perhaps his prayers or his blessing would help. The woman cried bitterly, but the *Baal Shem Tov* told her, 'I see that in Heaven they are not ready to accept my prayers. As much as I want to, I cannot help you.' Brokenhearted, the woman went home.

"As the *Baal Shem Tov's* wagon was leaving town, the woman came running after him. 'Rebbe, Rebbe, I took the last *kopeks* in my possession and I bought some material with which I made a robe for the Rebbe!' Overcome by the woman's gesture and all that lay behind it, the *Baal Shem Tov* blessed the woman that a

Why does the Torah refer to the *Akeidah* as a test of Abraham, rather than of Isaac? Isaac was 37 years old at the time, certainly old enough to refuse to be offered as a sacrifice; yet, he willingly followed his father. Furthermore, why is the *Akeidah* mentioned in the Torah, while Abraham's willingness to enter the furnace of Nimrod at Ur Kasdim is mentioned only in the teachings of our Sages?

According to *Divrei Shmuel*, the second question may answer the first. For spiritual giants like Abraham and Isaac, the willingness to make the "ultimate" sacrifice for God is not at all remarkable. To them, life is a vehicle to serve God, and if He asks them to give it up, they are ready. For Abraham, the *Akeidah* was more significantly a test of *faith*. When he was initially commanded to make an offering of Isaac, the Evil Inclination began to whisper in his ear, "First God said, 'through Isaac will offspring be considered yours' (*Genesis* 21:12); now He instructs you to take him and offer him as a sacrifice! What are you going to do?" Ever strong in his faith, Abraham replied, "I will not question God's command."

This test of faith in the face of an "obvious" contradiction was Abraham's and Abraham's alone. At Ur Kasdim and at the *Akeidah*, Abraham and Isaac were ready to give up their lives, since there was no ambiguity in the situation. But the *Akeidah* was a greater challenge of Abraham, because God seemed to be contradicting Himself.

Beis HaLevi offers a different perspective based on a deep psychological insight. Why is it that people who think little of transgressing a Torah precept when it interferes with earning some money, with the success of their children, or in order to achieve some pleasure or enjoyment are nonetheless ready to die in order to sanctify God's Name? The answer is that it is easier to lose everything and allow oneself to be slaughtered than to continue to live with a constant sense of deprivation.

Had Isaac been slaughtered, he would have died in one glorious moment of spiritual grandeur — but Abraham would spend the rest of his days mourning his loss, with a gnawing sense of deprivation at having lost his precious son, his only spiritual heir. Thus the *Akeidah* was primarily a test of Abraham. As the *Alter of Novardok* expressed it, "It is easier to die like a Jew than to live like a Jew."[14]

קַח נָא אֶת בִּנְךָ
Please take your son (ibid. 2).

According to *Rashi,* the expression *please* indicates that God pleaded with Abraham to withstand this final test, because otherwise people would say that his earlier sacrifices were without substance. *R' Shimon Schwab* questioned: How could anybody negate the value of the great trials that Abraham withstood just because he did not rise to the last and greatest one? He explained that while the earlier tests certainly displayed the exalted spiritual level of Abraham and his unflagging loyalty to his Maker, it was only his willingness to give up his only son for God that earned the

---

son be born to her, and in fact it came to be."

The *Kozhnitzer Maggid* looked at the woman who had come to him for a blessing and said to her, "And I am that child."

The woman began to scream. "Rebbe, Rebbe I also will make you a robe." The *Kozhnitzer* interjected, "You don't understand. There is a big difference between you and my mother. She didn't know this story."

For Jews of all the generations, Abraham serves as the prototype of devotion and self-sacrifice. But Abraham himself "didn't know the story."

14. **Unbearable Sight.** *Kiflayim L'Sushia* offers a parable. A person accused of treason was mercilessly tortured to force him to confess, but to no avail. The police were at their wit's end. Finally, someone suggested that the accused's child be tortured in front of his eyes. In but a few short moments he admitted everything.

Such is human nature. People can endure excruciating physical pain, but cannot withstand even the threat of their children's suffering. One will do anything to spare his child.

This was Abraham's test. Could his allegiance to God outweigh his parental instinct and love? For Isaac it meant personal sacrifice which, although it carried tremendous significance, was not nearly as severe a test as that of his father.

eternal existence of the nation of Israel, which proudly bears his message and continues to live according to his values.

Without the *Akeidah,* all of Abraham's righteousness might have been viewed as nothing more than momentary flashes of spiritual brilliance, which lack real substance. Therefore God pleaded with Abraham that he be strong once more, in order to assure the survival of the Divine charge to spread His message to the world.[15]

Rabbeinu Nissim (Derashos HaRan) explains God's pleading tone in a different light: "Please forgive Me My promise that 'through Isaac will offspring be considered yours' *(Genesis* 21:12)." In other words, God did not *command* him, He *asked* him. Had Abraham argued that "besides Isaac, You haven't given me children who are fit to be my spiritual heirs," he would have had a legitimate right to refuse to sacrifice Isaac and God would not have punished him for his refusal, because there was no direct command.

Abraham with his burning with love for God was ready to give away everything he had, even his beloved son, solely to please God, even if he could legitimately absolve himself.[16]

אֲשֶׁר אָהַבְתָּ

That you love (ibid.).

On *Erev Shabbos Parashas Vayeira,* 1935, R' Yitzchak Alter, son of the *Imrei Emes of Ger,* passed away just as the sun was setting. The grieving father had offered his own personal *Akeidah.* As the *Imrei Emes* spoke that Friday night to his followers, these were his words: "My grandfather, the *Chidushei HaRim,* explained that the trial of the *Akeidah* was that Abraham continue to love Isaac intensely — and still be ready to bring him to the altar, with the full intensity of parental love intact.

"God did not want Abraham to deny his emotions. He wanted Abraham to fully experience his love of Isaac and yet fan the flame of his love for God just a bit higher.

"While the Talmud *(Eruvin* 22a) teaches that Torah can only survive among people committed enough to sometimes display cruelty to children and family members in order to fulfill the Torah's dictates, here God was not looking for cruelty. Let Abraham draw the knife across Isaac's neck, and let it be with the complete warmth of soul and with a burning intense love, a love that wants only the best for his beloved Isaac.

"This is the true understanding of a puzzling Midrash which teaches that as Abraham lifted his hand to take the knife, tears poured from his eyes and in his heart he was happy to do God's will. Both are necessary; tears of pity and a joyous heart.

"Isaac called out to his father, 'Father,' in order to arouse his mercy *(Midrash),* not, God forbid, so that Abraham might be overcome with emotion and change his plans but rather so that even his love would be offered upon the altar."

The *Imrei Emes* explained the test of the *Akeidah,* but he was also expressing his own acceptance of the loss of his son.

God did not immediately reveal to Abraham the clear identity of the intended offering. The Talmud records the conversation as follows:

God said, "Take your son."

---

15. **Inspiring Evidence.** One should never seek honor or publicity for his good deeds, but one's children must realize what is substantial and real in life. By allowing them to see us devoting time to Torah study or allowing them to see us pray with feeling and warmth, we give our lives a substance that will endure when they follow our example.

16. **But . . .** According to my brother *R' Yussie Lieber,* this is the homiletic meaning of the words of confession recited on Yom Kippur, אֲבָל אֲנַחְנוּ חָטָאנוּ, *but we have sinned.* The greatest traps in life are the legitimate excuses. "I really want to spend Sunday mornings learning — *but* I have so many social and familial commitments." "I would love to give substantially to help a neighbor who has fallen on hard times — *but* I must honor *Yom Tov* by buying myself a new suit and hat." "I had intended to control my temper — *but* he really insulted me." The excuses may be valid, but they cause us to sin against ourselves and impede our spiritual growth. *But,* I have sinned.

It is the *buts* in our lives that bring us to sin. Abraham had every good reason in the world to refuse, yet he heeded God's plea that he *please* take his son without any ifs or buts.

"But I have *two* sons [Isaac and Ishmael]. Which should I take?"

"אֶת יְחִידְךָ, *your only one.*"

"But each of them is the only son of his mother."

"אֲשֶׁר אָהַבְתָּ, *whom you love!*" God answered.

"But I love them both."

"אֶת יִצְחָק, I mean *Isaac,*" God replied.

The slow unfolding of the offering's identity was to make the commandment more precious to Abraham, by arousing his curiosity and rewarding him for complying with every word of the command (*Sanhedrin* 89b; *Rashi* ad loc.).

God eased Abraham slowly, step-by-step, into the herculean task. First Abraham found in himself the emotional fortitude to sacrifice his son, whichever it was. Next, he garnered the tenacity and strength of commitment to offer his *only* son. In the third step, Abraham dug deep into the wellspring of his love for God and reached a pinnacle of love that superseded his great parental love, and came to terms with the fact that it was Isaac whom God expected him to offer. Why was this necessary? Why couldn't he immediately proceed to the ultimate level of self-sacrifice?

Sfas Emes explains: Everything recorded in the Torah about our forefathers has a monumental impact on our spiritual makeup. When Abraham displayed his unwavering allegiance to God and His word, time and time again, he implanted in his children the same ability. Therefore Abraham had to express his readiness to sacrifice for God in gradually increasing stages. By doing so, he erected a ladder for us so that any Jew can ascend to the heights of self-sacrifice. Even one not yet ready for a full commitment to Torah can gradually grow into it.

פרשת חיי שרה &·
Parashas Chayei Sarah

Background

The *parashah* opens with Sarah's death and Abraham's effort to provide her with an appropriate burial plot. This site, the Cave of Machpelah, was the final resting place of four couples: Adam and Eve, Abraham and Sarah, Isaac and Rebecca, and Jacob and Leah.

וַיִּהְיוּ חַיֵּי שָׂרָה מֵאָה שָׁנָה וְעֶשְׂרִים שָׁנָה
Sarah's lifetime was one hundred years, twenty years . . . (23:1).

Targum *Yonasan* (verse 22:20) explains the juxtaposition of Sarah's death and the *Akeidah* as an indication that she died when Satan told her that Abraham had actually slaughtered Isaac. Considering Sarah's exalted level of spirituality, however, the implication that she was heartbroken over her son's being offered as a sacrifice to God is somewhat difficult to accept.[1], [2]

The answer lies in the words of comfort once offered parents whose son died suddenly at the young age of 26 after having brought hundreds of young people back to Judaism. "Every Jew is sent to the world to illuminate it with God's Presence. Most spend seventy or eighty years striking matches which continually blow out, while other unique souls like your son may be compared to a shooting star that rockets across the sky for but a short time, all the while casting great light."

---

1. **Almost Not Good Enough.** *Rashi* (citing *Midrash Tanchuma*) writes that when Sarah was informed that Abraham *almost* slaughtered Isaac, she passed away. When Abraham was told at the last minute that God only wanted him to bring Isaac up on the altar but not to slaughter him, Sarah was not there. When she heard that Abraham only *almost* slaughtered Isaac, but that his desire to complete the offering had been thwarted, she passed away (*Binah L'Tushiah*).

2. **Emotional Acclimation.** Why was Abraham able to deal with the thought of his son being slaughtered while Sarah passed away upon hearing the news?

R' Chaim Shmulevitz offered two insights. First, human beings possess a phenomenal ability to become acclimated to the most deplorable situations. Slowly but surely, that which previously seemed incredible becomes reality.

When God commanded Abraham to offer Isaac up on the altar He broke the idea to him gradually, in stages (see *Rashi* 22:2). The natural ability to become accustomed to difficult situations helped Abraham confront the challenge. Sarah, however, was presented, without any forewarning, with the "fact" that her son was almost slaughtered. She could not bear it.

Secondly, when God tests a person, He provides him the strength to withstand it. For this reason, the Sages teach that one should never place himself in an overly challenging or tempting situation (*Sanhedrin* 107a); only when God places us in such a situation may we be assured that He grants us the spiritual and emotional wherewithal to "weather the storm." Not so, however, when the challenge is self-induced.

Since God tested Abraham at the *Akeidah,* He gave him the strength to succeed. Sarah, despite her spiritual greatness, was not fortified with the emotional reserves to survive the thought that Isaac was no longer alive.

When Sarah heard that she had succeeded in raising a son who was ready to make the ultimate sacrifice for God, she knew she had accomplished her purpose in life. She was now ready to die (*Zekan Aharon*).[3] [4]

❧

*R*ashi notes the separate reckoning of the years, explaining *100 years, 20 years* as teaching that she was the same at age 20 as at the age of 100.

Youth is a precious time. Young people are idealistic, emotionally excitable and impulsive (which can be a very positive trait), all of which bring enthusiasm and alacrity to life's tasks. On the other hand, certain very positive traits generally come only with age. Level-headedness, experience and its lessons, the ability to reign in one's passions and make logical decisions all come with maturity.

Sarah was at 20 like she was at 100; calm, level headed and totally in control of her desires.

Alternately, at the age of 100 she still had the fire of youth, idealism and emotional excitement

This rare combination of youth and age is the hallmark of greatness (*Maayana Shel Torah*).

שְׁנֵי חַיֵּי שָׂרָה
the years of Sarah's life (ibid).

*W*hy does the Torah repeat this phrase? To teach that all of Sarah's years were equally good (*Rashi*).

This assessment seems astounding. She suffered the pain of childlessness until the age of 90. The famine that forced her and Abraham out of the Promised Land and her debasing incidents with Pharaoh and Abimelech certainly don't qualify as "good times." How can the Torah say that all her years were equally good?

HaDerash V'Halyun and *R' Zusia of Anipoli* suggest that the Torah speaks of Sarah's perception of reality. Her motto throughout her years, no matter

---

3. **Never Beyond.** God only tests people only in those areas in which He knows they are strong enough to succeed (see *Ramban, Genesis* 22:1). With all his love for Isaac, Abraham was asked to sacrifice him because God knew he could do it.

God tested Abraham, but not Sarah, for He knew that it was beyond her ability to endure the anguish. God was not upset with Sarah's reaction to the *Akeidah* — He reckoned with it and never put her to that test (*Meilitz Yosher*).

According to *Chidushei HaRim,* this is the meaning of the Talmud's statement (*Kesubos* 33b) that had Nebuchadnezzar tortured Chananiah, Mishael and Azariah, they would have bowed to the statue set up by Nebuchadnezzar. They were strong enough to be burned to death, but not to withstand torture.

The Talmud does not mean to downplay the spiritual stature of these great men. Rather, it teaches that even great men are not given trials and tribulations beyond their abilities to endure. God tested their willingness to endure instant death by fire on His behalf. Aware that they could not bear torture, He did not allow the tyrant to put them to that test.

In the words of the *Vilna Gaon,* "It is a Divine miracle that He holds the evil inclination on a leash, not allowing him any more of a foothold in a person's life than the degree at which the person can still overcome him."

4. **Not Done Yet.** On the other hand, the fact that one has yet to fulfill his unique mission in life is a reason why he must still live. *Talmud Yerushalmi* (*Kiddushin* 1:7) relates that R' Tarfon was a paradigm of parental honor. Once, the laces on his mother's shoe ripped in the courtyard near her house, and she began hopping home. R' Tarfon quickly darted out to her and placed his hands under her foot so that she would not get dirty.

Once when R' Tarfon was sick the Sages came to visit him. His mother met them and implored them to pray on his behalf, saying that his merit was that he was extremely dedicated to her honor. She cited the previous incident as an example of his dedication. The Sages responded, "Even if he was a thousandfold dedicated to the mitzvah, he would not have achieved half of what one must do to honor parents."

Their answer is incomprehensible. Why did they make such short shrift of R' Tarfon's great achievements in this area? Furthermore, what kind of answer is this to a mother whose loyal son is deathly ill?

Avnei Nezer explains: When they heard of his extraordinary level of parental fidelity, they realized that R' Tarfon's special mission in life was the mitzvah of honoring parents. They feared that he had reached the ultimate in this mitzvah and therefore had finished his task in this world. As a prayer of sorts, they said that he had yet to reach the peak of honoring his mother, and therefore should be granted more years of life to fulfill his mission.

R' Yisrael Shimon Kostelanitz lived to a ripe old age. Often he would tell his grandchildren, "I'm not going to die yet. How do I know? Because I still need to do *teshuvah* (repent) before I die and I haven't done it yet."

the circumstances, was "this too is for the good." Whatever befell her, she followed the path advocated by our Sages, who taught that one should bless God for the perceived evil just as for the perceived good. Since all the circumstances of her life came from God, she viewed them all as equally good.[5]

Techeiles Mordechai offers a different perspective. Most people experience periods in their lives when they feel driven and motivated to serve God, as well as times when spiritual matters hold little appeal. They compartmentalize their activities into the convenient categories of mundane and spiritual. The truly righteous, however, understand the secret of King Solomon's words, *Know Him in all your ways* (Proverbs 3:6). *Rambam* (*Shemoneh Perakim* 5) explains that all of life's activities are opportunities to serve Hashem. Business affairs, sleeping, eating and all the other seemingly mundane pursuits can be transformed into vehicles for spiritual activity and growth. Music, art, humor and other seemingly worldly pleasures can be employed to place one in a frame of mind conducive to Torah study and mitzvah observance.

From this perspective, every minute of life can be used to attain the goodness of a close relationship with God.

All of Sarah's days were good because every moment of her life was filled with meaning.

וַיָּבֹא אַבְרָהָם לִסְפֹּד לְשָׂרָה וְלִבְכֹּתָה
and Abraham came to eulogize Sarah and to bewail her (ibid. 2).

The literal translation of לִסְפֹּד לְשָׂרָה is *to eulogize* [to] *Sarah;* לִסְפֹּד אֶת שָׂרָה, *to eulogize Sarah,*

would seem to be the more correct form.

People tend to exaggerate when eulogizing others. Rather than focusing on the person's true positive characteristics, they seek to "dress up" the deceased with superlatives that do not apply. In reality, they neither honor nor do justice to the memory of the departed, since neither the eulogizer nor the listeners believe the exaggerated praises.[6]

Abraham did not merely praise Sarah indiscriminately; he eulogized her by offering an authentic character portrait, describing the loss in a fashion that remained loyal to her true character, nature and good deeds.

Thus he eulogized *to* Sarah, for the picture truly portrayed reality (*Avnei Chen*).

The Torah teaches that Abraham eulogized Sarah and bewailed her passing. The order seems reversed; initially one bewails the immediate pain and only after achieving release is one able to mentally focus on the dimensions of the loss, offering eulogies of the departed and an assessment of the vacuum caused by her loss. The Talmud (*Moed Katan* 27b) in fact teaches that the first three days after a loved one's death are a time for crying, while the time for eulogies is up until seven days, for the pain during the first three days is so searing that one cannot find words to express the loss. Why, then, does the Torah speak first of Abraham *eulogizing* Sarah and only afterwards of *bewailing* her?

Kli Yakar explains that normally the most intense feeling of loss is at the beginning, immediately after the person dies. As time goes on, the sense of

---

5. **Who? Me?** *R' Zusia of Anipoli* explained the verse *and Hashem blessed Abraham with everything* (בַּכֹּל, lit. *all*) in this light. Abraham was blessed with the vision to see כָּל מַה דְּעָבִיד רַחֲמָנָא לְטַב עָבִיד, *all God did was good* (*Berachos* 60b).

R' Zusia lived this mind-set throughout his life, and he would interpret the blessing we recite every morning accordingly: Blessed . . . Who has provided me כָּל צָרְכִּי, *my every need*. R' Zusia explained, "Everything You did for me fills a need of mine, because everything You do to me is for my good."

Two young men visited the *Maggid of Mezritch* and asked him to explain the words of the Sages that one must bless Him for the bad just like one blesses Him for the good. "How is this possible?" they asked.

He sent them to ask the question of R' Zusia. They found him in tatters, sitting in pain near the furnace in the study hall and told him that the Maggid had sent them to ask him to explain the enigmatic Talmudic statement.

Replied R' Zusia, "Why did he send you to me? He must be mistaken. I can't answer you since I've yet to experience the taste of badness in my life."

6. **Mistaken Identity.** A wealthy miser passed away. At his funeral, the eulogizers spoke of his magnanimity, of his warm heart and open hand. His son — who knew his father for the miser he was — turned to his mother in middle of the eulogy. "Mom, let's get out of here. That can't be my father in the casket."

loss and pain decrease. Thus, initially one cries; after three days the pain recedes somewhat and the shock of the loss is lessened. Then one is able to eulogize, giving his emotions a more cerebral expression.

There are, however, losses that do not diminish with time; on the contrary the sense of a gaping void only grows stronger. Abraham sensed that with the loss of Sarah, who was not only his wife, but a great woman in her own right, the feeling of loss would increase with time. Therefore, after he eulogized her, he realized more and more the true dimensions of his loss. Then he really began to bewail her death.

An alternative approach is offered by *R' Elazar M. Shach*: People can bewail the death of a person only to the extent that they are able to truly assess the loss. Sometimes we do not cry because we do not really understand what we have lost.

Sarah died an old woman. People did not understand that with her death, Abraham's partner in all his spiritual endeavors was gone. Abraham therefore eulogized her first. He painted a word picture so that they would realize that it was Sarah who had brought so many women to authentic faith in One God. Only after his eulogy were people capable of mourning her loss.[7]

The כ of the word לִבְכֹּתָהּ, *to bewail her*, is written in a diminished form, the implication being that Abraham didn't cry very much over the loss of his beloved wife. How could this be? *Baal HaTurim* writes that since Sarah lived a long life, Abraham shed a minimum of tears over her death. This

seems incredible. Certainly one cries over the loss of his life's partner regardless of how old she was when she died!

The *Vilna Gaon* explained: Abraham knew that Sarah had fulfilled her entire mission in life. She had made full use of this world as a corridor which leads to the World to Come, and had prepared herself properly in the "lobby" so that she could enter the "banquet hall" (see *Avos* 4:21). Hence there was no reason for him to cry for her soul. The only reason to cry was over the loss of her physical presence. However, as the Torah teaches, *you are children to Hashem, your God — you shall not cut yourselves and you shall not make a bald spot between your eyes for a dead person. For you are a holy people to Hashem, your God* (*Deuteronomy* 14:1-2). As children of God and as a holy people it is inappropriate that we excessively bewail the loss of the body. We must realize that the state of the eternal soul should be our primary focus. Thus when Sarah died old and fulfilled, Abraham's tears were limited.

Bikkurei Aviv offers a different perspective, focused on why only the letter כ is written in the diminutive form.

The Sages interpret the repetition of *years* in the verse *one hundred years, twenty years and seven years* (23:1) as dividing Sarah's life into three periods, each with its own uniqueness, yet with shared qualities. She was as sinless at 100 as she was at 20; at 20 her beauty was as innocent and wholesome as when she was 7.

Thus the age of 20 is a symbol of both her righteousness and her beauty. Since the numerical value of כ is twenty, the Torah uses a small כ to teach us that Abraham's tears were diminished

---

7. **Assessing the Loss.** One who bewails a deceased cries for himself and for the departed. If, however, the departed put his earthly sojourn to a good use, then there is no reason to weep for the departed, who is going to a far better existence and, armed with the spiritual accomplishments in this world, stands only to gain by the change of venue.

In such a case we cry only for *ourselves*, who are no longer able to enjoy and benefit from the person's presence. Only when the person failed to make a spiritual success of life must we cry for him as well.

Thus we cry immediately for one who did not complete his earthly mission, since he has lost the opportunity to salvage his life. However, for one who filled his days in this world with spiritual content and meaning, there is no need to cry. In such a case we only cry for ourselves, and therefore must first eulogize so that we realize the magnitude of our loss.

Abraham did not cry for Sarah; he cried for himself and the people of his generation. He therefore first eulogized Sarah, focusing on what the world would be missing now that she was gone. Only then could he and they really cry (based on *Kli Yakar*).

since they were primarily for the the world's loss of her righteousness, not for her beauty.[8]

גֵּר וְתוֹשָׁב אָנֹכִי עִמָּכֶם
I am an alien and a resident among you (ibid. 4).

The righteous see themselves as aliens and strangers in this world. They are here only temporarily, on the way to a higher and far more meaningful existence. The wicked see life from the opposite perspective. In their eyes, this world is all that exists, and the here and now is their only permanent reality. Thus they live with the motto "eat, drink and be merry, for tomorrow we die."

This is what Abraham meant to tell the Hittites. "Our philosophies of life are diametrically opposed. The two of us are like an alien and a resident, for you see yourselves as permanent residents, in this world while I view myself as an alien sojourner. "Thus I ask you to give me a burial place, not one of the choicest plots among you but rather on the edge of Ephron's field. We are different and should remain separate" (*Dubno Maggid*).[9]

R' Eliyahu Meir Bloch, Rosh Yeshivah of Telshe, views this dual identity as a reflection of Abraham's clarity of vision. If one is intellectually and emotionally independent and oblivious to the winds of conformity, then one can be a "resident" with a strong sense of self, even while acting like an "alien" who knows that this world is really not his home. One who is firm in his commitment to truth sees a clear path in life. He is a resident, firm and unshakable in his outlook, all the while maintaining the position of a comfortable outsider.

וַיָּקָם אַבְרָהָם וַיִּשְׁתַּחוּ לְעַם הָאָרֶץ לִבְנֵי חֵת
Then Abraham rose up and bowed down to the members of the council, to the children of Heth (ibid. 7).

After returning from the *Akeidah* to find his beloved wife dead, Abraham had to deal with the wily Ephron and the other Hittites, in order to purchase a burial plot for her. Although they knew that Abraham would be granted this land by God, they wanted to delay his settling there as much as possible. They therefore concocted a story about a city ordinance which forbade granting burial space to outsiders. Bowed under the terrible grief of his loss and in the midst of eulogizing his illustrious wife, whose level of prophecy was even greater

---

8. **Woman of Valor.** The Midrash teaches that Abraham employed the text of King Solomon's ode to his mother (*Eishes Chayil,* "A Woman of Valor") when eulogizing Sarah.

The diminished crying, bewailing the loss of her righteousness but not of her beauty, comes to full expression in the concluding words of that paean of praise, *False is grace and vain is beauty, a God-fearing woman — she should be praised* (Proverbs 31:30).

9. **Permanently Temporary.** The *Dubno Maggid* interprets the verse *for you are sojourners and residents with Me* (*Leviticus* 25:23) in this vein. God says to man, "The two of us are a sojourner and a resident. If you see yourself as a permanent resident in this world and therefore expend your greatest efforts on worldly success, then I will be an alien sojourner in your life. If, however, you enjoy a healthy perspective and view your stay in this world as the fleeting passage of an alien who should devote himself primarily to Torah study, performing kind deeds and growing spiritually, then I will be a permanent presence in your life."

The *Chafetz Chaim* offered the following parable: A wealthy man commissioned an architect to draw up plans for a magnificent home. He asked the architect to plan for a large banquet hall, and to be sure that the corridor leading to it be very wide.

After measuring the proposed building site, the architect returned to his client and said to him, "The plot is clearly not large enough for both a lavish banquet hall and a large corridor. If we expand the corridor it will come at the expense of diminishing the size of the banquet hall. The choice is yours but if you want my suggestion, I think you should cut down on the corridor in order to make the banquet hall large enough. This is the prevalent style — to make the banquet room large and the corridor small. If you do the opposite, people will laugh at you. They will say, 'Look what that fool did; the banquet hall, where people should be able to sit comfortably, he made small but the corridor, which is merely a way to get into the hall, he made large.' "

We spend our entire lives building our homes in the World to Come. But, like the fool in the story, we insist on investing all our time and energy building a lavish corridor, i.e., our comforts in this world. In doing so, we limit the scope of the banquet hall (the World to Come), sacrificing our eternal home for a temporary one.

than his, Abraham would have been quite justified in expressing a less than gracious response to their cunning and trickery. But Abraham was a paragon of grace. He swallowed his pain and bowed to the Hittites in recognition that "no one else has to suffer because I am in pain" (*Michtav MeEliyahu*).[10]

בְּכֶסֶף מָלֵא יִתְּנֶנָּה לִי
Let him grant it to me
for its full price (ibid. 9).

Many reasons have been given for why Abraham insisted on paying full price for the burial plot. The *Steipler Gaon* offered the following insight:

Whenever someone does something on your behalf, you become indebted to repay the favor. The Sages (*Bereishis Rabbah* 58) teach that if someone served you a meal of beans, you must pay him back with a meal of meat, since he took the initiative of inviting you. Accepting favors from an evil person, therefore, can be dangerous since he will demand incessant repayment, viewing the recipient as "indentured" to himself. This can cause one to lose endless time from spiritual pursuits, as well as undermine the positive influence one might exert on others.

The Sages alluded to this when they said that even if an ignorant person respects a Torah scholar as a golden vase, once the scholar derives benefit from him, the ignorant person, he looks at the scholar as a clay jar. As soon as the Torah scholar becomes dependent on the ignorant, their respect for him is drastically reduced.[11]

Thus, Abraham wanted no gifts and no bargains. *Let him grant it to me for its full price,* he said. I don't want to be morally indebted to Ephron.

Rabbeinu Bachya notes that there are three sites in *Eretz Yisrael* that were bought for their full price. The first was the Cave of Machpelah, purchased by Abraham. The second was the site of Mount Gerizim and Mount Ebal, which Jacob bought for one hundred *kesitahs* (see *Genesis* 33:19). Finally,

---

10. **Why Should He Suffer?** The wife of *R' Avraham Grodzensky,* the *mashgiach* of the Slabodka Yeshivah, passed away at a very young age, leaving him with a large family including several young children. When he was sitting *shivah* a student came to tell him the good news that he had been exempted from being drafted into the Lithuanian army. R' Avraham stood up, kissed the young man and wished him *mazal tov.* His personal pain and tragedy did not impair his ability to rejoice with a friend.

This is not only true about honoring others under trying circumstances; one must be careful to maintain one's own self-respect even when experiencing a personal blow.

R' Chaim Yaakov Goldvicht went to console *R' Yitzchak Hutner,* when he sat *shivah* on the passing of his rebbetzin.

People waited in an anteroom and were allowed in to R' Hutner one at a time. When R' Goldvicht entered, he sat quietly waiting for R' Hutner to begin speaking. As R' Goldvicht put it, "The question hung in the air. What was the meaning of this remarkable practice of seeing people one at at time?"

R' Hutner related the following story by way of explanation: One of *R' Yisrael Salanter's* followers, a wealthy businessman, was sitting *shivah.* He asked the maid to bring him a glass of tea. Generally she served tea in a crystal glass, but under the circumstances, she felt that a plain glass would be more appropriate. When she brought the tea he said to her quietly, "Just because I suffered one blow, do I have to suffer another?"

"I," concluded R' Hutner, "never see groups of people. I need to talk with people individually so that I can give them my undivided attention. Now that I've suffered the terrible blow of losing my wife, must I suffer the additional blow of having to conduct mass entertainment?"

11. **Getting Off Cheaply.** [While it is certainly appropriate for laymen to give financial support to rabbis and Torah scholars, it is a grave error to allow laymen to think that all they owe their spiritual leaders is money.

Every layman is the beneficiary of his rabbi's wisdom, time, care and concern. Rabbis should make it clear that the main thing they expect from their congregants is upgrading their commitments to Halachah and Torah study.]

The *Brisker Rav* once spent a few days at a hotel when his youngest son got married. When he was about to leave, he approached the hotelier and asked for the bill. The proprietor refused to take money for the rav's stay.

"It is an honor and pleasure to have hosted the rav and his family," he said. The Brisker Rav insisted on paying nevertheless.

He later commented to a family member; "One always has to pay. The most inexpensive form of payment is money."

King David purchased the site of the Temple from *Araunah the Jebusite* for a hefty sum.

Mount Gerizim and Mount Ebal represent Torah, for it was there that the Jewish people re-ratified their commitment to the Torah. The Temple is the symbol of Divine service, while the purchase of a burial plot by Abraham was the ultimate in interpersonal kindness.

These three areas — Torah, service of God and kindness — are the basic foundations of the world (see *Avos* 1:2). We must be ready to expend whatever monies and resources are necessary in order to maintain these pillars of existence.

אֶרֶץ אַרְבַּע מֵאֹת שֶׁקֶל כֶּסֶף בֵּינִי וּבֵינְךָ מַה הוּא
Land [worth] four hundred silver shekels; between me and you — what is it? (ibid. 15).

Rashi explains *between me and you* as meaning, what is such a sum between two beloved [friends] like us?

Since when were Ephron and Abraham friends who loved one another?

R' Chaim Meir of Vizhnitz offered a lovely homiletical perspective.

Abraham and Ephron were both lovers, not of each other but of different things. Said Ephron, "I love money and can never have enough of it. For me, 400 silver *shekels* is an insignificant sum." As the Sages say, "One who has a 100 wants 200. Those who love money are never satiated with money." You, Abraham, on the other hand, love *mitzvos* and are ready to spend significant amounts of money in order to perform them.

Thus to each one of us (each according to his love), 400 silver *shekels* is a paltry sum."

וַיָּקָם שְׂדֵה עֶפְרוֹן
And Ephron's field . . . was confirmed (ibid. 17).

The Midrash interprets וַיָּקָם as *it rose,* for the property became elevated when it passed from the profane hands of Ephron to the holy ones of Abraham.

How can an inanimate item sense elevation?

R' Eliyahu Meir Bloch explained: From the Torah standpoint, acquisition is not merely a technical means of transferring property. One's property is an extension of self to the extent that the inanimate property is affected by the spiritual level of its owner.

Since God created everything in order to add to the greater glory of Heaven, the plot of land takes a definite step upward when it becomes linked to the destiny of a spiritual titan such as Abraham.[12]

Background

Sensing that his own trailblazing life was nearing its end, Abraham sought to perpetuate his legacy by finding a mate for his son Isaac. He made his servant Eliezer swear that he would search for Isaac's match among the members of the family in Charan rather than among the Canaanites.[13]

וְאַבְרָהָם זָקֵן בָּא בַּיָּמִים
Now Abraham was old, well on in years (24:1).

The term בָּא בַּיָּמִים may be rendered literally as *he came with the days.* R' Avraham of Slonim offered a homiletical interpretation.

Some people allow the day to precede them, while

---

12. **Carnivorous Ignoramous.** According to *Maharal,* this is the thrust of the Talmudic assertion that an ignoramus is forbidden to partake of meat (*Pesachim* 49b). When man ingests food in order to enhance his uniquely human and spiritual aspects, he elevates the food, turning vegetative and meat substance into part of the human being.

An ignoramus who does not accept the Torah as his guide to elevating the mundane and transforming it into the sanctified must refrain from eating meat. Rather than elevating the meat, he will be spiritually pulled downward by the animalistic nature that it arouses.

13. **Genetic Flaw.** Although the Charanite families were idolaters, Abraham saw them as a better place to look for a mate for Isaac than among the Canaanites who were ethically and morally degenerate.

Idolatry is a theological-intellectual flaw that views the powerless as powerful. Intellectual flaws are not passed from generation to generation, unlike ethical or moral imperfection which does carry over genetically.

Abraham, concerned over the spiritual orientation of his grandchildren and family, was more hesitant to marry his son to a maiden with inherent ethical and moral flaws than to have him marry the child of an idolater (*Kli Yakar, Avnei Nezer*).

others precede the day. The one who allows his day to precede him is a person who spends most of his day on futile, foolish pursuits and realizes only at the end of the day that it is about time that he did something in service of God and his own spiritual growth. On the other hand, and even worse, is someone who lacks firm faith in God, and therefore worries today about what will be tomorrow. Such a person allows his fears and faithlessness to precede his attitude toward each new day.

Abraham was like neither of the above. He came exactly with the day, for his service of God began as soon as the day arrived. Likewise, his firm faith never allowed him to worry about tomorrow even a minute before it came. Abraham came *with* his days.

Chidushei HaRim suggests a different perspective. Every day has its unique challenges and goals. The spiritual profit to be reaped today could not have been reaped yesterday, nor will it be available tomorrow. Today and only today can one seize the specific spiritual opportunities available to him. Abraham did not merely live the big picture; he came to the end of his life having made good use of every single day and its unique goal. He enlightened every day with spiritual light, making it *day*. Thus he approached his life with all of his days intact and fulfilled.

וַיֹּאמֶר אַבְרָהָם אֶל עַבְדּוֹ זְקַן בֵּיתוֹ
הַמֹּשֵׁל בְּכָל אֲשֶׁר לוֹ שִׂים נָא יָדְךָ תַּחַת
יְרֵכִי וְאַשְׁבִּיעֲךָ בַּה׳ אֱלֹקֵי הַשָּׁמַיִם
And Abraham said to his servant,
the elder of his household who controlled
all that was his: "Place now your hand
under my thigh. And I will have you swear
by Hashem God of heaven . . . " (ibid. 2-3).

Be'er Mayim Chaim offers a parable to explain why Abraham asked Eliezer to swear.

Normally the first time one visits a city he must ascertain where he may eat. A simple Jew looks for a kosher sign on a restaurant, and if he sees it, he is satisfied that he may go inside and eat. A Jew who takes his Judaism more seriously will approach another Jew in the marketplace and ask him where he may eat, relying on the Talmudic dictum (*Gittin* 2b) that in ritual (as opposed to monetary areas) one witness is sufficient.

A more vigilant person will go to the local synagogue or *beis midrash* and look for someone who looks like a respectable member of the community and ask him. Someone more careful will not rely on anyone other than the rabbi of the town.

If the same person came there to invest a large sum of money with a local businessmen and wanted to find out which ones were honest and trustworthy, he would not rely on any of the above-mentioned people. Instead, he would spend an extended period of time, getting to know the populace. Only when he personally felt confident that a person was honest would he be ready to do business with him. The testimony of any townsperson — be it layman, students of the *beis midrash* or even the local rabbi — would be insufficient in his eyes.

Even after he was sure he was dealing with an honest person, he would still demand a signed contract, guarantors and proof of financial stability.

This is the usual, albeit improper, difference in how people approach spiritual matters as opposed to fiscal ones.[14]

---

14. **Blind Trust.** *R' Yisrael Salanter* once came to a village inn. When the proprietor saw a Jew with a rabbinic appearance, he realized he might be able to save himself a trip to the *shochet* (ritual slaughterer) in the city. "Are you a *shochet*?" he asked R' Yisrael. "I have a cow I would like you to slaughter." R' Yisrael demurred, "I'm sorry, I am not a *shochet*."

A while later, R' Yisrael approached the innkeeper and asked if he could borrow a ruble. Replied the innkeeper, "This is the first time I've ever met you. How can I lend you money when I don't even know who you are or where you come from?" replied the innkeeper.

R' Yisrael turned to him, "Listen to your own words. When it comes to money you don't trust me for even one ruble, yet after a perfunctory 'hello' you were ready to rely on me to slaughter your animal, an act which entails many Torah prohibitions."

[An insightful educator once asked his students, "If you had a .00001 suspicion that some food contained arsenic, would you eat it? Of course not. So why, when in doubt, are you ready to say, 'It's probably kosher. Everybody eats it [there]' "? He then concluded, "Often when we inquire about the rabbinical supervision on an

Abraham, however, was of a different ilk with his priorities solid and clear. Although he was extremely wealthy, he deposited everything he had with Eliezer who *controlled all that was his.* With regard to his physical possessions, he trusted Eliezer implicitly. But when it came to the spiritual agenda of finding a wife for Isaac and a mother of the nation, he was skeptical and asked Eliezer to take an oath.

Shem MiShmuel offers a different approach, focusing on the power of an oath. Deep within himself, man possesses the power and ability to succeed in very difficult situations; however, he is generally unaware that such capabilities exist. When one swears and must therefore fulfill his commitment under any and all circumstances, he realizes that there is no way for him to evade his responsibilities. Then, his willpower surfaces, granting him the strength to surmount the insurmountable and honor his pledge.

Abraham knew how difficult it would be for Eliezer to succeed in his mission. Besides the obvious problem of Bethuel and Laban, Abraham was sure that all the antispiritual forces in the world would seek to derail the continuation of his family and his legacy. Thus he made Eliezer swear so that he could reach deeply into his recesses of strength and spirit to fulfill his holy mission.[15]

מִבְּנוֹת הַכְּנַעֲנִי אֲשֶׁר אָנֹכִי יוֹשֵׁב בְּקִרְבּוֹ
from the daughters of the Canaanites among whom I dwell (ibid. 3).

The implication is that had Abraham lived elsewhere he might not have disqualified a Canaanite maiden as a wife for his son Isaac. *Chasam Sofer* explains: Abraham believed that the power of his household and its values could influence any young maiden to follow the true religion's path of morality, ethics and righteousness. He feared only that were the maiden to be a local, she would have ready access to her family and its negative influence. He, therefore, told Eliezer not to select a maiden from the Canaanites *among whom I dwell. Rather to my land and to my kindred shall you go* (verse 4).[16]

וַעֲשֵׂה חֶסֶד עִם אֲדֹנִי אַבְרָהָם
that You do kindness with my master Abraham (ibid. 12).

Eliezer deeply admired Abraham. Why, then, did he ask God for success in his mission as a kindness to Abraham rather than due to Abraham's merit? *Chidushei HaRim* explains that this was reflective of the lessons Eliezer absorbed in Abraham's home and presence. The faith in Divine Providence was so powerful that all of

---

eatery or product we are not really interested in knowing if it is truly kosher. Rather, we just want to be sure that if it is not, then there is someone willing to burn in purgatory instead of us."]

15. **Pride on the Line.** A long-time smoker had tried many times, unsuccessfully, to quit smoking. Finally he hit on a plan. He told many of his friends that right after Tishah B'Av he would stop. The embarrassment he would experience if he did not make good on his pledge gave him the incentive and strength to succeed.

This strategy can easily be adapted to matters of the spirit. By putting one's ego and pride on the line, one can tap into hidden resources of strength he might otherwise not realized he had.

16. **Spiritual Surroundings.** According to *R' Moshe Feinstein,* this is the thrust of verse 6, in which Abraham warns his servant not to bring Isaac to the hometown of Bethuel and Rebecca. Abraham preferred that Isaac find a wife on a lower spiritual level than Rebecca, rather than leave *Eretz Yisrael* and move to Charan.

The powerful influence of one's surroundings and social interactions can never be underestimated. Even a holy couple like Isaac and Rebecca could not remain untainted or unaffected by the spiritual onslaught of Charan. Only by keeping them in his sphere of influence was Abraham confident that the next link in the chain would be strengthened sufficiently.

This teaches us the crucial nature of setting up a home in an area inhabited by Torah scholars or people who will serve as a positive spiritual influence.

[Even young people who do not intend to continue full-time learning after marriage should seek to settle in a *kollel* community. The values of the community will undoubtedly leave their mark on the couple, their household and eventually their family.]

Abraham's servants knew that human success, even that of one as righteous as Abraham, comes only due to God's kindness and abundant mercy. As the Midrash says, "Everyone needs God's kindness. Even Abraham who brought Godly kindness into the world needs His kindness."

וְהָיָה הַנַּעֲרָ אֲשֶׁר אֹמַר אֵלֶיהָ הַטִּי נָא
כַדֵּךְ וְאֶשְׁתֶּה וְאָמְרָה שְׁתֵה וְגַם גְּמַלֶּיךָ
אַשְׁקֶה אֹתָהּ הֹכַחְתָּ לְעַבְדְּךָ לְיִצְחָק

*"Let it be that the maiden to whom
I shall say, 'Please tip over your jug so
I may drink,' and who replies, 'Drink,
and I will even water your camels,'
her will You have designated for
Your servant, for Isaac"* (ibid. 14).

In order to ascertain if a maiden was fit to be the wife of Isaac and the progenitor of Abraham's family, Eliezer had to know that she possessed the trait of kindness (חֶסֶד).

The true definition of *chessed* is the ability to be sensitive enough to anticipate the needs of others.

When Rebecca met Eliezer at the well, she did not merely respond to his request; she sought to do more than he requested. Eliezer asked only that she let *him* have a drink of water, but she offered water to ten thirsty camels. A woman whose soul is woven from the fabric of *chessed* does not seek to do *chessed* merely because she is commanded to do so; rather, it is her very essence and calling in life. She is the proper woman to serve as the wife of Isaac and mother of the Jewish people (*Nesivos Shalom*).[17]

וַתְּמַלֵּא כַדָּהּ וַתַּעַל

She filled her jug and ascended (ibid. 16).

The Midrash interprets the "ascent" as referring to the water. So great was Rebecca's virtue that a miracle occurred and the water rose to meet her. When Eliezer saw this he ran toward her.

Ramban infers this from the language used here as opposed to verse 20 when it says she drew for all his camels. The implication is that when she originally came to the well, the water rose to meet her; however, when she went to get water for the camels she had to draw it herself. What is the difference between the two instances?

R' Levi Yitzchak of Berditchev sees here a fundamental lesson regarding the performance of *mitzvos*. When a righteous person has personal needs God may provide them in a supernatural way. However, when one does a mitzvah one must do it with one's own natural faculties; miracles do not occur to facilitate the performance of *mitzvos*. Thus when Rebecca went to the well, the water miraculously rose to meet her. When, however, she wanted water for Eliezer's camels, a miracle did not happen. It was her mitzvah to be done through her own effort.

אִם לֹא אֶל בֵּית אָבִי תֵּלֵךְ
וְאֶל מִשְׁפַּחְתִּי וְלָקַחְתָּ אִשָּׁה לִבְנִי

*Unless you go to my father's house, and to
my family and take a wife for my son* (ibid. 38).

There is a discrepancy between Abraham's initial charge and the way Eliezer relates the story to Bethuel and Laban. Abraham asked him to find a wife *for my son, for Isaac* (ibid. 4), yet here Eliezer

---

17. **Beautiful Eyes.** If Eliezer was seeking a woman who possessed all the positive character traits for Isaac, then why did he focus on חֶסֶד? The answer lies in the words of the *Mishnah* (Avos 2:13). *R' Yochanan ben Zakkai* asked his students to go out and discern which is the proper path to which a man should cling. Each disciple offered his view, with *R' Elazar ben Arach* claiming that a good heart is the proper path to follow.

R' Yochanan ben Zakkai concluded that a good heart is the trait which includes all the virtues mentioned by the other disciples. Thus Eliezer sought in Rebecca a good heart, for it is this virtue which encompasses all others (*Zichron Meir*).

Kli Yakar sees an allusion to *chessed* as reflective of one's total character in the words of the Sages that one need not check the degree of beauty of a bride if she has good eyes (*Taanis* 24a).

By "good eyes" the Sages refer to one who is magnanimous of spirit and treats others kindly, never begrudging them anything. This ability to desire the good of others without ever feeling that it takes away from oneself is the key to pristine character in all areas.

speaks only of taking a wife *for my son.*

Beis HaLevi explains: Abraham asked Eliezer to seek a bride who was fit to be both Abraham's daughter-in-law and Isaac's wife. She had to be an appropriate addition to Abraham's household as well as a fitting mate for one as righteous and holy as Isaac. He therefore charged him with finding a wife for *my* son, for Isaac.

Given whom he was dealing with, Eliezer realized that he would do best to highlight the fact that Rebecca would be Abraham's daughter-in-law but to ignore the fact that she needs to be married to one as holy as Isaac.

The situation is analogous to a wealthy man who sought a son-in-law. He told matchmakers that he sought the son of one of the greatest rabbis of the generation and was ready to spend serious money on such a match. A matchmaker approached him with the following proposition: "I have an even better match for you. If you are ready to incur the heavy price for the son of a great Torah scholar you must certainly be ready to pay for a young man who is himself an accomplished scholar. I have just such a young man for your daughter."

The wealthy man replied, "Not at all! Do you think I want my daughter to suffer the life of a rabbi's wife? I want her to be able to go out, enjoy the finer things in life, and not be tied down to her house and the monotonous existence of the rabbinate. I want my daughter to have the honor of being part of a great rabbi's family, but her husband should be a successful businessman and one adept in the ways of the world."[18]

Eliezer understood the mind-set of Rebbeca's family. They sought the honor of becoming part of Abraham's family but they really did not want their daughter and sister to marry someone as exalted as Isaac. Therefore, when speaking with them, Eliezer spoke only of taking a wife for Abraham's son without making a specific reference to Isaac.

---

18. **Not By Me!** [Many people display respect and even affection for Torah scholars yet are horrified at the thought that their own sons will follow that route. Similarly, under the guise of being concerned parents, people seek a son-in-law who will provide for their daughter in a comfortable style. But the truth is that if they really cared for their daughter, they would look for a young man who will provide a spiritual tone to his home that assures the level of *Yiddishkeit* of their grandchildren.]

פרשת תולדות ﭞ
Parashas Toldos

Background

The *parashah* begins with a description of the birth of Jacob and Esau, which resulted from the prayers of Isaac and his barren wife Rebecca, and then goes on to narrate Esau's sale of the birthright to Jacob.

וְאֵלֶּה תּוֹלְדֹת יִצְחָק בֶּן אַבְרָהָם, אַבְרָהָם הוֹלִיד אֶת יִצְחָק
And these are the offspring of Isaac son of Abraham, Abraham begot Isaac (25:19).

Rashi (*Genesis* 6:9) teaches that the primary offspring of the righteous are their good deeds, for one's worthwhile accomplishments are his primary legacy.

R' Menachem of Amshinov explained our verse accordingly. Isaac's spiritual achievements — his "offspring" — came about because he constantly remembered that Abraham was his father, and he was conscious that he had to live up to Abraham's legacy.[1]

וַיֶּעְתַּר יִצְחָק לַה׳ לְנֹכַח אִשְׁתּוֹ כִּי עֲקָרָה הִוא
Isaac entreated Hashem opposite his wife because she was barren (ibid. 21).

Why does the Torah speak of the prayer before mentioning what caused the need for prayer? Would it not have been more logical for the Torah to first mention that Rebecca was barren and then that Isaac prayed? The answer is that the Torah alludes here to the nature of prayer.

A surface understanding of the events leads one to conclude that Isaac and Rebecca's prayers were a result of their childlessness and barrenness. Actually, the correct order is reversed for the

---

1. **Barely Touching.** When discussing or reading about the spiritual giants of yesteryear we frequently feel dwarfed into insignificance, or — worse — into a lack of ambition for spiritual growth, because their achievements are beyond us.

R' Simchah Bunim of P'shis'cha addressed this issue. Our Sages teach that the spiritual chasm between us and our forefathers is so great that if they were like angels, then we are mortal men. And if we see them as mere mortals, then we are nothing more than senseless donkeys by comparison (see *Shabbos* 112b). How then can they tell us that one should always say, מָתַי יַגִּיעוּ מַעֲשַׂי לְמַעֲשֵׂי אֲבוֹתַי, *When will my deeds reach the level of those of my forefathers? (Tanna D'vei Eliyahu* 25). Explained R' Bunim: The word יַגִּיעוּ does not mean *reach,* for our deeds will never reach theirs. The word comes from the expression נְגִיעָה, a *touch.* If one looks at the forefathers as role models whom he should *attempt* to emulate and if he is ready to spiritually, emotionally and intellectually stretch his abilities and efforts to their true maximum, his deeds will just barely "touch" those of his forefathers. If, however, he tries merely to be "himself" as he perceives it, he will even fall short of his own true potential.

One who does not aspire to be a five-star general will not even succeed at being an adequate private.

While some see themselves as they are and ask, "Why?" the truly great personalities dream of a self that is not yet and ask, "Why not?"

Talmud (*Yevamos* 64a) teaches that Rebecca was barren since God desires the prayers of the righteous. God made Isaac and Rebecca barren because He knew they would respond to their plight with heartfelt prayer. Hence their future prayer is the end and Rebecca's barrenness only a means.

The Torah reveals this by first writing that Isaac prayed since that was the result desired by God. What was the means by which God elicited his prayer? *Because she was barren* (Rabbeinu Bachya, Aperion — R' Shlomo Ganzfried).[2]

וַיֵּעָתֶר לוֹ ה׳

*Hashem allowed Himself
to be entreated by him* (ibid.)

The implication is that Hashem responded to Isaac's prayer rather than to Rebecca's. According to *Rashi*, this teaches that the prayer of a righteous child of wicked parents (Rebecca) cannot be compared with that of a righteous child of righteous parents (Isaac). Seemingly the opposite should be true. Since Rebecca had to transcend her evil roots in order to achieve righteousness, would it not be reasonable to assume that her prayers should be the most potent?

Divrei Shmuel comments that the potency of one's prayer is directly linked to one's degree of humility. One who prays although he is sure that he deserves nothing is answered.[3]

Thus Isaac prayed *opposite his wife*, convinced that he did not deserve Divine help, but that they would be granted children in her merit. Rebecca, on the other hand, prayed that the merit of Isaac would bring them the blessing of children in spite of her (self-perceived) lowly spiritual status.

The humility of the righteous child of a righteous person is more meaningful than that of the righteous child of a wicked person, for the former is humble despite his lofty background while the latter has good cause for humility.

וַיִּתְרֹצְצוּ הַבָּנִים בְּקִרְבָּהּ

The children agitated within her (ibid. 22).

Rashi explains that when Rebecca passed the Torah academy of Shem and Eber, Jacob figuratively sought to leave the womb and hurry to the academy, and when she passed a temple of idol worship, Esau struggled to break out. [Thus וַיִּתְרֹצְצוּ is linked to the word רִיצָה, *to run*.]

The Talmud (*Niddah* 30b) teaches that while in the womb the unborn fetus is taught the entire Torah by an angel. While we can easily understand why Esau would want to escape such an environment, why should Jacob want to run out? It would

2. **He's Listening!** A similar sentiment is expressed in *Hallel*. King David says: *I love [Him] for Hashem hears my voice, my supplications. He inclined His ear to me ...* (Psalms 116: 1-2).

The order of the verse seems reversed since one first inclines his ears and only then hears. Why does King David change the natural order?

R' Yitzchak Hutner explained: The goal of prayer is the link of communication established between man and his Creator. God's actual fulfillment of our many requests is secondary and almost incidental. Thus King David speaks in ascending order of importance. "Hashem hears my voice and answers my prayer. It is not the fulfillment of my request that gladdens me so much as the fact that it proves to me that He inclined His ear to me and is listening."

[The surface understanding has it that prayer comes in order to solve problems. In truth, problems come in order to motivate us to pray. Pain and travail may be analogous to the child who goes away from home. What does a parent do if the child does not stay in touch? He stops sending money (and cancels the credit card). Eventually the child has no choice but to call home to ask for money. Likewise, when we fail to communicate with God, He forces us to "call home."]

The *Ponevezher Rav* used to say, "When prayers go unanswered it isn't because He doesn't listen. He listened and said, 'No.' " [The main purpose of prayer, communication, has been achieved. Whether the answer is yes or no is another issue.]

3. **Why Me?** A young man who dabbled in heretical ideas despite his ostensibly Orthodox lifestyle experienced personal tragedy. His response was, "After everything I did for God, this is what He does to me?" He went on to promulgate a "God is Dead" theology of Judaism.

Prayer entails the humility to realize that what we do for God is infinitesimal compared to what He does for us. Thus in prayer we come figuratively with "hat in hand," completely dependent on His infinite mercy.

seem that learning the entire Torah from an angel is about as idyllic a situation as one could want. *Chasam Sofer* explains: The negative effect of studying in the company of Esau is so powerful that one must flee, even if it means losing the opportunity to study under the tutelage of an angel.[4]

Jacob was unable to escape and go to the study hall because Esau blocked his exit. If so, why couldn't Esau leave to the temples of idol worship? Who would have stopped him? Certainly not Jacob, who would have been more than happy to see him leave. The answer, explains *R' Yechezkel of Kuzmir,* is that Esau is willing to forgo his own idol worship in order to insure that Jacob does not enter the Torah academy.[5],[6]

How did Jacob know, inside the womb, when his mother passed by the study hall? *R' Yerucham Levovitz of Mir* submits that the question seems plausible only because we do not view spiritual matters as reality. In truth, however, spiritual drives are even more real than physical ones.

Just as the compass always points to the north regardless of which direction it faces, so the soul is drawn automatically toward its intrinsic orientation. Jacob's soul, rooted in holiness, was automatically drawn toward the sanctity of the academy of Shem and Eber. Conversely, even before he was born, Esau instinctively turned to idolatry.[7]

וַתֹּאמֶר אִם כֵּן לָמָּה זֶּה אָנֹכִי

and she said, "If so, why am I thus?" (ibid.).

Aware of the spiritual conflict raging within her, Rebecca regretted having conceived. Why would a woman who had waited so long for children regret having received such a blessing?

R' Eliyahu Meir Bloch explains: The nature of an expectant woman changes. One example of this is the change in appetite and the craving for particular foods that many pregnant women experience. A

4. **Handpicked Classmates.** The *Chasam Sofer* took extreme care not only in choosing teachers for his children but also in assuring that they study with good children. [When selecting a school, one must investigate not only who the teachers are but, even more importantly, who are the students and classmates.]

5. **Spiritual Jugular.** The enemies of the Jewish people from time immemorial have always known that the key to destroying us is to prevent the yeshivah student from studying Torah. Even the Nazis understood this. In a memorandum dated October 25, 1940 and dispatched to the Nazi district governors in occupied Poland, *das Reichs sicherheits haupttamt* (the Central Office of the German Security Forces) instructed them not to grant exit visas to *Ostjuden* (Eastern European Jews). The reason behind this order is clearly spelled out: The Nazis feared that because of their *"Orthodoxen einstellung"* (Orthodoxy) these *Ostjuden* would provide *"die Rabbiner and Talmud lehrer"* (the rabbis and teachers of the Talmud) who would create *"die geistege Erneuerung"* (the spiritual regeneration) of the Jews in America and throughout the world.

Whoever the Germans would fail to kill physically they sought to annihilate spiritually.

6. **Maternal Molding.** Homiletically the Sages teach us that the values of children are formed primarily by their mothers. If the mother figuratively "passes the study hall" by holding Torah and Torah scholars in high esteem, then "Jacob will seek to run out" to the Torah academies. If, however, she degrades Torah and values secular culture and its models of success, she will produce an Esau who looks toward such goals as his life's destiny (*Iturei Torah*).

When *R' Aryeh Leib,* son of the *Chafetz Chaim,* was to be married, he had the local tailor make him a new suit as was customary. His mother accompanied him to the final fitting.

When the tailor finished his work, he wished the groom that he become a highly successful businessman. His mother was aghast and started screaming at the tailor. "That is a blessing?! That's a curse! Bless him that he become a great *talmid chacham* and a God-fearing Jew." It is the aspirations of the mothers that shape the destiny of their children.

[A great *rosh yeshivah* was once asked why Yiddish is considered in certain quarters to be a sacred tongue of sorts. "What makes Yiddish holy?" he was asked. "Is it anything more than a dialect of German?"

He replied, "When your grandmother and great-grandmother lit candles on *Erev Shabbos* and beseeched God that you grow up to be a *talmid chacham* and a good Jew, they prayed in Yiddish. It was those prayers that gave Yiddish its sanctity."]

7. **Roots.** *R' Tzadok HaKohen* writes that the place toward which a person is drawn in times of personal crisis indicates the spiritual orientation of his soul.

woman like Rebecca senses such changes on a spiritual level. Hence when she felt drawn simultaneously to the study hall and to the temple of idolatry, she suspected that she was carrying a child who suffered from spiritual schizophrenia. So much did this disturb her that she regretted the pregnancy. Only when she was informed that she was carrying twins was she reassured.

One righteous son and one evil son is preferable to one child wracked by inner conflict, for negative orientation can be reworked, but a child with a confused set of values is often beyond hope.

שְׁנֵי גוֹיִם בְּבִטְנֵךְ וּשְׁנֵי לְאֻמִּים
מִמֵּעַיִךְ יִפָּרֵדוּ . . . וְרַב יַעֲבֹד צָעִיר

Two nations are in your womb and two regimes from your insides will be separated . . and the elder shall serve the younger (ibid. 23).

The word גוֹיִם is written in the Torah scroll as גֵּיִים, *titans.* The Talmud (*Avodah Zarah* 11a) interprets this as a reference to R' Yehudah HaNassi, the redactor of the *Mishnah,* and his contemporary Antoninus Pius, the Roman governor of Palestine. Why don't the Sages explain the reference in its obvious context, as speaking about Jacob and Esau?

R' Gedaliah Schorr explains: On the words *and the elder shall serve the younger*, the Midrash adds "if he merits it." Most commentators understand this to mean that if the younger Jacob deserves it, he will be served by his older brother Esau. *Rashi,* however, (on the Midrash) suggests just the opposite: If *Esau* merits, then he will serve Jacob. Esau's key to success lies in his subservience to Jacob, by

providing his physical needs so that he can focus on his spiritual mission. If Esau has the wisdom to do so, he can achieve spiritual success. Isaac blessed Esau with a this-worldly blessing (see Chapter 27), in the hope that he would have the inner strength to subjugate himself to Jacob. Esau, however, refused to assume his appropriate role, instead insisting on being the dominant brother and the primary heir to his father.

Only during the times of R' Yehudah HaNassi and Antoninus Pius were the words of God finally fulfilled. The Talmud (*Avodah Zarah* 10b) relates that the two extremely wealthy and powerful men maintained a friendly relationship. When Antoninus came to visit he bent down and asked R' Yehudah to use his back as a footstool to climb up to his sofa. At first, R' Yehudah refused, insisting that Antoninus was royalty and that such behavior was beneath his dignity. Antoninus was adamant, however, expressing the hope that "I might serve as a mat under you in the World to Come!"

Thus the proper relationship between Jacob and Esau came to be only during the times of the unique relationship between their descendants.[8]

The national identities of Jacob and Esau are totally different from their very birth. Although all men are created in the image of God, Israel was chosen to be uniquely His. Not so the nations of the world, whose ethnic chauvinism causes them to love their countrymen and hate others. Thus *two regimes from your insides will be separated (Likutei Basar Likutei).*[9]

---

8. **Bitter Medicine.** The promise that Esau would serve Jacob seemingly has not come true. We suffer a long exile at the hands of Esau and his descendants; where is the promise that the older one will serve the younger one?

R' Elyah Lopian offered an analogy: A king appointed many attendants to serve his son. One person was in charge of his food, another of his wardrobe, and another attendant was the child's physician, assigned to care for his health. Sometimes the doctor has no choice but to prescribe bitter medicine or painful surgery. Yet he, too, was providing for the prince.

Esau always serves the needs of Jacob. If the Jewish people's spiritual "vital signs" are what they should be, then Esau serves him by providing for his physical needs. If, however, the Jews become spiritually ill, the nations of the world become their "surgeons," performing painful, but therapeutic, procedures.

9. **Inside Information.** A key difference between the descendants of Jacob and those of Esau relates to their "insides," namely their approach to food. A Jew is restrained in his consumption; not everything is kosher. Furthermore, the Jew turns eating and drinking into sacred acts. Shabbos and *Yom Tov* meals, for example, are but two of the many examples of food consumption as a form of serving God (*R' Leibel Eiger*). To the non-Jew, life is compartmentalized. Holy is holy and mundane is mundane and never the twain shall meet.

The Talmud underscores this fundamental difference when it teaches that a non-Jew may send an offering to the

וַיֶּאֱהַב יִצְחָק אֶת עֵשָׂו כִּי צַיִד בְּפִיו
Isaac loved Esau for game was in his mouth (ibid. 28).

Not only was Esau a hunter in the literal sense, he also cunningly trapped Isaac by asking questions which would make him seem exceptionally pious in Isaac's eyes. For example, he would inquire as to how tithes should be taken from salt and straw [although he knew that they were not subject to tithes] (*Rashi*).

Why did Esau pick these foolish topics to showcase his "piety"? Why not ask legitimate halachic questions?

Shem MiShmuel suggests the following: Everything in life has either a primary or auxiliary function. This world, for example, is of secondary importance to the World to Come and must serve as a means to achieve one's share in that world. Likewise, the six weekdays are meant to prepare for the Sabbath, which testifies to God's creation of the world. The same is true in the physical world, as well. A fruit's peel is of minor significance when compared to the fruit itself.

But even something that functions in a secondary role is important if it faithfully fulfills its mission. The mundane world is a very meaningful place if one uses it to prepare himself for the World to Come. The toil of the six weekdays is infused with sanctity if one uses them to provide for his Sabbath, when he focuses solely on his own spirituality. Likewise, with regard to the laws of impurity, the peel has the same halachic status as the fruit itself, since its function is to protect the fruit.

True, Esau was of secondary importance to Jacob; but he would have gained a high degree of prominence had he been willing to provide for Jacob's physical needs. In his arrogance, however, he refused to assume a supporting role, preferring to regard himself as the lead actor in his world.

Esau's questions regarding tithes reflected his arrogant mind-set. Salt is used to bring out the taste in food; its role is auxiliary. Likewise, straw is secondary to kernels of wheat. Esau wanted those items to be the tithe, elevated to importance. His questions were but a reflection of his unwillingness to assume his appropriate role.

R' Meir of Premishlan saw a different lesson in the verse, which tells of Isaac's love of Esau. The Talmud teaches that at the End of Days God will turn to each of the Patriarchs and say "your descendants have sinned." Abraham and Jacob will reply that the sinners should be punished accordingly. Only Isaac will defend the Jewish people, trying to prove that their sins are not as terrible as they seem (*Shabbos* 89b). Why of all the Patriarchs will Isaac be the one to come to our defense?

R' Meir explained that Isaac will say, "I, too, had a son who sinned grievously, yet I loved him and was ready to forgive him. You, Master of the world, certainly should love Your children and forgive them in spite of their sins." Hence Isaac's love for Esau will provide him with the appropriate plea in his defense of the Jews.

The verse should be therefore understood as follows: *Isaac loved Esau for* [this love was] *game in his* [Isaac's] *mouth.* It was his love for Esau, in spite of who Esau was, that provided him with the defense he will offer God on behalf of his people.[10]

Temple but only a burnt-offering (עוֹלָה), but he may not send a peace-offering, from which the Kohanim and the owners partake. The Talmud explains that a non-Jew can understand an offering that is brought totally to God. The idea that (as with a peace-offering) the owners and Kohanim eat and their actions elicit Divine atonement is incomprehensible to a non-Jew. Thus it is from their mother's *insides* that Jacob and Esau part ways.

10. **We're Not Worse.** *R' Chaim Shmulevitz* would occasionally go to *Yad Avshalom* (Absalom's Memorial) to pray. Since Absalom was the rebellious son of King David, who even tried to kill his father, people found R' Chaim's custom perplexing.

R' Chaim explained: "When he lamented Absalom's death, King David referred to him eight times as 'my son.' The Talmud (*Sotah* 10b) teaches that the first seven references lifted Absalom out of the seven levels of purgatory and the eighth mention pulled him into the World to Come.

"I go to *Yad Avshalom* and I say to Hashem, 'As much as Your beloved children rebel against You, it is certainly not as severe as the rebellion of Absalom against his father. Even after everything he tried to do to his father, King David still loved him enough to pull him out of purgatory and push him into the World to Come. Certainly You can have mercy on Your children.'"

וְרִבְקָה אֹהֶבֶת אֶת יַעֲקֹב
but Rebecca loved Jacob (ibid.).

Isaac grew up in the home of Abraham and Sarah, where he was never exposed to even the slightest tinge of falsehood. Having experienced perfect truth his entire life, he had no doubt that Esau's questions were an authentic expression of his desire to know the will of God. Not so Rebecca. Having spent her childhood in the company of such masters of deceit as her brother Laban, she was able to see through Esau's facade of righteousness. Thus while Isaac loved Esau, Rebbeca loved Jacob (*R' Naftali of Ropschitz*).[11], [12]

Shelah notes that Isaac's love for Esau is expressed in the past tense (וַיֶּאֱהַב) while Rebecca's love of Jacob is stated in the present (אֹהֶבֶת).

This is based on the *Mishnah* (*Avos* 5:19), which teaches that "Any love that depends on a specific cause, when the cause is gone the love is gone; but if it does not depend on a specific cause it will never cease." Isaac loved Esau because he brought him venison. Since Isaac's love depended on Esau's service, the love was not an enduring love, so it is written in the past tense. Rebecca's love, however, is in the present tense. It was constant and enduring for it depended on no specific cause whatsoever.[13]

וַיָּזֶד יַעֲקֹב נָזִיד
Jacob simmered a stew (ibid. 29).

Abraham had died on that day, and Jacob was preparing the stew as the traditional mourner's meal for his father, Isaac (*Rashi*).

Why did Jacob, not Rebecca, prepare the meal? *Meilitz Yosher* explains that lentil stew is a traditional mourner's dish, for the rounded shape of the bean symbolizes the cyclical nature of life — people are born and people die. Man's challenge is to make full use of his temporary interlude of life. Jacob wanted this lesson to penetrate his consciousness in the deepest way possible. Following the dictum of *Sefer*

---

11. **It Takes One to Know One.** The Talmud (*Yoma* 9b) reports that one could feel comfortable investing money with anyone with whom Reish Lakish would speak in public, and need not even have witnesses present at the transaction. The Talmud does not say this about R' Yochanan or any other contemporaries of Reish Lakish. They, who grew up among righteous people, had no inkling of the treacherous ways of the wicked. Reish Lakish, who in his youth was a highway robber, could immediately sense who was dishonest. If he spoke with a person publicly one could be sure that the person was honest.

As the popular adage has it, "It takes [a former] one to know one."

12. **He Needs It!** According to *Alshich*, Isaac understood the fundamental difference between Jacob and Esau. It was for this very reason that he sought to create a close relationship with Esau, eating from his prey and hoping meanwhile to bring him back to the proper path.

A fascinating incident about the *Alter of Slabodka* underscores this approach. Two friends, both of them exceptionally bright, learned in Slabodka. One was an assiduous student, while the other one did not really apply himself to learning. Remarkably, the Alter paid scant attention to the first one, while he showered the second with attention, concern, and even praise. The diligent student felt slighted, but he never questioned the Alter about the matter.

When the better student was sitting *shivah*, the Alter came to pay a condolence call. The student could no longer control his curiosity and asked the Alter to explain his behavior. The Alter replied, "You derive great satisfaction and self-fulfillment from your diligent and successful study. When you come to me looking for praise or honor, it is your *yetzer hara* (evil inclination) that brings you. I am not ready to supply such needs because there is no spiritual gain in it. Your friend, on the other hand, feels that his self-realization lays elsewhere than in the yeshivah. When he comes to me for attention, it is his *yetzer tov* (positive inclination) which is driving him. I am always ready to give him the attention."

R' Shlomo Wolbe relates that when he and R' Moshe Shmuel Shapiro started the yeshivah in *Be'er Yaakov*, they asked the *Chazon Ish* to speak to *roshei yeshivah* to send them "good" students. "Good *bachurim*," the Chazon Ish replied, "don't need a yeshivah. It is your job to help others *become* good."

13. **Present and Constant.** The Midrash (*Bereishis Rabbah* 63:6) reflects this perspective on the difference between Isaac's love for Esau and Rebecca's for Jacob. The Midrash explains that Rebecca kept loving Jacob more and more. Thus her love is described in the present tense, for the present never disappears; every present is succeeded by a new present. Isaac's love of Esau is described in the past tense, indicative of something here today and gone tomorrow (*R' Leibel Eiger*).

HaChinuch, which teaches that הָאָדָם נִפְעָל כְּפִי פְּעוּלוֹתָיו, *a person is conditioned by his deeds,* Jacob wanted to simmer the stew himself so that its lesson would become embedded in his soul.[14]

Rabbeinu Bachya views Jacob's preparation of the lentil stew as indicative of the contrast between the values of Jacob and the values of Esau. Esau wanted to buy the instant gratification of this world symbolized by the red lentil-stew, while Jacob understood it for what it was — merely a fleeting phenomenon symbolized by the round lentil shape, here today and gone tomorrow. Jacob wanted to change places with Esau, offering him this world in exchange for the birthright, the key to the World to Come.

הַלְעִיטֵנִי נָא מִן הָאָדֹם הָאָדֹם הַזֶּה . . .
עַל כֵּן קָרָא שְׁמוֹ אֱדוֹם.

Pour into me now [please]
some of that very red stuff . . .
He therefore called his name Edom (ibid. 30).

Lentils are red only when they are raw; once cooked they turn a different color. Why then did Esau ask for the very *red* stuff, when it was no longer red? Furthermore, the Sages note that unlike Jacob who spoke politely to Isaac, asking him *rise up, please sit and eat of my game* (27:19),

Esau addressed Isaac uncouthly; *Let my father rise and eat of his son's game.*

If Esau, whose parental honor was legendary, did not say *please* to his father, certainly he did not address his nemesis Jacob with such politeness?!

Chavos Yair submits that the word נָא be translated *raw* as in the context of the *pesach*-offering: *you shall not eat it* נָא, *partially cooked* (*Exodus* 12:9). Esau asked Jacob to pour the lentil stew into his mouth when it was still undercooked and red. He wanted the food *now* and had no patience to wait until it was fully cooked.[15]

It seems strange that Esau was called Edom due to this one-time use of the expression הָאָדֹם הָאָדֹם, *that very red.* [16]

However, this incident was not merely an isolated slip of the tongue; it reflected Esau's philosophy of life. Selling the birthright and its unique spiritual opportunities for nothing but a lentil stew illustrates the essence of an Esau, who barters eternity for fleeting momentary pleasure. Esau scorns anything with even the slightest connection to spirituality, viewing man (and himself) as nothing more than a consumer of pleasure. This narcissistic pursuit of the here and now came to the fore in Esau's call to *pour into me, now, some of this very red stuff* (*Skulener Rebbe*).[17]

---

14. **Multimessage Metaphor.** The *Chafetz Chaim* expresses this very perspective when commenting on Esau's comment, *Look I am going to die today, so of what use to me is a birthright* (25:32). "How ironic that the remembrance of death so energizes the righteous that it inspires them to repentance, good deeds and abstinence from excessive indulgence in worldly pleasures (see *Berachos* 5a), while the very same thought brings wicked people like Esau to react with 'eat, drink and be merry for tomorrow you shall die.'"

This is but an example of the words of *Hosea* (14:10), *For the ways of Hashem are straight; the righteous walk in them and the sinners will stumble over them.*

15. **Uncooked Fare.** Homiletically, the desire to eat uncooked food is symptomatic of Esau and his philosophy of life. According to *Mei HaShiloach* (*Beshalach*), Esau's statement *Look I am going to die, so of what use to me is the birthright* is a rejection of the belief that humans enjoy free choice and that their actions affect their destiny. This belief calls on man to take his God-given raw ingredients (talents, intelligence, etc.) and "cook them" into a life which is savory in His eyes.

One who rejects this belief and mission sees life as raw food, which exists only to be consumed (*Zekan Aharon*).

16. **Quick Reputation.** A good name is years in the making. Only at the age of 99, after decades of spiritual toil, did Abram become Abraham. Only after a fierce struggle with the angel of Esau did Jacob receive the appellation Israel (*Genesis* 32:29). A bad name, on the other hand, can be acquired in a moment. Esau merely said, "הָאָדֹם הָאָדֹם הַזֶּה", and he received the name Edom (*R' Shlomo Bloch*).

17. **Red Stuff.** *Maharal* often identifies physical and spiritual with the terms חֹמֶר (matter) and צוּרָה (form). Raw "matter" that has yet to assume defined dimensions is symbolic of existence without the restraint that provides people with the limitations that control their animal nature and shape it into a meaningful life. "Form" is raw matter that has been shaped into something constructive. Wood, for example, is matter. A chair is

Background

As he approached death, Isaac decided to bestow the Patriarchal blessings on Esau. For various reasons expressed by the commentators, he felt that Esau, despite his evil nature or perhaps because of it, needed these blessings. But through Divine Inspiration, Rebecca saw things differently and engineered a ruse so that Isaac would bless Jacob instead.

וַעֲשֵׂה לִי מַטְעַמִּים כַּאֲשֶׁר אָהַבְתִּי . . .
בַּעֲבוּר תְּבָרֶכְךָ נַפְשִׁי בְּטֶרֶם אָמוּת

Then make me delicacies such as I love . . . so that my soul may bless you before I die (27:4).

Isaac wanted to bless Esau with worldly success, that he would harness to the advancement of Jacob's spiritual pursuits, which was the only channel through which Esau could give meaning to his life. Isaac therefore asked Esau to harness his talent for hunting to the positive goal of honoring his father, thereby showing that all worldly abilities and resources should be dedicated to the ultimate service of Hashem.

Why did Isaac seek to bless only the firstborn Esau? Why didn't he give separate blessings to each of his sons, as Jacob did (*Genesis* 49)?

Had Isaac blessed Jacob, knowing who he was, Jacob's offspring would merit the blessing only if they followed in Jacob's ways. God wanted the Jewish people to be privy to the blessing under all circumstances, even when they are unworthy and, God forbid, seem almost like Esau. Therefore God wanted Isaac to think he would bless only Esau, so that the blessing would be relevant even when Israel behaved like Esau (*R' Yitzchak of Vorki*).[18]

According to *R' Elya Meir Bloch,* Isaac asked Esau to bring him food as a means to strengthen the emotional bond between them. In this way he hoped that his blessings would take root in Esau's soul. The Talmud (*Bava Kamma* 20a) relates an incident that highlights the power of personal service as a means of creating a spiritual conduit.

R' Chisda asked Rami bar Chama a very difficult question. Rami replied, "If you will serve me I will answer you," whereupon R' Chisda folded Rami's turban.

Why would Rami bar Chama reply only if R' Chisda made a gesture of subservience? R' Elya Meir explained: Rami bar Chama's answer would be complex and demand intense concentration for its nuances to be fully understood. He wanted to be sure that R' Chisda was ready to create the soul connection between teacher and student that was necessary to convey the subtlety of the Torah's words.

Here, too, Isaac wanted to cement the bond between him and Esau before giving him the blessing.[19]

---

wood that has been given a form.

Esau saw life only in its physical terms and referred to things that way. He did not call the food a stew, the particular form that the beans had assumed; he called it the *very red stuff,* a description based only on the external color of the raw matter (*Zekan Aharon*).

18. **Unconditional Blessings.** According to *Nesivos Shalom,* this is the intent of the Midrashic comment on the verse *And may God give you* (ibid. 28), יִתֵּן וְיַחֲזֹר וְיִתֵּן, *May He give and give again*. Not only before we sin and deserve the blessings will we receive them, but even if we sin and seemingly fall to the level of Esau, we will still receive the blessings.

19. **Overplayed Mitzvah.** Jacob was afraid that Esau would prevail over him due to the latter's pronounced commitment to the commandment of honoring parents (see commentators to *Genesis* 32:8). *R' Shimon ben Gamliel* said of himself that while he spent his entire life serving his father, it did not equal even 1 percent of the filial honor Esau displayed. Why then did this not influence Esau to change his evil ways?

R' Chaim Mordechai Katz related the following by way of explanation: "I remember as a young man that after World War I and the terrible destruction it left in its wake, there was a mass awakening with regard to Sabbath observance. The spirit of the words of the Sages that Sabbath observance is crucial to the Final Redemption captivated the masses. Organizations sprouted and rallies were held about Sabbath observance, with eloquent speakers traveling from town to town to arouse the population. There was even a proposal to hold a mass assembly in Berlin to strengthen Sabbath observance.

"Many students of Telshe went to discuss this phenomenon with our rebbe, the *Rosh Yeshivah* of Telshe, *R' Yosef Leib Bloch*. We were all excited about the prospect of a mass effort on behalf of Shabbos. We were shocked to hear his reply: 'I'm afraid this is but a new Zionism.' He then explained. 'We all know that settling the Land of Israel

אוּלַי יְמֻשֵּׁנִי אָבִי וְהָיִיתִי בְעֵינָיו כִּמְתַעְתֵּעַ

Perhaps my father will feel me and I shall be as a mocker in his eyes (ibid. 12).

The Talmud (*Makkos* 24a) interprets the phrase *one has no slander on his tongue* (*Psalms* 15:3) as referring to Jacob who did not want to lie, but was forced to do so by his mother (see *Rashi ad loc.*).

A cursory reading of our verse, however, indicates not that he did not *want* to lie, but that he was afraid to do so. Where do the Sages see unwillingness on Jacob's part?

The *Vilna Gaon* explains: The word אוּלַי means *perhaps* while פֶּן means *lest*. One uses the word *perhaps* regarding something he hopes will happen while the term *lest* is used when speaking of something one hopes will not occur. Thus, it would have seemed more appropriate for Jacob to say פֶּן, *lest*, since he certainly dreaded being caught at his ruse.

The answer is that Jacob's reluctance to lie was so strong that subconsciously he hoped that Isaac would detect him. He therefore said אוּלַי, *perhaps*, as if to say "I won't have to go through with the lie." It was Rebecca, under Divine guidance, who coerced him to do what he considered to be unthinkable.[20]

The words of Jacob seem to imply that he was less worried about telling a lie than he was about his father's perception of him as a mocker. *R' Noach Orlowek* offers an explanation based on a careful reading of a story in the life of Rav (*Yevamos* 63a). His wife was a difficult woman. Whatever dish he asked her to prepare, she would cook something different. If he asked for lentils, she would make bean soup; if he wanted beans, he would get lentils. When their son Chiya was old enough to understand what was happening, he devised a plan to help his father. If Rav wanted beans, Chiya would tell his mother that Rav wanted lentils, and vice versa. Rav was pleasantly surprised that the menu was now to his liking, and mentioned it to Chiya, who told him the secret of the change. Rav was upset. He said, "Stop doing that, for the prophet says *they train their tongue to speak falsehood*" (*Jeremiah* 9:4).

Why did Rav cite a verse from the Prophets rather than the Biblical source which prohibits falsehood, מִדְּבַר שֶׁקֶר תִּרְחָק, *Distance yourself from a false word* (*Exodus* 23:7)?

The key lies in the difference between doing and being. Although there are times when one is permitted to lie (see *Rashi* on *Genesis* 18:13), one may never become a "liar," in the sense that one is a habitual liar. While Chiya was right to find a way to please his father without arousing his mother's ire, Rav was afraid that by constantly doing so he would lose his sensitivity to truth and become a liar. While what he did was not a transgression of the commandment to distance himself from falsehood, it certainly might lead him to train his tongue to speak falsehood.

Similarly, while realizing that his mother was

---

is an extremely precious mitzvah. Nevertheless, it is a mistake to put all of our energies into one mitzvah, for eventually all other *mitzvos* are neglected. At a certain point, the Zionists began to believe that if one is dedicated to the resettlement of the Land, then his behavior in other areas is acceptable, even if it is not in accordance with the Torah.

"In truth, however, we have 613 *mitzvos* and one must at least *intend* to fulfill them all. Therefore, as important as Sabbath observance is, to put all of our energies into Sabbath observance is dangerous, for increased adherence in this area might very well cause a laxity in all other areas of Torah observance."

When Esau focused all his energies into filial respect, he turned it into "the entire Torah" and felt no obligation to pursue spirituality on any other level. Thus, although he was unique in honoring his father, it left no mark on the rest of his life or behavior.

20. **Impostor Uncovered.** *R' Moshe of Kobrin* offered a homiletical interpretation of this verse. One can never sure that he truly serves Hashem as one should. Even if we fulfill the *mitzvos*, to what extent do our actions express our true personality?

When Jacob spoke of his "father," he was referring to God. "Perhaps my Father in Heaven "will feel me? — i.e., perhaps He will inspect the spiritual quality of my life and deeds — and I shall appear to be a mocker in His eyes." God will ask me, "Is that the way one is to study Torah or pray? Is frozen, heartless fulfillment of the *mitzvos* sufficient?"

right that he had to deceive Isaac, Jacob was afraid that he might *become* a "mocker," and be recognized as such by his father.[21]

וְיִתֶּן לְךָ הָאֱלֹקִים מִטַּל הַשָּׁמַיִם . . .
And may God give you of the dew of the heavens . . . (ibid 28).

The word *and* seems misplaced since this verse is not a continuation of what was said earlier. *Rashi* (citing the Midrash, יִתֵּן וְיַחֲזֹר וְיִתֵּן) explains that the word *and* is meant to imply that God's blessing will be continuous: He will give you blessings again and again.

God is certainly able to give all the blessings at once; why did Isaac imply that He should give consistently in smaller amounts?

Wealth is a double-edged sword. On one hand one can do great things with wealth. Support of Torah, beautification of mitzvos, extensive charity and kindness are but a few of the positive uses to which one can put financial success. On the other hand, wealth is a challenge and a trial, often a source of much pain and anguish. It can even bring one to deny his dependency on God. Overnight riches are even more spiritually dangerous, leading one to arrogance and narcissism. Thus Isaac's blessing was that God should parcel out His blessings a little bit at a time (*Ksav Sofer*).

The *mussar* masters offer an alternative approach. Instant success or wealth does not lead to constant joy and contentment. One is happy for a day or two and then the thrill begins to fade. That is the nature of desire; one wants it and finds it attractive only when he doesn't have it. Once achieved, it loses its mystique. But one who achieves wealth or success in gradual but steady increments is able to enjoy constant happiness. Isaac therefore blessed Jacob that God give and give again, so that his life would be a string of successively joyous moments.[22]

According to *R' Shmuel Rozovski*, God's constant giving is His way of assuring that man maintain constant contact with Him. Were He to give only once, the ongoing relationship between God and man might dissipate. Thus He gives and gives again, making us constant beneficiaries and thus allowing us to continually realize and acknowledge our link to Him.[23]

Rashi notes that Isaac blesses Jacob that אֱלֹקִים, the Name of God that denotes strict justice, will bless him; if he deserves the blessing he will get it; if not, then he will not.

Shem MiShmuel asks the obvious question: If Jacob deserves prosperity, why does he need the blessing?

The answer is that the strict justice is not to

---

21. **Ugly Lie.** The Talmud (*Sanhedrin* 92b) equates deceit with idolatry, based on the common usage of the term "mockery" (see *Jeremiah* 10:15). Had Rebecca not known (through Divine inspiration) that Jacob's deceit was permitted, it would have been deemed a terrible sin, equivalent to that of idolatry.

Lying is intrinsically ugly and detestable. This is so not only when one lies in order to gain at the expense of others, but even when it is a "victimless crime" committed in the course of simple conversation. A person who occasionally speaks untruthfully still retains his humanity, but a habitual liar loses it (*Chazon Ish*).

22. **Recycling Divine Kindness.** R' Gedaliah Schorr contrasts the incremental blessing given Jacob with the blessing granted Esau: *Behold, of the fatness of the earth shall be your dwelling* (Genesis 27:39). When a Jew receives prosperity from God, he doesn't merely take it for himself; he gives it back to God in the form of support for Torah study, enhancement of *mitzvos*, or as charity for the needy. Thus when God gives blessings piecemeal; when He sees that a blessing was used properly, He gives more blessings. Esau, on the other hand, keeps his worldly bounty for himself. Thus the fatness of the earth shall be his dwelling, for it will remain with him.

At first, Isaac thought that Esau would dedicate his worldly prosperity to spiritual pursuits. When he realized that God had ordained that the blessing go to Jacob, Isaac knew that he was wrong about Esau.

23. **Guess from Whom?** According to *Avnei Nezer,* the homiletical meaning of וְיִתֶּן לְךָ הָאֱלֹקִים . . . , is *May you be given through God the dew of the heavens and the fatness of the earth.* When a Jew is granted prosperity, it is not the prosperity itself that is meaningful, but rather the fact that he received it from God; the relationship is more significant than the gift itself. To a Jew it is not *what* he received that is important as much as from *Whom* he received it.

determine whether or not we deserve blessings, but rather if they will truly benefit us or will lead us to spiritual apathy (or worse). If God determines that worldly success is dangerous for our spirituality, He will withhold it. As for Esau, however, if God were to withhold his blessings, Esau would respond with even greater heresy and rejection of Him. In order to forestall such a desecration of His Name, God provides for Esau under all circumstances.

פרשת ויצא ⊰
Parashas Vayeitzei

Background

At his parents' behest, Jacob flees from his home in Canaan and goes to the ancestral family home, birthplace of Rebecca and hometown of her father Bethuel and brother Laban. On the way, he is shown a prophetic vision that fortifies his resolve to spiritually survive the exile he is about to begin.[1]

וַיֵּצֵא יַעֲקֹב מִבְּאֵר שָׁבַע
Jacob departed from Beer-sheba (28:10).

According to the Sages, *Eretz Yisrael* is, in a spiritual sense, the highest of all lands. There-fore, leaving the Land is a descent. In this light, it would seem that וַיֵּרֶד יַעֲקֹב, *and Jacob descended,* would be the more appropriate phrase.

It is in answer to this question that *Rashi* cites the Midrash that "a righteous person's departure from a place leaves a void. As long as he lives in a city he is its glory, its splendor and its beauty; when he departs, its glory, splendor and beauty depart with him." The Land of Israel is elevated above all other lands, but for Jacob, leaving the Land was not a descent for he took its sanctity with him. When a righteous person like Jacob leaves Israel, all of its spiritual glory, splendor and beauty accompany him.

If "a righteous person's departure from a place leaves a void" (*Rashi*),[2] then why does the Torah

---

1. **Constantly Preoccupied.** According to the *Baalei HaMesorah,* the masters of Scriptural tradition, the *sidrah* of *Vayeitzei* contains no "paragraph" breaks in the text. *Sfas Emes* understands that this teaches us that although Jacob left the Land of Israel physically, he never severed his emotional ties with it. From the time he left (described at the beginning of the *sidrah*) until the time he returned (and the angels of Israel came to accompany him back into the Land, see 32:2 and *Rashi* ad loc.), his mind and heart were riveted on the Land. [As the *Baal Shem Tov* taught: In reality a person is wherever his thoughts are.]

In this way, Jacob fulfilled his mother's words that he flee to Padan Aram and *remain with him* (Laban) *a short while until your brother's wrath subsides* (27:44). Jacob remained with Laban for twenty years in addition to the fourteen years spent at the academy of Shem and Eber; how can thirty-four years be considered *a short while*? The answer is that love has a way of making time go quickly. Just as the Torah teaches that the first seven years that Jacob worked in order to marry Rachel *seemed to him a few days* (יָמִים אֲחָדִים) *because of his love for her* (29:20), so too, the thirty-four years he spent away from his beloved Land seemed *a short while* (יָמִים אֲחָדִים) because of his love for the Land. From the time he left until he returned, there were no gaps in Jacob's preoccupation with *Eretz Yisrael*.

2. **After the Fact.** *R' Itzikel of Brod* was forced to leave his position as Rav of Brod by the incessant harassment of the community leaders. Shortly before his departure, the members of the community tendered a farewell reception, at which they spoke lavishly of his praises and bemoaned the fact that he was leaving them.   With pain in his heart, R' Itzikel responded by quoting *Rashi* that the *departure* of the righteous leaves its mark. "Apparently, it is only when the righteous are about to depart a city that their presence is felt and appreciated. While he resides there, nobody takes any notice of him; on the contrary, they embitter his life. This explains an enigmatic verse, *The*

describe Abraham's departure to Egypt with the words וַיֵּלֶךְ אַבְרָם, *and Abram went,* rather than and Abram *left*? (See *Genesis* 12:4).

The *Chasam Sofer* explains that the departure of the righteous can leaves a void only if the people had appreciated his presence while he was there. Abraham's departure left little impression, since he lived among idolaters who saw him as some sort of fanatic at best. His departure meant nothing to them. Jacob, however, left his parents behind. Spiritually sensitive, they knew that much of the glory, splendor and beauty of the place had departed with Jacob.

Although our verse makes clear that in the case of Jacob, it was his departure that had an adverse affect on Beer-sheba, it often happens that a righteous person feels that the shortcomings of a place influences his decision to leave. A *tzaddik's* motivations for leaving a place of residence are not the same as other peoples. He does not choose to leave in order to seek greater financial success or a higher standard of living; generally, he leaves because the area's spiritual climate is no longer conducive to the type of life he wants for himself and his family. Thus, it is not as a result of his departure that the place loses its splendor, but rather that he feels the need to leave because the spiritual splendor has left already (*R' Yerucham Warhaftig*).

The Torah writes both of Jacob's departure from Beer-sheba and of his intended destination Haran, for each represents a meaningful goal on its own. He left Beer-sheba in obedience to his mother's request that he escape from the danger of Esau. His destination in Haran was the fulfillment of his father's request to travel there to find an appropriate mate.[3]

וַיִּפְגַּע בַּמָּקוֹם
He encountered the place (ibid. 11).

Although he was escaping Esau at the behest of his mother, Jacob was in no rush to leave the land of his fathers. Thus at the border, before leaving the Land, he *encountered the place* like someone who bumps into a wall that does not allow him to continue. He slept there and had a dream in which God consented to his departure and promised him that he and his children would one day return. Only then did Jacob *lift his feet* (see 29:1) and, reassured that Hashem would protect him and bring him back, continue his travels with alacrity and a lightness of heart [see *Rashi* ad loc] (*R' Yechezkel Abramsky*).[4]

Rashi offers two interpretations of the term וַיִּפְגַּע, *he encountered.* He explains the "encounter" as prayer, for it was then that Jacob instituted the evening prayer. In addition, Mount Moriah miraculously moved to where Jacob was, thus allowing him to encounter it.

---

angel of Hashem did not continue anymore to appear to Manoah and his wife; then Manoah realized that he was an angel of Hashem (*Judges* 13:21). Only when the angel left did Manoah realize he was an angel. While the angel appeared to them and dwelled in their midst, they did not realize that an angel was among them." [Referring to the two successive *sidras* of אַחֲרֵי מוֹת - קְדשִׁים, there is an old Yiddish maxim that only after people pass away (אחרי מות) are they considered holy (קְדשִׁים).]

3. **Leaving and Coming.** The *Steipler Gaon* viewed this formula of leaving from and traveling to as a model of our generation's need to send children away to yeshivah. In years gone by, a child could stay at home and remain a loyal Torah Jew. The home itself provided an environment of fear of Heaven, good character and a basic Torah outlook and lifestyle. Today, unfortunately, the pervasive lack of moral and ethical values obligates parents to send their children from home to the pure Torah atmosphere of the yeshivah.

For example, not all young men in Eastern Europe attended a yeshivah after a certain age. Financial realities forced all but the most intellectually superior students to leave the yeshivah. Nevertheless, the Jewish street was pure enough to produce fine, upstanding Jews. Today, however, everybody must go to a yeshivah. Even those who will not become outstanding scholars need the yeshivah to insure that they grow up to be loyal steadfast Jews.

While parents used to send their children *to* the yeshivah to grow in Torah under the tutelage of great Torah scholars, today they send them *from* the home in order to escape the spiritual pollution that surrounds and infiltrates it. If a young man wishes to succeed in becoming a true *talmid chacham,* he must both *leave* his home and *come* to the yeshivah (*Bircas Peretz*).

4. **Sad Farewell.** [Even when a Jew has to leave the Land of Israel he does it with a heavy heart. Sensitive Jews never say, "I'm going home," when returning to the Diaspora.]

Sfas Emes views both explanations as thematically related to each other. Even in times of spiritual darkness, when one does not sense the light of Hashem, he can still bring Godliness into his life through heartfelt prayer. If one really craves God's closeness, his prayer will pierce the darkness and allow God's light to shine through.

According to *Rashi,* Jacob had already arrived at Haran when he realized that he had passed Beth-El, the place where his forefathers had prayed. He regretted that he himself had failed to do so — and then he was miraculously returned to Beth-El.[5]

Considering that he was 63 years old at the time and after having spent fourteen sleepless years at the academy of Shem and Eber, it would have been perfectly understandable if Jacob had rested before returning to Beth-El. Nevertheless, fearful of the consequences of squandering the opportunity to pray, he returned immediately. As a result, he was granted the majestic vision of the angels going up and down the ladder, symbolizing the travails and eventual triumph of the Jewish people in exile.

We must learn from Jacob that the key to spiritual ascent and growth is to seize the moment (*Michtav MeEliyahu*).[6]

וַיֵּלֶן שָׁם כִּי בָא הַשֶּׁמֶשׁ
*and spent the night there
because the sun had set* (ibid.).

The Midrash (*Bereishis Rabbah* 68) interprets the words כִּי בָא as if they were one word spelled כִּיבָה, *He extinguished*, i.e., God "extinguished" the light of the sun, by making it set early so that He could talk privately with Jacob, as it were. This might be compared to a beloved subject who travels a distance to visit his king. The king said to his servants, "Extinguish the lights and put out the lamps so that I may speak with my beloved one in privacy." So too, God had the sun set early in order to speak to Jacob "in private."

What does the Midrash add to that which is written in the text? *R' A.M. Hershberg* suggests that the darkness was symbolically meant as a test of Jacob's loyalty to God: When darkness settled over his life, would he still remain God's beloved subject?

Zekan Aharon expands on this theme. On the threshold of exile from *Eretz Yisrael*, the Land of his father and grandfather, God assured Jacob that he would not only survive, but would actually grow spiritually from the experience. The Exile is God's way of "closing the lights" so that He can afford us spiritual opportunities so precious that they must be revealed in total privacy. Thus He creates *galus* so that the nations of the world will think that we Jews are in decline, while in truth He is offering us

---

5. **Providential Speed.** There are two instances in the Torah where the Sages teach that people were miraculously able to cover long distances in a very short while — and both are related to finding a suitable match. When Eliezer was going to find a match for Isaac and when Jacob was on his way to finding his life partner, they were blessed with קְפִיצַת הַדֶּרֶךְ, a *quickening of the way.*

This is a portent for all times. Many children reach marriageable age and their parents fear that by natural means, they cannot help their children get on their feet financially. How can they afford to make a wedding and give the young couple the minimum with which to set up a home? We must never despair. Like our forefathers, we must place our trust in Hashem and before we know it, we may arrive at our destination, ready to enjoy the *nachas* of children and grandchildren (*Bikkurei Aviv*).

6. **Burning Issue.** During a meal at the Yeshivah of Volozhin, someone asked a question of the student who was reputed to possess the broadest Talmudic knowledge in the yeshivah. The answer was given in a *Tosafos,* but the young man did not remember it. Devastated, he bolted from the table even before reciting the Grace After Meals. He went to a synagogue in a nearby small town and sat and learned for seven years straight. He eventually became one of the towering figures of the generation.

Many years later, a group of students asked *R' Chaim of Volozhin* about the incident. He replied, "What he did was certainly contrary to halachah since he failed to recite the blessings, but if had waited to do so, he would never have spent those seven consecutive years learning and he would have never become the great man that he is." To be great, one must seize the moment (*R' Chaim Shmulevitz*).

the greatest spiritual gifts imaginable, speaking to us in the intimate way which is only possible under the cover of darkness.[7]

וַיִּקַּח מֵאַבְנֵי הַמָּקוֹם וַיָּשֶׂם מְרַאֲשֹׁתָיו
he took from the stones of the place which he arranged around his head (ibid.).

According to *Rashi*, Jacob placed stones around his head as a protection against wild animals. This would seem to be an exercise in futility since the rest of his body was still exposed to attack. Jacob's initiative teaches that everything that is given to man, be it his sustenance or security, is a result of hidden miracles; all of man's efforts achieve nothing in themselves. Nevertheless, he is obligated to exert some type of effort to achieve his goals [הִשְׁתַּדְּלוּת] , all the while realizing that his success is dependent on God's will. Jacob knew that he would be protected from wild animals only if God willed it to be so. The stones were merely the token effort required of him (*Alter of Kelm*).[8]

Alternatively, *Rashi* explains that the stones began to quarrel with each other, as it were,

saying, "Upon me shall this righteous man rest his head." Thereupon God combined them all into one stone. This concept seems incredible. Inanimate stones can neither see nor understand, yet they vie for the privilege of serving the righteous man. How can this be?

Every molecule of Creation has the potential to serve as a source of God's glory, for "everything that God made, He made solely for His glory" (*Avos* 6:11). Each part of Creation yearns for man to provide it with the opportunity to realize its potential. Thus the stones competed for the chance to serve the righteous man (*Zekan Aharon*).

What was the purpose of fusing all the rocks together? Since Jacob's head could rest only on one part of the rock, wouldn't the rest of the rock still ask that he place his head on it? The *Imrei Emes* replies that unity overcomes jealousy and strife. When many elements unite, they are all part of a single whole, and there is no longer room for pettiness.[9]

---

7. **Intimate Words.** The Talmud interprets the verse *He has placed me in darkness* (*Lamentations* 3:6) as referring to the Babylonian Talmud (*Sanhedrin* 24a). The greatest revelation of Torah, the Talmud, which is the Jewish people's beacon of light, was revealed only from the darkness of the Exile. Jews must never despair, for God does not abandon us, even in exile. If we listen carefully, we will hear Him speaking to us, whispering words of intimacy and encouragement even while we are surrounded by darkness.

The *Nesivos Shalom* suggests that the chassidic custom of eating the third Shabbos meal in the dark is based on this Midrash. The time of the third meal is known in Kabbalistic literature as רַעֲוָא דְּרַעֲוִין, the time of the "desire of desire," i.e., the meal at which God infuses man with a powerful desire to cleave to Him. This intimate message is conveyed in the dark.

8. **Beyond Miraculous.** If everything is dependent on God, why must man make any effort at all? *R' Eliyahu E. Dessler* explained. Man must invest effort in order to create a trial of faith for himself: After he has done his best, will he still recognize that success is granted by God, or will he believe that his efforts made it happen? Thus it follows that the greater one's trust in God, the lesser the effort demanded of him.

During World War I, the future *Brisker Rav*, *R' Yitzchak Zev Soloveitchik*, found refuge in Warsaw. When the German bombardment of the city began, he went down to the basement of the building along with all the neighbors. However, when the assault intensified, he went back upstairs. His neighbors found his behavior incomprehensible: When the bombing was light and the danger was limited he stayed in the shelter, yet when the danger increased he left!

The Rav explained: "In truth, a person's trust in God should be so vibrant that he should make no physical effort to improve his situation. The *Ramban,* however, teaches that one must avoid having to rely on an obvious miracle. Earlier, when the bombing was light, I was obligated to go into the shelter, but now the bombing is so intense that even the shelter doesn't offer real protection. Since we are totally dependent on Him anyway, I might as well go back upstairs."

9. **Security in Unity.** *Zichron Shmuel* offers a homiletic interpretation synthesizing *Rashi's* two approaches: The unity of the Jewish people is its most potent weapon against the attack of the "wild beasts" (nations of the world) who seek to destroy us.

וַיִּשְׁכַּב בַּמָּקוֹם הַהוּא
and lay down in that place (ibid.).

The Sages infer that it was only here that Jacob lay down, but during his fourteen years at the academy of Shem and Eber, he never lay down to sleep, so preoccupied was he in preparing himself for the encounter with Laban and a culture antagonistic to the values of his parental home.[10]

Although Jacob could surely have found a more comfortable place to rest, he still preferred to do so upon the earth and stones. Homiletically, this offers two lessons. First, survival in an antagonistic environment is possible only if one remains aware of the inherent spiritual dangers. Second, this reflects the Jew's love for the Land of Israel, even when it is less than comfortable. In the spirit of King David, *for Your servants have cherished her stones and favored her dust* (Psalms 102:15).

וְהִנֵּה סֻלָּם מֻצָּב אַרְצָה וְרֹאשׁוֹ מַגִּיעַ הַשָּׁמָיְמָה
a ladder was set earthward and its top reached heavenward (ibid. 12).

The word סוּלָּם has the same *gematria* (numerical value) as מָמוֹן, *money* (136). While money is seemingly the most mundane of items (*set earthward*), in reality *its top reaches heavenward*, for money is among the most effective tools to advancing a spiritual agenda. Be it through charity, support of Torah scholars or money spent on other *mitzvos*, money can take man to dazzling spiritual heights. On the other hand, money can drive one to the lowest depths.[11]

This is the thrust of the Talmudic dictum that righteous people treasure their money more than their own bodies (*Sotah* 12a). Such people realize that without money, many opportunities are foreclosed to them. A body alone without resources is insufficient (*Baal Shem Tov*).[12]

According to *Yismach Moshe*, Jacob's ladder is a metaphor for man himself. Corporeal man, formed out of the ground, is *set earthward*. Nevertheless, he is blessed with a Godly soul; hence, the apex of his being *reaches heavenward*. When man allows his physical needs and existence to dominate him, they drag him downward and he becomes *set earthward*. If, however, he imbues his corporeal existence with meaning and infuses his life with the spirit of Torah, then the ladder can reach the greatest heights.

Furthermore, man's actions in this world affect what happens in Heaven. As *R' Chaim of Volozhin* explains, "Know what is above you" (*Avos* 2:1) homiletically means that one must know that whatever occurs in the Heavenly spheres is a result of his actions on earth. Thus man is *set earthward*, i.e., he lives an earthly life, but his actions unleash forces in the upper worlds and cause a cosmic flow from Heaven earthward. He is the ladder *set earthward* whose top *reaches heavenward* serving as the link between heaven and earth. *And behold!*

---

10. **Elevated Perspectives.** Since the Torah had not yet been given, what exactly did Jacob study for fourteen years at the academy of Shem and Eber? *Nesivos Shalom* explains that one must be a Jew before he can receive the Torah, for Torah can only be granted to a Jew. In order to merit the Torah, one must be permeated with the basic values of Judaism. In the academy of Shem and Eber, the curriculum consisted of developing one's character and learning how to be a Jew.

The *Mishnah* (*Avos* 5:22) enlightens us about the curriculum at the yeshivah of Abraham our forefather. His students — then and now — are recognizable because they possess a good eye, a humble spirit and a meek soul. These three areas, which encompass the entirety of the human personality, were studied in Abraham's yeshivah, in order to imbue the students with a uniquely Jewish character and orientation. The lectures taught how to achieve elevated perspectives in these three central areas.

11. **Squeezed Out.** *R' Meir of Premishlan* cried out to God, "Master of the world, I know that if You squeeze out the essence of all the Jewish prayers, only money will come out, because that is their most frequent request. But believe me, if You squeeze out the essence of their financial requests, Torah, *mitzvos* and acts of kindness will come out. Why does a Jew want money except to provide his children with a proper Torah education, to perform Your commandments in a beautiful manner and to help the less fortunate of Your children?"

12. **Up and Down.** *Baal HaTurim* notes that the numerical value of סוּלָּם, *ladder*, also equals that of עוֹנִי, *poverty*. Poverty and wealth are often cyclical and life is a ladder. Some climb up and realize מָמוֹן (money = 136), while others fall into עוֹנִי (*poverty* =136).

angels of God were ascending and descending on it (ibid.). Even the rise and fall of the angels is contingent on man; they ascend and descend בּוֹ, on *him*. If man serves God, they rise; if he abandons God, they fall.[13]

הָאָרֶץ אֲשֶׁר אַתָּה שֹׁכֵב עָלֶיהָ לְךָ אֶתְּנֶנָּה וּלְזַרְעֶךָ
the ground upon which you are lying, to you will I give it and to your descendants (ibid. 13).

Only those who are willing to exhibit self-sacrifice on behalf of the Land of Israel will merit to acquire a share in it and actually live there.

According to the *Kozhnitzer Maggid*, this is alluded to in this verse. The Land that will be granted to you and your descendants is the earth for which you were figuratively willing to "lay down on the ground."[14]

R' Leibish Charif relates this Divine promise to the next verse *Your offspring shall be as the dust of the earth* (ibid. 14). This explanation is based on the Talmud (*Gittin* 57a), which compares the Land of Israel to a deer. Just as a deer's skin expands or contracts to accommodate its growth, so the Land of Israel has an elasticity that allows it to expand or contract in order to accommodate all who want to live there. Thus God promised that even when *your offspring shall be as [numerous as] the dust of the earth*, still *Eretz Yisrael* will always make itself hospitable to them.

Rashi interprets *the ground upon which you are lying* as teaching that God folded all of *Eretz Yisrael* under Jacob, so that, in effect, he lay on all of the Land (*Chullin* 91b). This teaches that *Eretz Yisrael* is not defined by its physical borders. It exists wherever it is "folded under Jacob." Only when life is governed by Jacob's values and spirit is the Land truly *Eretz Yisrael*, the Holy Land. Thus, even the Diaspora may possess its sanctity — if it is imbued with Jacob's spirit (*R' Elazar M. Shach*).[15]

וְהָיָה זַרְעֲךָ כַּעֲפַר הָאָרֶץ
Your offspring shall be as the dust of the earth (ibid. 14).

According to *HaDerash V'Halyun*, this is a precondition for the blessing that the Jewish people *shall spread out powerfully westward, eastward, northward and southward*. Unlike the stars which are totally separated from each other, and unlike grains of sand which, while in close proximity, are separate entities, the dust of the earth is connected in clods. Only unity will engender the resurgence of the nation.

Sforno sees *the dust of the earth* as a metaphor for national degradation. Just as the primal light emerged from darkness (see *Genesis* 1:2-3), so the light of Israel will shine after what seems to be its total eclipse. As the Sages taught, "If you witness a generation when troubles come in riverlike torrents, await the coming of the Messiah" (*Sanhedrin* 98a).

---

13. **Keep on Moving!** The *Chafetz Chaim* expands on the analogy of man as a ladder. The ladder of life has very delicate rungs. One either continues to rise or he automatically falls. If one tries to stay on a single rung, it breaks and he plummets earthward. Everything is dependent on man; if he does not go up, he falls. The angels ascend or descend on *him*.

14. **Land Resuscitated.** In a homiletic rendering, *Elef HaMagen* views the verse as a promise of the resettlement of Jews in *Eretz Yisrael*. For generations, the Jews of the Diaspora viewed it as a place where old people came to live out their last years, die and be buried in its holy soil. Or they wanted their bodies to be brought there for burial. Thus it was the ground on which to lie down. Now, however, that so many young people abandon the glitter of the Exile and move to *Eretz Yisrael* in order to deepen their commitment to Judaism, it has become the Land of Israel and his [young] descendants.

15. **Roaming Sanctity.** This concept of "outposts" of *Eretz Yisrael* finds expression in the words of the Talmud: "In the future [Messianic era], the synagogues and study halls in Babylonia [the exile] will relocate to *Eretz Yisrael*" (*Megillah* 29a).

The *Chasam Sofer* interprets that even now, those places are like oases of *Eretz Yisrael* in the spiritual desert of the Diaspora. When the Messiah comes, they will go back home.

The *Chazon Ish* wrote, in the 1920's: "Poland is like *Eretz Yisrael*, since it is the home of established *yeshivos*, the righteous *Chafetz Chaim* and other great men of Torah reside there, and there is fear of Heaven there. All other lands are considered like the Diaspora" (*Collected Letters* I:77).

**כִּי לֹא אֶעֱזָבְךָ עַד אֲשֶׁר אִם
עָשִׂיתִי אֶת אֲשֶׁר דִּבַּרְתִּי לָךְ**

*for I will not forsake you until I have done
what I have spoken about you* (ibid. 15).

Are we to infer that after God fulfills what He has promised He *will* forsake us? This cannot be, for how can we survive for even a minute without His protection? Rather, it means that until the major salvation comes, He will provide us with minor miracles, allowing us to survive (*R' Menachem Mendel of Vizhnitz, R' Avraham of Slonim*).[16]

**וַיִּיקַץ יַעֲקֹב מִשְּׁנָתוֹ וַיֹּאמֶר אָכֵן
יֵשׁ ה' בַּמָּקוֹם הַזֶּה וְאָנֹכִי לֹא יָדָעְתִּי**

*Jacob awoke from his sleep and said,
"Surely Hashem is present in this place
and I did not know!"* (ibid. 16).

This implies that had Jacob been aware of the sanctity of the place, he would not have slept there. This statement seems astounding. At this holy place, Jacob experienced a pristine level of prophecy and the pinnacle of spiritual engagement; yet, he would have given it up in order not to sleep on such holy ground.

According to the *Alter of Slabodka*, this shows the importance of respectful behavior. Jacob was ready to forgo a prophecy and closeness to

Hashem if achieving it entailed disrespectfully sleeping in the site of the Abode of God and the gate of the heavens. Alternatively, since he realized that the Temple would be built there, he realized that reverence for the Temple, or, more accurately, toward the One whose Presence resides within, demanded that he not sleep there (*R' Yitzchak Zev Soloveitchik*).[17]

Nachlas Eliezer sees a practical lesson. Generally we are not content to expend only minimal efforts in order to achieve our physical needs. We want to give our all so that we will receive more and more. On the other hand, with regard to Torah and *mitzvos*, we tend to look for shortcuts, so that we can easily achieve what we perceive to be our spiritual needs. As the folk saying has it, "There are people who want to become the *Vilna Gaon* overnight, but they also want to sleep that night."

Jacob's perspective was the diametric opposite. With regard to his physical concerns, he prayed that God would provide him with nothing more than *bread to eat and clothes to wear* (ibid. 20). However, in matters of the spirit, he was unwilling to receive anything as a gift; all of his spiritual achievements had to be earned by his own efforts. Hence, when he woke up, he was upset. "Had I known the spiritual potential of this place, I would not have slept and let prophecy come to me unearned. I would have prepared for it so that when

---

16. **Help Until . . .** *R' Isser Zalman Meltzer* was fond of relating the following incident: In the waiting room of *R' Yisrael of Rizhin* sat a man, his forehead furrowed with worry, his appearance a picture of pain and travail. The Rebbe's young son Dovid Moshe (later to be the Rebbe of Tchortkov) turned to the Jew and asked him, "What do you want to request from my father?"

With a bittersweet smile, the Jew caressed the boy's flowing locks and said, "I need your father to bless me that I be saved from my many woes."

Suddenly the door opened and the Jew went in to the Rebbe. A short while later when he emerged and the youngster asked him what the Rizhiner had said. "He said that Hashem will help me," came the reply. "Fine," said Dovid Moshe, "but what will be until Hashem helps?" When the Jew did not have an answer, the young boy told him, "Go back inside and ask my father."

The Jew did just that. The Rizhiner then said to him, "Hashem will help until He helps. That's what He told Jacob, *for I will not forsake you until I have done what I have spoken about you*, meaning "Until I will help you, I will not forsake you." [ביז דער רבונו של עולם וועט העלפן וועט ער אויך העלפן.]

17. **Fully Awake.** Many people wake up in the middle of the night, as Jacob did, yet there is a world of difference between what a righteous person does when he wakes up and what others do. When a conscientious servant of God awakens, he immediately surges forward into pursuing his spiritual agenda. Ordinarily people turn over and go back to sleep. Thus, when Pharaoh had a dream that disturbed him and portended an upheaval in his country, he awoke and went right back to sleep (*Genesis* 41:4-5). Here, regarding Jacob, however, the Torah writes *Jacob awoke from his sleep and* [he immediately] *said, "Surely Hashem is present in this place"* (*R' Meir'l of Premishlan*).

Whenever *R' Simchah Zissel Broide* (*Rosh Yeshivah of Chevron*) woke up in the morning, irrespective of the hour, he would get out of bed and begin his day of intense Torah study.

it happened it would have been truly mine, a result of my preparation."[18], [19]

מַה נּוֹרָא הַמָּקוֹם הַזֶּה
"How awesome is this Place!" (ibid. 17).

Some hold that their spiritual achievements are products of their own talents, efforts and personal piety, while others understand that even their spiritual [and certainly corporeal] achievements are Divine gifts.

Although the Sages teach that Mount Moriah miraculously moved to meet Jacob, he himself was sure that the spiritual revelation he experienced was the result of the intrinsic sanctity of the place. *"How awesome is this Place!"* This is another example of the many kindnesses God shows the righteous. He saves the righteous from becoming arrogant by letting man be convinced that God led them to spiritual heights, even when the experience is really the result of man's own efforts (*Sfas Emes*).

The Talmud (*Chullin* 91b) teaches that Jacob had already arrived in Haran when he realized he had passed the site of the future Temple. He re-

buked himself, saying, "Is it possible that I passed by the place where my forefathers prayed and I did not utilize the opportunity to pray there?!" Miraculously God brought him back to the site of the Temple.

This implies that only because Jacob had passed by was it appropriate that he stop there to pray. He would not have been remiss had he failed to make a special detour to the site where his forefathers prayed. Once he passed by, however, he was remiss in not having capitalized on the chance to pray there.

According to *R' Eliyahu Meir Bloch*, this teaches that ignoring a spiritual opportunity leaves a negative mark on man's soul.[20] [This is worse than not seeking out spiritual growth for as the Sages taught, "Who is a fool? . . . one who destroys what has been given him" (*Chagigah* 3b).]

אִם יִהְיֶה אֱלֹקִים עִמָּדִי וּשְׁמָרַנִי בַּדֶּרֶךְ הַזֶּה
"If God will be with me, will guard me on this way that I am going (ibid. 20).

Since God had promised Jacob that He would protect him (verse 15), why does Jacob say, *If God will be with me*, as though he is in doubt?

---

18. **Effortless Torah?** *R' Chaim of Volozhin* writes in his preface to the *Vilna Gaon's* commentary to *Safra D'Tzniusa*: "He [the Vilna Gaon] told me that many times angels appeared to him in order to reveal to him many deep secrets of Torah, yet he always refused to listen to them. When one of these angels was persistent, the Gaon said to him, 'I want no gifts in learning the Torah. My eyes are raised in prayer to Hashem that whatever of His Torah He wants me to understand, He should personally reveal to me by allowing me to toil with my own intelligence until I understand. May He grant me an understanding heart and may my two kidneys function like two fountains of knowledge (see *Bereishis Rabbah* 61). Then I will know that I have found favor in His eyes. I want only what I worked on and have no interest in what angels want me to perceive without effort.' "

19. **Always Accessible.** The Midrash teaches that Jacob's flight from his paternal home symbolized the later exile of his children. God therefore showed him in his vision that the sanctity of the Temple would always be accessible to the Jewish people no matter where they are located. Just as God moved Mount Moriah, the location of the future Temple, to meet Jacob, so the spirit of the Temple will fill synagogues and Torah study halls. This is why Jacob said, *"Surely Hashem is present in this place* even while we are outside the Land and in exile, *and I did not know* that His Divine Presence will always be with my children" (*Melo HaOmer*).

20. **Grab the Opportunity.** When God appeared to Moses at the Burning Bush, he *hid his face for he was not to gaze toward God (Exodus* 3:6). Later, after the incident of the Golden Calf, he asked God, *Show me now Your glory* (ibid 34:19). God replied by telling him, "When I wanted [to reveal My glory at the bush], you didn't want to look. Now that you do want to, I no longer want to be revealed." At the bush, Moses was presented with an opportunity to experience a revelation of God, yet he let the opportunity slip by. For this he was punished, and when he wanted to experience the glory of Hashem, God was unwilling to reveal it.

A student who has the opportunity to grow from his teacher or yeshivah, or a congregant who can benefit from his rabbi, must never refrain from taking full advantage of the blessing when it is available to him (*R' Eliyahu Meir Bloch*).

R' S. R. Hirsch explains: The aforementioned promise of protection was that God would save him from physical harm, something that is completely in God's Hands. Here, however, Jacob sought assurance for his spiritual welfare. Since he knew that everything is in the hands of Heaven except for the fear of Heaven (*Berachos* 33b), Jacob was afraid that he might not merit the spiritual armor necessary to survive his sojourn with Laban. He therefore asked God to please protect him.

Imrei Emes embellishes on this approach, invoking the words of the Talmud (*Berachos* 11a) that the Biblical term דֶּרֶךְ, *way,* refers to activities that are neither permitted nor forbidden, but that are optional.[21] Accordingly, Jacob asked that God guard him on the דֶּרֶךְ, *way,* assuring him that even in such "mundane" areas as eating and drinking he be able to conduct himself in a fashion that enhances God's honor and glory.

which one cannot live. He writes: "As is well known, the pursuit of luxuries is often the cause of much heartache. Therefore, one who truly fears God and seeks to serve Him should be satisfied with his lot and curb his desire for luxuries, allowing his heart to find satisfaction and satiety in the fear of God.

"Know," he continues, "that if not for the innately evil desire to chase after wealth and honor in this world, it would be appropriate not to be at all concerned over not having these inconsequential 'extras.' One should ask of God only that which is absolutely necessary for whatever one *must* have will certainly be provided daily by Him. The very nature of the world attests to the fact that necessities are always provided, for the more necessary something is, the more readily available it is. [Air is always available, water almost always, bread usually, while delicacies are less accessible.][22]

וְנָתַן לִי לֶחֶם לֶאֱכֹל וּבֶגֶד לִלְבֹּשׁ
will give me bread to eat and clothes to wear (ibid.).

According to *Rabbeinu Bachya,* this request highlights the perspective of the righteous who ask God only for absolute necessities, without

Jacob's request for bread *to eat* and clothing *to wear* seems redundant. Is it not obvious that food is to be eaten and clothing to be worn?

Many answers have been offered to this question. According to *R' David of Lelov,* Jacob asked for enough bread *to eat* but not so much that he could save some for later. As the Sages teach, one who

---

21. **No Spiritual Switzerland.** There is no such a thing as spiritually benign optional activities. It is a mistake to assume that *mitzvos* are only those things God commands us to do, sins are those from which He commands us to refrain, and all other activities are neutral and make no difference to Him. "*Everything* that God created He made for His greater glory" (*Avos* 6:12). As *Chovos HaLevavos* maintains, every human activity can be used to further God's ends or to thwart them.

The true definition of optional activities is that unlike *mitzvos*, which always enhance His glory, and sins which always diminish it, optional activities are defined by how man uses them. For example, eating can be the equivalent of offering a sacrifice on the altar, if one eats in a refined way, to strengthen his body in the service of God. On the other hand, if one is not careful, it can be reduced to gluttony and gastronomic indulgence, which debases both man and his food. Thus it is optional, in the sense that whether it adds or diminishes from His honor is dependent on man (*R' Yitzchak Hutner*).

22. **Burdensome Luxury.** When a wooden floor was put down over the earthen surface in the *Chafetz Chaim's* home, he was upset. For him, the earthen floor was more than sufficient. One Friday when he saw a family member washing and polishing the floor he commented, "Tell me the truth! Wouldn't it be better to wash and polish our souls so that they be pure, instead of washing and polishing the floor?" When his Rebbetzin asked him why their home had no curtains while *R' Chaim Ozer Grodzenski's* home did, he replied, "Why don't you understand? R' Chaim Ozer is the leader of the nation about whom the Torah commands that his fellow Jews enhance his standing by enriching him. He has no choice but to bear the pain of having luxuries. I am a simple Jew who is not obligated to bear that burden."

According to *Maharal*, this perspective is reflected in the fact that matzah, the "poor bread," is a symbol of freedom. Possessions can be an imprisoning encumbrance if one feels he cannot manage without them. One who can subsist on the bare minimum is truly free. Thus matzah, made from the barest of necessary ingredients, is a sign of true freedom.

worries what he will eat tomorrow suffers from a diminished faith. Furthermore, he only asked for clothes *to wear,* not in order to fill the closet.[23]

R' *Shlomo Leib of Lenchno* offered the following prayer: "Master of the world, grant Jews bread they can eat. Provide them with the joy of the heart which engenders appetite, for when one is sad or in pain he cannot bring himself to eat. Let them wear the clothes that You give them and not have to give them to creditors as collateral for loans." Thus, Jacob hoped for bread *to eat* and clothes *to wear.*

Background

Jacob travels to Haran and comes upon a group of shepherds waiting at a well, until enough of them gather in order to remove the heavy boulder that covered the well. It is here that Jacob meets his future wife and mainstay of his home — Rachel. It is here that eleven of the twelve tribal ancestors will be born.

אַחַי מֵאַיִן אַתֶּם
My brothers, where are you from? (29:4).

Rashi (verse 7) notes that Jacob reprimanded the shepherds for loafing. He said to them, "If you are dayworkers, *look, the day is still long.*" How did Jacob, a guest and outsider who never met these people before, have the audacity to rebuke them? Even more fascinating is that they accepted the criticism and, rather than telling him not to meddle, they replied that they had to wait for more shepherds to help remove the large stone.

The *Ponevezher Rav* explained: Resistance to criticism is based on the perception that the person offering it is an adversary. However, when one senses authentic concern and feels that the criticism is an expression of love, one can swallow the most bitter of pills. When Jacob referred to the shepherds as "my brothers," he showed his heartfelt love for them and thus disarmed all resistance. From a "brother" they knew the criticism was meant constructively.[24]

According to R' *Yaakov Kaminetsky,* Jacob followed the advice of *Rambam,* that one who offers rebuke must do so privately, and speak in a calm, soft and respectful tone. He should make it clear that he criticizes only because he is concerned for the other person's welfare (*Hilchos Deios* 7:7). Thus he first called them "brothers," and only then offered his criticism.

לֹא עֵת הֵאָסֵף הַמִּקְנֶה הַשְׁקוּ הַצֹּאן וּלְכוּ רְעוּ
It is not yet time to bring the livestock in, water the flock and go on grazing (ibid. 7).

According to R' *Chaim Vital,* this is an allusion to the Final Redemption. It is not yet time to "bring in the livestock," to gather in the exiled Jewish people. The shepherds, the leaders of the people, must water the flock with the refreshing words of Torah and allow them to graze, fattening them with intense, vibrant faith. When all the flocks are gathered and the Jewish people united, they will be ready for redemption.[25]

---

23. **Money for Money?** Some people need money for their needs while others want money simply in order to have money. Jacob saw food and clothes as a means to provide him with the basic conditions necessary to spend his life serving God — not as a self-serving goal.

24. **Respectful Critique.** Criticism offered in a demeaning way is always intolerable and therefore rejected. One may never criticize in such a way that it delegitimizes *people*; only *behavior* should be condemned. Thus one should be pleasant toward others even when rebuking them, for criticism offered in a palatable way may be very productive. *Shelah* and *Alshich* interpret the verse in *Proverbs* (9:8) in this light: *Do not offer rebuke to a scoffer lest he hate you; chastise a wise man and he will love you.* When offering chastisement, one must take care not to be insulting to the target of his criticism, treating him as if he is a scoffer. Instead one should appeal to the other person's dignity, saying, "You are an intelligent and upstanding individual. Such behavior as you have exhibited in the past is below your dignity and does not befit somebody as wise and special as you." The person will then love you and accept your constructive criticism.

25. **In the Meantime.** R' *Meir of Premishlan,* in his love for his people, explained it thus; "Master of the world! Maybe it is not yet the time to bring in the sheep. In the meantime, please *water the flock,* provide them with sustenance and let them graze. Don't allow their sins to impede their ability to flourish until You redeem them."

הַפַּעַם אוֹדֶה אֶת ה'

This time let me gratefully praise Hashem (ibid. 35).

The name יְהוּדָה connotes Leah's gratitude to Hashem for having granted her more than her rightful share of Jacob's twelve sons. Since Jacob had four wives and was destined to have twelve sons, each of the Matriarchs expected to give birth to three. When Leah gave birth to her fourth, she named him Judah, from הוֹדָאָה, *thanks*, to express her gratitude to God. The Talmud (*Berachos* 7a) states that from the time of Creation, no one offered gratitude to Hashem until Leah. This seems perplexing, for certainly our forefathers offered thanks to God for everything He had done for them. What was so unique about Leah's gratitude?

Maayana Shel Torah explains: The word הוֹדָאָה bears two connotations; one is gratitude, but the other implies admission. One who is מוֹדֶה admits to something or somebody. When one is sure that his friend was wrong about something and then he realizes otherwise, he is מוֹדֶה and admits that his friend was right and he was mistaken. This is true regarding gratitude as well. There is a gratitude which expresses appreciation for a kindness. But a deeper, more profound form of gratitude is when one admits that what initially appeared as something detrimental was in reality a great favor.[26]

Initially Leah considered it a terrible personal tragedy that Jacob loved her less than Rachel. Ultimately she came to realize that it was because of this that God granted her the lion's share of the tribes. She therefore stated, *this time let me gratefully* admit that it was all really for my benefit and therefore *praise Hashem.*

In this type of הוֹדָאָה, Leah was the pioneer.

---

26. **Cathartic Pain.** The Chassidic masters render a verse in Hallel in this vein. אוֹדְךָ כִּי עֲנִיתָנִי וַתְּהִי לִי לִישׁוּעָה, *I thank You, for You have pained me and become my salvation* (*Psalms* 118:21). The pain that I had initially viewed as punishment was in reality the source of my salvation. I therefore thank You, Hashem, not only for the salvation but also for the pain.

According to *Sfas Emes,* this explains why at the Pesach Seder we eat *maror* (bitter herbs, ostensibly a symbol of servitude) after matzah, which reflects freedom. Only in hindsight do we realize that even the perceived bitterness is also a sign of freedom, for out of the pain was born the gain.

פרשת וישלח ⧉
Parashas Vayishlach

Background

Thirty-four years after he fled from Esau and his wrath over losing the paternal blessings, Jacob is on his way back to *Eretz Yisrael*. Esau's hatred has yet to subside, however, and he is leading an army to settle his old score with Jacob.

וַיִּשְׁלַח יַעֲקֹב מַלְאָכִים לְפָנָיו אֶל עֵשָׂו אָחִיו . . .

Then Jacob sent angels ahead of him to Esau his brother . . . (32:4).

Citing one of two Midrashic opinions as to the identity of Jacob's messengers, *Rashi* submits that they were really angels. The alternate opinion of the Midrash renders מַלְאָכִים as [human] emissaries.

According to *Divrei Yaakov*, the choice of angels rather than human emissaries was based on the advice of the *Mishnah,* "Distance yourself from a bad neighbor" (*Avos* 1:6). A person's character can be adversely affected by contact with wicked people, for the negative atmosphere will eventually rub off on him. Hence Jacob was wary of sending mere mortals to *Esau his brother,* a wicked person, and *to the land of Seir,* an evil place, for nothing less than an angel could survive the encounter unscathed.[1]

Alternatively, the need for actual angels was born of the sensitive nature of the mission. When Jacob sent the messengers, he was unsure of Esau's intentions. Was he seeking peace or war? Was he interested in being *Esau* or was he ready to be *his brother*? If Esau sought brotherhood and peace, then the messengers would respond in a conciliatory manner. On the other hand, if it was "Esau" who stood before them, then they would have to make it clear that just as Jacob survived Laban, he would survive Esau as well. Only angels

---

1. **Angelic Mitzvos.** Who were those angels? The *Mishnah* teaches that "He who fulfills even a single mitzvah gains himself an advocate" to plead on his behalf at the bar of Divine justice (see *Avos* 4:13). The commentators explain that every mitzvah creates a positive angel while every sin creates a negative angel, who condemns and prosecutes against the person.

Jacob sent the angels that were created by his *mitzvos*, so that they could simultaneously bring his message to Esau while pleading before God that he be saved from the bloody hands of his brother. [*Rashi's* expression is מַלְאָכִים מַמָּשׁ, *real angels*. The word מַמָּשׁ is an abbreviation for מַלְאָכִים מִמִּצְוֹת שֶׁעָשָׂה, *angels* [created] *from the mitzvos he performed*] (*R' Elimelech of Lizhensk*).

Alternatively, he sent them in order to cause Esau to repent (*Shem MiShmuel*).

Esau told Jacob, "*Look, I am going to die, so of what use is the birthright*" (*Genesis* 25:32), expressing the philosophy of "Eat, drink and be merry for tomorrow you shall die." In Esau's view, this world is an end in itself; there is nothing eternal or lasting that emerges from it. Jacob therefore sent the angels created by his performance of the commandments as a way of bringing Esau to the realization that *mitzvos* create eternity, thereby encouraging him to repent (*Zekan Aharon*).

could accurately ascertain Esau's agenda and respond appropriately (*Kometz HaMinchah*).[2]

עִם לָבָן גַּרְתִּי
I have sojourned with Laban (ibid. 5).

Rashi explains this as Jacob's way of telling Esau that Isaac's blessings had not been fulfilled; therefore, Esau had no reason to be jealous of or hate him. "I remained an alien sojourner and have not achieved princely status." Despite our father's blessings, I have remained a homeless man, dependent on the hospitality of others all these years.

According to the Midrash, the word גַּרְתִּי, which can be rearranged to spell תַּרְיַ"ג, the acronym for the 613 commandments, was meant to imply to Esau that in spite of having lived (גַּרְתִּי) with Laban, Jacob had remained committed to the 613 commandments (תַּרְיַ"ג) and did not learn from his host's evil ways.

Of what interest is this to Esau? *R' Tzvi Hirsch Farber* explained: When Isaac blessed Esau he said to him, *When you are aggrieved* [because Israel has transgressed the Torah and is undeserving of spiritual ascent, then] *you may cast off his yoke from upon your neck* (Genesis 27:40). Esau was sure that Jacob would be negatively influenced by his twenty years in the house of Laban — how could those pernicious surroundings not have a bad effect? —

and that Jacob would forsake his loyalty to Torah and God. Jacob therefore informed Esau that he had not lost his right to dominion. "Although I sojourned with Laban, I kept the 613 *mitzvos* and did not learn from his evil ways" (*Rashi*).[3]

According to *R' Moshe Feinstein,* Jacob wanted to make it clear to Esau that fidelity to God and Torah is a nonnegotiable factor in the quest for peace. "Under the worst of conditions, in the shadow of the crooked Laban, I was unwilling to compromise my Judaism, and I won't compromise it to make peace with you either. If your definition of 'peace' is assimilation of my children with yours, then I want no part of such a peace."

Peace between people is important, but loyalty to Torah means being at peace with God — and that is more important.

Even Azel offers a different perspective, based on the Midrash that suggests that Jacob feared Esau because the latter had fulfilled the mitzvah of living in the Land of Israel. Jacob therefore instructed the messengers to tell Esau, *I sojourned with Laban.* "Although you fulfilled the one mitzvah of living in the Land of Israel, I fought tenaciously against the spiritually insidious influence of Laban in order to educate my children to fulfill all 613 commandments. Your one mitzvah cannot outweigh my dedication to all of God's *mitzvos.*"[4]

---

2. **Personal Reconciliation.** *R' Shneur Zalman* (the *Baal HaTanya*) and *R' Baruch of Medziboz* were involved in a protracted disagreement. Many well-meaning people sought to mediate, but to no avail. R' Baruch commented: When Jacob wanted to make peace with Esau, he sent messengers; yet, his brother rebuffed the overture, as it says, *The angel returned to Jacob, saying, "We came to your brother to Esau; he is heading toward you, and four hundred men are with him"* (verse 7). Only when the brothers met personally were they able to achieve reconciliation. We see from this that messengers, even angels, cannot be relied on to make peace.

3. **Yearning to Do.** Did Jacob really keep all 613 *mitzvos* while in Laban's home? He was obviously unable to keep the agricultural *mitzvos* which can only be performed in the Land of Israel. Furthermore, as the Sages teach, Jacob did not fulfill the mitzvah of honoring his parents while he lived with Laban.

The *Chasam Sofer* sees the answer in Jacob's choice of words, וְתַרְיַ"ג מִצְוֹת שָׁמַרְתִּי, "and I *kept* the 613 *mitzvos,*" rather than קִיַּמְתִּי, "I fulfilled." The word שָׁמַרְתִּי may be rendered *I waited for* [as in וְאָבִיו שָׁמַר אֶת הַדָּבָר, *but his father kept the matter in mind* (Genesis 37:11), anxiously awaiting for Joseph's dream to be realized]. Jacob anxiously awaited his return to his Land and to his parents' home where he would finally be able to fulfill the *mitzvos* that could not be performed in Haran.

The dream and heartfelt desire to perform a mitzvah earns one reward as if he had actually fulfilled it (see *Berachos* 6a and *Shaarei Teshuvah* 2:10).

4. **Clean Bill of Spiritual Health.** [Often we hear people claim that they are "Jews at heart" although they are lax about practical fulfillment of the commandments. They fail to realize that as central as the heart is to the body, it cannot keep one alive if his kidneys, lungs, brain, or pancreas fail. One must enjoy health in all of his organs and limbs.

When the Sages teach that the 248 positive commandments correspond to the 248 limbs/organs of the body, they mean that one must maintain spiritual health in all areas.]

Jacob's claim that he kept the *mitzvos* and remained uninfluenced by Laban, even while living with him, seems uncharacteristically pompous for Jacob.

The *Chafetz Chaim* and *R' Meir Shapiro* submit a homiletical interpretation. Although Jacob kept the commandments, he regretted that he failed to fulfill them with zest and passion. "If only I could invest as much enthusiasm and feeling in my *mitzvos* as Laban does in his sins! I didn't learn from his evil ways the passion with which one must perform God's will."[5]

וַיִּירָא יַעֲקֹב מְאֹד וַיֵּצֶר לוֹ
Jacob became very frightened,
and it distressed him (ibid. 8).

According to *Rashi,* Jacob was *frightened* that Esau might kill him and was *distressed* by the possibility that, in defending himself or his family, he might kill others.

Jacob was *distressed* over the fact that he was *frightened.* He was bothered that he lacked the requisite degree of faith that allows one to fear no one but God. This is the thrust of the verse *Rescue me, please, from the hand of my brother, from the hand of Esau — for I fear him* (ibid. 12). That he feared Esau was an indication to him that his fear of Heaven was flawed, thus making him vulnerable; hence, he asked God to rescue him (*Orach LaChaim*).[6]

R' Menachem Mendel of Kotzk comments that there is a rule that a statement in the Mishnah made in the name of אֲחֵרִים , *others,* always refers to R' Meir. According to the Talmudic tradition, R' Meir was a descendant of Esau. Thus in our verses, Jacob expressed two fears. He was afraid that *he* might be killed. And if he were forced to defend himself and his family, he might kill "others," i.e., R' Meir, because if he killed Esau, the great sage R' Meir would never be born, and the loss to Torah knowledge would be incalculable.

וְהָיָה הַמַּחֲנֶה הַנִּשְׁאָר לִפְלֵיטָה
then the remaining camp shall survive (ibid. 9).

According to the Sages, וְהָיָה implies a joyful situation. Where is the joy in Jacob's acknowledgment that half of his family might die? Jacob prayed that throughout Jewish history, whenever Jews would suffer pogroms or massacres, they should find some comfort in the knowledge that other Jewish communities will be spared. As the Talmud (*Pesachim* 87b) teaches, it is an act of Divine kindness that God spread the Jewish people among the nations (*Maharsham*).[7]

---

5. **Truthfully True.** Someone once asked *R' Baruch Ber Leibovitz, Rosh Yeshivah of Kaminetz,* why those who seek to undermine the Torah way are so successful in their efforts. Since when does such falsehood deserve to meet such success?

R' Baruch replied, "They act on behalf of falsehood with earnestness and authenticity while we who act on behalf of truth often do so with motives which are less than pure and honest." [This may explain the seemingly redundant expression אֱמֶת לַאֲמִתּוֹ, *truthfully true.* One must do the right thing for the right reasons, and with dedication to the truth.]

6. **Futility Fearful.** *Chovos HaLevavos* writes of a pious man who found himself alone at night in the wilderness. When asked whether he was afraid of thieves or wild animals, he replied, "In the presence of God, I am embarrassed to fear any creature besides Him."

According to the *Baal Shem Tov,* Jacob's distress was rooted in the fact that his fear of Esau did not help him learn to fear God.

B'nei Yissas'char sees this as the message of the phrase from the *Hoshana* petitions of Succos, כְּבוּשָׁה בַּגּוֹלָה. לוֹמֶדֶת יִרְאָתֶךְ, *while vanquished in exile, she* [the nation of Israel] *learns Your awesomeness.* While in exile, the Jewish people take their fear of the host nations and transform it into a lesson on how to fear God.

7. **Sanctified Survival.** When Hitler rose to power in the 1930's and declared his goal of making Europe *Judenrein* (free of Jews), one of the *roshei yeshivah* of Radin asked the *Chafetz Chaim* what would happen to Jewry. The Sage of Radin replied: "He will not succeed! No one in history has ever or will succeed in totally annihilating the Jewish people. The Torah promises *If Esau comes to one camp and strikes it down, then the remaining camp shall survive.*"

The *roshei yeshivah* then asked, "And if he, God forbid, succeeds in destroying European Jewry, who will serve as the remaining surviving camp?" Answered the Chafetz Chaim, "The prophet *Obadiah* says, 'On the mountain

Jacob prepared for the confrontation in three ways. He readied himself and his camp for battle, he implored God for Divine mercy, and he sent a lavish tribute to appease Esau's anger (*Rashi*).

Niflaos Chadashos questions the need for all three. If prayer is efficacious, why bother with preparations for battle or the offering of tributes? The answer is that Jacob prayed that God allow him to succeed if battle should become necessary. But better yet, he prayed, let Esau be appeased by the tribute. Jews do not rely on miracles; they expend all necessary efforts to achieve success through natural means. And yet they pray, for they realize that no efforts will yield results without God's help.[8]

Nachlas Chamishah finds an allusion to this message in the order of Jacob's preparations. The reference to prayer is mentioned between battle and tribute, because both preparations must be accompanied by prayer. If one must go to war, one must pray for victory. And if one must resort to tribute, one must pray that it be accepted graciously.

Sfas Emes submits a profound understanding of Jacob's preparations, viewing his entire engagement with Esau as an exercise in loving God. The Torah teaches that one must love God with *all his heart, all his soul and all his resources* (see *Deuteronomy* 6:5). *Prayer* is the service of the "heart." When in *battle,* one risks his "soul," for one may be killed. One's material "resources" are expended in providing *tribute* to others. Jacob's love of God was so intense that he committed himself to the fight for spiritual life with battle, prayer and tribute.

קָטֹנְתִּי מִכֹּל הַחֲסָדִים וּמִכָּל הָאֱמֶת
אֲשֶׁר עָשִׂיתָ אֶת עַבְדֶּךָ
I have been diminished by all the kindnesses and all the truth that You have done Your servant (ibid. 11).

As much as we might feel we have done things for God, it pales into insignificance when compared to what He does for us. Hence the more one experiences God's kindness, the more humbly he begins to view himself.[9]

We even begin to suspect that perhaps our "good deeds" are not so great after all.[10]

Thus Jacob said to God, "The great kindness You have shown me has diminished my own perception of my spiritual status. I realize how terribly dependent I am on Your mercy. Therefore, I ask You to save me from Esau" (*Sfas Emes, Divrei Shmuel*).

Shemen HaMaor offers a perspective based on an interpretation of the *Vilna Gaon.*

The *Gaon* comments that a lender may demand payment of an outstanding debt only as long as it

---

of Zion shall be a place of survival and it shall be holy (*Obadiah* 1:17).' *Eretz Yisrael* will always be a place of refuge."

The Chafetz Chaim gave a parable. "Two small villages shared a fire engine. It went to whichever place had a fire. What if there were fires in both villages? Then it would first put out the fire in its hometown, and only then would it go to the next place. So it is in the world. *Eretz Yisrael* is God's hometown. He will not let it be destroyed."

Interestingly, the German army under General Erwin Rommel, its most brilliant general, swept across North Africa and was poised to invade Palestine, when its advance was halted at the battle of El Alamein. The Chafetz Chaim's vision was validated.

8. **Redeemed by Prayer.** The interfacing nature of "natural" causes and prayer is alluded to by the words of the Sages that one must place the blessing of redemption immediately before the beginning of the *Shemoneh Esrei* (*Amidah*) prayer, סוֹמֵךְ גְּאוּלָה לִתְפִילָה. Although redemption often seems to result from natural circumstances, in truth it can only result from heartfelt prayer.

9. **Spoiled by Success.** Wicked people see it the other way. Rather than seeing success as an indication of how much they need God and how dependent they are on Him, they look at it as a sign of their own prowess, which leads to an arrogant denial of God. King David expressed this in the words חֶסֶד לְאֻמִּים חַטָּאת, *the kindness of the nations is sin* (*Proverbs* 14:34). When God provides the nations with kindness, He gives them cause to sin (*Sfas Emes*).

10. **Good Deeds?** R' Yosef of Delatitch was reading the *Hataras Nedarim* (annulment of vows) formula on *Erev Rosh Hashanah.* When he reached the phrase, "I do not regret, Heaven forbid, the performance of the good deeds I have done," he stopped, thought for a moment and closed the *siddur.* "There must be a printing error here," he said. "What good deeds did I do?"

He looked into a second *siddur* which, of course, contained the same words. He began to sob, "Are my deeds the good deeds they are referring to?"

has not been paid. After that, the lender has no further claim. Not so one who receives a gift. Since it is purely a token of the giver's kindness and affection, the recipient may appeal continually to the giver for a further favor. Had all that we received from God in the past been earned by our good deeds, we should worry that He has paid us in full, leaving us no right to ask for more. However, since all that He gives us is far more than we can ever deserve, we feel entitled to throw ourselves on His mercy.

This is the meaning of the prayer, "Until now Your mercy has helped us and Your Kindness has not forsaken us. Do not abandon us, Hashem our God, forever" (from the Shabbos morning *Nishmas*). "Since everything You give us is a result of Your mercy and not our actions, we therefore beg You, 'Do not abandon us, Hashem our God, forever.' "

This was the thrust of Jacob's words: "Even though I was too small [in good deeds] to deserve all of Your kindnesses, You were still kind and merciful to me. Therefore, I ask You to save me from my brother, from Esau — even though I don't deserve it."

Rashi explains that Jacob was afraid that the kindnesses which Hashem showered on him were in payment for whatever merits he had and that now his merits had been diminished. In the interim since God promised to watch over him, Jacob feared that he had became "soiled by sin" and no longer deserved to be saved from Esau.

Meilitz Yosher explains the metaphor "soiled by sin" with the following analogy: A person who falls into a garbage bin feels horrible. He closes his nostrils against the wretched stench and quickly tries to brush off the stains from his clothing. Often the mere sight of the filth makes him nauseous. A baby, however, loves the freedom to roll around in the filth; the dirtier the place, the more the child enjoys himself. This is as true of the soul as it is of the body. Immature and evil people spend their lives in sin. Although their souls view sin as filth, they continue not only to "soil their souls" but, like children, revel in it.

To the righteous, however, transgressing God's word is comparable to falling into a garbage heap. They cannot bear the rancid odor of sin, and feel that they have been "soiled by sin."

הַצִּילֵנִי נָא מִיַּד אָחִי מִיַּד עֵשָׂו

Rescue me, please, from the hand of my brother, from the hand of Esau (ibid. 12).

Since Esau was Jacob's only brother, why does he say both *my brother* and *Esau?*

Beis HaLevi explains that this is another instance in which events in the lives of the Patriarchs serve as a harbinger of their descendant's future. The extended exile at the hands of Esau and his progeny will express itself in two forms. Wars, pogroms and persecutions are the "Esau" manifestation of exile, as our enemies seek the physical annihilation of the Jewish people. If this method fails, Esau adopts the loving face and kindly demeanor of *my brother,* seeking to lull us into a spiritual complacency which will allow him to gradually weaken and eventually unravel our faith and connection to God. This is a far more insidious form of exile, as the Sages taught, "One who causes another to sin is worse than one who murders him" (*Bamidbar Rabbah* 21:5).

Jacob prayed not only that *Esau* should not kill him, but more importantly, that he be saved from the spiritual danger inherent in a close relationship with *my brother.* Both prayers were answered, for immediately after they met, *Esau started back that day on his way toward Seir* (33:16).[11]

---

11. **Neither Sting nor Honey.** *R' Akiva Eiger* offers a homiletical interpretation of a *Mishnah* (*Berachos* 30b) which conveys this very idea.

The *Mishnah* teaches that "Even if the king greets one [during prayer], he should not respond. Even if a snake is poised by his heel [ready to bite], he should not interrupt."

Sometimes we are hosted by a ruler who ostensibly seeks our peace and welfare. Other times we find ourselves threatened by snakelike powers who are poised, ready to "bite" and deal us a fatal blow.

These situations are equally threatening to our Judaism and our spiritual link to God. The *Mishnah* teaches that we must never interrupt our ongoing dialogue with Him nor should we respond too warmly to brotherly overtures of peace and friendship.

R' Zalman Sorotzkin submits that in our times, the "Esau" threat comes from the east while the spiritual poison

וְאַתָּה אָמַרְתָּ הֵיטֵב אֵיטִיב עִמָּךְ
And You had said,
"I will surely do good with you" (ibid. 13).

Why the double expression הֵיטֵב אֵיטִיב, literally *good will do good*?

While Hashem bestows His goodness on both the righteous and the wicked, there is a world of difference between the two. He is good to the righteous to provide them with the means to serve Him. The wicked, however, receive His goodness as this-worldly payment for their good deeds, so that they will not have access to the World to Come. Hence their "good" is not truly good. God promised Jacob that the good He would bestow on Him would be "surely" good, both in this world and the next (*Kedushas Levi*).[12]

Just a bit earlier, Jacob expressed his fear that as a result of his sins, God's promises were no longer binding. Why then does he again invoke the promise that God made to "surely do good" with him?

Beis HaLevi offers the following: When man's actions "force" God to restrict the flow of His kindness, the truly righteous are not overly concerned about their personal loss. "If God deemed me unfit for His beneficence, so be it." What distresses them is that God, Who is the "Good One, Who seeks to bestow goodness on others," is, as it were, unable to do so, because of their unworthiness.

Jacob was primarily concerned that if Esau would come and strike him down along with his wives and children, what would become of God's promise? *And You had said, "I will surely do good with you and I will make your offspring like the sand of the sea."* His concern was not for himself but rather for God, the very essence of goodness.[13]

וְאֶת אַחַד עָשָׂר יְלָדָיו
and his eleven sons (ibid. 23).

Why are only the eleven sons mentioned? Where was Dinah? *Rashi* cites the Midrash that Jacob placed her in a box and closed it tightly so that Esau not fix his eyes upon her and want to marry her. For this Jacob was punished, for she might have caused Esau to repent.[14] Instead of marrying Esau, she was taken forcibly by Shechem (see *Genesis* 34).

Why was Jacob punished? He was merely following the dictum of the Sages who taught that one who gives his daughter in marriage to an ignoramus is deemed to have placed her at the mercy of a hungry lion (*Pesachim* 49b).

The *Chazon Ish* submits that someone like Jacob, blessed as he was with Divine inspiration, should have known that Dinah could cause even an Esau to repent. The failure to realize and act upon this was reason enough for him to be punished. Ordinary people, however, have no way of knowing if their child will influence others or will be influenced by them. We have no right to risk our

---

of brotherhood comes from the west. The hatred incited by Moslem fundamentalists from the east, as well as the more insidious destruction inherent in the lure of western values, both jeopardize Jewish integrity and survival.

12. **Graceless Success.** Success is not always a sign of Divine favor; it may be nothing more than a reward in response to something positive we have done, but it is given now in place of what would have been a much greater reward in the World to Come. Sometimes "you can tell how little God thinks of money by looking at whom He gives it to" may actually be true.

13. **Eternally Grateful.** When man is thankful and offers praise to God for his lot in life, God responds by generously providing for him. Whenever someone asks, "How are you? How do you feel?" one should respond positively, for then God will cause it to be so.

When a child boasts about how wonderful his father is, the father will not say, "It's not true, I'm a horrible person." Rather, he will do everything possible to justify his child's claims.

This is the homiletic lesson of this verse. And if you said הֵיטֵב, *He is good* (Thank God, everything is fine), then God replies, אֵיטִיב, *I will surely do good with you* (R' Asher of Stolin).

14. **Never Too Late!** Esau had been wallowing in sin for over a hundred years and yet Jacob was punished for not allowing him to marry Dinah, who might have been a good influence on him. How powerful is the hope that one can return and rectify a life previously lived with total recklessness! It is *never* too late (*Meilitz Yosher*).

children's purity for the doubtful spiritual improvement of others.[15]

R' Simchah Zissel of Kelm suggests that Jacob was far too adamant in his refusal to allow Esau to marry Dinah. He was right to hide her in the box, but why did he have to slam it shut? In other words, while it is true that one cannot take inordinate risks to bring others to repent, one should at least feel pain that others will be deprived because one is compelled to put the interests of his family first. [16]

Simchas Aharon suggests that there is a major difference between an Esau and an ignoramus. The Sages speak of the danger inherent in marrying an ignoramus. On a certain level, such a person is worse than someone like Esau, for an ignoramus suffers from spiritual apathy while a wicked person is alive and animated albeit in the wrong direction. To marry one's daughter to an ignoramus is to consign her to spiritual apathy and death, for her apathetic husband will almost certainly never change. Esau, however, was passionately dedicated to his evil ways; such passion might have been transformed into a force for good.

Background

Jacob remains alone on the other side of the brook of Jabok. There he meets the guardian angel of Esau, who is Satan, the embodiment of evil, and the two do battle. This is a cosmic event, the great struggle between good and evil.

וַיִּוָּתֵר יַעֲקֹב לְבַדּוֹ
Jacob was left alone (ibid. 25).

Having returned for some small earthenware pitchers, Jacob remained alone. The Sages derive from this that "to the righteous, their money is dearer to them than their bodies" (*Chullin* 91a).[17]

Why is their money so precious to them? Explains the *Arizal:* While wicked people often enjoy financial success as payment in this-worldly currency for their few good deeds,[18] the righteous receive only that which they need in order to serve God. [Sometimes that entails the bare necessities required to be able to function; other times, a righteous person may be challenged with the test of wealth.] Were they not to need it, God would not grant it to them.

Thus, Jacob returned for these items of negligible value since they were certainly necessary to his service of God. To ignore them, would have been to slight Divine Providence, for in His wisdom God had decreed that Jacob's mission on earth required him to have these "inconsequential" items.

R' Meir Shapiro submits that the reason the

15. **Cooling Off.** This very issue was the subject of debate between Abraham and Sarah. Abraham felt that if Ishmael remained with them he might eventually be warmed by Isaac's influence and become rehabilitated. Sarah disagreed, saying that rather than Isaac spiritually warming up Ishmael, Ishmael would cool off Isaac.

16. **Desirable Impossibility.** *R' Elazar M. Shach* augments this theme: Certainly Jacob acted correctly in not allowing Dinah to marry Esau. Nevertheless, he should have at least entertained the idea before dismissing it as too dangerous. Imagine bringing Esau, with all of his intelligence and talent, over to the side of sanctity and purity. It should have pained Jacob that he could not do the ultimate in spiritual kindness on behalf of his brother. Since he was complacent about it, he was punished.

17. **Righteous Perspective.** *R' Yisrael Salanter* said, "The righteous view their money as more valuable than *their own* bodies — but not more than someone else's physical comfort."

18. **Valuable Currency.** Why does God repay the wicked with the devalued currency of a temporal reward? The key to understanding this is in the realization that only man can determine the value of his *mitzvos*. If in one's heart his *mitzvos* are worthless, then they are in fact without value. As the Sages teach (*Kiddushin* 40b), one who regrets having performed a mitzvah loses his reward for it (*Rambam, Hilchos Teshuvah* 3:3).

Why is this so? The value of any commodity is determined by the law of supply and demand. If one has a monopoly, however, then he can dictate the price. Since every person has a monopoly on his own *mitzvos*, he can ask for them what he wants. Since worldly success is the most valuable thing in the eyes of the wicked, God rewards them in that currency. Righteous people, however, know that there is a far more valuable currency; they assess their *mitzvos* in terms of the World to Come (based on *Michtav MeEliyahu*).

The two ways to see how one evaluates his *mitzvos* are the joy with which one performs them and the difficulties one is ready to endure for their sake (*Pachad Yitzchak*).

righteous value their money more than their bodies is because they generally spend their money on spiritual rather than physical pursuits. They view their bodies as a mere tool in the advancement of their spiritual agenda and realize that there are spiritual attainments which cannot be achieved without money. The wicked, on the other hand, view physical pleasure as life's *raison d'etre.* For them, money is significant for it allows them to buy creature comforts with which to pamper themselves. Obviously, then, their bodies are more valuable to them than money, which is only a means to attain their goal of physical luxury and comfort.[19]

וַיֵּאָבֵק אִישׁ עִמּוֹ
and a man wrestled with him (ibid.)

That man was the guardian angel of Esau, the prime spiritual force of evil. The Talmud (*Chullin* 91a) describes him, saying that "He appeared either like a Torah scholar or like a thief."

Avnei Nezer explains that this portrayal reflects the two opposite tactics that the evil inclination employs to entrap people. Sometimes it displays sin openly, in all its ugliness, and attempts to arouse in its victim a passion so powerful that he succumbs. This is the "thief" who seeks to rob us of our morality.

At other times, the evil inclination wraps itself in a cloak of righteousness, rationalizing that not only is the proposed behavior not wrong, but that it might even be a mitzvah to do it. This is the "Torah scholar" who tries to rationalize away our conscience.[20]

וַיַּרְא כִּי לֹא יָכֹל לוֹ וַיִּגַּע בְּכַף יְרֵכוֹ
When he perceived that he could not overcome him, he struck the socket of his hip (ibid. 26).

When Esau's angel saw that Jacob cleaved so tenaciously to God that he could not be overcome, the angel struck the socket of Jacob's hip. According to the *Zohar,* this is an allusion to the potential supporters of Torah in future generations. They are compared to the hip socket, for just as the leg and hip support the body, so the supporters of Torah uphold the Jewish people. Without Torah, the Jewish nation cannot survive and, in the words of *Pirkei Avos* (3:21), "If there is no flour (sustenance), there is no Torah."

Here Esau succeeded in weakening the future generations for, as the verse teaches, *so Jacob's hip socket was dislocated.* The constant struggle to find financial support for Torah scholars and institutions and the flimsy excuses with which potential donors convince themselves that they are unable to do

---

19. **Rational Beings?** [We consider ourselves to be rational people, yet we often fail to follow our questions about life to their logical conclusion:

"Why do you work so hard?"

"In order to make a living."

"And why do you need to make a living?"

"In order to provide food and shelter for myself and my family."

"And why do you need food and shelter?"

"What do you mean? Should we starve to death?!"

"You mean you need to live. Why do you need to live?"

"Every Jew knows the answer to that question. We need to live in order to serve God and enlighten our *neshamos*."

Then why do so many who observe us get the impression that the last answer is a secondary, almost peripheral item on our life's agenda?]

20. **Strength and Light.** One of the joyous hymns of Simchas Torah reads נָגִיל וְנָשִׂישׂ בְּזֹאת הַתּוֹרָה כִּי הִיא עֹז לָנוּ וְאוֹרָה, *Let us exult and rejoice with this Torah for to us it is strength and light.*

R' Tzadok HaKohen of Lublin offers an explanation, based on the Talmud (*Kiddushin* 30b), that Torah is an antidote to evil. When the evil inclination tries to seduce us to sin by arousing lust and passion, the Torah provides us with עֹז, *strength,* to fight off the attack. And when the evil inclination uses guile to convince us that sinful conduct is meritorious, the Torah provides אוֹרָה, *light,* giving us a clarity of vision to see through the facade of our "Torah-scholar friend" who seeks to entrap our souls.

their share are all the result of the evil angel's partial success in wrestling with Jacob (*Chafetz Chaim*).[21]

וַיֹּאמֶר שַׁלְּחֵנִי כִּי עָלָה הַשָּׁחַר
Then he said, "Let me go,
for dawn has broken" (ibid. 27).

The angel told Jacob that from the day he was created until the day of their battle, his turn to sing in praise of God had not yet arrived. Only now did his time come. He therefore asked to be released to join the Heavenly choir (*Midrash*).

What was so special about this day that the angel's turn to sing praise had arrived? *Avodas Yisrael* explains that every angel has its own unique mission, which no other angel can accomplish. Only upon completion of its mission, when he has fulfilled the reason for its existence, may the angel sing God's praises. The angel of Esau, evil incarnate, was created in order to entice man to sin, so that man can spurn his advances and overcome the challenge. When man is strong enough to do so, the angel's task is complete.[22]

Until Jacob took on the forces of evil, no one else had beaten them back quite so successfully. Hence only now did the evil inclination truly fulfill its earthly mission, so the time had arrived for him to sing God's praises.

Jacob finally encounters Esau and, for the moment, Esau's feelings of brotherhood overcome his animosity. They part ways as friends, to meet again at the Final Redemption, when Esau will bow to Jacob's superiority.

וַיִּשְׁתַּחוּ אַרְצָה שֶׁבַע פְּעָמִים עַד גִּשְׁתּוֹ עַד אָחִיו
and [he] bowed earthward seven times
until he reached his brother (33:3).

What did Jacob intend to achieve with these prostrations? *Divrei Shmuel* explains that Esau's hatred was not total. There still remained a glimmer of brotherly love embedded deep within him, but it could not surface for it was encrusted with seven layers of spiritual impurity. By means of his seven prostrations, Jacob was able to symbolically strip away the seven layers of impurity and penetrate to the core of his brother's soul. At that level, Jacob stood in front of *his brother,* for the deeply embedded spark of brotherly love was able to emerge. At that point, Esau was so overwhelmed by his rediscovered emotion that he embraced and kissed Jacob.[23]

---

21. **Too Much for One Person.** The *Chafetz Chaim* viewed support of Torah and holy causes as a privilege which must be shared among many people.

R' Avraham Meyers, a wealthy American Jew, visited the Chafetz Chaim in the early 1930's in Radin. He noticed that the great sage seemed perturbed and asked him why. The Chafetz Chaim told him that in a certain town near Radin the *mikveh* was in total disrepair, and the Chafetz Chaim didn't know where to get the necessary funds for a new one. Mr. Meyers asked what the *mikveh* would cost in Polish zlotys, quickly calculated the dollar equivalent and wrote out a check for the entire amount. The Chafetz Chaim said to him, "My dear R' Avraham, for one Jew to have the entire *zechus* (merit) of a *mikveh* is too much. I can't allow you to have that *zechus* alone." When R' Avraham asked how big a share he could have, the Chafetz Chaim told him "half." He promptly wrote a new check for half the amount.

[His son, R' Daniel Meyers, went door to door and pieced together small contributions to build the first *mikveh* in the Far Rockaway/Bayswater area of New York].

22. **Cat and Mouse.** Serious Jews enjoy an ambivalent relationship with their evil inclination. On one hand they would prefer that he cease to exist so that they need not be faced with threatening spiritual challenges. On the other hand, they know that without an evil inclination one cannot grow.

The *Baal Shem Tov* submitted the following parable: A king who wanted to test the loyalty of his subjects sent some agents provocateurs to incite a rebellion. Most of his subjects were drawn into the snares of the seditionists. One shrewd individual, however, saw through the ruse. He told the rabble-rouser, "You are doing your job by inciting sedition, and I will do my job by not being ensnared in your insidious plot." We will let the evil inclination do his job as long as he lets us do ours.

23. **Penetrating Education.** If this is true with regard to someone as devoid of sanctity as Esau, certainly a Jewish child whose soul emanates from below Hashem's Holy Throne is reachable. Even if his soul is encased by a

וַיִּפֹּל עַל צַוָּארָו וַיִּשָּׁקֵהוּ
[Esau] fell on his neck and kissed him (ibid. 4).

The Midrash states that Esau tried to bite Jacob's neck, but it turned hard as marble. How shall we reconcile the Midrash with the words [he] *kissed him*?

The loving kisses of an Esau are spiritual poison for Jacob. While they seem to be kisses, they are deadly bites (*Chidushei HaRim*).

In the Torah scroll, there are dots over the letters of וַיִּשָּׁקֵהוּ, *and [Esau] kissed [Jacob]*. Such dots are meant to draws attention to the word. They point to a hidden meaning, often one that is different from the ostensible explanation of the word. In this case, the Sages disagree as to the meaning of the dots. Some hold that the dots imply that Esau's kisses were insincere while R' Shimon bar Yochai submits that although it is an ironclad rule that "Esau hates Jacob," at that moment his mercy was aroused and he kissed Jacob wholeheartedly.

While people seek to explain anti-Semitism, which seems to be pervasive and irrational, R' Shimon bar Yochai states simple that it is a "law," an inviolable rule of life. Jews are accused of being blood-sucking capitalists, autocratic communists and visionary socialists. They are accused of being too shrewd at business and secretly in control of the world, and at the same time parasites who are a financial drain on their host country. They are too conservative and too liberal; too revolutionary and champions of the status quo. None of these contradictions are the real reasons. "Esau hates Jacob" simply because he is Jacob. As the French philosopher Voltaire admitted, he hated Jews for no rational reason.[24]

Background

Jacob arrives back in the Land of Israel having physically and spiritually survived the manifold difficulties he encountered during his thirty-four years outside the Land.

וַיָּבֹא יַעֲקֹב שָׁלֵם עִיר שְׁכֶם
Jacob arrived intact at the city of Shechem (ibid. 18).

Jacob's triumphant return to the Land of Israel is the episode in the lives of the forefathers which foreshadows the eventual triumphant return of the Jewish nation to its Land. According to *B'nei Yissas'char,* the Torah teaches us the secret of Jewish survival in the exile and the key to our eventual redemption. The word שָׁלֵם is an acronym for שֵׁם, *name;* לָשׁוֹן, *language;* and מַלְבּוּשׁ, *clothing.* Although Jacob lived in the spiritually debilitating environs of Laban and underwent a harrowing encounter with Esau, he managed to maintain his unique values and identity. We, his children, will only survive the Exile if we maintain our Jewish integrity at all costs as symbolized by our Jewish names, by using a uniquely Jewish way of speaking and by distinct Jewish dress. It is through these measures that we will be assured of arriving back home spiritually intact.

---

seemingly impenetrable spiritual encrustation, a loving teacher can find a way to the inner recesses of his soul (*Nesivei Chinuch*).

24. **Jewish Depth.** R' Mordechai and R' Shmuel, two Hungarian rabbis, were walking in the street. Suddenly, several young gentile ruffians threw stones at R' Mordechai, but left R' Shmuel alone. When they had walked a bit more, R' Mordechai noticed that R' Shmuel was crying bitterly.

"Why are you crying?" he asked. R' Shmuel replied, "That Esau hates Jacob is a fact of life. If the ruffians chose you as their victim and not me, then I must conclude that the name 'Jew' is more deeply etched on your face than on mine. I see I must have sinned and weakened the Jew inside of me."

פרשת וישב &
Parashas Vayeishev

Background

After enduring a long and bitter exile, Jacob finally settles down in the Land of his forefathers. The tranquility that he sought, however, continues to evade him. The sibling rivalry among his children brings upon him the terrible tragedy of his beloved son Joseph being nearly killed and then sold into slavery.

וַיֵּשֶׁב יַעֲקֹב בְּאֶרֶץ מְגוּרֵי אָבִיו
Jacob settled in the land of his father's sojourning (37:1)

Jacob wished to settle down in tranquility, but the anguish of Joseph's disappearance pounced upon him. Although the righteous seek serenity, God decides otherwise. "Are they not satisfied with all that awaits them in the World to Come? Why do they expect to live at ease in this world as well?"(*Rashi*).[1]

According to *Chidushei HaRim,* this teaches us a cardinal lesson in how to confront the difficulties of life. There are those who see travails as unpleasant coincidences that one should try to avoid; however, the truly righteous do not seek tranquility in our world of turmoil and travails but look instead for meaning. The key to true serenity is faith that God has a master plan and that our difficulties are milestones on the road to happiness.

The *Chafetz Chaim* submits that one should accept life's difficulties and try to deal with them by improving oneself spiritually, rather than by seeking to run away from them. It is impossible to flee from God's wrath or his challenges. One who seeks figuratively to "dodge the bullets" may be compared to a prisoner bound by cuffs and leg irons. The more he tries to wriggle loose, the greater the pain as the chains cut deeply into his flesh.

---

1. **Not Yet Fulfilled.** Many great men (such as R' Yehudah HaNassi, R' Elazar ben Azariah and R' Ashi) enjoyed both worlds without experiencing anguish pouncing upon them. Even Jacob spent the last seventeen years of his life tranquilly in Egypt. What was wrong with his request?

R' Moshe Sternbuch suggests that Jacob did not seek creature comforts or wealth. He merely felt that his many travails over the years had been enough to bring him to the apex of his spiritual potential. God brought the anguish of Joseph upon him because he was capable of reaching still greater heights.

[Our attitude toward tests must be simultaneously wary and welcoming. King David asked God, בְּחָנֵנִי ה' וְנַסֵּנִי, *Examine me, Hashem, and test me (Psalms* 26:2), for there is no growth without trials. Nevertheless, we pray every day not to be tested, lest we fail. Although one should not seek difficult challenges, if they come, one should pray for God's help to overcome them. One must always realize that the King Who sends us to the battlefront certainly provides us with the ammunition to lead us to victory.]

אֵלֶּה תּוֹלְדוֹת יַעֲקֹב יוֹסֵף . . .
These are the chronicles of Jacob;
Joseph . . . (ibid. 2).[2]

The Torah's messages are eternal, applicable in all generations. According to the *Chafetz Chaim*, the story of Joseph and his brothers is really the historic saga of the Jewish people. Joseph, his father's most beloved child, was forced to leave his home and birthplace. He was taken to a faraway land where he was handed over to immoral and unethical people, who sought to do him in at every turn.

In spite of it all, Divine Providence turned everything around. The seeming tragedy of being torn from his father's home and sold as a slave was ultimately the cause of his rise to power. His master threw him into a dungeon, but it was there that he met Pharaoh's imprisoned butler, who became the catalyst for Joseph's meteoric rise to power, as sovereign over Egypt and savior of his family and the entire region.

God's Hand works in mysterious ways that man cannot fathom. Man often finds himself in terrible trouble, never dreaming that his seemingly hopeless situation is actually the springboard for his salvation.

The story of Joseph is the story of the chronicles of Jacob's children. Whenever they seem to hit rock bottom it is really God's way of preparing them for redemption. This is mirrored in the words of Isaiah, *You will say on that day, "I Thank You, Hashem, for You were angry with me"* (12:1). At the end of the day, we will realize that the pain and travail were really the initial steps to salvation.

בֶּן שְׁבַע עֶשְׂרֵה שָׁנָה . . . וְהוּא נַעַר
at the age of seventeen . . .
but he was a youth (ibid.).

The classical commentators are troubled by the phrase וְהוּא נַעַר, *but he was a youth*, since the term נַעַר, which usually refers to a child seems inapplicable to a 17-year-old. *R' Aharon (II) of Karlin* suggests that *youth* is a state of mind, not a chronological period. As King David said, *I have been a youth and also aged* (*Psalms* 37:25). Although I have [chronologically] aged, I have remained a youth [in spirit]. One must find a freshness of approach and a youthfulness of spirit in the service of Hashem. [The Jewish people are compared to [and calculate their calendar by] the moon, for it is the very symbol of youthful renewal.][3]

וַיָּבֵא יוֹסֵף אֶת דִּבָּתָם רָעָה אֶל אֲבִיהֶם
and Joseph would bring evil reports
about them to their father (ibid.).

Are we to believe that Joseph actually slandered his brothers to Jacob? *R' Mendel of Vorki* explained: When a parent has among his children one child who is unique and outstanding, he often points to him when trying to stimulate the others. "Why can't you be like your brother?" Joseph so outshone his brothers that his very presence inspired Jacob to rebuke them; their inevitable comparison to Joseph cast the brothers in a negative light. Why then was Joseph punished? Because the truly righteous [unless they need to

---

2. **Always Doing More.** *R' Mendel of Rimanov* offers a homiletical definition of Jacob's true spiritual offspring. The word יוֹסֵף can be rendered literally as *he shall add*. A Jew should never be content with his achievements; he should always look for ways to enhance his study of Torah and performance of the commandments.

Torah and *mitzvos* can be compared to food. The more one eats, the greater his appetite. Similarly, the more Torah one studies and the more *mitzvos* one performs, the greater his need to learn and do more; he can no longer survive on less (*R' Yitzchak Hutner*). [If אֹהֵב כֶּסֶף לֹא יִשְׂבַּע כֶּסֶף, *one who loves money is never satisfied with money,* certainly אוֹהֵב מִצְוֹת לֹא יִשְׂבַּע מִצְוֹת, *one who loves mitzvos is never satiated with the commandments one has performed.*] (See *Koheles Rabbah* 5:8.)

3. **Eternally Young.** When *R' Yisrael Shimon Kostelanitz* was well past 80, he traveled from Jerusalem to New York to participate in a granddaughter's wedding. On the same plane was *R' Yitzchak Hutner* who asked him how he found the strength to make such an arduous journey at his age. Replied R' Yisrael Shimon, "*Chassidim* explain the words וַיִּקַּח אֶת שְׁנֵי נְעָרָיו אִתּוֹ (*Genesis* 22:3) — which is rendered as *[Abraham] took his two youths with him* — as 'and he took his young years with him.' Abraham at the age of 99 went to the *Akeidah* with the alacrity and verve of a youngster."

serve as a role model for others] hide their good deeds, even from their parents.

In a halachic sense, Joseph's actions were justified, for the process of offering rebuke calls on one to first personally rebuke the wrongdoers. If they are unwilling to accept criticism, one may then bring a parent, teacher or other objective party into the process. However, when doing so he must meet two conditions: a) He must report the incident as it happened, without embellishment; and b) he must intend only to see the wrong rectified and not seek personal aggrandizement.

The Torah addresses all these issues. Since Joseph was friendly with the children of the maidservants, he was sure that the brothers would not heed his admonitions. Hence he turned to his father, yet he was careful to *bring the evil reports to Jacob just as they occurred* (like one who moves an object from one place to another). Finally he told it to *their* father, as if it wasn't his father with whom he could ingratiate himself by criticizing his brothers (*Afikei Yam*). In spite of his good intentions, however, his reports were tainted, for he should have judged them favorably. Thus the Torah calls it דִּבָּתָם רָעָה, *evil reports* (*R' S.R. Hirsch, Gur Aryeh*).[4], [5]

וְעָשָׂה לוֹ כְּתֹנֶת פַּסִּים
And he made him a fine woolen tunic (ibid. 3).

The Talmud (*Shabbos* 10b) teaches that the brothers' jealousy over Joseph's tunic caused them to eventually sell him to Egypt.

Rashi cites the Midrash (*Bereishis Rabbah* 84:8)

that the word פַּסִּים is an acronym for the terrible events that would befall Joseph as a result of his sale by his brothers: פּוֹטִיפַר, *Potiphar*, in whose home Joseph would undergo the trial of passion with his master's wife, and be jailed for a decade as a result; סוֹחֲרִים, the traveling *merchants*, to whom he would be sold; יִשְׁמְעֵאלִים, the nomadic *Arabs*, who would buy him from the merchants; and finally the מִדְיָנִים, *Midianites*, who bought him from the Arabs and sold him to Potiphar in Egypt.

וְלֹא יָכְלוּ דַּבְּרוֹ לְשָׁלֹם
and they could not speak to him peaceably (ibid. 4).

Hatred has a way of growing and snowballing. The more time passes, the deeper hatred becomes entrenched in one's heart. Were one to be honest with his friend and tell him why he is angry with him, the friend might apologize, explain, admit guilt or promise to mend his ways. Any one of these reactions would soften the hatred and eventually cause it to dissipate.

It is for this reason that the Torah commands us *You shall not hate your brother in your heart* (*Leviticus* 19:17). Do not allow your hatred toward a fellow Jew to simmer *within* your heart; rather, *you shall reprove your fellow* (ibid.). Tell him what is in your heart and mind and open channels of communication so that you can discuss the issues and reach an amicable resolution.

Joseph's brothers did not follow this dictum of the Torah. *They could not speak to him peaceably* and therefore were never able to conduct the dialogue that can end quarrels. They let their

---

4. **More Talk.** Once the *Chafetz Chaim* was a passenger on a horse-drawn coach, and he dozed off in midjourney. When he awoke he heard some of the people conversing quietly. Fearful that they were talking *lashon hara* (slanderous talk) he asked, "What are Jews talking about?" They answered "Foolishness. We are talking about the horses." The Chafetz Chaim replied "Good! Good! Better to talk about horses than about people." [My father ע"ה would always tell me, "Don't mention *menchen* (people)."]

When the Chafetz Chaim suffered from an acute hearing loss in his later years, he was visited by *R' Meir Shapiro*, who advised him to undergo surgery to correct the impairment. The Chafetz Chaim refused, saying, "When the ears are open a lot of *lashon hara* enters and penetrates. If Hashem did me the favor of making me unable to listen to *lashon hara*, shall I obstinately try to hear?"

5. **Mental Somersaults.** Everything God made has a purpose. What is the purpose of convoluted and crooked logic? *R' Simchah Bunim of P'shis'cha* answered that the commandment to judge others favorably sometimes demands that we perform mental somersaults, in order to put a positive light on evil behavior. Thus, sometimes we must think in a convoluted fashion.

hatred grow until it boiled over into a plot to kill their brother.[6]

וַיַּחֲלֹם יוֹסֵף חֲלוֹם וַיַּגֵּד לְאֶחָיו וַיּוֹסִפוּ עוֹד שְׂנֹא אֹתוֹ
Joseph dreamt a dream which he told to his brothers and they hated him even more (ibid. 5).

Although Joseph has not yet revealed the contents of the dream, the brothers already hated him even more. Only in the next verse does Joseph relate the content of a dream that made his brothers' hatred increase to an even greater degree. Why did they hate him now, when all he said was that he dreamed? According to *Ohr HaChaim*, their hatred was so intense that as soon as he said that he had dreamed, they told him that they were not interested in listening. He then implored, *Hear, if you please, this dream which I dreamt* (verse 6).

Since their hatred was pre-existing, why does the Torah describe their *increased* hatred as a result of his attempt to relate his dream? *Zekan Aharon* submits that just as expressing love increases love, so expressing animosity increases the intensity of hatred.[7]

הֲמָלֹךְ תִּמְלֹךְ עָלֵינוּ אִם מָשׁוֹל תִּמְשֹׁל בָּנוּ
Would you then reign over us? Would you then dominate us? (ibid. 8).

A king (מֶלֶךְ) *reigns* with the consent of his subjects while a ruler (מוֹשֵׁל) *dominates* them against their will (*Ibn Ezra*). The brothers countered that they would not willingly accept Joseph as their king nor would he succeed in forcing them to accept him as a ruler. According to the *Vilna Gaon*, this explains the verse appended to the end of אָז יָשִׁיר, *the Song at the Sea*, in the *Shacharis* prayer: כִּי לַה׳ הַמְּלוּכָה וּמוֹשֵׁל בַּגּוֹיִם, *For the sovereignty is Hashem's and He rules over the nations*. At this point in history, God is King only over the Jewish people, who willingly and lovingly accept His sovereignty. For the nations of the world, He is at present only a ruler who dominates them despite their unwillingness to accept Him.

In the End of Days, however, *saviors will ascend Mount Zion to judge Esau's mountain and the **kingdom** will be Hashem's* (Obadiah 1:21). *Then Hashem will be **King** over **all** the world*. In the future all nations will willingly proclaim God as their King.[8]

According to *R' Yitzchak Hutner*, this is the

---

6. **Therapeutic Venting.** Sometimes we become such prisoners of our own righteous indignation that we are unable to discuss our differences civilly. "I am right. He should make the first move," or "I won't talk to him. He'll get the message," are but two of the foolish ways in which we allow to poison our lives.

Tzvi LaTzaddik adds another perspective based on an interpretation of *Alshich*. When Moses prayed that the Jewish people be saved after the sin of the Golden Calf, the Torah says וַיִּנָּחֶם ה׳ עַל הָרָעָה אֲשֶׁר דִּבֶּר לַעֲשׂוֹת לְעַמּוֹ, *Hashem reconsidered regarding the evil that He declared He would do to His people* (Exodus 32:14). According to *Alshich*, the reason *Hashem reconsidered* is because *He declared*. When one expresses his anger and hurt, the very verbalization has a therapeutic effect, soothing and calming him. Since God spoke and vented His feelings, so to speak, it helped Him to achieve the "peaces" needed to forgive.

[Often people prefer to be angry rather than rid themselves of the anger. As *R' Gershon Henach of Radzin* said, "There are people who wake up in the morning angry. They merely need some time to figure out at *whom* they want to be angry."]

7. **Realistic Dreamer.** *Simchas Aharon* suggests that, in fact, Joseph told them nothing more than that he had dreamt, and yet this engendered increased hatred. Convinced that he suffered from fantasies and delusions of grandeur, they could not tolerate "the dreamer."

People often tell those with the courage to dream, "Be realistic," yet the "dreamers" are the ones who accomplish things in this world. When the *Ponevezher Rav* unveiled his plans for a huge yeshivah building in Bnei Brak, people thought the idea outlandish. Someone had the audacity to say to him, "Rebbe, you are dreaming!" He replied, "Yes, I am dreaming, but I am not sleeping."

8. **Eternal Kingdom.** This difference is further borne out by the verse in *Ashrei* (Psalms 145:13) מַלְכוּתְךָ מַלְכוּת כָּל עֹלָמִים וּמֶמְשַׁלְתְּךָ בְּכָל דּוֹר וָדוֹר, *Your kingdom is a kingdom spanning all eternities and Your dominion is throughout every generation*. Throughout the generations God is a "dominating" Ruler for all while for the Jewish people, He is King. However, this distinction will end when even the nations of the world will accept Him. Thus His kingdom is eternal while His dominion is only throughout the generations.

reason why the nations of the world were commanded the seven Noahide laws without any discussion as to whether they wanted them or not, while the Jewish people were asked if they wanted to accept the Torah. Accepting the Torah meant accepting God as our King, and kingship demands the willingness of its subjects. For the rest of the nations He is a ruler — it is unnecessary for them to willingly accept His decrees.

וַיְקַנְאוּ בוֹ אֶחָיו
So his brothers were jealous of him (ibid. 11).

After the first dream, the Torah says that the brothers hated Joseph. Why after the second dream does the Torah describe their reaction as jealousy rather than hatred?

Noting differences between the two dreams, *Beis HaLevi* explains: The first dream portrayed the brothers' financial dependence on Joseph, not that their bundles would bow to Joseph himself, but to his bundle (verse 7). The message was that they would be financially subservient to him. The second dream carried a far more powerful message. There Joseph spoke of the greatest natural forces *bowing down to me,* thus alluding to his vision of superiority over his brothers.

Joseph's first dream aroused hatred but not jealousy, for people like Joseph's brothers would not be jealous of financial success. When he began to dream of spiritual superiority, however, their jealousy was aroused.[9]

Background

Jacob sends Joseph to visit his brothers who are grazing the family's flocks. Convinced that he wanted to sow dissension and thus undermine the family's spiritual destiny, the brothers felt that he warranted the death penalty. Eventually they sell him to traveling merchants, and he ultimately becomes a slave to an Egyptian official.

וַיֵּלְכוּ אֶחָיו לִרְעוֹת אֶת צֹאן אֲבִיהֶם בִּשְׁכֶם
Now his brothers went to pasture their father's flock in Shechem (ibid. 12).

Rashi (based on *Bereishis Rabbah* 84:13) notes the dots which appear in the Torah scroll over the word אֶת and interprets them to imply that the brothers' intention was not to pasture their father's sheep, but rather to figuratively "pasture" themselves and their personal desires.

Having reached the point that they did not care about their father's property, it was no longer far-fetched that they would attempt to kill his son with no consideration for Jacob (*Haamek Davar*).

Chasam Sofer interprets the Midrash in a fashion less critical of the brothers. While they thought that they were going to pasture their father's sheep, in reality they were triggering a chain of events which would eventually benefit them, since it was Joseph's rise to power in Egypt that saved the family from the famine in Canaan. When Joseph finally revealed himself (*Genesis* 45:3) he focused them on this perspective. He said to them: *And now, be not distressed, nor reproach yourselves for having sold me here, for it was to be a provider that God sent me ahead of you* (ibid. 5).

לֶךְ נָא רְאֵה אֶת שְׁלוֹם אַחֶיךָ
Go now, look into the welfare of your brothers (ibid. 14).

Since Jacob must have known, at least to some extent, of the extreme animosity between Joseph and his brothers, why did he send Joseph to visit them and thus place him in danger?

According to *R' Simchah Bunim of P'shis'cha,* our verse provides the answer. Jacob told Joseph

---

9. **Jealousy.** According to *Rambam,* the only sin regarding which God is called "jealous" is the sin of idolatry. Jealousy connotes the feeling that someone else has usurped one's position and has occupied what is rightfully one's station in life. Hence while all sins express rebellion against God, idolatry means to replace Him. Thus He is a "jealous" God only regarding idolatry.

[We might accordingly suggest that the target of one's jealousy tells us much about the person. Is he jealous of a millionaire or of a *talmid chacham*? Do we envy the woman whose son is a doctor or the one whose son is a *rosh yeshivah*?]

to *look into the welfare of your brothers.* "Before, you brought me evil reports about them. Now, seek out their positive traits and the areas where they enjoy שְׁלֵמוּת, *perfection*. In this way you will disarm them and detoxify their hatred toward you."[10]

וַיִּשְׁלָחֵהוּ מֵעֵמֶק חֶבְרוֹן
So he sent him from the depth of Hebron (ibid.).

Hebron is on a mountain, not in the *depth* of a valley. *Rashi* explains that the verse refers figuratively to the fulfillment of the deep and profound design of the righteous Abraham, who is buried at Hebron [in the Cave of Machpelah].

What deep design was realized with the sale of Joseph? Abraham, who grew up in the idolatrous home of Terah, discovered the light of Hashem out of the darkness of his father's idolatry. As a spiritually self-made man, he constantly strove to discover the light which is beclouded by darkness. But he was afraid that his children, brought up in the sanctified atmosphere of his home, would become apathetic about the service of God, lacking the fire of his pioneering self-discovery. In a certain sense, he hoped that his children would experience the spiritual darkness of exile so that they too could recapture the excitement that one experiences when one discerns the light. In the Egyptian exile, Israel's yearning for God would reawaken and deepen, achieving an intensity undulled by the monotony of habit.[11]

וַיִּשְׁאָלֵהוּ הָאִישׁ לֵאמֹר מַה תְּבַקֵּשׁ
The man asked him, saying, "What do you seek?" (ibid. 15)

The "man" was the angel Gabriel disguised as a man, sent by God to lead Joseph to his brothers.[12] *Ramban* writes: "He wandered off the path, totally lost, and went into the first field he saw since he was looking for the place where they were pasturing. The Torah goes into great detail to show us that in spite of Joseph having had many reasons to return to his father and avoid the unpleasant confrontation with his hateful brothers, he continued on his mission in order to honor his

---

10. **Melted by Love.** Love and concern have an amazing power to soften people. One's most venomous enemies cannot continue to hate with the same intensity in the face of care, love and genuine interest. We must therefore seek to imbue ourselves with a positive eye, capable of seeing the good in our friends, spouses and children.

In the words of *R' Elimelech of Lizhensk* in his famous prayer: "Please put in our hearts that each one of us should see only the good points in our friends and not their faults."

11. **Retaining Freshness.** Human nature dictates that as things become habitual they lose their mystique and we become less excited by them. One who grew up in an observant home and knows no other lifestyle often loses his enthusiasm. His commitment becomes tepid and he does what he does because he *must*.

Maintaining a fresh perspective and a sense of excitement about Judaism is one of the most difficult challenges facing a person brought up in a traditional home. Such people would do well to look toward *baalei teshuvah* (returnees to Judaism), whose freshness of commitment is inspiring and hopefully contagious.

A young man who grew up in an observant home attended a yeshivah where most of the students were *baalei teshuvah*. Once, while visiting the *Lev Simchah of Ger*, he told the Rebbe, "I learn in a *baal teshuvah* yeshivah but I'm not a *baal teshuvah*." The Rebbe retorted, "Why not?"

12. **Spiritually Preoccupied.** Someone came to *R' Chaim of Sanz* with a tale of woe. His daughter was getting older and he lacked the necessary funds to marry her off. R' Chaim gave him a letter of introduction to one of his close followers, a wealthy scholar, asking him to collect funds on behalf of the unfortunate supplicant. When the rich *chassid* read the letter, he said to the poor man, "The study of Torah is more important than all other *mitzvos*. I can't give up the time from learning to help you." A few months later the wealthy *chassid* came to visit his Rebbe in Sanz. When he offered his hand to the Rebbe in greeting, R' Chaim refused to take it. R' Chaim then said to him, "When the Torah calls the person who met Joseph *the man*, *Rashi* explains that it was the angel Gabriel. When the Torah says that *"a man"* came to wrestle with Jacob (*Genesis* 32:25), *Rashi* identifies him as the the evil angel of Esau. In both cases, the Torah says only that it was a "man"; how does Rashi know which angel was which?

"The answer is that when an unknown man comes forward to help Joseph who is lost, we know that it must be a good angel, like Gabriel. When Jacob met a 'man' and asked for a blessing, the man answered, 'I have no time, I must go sing the praises of God' (*Rashi* ad loc.). Someone who has no time for others because he claims to be spiritually occupied can only be the angel of Esau."

father and his request. Furthermore, the story teaches us that God's decrees are true and lasting, while all of man's well-thought-out plans have no staying power. God brought Joseph a guide to cause him to unwittingly fall into his brothers' hands. This whole incident teaches us that *Many designs are in man's heart but the counsel of Hashem — only it will prevail* (Proverbs 19:21).

The word לֵאמֹר, *saying,* usually means that the statement is to be repeated to others. In our verse, to whom was the angel's question to be repeated?

R' Menachem Mendel of Kotzk offered a homiletic explanation of the verse. Joseph was leaving the holiness and purity of Jacob's home, and was about to be plunged into the moral filth and detestable culture of Egypt. How was he to survive all alone in his new surroundings? The angel taught

him that the key to his survival was to *say* [to himself] over and over, *"What do you seek?"* Only by constantly focusing on his goals in life would he survive Egypt.[13]

אֶת אַחַי אָנֹכִי מְבַקֵּשׁ
My brothers do I seek (ibid. 16).

Joseph sought the *brotherhood* of his brothers, for he was sure that if he could reawaken their brotherly love they would be ready to accept him and the message of his dreams.[14]

Even after the angel hinted to him that his brothers had abandoned the last vestiges of brotherly love and in fact planned to kill him, he still persisted in looking for them. Why was he so obstinate in his search?

Divrei Shmuel explains: The Sages (*Bava Basra* 16b) teach the axiom אֹו חַבְרָא אֹו מִיתוּתָא, *either friendship or death.* Joseph sought their brotherhood, for without it life is not worth living.[15], [16]

13. **Clarity of Vision.** This is the key to spiritual growth and survival for every Jew. In the words of *R' Moshe Chaim Luzzato,* "The foundation of saintliness and the source of all true and perfect service of God is that it should be clarified and validated to man what his obligation in his world are *and toward what he must place his focus and goal in all his toils during his entire life* (*Mesilas Yesharim*)."

14. **Praying for Others.** Homiletically this verse teaches that in prayer we should not only ask God for our own needs but also for the needs of our brothers. We should pray that we be answered along with all Jews who are in need. The Talmud (*Shabbos* 12b) submits that when praying for someone who is sick, we should ask that he be healed along with all other Jews who are ill. Thus we might read the verse אֶת אַחַי אָנֹכִי מְבַקֵּשׁ, "May I be helped along with all my brothers" (*Ohr HaTefillah*).

15. **Give Me Friendship or Give Me Death.** The original quote in the Talmud is אֹו חַבְרָא כְּחַבְרֵי דְּאִיֹּוב אֹו מִיתוּתָא, *either friendship like the friends of Job or death.* Why does the Talmud single out the friendship of Job's friends?

R' Shlomo HaKohen of Vilna explained: God gave Satan almost limitless power over Job. *"Only his soul must you guard"* (Job 2:6), he was instructed. Satan brought endless pain and travail upon Job. His children died, he suffered hunger and poverty, leprosy, boils and all types of physical ailments. The only thing Satan allowed him to retain was his good friends. Why didn't Satan take them away as well? The answer is that to do so would be deemed as taking his soul. "Either friendship or death."

16. **Friendship.** "Yesterday I received your letter. As I read it I inhaled the warm aroma of loyal friendship. In the last short while I have learned to recognize the value of the precious jewel called friendship. How much spiritual improvement and soul-enrichment it can create for one able to dive into its depths in order to retrieve the endless pearls to be found there!

"I must admit and openly confess that I never really understood this before. I am deeply indebted to 'friendship,' a serious part of my spiritual growth is a result of friendship.

"In truth all of this was a gift of 'friendship' without any serious effort on my part. Instead of taking the cup which friendship proffered to me, as I should have, grabbing it in my two hands and drinking it to its end in order that it be a source of blessing inside of me, I only dabbed my fingers in it. Only the little bit which stuck to my fingers remained with me. For example, regarding our relationship: Isn't it obvious that we could have doubled or tripled the amount of spiritually elevated times we spent together? How many areas of spiritual growth could we have undoubtedly reached and developed together had we only invested more energy into our friendship?" (*R' Yitzchak Hutner,* Collected Letters 171).

נֵלְכָה דֹּתָנָה
Let us go to Dothan (ibid. 17).

The Midrash (cited by *Rashi*) offers a homiletical interpretation. "They went to find a religious (דָּת) justification to kill you." Joseph, so sure of the power of their brotherhood, understood only the simple meaning of the angel's response; that they went to Dothan.

Why didn't brotherly love carry the day? The Midrash explains that the brothers acted with a powerful sense of self-righteousness. Considering themselves morally justified, they could not be stopped from performing the "mitzvah" of killing Joseph.[17]

וַיִּשְׁמַע רְאוּבֵן וַיַּצִּלֵהוּ מִיָּדָם
Reuben heard, and he rescued him from their hand (ibid. 21)

The Midrash teaches that had Reuben realized that if the Torah would record *and he rescued him from their hand*, he would have carried Joseph on his shoulders and brought him back to Jacob. This Midrash seems astounding. Do the Sages view Reuben as one who would do the right thing only for the honor of having his act recorded in the Torah?! Certainly Reuben wasn't a publicity hound!

Sfas Emes explains: Whenever an incident is written in the Torah it assumes a dimension of eternity. The Torah is not a history book;[18] any incident written in it holds an eternal lesson for the Jewish people. Thinking that his good deed was the act of a private individual with no cosmic or historic meaning, Reuben did not take it as seriously as he should have. Had he realized that the Torah would record his valiant efforts to save his brother, thus making it part of our national heritage, he would have done even more and carried Joseph on his shoulders back to Jacob.[19]

---

17. **Clear Conscience.** This self-righteous posture is borne out by the commentary of the *Sforno* on the words *they sat to eat food* (verse 25), after they threw Joseph into the pit. "They in no way viewed what they had done as a misdeed or a mistake which should cause them to refrain from eating." Their conscience did not bother them or even cause them to question what they had done. Convinced that they did what had to be done, they sat comfortably to eat.

R' Simchah Bunim of P'shis'cha saw this message in a *Mishnah* (Avos 2:17), which teaches "let *all* your deeds be for the sake of Heaven." *All* your deeds should be for the sake of Heaven — even the very fact that you are [ostensibly] acting for the sake of Heaven. In other words, a person may plan to do something, convinced that God demands it of him. That is a time when he should examine his motives and be certain that his religious zeal is untainted by personal considerations.

18. **Eternally Significant.** Certain stories appear in the Torah in great detail while there are eras that the Torah ignores completely. There is not a word in the Torah about Abraham from his youth until he was 70 years old. Likewise, Moses' biography ignores the years from 13 until 80. Only the Torah (and its Giver) can differentiate between a passing incident and one with eternal ramifications. Man, on the other hand, often views insignificant events as meaningful while he misses the true significance of actions which he views as peripheral.

One must pour all his energies into every good deed, since one never knows how it will affect him, his children, his environment and his community. He may think he is building a sand castle when in truth he is building entire worlds (*R' Eliyahu Meir Bloch*).

19. **Never Too Late.** When speaking of the Final Redemption the prophet writes: *I am Hashem, in its time I will make it come prematurely* (Isaiah 70:22). This would seem to be a contradiction in terms, for if it is in *its time*, it is not premature and if it is premature, it is not in its time. The Talmud (Sanhedrin 98a) explains that if we merit redemption it will come before its set time, but even if we don't merit it, it will still come by a certain Divinely predetermined time.

R' Tzadok HaKohen of Lublin (*Tzidkas HaTzadik* 50) submits that this is true on a personal level as well. "Its time" is when a person truly and acutely needs Divine salvation. He is desperately thirsty for God's help; he yearns for it and cannot continue without it. A premature deliverance is when God saves one even before he realizes how desperate his situation is.

To one who is meritorious, God provides salvation even before his situation becomes unbearable. [This is equally true of the Messianic redemption. When the Jewish people will be overcome by a collective burning thirst for his coming, and they realize that there is no other way for them to be saved, then "its time" will have arrived.]

However, even someone who does not merit this will be saved in "its time" — namely, before it becomes too late.

וְהַבּוֹר רֵק אֵין בּוֹ מָיִם
The pit was empty,
no water was in it (ibid. 24).

The redundancy implies that there was no *water* in it, but there *were* other things — serpents and scorpions (*Rashi*).[20] Why would Reuben suggest throwing Joseph into a pit with serpents and scorpions, which spelled almost certain death? Some commentators submit that Reuben and the brothers were unaware of the serpents and scorpions.

R' Yitzchak Zev Soloveitchik submits that Reuben was aware of the contents of the pit and nonetheless is considered to have saved Joseph by convincing the brothers to throw him into it. Reuben based his decision on the dictum that "Not the scorpion kills, sin kills" (*Berachos* 33a); the scorpion is nothing more than God's messenger to kill the guilty. Reuben was sure that due to Joseph's righteousness, he was safe from the snakes. He was right, and that was how he saved his brother.

Even Azel offers a homiletical interpretation of *Rashi:* The only way to overcome the evil inclination is through the study of Torah. One who does so develops God's mind-set and thought patterns, as it were, and can achieve clarity in understanding His Will. As the Sages teach (*Kiddushin* 30a), God says, "I created an evil inclination and I created Torah as its antidote." Without Torah, one is vulnerable to the figurative snake, the evil persuader. The Torah alludes to this by saying that the pit had no "water," i.e., Torah. It follows therefore

that it had snakes and scorpions, symbolic of the forces of evil, which seek to spiritually kill man in the absence of Torah.[21]

Background

The Torah interrupts the saga of Joseph to tell the story of Judah. He moved away from his brothers and married. In a fascinating turn of events he planted the roots of the Messiah and the Davidic dynasty.

וַיְהִי בָּעֵת הַהִוא וַיֵּרֶד יְהוּדָה מֵאֵת אֶחָיו
It was at that time that Judah
descended from his brothers (38:1).

The Midrash explains the juxtaposition of this incident with the saga of Joseph as based on the expression *Identify, if you please,* which occurs in both stories (see 38:25 and 37:32). The brothers and Judah, who was their leader, asked Jacob if he could identify Joseph's tunic. Judah was punished for this cruel hoax when his misadventure with Tamar was revealed through her request that Judah identify the security he had left with her.

Meshech Chochmah elaborates on the connection. Ultimately the sale of Joseph was a positive development, as he told his brothers *for it was to be a provider that God sent me ahead of you* (*Genesis* 45:5). Nevertheless, their intent was not pristine. *Although you intended me harm, God*

If one sees that God has yet to provide him salvation from his problems, he may rest assured that he still has the strength to bear the pain, for our Merciful Father would never push us over the brink. In "its time" He will save us.

20. **Positively Expansive.** The verse describes both the positive and negative aspects of this pit. The plus was that it had no water; the flaw was that it contained snakes and scorpions.

R' Zalman Sorotzkin notes that the Torah spells out the positive aspect explicitly, while it only alludes to the negative. If this how the Torah speaks of a pit, how much more so must we take care to follow this pattern when speaking of people. We must speak explicitly of their positive attributes, but even when we must mention their flaws, we should do so only by means of allusion.

21. **Spiritual Physics.** After delineating the precautionary steps one must take in order to avoid immoral behavior, *Rambam* writes: Greater than all of these [steps to prevent immorality], the Sages taught that one should turn his mind and preoccupation to words of Torah, allowing himself to expand his intelligence with wisdom. Thoughts of immoral behavior can overpower a heart only if it is devoid of wisdom (*Hilchos Isurei Biah* 22:21).

As in physics, the soul abhors a vacuum. When one's soul is empty of spiritual content, the heart, mind, and soul are inundated with immorality, heresy and illicit passion. The pit was empty; it had no water. Consequently it was filled with snakes and scorpions.

intended it for good (50:20). This is an example of people who had bad intentions when doing something that ultimately served a positive goal.

The Sages teach that one sin leads to another [similar] sin (*Avos* 4:2). Hence as a result of Judah's major involvement in the sale of Joseph (see *Rashi* to 38:1) he again became entangled in a sin of intent.

According to the Sages (*Makkos* 23), when Judah admitted his tryst with Tamar, a Heavenly voice called out, verifying that it was in accordance with God's plans for the emergence of the Davidic dynasty that Judah acted as he did. Nevertheless, his intentions were less than perfect. Here again God's aims were served by actions which stemmed from flawed motives. Thus the Midrash elucidates that the expression *Identify, if you please*, applies both to the sale of Joseph and to Judah and Tamar. A surface assessment of the stories yields one evaluation while under the surface the Divine tapestry is being woven.[22]

Malbim sees the story of Judah as the cure which God always creates before the malady. Since the sale of Joseph precipitated the Egyptian exile, the root and paradigm of all subsequent exiles, it was necessary to plant the roots of the ultimate redemption before the exile process began. As the Midrash puts it, before the first enslaver (the new Pharaoh — see *Exodus* 1:8) was born, the seeds of the ultimate redeemer (Messiah) were planted.

Rashi cites a Midrash explaining the juxtaposition of the sale of Joseph and the term *Judah descended from his brothers*. Judah's descent was figurative, since his brothers deposed him from his preeminence as their leader. They blamed him for the terrible grief Jacob suffered over the loss of Joseph. "You told us to sell him," they charged. "Had you advised us to send him back to our father we would have listened!"[23]

The Midrash expounds on this theme, teaching that from the role of Judah in the sale of Joseph we learn that one who begins a mitzvah and does not finish it is liable to see his wife and children die

---

22. **Choices not Actions.** These are two of many such instances in the Torah, where positive actions are rooted in tainted motives. Heaven has a way of making sure that its objectives are met, yet the person who advances the Heavenly plan is judged not according to his actions but rather according to his intent. In a seminal exposition of the concept, *Rambam* (*Genesis* 15:14), submits that even when God decrees that somebody will die in the coming year, the one who murders him is not absolved of guilt simply because he is fulfilling a Divine mandate. Since he acts out of personal motives, and not in fulfillment of the Divine Will, he will be punished. Only when a prophet predicts the demise or downfall of an individual or group, and someone undertakes to carry out the task purely because God commanded it, is he innocent. If, however, he acts for any other reason he is deemed guilty.

The classic example is Pharaoh's enslavement and persecution of the Jews. True, God informed Abraham that it would happen, but the individual Egyptian, from Pharaoh on down, acted on his own volition, not because God commanded him.

23. **It's Your Fault.** The idea that the brothers were angry at Judah is astounding. They wanted to kill Joseph; Judah wanted to save him. What right did they have to be upset with him to the extent that they deposed him?

The *Chafetz Chaim* would often relate the story of a Jew who was in the whiskey business. For years he evaded paying the alcohol tax and as a result became very wealthy. When he was finally caught, he was sentenced to fifteen years at hard labor in Siberia. As the police were escorting him in iron chains they passed his hometown of Rakov. He asked them for permission to see the rabbi, and his request was granted. The rabbi asked the prisoner, " How can I help you?" In a broken voice the prisoner replied, "I am going to Siberia for fifteen years and it is your fault, Rebbe. You certainly knew what I was doing; why didn't you say that flouting civil law is forbidden by the Torah (see *Gittin* 10b)? Why didn't you warn me what a terrible price I would have to pay for my misdeeds, that every thief is punished in the end? As rabbi of our town this was your job. Now I will have to toil as a slave because of you!"

Said the Chafetz Chaim: This man knew the severity of his crimes and was aware of the harshness with which the government might punish him, yet he blamed the rabbi for not rebuking him. Certainly when the Heavenly Court sentences sinners to punishments far worse than fifteen years in Siberia, a finger will be pointed toward those who could have guided the sinners toward the path of virtue, but did not.

It was Judah's duty to stop his brothers from selling Joseph, and he was punished for not having done so.

in his lifetime. Once he suggested that Joseph not be killed, he should have gone all the way and brought him back to his father.[24]

The implication is astounding: One who left the mitzvah unfinished is more culpable than one who did not even begin. The brothers wanted to kill Joseph; Judah at least saved him from certain death. Why is he to blame?

R' Yerucham Levovitz submits that once a person begins to do a good deed, he becomes emotionally attached to it. The mitzvah itself demands that it be brought to fruition and not be permitted to die. Since the main offspring of a righteous person are his good deeds, one who buries his spiritual offspring might eventually be forced, God forbid, to bury his physical offspring.

---

24. **Psychological Transference.** Why did they blame Judah and not Reuben who had initially suggested that they throw Joseph into the pit? A deep psychological insight of *Ralbag* provides the answer. The Torah teaches us how to wean people from a path fraught with spiritual danger. When one sees his friends ready to transgress a Torah prohibition he must assess how passionate they are in doing so. If they are firmly set on committing the sin, one will never be able to dissuade them in a one-time confrontation. They must be weaned from their resolve step by step.

It is true that Reuben wanted to save Joseph and bring him back to Jacob, but he knew that the brother's desire to kill Joseph did not allow for a head-on confrontation. They would not listen to him. He began by suggesting that rather than killing him directly they throw him into the pit. He thought that in this way he could soften their hatred of Joseph enough so that he could surreptitiously bring Joseph back to Jacob.

Reuben succeeded to the extent that when Judah suggested selling Joseph instead, they were receptive. Had Reuben proposed such an idea when the brothers were still in the heat of their hatred, they would have never accepted it. Thus, they were not angry at Reuben, for they themselves knew that they would have rejected his suggestion to return Joseph to Jacob. Once, however, Reuben softened their obstinate stand, they could have agreed to a plea from Judah to give Joseph a reprieve. The brothers were therefore upset with Judah for not forcing them to do the right thing.

פרשת מקץ ‎ఞ
Parashas Mikeitz

Background

This *parashah* marks the beginning of the chain of events that would bring Jacob and his children to Egypt, thereby setting the stage for the exile and servitude which would in turn lead to the Exodus and emergence of the Jewish nation. Pharaoh's dream is the catalyst for these historical milestones.

וַיְהִי מִקֵּץ שְׁנָתַיִם יָמִים
It happened at the end of two years to the day (41:1).

Exactly two years after the release of the Chamberlain of Cupbearers, Pharaoh had a dream. According to *Nachalas David,* the Torah notes the date in order to teach an important lesson. Pharaoh, who considered himself a deity, merited a prophetic dream so that Joseph would be freed from prison and be able to ascend to power in Egypt. The Torah emphasizes this by defining the moment at which he had his dream in terms of Joseph's imprisonment. Joseph was not freed because Pharaoh dreamed; Pharaoh dreamed, because the time had come to free Joseph.

In a homiletical vein, *R' Meir'l of Premishlan* rendered the verse as follows: וַיְהִי מִקֵּץ, and it happens at the end [when man senses that his end is near], שְׁנָתַיִם יָמִים, that man realizes he has spiritually slept (שֵׁנָה) away his days, never taking full advantage of life's opportunities. *R' Moshe Michel of Biala* added: *Pharaoh was dreaming.* At the end of a person's life, it frequently becomes clear that he has spent his life in a dreamlike trance. While he thought that he made good use of his years in this world, in the end he is faced with the realization that *behold he is standing at the river,* not even having begun to dip his toes into the water of life nor face up to its challenges.[1]

The Midrash interprets the verse *Praiseworthy is the man who makes Hashem His trust (Psalms 40:5)* as a reference to Joseph, who was punished by languishing in prison for an additional two years because he turned to the cupbearer to help him. This Midrash seems to contradict itself. If Joseph was a person who placed his trust in God, why did he ask for the help of mortal man? And if his human effort was legitimate, why was he punished?

The *Chazon Ish* in a short, but seminal, essay on

---

1. **Sleepingly Aware.** Once during a *tish, R' Moshe Avraham Berezovsky* was standing behind the *Slonimer Rebbe,* the *Divrei Shmuel.* To the Rebbe's right sat one of his most prominent *chassidim.* The Rebbe asked him, "What is Moshe Avraham doing at this very moment?" R' Moshe Avraham whispered in the *chassid's* ear, "Tell the Rebbe that I am sleeping." Immediately he said to the Rebbe, "Moshe Avraham says he is sleeping."

The *Divrei Shmuel* smiled and replied, "If he realizes he is sleeping, that is fine. Woe, however, to the person who is fast asleep and doesn't even realize it."

this question suggests that while man is obligated to attempt to solve life's challenges by expending human effort rather than by relying on miracles, such efforts are justified only if they stand a reasonable chance of success. When one is disheartened, depressed and downcast, he reaches for the flimsiest of straws in order to find encouragement. One who truly trusts in God should never fall into such despair that he relies on efforts that are unlikely to yield positive results.

Thus the legitimate extent of one's efforts is directly linked to his level of trust in God; the greater his trust, the lesser his efforts and vice versa. An ordinary person would have been justified in seeking the cupbearer's help, even though the chances of success were slight. The Midrash faults Joseph for doing so, because a person with his exceptional degree of trust in God should not have stooped so low as to beseech the cupbearer for help.

R' Menachem Mendel of Kotzk offers a different perspective. Punishment is meant as a "wake-up call," to arouse man from spiritual slumber and push him to begin pursuing the real agenda of life. Not everyone merits to be punished immediately for his misdeeds or misthoughts, so that he realizes the areas in which he must mend his ways. Joseph, who worked a lifetime on strengthening his trust in God, veered from his path when he asked for the cupbearer's help. It was only due to his elevated level of trust that he was punished almost immediately and given the opportunity to rectify his "sin." Because he was a *man who places his trust in God,* he *merited* to remain in prison for an additional two years.

וּפַרְעֹה חֹלֵם וְהִנֵּה עֹמֵד עַל הַיְאֹר
Pharaoh was dreaming that behold! — he was standing over the River (ibid.).

The verse is framed in present rather than in past tense. Pharaoh was *dreaming;* Pharaoh constantly fantasized that he was a deity that stood above all else. In his mind, *he was standing over* [and above] *the River* — he was even more powerful than the Nile River which was ostensibly the source of sustenance for all of Egypt. [2]

וַתִּרְעֶינָה בָּאָחוּ
And they were grazing in the marshland (ibid. 2)

According to the *Zohar,* Pharaoh's dreams were an allegory for the ongoing battle between good and evil. The only way in which good can overcome evil is if the forces for good are united. This is alluded to in the words *they were grazing* בָּאָחוּ, which may homiletically be related to אַחְוָה, *brotherhood.* This message is reiterated in Pharaoh's second dream where the seven ears of grain sprouted on a single stalk. [3]

Evil exists in separation, for each evil person has his own personal agenda. Even when the wicked attain a semblance of unity and friendship it is of the type described in *Pirkei Avos* as *love that depends on a specific cause* (5:19) and is not lasting. The good stalks were healthy and good; emotionally healthy themselves and good to others.

Sfas Emes sees in the dream an allusion to the tactics of the evil inclination. Initially he visits man infrequently, acting much like a passerby in man's

---

2. **Way Above?** The Midrash contrasts wicked people such as Pharaoh who view themselves as standing above their "god" with the righteous who, like Jacob, sense that *behold! Hashem was standing over him* (*Genesis* 28:13).

The righteous constantly seek to elevate themselves spiritually so that they may perceive some of God's greatness. The higher they rise, the more they realize how great the chasm is between themselves and God. Hence they always feel that He is far above them. The wicked, on the other hand, do not want to be subservient to God; they want to create a compromise so that their commitment to God need not interfere with their pursuit of a personal agenda of physical pleasure.

The wicked stand over their "god" waiting for him to "rise" to their standards and goals (*R' Eliyahu Meir Bloch*).

3. **Positive Prosperity.** *Rashi* explains that the beauty of the cows alludes to the years of plenty, when people view each other favorably and see beauty in one another. In good times people view life, and thus each other, in a positive light, but when poverty reigns, there is jealousy. According to *Likutei Yehoshua,* the imagery alludes to this. The cows grazed בָּאָחוּ, which can be homiletically rendered as *in brotherhood* [from אָח, *brother*], for when there is general prosperity, dissent declines, people see the good in each other and feel united in brotherhood.

life. Soon he becomes a frequent guest in our consciousness, and eventually he becomes the host who controls us. This is alluded to in the story of the ugly and scrawny cows. They emerged from the Nile, making their appearance gradually. Soon they were standing, exhibiting a more permanent presence. Eventually they devoured the robust cows, which are symbolic of the goodness in man.

וְאֵין פּוֹתֵר אוֹתָם לְפַרְעֹה
But none could interpret them for Pharaoh (ibid. 8).

When Pharaoh asked his advisers for an interpretation they were unable to provide one that satisfied him (*Rashi*). Why was it so hard for them to explain Pharaoh's dreams?

Chochmah Im Nachalah submits that Pharaoh's advisers believed that the world operates only within the laws of nature and therefore found the dream unbelievable. The idea that the robust cows were devoured by the gaunt ones flew in the face of "the survival of the fittest" which dictates that the weak fall into the hands of the strong.[4]

Educated in the home of Jacob, Joseph saw things differently. The rules of nature were created by God Who can bend and override them at will. He can bring victory to the weak and defeat to the strong. Thus it was Joseph who was able to provide Pharaoh with an acceptable interpretation.

וְשָׁם אִתָּנוּ נַעַר עִבְרִי עֶבֶד לְשַׂר הַטַּבָּחִים
And there with us was a Hebrew youth, a slave of the Chamberlain of Butchers . . .. (ibid. 12).

Cursed are the wicked, because even their favors are flawed and incomplete (*Rashi*). Although the cupbearer knew that Joseph saved him, he could not bring himself to speak positively about Joseph. He referred to him as an immature *youth*; as a *Hebrew* outsider who does not speak or understand our language; and as a *slave* who should never be allowed to gain power.

According to *Meilitz Yosher* and *Da'as Torah*, this emotional stinginess, which *Rashi* views as wickedness, was a subconscious reaction of the cupbearer. Although he knew how indebted he was to Joseph, he could not bring himself to acknowledge the favor.

Machazeh Eliyahu wonders why the Midrash considers the words of the cupbearer as merely an "incomplete favor" when in reality his description was a blatant lie. Certainly he must have recognized Joseph's great wisdom during the time they were together in prison. How could he call him an immature youth? The answer is that the cupbearer *did* tell the truth; Joseph was young at the time. [Although he was 28 years old when the cupbearer met him, that is very young for an adviser to the mightiest king of the time.] The charge against the cupbearer is that he well knew that the words young, Jewish, and slave, especially in combination, carry a very negative connotation. The unspoken innuendo was that he is a young, foolish and irresponsible slave, and no amount of explanation could undo the initial impression of these words. It is not enough to state facts, the way in which they are stated can be more harmful — and more dishonest — than lies.[5]

וַיְרִיצֻהוּ מִן הַבּוֹר
and they rushed him from the dungeon (ibid. 14).

Joseph's release from prison is a metaphor for the eventual redemption of the Jewish people. When the time arrives for something to happen, God does not delay; as soon as the time came for Joseph to leave the dungeon, he was whisked out. Likewise, taught the *Chafetz Chaim*, when the

---

4. **Believing Is Believing.** *Ramban* (*Leviticus* 16:8) describes Aristotle and his disciples as believing that whatever cannot be proven logically does not really exist. The Epicurean philosophy is the strongest expression of this world-view. Therefore, the miracle that symbolized the victory of the Jewish people over Greek culture was the lighting of the Menorah with a one-day supply of oil which lasted for eight days (*Zekan Aharon*).

Chanukah almost invariably coincides with *Parashas Mikeitz*. *Chanah David* suggests that the festival alludes to Pharaoh's dream. Just as the gaunt, weak cows devoured the robust, strong ones, so God gave the mighty Syrian-Greeks into the hands of the relatively weak Hasmoneans.

5. **Prejudiced Perceptions.** *Alshich* sees this power of initial impressions as the poison of slander. Once people are exposed to a negative evaluation of someone's character, it is nearly impossible to undo the damage. All the explanations in the world will not change the listener's first perception.

moment comes for the Messianic Redemption, God will immediately rush us home to His Land.[6]

וַיְגַלַּח וַיְחַלֵּף שִׂמְלֹתָיו וַיָּבֹא אֶל פַּרְעֹה
He shaved and changed his clothes and he came to Pharaoh (ibid.).

Rashi explains that Joseph shaved and changed as a sign of respect for royalty. After languishing in a dungeon for twelve years, we might expect that Joseph would spruce up his appearance a bit before coming in front of Pharaoh. What does *Rashi* mean to teach us?

R' Meir HaKohen offers the following: Having heard from the cupbearer of Joseph's phenomenal ability to interpret dreams, Pharaoh wanted to see him without delay. On one hand, Joseph thought that, since he had been punished for having groomed himself excessively (see *Rashi* to Genesis 37:2), perhaps he should avoid being concerned with his appearance when he was summoned by Pharaoh. On the other hand, he decided that since he came from Jacob and a house of royalty, it would be inappropriate for him to appear in public in a disheveled state. He therefore shaved and changed clothes as a sign of respect for his father, who was royalty.[7]

Background

Joseph offers a dazzling interpretation of the dream, accounting for all its details. He even

---

6. **Dovetailed Deliverance.** The Exodus from Egypt is but one example of this phenomenon. The Torah describes the moment of the Exodus with the words: *It was at the end of four hundred and thirty years, and it was on that very day that all the legions of Hashem left the land of Egypt* (Exodus 12:41). The Exodus was calibrated to dovetail with the Divine prophecy given Abraham (see *Genesis* 15:13). Isaac was born on the fifteenth of Nissan. It was then that the prophesied years of exile began, and the Jews were liberated four hundred years later to the day (See *Rashi* to *Exodus* 12:41). Thus the Torah describes the Exodus in terms of Israel being rushed out of Egypt (See *Exodus* 12:39).

R' Yerucham Levovitz contrasts Divine redemption with salvations brought about by human beings. Even after man decides to free his fellow, many prefatory stages must occur before he is actually freed. We see this constantly in history. A nation or an organization of nations may resolve on a major policy initiative, but it goes through debate, crafting and preparation before it can be put into effect. God's salvation, however, is always fully in place — as soon as He reveals it, it happens. A human ruler may grant his subject clemency, but the prisoner will languish in captivity until all the paperwork is prepared. Although officially he has been freed, it might take some time before he actually tastes freedom. God's salvation, however, happens not a moment too late.

7. **Appropriate Attire.** *R' Yitzchak Zilberstein* related that he was once in the home of *R' Aharon of Belz* when a painter in work clothes came and asked to be admitted to the Rebbe. "I have a terrible problem and I must speak to the Rebbe immediately," he said. *R' Shalom Fogel,* the Rebbe's *gabbai* (secretary), refused to let the man see the Rebbe. "You will not go in dressed this way!" he stated categorically. Even after the man tearfully poured out his tale of woe, *R' Shalom* was adamant. "Go home, change and come back. I will let you in without delay when you return, but I cannot let you in while you are dressed in such clothing."

In light of the fact that the Torah equates the honor we must afford Torah scholars with the honor to be granted to Hashem, we should pay attention to the clothes we wear while praying. For example, the plastic rain cover on a hat should be removed before prayer. Likewise, galoshes should be taken off.

Yalkut Meam Loez submits that our verse implies this principle. If one takes care to dress appropriately when coming in front of a mortal king, how much more so should people be properly dressed and groomed when they appear before the King of kings (See *Rambam, Hilchos Tefillah* 5:5).

The following famous incident underscores the need to approach God in prayer as if we stand before the King.
On *Rosh Hashanah,* the one who leads the congregation in *Shacharis,* begins by chanting a moving melody that builds up to a crescendo, at which point he proclaims with resonance, "*HaMelech!* (The King)!"

One *Rosh Hashanah* as *R' Aharon* of *Karlin* approached the lectern to lead this prayer, he chanted the word "*HaMelech,*" and promptly fainted. The people in *shul* immediately ran to revive him, and prayers continued. Afterwards people asked the *Rebbe,* "What was it that caused you to faint?"

He replied, "I thought of an incident recorded in the Talmud (*Gittin* 56a), which *R' Yochanan ben Zakkai* appeared before the Roman general Vespasian to plead on behalf of his fellow Jews. *R' Yochanan ben Zakkai* greeted the general by saying, 'Peace to you, O king! Peace to you. O king!'

Vespasian, surprised by this appellation, exclaimed, If I'm not the king your greeting is treasonous and if I am

---

suggests to Pharaoh that he appoint a wise and understanding person who would take charge of the Egyptian economy so that the country would prepare to weather the coming seven years of famine. Pharaoh makes the surprising decision that Joseph is the most qualified person.

וְעַתָּה יֵרֶא פַרְעֹה אִישׁ נָבוֹן
וְחָכָם וִישִׁיתֵהוּ עַל אֶרֶץ מִצְרָיִם

And let Pharaoh seek out a discerning and wise man and set him over the land of Egypt (ibid. 33).

Pharaoh asked Joseph only to interpret his dreams; why did Joseph offer unsolicited counsel as to how to react to the portending catastrophe? *Ramban* explains that Joseph's political advice flowed from the dream. He wondered why God would show Pharaoh the seven years of famine now, since this would seem to contradict the axiom that "it is sufficient to deal with suffering in its time" (see *Berachos* 9b). He therefore understood that the famine was revealed to Pharaoh so that he might plan ahead. Joseph therefore advised Pharaoh to seek the appropriate person now.[8]

Why was it necessary to appoint someone wise? Could not any grain merchant gather and store the produce, and be in charge of selling it at the appropriate time? *R' Shlomo Bloch* offers an explanation based on a personal experience: "I remember from my youth a famine in Vilna. Every day there were at least fifty funerals of people who were found in the streets dead of starvation. Had there been someone, years before, when there was plenty of food, who could have envisioned hungry people roaming the streets desperately searching for something to eat, he would have prepared for the bad times. Only someone with that vision could have convinced the people to save for the hard times to come. He would have been able to paint a picture so terrible that the masses would respond to the unthinkable but impending catastrophe, convinced that the issue is not one of more or less food, but rather one of life and death. As the Sages teach, 'Who is wise? He who envisions the future' " (*Tamid* 32a).

Joseph understood that during the years of plenty no one could imagine what lay ahead, and therefore would be incapable of understanding the need to make do with less in spite of the abundance of food. It was necessary to find a wise man who could inspire the populace with his vision of the future.[9]

---

indeed the king (and not merely a general), then how is it that you have not come to me until now?'

"That is what came to mind." said the *Rebbe,* still shaken. 'If *Hashem* is indeed the King, then why have I not returned to him, with repentance, until now?'

8. **Just for Me.** *R' Tzvi Hirsch Farber* offered a different approach based on an amusing parable. Two princes, both obsessed with themselves and their honor, were traveling on the same train. When they arrived at the station they were met by an orchestra. Each one in his own "humility" was convinced that the musicians were there in his honor. Unable to agree, they decided to ask a Jew who lived nearby. The Jew, who had not a penny for the forthcoming Pesach holiday, was shocked when the two noblemen asked him to arbitrate their argument. He asked them for fifty rubles as his arbitration fee and then told them, "The musicians came not for you nor for you. They came for me so that I would have the money I need for the holiday."

Joseph though to himself, "God could very well bring either plenty or famine without granting Pharaoh a form of prophecy. Why did He communicate with Pharaoh through this dream? The whole episode could only be in order that I rise to power." He therefore offered advice, which Pharaoh accepted.

9. **Distracting Overture.** *R' Elyah Lopian* compares this world to the years of plenty, and the Next World to the years of famine. Only in this world does one have almost endless opportunities to study Torah and perform its commandments. In the Next World, no such opportunities exist; it is a time of famine. We tend to think that this life is forever and we will always be able to do *mitzvos* and store away spiritual provisions for later. It takes wisdom to envision a time when we will not be able to add to our storehouse of merit. If we remember the famine for *mitzvos* that exists in the Next World, we will use our time in this world wisely. A famous parable brings this point home.

An extended war was ended when a general devised a victorious strategy. The king had promised that the victor would be rewarded with an opportunity to spend an hour in the royal vault, free to take whatever he wished. As the great day approached, the king was worried. He had to honor his promise, but he was afraid that the general would take too much valuable treasure from the vault. He asked his advisers for an idea.

One of them said, "I have an idea, which will allow you to honor your promise without losing much wealth. I know

מְנַשֶּׁה כִּי נַשַּׁנִי אֱלֹקִים אֶת כָּל עֲמָלִי וְאֵת כָּל בֵּית אָבִי . . . אֶפְרַיִם כִּי הִפְרַנִי אֱלֹקִים בְּאֶרֶץ עָנְיִי

Manasseh for "God has made me forget all my hardship and all my father's household" . . . Ephraim, for "God has made me fruitful in the land of my suffering" (ibid. 51-52).

Malbim views Joseph's choice of names as an expression of his desire to always remember the hard times that preceded his rise to power and greatness. Even now, after he became fruitful in the land of Egypt, he gave his first son a name that would always remind him that although God's gift of good fortune would make it easy for him to forget his hardship and his father's home, he would never do so.[10]

The name of Joseph's second son, Ephraim, symbolized that despite his new eminence, Joseph viewed Egypt as a land of suffering.[11]

R' Zalman Sorotzkin offers a different perspective. Joseph began by praising God for having allowed him to leave his imprisonment and to become the viceroy of Egypt. He said, "God made me forget all my [previous] hardship [in Egypt] and all [the travail I underwent in] my father's household." Then, after thanking God for His kindness, Joseph began to remember his father's home. He would have preferred to suffer the hatred of his brothers, but remain in his father's shadow, than to rise to the height of grandeur in Egypt. *God has made me fruitful* but, unfortunately, it is *in the land of my suffering*.[12]

Background

Due to the famine in Canaan, Jacob feels compelled to send the brothers to Egypt to buy food. There they will unwittingly be reunited with

---

that the general is a great lover of music. On the day he is supposed to enter the vault, place the best orchestra in the land inside and have them play. The general will be captivated by the music and forget why he came to the vault." The idea caught the king's fancy and he brought the orchestra to the vault on the appointed day.

The general appeared at the palace gate. The door to the vault opened and he entered. He was mesmerized by the beautiful, enchanting music. For a moment he stood still, enraptured. Quickly, however, he remembered why he was there. He hurried inside, ready to fill his briefcase and pockets. Suddenly the intensity of the music increased and again he stopped in his tracks, listening to beautiful music. After a minute or two he began to figuratively scream at himself, "Fool! This is a golden opportunity; do not miss it because of your love for music!" At that very moment, however, the orchestra picked up its intensity, and again the general forgot where he was there. Suddenly a hand grabbed the collar of his shirt and pulled him out of the vault. "Your time is up!" a voice told him. "It's time to leave."

We are all given time in this world to grab treasures by studying Torah and performing God's commandments. Compared to the next, eternal world, this world is like a mere hour, but it is in these "sixty minutes" that we can grab endless spiritual wealth. The evil inclination, in an effort to make us forget why we are here, bombards us with all kinds of lovely, enchanting distractions. Let us close our ears to this world's "music" and take more and more spiritual treasures from the vault of life.

10. **The Blessing of Forgetfulness.** *R' Eliyahu Meir Bloch* lost his wife and family in the Nazi Holocaust. Miraculously he and his brother-in-law *R' Chaim Mordechai Katz* escaped and rebuilt the Telshe Yeshivah in Cleveland. In 1943, Rabbi Bloch wrote the following: "In what fashion does the name of Manasseh, implying that Joseph had forgotten his father's household, commemorate God's kindness toward him? Certainly it was pain and hardship that made him forget his glorious past.

"Sometimes it is a blessing to forget one's past. Rather than falling into a debilitating depression, Joseph, with God's help, was able to block out the memories of a beautiful past so that he could serve God in the spiritual misery of Egypt. These are our feelings now in our present situation."

Rabbi Bloch wrote that he felt blessed by Hashem that the memory of his destroyed yeshivah and murdered family did not paralyze his efforts to rebuild the glory that had seemingly been lost.

11. **Pain for Gain.** On Pesach we eat matzah, a symbol of freedom, and then *maror* (bitter herbs), a symbol of slavery. This sequence is seemingly out of order. According to *Malbim* and *Sfas Emes,* this teaches that the pain is really the catalyst for the gain, that the pain of exile is the source of redemption. Since we realize this only in hindsight, we first eat the matzah. Only after having tasted freedom can we realize that the *maror*, too, was part of the trek to freedom.

12. **Alien Survivors.** According to the *Netziv,* the key to survival in exile is to never feel comfortable there. This is alluded to in God's words to Abraham, *Know with certainty that your offspring shall be aliens in a land not their own . . . and afterwards they will leave . . .* (Genesis 15:13-14). The realization that we are aliens in a land not our own allows us to make our way through the night of exile.

Joseph, although it will take more travails before they realize who the viceroy of Egypt really is.

וַיַּרְא יַעֲקֹב כִּי יֶשׁ שֶׁבֶר בְּמִצְרָיִם
Jacob perceived that there were provisions in Egypt (42:1).

The use of the term "perceived" seems to be inaccurate, since knowledge that provisions are available in Egypt is a matter of receiving information, not perception. Furthermore, וַיַּרְא means *he saw;* certainly Jacob did not physically see what was going on in faraway Egypt! *Rashi* therefore interprets שֶׁבֶר as שֵׂבֶר, *hope.* Jacob saw prophetically that there was *hope* in Egypt, though he was not shown that the hope was Joseph.

In its plain meaning, the verse refers to food, but the Sages understood it homiletically to mean hope, as well. What is the relationship between the *p'shat* (plain meaning) and the *d'rash* (homiletic interpretation)?

Jacob sensed that there had to be something special and holy about the fact that Egypt was privileged to be the sole provider for the entire civilized world. "How is it possible," he wondered, "that this base and immoral nation was chosen to be the savior of the world?" Such behavior can only come from a holy and elevated source. When Jacob saw that there was שֶׁבֶר, *food,* in Egypt, that the Egyptians were ready to share with others, a spark of שֵׂבֶר, *hope,* began to flicker in his mind and heart. Maybe it was his son Joseph who stood behind this humanitarian effort. Maybe it was his influence that brought it all about (*Karnei Ohr*).[13]

Meor Einayim submits an alternative approach based on the Midrashic teaching that before God created our world, He created and destroyed many other worlds. This process is known in Kabbalistic literature as the "breakage before the *tikkun* (perfection)." The descent of Jacob's family to Egypt, too, was the preliminary "breakage" from which perfection of the Jewish nation emerged. The descent prepared the Jewish people for their eventual ascent to Mount Sinai, where they received the Torah. In this sense, Jacob saw שֶׁבֶר, *breakage,* in Egypt, but he understood that his family's sojourn there was a temporary breakage meant to prime them for spiritual grandeur.[14]

וְיוֹסֵף הוּא הַשַּׁלִּיט עַל הָאָרֶץ הוּא הַמַּשְׁבִּיר לְכָל עַם הָאָרֶץ
Now Joseph — he was the viceroy over the land, he was the provider to all the people of the land (ibid. 6).

This verse means to present a contrast. Even though Joseph was the viceroy of Egypt and could have appointed functionaries to distribute the food, he served personally as the provider for the people. Why did he insist on doing it himself? First, he wished to be sure that each person received exactly what he deserved. Secondly, Joseph sought to teach the people that mercy is not simply an emotion to which one pays lip service with a sigh. One must act personally to alleviate his fellow's suffering (*Sifsei Kohen*).[15]

The Midrash notes that throughout the years of

---

13. **Not Beyond Hope.** In a homiletical spin, *R' Elimelech of Grodzisk* explains the verse as a lesson for life. יֶשׁ שֶׁבֶר בְּמִצְרָיִם, there is hope even in מִצְרָיִם. The word מצרים can be read מְצָרִים, *narrow, constricting straits.* Even when one suffers spiritual constriction and lives with a narrow perspective, let him never forget that there is שֵׂבֶר, *hope.* In the words of King David, *Fortunate (or happy) is one whose help is Jacob's God, whose hope is in Hashem, his God (Psalms* 146:5).

14. **Brokenhearted Completeness.** *R' Muttel of Slonim* was sitting with a group of *chassidim* on *Erev Yom Kippur.* Crying brokenheartedly he said to them, "What shall we take with us as we enter the holy day? Maybe our brokenheartedness will protect us and we will emerge purified?"

After a few moments he felt encouraged. "Jacob prophesied, although he was not fully aware of what he was saying. He suddenly perceived that somewhere in Egypt there was a person whose heart is broken (שֶׁבֶר) over not doing enough for God. While he did not know who that person was, it gave him hope that his family could likewise spiritually survive a sojourn in Egypt."

15. **Don't Bother.** Once the *Chafetz Chaim* was making the bed for a guest. The visitor protested. "Rebbe, why should you take the trouble? I can do it myself."

The next day at the morning *Shacharis* prayers, the Chafetz Chaim offered to put on *tefillin* on behalf of the guest. Surprised, the visitor said, "Rebbe, it is my mitzvah, you can not do it for me." Countered the great sage, "*Hachnassas orchim* (hospitality) is *my* mitzvah. Why did you think you could do it on my behalf?"

famine, Joseph waited until the end of each day before tasting any food; he finished providing for the last of the day's supplicants before he allowed himself to eat.[16]

וַיַּכֵּר וַיִּתְנַכֵּר אֲלֵיהֶם
and he recognized them but he acted like a stranger toward them (ibid. 7).

Why did Joseph conceal his identity from his brothers? *Kedushas Levi* sees this as an expression of Joseph's sensitivity toward their feelings. People are rarely good losers. The feeling that one is compelled to be subservient to someone else is a bitter pill to swallow. Certainly one dreads that such an experience be witnessed by a close friend or family member. Had the brothers known that Joseph was one to whom they humbly bowed and that he was witnessing the fulfillment of the dream they had scorned, they would have felt deep psychological pain and suffering. In order to save them from such mental anguish, Joseph concealed his identity.

A lesser person might have reveled in the sweet revenge and preferred that his "enemy" feel the degradation of downfall to the fullest. Joseph did the opposite. While his brothers had to bow in fulfillment of his dream, there was no need for them to undergo the shame of being vanquished. Joseph saved them that pain.[17]

אִם כֵּנִים אַתֶּם אֲחִיכֶם אֶחָד יֵאָסֵר בְּבֵית מִשְׁמַרְכֶם
If you are truthful people, let one of your brothers be imprisoned in your place of confinement (ibid. 19).

Rashi asks why Joseph refers to the prison as "your place of confinement," and explains that he means the place where they were confined at that moment. *Ohel Moed* offers the following, based on the words of R' Zeira (*Megillah* 28a), who said, "I did not exult in the failure of my friend." Basic human decency dictates that one not rejoice at the expense of a friend; why does R' Zeira mention that he did not do something that is obviously wrong? Explained *R' Yitzchak of Vorki*: R' Zeira was so sensitive to the plight of his friends that he sensed their pain as his own. When a friend was hurting, R' Zeira could not bring himself to rejoice about *anything*, even about sources of personal joy.

It was to this sense of brotherhood that Joseph appealed. He wanted his brothers to feel that if one of them were to sit in prison, then in essence they would all be incarcerated.

וַיֶּחֶרְדוּ אִישׁ אֶל אָחִיו לֵאמֹר מַה זֹּאת עָשָׂה אֱלֹקִים לָנוּ
and they turned trembling one to another, saying, "What is this that God has done to us?" (ibid. 28).

This verse implies that the brothers were fearful and concerned for one another, not each one for himself. The Sages teach that a person should bless God for the seemingly bad things that happen to him just as he does for the good (*Berachos* 54a), since (in the words of *Ramban*) whatever God does is ultimately for the good. However, one must adopt this perspective only with regard to one's own personal difficulties. With regard to others, one must empathize with them and try to help them, but not preach that they should have faith in God's ultimate goodness.

Accordingly, the Torah reports that each turned and trembled toward his brother. With regard to themselves, they made peace with Divine justice, sure that whatever God does is for the good. But toward their brothers, they showed care and concern (*Iturei Torah*).

Were we to be in a similar situation and suddenly

---

16. **Popular Providers.** *R' Aharon Levin of Reisha* commented that such a level of concern helps a leader win the loyalty of the populace and consolidate his authority over them. Some rulers control their people by force while others strengthen their hold with kindness and generosity to their subjects. Our verse teaches that Joseph was the viceroy *because* he was the provider to all the people of the land.

17. **Sympathetic Outsider.** On the words "but he acted like a stranger toward them," *Onkelos* adds *He thought about what to say to them. Divrei Yechezkel* explains: An interested party finds it hard to be objective; to react appropriately to a situation and offer sound advice, one must be able to approach it as an outsider. Joseph knew that his mission was twofold: to let his brothers achieve atonement for having sold him, and to allow for the fulfillment of his prophetic dreams. He *acted as a stranger toward them* in order to try and achieve the objectivity that would enable him to think clearly about what to say.

found money in our sacks, we would have had mixed feelings. On one hand, we would be excited over the windfall; on the other hand, we would be fearful of the consequences from the viceroy, to whom the money belonged. The brothers, however, had only one thought: *What is this that God has done to us?* It was clear to them that the viceroy and his servants were irrelevant. The brothers did not even mention them, so clearly did they see the Hand of Providence.

When Joseph revealed himself, he reinforced this clarity of vision by reassuring his brothers that he did not intend to take revenge: *And now: it was not you who sent me here, but God* (45:8). "Why should I blame you when it was God Who sent me here? At best, you were His pawns" (*R' Yerucham Levovitz*).

וְאֵל שַׁדַּי יִתֵּן לָכֶם רַחֲמִים
And may El Shaddai grant you mercy (43:14).

If one wants God to show him mercy, he must first become capable of showing mercy toward others. As the Sages taught, כָּל הַמְרַחֵם עַל הַבְּרִיּוֹת מְרַחֲמִים עָלָיו מִן הַשָּׁמַיִם, *Whoever is merciful to others, they will be merciful to him from Heaven* (*Shabbos* 151b). Jacob prayed that God would imbue his children with mercy, so that they — by being compassionate people — would deserve God's compassion for themselves. God is man's shadow (see *Psalms* 121:5), meaning homiletically that He reflects people's behavior by acting toward them as they act toward others. Thus, the best way for Jacob to invoke God's mercy upon his childrem was to pray that they be merciful to others (*Aish Dos*).

The Midrash explains why Jacob invoked the Name *El Shaddai*, which means *He Who is sufficient*. Jacob referred to the time of Creation, when the universe was expanding as it came into being. When it reached the size that God desired, He declared, "It is sufficient," as it were, and it stopped growing. Now Jacob prayed, "May He Who said to the world, 'Enough,' now declare that my troubles are enough."[18]

Yesod HaAvodah explains the parallel. Although we firmly believe that all the difficulties and travails that You bring upon us are truly acts of Divine Kindness that are for our ultimate benefit, we still ask You to say "enough" to our troubles. We ask You to follow the pattern of Creation. Although the entirety of Creation was an expression of Your lovingkindness, You still, at a certain point, set limits on the expansion of this world.

Likewise we implore You to say "enough" to the hidden kindnesses You show us by putting an end to our troubles.[19]

---

18. **Enough!** *R' Gedaliah Schorr* offers a penetrating perspective on the concept of sufficiency. God created the world from a primordial, spiritual essence that, He decreed, should become continuously more physical until it assumed the form of the universe as we know it. Had it remained in its pristine form, God's Presence would have been so obvious that man would have had no choice but to recognize Him. If so, there could not be freedom of choice, any more than one has the freedom to choose whether or not to put his arm into a flaming furnace. God therefore allowed His sanctity to assume physical dimensions, regulated by the laws of nature so as to becloud His Presence. Then, man could — as people do — err that there is ח"ו no God. One *can* find God in this world, but one must search and exercise honest judgment.

On the other hand, had God allowed the world to become any more physical, it would have become impossible to penetrate the veil and discover Him. He therefore said to the world, "Enough!" The process of quantification must stop before the world become so grossly physical that it will be impossible to recognize God.

Personal woes and troubles also serve to create the balance necessary for true free choice, with regard to recognizing God and performing His will. Were every deserving person to be immediately rewarded, man's inherent logic would leave him no choice but to do the right thing. The existence of the righteous person who suffers creates doubt in man's mind as to whether to do God's will. [Furthermore, pain and travail often force us to reengage with Him.] Nevertheless, if our troubles become totally overwhelming, we may, God forbid, break and lose our spiritual and emotional stability. We therefore ask God to say "enough" to our troubles: May He Who said to the world, "Enough," declare our troubles to be "enough."

19. **Fully Satiated.** Shortly before he died, the *Damesek Eliezer of Vizhnitz* underwent surgery. On the Sabbath before the operation, he offered the following interpretation to the words of our prayer שַׂבְּעֵנוּ מִטּוּבֶךָ, *satisfy us from Your goodness.* "We firmly believe that everything You do is for the good, even when You inflict pain upon us. Nevertheless, the hidden kindness cannot provide us with satisfaction for, as the Sages teach, 'the blind eat but are never satisfied' (*Yoma* 74b). In order to achieve satisfaction, one must see the food. Likewise with Your kindness; we implore You to *satisfy us from Your goodness.* Grant us Your kindness in ways that we can see it and thus achieve satisfaction and satiety."

פרשת ויגש ‎⧉
Parashas Vayigash

Background

After Benjamin is caught with the viceroy's goblet, Judah steps forward to plead the case for his younger brother's freedom. With simple, straightforward arguments, he penetrates Joseph's heart and causes him to reveal his identity and to proclaim his undying love for his brothers, in spite of what they did to him.

וַיִּגַּשׁ אֵלָיו יְהוּדָה
Then Judah approached him (44:18).

It is customary to step three steps back and then three steps forward before beginning the silent *Amidah*. According to the *Rokeach*, the source for this custom is rooted in the three Biblical verses that speak of "approaching": *Abraham came forward (Genesis* 18:23) when he implored God to save the inhabitants of Sodom; *Judah approached him*; and *Elijah the prophet approached (I Kings* 18:36).

When speaking to a human being, it is natural that one approaches him, hence Judah stepped forward even though he was already standing in front of Joseph. But how does this explain why we take three steps forward in prayer; certainly we come no closer to God by "moving toward" Him. That we do so indicates that the very essence of prayer is the desire to achieve greater closeness to God. When one wants to ask for something in prayer, he must feel a burning desire to actively bring himself closer to the One Above. Although this "closeness" is in spirit, not space, one gives this emotion concrete expression by stepping closer to Hashem (*R' Aharon Leib Steinman*).[1]

A careful reading of Judah's entreaty makes one realize that he added no new plea; he merely repeated the chain of events that had transpired up until this point. What did he seek to gain by this?

According to *Sfas Emes*, painful and stressful situations last only until one realizes that everything is the will of God, Who does only what is good for people— even when they cannot perceive it. This was Judah's purpose in rehashing the events; he wanted to bring himself to the realization that God had engineered it all for the benefit of Jacob's family and the emerging Jewish people.[2]

---

1. **Really Good.** *Mesilas Yesharim* (Chapter 1) writes: "True perfection is found only in cleaving to God. This is what King David meant when he said, *But as for me, God's nearness is my good (Psalms* 73:28) . . .. Only this is true goodness. All other things which people consider good are nothing more than hollow, meaningless foolishness."

2. **Pulling Strings.** When Jacob wanted the brothers to go back to Egypt for more food, they said they could not return without Benjamin. Jacob replied, *Why did you treat me so ill* by telling the man that you have another brother? The Midrash (*Bereishis Rabbah* 91:10) comments that Jacob never spoke inappropriately except for here. Hashem said, as it were, "I am busy establishing a kingdom over Egypt and he says, 'Why did you treat me so ill?' "

A great *rosh yeshivah* once told his students, "Whenever I see this Midrash, I know I must repent. When I began the yeshivah, there were days that I met such failure in raising funds and recruiting students that I said to myself,

Alternatively, when a Jew stands in front of a despot, pleading with him on behalf of another Jew or the Jewish people at large, in his heart of hearts, he is really praying to God. A Jew knows that the mortal ruler is nothing more than God's messenger, and that destiny is in His hands alone.[3]

According to the *Vilna Gaon,* this explains an enigmatic comment of the Talmud. When Queen Esther was ready to expose Haman as the one who wanted to exterminate her nation, King Ahasuerus asked her to identify the culprit. She exclaimed, *"A man who is an adversary and an enemy! This wicked Haman!"* (*Esther* 7:6). The Talmud (*Megillah* 16a) teaches that initially when she said *This wicked,* she pointed toward Ahaseurus, whereupon an angel pushed her hand in the direction of Haman. How could Esther have done such a potentially fatal thing? She had her chance to foil Haman and his genocidal decree by pointing directly at him; why would she have wanted to arouse Ahaseurus' ire by accusing him?

The *Vilna Gaon* explains: One's imagination is a powerful force. If someone has a particular person in mind, one may be speaking to Daniel and call him David, because at that moment David is on his mind; while consciously he is aware that he is speaking to Daniel, in his subconscious he is talking to David. Sometimes the subconscious comes to the fore and overwhelms the conscious.

Likewise, when the truly righteous stand in front of a mortal king, a judge, or anyone in a position of great power, they are consciously aware of whom they are facing, but deep inside their hearts they are pleading with God. Their external entreaties are addressed to the mortal king, while their internal cry is directed toward the true King. While their words are couched in terms understood by the despot, their inner meaning is transmitted to God.

Esther forgot for a moment that she was speaking to Ahaseurus; in her most inner self she stood in front of Hashem. Speaking to Him, she pointed to Ahaseurus, the true culprit. Only by grace of the angel pushing her hand was she saved from making a fatal error.

The same was true when Judah approached Joseph to plead for Benjamin. In the physical sense,

---

'Why am I doing this?' Hashem was busy putting all the pieces together and I could only say, 'Why did you treat me so ill'?"

3. **Public Servant.** When one realizes that success is ultimately dependent on one's relationship with God rather than on his efforts to persuade the powers that be, he is not disappointed when his lobbying efforts are less than effective.

In a moving letter to *R' Moshe Sherer, R' Yitzchak Hutner* places all this in perspective.

My dear and beloved . . .

At the very moment that I read of the negative decision of the U.S. Supreme Court [regarding federal aid to parochial schools] your image came before my eyes; the image remained there even after I put the newspaper down. From afar I felt your heartbeat; every tremor of your soul sent waves of trepidation through my spine. I felt powerfully compelled to speak to you words of encouragement and strengthening thoughts. I was unable to find relief until I picked up my pen to write to you a few words.

I mentioned to you the well-known adage of *R' Yisrael Salanter,* "One involved in public service must be committed to three principles. Never to be upset and angry, never to tire, and never to want to accomplish." Regarding the first two commitments you have succeeded outstandingly. I can personally testify that in the past you neither got angry nor tired. Now you must withstand the trial of remaining firm in the third commitment, not to want to accomplish [man must do, Hashem accomplishes].

"I likewise mentioned to you that we must always remember that all of the prayers and entreaties which we offer in merit of the *Akeidah* are based on an event which never came to fruition. The entire Jewish nation places its hopes and prayers on the *Akeidah,* but its merit is in no way diminished by the fact that it remained, in the practical realm, an unfulfilled idea.

I pray for you that Hashem provide you with encouragement and strength. I beg of you not to allow any softening of resolve or emotional distress to enter your camp. May your intensity of purpose remain strong and may you merit to be our and God's agent in your holy work.

With hope for the elevation of the honor of those who loyally pursue public service.

With love,
Yitzchak Hutner

he was speaking to the Egyptian viceroy, but deep in his heart, Judah approached God, praying that He would save him from losing his portion in this world and the next (*Zekan Aharon*).[4]

The Midrash (*Bereishis Rabbah* 93) reports that when Joseph seized Benjamin and told the brothers, *"The man in whose possession the goblet was found, only he shall be my slave,"* Judah responded by saying, "If you will seize Benjamin, what will be with the peace in our father's home?" Judah became angry and began to scream so loudly that even Chushim son of Dan, who was hearing impaired, heard Judah's screams and joined in.

Avnei Azel interprets this Midrash homiletically. Benjamin symbolizes the Jewish youths who have been torn from their heritage and from their Father in Heaven by an education antagonistic to the spirit and lifestyle of Jacob. While most people stand by apathetically, accepting this outrage as a fact of life rather than viewing it as a heartrending tragedy, there arise the Judahs of the nation, those who feel a personal sense of responsibility for the spiritual future of the Jewish people. They cannot sit by in peace, for they are *the servant who took responsibility for the youth* who see the loss of the youth as an unbearable catastrophe. When "Benjamin" is seized by those who seek to assimilate him into a foreign culture, the "Judahs" of the nation cry out, "What will become of the peace in our father's home?" Out of his deeply felt responsibility for the future of the nation and its youth,

"Judah" fights valiantly and pleads for their spiritual survival. His earth-shattering cries awaken even the "Chushims," those who are generally deaf to the spiritual plight of the nation, and arouse them from their apathetic slumber.[5]

וְהָיָה כִּרְאוֹתוֹ כִּי אֵין הַנַּעַר וָמֵת
It will happen that when he sees the youth is missing he will die (ibid. 31).

Rashi explains that the verse refers to Jacob, who would die of grief. Why did not Judah mention the grief that Benjamin's ten children would experience if something happened to him? The answer lies in the truism that the feelings of a parent for his child are much stronger than the feelings of a child for his parent. A Talmudic rule (*Sanhedrin* 72b) bears this out. If a father breaks into his son's home at night to commit robbery, the son may not kill his father in self-defense since we can be sure that the father comes only for money but would never kill the son, even if he tried to defend his property. Only if we clearly know otherwise may the child kill in self-defense.

On the other hand when the roles are reversed, the father may assume that the child will kill him if he resists (unless we know otherwise) and therefore the father may react accordingly. (See *Rambam Hilchos Geneivah* 9:10). Hence when Judah appealed to Joseph, he framed his plea in terms of what Benjamin's loss would do to Jacob rather than what it would do to Benjamin's children (*R' Menachem Mendel of Kotzk, R' Yerucham Warhaftig*).[6]

---

4. **Jewish Approach.** In this light, *Divrei Yisrael* offers a homiletical rendering of the verse: "And Judah approached Him." A Jew must always approach Hashem and say of himself, "Judah," — no matter what happens to me, I am a loyal Jew, and I will remain so forever."

5. **Torah Pioneer.** *R' Dov Lesser* spent the best years of his life traveling across North America, eliciting sympathy and support for Torah institutions and establishing community day schools, yeshivah high schools and *kollelim*. He once offered an insight that expressed his commitment to spreading Torah.

Jacob chose only Judah to be a pioneer in Egypt and establish a house of study in Goshen (see 46:28). Why did he single out Judah? Explained R' Dov, "Only someone who declares *I will personally guarantee him; of my own hand you can demand him* (43:9) can be entrusted with the building of Torah and the spiritual security of the people."

6. **Parental Care.** An old Yiddish maxim says that one mother can care for ten children but ten children cannot care for one mother.

R' Yechiel Meir of Ostrovtze explained why this is so. Many personality traits are universal, passed from generation to generation. The first parents, Adam and Eve, had biological children but no biological parents. Hence they passed on to all generations the trait of parental compassion for children, but having never experienced

כִּי עַבְדְּךָ עָרַב אֶת הַנַּעַר
For your servant took responsibility for the youth (ibid. 32).

To explain to the viceroy why only he stepped forward and argued so vehemently for Benjamin's release, Judah said that he alone had undertaken responsibility for Benjamin's return.

The Talmud teaches, כָּל יִשְׂרָאֵל עֲרֵבִים זֶה בָּזֶה, *All Jews are responsible for one another"* (*Shevuos* 39a). This is the basis for the duty to offer rebuke to a fellow Jew who engages in improper behavior. The word עָרַב, *took responsibility,* also means sweet. Only when we truly love a fellow Jew and see how sweet and pure he is can we offer constructive criticism. Only when spoken out of love and true concern can rebuke engender change.

The word also is related to תַּעֲרֹבֶת, *a mixture.* All Jews are elements of a huge compound called עַם יִשְׂרָאֵל, *the Jewish nation.* Every Jew has a vested interest in the physical and spiritual condition of his fellow Jew. Judah taught that responsibility to all Jews, for all time (*R' Menachem Mendel of Lubavitch*).

כִּי אֵיךְ אֶעֱלֶה אֶל אָבִי וְהַנַּעַר אֵינֶנּוּ אִתִּי
For how can I go up to my father if the youth is not with me (ibid. 34).

In a homiletical sense, this verse teaches the soul-searching that every Jew must do. "How can I go up to my Father in Heaven after my earthly sojourn, and my youthful years are no longer with me, having been wasted on mundane pursuits?" (*R' Yaakov Yosef of Polonoye*).

Likewise, every Jewish father must say to himself, "How can I leave this world and go up to my Father if my children are not with me, because I did not do enough to imbue them with the ideals of Torah and authentic Judaism?"[7]

R' Meir of Premishlan embellishes on this theme based on the Midrashic teaching that when God wanted to give the Torah to the Jewish people He asked for a guarantor who would vouchsafe that Jews would observe the commandments. The only guarantor God accepted were the young ones of the Jewish nation throughout its history. How then are we to come before God when our young ones have not been taught to study Torah and observe it? We, as God's servants, took responsibility through the loyalty of our youth. How then can we allow our children to become spiritually bankrupt?

פֶּן אֶרְאֶה בָרָע אֲשֶׁר יִמְצָא אֶת אָבִי
lest I see the evil that will befall my father (ibid.).

Initially Judah made his case with the viceroy based on the personal responsibility he undertook for Benjamin and that he, Judah, would lose his share in this world and the Next World if he did not honor his pledge. In conclusion, he focuses on the terrible pain the loss of Benjamin would cause his father.

Sfas Emes comments that in Judah's scale of values, the pain of his father was far more meaningful than his personal woe. He spoke of his personal vulnerability and then moved on to the issue of his father's anguish in order to impress upon the viceroy how deeply he felt about his father. When this became the major issue, the time was ripe for the crisis to finally resolve itself by Joseph revealing himself to his brothers.

This approach teaches how one should serve God. While it is acceptable to serve Him in order to merit success in this world and the Next World, the ultimate concern should be to do His will, "lest I

---

feelings of compassion toward biological parents, they could not pass this trait on to their children.

R' Menachem Mendel of Kotzk added: We are not nearly as concerned about the pain God suffers as He is about our pain. [When forced to choose between our desire to please our Father and yielding to our children's demands for things that pain God, we must take great care not to allow our parental "compassion" to win out.]

7. **Lost Youth.** Languishing in the Warsaw ghetto, with his world crumbling around him, *R' Klonymous Kalman of Piaczetzna* said to his followers: "Soon we will be taken to the *Akeidah*. How can we go up to our Father in Heaven when our youth are not with us? Many of them left the path of Torah because we stopped our efforts to educate them in the Torah way. We said to ourselves, 'The Nazis will anyway put them in the gas chambers.' How did we do such a thing?"

see the evil that will befall my Father" if I stray from His path.[8]

Background

Finally convinced that his brothers are truly concerned for his brother Benjamin and their father, Joseph decides that the time has come to reveal his true identity.

וְלֹא יָכֹל יוֹסֵף לְהִתְאַפֵּק לְכֹל הַנִּצָּבִים עָלָיו

Now Joseph could not restrain himself in the presence of all who stood before him (45:1).

Joseph ordered that everyone except his brothers should leave the room because he could not bear to embarrass his brothers in the presence of so many bystanders (*Rashi*). *Rashbam* disagrees, viewing the issue as one of self-image. Joseph did not want the royal entourage to see him crying.

How was *Rashi* so sure that Joseph was concerned with his brothers' honor and not his own? *Iturei Torah* notes that the next verse states that Joseph's crying was heard throughout the capital city and in the palace of Pharoah. Had his own honor been his primary concern, he would have controlled himself and not cried so loudly. Obviously, therefore, Joseph's concern was to save his brothers from embarrassment.

אֲנִי יוֹסֵף הַעוֹד אָבִי חָי וְלֹא יָכְלוּ אֶחָיו לַעֲנוֹת אֹתוֹ כִּי נִבְהֲלוּ מִפָּנָיו

"I am Joseph. Is my father still alive?" But his brothers could not answer him because they were left disconcerted in front of him (ibid. 3).

The Midrash teaches in the name of Abba Kohen Bardala: "Woe to us regarding the day of judgment; woe to us regarding the day of rebuke. Joseph was [almost] the youngest of the brothers, yet they could not respond to his rebuke. Certainly when God will rebuke each of us according to who he is, we certainly will be shocked into silence."

The Sage uses two terms: "the day of judgment" and "the day of rebuke." What is the difference between the two? Furthermore, what does the Midrash mean that "God will rebuke each of us *according to who he is*"? Lastly, after the brothers had consistently spoken of their father and the effect Benjamin's absence would have upon him, why did Joseph ask his brothers if Jacob was alive?

Beis HaLevi explains: Man lives with so much inconsistency and, in many ways, he is almost schizophrenic. "The day of judgment" refers to the time when man will be called before the bar of Divine Justice to account for his deeds, good and bad. "The day of rebuke" refers to the time when the glaring inconsistencies in our lives will be shown to us.

Often we have legitimate reasons and mitigating circumstances that, to some extent, justify our shortcomings. For example, when we are approached to contribute to a charitable cause or to help a friend in need, we may claim that times are hard, money is tight, and our obligations to family simply do not allow us to help others. Such excuses would be acceptable were we not to undermine our claims by our own behavior. We claim we cannot afford to help others, but the funds are there for a lavish vacation, home renovations, a new wardrobe, or a new or second car. On the day of rebuke, we will be shown *from our own actions* the flimsy quality of these self-justifications. Thus the Midrash speaks of God offering rebuke to each of us *according to who he is*.

Such was the rebuke offered by Joseph to his brothers. Their plea on behalf of Benjamin was based on the fatal effect it would have on Jacob. But Joseph said to them, *"I am Joseph! Is my father still alive?* If you are so concerned with your father's health and welfare, and you are so worried about what the loss of Benjamin will do to him, then why did you sell me?! I am Joseph whose disappearance was heartbreaking to my father! Is my father still alive? When you were ready to kill me, and then decided to sell me, did you consider whether our father would survive the shock?" Indicted by their own actions, the brothers were shocked into silence.

---

8. **Reputation on the Line.** *R' Eliyahu Meir Bloch* explains why Judah put his two worlds at risk in promising to return Benjamin to Jacob. He knew that the extra emotional pressure that is created when one has a strong personal stake in an outcome goes a long way in propelling one to exert himself beyond ordinary limits. While pride is often spiritually detrimental, it can sometimes spur one on to achievements that he might otherwise never reach.

Certainly when we will stand in front of God and He will rebuke us on the basis of our own inconsistencies, we, too, will be speechless.[9], [10]

Sfas Emes offers a different approach. The brothers were convinced that Joseph was a fantasizer, obsessed with delusions of grandeur. They understood his excessive concern with personal grooming (see *Genesis* 37:2, *Rashi* ad loc.) as indicative of narcissism. When Joseph revealed himself and proved to them that he was unaffected by the immoral climate of Egypt, they were embarrassed over how they had misjudged him. This is the very shame we will suffer on the day of rebuke, when we realize how mistaken we were in treating this world as an arena for physical pleasures, when in reality it was a land of spiritual opportunities. But then, it will be too late.[11], [12]

וְעַתָּה אַל תֵּעָצְבוּ וְאַל יִחַר בְּעֵינֵיכֶם כִּי מְכַרְתֶּם אֹתִי הֵנָּה כִּי לְמִחְיָה שְׁלָחַנִי אֱלֹקִים לִפְנֵיכֶם

And now, be not distressed nor reproach yourselves for having sold me here, for it was to be a provider that God sent me ahead of you (ibid. 5).

Joseph reiterates this point in verse 8: *And now it was not you who sent me here but God.* On the surface this seems to be an expression of kindness. Sensitive to the fact that his brothers were

---

9. **Innocent Bystander.** *R' Jacob Yuzef* offers a variation on this approach. When one combats a foe, one should be careful not to harm innocent bystanders. Certainly one would avoid hurting a relative or friend. Even the bloodthirsty Esau, who wanted to avenge himself against Jacob, refrained from doing so while their father was still alive. *And Esau thought, "May the days of mourning for my father draw near, then I will kill my brother Jacob"* (*Genesis* 27:41). Joseph rebuked his brothers on this very point. "*I am Joseph,* whom you all deemed worthy to be put to death. But why did you not have the decency to spare our father the pain of losing me? Was not my father still alive? Was not that important to you?"

10. **Insubordinate Misappropriation.** When one sins, he should be overcome with a terrible sense of shame. "God gave me the life, strength, ability and resources to serve Him. How could I have used His gifts against Him?" (*Sfas Emes*).

11. **Forgetting Father.** *R' Meir Shapiro* interpreted the verse homiletically. As Joseph listened without protest to Judah repeatedly referring to Jacob as "your servant my father," Joseph began to wonder, "Have I become desensitized to my father's honor? Has my love for him been extinguished?"

He therefore said to them, "*Is my father still alive* inside of me? I forgive you for having sold me as a slave to the Ishmaelites. I can rise above my terror when you threw me into a pit of snakes and scorpions. I can forgive you for putting me through all the travails I experienced in Egypt. But I cannot forgive you for separating me from my father for twenty-two years and extinguishing his love from my heart!"

[The Jewish people can accept the terrible pain that it experienced in the dark and bitter exile, but one thing we can never forgive: that its persecutions caused many of us to lose our love of our Father as a result of our separation from Him.]

12. **Horsemen.** Giving and receiving rebuke is a subtle art. As a rule *R' Yerucham Levovitz* spoke publicly only to his students in the Mirrer Yeshivah. Once he made an exception to this practice, but later regretted it. This happened when he visited a town and the head of the community said, "Rebbe, the Jews of this town are fine, upstanding people. Would you honor us with words of *mussar* in our synagogue?" R' Yerucham was in a quandary. On one hand, it was hard to refuse the request; on the other hand, he was sure that his tone and style might be too sharp for the people, even if he would attempt to soften them. Sure enough, as he spoke his heartfelt words, people started drifting out of the synagogue until very few were left.

Years later, he related the incident to his students and explained what happened. "Why do you think the townspeople took my words so personally that they left the synagogue, while you in the yeshivah soak up every word? I'll explain with a parable: When the first explorers landed on the American continent they brought horses with them. The natives, who had never seen horses before, were shocked to see this miraculous hybrid which was a combination of a four-legged animal on the bottom with a two-legged human on top. Before they recovered from their initial surprise, they were even more shocked to see the rider jump off the horse, thus making it clear that the person and the animal were two separate entities.

"Here in the yeshivah we know that the physical body is not the essence of man; the body is merely the horse upon which the soul rides. Those Jews, fine as they were, thought that the man and the horse were the same being. Thus when I spoke to their horse asking it to reign itself in, they were insulted and left."

suffering guilt feelings for having sold him and having wanted to kill him, Joseph calmed their consciences by minimizing their misdeeds and showing how he ultimately gained fame and power as a result of their actions.

In a deeper sense, Joseph's attitude may be seen as a reflection of the principle taught by the *Ramban* (*Exodus* 18:11, *Genesis* 15:14). In discussing the question of why the Egyptians should have been punished for enslaving the Jews when they were only carrying out God's decree, *Ramban* explains that they were punished only because they went beyond the Divine mandate and oppressed the Jews excessively. Had they merely enslaved the Jews but not treated them cruelly, the Egyptians would not have deserved punishment, for they would have been acting as God's messengers.

Understood in this light, Joseph was not merely seeking to assuage his brothers' consciences; he earnestly believed that his brothers were nothing more than God's agents to bring him to Egypt. They did nothing; God acted through them. Thus, one who suffers at the hands of another should consider his oppressor to be nothing more than God's enforcing arm, sent to carry out the Divine decree.

King David reacted in this fashion when he was forced to flee Jerusalem because of Absalom's rebellion (see *II Samuel* Ch. 16). As he trudged from his capital, Shimei ben Gera cursed him and pelted him with stones. Outraged, David's loyal follower Avishai wanted to kill Shimei for his cowardly and rebellious behavior, but David would not permit it. He told Avishai that "God told him [Shimei] to curse David" (ibid. v.10). *Sefer HaChinuch* (*mitzvah* 241) teaches this is the underlying reason behind the Biblical prohibition against taking revenge. Since whatever befalls man is the will of God, he has no reason to get angry at someone who is nothing more than the stick that God is using to strike him.

Why should one be angrier at the person who pained him than he is at the stone that was thrown at him? (*R' Yerucham Levovitz*)[13]

The Midrash teaches that the word וְעַתָּה, *and now*, is an expression of repentance. While the brothers had expressed regret earlier (42:21), it was not true repentance out of love and a desire to do the right thing as much as a reaction to the viceroy's demand that they bring Benjamin to him. Here, however, they experienced true repentance, which transforms sin into merit. What they had done to Joseph was done out of their personal animosity toward him, but now that they repented and changed their attitude toward him, all that was left was the act itself. That act, Joseph now told them, was an act of God. Thus they had no reason to be upset or to reproach themselves (*Simchas Aharon*).[14]

וְהִגַּדְתֶּם לְאָבִי אֶת כָּל כְּבוֹדִי בְּמִצְרָיִם
Therefore, tell my father of all my glory in Egypt (ibid. 13).

It seems odd that Joseph should be proud of the honor he received in Egypt and want to convey it to Jacob. *Be'er Moshe* interprets the verse as teaching that Joseph attributed all the honor he received in Egypt to the merit of Jacob. As the Sages teach, it was so imperative for Jacob to come to Egypt that had Joseph not been in Egypt to orchestrate his father's arrival, Jacob would have had to be dragged there in chains (*Midrash Rabbah* 86:2, see also *Shabbos* 89b). In order to spare Jacob this pain, his son rose to great power in Egypt. Thus, Joseph wanted Jacob to know his son's honor was entirely in his merit.

Ohr Yitzchak offers a variation on this theme. Joseph realized that his great rise to power in Egypt was because he had withstood temptation when Potiphar's wife tried to seduce him (39:12). According to the Sages, at the moment when his resistance was about to break, the image of his father appeared to him at the window and gave him the strength

---

13. **Personal Vendetta.** [This does not absolve the perpetrator of responsibility for his actions, since he did not act as he did simply to be God's agent. He had his own personal agenda, for which he will deservedly be punished.]

14. **Down the Road.** The implication of *and now* is that at some other point in time, they would have renewed reason to be upset over having sold Joseph. According to *Tzror HaMor*, this alludes to the Ten Martyrs who were killed during the Hadrianic period as a punishment for the sale of Joseph (as told in the *Yom Kippur Mussaf* service and in the *Kinnos* of *Tishah B'Av*).

to tear himself loose from her seductive charm (*Sotah* 36b). Hence all his honor came from his father.

R' Simchah Bunim of P'shis'cha viewed Joseph's words from a different perspective. Honor is a fantasy that makes us dependent on others for our own self-esteem. Nevertheless, as a wise student of human nature noted, when the *Mishnah* (*Avos* 4:28) speaks of jealousy, lust and glory as the traits that remove a man from the world it lists glory last, in accordance with the maxim אַחֲרוֹן אַחֲרוֹן חָבִיב, *the last is the most precious.*

Joseph's message to Jacob was that he had reached the point of spiritual maturity where honor was meaningless to him. That allowed him to be honored without becoming proud."[15]

וַיִּפֹּל עַל צַוְּארֵי בִנְיָמִן אָחִיו וַיֵּבְךְ וּבִנְיָמִן בָּכָה עַל צַוָּארָיו

Then he fell upon his brother Benjamin's neck and wept; and Benjamin wept upon his neck (ibid. 14).

Rashi comments that Joseph and Benjamin wept over the destruction of the sanctuaries that would be built in their respective territories. Joseph wept over the two Temples that would be built in Benjamin's portion of Jerusalem, while Benjamin wept over the Tabernacle at Shiloh, which would be erected in the portion of Joseph's son Ephraim (see *Megillah* 16b).

The analogy of the neck to the Sanctuary is based on the Sages' interpretation of the verse *As stately as the Tower of David is your neck* (*Song of Songs* 4:4) as a reference to the Temple (see *Berachos* 30a). *Avnei Nezer* explained that the neck connects the head to the rest of the body, symbolic of the connection between the spiritual soul (ensconced in the brain) and the physical body. The function of the Temple was to connect the spiritual and the physical, heaven to earth.[16] Prayers ascend to heaven by way of the Temple and God grants blessings to the Jewish people through the same conduit.[17]

Why at this moment of joy did Joseph and Benjamin see fit to cry over the destruction of the

---

15. **Phantom Chase.** The Sages teach (see *Eruvin* 13b) that honor chases after the one who runs away from it. Why should he be punished by having to accept honor when he so obviously does not want it? Answered *R' Menachem Mendel of Kotzk:* One who runs away from honor obviously views it as something to be reckoned with; otherwise he would ignore it. His punishment is that honor pursues him. One should view honor as something so foolish and detestable that it is not even to be reckoned with. Why run away from a phantom?

16. **Neck and Neck.** Two incidents, one in the Torah and one in the Prophets, assume new significance in light of the concept of the *Avnei Nezer*. When Esau encountered Jacob on the latter's way back from Laban, Esau kissed him. In the Torah scroll, there are dots over the word, *he kissed him,* indicating that there is a meaning beyond the literal one. The Midrash interprets this to mean that Esau sought to bite Jacob's neck, but, miraculously, Jacob's neck turned granite hard and Esau was unable to hurt him. The reason he tried to bite the neck was because, from Esau's perspective, there was an impregnable barrier between this world, which was Esau's, and the Next World, which was Jacob's. Jacob, however, "stole" the this-worldly blessings of Isaac because the purpose of life is to connect the spiritual and the temporal, imbuing the latter with the former. Thus Esau tried to bite Jacob's neck, which symbolized the connection of the spiritual and the physical.

When Eli, the Kohen Gadol and Judge of the Jewish people, was informed that the Ark had been captured by the Philistines, he fell backward and fatally broke his neck (*I Samuel* 4:18). He realized that without the Ark, the Sanctuary could no longer fully serve as the link between heaven and earth, a realization that was given physical expression by his broken neck (*Simchas Aharon*).

17. **Our Rain.** The prayer for rain is recited on *Shemini Atzeres*, the festival before the rainy season in *Eretz Yisrael*. Seemingly, this prayer should be recited in each country before its own rainy season. Nevertheless, all Jews pray for rain on the basis of the season in *Eretz Yisrael*, regardless of their place of residence. *R' Aryeh Tzvi Frommer* (*Eretz Tzvi*) explains: The Torah refers to *Eretz Yisrael* as "a Land that Hashem, your God, seeks out; the eyes of Hashem, your God, are always upon it from the beginning of the year to year's end" (*Deuteronomy* 11:12). Though God is omniscient and oversees the entire universe, His principal attention is focused on *Eretz Yisrael*, while the rest of the world enjoys His blessing on a secondary level. *Eretz Yisrael* serves as the conduit for God's beneficence on earth, and only after attending to its needs does He bless other lands (see *Rashi* ad loc.). The key to rain and prosperity around the globe lies in God's blessing the Land of Israel; therefore we pray that He grant rain to the Holy Land and that the blessing of rain flow from it to the rest of the world.

sanctuaries? Furthermore, why did each one of them weep over the destruction of the sanctuary found in the other one's territory?

R' Yechezkel of Kuzmir explained: When the two brothers were finally reunited, they realized that their twenty-two painful years of separation resulted from baseless hatred. Furthermore, they understood that hatred is so powerfully destructive a force that it would one day cause the destruction of the Temple.

The way to rectify hatred without cause is through love without cause. The most vibrant indication of such love is the ability to be moved by someone else's troubles more than by one's own. Likewise, one who truly loves another rejoices in the other's success more than in one's own.

Joseph and Benjamin cried over each other's tragedy to show that such tears are the remedy for tears brought on by baseless hatred. Just as שִׂנְאַת חִנָּם, *baseless hatred,* caused our exile, so אַהֲבַת חִנָּם, *baseless love,* will bring our redemption.[18]

וּלְבִנְיָמִן נָתַן שְׁלֹשׁ מֵאוֹת כֶּסֶף וְחָמֵשׁ חֲלִפֹת שְׂמָלֹת
but to Benjamin he gave three hundred pieces of silver and five changes of clothing (ibid. 22).

The Talmud (*Megillah* 16b) wonders why Joseph, who was a victim of the jealousy his father aroused by giving him a fine woolen tunic (see *Genesis* 37:3), would have aroused their jealousy again by giving his brother Benjamin a more lavish gift than he gave the others. The answer may lie in the *Rambam's* definition of perfect repentance. "When a person is presented with the opportunity to repeat a sin that he previously committed, yet he refrains as an act of repentance — although he finds himself in the same situation and circumstances — this is complete repentance" (*Hilchos Teshuvah* 2:1).

Sure that his brothers had repented their sin, Joseph created the same potential for jealousy so that, by not being jealous of Benjamin, they would demonstrate true and complete repentance (based on *Iturei Torah*).[19]

וּלְאָבִיו שָׁלַח כְּזֹאת עֲשָׂרָה חֲמֹרִים נֹשְׂאִים מִטּוּב מִצְרָיִם
And to his father he sent the following: ten he-donkeys laden with the best of Egypt (ibid. 23).

Why does the Torah emphasize that Joseph sent ten donkeys? *Maharal* (*Gevuros Hashem* 10) suggests that Joseph sought to imply that Jacob should not be angry with the brothers. The ten brothers who had sold him were like ten donkeys. Just as a donkey carries a load even though it is unaware of why it does so, likewise the brothers had no inkling of the Divine purpose that caused them to sell Joseph into slavery. They did so to bring the family in the preordained exile and eventually be redeemed and leave the country *with the best of Egypt.* (See *Genesis* 15:14, *and afterwards they will leave with great wealth.*)

According to *Rashi,* the phrase *the best of Egypt* refers to aged wine, which is pleasing to older people. What did Joseph symbolize with the gift? *Maayana Shel Torah* explains. R' Meir says: "Do not look at the vessel but what is in it; there is a new vessel filled with old wine" (*Avos* 4:27). Joseph wanted to tell his father that he was the personification of this *Mishnah.* His exterior was that of the viceroy of Egypt, but inside he remained the son of Jacob he had always been. The old and heady wine, the tradition and values he had observed in Jacob's

---

18. **Causeless Love.** The Talmud (*Berachos* 6b) teaches that one who brings joy to a bride and groom is considered to have rebuilt one of the ruins of Jerusalem. The bride and groom do not need others to bring them joy; they are happy anyway. On the other hand, the guests have no personal reason to rejoice; they do so only on behalf of the bride and groom. One who rejoices with them exhibits love without cause and is deemed as if he had rebuilt the ruins of Jerusalem, which was destroyed due to hatred without cause (*Yalkut Lekach Tov*).

19. **Déjà Vu.** When man truly repents, God provides him with the opportunity to commit the same sin, so that he can prove that his repentance is complete. Obviously, man may not voluntarily place himself in a situation of such great temptation, since he can never be certain that his passion will not overcome him again. Rather, God re-creates the same scenario for him, since God is confident that now, unlike the last time, the person has developed the spiritual fortitude to withstand the trial (*Tzidkas HaTzaddik* 73).

home, filled his very essence. Aware that his father was concerned that he may have been irreparably damaged in the immoral atmosphere of Egypt, Joseph meant to reassure him that only the vessel was new; the wine had not soured. He therefore sent aged wine, which is pleasing to those of an earlier era.[20]

Background

After receiving the news that Joseph is still alive, Jacob leaves the Land of Israel to go to Egypt, for what he initially thought would be a temporary stay. God reassures him that he need not fear going to Egypt, for God Himself would, as it were, accompany him to Egypt and accompany his children back to the Land of Israel.

וַיִּסַּע יִשְׂרָאֵל וְכָל אֲשֶׁר לוֹ וַיָּבֹא בְּאֵרָה שֶּׁבַע
וַיִּזְבַּח זְבָחִים לֵאלֹהֵי אָבִיו יִצְחָק

So Israel set out with all that he had and he came to Be'er-sheba where he slaughtered sacrifices to the God of his father Isaac (46:1).

Why did Jacob travel to Be'er-sheba on foot, unlike later when *the sons of Israel transported Jacob their father . . . in wagons* (verse 5)? Secondly, why did Jacob offer sacrifices to God specifically as the God of his father Isaac?

R' Moshe Mordechai Epstein explains: Jacob was afraid of leaving the Land of Israel to go to Egypt, terrified by the possibility that his children might assimilate into Egyptian culture and lose their emotional connection to the Land. He therefore traveled to Be'er-sheba to offer sacrifices to the God of his father Isaac who, unlike Abraham, never left the Land. He wanted to seek God's guidance as to whether he should follow his father's practice and remain in the Land at all costs.

Until he was sure that he was traveling to Egypt with God's approval, he felt it was wrong to make use of the wagons Pharaoh sent him specifically for that purpose. Only after receiving Divine approval to descend to Egypt did he travel by wagon.[21]

Sidduro Shel Shabbos offers another explanation as to why Jacob sacrificed to the God of Isaac. There are two ways one may react to having been saved from pain and trouble. One way is to be thankful to God for having saved him, although one would prefer to have never experienced the difficulty. A more elevated perspective is to realize that one's very suffering created the opportunity for God's Name to be sanctified by means of the salvation. One who shares this approach is happy over the pain as well, for he appreciates God's expressions of judgment just as he appreciates His expressions of Divine mercy. When the torturous saga of Joseph came full circle, Jacob sacrificed to the God of his father Isaac, the very embodiment of Divine justice.

כִּי תוֹעֲבַת מִצְרַיִם כָּל רֹעֵה צֹאן

Since all shepherds are abhorrent to Egyptians (ibid. 34).

Joseph gave his brothers advice that would serve the Jewish people well throughout their experiences in the exile. "Don't try to find favor in the eyes of your non-Jewish hosts. Don't seek to imitate their lifestyle or to become involved in their culture. The secret of Jewish survival in exile is to remain outsiders."

---

20. **Vintage Wine.** Old wine improves with age only if it was originally of high quality. If the wine was of inferior quality to begin with, it gets more and more spoiled as time goes on. One who brewed a life of spiritual quality while young can expect to improve with time. If his younger years were cheapened, it is rare that with age he will turn into an aromatic spiritual vintage (*R' Shloima Alter*).

R' Yitzchak Hutner explained why elderly people appreciate aged wine. Generally, time causes things to break down and disintegrate. Wine is one of the rare things that gets better with age. Old people, who are often made to feel obsolete, appreciate aged wine, for it encourages them to feel that they too get better with every day.

21. **Sighful Departure.** Even when a Jew must leave *Eretz Yisrael*, he is in no rush to do so. Although Jacob had been commanded to go to Egypt, and was coerced to abandon the palace of the King, he traveled by foot, unwilling to leave the Land a minute earlier than necessary. There are things one must do in life; nevertheless, he should do them with a sigh of resignation (*Zekan Aharon*).

Given the prosperity that he himself brought the country by serving the government, Joseph was sure that Pharaoh would try to enlist his brothers in governmental service. He therefore told Pharaoh openly that they were shepherds. Since all shepherds are abhorrent to Egyptians, Joseph ensured that Pharaoh would isolate them in Goshen (*Chidushei Harim*).[22]

22. **Eternal Outsiders.** According to the *Netziv*, this is the underlying philosophy expressed in the words of the Haggadah, "It is this that has stood firm by our fathers and us, for it was not one [nation] alone that rose against us." "This" refers not to God's promise of salvation and protection but to Israel's exile status as strangers and sojourners, for it is this quality that allows us to survive the spiritual ravages of exposure to foreign and often degenerate cultures. God's promise to Abraham that his *offspring will be aliens in a land not their own* (*Genesis* 15:13) was the greatest insurance against assimilation. Israel's refusal to allow its personal and national identity to be obliterated in the melting pots of exile has proven to be its most successful survival tactic. A Jew in exile should never feel completely at home or at ease; wherever he is, he must sense that he is not truly at home. This perception has saved us from disappearing from the stage of history.

Meshech Chochmah submits that this ability to remain separate from our host environment is alluded to by our raising of the cups when reciting "It is this." The decree to forbid wine touched by gentiles (see *Shabbos* 17b and *Yoreh Deah* 123:1) was intended to prevent intermarriage by limiting fraternization between Jews and non-Jews. Thus the very wine in our cups provided spiritual protection from our enemies. We offer praise to the wine itself, symbolic of our separatist posture while in exile among the nations. We are different and must never forget it!

As *R' Chaim of Volozhin* said, "If a Jew doesn't make *Kiddush* (to sanctify himself by maintaining a distinctly Jewish lifestyle), then the non-Jew will make *Havdalah* for him (by making the Jew realize he is truly different)."

פרשת ויחי 🙠
Parashas Vayechi

Background

Shortly before his death, Jacob summons Joseph and asks him to swear that he will bury him in the Cave of Machpelah where his forefathers were interred. Jacob then blesses Joseph's sons, Ephraim and Manasseh, granting them the status of tribes, but giving primacy to the younger Ephraim over the older Manasseh.

וַיְחִי יַעֲקֹב בְּאֶרֶץ מִצְרַיִם
Jacob lived in the land of Egypt (47:28).

R' *Amiel* notes that both *parshiyos* which focus on the death of great people begin with and are named for expressions of life with which they begin. The *parashah* that speaks of Sarah's death is called *Chayei Sarah* (the life of Sarah), while our *parashah*, which describes the death of Jacob, is entitled *Vayechi* (Jacob lived).

The good deeds of the righteous live on, making them immortal. Their lives exert a lasting influence on ours, their life's work is the spiritual heritage of generations to come, and it is from them that we inherit our authentic Torah culture. As the Sages taught, "Even in [physical] death the righteous live on" (*Berachos* 18a).[1],[2]

Rashi notes that the *parashah* is סְתוּמָה, *closed,* meaning that the Torah scroll leaves no space between this and the previous *parashah*. R' *Tzadok HaKohen of Lublin* explains why this is so. Much of this *parashah*'s subject matter is beyond human comprehension. Jacob had been in exile before — fleeing from Esau and living with Laban — and had returned to the Land of Israel after surviving them both. Why did he have to descend to the immoral climate of Egypt so that his descendants would be able to return to the Land in triumph? Why did the spiritual gestation of the nation of Israel have to occur in decadent Egypt of all

---

1. **Really Living.** *Oznayim L'Torah* presents another perspective. In a sense, "real life" begin only after one's physical demise. The righteous, who live with the perspective that this world is like a lobby before the "banquet hall" of the World to Come (see *Avos* 4:21), understand that only after they leave this world do they really come alive.

2. **Hidden Treasure.** This holds a profound lesson that teaches a survival tactic with which to weather our long exile. The spiritual descent of our people seems to worsen with each generation, making us wonder how we will ever merit redemption. The answer lies in realizing how much of our spiritual treasures were granted us in the exile. Whether the Torah in the desert or the Talmud in Babylonia, the *Rif* in North Africa or the *Rema* in Poland, some of the greatest revelations of Torah occurred under the dark cloud of the Diaspora.

As R' *Simchah Bunim of P'shis'cha* said: "While the spiritual dimensions of the souls shrink with succeeding generations, the point of truth (*pintele emes*) in the hearts of the Jewish people becomes purer and more refined as time goes on."

places? Why did the Jewish people have to receive the Torah in the desert? Would it not have been more appropriate for them to receive it in the Holy Land?

The *parashah* is סְתוּמָה, *closed*, because the answers to these questions are beyond the human intellect. As the Sages taught, the spaces in the Torah between paragraphs and chapters served to provide Moses with a pause, in order to contemplate the previous text (see *Rashi, Leviticus* 1:1). But in our case, such contemplation would be futile and was therefore unnecessary.

Rashi suggests that upon Jacob's death, the hearts of the children of Israel "closed," in expectation of the impending bondage. Although the actual, physical bondage began only upon the death of Joseph and all his brothers over seventy-five years later, the spiritual aspect of exile began when Jacob died. Their eyes and hearts became callous to the eternal truth that emanates from the soul. Their vision became so beclouded that they began to view themselves and their lives from a shallow, physical perspective. This narrow, mistaken perception of life is the very essence of exile (*Sfas Emes*).[3]

Taam V'Daas offers a different viewpoint. As long as Jacob was alive, he and his children remained aware that they were living only temporarily in a foreign land with "foreign" values. When Jacob passed on, however, his descendants became enamored by the wealthy, leisurely atmosphere of Egypt. Their eyes became blinded and their hearts desensitized to the fact that they were really living in a spiritual snake pit.[4] This blindness was symptomatic of real exile, for a truly free soul senses, even in good times, that a Jew has no real place in Egypt and rightfully belongs only in the Land of Israel.

Even the best exile breeds spiritual blindness and insensitivity. When we reach the point where we feel totally at home, we should know that we are really in exile.

וַיִּקְרְבוּ יְמֵי יִשְׂרָאֵל לָמוּת
The time approached for Israel to die (ibid. 29).

When referring to Jacob's life, the Torah says *Jacob lived*, yet here it speaks of *Israel's* impending death. Why does the Torah use different names? *Rabbeinu Bachya* suggests that the

---

3. **Blindly Insensitive.** In good times, when the Jewish people act in accordance with their status as children of Hashem, God says to them: *My child, give your heart to Me, and your eyes will desire My ways (Proverbs 23:26).* He calls upon them to focus their eyes and hearts heavenward, ready to receive the Presence of God in their lives and hearts. Once Jacob died and the spiritual impurity of Egypt invaded their systems, the Jews began to fall into the trap of following their hearts (heresy) and their eyes (immorality). Thus their eyes and hearts were closed to the message of Godliness and sanctity. This spiritual blindness and callousness of heart is the very essence of exile. Our redemption is impeded to this very day by this spiritual blockage (*Nesivos Shalom*).

4. **Too Comfortable.** If *Vayechi* is "closed" due to the death of Jacob, it would seem more appropriate that the space between the end of *Vayechi* (when Jacob actually died) and the beginning of *Shemos* be closed. Why is the closure between *Vayigash* and *Vayechi*?

She'aris Menachem suggests that it was at the end of *Vayigash* that the Jews began to feel comfortable in Egypt. The verse *Thus Israel settled in the land of Egypt in the region of Goshen; **they acquired property in it** (47:27)* indicates that they no longer viewed themselves as aliens who were sojourning in Egypt but rather as permanent residents. This was indicative of the closure of their spiritual eyes and hearts; thus, the end of *Vayigash* is closed (*Kli Yakar*).

R' S.R. Hirsch sees this as the underlying theme of *Rashi*'s explanation as to why Jacob asked to be interred in the Land of Israel. Rashi cites three reasons why Jacob did not want to be buried in Egypt. First, he did not want to be subjected to the lice that would plague Egypt during the ten plagues. Second, he wished to avoid the painful process of arriving in Israel in order to be resurrected in the End of Days. Lastly, he feared that were he to be buried in Egypt, his tomb would be enshrined and worshiped by the Egyptians. Why doesn't *Rashi* simply explain that Jacob wanted to be buried near his forefathers in the Cave of Machpelah? *Rashi* understood that Jacob intended to demean the Egyptian sojourn in the eyes of his offspring, as if to say, "You want to live in Egypt?! I don't even want to be *buried* there!" Once Jacob was gone, this lesson was lost. Complacent in Egypt, the Jews left themselves open for the worst.

name "Jacob" refers to his physical existence, while "Israel" denotes his spiritual life. Although one's spiritual life is his primary realm of existence, one may not neglect his physical dimension since life in this world is not viable without it. [It is in this vein that the Sages taught that Jacob was given the new name Israel. The name Jacob was not removed from him; rather, Israel would become his primary name, and Jacob his secondary one (*Berachos* 13a).] On the other hand, one who makes his physical needs primary and his service of God secondary misses the very essence of life.

When speaking of life in this temporal world, the Torah uses the term *Jacob lived.* Only when he was on the threshold of death, just before his body was about to expire and his soul to ascend to a more pristine level of existence, does the Torah call him *Israel.* [5]

Our verse might be rendered "the *days* of Israel (rather than Jacob himself) came close to dying." The righteous imbue every moment of life with eternity. Thus the Sages teach that the righteous live on even in death, because they live on in their legacy of deeds, teachings, children and students who follow their path. Only their days in this world expire; but their essence lives on forever! (*R' Eazer Shach*).

חֶסֶד וֶאֱמֶת
Kindness and truth (ibid.).

The kindness shown to the dead is true and purely altruistic, for the benefactor does not expect repayment (*Rashi*).[6] Although kindness shown to the dead *is* repaid, in the sense that "One who eulogizes others will be properly eulogized, one who arranges for the burial of others will himself be buried" (*Moed Katan* 28b), nevertheless this is not the type of repayment that one eagerly awaits. According to the *Skulener Rebbe,* Joseph performed both kindness and an act of truth by not burying Jacob in Egypt. By saving him from the plague of lice and the degrading after-death return to Israel, he acted kindly toward his father. Furthermore, he served truth by assuring that Jacob's tomb not be turned into a shrine for idolatry.

According to *Sfas Emes*, Jacob said that burying him in *Eretz Yisrael* was not only an act of *kindness*, but also an acknowledgement of the *truth*. Unlike people who spend their entire lives outside the Land yet want to be buried there, Jacob said, "My emotional attachment to the Land has never been severed. Even when Providence forced me to leave, it was always a temporary leave of absence, for my heart never left the Land. To bury me in Israel is not only kindness but also the truth."[7]

---

5. **Truly Free.** We speak of someone who died as having been נִפְטָר (from the root פָּטוּר, *free* or *absolved*), i.e., he has been freed from this life. While this physical world is the only place where man can grow spiritually, its temporal existence is still a terrible burden for the soul to endure. Furthermore, as long as one is alive, he must bear the pressure of the ongoing battle with his evil inclination. When he dies, he is finally exempted from these travails; he is נִפְטָר (absolved) from the yoke of this temporal world (*R' Yaakov Aharon of Aleksander*).

6. **True Kindness.** The Torah is called truth (*Malachi* 2:6) and kindness (*Proverbs* 31:26). Our involvement in Torah and *mitzvos* should be an altruistic expression of our love for God and our gratitude to Him. We should not be awaiting reward [see *Avos* 1:3] (*R' Yisrael of Modhzitz*).

7. **Deserving the Land.** Shortly after learning that he was terminally ill, *R' Meir Kotler* wrote his brother about his thoughts concerning *Eretz Yisrael*. "Let me reveal to you the reasons why I want to go [to *Eretz Yisrael*] now. First, I don't know how much time I have left to be among the 'sons of Zion.' Second, but primarily, I want to fulfill many of the *mitzvos* before . . . Some can be fulfilled only there, while others, although not intrinsically linked to the Land, are much easier to fulfill there, where the conditions for fulfillment are more readily available. One must fulfill every mitzvah at least once in his lifetime and 'one who prepares on *Erev Shabbos* will [have food to] eat on Shabbos. This is true regardless of whether it is a long *Erev Shabbos* in the summer or one of the short winter Fridays. One who prepares will eat; one who doesn't prepare won't eat.

"There is yet another reason why I want to travel to *Eretz Yisrael*, although I am terribly embarrassed to put it to paper: I remember when *R' Meir Feist zt"l* passed away and it became known that he wanted to be buried in America. We all were surprised that one with such a deep love for Zion would not want to be buried 'beneath the Altar' [in Jerusalem]. I believe, and our father *shlita* (R' Schneur Kotler) agreed with me, that his decision to be buried in America was based on the Midrash which teaches that Hashem says you came and defiled My Land. In

וְעַתָּה שְׁנֵי בָנֶיךָ הַנּוֹלָדִים לְךָ בְּאֶרֶץ מִצְרַיִם עַד בֹּאִי אֵלֶיךָ מִצְרַיְמָה לִי הֵם אֶפְרַיִם וּמְנַשֶּׁה כִּרְאוּבֵן וְשִׁמְעוֹן יִהְיוּ לִי

And now your two sons who were born to you in the land of Egypt before my coming to you in Egypt shall be mine; Ephraim and Manasseh shall be mine like Reuben and Simeon (48:5).

Maharal explains that Jacob's lengthy description of Ephraim and Manasseh captures their uniqueness. To be able to withstand a hostile environment is a considerable feat, but it is even more remarkable when one lacks any living link to the tradition. Ephraim and Manasseh grew up in Egypt, the very antithesis of Jewish purity. If they had had at least some exposure to Jacob, they might have been expected to survive as loyal Jews, but, as Jacob said, they were born *before my coming to you in Egypt,* yet they were still as pure as Jacob's own children. He therefore elevated them to that same status: *Ephraim and Manasseh shall be mine like Reuben and Simeon.*

For this reason, the Torah teaches us to bless our children to be like Ephraim and Manasseh, rather than like Abraham, Isaac and Jacob. As R' Shmuel Hominer explains, we bless every Jewish child that he be able to emulate Ephraim and Manasseh by rising above the negative influence of his surroundings and linking himself to his heritage.[8]

וַאֲנִי בְּבֹאִי מִפַּדָּן מֵתָה עָלַי רָחֵל . . .

But as for me — when I came from Paddan, Rachel died on me . . . (ibid. 7).

Jacob sensed that Joseph might not be willing to bury him in the Cave of Machpelah, since

Jacob himself did not do so for Joseph's mother Rachel. Jacob explained that God commanded him to bury Rachel on the roadside so that her soul could help the Jewish people when Nebuzaradan, the chief general of King Nebuchadnezzar of Babylon, led them into captivity after the fall of the First Temple (see II *Kings* 25:8). When the Jews were trudging into exile along the road to Bethlehem, tormented, hungry and exhausted, they passed Rachel's grave. Her soul came to God, as it were, and wept for her children.

The other Patriarchs and Matriarchs, too, prayed, but only her tears were accepted by God.

The Midrash (*Eichah Rabbah—Introduction*) explains: Rachel said to God, "What did my children do that You brought such terrible calamities upon them? Is it because they introduced idolatry into their homes, which is equivalent to a disloyal husband who brings another wife into his home? I deeply loved my future husband Jacob; he worked for seven years in order to marry me. We suspected that my father Laban might substitute my sister Leah for me, and we decided on a secret password and signal so that he would know if there was any chicanery. Laban *did* try to trick Jacob, but I knew my sister would be humiliated if Jacob found her out. I took the initiative and willingly told her the secret signal. If I, a mere mortal, had mercy on my sister and allowed 'another woman' into my home, certainly You Who are a Merciful King should have compassion on Your children!"

God responded, "*Your work will be rewarded . . . and your children will return to their border.*" (*Jeremiah* 31:15-16).

Only Rachel could utter such words of defense

---

your lifetime you didn't come and now in death you come?" Since ultimately he did not merit to attach himself to the Land, he felt it improper to be buried there.

"Even though I am as worthless as I am — would it be that I was as careful about explicit commandments — nonetheless this issue worries me. If I would be able to be in *Eretz Yisrael* before, I would feel much better [about being buried there]. . ."

8. **Bridging the Gap.** R' Shmuel Yaakov Borenstein adds that it is almost axiomatic that there is spiritual attrition as we pass from one generation to the next. "If the earlier generations were angels we are mere mortals. If they were mortals then we are donkeys," teach the Sages (*Berachos* 38b). Ephraim and Manasseh were exceptions to the rule. Although they were born into a later generation, they succeeded in reversing the spiritual downturn and linking themselves to an earlier time. Although they were not born as tribal ancestors, they reached the spiritual level of those who were. Thus we bless our children, "May you supersede the natural limitations of your time and link yourselves to the spiritual level of your predecessors."

on behalf of her children. God knew this and wanted it to happen. That is why He wanted her buried on the roadside.[9]

וַיַּרְא יִשְׂרָאֵל אֶת בְּנֵי יוֹסֵף וַיֹּאמֶר מִי אֵלֶּה
Then Israel saw Joseph's sons and he said, "Who are these?" (ibid. 8).

Rashi explains Jacob's question as meaning, "Where did these children who are unfit for blessing come from?" Such a question seems hard to understand. Jacob had been with Ephraim and Manasseh for seventeen years in Egypt; why now did he suddenly find them unworthy of blessing? *R' Zalman Sorotzkin* offers the following perspective:

Certain types of behavior, while appropriate for the average person, do not befit one who is more prestigious and refined. One who occupies a position of leadership must set an example for others and maintain higher standards.[10] This is the thrust of the prayer's description of Rosh Hashanah as a day of judgment of מַעֲשֵׂי אִישׁ וּפְקֻדָּתוֹ, *the actions of man and his appointment*, i.e., his position in life. When God judges man, He takes into account not only the deeds themselves, but also his station in life and the community.[11]

As long as Ephraim and Manasseh were merely Joseph's sons, their behavior pleased Jacob. Now that he had granted them the elevated status of tribes, however, they were answerable to a higher standard. Viewed in this new light, Jacob thought them unfit for blessing. Joseph reassured his father that they were fit for blessing in spite of the wicked descendants who would emerge from them. (Jeraboam and Ahab from Ephraim; Yehu and his sons from Manasseh. See *I Kings* 11:26-14:20, 16:28.)

Joseph replied to Jacob's question: *They are my sons whom God has given me here* (ibid. 9). His intention was to apologize for his sons and to explain that perhaps it was because they were exposed to Egyptian culture that they were less than what one might expect from Jacob's grandchildren. Jacob replied, *Bring them to me if you please and I will bless them* (ibid.). Let them become close to me and I will raise them spiritually to the point that they will be fit for my blessing.

Joseph told Jacob, "They are *my* sons, educated

---

9. **Tears of a Mother.** *R' Chaim Shmulevitz* would frequently go to pray at Rachel's tomb. He related to his students what he said to "Mother Rachel." He said, "Mother, the prophet asked you to stop crying but I, your son Chaim, say, ''וויין מאמע וויין, Cry Mother, cry! Cry for your children and beg God to have mercy on them!''

10. **Filling a Role.** According to *Malbim,* the difference between one's private behavior and his public persona is the key to understanding the difference between the sin of King Saul and that of King David. The Sages teach that David sinned more than once, yet he retained his throne, while Saul sinned only once (in not killing the Amalekites), yet his was a fatal flaw.

David's "misbehaviors" were on a personal level and did not affect the status of his kingdom, while Saul misbehaved *in his role as king*, and as such lost the monarchy. David was judged on *the actions of man* while Saul was indicted for his failure with regard to *his appointment*.

[Parents and teachers must always know that their behavior is not merely a matter of personal choice. They serve as a moral and ethical compass for their children, subtly imbuing them with standards for life. They must judge themselves not only in terms of *the actions of man*, but even more so in relation to *his appointment*.]

11. **Saving Grace.** *R' E. E. Dessler* views this judgment in terms of one's position as frequently providing one with a saving grace. The *Zohar* writes that on the first day of Rosh Hashanah, God judges with "severe judgment," while on the second day, He exercises "softened judgment." R' Dessler explains that on the first day, God judges us according to our actions and behavior. If we are not found meritorious on a personal level, God judges us again, on the second day, taking into consideration the role we play in providing benefit to others or to the community at large.

For example, one's personal life may leave much to be desired, but if he provides support for a Torah scholar whose teachings inspire many to live a Torah life or whose Torah learning provides existence to the world, he may be judged kindly. Similarly, one's role in the community or even something that God knows he or his offspring will do in the future may be enough to earn him mercy in God's judgment. Thus while his *actions* are not enough, he may be saved because of *his appointment*.

in the same spirit that you educated me." By making the utmost effort to educate his sons in his father's path, despite the hostile environment of Egypt, Joseph succeeded in making them fit for blessing; thus, Jacob agreed to bless them (*Chafetz Chaim*).[12]

וַיִּשְׁלַח יִשְׂרָאֵל אֶת יְמִינוֹ וַיָּשֶׁת עַל רֹאשׁ אֶפְרַיִם וְהוּא הַצָּעִיר

But Israel extended his right hand and laid it on Ephraim's head and he was the younger (ibid. 14).

The *Chafetz Chaim* suggests rendering וְהוּא הַצָּעִיר as *for he was the younger.* The reason Ephraim was blessed before Manasseh was *because* he was the younger. His humility, his ability to view himself as the younger and less significant than his brother made him fit for blessing.

Jacob reiterated this point when he said *yet his younger [smaller] brother shall become greater than he* (verse 19). By making himself small (humble), Ephraim became truly great.[13]

In Jacob's use of both his right and his left hands, the verse has a homiletical message on how to raise young people. The Sages teach that one should bring young ones close with his right (stronger) hand while pushing them away with the left. This implies a dual approach; one must show much love and encouragement, but also firmness and restraint. In seeking to inculcate our children with Torah values we must make a strong effort to offer them a warm, caring sense of closeness. On the other hand, this must be tempered by a sense of reverence so that familiarity does not breed contempt and so that they know they must earn approval. Thus Jacob sent out his right, stronger hand toward Ephraim for he was the younger one. Our full strength must be dedicated to reaching out to our youth (*Likutei Amarim*).[14]

---

12. **Not Enough.** A mother asked the *Chafetz Chaim* for a blessing that her son become a great *talmid chacham*. He became uncharacteristically agitated. "You are mistaken if you think that my blessing can accomplish this. For success at Torah, blessings are not enough — one must act. Send you son to a good yeshivah and let him labor at Torah study under the tutelage of God-fearing teachers. Let him be surrounded with good friends with whom he can study and grow, and who will be a good influence. Then — maybe then — you will merit a son who is a true scholar. My blessing is not enough."

13. **Smaller Is Better.** *Maharal (Gur Aryeh, Numbers* 21:35) explains that physical size is indicative of dimensions, a symbol of corporeal things, while the spiritual takes up no space. Hence Jacob is called "her young [small] son" (*Genesis* 27:15), for his physical smallness is symbolic of his spiritual orientation.

14. **Far Yet Close.** In his short volume on education, the late *Slonimer Rebbe* dealt with this teaching of the Sages. By saying that we must bring students close to us "with the right hand" yet simultaneously we must push them back and distance them "with the left," the Sages offered a powerful insight into the art of education. These two fundamental approaches seem to contradict each other. On the one hand, successful education is to a great extent contingent upon the student loving and consequently trusting his teacher. When a student is confident that his success and well-being are the teacher's foremost concerns, the teacher's words and expectations have the maximum effect. Otherwise, the chances of success are negligible. On the other hand, there must be a certain sense of fear in students, since proper discipline and respect are crucial to success.

The resolution of this apparent contradiction is the instruction to use both "right" and "left" in relating to students. There must be a proper balance of the two, so that the right hand, which symbolizes love, is balanced by the left, which symbolizes the ability to maintain the proper respect and discipline. This calls for a delicate combination, with love being the more dominant emotion and fear the weaker but necessary counterbalance. Even when disciplining one's charges, it is critical that the child's love remains strong enough to survive the temporary distancing. Furthermore, even when he disciplines, the teacher must be sure that the students know he still loves them. Children are very perceptive; they know who truly loves them and who only says so. This is one of the most difficult challenges in education — to continue to love even students who are annoying, aggravating and impudent.

If the teacher cannot maintain this balance, it is better to err on the side of giving too much love rather than engendering too much fear. Without love between teacher and student, successful education is simply not viable (*Nesivos Shalom — Nesivei Chinuch*).

[124] ספר בראשית: פרשת ויחי

וַיְבָרֶךְ אֶת יוֹסֵף
He blessed Joseph (ibid. 15).

The *Zohar* questions why the Torah speaks of blessing Joseph, when what follows is a blessing to Ephraim and Manasseh. He explains that the greatest blessing one can grant a parent is to bless his children.

Likutei Ritzba elaborates: When one's children follow in one's righteous footsteps, he is proud that they bear his name. But if they abandon their heritage, their parents become uncomfortable with the association. Here Jacob blessed Ephraim and Manasseh that they would bear his name and the name of his forefathers. This was the greatest blessing that Joseph could receive.

הָאֱלֹקִים הָרֹעֶה אֹתִי מֵעוֹדִי עַד הַיּוֹם הַזֶּה
God, Who shepherds me from my inception until this day (ibid.).

Malbim explains the shepherding metaphor. A shepherd tends his flock without checking to see if their behavior justifies it. So God shepherds man, granting him sustenance even when he doesn't deserve it.[15]

Ramban renders הָרֹעֶה אֹתִי as [God] *Who was my friend,* relating it to רֵעֲךָ as in *Do not forsake your friend and the friend of your father* (Proverbs 27:10).

Our forefathers sense of unity with God gave them an almost friendlike relationship. They sensed that, like a close friend, God "walked" alongside them, helping them on their way through life.[16]

וַיִּקְרֵא בָהֶם שְׁמִי וְשֵׁם אֲבֹתַי אַבְרָהָם וְיִצְחָק
and may my name be declared upon them and the names of my forefathers, Abraham and Isaac (ibid. 16).

The Talmud teaches that once a family has three consecutive generations commited to Torah, the Torah always "returns" to the family (*Bava Metzia* 85a). If so, since all Jews are descendants of the three Patriarchs, how can so many be ignorant of the Torah?

R' Chaim of Volozhin answered with a parable. A prestigious minister used to make an annual trip to a certain village, where he stayed at the same lodgings every year. When his host passed away, he returned to the same home, confident that the heirs would welcome him as joyously as their father had. The minister arrived and knocked on the door. No one came out to greet him. Understanding that he was no longer welcome, he sought accommodations elsewhere.

Similarly, it is true that the Torah *returns* to its lodgings generation after generation as long as it is made to feel welcome. However, if its erstwhile hosts are not home for it, it must go elsewhere.

בְּךָ יְבָרֵךְ יִשְׂרָאֵל לֵאמֹר יְשִׂמְךָ אֱלֹקִים כְּאֶפְרַיִם וְכִמְנַשֶּׁה
By you shall Israel bless saying, "May God make you like Ephraim and Manasseh" (ibid. 20).

While most commentators view the blessing as "May God make you like Ephraim *or* Manasseh," *Igra D'Kallah* interprets it as Ephraim *and* Manasseh.

---

15. **Sustained by the Shepherd.** *Taam V'Daas* takes the simile a step further. Just as it never occurs to the sheep that they might graze on their own, and they are sure that it is the shepherd that sustains them, so we must realize that our financial success and sustenance are not really in our hands, but come from our Shepherd. As King Solomon says, *nor does bread come to the wise* (Ecclesiastes 9:11). Experience shows that many people have finely honed business acumen yet lack basic necessities, while others come into great wealth with no business sense at all.

16. **Symbiotic Sensitivity.** This sense of unifying friendship underlies the appellation רֵעִים הָאֲהוּבִים, *the beloved companions,* used in the Seven Blessings recited under the *chuppah.* Husbands and wives do not regard their spouses as an "other," but rather as complementary parts of themselves. *R' Aryeh Levin's* wife once felt pain in her foot. When they went to the doctor, R' Aryeh said, "Our foot hurts."

We enjoy this type of relationship with God, as the prophet says, *In all their [Israel's] pain it is painful to Him* (Isaiah 63:9). The contrary is also true, for a Jew feels God's pain when man fails to carry out His will.

The joy that comes with life's blessings is frequently dampened by the jealousy others feel toward the blessed one. Furthermore, the one chosen to receive blessings may become haughty and arrogant. Jacob blessed the younger Ephraim first and only afterwards did he bless Manasseh. Nevertheless, Ephraim did not become arrogant, nor did Manasseh become jealous. This was unlike Jacob's blessing to Joseph, which spawned jealousy. We therefore bless our children that all of life's gifts and blessings bring them joy without generating jealousy or arrogance.

אֲשֶׁר לָקַחְתִּי מִיַּד הָאֱמֹרִי בְּחַרְבִּי וּבְקַשְׁתִּי
which I took from the hand of the Emorite with my sword and with my bow (ibid. 22).

Targum Onkelos (see *Bava Basra* 123a) explains that the *sword* alludes to prayer, and the *bow* to prayer. "Why," asks *R' Avraham Aharon of Constantin*, "does the *Targum* not interpret the verse literally, as referring to the weaponry Simeon and Levi used in the battle against Shechem?" He explains, that in war, the first ones to fight are the archers — like modern artillery or bombers — and afterwards the infantry joins the fray. Thus, if Jacob was referring to the military engagement, he should have mentioned the *bow* before the *sword.* Obviously, therefore, the weaponry is meant symbolically.

Alternatively, man is born with an evil inclination that is part of his psyche and therefore dwells at close quarters. The first step in battling evil is to move it out of one's immediate territory. After one succeeds in doing so, he is ready to force the evil inclination to retreat without any possibility of counterattack. Thus man must first attack evil with the *sword* intended for face-to-face combat. Only afterwards is he ready to fire his *bow* from afar, endeavoring to keep his evil inclination from coming back upon him. Jacob viewed his capture of Shechem as a result of his battle with evil which he fought with his sword and then with his bow. He evicted the evil persuader and then succeeded in keeping him at bay.[17]

The commentators see multiple allusions in the warfare/prayer nexus. According to *R' Yitzchak Zev Soloveitchik of Brisk*, the two similes (sword and bow) refer to two types of prayer. The regular prayers established by the Men of the Great Assembly are like a sword which is so sharp and lethal that it wounds, if not kills, almost on contact. Personal petitions are like a bow. Not imbued with the power of the Men of the Great Assembly, who composed the standard prayers, the personal petition is only as powerful as the concentration and intent we put into it. The arrow itself is not sharp and in itself can do little damage. Its power lies in the strength of the archer who pulls the bow tightly and shoots the arrow speedily toward his target.[18], [19]

Maharsha views the two similes for prayer as

---

17. **Spiritual Strategy.** The *Netziv* presents the simile from a different angle. When an army targets a general or some other important personage, there are two stages in taking the prey. First, they use their swords to clear the area and thus expose the target. Only then can the snipers take aim and shoot. The same is true of prayer. Our "target" is that God answer our prayers and grant our requests, but sometimes our spiritual stature is such that many negative forces impede our prayers. We must therefore pray that He first remove that which stands in the way of our prayers, and only then can we hope that our requests will come before God. Initially our prayers must function as a sword; only afterwards can they be effective as a bow.

18. **Standard Prayer.** The standardized prayers are effective, regardless of who is praying. Only when one makes a personal request does one's spiritual strength make a difference. It is for this reason that the Sages teach that one who has a sick person at home should ask a Torah scholar to pray on his behalf (*Bava Basra* 116a).

19. **Shooting in a Second.** *R' Menachem Mendel of Kotzk* explains why prayer is like a bow. The tighter one pulls on the bow, the higher and farther the arrow flies. Likewise, the tighter one stretches his mind and emotions in concentrating on his prayers, the further the prayer will carry and the more it will penetrate the gates of prayer.

R' Shlomo of Belz elaborates: The preparation of the sword or the bow for use is often far more time consuming than the fateful act itself. One can spend hours sharpening the sword or aiming the bow and arrow, while the flaying or shooting takes less than a moment. The Sages teach (*Berachos* 30b) that devout people in earlier times would prepare for an hour before beginning to pray. By doing so, they focused their thoughts on the upcoming prayer. Thus prayer and petition are like the sword and the bow.

Avnei Nezer spent extensive time reciting all the prayers before reaching the silent *Amidah,* which he prayed

symbolic of the power of our prayers to vanquish our enemies. Isaac blessed Esau saying, *By your sword you shall live* (Genesis 27:40), yet the "sword" with which Jacob defeats Esau is prayer. As the Sages teach, "When the voice is the voice of Jacob['s prayer], the hands are not the [successful murderous] hands of Esau" (*Bereishis Rabbah* 65:20).

Our requests, symbolized by the bow, neutralize the power of Ishmael, about whom the Torah writes *he dwelt in the desert and became an accomplished archer* (Genesis 21:20).

הֵאָסְפוּ וְאַגִּידָה לָכֶם אֵת אֲשֶׁר
יִקְרָא אֶתְכֶם בְּאַחֲרִית הַיָּמִים

Assemble yourselves and I will tell you what will befall you in the End of the Days (49:1).

According to *Rashi,* Jacob sought to reveal to his children the time when the Final Redemption would occur, but the Divine spirit left him and he was unable to do so.

Many interpretations have been offered as to why Heaven prevented Jacob from revealing the time of the Messianic era.

R' Simchah Bunim of P'shis'cha submits that Jacob wanted to describe the spiritual climate that would precede the End of the Days, the low level of leadership the Jewish people would suffer and the terrible brazenness[20] and ignorance that would characterize the times. The Divine Presence left him because It does not suffer well the besmirching of the Jewish people.

R' Yaakov of Sadigura invokes a similar theme. The Sages teach that there are two times for the coming of the Messiah. If Israel repents, he will come sooner. If we do not repent, then God will create circumstances that will force us to repent, because there is a deadline beyond which the Messiah will not delay. Which end did Jacob want to reveal? It could not have been the time of Jewish repentance, for that is totally dependent on free choice. Rather, he wanted to reveal the deadline beyond which Jewish suffering will not continue, even if the people don't repent. By doing so, Jacob would have done the unthinkable — to suggest that the Jewish people would not repent. The Divine Presence would not tolerate this.[21]

Sfas Emes adds: In order for God to grant us true goodness, our souls must be pure. Exile is meant to purify us of the negative impact that sin leaves upon our souls. Were we to know when the Redemption will come, it would take away much of the exile's sting and pain, for any kind of suffering is more bearable if one knows when it will end. Thus Jacob could not reveal the end of the exile, for that would have defeated its purpose.[22]

---

very quickly. To explain this practice, he cited the *Targum.* "Prayer is like a bow. You aim, pulling the bow tighter and tighter, trying to shoot perfectly straight. This might take hours. The shooting itself takes just a second."

20. **What a Chutzpah!** *R' Akiva Eiger* and *R' Yaakov Loberbaum* (author of *Nesivos HaMishpat*) were walking one day in Warsaw, engrossed in Talmudic debate, while two young upstarts sat on a bench laughing, instead of rising in their honor. R' Yaakov turned to R' Akiva Eiger and said, "This is what the Sages meant when they said that 'before Mashiach comes brazenness will abound' " (*Sotah* 49b).

"No, no, my friend," replied R' Akiva Eiger. "Before Mashiach comes, two Jews like us will be sitting on a bench and two young men like them will pass by. When we do not rise in *their* honor, one will say one to another, 'It's the time of Mashiach, *chutzpah* is rampant.' "

21. **Fearful Fearlessness.** *Sfas Emes* offers a penetrating analysis of prayer based on this incident. *Tanna D'Vei Eliyahu* states about the verse *Fear not, Abram* (Genesis 15:1): "God says, 'Fear not,' only to someone who is truly God fearing." When He assures man that there is nothing to fear, there truly is nothing to fear. This sense of security, however, might very well undermine one's desire to pray. Why pray when there is nothing to fear? Therefore God says, "Fear not," only to someone who is so God fearing that the primary function of prayer, in his mind, is to strengthen the link between God and man. Jacob could know the exact time when the Messiah would come, yet pray for and anxiously await it. His children were not on that level. They had to be kept in the blind so that they would anxiously await the Messiah's arrival.

22. **Sad.** *R' Naftali of Ropschitz* offered a different perspective. Jacob wanted to reveal when the Messianic Age would begin, but when he began to contemplate the terrible travails that would befall the Jewish people, he became depressed, empathizing with his descendants. Since God's Presence does not rest in sadness, It departed from Jacob.

ספר
שמות

SHEMOS/EXODUS

פרשת שמות ﬣ
Parashas Shemos

Background

The Book of *Exodus* begins with the death of Joseph and his generation and the start of the Jewish people's gradual enslavement. The enslavement was a ruse; in truth, Pharaoh sought nothing less than the annihilation of the Jewish people, whom the Egyptians perceived as a threat.

וְאֵלֶּה שְׁמוֹת בְּנֵי יִשְׂרָאֵל הַבָּאִים מִצְרָיְמָה
And these are the names of the Children of Israel who were coming to Egypt (1:1).

The Torah refers to the Jews as those *who were coming,* but since they had arrived years before, it would seem more accurate to say *who came.* The truth is otherwise. In all the years that the Children of Israel were in Egypt, they never lost the emotional and psychological feeling that they had just recently arrived. They lived with a deep yearning for *Eretz Yisrael* and refused to allow themselves to feel established in Egypt.[1] It was only when that generation died, and there arose a new generation that never knew the Land of their forefathers, that the real subjugation began (*R' Yissachar Dov of Belz, Ksav Sofer*).

Rashi notes that although the names of the tribes had been mentioned during their lifetime, the Torah repeats them upon their death as an expression of endearment.[2] They are likened to the stars, which God brings out in numbers and by name (see *Isaiah* 40:26).

Stars seem smaller than they really are because they are so far away. Every Jew must know that he is really a source of phenomenal light; it is only because he is far from God that he fails to illuminate the world. If he would only come closer, he would really begin to shine (*Zekan Aharon*).

---

1. **Unwelcome Upstarts.** According to *Chizkuni,* the phrase *who were coming* refers to the attitude of the Egyptians, and aptly captures the spirit of exile. Wherever Jews go, they remain strangers and outsiders. Even if they live somewhere for an extended period of time, become well established, and add to the prosperity and welfare of their host country, they will always be perceived as foreigners who have only recently arrived.

2. **How Dear.** To whom exactly does God want to express how dear He holds the Jewish people? To the Jews themselves. Every Jew must know how precious he is to God and how much God loves him. We can be compared to the stars. Just as God created the stars in order to illuminate the darkness, so He created the Jewish people to spread His light in the spiritually darkest places and situations.

Every Jew has his own name. Much like the angels whose names define their unique mission, every Jew has a unique mission in life — one that only he can fulfill. We must therefore search to discover our uniqueness and strive at all costs to remain authentic rather than seeking to copy someone else (*Sfas Emes*).

Why does the Torah speak of the *names* of the Children of Israel who were coming to Egypt? Let the verse state simply that *these were the Children of Israel,* and then list their names, without stressing the word "names."

R' Yehudah Leib Fein explained with a parable. In every large city in Poland there was a prison specifically meant to hold those who did not sweep the patch of street in front of their homes. In order to spare these "criminals" from being held with thieves and murderers, the government established separate sanitation prisons. Shrewd people who were supposed to be incarcerated there bribed the wardens to write their names in the prison roster, as being present. When their sentences were over, the wardens would simply erase their names and be done with it. Thus, the "names" served out the sentence, while the transgressors were free.

The family of Jacob went into exile in name only; in their essential selves, they remained free men. Strongly attached to God and His values, their souls were never shackled by the chains of exile. Thus the Torah speaks of the *names* that went to Egypt. At the very outset, the Torah teaches us that every Jew, regardless of the physical exile in which he lives, is imprisoned in name only. By remaining deeply attached to God and Torah study, he remains internally free, the master of his soul and destiny. Only in name will he be in exile, while his spirit roams free in the world of Torah.[3]

אֶת יַעֲקֹב אִישׁ וּבֵיתוֹ בָּאוּ

With Jacob each man and his household came (ibid.).

Why does this verse stress that *each man and his household* came with Jacob, when the Torah makes specific mention of them in the next verses? *Chafetz Chaim* explained: The tribes would never have agreed to come with their families to the morally decadent climate of Egypt if Jacob had not agreed to come along with them. Only when the tribes realized that their father Jacob would accompany them were they ready to go, confident that his influence would protect them and their children from the spiritual contamination of Egypt. Thus the Torah teaches that *with Jacob* they were ready — that *each man and his household came.*[4]

HaDrash V'Halyun elaborates: Generally, when a person leaves a small town with a solid Torah atmosphere for a large city with looser standards, he retains the standards he absorbed in his childhood, but his children are often casualties of the move, since they slowly but surely adapt to the standards of their new home. Here the Torah teaches the secret of maintaining familial standards in exile. Although the Children of Israel moved from their sanctified home to Egypt, they came as a unit with a vibrant intergenerational connection: *a man and his household came* — with no generation gap.

3. **Essential Torah.** Exile can obliterate one's essential character and spiritually absorb one into the prevailing culture. Thus one loses his name (symbolic of his essence) in exile. The essential character of a Jew is his burning desire to fulfill the will of God and leave its imprint on his surroundings. Thus, as the Jews went into their first exile, God indirectly divulged the secret of retaining their names. *These are the names of the Children of Israel.*

Many commentators note that the word שְׁמוֹת, *names,* is an acronym for שְׁנַיִם מִקְרָא וְאֶחָד תַּרְגוּם, the halachic obligation to read the text of the weekly *sidrah* twice, and the *Targum Onkelos* translation once. (See *Shulchan Aruch, Orach Chaim* 285). By reading the *sidrah* twice, deeply internalizing the lessons of Torah and then translating them into everyday life, we can survive the exile with our names, and essence, intact (*Simchas Aharon*).

4. **Sagacious Restraint.** In his later years, the *Chafetz Chaim* wanted to leave Poland and move to *Eretz Yisrael.* Preparations were made in both locations; in fact, a special synagogue was built for him in Petach Tikvah, but his wife's health prevented his departure.

Fearing that the communities and the *yeshivos* would suffer in his absence, *R' Chaim Ozer Grodzenski* spoke in the name of the great *roshei hayeshivah* and rabbis imploring him to stay. The Chafetz Chaim replied, "As long as I still had the strength, I was ready to wage the battle for the supremacy of Torah. Now, however, I'm an old man, and I'm no longer able to wage the fight. My absence will not cause any harm."

R' Chaim Ozer responded, "R' Yisrael Salanter would often say, 'As long as the grandfather sits at the table, the little ones behave themselves.' "

The verse refers to the Jews as the *Children of Israel,* yet it speaks of their father as *Jacob,* rather than Israel. *Shem MiShmuel* sees the two names as a prescription for national survival. The name יִשְׂרָאֵל (Israel) spells לִי ראשׁ, *the head is mine,* for the Jewish people must stand head and shoulders above all others in their spiritual and moral standards. Only when Jews recognize their potential for spiritual supremacy can they avoid the plague of assimilation. On the other hand, we must always remain יַעֲקֹב (related to עֵקֶב, *heel*), humble in our relationship to God. By combining humility with pride, and fusing firm resolve with patience, we can survive any exile.

וְיוֹסֵף הָיָה בְמִצְרָיִם
And Joseph was in Egypt (ibid. 5).

Why does the Torah mention something so obvious? *Rashi* explains that this teaches us that Joseph retained his righteousness, whether as his father's shepherd and student or as the viceroy of Egypt. Whether tested with poverty and humiliation as a shepherd or with grandeur and wealth as a statesman, Joseph remained loyal to God.

Poverty can be debilitating, causing one to (God forbid) question Divine fairness, while wealth can lead to an arrogant denial of God. One must emulate Joseph, for he withstood both tests. This ability to remain true to oneself under all circumstances is the real sign of greatness.[5]

וַיָּמָת יוֹסֵף וְכָל אֶחָיו וְכֹל הַדּוֹר הַהוּא
Joseph died and all his brothers and that entire generation (ibid. 6).

Ohr HaChaim views this verse as a description of the spiritual downward spiral that precipitated the exile and enslavement. Joseph's passing

meant that the Jews were no longer regarded with respect by the average Egyptian; rather, the Egyptians viewed them as equals. Once all the brothers had died, the Egyptians began to display scorn toward the Jews. But it was only after the death of that entire generation that they felt ready to begin the enslavement.

R' Chaim Shmulevitz explained that although the Egyptians had no ethical qualms about subordinating others, they could not bring themselves to do so as long as they still admired the Jews as prestigious and honorable people. Only when their prestige declined to the point that they looked down on them were the Egyptians emotionally able to enslave them.

The relationship between respect and enslavement works both ways. An oppressor cannot enslave a nation unless he views it with disdain and even contempt. Similarly, a nation will not submit passively to subordination unless it views itself as inferior to the oppressor. The Jews became vulnerable only when they saw themselves as inferior to the Egyptians.[6]

וּבְנֵי יִשְׂרָאֵל פָּרוּ וַיִּשְׁרְצוּ . . .
וַתִּמָּלֵא הָאָרֶץ אֹתָם
The Children of Israel were fruitful, teemed . . . and the land became filled with them (ibid. 7).

According to *Binah L'Itim,* this verse signals a radical departure from Jacob's exile-survival strategy. He told Pharaoh that his children were shepherds, so that the Egyptians — who worshiped sheep — would not want to have any connection with them. As a result, Pharaoh agreed to Joseph's desire to settle the Jews in Goshen, effectively curtailing social contact between Jews and Egyptians. Once Joseph died, however, *the Children of Israel multiplied . . . and the land became*

---

5. **Forever Joseph.** *R' Levi Yitzchak of Berditchev* put it succinctly: Although Pharaoh gave him the Egyptian name Zaphenath — Paneah, Joseph remained Joseph, even in Egypt.

6. **Sinful Self-Debasement.** *R' Chaim Shmulevitz* continues: This lack of self-respect opens the door for the evil persuader to ruin man's life. Initially he does not seek to cause a good person to sin; rather, he tries to make him lose his self-respect within the confines of permitted behavior. Once a person feels cheapened, he is fair game for the evil inclination. Held captive by his own desires, man can be brought to the lowest of sins.

Conversely, the most effective counterattack against evil is to view oneself as too honorable and prestigious to give up his exalted status by sinning. Out of fear of demeaning himself and his royal station in life, man can find the strength to resist degrading temptation.

filled with them. Discarding their low profile, they were seen all over the land, seeking to socialize with the Egyptian upper class. Suddenly the Egyptians were exposed to the financial success of the Jews, and in foreshadowing many oppressors to come, the Egyptians imagined that the foreigners were succeeding at their hosts' expense. This mentality spawned tremendous Jew-hatred, and the masses began to claim that "the Jews are numerous and strong at our expense" (see verse 9).[7]

וְכַאֲשֶׁר יְעַנּוּ אֹתוֹ כֵּן יִרְבֶּה וְכֵן יִפְרֹץ
But as much as they would afflict it,
so it would increase and so it
would spread out (ibid. 12).

The phrase וְכַאֲשֶׁר יְעַנּוּ, *as much as they would afflict it,* is in future tense. According to *Orach Chaim,* this is a promise regarding the benefits of future exiles. Whenever and wherever the Jews will be oppressed, the oppression will ultimately yield positive results. Throughout their bittersweet history, the Jewish people always emerged from their torment, strengthened and toughened by the experience.[8]

Maharal views this concept in spiritual terms. The blessing implied in this verse is not merely a reward for having borne the torment of the Egyptians; rather, it is a direct result of the physical oppression. The physical and spiritual elements that compromise man constantly vie for supremacy in his life. When one's physical dimension is diminished it makes his spirit ascendant, and vice versa. The physical oppression of the Jews set in motion a process that began to purge the physical, so that the spiritual would dominate. Thus the more the Egyptians would afflict the bodies of the Jews, their souls and sanctity would increase and expand.

It is true in all generations that physical oppression brings out the beauty of the Jewish spirit. The greatest elucidation and development of the Oral Torah occurred in the darkest periods of exile. For example, the Sages explain the verse *He has placed me in darkness like the eternally dead* (*Lamentations* 3:6) as referring to the Babylonian Talmud (see *Sanhedrin* 24a). It was in the darkness of the Babylonian exile, when the light of the world, the Temple, lay in ruins that the Jewish people created the Talmud. Whether Germany and France during the Crusader period, Spain before the Inquisition, Provence with its bloodbaths, or Russia's rampant anti-Semitic pogroms and oppression, they all spawned great outpourings of Torah literature. *For as they would afflict it, so it would increase and so it would spread out* (R' Yitzchak Hutner, R' Chaim Zimmerman).[9], [10]

---

7. **Invasion = Isolation.** *Yalkut Shimoni* comments that when the theaters and entertainment spots became filled with Jews, the Egyptians instituted apartheid decrees to segregate them. *Maayana Shel Torah* adds: The more Jews seek to infiltrate the cultural world of non-Jews, the greater the latter's hatred becomes. They seek to promulgate laws to isolate Jews and distance them. *R' Elchanan Wasserman* put it this way: "People say it is hard to be a Jew; it is even harder to be a gentile," because our non-Jewish countrymen resent it.

8. **Exile Tough.** *R' Meir Shapiro* interpreted the custom to eat hard-boiled eggs at the Seder as reflective of this idea. The longer one boils an egg the harder it becomes. This mirrors the Jewish people, whose commitment to God becomes stronger and more fierce in direct proportion to the "hot water" of exile.

9. **Gain with Pain.** Personal success in Torah study is also linked to the travail that accompanies it. The *Rashash of Vilna* encountered difficulty in understanding the comments of a particular *Tosafos* in the tractate of *Yevamos.* For many years he was unable to penetrate its meaning. Once the *Netziv of Volozhin* was in Vilna and visited the Rashash. The Rashash was overjoyed and, in the course of the visit, presented the Netziv with the difficulty. The Netziv read and reread the *Tosafos* a few times and arrived at an explanation that satisfactorily resolved the Rashash's questions.

On one hand, the Rashash was thrilled to have an answer; on the other hand, he was upset that while he had unsuccessfully struggled with the *Tosafos* for years, the Netziv was able to grasp it in such a relatively short time. The Netziv sought to comfort the Rashash and said to him, "You are, thank God, a very wealthy Jew who learns Torah without the oppressing worries of making a living, while I study Torah in poverty and have to worry about meeting the budget of the yeshivah, as well. It is for this reason that I merited to answer your question."

10. **Local Development.** According to *Chida,* one of the reasons for our protracted exile experience is that there are ideas in the Torah that must be developed within particular locations. Once the Torah of a particular locale is developed, the Jews have no reason to remain there and in fact are exiled. The Talmud in Babylonia, the Geonim

וַיָּקֻצוּ מִפְּנֵי בְּנֵי יִשְׂרָאֵל

And they became disgusted because of the Children of Israel (ibid.).

This disgust was a blessing in disguise. According to *Sfas Emes* and others, the Egyptians suddenly felt an intense hatred toward the Jews. It overtook their emotions almost against their will, for this was the manner in which Divine Providence sought to guarantee that the Jews would remain isolated from the Egyptians and not assimilate. Regarding this, King David writes הָפַךְ לִבָּם לִשְׂנֹא עַמּוֹ, *He turned their hearts to hate His nation* (*Psalms* 105:25).[11]

R' Mordechai Gimpel of Ruzinoi adds: When God told Abraham that his children would be sojourners in a land *not their own,* He blessed the Jews with the ability to remain outsiders in Egypt. No matter how long they would live there, they would always feel that Egypt is not really their place.

שֵׁם הָאַחַת שִׁפְרָה וְשֵׁם הַשֵּׁנִית פּוּעָה

The name of the first was Shifrah and the name of the second was Puah (ibid. 15).

According to the Sages (*Sotah* 11b), these midwives were really Jochebed and Miriam, the mother and sister of Moses. One was called Shifrah for she beautified, מְשַׁפֶּרֶת, the newborn babies, while the second was called פּוּעָה for she would coo to them, calming them when they cried.

Jochebed and Miriam were prophetesses, women of supreme spiritual stature. Nevertheless the Torah praises them for their nurturing skills rather than for their spiritual qualities.

According to *R' Shmuel Rozovsky,* the Torah means to emphasize that the power to nurture children is a blessing and a privilege that God grants women. Jochebed and Miriam did not seek to become great *men;* they became great *women* and utilized their Divinely given instincts and skills to serve others. The Torah underscores this by giving them names that signify their special ability as child-rearers.[12]

R' Yerucham Levovitz sheds light on a different aspect of these names. In the Torah, names indicate essence. Those characteristics that we view as important are often not the truly defining character of a person. His essence may find expression in what seems to us to be an insignificant detail. When the Torah calls Jochebed and Miriam by the new names of Shifrah and Puah it teaches us that the kindness they exhibited in their role as midwives is their defining quality, the one that made them great.[13]

---

in Iran-Iraq, R' Yitzchak Alfasi in North Africa as well as the Rishonim in Spain and the Tosafists in France and Provence are all examples of this phenomenon.

11. **United by Hate.** In a small town in New Jersey, populated by many Holocaust survivors, vandals painted a swastika and other anti-Semitic epithets on the wall of the synagogue. Contrary to popular sentiment, the rabbi left the offensive writing on the wall for a few days before having it removed. When Holocaust survivors protested that the daily visual reminder of their loss was too painful, he explained, ''You are right! But it is important for our children to know that there is anti-Semitism in the world. It sensitizes us to our role in life and unites us, forcing us to realize who we really are.''

12. **Insulted Identity.** People tend to become jealous of who and what *others* are, and they fail to appreciate their own God-given uniqueness. How ironic that those who seek to turn women into men in a quest for ''equality'' are called feminists. Everyone understands that an orchestra must be comprised of many different instruments and that it would be ridiculous if the violinist were to resent the kettle drum because its sound is much louder and more prominent. Yet some groups measure women's unique qualities by a male yardstick, and seek to denigrate that which is uniquely feminine in favor of masculine characteristics and attitudes.

13. **Big and Little.** A wise man once said that big people are big in the little things in life; it is man who makes things big or small. A great person utilizes seemingly little things in important ways, while spiritual midgets can debase even the most significant things. Money, which is often a lethal spiritual poison, can be the source of intense love of God, in the spirit of *You shall love Hashem your God . . . with all your resources* (*Deuteronomy* 6:5). When the Roman emperor, Turnus Rufus, asked R' Akiva why God created paupers, R' Akiva answered, ''In order to save the givers from *Gehinnom*'' (*Bava Basra* 10a), by giving them the opportunity to dispel the gloom of poverty from the needy. The very same money that can destroy a person can also offer salvation for his soul.

Similarly, the selfsame drive which can make man a partner with God in creating new life (see *Kiddushin* 30b)

וַתִּירֶאןָ הַמְיַלְּדֹת אֶת הָאֱלֹקִים . . . וַתְּחַיֶּיןָ אֶת הַיְלָדִים

But the midwives feared God . . .
and they caused the boys to live (ibid. 17).

Even though murder is a crime for Jews and non-Jews alike, the midwives are praised for not killing the boys. *R' Shlomo of Lutzk* submits that Jochebed and Miriam could have refused the royal appointment to serve as the Jewish midwives, but they were afraid that someone else who accepted the job might not have the strength of character and the tenacity of spirit to stand up to Pharaoh and ignore his directive. They therefore willingly placed themselves in jeopardy in order to thwart Pharaoh's diabolical design. This was fear of Heaven at its best.[14], [15]

R' Elyah Lopian notes the Torah's priorities in describing the greatness of Shifrah and Puah. The public acclaim awarded a person who has saved thousands of people is fantastic. If someone were to ask, "Is he a God-fearing person?" the reaction would be, "What difference does it make when he saved so many people?" In contrast, the Torah sees Jochebed and Miriam's fear of God as their primary virtue; the saving of so many Jewish lives was simply the tangible expression of that fear.[16], [17]

---

can be degraded to become nothing more than base, sensual indulgence.

It is man who either makes the small big or, unfortunately, turns the big into small. [See *Rambam, Shemoneh Perakim* 5] (*R' Yerucham Levovitz*).

14. **Afraid to Ruin the Love.** Fear of Heaven does not mean only fear of sin. One motivated to prevent an occurrence that, while not technically a sin, would not be pleasing to God, also displays fear of God.

R' *Asher of Stolin* became the Rebbe at a very young age. A close friend of his, who now found himself a *chassid,* suddenly felt very awkward with the relationship. Once R' Asher asked him directly, "Are you afraid of me?" When the *chassid* did not reply, R' Asher asked again. Finally the *chassid* blurted out, "I am afraid of doing anything which might ruin the love between us." R' Asher was angered. "*Sheigitz* (scoundrel)! That is the true definition of Fear of Heaven."

15. **Cautiously Competent.** *R' Yisrael Salanter* recommended to a young man that he accept a rabbinical post that was offered to him. The young man was hesitant, claiming to be fearful of issuing inaccurate halachic decisions. Said R' Yisrael, "Who then should accept rabbinic posts; those who are not afraid?"

16. **Unique Roles.** Just as one's efforts to acquire material security are the fulfillment of an obligation [that one must work for a livelihood], and one may never think that success is due to his strength and the might of his hand, so it is with regard to securing children's spiritual "safety." All of our efforts are in order to fulfill our mitzvah to try; but we must remember that in reality we cannot achieve anything [on our own]. It is through our efforts that we open the gates of Divine mercy so that our actions be blessed and achieve their objective. One who prays and supplicates intensively regarding other people's spiritual improvement can be more effective than one who is tangibly involved.

Nevertheless, the question of how to proceed, whether through prayer or practical effort, must be weighed carefully. For if practical efforts are called for, then one who refrains from action transgresses the prohibition of *you shall not stand aside while your fellow's blood is shed* (*Leviticus* 19:16).

One who sees a friend drowning and, rather than actively diving in to save him, stands aside and prays for him, is nothing short of a murderer. On the other hand, if he is unable to physically rescue his friend yet does not pray on his behalf, he is considered among those who have restrained someone who wishes to save a life . . .

Just as the human body and its limbs are divided according to function, with the eyes to see, the ears to hear and the arms to act, so the national corpus is like one body, with every individual a separate part. Each person has to fill his particular function and role. If the Torah students were to truly toil in Torah, they would, through their outpouring of sanctity, rescue many children and adults from sinful thoughts, heresy and the like through the spirit of purity with which they imbue the world. Anyone who has been in close proximity to a true Torah personality knows that there is visible evidence of his exceptional influence upon many people. This degree of influence could never be achieved by practical measures. Furthermore his impact is felt even far from his actual physical location although due to its subtlety it remains invisible to the eye (*Chazon Ish, Collected Letters* 3:62).

17. **Reverent Deterrent.** The Torah stresses the fear of God that brought the midwives to defy Pharaoh's decree. The moral ugliness of ignoring God's will is compounded by the fact that it is He Who grants us the ability to act contrary to His will. This itself is sufficient reason to refrain from doing that which He forbids. One therefore deserves no special reward for not transgressing His word. Rather, one earns reward for cultivating the Fear of Heaven that makes one realize the audacity of sin (*R' Elazar M. Shach*).

כָּל הַבֵּן הַיִּלּוֹד הַיְאֹרָה תַּשְׁלִיכֻהוּ

"Every son that will be born — into the River you shall throw him! . . ." (ibid. 22).

Although the verse does not specifically mention Jewish boys, *Targum Onkelos* translates the verse as "Every son born *to the Jews* shall be cast into the River." Where did Onkelos see that the decree was exclusively meant for the Jewish boys?

While *R' Meir Shapiro* was rav of Lublin, he also served as a deputy in the Polish Sejm (parliament). Once he discussed the fact that while the law ostensibly grants Jews equal rights, in practice the laws are interpreted in ways that effectively strip the Jews of their constitutional privileges. "This practice is an old one. Pharaoh officially decreed death on all male babies yet those in charge of implementing the law understood full well that the idea was to kill only the Jewish boys."

Onkelos, who was a proselyte and a relative of the Roman emperor, knew from his experience that official edicts might be phrased in general terms, but in practice the Jews are to be singled out.

Background

In the face of the terrible edict of infanticide, many Jewish couples separate out of despair, among them Amram and Jochebed. Their daughter Miriam convinces her parents to remarry. She argued that their "decree" was even worse than Pharaoh's, since Pharaoh's was directed only against the boys, but if Jewish couples were to divorce, no girls would be born. Her parents acknowledged that she was right and they remarried. From their renewed union, Moses is born. Thanks to the intervention of Pharaoh's daughter, he is saved from drowning and grows up in the royal palace.

וַיֵּלֶךְ אִישׁ מִבֵּית לֵוִי וַיִּקַּח אֶת בַּת לֵוִי

A man went from the house of Levi and he took a daughter of Levi (2:1).

Why does the Torah speak in such a cryptic fashion rather than clearly stating that Amram and Jochebed remarried? *Kehillas Yitzchak* suggests that the Torah mentions Moses' parents anonymously in order to emphasize that the greatest of all prophets, the man of God, was born to "ordinary" flesh and blood parents. Let no one claim that he was some kind of heavenly creature; he was born to corporeal parents, yet he rose to be the messenger of Hashem, to redeem His people and give them the Torah.

R' S.R. Hirsch adds: While Amram and Jochebed were obviously great people, the Torah omits this fact when portraying Moses' birth. Any child born in sanctity and purity can strive to reach the highest levels of spiritual achievement. As *Rambam* (*Hilchos Teshuvah* 5:1-2) writes: "Do not entertain the thought . . . that God decreed on a person from conception whether to be righteous or wicked. This is not so. Rather any person could be fit to be as righteous as Moses our teacher . . .."[18]

וְלֹא יָכְלָה עוֹד הַצְּפִינוֹ

She could not hide him any longer (ibid. 3).

Ibn Ezra writes that while God could have helped Moses' family to hide him successfully, He wanted the child to grow up among royalty so that he could emotionally rise above the slave mentality of the Jews in bondage. Furthermore, living in the palace would grant him the self-confidence to kill the Egyptian for having abused a Jew (see *Exodus* 2:12). Even at the well in Midian he had the strength of character and conviction to stop the shepherds from taking advantage of Jethro's daughters (ibid. 17).

Yet another reason why it was crucial that he not

---

18. **Believing in the Future.** The story of the remarriage of Amram and Jochebed conveys a lesson which Jews learned and relearned throughout their history. In the worst of times, when political conditions and anti-Semitism made the chances for Jewish survival very slim, Jews never refrained from marrying and bringing children into the world. *R' Yechiel Yaakov Weinberg,* who lived in the Warsaw Ghetto, testified that despite the subhuman conditions in the ghetto and the daily deportations to the human slaughterhouses, Jews continued to marry and have children. Tragically, most of those parents and children were sent to the death camps. They sanctified God's Name in life and in death.

grow up among his brothers was so that when he would eventually come to free them, they would respect and revere him rather than see him as "just" another Jew.

R' Zalman Sorotzkin suggests a different approach, based on a comment of his mother. When her other son, R' Yoel, was a student at Volozhin, he was inducted into the army. An assiduous student and already an accomplished and God-fearing scholar, it was truly a tragedy that he would have to spend his best years in the military. Rebbetzin Sorotzkin said: "I am sure that he will be freed. The Mishnah (Pirkei Avos 3:6) guarantees that whoever accepts the yoke of Torah upon himself will be freed from the yoke of the government. The only reason he was inducted in the first place is because, as a future leader of the nation, it is imperative that he experience, even temporarily, the bitter taste that all the other young men are forced to swallow."

Concluded R' Zalman: Although God could have saved him in many ways, Moses had to be thrown into the river temporarily in order that he share, and thus identify with, the experience of the nation. He too had to taste the bitter experience of Pharaoh's decree.

וַתֵּתַצַּב אֲחֹתוֹ מֵרָחֹק לְדֵעָה מַה יֵּעָשֶׂה לוֹ
His sister stationed herself at a distance to know what would be done with him (ibid. 4).

The *Chafetz Chaim* invoked this verse when discussing the miraculous survival of the *yeshivos.*

In the story of the מְקֹשֵׁשׁ עֵצִים, *the Jew who gathered wood on the Sabbath,* the Torah writes that he was temporarily jailed *for it had not been clarified what should be done to him (Numbers 15:34). Rashi* (ad loc.) explains that they knew that he was subject to the death penalty, but were unsure which of the four forms of capital punishment was to be administered. Here, too, Miriam had no doubt that her brother, born to save his people, would survive. She stationed herself nearby in order to see *how* this would happen.

"The *yeshivos,*" concluded the *Chafetz Chaim,* "are the key to the survival of the Jewish people. Their survival is not in question. However, in what way God will bring it about — that we don't know."[19]

וַתִּשְׁלַח אֶת אֲמָתָהּ וַתִּקָּחֶהָ
she sent her maidservant and she took it (ibid. 5).

Rashi, citing *Sotah* 12b, explains that she extended her arm in order to retrieve the basket. Although it was too far away for her to reach it, her arm stretched miraculously until she was able to pull the basket in. Why did she stick out her arm when she could not reach the basket? *R' Menachem Mendel of Kotzk* learns from this that when seeking to do the right thing, one should not reckon with "natural" limitations. One must do his best — and then leave the rest to God. Action is our duty; accomplishment is in the hands of God.[20]

---

19. **Our Share.** When the few surviving *roshei yeshivah* came to Israel after the Holocaust, they called an emergency meeting to discuss how to resuscitate the charred remains of the great European citadels of Torah, whose best sons went up to Heaven in flames.

R' Yosef Kahaneman, the *Ponevezher Rav,* addressed the gathering. "Dear colleagues!" he said. "We are gathered here for naught; it's a shame to waste our time and strength. What do we want to do? Save the Torah? God already promised us that it will not be forgotten from the mouths of our offspring (see *Deuteronomy* 31:21). Do *we* have to save it?! Does God need *our* help in keeping His promise? If this is our goal, let us adjourn now."

"With one word, however, we can turn this into a practical and productive meeting. The question is not *how* to save the Torah. Torah will flourish; God's promise will become a reality as the *yeshivos* will fill up with students. We must gather to figure out how we will merit to become part of that wondrous world of Torah that will rise here. How will we be able to have a share in a reborn Torah world?"

20. **Major Generals.** We often fall into the trap of thinking that if we can not be perfect, then we should do nothing. Many yeshivah students think that if they cannot become *roshei yeshivah,* then their efforts are worthless.

An Orthodox Israeli taxi driver, who was fortunate to have driven the *Steipler Gaon,* related the following incident: "Once, the Steipler asked me if I find time to learn or attend a *shiur* (Talmud class) after a long, tiring day of driving. I told him that I regularly attend a *Daf Yomi* class, but it pains me to admit that I usually fall asleep within a few minutes and wake up only when the lecturer finishes the *shiur.* I explained to him how painful it is to

**וְהִנֵּה נַעַר בֹּכֶה וַתַּחְמֹל עָלָיו
וַתֹּאמֶר מִיַּלְדֵי הָעִבְרִים זֶה**

*and behold! a youth was crying.
She took pity on him and said,
"This is one of the Hebrew boys"* (ibid. 6).

How did she know that the child was Jewish? And once she realized that he was, why did she take pity on him when her own father had decreed that all Jewish boys be killed? The answer lies in the order of what transpired. First Pharaoh's daughter took pity on the child. Realizing that his cry aroused in her an unnatural compassion, one that ran contrary to her home and upbringing, she concluded that it must be a reflection of the natural sense of mercy that is the heritage of the Jews. The crying child aroused a spark of mercy inside her that came to fruition when she converted to Judaism (*R' Aharon of Sanz*).

R' Mordechai Chaim of Slonim offered a different approach. A non-Jew cries with a sense of despair, but when a Jew weeps, there is hope behind the tears. When the Egyptian princess heard the baby's cry, and recognized the hope within it, she realized that he was one of the Hebrew boys.[21]

אִשָּׁה מֵינֶקֶת מִן הָעִבְרִיֹּת

a wet nurse from the Hebrew women (ibid 7).

Rashi explains that Moses refused to nurse from the Egyptian women. "Shall I, who will converse with the Divine Presence, ingest impure milk?" he said. Although it was permitted for him to nurse from an Egyptian mother, Moses refused to do so. He had such a clear sense of himself as a Jew and as one with whom the Divine Presence would converse that he could not bring himself to demean such a soul by nursing from an Egyptian wet nurse.

We too are Hashem's precious children; we too speak with the Divine Presence, every day. When we in our prayers say, "Blessed are You," we address God Himself. Were we to realize how elevated an existence we enjoy, we would never demean ourselves by seeking impure or meaningless desires.

R' Yaakov Kaminetsky offers further perspective. Rema (*Yoreh Deah* 81:7) rules that it is preferable that Jewish children nurse only from Jewish women, since "milk of a non-Jewish woman contaminates the heart of the child, imbuing him with a negative nature." Citing *Rashba*, the *Vilna Gaon* points to the case of Moses as the source of this ruling. This source would seem to be inappropriate, however, since Moses' reticence was based on his particular set of circumstances. He knew that he was destined to converse with the Divine Presence. If so, then why must all Jewish children refrain from digesting the milk of a non-Jewish mother?

The answer is that parents must view every Jewish child as someone with the potential to converse with the Divine Presence. We must therefore educate all our children toward this goal — that they be fit to converse with God.

---

me that I can't remain awake, nor do I ever get to understand the *daf.*

"The Steipler smiled to me and encouraged me. When he was leaving the taxi he caressed my face and said, 'Know that in this world you don't consider yourself to be significant, but I can assure you that in Heaven you are a major general. Do your best; you can't do more. Keep going to the *shiur,* even if you fall asleep over the *Gemara.* In Heaven they consider you a great and righteous person.' "

God does not demand of us any more than we are capable of doing. If we make our utmost efforts, then in God's eyes we are major generals.

We must do ours and then He will make it happen!

21. **Return to the Crib.** *R' Dov Ber of Lubavitch* was so engrossed in his learning the he did not hear his crying baby, who had fallen out of his crib in the next room. R' Dov Ber's father, *R' Schneur Zalman of Liadi,* the *Baal HaTanya,* lived on the floor above his son. He, too, was engrossed in learning, yet he heard the child's cries. He went downstairs, lifted the child, soothed him and put him back to sleep in the crib. Later he told his son: "Even when one is totally involved in his own learning he must never be oblivious to a child's cries."

R' Menachem Mendel of Lubavitch expounded: "Even if a person is totally preoccupied with his own spiritual growth he may never become callous or oblivious to the cry of a Jewish child who needs help. The Jewish child who is lost among the nations must be picked up, soothed and returned to his crib. How many Jewish children, in our times, have fallen out of the crib?!"

Background

Moses assumes the role of shepherd for Jethro's sheep, which was the training ground for his future role as "the loyal shepherd" of God's flock. While he is in the desert with the sheep, God appears to him in the Burning Bush.

וּמֹשֶׁה הָיָה רֹעֶה אֶת צֹאן יִתְרוֹ

*Moses was shepherding
the sheep of Jethro (3:1).*

The Midrash relates that one of the sheep once strayed from the rest of the flock. Moses ran after it, searching until he was able to find it and bring it back.

How did Moses allow himself to chase after a solitary sheep thereby abandoning the entire flock?[22]

Moses knew that the unity among the rest of the flock would protect it from danger. The lost sheep lacked that advantage, and therefore it was truly in jeopardy. Furthermore, he knew that the loss of even one sheep could potentially create dissension within the entire flock. Lastly, Moses knew full well that it was not the poor sheep's fault that it had wandered off; rather, the shepherd was to blame.

Unity among Jews protects every individual; when a Jew is cast asunder from his fellow Jews he is in spiritual jeopardy. Every effort must be made to reunite him with the rest of the flock. Concomitantly, the loss of any individual undermines the strength of the nation. Finally a true leader knows that if a Jew leaves the fold the ultimate responsibility lies with the leader (*Sfas Emes*).[23]

---

22. **Individualistic Unity.** Authentic Jewish leadership recognizes that it is unacceptable to sacrifice the individual for the sake of the group. No individual may be written off to serve the needs of the group.

R' Ozer Kesserman suggests an allusion to this concept in the less-famous ending of a well-known comment. Regarding the unity of the Jewish people at Sinai, *Rashi* comments that they were כְּאִישׁ אֶחָד בְּלֵב אֶחָד, *as one man with one heart*, says *Rashi*. He continues: *However, all the other encampments* [of the Jews in the wilderness] *were fraught with strife and arguments.* Why does *Rashi* besmirch the Jewish people? Explained R' Ozer: While unity is important, the differences of opinion that reflect individuality are crucial to maintaining a spiritually healthy nation.

23. **Never Alone.** When the masses are not loyal to Hashem and His Torah, the Torah leader sees himself responsible and does whatever he can to bring the stray members back into the fold. When a Jew is all alone he is spiritually vulnerable. Everything possible must be done to bring him back to his spiritual home.

פרשת וארא ﬤ
Parashas Va'eira

Background

Following his disappointing encounter with Pharaoh, Moses reports back to God, describing the worsening fate of the Jews and questions Him as to why He has not yet redeemed them. God responds by rebuking Moses on one hand, but simultaneously reassuring him that the redemption is at hand.

וַיְדַבֵּר אֱלֹקִים אֶל מֹשֶׁה וַיֹּאמֶר אֵלָיו אֲנִי ה'

God spoke to Moses and said to him, "I am Hashem" (6:2).

Rashi interprets וַיְדַבֵּר, *spoke*, as meaning that God spoke harshly in response to Moses' complaint at the end of the previous *parashah*. This understanding is supported by the use of God's Name אֱלֹקִים, indicative of His attribute of strict justice, as opposed to "Hashem" which connotes Divine mercy.

The *Steipler Gaon* notes that both Divine Names appear in this verse, implying that God's response included both justice and mercy. He responded as אֱלֹקִים, the God Who exhibits justice, and He told Moses that *I am Hashem* — what appears to you to be strict justice is in fact Divine Mercy.[1]

In his role as the loyal shepherd of his people, Moses complained to God about their suffering, to which God answered, *I am Hashem.* Believe me, He told Moses, I am the Master of Mercy. If they need mercy, I will provide it. If I don't, then you must understand that they are getting whatever they need (*R' Yosef Chaim Sonnenfeld*).

וָאֵרָא אֶל אַבְרָהָם אֶל יִצְחָק וְאֶל יַעֲקֹב

I appeared to Abraham, to Isaac and to Jacob . . . (ibid. 3).

Rashi comments: "I appeared to the אָבוֹת (Patriarchs)." This would seem to be rather obvious, since the names of the Patriarchs are clearly mentioned in the verse. What additional under-

---

1. **Silver Lining.** *Shaarei Simchah* explains the silver lining of mercy contained within the cloud of scrupulous justice. According to God's promise to Abraham, the Jewish people were to be enslaved in "a land not their own" for four hundred years. In reality, however, they were enslaved in Egypt for only two hundred ten years. The commentators explain that since the Egyptians oppressed them excessively by increasing the workload to inhumane proportions, the ordained suffering of four hundred years of enslavement was condensed into two hundred and ten years. Consequently, the Egyptian refusal to give straw to the Jewish slaves, which seemed to be an exhibition of Divine stringency, was in truth an act of mercy, since it caused a hastening of the Exodus.

[To the uninitiated outsider, the surgeon who performs open-heart surgery seems to be nothing less than a savage. Only one who understands the process realizes that a life-saving act of mercy is taking place before his eyes. To man, God appears to be אֱלֹקִים, dispensing justice rather than mercy. Were we to truly understand the process, we would realize that *I am Hashem.*]

standing is Rashi offering? *Chasam Sofer* suggests a homiletic interpretation, rendering the word אָבוֹת as those with desire (see *Deuteronomy* 29:19). God appears only to those who desire that He become a presence in their lives. The Patriarchs had a deep-seated desire to bring Him into their lives. He therefore "complied" and appeared to them.

Rambam explains the words אֶהְיֶה אֲשֶׁר אֶהְיֶה, *I shall be as I shall be* (*Exodus* 3:14), in this vein. *I shall be* with those who desire that *I shall be* with them.[2]

R' Meir of Premishlan suggests that Rashi's comment teaches that Isaac and Jacob were Patriarchs in their own right, and not merely because they were Abraham's progeny. Each was a father of the Jewish people in his own merit, not merely someone's son.[3]

וּשְׁמִי ה׳ לֹא נוֹדַעְתִּי לָהֶם
but with My Name Hashem I did not make Myself known to them (ibid.).

Rashi explains that the name יְ־ה־ו־ה signifies God as One Who honors His pledges. God revealed it now to Moses, to signify that He was now ready to fulfill His promise to free His children and bring them to the Land of Israel.

This Four-letter Name is traditionally understood to signify that God is הָיָה, הֹוֶה, וְיִהְיֶה, that He *was, is* and always *will be*, which represents the fact that God is not limited by the strictures of time. In addition, it implies הַוְיָה, that He brought, and continues to bring, the entire universe into existence. *R' Yitzchak Hutner* explains how these two explanations are integrated with Rashi's statement.

With the best of intentions, mortal man is limited in his ability to honor a promise. Who can say that he will still be alive when the time comes for him to do so? Furthermore, even if he is alive, who can be sure he will have the resources, the health, or the ability to do so? God, on the other hand, is eternal; He existed, exists and always will exist. Furthermore, He brought everything into existence and exercises absolute power over all forces in the world; no power can prevent Him from honoring His word. Thus the Four-letter Name signifies that God carries out His promises.

וְגַם אֲנִי שָׁמַעְתִּי אֶת נַאֲקַת בְּנֵי יִשְׂרָאֵל אֲשֶׁר מִצְרַיִם מַעֲבִדִים אֹתָם וָאֶזְכֹּר אֶת בְּרִיתִי
Moreover, I have heard the groan of the Children of Israel whom Egypt enslaves and I have remembered My covenant (ibid. 5).

Why did the groan of the Jewish people cause God to remember His covenant? *R' Yehoshua of Ostrovtze* suggests that the pain of the Egyptian exile was spiritually beneficial for the Jews, for they had to be purged of their impurities in order to become fit for the spiritual treasures of Torah

---

2. **Let Him in!** A young man was standing near the *Kotzker Rebbe* when the Rebbe sharply asked, "Where is God to be found?" Startled by the question, the young man replied, "His glory fills the entire world." The retort came immediately. "No, no! He is to be found wherever we let Him in." King David gives expression to this sentiment by saying, *Hashem desires those who fear Him, those who yearn for His kindness* (*Psalms* 147:11).

This is true of Torah, as well. Only one who earnestly desires to understand the word of God will succeed in doing so. *Vilna Gaon* cites the verse *O all who are thirsty, go to water* (*Isaiah* 55:1) as the Scriptural source for the words of the *Mishnah* "and you shall drink in the words [of the Sages] thirstily" (*Avos* 1:4). *R' Yitzchak Hutner* explains the analogy of Torah to water. One must recite a blessing before drinking any beverage, even if he is not thirsty, because he enjoys its taste. An exception to this rule is water. In the case of water, only if one is thirsty must he recite a blessing (see *Shulchan Aruch* O.C. 204:7,8; M.B. §40), because one derives enjoyment from water only if one is thirsty for it. It is the same with Torah learning; in order to get the maximum benefit from it, one must be thirsty for it.

3. **Like Son, Like Father.** According to *R' Menachem Mendel of Kotzk*, this is the thrust of the verse, *This is my God . . . the God of my father* (*Exodus* 15:2). One must first create a personal relationship with God and then connect it to his parental heritage.

It has been said that parental or familial lineage is like a string of zeros. If one puts something in front of them, even a one, then they are worth a lot. If one does not put anything in front of them, then no matter how many there are, they still remain zero.

and *Eretz Yisrael.* [4], [5] However, the Egyptians who served as God's messengers in inflicting the suffering did not realize that they were merely God's proxies. They questioned where God was while His people were suffering, and thus the enslavement caused a desecration of His honor. When God heard the groan of the Jews that *Egypt enslaves,* He remembered His covenantal relationship with them and that it was their mission to sanctify His Name in the world. Therefore the time had come to redeem them, and thereby end the desecration.

Divrei Shaul sees the connection in a different context. The cause of the world's hatred toward the Jews is rooted in our separatism. Because we enjoy a covenantal bond with God — and a covenant is exclusionary by definition — non-Jews are outsiders, and the Egyptians viewed this separatism as an expression of arrogance and hated the Jews for it. Thus when our forefathers groaned, God heard them and remembered that His covenant was the cause of the hatred that led the Egyptians to enslave His people.[6]

וְהוֹצֵאתִי אֶתְכֶם מִתַּחַת סִבְלֹת מִצְרָיִם
And I shall take you out from under the burdens of Egypt (ibid. 6).

The first step toward redemption is to view enslavement as unbearable and to psychologically rebel against it. Homiletically, the word סִבְלֹת, *burdens,* can be rendered, like סַבְלָנוּת, *forbearance* or *tolerance.* As long as one is not disgusted and "fed up" with the exile, as long as one is resigned to tolerate it, he is not ready for redemption. Moses told the Jewish people that God would end their willingness to bear the enslavement and immorality of Egypt, so that the process of

---

4. **Painful Passport.** The *Chasam Sofer* explains the flow of the verses in this light. Since *I have heard the groan of the Children of Israel . . .* indicating that the nation had been purged by its suffering, *therefore . . . I shall take you to Me for a people* (verse 7) at Mount Sinai when I give you the Torah and *I shall bring you to the Land . . .* (verse 8).

5. **Leave the Room.** The *Chafetz Chaim* was once discussing why God has not sent prophets to His people during the long exile to strengthen and encourage them as He did in bygone days. He explained that the pain of the Jewish people had been maximized before God sent Moses to free them. Moses, who witnessed their pain personally, tried to alleviate their suffering. As *Rashi* explains: Moses observed their burdens in order to see their suffering and grieve with them (see *Rashi* to *Exodus* 2:11). Furthermore, he pleaded that God stop worsening their plight. God knew, however, that it was ultimately beneficial that they endure the exile and the travail of enslavement, for only when they were sufficiently purified could they be truly redeemed. It was necessary, therefore, for God to choreograph events so that Moses would flee to Midian. Then God could increase the suffering that would eventually lead to redemption.

We, too, concluded the Sage of Radin, must undergo a certain amount of cathartic suffering before God can fully redeem us. Were we to have prophets, they would turn over worlds in order to soften or alleviate the exile. Hence God does not send us prophets so that through our suffering we atone for all our sins and thus become fit for eternal salvation.

R' Moshe Landynski, who was present when the Chafetz Chaim said this, added: When the Temple was destroyed Jeremiah had already left Jerusalem. Had he been present, he would have implored God not to destroy it. God caused Jeremiah to leave, because He knew that if the Temple would not be destroyed, He would have no choice other than to pour His wrath onto the people. This is similar to a child who must undergo a painful but life-saving operation. Were the child's mother to be present, she would be unable to bear the sight and would attempt to stop the surgeon from doing what must be done. She is therefore sent out of the operating room. Moses had to be sent away from Egypt and Jeremiah from Jerusalem so that the Surgeon could go about healing His children.

6. **Not Too Salty.** The Sages (*Berachos* 5a) teach that both suffering and salt are referred to as a covenant (see *Deuteronomy* 28:69 and *Leviticus* 2:13). Just as salt brings out the best in meat, so suffering atones for one's sins, bringing out the best in him.

R' Mendel of Rimanov expanded on the analogy: Salt adds flavor to meat only if it is sprinkled in limited amounts. Too much salt ruins the meat and makes it inedible. The same applies to suffering. Inflicted sparingly, suffering tenderizes man's heart, stimulating spiritual stirrings. Too much suffering, however, is debilitating; it breaks man and causes him to rebel against his Creator. Thus, when the Jews groaned, God remembered His covenant.

emancipation could begin (*R' Menachem Mendel of Kotzk, Chidushei HaRim* et al.).

This is true on a personal level as well. We are all too quick to make peace with a devalued level of spirituality and tend to believe that it is the natural state of things. "That is just the way I am. I was always like this," we say to ourselves. We accept the unacceptable status quo. When we reach that point of indifference, God must quickly redeem us before it is too late (*Zekan Aharon*).[7]

וְלָקַחְתִּי אֶתְכֶם לִי לְעָם . . . וִידַעְתֶּם כִּי אֲנִי ה׳ אֱלֹקֵיכֶם הַמּוֹצִיא אֶתְכֶם . . .
I shall take you to Me for a people . . . and you shall know that I am Hashem your God Who takes you out . . . (ibid. 7).

How can the verse promise that we will *know* God, whose essence is unfathomable to human intellect? The answer is that we can access the light of God's Presence through Torah and *mitzvos*. As the *Zohar* explains, the first word of the Ten Commandments, אָנֹכִי, is an acronym for אֲנָא נַפְשִׁי כָּתָבִית יָהָבִית, *I presented My soul in writing*, i.e., the most intense concentration of Godliness is in His written Torah.

I shall take you to Me for a people at Sinai. By giving you the Torah, *you shall know that I am Hashem* (*R' Levi Yitzchak of Berditchev*).[8]

Sfas Emes sees *and you shall know that I am*

Hashem your God Who takes you out as the ultimate goal of the redemption. To become free is not enough; more importantly, we will realize and see clearly that only God is the Redeemer. The main function of freedom is the strength of faith with which it enables us to recognize the true Savior.

וְנָתַתִּי אֹתָהּ לָכֶם מוֹרָשָׁה
and I shall give it to you as a heritage (ibid. 8).

Eretz Yisrael is our heritage — not only when we reside in it, but also when we are in exile. The Jewish people are like a landowner who was forced to abandon a familial plot. Although physically absent, his spirit is constantly preoccupied with the land, trying desperately not to forget its unique qualities and praying that one day he will merit to regain it (*Netziv*).

The term מוֹרָשָׁה appears only twice in the Torah. It is used in our verse regarding *Eretz Yisrael,* and Moses uses it again in reference to the Torah, as part of his final blessings to the Jewish people (see *Deuteronomy* 33:4). These two gifts are inextricably linked, for the inheritance of the Land of Israel is contingent upon our fidelity to the Godly heritage of Torah. In the words of King David וַיִּתֵּן לָהֶם אַרְצוֹת גּוֹיִם . . . בַּעֲבוּר יִשְׁמְרוּ חֻקָּיו וְתוֹרֹתָיו יִנְצֹרוּ, *And He gave them the lands of the nations . . . so that they may safeguard His statutes and observe His*

---

7. **Unbearable Exile.** *R' H.,* a wealthy manufacturer in New York, refuses to own a house in America. He recognizes the danger of finding the exile to be so comfortable that we consider it the natural order of things. *R' H.* says, "The only people who can justifiably own a home in the Diaspora are the Jewish educators who need security and equity in order to function as worry-free as possible in their sanctified calling. What, however, is our justification to feel ourselves permanent in *galus*?" *R' Yaakov Shimshon of Shpitivka* put it succinctly: "It is easier to take the Jews out of exile than to take the exile out of the Jews."

8. **Now I Know.** Previously (verse 6) Moses had been commanded to tell the Jews, "*I am Hashem.*" Here the Torah promises that they will *know* that He is Hashem. Before God took us as His people at Sinai, we only *heard* that He is Hashem. Once He granted us the Torah, however, we *know* that He is Hashem (*R' Yechezkel Abramsky*).

One of the early chassidic masters was originally an opponent of the new movement, as were his in-laws, with whom he lived. He became curious and then sympathetic to the new movement, and went to study for an extended period of time under the *Maggid of Mezritch,* the successor of the *Baal Shem Tov,* as the leader of *chassidim.* When the young man returned home, his annoyed father-in-law asked sarcastically what he had learned there. "I learned that there is a God," the new *chassid* replied.

Taken aback, his father-in-law called in the maidservant and asker her, "Is there a God in the world?" Surprised, she said, "Of course! why do you even ask?"

The exasperated man turned to his son-in-law and said, "*Nu!*?"

The young man replied, "She *says* there is a God, but after being with the *Maggid,* I *know* it."

teachings (*Psalms* 105:44-45, *Yalkut HaChadash*).[9]

Ohr HaChaim views this principle as the reason that after the first four expressions of redemption (וְהוֹצֵאתִי, וְהִצַּלְתִּי, וְגָאַלְתִּי, וְלָקַחְתִּי) — *I shall take you out, I shall rescue you, I shall redeem you, I shall take you to Me*) the Torah writes *and you shall know that I am Hashem*. Only if you know this does God's next promise go into effect: *I shall bring you to the Land.* Entering *Eretz Yisrael* is contingent upon knowing Him intimately through following the path of those from whom we inherited our right to the Land.[10]

וְלֹא שָׁמְעוּ אֶל מֹשֶׁה מִקֹּצֶר רוּחַ וּמֵעֲבֹדָה קָשָׁה
But they did not heed Moses, because of shortness of breath and hard work (ibid. 9).

Why were the Jews unwilling to accept Moses' message that they would be freed? *Meshech Chochmah* submits that a person who is suffering senses the pain of the present so vividly that he cannot be consoled by promises of a bright but distant future. The Jews, so short of breath due to the backbreaking toil, were incapable of absorbing Moses' message of a rosy future that included receiving the Torah and entering the Land of Israel. They needed instant relief from their present purgatory. God therefore instructed Moses again *to take the Children of Israel out of the land of Egypt* (verse 13).

Sfas Emes interprets *shortness of breath* homi-letically. Inspiring messages and prophetic words can be received only by someone with the power of spiritual reception. One whose physicality has firm control over him does not possess the spiritual "ears" to absorb such concepts. It is one's soul, breathed into one by God, that provides man with this spiritual receptivity. Having undergone extensive exposure to the impurity of Egypt, the Jews suffered from shortness of *Godly* breath; they could not hear what Moses had to say.[11]

Background

God commands Moses to speak to Pharaoh about freeing the Jews. Moses protests, claiming that if the Jews had not been receptive to his message of freedom, then certainly Pharaoh will reject his demands.

הֵן בְּנֵי יִשְׂרָאֵל לֹא שָׁמְעוּ אֵלַי וְאֵיךְ יִשְׁמָעֵנִי פַרְעֹה וַאֲנִי עֲרַל שְׂפָתָיִם
Behold, the Children of Israel have not listened to me, so how will Pharaoh listen to me? And I have sealed lips! (ibid. 12).

Rashi notes that this is one of ten instances where a *kal v'chomer* (a fortiori) argument appears in the Torah.

The commentators suggest that in this case the argument is flawed, since the Torah explains earlier

---

9. **Linked Heritage.** The so-called "Secular Revolution" declared by secular Israeli politicians in the year 2000 never took place, since the Palestinian *intifada* broke out almost immediately. When Jews declare that the heritage of Torah is not theirs, others declare that the heritage of *Eretz Yisrael* is not theirs either.

10. **Deserving Heirs.** *L'Nefesh Chayah* offers a beautiful parable. The city elders decided to build an ornate mansion for the rav and his family, including a chamber for the proceedings of his *beis din*. Before the project could be completed, however, the rav passed away. His children claimed that, as heirs, they were entitled to the mansion. The city elders countered, "Were one of you fit to succeed your father as rav, you would have a legitimate claim to the property. But, since none of you follow in your father's footsteps, why should you inherit it?"

God promises to give us the Land He promised to our ancestors, but only if we make ourselves worthy heirs to their way of life and their loyalty to God have we a claim to the palace. If, however, we do not follow the Torah, what is the legitimacy of our claim?

Ramban notes that when Moses prayed for the Jews in the wake of the episode of the spies he did not invoke the merit of the Patriarchs. Since the people had repudiated their fathers' fervent longing for the Land and rejected the heritage they were to receive from them, it was inappropriate to invoke their merit (see *Ramban* to *Numbers* 14:18).

11. **Looking to Be Moved.** [We often listen to rabbis who try to arouse us to greater adherence to Torah and *mitzvos,* and yet we remain the same. Our initial reaction is to blame the speaker; he was not powerful or dynamic enough. In reality, however, we lack the basic orientation for growth and change. We go to an address meant to inspire and effect change, but we sit as spectators waiting to be entertained. Much as one who attends an art exhibit, we are impressed with the beauty of the presentation yet make no effort to be authentically moved by the experience.]

that the Jews did not listen to Moses due to short-ness of breath and hard work, obstacles which were most definitely not applicable to Pharaoh. Many approaches have been submitted to resolve this issue.

According to *Sfas Emes*, the spiritual climate among the nations of the world is directly linked to that of the Jews.[12] If the Jews are not receptive to spirituality, then the non-Jews will definitely be unreceptive. Thus Moses claimed that if the Jews (even though it was due to hard labor and shortness of breath) are unable to relate to Moses' words, certainly Pharaoh will not listen.

Alternatively, this teaches us the reciprocal relationship between Jews and their leaders. The receptivity of the Jews to the words of their leaders endows the leaders with the power to influence others.[13] When Jews refuse to listen, their leaders lose the ability to influence anyone — even non-Jews. Hence Moses claimed that if the Jews are unwilling to listen, then he will be unable to influence Pharaoh. Thus he concluded, *And I have sealed lips!* As a result of the Jews not believing in him, he truly lost his ability to influence through speech.

R' Yosef Leib Nendik offers a *mussar* approach based on *Ibn Ezra*'s rendering of the verse אִישׁ אוֹ אִשָּׁה כִּי יַפְלִא לִנְדֹּר נֶדֶר as *A man or woman who will do something astounding to take a* [Nazarite] *vow* (*Numbers* 6:2). While most people obsessively chase after the physical pleasures of the world, the person taking a Nazirite vow does the opposite. Most people are servants of their passions, but the truly free person is the one who can control his desires.[14]

When the Sages taught "Only one involved in Torah is truly free" (*Pirkei Avos* 6:2), they meant to say that only Torah allows one to free himself from the shackles of desire and to truly exercise free choice. Without Torah, one is not free at all, he is a slave, controlled by a master foreign to his better instincts. While intellectually he might have correct ideas of how to live, ultimately his master — his passion — will force him to act otherwise. Moses argued that if the Jews, enslaved by Pharaoh, could not listen, then certainly Pharaoh, enslaved by evil and desire, will insist on keeping the Jews in his land.

וַאֲנִי עֲרַל שְׂפָתָיִם
And I have sealed lips! (ibid.).

Why was Moses' power of speech impeded? *Derashos HaRan* writes: Although Moses possessed all the prerequisites for prophecy (see *Rambam, Hilchos Yesodei HaTorah* 7), he lacked the ability to speak clearly. God gave him this handicap so that no one would ever be able to claim that the Jewish people and their leaders were attracted by Moses' personality and were induced to accept the Torah thanks to his charismatic eloquence. Throughout history, many demagogic orators have succeeded in convincing the masses to follow them and accept their lies as truth. God gave Moses "sealed lips" so that everything he taught would be accepted solely because of its intrinsic truth, and not because of his oratory.

Maharal explains Moses' sealed lips as reflective of his uniqueness. Man is a synthesis of the physical and spiritual, who became alive when God *blew into his nostrils the soul of life; and man became a living being* (*Genesis* 2:7). *Targum Onkelos* defines *a living being* as "a speaking spirit"; namely, possessing the power of intelligent speech. Thus the power of speech is the result of the fusion of body and

---

12. **Best of Times.** A wise student of history once commented, "The best situation is when the Jews are religious and the non-Jews are not. The worst situation is when the non-Jews are religious and the Jews are not."

13. **Communally Empowered.** Homiletically, this is the meaning of the words "Make for yourself a teacher" (*Avos* 1:6). It is the student who endows the teacher with influence and empowers him to teach and leave a mark. One must make himself a student, for by doing so he makes the teacher a teacher.

 R' Chaim Shmulevitz once said, "There is a Jew in Jerusalem (the *Beis Yisrael* of Ger) about whom people say that he performs miracles. It's true; he *does* do miracles. If my students believed in me as his *chassidim* believe in him, I too could effect miracles."

14. **Eyes in Hand.** The *Sanz-Klausenberg Rebbe* once stayed at the home of *R' Levy* of Panama City. Many years later, R' Levy's son asked the elderly gentile maid what she remembered about his visit. She replied, "He was a truly holy man. I saw that his eyes were not in his sockets; rather, he held his eyes in his hands, moving them at will. He sees only what he wants to see and does not allow his eyes to see what he doesn't want them to see."

soul, physical and spiritual. In ordinary human beings, where the relationship between man's physical and spiritual components is fairly balanced, the result is normal speech. Moses had flawed speech because he was disproportionately more spiritual than physical.[15]

וַיְדַבֵּר ה' אֶל מֹשֶׁה וְאֶל אַהֲרֹן וַיְצַוֵּם
אֶל בְּנֵי יִשְׂרָאֵל וְאֶל פַּרְעֹה מֶלֶךְ מִצְרָיִם
לְהוֹצִיא אֶת בְּנֵי יִשְׂרָאֵל מֵאֶרֶץ מִצְרָיִם

Hashem spoke to Moses and Aaron and commanded them regarding the Children of Israel and regarding Pharaoh, king of Egypt, to take the Children of Israel out of the land of Egypt (ibid. 13).

What exactly did God command Moses and Aaron regarding the Children of Israel? Regarding Pharaoh He told them to order him to free the Jews from Egyptian bondage. What impact did this command have on the Jews?[16]

R' Levi Yitzchak of Berditchev sees this as revealing a cardinal idea regarding Divine beneficence. God, the Ultimate Good, deeply desires to shower His kindness on the Jewish people. Whenever they act in a way that justifies such an outpouring, they please Him. This is what the Sages meant when they said "The reward of a mitzvah is a mitzvah" (*Pirkei Avos* 4:2), for the fact that one's good deeds give God the opportunity to reward him is in itself a mitzvah. Thus God told Moses and Aaron to arouse the Jews to make the necessary preparations for the Exodus so that He could actually redeem them. These preparations are the mitzvah that God told Moses and Aaron to teach the children of Israel.

R' Henach of Aleksander links this verse to the next one, which speaks of the heads of the Jewish people. God told Moses and Aaron to focus the people on their roots. "Remember that you are descendants of the Patriarchs and the tribal ancestors, all of them holy people. Slavery and its resultant debasement are not fitting for you!"[17]

---

15. **Synthesized Speech.** *Rema* (*Shulchan Aruch, Orach Chaim* 6:1) explains the אֲשֶׁר יָצַר blessing, which thanks God for creating the human body in such a way that it can perform all the internal functions necessary for life and health. It concludes with the words *Blessed are You, Hashem, Who heals all flesh and* מַפְלִיא לַעֲשׂוֹת *acts wondrously. Rema* explains that the greatest wonder of all is that God blends the physical body with the spiritual soul. As *Onkelos* notes, speech is the product of this synthesis between body and soul. This explains why the section of *Rambam's Mishneh Torah* dealing with laws that require verbal enunciation (Vows, Nazirism, Oaths, etc.) is called *Sefer Haflaah,* the Book of Verbal Expression, which can also be rendered the "Book of Wondrousness" (*R' Yitzchak Hutner*).

16. **On the Heart.** Although the Jews did not listen to Moses due to the debilitating enslavement, God instructed him to continue speaking to them. The word of God is described by the prophet as follows: *For just as the rain and the snow descend from heaven and will not return there, unless it waters the earth and causes it to produce and sprout . . . so shall be My word that emanates from My mouth, it shall not return to Me unfulfilled unless it will have accomplished what I desired and brought success where I sent it* (Isaiah 55:10-11). The word of God will always leave its mark, if not immediately, then certainly eventually. Sanctified words do not go for naught; sooner or later they will be heard (*Sfas Emes*).

R' Menachem Mendel of Kotzk heard this message in the words from the first paragraph of the Shema: וְהָיוּ הַדְּבָרִים הָאֵלֶּה . . . עַל לְבָבֶךָ, *And these matters [that I command you today] shall be upon your heart* (Deuteronomy 6:6). The Torah speaks of the words *upon* your heart rather than *in* your heart. Often our hearts are not ready to absorb the word of God and the messages of Torah. Nevertheless, we are commanded to place the words *upon* the heart, i.e., not to ignore or forget them, even though they have not yet penetrated our hearts. The moment may yet come when the heart will be receptive and open to those words. [Parents and teachers often become frustrated, convinced that the messages they convey to their children or students are falling on deaf ears. Nevertheless, they should continue talking to the young, placing the words of Torah *upon* their hearts, for eventually they will penetrate.]

17. **Overwhelmed by Unity.** *R' Zusia of Anipoli* homiletically renders וַיְצַוֵּם as *and unite them* (as in צַוְותָא, *companionship*). God told Moses and Aaron to bring a spirit of unity into the nation. Bring their hearts closer to one another and let them yearn as one for true freedom. Pharaoh will have no choice but to free them.

Simchas Aharon adds: let every Jew pray that his fellow Jews be freed. When each individual prays for the rest of the nation, then prayers will be answered, for God never rejects the prayer of the congregation or the nation. Furthermore, every Jew's prayer will be answered, for, as the Sages said, "One who prays on behalf of his friend when he himself is in need of the same thing will be answered first" (*Bava Kamma* 92a, *Simchas Aharon*).

Talmud Yerushalmi (*Rosh Hashanah* 3:5) states that Moses taught the Jews the laws pertaining to the freeing of slaves. According to the *Rogatchover Gaon*, this is alluded to in the verse *and commanded them regarding the Children of Israel and regarding Pharaoh . . . that he send the Children of Israel.* Both the Children of Israel (in the future) and Pharaoh (now) must send away the Children of Israel.

Why was it so important that they learn these laws at this particular juncture? According to *Shir HaShirim Rabbah* (4:15) the tribes of Reuben, Simeon and Levi themselves had Jewish servants while in Egypt, and Moses could not demand that Pharaoh free the Jews while there were Jews who were still subjugating their own brothers (*Meshech Chochmah*).[18]

Mikdash Mordechai notes the words of King Solomon, *One who mocks a pauper insults his Maker; one who rejoices over another's misfortune will not be exonerated* (*Proverbs* 17:5), which teaches that one should not mock those who are helpless. Accordingly, it is strange that God would command the Jews about freeing their servants when they themselves are suffering under the yoke of painful servitude; it seems to be a cruel mockery. He explains that this was actually the perfect time to address the issue. The natural desire for power is so strong that people often tend to abuse their authority and treat their subordinates harshly. A master views himself as the exclusive owner of the slave, body and soul.

Precisely then, when the Jews were experiencing the taste of cruel oppression on their own flesh, was the most opportune moment to impress upon them the Torah's standards about how one must treat his servants. While the bitter taste of slavery was still in their mouths, they would best

be able to understand that "one who buys himself a servant in truth buys himself a master" (*Kiddushin* 22a).

Background

The Torah now traces the genealogy of Moses and Aaron. The redeemers of the nation were mere mortals born of mortals, who rose to greatness through their own efforts.

וְאֵלֶּה שְׁמוֹת בְּנֵי לֵוִי
These were the names of the sons of Levi (ibid. 16)

When listing the descendants of Reuben and Simeon the Torah speaks of *the sons of,* but when referring to Levi the Torah adds the phrase *the **names** of the sons.* According to *Shelah,* this alludes to a special quality of Levi — the ability to empathize with the plight of others. Although the tribe of Levi was not enslaved, nonetheless, it was Divinely inspired to envision the enslavement years before it began. As a result, the names Levi gave his sons reflected their emotional identification with their brothers' pain. The name גֵּרְשׁוֹן, *Gershon* [from גֵּר, *stranger*], reflects the status of the Jews as strangers in Egypt; קְהָת, *Kehath,* was named so to focus on the fact that the teeth of the Jews were put on edge [as in הִקְהֵה אֶת שִׁנָּיו, *blunt his teeth,* in the Pesach Haggadah] as a result of the painful exile. Finally, the name מְרָרִי, *Merari,* referred to the bitterness (מֵרוּר) of slavery. Thus the Torah teaches that even if one does not personally experience pain and travail, one must identify with the pain of others, and certainly with that of his brothers.[19]

---

18. **Classless Liberty.** The commandment regarding the freeing of servants was intended to create unity among the Jews. As long as there were servants and masters, upper- and lower-class citizens, they would lack the unity necessary for true freedom (*Zekan Aharon*).

19. **How Can I?** During World War I, the *Chafetz Chaim* was constantly restless, plagued by the suffering of Jewish communities in the path of the warring German and Russian armies. One night his wife woke up and saw that he was not in his bed. She went to the next room and found him lying on some hard wooden chairs, his head resting on one of his arms. She asked why he was sleeping there. He replied, "When young Jewish boys are in foxholes at the battlefront, suffering cold and hunger and facing death at any moment, how can I sleep comfortably?"

הוּא אַהֲרֹן וּמֹשֶׁה . . . הֵם הַמְדַבְּרִים
אֶל פַּרְעֹה מֶלֶךְ מִצְרַיִם לְהוֹצִיא אֶת
בְּנֵי יִשְׂרָאֵל מִמִּצְרָיִם הוּא מֹשֶׁה וְאַהֲרֹן
*This was Aaron and Moses . . . They were
the ones who spoke to Pharaoh, king of Egypt,
to take the Children of Israel out of the land of
Egypt; this was Moses and Aaron (ibid. 26-27).*

The Sages note that in some verses Aaron is mentioned before Moses while in others the order is reversed. This teaches that they were equally great.

The Sages (*Berachos* 58a) teach that just as no two faces are the same so the opinions of no two people are the same.[20] How then can the Sages say that Aaron and Moses were equal? The *Chozeh of Lublin* views their self-effacement as the key to their equality. Ordinary people, each of whom values his own opinions over those of others, can never see one another as equals. Moses and Aaron, who said of themselves *for what are we (Exodus* 16:7), were so humble that each was able to see the other as greater than himself. Hence they were equal.

Chasam Sofer views the verses as teaching that loyalty to God and Torah is what grants Jewish leaders legitimacy to represent Jewish interests in the halls of government. Aaron and Moses, to whom the word of Hashem is inviolable, *were the ones who spoke to Pharaoh,* representing the nation and its true interests in front of the Egyptian monarch. One cannot be a Jewish leader unless he is intimately linked to the God of the Jews and His Torah.

Be'er Mayim Chaim sees the ability of Moses and Aaron to function in the corridors of power without becoming corrupt as reflected in this verse. Aaron and Moses who came before Pharaoh remained the same Moses and Aaron even after repeated encounters with the immoral atmosphere of the Egyptian royalty.

Moses brings the plagues upon Pharaoh and Egypt in order to bring them to the recognition that *I am Hashem in the midst of the earth* (*Exodus* 8:18), totally involved and in control of human destiny.

וְשָׁרַץ הַיְאֹר צְפַרְדְּעִים . . . וּבְתַנּוּרֶיךָ
*The River shall swarm with frogs . . .
and into your ovens (7:28).*

The Talmud (*Pesachim* 53b) teaches that Chananiah, Mishael and Azariah went willingly into the furnace, having derived the obligation to do so from the frogs who willingly went into the ovens. According to *Chasam Sofer,* this is reflected in *Perek Shirah,* which lists the songs of praise that every part of Creation figuratively sings to God. The frog's song is, בָּרוּךְ שֵׁם כְּבוֹד מַלְכוּתוֹ לְעוֹלָם וָעֶד, *Blessed is the Name of His glorious Kingdom for all eternity.* Our duty to declare His Kingdom forever is derived from the willingness of the frogs in Egypt to die in order to sanctify His Name.

לְמָתַי אַעְתִּיר לְךָ . . . וַיִּצְעַק מֹשֶׁה אֶל ה'
*for when shall I entreat for you . . .
Moses cried out to Hashem (8:5,8)*

The Torah uses many different expressions when describing the prayers of Moses for the people; for example, groaned, cried out, outcry (2:23), moaning (ibid. 24), to name a few. The Midrash (*Devarim Rabbah* 2:1) describes a total of ten expressions of prayer. According to *Arizal,* the uniquely human power to speak and pray was suppressed in the Egyptian exile. The ten plagues

---

20. **Individual Faces.** *R' Menachem Mendel of Kotzk* explained the comparison of faces to ideas. One may venture an opinion about somebody else's face; one may feel that his own face is prettier than his friend's. One thing, however, one cannot do — to claim that his friend's face is not a face. This is analogous to opinions. One may agree or disagree with a friend's opinion; one may be sure that he is right and his friend is wrong. However, one should not demean his fellow by saying, "My friend's opinion is not an opinion." One must respect someone else's point of view. [While there is objective truth found only in the Torah, one may never discount another's opinion. Disagree, but realize that unless you are a great Torah scholar privy to the depths of Torah, you are as fallible a human being as your friend.]

that freed the people from exile also freed them to speak openly to God in prayer. Thus the process of the ten plagues parallels the ten expressions of prayer.[21]

---

21. **Freedom of Speech.** According to the Kabbalists, the word פֶּסַח (Passover) is a contraction of פֶּה סָח, ''The mouth speaks.'' Man was created as a physical being into which God blew a living soul. As a result of this fusion, man was granted the power of speech. Speech is a way for him to give concrete expression to his intelligence.

When the Jews were swallowed up in the spiritual quagmire of Egypt and became caught up in the physical preoccupations of Egypt, they lost their unique synthesis of body and soul, and could no longer turn to God in prayer and share their burdens with Him. Only with the defeat of Egypt and its alluring culture was the Jewish soul able to reassert itself and find expression in the many aspects of prayer.

Sometimes we are so overwhelmed by the difficulties of life that we are emotionally unable to pray. We think, ''If only I could pray, then God would save me from my troubles.'' In truth, however, the converse is also true. If only the pain would subside, we might actually be able to pray. Let us pray that we be spared pain so that we may really pray (*Simchas Aharon*).

פרשת בא ‎€
Parashas Bo

Background

As the Exodus draws near, God sends Moses to Pharaoh once again. This time God promises that He will make a mockery of Pharaoh, which will strengthen the faith of the Jews.

וַיֹּאמֶר ה׳ אֶל מֹשֶׁה בֹּא אֶל פַּרְעֹה
*Hashem said to Moses,
"Come to Pharaoh" (10:1).*

It would seem that the words "**Go** to Pharaoh" would have been more accurate. *R' Menachem Mendel of Kotzk* explains that the term "go" would have been inappropriate, since one never leaves the presence of God Whose glory fills the world. God said to Moses, "Come with Me to Pharaoh. There is no need to be afraid of him, for I am with you."

כִּי אֲנִי הִכְבַּדְתִּי אֶת לִבּוֹ וְאֶת לֵב עֲבָדָיו
for I have made his heart and the heart of his servants stubborn (ibid.).

The classic commentators question how God could punish Pharaoh for stubbornly refusing to free the Jewish people. Since God Himself imposed this stubbornness upon the king how could he be held responsible for his recalcitrance?.[1]

Beis HaLevi and others maintain that by hardening Pharaoh's heart God did not take away his free choice; on the contrary, He *restored* it. Pharaoh did not want to free the Jews, but as a result of the incessant battering of the plagues, his resolve began to weaken, not because he acknowledged the existence and power of Hashem — which he denied when Moses first came to him — but because the pain had become too great. But the Divine goal was for Pharaoh to recognize God's

---

1. **Fraught with Danger.** *Rambam* writes: "There are times when one commits a great sin or many transgressions and the True Judge decrees that the appropriate punishment is that he will not be allowed to repent, in order that he die as a result of his many sins. This is what the Torah means when it writes 'And I will make Pharaoh's heart stubborn.' Since he initially sinned willingly and out of free choice and volition, God took away from him the ability to repent, so that eventually he would be punished for all his sins" (*Hilchos Teshuvah* 6:3).

Free choice is a double-edged sword. If one uses it properly, it can be a great blessing; if not, it is a curse. It might be compared to the concept of a "designated driver." If one knows that he will be drinking and might become inebriated, he must give his car keys to someone else so that he will not drive drunk and cause an accident. So too, if we abuse our free choice, God, as it were, takes the keys back.

But why was Pharaoh culpable for what he did after his free choice was removed? *Rambam* explains that since Pharaoh's own free choice caused him to be deprived of his free choice, he is held responsible for what he does. This is analogous to someone who far exceeded the speed limit, and lost control of the car he had borrowed. Obviously he is responsible for any damage that occurred while the car was out of control since his own negligence caused it to happen. Pharaoh brought himself to the point that he lost control of his life. It was his own fault and he had to pay the price (*Zekan Aharon*).

omnipotence and total control of nature. For the king to yield only because he could no longer endure the suffering of the plagues would have meant that Pharaoh recognized the stick, rather than the One Who wields it. God hardened Pharaoh's heart and strengthened his resolve in order to neutralize the effect of the plagues so that he really would have free choice in deciding whether or not to "let His people go."[2]

The verse seems to imply that God told Moses to go to Pharaoh *because* He had hardened his heart. *R' Yechiel Meir of Gostinin* explains that Moses was reluctant to go to Pharaoh and provide him with the opportunity to display his tenacity yet again. Such dedication would be an indictment against the Jews: Were they as dedicated to serving God as Pharaoh was to rebelling against Him? God consoled Moses, saying "Don't be impressed with Pharaoh's tenacity; it is not because of his strength of character, *for I have made his heart and the heart of his servants stubborn.*"

וּלְמַעַן תְּסַפֵּר בְּאָזְנֵי בִנְךָ וּבֶן בִּנְךָ
And so that you may relate in the ears of your son and your son's son (ibid. 2).

Why does the Torah command us to relate the story of the miraculous Exodus specifically to children and grandchildren? *Aperion* offers a homiletical lesson: Some people are committed to

Torah and *mitzvos*, and maintain the highest standards of Halachah for themselves, but do not want to impose such strict standards upon their children. They provide them with an education that stresses other subjects more than Torah, and believe, wrongly, that they will succeed in producing generations dedicated to Torah and *mitzvos*.

This is a fatal error. Even if (through some miracle) their children will not reject the Torah, they will certainly be less observant than their parents. *Their* children will lapse even further from authentic Judaism. The Torah therefore insists that we teach the message of faith to our children in its full vibrancy, so that they in turn will be able to educate *their* children in this very spirit.[3]

וִידַעְתֶּם כִּי אֲנִי ה'
That you may know that I am Hashem (ibid.).

The verse begins by saying that parents must inculcate their children with faith, but then it turns to the parents and says that *they*, the parents, are to know Hashem. *R' Yehoshua of Belz* explains that the commitment of parents is a precondition for teaching children to believe in God. If one wants his messages to be taken seriously by his children, then he himself must firmly believe. In order to successfully relate the messages of faith *in the ears of your son . . .* you yourself must *know that I am Hashem.* [4]

In contrast, *R' Yehoshua of Kutna* views the

---

2. **Restoring Balance.** *Chavos Yair* offers a lovely parable. A Jew and a non-Jew had a business disagreement and were scheduled to appear before a gentile judge, who was well known for his anti-Semitism. The Jew sent the judge a sizable bribe. The judge summoned the Jew privately and said, "I don't understand you. Your Torah forbids bribery, which makes sense, since the judge will be influenced to rule on behalf of the one giving the bribe. How could you do such a thing?"

The Jew mustered the courage to tell the truth. "Had you been a Jew and my opponent was also a Jew, you would have been impartial. In such a case, it would be wrong of me to offer a bribe and undermine your objectivity. But since my opponent is a gentile and you are a known anti-Semite, you would be prejudiced against me. All my bribe can accomplish is to make you impartial, as a judge should be. On one side is your anti-Semitism; on the other side is my bribe. Now the scales are even and you can be objective."

3. **Multigenerational Faith.** *And may you see children [born] to your children (Psalms* 128:6) is not merely a blessing that one merit to see grandchildren. King David also means to bless us that we be successful in endowing our children with a powerful Jewish education, one strong enough to one day ignite the souls of their children.

4. **Parental Spill-Off.** According to the *Chafetz Chaim,* this message resonates in the words of the *Shema* : *Let these matters that I command you today be upon your heart. Teach them thoroughly to your children . . . (Deuteronomy* 6:6). The degree to which one can educate his children is directly related to how deeply the message of Torah and its values has penetrated his heart. One who pays mere lip service to Torah cannot expect to successfully raise his children to be undyingly loyal to it. One whose heart is suffused with dedication to the Torah will sacrifice everything in order to educate his children to be loyal, vibrant Jews.

verse's end — the faith of the parents — as the outcome of the process. By repeating the timeless truths about the Exodus and its lessons, one strengthens his own faith. By teaching your children, *you may know that I am Hashem*. [5], [6]

עַד מָתַי מֵאַנְתָּ לֵעָנֹת מִפָּנָי
Until when will you refuse to be humbled before Me? (ibid. 3).

When a committed Jew sins, he feels brokenhearted, full of regret for "disappointing" God and not having been strong enough to rise to the test. Deep in his heart he yearns for God's closeness and prays for the fortitude to continue to live according to His will. He "wants to want" the right thing, and it hurts him that his desire is not as strong as he knows it should be.

Pharaoh was just the opposite. Not only did he flout God's will without compunction, he didn't even feel guilty for not feeling guilty. Totally complacent and satisfied with himself and his rebelliousness, he felt no need to humble himself to God. God sent Moses to tell him, *Until when will you refuse to be humbled before Me?* "Your major offense is that you do not not even care to humble yourself" (*Sfas Emes*).[7]

בִּנְעָרֵינוּ וּבִזְקֵנֵינוּ נֵלֵךְ
With our youngsters and with our elders we shall go (ibid. 9).

Pharaoh wanted to allow only the adult males to go and serve Hashem. Like many throughout the generations, Pharaoh understood that if he were to consign religion to the "old folks" and succeed in cutting off the youth from its tradition, he would eventually sever the people's connection to God.

R' Yosef Tzvi of Yafo elaborates: Moses mentioned the youth before the elders so that Pharaoh would understand clearly that their participation in God's service was primary. Pharaoh was willing to allow the elders to conduct a festival for God as long as the youth would remain behind. On a practical level, he realized that young manpower could build Egypt. On a spiritual level, he wanted to keep the youth behind since they were the most susceptible to the temptations of Egypt's immorality.

Moses, too, knew that, having not yet achieved a steady course in life, the youth were vulnerable to the magnetic pull of the Egyptian culture. He wanted to harness their youthful vibrancy and energy to the service of God; therefore, his first concern was for the youngsters.[8]

---

5. **Reciprocal Strength.** [How frequently the commitment of parents to Judaism is strengthened by their efforts to educate their children. Intelligent, sensitive and truly loving parents are ready to change their lifestyles and upgrade their own commitment so that their children will not be subjected to contradictory messages, one from the home and one from the school.]

6. **Faith Talk.** *R' Avraham of Slonim* suggests a homiletical allusion to the principle that faith is strengthened by constant verbalization. The Psalmist says, *I believed because I spoke* (Psalms 116:10) to the heart and emotions those eternal truths that are essential to one's faith. Verbal expression of the eternal certitudes of faith helps them penetrate to the deepest recesses of our conscious and subconscious. In this vein he interprets the verse *Faith is forgotten; it is detached from their mouths* (Jeremiah 7:28). People's faith became weakened because they stopped talking about it. (This may be the reason why many people have the custom of reciting the Thirteen Principles of Faith [אֲנִי מַאֲמִין] every day after the morning prayers.)

7. **Impenetrable Barrier.** Pure character and the excision of egocentricity and evil from the human personality are a goal in themselves, not merely important means to improve oneself. According to the *Baal Shem Tov*, the verse "I was standing between Hashem and you" (*Deuteronomy* 5:5) reflects the spiritual ugliness of arrogance. The "I" — the inflated ego, which is the source of all negative character traits — stands as a barrier between "Hashem and you" (*Nesivos Shalom, Nesivei Chinuch*).

8. **Orphaned Generation.** A community that ignores the spiritual plight of its young and focuses only on the old people is like an old-age home. Conversely, one that shunts aside its elders in favor of the young is like an orphanage. Fortunate are the young who view the wisdom of their elders as a beacon of light by which to make their way through life; blessed are the elders who are strengthened by the alacrity and verve of the young (*Hagigei Asher*). The *Ponevezher Rav* put it this way: "An orphaned child is one without parents; an orphaned generation is one without children."

רְאוּ כִּי רָעָה נֶגֶד פְּנֵיכֶם. לֹא כֵן לְכוּ נָא הַגְּבָרִים

Look — the evil intent is opposite your faces.
Not so; let the men go now (ibid. 10-11).

Ridbaz offers a novel interpretation. Pharaoh was ready to allow the men to travel but refused to send the young children, ostensibly out of fear that the trip would be dangerous for them. What about the women? Up to now Pharaoh would not allow the men to go serve God, fearful that the experience would spark a spiritual revolution that would cleanse them of the idolatry and immorality to which he had exposed them. Now that he was forced to accede to Moses' demand, Pharaoh hit on a plan that would nullify the spiritual gain of the festival of serving Hashem. By claiming to be concerned for the welfare of the children, he would force the women to remain in Egypt. His insight into the makeup of the Jewish home was such that he knew that whatever spiritual gain the men might have from the experience would quickly be undone by the women who did not experience the festival.[9]

Background

The penultimate plague, Darkness, envelops the Egyptians in a tangible supernatural darkness. This plague served a dual purpose; (a) to provide the Jews with the opportunity to determine where the Egyptian wealth was to be found. Later, before the actual Exodus, they would ask the Egyptians to "lend" them these valuables; (b) the assimilated Jews who did not deserve to leave Egypt could die during the darkness, out of sight of the Egyptians, thus not enabling them to claim that the Jews were subject to the plagues.[10], [11]

לֹא רָאוּ אִישׁ אֶת אָחִיו וְלֹא קָמוּ אִישׁ מִתַּחְתָּיו

No man could see his brother nor could anyone rise from his place (ibid. 23).

Homiletically, *Chidushei HaRim* interprets this verse as a description of the blindness induced by egocentricity, the darkness that falls when someone is oblivious to his fellow and cannot sense

---

9. **Rescuing Our Roots.** This insidious phenomenon of the men being more involved in observance than the women took a heavy toll on European Jewry, until the visionary *Sarah Schenirer* founded the Bais Yaakov school system. While the men received a solid Torah education from their youngest years and, for the most part, remained God-fearing Jews, women's Torah education was ignored. Most young women were educated in public schools or, even worse, in schools that preached an anti-Torah philosophy. In many cases, the Jewish identities of many such women fell victim to this lack of Torah education. Not only were their minds and hearts poisoned with anti-Torah propaganda, they passed this poison on to siblings, husbands and children, bringing down entire families and eventually communities. Of what value is it to educate the men without insuring that the women and girls remain loyal to God and His Torah?

R' Aharon Kotler is reported to have said, "If not for Bais Yaakov, all the *yeshivos* would be forced to close." R' Elyah Lopian said, "The *yeshivos* are very important but Bais Yaakov is more important. Without Bais Yaakov, the *yeshivos* could not exist." In the words of R' Yitzchak Hutner, "If you take a בַּת יִשְׂרָאֵל (Jewish woman) and place the *yud* (Jew) inside, you gain an entire בַּיִת (household)."

10. **Unwillingly Imprisoned.** The Midrash (*Shemos Rabbah* 14:3) identifies the Jews who died as those who had become so integrated into Egypt that they did not want to leave. Although they claimed to want freedom like the other Jews, God, Who searches one's innermost thoughts and motives, knew their true desire. *Taam V'Daas* submits that this will occur again before the Final Redemption. Those who are comfortable with their existence and their business and political connections, and really do not want to be liberated, will, God forbid, not merit to see it. Not only must we believe that the Final Redemption will come, we must also anxiously await it.

11. **No Such a Mitzvah.** A Jew who reported a fellow Jew to the Russian government was severely reprimanded by R' Chaim of Sanz. The informer justified himself by claiming that the fellow was wicked and a heretic, and that it was a mitzvah to bury him. R' Chaim replied: "I'll prove to you that there is no special mitzvah to bury a wicked person. The Midrash teaches that the assimilated Jews in Egypt died and were buried during the three days of darkness. Nevertheless, the *Mechilta* says that when the time came to liberate the Jews they had no *mitzvos* to speak of. God commanded them to circumcise themselves and bring the Pesach offering so they would have the merit of these *mitzvos*. If you are right, they already had the mitzvah of burying the wicked. The answer is that there is no such a mitzvah."

his pain. As a result of *No man could see his brother,* one's emotional faculties can become so desensitized that no one *could rise from his place.* Unable to feel for others, people lose the ability to grow and become better. In this light, *Avnei Azel* understands the *Midrash* that the darkness was as thick as a golden *dinar* coin. The incessant and obsessive chase after money causes one to become so totally self-centered that he becomes blind to the needs of others. One simply sees no one but himself.

וּלְכָל בְּנֵי יִשְׂרָאֵל הָיָה אוֹר בְּמוֹשְׁבֹתָם
but for all the Children of Israel there was light in their dwellings (ibid.).

Rashi (*Genesis* 1:4), citing the Midrash, teaches that the original light of Creation was intensely spiritual. God saw that the wicked were unworthy of enjoying it, and therefore He set it aside for the righteous of future generations.

According to *R' Menachem Mendel of Kotzk,* this was the light that the Children of Israel had in their dwellings during the plague of darkness, when the wicked had no light.[12]

Midrash Rabbah defines this light with the words of King David, *Your word is a lamp for my feet and a light for my path* (*Psalms* 119:105), a reference to the light of Torah. *R' Shmuel Rozovsky* explains: In the deep darkness of Egypt, which was so thick that it could be touched and no light could penetrate, the only source of light was the light of Torah — *for all the Children of Israel there was light in their dwellings* — for among the Jews the light of God's Torah burned brightly. The word of God is so illuminating that it can pierce the thickest darkness.

וְגַם מִקְנֵנוּ יֵלֵךְ עִמָּנוּ . . . כִּי מִמֶּנּוּ נִקַּח לַעֲבֹד אֶת ה' אֱלֹקֵינוּ
And our livestock, as well, will go with us . . . for from it we will take to serve Hashem, our God (ibid. 26).

First the verse says that the livestock will *go,* implying that they will go on their own, and

then it says that they will be *taken. Malbim* comments. When Elijah challenged the prophets of the Baal at Mount Carmel (*I Kings* 18), the bull he was to offer willingly stretched out its neck to be slaughtered as an offering for God's honor. Here, too, the livestock will go with us, ready to do their part in the service of Hashem. The verse continues, *from it we will take to serve Hashem,* meaning that the livestock will serve as an example to us, as a role model that we should emulate by being ready to sacrifice ourselves on God's behalf. In this sense, the Jewish people are described in the *Tachanun* prayer with the words, "we are regarded as the sheep led to slaughter."

According to the *Yid HaKadosh of P'shis'cha,* the verse relates to the age-old debate of intellectual/emotional as opposed to active religion. Pharaoh argued that the Jews could serve God without bringing offerings. "Serve with your hearts," he argued. Moses retorted that intent is only meaningful if it translates into action. Our livestock will go with us as well, for only through tangible action can one achieve true connection with God.

וַאֲנַחְנוּ לֹא נֵדַע מַה נַּעֲבֹד אֶת ה' עַד בֹּאֵנוּ שָׁמָּה
and we will not know with what we are to serve Hashem until our arrival there (ibid.).

Offerings have two basic functions. They are brought either to gain atonement for past sins or as an expression of gratitude for God's constant miracles. Sure that their entire journey from slavery through Exodus until the receiving of the Torah would be accompanied by miracles, the Jews did not know how extensive their gratitude would have to be. Hence they said that they would not know with what to serve Him until they arrived at Sinai (*Ksav Sofer*).

Alternatively, the verse points out the fallacy of free expression in religious experience. The form through which we must serve God is clearly defined by Torah. Just as an intricate computer system needs every microcomponent to be in place in order to function properly, so every detail

---

12. **Light Capsules.** According to the *Baal Shem Tov,* God ensconced the primordial light in the Torah (see *Midrash Tanchuma, Noach*). Hence while the wicked Egyptians wallowed in darkness, the Jews were able to access the primordial light hidden inside the word of God (*Zekan Aharon*).

of our service of God is precisely delineated in the Torah. We will not know how to serve Him until we arrive at Sinai and receive His detailed instructions (*Simchas Aharon*).

Chidushei HaRim views the word *there* homiletically, as a reference to the Heavenly court, which everyone must one day face. In life, one may never know the true value of his good deeds. Were they done properly, with correct intent and purity of motive, or were they tainted and cheapened? Were they done for the sake of Heaven or with ulterior motives? We will truly not know with what to serve Hashem *until our arrival there*. [14]

Background

The time of the Exodus is rapidly approaching, and the final plague, the death of the firstborn, is about to take place. God conveys to Moses the full details of this miraculous plague to be related to Pharaoh, who nonetheless continues his obstinate refusal to free the Jews.

כְּשַׁלְּחוֹ כָּלָה גָּרֵשׁ יְגָרֵשׁ אֶתְכֶם מִזֶּה
When he sends forth it shall be complete —
he shall drive you out of here (11:1).

Why was it insufficient for Pharaoh to simply allow them to leave? Why did he have to forcibly drive them out of Egypt? *Sfas Emes* explains that when God liberated the Jews from

Egypt, He wanted not only to free them from exile in Egypt, but also to free them of every vestige of Egyptian influence. By having Pharaoh drive them away, God assured that he would sever any connection between Egypt and the Children of Israel. This would allow the Jews to be spiritually unencumbered and able to rise to the heights necessary to receive the Torah and enter the Land of Israel. Had Pharaoh freed them willingly, they would have remained morally indebted and spiritually tied to Egypt, unable to be truly free.

R' Yitzchak Zelig of Sokolov embellishes on this approach. Whenever one shows kindness to another, it forges a link between them and creates mutual love. Had the Jews left Egypt as a result of Pharaoh's goodness, they would have felt a sense of gratitude toward him and his people, and perhaps even a subconscious yearning to return. God therefore had Pharaoh eject the Jews from his land.[15]

דַּבֶּר נָא בְּאָזְנֵי הָעָם וְיִשְׁאֲלוּ אִישׁ מֵאֵת
רֵעֵהוּ וְאִשָּׁה מֵאֵת רְעוּתָהּ כְּלֵי כֶסֶף וּכְלֵי זָהָב
Please speak in the ears of the people: Let each man request of his fellow and each woman of her fellow silver vessels and gold vessels (ibid. 2).

God asked Moses to *please* prevail upon the Jews to request valuables from their Egyptian hosts so that the soul of Abraham would not claim that God fulfilled the part of His promise which called for exile and oppression, but failed to fulfill His guarantee that they would leave with great

---

14. **Personalized Mission.** *R' Yisrael of Rizhin* added a personal perspective: Everyone is sent to this world with his unique soul in order to perfect a specific aspect of Creation. Everyone has his unique mission in life that only he can fulfill. One may spend his whole life doing good things (studying Torah, fulfilling *mitzvos,* praying, helping others) and yet may not have fulfilled his unique mission. One must pray for the insight to know why he was sent to the world; otherwise *we will not know with what we are to serve Hashem until our arrival there.*

Zekan Aharon submits that *there* refers to *Eretz Yisrael.* This interpretation is based on the *Sifre (Deuteronomy* 11:7) that the most meaningful fulfillment of the *mitzvos* is in the Land of Israel (see *Ramban* to *Leviticus* 18:25). As the Sages taught "there is no Torah like the Torah of *Eretz Yisrael"* (*Bereishis Rabbah* 16:4), for the level of service of Hashem that one can achieve there is unparalleled in the Diaspora. Therefore the Torah teaches that we will not truly know how to serve Him *until our arrival there.*

15. **Total Severance.** Although this severance of ties had to be in such a way that the Jews would feel no gratitude toward the Egyptians for granting them liberty, the Torah commands us not to reject an Egyptian, *for you were a sojourner in his land* (*Deuteronomy* 23:8). Even though they brutally enslaved us, we must be grateful to them for welcoming our forefather Jacob and his family, and even for hosting us while we were enslaved.

This teaches us an important lesson with regard to our attitude toward our hosts in exile. On one hand we must be thankful for all they do — even if they do so for their own benefit. However, we may not allow our gratitude to create an emotional link between us and those whose culture and values are spiritually detrimental (*Simchas Aharon*).

wealth (*Rashi*). The Sages' words are surprising. Is God less bound than humans to keep His word? Why do the Sages frame it in terms of preventing Abraham from complaining?

HaBe'er offers the following: Both wealth and poverty pose trials to one who wishes to serve God. Poverty can cause one to stray from the Godly path and resort to dishonesty, while wealth can bring one to reject God completely. In fact, the test of wealth is the more difficult of the two. Moses had to beg the Jews to take gold and silver from the Egyptians since they feared the trial of wealth. Abraham had undergone and withstood both tests. He was faced with poverty when he left his father's house with nothing and was subject to the trial of wealth when he returned from Egypt, rich in cattle, silver and gold. Abraham had conquered wealth; he did not fear it. He would therefore insist that God keep His promise to grant wealth to his descendants.[16]

The *Maggid of Dubno* offers a different perspective. Beyond freedom from physical bondage, the Jews achieved tremendous spiritual wealth as a result of the Exodus. The spiritual sophisticates among them certainly viewed this as the fulfillment of the Divine promise that they would leave with great wealth. Abraham, however, might claim that the simple Jew must be reckoned with as well. Just as he experienced the servitude and oppression in its most literal sense, so should he taste wealth in its most basic form.

R' Yehoshua of Horodna sees in this an indication of the spiritual refinement of the Jews and their unwillingness to be involved in anything less than perfect honesty. Although the Jews realized that they were entitled to the wealth of the Egyptians as compensation for their years of backbreaking labor, they were nevertheless extremely uncom-

fortable with the unsavory method of acquiring it. Moses asked them to "borrow" valuable objects from the Egyptians, objects that the Jews knew would not be returned. As the prophet says, *The remnant of Israel will not commit corruption* (*Zephaniah* 3:13). God therefore asked that they *please* allow him to fulfill His promise.

Peninei HaTorah explains differently. The Talmud (*Kiddushin* 31a) teaches that one who is obligated to do a mitzvah receives greater reward than one who does so only voluntarily. *Tosafos* (s.v. גדול המצווה) explains that when one is obligated, the evil inclination seeks to dissuade him from fulfilling his obligation; there is a natural tendency to rebel against coercion. One who volunteers, on the other hand, does not have to overcome this resistance and therefore does not earn the reward that goes to one who has to fight his evil inclination. Had God commanded the Jews to take riches from the Egyptians, it would have become a mitzvah, along with its accompanying evil inclination. Therefore God asked Moses to implore the Jews to *please* take the wealth.[17]

עַד בְּכוֹר הַשִּׁפְחָה אֲשֶׁר אַחַר הָרֵחָיִם
To the firstborn of the maidservant who is behind the millstone (ibid. 5).

Rashi notes that even the lowliest Egyptians enslaved the Jews or, at the very least, derived enjoyment from their suffering and therefore deserved punishment. This is a recurrent pattern in our history. Even those nations that do not actively persecute us consider us to be threatening outsiders. They are therefore happy when others try to eradicate the Jews.

When Hitler ימ״ש almost succeeded in wiping out

---

16. **Spiritual Ambush.** In fact, the wealth turned out to be a spiritual boomerang since it served as the means to make the Golden Calf. Moses claimed later that, to a certain extent, God Himself was to be blamed for the Golden Calf, since He wanted the Jews to have such wealth and asked Moses נָא, to *please* tell the Jews to ask the Egyptians for precious objects. Accordingly, when Moses pleaded with God to forgive the Jews for the Calf he said that if God was unwilling to do so then, מְחֵנִי נָא מִסִּפְרְךָ, *erase me please from Your book* (*Exodus* 32:32). Homiletically, this can be interpreted to mean "Erase the word נָא, *please,* from Your Torah, for it was Your *please* which caused the Jews to have the wealth out of which arose the Golden Calf."

17. **No Way Back.** *R' Moshe of Lelov* offered a humorous explanation as to why it was so important to God that the Jews "borrow" gold and silver from the Egyptians. Fearful that the Jews would lose their courage in the Wilderness and would seek to return to Egypt, God wanted to give them a vested interest not to do so. Since much of their wealth had been "borrowed," the Egyptians would demand repayment, so the Jews would have less inclination to return.

the Jewish people, he found many allies who were just as enthusiastic about murdering Jews as he was, if not even more so. Even those who were not actively involved gave tacit approval through their deafening silence, and in their heart of hearts were happy that Hitler had finally begun to do "what should have been done a long time ago" (*Taam V'Daas*).[18]

Background

After receiving the mitzvah to sanctify time by declaring the beginning of the new lunar cycle as Rosh Chodesh, Moses is commanded with regard to the laws of the Pesach offering, the offering that would initiate the Jewish people as a nation.[19]

וַאֲכַלְתֶּם אֹתוֹ בְּחִפָּזוֹן

you shall eat it in haste (12:11).

The haste with which the Jews were commanded to eat the Pesach offering symbolized that they were at the brink of spiritual destruction due to their prolonged exposure to the immorality of Egypt. In the words of the *Zohar*, they were wallowing in the forty-ninth level of impurity. Had they remained in Egypt any longer, they might have fallen to the fiftieth level, from which redemption would have been impossible. They had to be redeemed quickly, therefore, before it was too late.[20]

The obvious question arises: Why did God wait so long before extricating them from the impurity of Egypt? Why didn't He save them from the

---

18. **Moral Dilemma.** Enjoying someone else's pain when it is to your own benefit can be a moral dilemma. *R' Yitzchak Zilberstein* relates the following incident. "A Jew told me that he was afraid that in Heaven he would be brought to justice for having said בָּרוּךְ הַשֵּׁם (Thank God). For a moment I thought that I did not hear correctly. For saying בָּרוּךְ הַשֵּׁם?! He told me the following story: 'I was involved in a fatal car accident, which was not my fault. Nevertheless, I was fearful that the one person who witnessed it would report me and that I might be subject to imprisonment. A while later, the witness himself was unfortunately killed in an automobile accident. When I heard about it, the words בָּרוּךְ הַשֵּׁם slipped out of my mouth. Obviously I didn't mean that I was happy over his death, God forbid; I was merely relieved that I was no longer under the threat of imprisonment.'

"The Jew asked me if what he did was a sin and if so, how he could atone for it. I told him that a similar question was posed by a *kapo* who was in charge of unloading transports of people shipped to Auschwitz. Toward the end of the war, as the frequency of the transports decreased, this *kapo* began to fear for his life since he had no doubts that once the Germans ש"י had no need for his 'services' they would kill him. After a lengthy period during which no transports arrived, he saw a line of cattle cars approaching the camp. He issued a sigh of relief and said בָּרוּךְ הַשֵּׁם, since the transport extended his lease on life.

"*R' Ephraim Oshry*, in his *Teshuvos MiMaamakim*, which discusses halachic questions that arose under the Nazis, writes that he was asked by the *kapo* if this was a sin and what he could do about it."

R' Zilberstein answered the question by citing *Tosafos* (Yoma 22b s.v. *v'haamar Rav*) which teaches that King David was considered only an *inadvertent* sinner, when he composed a song of praise to God over the fall of King Saul. Since one cannot be blamed for inappropriate behavior exhibited in a time of pain and stress, King David's sin is treated mildly. Because King Saul had tried to kill him, King David's blame is mitigated. "This shows," concluded the rabbi, "that one who says בָּרוּךְ הַשֵּׁם when saved at the expense of another is considered to be only an inadvertent sinner. One is not judged harshly for what he does in a stressful moment."

19. **Excise by Default.** *B'nei Yissas'char* notes that there are only two *positive* commandments which warrant *kares* (spiritual excision) if one fails to fulfill them — the Pesach offering and circumcision. *Kares* means that one severs his life-giving link to the Jewish people. One who fails to fulfill the mitzvah of Pesach lacks the basic national connection while one who purposely remains uncircumcised fails to link himself to the Jewish people on a personal level. In these two instances he, by default, suffers *kares*.

20. **Grab the Moment.** *R' Tzadok HaKohen of Lublin* writes: One's personal initiation into the service of God must be done hastily, like the haste of the national initiation. When one seeks to sever the binding ties to physical, this-worldly pleasures, he must wait for the moment when the desire to connect with God's Will is aroused in him and then seize that opportunity to escape. Having made the break, he should then seek to grow gradually, step by step, similar to the Pesach offering brought in the generations that followed the Exodus (*Tzidkas HaTzaddik* 1).

[Emotion is fleeting and lacks a sense of permanence. When one experiences spiritual inspiration, one should concretize it before it dissipates. Once one has embarked on a course of growth, he may proceed in an orderly, methodical manner, being sure at each stage that he is on firm footing before proceeding further.]

---

spiritual quagmire when they reached the forty-eighth level of impurity, and alleviate the need for such haste?

Divrei Shmuel explains: When a seed is planted in the ground it must disintegrate before anything can sprout, but if the disintegration is total, nothing will grow. For example, if rotten wheat kernels are planted in the ground, they will yield nothing. Only at the stage immediately before total rot can growth occur. The Egyptian exile was the greenhouse into which the Jewish nation was born. Before it could be created, it had to reach the stage just before total disintegration. Only when nothing but the very last spades of spiritual life still burned could the creation of this new nation occur. Thus it was in the very last minute when the regeneration process could occur that the Jews were ready for redemption. At that moment, haste was crucial.[21], [22]

---

21. **The Edge of Health.** *Sfas Emes* offers a different perspective. Just as a child receives his immune system while in the womb, so the Jewish people developed their spiritual antibodies while they were in Egypt. They were exposed to the fullest survivable combination of spiritual impurity so that when they emerged they would be immune to whatever spiritual impurities they might encounter throughout the Exile.

Much like an innoculation, which introduces a strain of the disease that is neither too weak to produce antibodies nor too powerful for the body's immune system, so it is with spiritual inoculation. Had they left Egypt before falling to the forty-ninth level of impurity, they would not have been fully inoculated. God took them to the brink and then hastily saved them, before it was too late.

22. **Down and Up.** The greatest mussarists spoke of a spiritual descent that is the necessary prelude to spiritual ascent (יְרִידָה לְצוֹרֶךְ עֲלִיָּה). This parallels the growth process described here. Before a person is able to make a quantum leap of spiritual growth, it is necessary to have the seeds of that growth approach the stage of spiritual breakdown.

פרשת בשלח ﷽
Parashas Beshalach

Background

Finally freed from Egyptian bondage, the Jew-ish people leave Egypt on a circuitous route in order to avoid a confrontation with the Philistine warriors who would surely attack the Jewish "invaders" crossing their territory. Convinced that the Jews lost their way in the desert, Pharaoh chases them down at the Sea of Reeds, where conclusive defeat awaits him.

וַיְהִי בְּשַׁלַּח פַּרְעֹה אֶת הָעָם
It happened when Pharaoh sent out the people (13:17).

The term וַיְהִי generally precedes the description of a sad event. What was sad about the Jews leaving Egypt? The Midrash interprets וַיְהִי as if it read וַי, *woe*. Even after everything that befell the land of Egypt and its citizens, Pharaoh still felt a sense of pain over letting the Jews go.

Based on *Ramban's* observation, *Igra D'Kallah* explains that the word הָעָם, *the people,* refers to the spiritually inferior members of the nation, specifi-cally the *eirev rav,* the Egyptian rabble that flocked to join the Jews when they left Egypt. They were the ones who later incited the catastrophe of the Golden Calf (see *Exodus* 32). Thus it was a tragedy that *the people* — i.e., the *eirev rav* — left Egypt and provoked the righteous Jews to such a terrible sin.[1]

R' Tzadok HaKohen of Lublin adds two novel perspectives: God's main goal in inflicting the plagues upon the Egyptians was to implant within the Jews a yearning to be free from the spiritual impurity of Egypt. But even after witnessing so many miracles, they were still not ready to leave willingly; Pharaoh had to send them out. How sad

---

1. **Missing the Point.** Because of our belief in the effectiveness of the political process and our own human efforts, we often forget that our successes (and failures) result from Divine intervention. Whether linked to our own spiritual state, or related to an unknown Divine agenda, the path of our lives is determined by God alone. How unfortunate we are when we fail to realize this. According to *R' Yehoshua of Belz,* this failure is behind the expression of sadness, וַיְהִי. After witnessing the miraculous Hand of God, there were still people (הָעָם, the spiritual riffraff) who saw the whole story as *Pharaoh sent out the people.*

Sfas Emes offers a different perspective based on the difference between the Exodus and the Splitting of the Sea. God liberated us from Egypt in an act of total mercy. Since we did not deserve to be redeemed, Divine justice could not be fully employed, for if it were, the judgment would have been directed against us as well — and this similarity between Israel and Egypt caused distress to God. Only at the Sea, when Israel exhibited courageous faith in God by willingly going into the water, was there cause for joy, as God vanquished those who were both His enemies and ours.

[Only when we earn something does God rejoice. While He mercifully provides for us even when we are undeserving, He is joyous, as it were, when He can bestow upon us that which is rightfully ours.]

it is when Jews don't want to save themselves from spiritual suffocation.[2]

Alternatively, the very fact that Pharaoh chased after them indicates that some emotional tie still existed between them. The fact that Pharaoh wanted to force them to return demonstrated clearly that there still existed a spiritual attachment. This was the true tragedy.

וְלֹא נָחָם אֱלֹקִים דֶּרֶךְ אֶרֶץ פְּלִשְׁתִּים
that God did not lead them by way of the land of the Philistines (ibid.).

The shorter route from Egypt to *Eretz Yisrael* was through the territory of the Philistines, but while it offered the advantage of readily available provisions, it entailed coming in close contact with the belligerent Philistines. Such an encounter might have influenced the Jews to want to return to Egypt. The longer route through the desert held little in the way of provisions, but avoided the negative impact of confrontation with the Philistines.

This, says the *Chafetz Chaim,* provides an answer to those who sell their souls by pursuing a livelihood through involvement in settings or occupations that run contrary to the spirit of Torah and Halachah. Let anyone contemplating such a step consider that if God preferred to take the Jews from Egypt through the circuitous, rather than the direct, way, apparently the risk of losing business is less of a threat than spiritual assimilation. If God could provide for three million Jews in the Wilderness, He can certainly take care of one Jew who

possesses the strength of character to stand up to the test.

According to *Sfas Emes,* God took the Jews on a circuitous path as a symbol for generations of Jews to come. Jews must know how to traverse spiritually rugged terrain and make their way through inhospitable places in order to survive the travails of exile. It was on their way out of Egypt that they learned this lesson in survival.[3]

כִּי קָרוֹב הוּא . . . וְשָׁבוּ מִצְרָיְמָה
because it was near . . . and they will return to Egypt (ibid.).

Since the land of the Philistines was close to Egypt, God feared that upon encountering war with the Philistines, the Jews would seek to return to the land of their bondage (*Rashi*).

Imrei Shefer (following the comment of the *Daas Zekeinim Baalei HaTosafos*) interprets כִּי קָרוֹב הוּא as *because He [God] is close* [to His people]. When a stranger gives someone a gift and it is rejected, it makes little difference to the giver. A father, however, cares deeply when his child refuses to accept his gift. Since God is our Father and wanted us to accept His gift of freedom, He did not take us by way of Philistia, where we might have been attacked and decide to return to Egypt.

In a different approach, *because it was near* is understood as referring to the Land of Israel. God did not want to bring the Jews to the Land of Israel immediately, while they were still under the influence of Egyptian culture, and their habits and character were still Egyptianlike. Furthermore,

---

2. **Divine Denial.** Spiritual blindness allows us to see God's Hand clearly and yet to psychologically deny its reality. An old Yiddish saying comes to mind: "A fool is the person who looks at the finger when you point to the moon."

3. **Roundabout Route.** Let us never be dismayed and lose hope when the path to the ultimate Redemption seems to take a seemingly endless, roundabout route. Just as our first liberation did not take us directly to the Promised Land, so the Final Redemption will come only after a circuitous sojourn throughout the inhospitable lands of exile (*Zekan Aharon*).

The word *hakafah,* "circuit" (as in the *Hakafos* of *Simchas Torah*), can be considered a metaphor for the entire history of the Jewish people. In the centuries of our exile, we took the Torah with us from country to country. Following a circuitous route, we started in Babylonia, where the *Talmud Bavli* developed. From there we traveled from country to country, continent to continent, and hemisphere to hemisphere, all the while doing our best to carry the Torah proudly aloft. This wandering from place to place will hopefully end soon, when God will allow the joy and light of Torah to guide us to a final, tranquil port of destination — *Eretz Yisrael,* from where our odyssey began — with the coming of *Mashiach,* speedily in our days (*R' Meir Shapiro*).

the slave mentality was so deeply rooted within them[4] that they were not yet ready to enter the Land where man must experience the true freedom of serving God. They therefore had to take the long route to *Eretz Yisrael,* rather than pass through the land of Philistines *because it was near* [the Land of Israel] (*R' Yehudah Leib Graubart*).

Finally, the *Steipler Gaon* submits that had they encountered battle with the Philistines, the combination of geographical and spiritual proximity to Egypt would have caused them to go back. It was necessary for them to make the unalterable decision that they could never bring themselves to return to the abominations of Egypt.

This teaches us that one should invest time and energy in distancing oneself from sin. It was worthwhile to spend the time and energy to travel the long route through the desert so as to avoid leaving themselves a way back to the impurity of Egypt (*R' E.E. Dessler*).[5]

וַחֲמֻשִׁים עָלוּ בְנֵי יִשְׂרָאֵל מֵאֶרֶץ מִצְרָיִם
The Children of Israel were armed when they went up from the land of Egypt (ibid. 18).

Rabbeinu Bachya writes that the Jews took weapons with them even though they were under God's direct protection, for God intervenes only after man has expended a certain degree of

natural effort. As the Sages teach, "We do not rely on miracles" (see *Pesachim* 64b and *Ramban* to *Genesis* 6:19).

If so, and since they were armed, why did God not command them at the Sea of Reeds to fight the Egyptians with the armaments they had taken with them? Why did He produce a miracle rather than allow them to engage in conventional warfare? What was the use of bringing weapons if they were never meant to use them?

Chasam Sofer explains: The Jews had no moral right to fight the Egyptians since they owed them a debt of gratitude for having been hosts to Jacob their forefather and his descendants. This moral obligation is the ethical underpinning of the Torah's prohibition against rejecting Egyptian converts after three generations: *You shall not reject an Egyptian for you were a sojourner in his land* (*Deuteronomy* 23:8). Furthermore, we are taught that "one should never throw stones into the water pit from which he drank" (*Bava Kamma* 92b). That is why God told the Jews to plunge into the sea without putting up a fight against the Egyptians, for *Hashem shall make war for you, and you shall remain silent* (*Exodus* 14:14).

Through this incident, the Torah teaches that even unwitting kindness deserves a positive response. Although we left Egypt ready to fight the Egyptians rather than rely on miracles, Hashem forbade us to do so in order to show our appreciation. In a sense, the reason we were armed was to

---

4. **Slavish State of Mind.** According to *Ibn Ezra,* it was this slave mentality that caused the 600,000 Jews not to fight back when the Egyptians chased them to the Sea of Reeds. Slavish servility may last long beyond the actual physical bondage. It was only because the generation that entered the Land was never enslaved that it had the courage to fight the Canaanites and conquer the Land. Likewise, according to *Ibn Ezra,* one of the reasons God caused Moses to grow up in Pharaoh's home was so that he would not acquire a servile mentality. Raised as royalty, he was able to speak to Pharaoh as an equal and to take a firm stand, as he did when he killed the Egyptian who was beating a defenseless Jew (*Exodus* 2:12), and when he protected Jethro's daughters from the Midianite shepherds (ibid. 17).

5. **Entrapped by Ego.** There are many ways to prevent oneself from returning to sin. One of the most effective ways is to tell all one's friends of his decision to change. Even when one's basic willpower fails him, the mere thought of looking foolish in the eyes of his friends can reinforce his resolve to do the right thing.

R' Yitzchak Zilberstein once discussed the importance of not talking during the prayers in the synagogue. He cited the *Beis Yisrael* who explained the verse *Hashem shall make war for you, and you shall remain silent* (*Exodus* 14:14) as referring to proper conduct while in the synagogue. If you *shall remain silent,* speaking in the synagogue only words of prayer, then *Hashem will make war* against your enemies. Rabbi Zilberstein then suggested that his congregants tell their friends that they have decided to stop talking during the prayers or the Torah reading. By doing this, he said we burn the bridge that leads back to that uncouth habit, for even if we have the urge to talk, the potential embarrassment and social pressure will stop us.

show that we would *not* use the armaments against our benefactors.[6]

According to *R' Yosef Ber Soloveitchik of Brisk-Jerusalem* this verse is connected to the next one, *Moses took the bones of Joseph with him*, for Joseph's bones were their armaments, granting them victory against the Egyptians at the Sea. As *Yalkut Shimoni* states, "the Sea split upon seeing the bones of Joseph."

The *Chozeh of Lublin* views the power of prayer as the armaments that the Jews took with them. *Targum Onkelos* explains the verse *which I took from the hand of the Emorite with my sword and with my bow* (*Genesis* 48:22) as "with my prayer and with my request." The most powerful weapon in a Jew's arsenal is prayer, for the ability to conquer is directly linked to the state of our spirituality. When the Jews came to the Sea they did battle, not with physical armaments but with prayer, as the verse states, *the Children of Israel cried out to Hashem* (14:10).[7]

וַיִּקַּח מֹשֶׁה אֶת עַצְמוֹת יוֹסֵף עִמּוֹ
Moses took the bones of Joseph with him (ibid. 19).

While the rest of the Jews were busy taking the wealth of the Egyptians, Moses removed Joseph's remains from the bottom of the Nile. The difference between their actions and his is reflected in the term *with him*, implying that they remained with him always. Indeed, one's *mitzvos* and good deeds are what he takes with him when he passes on to the next world, while one's material wealth is left behind. As King David said (*Psalms* 49:17-18), *Fear not when a man grows rich, when he increases the glory of his house; for upon his death he will not take anything, his glory will not descend after him* (*Kli Yakar*).

The Midrash interprets King Solomon's words *the wise of heart takes* [i.e., chooses the performance of] *commandments* (*Proverbs* 10:8) as a reference to Moses, who took Joseph's bones while the other Jews were gathering wealth. Why does the Midrash imply that Moses was involved in a mitzvah while the rest of the Jews were not? Wasn't "requesting" the valuables of the Egyptians also a mitzvah since God had instructed them to do so?

Avnei Nezer explains: Certain *mitzvos* are accompanied by personal physical pleasure or gain while other *mitzvos* are performed purely in fulfillment of God's will and provide no personal this-worldly gain at all. While taking the riches of the Egyptians was certainly a mitzvah, it was difficult to do it with totally altruistic motives. In contrast, the wisdom of heart that Moses displayed

---

6. **Endless Gratitude.** The Talmud (*Bechoros* 5b) teaches that a firstborn donkey (as opposed to a firstborn horse or camel) is subject to the mitzvah of redemption in reward for having helped the Jews carry the vast wealth they took with them when they left Egypt. Certainly the donkeys, who have no free choice, did not intend to help the Jews. Why are they rewarded by taking part in a mitzvah? Furthermore, why are all donkeys throughout the generations rewarded for the deeds of their "ancestors"?

According to *Sifsei Chaim*, this teaches that gratitude must be shown even when the favor was done unwittingly and even when the benefactor was forced to do the favor. Even a favor done by an inanimate object deserves recognition and response. When God commanded Moses and Aaron to bring the plagues of blood, frogs and lice, Aaron was the one who smote the Nile and the earth, since Moses owed them gratitude for having saved his life (the Nile when he floated on it as a baby, the earth when he quickly buried the Egyptian whom he killed).

One is rewarded even for doing a passive favor by not ruining an existing situation. As *Rashi* teaches, "In reward for not barking when the Jews left Egypt (*Exodus* 11:7), the dogs were rewarded when God commanded us to dispose of flesh torn in the field by giving it to the dogs." (See *Rashi* to *Exodus* 22:30.)

Ultimately all our benefactors, be they human, animal or inanimate, are messengers whom God employs to send us what He wants us to have. Nevertheless, they are worthy of reward for carrying out His wishes.

7. **Prayerfully Negated.** The Sages commented on the verse *The voice is Jacob's voice, but the hands are Esau's hands* (*Genesis* 27:22) that when the voice is the voice of Jacob, then the hands are not the hands of Esau. When Jacob engages in prayer, the hands of Esau are powerless to harm him.

was to choose a pure mitzvah that brought him no personal gain in this world.[8]

לִפְנֵי בַּעַל צְפֹן
before Baal-zephon (14:2).

According to *Rashi,* Baal-zephon was the sole surviving Egyptian idol; all others had been destroyed before the Exodus. *Mechilta* indicates that the national wealth in gold and silver was stored in Pithom, now known as Pi-hahiroth. Hence the idol was called Baal-zephon, for it was the master, so to speak, of the צָפוּן, *the hidden treasure.* The final victory against the Egyptians occurred here, for wealth was the last stronghold that made them think they were still invincible.

According to *Taam V'Daas,* this holds an eternal lesson about the limited security provided by fiscal wealth. People devote their best years to accumulate fortunes, sure that money will save them from evil, pain and trouble. Eventually they become indentured slaves to their pursuit of money; it becomes their last idol. They don't realize how futile and inadequate it is. But sooner or later, that idol, too, fall.[9]

וַה׳ הֹלֵךְ לִפְנֵיהֶם יוֹמָם בְּעַמּוּד עָנָן לַנְחֹתָם הַדֶּרֶךְ וְלַיְלָה בְּעַמּוּד אֵשׁ לְהָאִיר לָהֶם
Hashem went before them by day in a pillar of cloud to lead them on the way and by night in a pillar of fire to give them light (ibid. 21).

This verse speaks not only of how God led the Jews out of Egypt but also of how He guides us constantly, until this very day. During the day, which symbolizes the times when everything in life is going well, Hashem goes before us, keeping us on the proper path, never allowing our successes to "go to our head" and cause us to reject Him. At night, in troubled times when we find ourselves in what seems to be an impenetrable darkness, Hashem serves as a beacon of light, letting us see beyond our pain to the truth that He provides light (*Oznayim L'Torah*).

Background

In order to lure Pharaoh into chasing after the Jews, God commands them to turn back, thus giving the impression that they were trapped in the Wilderness and therefore were vulnerable. This caused Pharaoh to regret having set the Jews free and to pursue them until the Sea of Reeds. There, God would perform the great miracle of the Splitting of the Sea, permitting Israel to march to freedom. Then He would drown the Egyptians, showing once and for all that only He controls nature and human destiny.

וַיֹּאמְרוּ מַה זֹּאת עָשִׂינוּ כִּי שִׁלַּחְנוּ אֶת יִשְׂרָאֵל מֵעָבְדֵנוּ
and they said, "What is this that we have done that we sent away Israel from serving us?" (ibid. 5).

Did the Egyptians really believe that it was *they* who had sent away the Jews? Did they forget that God had, figuratively, brought them to their knees with the ten plagues?

This underscores the reality that man's intellectual perceptions often mirror his emotional bias.

---

8. **Leaderly Patience.** As Moses left Egypt, about to lead the Jewish people through the Wilderness to the Promised Land, he took the עַצְמוֹת יוֹסֵף, which can be rendered homiletically *the essence of Joseph,* as his guiding principle of leadership. Just as Joseph responded to his brothers' mistreatment with kindness, so Moses committed himself to exhibit the same type of patience with his flock, responding to their obstinate and provocative behavior with care and concern (*Iturei Torah*).

9. **The High and Mighty.** *Humankind's haughtiness will be humbled and men's arrogance will be brought down; and Hashem alone will be exalted on that day* (Isaiah 2:17). In a letter written the day after "9/11," R' Michel Yehudah Lefkowitz wrote, "Now that we have heard the terrible tragedy that occurred, that Hashem has shown that even places that the nations of the world viewed as safe havens are unable to guarantee their own safety, we see clearly that everything is totally in His hands. The least intelligent person alive can no longer mistakenly think that any human force can truly protect us. Clearly it is He Who decides who will live and who will die.

"Our only hope is to strengthen ourselves in heartfelt prayer, to pray with pristine faith and [to engage] in Torah study and acts of kindness toward others. We must distance ourselves from interpersonal strife and animosity so that Hashem too will show His compassion toward us and allow us to live."

Upset over the loss of their slaves, the Egyptians forgot the plagues, forgot their dead firstborn and psychologically blocked out the terrible screaming which had occurred but a few days earlier. Blinded by psychological denial, they could say without reservation that *we sent away Israel from serving us.*

וּבְנֵי יִשְׂרָאֵל יֹצְאִים בְּיָד רָמָה
and the Children of Israel were going out with an upraised arm (ibid. 8).

Targum Onkelos renders בְּיָד רָמָה as *openly.* The Jews did not leave arrogantly, ready to avenge themselves against their oppressors. They left with the pride of free men, fearing no one and ready to chart their course in life independent of any influence except for God's will (*Mei HaShiloach*).

וּפַרְעֹה הִקְרִיב
Pharaoh approached (ibid. 10).

The literal meaning of הִקְרִיב is *[Pharaoh] caused someone to approach,* not that he himself approached. The Midrash (*Shemos Rabbah* 21:5) explains that his actions moved the Jews to true repentance and thus brought them closer to God. The Midrash likens this to a king who was traveling on the road when he heard a princess cry out, "Save me from the bandits!" He stopped and rescued her. A while later he decided to marry her and desperately wanted her to speak with him. When she refused to do so he sent bandits to attack her so that she would again cry out for his help. When she did so he said, "This is what I was waiting for."

In Egypt the Jews cried out for God to relieve their suffering, which He did. But God wanted to hear from them even after He liberated them. Since they did not do so, He sent the Egyptians to chase after them. Terrified, they again cried out for God's help. Thus it was Pharaoh who brought them closer to God.[10]

וְהִנֵּה מִצְרַיִם נֹסֵעַ אַחֲרֵיהֶם
and behold, Egypt was journeying after them (ibid.).

The Torah describes the Egyptian army in the singular [נֹסֵעַ] rather than in the plural [נֹסְעִים] because they were united in their pursuit of the Jews. In the words of *Rashi,* they were בְּלֵב אֶחָד כְּאִישׁ אֶחָד, *with one heart like one man.* This is reminiscent of the Sages' comment that the Jews at Sinai were כְּאִישׁ אֶחָד בְּלֵב אֶחָד, *like one man, with one heart* (See *Rashi* to *Exodus* 19:2) . What are we to learn from the reversal of the phrase?

R' Yitzchak Hutner explains: When we speak of one person, it is reasonable to assume that both his right and left hands intrinsically desire the same thing. However, when we speak of two people, there exists no intrinsic unity of purpose. Only when they decide to join forces can we speak of synthetic unity. The Jewish people are intrinsically one, for Torah and God unite them at their roots. Separation is an unnatural result of artificial divisiveness. When things are as they should be, we are one person; hence, automatically we are of one heart.[11]

Non-Jews, however, are basically divided. It is only out of pragmatic concerns that they can unite to pursue a common agenda. In their fanatic hatred of their former slaves, the Egyptians were able to rise above their basic divisiveness and unite in pursuit of the Jews. Since they were of one heart,

---

10. **What a Shame!** Prayer is not meant to alleviate suffering; rather, suffering is intended to cause prayer. When Pharaoh chased the Jewish people he served as God's agent to get them to turn to Him. *R' Meir Yechiel of Mogilnentza* said, "Isn't it a shame that the Jewish people needs Pharaoh to get them to pray to God and communicate with Him, and are not wise enough to do so on their own?"

According to *Avnei Azel* it is for this very reason that the Jews cried out to God. It was as if they said, "How sad indeed that we have sunk so low that only Pharaoh can get us to pray and repent."

Anti-Semitism has an uncanny ability to unite the Jewish people. When it becomes clear just how uncordial our hosts are, we look to each other for the strength to withstand the onslaught. Thus וּפַרְעֹה הִקְרִיב, Pharaoh and his venomous hatred brought the Jews closer to each other (*Simchas Aharon*).

11. **Intrinsic Unity.** For this reason the Torah refers to the seventy members of Jacob's household who descended with him to Egypt as נֶפֶשׁ (singular) while the six children of Esau are called נְפָשׁוֹת (plural). We who serve one God are intrinsically united (see *Rashi* to *Genesis* 46:27).

they acted as one man. For Jews, there exists a unity of essence; for others, it is merely a unity of purpose and objective.[12]

וַיִּצְעֲקוּ בְנֵי יִשְׂרָאֵל אֶל ה׳
The Children of Israel cried out to Hashem (ibid.).

Rashi comments that the Jews prayed because they "grasped the practice of their forefathers." *Maharal* notes that just a moment earlier they had complained that Moses had taken them out of Egypt to die in the desert, which indicates their low level of faith. Nevertheless, they instinctively resorted to prayer. They knew from their forefathers that when a Jew is in trouble he must cry out to God.[13]

The *Baal Shem Tov* understood their cry in a more positive light. Pain and suffering don't just "happen" to a person. One who thinks he can run away from them is like a woman in labor who ran away, thinking she could escape from the pain. She quickly found out that they stayed with her. The only thing to do about difficulties is to approach God in prayer. When the Jews saw Pharaoh and his armies hot on their heels, they realized that their only hope was prayer.[14]

R' Muttel of Slonim put it this way: When one whips a horse to make it run faster, the horse complies because it thinks that it is running away from the whip. The horse does not realize that the one whipping him is riding along on his back. But when a person is whipped, he must turn around and see who is whipping him. Jews must realize that it is God's stick that is hitting us. This realization itself is comforting, for as King David said, "*Your rod and Your staff, they comfort me*" (*Psalms 23:4*).

וַיִּירְאוּ מְאֹד וַיִּצְעֲקוּ בְנֵי יִשְׂרָאֵל
and they were very frightened; the Children of Israel cried out (ibid.).

A truly God-fearing person is ashamed of fearing anyone or anything besides God. They cried out in embarrassment that they were very frightened of mortal men (*Maor V'Shemesh*).

ה׳ יִלָּחֵם לָכֶם וְאַתֶּם תַּחֲרִשׁוּן
Hashem shall make war for you, and you shall remain silent (ibid. 14).

Unlike the period preceding the Exodus when the Jews needed the merit of the Pesach-offering,

---

12. **Exile Appropriation.** *R' Menachem Mendel of Kotzk* sees this unity of the Egyptians as symptomatic of the exile. When the non-Jew adopts the positive attributes of the Jew, we are truly in exile.

13. **Foxhole Atheist.** *R' A.* was a member of a group of students at *Telshe Yeshivah* who visited the Jewish sick in the local hospital every Friday. Once he visited a man scheduled for surgery the following Tuesday. In the course of the conversation the man said, "I'm an atheist. I don't believe in God." R' A. said, "I'll make you a bet. I wager that at some point before your surgery you will turn to God. If you don't, I will give you $5; but if you do, then you have to donate $10 to the yeshivah. When I come to visit next Friday, you'll tell me what happened." After wishing the man well, R' A. left.

The next Friday, the patient handed R' A. an envelope. "Enclosed is a $10 bill for the yeshivah," he said. "I didn't turn to God the entire time, but as I saw the anesthesiologist standing over me, I said, 'God help me!'"

He "grasped the practice of his forefathers."

14. **Divine Doctor.** *Dr. Guardia,* the personal physician of the king of Prussia, became a full-fledged *baal teshuvah* and a disciple of the *Maggid of Mezritch,* the *Baal Shem Tov's* successor. One day a distraught young girl came running into his house and pleaded with him in a trembling voice to come and save her father who was in critical condition. He stood up as if to leave and slowly, carefully, took his coat out of his closet. He shook it out, brushed his hat and polished his shoes at leisure; he seemed to be in absolutely no rush, whatsoever.

Knowing that every second was crucial, the girl stood anxiously, wringing her hands. Finally, in total despair, she issued a heart-rending cry. "Master of the world! Since the doctor is in no rush, You save my father by Yourself!"

Dr. Guardia turned to her and said, "Go home. Your father's condition has improved; he will be fine." And so it was.

When asked how he knew, the doctor replied, "From the young girl's words I was able to realize that the situation was hopeless by human standards. Only God could help her father. I did what I did in order to break her heart even more so that she would cry out to God. He, I knew, would not reject her brokenhearted prayer."

at the sea they didn't need to do any mitzvah, just wait quietly for God's salvation. When Jews are ready and willing to exhibit self-sacrifice on God's behalf, such as going into the Sea of Reeds, nothing more is necessary for God to save them. The merit of such total dedication is greater than the greatest deeds (*Avnei Nezer*).

Chidushei HaRim elaborates: When the Jewish people cry out to God, expressing their faith in Him and their sense of closeness to Him, they no longer need to pray. They are His children and He must save them. By the mere fact that they turn to God in prayer, certain that He is their only source of salvation, they arouse His Fatherly love and compassion. He therefore says to them, *Why do you cry out to Me?* (ibid 15).[15]

Meshech Chochmah sees this verse as Moses' reassurance to the Jewish people that God would always protect them. God shall always make war for you. You may expect His help; not only now, when you have a legitimate right to ask it of the One Who took you out of Egypt to a desolate wilderness, but even when you have no justification for why God should save you — He will still wage war on your behalf. Even when we must admit that "God is just and we are embarrassed" over our sins and lack of merit, He will still save us from our enemies.[16]

דַּבֵּר אֶל בְּנֵי יִשְׂרָאֵל וְיִסָּעוּ
Speak to the Children of Israel
and let them journey forth (ibid. 15).

There are times in life when prayer is not enough; we must give concrete expression to our faith in God in order to arouse His mercy. God told Moses that the encounter at the Sea of Reeds was such an occasion. Only by entering the Sea before it split and relying on God that He would miraculously save them could they in fact merit that God would do so. Nothing, not even the raging

---

15. **Insidious Heresy.** At the Sea, God told the Jews to be totally passive. Not only were they not to fight; they were not even to pray. In contrast, at the end of the *sidrah,* the Torah relates that at the battle with Amalek they were enjoined to fight and Moses ascended the mountain to pray. Why the difference in approach? *Mei HaShiloach* differentiates between two types of heresy. Pharaoh and the mighty Egyptian empire simply claimed that God does not exist and that all success is the result of human endeavor. The response to such a belief is to underscore the futility of human effort and to show clearly that everything is in the hands of Heaven. God therefore had us assume a passive posture against Egypt, neither fighting nor praying. God would do everything.

Amalek, a descendant of Esau, preaches a far more insidious form of nonbelief. The Amalekites claim that everything is in the hands of Heaven — even one's fear of Heaven. Seeking to shirk responsibility, they claim that everything is predetermined and that man has no control over his destiny. In the words of Esau, *Look, I am going to die, so of what use to me is the birthright* (Genesis 25:32). "Since I will die in the end anyway, I might as well eat, drink and be merry." The deterministic philosophy of Esau is to rationalize that whatever evil he does must be the will of God, for if not he would be unable to do it, Esau (and Amalek) refuse to bear responsibility for their actions. God told us to combat this brand of heresy by showing clearly that only through our efforts (prayer and action) will we deserve Divine intervention.

[Much of the permissiveness of Western society is linked to this rejection of the cardinal principle of free choice; people claim to have been molded by and subjected to forces that are beyond their control, and hence they shirk personal responsibility. This is the last form of heresy before the coming of *Mashiach* (R' Yitzchak Hutner).]

16. **Silent Warriors.** When the forces of negativity in Heaven seek to indict the Jewish people, there always exists the mitigating argument, "The travails of the exile caused the Jews to sin. Had the non-Jews undergone such terrible tribulations, their behavior would have been much worse." There is, however, one area in which Jews are vulnerable. The Heavenly Prosecutor can claim that while non-Jews act with decorum and do not chatter in their houses of worship, the Jews show less reverence while in the synagogue.

Homiletically, our verse addresses this issue. God promises that He will fight for us, refuting Satan's claims. But it is up to us, however, to refute his one legitimate claim. If we want Him to wage our wars, we must *remain silent* in the synagogue (R' Yonasan Eibeschutz).

[In a humorous vein, R' Yonasan once explained to a priest why Jews pray loudly in the synagogue while almost complete silence reigns in the churches. "Very simple! We Jews pray to a very old God. Since oldsters are often hard of hearing we must raise our voices in prayer. You, however, who pray to a much younger 'deity,' can speak in a much softer tone."]

sea, can stand in the way of true faith (*Ohr Ha-Chaim, Nefesh HaChaim*).[17], [18]

Background

When the Jewish nation advanced into the Wilderness they protested that they had no food and were in danger of starvation. They claimed that they were better off in Egypt than in the Wilderness. God gave them manna, heavenly food, thus proving that man lives not by bread alone but rather by the word of Hashem.

לְמַעַן אֲנַסֶּנּוּ הֲיֵלֵךְ בְּתוֹרָתִי אִם לֹא

so that I can test them, whether they will follow My teaching or not (16:4).

R' Shimon bar Yochai said: "The Torah was given only to those who ate the manna" (*Mechilta*). R' *Menachem Mendel of Kotzk* explained, Torah is not given to those who rely on their wealth to provide for all their future needs. To the contrary; excessive wealth often leads to the abandonment of Torah. As the Torah teaches: *Jeshurun*

became fat and kicked . . . and it deserted God, its Maker (Deuteronomy 32:15). The manna fell daily to teach us that one must be satisfied when his present needs are met and not worry about tomorrow. This clarity of vision that Hashem is our real Provider is what makes Torah viable as a way of life, rather than just as a mere code of conduct.

According to R' *Dov Ber of Mezritch*, it was the security of being provided for that served as a test. People in need are quick to believe in God. Would they believe in Him even though they lacked nothing?

וְהוּא כְּזֶרַע גַּד לָבָן וְטַעְמוֹ כְּצַפִּיחִת בִּדְבָשׁ

it was like a coriander seed, it was white and it tasted like a cake fried in honey (ibid. 31).

Rashi (ad loc.) explains that since every Jew was afraid that no manna would fall the next day, they dedicated their hearts to God. R' *Reuvain Melamed* explains that a master is obligated to provide for his indentured servant even if he does not deserve it. By making themselves servants of God, the Jews were assured that their Master would provide for His servants.

---

17. **Going Beyond.** The words נֵס, *miracle,* and נִסָּיוֹן, *test,* stem from the same root. *Sfas Emes* explains: Tests of faith call upon us to transcend our natural fears and logical considerations and to rely on our knowledge that whatever God demands of us is for our own benefit. We must figuratively "go the extra mile" for Him. In response, He performs miracles on our behalf, going beyond the limitations imposed by His rules of nature and doing the supernatural. When we display faith beyond the norm He responds in kind.

18. **Saved by Faith.** A young Jerusalemite told the following story: "As I sat in the hospital waiting room while my wife gave birth, the doctor came out with a worried look on his face. He told me that while the baby was fine, my wife's life was in danger and she needed immediate surgery. All throughout the surgery, the doctors kept sending me to the blood bank for more and more units of blood. Frankly, I felt my heart ready to burst from fear during the almost two-hour operation. Suddenly I remembered the words of R' Chaim of Volozhin, that if one focuses his thoughts on the reality that אֵין עוֹד מִלְבַדּוֹ, *no other force exists in the world besides Him,* he will be saved from the gravest circumstances. I unreservedly concentrated on this truth that only God has power and that no one or nothing can do anything to me, my wife or my family unless God makes it happen. Everything is in His hands.

"I repeated this to myself again and again, and I felt my faith growing stronger. When I returned to the operating room the smiling doctors were standing outside, waiting to give me the good news. 'Believe us, we don't know how we were able to stabilize your wife's condition, but the crisis has miraculously passed. We wrote on your wife's medical chart: a medical miracle.'

"When I heard this I could no longer control myself and broke out in tears, crying uncontrollably like a baby. The doctors were shocked since I had maintained my composure throughout the entire crisis. I couldn't bring myself to explain it to them, although I'm sure they would have been moved had I done so. It was faith and total faith that helped me tap into the One for Whom nothing is impossible."

"It is truly a wondrous *segulah* to disarm any other powers from impacting on one's life and to establish deeply in one's heart that aside from God, there is no other force or power in the world. When one so fully identifies with God's unlimited power, He, in turn, will ensure that no other force can harm him" (*Nefesh HaChaim* 3:12).

The Talmud (*Yoma* 75a) teaches that the manna was white since it cleansed Jews of their sins and it could show who was telling the truth. If two people were to appear before Moses, each claiming to own a particular servant, he would tell them to return the next day. The next morning, Moses would send someone to see where the servant's portion of manna fell. Based on whose tent had the extra portion of manna, Moses knew which litigant was telling the truth.

When a Jew knows that he can no longer hide behind his lies it forces him to figuratively "clean up his act." Thus the manna cleansed the Jews of their sins.[19]

וּבְנֵי יִשְׂרָאֵל אָכְלוּ אֶת הַמָּן אַרְבָּעִים
שָׁנָה . . . עַד בֹּאָם אֶל קְצֵה אֶרֶץ כְּנָעַן
*The Children of Israel ate the manna
. . . until their arrival at the border
of the land of Canaan (ibid. 35).*

While in the Wilderness, the Jews were provided with the manna in the merit of Moses. Once they entered the Land of Israel, the manna stopped and in place of bread from heaven they were commanded to work the land. Homiletically this teaches that although their sustenance in the desert came directly from heaven and was not due to any merit of their own, God really wanted them to serve Him in their mundane occupations, thereby bringing holiness into their everyday life. Then they would be deserving of sustenance (*Simchas Aharon*).

Alternatively, the manna and its daily distribution was a training ground for the Jews to learn faith in God and total reliance on Him. Once they learned the lesson, they were sent into the Land where they had to apply it. Ostensibly they would be earning their sustenance through work in the fields and commerce, but their challenge was to understand that even then, one lives only through the word of God (*Zekan Aharon*).[20]

---

19. **Intelligent Taste.** *R' Shimon Schwab* once spent a Shabbos with the *Chafetz Chaim*. Among the gems he heard from him on that Friday night was the following: The Sages teach that when one ate manna, he could enjoy any taste that he wanted. "What happened," asked the Chafetz Chaim, "if he didn't think about any food while he was eating? What taste did the manna have then?"

The assembled people waited for his answer. "If one did not think when he ate the manna, it had *no* taste. Spiritual things only have a special character only if one thinks about them, values them and gives them a taste."

"What is more enjoyable than a piece of Gemara?" continued the Chafetz Chaim, licking his fingers to dramatize his point. Nevertheless if one does not think about what he is learning, it has no taste to it at all.

"Even the extent to which one will experience the sweet taste of *Mashiach's* coming depends on how much one wants him to come. Those who don't wait for him impatiently, and who don't appreciate what his coming will mean for the world and all its individuals, will taste nothing special."

20. **Expanding Horizons.** *R' Yitzchak of Vorki* asked: Since every Jew received his sustenance directly from God, how did Jews find opportunities to practice charity and interpersonal kindness while in the Wilderness? He explained, that one can practice kindness by expanding another's horizons. Although every person could taste in the manna whatever food he desired, what might a poor person think about — a piece of hard bread with an onion!? The wealthy, accustomed to delicacies, could teach the poor to broaden their horizons to include fish and meat, at the very least.

This holds a powerful lesson for teachers and spiritual leaders. As important as it is to change people's behavior so that they comply with the Torah's expectations, it is even more important to raise their perceptions, goals and spiritual horizons. Just as manna had any taste one wanted, so in Torah one can taste whatever spiritual taste he wants; he only has to desire to achieve it and God will put the taste in his mouth.

[An insightful educator once said: To change behavior is hard but changing one's perceptions and raising his spiritual goals and vistas is far more difficult.]

פרשת יתרו ֶּֿ
Parashas Yisro

<hr/>

Background

The *sidrah* opens with the arrival of Jethro at the Camp of the Israelites. Jethro, Moses' father-in-law, who was once a religious leader in Midian and before that an adviser to Pharaoh, leaves it all behind and casts his lot with the Jewish nation.

וַיִּשְׁמַע יִתְרוֹ כֹהֵן מִדְיָן חֹתֵן מֹשֶׁה
Jethro, the minister of Midian,
the father-in-law of Moses heard (18:1).

Rashi asks: What did Jethro hear that made him join the Jewish people? He heard about the Splitting of the Sea and the battle with Amalek. Although these are two (of three) independent opinions in the Talmud (*Zevachim* 116a), Rashi combines them, thereby conveying a homiletic message. It was the combination of these two events which led Jethro to come out to the Wilderness. The entire civilized world heard of the miraculous Splitting of the Sea. The supernatural salvation of the Jewish people and the vanquishing of the Egyptians struck terror in the hearts of the nations (see 15:14-16), but the Amalekites chose to mount a sneak attack against the Jews. Jethro realized that one can see miracles and remain apathetic (or worse). He therefore felt that he could not merely stay home; he had to act on his convictions and join the Jewish people and its teacher, Moses (*R' Elyah Lopian*).[1], [2]

Why did Jethro wait until he heard about the Splitting of the Sea and the battle with Amalek? Why didn't the Exodus itself succeed in moving him to convert?

<hr/>

1. **Perspective.** *R' Yechiel Mordechai Gordon* notes that *Rashi* mentions the Jews' *battle* with the Amalekites rather than their victory over them. It was the Amalekite brazenness in attacking the Jews that motivated Jethro's decision. Jethro realized that it is not enough to know that God is great; one must act positively upon the knowledge.

Amalek and Jethro both heard about the Exodus from Egypt. Why did they have such polar reactions to the same event?

R' Yosef Leib Nendik submits that it is human nature for people to react differently to the same occurrence. If someone suddenly becomes wealthy, his friends and relatives rejoice for him. Poor people are glad that they have a new address for financial assistance or loans. Businessmen are excited over the prospect of a new investor and local thieves drool over a new potential victim.

Likewise with regard to the Exodus. Nearly all the nations were petrified. Amalek thought that the answer to the perceived threat of the Jews lay in "offense is the best defense." Only Jethro heard the inner message that called him to come out to the desert and convert to join the Jewish nation.

2. **Recurrent Battle.** *R' Eliezer Yudel Epstein* views this combination of events as mirroring the ongoing battle against the evil inclination. "When I go to the synagogue I experience such a clear sense of my relationship with God that I feel as if I was at the Splitting of the Sea where even the lowliest maidservant experienced Godliness. Nevertheless, when I get home, the war with Amalek (the evil impulse) begins again."

Maayana Shel Torah explains: Jethro initially thought that to be a Jew meant to live without an evil inclination, to be almost angelic. Then he heard that even a lowly maidservant experienced a revelation of God at the Splitting of the Sea, and yet the Jews were still vulnerable to the attack of Amalek (the archsymbol of evil). This implied that the evil inclination does not desist from tempting people who have attained spiritual heights. Thus, he realized, being Jewish entails battling evil with one's full strength — and meriting God's help to be victorious. He then decided that he should become a Jew.[3]

Why is the *sidrah* which contains the revelation at Sinai named after Jethro? Would it not have been more appropriate to name it after Moses, who brought the Torah to the Jewish people?

R' Yaakov Perlow, the *Novominsker Rebbe,* offers the following: *R' Yonah (Shaarei Teshuvah* 2:12) cites a Midrash that one who fell from a roof and smashed many bones needs a separate cast for each one, but a sinner, who figuratively "smashes all his bones," can be cured by one "bandage"; namely, the ability to listen to and accept reproof. Thus the prophet says, *Incline your ear and come to Me; listen, and your soul will be rejuvenated (Isaiah* 55:3).

At Mount Sinai the Jews saw the revelation of God and His word. Such an experience can make an effective connection between the Torah and those who are already close to it. But how can people who are emotionally removed be brought closer to it? Jethro, drawn to Torah by *hearing* from a distance, provided the link for those too far away to *see* the glory of God. Jethro *heard* and came, so that others throughout the generations could follow.

כֹּהֵן מִדְיָן חֹתֵן מֹשֶׁה
The minister of Midian, the father-in-law of Moses (ibid.).

Here the Torah mentions Jethro's position as the minister of Midian, while in the next verse he is described only as the father-in-law of Moses. Why the difference? Furthermore, it is inappropriate to mention a convert's past. [In the words of *Maseches Gerim* (4:1): "One may never say to a proselyte 'previously you served total vanity with pig meat between your teeth' "] (see *Rashi* to verse 9). Why, then, did the Torah deem it necessary to inform us that Jethro had been a Midianite religious minister?

R' Menachem Cohen submits that the Torah wants to showcase the greatness of Jethro's conversion. Although he heard the news while basking in the honor and prestige of the ministry of Midian, he walked away from it all in order to come close to God and His people. Once the Torah makes this point, it never again mentions that Jethro was once the minister of Midian. As the Midrash (*Bamidbar Rabbah* 3:15) teaches, "A proselyte who converts and is occupied with Torah is like a Kohen Gadol."[4]

---

3. **Heaven On Earth.** This message is reflected in Moses' answer to the angels, who wondered why God wished to give the Torah to humans rather than to angels. "Do you have an evil inclination among you?" Moses asked. "Do hatred, jealousy, passion or the like exist among you?" The Torah is not for angels. Its purpose is to elevate man above the pettiness of the world and to edify him. "The heavens are God's and the earth He gave to man" (*Psalms* 115:16). Said the *Chidushei HaRim,* "He gave the earth to man so that man should make it Heavenly."

4. **On Top of the World.** *R' Shlomo Ganzfried* offers a halachic perspective: The Talmud (*Yevamos* 24b) teaches that converts are accepted only during historical periods when the Jewish people is downtrodden. For example, during the reigns of King David and King Solomon, when the Jews enjoyed political autonomy and financial prosperity, no converts were accepted, since they were likely motivated by a desire for personal security and monetary gain. Likewise, proselytes will not be accepted in the Messianic era. How then was Jethro allowed to convert while the Jews enjoyed an idyllic existence in the Wilderness?

The answer lies in the Talmud's explanation of why Pharaoh's daughter was allowed to convert during the reign of King Solomon. Since she was a princess who enjoyed the good life anyway, there was no fear that she converted in order to improve her political or financial standing. (*Yevamos* 76a).

The same principle applied to Jethro. He was a well-placed cleric in Midian, with position and money. He had nothing to gain and everything to lose by joining the Jewish people; thus his conversion was sincere and not to improve his material position in life. To make this point, the Torah notes his prestigious past.

אֲשֶׁר שֵׁם הָאֶחָד גֵּרְשֹׁם כִּי אָמַר גֵּר הָיִיתִי בְּאֶרֶץ נָכְרִיָּה. וְשֵׁם הָאֶחָד אֱלִיעֶזֶר כִּי אֱלֹקֵי אָבִי בְּעֶזְרִי וַיַּצִּלֵנִי מֵחֶרֶב פַּרְעֹה

of whom the name of one was Gershom, for he had said, "I was a sojourner in a strange land"; and the name of the other was Eliezer, for "the God of my father came to my aid, and He saved me from the sword of Pharaoh" (ibid. 3-4).

Moses had been saved from the sword of Pharaoh before he *was a sojourner in a strange land,* i.e., Midian. Why, then, did he name his first son in commemoration of his status as a sojourner and only afterward give expression to his salvation from Pharaoh?

R' Moshe Feinstein explained: Someone as talented as Moses could easily have integrated himself into the society of Midian and might have risen to the higher echelons of commerce or government. Aware of this possibility and fearful of the effect it might have on his children, Moses made every effort to maintain his status as a sojourner among the Midianites. He named his first child "Gershom" as an expression of thanks to God for granting him the clarity of vision to see how important it was to remain an outsider.[5] Without this perspective, the value of his salvation from Pharaoh would have been negligible. Of what use would his salvation have been if he had traded the Egyptian palace for a prestigious position in Midian? He therefore named his first son Gershom and only afterward did he thank God for having saved him from Pharaoh's sword.

R' Yonasan Eibeshutz reveals another side of the coin. Nothing is as unbearably painful to a Jewish leader as having to witness the pain of his people. A true shepherd of the nation would rather die than witness the oppression of his flock.

When Moses' first son was born, the Jewish people were still suffering exile in Egypt with no end in sight. For a man like him, death might have been preferable to the knowledge of what his brethren were going through in Egypt, and therefore he could not give thanks for his salvation from Pharaoh. Only when his second son was born, after God told him at the Burning Bush that He would redeem His people, could Moses fully thank Hashem for saving him from Pharaoh's sword.

אֶל הַמִּדְבָּר אֲשֶׁר הוּא חֹנֶה שָׁם הַר הָאֱלֹקִים
To the Wilderness where he was encamped by the Mountain of God (ibid. 5).

Why does the Torah first tell us that Moses encamped there and only afterwards teach us that it was the Mountain of God? *Chasam Sofer* cites the dictum of the Sages (see *Taanis* 21b), "it is the man who sanctifies the place," rather than the place that sanctifies the man. Because Moses himself was qualified to receive God's Presence, that place became the Mountain of God.

---

5. **Safe Trip.** *Shelah* defines the term עַם הָאָרֶץ (an ignorant, coarse person) as describing someone who views the אֶרֶץ, this world, as his true home. Such a person is called an עַם הָאָרֶץ, literally a *nation of the earth,* since his basic orientation is this worldly. One must develop the feeling that he is a stranger in this world. The more one views himself as a stranger, the less likely he is to become an עַם הָאָרֶץ.

In this vein *R' Chaim Shmulevitz* explained the appellation בֶּן עוֹלָם הַבָּא (literally a "son of the World to Come"). A person who sees himself as temporarily displaced in this world, with his real home the World to Come, is a true בֶּן עוֹלָם הַבָּא. For example, a tourist in Israel is referred to as "the foreigner" for it is obvious that he is there only temporarily. Likewise, one whose demeanor and behavior make it clear that he is only passing through this world is called a בֶּן עוֹלָם הַבָּא, a citizen of the World to Come.

R' E.E. Dessler once accompanied a student who was leaving the yeshivah to the train station. When they got there, the student asked him for a blessing. R' Dessler replied, "I wish you from the bottom of my heart that you find a comfortable seat on your trip." The student was aghast. "Rebbi, I asked you for a blessing that might accompany me through life. Why did you only bless me that I have a comfortable trip!" R' Dessler responded, "I did bless you for life, since life itself is one long arduous journey with the Next World its ultimate destination. I bless you that throughout the journey of life you enjoy conditions that will enable you to arrive safely at your destination."

This is the message of the name "Gershom." Someone who understands that life is a journey, in which one spends a night here and a night there with no permanence anywhere, is not fazed by difficulties or inconveniences, for it is all but a passing stage.

וַיַּחַדְּ יִתְרוֹ עַל כָּל הַטּוֹבָה אֲשֶׁר עָשָׂה ה׳ לְיִשְׂרָאֵל

Jethro rejoiced over all the good that Hashem had done for Israel (ibid. 9).

וַיֹּאמֶר יִתְרוֹ בָּרוּךְ ה׳ אֲשֶׁר הִצִּיל אֶתְכֶם מִיַּד מִצְרַיִם

Jethro said, "Blessed is Hashem, Who has rescued you from the hand of Egypt" (ibid. 10).

*O*hr HaChaim renders וַיַּחַדְּ as *prickles of joy.* Jethro's happiness over what God did for the Jews was so intense that he felt physically overcome with emotion. *Rashi,* however, cites the Midrash, which renders וַיַּחַדְּ as *prickles of unease* over the demise of the Egyptians. Why did the Sages interpret וַיַּחַדְּ in a negative sense when it could have easily been understood positively?

R' Yehoshua of Kutna explains that חֶדְוָה, which is one of many expressions of joy,[6] connotes the joy one experiences in spite of having legitimate cause for sadness. Although one wants to cry, he finds in himself the ability to be happy. For example, when the exiles returned from Babylon and remembered the lost glory of the First Temple, Nehemiah exhorted them to overcome their emotions and rejoice over their return. He said to them, וְעַל תֵּעָצֵבוּ, *Do not be sad for the* **enjoyment** כִּי חֶדְוַת ה׳ הִיא מָעֻזְּכֶם. *of Hashem is your strength* (Nehemiah 8:10).

This is why the Torah speaks of Jethro's happiness in terms of חֶדְוָה. Although he was a proselyte who had lived in Egypt, and therefore felt pain over the demise of his former countrymen, he still rejoiced over everything God had done for His people, Israel. His initial reaction was to feel prickles of unease. Nevertheless, prickles of joy replaced them as *Jethro rejoiced over all the good that Hashem had done for Israel.*

*T*he Talmud (*Sanhedrin* 94a) sees this verse as a criticism of Moses and the Jewish people, who up until this time did not bless God, while Jethro, the outsider, did bless Him. This comment is puzzling, for Moses and the Jews had praised God lavishly with the Song at the Sea.

Tiferes Shlomo explains that there is a fundamental difference between the cases of Jethro and the Jewish people. The Jewish people praised God at the Sea for what He did *for them.* Admirable as that is, its significance is diminished when compared to Jethro who praised and blessed God for what He did for others. *Blessed is Hashem, Who has rescued you.* [7]

כִּי בַדָּבָר אֲשֶׁר זָדוּ עֲלֵיהֶם

for in the very matter in which [the Egyptians] had conspired against them . . .! (ibid. 11).

*R*ashi sees this as an expression of Divine justice being meted out "measure for measure," מִדָּה כְּנֶגֶד מִדָּה. In order to make it clear that the Egyptians were being punished for conspiring to drown the Jewish male babies, they themselves were drowned in the Sea of Reeds.

Ramban renders בַדָּבָר אֲשֶׁר זָדוּ as *the area where their intent was purposely wicked.* Although God decreed that a foreign nation would enslave and

---

6. **Rediscovering Joy.** Two additional expressions of joy are שָׂשׂוֹן and שִׂמְחָה. The latter connotes joy over something new that one had not experienced before, while the former refers to happiness associated with something one had lost and now rediscovered.

The Sages (*Kiddushin* 2b) describe one's wife as his lost "object" for which he must search, since Eve was formed from Adam's rib. It is as if Adam's experience symbolizes every man. An integral part of every man is "missing." Something, is missing, as it were, and he searches for the wife whose companionship replaces it. Thus, the seventh blessing of the wedding ceremony states: אֲשֶׁר בָּרָא שָׂשׂוֹן וְשִׂמְחָה חָתָן וְכַלָּה, *Who created joy and gladness, groom and bride.*

The groom experiences שָׂשׂוֹן, for he rediscovers his missing part. The bride, who rejoices over an element of her life she does not yet know, has שִׂמְחָה, the joy of something totally new to her (*R' Yehoshua of Kutna*).

7. **Nothing in It for Me.** Rejoicing over someone else's success is an admirable trait, for one who praises God for having helped another person truly loves his fellow. Additionally, thanking God for being kind to others has special meaning, for a truly committed servant of God is happy when God has an opportunity to shower His beneficence upon man. This joy is even more meaningful when the person himself is not the beneficiary of God's gift, but rather a passive bystander.

Jethro rejoiced that God was able to show kindness and that the Jewish people benefited from His kindness — even though he personally had no gain (*Simchas Aharon*).

oppress the Jewish people, the Egyptians went far beyond the Divine mandate by, among other things, decreeing the murder of the male babies. They overstepped the parameters of the Divine will, and therefore made themselves subject to punishment. Hence their wicked intent was the key factor in causing their punishment.[8]

R' Yitzchak Zev Soloveitchik of Brisk submits a different approach. Since God punishes non-Jews even for mere sinful thoughts (see *Kiddushin* 39b, *Tosafos* ad loc. s.v. *machshavah* and *Talmud Yerushalmi Pe'ah* 1:1), the Egyptians were punished even for evil plans that never came to fruition. Balaam, Job and Jethro served as advisers to Pharaoh and were involved in (or at least aware of) the evil decree to kill the male Jewish babies. Hence Jethro was aware of all the designs that the Egyptians considered promulgating against the Jews. The Talmud (*Sanhedrin* 106a) teaches that the Jews themselves did not understand the full scope of the punishments meted out to Egyptians, since they were unaware of all their

sinister musings — but Jethro knew the whole truth. Hence he *rejoiced over **all** the good that Hashem had done for Israel* and realized that the Egyptians were punished even for what they had *conspired against them.* [9]

Background

At Mount Sinai, God raised the entire Jewish nation to the level of prophecy, so that they could personally witness and vouch for the veracity of Moses' prophecy. There, the Jews were taught the Ten Commandments, which, according to *R' Saadiah Gaon,* incorporate all 613 commandments.

The Ten Commandments are inscribed on two tablets, five commandments on each. The first five utterances relate to obligations between man and God, and the other five relate to interpersonal *mitzvos,* between man and his fellow man. This demonstrates that both categories are equally essential to a Torah-oriented lifestyle.

---

8. **Self-Mirror.** *Pardes Yosef* offers a variation on *Rashi's approach,* based on an insight of the *Baal Shem Tov.* When Nathan the Prophet rebuked King David, he began with a parable of two citizens, one wealthy and one poor. The rich man owned much cattle, while the poor man had only one small sheep; but the rich man stole the single sheep from the poor man. When David heard this story, he was appalled. "Let the man who did this die," he declared passionately. Only then did Nathan explain that this was parallel to David's own treatment of Bath-sheba, whom he had taken from her husband, Uriah the Hittite. "You are the man," Nathan said to King David. In this way David indicted himself. [For someone on King David's exalted spiritual level this was deemed a sin although legally, he had not sinned (See *Shabbos* 56a).]

So, taught the *Baal Shem Tov,* does man decide his own punishment for his transgressions. He is given the opportunity to view someone else doing what he did, in a slightly camouflaged form, and in a fit of righteous indignation he passes sentence. Only then is the smokescreen lifted, and he realizes that he has decreed his own punishment. For this reason we are taught to judge everyone favorably. One should not be in a rush to condemn his fellow, for he may be passing judgment on himself. The reverse is also true; one who judges others favorably effects a favorable judgment for himself.

Our verse alludes to this. The very manner in which the Egyptians conspired against others was ultimately turned against them.

9. **Foiled Conspiracies.** At a meeting in St. Petersburg, a Russian minister asked *R' Yitzchak of Volozhin* to explain the words of King David, *Praise Hashem, all nations; praise Him, all the states! For His kindness has overwhelmed us* (*Psalms* 117:1). "Why," asked the minister, "should *non-Jewish* people and nations praise God for overwhelming *Israel* with Divine Kindness?"

R' Yitzchak replied, "For every anti-Jewish decree that you and your cohorts succeeded in promulgating, there were another ten which you wanted to decree but were unsuccessful. Only you, the heads of the ministries, know how much you wanted to harm us and how God, in His infinite mercy on His people, foiled your plans. Thus only you can praise God for the overwhelming kindness He showed and continues to show His children."

[This may also be David's allusion when he offers praise *to Him Who alone performs great wonders* (*Psalms* 136:4). God performs countless wonders *alone* on our behalf, with hardly a soul — not even the beneficiaries — being aware of His kindness.]

אָנֹכִי ה' אֱלֹקֶיךָ

I am Hashem, your God (20:2).

Rambam (*Sefer HaMitzvos, Positive Commandment* 1) reckons this as the first of the six hundred and thirteen Biblical commandments: "One must know [and believe] that there is One God."

Other commentators agree that one must have faith in God, but they do not count it as a separate mitzvah. *Ramban* explains: *Mitzvos* are actions that God commands us either to do or not do. But the necessary prerequisite to commandments is the acceptance of the Commander; only then can He issue His decrees. Only through faith can one subjugate himself to God and obey His commands.

Rambam agrees that intellectual faith cannot be a mitzvah, since it is the bedrock of all *mitzvos*. The faith that the Torah commands us to have is emotional faith. We are enjoined to make our faith in God a live and vibrant entity that permeates every fiber of our bodies and informs every step of our lives (*Nesivos Shalom*).[10]

Nesivos Shalom adds perspective: There is no special mitzvah to be a Jew; rather, one who is a Jew is obligated to fulfill God's *mitzvos*. Likewise, faith is not a specific mitzvah; it is what makes a Jew into a Jew.

Faith is an emotion, a conviction; how can the Torah command us to believe?

Man's soul is like a small bird. Entrapped in the narrow confines of a corporeal body and a mundane society, the Jewish soul strives instinctively for a broader spiritual existence. Faith is an expression of the soul's yearning for something beyond the physical limitations of the body. Like an unhatched bird pecking on the wall of the egg, instinctively yearning to break free, the soul struggles for spiritual freedom. The mitzvah of *emunah* (faith) calls on a Jew to allow his natural yearning for God to burst forth and let him become himself (*MiMayanos HaNetzach*).[11]

---

10. **Until Then.** A story about *R' Yisrael of Rizhin* illustrates the immense gap between intellectual and emotional faith.

A brokenhearted Jew once poured out his woes. "Rebbe, I must have your blessing; I need a major salvation," the Jew cried. The Rebbe replied, "The Master of the universe will help." Satisfied that things would work out, the Jew left the Rebbe's room, and encountered the Rizhiner's young son, David Moshe (later the *Rebbe of Tchortkov*) sitting outside the room. "Tell me, what did my father say?" he asked the Jew. "The Rebbe said, 'The Master of the universe will help,'" replied the *chassid*. "Fine," retorted the future Tchortkover, "but what will be *until* He helps?" The Jew looked at him, dumbfounded. "Go back to my father," David Moshe said, "and ask him." The Jew went back to the Rizhiner's room and returned to the Tchortkover shortly thereafter. "Your father said that *until* the Master of universe helps, the Master of the universe will help."

Sometimes one truly believes in God's ability to help. Nevertheless, the fear of how one will survive until that happens can itself be overwhelming. The Rizhiner's first answer spoke to the distraught Jew's mind; the second kindled a faith in his heart that would carry him until he witnessed God's helping hand.

11. **Intrinsic Love.** To bear witness to the consequences in store for the Jewish people if they abandon the Torah, God, through Moses, invokes heaven and earth (*Deuteronomy* 31:28), for He wants us to draw a lesson from them. Though heaven and earth are neither rewarded nor punished, they never deviate from performing the functions God ordained for them. Certainly Jews, who are rewarded for performing His will and are subject to punishment for disobeying it, must be zealous in fulfilling His Torah (*Rashi* ad loc.).

The analogy seems flawed, however. Heaven and earth have no choice but to function according to God's will, but man has free choice and therefore has the option of choosing the wrong path in life. If so, how does the example of heaven and earth apply to man?

The answer lies in the words of *Rambam*: "One who is under attack from his evil inclination to ignore performing a mitzvah or to transgress a prohibition, and is coerced by physical force to perform the mitzvah or to refrain from transgression, is not deemed to have acted under duress . . . Since he wants to be a true Jew, [his natural inclination] follows the *mitzvos* and refrains from transgression; it is his evil inclination that impedes him [from expressing his inner will]" (*Hilchos Gerushin* 2:20).

Apparently, concludes *Sfas Emes*, allegiance to God is part of man's nature. If he rids himself of the exterior pressures and distractions that pull him toward evil, his basic tendency toward faith and fidelity will assert itself. Thus man's own free choice orients him to believe in God. God simply commands us to follow our intrinsic intuition and believe.

אָנֹכִי ה' אֱלֹקֶיךָ אֲשֶׁר הוֹצֵאתִיךָ מֵאֶרֶץ מִצְרָיִם
I am Hashem, your God, Who took you out of the land of Egypt (ibid.).

The commentators discuss the reasons why God identified Himself as the One *Who took you out of the land of Egypt* rather than as the Creator of the world (see *Ramban, Kuzari, Rabbeinu Bachya* et al.). *R' Simchah Bunim of P'shis'cha* offers the following: Had God identified Himself as the Creator, man might have been overwhelmed. "How am I, an insignificant cog in the infinity of creation, supposed to relate to an unfathomable and Almighty God Who created all? How dare I seek His closeness?"

To allay such fears, God introduces Himself as "I am God Who pulled you out of the filth of Egypt. I was ready to descend to Egypt's impurity for your sake because I am always with you. Believe in Me and follow My Torah."

Nesivos Shalom adds: It is not enough for a Jew to believe in God in the abstract. He must also realize that Hashem is his *personal* God, at all times and in all situations — *I am* אֱלֹקֶיךָ, **your** *God,* and I remain your God even if you rebel against Me. Even as Israel wallowed in the forty-ninth degree of impurity in Egypt, God was still with us.

Only when man has broken the shackles of servitude and freed his spiritual self from the chains of his passion is life meaningful. Man was not created to be a slave to slaves. Thus God presents Himself, not as the Creator of life, but as the One Who gave life meaning by providing us with the freedom to truly live (*Kli Yakar*). Had God spoken of His role as Creator, the Jews would not have understood why of all the nations of the world it was they who were picked to receive God's greatest gift, His Torah. They might even have viewed it as a burden that they must grudgingly bear.

Therefore God refers to Himself as the Liberator Who expressed His powerful love for His people by redeeming them from bondage. The gift of Torah is one more demonstration of His love for us. As the Talmud teaches, "God wanted to grant merit and purification to Israel, He therefore increased for them [the opportunities for] Torah and *mitzvos*" (*Makkos* 23b). It is only through Torah that one can achieve true freedom (*Chizkuni, Oznayim L'Torah*).

Though addressed to the entire nation of Israel, the Ten Commandments are phrased in the singular, as if addressed to each individual Jew. What lesson does this hold for us? The commentators offer a plethora of explanations:

❏ The Sages teach that the Jews achieved a heightened sense of national unity at Sinai and become as "one man with one heart" (see *Rashi*). Thus God spoke to us as one person, in the singular.

❏ The *Chozeh of Lublin* said, "Even if all those around you abandon the Torah way, even if the whole world refuses to follow the Godly path, do not despair. God is *your* God, ready to help you swim against the tide and follow your own conscience."

❏ In an elaboration on this theme, *R' David Deitch* submits that the Torah alludes to the significance of each individual. Let one not say, "Even if I don't study and fulfill the Torah, there are many righteous people ready to do God's work. The world will survive without my Torah study and *mitzvos*." The singular expression speaks to the individual. as if to say, "God has only one soldier and you are he!" *I am Hashem, your God* — as if you are My only subject.

❏ Every Jew is equally commanded to follow the dictates of the Torah, but each of us perceives God's Presence in the world and in our own lives in a different way. I am Hashem, *your* [personal] God (*Sfas Emes*).

❏ Let one never think that the Torah is only a national obligation; every Jew is personally obligated to serve God (*Sifsei Kohen*).

אָנֹכִי ה' . . . לֹא יִהְיֶה לְךָ
I [am Hashem] . . . You shall not have . . . (ibid. 2-3).

The Sages taught that when the Children of Israel heard the first two of the Ten Commandments from God Himself, their souls temporarily left their bodies (*Shir HaShirim Rabbah* 6:3). Why was this necessary? Surely, God, the All-Powerful, could have allowed them to experience this personal revelation without having their souls depart. This teaches that true commitment to God and His Torah calls for a willingness to sacrifice; one must be ready to give his heart and soul for the sake of the Torah and the Jewish people (*Sfas Emes*).[12], [13]

לֹא יִהְיֶה לְךָ אֱלֹהִים אֲחֵרִים
You shall have no other gods (ibid. 2).

King David teaches סוּר מֵרָע וַעֲשֵׂה טוֹב, *Turn from evil and do good* (*Psalms* 34:15). One must first abandon evil and only then will he be able to pursue the path of good. Man cannot rise to good if his spirit is weighted down by evil. Why, then, did God first speak of accepting Him as our God and only then of rejecting idolatry?

R' Tzadok HaKohen explains: By focusing on God's omnipresence and developing a vigorous and dynamic faith in Him, one merits to be saved from all forms of idolatry to the point that his faith will rescue him from transgressing God's will. Just as the Sages teach that when one performs a mitzvah, an angel is created that watches over him, so one who develops faith in God merits that God Himself will protect him from any spiritual or even physical harm.

All the other *mitzvos* were taught to us by Moses, God's agent. When we perform them, therefore, we are protected by God's agents, the angels. The mitzvah to believe in Him, however, was taught to us by God Himself. Thus He offers us His personal protection in response to our faith.[14]

לֹא תִשָּׂא אֶת שֵׁם ה' אֱלֹקֶיךָ לַשָּׁוְא
You shall not take the Name of Hashem, your God, in vain (ibid. 7).

Homiletically, the verse calls for honesty in how one projects his public image. Do not bear God's Name in a false and counterfeit fashion. Do not mislead others into thinking that you are more upright or God-fearing than you actually are (*Ohr HaChaim*).

כִּי לֹא יְנַקֶּה ה' אֵת אֲשֶׁר יִשָּׂא אֶת שְׁמוֹ לַשָּׁוְא
for Hashem will not absolve anyone who takes His Name in vain (ibid.).

"But doesn't repentance absolve one of his sins?" asks *R' Meir of Premishlan*. "Why is this sin different from the others?" He replied: "All of man's actions are recorded in a Heavenly ledger (*Pirkei Avos* 2:1). For example, if, God forbid, one eats nonkosher food, then the verse which forbids it is written down next to his name. When he repents, the verse is erased. However, even if man repents

---

12. **Reinvigorated Spirit.** The Sages continue, explaining that God resuscitated the Jews after their souls expired. *Zekan Aharon* suggests that one who is ready and willing to sacrifice himself and his desires on behalf of God will be granted a renewed life, with a more vibrant and invigorated spirit.

13. **One and Two.** *R' Yosef Yitzchak Schneerson*, the Lubavitcher Rebbe, was arrested in Russia for the "heinous crime" of spreading the teachings of Judaism, but he refused to comply with demands that he cease his activities. One of his interrogators threatened him with a pistol. "This little toy has a powerful effect on people. It has changed many minds," the officer snickered.

The Rebbe serenely replied, "That little toy can frighten a person with many gods and one world. I have only One God and two worlds (this and the World to Come). To me, your toy means nothing."

14. **Nothing Else but You!.** The relationship between absolute faith and Divine protection has proven itself to those who have such faith. *R' Chaim of Volozhin* writes that one who concentrates on Hashem's total control of everything will be protected from all danger. An episode in his own life highlights how R' Chaim lived by his own words.

One year, due to the Cossack bands who roamed the countryside, Reb Chaim was unable to travel to his rebbe, the *Vilna Gaon*. The main road between Volozhin and Vilna was considered far too dangerous for travel. Reb Chaim waited until the danger had abated, and only then did he set off for Vilna. As his carriage made its way to its destination, the calm was suddenly disturbed by the sound of hooves galloping at breakneck speed. The equestrian expertise and garb of the fast approaching rider identified him as a Cossack. In his raised hand he held a sword, poised menacingly to strike.

Our Sages tell us that even when the executioner's sword is at our throat we should not despair, and Reb Chaim did not. No cries for mercy escaped his lips. Rather, he shut his eyes and with all his powers of concentration, he focused on the one sublime truth: אֵין עוֹד מִלְבַדּוֹ, *there is nothing other than Him*, i.e., Hashem is the Eternal God, and there is no power in the world other than Him. As Reb Chaim sat, his eyes closed in concentration, the Cossack returned his weapon to its sheath and rode past as if he had never intended to harm anyone.

for the sin of taking God's Name in vain it is impossible to totally erase the verse since it contains God's Name. Thus one is never able to be fully absolved from the sin of taking God's Name in vain.

The Sages teach (*Shevuos* 39a) that the entire world shook when God said, "You shall not take the Name of Hashem, your God, in vain." What was so momentous about this commandment? *Haflaah* explains: When the Jewish people accepted the Torah they took an oath that they would always fulfill it. One who is lax regarding oaths and takes God's Name in vain indicates that his oath is of negligible value, including his oath to keep the Torah. But without Torah, the world would cease to exist. Thus, the entire world shook at the sound of God's words "You shall not take the Name of Hashem, your God, in vain."

זָכוֹר אֶת יוֹם הַשַּׁבָּת לְקַדְּשׁוֹ
Remember the day of Shabbos to sanctify it (ibid. 8).

Surprisingly, our Sages explain this commandment as a call to eat fine food and delicacies and to wear special clothes in honor of the Sabbath. One might have supposed that the Torah would instruct us to pursue a more sacred agenda on this most hallowed of days.

The *Baal Shem Tov* offered a relevant parable: A prince was kidnapped and held captive by ruffians. One day he received a letter from his father, the king. Overwhelmed with joy, he felt a powerful urge to dance. But how could he do so when his captors, unable to appreciate his emotions, would ridicule him for his senseless dancing? He offered them liberal drinks of whiskey until they became intoxicated and began to dance in drunken revelry. While they danced because of their liquor, he danced over his father's letter.

The Torah teaches us to indulge our bodies on the Sabbath so that it will rejoice, free of sadness or depression. That will allow the soul, the royal prince inside every Jew, to rejoice over its renewed connection to its Father, the King.

לֹא תַחְמֹד
You shall not covet (ibid. 14).

This prohibition seems unreasonable. How can one be forbidden to entertain a natural desire? *Ibn Ezra* comments that a peasant may long to marry the wench from the next farm, but he will not even dream of marrying a princess, because she is completely removed from his world. So too, if one were to understand that what God gave him is his and what God gave someone else is foreclosed from him, he would not even desire something that was ordained for someone else. This prohibition obligates man to attain a level of faith that makes us view personal property as something beyond the pale of our wildest dreams.

Beis HaLevi submits a different approach, suggesting that it is fear of Heaven which underlies this prohibition. For example, someone driving on a scenic route may be distracted from the road and drawn to look at the lovely scenery. If, however, the car suddenly hits a patch of ice and skids toward a steep cliff, fear of the imminent danger so overwhelms the driver that he cannot think of anything else. Our fear of Heaven should not allow us to focus on someone else's property.[15]

---

15. **Impenetrable Barrier.** *Sfas Emes* related that, as a child, his grandfather the *Chidushei HaRim* took him to Kotzk. One day he heard his aunt, the Kotzker Rebbetzin, complaining to the Rebbe's attendant, *R' Feivel,* that many items had disappeared from the house. Since they had apparently been stolen, R' Feivel said to the Rebbetzin, "Why shouldn't people steal here? Everything is open and available for the taking." The Rebbe inside his room overheard the conversation and let out a roar. "Why shouldn't they steal? Because the Torah says 'You shall not steal.' " "That roar penetrated deep into my heart," said the *Sfas Emes.* "For the rest of my life I envisioned a huge wall which stops people from stealing. How can anyone climb over that barrier and bring himself to steal?"

The *Ohr Pnei Moshe* was a renowned scribe. When he passed away, he left three pairs of *tefillin* he had written. *R' Menachem Mendel of Kotzk* scraped together his last pennies to buy one of them from R' Moshe's widow. He asked one of R' Moshe's *chassidim* to bring him the pair of *tefillin.* When the *chassid* brought them, he mentioned to the Rebbe in passing that he had transgressed the commandment "You shall not covet" and put on the *tefillin.* "I couldn't control myself," he said. The Rebbe replied, "Keep the *tefillin.* I have no use for *tefillin* that caused a Jew to transgress the prohibition to covet someone else's property."

⚜ פרשת משפטים ⚜
Parashas Mishpatim

Background

This *sidrah*, which deals primarily with civil law and damages, gives practical application to the Divine revelation at Sinai. The way in which one treats his servants and the respect he accords to his fellow man's property are issues no less sanctified or sublime than the great principles of belief promulgated at Sinai.

וְאֵלֶּה הַמִּשְׁפָּטִים
And these are the ordinances (21:1).

The previous *sidrah* ended with laws of the Altar while this one begins with the ordinances that the Sanhedrin must enforce. The *sidrah* begins with the conjunction *and,* indicating that the Altar and the Sanhedrin are linked. This teaches that the Great Sanhedrin must be located at the Temple near the Altar (*Rashi,* citing *Tanchuma*).

According to *R' Tzvi Pesach Frank,* the San-hedrin and the Altar share a common theme, for both are peacemakers. The Altar upon which we bring offerings helps us achieve atonement for our sins thus making peace between Israel and God. Justice (enforced by the Sanhedrin) brings truth and peace between men. Hence the Sanhedrin sat near the location of the Altar.[1]

Avnei Azel views the connection as a lesson in the fundamental difference between Torah and secular civil law. The latter has no religious or intrinsic moral basis. Rather, it is the product of the need for a social contract that will enable society to function. The Torah's civil law, however, is part of God's mandate and is endowed with the same sanctity as all other *mitzvos.* This equality is expressed in the fact that the Torah refers to the Tablets which contained the Ten Commandments as לֻחֹת הַבְּרִית. Although it is pronounced לוּחוֹת, in the plural, it is spelled לֻחַת, in the singular, for the first five "ritual" commandments and the second five "social" edicts are a seamless expression of equal sanctity.

---

1. **Divine Proxy.** The power of the Sanhedrin to adjudicate is rooted in its sanctity as God's proxy. The judges are referred to in the Torah as אֱלֹהִים, which is a Name of God (see verse 6), because they are His agents in administering the justice that is really His (See *Ibn Ezra* ad loc and *Deuteronomy* 1:17).

In 1956 the State of Israel invested *dayanim* (rabbinic judges) with legal status and had them swear allegiance to the state and its laws. At the time, *R' Yitzchak Hutner* told his students: "When I first heard about this I cried like a baby. What kind of insanity is this, that a *dayan* should pledge allegiance to a country, a person or any other body, other than to uphold the laws of the *Shulchan Aruch*?! This is nothing more than a cheap imitation of the Anglo-Saxon investiture ceremony, when one is appointed to a government position."

The Sanhedrin and the Altar are adjacent to each other because just as the offerings in the Temple are holy, so the laws that govern the marketplace and civil society are holy.[2]

*R*ashi offers another perspective on the connection between the civil laws and the building of the Altar. Just as those commandments were given at Sinai, so these were from Sinai.

Since much of civil law is reasonable and logical, one might perceive it as the creation of the human mind. The Torah therefore testifies that just as those laws whose reasons are unknown to us are from Sinai and are the product of Divine wisdom, so these "rational" civil practices are also Godly precepts revealed to us at Sinai (*Chidushei HaRim*).[3]

According to *Rav*, the first *Mishnah* of *Pirkei Avos*, which traces the chain of Torah tradition from Sinai, seeks to convey this theme. Since *Pirkei Avos* basically deals with ethics, one might view it as the Jewish counterpart of ethical tracts authored by some of the world's greatest non-Jewish moralists.

The *Mishnah* therefore begins with "Moses received the Torah from Sinai" in order to emphasize

---

2. **Restoring Equality.** *R' Yisrael Salanter's* major goal in founding the Mussar Movement was to restore this balance between the two parts of Torah. His students found it significant that his *yahrzeit* always falls around the week of *Parashas Mishpatim*.

After the long list of laws in the *sidrah*, the Torah (24:1) records the covenant of Torah executed by Moses, in which he took the blood of the offerings and sprinkled it partly on the Altar and partly on the people. According to *Zekan Aharon*, Moses captured the spirit of the Torah by showing that the essence of its covenant is about the connection between the Altar (commandments between man and God) and the people (commandments between man and man).

The call of Sinai is complete only when it reaches, and informs, the most mundane details of life.

3. **Us and Them.** Even the "rational" laws whose reasons are accessible to us must be performed only because God commanded them, and not because we consider them to be logical. This is the underlying reason behind the commandment that disputes must be brought before Jewish courts, even in instances where a gentile court would rule exactly like its Jewish counterpart. By doing so, one emphasizes that his commitment to justice is a commitment to God, and not to human reason (*R' Menachem Mendel of Lubavitch*).

A non-Jewish notable once confronted *R' Avraham Yehoshua of Apt*, arguing for the superiority of the secular judicial system. "In our system if someone wants to make a claim against a friend he presents the court with a legal brief containing his arguments and claims, and the magistrate sets a date for a court appearance. In the interim the judge has time to study the relative merits of the case. When the case finally comes before the court, each side is represented by an attorney who argues on behalf of his client. Finally, the magistrate issues his ruling, which is subject to appeal. Such a system gives the parties maximum opportunity to be heard and vindicated. You Jews, however, have a primitive system. The two parties come to the rabbi, present their arguments and the rabbi almost always rules immediately. How do you expect to achieve equitable justice with such a system?"

The Apter Rav replied, "Let me explain with a parable. A wolf once chased a sheep. Just as he was ready to eat the sheep a lion came and grabbed it away. The wolf screamed, 'You are a thief!' The two animals decided to settle the matter by appearing before the fox, who ruled that they should split the sheep. Who would split it properly? The fox. He split the sheep in half and checked to see that the two halves were equal. Since one piece looked larger than the other, he bit off a piece to equal things out. Unfortunately, the previously smaller piece was now larger than the half he had bitten from. He now bit off some of the larger piece, attempting to create two equal pieces, but again he miscalculated. After a few more 'corrective' bites there was nothing left for either of the litigants, neither for the lion nor for the wolf.

"This," said the Apter, "is what happens in your judicial system. Things drag on, court costs mount, lawyers take the 'lion's share' of the money and before you know it the litigants are left penniless. In our system the rabbi tries to rule quickly or to facilitate a compromise so that the two sides truly receive equitable justice."

---

that the moral and ethical code is no less Divine than ritual law.[4], [5]

The Midrash (*Shemos Rabbah* 30:1) records a fascinating comment: "Due to the ordinances You gave them, they argue among themselves. Eventually they come to court and make peace."

The Midrash seems to have the order backwards. The ordinances do not cause arguments; to the contrary, God granted us ordinances so that we may adjudicate and solve the arguments.

R' Yaakov Naiman views the Midrash as highlighting the extreme sensitivity of the Jewish people. Just as we are careful regarding ritual matters, so we are cautious in interpersonal monetary issues. When God gave us the ordinances He sensitized us to the Divine mandate to safeguard other people's money. Jews began worrying, "Maybe I am holding money to which I am not legally entitled." Thus, the law caused Jews to argue, each claiming, "The money is his, not mine!"

Eventually they would make peace by asking the *beis din* to rule who is right.[6]

כִּי תִקְנֶה עֶבֶד עִבְרִי
If you buy a Jewish bondsman (ibid. 2).

Why does the Torah begin the civil ordinances with the laws pertaining to a thief who was sold into bondage in order to raise funds to pay his victims? The laws of people who do favors on behalf of others, such as lenders (22:24) or unpaid custodians (22:6-7), would have seemed to be a more appropriate beginning.

R' Yisrael Salanter explained with a parable. A man has two sons. One is a fine, upstanding, respectable and successful citizen, who brings joy and honor to his father. The other son steals and lies, consorts with riffraff, and his reputation is unsavory at best. About whom does the father think constantly and toward whom are his efforts primarily focused? Obviously on the ne'er-do-well. The father is busy day and night, willing to try any possible tactic in order to put his son back on track.

Every Jew — even a thief — is a child of God. The Torah therefore begins the ordinances with the law of a thief sold as a bondsman. Our Merciful Father says, "My dear child, even though you stole and were sold as a slave, even though you abandoned Me and My Torah, you still remain the major subject of My concern to whom I devote My fullest efforts."

How does God hope to get His thieving son back on the right path? Were the thief to be imprisoned, he would be influenced by his fellow inmates. Furthermore, how can we expect him to stop stealing upon his release from prison if he will have no other way of supporting his wife and children?

---

4. Implanted Justice. *R' Gedaliah Schorr* expands on this theme. The very fact that human intellect perceives the logic and justice inherent in civil laws, such as the prohibition to steal or to murder, is because God has implanted such perceptions in the human mind. As King Solomon taught, *He also put the world into their minds* (*Ecclesiastes* 3:11), meaning that God imbued man with innate intelligence to understand the laws and conventions necessary to create a functional society. Hence even these laws are ultimately God given.

King David captured this message when he wrote *Mighty is the King, Who loves justice. You founded fairness* (*Psalms* 99:4). Although human beings have standards of fairness, we should not delude ourselves into thinking that such ideals are of human origin. Even so-called "human decency" was ingrained in man by God (*Chidushei HaRim*).

5. Obvious, My Dear . . . . This, explains *Imrei Emes,* is why the Talmud frequently states that מִילְתָא דְאַתְיָא בְּקַל וָחוֹמֶר טָרַח וְכָתַב לָהּ קְרָא, although a law might be derived from logical reasoning [a קַל וָחוֹמֶר, a *fortiori* argument], nevertheless the Torah took the trouble to record it (see *Pesachim* 18b). The Torah did so in order that man understand that the ultimate truth emanates from God — not from human intellect.

6. Blindly Convinced. A *chassid* came to the *Imrei Emes* with a complaint. "My friend and I appeared before *beis din* regarding a monetary dispute. Before I went to the court I studied all the pertinent chapters in the *Shulchan Aruch* and the commentators. I was sure I was right, yet the *beis din* ruled gainst me."

The *Imrei Emes* responded, "I now understand the Midrash that states that Jews get into arguments as a result of the ordinances. Once God gave us the law, each person studies it and his self-interest convinces him that his claim is justified and accurate. Thus they become embroiled in major strife. The true way of the Torah is to seek truth — not victory."

Therefore the Torah prescribes that he be sold to a respectable person who can serve as a positive role model. In such an environment, he will be cared for and made to feel like a functional and upstanding human being, until he actually grows into the role. Before he is freed, the Torah helps him become established financially by commanding his master to grant him substantial financial gifts (*Deuteronomy* 15:14). In this way, he can be rehabilitated and start his life afresh.

God cares for all His children — even if they are thieves.[7], [8]

כִּי תִקְנֶה עֶבֶד עִבְרִי
If you buy a Jewish bondsman (ibid.).

Why does the Torah refer to the bondsman as an עֶבֶד עִבְרִי, *Hebrew servant,* rather than an עֶבֶד יִשְׂרָאֵלִי, *Israelite servant?*

The appellation עִבְרִי comes from the word עֵבֶר, *side* or *[riverbank],* that was first applied to Abraham (see *Genesis* 14:13), because he originated on the *other side* of the Euphrates River. However, it also referred to Abraham as a person who, with Sarah, was on one side of a moral and spiritual divide, firmly rooted in his faith in One God, while the rest of the world was on the other. A Jew must be ready to endure that type of isolation, for while popularity is appealing, it can also be a trap. The desire to win the approval of others can easily lead one to compromise his principles.

The ability to be on the "other side" is the truest form of freedom, for one should not feel bound or answerable to anything or anyone outside of the truth. One must tenaciously embrace what he understands to be the truth and not be swayed from it.

A Jewish bondsman is enslaved for six years, and then he goes free, because, as a Jew, he is intrinsically free and cannot be indentured to other slaves. In spite of his temporary servitude, he is truly an עִבְרִי, free to live according to his own truth and not that of others (*Avnei Nezer*).[9]

וּבַשְּׁבִעֵת יֵצֵא לַחָפְשִׁי חִנָּם
and in the seventh he shall go free (ibid.).

Talmud Yerushalmi (*Rosh Hashanah* 3:5) teaches that the Jewish people were taught this law while still enslaved in Egypt. *Jeremiah* (34:13-14) alludes to this, saying: *I sealed a covenant with your forefathers on the day I took them out of the land of Egypt . . . each of you shall send forth his Hebrew brother who will have been sold to you.*

The Jews were still in Egypt when God commanded them about freeing slaves — though this would not apply until they entered the Land and kept the Sabbatical year, over 50 years later. On the other hand although they would begin keeping the Sabbath immediately after the Exodus, they learned nothing about it until after they left Egypt.

R' Chaim Shmulevitz finds a powerful lesson in this. Setting one's slaves free is an emotionally difficult task. One enjoys being a "master" with

---

7. **Dignity.** Divine concern for human dignity — even that of a thief — is underscored by law that one who steals an ox or a sheep and sells or slaughters it must pay five times the value of the ox and four times the value of the sheep (*Exodus* 21:37). According to R' Yochanan ben Zakkai, the payment of the one who steals the sheep is reduced since the thief suffered the embarrassment of carrying it on his shoulders as he made his escape.

While people might say, "Why have compassion on a thief? He should not have stolen!" God says otherwise. "He is my child. Even though he sins, I have compassion on him."

If that is the degree of God's compassion towards a thief, how compassionate must He be toward those who try to do the right thing? (*R' Yaakov Naiman*).

8. **A Crooked Mitzvah.** Who would be foolish enough to bring a thief into his home? The answer is that there are Jews with money who are always in search of *mitzvos.* Just as a Jew can use his money to buy a Torah scroll to fulfill a *mitzvah,* so there are Jews willing to purchase a Jewish bondsman in order to fulfill a *mitzvah.* Just as God cares for His thieves, so there are Jews who care for them (*R' Isaac Sher*).

9. **Personal Tradition.** The tradition we receive from our parents and grandparents is not meant, God forbid, to be an imprisoning encumbrance. Every Jew should come freely to a vibrant personal relationship with God. Only then does he become a link in the golden chain of tradition. In the words of *R' Menachem Mendel of Kotzk,* one must first say, *This is my God* (*Exodus* 15:2), and only afterwards, *the God of my father* (ibid.).

power over "servants." Although the servant yearns for freedom, the master is oblivious to anything besides maintaining his own position. That is why God taught Israel about freeing slaves at the moment when they tasted the intense joy of freedom. At that moment when they could fully empathize with the plight of the slave and experience the joy of freedom, they accepted upon themselves the obligation to provide their slaves with this very experience.

This is true in all areas of life. One must seize the moment of intense emotional meaning and use it to commit himself to the underlying message of the experience.

וְרָצַע אֲדֹנָיו אֶת אָזְנוֹ בַּמַּרְצֵעַ
and his master shall bore through his ear with the awl (ibid. 6).

The Sages explain why boring the earlobe symbolizes the servitude of the bondsman who spurns freedom and insists on remaining indentured. The ear that heard at Sinai the prohibition not to steal, yet did so regardless, deserves to be bored. Likewise, the ear that heard God say *the Children of Israel are . . . My servants* (*Leviticus* 25:55), yet chose to be the servant of a mortal human being, must be bored.

Since the bondsman discussed in this chapter was sold into slavery by the court to pay for the theft, he became a slave because of the legs that went to steal and the hands that committed the theft; why should the ear be punished?

R' Tzvi Pesach Frank submits two approaches:

When one hears the word of God it must penetrate deeply, leaving its mark on the total person. One who hears in this fashion is driven to follow the will of God. If he is not driven to practical commitment, however, then it is obvious that he heard only superficially, with God's words going in one ear and out the other. Since the lesson left no impact on the rest of the person, it was only the *ear* that heard God speak. Thus it is the ear that heard God say not to steal that must be punished for not spreading the message throughout his entire person.

Alternatively, the Torah describes the revelation at Sinai as *a great voice, never to be repeated* (*Deuteronomy* 5:19). *Targum Onkelos* renders it as *a great unending voice.* The voice of God at Sinai continues throughout Jewish history, constantly speaking to every Jew and encouraging him to follow the Torah. One who ignores this recurrent message basically claims that Sinai was an isolated event. He heard the words at *Sinai* yet he did not take them with him. Hence his ear must be bored.[10]

If the reason his ear is bored is because he rejected the message that we are servants of God and not of man, why do we bore his ear only after he decides to remain with his flesh-and-blood master? Why don't we do so as soon as he sells himself to another human being?

According to *R' Yechezkel Levenstein,* the Torah teaches the dynamics of sin and repentance. When a person's spiritual brakes first begin to fail and he starts to lose control, he is in great peril. Downward momentum, driven by spiritual gravity, turns into a

---

10. **Wrong Frequency.** *Imrei Emes* embellishes on this theme. Just as a radio receiver picks up signals that are within its frequency range, so the human ear is attuned to specific sounds. If the ear was unable to hear the message of the ugliness of thievery or the degradation of being enslaved to a human being, then apparently it is attuned to a different frequency. Foul language, mockery and the like have apparently desensitized such an ear to the word of God.

Since the earlobe was created so that man could use it to close his ear to negative and spiritually damaging messages (see *Kesubos* 5b), one who failed to use it properly and allowed aural pollution to infiltrate himself is faulted for not hearing the word of God.

Sfas Emes comments that when the Jewish people stood at Sinai and accepted the Torah they proclaimed נַעֲשֶׂה וְנִשְׁמַע, *we will do and we will hear.* A Jew seeks not only to do what he knows God asks of him, he looks for opportunities to hear more things that he can do for God. *We will do* expressed the Jews' readiness to do God's will. *We will hear* is the Jews' call that they "accept Your sovereignty and look for every opportunity to serve You."

The Jewish bondsman continues to perform the *mitzvos* even after being sold. What he lacks is the ability to fully assume the yoke of Heaven since he is beholden to his master. He can proclaim *we will do,* but his declaration *we will hear* rings hollow due to his servitude to a mortal. When he prefers to remain enslaved, he undermines his commitment to נִשְׁמַע, *we will hear;* hence it is his ear that must be bored.

powerful, unstoppable force. On the surface the person seems to be spiritually healthy, but in reality he is in great danger. On the other hand, one who has fallen very far, and begins to take the initial steps toward spiritual rehabilitation is, to a great degree, in a far better position. He has begun the uphill battle and taken the first steps toward overcoming his negative impulses. With time his upward momentum will increase and intensify to the point that he will eventually succeed.[11]

While one is on a spiritual slide, it is almost impossible to reason with him or convince him to change his ways. He is so caught up in his passion that he is deaf to any positive message. Only when he hits rock bottom and is wallowing in evil can he be awakened. His passion spent, he is able to realize how far he has fallen. Now he is ready to pick himself up and attempt to climb the mountain to repentance.

When the Jewish bondsman initially sells himself, his downward momentum is so great that the message inherent in boring his earlobe will be lost on him. Only after six years of servitude to another human being and only when he has fallen so low that he loves the non-Jewish maidservant he was coupled with more than his Jewish wife, and prefers his mortal master to freedom, is he ready to begin the trek to rehabilitation. Only then can he begin to save his soul.

Sfas Emes answers the question from a different perspective.

We often fool ourselves into believing that we can successfully maintain dual loyalty, serving God and man simultaneously. When the Jewish bondsman sells himself to a mortal master, he naively believes that his subservience to his master will not impede his sense of servitude toward God. He thinks he can accommodate both. Thus we may soften our judgment of him for having sold himself. Once, he has experienced six years of servitude, however, he should know better. If he still insists on not taking the opportunity to be free to truly serve God, he deserves to be punished.[12]

וְכִי יִמְכֹּר אִישׁ אֶת בִּתּוֹ לְאָמָה לֹא תֵצֵא כְּצֵאת הָעֲבָדִים

If a man will sell his daughter as a bondswoman, she shall not leave like the leave-taking of the slaves (ibid. 7).

The *Zohar* interprets this verse allegorically. When the time comes for the soul to descend to this world, it begs God to be spared the ordeal. "Why should I descend to the lower world where I will become soiled by sin?" God responds, "You were created for the purpose of helping a Jew survive the lure of the physical world." The soul has no choice but to comply. The Torah shows man and his soul how to survive the challenge of this world. "God gave you a gem [the soul] to help you make your way safely through life. Thus the Torah teaches that *if a "man"* [God] *sells His daughter* [the soul] *as a bondswoman,* to be tempted by the corporeal desires surrounding it, one must be careful

---

11. **Downward Spiral.** In Kelm they used to say that one who prayed without concentration and then began focusing on but a few words of his prayer is better off than one who always prayed with concentration and recently began to slack off. While the first person is on an upward swing, the second is on the way down.

R' Yisrael Salanter lived in Paris in his later years, intent on spreading his *mussar* teachings and seeking to spark a spiritual revolution among French-Jewish youth. He even encouraged a project to translate the Talmud into French.

Some of his disciples questioned him "Why move to France; have you finished the task of remaking Polish and Lithuanian Jewry?" R' Yisrael replied, "A wagon that is rolling down a mountain moves so rapidly that it futile for one to try to stop it. One must wait until the wagon reaches the level ground at the foot of the mountain. Then one can slow it, stop it and reverse its course. Polish and Lithuanian Jewry are spiritually plunging downhill; I cannot reverse the process. But France has hit rock bottom. Now we can begin the process of spiritual ascent."

12. **Breaking the Shackles.** One might counter that six years of functioning with a slave mentality should mitigate the severity of censure against a slave who chooses to extend his bondage. Nevertheless, the basic urge for freedom should be so strong that the servant should feel compelled to break loose from his slavery. If he does not, he is subject to punishment. He may claim that he was forced to sell himself due to pressing financial circumstances, but he contradicts that defense when he rejects the chance to go free. Then he is punished retroactively for initially selling himself into bondage (*Sfas Emes*).

that *she shall not leave like the leave-taking of the slaves,* soiled by the sins of this world. Rather, she should maintain her intrinsic freedom at all costs so that when the "Man" receives His "daughter" upon her return, she is in at least, the same state of purity as she was when she "left."

Background

Murder, manslaughter, personal and property damages all fall within the purview of Divine justice. The Torah prescribes how to deal with both victim and perpetrator.

אִם יָקוּם וְהִתְהַלֵּךְ בַּחוּץ עַל מִשְׁעַנְתּוֹ
וְנִקָּה הַמַּכֶּה רַק שִׁבְתּוֹ יִתֵּן וְרַפֹּא יְרַפֵּא

If he gets up and goes about outside under his own power, the one who struck is absolved. Only for his lost time shall he pay, and he shall provide for healing (ibid. 19).

The Talmud (*Bava Kamma* 85a) derives from this verse that doctors have Divine permission to practice medicine and heal the sick. The relationship between seeking medical help and relying on God to heal is a very delicate issue.

R' Elyah Lopian related that when *R' Simchah Zissel of Kelm* was ill, he would summon a paramedic rather than a full-fledged doctor. When asked to explain this practice he replied, "I am not ready to rely totally on my trust in God since I am unsure as to whether it is pure enough to merit Divine intervention. On the other hand, I am afraid to call a doctor since I might rely on him and his knowledge rather than on God. I therefore struck on a compromise — the paramedic. On one hand, he makes some type of effort so that I do not depend on a total miracle; on the other hand, his medical skills are so rudimentary that I know I can not rely on him and I must rely on God. I therefore pray to God that the paramedic will do the right thing."[13]

Taam V'Daas submits that the requirement to balance the use of medical science with the belief that it is God Who truly heals is alluded to in the double expression וְרַפֹּא יְרַפֵּא in the verse, which mandates that one seek medical treatment. Such double terms are often interpreted by the Sages as conveying a constant and recurrent obligation. For example, הָשֵׁב תְּשִׁיבֶנּוּ, *you shall return it to him repeatedly* (*Exodus* 23:4), means that the Torah requires one to return a lost item even if it is lost time after time. The finder may not ignore it on the grounds that the owner is apparently careless (See *Bava Metzia* 30b). Likewise, if one course of medical treatment did not succeed, he should not despair. Rather, he should seek alternative therapies until, with God's help, he will be cured.[14], [15]

R' Yisrael of Rizhin offered a homiletical interpre-

---

13. **Faithful Medicine.** The *Chazon Ish* writes: "I personally view normal efforts in health-related matters as an obligation and a mitzvah, one of the obligations incumbent upon us in order to maintain the human being and his stature as God created him. Many of the Talmudic Sages used the offices of non-Jewish and even heretical doctors (see *Avodah Zarah* 27b), as well as many herbs and living creatures which were created with healing qualities. The human intellect with its ability to devise medical cures is also one of God's creations.

"Although there exists a legitimate spiritual path in life which allows one to skip over natural means and certainly to avoid excessive efforts in that direction [and to rely totally on God for a cure] one must weigh the matter very carefully [before embarking on such a path]. Veering away from the true path in either direction is wrong. For one to rely on God to a degree that is beyond his true level of trust or to exhibit excessive belief in human efforts are both distortions of truth.

14. **Doctor Divine.** Although a doctor cures many patients, his success is not necessarily related to his expertise. Just as there is a Heavenly decree that a particular medicine will cure a specific disease, so it is decided in Heaven which doctor will cure it. The decree causes the doctor's success. Hence if one doctor's treatment is unsuccessful, one should try another doctor — perhaps he is the messenger to whom God granted the ability to cure the disease (*Chazon Ish*).

A sick relative of the *Chozeh of Lublin* asked that he pray on his behalf. "The doctors have given up hope. They claim I won't live out the year," he said. The Chozeh became upset. "The Torah gave them permission only to heal the sick, not to decide that they are beyond help!"

15. **Root Cause.** When *R' Yechezkel Sarna* was hospitalized in Switzerland he wrote in his diary: "Every physical ailment has a spiritual cause. Hence it is possible that as a result of some spiritual merit one will be cured of the

tation to the entire verse based on the words of the Sages that one's money is what figuratively puts him on his feet (*Pesachim* 119a). *If he gets up* and becomes wealthy *and goes about outside,* living beyond the pale of a Torah lifestyle, because he feels that his destiny falls *under his own power,* thinking he can control his own life with his wealth then if he wants *the one who struck* (i.e., himself) to be *absolved* and achieve atonement, there is only one sure way to repent. *Only for his lost time shall he pay,* by giving charity, *and* thus *he shall provide for healing* to his ailing soul.

עַיִן תַּחַת עַיִן
an eye for an eye (ibid. 24).

While a literal reading of this verse indicates that one who blinds someone must himself be blinded in retaliation, this is not and never was the correct interpretation. The Sages teach that in fact one must pay the monetary equivalent of the eye, meaning that he must pay the victim damages for his lost eye. *HaKsav V'HaKabbalah* submits that a careful reading of the text leads directly to the Sages' interpretation. Generally the Torah speaks first of the crime and then spells out the appropriate punishment. Thus עַיִן, for taking someone's eye (the crime), תַּחַת עַיִן; one must pay *instead of the eye*, namely its monetary value.[16]

If the Torah is referring to monetary payment, why is the verse written in a way that it implies the literal taking of *an eye for an eye*? *Chazon Ish* explained that aside from the technical, legal meaning of a law, it also means to convey an ethical lesson.

For example, the Sages taught that a Sanhedrin that administers the death penalty even once in seventy years is deemed a "murderous" Sanhedrin (*Makkos* 7a). Likewise, capital cases require a sanhedrin of twenty-three members, who must

keep in mind a myriad of halachic requirements in order to issue an accurate ruling. These regulations are intended to magnify the inestimable value of human life and to teach us how vital it is for the judicial system to avoid killing someone through a mistaken ruling. The laws of judging an alleged murderer are not intended merely to address the immediate issue of homicide, but, more importantly, to convey a clear understanding of how precious human life is to God — even when dealing with the life of a murderer.

Likewise here. Although in practice one who has blinded another does not have his own eye taken out, the Torah still emphasizes the severity of the crime by describing the punishment in stark terms. While he pays only money, in the Torah's scale of values, the crime is as morally reprehensible as if it were punishable by literally taking *an eye for an eye.*

כִּי יִכְרֶה אִישׁ בֹּר . . . בַּעַל הַבּוֹר יְשַׁלֵּם כֶּסֶף יָשִׁיב לִבְעָלָיו
if a man shall dig a pit . . . the owner of the pit shall make restitution. He shall return money to its owner (ibid. 33-34).

Sfas Emes suggests a homiletical reading of the verse, in which he interprets the digger of the pit as a generic reference to a sinner and relates the word כֶּסֶף, *money,* to its other, less common meaning, כִּסּוּפִים, *yearning.* When a man sins, he does not affect only his own life, he affects others as well, either by desecrating God's Name, by being a negative role model, or simply because sin pollutes the spiritual atmosphere and can even tip the cosmic balance of merit and sin. Thus a sinner is like someone who digs a pit in public property, because he creates a hazard to others. The sinner must repent and make restitution to God. How? *He shall return* כֶּסֶף, his yearning, *to His owner.*

---

physical symptoms, yet the underlying spiritual cause of the disease still remains. Such a cure is healing (רְפוּאָה) without salvation (יְשׁוּעָה), for without dealing with the root cause, one is vulnerable to a relapse.

"We therefore pray (in *Shemoneh Esrei*), רְפָאֵנוּ ה' וְנֵרָפֵא הוֹשִׁיעֵנוּ וְנִוָּשֵׁעָה, *Heal us Hashem* [of the symptoms] — *then we will be healed; save us* [from the spiritual root cause] — *then we will be saved.*"

16. **Right Under the Eye.** The *Vilna Gaon* sees an allusion to the Sages' interpretation in the use of the words עַיִן תַּחַת עַיִן (lit. *an eye under an eye*) rather then עַיִן בְּעַד עַיִן (*an eye in return for an eye*). The letters that come after (or are *under*) the letters of the word עַיִן are פכס. When rearranged they spell כֶּסֶף, *money.* Thus one who takes an eye pays with what is under (תַּחַת) the עַיִן, namely כֶּסֶף, *money.*

He must take his yearning for sin and redirect his passions toward God, by striving to serve Him.

כִּי יִתֵּן אִישׁ אֶל רֵעֵהוּ כֶּסֶף אוֹ כֵלִים לִשְׁמֹר וְגֻנַּב מִבֵּית הָאִישׁ אִם יִמָּצֵא הַגַּנָּב יְשַׁלֵּם שְׁנָיִם

If a man shall give money or vessels to his fellow to safeguard and it is stolen from the house of the man, if the thief is found he shall pay double (22:6).

Like many of the civil laws included in the Torah, this verse may be understood on a spiritual plane. If a *"man"* (meaning God, Who is called a *Man of war* — see *Exodus* 15:3) gives *money or vessels, to his fellow,* meaning that He provides faculties and physical needs to be safeguarded and used only for sanctified purposes, and they were stolen *from the house of the Man,* i.e., they were misappropriated for mundane or sinful purposes and *the thief,* i.e., the sinner, *was found* unwilling to repent, then he will have to pay double, both for the sin and for not having repented. If, however, *the thief is found,* namely that the sinner seeks to repent, then he will come close to הָאֱלֹהִים (lit. the court), God, for one who repents reaches a higher spiritual level than one who never sinned (*Chasam Sofer* citing *R' Nosson Adler*).[17]

וְכִי יִשְׁאַל אִישׁ מֵעִם רֵעֵהוּ . . . שַׁלֵּם יְשַׁלֵּם . . . אִם בְּעָלָיו עִמּוֹ לֹא יְשַׁלֵּם

If a man shall borrow from his fellow and it shall become broken or shall die . . . he shall surely make restitution. If its owner was with him, he shall not make restitution (ibid. 13-14).

Man was granted his soul and all his faculties by God and, like a borrower, he has free reign to use them as he pleases. However, also like a borrower, he is responsible even if he sins accidentally. The only way one can be absolved of such responsibility is if he is so thoroughly dedicated to God that the "Owner" is always with him. Even when he sins inadvertently he is pained by his actions and continues to yearn for God's closeness. Hence the Owner is with him all the time.

The reason one is culpable for his inadvertent sins is that they ultimately stem from a negligent attitude toward accepting the yoke of God's sovereignty. One who truly has God with him at all times may legitimately claim that his transgressions were unintentional (*Sfas Emes*).

כָּל אַלְמָנָה וְיָתוֹם לֹא תְעַנּוּן

You shall not cause pain to any widow or orphan (ibid. 21).

Why is the word תְעַנּוּן, *to cause pain,* written with an additional *nun*? *Ibn Ezra* explains that anyone who witnesses the mistreatment of a widow and orphan and does not try to defend them is himself deemed to be complicit in the pain. According to the *Netziv,* this idea is clearly stated by the prophet (*Isaiah* (64:11): *Will You restrain Yourself in the face of all these, Hashem, and be silent and impose upon us so much suffering?* Silence in the face of mistreatment is the equivalent of imposing suffering.[18]

---

17. **Custodical Care.** *Sfas Emes* expands on the analogy. God gives man כֶּסֶף, yearnings and desires, and כֵּלִים, the physical tools to navigate life. Man must protect these gifts for the evil inclination, the primary thief, seeks to rob him of his values and even his soul. If one catches the thief after he stole, and returns the stolen goods, the thief pays double. Allegorically this means that if a sinner repents and returns the stolen goods, he is paid doubly, for he achieves the special closeness to God that is reserved for those who repent.

Sometimes circumstances in life are so difficult that one inadvertently falls into sin. Here, too, the law of a custodian applies. If one was careful not to lay his hand on his fellow's property, meaning that he did not use God's gifts for his personal enjoyment, then he can legitimately expect to be forgiven for any accidental, inadvertent sin.

18. **My Book.** Once a group of prominent rabbis met at the home of *R' Chaim Ozer Grodzenski of Vilna* to discuss communal matters. In middle of the meeting a woman burst into the room and began banging on the table and screaming, "If the Rav won't give me a letter of recommendation to the charity fund, I will smash all the furniture in the room!"

R' Chaim Ozer tried to calm her down and offered her money, but to no avail. She continued to scream and even began speaking rudely to him. Some of the rabbis in attendance began to berate her for her impudence. R' Chaim Ozer cut them short. "Leave her be. She's a widow!"

R' Chaim Ozer once said, "When I was younger I was sure that the most significant thing I could do was write

אִם עַנֵּה תְעַנֶּה אֹתוֹ כִּי אִם צָעֹק
יִצְעַק אֵלַי שָׁמֹעַ אֶשְׁמַע צַעֲקָתוֹ

If you dare to cause him pain . . .!
for if he shall cry out to Me,
I shall surely hear his outcry (ibid. 22).

While normally one who complains to God about another Jew rather than summoning him to a *beis din* is Divinely punished, the rule changes in the case of orphans and widows. If they shall cry out to Him rather than turn to a tribunal of mortals, God will still heed their cry. Since He is the Father of all orphans and the Judge of all widows, He listens. How can one be upset with a child who calls out to his father for help in hard times? (*Alshich*).[19]

R' Menachem Mendel of Kotzk notes that each of the three verbs in the verse is doubled. When one mistreats orphans or widows, the pain is compounded because they are reminded of their unfortunate state and are convinced that others feel free to abuse them because of their helplessness. Their outcry contains a double dose of bitterness which God does not ignore.[20]

Torah novella. Now I know that helping widows and orphans is more important.''

When he published his magnum opus *Achiezer*, he presented a copy to *R' Elya Chaim Meisel*, the Rabbi of Lodz, Poland and said to him, ''R' Elya Chaim, when will we see your book printed?'' R' Elya Chaim showed him an envelope full of loan agreements that he had co-signed and ultimately had paid when the borrower could not pay. The loans were granted to indigent Torah scholars and poor widows and orphans. ''This is my book,'' said R' Elya Chaim. R' Chaim Ozer began to sob uncontrollably.

19. **Sown with Tears.** The tears of any Jew can shake the heavens and bring blessing to the world, especially the tears of a widow or an orphan.

For many years after the death of *R' Tzvi Pesach Frank*, Jerusalem had no official chief rabbi. Finally it was decided to hold elections and *R' Chaim Yaakov Levin* was asked to be a candidate for the position. He asked those pressuring him to run who the other candidates were. When he heard that *R' Betzalel Zolty* was one of them, he immediately withdrew from the race; nothing could sway him from his decision. When asked to explain he replied, ''My father (*R' Aryeh Levin*) once told us that he was walking one evening on a narrow Jerusalem street when he saw a woman sitting next to a small dim lamp, darning socks. 'Why do you bother with fixing socks and by such dim light?' he asked her. She answered, 'I am a widow and with the little bit of money I earn I am able to pay my orphaned son's tuition.' As she spoke tears rolled down her face and onto the socks.

''Do you know who that woman was? She was R' Betzalel's mother, and she supported her son by darning socks. Is it possible to compete with the tears of a widow? A *talmid chacham* like R' Betzalel Zolty who grew from a field irrigated with the hot tears of a widow deserves to be the rav of Jerusalem.''

R' Hirsch Broide of Kelm employed a young orphan girl who performed many of the domestic chores in his home. At a certain point the house was plagued with many thefts and the rebbetzin suspected that the girl, unable to resist temptation, had stolen money and valuables. When the rebbetzin asked R' Hirsch if she was allowed to summon the girl to a *din Torah* (rabbinic court), he said yes, and she went to have the court set a date for the hearing.

When the hearing date arrived and the rebbetzin was preparing to leave for the *beis din,* she noticed that R' Hirsch was putting on his coat, preparing to leave as well. ''Where are you going?'' she asked, to which he replied, ''To the *beis din.* '' Sure that he was coming to help her argue her case she said, ''It's not necessary; I can present my case alone.''

R' Hirsch responded. ''I'm not going to help you. Since the girl has no one to help her, I'm going to help argue her case.''

The rebbetzin decided to stay home.

20. **A Widowed Heart.** *R' Yechezkel Abramsky* related that *R' Chaim Soloveitchick* never referred to himself as the Rav of Brisk nor did he sign his name as such. In his humility he viewed himself as undeserving of such a title and would not use it. Only once did he make an exception.

One of his students told him about a widow in Brisk who was downtrodden and in need of encouragement. He immediately decided to go visit her and asked his student to go quickly to her house and tell her that the Rav of Brisk was on the way. In order to bring joy to a brokenhearted widow, R' Chaim was ready to do something he found very distasteful and have himself announced as the Rav of Brisk.

R' Yechezkel himself had this type of sensitivity to the plight of widows. An eyewitness related that he was sitting with R' Yechezkel in the last year of his life when there was a knock at the door. The rebbetzin opened the door and a neighbor, a widow, entered. The lonely woman had come to visit the rebbetzin. In spite of his age and ill

כִּי תִרְאֶה חֲמוֹר שֹׂנַאֲךָ רֹבֵץ
תַּחַת מַשָּׂאוֹ . . . עָזֹב תַּעֲזֹב עִמּוֹ
*If you see the donkey of someone you
hate crouching under its burden . . .
you shall help repeatedly with him (23:5).*

The Torah speaks about helping one's enemy. The Talmud explains that if one is confronted with the choice between helping a friend unload his overburdened donkey and helping his enemy to load his donkey, one must give precedence to his enemy. The reason is that by helping one's enemy, he subdues the evil inclination that encourages him not to help (*Bava Metzia* 32b-33a).[21] The Talmud questions this premise, since allowing the overloaded animal to bear its burden constitutes צַעַר בַּעֲלֵי חַיִּים, *cruelty toward living creatures,* which, according to some opinions, is a Biblical prohibition. How can an exercise in self-improvement —

such as subduing one's evil inclination — overrule a Biblical prohibition? Nonetheless, concludes the Talmud, subduing that evil streak is more important.

R' Yitzchak Blazer explained that the requirement to help with an enemy's donkey is no different than the slaughter of animals for food or the use of animals for work. There, too, one might ask why such uses do not constitute cruelty to animals. The answer is that animal life was created to serve man. Whether as food, clothing, or to meet any other real human need, the animal is there for man's benefit. If this is true on a physical level, how much more so does it apply to man's spirituality. If the donkey of one's friend will suffer so that one can subdue his evil inclination by helping his enemy, so be it. As crucial as food is to man, subduing his baser instincts is truly a matter of life and death.[22]

---

health, R' Yechezkel got up and wished her "a *Gut Shabbos.*" He then said to her, "May I ask you a favor? This week I bought a new frock coat. Would you mind looking at it and giving me your opinion about the quality and the fit?" The woman was honored beyond words that the great man was asking her opinion. He thus graciously fulfilled the verse, *I would bring joyous song to a widowed heart (Job* 29:13).

A young widow once came to *R' Shlomo Zalman Auerbach.* Her husband had died recently, leaving several orphans, and she could find no peace. Her question was what could she do as a merit for her husband's soul.

R' Shlomo Zalman said, "Buy toys. Play with your children and make them happy. That is the best thing you can do for your husband's soul."

21. **Unloading the Heart.** *Targum Onkelos* alludes to this sense of precedence in his translation of the double עָזֹב תַּעֲזֹב, rendering it as *abandon whatever* [animosity] *you have against him in your heart* and help him unload.

22. **Short Circuit.** How does one know if the person who needs his help is hated to the extent that he must subdue his hatred and help nonetheless? According to *Imrei Yaakov,* this is the thrust of the Torah's words *would you refrain from helping him?* If one feels an urge to refrain from helping a fellow Jew, it indicates that in his heart he hates him, even if he doesn't realize it consciously. The urge not to help is the telltale sign. If you really don't want to help a Jew — help him!

Tosafos (Pesachim 113b) submits that the hatred discussed here cannot be ordinary hatred, since the Torah forbids one to hate a fellow Jew *(Leviticus* 19:17). Rather it refers to someone who persists in brazenly committing sins despite repeated warnings. Such a person should be hated in the spirit of King David who said, *Lovers of Hashem hate evil (Psalms* 97:10).

Why then does the Torah command us to help him? Because human relationships are reciprocal. As King Solomon taught, כַּמַּיִם הַפָּנִים לַפָּנִים כֵּן לֵב הָאָדָם לָאָדָם, *As water reflects a face back to a face, so one's heart is reflected back to him by another (Proverbs* 27:19). If I hate someone because of his sins then he will automatically reciprocate the hatred for motives not as pure and legitimate as mine. I, in turn, will respond to his hatred with personal, rather than altruistic, resentment. In short order we will hate each other with no Heavenly intent at all. In order to prevent this conflagration of hatred, the Torah commands us to help even someone whom we may legitimately consider an enemy.

פרשת תרומה ‎⊰
Parashas Terumah

Background

In order to maintain the Divine Presence that descended to Mount Sinai at the giving of the Torah, God commands the Jewish nation to create a Tabernacle (*Ramban*). God asks that an outpouring of magnanimity provide the necessary raw materials from which the people would fashion His earthly footstool (see *Isaiah* 66:1).[1], [2]

The *sidrah* that discusses the building of the Tabernacle was preceded by *Mishpatim*, which contain laws governing interpersonal relationships and the protection of private property. However, the specific commands to build the Altar made of earth (the copper Altar in the Tabernacle) and the stone Altar (in the Temple) appeared at the end of *Yisro*, before the civil law.

R' Zalman Sorotzkin explains: Earth and stones are plentiful and easy to come by. Gold, silver and copper, however, are expensive and not always affordable. Thus before commanding us to donate these valuable items for the Tabernacle the Torah interjects to teach us the laws of personal property. We must be sure that whatever we donate for the Tabernacle is halachically "kosher" money.

Beis HaLevi elaborates: Charity given from money that is not earned honestly is not deemed a *mitzvah* but rather a sin, just as one who takes a stolen lulav does not fulfill the *mitzvah* since it is deemed a מִצְוָה הַבָּאָה בַּעֲבֵירָה, *a mitzvah performed through transgression* (See *Succah* 30a). Only after studying *Parashas Mishpatim* and learning to differentiate between "kosher" and "nonkosher" money can one separate *terumah* (a portion) of his money to build the Tabernacle.[3]

---

1. **Magnanimity.** Since the Tabernacle was to be the ongoing continuation of Sinai, it had to be built with voluntary donations. Just as the Jewish people declared נַעֲשֶׂה וְנִשְׁמָע, *we will do and we will hear,* at Sinai, voluntarily committing themselves to the word of God, and proclaimed, "We desire to see our King" (see *Rashi* to *Exodus* 19:9), so the Tabernacle, the place where God's Presence would remain with us, could be created only by a similar spirit of heartfelt personal motivation (*Zekan Aharon*).

2. **Spiritual Elevator.** *Terumah* literally means *an elevation.* R' Hirsch of Rimanov notes that תְּרוּמָה spells the word תּוֹרָה with an additional מ, which has the numerical value of 40. The Torah, which God gave to Moses when he went up to Heaven for forty days, is the key to elevating every aspect of life.

3. **Justly Given.** *Isaiah* (56:1) captures this message. *So said Hashem: Observe justice and perform* צְדָקָה, *righteousness.* Only through strict adherence to justice in monetary matters is one truly able to perform righteousness and charity. Unless one carefully scrutinizes the "cleanliness" of his money before donating to charity, he often jeopardizes his chances of fulfilling the mitzvah. According to the *Zohar*, the prophet conveys this sentiment when he says, *Surely you should divide your bread with the hungry* (Isaiah 58:7). It does not say "divide bread" but rather "divide *your* bread." Charity given from money not one's own is really a sin.

Maharsha (*Kesubos* 67a) writes: "Many in our generation have amassed their wealth in a less than truthful

וְיִקְחוּ לִי תְּרוּמָה
Let them take for Me a portion (25:2).

The Midrash (*Shemos Rabbah* 33:1) renders this phrase as *let them take Me as a portion*. Unlike a regular acquisition in which the buyer buys the item but does not acquire the seller, when God "sold" us the Torah we acquired Him along with it. This may be compared to a princess who married a prince from a faraway land. After the young couple resided for a while in the home of the bride's father, the time came for the prince and his princess to return to his homeland. The bride's father was heartbroken over the prospect of separation from his precious daughter. On the other hand, he realized that he could not demand of the prince that he remain. He therefore asked the newlyweds to build a small chamber for him wherever they live, so he would be able to stay with them.

The Torah is God's precious "daughter" whom He gave to her groom, the people of Israel. When they finally left Sinai, He couldn't bear the separation, as it were. He asked them to build a Tabernacle so that His Presence could travel along with them. Thus when they acquired the Torah at Sinai they acquired God with it. The way in which they held on to His Presence was by building Him a small Tabernacle.[4]

The term וְיִתְּנוּ, *you shall give,* would seem to be more appropriate than וְיִקְחוּ, *you shall take.* Why does the Torah refer to giving the portion as taking? *Alshich* invokes a halachic analogy. One seeking to marry a woman must give her a ring or something of value to effect the new relationship;

if she gives the man something, the marriage does not take effect. However, if the man is a prestigious person, she is deemed married even if she gave him the money (see *Kiddushin* 7a), because it is considered an honor for him to have accepted the gift from her. Such an honor has monetary value, and is the same as his actually giving her something. When we give our donations to God in order to build Him a Sanctuary we are really taking, not giving.

Sfas Emes elaborates: What can man give God, Who needs nothing? God provides us with a way to earn merit by displaying our willingness to give. Hence when we give, in reality we *take* for ourselves the merit of giving.[5]

Malbim offers an explanation based on the *Mishnah* (*Avos* 3:8) that teaches, "Give Him from His own, for you and your possessions are His." One must never be stingy in matters of charity or expenditures for *mitzvos.* One must realize that he is spending God's money and not his own, and therefore give happily and magnanimously. Hence man *takes* his livelihood from God so that he will be able to contribute to worthy causes.

This might be compared to a parent who showers a child with all kinds of wealth and gifts, and then asks the child to share it with him. Although it was the parent who gave the gifts in the first place, it is a source of joy to him when the child shares it. Likewise, although God granted us the wealth, He rejoices when we *take* and then give it back to Him.[6]

Beis HaLevi compares man and his possessions to a jar that contains a piece of sugar and a large fly. The fly moves around in the jar and from time

---

fashion or by desecrating God's Name through stealing from non-Jews and then contributing from those funds in order to acquire honor, public accolades, posterity and the blessings of the congregation. In reality this is a travesty, a sinful mitzvah."

4. **A Little House.** *R' Elya Meir Bloch* suggests that just as the nation at large needs a small house where our Father can reside with us, so every individual must create a little compartment in his heart and life where he can vibrantly sense the Presence of God. The way to do this is to set aside a special time daily, or at least weekly, to ponder the all-pervasive greatness of God and to make Him an integral part of our lives.

5. **In His Shoes.** *R' Yoel Baranchik* sees a different message in the Torah's referring to the contributions as taking. One who gives must emotionally put himself in the place of the recipient and be sensitive to his feelings. By doing so he will to a certain degree ameliorate feelings of shame and dependency on the part of the recipient, and allow him to receive his gift painlessly and pleasantly.

6. **Now You May.** The term *terumah* is applied to charitable gifts, for just as the *terumah* taken from one's crop permits one to eat the entire pile of grain, so charity elevates one's remaining money, making it permitted for personal use (*Taam V'Daas*).

to time licks the sugar. May the fly brag of its wealth, as the owner of the sugar? Of course not. Although it can lick the sugar, it cannot flee the jar and take the sugar with it. Man enjoys wealth and pleasure in this world, but when he dies, his wealth remains behind. Only that which he invested in charity or *mitzvos* is he able to take with him. Hence when man gives to charity, he is taking rather than giving.[7]

וְיִקְחוּ לִי תְּרוּמָה
Let them take for Me a portion (ibid.)

R*ashi* comments that the term *for Me* indicates that people should contribute to the Tabernacle purely for the sake of God's Name. *Chidushei*

HaRim submits that the Torah teaches us the extent to which one's motives should be altruistic when performing a *mitzvah*. Although one receives spiritual gain from fulfilling God's will, the motivation should be purely to please God. [One should not view *mitzvos* as a vehicle to increase one's prestige or social standing.]

Oznayim L'Torah notes that although *Rashi* makes a similar comment with regard to the verse וְעָשׂוּ לִי מִקְדָּשׁ, *they shall make a Sanctuary for Me* (25:8), he nonetheless underscores the necessity for pure motives here, when discussing the contributions. Not only must the act of building the Tabernacle be the result of pristine motives; even the preparatory stages must be informed by that spirit.[8]

---

7. **Giving of Oneself.** When R' Chaim Soloveitchik was a *rosh yeshivah* in Volozhin, the yeshivah was in extremely difficult financial straits. In order to assist the yeshivah, R' Chaim went to Minsk, the home of R' Baruch Zladowitz and R' Dov Ber Pines, two wealthy and learned Jews who functioned as the local committee for the yeshivah. R' Chaim went to R' Zladowitz's home and explained why he had come to Minsk. In spite of the sizable sum necessary to cover the yeshivah's debts, R' Zladowitz promised to try his best to ease the situation. R' Chaim took up lodgings at the Zladowitz home and spent all of his time deeply engrossed in learning. After a few days he asked R' Baruch if he had succeeded in making progress in raising the necessary funds. When R' Baruch told him that he had already raised half the needed sum, R' Chaim was pleased and went back to his learning. After almost a month since his arrival, R' Chaim inquired again of R' Baruch, and was told, "Thank God, I now have the entire sum. The Rav can go back to the yeshivah." R' Chaim thanked him, traveled back to Volozhin and paid off the creditors.

A few days later two gentlemen arrived in Volozhin in order to present a *din torah* (monetary case) to R' Chaim. R' Baruch Zladowitz and R' Dov Ber Pines wanted him to settle a dispute between them. R' Dov Ber claimed that R' Baruch had mistreated him. Since they had been partners throughout the years in all their charitable activities, R' Dov Ber demanded to know why R' Baruch was entitled to pay off the entire debt of the yeshivah from his own pocket and not allow R' Dov Ber half of the mitzvah. Why should they not have share equally in saving the yeshivah of Volozhin?

Upon hearing that R' Baruch had not raised funds but had given his personal funds, R' Chaim asked, "Why did you make me stay in Minsk for a month rather than allow me to return to my students as quickly as possible?"

R' Baruch replied, "Even the first half of the money was not easy for me. I had to work on myself for a few days until I was able to overcome my desire to keep the money. Only then could I commit to giving the first half. What can I say, Rebbe; it took me another few weeks to be ready to give the rest of the money."

This, explained R' Zalman Sorotzkin, is why the Torah teaches that one should *take* a portion. A person has to work on himself until he is ready to *take* a portion of his wealth and give it to God.

8. **Pure from the Outset.** The Talmud (*Bava Metzia* 85b) relates that R' Chiya claimed that if Torah were to be forgotten among the Jewish people, God forbid, he would be able to restore it. He would plant flax, make nets from its fibers, and catch deer. He would give the venison to Torah scholars and make parchment from the deerskins. He would write the Five Books of Moses on five parchments, and the six orders of *Mishnah* on another six parchments. He would then teach each of five children one of the books of Moses and each of six children an order of *Mishnah*. He would then have each child teach the others, and in that way spark a renaissance of Torah.

Why, asks the *Vilna Gaon*, couldn't R' Chiya save time by buying parchment? The Gaon explains that in order to produce a pure product, one must make sure that pure motives accompany every step of the process. R' Chiya therefore began the holy process in absolute sanctity from the earliest stage.

[In the spirit of R' Chiya, R' David Sitnick taught students in a summer bungalow colony in a gazebo that he built with his own two hands. By imbuing the physical structure with a purity of heart, one can teach Torah in a totally different way.]

The requirement to contribute with pure motives seems to contradict the Talmud's comment that one who gives charity on condition that his sick son shall live is considered to be a righteous person (*Rosh Hashanah* 4a). *R' Shalom of Kaminka* suggests that the Torah does not speak to the contributors, but rather to the public officials in charge of *taking* the contributions. They must do their job out of a sense of duty toward God, and not use their position to achieve honor, fame or power.

מֵאֵת כָּל אִישׁ אֲשֶׁר יִדְּבֶנּוּ לִבּוֹ תִּקְחוּ אֶת תְּרוּמָתִי

from every man whose heart motivates him you shall take My portion (ibid.).

Since all the gold and silver in the world really belongs to God, man cannot "give Him" what is already His. The only thing one can truly offer God is one's heart and emotions. We give Him the desire to give of ourselves. One who donates money begrudgingly really contributes nothing to God. Therefore the Torah teaches that only from a man *whose heart motivates him shall you take My portion* (*Chasam Sofer*).

The foundation of the Tabernacle is the Presence of God in every Jewish heart. As *Alshich* taught, וְשָׁכַנְתִּי בְּתוֹכָם, *so that I will dwell among them* (verse 8), means that God's Presence will dwell within every Jew. Just as God gives us His blessings willingly and without reservation, so when we build a Tabernacle we must do so with total commitment (*Simchas Aharon*).

The *Midrash* teaches that Moses asked if the Jewish people could build a Tabernacle for God. God replied, "Even one of them can do it. As the verse states, *from every man whose heart motivates him.*" This Midrash seems incomprehensible; how could one Jew build the Tabernacle singlehandedly?[9] *R' Shlomo Kluger* explains: Moses was concerned that every Jew would wish to participate in what he perceived to be the central elements of the Tabernacle. They would all want to contribute to the Ark or the Table, rather than to those objects which they viewed as less significant. God reassured him that even if one Jew paid for the entire Sanctuary, no one would be jealous. On the contrary, they would rejoice that God's will was done, even if someone else did it.[10]

Rashi notes that the term תְּרוּמָה, *portion* or *offering,* occurs three times in the first two verses. The first *terumah* refers to the half-shekels used to make the silver sockets that housed the planks of the Tabernacle. The second refers to the half-shekels used to purchase public offerings. Both of the above contributions had to be half-shekels, from rich and poor alike. The third *terumah* refers to the unlimited contributions used to build the Tabernacle.

Of the contributions used for the construction of the Tabernacle, one — the silver for the sockets —

---

9. **What's in It for Him.** This attitude of being concerned with how one can benefit God, rather than what one can gain for oneself is reflected in the following short essay of the *Chazon Ish*: A righteous man once invited a guest to join him for the Shabbos meals. The members of his household were emotionally prepared to welcome him since they too enjoyed having guests. However, the person in the synagogue who was in charge of assigning guests to hosts was unaware of the righteous man's invitation and sent the guest elsewhere. Consequently, when the righteous man came home from the Friday night prayers, he was alone. His family was deeply disappointed. The man turned to them and said, "A guest is not property with which one does business. My only concern was that the guest's needs be met and that he have his Shabbos meals. It makes no difference to me if he received them from me or from someone else." This is not the attitude of many people. While they enjoy doing good, they are not beyond "stinginess" and are upset to see others competing with their "business" (*Emunah U'Vitachon*).

10. **Built Together.** When the *Chafetz Chaim* was contemplating the construction of a new building for his yeshivah in Radin, a wealthy Jew offered to underwrite the entire expense. "God has granted me wealth and I want the merit of erecting the yeshivah building." The Chafetz Chaim replied, "While your intentions are honorable and God will certainly reward you, I cannot accept your offer. Every Jew must have the *zechus* to participate in the mitzvah; no individual can do the whole thing. We see this from the Tabernacle. Although the Sages teach that even one Jew could have built the entire structure, nevertheless the Torah says to take *from every man whose heart motivates him.* Every Jew must be involved."

was clearly defined as a half-shekel, while all the others could be as much or as little as the donor wished. Why the difference?

Eish Dos explains that in addition to voluntary and unrestricted magnanimity, it is also important for one to develop a sense of duty and obligation in serving God. This idea is reflected in the Talmud which teaches that a mitzvah done by one who is commanded to do so is greater than that of one who does so voluntarily, because the evil inclination battles against the fulfillment of what one is obligated to do (*Avodah Zarah* 3a; *Tosafos* ad loc.). True, God wanted the Tabernacle built as a result of altruistic generosity, but He also wanted that Jews should struggle with and overcome the evil inclination. He therefore enjoined Israel to give exactly a half-shekel for the sockets.[11]

זָהָב וָכֶסֶף וּנְחֹשֶׁת
gold, silver and copper (ibid.).

These three elements are mentioned again when King David describes his preparations to build a Temple: *With all my might I have prepared for the Temple of my God — gold for golden things, silver for silver things, copper for copper things* (I Chronicles 29:2).

The *Dubno Maggid* comments that God asked for gold, silver and copper not because He needs these precious metals, God forbid. He chose them because man views them as valuable and precious. When man contributes something that is of value to him, that item is an expression of his love of God. While it is such devotion that truly builds a Tabernacle in which God's Presence

may reside, God asks for tangible expressions of those emotions.[12]

וְעָשׂוּ לִי מִקְדָּשׁ וְשָׁכַנְתִּי בְּתוֹכָם
They shall make a Sanctuary for Me — so that I may dwell among them (ibid. 8).

Rashi renders the verse *you shall make a house of sanctity dedicated to Me*. A Jew must infuse his home with sanctity. His private life and the atmosphere in his home should be saturated with holiness. Such a home is truly a sanctuary for God's Presence (*R' Menachem of Amshinov*).

The Midrash teaches that when God told Moses *they shall make a Sanctuary for Me*, Moses was shocked at the idea. "How can man make a home for God?" he asked. "*Would God truly dwell on earth? Behold, the heavens and the highest heavens cannot contain You*" (I Kings 8:27). God replied, "I don't ask them to do [anything] according to My standards and abilities, but rather according to their abilities."

The *Chafetz Chaim* saw in this Midrash a powerful message about God's expectations of us. God does not make unreasonable demands, nor does He expect us to do the impossible. As King Solomon said, *Whatever you are able to do with your might, do it* (Ecclesiastes 9:10). God asks only that you do with *your* might, i.e., that you serve Him to the best of your ability, not more. If we do so, then God will reward our efforts by increasing our capabilities, so that we will be able to do even more. It follows, therefore, that every Jew must have fixed times to study Torah according to his abilities. One who can study Talmud should do so,

---

11. **Root Obligation.** Of all the parts of the Tabernacle, only the sockets were made from silver that Jews were *obligated* to give. The Tabernacle's walls were supported by the sockets; they were its basis and foundation. This symbolizes for us that the fundamental element of one's service of God must be the irrevocable sense of duty, an attitude that "I *must* do His will." As King David teaches, *Turn from evil and do good* (Psalms 34:15). Before moving on to volunteerism we must be firmly rooted in the nonnegotiable character of our obligations to God (*Eish Dos*).

12. **Torah Is Gold.** The *Chasam Sofer* submits that the words זָהָב כֶּסֶף נָחֹשֶׁת allude to the days when the Torah is read in the synagogue. ז alludes to the seventh day, the Sabbath; ה to the fifth day of the week, Thursday, and ב to Monday, when the public Torah reading is held; כ stands for כִּפּוּר (יוֹם), ס for סוכות, פ for פּוּרִים; נ alludes to נֵרוֹת (candles for Chanukah), ח to חוֹדֶשׁ (ראשׁ) including Rosh Hashanah, which is the Rosh Chodesh of Tishrei; שׁ stands for שְׁבוּעוֹת, שְׁמִינִי עֲצֶרֶת, שִׂמְחַת תּוֹרָה; and ת represents תַּעֲנִית, the fast days.

The essence of the Tabernacle is that God is a constant presence in our lives. This can happen only when we make Torah study and its public reading an essential element of our existence.

while one who finds that too difficult should study *Mishnah*. If this is also proves to be too hard, let him study Halachah or *Chumash*. No one may claim that Torah study is beyond his ability.[13]

Background

After commanding the Jewish people to contribute for the Sanctuary, the Torah discusses the various components and vessels to be kept there. Since the Tabernacle was the embodiment of the Revelation at Sinai, the first to be described is the Ark, which contained the Tablets with the Ten Commandments.

וְעָשׂוּ אֲרוֹן עֲצֵי שִׁטִּים
They shall make an Ark of acacia wood (ibid. 10).

Unlike other components (Table, Menorah etc.) regarding which the Torah commands וְעָשִׂיתָ, *and you* (singular) *shall make,* here the Torah states וְעָשׂוּ, *and they shall make.* While the crown of priesthood is available only to Aaron and his descendants, and the crown of kingdom to David and his descendants, the crown of Torah can be acquired by any Jew who is ready to dedicate himself relentlessly to its study. As the Sages teach (*Horayos* 13a), "A *mamzer* who is a Torah scholar takes precedence over an ignorant Kohen Gadol" (*Alshich*).

The *Chafetz Chaim* submits that every Jew has a portion in Torah, symbolized by the Ark. Those who are found to be truly meritorious are able to study Torah and reveal its depths, while others can attach themselves to the Tree of Life by supporting Torah scholars. Thus Torah, as symbolized by the Ark, is a collective effort.[14] According to *Zekan Aharon,* the plural expression underscores the fact that Torah is a gift that God granted to the nation *as a whole,* not to any particular individual. This, explains *R' Aharon Kotler,* is reflected in the words of the Sages (*Nedarim* 55a), that the Torah was given in the Wilderness. One must make himself "ownerless" like the Wilderness in order to merit the gift of Torah. *Rivan* (ad loc.) explains that this calls on the Torah scholar to understand that Torah belongs not to him personally but to the nation at large, and therefore no individual can expect someone else to pay for the privilege of having Torah taught to him. (See *Shulchan Aruch Yoreh Deah* 246:21 for an explanation of why Torah teachers in our times are permitted and even obligated to be paid for their services.)

אַמָּתַיִם וָחֵצִי אָרְכּוֹ וְאַמָּה וָחֵצִי רָחְבּוֹ וְאַמָּה וָחֵצִי קֹמָתוֹ
two and a half cubits its length, a cubit and a half its width and a cubit and a half its height (ibid.).

All the Ark's dimensions were of partial measurements, with half cubits in each one. According to *R' Nosson Adler,* this teaches anyone who studies Torah that while he tries to understand the profundity of Torah, he must also know that full, true perception of God's is beyond man's ken.

The half cubits also reflect the concept that humility is a precondition to the comprehension of Torah. One who considers himself to be whole lacks the basic prerequisite to knowledge of the

---

13. **Need to Know.** *Tanna D'Vei Eliyahu* (*Zuta* 14) relates the story of an encounter between Eliyahu HaNavi and a man who was totally ignorant of Torah knowledge. Eliyahu asked him, "What will you answer God on the Day of Judgment?" The man replied, "I will tell Him that I lacked the intelligence and insight to study Torah." Eliyahu retorted, "What do you do for a living?" When the man told him he was a fisherman, Eliyahu asked him, "Who taught you to bring linen and weave nets, to throw them into the ocean and to catch fish?" The man responded, "God in Heaven gave me the intelligence to understand how to do these things," to which Eliyahu responded, "Do you really think He gave you intelligence for that but not so that you could understand His Torah?"

14. **Matching Needs.** Based on this "partnership," *Pnei Yosef* offers a novel interpretation to the blessing of בּוֹרֵא נְפָשׁוֹת, which is recited after eating. We praise God as בּוֹרֵא נְפָשׁוֹת רַבּוֹת וְחֶסְרוֹנָן, *(He) creates many souls and the things they lack.* i.e., He creates both the Torah scholar who lacks a way to sustain himself, and a businessman who has no real connection to Torah study. The first needs physical sustenance, while the second needs spiritual sustenance. Bringing them together is His way לְהַחֲיוֹת בָּהֶם נֶפֶשׁ כָּל חָי, *of giving life to the souls of all living creatures.*

Torah. Therefore it was Moses, the humblest of men, who merited to receive the Torah at Sinai, which was the lowliest of mountains.

Olelos Ephraim views the half cubits as reflecting the interdependent teacher/student relationship that is crucial to success in Torah study. One cannot truly become great in Torah from independent study alone; receiving the tradition from a teacher and learning the proper intellectual approach from him is imperative. On the other hand, the dictum of the Sages that one learns more from students than from teachers or colleagues (*Makkos* 10b) indicates clearly that students are integral to the growth of a teacher. Growth in Torah knowledge is a shared proposition.

The Sages teach that the Ark miraculously took up no physical space. Various homiletic interpretations have been put forward to explain this concept.

The *Chasam Sofer* submits that the Torah is not dependent on a particular place; rather, one must be committed to Torah living and study at all times and in every location.[15]

Maayana Shel Torah suggests that the financial survival of Torah scholars is miraculous. While everything in life seems to have its place, the lofty souls who maintain the existence of the world by studying Torah don't seem to occupy a very prominent position in the communal hierarchy of values. Procuring support for them is an ongoing struggle. The Ark, symbolic of Torah, occupies "no space," yet it miraculously survives.

According to *R' Aaron Levin*, the reason the Ark occupies no space is to teach us the humility expected of a true *talmid chacham*. Although he is the embodiment of the Tablets which rest in the Ark, he does not seek any special place for himself.[16]

וְצִפִּיתָ אֹתוֹ זָהָב טָהוֹר מִבַּיִת וּמִחוּץ תְּצַפֶּנּוּ
You shall cover it with pure gold, from within and without you shall cover it (ibid. 11).

The Sages derived from this verse that any Torah scholar whose inside is not like his outside, i.e., his true spiritual level is not as elevated as the image he projects, is not considered a *talmid chacham* (*Yoma* 72b). Clearly, the noble appellation "Torah scholar" implies more than the scope and depth of his Torah knowledge. *Taam V'Daas* explains that the term is not limited to one's knowledge but rather includes one's essence. The Torah must reform and influence a person internally and externally. Just as food affects a person both internally and externally, so the Torah, the food of the soul, must affect a person both internally and externally.[17]

A Torah scholar whose inside is not like his outside clearly has not digested his spiritual food. If his character is flawed or he lives with moral and ethical inconsistencies, it is apparent that his Torah knowledge has not been absorbed into his blood. Such a person is not a true *talmid chacham*.

While this appears to teach that one cannot suffer from moral hypocrisy, since the Ark was golden on the inside and the outside, the analogy seems flawed. The Ark was composed of *three* boxes, a wooden one set inside a golden one, and a golden one inside the wooden one.

Yitzpan LaYesharim Tushiah offers the following: Externally, the scholar must carry himself respectfully in order to enhance the prestige of Torah in the eyes of the masses. Furthermore, he must display a certain air of firmness and self-confidence in order to leave his mark on his community and surroundings. Inside his heart, however, he must be humble like the simple wooden box, taking care

---

15. **Nothing's Changed.** Before World War II, there was an attitude of hopelessness in the United States, a resigned feeling that age-old dedication to Torah study and the performance of the commandments could never take root in America. Then, great Torah leaders from the yeshivah and chassidic worlds arrived, and they declared unreservedly that "America is not different!" Convinced of the eternal power of Torah to reshape landscapes and hearts, they sparkplugged a revolution both in practice and in values.

16. **Outstandingly Simple.** R' Avraham Pam was *rosh yeshivah* of Torah Vodaath and a member of the Moetzes Gedolei HaTorah, yet he never sat by the front wall of the *beis hamidrash*. Instead, he sat among his students.

17. **Unrefined Donkey.** The Sages coined a phrase that captures the sentiment: חֲמוֹר טָעוּן סְפָרִים, "A donkey laden with books." All the books in the world will not succeed in making him anything more than a donkey.

not to have an exalted opinion of himself, but rather as one who studies Torah simply because that is the purpose of life. At an even deeper, interior level, there is another golden box, representing his potential, which is he is challenged to fulfill. As the *Alter of Slabodka* taught, "True humility is rooted in the recognition of one's potential; compared to what I could be, what I am doing presently is but a drop in the bucket."[18]

בְּטַבְּעֹת הָאָרֹן יִהְיוּ הַבַּדִים לֹא יָסֻרוּ מִמֶּנּוּ

The staves shall remain in the rings of the Ark; they may not be removed from it (ibid. 15).

The staves represent the supporters of Torah and must be inseparable from the "Ark," i.e. those who dedicate their lives to Torah study. Likewise, Torah scholars must maintain constant contact with their benefactors, ready to offer them spiritual support in exchange for their financial assistance.[19]

The Sages interpreted the verse חֶרֶב אֶל הַבַּדִּים, *A sword against the sorcerers* [lit. the staves] (*Jeremiah* 50:36), as a reference to Torah scholars who study Torah exclusively on their own (*Taanis* 7a). This means that one who studies Torah in solitude, rather than with others who can bring out the best in him, deserves condemnation.

Homiletically this teaches that when Torah scholars valiantly try to grow in Torah while simultaneously providing for their families, it is the potential supporters of Torah, the symbolic staves, who must accept blame. The sword rests on the *staves* when the scholars study alone, with no one to provide them with moral or financial support (*Chasam Sofer*).[20], [21]

---

18. **Reshaped by Torah.** At the dedication of the *beis midrash* in Ger, the *Chidushei HaRim* commented on a story in the Talmud regarding R' Gamliel and R' Elazar ben Azariah (*Berachos* 28a). During R' Gamliel's tenure as *Nasi*, his policy was to admit to the study hall only students whose "inside was like their outside." When R' Gamliel was deposed, the new *Nasi*, R' Elazar ben Azariah, had the doorman removed, so that students who did not meet this exacting standard could enter. The Talmud reports that it became necessary to add many benches to the study hall. When R' Gamliel saw this he began to fear that he might be subject to Divine punishment for having caused so many people to refrain from Torah study during his tenure.

"What," asked the Chidushei HaRim, "caused R' Gamliel to reassess his position?" Looking around the crowded newly built *beis midrash,* the Chidushei HaRim explained "When the students excluded by R' Gamliel were permitted to enter the study hall, they were transformed and their 'inside became like their outside.' The Torah had such a powerful effect on them that they changed almost immediately. R' Gamliel realized that although one must be fit for Torah, sometimes the experience of study makes one fit. He therefore regretted not having given them the opportunity to change."

[The Yiddish maxim has it that sometimes "the appetite comes with the eating." The *Chazon Ish* was opposed to elitist standards regarding who should be admitted to a yeshivah. When *R' Shlomo Wolbe* asked him to recommend "good boys" to his yeshivah, the Chazon Ish said, "Good boys don't need a yeshivah." As long as there is no risk of a poor student negatively influencing others, they should be admitted, since they may become "inside like outside."]

19. **Returning the Favor.** *R' C.,* a sensitive scholar and *rosh kollel* in Jerusalem, often travels to the United States and England on fundraising trips. Over the years, he has developed an interesting practice that stems from his feeling that he must give something back to his benefactors. He asks his larger contributors when and what they would like to learn with him while he is in their locale. At all hours of the day and night, R' C. can be found learning with the *kollel's* supporters. He might be learning *Chumash* with someone from 2:30 to 3:30 a.m., and from 6 to 7 a.m. a *shiur* in Talmud, etc. In this way he fulfills the verse *The staves shall remain in the rings of the Ark; they may not be removed from it.*

20. **Slaughtered in Silence.** At the second *Knessiah Gedolah* of *Agudath Israel* (1929), a *siyum* was held on the tractate *Zevachim,* which had been studied in the *Daf Yomi* cycle. R' Meir Shapiro, innovator of the *Daf Yomi,* addressed the crowd. Citing a *Mishnah* in Zevachim (5:1), he offered the following homiletical interpretation. קָדְשֵׁי קָדָשִׁים, "The *holiest of the holy* Jews that we have are those who toil at Torah study. How many of them unfortunately escape our notice and therefore our concern and care? שְׁחִיטָתָן בַּצָּפוֹן, *they are slaughtered* (lit. in the *northern part* of the Temple courtyard,) when they are hidden. *Shielded from* (צָפוּן) the limelight, they suffer deprivation and poverty, figuratively slaughtered for Torah."

21. **Clear Vision.** *R' Y.F.* is a highly successful manufacturer who does millions of dollars of business every year.

וְעָשִׂיתָ שְׁנַיִם כְּרֻבִים זָהָב

You shall make two Cherubim of gold (ibid. 18).

Mechilta (*Yisro* 10) teaches that although the rest of the Temple vessels may be constructed from other metals if gold is unavailable, the Cherubim must only be made of gold. Why is it forbidden to use other metals? Homiletically, *R' Meir Shapiro* explains: The Cherubim had the faces of young children because they symbolize Israel's young. They were positioned on top of the Ark to underscore that the primary preoccupation of the Jewish people must be to connect their children to the Ark by educating them to study and practice Torah, and feel a deep connection to it. In other areas we might allow ourselves to limit the size of our contributions, but to provide our children with the best educational opportunities[22] we must spend generously. For the Cherubim, nothing less than "gold" is sufficient.

R' Yisrael Salanter takes another view of the message inherent in the placement of childlike Cherubim on the Ark, based on the *Baal HaTurim* who cites the verse *When Israel was a lad I loved him* (*Hosea* 11:1). A Jew must always view himself as a child, who is like a clean, smooth piece of paper that can easily be written upon. God loves the Jew who allows himself to be spiritually

molded and shaped like a child. The Torah commanded us to put childlike figures on the Ark as a perpetual reminder that in order to be linked to Torah we must view ourselves as children who are not encumbered by bad habits and are easily able to change and grow.[23]

According to the *Vilna Gaon*, the symbolism of the Cherubim emphasizes trust in God as the key to bringing the Divine Presence into our lives. The Midrash cites the following analogy: Young chicks are obviously fed by the mother hen, but if a fully grown chick comes to its mother for food, the mother will push it away, since it is no longer helpless and can fend for itself. Likewise, when a man is young, he trusts God and relies heavily upon Him, and God responds in kind. As one grows older and becomes self-reliant, he feels less need to rely on God, Who consequently becomes less involved in his life.

This is true on a national level as well. Before the Jewish people passed through the Sea of Reeds, they felt a strong need to rely on God. Later, as this sense of need diminished, so did His involvement. When we want God to become a greater part of our lives, we must become child-like in our total reliance on Him. Hence the Ark where His Presence was to reside was adorned with the Cherubim.[24]

Recently he met an old friend who had been in a similar business for many years but had given it up to become a highly influential educator. R' Y.F. said to his friend, with a tinge of sadness in his voice, "I'm still in *shmattes* (rags, i.e. clothing manufacturing), while you are affecting lives." R' Y.F.'s support of Torah is not only financial, it is also emotional and moral. By recognizing the importance of his friend's work, he made the educator feel that what he was doing was vital.

22. **Golden Opportunity.** [This attitude regarding the necessity to spend "gold" on the education of our "cherubim" should inform our approach to paying our children's *rebbeim* and *moros* (teachers). Given the amount of time our children spend with their teachers and mentors, we should seek the most competent, talented and inspiring people — and pay them commensurately.]

23. **Self-Imprisonment.** We are often imprisoned either by our own self-image or the perceptions of others about who we are. Z. was a student at a certain yeshivah where he was viewed as the class clown. Later on he went to Israel and studied at the Mirrer Yeshivah, where he began to come into his own as a serious student. When the time came for him to return to the United States he contemplated going back to his *alma mater*. A close friend told him, "In your old yeshivah, you will always be known as Z. the clown. Even if you learn 25 hours a day it won't help you shed your old image. Go to a new yeshivah and start off as a good student who just came back from Israel."

24. **Devils or Angels?** *R' Moshe Mordechai Epstein* notes that the word Cherubim appears twice in the Torah. In *Genesis* (3:24) the Torah states that God stationed the Cherubim at the east of the Garden of Eden to guard the way to the Tree of Life. *Rashi* (ad loc.) explains that they were destructive angels who were charged with preventing Adam from reentering the Garden. Here, however, the Cherubim were angelic childlike figures.

וּפְנֵיהֶם אִישׁ אֶל אָחִיו
Their faces toward
each other (ibid. 20).

This verse states that the Cherubim faced each other, while in *II Chronicles* (3:13) the verse teaches that they faced away from each other, toward the walls of the Temple. The Talmud (*Bava Basra* 99a) resolves the contradiction by teaching that when Jews do the will of God the Cherubim face each other as a sign of closeness and love; when they fail to do His will, the Cherubim face away from each other.

Pardes Yosef and *R' Yitzchak Elchanan Spektor* submit the following: One who truly wants to fulfill the will of God cannot focus only on his own physical and spiritual needs. He must be concerned about his fellow Jew and do everything possible to help him achieve success. Not only does he try to assure that his own son studies Torah, he is equally concerned about his friend's son. Hence when Jews sought to do the will of God, the Cherubim faced each other, because they were concerned for each other. But when one is concerned only about his own life, when he figuratively turns his face away from his friends, it is clear that he is not performing the will of God.

Ritva (*Yoma* 54b) questions how the phrase *their faces toward each other* can refer to a time when Jews do God's will in light of the report that when the gentiles entered the First Temple, just before it was destroyed, they saw the Cherubim embracing each other (ibid.). Certainly the Jews could not have been performing God's will at the

time of the destruction![25] *R' Mordechai Yehudah Leib Zaks* submits that the will of God referred to in this verse is the maintenance of interpersonal relationships among Jews and the fulfillment of the *mitzvos* that govern the interaction of Jew with Jew. During the First Temple era, the sins that brought about the destruction were between God and man, not between man and man. Hence the Cherubim hugged each other, symbolic of the loving interpersonal bond between Jews. [It was the Second Temple that was destroyed due to interpersonal strife and baseless hatred (see *Yoma* 9b).]

וְשַׂמְתָּ אֶת הַשֻּׁלְחָן מִחוּץ לַפָּרֹכֶת
You shall place the Table
outside the partition (26:35).

The Talmud (*Yoma* 33b) delineates the locations where each of the items in the Tabernacle stood. The Table stood on the north side, the Menorah on the south and the Altar in the middle. *Chasam Sofer* (*Responsa Orach Chaim* 28) sees this as the source for the traditional layout of the synagogue with the *bimah* placed in the middle of the synagogue, rather than up front near the Ark. (See *Rambam, Hilchos Tefillah* 11:3 and *Rema* O.C. 150:4.)

He writes: "The *bimah* where we read the portions about the offerings is the equivalent of the Altar. For this reason we make circuits around the *bimah* on Succos (with the four species), in commemoration of the circuits which were made around the Altar in the Temple. The Sages teach that when the Temple stood we achieved

---

Why does Rashi offer two different renderings of the same word?

The lesson for us is that when one gives a Jewish child a proper education, one that connects him to the Ark of Torah, he will grow up almost angelic with his wings spread over the Ark. When, however, he is not educated along the Torah path he can become a destructive angel.

25. **The Slap of a Father.** *R' Yisrael Chaim Prager* suggested a resolution based on a comment of *R' Menachem Mendel of Kotzk.* Why is the month in which both Temples were destroyed called *Av,* which means *father?* Answered the Kotzker, "When someone caresses a child's face in the synagogue, he may or may not be the child's father. However, if you see someone slap the child, you can be sure it is his father." Only a father cares enough to slap the child so that he will change his ways. When God allowed the Temples to be destroyed He showed us that He is our loving Father Who really cares.

At that moment the Cherubim hugged each other, symbolizing the all-embracing love between us and our Father. The enemy then realized that it was God Who was bringing this upon the Jews to cause them to repent, it was not they who were punishing Israel.

atonement by means of the offerings brought on the Altar, while today reading Torah takes the place of the offerings. We therefore read the Torah publicly on the *bimah,* which is placed in the center of the synagogue just as the Altar was in the Temple."[26]

26. **The Last Remnant.** *R' Michel Shurkin* submits that the *bimah* is not merely a commemoration of the Altar but is actually a remnant of the Temple itself. As we say in the *Selichos* recited at *Ne'ilah* on *Yom Kippur:* "The Holy City and the suburbs have become a disgrace and been looted . . . and there is nothing left but this Torah." According to *Avnei Nezer,* this is why, if one completes a Talmudic tractate, the restrictions against drinking wine and eating meat during the Three Weeks preceding Tishah B'Av are suspended. The Talmud states (*Berachos* 8a) that since the destruction of the Temple, the only place God still has in the world is the four ells of Halachah [and Torah study]. This means that the destruction did not penetrate the place where Torah is studied. Hence completing a Talmudic tractate is the equivalent of moving to a place that is not subject to the Temple destruction. It is therefore permitted to eat meat and drink wine.

R' Shlomo Freifeld once said: "If Torah and destruction are truly exclusive, how are we to understand the presence of a depressed student in a yeshivah? They are a contradiction in terms!"

פרשת תצוה ⊰
Parashas Tetzaveh

Background

The laws regarding the erection of the Tabernacle are followed by those relating to the Kohanim, those who would perform the service in the Tabernacle. In the words of the Talmud (*Yoma* 19a), the Kohanim are both God's agents and ours.

The commentators note that Moses' name is not mentioned in this *parashah*, something that does not occur in any other *sidrah* from the time of Moses' birth until *Deuteronomy*, which he wrote in first person. *Baal HaTurim* submits that God omitted Moses' name from this *sidrah* in response to his prayer at the Golden Calf: *And now if You would but forgive their sin! — but if not, erase me now from Your book that You have written* (*Exodus* 32:32). Although God did forgive their sin, Moses' curse still came to be in part, for the curse of a righteous person is fulfilled even if uttered on a conditional basis. (See *Berachos* 56a.)

Why did the omission occur specifically in this *sidrah*? The *Vilna Gaon* submits that the omission alludes to the seventh of Adar, the day of Moses' death, which almost always occurs during the week when *Tetzaveh* is read in the synagogue. It was then that Moses was physically erased from the land of the living, and so it is from this *sidrah* that his name is "erased," as well.[1]

R' Shimon Sofer views the omission not as punishment but as a reward for Moses' willingness to "confront" God out of loyalty to his beloved flock. In Moses' mind, if he failed to secure a merciful pardon for his people, he was a failure as a leader and did not deserve to be mentioned in the Torah. A parable might help us understand the nature of the reward: An officer exhibited extreme loyalty and self-sacrifice on behalf of the king — how could the king reward him? He gave him the royal scepter for a time, and as long as he held it, he was entitled to promulgate any law he wished.

God rewarded Moses for his undying loyalty to

---

1. **Permeating Presence.** The *Vilna Gaon* elaborates: Although Moses' name is not mentioned openly, there is a hidden allusion to him in the *parashah*. *Tetzaveh* contains 101 verses, the gematria equivalent of the hidden letters in Moses' name. When the individual letters of his name are spelled out, משה is מֵם שִׁין הֵא. The revealed letters in his name are משה while the hidden ones are א + ין + ם, which equal 101.

The hidden and revealed aspects of Moses' name allude to the dual aspects of his death. The body, the *revealed* aspect of Moses, died and ceased to exist, but his *unseen* spirit lives on forever in the hearts and minds of all Jews. Thus his name is not found in the *sidrah* but the hidden aspect of his life permeates its entirety.

Oznayim L'Torah offers a variant approach as to why we find Moses' name missing in this *sidrah*, which in the weekly Torah reading cycle nearly always coincides with the anniversary of his death. Unlike other religions, which endow the birthday or date of demise of a leader with religious significance, Judaism has no such anniversaries to commemorate the lives of our great leaders. To demonstrate this, on the week that Moses was born and died his name is omitted from the *sidrah*.

His people by "handing him the scepter" and allowing him to be the one who issued the command, by beginning this *sidrah* with the words *Now you* [Moses] *shall command the Children of Israel.* There is no need to mention Moses' name because he is the one who is issuing the commands.[2]

שֶׁמֶן זַיִת זָךְ כָּתִית לַמָּאוֹר
pure, pressed olive oil for illumination (27:20).

Midrash Tanchuma infers from this verse that the only oil that had to come from olives that were lightly pressed, rather than crushed, was the oil for lighting the Menorah.[3] The light pressing would insure that the few drops of oil that came from each olive would be perfectly pure from the outset, rather than having sediment and impurities that would later be filtered out. The oil put into meal offerings, on the other hand, need not be quite so pure.

R' Eliyahu Meir Kovner explains the difference between the two as related to personal issues as opposed to communal ones. The meal offerings eaten by individuals need not be so impeccably pure that they could never have impurities. The oil for the Menorah, however, whose illumination testified to the Presence of God among Israel, must be pristinely pure from the very first moment. This holds a lesson for those who seek to spread the word of God among the masses and cast their influence on a broader spectrum. One can spread the light only if he himself possesses a truly pure heart.

Avnei Nezer views the higher degree of purity required for the Menorah as related to the unique quality of Torah. The Menorah and its light are symbolic of Torah knowledge. As the Sages taught, "One who seeks wisdom, let him turn [at prayer] to the south, for the Menorah was in the south [side of the Temple]" (*Bava Basra* 25b). Torah is a spiritual commodity that must remain purely spiritual. Just as sediment beclouds the oil and detracts from the clarity of its flame, so preoccupation with temporal matters takes away from the clarity of Torah intelligence.[4]

לְהַעֲלֹת נֵר תָּמִיד
to kindle the lamp continually (ibid.).

The Midrash (*Shemos Rabbah* 36:2) comments that God says, "It is not that I need your light. Rather, I want you to light [the Menorah] for Me as I lit [your way] for you." This, continues the Midrash, is analogous to a sighted person who walked with a blind man. The sighted person said, "Let me support you and help you along the way." When they arrived at their destination, the sighted person said to his blind friend, "Could you please turn on the lights for me?"

The sighted person is of rare quality. Not only does he take care of his blind friend, he also asks for his help as if he were the dependent one, in order to spare his friend the painful feeling of dependency.

This is exactly how God treats His nation, Israel.

---

2. **Joyful and Brisk.** *Sfas Emes* cites the Midrash that the word תְּצַוֶּה connotes a call for alacrity (see *Rashi* to *Vayikra* 6:2). God instructed Moses to teach the people that they must show alacrity in fulfilling the Torah. The key to achieving this lies in arousing joy over the unique privilege of being allowed to do His bidding. How special it is that the actions of a mortal human being bring joy and happiness to God and leave an impact on all levels of existence.

3. **Pure Oil.** Just as oil can be taken from the olive by pressing it, so in order for the illumination of one's soul to cast its rays it is necessary that one attempt to squeeze all the illicit passions out of his psyche (*R' Nosson of Breslov*). The Midrash (*Shemos Rabbah* 36) views the pressing process as symbolic of the travails of the Jewish exile. Just as the squeezing results in pure oil, so the exile will result in repentance and the emergence of the pure unadulterated Jew.

4. **Foul Odor.** *R' Leib Malin* was once told about a certain professor in Brooklyn who was knowledgeable in, and lectured on, many areas of the Torah, thus giving the impression that Torah and other disciplines were of equal importance. R' Leib responded with the following parable: In small villages there exists a general store which sells all kinds of merchandise. Hammers, nails, shirts, pants and herring can all be found in the same store. In large cities this is not the case. Pants and shirts are found in a clothing store while for nails and hammers one must go to the hardware store; herring, on the other hand, can only be purchased at a delicatessen or fish store.

At first, it would seem that people of the village have it better since they can buy whatever they need in one place. The truth, however, is that in the general store the pants smell from herring and the shirts have rust stains from the nails. Torah must be pure! (*R' Michel Shurkin*).

He illuminates the world on behalf of its inhabitants and provides them with all their needs, yet He allows people to feel that are helping Him by lighting the Menorah.[5]

According to the *Baal Shem Tov*, this concept is the key to understanding a perplexing verse in *Psalms* (62:13): *And Yours, O Lord, is kindness, for You repay each man according to his deeds.* If God rewards man according to what he deserves, why does the verse refer to this an act of Divine *kindness*? The answer is that we have no right to expect reward even for the good deeds that we do. Could we have performed those deeds if God had not granted us life, ability, strength and resources? Without Him, we would not even be able to lift a finger. Accordingly, even when God repays each man according to his deeds, it is an act of kindness on His part. He allows us to feel that our deeds were a service to Him, when in truth whatever we do is only because He empowers us to do it (*Taam V'Daas*).

R' Elya Meir Bloch focuses on a different aspect of the Midrash. Although God provides us with illumination, He wants us to do our part as if it were dependent on our efforts. So it is in all areas of life. Although we know that the truth of Torah and God will eventually triumph, we must never tire of our own efforts to build and plant outposts of Torah to the best of our ability.

The Talmud (*Menachos* 99b) teaches that even if one merely read the *Shema* morning and evening he has fulfilled the obligation that *This Book of the Torah shall not depart from your mouth* (*Joshua* 1:8). [The Talmud, cautions, however, that this should not be widely taught, lest it be used as a pretext to refrain from learning.] This seems strange — how can the few minutes one takes to recite the *Shema* twice daily be deemed equivalent to Torah study "day and night"?

Our verse provides the answer. The Torah enjoins us to kindle the lamp continually, yet in reality it takes the Kohen but a few seconds to do so. Nevertheless, since it remains lit the entire time as a result of the Kohen's act, the Torah deems it as if the Kohen constantly lit it; likewise, with regard to our connection to Torah. One who recites *Shema* with intensity and reverent concentration ignites in his heart at that moment a fire of love for God and His Torah, which burns constantly — day and night (*Chidushei HaRim*).[6]

There are many homiletical interpretations of

---

5. **Make/Take.** The parable is really the story of our existence in this world. God supports all of creation, from the largest animals to the eggs of lice. In reality, those who toil to earn a living do nothing more to effect their survival than those who exert no effort. Nevertheless, like the healthy person in the parable, God in His kindness allows us to feel that we are actually *making* a living although in truth we *take* a living (*Taam V'Daas*).

6. **Charging the Batteries.** This concept is reflected in Moses' blessing in which he combined the tribes of Issachar and Zebulun (see *Deuteronomy* 33:18). The merchant tribe of Zebulun assumed the responsibility of supporting the Torah study of Issachar, so that Issachar's accomplishments in the study hall were possible thanks to the commercial excursions of Zebulun. When one leaves a meal and then returns, he need not recite a new blessing for his food as others remained at the table (see *Shulchan Aruch* O.C. 178:2). Likewise, when a Zebulun — a patron of Torah scholars — goes on business trips, he has a right to rejoice because his Issachar remains in the study hall. In this way, the businessman and the scholar are attached to one another. *Sfas Emes* suggests that the way for Zebulun to maintain that connection is to learn with his brother Issachar before going out to business. [Those who find themselves in the world of commerce would do well to "sit themselves at the table" of the *beis midrash* before going out to work. By maintaining a steady learning session in the morning before going to work or by using Sunday morning for learning before starting the next workweek, one is linked to the *beis midrash* at all times.]

Simchas Aharon contends that this is the underlying theme of Simchas Torah. It is a day that reminds us of the priorities that tend to become blurred in the daily struggle to earn a living. We tend to forget that earning a livelihood is a means, not an end in itself. *Rambam* rules עֲשֵׂה תּוֹרָתְךָ קֶבַע וּמְלַאכְתְּךָ אֲרַעי, *Make your Torah study permanent and your occupation temporary* (*Hilchos Talmud Torah* 3:7). This reminds us not only to make Torah study a fixture of our schedule, but also to make it the primary focus of our lives. Simchas Torah, with its heartfelt joy, inspires us always to recognize that our roots are in Torah. Even the most overworked businessman, preoccupied with his many distractions, will retain his strong ties to Torah if he sincerely and joyously makes a commitment to its study on Simchas Torah.

the words לְהַעֲלֹת נֵר תָּמִיד, *to kindle the lamp continually*. *R' Avraham Yaakov of Sadigura* says that the way to keep the flame of the Jewish soul kindled is to focus on something that must be done תָּמִיד, *continually;* namely, שִׁוִּיתִי ה׳ לְנֶגְדִּי תָמִיד, *I have set Hashem before me continually* (Psalms 16:8).

Maayana Shel Torah adds that a Jew must see to it that the flame of Torah burns constantly and brightly in his heart and soul, so that it illuminates his life, even in times of spiritual darkness.[7]

בְּאֹהֶל מוֹעֵד מִחוּץ לַפָּרֹכֶת
In the Tent of Meeting, outside the partition (ibid. 21).

The constant flame that burns in the heart of a Jew must find expression not only in the synagogue and study hall (*Tent of Meeting*) but also in mundane areas (*outside the partition*). The same spirit that informs our prayers and Torah study must permeate our business affairs, our conduct with others and the way we act at work or play (*Pardes Yosef*).

R' Aharon of Karlin sees this as a call to the Kohanim, those entrusted with the task of imbuing the Jewish people with the light of Torah. Not only those who are already in *the Tent of Meeting* but even those who are still *outside the partition* must be provided with the spark to ignite their souls.

Background

The Torah now delineates the vestments to be worn by the Kohanim when serving in the Tabernacle and, later, in the Temple. These vestments set the Kohanim apart and clearly indicate that they are servants of God.

וְעָשִׂיתָ בִגְדֵי קֹדֶשׁ לְאַהֲרֹן אָחִיךָ לְכָבוֹד וּלְתִפְאָרֶת
You shall make vestments of sanctity for Aaron your brother for glory and splendor (ibid. 28:2).

Clothes serve both to accentuate a person's beauty and to cover up one's nakedness. This is true in a spiritual sense as well. The Sages teach (*Zevachim* 88b) that each of the priestly vestments provided the nation with atonement for a particular type of sin. The tunic atoned for an unpunishable murder; the breeches for amoral behavior; and the turban for excessive arrogance. The Talmud (ibid.) elaborates on each of the vestments and the sins for which they atone. Thus the clothes of the Kohanim were able to "cover" the collective nakedness of the nation.

Here the Torah expresses the hope that the Jewish people will not sin and therefore will have no need for atonement. Rather, the vestments should function to highlight the spiritual splendor of the people *for glory and splendor.*

Ksav Sofer views the *glory and splendor* from a different vantage point. Unique attire generally serves a dual purpose. First, it reminds the one who wears it that he occupies a special position and must not allow himself to be dragged down by mixing with the wrong company. Second, unique attire or uniforms send a message to others to recognize the wearer's status and to afford him the appropriate respect. With reference to Aaron's vestments, the Torah speaks only of *glory and splendor.* This is a compliment to Aaron's infinite righteousness. His clothing was not needed as a reminder to him personally to live up to his position; he needed no such reminder. Rather, his priestly vestments were in order that others should accord him the proper respect. They were *for glory and splendor.* [8], [9]

---

7. **Fanning the Spark.** *Sichos Tzaddikim* elaborates: The fire of Torah and Godliness burns deep inside the soul of every Jew. No matter how much a Jew sins or how far he strays from the Torah, he will never succeed in totally extinguishing that point of spiritual light. One must fan the spark and seek to ignite it once more. Those who make the effort will be rewarded to see the fire of their souls ignite into a brilliant torch of sanctity.

8. **Reworking Degradation.** The Jews in Egypt retained their distinct clothing as a means of preventing assimilation. The *streimel* fur hat worn by many *chassidim* on Shabbos was originally imposed on Jews by anti-Semitic Eastern European gentiles in order to degrade them. In typical Jewish fashion, the Jews turned the hat into a sign of prestige and Jewish pride.

9. **Trapped by Trappings.** Unfortunately, most people are influenced by appearances in their perception of other

וְאַתָּה תְּדַבֵּר אֶל כָּל חַכְמֵי לֵב אֲשֶׁר מִלֵּאתִיו רוּחַ חָכְמָה

And you shall speak to all the wise-hearted people whom I have invested with a spirit of wisdom (ibid. 3).

The syntax in this verse appears to be flawed. מִלֵּאתִיו means *I invested **him**,* not *them,* which would seem to be the appropriate form. *Malbim* explains by defining the elusive term *wise-hearted people.* Intelligence does not always affect one's inner world. One's behavior may be the result of his intelligent judgment that it is in his self-interest or the good of the group to act a certain way, yet within his heart a fierce battle may rage between evil and good. A wise-hearted person is one whose intelligence has been so thoroughly internalized that it becomes part of his essence. When such intelligence totally fills the person, there is no room for evil. It is not the *people* whom God invested with the true spirit of wisdom — it is the *heart.* In the heart of the wise hearted there is nothing but the Godly spirit.

R' Chaim of Volozhin elaborates, based on the Talmud (*Berachos* 55a) which teaches, "God grants wisdom only to those who have wisdom, as the verse states, *and I have endowed the heart of every wise-hearted person with wisdom*" (*Exodus* 31:6).

If God endows only the wise hearted with wis-

dom, from where do they get the initial dose of wisdom? Explains R' Chaim: The initial wisdom is the fear of God, which is the receptacle into which God pours wisdom. Only man can provide fear of God, as the Sages taught, "Everything is in the hands of Heaven except for the fear of Heaven" (*Berachos* 33b). Thus God invested those wise-hearted (God-fearing) people with a spirit of wisdom.[10]

People often possess deep resources in terms of intelligence, aptitude, talent and ability, yet are unaware of them, so they never aspire to make themselves great. "Who am I to attempt to become a great scholar or to become truly close to God?" Consequently, they never realize their potential, taking it with them to the grave. Paraphrasing *Chovos HaLevavos* (Introduction), *Chasam Sofer* gives expression to this phenomenon: "Wisdom is planted in the hearts of men. If someone or something arouses them, they can excavate the treasure; if not, it will be lost. It is similar to a seed; if one hoes and plows, it grows — if not, it rots." God enjoined Moses to address the people who, while intrinsically *wise-hearted people,* were unaware of their potential. Speak to them, tell them that *I have invested* [them] *with a spirit of wisdom* and that I am waiting for them to draw it out.[11]

---

people and their importance. It therefore becomes necessary to create external trappings for the purpose of engendering respect.

R' Yitzchak Hutner writes of this phenomenon in a short monograph. "When we spoke for the first time, I heard him say, 'When no one took King Solomon's self-proclamation as king seriously, he could do nothing but rule over his walking stick.' As we got to know each other better, it became clear to me that this man was a careerist.

"I later met someone who said the following: 'At the time when nobody recognized him, was not King Solomon the same Solomon as before?' I later came to know this person as a man of spirit in the fullest sense of the word" (Collected Letters 7).

10. **Wise Hearted.** *Baal HaTurim* notes that חַכְמֵי לֵב אֲשֶׁר equals 611, the numerical equivalent of יִרְאַת. *Divrei Shalom* suggests that *wise-hearted people* are those who realize that their wisdom has been *invested* in them by God.

According to *R' Chaim Shmulevitz* the reason God imbues them with wisdom is because they have a passionate thirst for it.

The key to wisdom is the single-minded desire for it, above all else. When the young King Solomon was given the opportunity to ask for his heart's desire, he requested wisdom. God said that since he asked for wisdom instead of longevity or wealth or triumph over his enemies, he would be granted his wish and be the wisest of all men — and in addition he would be given longevity, riches and victory (*I Kings* 3:5-14).

Rambam captures this sentiment in his pithy explanation as to why a teacher sent to a city of refuge for inadvertent murderers must be accompanied by his students. "Without the study of Torah, the life of those involved in wisdom and those who seek it is equivalent to death" (*Hilchos Rotzeach* 7:1).

11. **Really Know Yourself.** *Yesod HaAvodah* underscores the need for man to know his potential, based on a homiletical interpretation of *To inform human beings of His mighty deeds* (*Psalms* 145:12). He renders it "to inform

וְאֵלֶּה הַבְּגָדִים אֲשֶׁר יַעֲשׂוּ חֹשֶׁן וְאֵפוֹד
These are the vestments that they shall make: a Breastplate, an Ephod (ibid. 4).

Rashi writes: "I found no explanation in the *baraisa* nor did I hear from anyone a description of the *Ephod*. My heart tells me that it looks like the apronlike garment worn by regal women while riding horseback." People wonder what led Rashi to associate the *Ephod* with women riding side-saddle. *R' Yechiel Meir of Gostinin* suggests that Rashi was puzzling over the definition of the *Ephod* when he suddenly looked up and noticed French noblewomen wearing aprons and riding on horses. He was perturbed over having been exposed to such a sight. Then he became convinced that it was not for naught that he saw them. From Heaven he had been taught what the *Ephod* looked like.

וְנָשָׂא אַהֲרֹן אֶת שְׁמוֹתָם לִפְנֵי ה' עַל שְׁתֵּי כְתֵפָיו לְזִכָּרֹן
Aaron shall carry their names before Hashem on both his shoulders as a remembrance (ibid. 12).

Be'er Mayim Chaim points out that Aaron carried the names of the people specifically on his shoulders. This teaches the quality of Jewish leadership that allows God to focus on and remember the righteousness of His people. Just as a father carries his child on his shoulders in order to protect him from wild beasts, stumbling blocks and anything else that might harm him, so Aaron, as a prototype Jewish leader, must lift his flock and figuratively carry it on his shoulders. By sharing his personal merit with the people and elevating them spiritually, he can cause God to view His nation as righteous and worthy of His protection.[12]

וְלֹא יִזַּח הַחֹשֶׁן מֵעַל הָאֵפוֹד
and the breastplate will not be loosened from upon the Ephod (ibid. 28).

According to the Sages (*Arachin* 16a), the Breastplate atones for miscarriages of justice while the *Ephod* atones for idolatry. This verse seems to suggest that the two sins are in some way connected. According to *Chasam Sofer* this is the source for the Sages' comment that appointing a corrupt judge is the equivalent of planting an *asheirah* tree (a tree worshiped as an idol) near the Altar (*Sanhedrin* 7b).

What is the connection between the two sins? *R' Moshe Feinstein* submits that at their root the two sins are actually one — a lack of real faith. When people justify dishonest behavior in their business affairs, they do so due to lack of faith; likewise, a corrupt judge. If people truly believed that man earns only that which God grants him, they could never sin with regard to money, since they would believe that one cannot earn a penny more or less than that which is Divinely decreed.

One who seeks atonement for a miscarriage of justice must ultimately be forgiven for the "idolatry" of thinking that there are powers that can overrule the Divine decree. Hence the Breastplate atones for the act of injustice while the *Ephod* atones for the idolatry that lies behind it.

וְעָשִׂיתָ אֶת מְעִיל הָאֵפוֹד כְּלִיל תְּכֵלֶת
You shall make the robe of the Ephod entirely of turquoise wool (ibid. 31).

The robe atoned for *lashon hara* [slander] (*Arachin* 16a). According to *Kli Yakar*, the turquoise color of the robe is related to the atonement. Turquoise blue, reminiscent of the sea, reminds man

---

the human being of *his* might." To the person who feels overwhelmed by the power of evil inside himself, God says that he *can* vanquish his evil inclination. If man would only realize how powerful he is, he would break down all the barriers that stand between him and God.

12. **Sensitive Heart.** Later (verse 30) the Torah states, *and Aaron shall bear the judgment of the Children of Israel on his heart constantly before Hashem.*

As one who "loved peace, chased peace, loved the people and sought to bring them close to Torah" (see *Pirkei Avos* 1:12), Aaron was the heart of the people, hypersensitive to their pain and their needs. He therefore bore their judgment (and names) on his heart, constantly pleading their case before Hashem (*Be'er Mayim Chaim, R' Shmuel Rozovsky*).

that just as God placed limits on the extent of the vast oceans, so He provided man with a fence and lock to his tongue in the form of lips and teeth. Furthermore, just as the sea does not go beyond its boundaries, so man must keep his speech within the confines of the permitted. In addition, turquoise alludes to the sky above and reminds us of God's constant Presence. The gold bells and pomegranates also allude to the sin of *lashon hara.* On one hand, the pomegranates allude to the silence one must generally maintain, particularly with regard to talking about others. As the Sages taught, "What must one's trade be in this world? Let him act like a mute" (*Chullin* 89a). On the other hand, the bells symbolize the positive power of speech one must employ in Torah study, prayer and in doing favors for others. If one uses his speech sparingly and selectively, the Torah promises that his prayers will be answered. *Its [his] sound will be heard when he enters the Sanctuary before Hashem* (28: 35) (*Chafetz Chaim*).[13]

שָׂפָה יִהְיֶה לְפִיו סָבִיב
its opening shall have a border all around (ibid. 32).

The *Yid HaKadosh of P'shis'cha* saw this verse as a call for self-control in speech. The word פִּיו literally means *his mouth.* One must erect a border around the opening of his mouth, limiting his speech to what is necessary and permitted.[14]

The Sages homiletically allude to this when they teach, "If he found it closed, there is certainly a man inside; if he found it open, it is certain that there is no man inside" (*Tamid* 26a). This means that one who keeps his mouth closed, limiting his speech to the permitted and sanctified, is truly a man of distinction. There is a man inside of him. On the other hand, one whose mouth is always open and who speaks indiscriminately is far from the man he could be.[15]

---

13. **Heart and Mouth Connection.** In a more homiletical vein, *Degel Machaneh Ephraim* suggests that this mitzvah can be fulfilled even now, in the absence of the Temple and functioning Kohanim. The Breastplate which rested on Aaron's chest alludes to the heart, while the *Ephod* is symbolic of the mouth (אֵפֹד and פֶּה, *mouth,* each equal 85 in gematria). Every Jew is obligated to insure that his heart never be separated from his mouth, meaning that what he says should express what he truly feels in his heart.

R' Yaakov Kaminetsky was a paragon of this total mouth/heart consistency. While a student in Slabodka, R' Yaakov was invited to spend Pesach with a certain family. He had a good reason not to do so, but in order to spare the feelings of his would-be host, he said he was forced to decline the invitation because it was his custom not to eat *gebroks,* foods which contain matzah and liquids. Actually, R' Yaakov's family did eat *gebroks* and until that year he did so, too. But from the time he uttered the words until he passed away, R' Yaakov never again ate *gebroks,* though he permitted his family to do so.

14. **Speech to Silence Ratio.** *Alshich* questions why the Torah speaks of the bells being between the pomegranates. Describing them as a pomegranate between two bells would be equally accurate, since they alternate. The Torah is teaching us a lesson about silence. The bell is symbolic of the mouth, with its knocker like the tongue, moving around inside and making noise. The bell that emits sounds when the Kohen Gadol enters the Sanctuary is the equivalent of one's power of speech. The pomegranates, on the other hand, symbolize the mouth closed in silence. By speaking of a bell surrounded by two pomegranates, the Torah teaches the proper proportion between speech and silence. Let one not think that every incident of silence should be paralleled by two instances of speaking. On the contrary, every bell (speech) must be surrounded by two pomegranates (silence).

Thus the verse concludes *Its sound shall be heard when he enters the Sanctuary before Hashem* (28:35). When the Kohen reserves his speech exclusively for Torah and prayer and does not defile his mouth with slander, inappropriate language, or the like, his voice will be heard when he enters the Sanctuary to pray on behalf of His people.

15. **All Kinds of Talk.** *Rambam* (*Commentary to Pirkei Avos* 1:17) categorizes five types of speech: (a) *Mitzvah* — Torah reading and study, and prayer. (b) *Forbidden* — false testimony, falsehood, talebearing, cursing, foul language and *lashon hara* (harmful gossip). (c) *Tasteless* — idle talk, general gossip and the like, or speaking disparagingly of positive ethical behavior. (d) *Worthwhile* — praising intelligent or virtuous character, degrading negative conduct or personality traits [of course, without referring to specific people]. (e) *Permissible* — business discussions, domestic issues (food, budget, etc.).

פַּעֲמֹן זָהָב וְרִמּוֹן
a gold bell and a pomegranate (ibid. 34).

According to *Peninim Yekarim*, the pomegranate alludes to one whose life is filled with Torah and *mitzvos*. As the Sages taught, "Even the unworthy among the Jews are as full of merit as the seeds of the pomegranate" (*Berachos* 57a). The verse teaches that the gold bell, symbolic of the boisterous ring of wealth, is meaningful only if it is used to fill one's life with Torah and *mitzvos*.

וְנִשְׁמַע קוֹלוֹ בְּבֹאוֹ אֶל הַקֹּדֶשׁ
Its sound shall be heard when he enters the Sanctuary (ibid. 35).

While humility and a low profile are positive attributes for all people, and certainly for the great men of the generation, this is true only with regard to mundane matters. With regard to issues that relate to the sanctity of the nation and the lives of its members, the voice of leadership must be loud and clear. When vital decisions must be made, humility and a low profile are out of place. Under such circumstances, leaders must speak with strength and the power of conviction. *His sound should be heard when he enters the Sanctuary* (*Chasam Sofer*).[16]

The *Mesorah*, tradition, links our verse to the verse *And Esau raised his voice and wept* (*Genesis* 27:38). What is the connection? *Oneg Shabbos* offers an explanation based on the *Zohar*, which teaches that "All the pain and travails that the Jewish people suffer in exile are due to the tears Esau shed over losing Isaac's blessing. When the Jews will nullify the tears of Esau with their own tears, the Messiah will come."

The words of the *Zohar* are astounding. Have not the Jewish people shed enough tears throughout their tragedy-filled exile to nullify those of Esau? *Arvei Nachal* understands the *Zohar* in light of the

rule of *kashrus* that things of like quality do not nullify each other (מִין בְּמִינוֹ אֵינוֹ בָּטֵל); rather, they reinforce each other (see *Chullin* 98b). Esau cried over losing physical, this-worldly blessings. Therefore as long as Jews' crying is over their physical persecution, their tears cannot nullify those of Esau, since they are of the same type. Only when Jews cry to God over their spiritual needs and desires will Esau's tears be nullified and the Final Redemption take place. This, submits *Oneg Shabbos*, is the meaning of the *Mesorah* comparison of Esau's voice to the sound of the Kohen Gadol when he enters the Sanctuary. We can nullify Esau's tears — and bring the Redemption — only when Jews really begin to cry to God for the restoration of the sanctuaries of their lives and of their families.

וְעָשִׂיתָ צִּיץ זָהָב טָהוֹר וּפִתַּחְתָּ עָלָיו פִּתּוּחֵי חֹתָם קֹדֶשׁ לַה׳
You shall make a Headplate of pure gold, and you shall engrave upon it, engraved like a signet ring, "Holy to Hashem" (ibid. 36).

According to the Talmud (*Arachin* 16a), the Headplate atones for brazenness. The *Zohar* explains that when the Kohen Gadol wears the Headplate on his forehead, he subdues the brazen people of the generation. In this light we may explain a perplexing *Mishnah* (*Avos* 5:24): "Yehudah ben Teima used to say: The brazen faced goes to *Gehinnom* but the shame faced goes to *Gan Eden*. May it be Your will, Hashem our God and the God of our forefathers, that the Holy Temple be rebuilt speedily in our days, and You grant us our share in Your Torah." The connection between the two clauses of the *Mishnah* and the prayer seems unclear. *Tzvi L'Yisrael* explains that when Yehudah ben Teima mentioned the brazen faced, he began to contemplate the suffering they cause to the truly righteous and upright. Pained by this state of affairs, his heart cried out in prayer, "May God speedily rebuild the Temple so that the Kohen Gadol's Headplate can subdue the brazen and

---

16. **Talk but Talk Right.** Guarding one's mouth does not necessarily entail remaining silent. The *Chafetz Chaim*, famed for his personal example with regard to guarding his tongue, was an engaging conversationalist who could talk *with* people for hours without talking *about* people.

negate the damage they inflict upon spiritual growth." Furthermore, the Talmud (*Beitzah* 25b) teaches that the Torah was granted to the Jewish people in order to temper their natural brazenness. Hence Yehudah ben Teima concluded his prayer with the words "grant us our share in Torah" so that our brazenness will be contained.

Chidushei HaRim submits that one rectifies the negativity of a trait by harnessing it for positive goals. King Solomon calls the evil inclination "an old foolish king" (*Koheles* 4:13). Since Solomon's time, the "king" has only become older, and it would be most brazen to be disrespectful to the elderly king — as when one looks the evil inclination in the eye and says, "You old and evil rogue, get out of my life!" Such use of brazenness is sacred. By looking at the Headplate we are inspired to adopt this sanctified obstinence.

That the Headplate atones for brazenness is alluded to by its Hebrew name, צִיץ, a word whose literal meaning is to *stare*. The Headplate inspires us to stare the evil inclination in the face and say, "No!" The words "Holy to Hashem" that were inscribed on the Headplate indicate that, although brazenness is generally a negative character trait, with regard to things that are "Holy to Hashem" one must be bold and outspoken (*Chasam Sofer*).[17]

The *Tur* (*Orach Chaim* 1) states this clearly, interpreting the words of *Pirkei Avos* (5:23) as follows: "Yehudah ben Teima begins with the words *be bold as a leopard* to serve God, since this is a cardinal principle of Judaism. Very often, one wants to perform a mitzvah but refrains from doing so because of people who scorn him. Therefore he is enjoined to assume an air of obstinacy against such scorn, and not refrain from performing the mitzvah."

וְשָׁכַנְתִּי בְּתוֹךְ בְּנֵי יִשְׂרָאֵל וְהָיִיתִי לָהֶם לֵאלֹקִים

I shall rest My Presence among the Children of Israel and I shall be their God (ibid. 45).

The name אֱלֹקִים connotes God's attribute of strict justice. Why will this attribute be the result of God's resting His presence among the Children of Israel?

R' Dov Ber, the renowned *Maggid of Mezritch*, explains by means of a parable. A father who deeply loves his son makes great efforts to protect him from harm. If someone even tries to hurt the son, the father will punish the attacker severely, not to mention what will happen if that someone actually succeeds. God tells us that since He will rest His Presence among us and display His overwhelming love for us, He will "have no choice" but to exact strict justice and retribution against those who seek to harm us.[18]

R' Henach of Aleksander focused on a different facet of the verse. He related, "I spent many years in the presence of someone whom people consider a great man. The closer I got to him, the less I felt connected to him. He simply shrunk in my eyes. Once I met the Kotzker Rebbe, however, it was just the opposite — the longer I stayed with him and the more I observed him, the deeper my respect and reverence for him became. "This is what the Torah means," said R' Henach. "Foreign goals and

---

17. **Step Forward.** *Tzvi Tzaddik* submits that the verse calls upon those who possess the ability to teach Torah to come forth and do so. The Sages (*Yevamos* 97a) teach that the lips of the deceased move in the grave, as it were, when people quote his Torah thoughts. A person should make every effort to teach others so that when he enters the Divine Sanctuary in Heaven after his demise, his voice will still be heard through the Torah study of his students, who will quote his teachings.

[When asked why he did not pursue a more lucrative career, a certain Torah teacher replied, "First, I can't think of anything more meaningful and lasting to do with my life than to show others the beauty of Torah. Second," and here he smiled, "the Sages teach that sometimes the teacher really deserves to go to *Gehinnom*. However, since it is inappropriate for the student to be in *Gan Eden* while his teacher is in *Gehinnom,* they let the teacher into *Gan Eden*" (*Yoma* 87a)].

18. **Vindictive Kindness.** In the hymn for Friday night, כָּל מְקַדֵּשׁ שְׁבִיעִי, we say: "Draw Your kindness on those who know You, jealous and vindicative God." The combination seems incongruous; what do kindness and vindictiveness have to do with each other? *Maayana Shel Torah* explains that God's kindness to the Children of Israel who seek to know Him and His ways will motivate Him to protect them jealously and take revenge against those who have the audacity to try and harm them.

heroes are impressive only from a distance; once you get close, the mirage of greatness disappears. Not so Hashem. As soon as He rests His Presence among us we begin to truly recognize His awesomeness, from up close. Then he really becomes our revered God."[19]

---

19. **Permanent Resident.** The *Chafetz Chaim* notes that the Torah speaks of God's Presence residing among (lit. *in*) the Children of Israel rather than *by*, i.e., near them. God is involved with every molecule of Creation, but since non-Jews are unwilling to accept His sovereignty, He figuratively hovers over them, never being among them. The Jewish people, who willingly accept God and welcome Him into their lives, merit that He resides in and among them.

Background

The *sidrah* opens with the laws of how to conduct a census. The Torah forbids Jews to be counted by means of a head-count, therefore the census was conducted by an indirect means. Every Jew included in the census was to give a silver half-shekel. The coins were counted to determine the number of Jews, and then were used for the construction and upkeep of the Tabernacle.

כִּי תִשָּׂא אֶת רֹאשׁ בְּנֵי יִשְׂרָאֵל לִפְקֻדֵיהֶם
When you take a census of the Children of Israel according to their numbers (30:12).

The literal meaning of the word תִשָּׂא is *elevate*; therefore, the phrase may be rendered *When you elevate the head(s) of the Children of Israel.* The commentators offer a plethora of explanations as to why the census is deemed an "elevation" of their heads.[1]

According to *Avnei Azel*, the blending of disparate individuals into a combined communal force grants them the ability to figuratively "raise their heads." A solitary individual is almost power-less to affect public policy and communal life. Once he becomes part of a larger community, a limb of the communal corpus, he can make his influence felt. Thus by being counted as part of the nation, each individual is able to figuratively raise his head.

S'deh Margalis offers an explanation based on the nature of Jewish charity. The Talmud (*Bava Basra* 10b) teaches that the words of King Solomon, *Charity will uplift a nation, but* וְחֶסֶד לְאֻמִּים חַטָּאת, *the kindness of the regimes is a sin (Proverbs 14:34)*, refer to two separate groups. The charity that Jews give elevates them, while that of the non-Jews misses the mark (חטא from the expression הֶחֱטִיא אֶת הַמַּטָּרָה, *he missed the mark*). Jews view charity as צְדָקָה, *justice,* for it is the moral obligation of the more fortunate to provide for those in need. On the other hand, non-Jews see charity as חֶסֶד, a totally voluntary act emanating from their good hearts and philanthropic spirit. When a Jew helps a fellow Jew he elevates himself, for by realizing that he is obligated to care for all Jews he rises above his personal narrow existence and truly becomes a man of the people. On the other hand, those who consider charity to be an expression of their own goodness are subject to

---

1. **Honest Accounting.** Homiletically, *Ohr Pnei Moshe* renders the word לִפְקֻדֵיהֶם (lit. *according to their numbers*) as *on their shortcomings* (see *Numbers* 31:49). Only one who takes honest stock of his spiritual deficiencies and realizes how little of his life's mission and goals he has accomplished can truly become spiritually elevated. One who is spiritually complacent and feels that he has no more room in his life for growth will never be able to rise above himself. Thus the Torah teaches *When you want to elevate the heads of the Children of Israel,* to help them rise to even greater spiritual heights, let them focus לִפְקֻדֵיהֶם, *on their shortcomings.* Once one defines the areas that need improvement, he may begin the trek upward.

pride and tend to belittle those who are dependent on them.

R' Yitzchak Hutner submits a different perspective. There are two methods of counting. The first is to add all the figures in a column until one reaches the sum total, which appears at the bottom. The alternative is to start with the total, a figure at the top of the sheet and then break it down into component parts. The nation of Israel can be viewed in both ways.

We count the Jewish people as individuals to arrive at a total, and then we "elevate" the totality figuratively to the head of the column. We count each Jew to allow him to realize that he is an integral component of the nation as a whole.[2], [3]

וְנָתְנוּ אִישׁ כֹּפֶר נַפְשׁוֹ
every man shall give Hashem an atonement for his soul (ibid.).

Here *Alshich* sees a homiletical prescription for the type of self-sacrifice which Jewish leadership must display. When you raise the head of the Children of Israel by appointing a leader for them, appoint only someone willing to serve as an atonement for them — someone who is ready to sacrifice his life and personal interests on their behalf.

Baal HaTurim notes that the word וְנָתְנוּ, [every man] *shall give*, may be read forwards and backwards. This implies that charity is not only something that leaves the donor, never to be seen again; it is an investment. Whatever one gives will eventually come back to him as God's blessing; one loses nothing when he gives to others.[4]

Regarding the verse עַשֵּׂר תְּעַשֵּׂר, *You shall tithe* (Deuteronomy 14:22), our Sages tell us that the double expression teaches עַשֵּׂר בִּשְׁבִיל שֶׁתִּתְעַשֵּׁר, *tithe so that [in reward] you will become wealthy.* Contrary to popular claims that giving charity depletes one's fortune, the Torah tells us that benevolence produces wealth.

Ben Ish Chai sees this as analogous to a nursing mother. As long as she continues to nurse and

---

2. **Too Many Chiefs.** *Otzar Chaim* submits yet another perspective on the makeup of the community. Rather than speak of counting רָאשֵׁי בְּנֵי יִשְׂרָאֵל, the **heads** (plural) *of the Children of Israel*, the Torah states כִּי תִשָּׂא אֶת רֹאשׁ בְּנֵי יִשְׂרָאֵל, *when you will count the* **head** *of the Children of Israel*, in the singular. A nation is blessed if it has many heads, i.e., bright and intelligent people. However, if the nation is comprised entirely of "heads," than each one feels that he deserves to stand at the head of the nation. Thus, too many "heads" are detrimental to effective leadership and a functional community.

A community might be compared to a royal palace. Although meant to house royalty, it is built with simple materials. The rough stones of the foundation allow the entire building to stand. Cement, simple bricks, stones and the like combine to build the palace. Only afterwards does the builder add precious stones and luxurious materials as adornments; likewise the nation. It must not have only intelligentsia, but also people of means, people of action and alacrity and people who follow their leaders and carry out their instructions. The upper levels cannot stand without the support of the lower ones.

3. **Be Big!** *Simchas Aharon* summits a homiletical interpretation. In order to help Jews overcome פְּקֻדֵיהֶם, their faults and flaws, and to rectify their shortcomings in their service of God, they must be lifted up. By imbuing a Jew with the realization that he is an elevated being and a child of God, one can help him save himself from sin. As *R' Shlomo Freifeld* would often say, "Don't be strong, be big!" In frontal combat with our evil inclination, we often aren't strong enough to be victorious. However, when we view ourselves in the proper elevated light, we may realize that the tempting desire is beneath us; we are bigger than it.

4. **Reciprocal Charity.** *Chida* submits that the benefactor and recipient enjoy reciprocal benefit. The rich person helps the poor man by giving, and the poor person benefits the rich one by providing him with the opportunity to be magnanimous. This is alluded to by the את בש system of letter relationships [in which the first letter (א) is parallel to the last letter (ת); the second (ב) with the next to last (ש), and so on]. In this letter system, the word צְדָקָה still spells צְדָקָה, for צ and ה are interchangeable as are ד and ק. The rich and the poor make an even swap.

The *Vilna Gaon* sees another message in the fact that וְנָתְנוּ can be read identically backwards and forwards. One who gives may become the victim of changing fortunes and be forced to receive help from others. Thus, charity is an investment, as R' Chiya told his wife (*Shabbos* 151b), "Give bread to a poor man so that he will give to your children." When she claimed that he was cursing their children, he replied, "Poverty is a cycle in the world." One who helps others will be saved from having to be helped by others.

provide her child with milk, her supply is replenished and increased. Only when she stops nursing does the flow dry up. Likewise, as long as men of means provide for God's less fortunate children, He will replenish and increase their wealth. If, however, they stop giving, so will God; eventually, their fortunes might dry up.[5]

זֶה יִתְּנוּ כָּל הָעֹבֵר עַל הַפְּקֻדִים מַחֲצִית הַשֶּׁקֶל
This they shall give — everyone who passes through the census — a half-shekel (ibid. 13).

Rabbeinu Yonah (*Shaarei Teshuvah* 1:47) teaches that charity has the power to protect one from suffering pending his repentance from sins. As King Solomon said, *Through kindness and truth, iniquity will be atoned* (*Proverbs* 16:6). Furthermore, it can even delay a Divine death sentence from being carried out. Again in the words of *Proverbs* (10:2), *but charity rescues from death.*

Accordingly, our verse may be rendered homiletically as כָּל הָעֹבֵר עַל הַפְּקֻדִים, whoever transgresses (passes over) *the Divine commandments* should give a half-shekel. By giving charity one can earn himself a temporary stay of the punishment he deserves for his sins, thus allowing him time to truly repent (*Simchas Aharon*).

Panim Yafos views the verse as a primer to repentance. One who is עֹבֵר עַל הַפְּקֻדִים, "transgresses the commandments," is called upon to give a half-shekel. Rather than falling into debilitating depression that he is spiritually beyond repair, let him view himself from the perspective of "half" as conveyed in the words of the Talmud: "Let one view himself as half meritorious and half guilty. If he does but one mitzvah, he can tip the Heavenly scales toward merit" (*Kiddushin* 40a-b). Repentance

is not an insurmountable task; it calls merely for the courage to take one step forward.

Zekan Aharon adds another perspective, based on the interpretation of *Maharal* regarding the forty lashes one is liable to receive for transgressing certain kinds of negative commandments. Through Scriptural interpretation, the Sages derived that the sentence was to receive thirty-nine lashes, not forty. How, and why, may they do so? Explains *Maharal*: The forty lashes parallel the forty days during which the human embryo is formed. It takes thirty-nine days to form the embryonic body; on the fortieth day, it is imbued with a soul.

When a person sins, all forty elements are involved, since the soul is inseparable from the body. Therefore, forty lashes of cathartic punishment are called for. In reality, however, the soul always maintains its purity and is not tainted by sin. Hence once the body receives its thirty-nine lashes, the soul returns to its intrinsic, pristine state. Thus although the Torah mentions forty lashes, only thirty-nine are actually needed.

We might interpret the half-shekel in this light. When man must atone for his sins, it is because his physical "half" brought him to sin. Once it is cleansed, the spiritual "half" — the soul — begins to shine again. We are called upon to bring a "half" shekel to atone for our souls, so that their luster can be restored.

According to the *Alshich,* we bring only a half-shekel so that we realize that a Jew alone is merely a fragment. Only by linking ourselves to others can we find completeness. *Toldos Yaakov Yosef* embellishes on this theme, based on the injunction "*The wealthy shall not increase and the*

---

5. **Redemptive Care.** According to *Damesek Eliezer,* the Torah alludes to the words of the Sages that the Jewish people will be redeemed in the merit of charity (*Shabbos* 139a): לִפְקֹדֵיהֶם, if they want to be *visited* (see *Genesis* 2:11) and redeemed by God, then וְנָתְנוּ, *let them give* charity. When we give to others, we demonstrate our ability to care and be kind even to those who may not deserve what we give them. God responds by redeeming us even if we have not truly earned it.

This is the thrust of our prayers when we bless the new month. "He Who performed miracles for our forefathers and redeemed them [in Egypt] from slavery to freedom — may He redeem us soon." The Jews in Egypt were at the lowest level of spiritual impurity, and were entirely undeserving of redemption. Nevertheless, God miraculously freed them. Similarly, we take the liberty of beseeching Him to bring the Final Redemption — even if we don't deserve it (*R' Tzadok HaKohen of Lublin*).

When we are merciful toward others, God will have mercy on us.

destitute shall not decrease from half a shekel (ibid. 15). In the plain sense, the verse means that all Jews must contribute no more and no less than the prescribed half-shekel. In a deeper sense, the Torah says that one should not think that since he is wealthy in Torah and *mitzvos*, he plays a more significant role than his spiritually destitute brother. Likewise, let the spiritually destitute never denigrate the significance of their contribution to the spiritual welfare of the nation. Every Jew plays a unique role in the nation that only he can fulfill; every Jew brings only a half-shekel, fully cognizant that his fellow Jew will compliment his role by bringing the other "half."[6]

Finally, *Nesivos Shalom* interprets the half as a reference to the heart of a Jew. How is one who is עֹבֵר עַל הַפְּקֻדִים, *who transgresses the commandments* and moves away from God, to find his way back? By giving a half-shekel. One who approaches God with a heart broken in "half," truly pained that he has

violated God's love for every Jew, will be granted the ability to atone for his soul. As King David taught, *Hashem is close to the broken hearted and those crushed in spirit He saves (Psalms 34:19).*[7]

הֶעָשִׁיר לֹא יַרְבֶּה וְהַדַּל
לֹא יַמְעִיט מִמַּחֲצִית הַשָּׁקֶל

The wealthy shall not increase and the destitute shall not decrease from half a shekel (ibid. 15).

Divrei Asher offers a mussarist approach to this verse. Let the wealthy not think that by refraining from giving charity they will increase personal fortunes; for *the wealthy shall not increase.* Likewise, the poor who give small amounts of charity to the even less fortunate should never entertain the thought that their ability to survive will be adversely affected by their giving; *the destitute shall not decrease.* [8]

A more homiletical approach explains the verse

---

6. **Real Help.** *R' Yitzchak Elchanan Spektor,* the Rav of Kovno, once went to request a donation from a well-known Torah scholar who was famed for both his wealth and his stinginess. The scholar refused to contribute, claiming that he paid his dues to Heaven by studying Torah and was therefore absolved from giving charity. "Philanthropy is for the ignorant or the wicked, to let them do something for God," he claimed, citing our verse as a proof. *Thus they shall give, all who transgress on the commandments.* R' Yitzchak Elchanan replied with a story: "After the Crimean War, a Russian general traveled the length and breadth of his country, raising funds to expand the country's navy. In one village, everyone made his contribution, when one of the villagers, known as a very poor person, stood up and pledged a hundred rubles, a fantastic sum. His neighbors were shocked. Unable to contain their curiosity they asked him to explain. He replied, 'Not long ago I was fined one ruble for an infraction of the law. Since I was unable to pay, the commissar sent me to jail for a week. Now that the homeland needs me, I am willing to sit in jail for a hundred weeks.'

Concluded the Rav of Kovno, "You are just like that villager. You want to fulfill your obligation to save a Jew by learning Torah. The poor will benefit as much from your Torah as the Russian navy would gain from the peasant sitting in jail. Moses didn't count the people according to how many pages of *Gemara* they learned; rather, he counted them by means of the half-shekels they donated."

7. **Completely Shattered.** "There is nothing as complete as a broken heart" (*R' Menachem Mendel of Kotzk*). As the Midrash teaches, "Unlike a mortal who makes use only of complete vessels, [and throws away the broken ones] God cherishes broken vessels" (*Yalkut Shimoni, Psalms* 51:§766). Only one who realizes that he is lacking and needs God's help and mercy to become complete stands a chance of achieving that completion. One who is sure that he lacks nothing spiritually — lacks everything.

8. **Not Likely.** The Talmud reports that in Usha, the Sages instituted that one may not spend more than one-fifth of his resources on charity (*Kesubos* 50a — See *Shulchan Aruch, Yoreh Deah* 249:1). Why did the Torah use an explicit verse to prohibit the wealthy from giving too much to the Tabernacle, yet sufficed with a Rabbinic enactment to prohibit them from giving too much to the poor?

R' Eizel Charif explained: Contributions to the Tabernacle were given publicly. Hence the Torah feared that the wealthy would give extravagantly in order to earn public recognition and honor. To prevent that, it instructed *the wealthy shall not increase.* Personal support of the poor, however, is generally done in private. In most cases there is no reason to fear that the wealthy will give too much, since they will have no ulterior motives for giving. Consequently, a Rabbinic prohibition is more than enough for the few altruistic, wealthy Jews who might privately give too much.

as follows: One who enjoys spiritual wealth in Torah and *mitzvos* should not deceive himself into thinking that he has accomplished everything he needs to. He must realize that he has given only "half," and has much more spiritual growth still to achieve. On the other hand, let the spiritually destitute never discount what they have done and fall into despair over their relatively low spiritual standing. As the saying goes, their glass is half full; they have accomplished half, and have *only* half way to go in order to give their assigned portion to Hashem (*Noam Elimelech*).

The Sages taught, "Whether one gives more or less, as long as he gives for the sake of Heaven" (*Menachos* 110a). *R' David of Kotzk* explained: Those who are destitute and give a minimal amount certainly give for the sake of Heaven. The wealthy, however, can give much and think of themselves as great people who deserve to be honored for their magnanimity. For them it is difficult to give purely for the sake of Heaven; they have too large a personal agenda involved in their giving. Therefore the Sages warned the one who gives a lot that he too must give for the sake of Heaven.

It is this message which the Torah seeks to convey when it teaches *the wealthy shall not increase* his giving; it is more important for him to upgrade his motives.[9]

Background

Before beginning their service in the Tabernacle (and later the Temple), the Kohanim had to wash their hands and feet from the copper Laver, which stood in the Courtyard. As part of the daily service, they were also commanded to offer incense.

וְעָשִׂיתָ כִּיּוֹר נְחֹשֶׁת
You shall make a copper Laver (ibid. 18).

Shem MiShmuel explains the juxtaposition of the section regarding the half-shekels and the making of the Laver. The Laver symbolizes man's efforts to cleanse himself of sin. One can succeed in doing so only if he unites with other Jews, as symbolized by the giving of a *half-*, rather than a full, shekel.[10]

[Although one sometimes lacks the fortitude to withstand the temptation of sin, or the courage to do what is right in the face of ridicule or opposition, one can triumph by becoming part of a community and tapping into its collective strength. Thus the Laver is created by the unity which the half-shekel symbolizes.]

Baal HaTurim submits that the juxtaposition of these two issues alludes to the dictum that God withholds rain from His people when people do not honor their pledges to charity (see *Taanis* 8b). [To raise the hopes of the poor by pledging, and then dashing their hopes of support is worse than simply not giving.]

R' Chaim Zaitchik sees an important lesson in this allusion. A person's responsibility is gauged subjectively, according to his level and perceptions. One who is emotionally deaf to the plight of others and feels no need to give of his resources to help the needy is an unfortunate soul; God does not expect much of him since he is incapable of mustering compassion for others. But one who has the emotional sensitivity to the plight of others and even pledges to help them, yet nevertheless lets his heart and emotions cool off to the point that he fails to honor his commitment — such a person causes God to withhold rain.

---

9. **Safe Arrival.** *R' Simchah Bunim of P'shis'cha* was asked "Since they (the wealthy and the poor) both give for the sake of Heaven, why isn't it better to give more?" He replied with a story: Two friends set out from their town to the regional fair. One arrived on Tuesday while the other arrived a few days later, on Friday. The early arrival asked his friend, "Why did you only arrive only now?" Replied the friend, "What difference does it make? The main thing is that I arrived."

For some it takes little in the way of action in order to attain the goal of acting for the sake of Heaven; for others, it takes more time and doing. The point, however, is to arrive at the destination — to act for the sake of Heaven.

10. **Collective Atonement.** We begin the *Kol Nidrei* service on Yom Kippur with a declaration permitting sinners to join the community in prayer. This practice is based on the words of the Talmud: "Any public fast that does not include sinners is not considered a true fast" (*Kerisos* 6b). The full atonement of Yom Kippur can be accessed only through the nation as a whole. The congregation is the conduit through which God washes away our sins with His pure waters. The word צִבּוּר, *congregation,* is an acronym for צַדִּיקִים, בֵּינוֹנִים, וּרְשָׁעִים (the *righteous*, *ordinary* and *wicked people*). Only by unifying all elements of the nation can we merit God's purifying atonement (*Zekan Aharon*).

וְרָחֲצוּ אַהֲרֹן וּבָנָיו מִמֶּנּוּ אֶת יְדֵיהֶם וְאֶת רַגְלֵיהֶם

From it Aaron and his sons shall wash their hands together with their feet (ibid. 19).

The word "washing" carries the connotation of removing oneself from personal involvement [hence the expression "washing one's hands of the affair"], as we find in the section regarding the axed heifer brought if a corpse is discovered in the field or on the road (see *Deuteronomy* 21). *All the elders of that city, who are closest to the corpse, shall wash their hands over the heifer . . . and say,* "*Our hands have not spilled this blood . . .*" (verses 6-7). Before the Kohen begins his service of God, he must set aside any personal considerations and commit himself wholeheartedly to doing God's will. Likewise, before we begin to eat, we wash our hands as a symbol of our desire that our eating (as well as our fulfillment of all our physical needs) be dedicated solely to God's service, and not to personal pleasure. By washing our hands, we symbolically request of God that if we find ourselves drawn to physical activities that do not conform with His will, He should cleanse us of that desire. The custom of reciting the Biblical section about the Laver before *Shacharis* and *Minchah* express a silent prayer that we be saved from praying for anything that God does not want us to have (*Mei HaShiloach*).[11], [12]

קַח לְךָ סַמִּים . . . וְחֶלְבְּנָה

Take for yourself spices . . . galbanum (ibid. 34).

Galbanum had a foul aroma; yet, it was included in the incense. The Sages infer from this that sinners must be included in our prayers and fast days (*Kerisos* 6b).[13] *Perishah* submits that when the wicked join in the communal prayers, their presence and their feelings of repentance make our prayers all the more effective. *Derashos HaRan* sees the wicked as a catalyst for the righteous to pray with greater intensity. [Were only the righteous to participate, they might not truly understand how desperate the nation's situation is. The presence of the wicked forces the righteous to realize how crucial their prayers are.]

Maharsha, however, notes that there were eleven types of spices in the incense; ten sweet-smelling and *galbanum* with its foul aroma. This teaches that only once there is a full quorum of ten it is necessary to bring in the spiritually foul "aroma" of the wicked. However, when there is not yet a solid core of good people, the participation of evil can be very harmful.[14]

Background

After completing the instructions on how to build the Tabernacle, God turns to Bezalel to

---

11. **Pray Carefully.** One must be very careful about what he prays for, since we may be granted our wishes even though they are to our detriment. *Chassidim* explained the prayer חַיִּים שֶׁיְּמַלֵּא ה' מִשְׁאֲלוֹת לִבֵּנוּ לְטוֹבָה, *a life in which Hashem fulfills our heartfelt requests for the good (Blessing of the New Month)*, in this light. We don't simply ask that He fulfill our heartfelt requests, since they are often not for the good. Implied in our prayer is faith that God knows what is best for us, and we ask Him to fulfill only those wishes that are for our benefit.

12. **Spiritual Wash Up.** In order to serve God properly, one must purge himself of negative character traits and wicked deeds. One must figuratively wash and cleanse his "hands," and free himself from the pull of his bad habits [הֶרְגֵּל as in רַגְלֵיהֶם, *habit*] (*R' Moshe of Kobrin*). *Divrei Binah* offers a different homiletical approach. Service of God is predicated on the realization that all success, even spiritual success, is a gift from Heaven. One must cleanse himself of the attitude that *my strength and the might of my **hand** made me all this wealth (Deuteronomy 8:17).*

13. **Interwoven Nation.** The Hebrew word for fast day is צוֹם. *R' Joseph B. Soloveitchik* submits that it is related to צַמָּה, *a braid* (see *Song of Songs* 4:3), for just as a braid is comprised of different strands of hair interwoven together, so the completeness of the Jewish people is achieved by weaving different types of Jews into a unified nation, with each element contributing its part.

14. **Communal Core.** [The great success of community *kollelim* is based on this premise. When lone individuals move to locations where Torah has yet to leave its mark on the local Jewish population, they are often influenced by their surroundings more than they influence it. When, however, a group of *kollel* members moves together and remains united, they can safely incorporate those removed from Torah into their community and remain untainted themselves.]

execute them. Never trained in any of the skills needed to erect the Tabernacle or create its vessels, Bezalel was uniquely blessed with a Godly spirit that gave him the ability to fulfill his mission.[15]

רְאֵה קָרָאתִי בְשֵׁם בְּצַלְאֵל

See, I have called by the name: Bezalel (31:2).

The Talmud (*Berachos* 55a) records a conversation between Moses and Bezalel. When Moses

---

15. **Long-Term Dividends.** *Mr. Irving Bunim* related: "One Friday night, when I was privileged to have *R' Elchanan Wasserman* as my guest, he was invited to make an appeal on behalf of his yeshivah, in one of the larger synagogues. Generally speaking, he was successful in his public appearances, and usually raised at least $1,000 in a synagogue appeal. Not this time, however. Even before he left my home he asked, 'Who will be in charge of the appeal here?' I answered, 'It is the custom that the rabbi announces the names of the donors and the amounts.' 'Then I fear then that we will not have success,' he said to me. 'That rabbi is anxious to conserve the money of his members.' I said: 'Perhaps he will try to impress *us* this time.' R' Elchanan held to his opinion: 'He may have that ambition, but the inclination to protect his members' money will prevail.'

"After *Kabbalas Shabbos,* R' Elchanan addressed the congregation for some three-quarters of an hour, devoting a substantial part of his remarks to the dire situation in the Baranovitch Yeshivah. 'All I ask is a slice of bread for those who toil in Torah.' He proposed that individual donors undertake to support the yeshiva for a week (the cost was $80 in those days); those who could afford less might donate $11.43, the budget for a single day. Whoever contributed would acquire for himself the merit of a week's or a day's learning by hundreds of *bachurim*. The reward for that week or day would be his alone.

"His proposal elicited a favorable response. The congregation became enthused, for this was an excellent business proposition. A whole week of Torah for $80; a whole day of Torah for $11.43! The the rabbi approached the pulpit. Instead of reinforcing R' Elchanan's remarks, he spoke for fifteen minutes on an unrelated topic. The powerful impact of R' Elchanan's speech weakened. The rabbi cooled the atmosphere, and concluded his remarks by stressing that 'every *single* dollar contributed to the yeshivah is sacred, *even one dollar.*' Contrary to the $80 mentioned by R' Elchanan, he extolled the value of single dollars. As a result the sum raised was negligible — less than $150 from the entire congregation — a flagrant insult."

Later that evening, the rabbi and other dignitaries came to the Bunim home. The rabbi tried to excuse himself: "You probably blame me for the meager results of the appeal." To everyone's surprise R' Elchanan broke into a smile and answered pleasantly: "Not at all. Tomorrow we shall read the passage, 'See I have called by name Bezalel ben Uri ben Hur of the tribe of Judah.' Now let us imagine this scene: Moses walks into the street, meets a Jew and says, 'We have to build the Tabernacle. Are you perhaps Bezalel ben Uri?' 'No,' the man answers, 'I am Reuben ben Jacob.' So he is not the right person. Moses walks further and meets another Jew. Again he asks, 'We have to build the Tabernacle. Is your name perhaps Bezalel ben Uri?' 'No,' the second man apologizes, 'I am Shimon ben Jacob.' Now is it conceivable that our teacher Moses should be angry at those two Jews for not being Bezalel ben Uri and not building the Tabernacle? What could they do? They were not chosen to build the Tabernacle — only Bezalel was. How can I blame you if your synagogue simply was not chosen to be among the builders of Torah in this age — if you do not have the merit of supporting the sanctuary?" (From *Reb Elchanan,* ArtScroll/Mesorah Publications).

The opportunity to support Torah in reality provides one with a unique chance to support oneself.

R' Yechezkel Sarna was once in the United Sates on a fundraising trip for Yeshivas Chevron. When perusing the list of potential donors to be invited to a parlor meeting, R' Yechezkel noticed the name of a Mr. Schiff who, in the 1920's, had underwritten a major portion of the cost of relocating part of the yeshivah from Slabodka, Lithuania to its new home in Hebron. In the interim, Mr. Schiff had fallen upon very hard times and was literally struggling to put food on his table. R' Yechezkel decided to save Mr. Schiff any embarrassment and therefore instructed the yeshivah office not to send him an invitation.

During the course of the meeting, Mr. Schiff suddenly made an unannounced appearance and asked to say a few words: "My dear brothers and friends: Life is cyclical; I was once a very wealthy man but now things have taken a turn for the worse and I literally struggle for basic necessities. From my gorgeous home I have fallen to living in a basement. The only thing left of my wealth is the money I contributed in order to bring the yeshivah to Israel. That merit I am unwilling to sell for any amount.

"Out of personal experience I want to make a suggestion. Whatever charity you can give, give it now; do it quickly, don't wait. No one knows what the future holds in store, or what type of resources he'll have tomorrow. Whatever you grab now is what lasts for eternity."

Moved by his words, those present contributed generously.

told Bezalel to build the Ark, the rest of the vessels and the Tabernacle, in that order, Bezalel replied, "Where am I to put the vessels that I build? Perhaps God instructed you [in the opposite order, namely] build the Tabernacle and then the Ark etc.?" Acknowledging that Bezalel's surmise was correct, Moses replied in a play on the name Bezalel, which is a combination of two words, בְּצֵל אֵל, *in the shadow of God*, "Were you perhaps in the shadow of God (בְּצֵל אֵל), that you know what He told me?"

But if God told Moses, as Bezalel suggested, that the Tabernacle should be built before the vessels were made, why did Moses reverse the order when he relayed the commandment to Bezalel? Commentators suggest that the answer can be found in a stich of the *L'chah Dodi* hymn, which is recited to usher in Shabbos: סוֹף מַעֲשֶׂה בְּמַחֲשָׁבָה תְּחִלָּה, *Last in deed, but first in thought*. This concept mirrors one that is common in everyday life. When a family plans to build a new home, their first thoughts are about what they will do in the house: raise children, study, have guests and so on. The architect's plans will be drawn to accommodate the uses of the house, not vice versa. Naturally, however, the construction will take place before the furniture and accessories can be purchased; so too with the Tabernacle. Of course, God told Moses that the structure should be built before the Ark and the other vessels were fashioned. But Moses understood that the purpose of the Tabernacle was to house the Ark with the Tablets of the Law, the Menorah that would symbolize the spiritual illumination of the Torah, and so on. This is what he related first to Bezalel. As the one who would supervise the actual construction, Bezalel, rightly, thought of the physical order of the project.

What did Bezalel understand that Moses didn't? The *Sokolover Rebbe* once visited a Polish town seeking to organize the local Orthodox community under the banner of Agudath Israel. Those who resisted his efforts claimed that there was no reason to factionalize the community. "The entire congregation is holy," they insisted, "why do we need an organizational structure?"

The Rebbe responded, "Our argument mirrors the difference in perspective between Bezalel and Moses. Moses couldn't imagine that any Jew would harm the Ark if it was left out in the open until a Tabernacle was built. Why not simply create the Ark and wait patiently for the erection of the Tabernacle?

"Bezalel replied, 'I understand the people better than you. Unless we first build a Tabernacle to house the Ark, it is a danger. We must first put up a secure and solid structure to serve as the home of the Ark.' " Bezalel understood the shadier side of human nature. An Ark is safe only if it has a permanent home. The Torah left in the open is vulnerable. We must create organizational structures in order to provide it with a safe haven.

וּבְלֵב כָּל חֲכַם לֵב נָתַתִּי חָכְמָה
and I have endowed the heart of every wise-hearted person with wisdom (31:6).

The Talmud (*Berachos* 55a) derives from this verse that God grants wisdom only to those who already possess wisdom. The obvious question presents itself: How does the process begin? If God does not give wisdom to those who do not have it, how do they have the initial wisdom needed in order for God to give them more wisdom? *R' Chaim of Volozhin* and *R' Yissachar Dov of Belz* explain: Fear of Heaven is the most basic form of wisdom. As Job said (28:28). *Behold, the fear of the Lord is wisdom.* According to the Talmud (*Shabbos* 31a), fear of Heaven protects one's Torah wisdom and keeps it vibrant and alive. God gives wisdom to those who, through their fear of Heaven, can ensure that God's wisdom will not be granted for naught (*Nefesh HaChaim* 4:5).[16]

[Just as one will not pour from a bottle of vintage wine unless he sees a glass in front of him, ready to receive the wine, so God will not pour the "heady wine" of Torah unless man presents a receptacle equipped to hold it. Fear of Heaven

---

16. **Safe Storage.** Based on this interpretation, we may resolve two disparate statements in the Talmud. On one hand, the Sages teach (*Berachos* 8a) that all God has in His world are the four ells of Halachah (i.e., Torah learning). On the other hand, they state that the only thing He has is a storehouse of fear of Heaven (ibid. 33a). The resolution is that the four ells of Halachah can be maintained only by placing them in the storehouse called fear of Heaven. As the *Mishnah* teaches, "Anyone whose fear of sin takes priority over his wisdom, his wisdom will endure" (*Avos* 3:12).

turns man into that receptacle.][17]

R' Simchah Bunim of P'shis'cha wondered: Why should God give wisdom to the wise, don't foolish people need the gift more than those who already have wisdom? He answered that wise people will use the Heavenly gift wisely. Fools will abuse it.

R' Elya Meir Bloch has a different perspective on the meaning of *wise-hearted*. The Talmud (*Niddah* 30b) teaches that before one is born he is taught the entire Torah in utero, and upon entering the world he forgets it. Nevertheless, his mind and heart are now spiritually primed, able to truly perceive Torah. Torah knowledge is not something one learns from external providers — it is learned by listening with one's heart. [As we say in our prayers, "Who . . . implanted eternal life within us" (*U'va L'Tzion*).] One who is *wise-hearted* allows himself and his heart to listen to the Torah that resides deep inside his soul. By preparing his heart, he can allow the words of his teachers to resonate from the recesses of his heart and soul.

Background

While teaching the laws of building the Tabernacle, the Torah repeats the commandment to keep the Sabbath. This underscores how crucial the Sabbath is to our nationhood. Even as exalted a spiritual endeavor as building a Sanctuary for God's Presence cannot override the observance of the Sabbath. Hence, even while erecting the Tabernacle, the nation worked on the sixth day and rested on the seventh.[18]

אַךְ אֶת שַׁבְּתֹתַי תִּשְׁמֹרוּ . . .
לָדַעַת כִּי אֲנִי ה' מְקַדִּשְׁכֶם
However you must observe My Sabbaths . . . to know that I am Hashem, Who makes you holy (ibid. 13).

The term אַךְ (however) indicates an exception. From here the Sages derive that there are limitations to the obligation to observe the Sabbath. In order to save a Jewish life one may, and must, desecrate the Sabbath. According to *Ohr HaChaim,* this message is conveyed in the flow of the verse. Although the Sabbath is important, it is not as important as a Jewish soul. Hence, in order to save a Jewish soul we are commanded to desecrate the Sabbath.

It is the exceptional אַךְ which reminds us that *I am Hashem, Who makes you holy.* [19], [20]

The Torah speaks of *My Sabbaths.* According to the *Chafetz Chaim,* the plural *Sabbaths* teaches that it is not enough that one himself observes the Sabbath; he must invest energy, time and

17. **Primary Wealth.** King Solomon teaches *for to sit in the shelter of wisdom is to sit in the shelter of money* (*Ecclesiastes* 7:12). Just as one must have wisdom to be granted wisdom, so God grants wealth to the wealthy. From where does one take the original wealth? The *Mishnah* (*Avos* 4:1) provides the answer: "Who is rich? He who is happy with his lot" (*R' Moshe Midner*).

18. **Preempted Space.** Sabbath, a sanctuary in time, precludes the need to create a sanctuary in space. Hence building the Tabernacle is overridden by the need to observe the Sabbath. The Sabbath itself is a sanctuary, thus the thirty-nine forms of labor that went into the construction of the Tabernacle are unnecessary, and therefore prohibited on the Sabbath (*Simchas Aharon*).

19. **Above All.** *R' Shmuel of Kaminka* once explained the special *Mussaf* prayer for Sabbath-Rosh Chodesh in light of the commandment to save a Jewish life even at the cost of performing labor otherwise forbidden on the Sabbath. "You fashioned Your world from old" and therefore Creation is quite meaningful. Even more significant is that "You completed your work on the Seventh Day" and thus granted us the holy Sabbath that testifies to You as the Creator. Even greater than this, however, "You chose us from all the peoples, You loved us and found favor in us." Hence saving a Jew supersedes the Sabbath.

20. **Rust-free.** *Sfas Emes* offers a different perspective on the word אַךְ, *however.* On the verse אַךְ אֶת הַזָּהָב, *[However] the gold . . .* (*Numbers* 31:22), which teaches how vessels are purged of nonkosher absorptions, the Sages interpreted that the gold itself must pass through fire. Therefore it is necessary to remove any rust on the vessel before subjecting it to the fire. Likewise here, in order to benefit from the edifying and purifying quality of the Sabbath, one must first remove the spiritual rust and decomposition from his soul. Only then can one truly observe the Sabbath.

money[21] to see that other Jews observe it as well. This is important not only to ensure the other person's spiritual state but also for oneself. Sabbath observance calls for a certain atmosphere. Even if one observes Sabbath, the sanctity of the day is adversely affected if those around him do not. Therefore the Torah calls on us to observe *My Sabbaths;* both your own and that of your fellow Jew.

R' Shmuel Eliyahu of Modzhitz focuses on the possessive *My Sabbaths* based on the dictum of the Sages, "Make your Sabbath like a weekday rather than becoming dependent on others" (*Shabbos* 118a). This teaches that one should eat a simple weekday style meal on the Sabbath rather than become dependent on charity for his Sabbath fare. When the question is the physical aspect of the Sabbath (namely food and drink, etc.) we are told "make **your** Sabbath like a weekday . . ." However, when it comes to *My Sabbaths,* namely the spiritual elements of the Sabbath (prayer, Torah study and other spiritual delights) which feed the soul, we are told "*you must observe it* at all costs."

The Talmud (*Beitzah* 16a) teaches that God told Moses, "I have a very special gift in My treasure house — its name is Shabbos. I want to give it to the Jews; go and tell them." From this we derive that one who gives a friend a gift must apprise him of the fact so that he realize its value.

A pauper once came to the home of *R' Shmelke of Nikolsburg,* asking for a donation. R' Shmelke searched high and low in his home for something to give him, since he had no cash at that moment. Suddenly he noticed one of the *rebbetzin's* rings, which he promptly gave to the pauper. When she returned home and noticed that the ring was missing, she cried out, "It is an expensive ring! It is worth at least 25 gold coins!"

R' Shmelke heard his wife's words and quickly ran after the pauper. When he saw the rabbi chasing him, he began running, sure that he would be asked to return the precious ring. R' Shmelke quickened his pace and finally caught up with the pauper. He said, "I just wanted to tell you that the ring is worth at least 25 gold coins. Don't sell it cheaply."

That Shabbos, R' Shmelke told his congregation the story. "This," he said, "is what God told Moses. 'I have a precious gift in My storehouse to give the Jewish people. Its name is Shabbos. Go apprise them of its value (see *Shabbos* 10b) so that they don't sell it cheaply by wasting the day, dedicating it exclusively to eating, sleeping, or engaging in idle conversation and foolishness!' "

וְשָׁמְרוּ בְנֵי יִשְׂרָאֵל אֶת הַשַּׁבָּת לַעֲשׂוֹת אֶת הַשַּׁבָּת בְּרִית עוֹלָם לְדֹרֹתָם
The Children of Israel shall observe the Sabbath to make the Sabbath an eternal covenant for their generations (ibid. 16).

In the last three verses, the Torah uses the term שְׁמִירָה, *observance* (literally watching or guarding), three times with regard to the Sabbath. According to *R' Samson Raphael Hirsch,* this alludes to the fact that one must relate to the Sabbath as a watchman relates to his responsibilities. The Torah obligates a watchman to do three things. He may not make personal use of the object under his care; he may not be negligent in guarding it; and he is held responsible (in certain cases) if it gets lost.

Since the Torah has appointed us to safeguard the Sabbath, we may not abuse or misappropriate it by using it for mundane activities or pursuits. We may not be negligent in observing its laws and prohibitions.[22] Finally, we must be conscious at all

---

21. **Steps to Sanctity.** On a visit to New York, *R' Chaim Kreiswirth* entered a Jewish-owned shoe store. In the course of a conversation with the owner, R' Chaim realized that the store remained open on Shabbos. R' Chaim asked the owner, "How much do you make on an average Sabbath?" When the owner quoted a large sum R' Chaim replied, "I am writing you a check for the next three Sabbaths. Close the store and I promise you that your weekday profit will increase to cover the Sabbath income." And it did!

22. **Eternal Sabbath.** One who wishes to ensure that his children will observe the Sabbath properly must be careful not to show any laxity in following its laws. When children see their parents less than perfectly careful regarding even the less stringent Sabbath laws, they feel justified in taking even greater liberties. If we observe the Sabbath carefully, then it will be an eternal covenant for their generations (*R' Yehoshua of Kutna*).

times of our responsibility as watchmen of the Sabbath, not only on the holy day itself, but even during the week.[23]

Ohr HaChaim renders וְשָׁמְרוּ as *and they await* (see *Genesis* 37:11 and *Rashi ad loc.*). We must view the Sabbath as a pleasure for which we wait impatiently the entire week. *Rambam* writes: "What constitutes honoring the Sabbath? This is what the Sages taught: It is a mitzvah for one to wash [at least] his face, hands and feet in warm water on Friday as an expression of honor for the Sabbath. One should then don a *tallis* and sit with a serious demeanor, waiting expectantly to receive the Sabbath, much as he would welcome a king" (*Hilchos Shabbos* 30:2).

Background

Moses goes up to Mount Sinai, and from there he ascends to Heaven in order to receive the Torah. When it seems that he is not going to descend, the people ask for a different intermediary between them and God. In an attempt to stall for time, Aaron tells them to bring jewelry in order to make a replacement. The tragic result is the Golden Calf. For their precipitous downfall, God wishes to annihilate them and begin anew with the descendants of Moses. Moses prays on their behalf and God cancels the decree.

וַיִּנָּחֶם ה' עַל הָרָעָה אֲשֶׁר דִּבֶּר לַעֲשׂוֹת לְעַמּוֹ
Hashem reconsidered regarding the evil that He declared He would do to His people (32:14).

The term *reconsidered*, in its usual sense, is inappropriate with reference to God, since it implies that His original intention was in error or that He was unaware of changes in future conditions. Obviously such considerations are impossible.

R' Yitzchak Hutner explains that in giving man free choice, God ultimately gave man the ability to, in a certain sense, influence and control the Divine conduct of the universe. For example, man's free choice can create such a pervasive aura of evil that it will bring destruction on the world, as happened in the time of Noah, when God declared that as a result of human corruption He would bring the Flood, destroy the world, and then begin anew. The sins of Israel caused God to permit the destruction of the Temples and virtually remove His Presence from Creation. After the Flood, He made a בְּרִית, *covenant*, that He would no longer curse the earth because of man's sins (see *Genesis* 8:21). Thus, before the Flood, God said that He *reconsidered* having made man (see *Genesis* 6:7), i.e., that He permitted man to cause the destruction of the world. From then on, He limited the potential effect of man's free choice. Similarly, before the sin of the Golden Calf, the behavior of the Jewish people could cause their own obliteration. Now, as it were, God "reconsidered" and made a covenant that the Jewish people would always exist, whatever their misbehavior.

Why did God forgive the Jews the sin of the Golden Calf although they did little in the way of repentance, while He was unwilling to forgive the sin of the spies, in spite of their open expressions of regret and repentance? *R' Menachem Mendel of Kotzk* explains that when a Jew sins out of a misguided desire for spiritual growth, God can be understanding. However, when the misdeed is about nothing more than physical comfort, one must repent deeply before he can hope for Divine forgiveness. When the Jews thought that Moses would not return, they sought an alternative leader. Obviously this was a grave sin, but their motive was not self-serving. But, at the time of the spies, when they showed that they lacked faith in God and feared the physical difficulties of entering the Land, God was loath to forgive them.

---

23. **Shame to Waste It!** *R' Nota of Avritch* never slept on the Sabbath, preferring to spend his time praying or studying Torah. When asked to explain his custom he replied, "It says that we should guard the Sabbath (וְשָׁמְרוּ). I have yet to hear of a guard who goes to sleep while on duty." Once he put it this way: "Napoleon Bonaparte slept very little when he was emperor. He claimed that it was a shame to waste even a moment of royalty. On the Sabbath every Jew is royalty, a child of the King. Why would one appointed to be a prince for twenty-four hours want to waste even a minute of the time?"

Nesivos Shalom embellishes on this theme: There is a world of difference between one who sins out of weakness and one who rejects a relationship with God. The Golden Calf is an instance of the former, for it was out of weakness and despair that they sinned. When, as the Midrash teaches, Satan conjured up an image of a dead Moses floating in the air, they lost their emotional equilibrium and declared *this man Moses who brought us up from the land of Egypt — we do not know what became of him* (32:1). Such a sin, severe as it may be, is pardonable. In the instance of the spies, however, there was a conscious desire to distance themselves from God. The Torah refers to their sin as a provocation of God (*Numbers* 14:11) for they hated that which God loved. God chose the Land of Israel as His gift to His children; yet, they rejected His gift.[24]

---

24. **Unpardonable Deprivation.** *Nachlas Yaakov Yehoshua* notes another difference between the two sins. The Golden Calf was a sin between man and God. Such a sin is pardonable. By slandering the Land, however, the spies hurt other Jews who would never enjoy the Land, which God attests is very, very good. To deprive another Jew is unpardonable.

פרשת ויקהל &
Parashas Vayakhel

Background

Moses summons all the people to charge them with building the Tabernacle. It happened the day after Yom Kippur, when Moses came down from Mount Sinai with the Second Tablets, an indication that God had granted them atonement for the sin of the Golden Calf.[1]

וַיַּקְהֵל מֹשֶׁה אֶת כָּל עֲדַת בְּנֵי יִשְׂרָאֵל
Moses assembled the entire assembly of the Children of Israel (35:1).

Ostensibly Moses gathered all the people to instruct them about building the Tabernacle and so that they would have an equal opportunity to contribute their talent and the necessary raw materials.

Ohr P'nei Moshe adds a homiletical twist: Moses saw through Divine inspiration that the Second Temple would be destroyed because of unbridled and senseless hatred among Jews. He therefore gathered the Jews together to imbue them with the sense of unity and mutual concern that is the bedrock of the Tabernacle and a prerequisite for God's Presence to reside among them.

Avnei Nezer sees this as the underlying reason why private altars (בָּמוֹת) were permitted only until the Tabernacle was erected. Once the Tabernacle was built, it became the force uniting the nation. Moses therefore summoned all the people in order to fuse them into a unified whole.[2]

According to *Rashi*, this gathering of the people

---

1. **Rekindled Romance.** *Tur (Orach Chaim* 625) discusses why the holiday of Succos is scheduled during Tishrei, although it commemorates an event that occurred immediately after Pesach, in Nissan. He explains that to leave one's home for an outdoor hut during the warm spring and summer indicates no real dedication to God's word. The Torah therefore commanded us to leave our homes and move outside just as the colder weather begins and everyone else is moving back inside.

The *Vilna Gaon (Commentary* to *Shir HaShirim* 1:4) offers a different approach based on the events described in our *sidrah.* The *succah* commemorates the Clouds of Glory that accompanied the Jewish nation in the Wilderness. After the people sinned with the Golden Calf, the clouds departed. When Moses descended on Yom Kippur with the second Tablets, the Jews knew that they had been forgiven, and on the following day (11 Tishrei), Moses issued the call for them to bring gold, silver and whatever else was needed for the building of the Tabernacle. For the next two days (12 and 13 Tishrei) the Jews brought their contributions; on the fourteenth the building of the Tabernacle began. The following day (15 Tishrei) the Clouds of Glory returned. Thus, the *Vilna Gaon* comments, we celebrate Succos in commemoration of the Clouds of Glory, which were reinstated after the Golden Calf incident, for they symbolize that when we repent our sins, God embraces us as fully as He did before we sinned.

2. **Revealed Unity.** According to *Ramban (Terumah)*, the function of the Tabernacle was to provide a permanent abode for the Divine Presence that was manifest at Sinai when we received the Torah. Just as at Sinai, God revealed Himself to the unified nation which was, in the words of the Sages, "like one man of one heart," so the Tabernacle

in order to erect the Tabernacle occurred the day after Yom Kippur, when God granted them the Second Tablets, indicating that He had forgiven them for the sin of the Golden Calf. Why didn't Moses issue the instructions on the day he descended from the mountain?

She'aris Menachem suggests that the Tabernacle could not be properly erected without the atonement of Yom Kippur. Since the Tabernacle had to be built with money that was untainted by even the slightest bit of dishonesty, it was necessary to give the Jews a day to repent from their sins, return what may not have been legitimately theirs, ask forgiveness of one another and spiritually "launder" any tainted money. Only then could Moses summon them to contribute to the Tabernacle.

Olelos Ephraim sees a homiletical lesson in the assembly of the people on the day after Yom Kippur. It is not enough to beg forgiveness and seek interpersonal harmony and peace on Yom Kippur itself. We must devise means and strategies so that this spirit will spill over to the rest of the year. Then we will be able to continue to assemble the *entire* assembly of the Children of Israel.[3]

אֵלֶּה הַדְּבָרִים אֲשֶׁר צִוָּה ה׳ לַעֲשֹׂת אֹתָם
These are the things that Hashem commanded, to do them (ibid.)

Every mitzvah is comprised of two elements: action and intent. In the area of action, all Jews are alike; for example, everyone takes the *esrog* and *lulav* in basically the same way. But in the area of intent, emotion and understanding, every person performs his *mitzvos* differently, for no two Jews are on the exactly same spiritual level. Thus the ability to uniformly summon and unite the people is enhanced when the goal is *to do them* (R' David Moshe of Tchortkov).[4]

The expression *to do them* seems incongruent, since the fulfillment of Sabbath is for the better part passive; one simply refrains from work on the Sabbath. *Divrei Shmuel* offers a homiletical approach: One must spend his week doing things that bind him emotionally and intellectually to the Sabbath. Since it is a bond between the Jewish people and God, we must become more "Jewish" in the course of the week, in order to prepare ourselves for, and truly benefit from, the Sabbath.

שֵׁשֶׁת יָמִים תֵּעָשֶׂה מְלָאכָה
On six days work may be done (ibid. 2).

The word תֵּעָשֶׂה is passive: work *will be done*. It would seem that תַּעֲשֶׂה, *you shall do*, would be a more appropriate term. Many approaches to this question have been presented. According to *Aperion*, the Torah sheds a perspective on the relationship between effort and success. One who firmly believes that success is granted by God, not caused by man's effort, has no emotional difficulty

---

had to result from a call to unity, in order to retain that degree of Divine Presence. Hence Moses *assembled the Children of Israel* (*Simchas Aharon*).

3. **Restoration.** According to *Taam V'Daas*, the significance of the morrow of Yom Kippur relates to the Sabbath laws that God taught at that time through Moses. Although God had informed the Jews of the Sabbath a few weeks after the Exodus, at Marah, Moses delineated the laws only now, after the atonement of Yom Kippur. Under the albatross of sin one finds it hard to bear the yoke of Heaven, but atonement cleanses the soul and sensitizes it to the will of God. As King David said, *For with You is forgiveness, that You may be feared* (*Psalms* 130:4). Since the laws of Sabbath are complex and constraining, Moses waited until the people were ready and able to assume the yoke.

This might be why we celebrate Simchas Torah after Yom Kippur, rather than on Shavuos when we received the Torah. One whose soul is encrusted with the residue of sin is unable to appreciate the Torah or rejoice over it. Only after Yom Kippur can we truly rejoice with the Torah.

4. **United in Action.** Unity in and of itself is not a value; it is significant to the degree that it enhances Israel's ability to strengthen its commitment to the Torah. In the hands of the wicked, unity can be extremely dangerous. The Tower of Babel (*Genesis* 11) is a perfect example of unity gone awry. *The whole earth was of one language and one common purpose* (ibid. 1), yet they used that unity to rebel against God. When Moses assembled the people, the first thing he told them was that this assembly is valuable insofar as it allows us to strengthen our resolve to follow the commandments *that Hashem commanded, to do them* (R'Aaron Levine of Reisha).

observing the Sabbath. For the less faithful, who think that their efforts are the true cause of financial success, the Sabbath presents a formidable test. The Torah teaches, therefore, שֵׁשֶׁת יָמִים תֵּעָשֶׂה מְלָאכָה, success *happens*, not through your efforts, but through the Hand of God.[5] Therefore *the seventh day shall be holy for you*—realize that you are not the cause of your success, and you will recognize that you do not lose by refraining from work on the Sabbath.

R' Yerachmiel of Ostrovtza views the cause-and-effect relationship conversely. One who is careful regarding the laws of the Sabbath will merit to earn a living easily, with a limited amount of strain and exertion. Thus the Torah teaches תֵּעָשֶׂה מְלָאכָה, your work will happen almost by itself. You will enjoy success that is disproportionate to your efforts. As the *Zohar* (2:85) teaches, "All blessings, both earthly and heavenly, are dependent on the Sabbath."[6]

R' Elya Meir Bloch adds another perspective, based on an understanding of a fundamental difference between the nation of Israel and all others. The function of the people of Israel is to infuse the world with holiness. For them, mundane work is at best a means to create an arena for sanctity. Thus for a Jew to invest excessive physical, and certainly emotional, energy into his mundane endeavors is to ignore his *raison d'etre.* Hence the Torah teaches תֵּעָשֶׂה מְלָאכָה — during the six weekdays, a Jew must let his work "happen," almost on its own, without investing his "self" in it. However, *the seventh day shall be holy*

for you. The Sabbath and its ability to infuse time with sanctity is for *you,* for this is the true goal of a Jew's life.

The implication of this verse is that we are *obligated* to work six days. This seems puzzling, since one who is independently wealthy is surely not commanded to work.[7] According to *Rabbeinu Bachya,* this teaches that one should conduct all of his weekday work and affairs in order to enhance God's honor in this world.

Why is this call to have "all of your actions be for the sake of Heaven" appended to the mitzvah of observing the Sabbath? *R' Yitzchak Hutner* explains: We abstain from performing the thirty-nine *melachos* (types of labor) that were needed in the construction of the Tabernacle, and God rested from His creation of heaven and earth. Where is the parallel between our Sabbath and His? The answer is that just as God created the entire cosmos so that man would have a place to serve Him, so the Jewish people created the Tabernacle, a microcosm that provides us with a unique place to serve God. Thus our Sabbath parallels His.

When we work six days with the attitude that all we do is for the sake of Heaven, we recognize that this world was created as an arena for Divine service. From this perspective our resting from the thirty-nine *melachos* of the Tabernacle becomes meaningful. Just as God rested from His creation of a place to serve Him, so we rest from

---

5. **Sanctified Leisure.** *Rema* (*Orach Chaim* 290:2) writes: "Working people who are unable to engage in serious Torah study during the week should devote more time on the Sabbath to Torah study than Torah scholars who are occupied full-time with Torah during the week. The Torah scholars should engage in a bit more physical enjoyment, such as eating or drinking, etc." According to *R' Tzvi Hirsch of Dinov,* our verse alludes to this idea. The Torah addresses those who follow the path of R' Shimon Bar Yochai (see *Berachos* 35b), applying themselves singlemindedly to Torah and trusting that their work (and sustenance) will be accomplished by others. Six days your work will be done almost by itself. On the seventh day יִהְיֶה לָכֶם קֹדֶשׁ, *your physical pleasure* (לָכֶם, lit. *what is yours*) *will be holy.*

6. **Source of Blessing.** *R' Shlomo Alkabetz* conveys this thought in the *Lechah Dodi:* לִקְרַאת שַׁבָּת לְכוּ וְנֵלְכָה כִּי הִיא מְקוֹר הַבְּרָכָה, *To welcome the Sabbath come let us go, for it is the source of blessing.*

7. **Human Abode.** The Sages derive that building the Tabernacle is forbidden on the Sabbath from the fact that the mitzvah of the Sabbath precedes the command to build a Tabernacle. *Chasam Sofer* sees an important lesson in this, one that teaches that every Jew is precious. The mitzvah to build a resting place for the Divine Presence does not override the Sabbath. Nevertheless, even a slight chance to save a Jewish life overrides the Sabbath. [A Jew is where the Divine Presence is most strongly rooted.]

our physical labors that create the surroundings in which we can serve Him.[8]

וּבַיּוֹם הַשְּׁבִיעִי יִהְיֶה לָכֶם קֹדֶשׁ
but the seventh day shall be holy for you (ibid.).

In the *zemiros* for Friday night we say כָּל מְקַדֵּשׁ שְׁבִיעִי כָּרָאוּי לוֹ, כָּל־שׁוֹמֵר שַׁבָּת כַּדָּת מֵחַלְּלוֹ, שְׂכָרוֹ הַרְבֵּה מְאֹד עַל פִּי פָעֳלוֹ, *Whoever hallows the Sabbath as befits it, whoever safeguards the Sabbath properly from desecration, his reward is exceedingly great in accordance with his deed.*

There are two types of Sabbath observers. Some people understand the sanctity of the Sabbath and infuse it with holiness by engaging in prayer, Torah study and other spiritual pursuits, in addition to the Sabbath meals. These are the people who hallow the Sabbath as befits it. Others safeguard the Sabbath properly by refraining from forbidden labor, but make it a day of eating, drinking, sleeping and social activities. Both types are rewarded — *his reward is exceedingly great* — but their rewards are not the same. Each

is granted recompense *in accordance with his deed* (*Chafetz Chaim*).[9]

The Midrash (*Shemos Rabbah* 25:16) teaches that Sabbath observance is equivalent to all the *mitzvos* of the Torah. God says, "If you merit to truly observe the Sabbath, I will deem it as if you kept all the *mitzvos* of the Torah. But if you desecrate it, I will deem it as if you transgressed all of my *mitzvos*."

On an elementary level, the reason Sabbath observance is so fundamental is because it bears testimony that God is the Creator and, therefore, all of His creatures are bound by His commandments. The *Chafetz Chaim* adds a perspective based on the words of the Talmud (*Shabbos* 10b): "God told Moses, 'I have a special gift in My treasury; its name is Shabbos. I want to give it to the Jewish people.'" Shabbos is the gift that God, the allegorical groom, gave to His bride, the nation of Israel. If a bride returns the gifts to the groom,

---

8. **Scriptural Destiny.** When the *Chafetz Chaim* visited Tchernigov, Russia, he was told about a Jew whose factory remained open on the Sabbath. When he attempted to convince the factory owner to close his business on the Sabbath, the Jew replied, "I earn a 4,000-ruble profit every day. Do you want me to lose that kind of money every Shabbos?" Retorted the Sage of Radin, "Would you prefer to lose the entire factory because of your desecration of the Shabbos? Look in the Torah. *On six days work may be done but the seventh day shall be holy for you.* Why does the Torah tell us what to do on the weekdays? Wouldn't it have been sufficient to simply forbid work on the Sabbath? The answer is that only one who carefully guards the sanctity of the Shabbos is granted the ability to work on the other six days."

Scornfully, the industrialist answered, "Does the Rebbe think that a verse in the Torah is what keeps my factory running?" With that, the Chafetz Chaim left, disappointed at having failed to convince the Jew.

When the Communist Revolution took place, the Bolsheviks seized the factory from its owner. Penniless and destitute, he sent a letter to the Chafetz Chaim. "Now I know," he wrote, "that you were right. The verse in the Torah decided the fate of my factory."

9. **Designated Holiness.** *Chasam Sofer* and *Maharsham* explain an enigmatic *Zohar*, based on a different understanding of the two types of Sabbath observers. "The Divine Presence never left the Jewish people on the Sabbath or Holidays — even on a weekday Sabbath" (*Zohar, Korach* 179). What is a "weekday Sabbath"? The Talmud (*Shabbos* 69b) teaches that if one is traveling in the wilderness and loses track of which day is the Sabbath, he should count six days and observe the seventh as the Sabbath. Thus although in reality it may be a weekday, it is his Sabbath. The Divine Presence resides with a Jew even on this "weekday Sabbath."

Thus there are two types of people. One *who hallows the Sabbath as befits him* although in reality it may not be the true Sabbath, and one who *safeguards the Sabbath properly* in its appropriate time. Both are amply rewarded for their efforts to observe the Sabbath to the best of their abilities.

R' Yechiel Mordechai Gordon explained another prayer in this light. *They shall rejoice in Your Kingship — those who observe the Sabbath and call it a delight. The people that sanctifies the seventh [day] — they all will be satisfied and delighted from your goodness (Mussaf of Shabbos).* Those who observe the Sabbath in its proper time and even those who sanctify the seventh day [which may not truly be the Sabbath] — they will all be satisfied and delighted from Your goodness.

the message is clear — the wedding is canceled. One who desecrates the Sabbath tells God, in effect, that the "marriage" between them is off. Thus Sabbath observance is equivalent to all the *mitzvos* of the Torah.

לֹא תְבַעֲרוּ אֵשׁ בְּכֹל מֹשְׁבֹתֵיכֶם בְּיוֹם הַשַּׁבָּת
You shall not kindle fire in any of your dwellings on the Sabbath day (ibid. 3).

Chasam Sofer offers a homiletical rendering of the verse, underscoring the necessity to prepare oneself spiritually in order to derive maximum spiritual benefit from the Sabbath. Within the soul of every Jew burns a fire of love for Hashem and a desire to achieve closeness with Him. One who invests energy to fan that flame during the weekdays, so that it will burn strongly, will not have to begin "from scratch" on the Sabbath. However, one who wastes his weekdays on foolishness, entering the Sabbath ill prepared, will have to begin to ignite the flame — *kindle* a spiritual *fire* — on the Sabbath. Thus the Torah teaches: *You shall not kindle fire . . . on the Sabbath day.* Don't wait until Sabbath to kindle your soul; keep it warm all week long, so that the flame can peak on the Sabbath.[10], [11]

The Sadducees claimed that this verse must be understood literally, to prohibit any benefit from fire on the Sabbath. As a result, they would sit in the dark throughout the day. [The custom of eating *cholent* (or any dish kept warm overnight on the fire kindled before the Sabbath) derives from a desire to express rejection this heretical view, which denies the validity of the Masoretic and rabbinic traditional interpretation.] *Beis Yosef* refutes the Sadduceean approach from the verse itself. Since the subject under discussion is the Sabbath, why does the verse repeat *on the Sabbath day*? The Torah means to stress that one may not kindle fire *on the Sabbath* **day** — but one may kindle it before the Sabbath and derive benefit on the Sabbath.[12]

זֶה הַדָּבָר אֲשֶׁר צִוָּה ה׳ לֵאמֹר
This is the word that Hashem has commanded, saying (ibid. 4).

Rashi adds a few enigmatic words: that this is what God commanded Moses to say to the people. What does *Rashi* add to the plain meaning of the verse? *Maayana Shel Torah* (based on the Midrash) submits that Moses was upset that he was not given an opportunity to contribute to the building of the Tabernacle. God told him, "Your words are more precious to Me than all else." Thus

---

10. **Burning Etiquette.** R' Yosef Chaim Sonnenfeld was sitting at home one Sabbath when someone came to tell him that a man had lit a fire in his house and was cooking on the Sabbath. The rabbi ran to the house and entered without knocking, to protest the desecration of the Sabbath. The lady of the house asked him indignantly, "Is this the way a Torah scholar behaves, barging into someone else's home uninvited?" He replied incredulously, "Since when is one careful about etiquette when his friend's home is on fire?"

11. **Emotional Inferno.** *Shelah* interprets אֵשׁ, *fire,* as a reference to anger and strife. Don't allow the conflagration of anger or strife to burn on the Sabbath. Why is the prohibition to become angry especially relevant on the Sabbath? According to the Sages, the fire of *Gehinnom* does not burn on the Sabbath. One who gets angry causes God to let that fire burn him. As the Sages taught, "One who gets angry is subject to all types of purgatory" (*Nedarim* 22a).

Zekan Aharon adds: Sabbath is a time of peace. As *Ramban* writes (28:2), the *Mussaf* offering of Sabbath, unlike other *Mussaf* offerings, does not include a sin-offering "for Sabbath and the nation of Israel are mates, and peace reigns between them." Just as peace reigns on Sabbath between man and God, so must peace reign between man and man. Thus no fire of anger or strife may burn in any of your dwellings on the Sabbath day.

Akeidas Yitzchak offers a practical interpretation. On the Sabbath, when people do not go to work, the leisure time affords them an opportunity for casual conversation. It almost natural that such conversations will turn to forbidden talk about business matters, criticism of the rabbi and *chazzan,* and the local institutions and their employees. Unfortunately, such discussions have a way of causing hatred and strife. Thus the Torah warns us not to kindle the flame of hatred on the Sabbath; it was given for far more productive purposes.

12. **Double Light.** By lighting Shabbos candles and enjoying their light, we simultaneously increase peace and harmony in the home (see *Shabbos* 23b) and reject the heretical interpretation of the Sadducees (*Simchas Aharon*).

Moses told the people, *This is the word that Hashem has commanded* **me to say to you.** "My share in the Tabernacle are the words I speak to you, which will arouse you to have a share in the Tabernacle"

[It is often easier to give than to ask others to give. Often people are reluctant to solicit from others because they do not want to become indebted. Moses, the leader, was given the task of asking others.][13]

Why does the Torah repeat all the details of how the Jewish people built the Tabernacle? Since all of the minute details were already spelled out in the *parshios* of *Terumah* and *Tetzaveh*, wouldn't it suffice for the Torah merely to state that they did as they were commanded?

The *Brisker Rav* offers an explanation based on the teaching of the Sages (*Bechoros* 17b) that the vessels of the Tabernacle did not necessarily adhere exactly to the measurements mentioned in the Torah; a margin of error was permitted because human beings cannot be accurate to the minutest degree. The Torah repeats the details of the construction in order to stress that although a margin of error was permissible, the Jewish people did in fact do *exactly* as they were commanded.

R' Yitzchak Hutner suggests a more homiletical interpretation: Generally, when one seeks to translate an abstract idea into a physical reality, the concept becomes diluted when one focuses on the

execution of its physical aspects. Here the Torah repeats all the details to teach that the people retained the spiritual content of every artifact *as Hashem had commanded Moses.*

קְחוּ מֵאִתְּכֶם תְּרוּמָה לַה'
Take from yourselves a portion for Hashem (ibid. 5).

Seemingly תֵּנוּ, *you shall give,* would seem to be more appropriate a phrase than קְחוּ, *take.* Furthermore, how does the call to *take* fit with the idea that the contributions were to be rooted in heartfelt motivation? *R' Zalman Sorotzkin* suggests that even when giving an unsolicited contribution, one must overcome the natural resistance to part with hard-earned personal funds. One must *take* from himself in order to give with heartfelt motivation.

Otzar Chaim submits that the Torah calls on all to contribute, even those who are experiencing hard times. *Take from yourselves,* even if your contribution comes at personal cost. True charity means giving when it hurts. The Talmud (*Bava Basra* 10b) alludes to this idea. King Solomon was asked, "What is the power of charity" [i.e., what is its reward]? He replied, "Look at the words of my father: *He gave a distribution to the destitute; his righteousness endures forever, his pride is exalted with glory*" (*Psalms* 112:9). Why did King Solomon feel a need to answer with his father's word? Didn't he himself have what to say on the subject? During the Solomonic era, when the nation's prosperity was unprecedented, it was easy for people to be generous. Only during the time of King David,

---

13. **Enough Merit?** In addition to his great stature as a Torah scholar, *R' Chaim Kreiswirth* was a living legend in personal *chessed* and in encouraging others to become involved. The following two incidents highlight his view of asking others for charitable donations.

R' Alexander Heiden was old and infirm when the committee of the *Jesode HaTorah* school in Antwerp, Belgium asked him and his wife to serve as guests of honor at their first dinner. R' Alexander graciously refused four or five delegations from the school. Finally, R' Kreiswirth came to speak to him. "R' Alexander, if you were offered to become a partner with someone over 100 years old who is still extremely productive and profitable, would you agree?" "Of course," replied Mr. Heiden. "*Jesode HaTorah* is over 100 years old and it is still producing profits," concluded the Rav. Mr. and Mrs. Heiden became the guests of honor.

Another incident had a less happy ending. R' Kreiswirth asked someone to contribute a sizable sum toward the cost of marrying off an orphan. "It is a great *zechus* (merit) for you to participate," said R' Kreiswirth. The Jew responded, "I don't lack merits; I don't want to participate." R' Kreiswirth left, shocked that a Jew could actually feel that he had enough merits and needed no more. Shortly afterwards, that Jew died in a plane crash. When R' Kreiswirth heard the news he cried, "Who knows? Had he contributed, maybe that merit would have saved him and the rest of the passengers?!"

when wars ravaged the Land and people often suffered hunger and deprivation, could the true value of charity be gauged.[14]

כֹּל נְדִיב לִבּוֹ יְבִיאֶהָ אֵת תְּרוּמַת ה׳
everyone whose heart motivates him shall bring it as the gift for Hashem (ibid.)

One must bring the heartfelt motivation along with the gift. It is this spirit of giving which is the bedrock of the Tabernacle (*Sfas Emes, R' Shmuel Rozovsky*).

Only God can know if someone gives from the heart or if it is only to impress others or as a "business expense." God sees into one's heart and emotions. *Otzar Chaim* finds a way to determine a donor's motivation in the end of this verse: *[he] shall bring it as the gift for Hashem.* One who voluntarily takes the initiative to bring his contribution, rather than waiting for the collectors to solicit him, indicates that his heart motivates him.[15]

R' Bentzion of Bobov sees the human spirit of magnanimity as the key to receiving God's blessings. *Every one whose heart motivates him* to give

will be blessed. He will bring upon himself the gift of Hashem.

וְכָל חֲכַם לֵב בָּכֶם יָבֹאוּ וְיַעֲשׂוּ אֵת כָּל אֲשֶׁר צִוָּה ה׳
Every wise-hearted person among you shall come and make everything that Hashem has commanded; (ibid. 10).

Igra D'Kallah cites the masters of Kabbalah that although all Jews contributed to the Tabernacle, the gifts given with a greater spirit of heartfelt intent were used for more sanctified artifacts, while those gifts given with less heart were relegated to less holy purposes. Thus the gifts that were made with the purest intent went toward the Ark or the Holy of Holies, while those given with less pure motives were used for one of the lesser vessels in the Tabernacle, or for the hooks or sockets.

Who determined the relative quality of the hundreds of thousands of gifts? The *wise-hearted among you*, those who had the wisdom of heart to be able to penetrate *among you* and sense the purity of each person's motives. They were commanded to *come and make everything* that *Hashem has commanded.*[16]

---

14. **When It Hurts!** *Mr. Y.*, a well-known philanthropist, once went through a very sharp downturn in his business and was operating at a loss. Nevertheless, he took out bank loans at interest in order to meet his *tzedakah* commitments. He took from himself.

15. **Too Precious.** The townspeople in Sassov once saw their *Rebbe, R' Moshe Leib,* carrying a large pile of firewood on his shoulder. Curious, they followed him as he took the pile to the home of a poor woman who had just given birth.

They said to him: "Rebbe, it is a lack of honor for the Torah for you to be this poor woman's delivery boy. We will hire a gentile porter to deliver the wood." Replied R' Moshe Leib, "You want me to give away a great mitzvah like this to that Ivan, and even pay him to do it?"

A young man from Antwerp, Belgium was driving near the bus station in Brussels when he saw *R' Chaim Kreiswirth* standing with two large overstuffed bags, waiting for the bus back to Antwerp. The young man pulled up beside the rabbi and offered him a ride home. Rabbi Kreiswirth agreed and the young man took the packages to put in the trunk of his car. He could barely lift them. The rabbi told him that he knew someone in Brussels who was willing to sell him fabric remnants at a very reasonable price. "I send them to an orphanage in *Eretz Yisrael* where the girls sew their own clothes." When the young man asked him why he went by bus instead of spending $50 for a taxi, the rabbi replied, "If I had another $50, I would buy more fabric."

16. **Powerful Motives.** *R' Zekel Pollack* relates that *R' Chaim Kreiswirth* once told him, "One can participate in any charity endeavor without having great merit or purity of motive. But in order to give for Torah study, one must deserve the opportunity. Whenever you consider asking someone to contribute to your *kollel,* think carefully if the person has the merits and purity of purpose to give for Torah. If you are confident that he does, then approach him; you will be successful."

A story about the *Brisker Rav* underscores this point with regard to all charities. Once there was a pogrom in Brisk, during which many Jews were killed and much Jewish property went up in flames. Shocked by the tragedy, Lithuanian Jewry created a rescue committee with many prominent rabbis serving as members of the committee.

HaDerash V'Halyun sees a lesson in the danger of procrastination. If one wants to do a mitzvah, he should do so with alacrity, as soon as he feels the urge. By talking about and discussing the mitzvah, one wastes time, allowing pitfalls and digressions to pop up. Before long, one realizes that he has lost the opportunity or the desire. *Every wise-hearted person among you* does not allow his enthusiasm to wane. Rather, *you shall come and make everything that Hashem has commanded,* without delay.[17]

וַיֵּצְאוּ כָּל עֲדַת בְּנֵי יִשְׂרָאֵל מִלִּפְנֵי מֹשֶׁה
The entire assembly of the Children of Israel left Moses' presence (ibid. 20).

Obviously they left Moses' presence; why does the Torah mention this? *R' Simchah Zissel* of *Kelm* comments that while learning Torah from Moses is extremely significant, what is more impressive is that even after the people had left, their behavior and demeanor demonstrated that they had been in his presence. Every move they made while "on leave" from Moses was as if it had been in *Moses' presence.*

This carries an important lesson. When students leave the yeshivah for intersession, or when people leave their spiritual mentor, they must be sure to take the "presence" of the yeshivah or mentor with them.[18]

וַיָּבֹאוּ כָּל אִישׁ אֲשֶׁר נְשָׂאוֹ לִבּוֹ
Every man whose heart inspired him came (ibid. 21).

Literally, נְשָׂאוֹ לִבּוֹ means *his heart lifted him.* According to *Ramban,* this phrase teaches that

---

A woman with a large family whose husband was killed in the pogrom applied to the committee for help, but it was not forthcoming. Distressed, she approached the Brisker Rav and asked him to intervene.

He met with the committee and said to them, "Why is it that after such an incident people are ready to organize a rescue committee, yet the thousands of poor and destitute Jews in Poland and Russia are still starving, and nobody does anything about it? The answer is that the intent of the founders of the committee is to fight anti-Semitism by making a statement that Jews will not allow themselves to be driven out. 'We will rebuild and remain here' is the message they want to send to the Gentiles. While this is a positive thing, the basic desire to help Jews in need is missing. Since the intent behind the giving is not in order to help people, the money is not helping. This widow did not receive support because of the misplaced motivations of those who give."

17. **Wise and Quick.** The *Vilna Gaon* interprets the words of King Solomon in this vein: *The wise of heart will seize good deeds, but the foolish one's lips will become weary (Proverbs 10:8).*

A wise-hearted person wastes no time and immediately seizes the first opportunity to fulfill the mitzvah; therefore, he is assured that no obstacles will impede his mitzvah-performance. The foolish person, however, *talks* about doing the mitzvah, procrastinating and delaying until he finds reason to reconsider and reassess the situation. The end result is that the mitzvah remains unperformed.

Alacrity in performing *mitzvos* is not merely an admirable trait; the lack of it has a negative impact upon the mitzvah. This is borne out by the parallel the Sages employ to teach us about it: *You shall safeguard the matzos (Exodus* 12:17). From the fact that the word מַצּוֹת and מִצְוֹת are spelled alike, the Sages teach, "If a mitzvah comes to your hands do not allow it to become 'leavened' by delaying its performance" (see *Rashi* ad loc.). When one causes a delay during the preparation of matzah, he doesn't merely lower the quality of the matzah; he turns it into leavened *chametz,* which is forbidden. Likewise, delaying the performance of a mitzvah makes it "sour" (*Pachad Yitzchak, Pesach*).

An elementary understanding of this is that one must view Torah and *mitzvos* as crucial to life. One panting for oxygen would never dream of saying, "I'll get it later." Should our approach to *mitzvos* be any different? Alternatively, when a parent asks a child to do something and the child answers, "Not now, I'll do it later," it is a sign of disregard on the child's part. When we delay doing a mitzvah we are telling our Father the same thing (*Zekan Aharon*) [see *Pachad Yitzchak,* ibid., for another explanation of the *chametz*/delay parallel].

18. **Full to the Top?** When a pot of water is boiling, it bubbles so much that one cannot ascertain how much water is in the pot. Only when it is removed from the fire and the bubbling recedes can one know the actual contents of the pot. When one is in the yeshivah or at the Rebbe's court, he is "on the fire," it is hard to know how much Torah and fear of God he has within himself. Only during intersession, when he is away from the yeshivah can we know his inner caliber (*R' Yitzchak Hutner*). [Vacation is not "time off from Torah," but rather as an opportunity to ascertain what we have really gained from our spiritual investments.]

as slaves in Egypt, the Jews had never been trained as artisans in the fine arts necessary to manufacture the various items for the Tabernacle. Nevertheless, *their hearts lifted them*, i.e., they had the courage to step forward and volunteer, confident that God would help them use their natural, raw talent to successfully produce the vessels He desired.

When one earnestly wants to do God's will, his natural "limitations" need not stand in his way. His yearning to please God will "trigger" Divine help that will allow him to transcend his "natural" abilities (or lack thereof). His "heart" will lift him above all obstacles. An outsider who doesn't know this secret will be sure that the work is that of an experienced craftsman (*R' Yechezkel Levenstein*).

R' Yerucham Levovitz of Mir elaborates: This holds true even in mundane areas of life. The key to achieving great success is the ability to think expansively and throw oneself into endeavors that are seemingly beyond one's resources and abilities. Those who think small remain small; those who dream big achieve greatness.[19]

וְהַנְּשִׂאָם הֵבִיאוּ אֵת אַבְנֵי הַשֹּׁהַם
The leaders brought the shoham stones (ibid. 27).

Rashi notes that the word נְשִׂאָם is spelled defectively: in this verse, since it usually contains two *yuds* (נְשִׂיאִים). This omission in the leaders' title indicates censure for them. Instead of leading the people in bringing gifts for the Tabernacle, the tribal leaders decided to wait. Let the people bring their contributions and the leaders would bring whatever was still missing. In fact, the people's response was overwhelming, and the *shoham* stones were the only things left for the leaders.

Although their intent was logical, the deficient spelling of their title is an implied rebuke for their lack of enthusiasm. The leaders, like all Jews, were commanded to contribute toward the building of the Tabernacle; not to try and calculate what was needed from them. When one has the opportunity to perform a mitzvah, no considerations, even altruistic or sacred ones, should prevent one from performing it with alacrity (*Brisker Rav*).

R' Reuvain Grozovsky offers a profound explanation of the "sin" of the leaders. Man's mission in life is not to perfect the world or provide it with that which it lacks. His job is to perfect himself. Alacrity is a sign of man's dedication to Divine Service as a primary agenda in life. When the Jewish people were commanded to offer contributions and to erect a Tabernacle, the goal was not the building; that God could provide without them. Its construction was the means through which each person could achieve his goal of striving toward spiritual perfection, by unleashing in himself a spirit of giving. By being "lazy," the leaders failed to distinguish between the means and the goal. They tried to anticipate what they should do to complete the building rather than what they should do in order to "complete" themselves.[20]

Background

The Laver was made from the copper mirrors contributed by the women. Since these mirrors were used to entice the men in Egypt to continue normal family life, the Laver was later used to bring peace between man and wife. (See *Numbers* 5:17-28.) The women understood that the Tabernacle itself served a similar function: to bring peace between God and His People (*Simchas Aharon*).

---

19. **Courageous Dreams.** A non-Jewish leader once said, "Some people see things as they are and ask, 'Why?' I dream of things that weren't yet — and say 'Why not?' "

20. **Means and Goals.** *R' Shneur Kotler* adds: The commentators question why, in *Parashas Terumah* (*Exodus* 25:2;8), the Torah speaks of the *mitzvah* to contribute wholeheartedly (verse 2) and only then of the purpose of the Tabernacle *you shall make a Sanctuary for Me — so that I may dwell among them* (ibid. 8). Shouldn't the purpose be mentioned first? This indicates that engendering the spirit of giving was the true goal; the building was the means of channeling that exalted emotion. The Tabernacle lacks nothing; it is the sum total of all of the sincerity and generosity that went into the giving. The leaders sinned by failing to realize that what seemed to be the means was really the goal.

וַיַּעַשׂ אֵת הַכִּיּוֹר נְחֹשֶׁת . . . בְּמַרְאֹת הַצֹּבְאֹת אֲשֶׁר צָבְאוּ פֶּתַח אֹהֶל מוֹעֵד

He made the Laver of copper . . . from the mirrors of the legions who massed at the entrance of the Tent of Meeting (38:8).

Why was the Laver made of mirrors? *Toldos Yaakov Yosef* explains: People are too subjective to see their own flaws. As the Sages teach, "A person cannot observe [i.e., judge] his own *tzaraas* afflictions [to determine their status]." Homiletically this means that one is oblivious to his own shortcomings. Furthermore, as the *Baal Shem Tov* taught, the flaws one sees in others are a reflection of his own personal flaws. [In psychology, this is known as projection, meaning that one "projects" his own shortcomings into his perception of others.] Just as a mirror reflects the ugly things about us, so when we see ugliness in others it is really a reflection of ourselves. This is one aspect of the Sages teaching, "Who is wise? He who learns from every person" (*Avos* 4:1). When the Kohanim came to wash before beginning the service, they sought to cleanse themselves not only of physical dirt but also of spiritual filth and uncleanliness. The Laver was therefore made of mirrors so that the Kohanim would be reminded to figuratively look themselves in the mirror and recognize which areas needed spiritual cleansing. By scrutinizing the way they view others, they would discover where they themselves needed improvement.[21]

---

21. **Mirror Image.** The *Baal Shem Tov* once saw a Jew desecrating the Sabbath. As upset as he was about the Sabbath desecration, he was also upset at himself. "How is it," he wondered, "that I can see Sabbath desecration? It must be that I, in some way, have a personal connection to such a terrible sin." Suddenly he remembered that he once was present when somebody degraded a Torah scholar and that he, the Baal Shem Tov, he did not protest as strongly as he should have. Since in the words of the *Zohar*, a Torah scholar is the human embodiment of the Sabbath, he had, figuratively, violated the Sabbath. As a result he witnessed someone else's desecration of the Sabbath.

It is this mirror quality which underlies the Baal Shem Tov's comment about the bitter waters (*Exodus* 15:22-27). The verse states *they could not drink the waters of Marah because they were bitter.* In the plain sense, *they* refers to the waters. The Baal Shem Tov, however, says that *they* refers to the people. When someone is bitter, everything around him seems bitter. The water is bitter, the neighbors are bitter, life is bitter. This is not merely an example of projecting one's feelings onto others; rather, it reflects the fact that one discovers his true self and feelings in others. The water was bitter because it reflected their own bitterness.

פרשת פקודי ≈
Parashas Pekudei

Background

The *sidrah* opens with a very exact accounting of all the gold, silver and copper that was donated for the Tabernacle and delineates precisely the purposes for which it was used. This serves as a prime example of how careful leaders must be very to account for public funds that pass through their hands. Although there was not even a shadow of a doubt as to Moses' integrity, he was careful to fulfill the Biblical dictum וִהְיִיתֶם נְקִים מֵה׳ וּמִיִּשְׂרָאֵל, *then you shall be vindicated from Hashem and from Israel (Numbers* 32:22).[1], [2]

אֵלֶּה פְקוּדֵי הַמִּשְׁכָּן מִשְׁכַּן הָעֵדֻת
These are the reckonings of the Tabernacle, the Tabernacle of Testimony (38:21).

Rashi (citing *Midrash Tanchuma*) comments that the word מִשְׁכָּן can be vowelized and read מַשְׁכָּן, *a collateral*. The repetition of the word alludes to the two Temples, which God took away and holds figuratively as collateral for the sins of the Jewish people. Only when we pay our debts by repenting will the collateral be returned in the form of the Third Temple.

Toldos Adam questions how the Temple could be taken as a collateral. The Torah states clearly

---

1. **Losing on a Bad Investment.** Why did the people expect a reckoning of the contributions to the Tabernacle, yet demanded no accounting of the funds given for the Golden Calf? *R' Zalman Sorotzkin* submits that this testifies to the pure motives of the Jewish people. Deep inside, every Jew wants to do the right thing; it is the enemy within that causes him to sin (see *Rambam, Hilchos Gerushin* 2:20). When a Jew contributes to something truly holy, he wants to be sure that every cent is dedicated to the cause. But if the evil inclination seduces him into contributing toward a sinful cause, the Jew is distraught and hopes that the money was ultimately misappropriated by the collectors. That way, his money will not be used for sinful purposes. Thus for the Tabernacle they wanted a full accounting; not so for the Golden Calf.

2. **Community and Individual.** During most years, *Vayakhel* and *Pekudei* are read together. *Vayakhel* means "to gather," indicative of the importance of gathering together all the individuals and creating a community. *Pekudei*, on the other hand, calls upon us to count every detail separately, and symbolizes the value of the individual. This teaches us an important outlook on the relationship between the individual and the community at large. Generally there are two distinct philosophies. One view has it that the community is the most important, that the individual has no intrinsic value other than as a cog in the huge communal machine. According to this outlook, the individual's needs must fall to the wayside when they interfere with the benefit of the community. The opposite view sees the community as a means to serve the individual. The former is communism; the latter, anarchism.

   The Torah sees neither extreme as correct. Rather, it calls for a balanced combination of the two. On one hand, the Sages teach that one who saves one Jewish soul has saved an entire world (*Sanhedrin* 37a); on the other hand, *Who is like Israel Your people, one [united] nation (I Chronicles* 17:21). A unified nation in which every individual is a world for himself is a nation in perfect harmony. Hence we read *Vayakhel* and *Pekudei* together, for they symbolize the ideal blend which makes for a unified nation of individuals (*R' Shlomo Yosef Zevin*).

that one may not take as collateral anything the debtor needs for his livelihood, for to deprive a person of his means of support is tantamount to taking his life. Certainly there is nothing we need for our spiritual livelihood more than the Temple! How, then, could God take the Temples as collateral for our sins? *Toldos Adam* finds the answer in a parallel verse in *Exodus* (22:25-26), where the Torah forbids a creditor to take his debtor's blanket at night, as collateral. The Torah then states *so it will be that if he cries out to Me I shall listen for I am compassionate.* If the debtor feels so deprived that he cries from the depths of his heart, then the creditor must return the collateral. Likewise, with regard to the Temple; God waits, hoping that we will feel so deprived of our spiritual livelihood that we will cry out sincerely, begging Him to return it. When we do so He will give us back the Temple.[3]

Where in the text or context is the allusion to the fact that the Temple (Tabernacle) would be taken as collateral? *Oheiv Yisrael* submits the following: When a person has his possessions assessed, it is reasonable to suspect that he plans on using them as collateral. The fact that the Torah spells out in such detail the amounts of gold, silver and copper that went into the Tabernacle indicates that eventually it or its successors would serve as collateral against the sins of the Jewish people.

The words of the Sages regarding the blessing of Balaam bear out this explanation. On the words *How goodly are your tents, O Jacob, your dwelling places O Israel* (*Numbers* 24:5), the Sages comment that from the blessings that God forced the evil Balaam to utter, we may understand which curses he really wanted to proclaim (*Sanhedrin* 105b). Balaam's words revealed his inner intent. When a person buys precious items and shows them to a friend, the friend blesses him: "May you use them at joyous occasions." An enemy, however, wishes that their owner will fall on hard times and be forced to use the items as collateral. Balaam spoke of the goodness of the tents of Jacob [a metaphor for the Tabernacle and Temples], yet he wished מִשְׁכְּנֹתֶיךָ יִשְׂרָאֵל, that they serve as a מַשְׁכֹּן, a surety for the sins of the Jews.[4]

מִשְׁכַּן הָעֵדֻת
the Tabernacle of Testimony (ibid.).

According to *Rashi*, the Tabernacle bore tangible witness that God had forgiven the sin of the Golden Calf. How did the Tabernacle testify that God had granted atonement? *Rabbeinu Yonah* explains that one knows his repentance has been accepted when he once again enjoys the same closeness with God that he had before he sinned. As King David implored God, הָשִׁיבָה לִי שְׂשׂוֹן יִשְׁעֶךָ,

---

3. **Are We Really Waiting.** The *Chafetz Chaim* related what happened when the heads of the Jewish community of Brisk asked *R' Yosef Dov Soloveitchik* (*Beis HaLevi*) to become their rabbi. Initially the Beis HaLevi refused, feeling that he was not worthy to occupy the pulpit that had been held by the revered *R' Yehoshua Leib Diskin.* One of the community elders said to him, "Rebbe! How can you refuse us? Twenty-five thousand Jews in Brisk are waiting for you." R' Yosef Dov was moved by the man's sincere words. He ran quickly to the Rebbetzin and asked her to give him his rabbinic garb. "I must go!" he cried. "How can I disappoint twenty-five thousand Jews!" The Chafetz Chaim sighed deeply when relating the story. "If R' Yosef Dov couldn't refuse the request of twenty-five thousand people, how much more so would the Messiah not refuse the sincere request of millions of Jews! If he knew that they were truly waiting for him, he would come immediately. The tragedy is that we aren't really waiting for him. We mouth the words in our prayers 'for we are waiting for You' (*Kedushah of Shacharis — Sabbath*) but in our hearts, are we really waiting?" The great sage sighed deeply and began to cry, "Are we really waiting?"

4. **Hidden Collateral.** The numerical value of אֵלֶּה is 36, an allusion to the thirty-six hidden saints in whose merit the world survives. Today, when we no longer have a Temple or a Tabernacle, they are the collateral that God takes from us in order to ensure that we will make good on our indebtedness, which comes as a result of sin (*Pardes Yosef*).

Why is sin a cause of debt? God gives us all of our talents and the opportunities to use them in His service. When, instead, we use His gift against His wishes, we must return to Him that which is His. Thus we are indebted to Him. The thirty-six *tzaddikim* create an atmosphere of sanctity that allows us to thrive spiritually, for God's Presence resides in them. When we sin and reject God, He withdraws His "ambassadors," taking them as collateral in order to insure that we will repay our debts (*Zekan Aharon*).

Restore to me the joy of Your salvation (*Psalms* 51:14). When God rested His Presence in the Tabernacle, He indicated that He was ready to reinstate His bond with His beloved people. This renewed closeness testified that He had forgiven them for the Golden Calf (*Simchas Aharon*).

Kiflayim L'Tushiah sees Moses' reckoning of the components of the Tabernacle as indicative of atonement. When one is ravenously hungry, he eats with wild abandon, gorging himself until he is sick. But when a doctor prescribes medicine, it is administered in exact, measured doses. When the Jews gave money for the Golden Calf they did so in a gluttonous fashion, forcibly removing the rings from the ears and fingers of their wives and children. In contrast, when they contributed to the Tabernacle, the amounts were exact and fully accounted for. Thus the giving to the Tabernacle was the "prescription medicine" meant to cure the spiritual ills caused by the wanton giving to the Golden Calf.

Malbim gives another perspective. Moses' reckoning must have been flawless; otherwise, God, Who hates theft, would never have rested His Presence there. Thus the Tabernacle testifies to the fiscal propriety of all those involved in its construction.[5]

בֶּקַע לַגֻּלְגֹּלֶת מַחֲצִית הַשֶּׁקֶל בְּשֶׁקֶל הַקֹּדֶשׁ
a beka for each head, a half-shekel in the sacred shekel (ibid. 26).

These half-shekels were melted down to make the sockets that held up the planks of the Sanctuary walls. Just as those contributions supported the Tabernacle structure, so the laity throughout the generations sustain those who study and teach Torah, thus giving all Jews a share in their holy work.

Because this partnership is so essential, the evil persuader invests vast amounts of time and energy to derail it. He begins by trying to distract the learners from putting their intellectual and emotional resources into Torah study. If this tactic fails, he targets the supporters of Torah, persuading them that their magnanimity is not needed or could better be directed elsewhere. ["There are plenty of *yeshivos*" or "They aren't really fully dedicated to Torah study; why support them?" "There are more important causes that deserve your help" — these are but some of the "reasons" why people fail to support Torah in accordance with their means] (*Chafetz Chaim*).[6]

Chidushei HaRim relates the one hundred sockets of the Tabernacle walls to the hundred daily blessings that a Jew should recite every day (See *Menachos* 43b). The word אֶדֶן, *socket*, is related to אָדוֹן, *master*. Just as the sockets were the foundation of the physical Tabernacle, so the hundred blessings that express our recognition of God's Mastery are the foundation of the Jew's internal Tabernacle.

Background

The Torah continues the accounting with the coverings of the Tabernacle and the royal vestments of the Kohanim.

כַּאֲשֶׁר צִוָּה ה' אֶת מֹשֶׁה
as Hashem had commanded Moses (39:1).

This phrase repeats itself no less than eighteen times in the *parashah*. *R' Yosef Leib Nendik* comments that man's every action leaves its im-

---

5. **Pure at the Base.** The purity which informs the creation of an edifice for sanctity effects the quality of spirituality that can be achieved there. The *Vilna Gaon* said that if a synagogue was built properly — if the axe used to cut the wood for the beams was made with pure intentions — it would be impossible to pray there with any negative thoughts or emotions (see *Bava Metzia* 85b).

6. **Backwards Logic.** A wealthy Jew excitedly told the *Chafetz Chaim* about his last will and testament. "I gave away my library to a certain yeshivah and left my money to my children." Replied the Chafetz Chaim, "You have it backwards. Your children need your books; maybe they will learn some Torah and be affected by it. The yeshivah has plenty of books; they don't need your library. On the other hand, the money would be much better spent if you would give it to provide Torah scholars with a living."

He explained the verse in *Ecclesiastes* (9:11) *nor does bread come to the wise, riches to the intelligent* in this vein. If the wise students of Torah lack bread it is symptomatic of the fact that wealth does not reside among the intelligent. Were the wealthy to be wise, they would see to it to support the impoverished scholars.

print on his surroundings, on the cosmos and on himself. God commanded the Jewish people to build a Tabernacle in total fidelity to the concept of "as Hashem had commanded Moses," so that there would be one small oasis of pristine purity, which would leave its mark and influence on the entire cosmos. In order to convey such untainted spirituality, it was imperative that the source of the influence remain unaffected by the downward trend that seems to infiltrate most human activity. Even the planks were made from trees that Jacob planted with sanctity and purity and which he took with him on his sojourn to Egypt. Thus it was important to stress repeatedly that the Jewish people created this tiny sector of sanctity exactly *as Hashem had commanded Moses.* [7]

Zichron Meir offers an alternative approach. It is not hard to create approximates, but difficult to create something authentic. One can be "almost" a proper Jew, "approximately" a God-fearing person, "nearly" a refined personality or "almost" a dedicated student of Torah, but it is much more demanding to be perfect. We must remember that service of God is how we repay Him for all He has given us. Just as one who "almost" repaid his debt is still indebted, so one who "almost" meets God's expectations is still spiritually "in the red." When the Jewish people made an earthly abode for Hashem it could not be almost perfect; it had to be *as Hashem had commanded Moses.*

וְלֹא יִזַּח הַחֹשֶׁן מֵעַל הָאֵפֹד
and the Breastplate would not be loosened from above the Ephod (ibid. 21).

One who loosens the Breastplate's connection to the Ephod transgresses a Biblical prohibi-

tion (*Yoma* 72a). *Peninei HaTorah* offers a homiletical explanation based on the Talmud (*Arachin* 16a), which teaches that the Breastplate atones for miscarriages of justice[8] while the Ephod brings forgiveness for idolatry. Idolatry is the fundamental sin between man and God while miscarriage of justice undermines all interpersonal relationships. By requiring that the Breastplate and Ephod remain connected, the Torah alludes to the inseparable link between interpersonal *mitzvos* and the *mitzvos* between man and God.

וַיָּבִיאוּ אֶת הַמִּשְׁכָּן אֶל מֹשֶׁה
They brought the Tabernacle to Moses (ibid. 33).

Rashi comments that the workmen were unable to erect the Tabernacle due to its massive weight, and brought the problem to Moses. When he told God that it was impossible to erect it, God said, "You attempt to do it and it will stand up on its own."

Only Moses, in his humility, was able to attempt to erect the Tabernacle with his own strength and yet simultaneously know in his heart that it only stands up on its own as a result of God's intervention (*Darkei Emunah*).

וַיְבָרֶךְ אֹתָם מֹשֶׁה
And Moses blessed them (ibid. 43).

Moses' blessing was, *"May the Divine Presence rest upon your handiwork"* (*Rashi*). May the pleasantness of the Lord, our God, be upon us — our handiwork, establish for us; our handiwork , establish it" (*Psalms* 90:17).

Ksav Sofer notes that the blessing does not say,

---

7. **Pure Oil.** *R' Nosson Wachtfogel* related that in the early years of Beth Medrash Govoha in Lakewood it was difficult to attract students. *R' Aharon Kotler* had to travel long, hard hours in order to enroll even one student. Once R' Nosson asked him, "Why does the *rosh yeshivah* exert himself so much and even incur degradation in search of students? Let's start a yeshivah high school (including a secular studies curriculum) as part of the yeshivah and thus have a natural 'feeder' of students." Replied R' Aharon, "I want there to exist at least 'one untainted flask of oil' in all of America from which we will be able to enlighten the rest of the country with pure unadulterated Torah."

8. **Joyous Heart.** Far from feeling slighted that Moses was chosen over him to be Israel's redeemer, Aaron rejoiced over the success of his younger brother. As a reward for his joyous heart at Moses' success, he was granted the privilege of bearing the Breastplate on his heart (see *Rashi* to *Exodus* 4:14).

Aaron's heart sought the good of others even at "personal" expense. There is no better place for the Breastplate, which atones for miscarriages of justice to rest (*Simchas Aharon*).

"May it be God's will," for it was assured that God would rest His Presence there. Moses blessed them that they truly desire that God's Presence rest in their Tabernacle. After all of their hard work they needed to add the crucial element: their desire to have God with them.[9]

Divrei Asher interprets "handiwork" as a reference not to the Tabernacle, but to man's ordinary, secular labors. Moses' prayer was, "May it be God's will that His Presence rest not only in your prayers, Torah study and mitzvah performance, but even upon your business and social activities." *Toras Maharitz* views Moses' blessing as related to so-called "cardiac Judaism." There are those who see no need to express their relationship with God through the performance of the commandments; they are content to be "a Jew at heart." Moses blessed them that they not allow themselves to think that their heartfelt donations were enough. "May the Divine Presence rest upon your **handiwork**."[10], [11]

בְּיוֹם הַחֹדֶשׁ הָרִאשׁוֹן בְּאֶחָד לַחֹדֶשׁ תָּקִים אֶת מִשְׁכַּן אֹהֶל מוֹעֵד
On the day of the first new moon, on the first of the month you shall erect the Tabernacle, the Tent of Meeting (40:2).

The Tabernacle was intended to be a place where the Divine Presence would rest, just as the world was meant to be when He created it. Just as מְלֹא כָל הָאָרֶץ כְּבוֹדוֹ, *The entire universe is full of His*

honor (Isaiah 6:3), so וּכְבוֹד ה׳ מָלֵא אֶת הַמִּשְׁכָּן, *and the glory of Hashem filled the Tabernacle (Exodus 40:35).* The Tabernacle was a microcosm of Creation. That is why the commandment to build the Tabernacle was given in the month of Tishrei and it was actually erected in *Nissan* — just as the idea to create the world arose in Tishrei while the actual creation occurred in Nissan. [See *Rosh Hashanah* 27a and *Tosafos* ad loc. s.v. כמאן מצלינן] (*Melo HaOmer*).

וְשַׂמְתָּ שָׁם אֵת אֲרוֹן הָעֵדוּת
There you shall place the Ark of Testimony (ibid. 3).

The Talmud (*Yoma* 52b) teaches that after the reign of Josiah (toward the end of the First Temple era), the Ark was hidden along with the jar of manna which commemorated that God had provided sustenance to His people in the Wilderness (see *Exodus* 16:33). According to *R' Aharon Levine* the linkage teaches us that our physical sustenance, represented by the jar of manna, is directly related to our connection to Torah, which is symbolized by the Ark. As the *Mishnah* teaches, "If there is no Torah, there is no flour (i.e. physical sustenance)" (*Avos* 3:17).

וַיָּקֶם מֹשֶׁה אֶת הַמִּשְׁכָּן
Moses erected the Tabernacle (ibid. 18).

The Sages taught that Moses erected and dismantled the Tabernacle on each day of the

---

9. **Let Him In.** Where is God to be found? Wherever man lets Him in (*R' Menachem Mendel of Kotzk*). [God enters man's life only if man makes him feel welcome. Just as one who wants a prestigious guest to visit his home makes sure that his guest will be comfortable, so we must conduct our lives and homes so that God will feel "comfortable" in our presence.]

10. **Complete Health.** [While the heart is a crucial organ, a person with a healthy heart cannot survive if the rest of his organs are not in good working order. The 248 *mitzvos* correspond to the parts of the human body, because true health means total functioning.]

11. **Balanced Effort.** *R' Aharon Bakst* wrote a letter to his son who was about to enter the world of business. "The Torah concludes the story of Creation with the words *which God created to make (Genesis 2:3)*. Creation waits for man to complete it by doing his share in the creative process. When man does so, God blesses his efforts with success.

"Whatever you do in life and in your business endeavors, weigh your course of action carefully and assess whether it is the right or wrong thing to do. If you do too much you will be flawed in your faith in God. On the other hand, too little effort may be an expression of laziness rather than one of trust in God. In either case, God's Presence will not be with you. Moses blessed the Jews that the Divine Presence rest upon *all* their actions."

seven-day dedication ceremonies. It was only on the eighth day that he left the Tabernacle standing (*Rashi, Leviticus* 9:23).[12] *Imrei Emes* sees this in a historical perspective. Altogether, the Tabernacle and the Temple were destined to fall or be permanently dismantled a total of seven times: the Tabernacle five times — in the Wilderness, in Gilgal, Shiloh (where it was destroyed by the Philistines), Nob and Gibeon — and the First and Second Temples each of which was destroyed. In order to assure that all seven fallings would only be temporary, Moses erected the Tabernacle seven times. Every time he re-erected it, he imbued the Jewish people with the ability to rebuild an Abode for God. King Solomon alludes to this in *Proverbs: Do not lurk, O wicked one, near the habitation of the righteous one; do not plunder his resting place . . . For though the righteous one may fall seven times, he will rise . . .* (24:15-16).

According to *Be'er Mayim Chaim,* the people and the artisans brought the physical structure of the Tabernacle to Moses, who would imbue the building with its spirit — the sanctity and the Presence of Hashem. This could not be achieved by anyone but Moses.[13], [14]

וַיִּקַּח וַיִּתֵּן אֶת הָעֵדֻת אֶל הָאָרֹן
He took and placed the testimony into the Ark (ibid. 20).

The clause *He took* seems superfluous. Why doesn't the verse simply say that he placed the Testimony in the Ark? According to its plain meaning, the verse teaches that Moses took the Tablets from the wooden ark where they were temporarily housed until the permanent Ark of gold was built. Once it was completed, Moses took the Tablets from their temporary location and placed them in their permanent one (*Ramban*).

Many commentators illuminate homiletical aspects of the verse, based on the fact that the Tablets and the Ark are symbolic of Torah.

According to *R' Moshe Midner,* the verse teaches that the study of Torah is a reciprocal process. One must study, but he must also endeavor to impart his Torah to others; he must give as well as take. Moses *took* the Torah from God, but he also *gave* it, by placing it in the hearts of the Jewish people.

Toras Chaim views the reciprocity in the very act of teaching Torah. One who teaches Torah generally receives, since his own knowledge is deepened

---

12. **Fall and Rise.** This is true on a personal and communal level as well. The goal of every Jew is to turn himself and his life into a comfortable abode for the Divine Presence, but the road to success is punctuated by failure. The righteous will fall seven times, but rise again each time (*Proverbs* 24:16); people must learn from their experience, so that each fall is but a step forward toward ultimately rising to lasting spiritual greatness. When Moses erected and reerected the Tabernacle, he invested every Jew with the resilience to rise again and again after setbacks (*Zekan Aharon*).

13. **Empty Temples.** When *R' Samson Raphael Hirsch* assumed the spiritual leadership of his Orthodox community in Frankfurt, he insisted on building a school before a synagogue; without a young generation loyal to the Torah, the synagogue building would have become an empty shell, without the spirit of God.

14. **Honorable Put Down.** One of the great Talmudists, a contemporary of *R' Simchah Bunim of P'shis'-cha,* criticized the latter's practice of asking his students, some of whom were great scholars, to perform menial tasks as a way to develop humility. "How do you allow yourself to demean the Torah's honor?" he challenged. R' Simchah Bunim responded by citing the Talmudic teaching (*Nedarim* 38a): "God rests His Presence only on one who is physically strong, wealthy, wise and humble." All these qualities were present in Moses. He was physically strong as it states, *He spread the Tent over the Tabernacle* (*Exodus* 40:19).

"While the need for one to be wise and humble in order to merit God's Presence is obvious, why must he be strong and wealthy? The answer is that the main quality needed is humility. One who is weak and poor, however, has no problem acquiring humility; he has nothing to be arrogant about. Only one who is humble in spite of his wealth, strength and intellect is truly humble. The scholars who come to me in P'shis'-cha are strong, rich and bright. If they don't learn to demean their own honor, how will they ever be humble?"

and clarified. As the Sages teach, "I learned much from my teachers, even more from my colleagues, and from my students more than from them all" (*Makkos* 10a).[15]

וַיָּשֶׂם אֶת הַבַּדִּים עַל הָאָרֹן
and inserted the staves on the Ark (ibid.).

The Sages taught that the Ark bears its bearers (*Sotah* 35b). The staves were not really made to lift the Ark, since the Ark raises its bearers. Those who financially support Torah, symbolized by the staves, do not raise the Torah and define its standards; rather, the Ark will raise its supporters to its own elevated level (*R' Aharon Levine*).

The Tablets allude to the Torah scholars who toil relentlessly in order to understand God's most precious gift. The staves are symbolic of the people of means who dedicate their wealth to support and carry the Ark of Torah study and education. Moses placed the Tablets in the Ark, granting the Torah scholars the ability to interpret the Written Torah that he brought to the people. As a loyal shepherd, he made sure that even those who were unable to dedicate their lives to full-time Torah study could be involved in the learning process. He gave them the role of staves with which the Ark can be carried (*Simchas Aharon*).[16]

וַיִּתֵּן אֶת הַשֻּׁלְחָן בְּאֹהֶל מוֹעֵד עַל יֶרֶךְ הַמִּשְׁכָּן צָפֹנָה
He put the Table in the Tent of Meeting on the north side of the Tabernacle (ibid. 22).

"One who desires monetary wealth should face northward [in his *Shemoneh Esrei*], for the Table [symbol of bread and prosperity] was located in the north. One who desires wisdom should face southward, for the Menorah [symbol of wisdom] was located in the south" (*Bava Basra* 25b).

What happens if one desires both wealth and wisdom? Where should he focus? *Zekan Aharon* submits that, with rare exceptions, one cannot acquire both wealth and wisdom simultaneously. As King Solomon writes, *nor does bread come to the wise* (*Ecclesiastes* 9:11). *Rambam* states clearly, "Lest one say, 'I will first gather wealth and then return to my Torah studies; I will purchase everything that I need and when I am free I will dedicate my time to Torah.' If such a thought enters your heart you will never merit the crown of Torah. Rather make Torah your main preoccupation and your work of secondary importance. 'Do not say when I am free I will study, for maybe you will never be free' " (*Hilchos Talmud Torah* 3:7).

Alternatively, one who *desires* wealth and *desires* wisdom cannot enjoy both. R' Yehudah HaNassi, who did have both, raised his ten fingers and

---

15. **Heart to Heart.** *Divrei Yisrael* adds another perspective: A teacher's influence on his students [and a parent's on children] is directly linked to how deeply the Torah has penetrated his heart. As *R' Moshe ibn Ezra* taught, דְּבָרִים הַיּוֹצְאִים מִן הַלֵּב נִכְנָסִים אֶל הַלֵּב, *Words coming from the heart penetrate the heart* (*Shiras Yisrael*). Thus one must take the Torah from his heart and place it in the Ark, namely his students.

16. **What About this World?** Nevertheless, one may never absolve himself from Torah study due to the financial support he extends to Torah scholars or even to his children so that they may learn (see *Rambam, Hilchos Talmud Torah* 1:4). *R' A.* is one of Jerusalem's most respected Torah scholars. When he was a young boy, he was asked if he would be willing to change places with someone who supports Torah, if he could be guaranteed to receive the same Heavenly reward he receives for his Torah study. *R' A.* replied with uncharacteristic bravado. "Even if I would get greater reward I wouldn't agree. I would have the reward, but I wouldn't have the Torah."

One who supports Torah will certainly receive great reward in the World to Come. But for one to truly reap the benefits Torah offers in *this world,* by enhancing the lives of those it touches, it is not enough to support Torah — one must actually study it.

R' Elazar M. Shach once told a world-famous philanthropist, "I envy your share in the World to Come for while I have doubts about the quality and sincerity of my Torah study, I know that you wholeheartedly support Torah scholars and scholarship. But how are you going to enjoy this world? I at least have my Torah learning, but what do you have?"

declared that he had not *enjoyed* even a finger's worth of his wealth. To him, wealth was a means to do great things, not his goal in life.

וּכְבוֹד ה׳ מָלֵא אֶת הַמִּשְׁכָּן
and the glory of Hashem filled the Tabernacle (ibid. 35)

Every element of the Tabernacle, down to the smallest accouterment, was a vibrant expression of Israel's love for God, resulting from the heartfelt sincerity of their donations and their yearning to be close to Him. In response, God showed the Jews an intense love that embraced every element of the Tabernacle, filling it with His Presence. When the Jews' commitment allowed no place for a vacuum in their hearts, God responded in kind, by not leaving even the smallest space devoid of His Presence. Therefore the glory of Hashem *filled* the Tabernacle (*R' Yaakov of Radzimin*).[17]

Tosafos notes that the Torah does not state that "the Tabernacle was full with the glory of Hashem" but rather that *the glory of Hashem filled the Tabernacle.* The former might imply that the entire glory of Hashem was enclosed by the Tabernacle. This is of course impossible, since "God is the place of the world; the world is not His place" (*Bereishis Rabbah* 68:10). Rather, *the glory of Hashem filled the*

Tabernacle, but there was still infinite Divine glory outside of it.

כִּי עֲנַן ה׳ עַל הַמִּשְׁכָּן יוֹמָם וְאֵשׁ תִּהְיֶה לַיְלָה בּוֹ לְעֵינֵי כָל בֵּית יִשְׂרָאֵל בְּכָל מַסְעֵיהֶם
For the cloud of Hashem would be on the Tabernacle by day and the fire would be on it at night before the eyes of all of the House of Israel throughout their journeys (ibid. 38).

One who lives as a Jew should, allows God to be a Presence in his life, and is a living Tabernacle. When the sun of success shines upon him, he should realize that it might not last forever and that clouds may block that light. On the other hand, when night, symbolic of difficult times, darkens his life, let him never forget that there is a fire with which God can, in but an instant, light up his life (*Yalkut Eliezer*).

Arono Shel Yosef views the verse as a primer for survival in exile. Clouds are meant to obstruct our vision and to make things look dark while fire sheds light on an object, allowing one to see it clearly. In all of their journeys throughout the exile, Jews should recognize that cultures that oppose the Torah are like a dark cloud that will dissipate, and they should never forget that the Torah is like a fire that enlightens and warms.[18]

---

17. **Unwelcome Guest.** *Maharatz Chayes* was walking in Vienna when he saw a "progressive" temple with the words *and the glory of Hashem filled the Tabernacle* inscribed in gold letters above the entrance. He commented, "They forgot to write the beginning of the verse: *Moses could not enter the Tent of Meeting.* In such a Temple where Moses' Torah is not accepted, he is not welcome."

18. **On the Road.** *Rashi* writes that even the places where the people camped are referred to as *journeys.* Though Jews reside peacefully in the seemingly benevolent surroundings of their hosts in exile, they should always realize that what seems like an encampment is really a temporary stop on their journey back to the Land of Israel, with the coming of the true Redeemer, speedily and in our days (*Yalkut Yehudah*).

ספר
ויקרא
VAYIKRA/LEVITICUS

פרשת ויקרא ⊷
Parashas Vayikra

Background

The Torah has now completed describing the Tabernacle and its contents; and it is about to discuss the laws of the sacrifices that were offered inside. Before detailing those laws, we are taught a lesson about *how* an offering should be brought.[1]

וַיִּקְרָא אֶל מֹשֶׁה
He called to Moses (Leviticus 1:1).

The letter א of the word וַיִּקְרָא is written diminutively. The term וַיִּקְרָא connotes a friendly calling, while the word וַיִּקָר, which is used when God appeared to Balaam, implies a chance or forced meeting.

God had ordered Moses to write וַיִּקְרָא, but Moses, the most humble of men, wanted to use the less complimentary וַיִּקָר. To fulfill God's command, he wrote the א, but he wrote it smaller than the rest of the word (*Baal HaTurim*).

R' Yisrael of Rizhin notes that the letters י-ק-ר spell both קְרִי, *impurity* and יְקָר, *glory*. A person who believes that his spiritual achievements are intended to bring him glory is impure. One who always feels undeserving is beloved by God.

Because Moses wanted to write וַיִּקָר, God lovingly called to him to come close.[2]

Moses' desire to write וַיִּקָר in order to avoid

---

1. **Starting Point.** In many communities there is a custom for youngsters to begin their study of *Chumash* with *Parashas Vayikra.*

This custom is explained by the Midrash (*Vayikra Rabbah* 7:3): "Why, when we begin teaching children, do we begin with *Toras Kohanim,* the section of the Torah that deals with the Temple service? Because children are pure of sin, and the offerings purified those who brought them. Let the pure children come and involve themselves in the study of the purifying offerings."

Avnei Azel suggests that we begin a child's Torah study with the portion that discusses sacrifices in order to inspire parents to willingly make sacrifices on behalf of their children's growth in Torah. If they want to inculcate their children with a passion for and commitment to Torah and *mitzvos,* the parents must be willing to show sacrifice. Parents must be prepared to bear the effort and the cost that goes into educating their children, even if it means forgoing pleasures, comforts or even some "necessities."

The Sages teach, "Be careful with the children of the poor, for it is from them that Torah will emerge" (*Nedarim* 71a). *R' Meir Shapiro* explains that the self-sacrifice poor parents endure to enable their children to study Torah inspires the children and fuels their success.

2. **Truly Humble.** *R' Simchah Bunim of P'shis'cha* offered the following insight into how Moses maintained his humility even as he reached the pinnacle of prophecy.

A person standing at the peak of a mountain realizes that he is not really taller than everyone else; it is the mountain that holds him high. Moses recognized that his many achievements were not of his own doing — God had granted them to him.

The *Steipler Gaon* offered a similar analogy: A destitute woman who borrows an elegant ball gown for a wedding

recognition and God's insistence that he write וַיִּקְרָא is an example of the teaching that "One who seeks prestige will have it escape him, while one who flees from prestige will have it follow him."

While we understand why it is appropriate for honor to avoid those who pursue it, why is the person who truly does not want prestige subjected to it?

Honor comes to the person who truly does not want it,[3] observes *Sfas Emes,* because Honor itself wants to be properly used.

When the person who flees recognition is, in fact, given honor, he recognizes that it is really being given to God, Who granted him the ability and the wherewithal to achieve.[4]

R' Menachem Mendel of Kotzk remarked: "If a flea is chasing someone, does the person run away? Of course not. The flea is too insignificant.

"A person with proper vision would view honor the same way — as too insignificant a threat to justify his fleeing. When one runs away from recognition, he indicates that he holds honor in too high a regard. His punishment is that honor pursues him."

Maayana Shel Torah offers a homiletic interpretation of the diminished א: The word אַלֵף, *aleph,* means to teach or learn. One who wants to understand Torah must be prepared to diminish himself. Moses, the paragon of humility, was the person God chose to transmit His Torah to mankind.

Rambam teaches: "Torah is compared to water, as it says 'Let all who are thirsty come to water.' Just as water does not gather at the top of an incline, but only at the bottom, so too Torah cannot be found among the haughty and the arrogant, but only among the downtrodden and humble who wallow in the dust of the scholars" (*Hilchos Talmud Torah* 3:9).[5]

The commentators note that that whenever God spoke to Moses with the terms "to speak," "to say," or "to command," He first called his name twice, as an expression of endearment (see *Gur Aryeh*).

---

does not spend the evening bragging about "her" dress. She is well aware that it is not hers, and that she will soon be returning it. God endows man with abilities and talents, but they are all on loan.

Humility does not mean being oblivious to our unique talents and achievements; it means that we recognize that they are not of our own doing — and they therefore cannot justify any personal pride.

3. **Looking Back.** Someone once asked *R' Simchah Bunim of P'shis'cha,* "Our Sages taught that honor pursues the person who flees from it. Yet although I constantly flee honor, it does not seem to pursue me!" R' Simchah Bunim replied, "Apparently, when you flee honor you keep looking over your shoulder to check if it is pursuing you. The honor, which is right behind you, sees you turning and suspects that you suddenly intend to chase it. So it turns on its heel and flees."

4. **Embarrassing Honors.** *R' Yisrael of Rizhin* offered the proper perspective toward honor with a parable: There was a royal minister who frequently traveled throughout the kingdom, managing the king's many interests. Wherever he went, he received recognition and honor from officials and commonfolk alike.

This minister once had occasion to travel with the king, who usually stayed in his palace. The minister was given treatment befitting an emissary of the king — people accorded him him great honor, offered him tributes, and even bowed to him. The king, on the other hand, was generally unknown to the public. They assumed he was merely an officer sent to accompanying the minister and they generally ignored him.

How embarrassed the minister was to be accorded such honor while his master was ignored!

Similarly, it is only the King of the universe Who truly deserves honor. How embarrassing it is when we forget that the King is with us and take the honor for ourselves!

5. **The Mountain of Humility.** The Talmud (*Sotah* 5a) teaches that God chose Mount Sinai as the site for the Giving of the Torah because it was low, symbolizing humility.

Elsewhere (*Megillah* 29a, see *Maharsha*) the Talmud tells us that the larger mountains accused Sinai of usurping their role, asserting that the Torah should actually have been chosen. "Because of your loftiness," a Heavenly voice replied, "all of you are blemished compared to Sinai." Rav Ashi commented: This illustrates that one who is haughty is blemished."

Moses mirrored this quality of Sinai. Indeed, the *Mishnah* (*Avos* 1:1) teaches: "Moshe received the Torah from Sinai."

It was through the lesson of Sinai, the lesson of humility, that Moshe merited to receive the Torah (*Tiferes Yisrael*).

In practice, it would seem that calling a friend by name shows affection. This affords us frequent opportunity to fulfill the mitzvah of וְאָהַבְתָּ לְרֵעֲךָ כָּמוֹךָ, *you shall love your fellow as yourself* [*Leviticus* 19:18] (R' Yechezkel Sarna).

Taam V'Daas questions why the Torah does not explicitly state Who called to *Moses,* or what He said when He called to him.

He suggests that before God would address Moses, he would experience an intense desire to cleave to God. This was the affectionate "calling" that prepared the mortal Moses to hear the Divine word of God. This indirect "calling" was God's expression that "I love you, and want you to be fit to hear My words."[6]

Every Jew, at times, experiences this expression of Divine love, the sense that the Divine Presence is immanent, inspiring us to draw ourselves closer.

One might suddenly sense a special connection with God during prayer, and his words take on added meaning, or a person may suddenly be struck by the futility of his daily preoccupations and feel the impetus to refocus his life.

One never knows when they will come, but these experiences are God calling to man without words. Man must respond by taking advantage of the inspiration to improve himself and rededicate himself to God's service.[7], [8]

אָדָם כִּי יַקְרִיב מִכֶּם קָרְבָּן לַה׳
When a man among you brings an offering to Hashem (ibid. 2).

The literal translation of this phrase is *A man who brings, from among you, an offering to Hashem.* The unique choice of phrasing teaches that when

---

6. **Repetitive Affinity.** The Midrash teaches that when God repeats a person's name twice, it is a sign of particular affinity. *Simchas Aharon* explains: When someone calls his friend by name, it serves to attract the other person's attention. The reason he repeats the name is that he likes the other person so much, he simply enjoys saying his name.

By repeating Moses' name, God was sending a message that He loved Moses so much that He enjoyed just saying, "Moses."

Alternatively, the second time He called Moses' name He was saying, "My words are directed especially to you" (R' Nosson Geisler).

7. **Concretization.** The verse in *Song of Songs* (2:7) reads הִשְׁבַּעְתִּי אֶתְכֶם . . . אִם תָּעִירוּ וְאִם תְּעוֹרְרוּ אֶת הָאַהֲבָה עַד שֶׁתֶּחְפָּץ, *I have abjured you . . . should you wake or rouse the love until it pleases. Ramban* (*Emunah U'Vitachon*) interprets the word שֶׁתֶּחְפָּץ as related to the word חֵפֶץ, *object.* We are cautioned not to let inspiration pass without making positive changes. We must objectify the experience and translate it into action.

8. **Knowledge Without Wisdom.** The Sages teach that had Moses entered the Sanctuary without being summoned, he would have been classified as a Torah scholar who has no דַּעַת (lit. intelligence). Such a scholar is characterized as being inferior to an animal carcass (*Yalkut Shimoni*).

דַּעַת has two opposite implications. On the one hand, it implies connection — וְהָאָדָם יָדַע אֶת חַוָּה אִשְׁתּוֹ, *Now the man had known his wife Eve* (*Genesis* 4:1). On the other hand, it connotes the wisdom to separate — "Why was *Havdalah* (the additional prayer recited at the end of the Sabbath and festivals to separate between these holy days and the weekdays) inserted into the blessing in *Shemoneh Esrei* where we ask for intelligence? Because without דַּעַת, *wisdom,* one cannot know how to distinguish (between the sacred and the mundane)" (*Yerushalmi Berachos* 5:2).

When one has דַּעַת, he can discern when he should draw close and when he should stay away. One who lacks the sensitivity to refrain from entering a place uninvited lacks דַּעַת (R' Yitzchak Hutner).

Why is a scholar without דַּעַת worse than an animal carcass?

One is permitted to write *mezuzos* or *tefillin* on parchment made from the skin of an unslaughtered animal, so long as it is of a kosher species. The words of Torah can sanctify the skin even of a carcass.

The scholar who lacks דַּעַת has been exposed to Torah. Yet the Torah did not succeed in elevating him and imbuing him with fear of God. Thus, a carcass is better — more susceptible to spirituality — than he is (*Maayana Shel Torah*).

What is true דַּעַת? In response to *maskilim* who sought to interpret דַּעַת as secular knowledge rather than fear of Hashem, *Noda BiYehudah* cited our Midrash and explained it as follows: A scholar who lacks fear of Heaven still projects the air of a true Torah personality. As a result, people follow him, unaware of the spiritual threat he poses. The putrid odor of a carcass, on the other hand, announces that it is rotten, and cautions people to stay away.

a person wants to come close to Hashem (קָרְבָּן relates to the word קָרַב, *to approach*), he must first bring an offering מִכֶּם, *of himself.* Let him sacrifice the animal within him, the evil inclination (*R' Schneur Zalman of Liadi*).[9]

The Talmud (*Chullin* 13b) derives from the word אָדָם, *a man*, that any man, even a non-Jew, may bring a voluntary offering to the Temple. As it sets out to teach the laws of offerings, the Torah makes it clear that all who feel the need to turn to God may bring a voluntary offering. In the words of *Isaiah* (56:7): *For My House will be called a house of prayer for all the nations* (*R' S.R. Hirsch*).

Bringing an offering demands humility — *a broken spirit is an offering to God* (*Psalms* 51:19). One who views himself as superior to others cannot really bring a proper offering. *Mei HaShiloach* suggests that this is the lesson of our verse: *When a man among you* — when a person does not consider himself above others — he can *bring an offering to Hashem.* [10], [11]

מִן הַבָּקָר וּמִן הַצֹּאן תַּקְרִיבוּ אֶת קָרְבַּנְכֶם
from the cattle or from the flock shall you bring your offering (ibid.).

One can learn from the cattle and flock how to offer himself to God. A regular animal is deemed an offering for God, because a Jew simply designated it as such. Similarly, if a Jew sincerely says of himself, "From now on I will be holy.

Whatever happened in the past is over, and now I am dedicating myself to Hashem," he has elevated himself and made himself worthy of Hashem, which is the greatest of spiritual achievements (*Tiferes Shlomo*).

Shem MiShmuel notes that *cattle* is symbolic of arrogance and strength, while *flock* (sheep) symbolizes meekness and humility.

A person must use both of these traits to succeed. One must be proud and unintimidated by those who ridicule his service of God. This kind of arrogance enables one to do what is right, even if it is unpopular. Humility, on the other hand, allows one to submit to the will of God.

We must bring offerings from *the cattle* and *the flock.* We must properly employ each one's characteristics in our service of God.[12]

Midrash Tanchuma tells us that the verse's use of the word אָדָם implies one who sins should take a lesson from Adam, who also sinned, and he should therefore bring an offering.

What is the comparison with Adam supposed to teach the sinner?

An offering is supposed to bring us to truly regret having sinned, and lead us to repent.

By studying the sin of Adam one realizes the destructive impact of sin. Adam sinned once — and as a result he brought the curses of hard labor and death to the world. The full impact of that sin is beyond our ken.

---

9. **Misplaced Self-Sacrifice.** People often sacrifice their lives for the ephemeral. Workaholics, for instance, forfeit family and spiritual pursuits in their effort to amass fortunes.

    The Torah teaches us that when a man offers מִכֶּם קָרְבָּן, *of himself a sacrifice,* let him be certain that it is לַה' *for Hashem,* and not for some worthless cause (*R' Y. Eiger*).

10. **"Me" Between Us.** *Yesod HaAvodah* sees this message reflected homiletically in the verse אָנֹכִי עֹמֵד בֵּין ה' וּבֵינֵיכֶם, *I was standing between Hashem and you* (*Deuteronomy* 5:5). It is the "I," the ego, that separates you from Hashem.

11. **Humble Conglomerate.** According to *R' Baruch of Medziboz*, the word אָדָם can be understood as an acronym that alludes to the humility which must underlie every true offering. These people expressed their true humility: Abraham (אַבְרָהָם) said, *I am but dust and ash* (*Genesis* 18:27); King David (דָּוִד) stated, *I am but a worm, not a man* (*Psalms* 22:7); and Moses (מֹשֶׁה), the humblest of men, saw himself as totally insignificant, *for what are we?* (*Exodus* 16:8).

12. **Appropriate Pocket.** *R' Simchah Bunim of P'shis'cha* said: "Every Jew must have two pockets, each with a slip of paper inside. In one pocket he must carry the verse *I am but dust and ash* (*Genesis* 18:27); in the other, the teaching of the Sages, 'One must say the world was created on my behalf' (*Mishnah Sanhedrin* 4:5). The art of life is knowing when to reach into which pocket."

The Midrash teaches us to recognize the gravity of sin, and the scope of its damage. This will lead us to complete repentance.

According to *Taam V'Daas*, the broad impact of sin is alluded to in our verse. The verse begins in the singular, *when a man* (אָדָם) *among you*, yet it concludes in the plural *shall you bring* (תַּקְרִיבוּ) *your offering*. One man sins, but his act affects everyone.

The Sages compare a sinner to a person drilling a hole in a boat. Although he may be making the hole in his own cabin, his actions will sink the entire ship.

When an individual sins, every Jew is affected. When he brings an offering, it atones for him and undoes the impact he had on others. Thus *when a man among you* brings an offering, all of you are elevated.

אֶל פֶּתַח אֹהֶל מוֹעֵד יַקְרִיב אֹתוֹ לִרְצֹנוֹ לִפְנֵי ה׳

he shall bring it to the entrance of the Tent of Meeting, voluntarily, before Hashem (ibid. 3).

Rashi, citing *Sifre*, notes that the words *he shall bring it* indicate that we compel him to bring the offering, while the word *voluntarily* seems to preclude such coercion. *Sifre* explains that "we force him until he is willing."

Many explanations have been offered for this enigmatic ruling (see *Rambam Hilchos, Geirushin* 2:20).

The *Chasam Sofer* offers the following interpretation: A Jew who lives far from Jerusalem, and spends his days working in the fields and tending to his livestock can lose his reverence for spiritual matters. Such a Jew may view spending his day studying Torah and serving God as a terrible punishment. However, when this Jew arrives in Jerusalem, the most beautiful city in the Land, and witnesses how people live happily, even as their lives are focused on Torah and *mitzvos*, his perspective will change. Uplifted by the majesty of the Temple service, caught up in the spirit of sanctity that permeates the air, he will change. He will want to be part of that way of life — and he will voluntarily bring his offering. Initially, *he shall* be forced to *bring it to the entrance of the Tent of Meeting*. Once there, however, he will offer it *voluntarily, before Hashem*. [13]

When a Jew truly desires to bear the yoke of Heaven, he is granted Divine assistance to overcome obstacles, and he is even granted situations where he has no choice but to do what is proper.

Although these circumstances were brought about by God, they were the result of the person's own desire and commitment. In these cases, the coercion *he shall bring it* is really an expression of his having *voluntarily* chosen to be *before Hashem* (*Sfas Emes*).[14]

When the Jews expressed fear of Heaven upon hearing God say the first two of the Ten Commandments, God told Moses, *Who can assure that this heart should remain theirs to fear Me and observe all My commandments* (*Deuteronomy* 5:26). The Sages (*Avodah Zarah* 5a) comment, "They should have said, 'You assure it.' "

The *Chazon Ish* explains: "If man prays that God draw him close and the prayer is accepted, the result is considered to be a result of the person's free choice (see, however, *Maharsha, Berachos* 10a). This is what the Talmud means, 'They should have said, "You assure it," for that would have allowed Him to draw us closer.' "

---

13. **Opportunities for Spiritual Growth.** When considering where to settle, families must consider not only employment opportunities, but also whether the place they are planning to move to will inspire them to grow in *Yiddishkeit*.

Jobs come and go, but over dedication to Torah and *mitzvos* is forever.

We may have to force ourselves to come to the Tent of Meeting, a vibrant Torah community, so that we will willingly bring our offering before Hashem.

14. **Consensual Coercion.** This is the very process that took place at Sinai. The Sages teach that the verse וַיִּתְיַצְּבוּ בְּתַחְתִּית הָהָר, *And they stood at the bottom* (lit. under) *of the mountain* (*Exodus* 19:17), tells us that God held Mount Sinai over the heads of the Jews and said, "If you accept the Torah, fine, and if not, your burial place will be here" (*Shabbos* 88a). The word וַיִּתְיַצְּבוּ literally means *they presented themselves* under the mountain. The Jewish people willingly gave God the right to force them to follow Torah (*Maskil L'Shlomo*).

וְהִקְרִיבוּ בְּנֵי אַהֲרֹן הַכֹּהֲנִים אֶת הַדָּם וְזָרְקוּ אֶת הַדָּם עַל הַמִּזְבֵּחַ
the sons of Aaron, the Kohanim, shall bring the blood and throw the blood on the Altar (ibid. 5).

Later, in verses 8-9, the Torah commands the Kohanim to place the fats on the Altar as well. Why did the Torah command that the blood and fat be offered on the Altar?

Glilei Zahav suggests a homiletic rendering: People can be warm and excited about things, or they can be cold and casual. Excitement should be used for Torah study, *mitzvos* and helping others. Coldness and disinterest are appropriate responses to temptation to sin. As humans, however, we sometimes pour all our passion into sin while we remain untouched by opportunities to perform *mitzvos*.

We therefore place both the blood — symbolic of heat and passion — and the fat — emblematic of that which weighs us down and makes us lazy — on the Altar. We ask for atonement for misappropriating both of these characteristics.[15]

וְהִקְטִיר הַכֹּהֵן אֶת הַכֹּל הַמִּזְבֵּחָה
the Kohen shall cause it all to go up in smoke on the Altar (ibid. 9).

Unlike the *chatas* and *asham* (the sin-offerings) or the *olah*, the elevation- or burnt-offering is burnt on the Altar in its entirety.

The *olah* is brought to atone for one's inappropri-ate thoughts and emotions, while the *chatas* and the *asham* atone for a person's sinful acts.

No one's actions can always be perfect for "there is no righteous man in the land that does good without sinning" (*Ecclesiastes* 7:20). However, one's will must always be totally dedicated to God. A Jew must always feel, "I want only to do God's will, if I only could." Thus the *olah*, representing our thoughts, are burnt on the Altar in its entirety (*Tzvi LiYisrael*).

אִשֵּׁה רֵיחַ נִיחֹחַ לַה׳
a fire-offering, a satisfying aroma to Hashem (ibid.).

God does not need our offerings; He neither eats nor drinks. It is "the fire" of the mitzvah, — the excitement and joy with which we imbue it — that causes the satisfying aroma to Hashem. (*R' Chaim Chaikel of Amdur*, cited in *Nesivos Shalom*).

Chidushei HaRim explains the significance of the term "aroma to God"; certainly God does not smell.

A person can smell something long before he actually sees the item which produces the smell. The offering is only meaningful if it has an aroma — the precursor of a new beginning and the signal that proper behavior will follow.[16]

Background

The Torah now discusses an elevation-offering of fowl. Although such an offering is of less

---

15. **Getting It Backwards.** *Kiflayim L'Tushia* tells a parable: One morning a businessman went to the *beis midrash* to pray, recite *Psalms* and study Torah. While he was gone, a good customer came to his home to make a sizable purchase. Since his wife was unable to help the man, he took his business elsewhere. When the businessman returned home, he was extremely upset. "If this happens again, you must call me from the *beis midrash.*" Several weeks later, a tax collector came to their home while the husband was in the *beis midrash.* The woman ran quickly to call her husband. He rushed home, only to be surprised by his visitor. The husband turned to his wife and said, "When a good customer came you were in no rush to call me, yet now that the tax collector is here you summon me immediately?!"

When a mitzvah opportunity comes along, we are often in no rush to do the right thing. Yet, when sin beckons — and laziness would be the best response — we are suddenly energized. We confuse the blood and the fat, and they must therefore be brought on the Altar — a reminder to keep our priorities in order and a commitment to dedicate our traits to God.

16. **New Beginnings.** How are we to atone for our sins now that we can no longer bring offerings?

Mabit explains: While the Temple stood, God's Presence was revealed. In that environment, the effect of sin was so catastrophic that one could not achieve full atonement without bringing a sacrifice. Now, however, when God's Presence is hidden, the effect of sin is not as pronounced, and man is somewhat less culpable. Therefore, one can achieve atonement through repentance, heartfelt prayer and Divine service.

monetary value than an animal brought as an elevation-offering, it is no less pleasing to God. The Sages taught, "The one who give a lot and the one who gives little are equal, as long as the person bringing the offering focuses his heart toward Heaven" (*Menachos* 110a).

וְאִם מִן הָעוֹף עֹלָה קָרְבָּנוֹ לַה׳
If one's offering to Hashem is an elevation-offering of fowl (ibid. 14).

Earlier, an animal brought as an elevation-offering is called *an offering*, yet the fowl is referred to as an *offering to Hashem*. *Ohr HaChaim* explains: The fowl is brought by a poor person, who is generally embarrassed and humbled by the fact that he cannot afford an animal offering. Isaiah tells us that God says, *"I abide in exaltedness and holiness — but am with the contrite and lowly of spirit"* (Isaiah 57:15). It is with this humbled person that God resides.

Alshich adds that the meager offering of a poor person who comes before God with a broken heart is on a higher level than the larger offering of the wealthy. It is for this reason that fowl must be slaughtered by a Kohen, while animal offerings may be slaughtered even by a non-Kohen.

וְשִׁסַּע אֹתוֹ בִכְנָפָיו לֹא יַבְדִּיל
He shall split it — with its feathers — he need not sever it (ibid. 17).

Although the feathers cause a terrible odor when they burn, they are not removed before the bird is placed on the Altar. Offerings of fowl are brought by the indigent. Without the feathers the bird would look tiny and insignificant. God wants the feathers to remain, so that the person feels his offering is more substantial. "Better to endure the smell," says God, "and make the poor man feel good" (*Rashi*).

This lesson has practical implications. By nature, people enjoy the company of well-groomed wealthy people while they tend to avoid the unwashed and unkempt indigent.

God, however, wants us to emulate His ways. He wants us to show special regard to the needy person, even if he is undergroomed and unpleasant. He wants us to try to make this man feel good about himself. We must certainly never indicate in any way that we feel even slightly uncomfortable around him.

Furthermore, we are commanded to honor him, for the Divine Presence is with him. When we honor him, we honor God; when we avoid him we show disdain for someone whose offering adorns the Altar (*R' Yerucham Levovitz of Mir*).[17]

רֵיחַ נִיחֹחַ
A satisfying aroma (ibid.).

The Torah describes the small fowl offering and the large animal offering as having *a satisfying aroma*. As mentioned, the Sages learn from here that "The one who gives a lot and the one who gives a little are equal as long as the person bringing the offering focuses his heart toward Heaven" (*Menachos* 110a).[18]

---

17. **Less Successful Brothers.** It is easy for a person to treat a well-mannered and successful child respectfully. But it is so much more meaningful to a parent when someone treats even his difficult and unpleasant children with love. When we honor a wealthy Jew God is happy that his children care for one another. However, God's joy is even greater when we properly treat His less successful child.

There is a custom to set a special table at a wedding for the poor, or at least to allow them to pass among the guests to solicit contributions. In many communities, this custom has been discontinued. Some people give the poor person a large contribution on condition that they not go around collecting so as not to trouble the guests.

The burning of the feathers teaches that God loves the beggars, and is honored even by their offensive odor. We too should not push them away.

Imagine how a father feels if one of his sons makes a wedding and does not allow another of the siblings to attend. That is how God feels when we keep out the poor (*Zekan Aharon*).

18. **When Quantity Counts.** One who brings a smaller offering is equal to one who brings a larger one, explains *R' Noach of Lechovitch*, because to God there is no difference between a lot or a little. With regard to charity, however, intent itself is not sufficient. The more one gives, the more praiseworthy he is.

Turei Zahav asks: If both of them equally focus their hearts toward God, why is the greater action no more significant?

R' Simchah Bunim of P'shis'cha offered a parable: Two merchants from the same town traveled to a fair. Although they both left at the same time, one of them encountered some difficulties along the way and arrived a few days after his friend. When the second fellow arrived, the first one asked him, "What took so long?" Answered his friend, "What difference does it make? The main thing is that I arrived on time for the fair."

The goal of an offering is the closeness to God that it engenders. It is the focusing of one's heart Heavenward that is the goal; the sacrifice is merely a means. Whether one brings a large sacrifice or a small one is immaterial, as long as the objective is achieved.

She'aris Menachem views the Sages' comment as directed to the wealthy. One who is able to bring only a bird feels inadequate, and realizes he is dependent on God's mercy. The person who brings the large animal, however, might feel that he has done "so much for God" that God owes him forgiveness. The Sages therefore tell him that in order for his offering to be accepted he too must focus his heart toward Heaven.

Background

The meal-offering, brought by those who suffer extreme deprivation, is especially meaningful to God. He views it as if the pauper offered his soul.

כָּל הַמִּנְחָה אֲשֶׁר תַּקְרִיבוּ לַה' לֹא תֵעָשֶׂה חָמֵץ כִּי כָל שְׂאֹר וְכָל דְּבַשׁ לֹא תַקְטִירוּ מִמֶּנּוּ אִשֶּׁה לַה'. קָרְבַּן רֵאשִׁית תַּקְרִיבוּ אֹתָם לַה'

Any meal-offering that you offer to Hashem shall not be prepared leavened, for you shall not cause to go up in smoke from any leaving or fruit-honey as a fire offering to Hashem. You shall offer them as a first-fruit offering to Hashem (2:11-12).

Chametz and leaven are symbols of arrogance. Honey which is extremely sweet represents the pursuit of sensual pleasures. Offerings to God may not be tainted by these two characteristics. One must not study Torah and fulfill *mitzvos* in order to gain fame and honor, nor should he do so in order to enjoy reward in this world.[19]

While this is the ideal, one who is setting out to truly serve God may motivate himself using these inducements. Indeed, the Sages tell us, "One may labor in Torah and *mitzvos* even not for their own sake, for he will ultimately come to do so for their own sake" (*Pesachim* 50b).

Thus the verse teaches, *you shall offer them as a first-fruit offering to Hashem* — when one is starting out, he may rely on these incentives (*Kli Yakar*).[20]

עַל כָּל קָרְבָּנְךָ תַּקְרִיב מֶלַח
on your every offering shall you offer salt (ibid. 13).

Why is salt acceptable while leaven and honey are not? It would seem that all three are

---

19. **Truth for Truth's Sake.** *Rambam* writes: "One who serves God out of love is involved with Torah and *mitzvos* and pursues wisdom not to achieve any goal in the world. He acts this way neither out of fear of punishment nor in order to attain the good life; rather, he practices what is true because it is true, and good will eventually come as a result." He continues: "One involved in Torah in order to receive reward or avoid punishment is doing so not for its own sake. The one who labors in it not out of fear or a desire for reward, but rather out of love for the Master of the world, is considered to be involved in it for its own sake (*Hilchos Teshuvah* 10:2, 10:5).

20. **Radical Departure.** *Rambam* (*Hilchos Deios* 2:2) teaches that in every trait, except humility, a person should not be extreme rather, he must seek to act in a balanced fashion. However, one who has gone to the bad extreme may have to temporarily behave in the other extreme in order to eventually arrive at the medium.

Divrei Shaul suggests that the verse alludes to this principle, by calling on us to refrain from offering leaven and honey — the extremes of sour and sweetness. The proper approach to God is in the middle. However, *you shall offer them as a first-fruit offering to Hashem.* One who is acting inappropriately and wishes to change himself may have to, at the outset, engage in extreme behavior. Only then will he achieve his goal of balance.

ingredients that enhance the product to which they are added.

She'aris Menachem explains: Leaven tends to cause everything around it to rise and expand indiscriminately. Likewise, honey imparts its own flavor into the food to which it is added.

Salt, on the other hand, has the ability to enhance the flavor of the food to which it was added. Used in proper measure, the salt's own taste is indistinguishable. It totally negates itself to help the food.

So while leaven and honey, which promote themselves, are prohibited, *on every offering shall you offer salt* — we add salt, which teaches to work only to help others. [21]

R' Uziel of Richival sees salt as a vital ingredient in our service of God. Food without salt is bland and unappetizing and *mitzvos* performed without emotion and spirit are bland and unappetizing to God.

The Sages taught that the term בְּרִית, *covenant,* is used with regard to both salt and to pain. Just as salt tenderizes meat, so pain spiritually tenderizes man. Added *R' Mendel of Rimanov:* Just as too much salt ruins food, too much pain spiritually cripples man.

---

21. **No Clones.** Sometimes, helping others is really a way of exercising power over them. One who invites a guest must be sure not to overwhelm him with attention. The *Mishnah (Avos* 1:2) teaches, "Treat the poor as members of your household." Be there to provide for them, without making them feel less at home than the members of your own family. A host must be like salt, bringing out the best in others without being overpowering.

Teachers, too, must seek to bring out the uniqueness of each student, rather than trying to recast the student in their own mold. *R' Yerucham Levovitz* once visited the *Alter of Slabodka.* They entered a room and carried on a heated debate that lasted hours. Someone listening on the outside heard the Alter, who was famed for the many unique students he produced, complained to R' Yerucham, "What is the big deal in [mass-] producing Cossacks?!"

פרשת צו ⊱
Parashas Tzav

Background

Now that the Torah has taught us about various offerings and told us who brings them, the Torah addresses the Kohanim, and explains the procedure for the various sacrifices.

צַו אֶת אַהֲרֹן וְאֶת בָּנָיו לֵאמֹר
Command Aaron and his sons, saying (6:2).

The use of the more emphatic צַו, *command,* rather than אֱמֹר, *say,* or דַּבֵּר, *speak,* implies that this is a charge to the Kohanim of that time, and for future generations, to perform the sacrificial service with alacrity. This is especially true regarding commandments which entail a monetary loss, such as the elevation-offering discussed here (*Rashi*).

Many homiletic insights have been offered on this comment. *Sfas Emes* notes that the Jews in exile face constant harassment and frequent efforts to preclude them from doing business. Discriminatory taxes and restrictions often made it extremely difficult for Jews to support their families. As the Jew is threatened to be overcome by these financial pressures, he needs ongoing reinforcement to maintain zeal in his service of God.

Chasam Sofer sees a special need for reinforcement because this mitzvah is constant — "for now and for generations." *Mitzvos* that are performed regularly are often done by rote. The Torah teaches that *the fire on the Altar shall be kept burning on it, it shall not be extinguished; and the Kohen shall kindle wood upon it every morning* (verse 5) — the *Kohanim* must keep their own "fire" for the mitzvah "burning." The Torah's use of צַו, *command,* highlights the need for constant rededication to these ongoing *mitzvos.* [1], [2]

According to the Sages, the sacrificing of the *olah*-offering requires particular alacrity because it is a mitzvah which involves חֶסְרוֹן כִּיס, *a monetary loss.* All of the *olah* is burnt; the Kohen eats none of its meat. The Torah tells us that he must therefore make a special effort to

---

1. **A Declaration Born of Love.** *Chasam Sofer* explains one of our daily prayers in this light. "We are fortunate — how good is our portion, how pleasant our lot . . . we unify Your Name each day, continually, and proclaim twice with love, Hear O Israel . . . (*Daily Shacharis*).

   We rejoice and view our lot as good because although we recite the *Shema* twice daily, we do so out of love for Hashem, and not merely out of rote.

2. **Zealously Connected.** The word צַו can be understood as related to צַוְותָא, *connected.* Homiletically, the Torah is calling for us, in every generation, to zealously protect our unity. Maintaining unity takes constant reinforcement and effort. Often, unity requires that we spend money on others or forgo monetary gains. Thus צַו calls for alacrity, even at the price of monetary loss (*Simchas Aharon*).

maintain his enthusiasm.[3]

Literally, the words כִּיס חֶסְרוֹן can be translated as *lack of a cover*. Homiletically, *Chidushei HaRim* explains: Most of man's limbs come with a cover or restraining device. The eyelid covers the eye, preventing it from seeing that which it should not see; the mouth and lips keep the tongue from abusing the power of speech; the ears have earlobes that man can use to cover his ears and block out spiritually detrimental speech (see *Kesubos* 5a). The mind, however, has no cover. It is susceptible to spiritual harm — it can only be protected through a person's own exceptional zealousness.

The elevation-offering is brought to atone for sinful thoughts. This, the Torah stresses, *lacks a protective cover*, and warrants exceptional care.

Divrei Menachem offers a similar insight: The covers of other limbs can restrain the limb from becoming involved in sin. The opposite is true, however, of the heart, the seat of the emotions; its cover causes it to become spiritually insensitive: *You shall cut away the barrier of your heart and no longer stiffen your neck* (*Deuteronomy* 10:16). In the case of the heart, the כִּיס, *cover*, is a חֶסְרוֹן, *detriment,* and it is imperative that we remain constantly vigilant.

Hadranei Asher offers another perspective: When business is going well, people are quick to bring offerings, contribute to charitable causes and sup-port Torah study. When business slows, however, and people face monetary losses, the first cuts in expenditures are often their charitable contributions. The Torah teaches that the need for zealousness and reinforcement is especially important when confronted with monetary loss.[4], [5]

וְאֵשׁ הַמִּזְבֵּחַ תּוּקַד בּוֹ
and the fire of the Altar shall be kept aflame on it (ibid.).

The father of *Rabbi Yehudah Aryeh Leib Alter,* (*Sfas Emes*), died when he was a young child and he was raised by his grandfather, the *Chidushei HaRim*. The grandfather would test the young boy on his studies every week. When they reached this verse, the young Leibel explained, וְאֵשׁ הַמִּזְבֵּחַ תּוּקַד בּוֹ, "*and the fires of the Altar shall be kept aflame in him* — in the heart of the Kohen."

This is reflected in the statement of a *Mishnah* (*Avos* 5:7). We are told that among the ten miracles that occurred in the Temple, "The rains (גְּשָׁמִים) did not extinguish the fire on the Altar pyre."

The word גְּשָׁמִים may also be read as גַּשְׁמִים, *physical* or *mundane*. The fact that the Kohanim partook of the flesh of the offerings in no way diminished the fire of the Altar that burned in their hearts. On the contrary, even the physical was

---

3. **Crazy over Money.** Man's obsession with money and its hold over him is amazing. The Kohen Gadol was among the most spiritually elevated people in the nation. He was also the wealthiest of the Kohanim (see *Yoma* 18a). Despite this, the Torah here addresses "Aaron and his sons" — even the Kohen Gadol and his children — and tells them not to allow the fact that they will not eat of the *olah's* meat affect their service. Will a little bit of meat affect the saintly — and wealthy — Kohen Gadol?

Yes, says the Torah. Money's hold over man defies logic. Though a man of spirit and of means, one can be influenced by financial considerations (*R' Yechezkel Levenstein*).

4. **First In, First Out.** An insightful *rosh yeshivah* was once discussing marriage prospects with one of his students. The young man foolishly believed that the key to his remaining dedicated to Torah learning lies with his marrying the daughter of a wealthy man.

The *rosh yeshivah* offered the following advice: "While there are obviously exceptions to this, let me tell you what my experience has been. You can marry a girl from a wealthy home or marry a young woman whose father is not wealthy but who is a *talmid chacham*. As long as the financial climate is good, you may be better off with the rich man's daughter. However, if the financial climate deteriorates, you will likely be the first one laid off the rich man's payroll, but the last one off the *talmid chacham's*."

5. **No Cash Charity.** *R' Mendel of Kossov* interprets כִּיס חֶסְרוֹן as *a missing pocket*. As long as the Temple stood, a Jew could achieve atonement through offerings. Now that we no longer have a Temple, we can achieve atonement by giving charity and helping others who have less than we do. But what can we do on the Sabbath when our "pockets" are "missing" because we cannot give money to those less fortunate? We can invite needy guests to our Sabbath table to practice charity even on the Sabbath.

צַו, *command,* indicates a call for zealousness [in charity], even on the Sabbath when the "pocket" is missing.

elevated through the sanctified heat and warmth of that flame (*Sfas Emes*).[6], [7]

R' Chaim of Volozhin offers a similar comment on the *Mishnah*:

No matter what challenges a person may face, he must always be sure that the torch of his commitment to Torah burns strongly. People often claim that their need for sustenance stands in the way of their serious involvement in Torah study. The lesson of this miracle in the Temple is that one's physical needs and desires, his גֶשֶׁם, must never, God forbid, hamper his spiritual pursuits.

וְהוֹצִיא אֶת הַדֶּשֶׁן אֶל מִחוּץ לַמַּחֲנֶה אֶל מָקוֹם טָהוֹר

and he shall remove the ash to the outside of the camp to a pure place (ibid.).

Beis Yaakov offers the following interpretation: The spiritual leaders of the nation, "the Kohen," must always attempt to raise the "ash," those

without spiritual achievement, and "place them near the Altar," giving them a connection to sanctity. Even if they "have left the camp," the leaders must make sure to provide them with "a pure place." We must never believe that a Jew's spiritual embers are completely extinguished. We must provide them with an environment that will help them come alive.[8], [9]

אֵשׁ תָּמִיד תּוּקַד עַל הַמִּזְבֵּחַ לֹא תִכְבֶּה

The fire on the Altar shall be kept burning on it, it shall not be extinguished (ibid. 6).

The extraordinary yearning for God that burns intensely in the heart of a Jew may never be extinguished. If one who extinguishes even a single coal on the Altar transgresses a Torah injunction (see *Zevachim* 91b based on this verse), how much greater is the sin for extinguishing the embers that burn on the altar of one's soul!

---

6. **Head Above Water.** *R' Menachem Mendel of Kotzk* tells us that this verse instructs parents to train their children not to allow pedestrian concerns to extinguish their flame of love and fear of God.

The Talmud (*Kiddushin* 29a) states that a parent is obligated to teach his child a trade, so that the child will be able to support himself and his family, and he must teach him to swim. What is the connection between the two?

The Kotzker Rebbe explains that involvement in a trade can easily take over a person's life. To maintain proper balance, it is imperative for a person to take a cue from swimming. When one swims, his entire body is immersed in the water — but survival depends on his ability to keep his head *above* the water. The same is true in business. While one might throw himself totally in commerce, to spiritually survive he must keep his head out of it.

King David said (*Psalms* 128:2), "When you eat the labor of your hands you are praiseworthy, and all is well with you." "You are praiseworthy and all is well when your labor is limited to your hands," commented the Kotzker. "When your head and heart get involved in your business, all is not well."

7. **Private Property.** *Sfas Emes* notes that the fire of the soul *must burn in him*, inside, not to be displayed.

The Talmud (*Succah* 28a) teaches that Hillel had eighty students. The greatest of them was R' Yonasan ben Uziel, while the smallest was R' Yochanan ben Zakkai — who had mastered all of Torah and every area of knowledge. The Talmud relates that when R' Yonasan ben Uziel was learning Torah, any bird that passed over him would be consumed by fire.

"If that was the student," a *chassid* asked the *Sfas Emes*, "what happened when Hillel the Teacher studied?"

"When Hillel learned," explained the Sfas Emes, "the bird was *not* consumed, because Hillel was great enough to keep the fire inside his body, with no manifestation on the outside."

8. **Still Burning.** *R' Moshe Sternbuch* sees this verse as advice to those who allow — or place — their children in whereabouts where they are subject to spiritual harm, for whatever reason, asserting that their children will anyway not succeed in Torah.

Every Jewish child deserves to be educated in Torah and *mitzvos,* regardless of the child's shortcomings or disabilities. Even the burned ashes must be placed in a pure place — they, too, are an intrinsic part of a sanctified offering, the people of Israel.

9. **Before It's Too Late.** *Marginisa D'Rebbi Meir* interprets the verse as a call to repentance.

A person must remember that he will not live forever. When his time comes, *He shall remove his* [regular] *garments and don other garments* [shrouds] *and he shall remove the ash* [his body with the fire of the soul removed] *to the outside of the camp* [the cemetery]. The soul, however, will go *to a pure place,* i.e., before God, to give a reckoning of what man did with his life.

The Talmud (Yoma 21b) teaches that although a Heavenly fire descends upon the Altar, we must add wood to the Altar each day to provide the fire on our own.

This bears a lesson for us in our own lives. It is not enough to rely on the natural "fire" for spirituality that burns within our souls. We must add to that flame by studying Torah, performing *mitzvos* and practicing kindness. This will enable us to rise ever higher (*R' Avraham of Boisk*).

Talmud Yerushalmi (*Yoma* 4:6) teaches that even when the Jewish people dismantled the Tabernacle and traveled, the fire on the Altar continued to burn.

HaDerash V'Halyun offers a metaphorical explanation:

When one is at home, his family and friends, who are observant, help to keep him from straying from the path of Torah. The force of habit and the fact that he is being seen by those he loves helps insure that he lives his life properly. When one is on the road, however, stripped of societal and cultural restraints, he has a greater chance of lapsing in his observance.

King David alludes to this when he says *Praiseworthy is each person who fears God, who walks in His ways* (*Psalms* 128:1). One who fears God even when traveling on his way is praiseworthy, for he is truly God fearing. The Torah teaches us that a *constant* fire must burn on the Altar of the Tabernacle — and within each of us. It must never be extinguished, not when encamped at home or even when traveling.[10], [11]

Zohar explains the *constant fires* as referring to the special power of Torah study. While sin can extinguish the merit of a mitzvah, the merit of Torah study is eternal.

For a mitzvah is a candle and Torah is light (*Proverbs* 6:23). *The candle of God is the soul of man* (ibid. 20:27). One who extinguishes the mitzvah candle by sinning temporarily extinguishes his own candle, and plunges himself into spiritual darkness. Torah, however, is an everlasting light which darkness can never vanquish.

מִצוֹת תֵּאָכֵל בְּמָקוֹם קָדֹשׁ
*it shall be eaten unleavened
in a holy place* (ibid. 9).

R' *Chaim Meir of Vizhnitz* sees this verse as an allusion to the matzos we eat on Pesach. We must make sure that those matzos are eaten in a holy place. Where is that holy place? In a mouth that is free of forbidden talk and does not indulge in gluttonous eating.

Many preface the daily *Pesukei D'Zimrah* praises of God with the declaration: "I now prepare my mouth to thank laud, and praise my Creator."

Just as one who designates an item for the Temple treasury may not use it for personal use — and certainly not for profane purposes — so we express our intent to sanctify our mouths, dedicating them only to use as God sees fit (*Simchas Aharon*).

לֹא תֵאָפֶה חָמֵץ
It shall not be baked leavened (ibid. 10).

Leaven is a metaphor for the evil inclination. Just as leaven causes dough to rise, so the evil inclination inflates one's ego, to the point that one does not feel beholden to God. An ingredient symbolic of an impediment to spiritual

---

10. **Protecting the Fire.** How did the Jews make sure that the fire was not extinguished as they traveled? The *Yerushalmi* explains that they constructed a copper hood to cover the fire and allow it to continue burning.

R' M. Rotenberg sees in this a description of how the Jews have survived the travels and the challenges of the exile. Wherever Torah-true Jews have gone, they have created mechanisms, institutions and structures to cover them, to keep them apart, to ensure that the fire of Torah not be extinguished. Where those coverings were breached, the fire was extinguished. Reformers of all types, from the Sadducees to our own times, have undermined the commitment of their adherents — and caused a loss of Jewish identity — by foolishly attempting to keep the fire without any protective cover.

11. **Completely at Home.** *Meiri* offers a converse approach in his novel interpretation of the *Mishnah* "do not judge your fellow until you have reached his place" (*Avos* 2:5). Do not judge someone when he is away from his city, because people sometimes act more piously when they are among strangers, trying to make a positive impression. If you want to know what someone is *really* like, *do not judge your fellow until you have reached his place* of residence; there, his guard is down and he will behave naturally, showing his true character.

growth has no place in the sacrificial service.

Why, then, do the two breads offered on Shavuos contain leaven?

Kli Yakar explains: When Moses went up to Heaven to be taught the Torah, the angels protested. "Why give the Torah to a mortal? Why not keep it here, in Heaven?" they asked. God told Moses to reply, and Moses said, "Do you have an evil inclination which tempts you to sin? You do not need the Torah; we mortals do!" (see *Shabbos* 88b-89a).

On Shavuos, the day we received the Torah, we acknowledge the existence of the evil inclination, as represented by the leaven.

קֹדֶשׁ קָדָשִׁים הוּא כַּחַטָּאת וְכָאָשָׁם

it is most holy like the sin-offering and like the guilt-offering (ibid.).

A meal-offering is considered קֹדֶשׁ קָדָשִׁים, *most holy,* even when it is brought voluntarily. A voluntary peace-offering, however, is considered קָדָשִׁים קַלִּים, of *lesser holiness.* Why the difference? Furthermore, why does the Torah choose the sin and guilt offerings as examples of most holy sacrifices, rather than an elevation-offering?

The meal-offering is typically brought by a poor person who cannot afford a more expensive sacrifice. He feels inadequate, and he comes before God humbly and with contrition. His meal-offering is therefore most holy.

This type of offering is comparable to a sin- or guilt-offering, which are brought to atone for sin. These offerings are most holy because, unlike a person who was always righteous, the penitent has struggled to reconnect with God. "Even the completely righteous cannot stand where the penitent stands" [*Sanhedrin* 99a] (based on *Kli Yakar* and *Abarbanel*).[12]

עֲשִׂירִת הָאֵפָה סֹלֶת מִנְחָה תָּמִיד

a tenth-ephah of fine flour as a continual meal-offering (ibid. 13).

A regular Kohen offers this as an initiation rite, the first time he serves. The Kohen Gadol must offer this each day.

The elevated status of the Kohen Gadol requires that he live each day with a sense of freshness, as if he were performing his duties for the first time (*Ohr HaNefesh*).

Abarbanel suggests that the Kohen Gadol brings this special meal-offering every day because he is the representative of the Jewish people. For him to achieve atonement for the people, he himself must be free of sin. Since no man is totally without sin (see *Ecclesiastes* 7:20), the Kohen Gadol is enjoined to achieve personal atonement by means of his daily offering.

בִּמְקוֹם אֲשֶׁר תִּשָּׁחֵט הָעֹלָה תִּשָּׁחֵט הַחַטָּאת

in the place where the elevation-offering is slaughtered shall the sin-offering be slaughtered (ibid. 18).

The comparison of the elevation-offering to the sin-offering encourages the penitent. "Do not be depressed by the fact that you have sinned," says the Torah. "Now that you have repented, you are as worthy as the righteous person who brings an elevation-offering." As the *Rambam* (*Hilchos Teshuvah* 7:4) teaches, "Let the penitent not think that he is far from the level of the righteous as a result of his sins. This is not so. Rather, he is as beloved and desirable before Hashem as if he had never sinned.[13] Not only this, but later their reward is greater, since, after having experienced sin, they were able to keep away from it and overcome their

---

12. **Spiritual Overconfidence.** The Sages contrast the *completely* righteous to those who repent. *R' Simchah Bunim of P'shis'cha* explains why a penitent is considered greater. One who is *completely* righteous is certain of his spiritual perfection. While his behavior is fine, he is stagnant. The penitent, however, is remorseful over his failures toward God. He constantly strives to elevate himself above his failings, and so he scales the greatest heights.

13. **Resurrective Dew.** The Midrash (*Bereishis Rabbah* 39:8) relates that Abraham was concerned about the sins he had committed before he discovered the true God. When he expressed his fears to Hashem, He replied, "לְךָ טַל יַלְדֻתֶיךָ", *To you is the dew of your youth* (Psalms 110:3). Just as dew evaporates and goes upward, so your youthful sins will dissipate."

Why is dew the metaphor for old sins?

The Talmud (*Taanis* 4a) teaches that the Jewish people asked God to shower them with spirituality like rain. God

evil desire. The Sages said that the completely righteous cannot stand where the penitents stand. This is because their spiritual level is greater than that of people who never sinned, since they conquer their evil inclination to a greater degree."

Noam Elimelech sees this parallel as a lesson to the sinner. One who physically does a transgression usually knows that God is aware of his misdeed. A person who sins in thought, however, may delude himself into thinking that not even God is aware of his misdeed. The Torah tells him to slaughter the elevation-offering — for improper thoughts — in the same place as the sin-offering. Realize that God sees our thoughts and emotions just as clearly as he sees our actions.

Alternatively, the equation tells a person who transgressed by doing an act not to fool himself into thinking that only his body sinned; his thoughts and emotions are still pure. The verse tells us that thought and action go together — a pure heart leads to proper behavior (*R' Feivel Schlesinger* based on *Shem MiShmuel*).

The Talmud teaches that the *Shemoneh Esrei* prayer is recited silently so as not to embarrass those who confess their sins while praying (*Sotah* 32b). This halachah is derived from the Torah's directive that the sin and elevation-offerings are slaughtered in the same place. Just as it was impossible for someone watching the slaughtering of an animal to discern whether it is a sin-offering or an elevation-offering, so too, in prayer, we must not be able to identify who is confessing his sins.[14]

וְזֹאת תּוֹרַת הָאָשָׁם קֹדֶשׁ קָדָשִׁים הוּא
This is the teaching of the guilt-offering; it is most holy (7:1).

The Torah describes the Red Heifer as one *which is without blemish and upon which a yoke has not come* (*Numbers* 19:2). The *Maggid of Kozhnitz* comments that one who views himself as being *without blemish* — a person who thinks himself perfect — is a person *upon which a yoke has not come*, who has yet to assume the yoke of Heaven.

Based on this, *Atzei Levonah* homiletically interprets our verse: *This is the Torah* — the mind-set — *of the* [one who must bring a] *guilt-offering*. What caused him to sin? *It is most holy* — his own sanctimoniousness.[15]

R' Yehoshua of Kutna offered a similar insight on the Talmudic statement that "even the emptiest of Jews is as full of *mitzvos* as a pomegranate is of seeds" (*Berachos* 57a).

While a person who is righteous senses that he has fallen short in his service of God, the "empty people" feel that they are full of mitzvos as a pomegranate is of seeds.

---

replied that rain is not always a positive force. Rather, He would be like dew for them, because dew is always beneficial. *I shall be like dew to Israel* (*Hosea* 14:6).

Explains *Avnei Nezer*: Rain showers the earth, providing sustenance. Dew, on the other hand, causes the earth to release its own nutrients. Dew is the catalyst for the earth to achieve its potential. The Jews asked God to grace them with lofty levels of spirituality. God replied that He would be like dew. He would help them develop their own spiritual potential, so that they could become "all that they could be."

Simchas Aharon adds that sin, too, can function like dew. Repentance for sin causes us to reach deeply into our souls to reconnect with God. On the journey back from sin, we must overcome spiritual obstacles, an exercise that leaves us spiritually stronger and healthier.

14. **Ensuring Comfort.** Although he knew the words of *Kiddush* by heart, the *Taz* always recited it from a *siddur*. He did this so that others there, who had not memorized the text, would feel comfortable looking in as well.

15. **Healthy Suspicion.** The Talmud teaches, "One should *always* study Torah even if it is not for its own sake, because through studying it not for its own sake will lead to studying it for its own sake" (*Pesachim* 50b).

How can one *always* study for the wrong reasons yet end up studying for the right reasons?!

The answer is that the one who constantly suspects that his motives are impure will seek to refine his commitment and will come to study with the purest of motives.

This is the Torah — the proper way to study Torah is with *a guilt-offering*, scrutinizing one's purity of heart. One who does so will become *most holy* (*Atzei Levonah*).

וְכָל מִנְחָה בְלוּלָה בַשֶּׁמֶן וַחֲרֵבָה לְכָל בְּנֵי אַהֲרֹן תִּהְיֶה אִישׁ כְּאָחִיו

And any meal-offering that is mixed with oil or that is dry, it shall belong to all the sons of Aaron, every man alike (ibid. 10).

Voluntary meal-offerings, which contain oil, and dry meal-offerings, which come for a sin, are equally divided among the Kohanim (*Rashi*). *Tiferes Shlomo* taught that the sons of Aaron, the leaders of the nation, must have warmth for all types of Jews. Those who are completely loyal to Torah, symbolized by the voluntary offering mixed with oil, and the sinners, symbolized by the dry offering, must be treated as brothers.

אִם עַל תּוֹדָה יַקְרִיבֶנּוּ

If he shall offer it for a thanksgiving-offering (ibid. 12).

Why is the thanksgiving-offering mentioned here, among the offerings of the Kohanim, and not in *Parashas Vayikra,* where the other general offerings are described?

Chasam Sofer explains that most people bring thanksgiving-offerings only upon being miraculously saved from disaster. Kohanim, however, are more spiritually sensitive, and realize that we benefit from miracles daily. Their thanksgiving-offerings are brought to thank God for His ordinary, hidden, miracles.[16]

Since God does not want Jews to experience danger, He chose to mention the thanksgiving-offering among the sacrifices of the Kohanim.[17]

The Sages note that although other offerings will be discontinued during the Messianic age, the thanksgiving-offering will exist forever (*Midrash Tanchuma, Emor*).[18]

Maharal suggests an explanation based on a Midrash (*Devarim Rabbah* 2:1). "There are ten expressions of prayer, but Moses chose to pray with תַּחֲנוּנִים (supplication for an undeserved gift). This teaches us that no one has any legitimate claim on the Creator."

People may think that while we must thank God for the goodness he grants us now, what we will reeive in the Messianic era was earned by us. The fact is, however, that even if we did earn it, it was only God's grace that gave us the opportunity to do so. When all other offerings will be irrelevant, the thanksgiving-offering will remain.

The word הוֹדָאָה (or תּוֹדָה) has two connotations, *thanks* and *admission.* By nature, people want to be independent. When a person expresses gratitude, he is admitting that he had no choice but to be dependent on someone else.

This is not only true with regard to other people, but also in our relationship to God. Man's arrogance leads him to think *My strength and the might of my hand made me all this wealth!* (*Deuteronomy* 8:17). For man to admit that he needs God requires a degree of humility. When we thank

---

16. **Constant Miracles.** Generally, sacrifices of "lesser holiness" (קָדָשִׁים קַלִּים) are eaten for two days and the intervening night. The thanksgiving-offering is an exception; it may be eaten only the day it is offered and the following night. Why the difference?

Imrei Emes explains: The thanksgiving-offering is brought in response to a miracle. We all experience miracles daily, so how can we celebrate yesterday's miracle today, when today's miracle calls for an offering of its own?

17. **Thanks for Saving Me.** *Divrei Shaar Chaim* offers an interpretation of the Midrash, applying it to our own times as well. One who succeeds in avoiding even inadvertent sin, and therefore "discontinues" other offerings, has good reason to be thankful. The thanksgiving-offering expressed gratitude to God for having saved us from the need to bring a sin-offering.

18. **Ultimate Kindness.** The refrain כִּי לְעוֹלָם חַסְדּוֹ, *for His kindness endures forever,* appears 26 times in *Psalms* 136. The Talmud (*Pesachim* 118a) correlates those 26 times with the 26 generations that lived from Creation until the Torah was given, for during all those generations God sustained the world as an act of kindness. The apparent question is: And is the sustenance of the world after Sinai not a result of Divine kindness?!

R' Yitzchak Hutner explains that God's kindness before Sinai is different from His kindness since. Providing for another's needs is a wonderful act of charity. It pales, however, in comparison to the kindness involved in providing a person with the opportunity to earn his own living.

Until Sinai, God's kindness was a handout. When God gave us Torah and its *mitzvos,* though, He provided us with an opportunity to earn our right to exist. That is a much greater act of kindness for which we must thank Him.

God, we admit our own limitations.

These two meanings are both used in the *Modim* prayer. One admits *that* and he thanks *for*: "We *admit that* You are Hashem our God . . . We *thank You . . . for* our lives . . ."

Jews are called *Yehudim*, based on the verse that describes the naming of *Yehudah*, Judah: "*This time let me gratefully praise Hashem; therefore she called him Judah*" (*Genesis* 29:35). A Jew realizes that whatever God grants him is far more than he deserves, and willingly admits and thanks Him for everything (*R' Yitzchak Hutner*).

וְהַנּוֹתָר מִבְּשַׂר הַזָּבַח . . .
בָּאֵשׁ יִשָּׂרֵף . . . פִּגּוּל יִהְיֶה
What is left over from the flesh of the feast-offering shall be burned in the fire . . . it remained rejected (ibid. 17-18).

Both נוֹתָר, sacrificial meat that was not eaten within its allotted time period, and פִּגּוּל, an offering disqualified through specific improper intentions by the Kohen performing the blood service, cause the hands of a person who touches them to become *tamei* (ritually unclean). According to one opinion, this decree was enacted in order to prevent a Kohen from purposely thinking improper thoughts with an offering that belongs to someone he dislikes. The fact that he would have to immerse his hands if he did so might prevent him from disqualifying the offering (*Pesachim* 85a and *Rashi* ad loc.).

But will the need to wash his hands deter a Kohen whose hatred for another person is so intense that he has no compunctions about sinning against God and man in ruining a sacrifice?!

The answer is that laziness and the desire to avoid even small personal inconveniences can stop a person from committing severe and enticing crimes. A person may forgo the fulfillment of his desire simply to avoid troubling himself even a bit (*R' Avraham Grodzinsky of Slabodka*).

וְהַבָּשָׂר אֲשֶׁר יִגַּע בְּכָל טָמֵא לֹא יֵאָכֵל
The flesh that touches any contaminated thing may not be eaten (ibid. 19).

Why is it that when a contaminated object comes in contact with a pure object, the pure object gets defiled? Why can't the reverse be true?

R' Menachem Mendel of *Kotzk* explained: When an object is rendered impure, it is impure without a doubt. So it has the power to make something else impure. It is unclear, however, whether anything in this impure world can be confirmed to be 100 percent pure?[19]

זֶה הַדָּבָר אֲשֶׁר צִוָּה ה׳ לַעֲשׂוֹת
This is the thing that Hashem commanded to be done (8:5).

Moses does not specify which "thing" he speaks of. *Yechahein Pe'er* explains: In the previous verse, Moses was told, *Gather the entire assembly to the entrance of the Tent of Meeting*. *Rashi* notes that although the entire assembly consisted of millions of people, the small area was miraculously able to contain them.

The lesson to be learned is that when Jews lovingly unite there is enough room for everybody. With unity and love, there is always enough

---

19. **Penetrating Contact.** Word reached the *Baal HaTanya* that a young man who often came to see him had begun to keep company with *maskilim,* people who advocated the abandonment of Jewish observance and embraced secularization. The *Baal HaTanya* summoned the young man and explained the great dangers of this association. "Your contact with them may influence you to leave the proper path," he said.

"It is not so easy to influence me," the young man replied. "I'll prove it to you. I've spent much time with *chassidim,* yet I have not become a *chassid.*"

"Your comparison is flawed," the Rebbe retorted. "When something contaminated touches a pure item, it defiles it by contact. Nevertheless, when the Torah speaks of something affected by the meat of a sacrifice, the Torah says *Whatever touches its flesh becomes holy* (6:20). *Rashi* explains that touching here means absorption of the offering's taste. For sanctity to influence other objects, it must be absorbed. Contact alone is insufficient."

Concluded the *Baal HaTanya,* "You will not be influenced by the *chassidim* unless you absorb what they have to offer, but you are endangering your soul by mere contact with the *maskilim.*"

room, and even a small space can accommodate many.[20]

This is "*the thing*" God commanded Moses to be done. Let Jews always love each other, so that through their unity there will always be place for everyone.

---

20. **Room for Everybody.** One of the ten miracles that occurred in the Temple was that the people stood crowded together, yet there was ample space when they prostrated themselves (*Avos* 5:7). *Shelah, Ruach Chaim* and *R' Aharon of Karlin* all offer the following homiletical insight: When people "stand" tall, with pride and selfishness, they feel "crowded"; everyone seems to be in their way. However, when they prostrate themselves, acting humbly and bending to the needs of others, they find that there is ample room for everyone.

פרשת שמיני ‎&
Parashas Shemini

Background

During the seven-day inaugural period for the Tabernacle, Moses erected and disassembled the Tabernacle daily, and he served as the Kohen Gadol. Now it was time for the Tabernacle to be permanently established. The Torah describes the eighth day, when the Kohanim performed a special service initiatng their new roles as those eligible to serve in the Tabernacle, and, later, in the Temple.

וַיְהִי בַּיּוֹם הַשְּׁמִינִי
It was on the eighth day (9:1)

The Talmud (*Megillah* 10b) explains that the term וַיְהִי, *and it was,* indicates an unpleasant occurrence while וְהָיָה, *and it will be,* connotes a joyous happening.

The *Dubno Maggid* explains why the words are used in this way: הָיָה, *it was,* in past tense. By adding a ו to make וְהָיָה, it is transformed into future tense. When something brings us happiness, we hope that it will continue on into the future. On the other hand, יְהִי means *will be,* in the future tense. The added ו

makes וַיְהִי past tense. The prospect of an unhappy event makes us want to quickly move into the past.[1]

The Talmud (ibid.) also teaches that the day the Tabernacle was established was, for God, as joyous a day as the day that He created heaven and earth. Why then is the term וַיְהִי, expressing unpleasantness, used?

The following parable can help us understand:

A young man was in a terrible car accident. After hours of toil, medics succeeded in extricating the man from the wreckage, thankful that he was still alive. One of his legs was so mangled, however, that it had to be amputated. The man was later fitted with a prosthetic leg, and after months of rehabilitation, he was finally able to walk. Though he made a grand party to celebrate his recovery, his joy was dampened by the fact that his leg had been replaced by an artificial device.

When God created the world, the entire universe was to be His Sanctuary. As a result of Adam's sin, the world could no longer serve in that capacity.

2448 years later, when the Jewish nation accepted the Torah, at Sinai, the world was to be reinstated to its original state. However, as a result of the sin of the Golden Calf, this too was not to be.

---

1. **New Beginnings.** *R' Chaim Meir of Vizhnitz* comments that it is a general "eighth day" that denotes unhappiness.

There are seven days in a week. On the first six days, the Jew is engaged in the mundane, causing his soul's spiritual brilliance to become dulled and sullied. On the seventh day, the holy Sabbath, a Jew has the opportunity to cleanse and burnish his soul. On the Sabbath, the Jew can be granted a fresh start. Indeed, the letters of שַׁבָּת are the same as תָּשֻׁב, to repent. Thus, the next day is not *the eighth* day but rather the first day of a new cycle.

But for a Jew who does not take advantage of the purifying powers of the Sabbath, the day after Sabbath is simply a continuation of the previous week. It is an eighth day during which their soul unabatedly continues its corruption. It is truly וַיְהִי, a sad occasion, when a Jew experiences יוֹם הַשְּׁמִינִי, an eighth day, without the balm of the Sabbath.

Instead, God granted us the ability to create a miniature world, the Tabernacle, where His Presence would "reside."

On one hand, the day the Tabernacle was erected caused God to rejoice as on the day of Creation, for it was a Sanctuary for His Presence. But it was joy tinged with sadness, for the Tabernacle was only a replacement of the original intent (*Zekan Aharon*).

קָרָא מֹשֶׁה לְאַהֲרֹן וּלְבָנָיו וּלְזִקְנֵי יִשְׂרָאֵל
Moses summoned Aaron and his sons, and the elders of Israel (ibid.)

"R' Akiva says: The Jewish people are compared to a bird. Just as a bird cannot fly without wings, so the Jewish people are helpless without their elders" (*Vayikra Rabbah* 11:8).

The Midrash (*Bereishis Rabbah* 65:4) teaches that originally Isaac looked exactly like his father Abraham. Abraham asked God to make him look older, so that people would not confuse the two. He said, "Master of the world! When a man goes someplace with his son, people will not know which of them to accord honor. If the elderly are crowned with signs of age, people will know to respect them." God replied, "Your argument is correct, and I will begin with you." This is the meaning of the verse *Now Abraham was old . . . and Hashem blessed Abraham with everything* (Genesis 24:1).

Was it important to Abraham that people accord him honor? He was the one who would himself wash the feet of his guests! He was the one who personally made sure that all their needs were met! How are we to understand his seeking respect?

Kehillas Yitzchak explains that Abraham saw a danger in young and old being indistinguishable. The wisdom and life experience of older people gives them the ability to guide and advise with wisdom and reason. Young people lack this insight.

Abraham was afraid that if the young and the old looked alike, people might unwittingly seek counsel with the young. In order to ensure his progeny would seek guidance from the proper people, Abraham asked God to provide man with signs of age.

The Jewish people are like a bird. Just as a bird's ability to soar depends on its wings, the ability of each generation to successfully rise above its challenges depends on its elders offering guidance and direction.[2]

When the *Noda BiYehudah* passed away, the town elders of Prague met in order to decide upon a successor. *R' Yaakov Landau,* a son of the late Rav, recounted that before his father's demise, he had asked that his son *R' Shmuel* succeed him. One of the local *dayanim* (rabbinic judges), who had desired the position, said that he did not believe R' Yaakov.

R' Yaakov responded: "Even though the command regarding the offerings was relevant only to the Kohanim, Moses summoned the elders as well. *Rashi* states that he did this to make it clear that

---

2. **Generational Link.** In the *Shemoneh Esrei* prayer we ask that God show compassion to "the righteous, the devout, the elders . . . and on the remnant of the scholars of the Jewish people." Who is the "*remnant* of the scholars" that is not included in the first three categories?

R' J.B. Soloveitchik observes that the chain of tradition is viable only if every generation has bridge-figures who are remnants of an earlier time. These people are the living link between the past and the present; they are the "remnant of the scholars of the Jewish people." The significance in protecting these remnants goes beyond their simply being "righteous, devout, or elders." It lies in their being the remnants of an earlier generation.

The Talmud (*Megillah* 31b) states: R' Shimon ben Elazar says: "If old men advise you to demolish and young men advise you to build, demolish and do not build, because the demolishing of old men is really building." The demolishing of the elders is constructive and the building of youth is actually destructive.

The story of Rechavam, son of King Solomon, illustrates this point.

When Rechavam ascended his father's throne, the people petitioned him to repeal some of his father's more difficult decrees. Rechavam took counsel with the elders, who advised him to accede to the people's wishes. Afterward, however, he conferred with his own colleagues, who urged him to rule with an iron fist. Rechavam accepted their advice, and the people revolted. As a result, Jeroboam was able to establish the kingdom of Israel (see *I Kings* 12:1-17).

Parents must remember that they are there to guide their children. While the relationship between parent and child be infused with warmth, love and respect, it is a mistake for parents to think that they are their child's friend. If parents think they are merely friends, they deprive their children of elders who can provide guidance based on seniority and life experience.

God had commanded Aaron to serve as Kohen Gadol, and that he had not seized the office on his own.

"If they were not going to believe Aaron, however, why should they believe Moses?

"The answer is that Aaron had a vested interest in claiming that he was appointed Kohen Gadol. Moses, however, had no direct interest. If he wanted to lie, he would have said that God appointed *him* Kohen Gadol. When he spoke on behalf of his brother, they believed him.

"Had I been lying," concluded R' Yaakov, "I would have claimed that my father asked that *I* become Rav."

וְאֶל בְּנֵי יִשְׂרָאֵל תְּדַבֵּר לֵאמֹר
And to the Children of Israel speak as follows (ibid. 3).

The term דִּבּוּר indicates a harsh manner of speaking, while אֲמִירָה connotes soft words. Here the verse directs Moses to address the people with both hard (תְּדַבֵּר) and soft (לֵאמֹר) words.

Effective leadership calls for different approaches to different situations. While sometimes soothing talk is in place, there are other occasions when harsh words are called for (*Oznayim L'Torah*).[3]

וְאֶל בְּנֵי יִשְׂרָאֵל תְּדַבֵּר לֵאמֹר קְחוּ שְׂעִיר עִזִּים לְחַטָּאת
And to the Children of Israel speak as follow. Take a he-goat for a sin-offering . . . (ibid.)

Toras Kohanim tells us that the Jewish people were required to bring a more sizable offering than Aaron, for he sought forgiveness for the sin of the Golden Calf, while they needed atonement

for the sale of Joseph as well.

Meshech Chochmah explores the connection between the sale of Joseph and the sin of the Golden Calf.

When Joseph slandered his brothers to their father, the brothers complained. "If you want to rebuke us, tell us directly. We can handle constructive criticism," they claimed.

What took place at the time of the Golden Calf refuted this assertion. When Hur, son of Miriam, attempted to stop the Jewish people when they created the Golden Calf, they killed him in cold blood. This highlighted that they were unable to handle direct rebuke.

The brothers' justification for selling Joseph was disproven by the actions of their children. Now they needed atonement for both sins.[4]

וַיֹּאמֶר מֹשֶׁה זֶה הַדָּבָר אֲשֶׁר צִוָּה ה׳ תַּעֲשׂוּ וְיֵרָא אֲלֵיכֶם כְּבוֹד ה׳
Moses said: This is the thing that Hashem has commanded you to do; then the glory of Hashem will appear to you (ibid. 6).

While the Jews desired to build a Tabernacle so that God would rest His Presence in *it*, Hashem sought to rest His Presence in *us*. Thus Moses said, *This is the thing that Hashem has commanded you to do* — fulfill the *mitzvos* of the Torah — *then the glory of Hashem will appear to **you*** — you yourselves will become human tabernacles (*Chozeh of Lublin*).[5]

Toras Kohanim interprets this verse as Moses telling the Jews, "Remove the evil inclination from your hearts and the glory of Hashem will appear to you." To what was Moses referring?

---

3. **Tough Love.** While a teacher or rabbi should *seek* to have his students or congregants like him, he cannot be fully effective if he has a *need* for them to like him. A "leader" who needs to be liked is unable to lead — because he is unable to tell his "followers" things they may not want to hear. A sign of true love is the ability to tell a person what he *needs* to hear, even if he does not *want* to hear it.

4. **Rectifying Disunity.** *Simchas Aharon* sees the need to atone for the sale of Joseph as being related to the erection of the Tabernacle. According to *Ramban* (*Exodus* 25:1), the Tabernacle was a permanent expression of the Divine Presence which had been revealed at Sinai. There, the nation stood "as one man with one heart." This spirit of unity was reflected in everyone's contributing to the construction of the Tabernacle. When the Tabernacle was erected, there was a need to redress the sale of Joseph, a fundamental instance of Jewish disunity.

5. **Cardiac Arrest.** *R' M. Cohen* sees in this verse a repudiation of the philosophy that all that Judaism asks is an emotional and intellectual attachment to God, and that adherence to *mitzvos* is really unimportant. *This is the thing that Hashem commanded — do!* It is only through doing that *the glory of Hashem will appear to you.*

Ksav Sofer observes that the evil inclination first seduces man to sin, and then he convinces man to give up hope of repenting.

When, for the first seven days, the Heavenly fire did not descend upon the Altar, the Jewish people began to think that their efforts were for naught. "We thought that the Divine Presence would reside among us, indicating that God had forgiven us for the sin of the Golden Calf. In truth, He has not," they said.

Moses therefore told them: "Be rid of that evil inclination that sows despair and convinces man that he can not repent. God *will* forgive you! Then *the glory of Hashem will appear to you*, for His greatest glory is that He accepts sincere repentance."[6]

וַיֹּאמֶר מֹשֶׁה אֶל אַהֲרֹן קְרַב אֶל הַמִּזְבֵּחַ

Moses said to Aaron: Come near to the Altar (ibid. 7).

Rashi comments that Aaron was hesitant to approach the Altar, embarrassed by the role he had played in the sin of the Golden Calf. Moses told him, "Why are you hesitant? לְכָךְ נִבְחָרְתָּ — For this you were chosen!" Understood simply, לְכָךְ, *for this*, refers to the position of Kohen Gadol. The *Baal Shem Tov*, however, explains that Moses told Aaron that the reason that he was chosen to be Kohen Gadol was because *of this* — his hesitation and sense of unworthiness. *Sfas Emes* notes that a person must strike a delicate balance when approaching a mitzvah. On the one hand, he must think, "Am I, a mortal tainted with sin, worthy of performing God's will?" However, this feeling must never restrain the person from meeting his responsibilities. He should be heartened by the fact that God commanded *him* to do His will, and he must therefore step forward and joyously perform the mitzvah.

Properly utilized, humility and shame for our misdeeds do not cause despondence, nor do they prevent a person from doing what he should. On the contrary, the recognition of one's inadequacy as he approaches to serve God engenders happiness and

---

6. **A Lost Cause.** *Rejoice, young man, in your childhood; let your heart cheer you in the days of your youth; follow the path of your heart and the sight of your eyes — but be aware that for all these things God will call you to account* (*Ecclesiastes* 11:9). The opening of the verse seem to be the sweet-sounding seduction of the evil inclination: "Enjoy, be cheerful, follow your heart and your eyes!" The conclusion, however, seems to be the rejoinder of the good inclination, *be aware that for all these things God will call you to account.*

Not so, taught the *Dubno Maggid*. In fact, the entire verse is the message of the evil inclination. He illustrated his point with a parable.

A poor, hungry man wandered through the streets wondering how he would get his next meal. Suddenly, a well-dressed man approached him. "My dear sir, you look hungry. Come with me to the restaurant, and I will treat you to a meal," he offered. They sat down together and proceeded to enjoy a sumptuous dinner. Toward the end of the meal, the rich man excused himself and absconded. After a long wait, the owner of the restaurant came to the table and demanded payment. "I have no money," pleaded the poor man. "That scoundrel tricked me and left."

The restauranteur noticed a watch on the man's wrist. "Give me the watch as payment," he said. "If you come back and pay me, I'll return the watch." The poor man complied and left the restaurant, embarrassed and upset.

Several days later, the poor man encountered his benefactor. The poor man lost no time in venting his fury upon him. "How could you do such a thing to me?" he cried.

To appease him, the wealthy man offered to take him to the restaurant again, and to pay both the old and the new bills. But again the rich man pulled the same ruse, leaving the poor person with the bill. The proprietor came to request payment, and the poor man could do nothing but repeat his tale of woe.

"You know what?" said the proprietor. "You may as well continue to eat and enjoy, since you will never succeed in redeeming your watch anyway."

"This is how the evil persuader works," explained the *Dubno Maggid*, "First he seduces and encourages us to enjoy the good life, since we live but once. We surrender our souls in payment to this master manipulator, much as the poor man gave his watch. But when we contemplate repentance, he tells us, 'You are beyond hope. *Be aware that for all these things God will call you to account* — you will never achieve repentance. You might as well continue your hedonistic ways.'

This is why the *Mishnah* cautions, *Do not despair of retribution* (*Avos* 1:7). No matter how deeply you have fallen into sin, you can still repent and avoid the punishment."

joy at the opportunity to, despite our shortcomings, be servants of the King of kings.

Divrei Shaarei Chaim and *Minchah Belulah* quote a Midrash (cited in *Ramban*) that when Aaron looked at the Altar, he conjured up an image of a calf. He lived, *my sin is constantly before me* (*Psalms* 51:5), always embarrassed by what he had done.

Who is better qualified to achieve atonement for the repentant of Israel than a person preoccupied with repentance?[7]

וַיָּבֹא מֹשֶׁה וְאַהֲרֹן אֶל אֹהֶל מוֹעֵד
*Moses and Aaron came to
the Tent of Meeting* (ibid. 23).

When Aaron saw that after the inauguration service the Divine Presence had still not descended on the Tabernacle, he was distraught. He was certain that this was a result of his participation in making the Golden Calf. Moses joined Aaron as they entered the Tent of Meeting to pray that God's presence descend (*Rashi*).

By nature, people blame others for tragedies that strike, especially when they are communal tragedies.

When Aaron saw that the Divine Presence failed to rest on the Tabernacle he was sure that he was the culprit. Although others had sinned more grievously, he assigned the blame to himself[8] (*R' Yerucham Levovitz of Mir*).

The climactic celebration of the inauguration of the Tabernacle was dashed by the death of Nadab and Abihu, Aaron's oldest sons. Aaron's exemplary response to the tragedy earned him the privilege of having God directly teach him the prohibition against serving in the Tabernacle and the Temple while intoxicated.

אֵשׁ זָרָה אֲשֶׁר לֹא צִוָּה אֹתָם
*an alien fire that He had not
commanded them* (10:1).

According to *Chidushei HaRim*, Nadab and Abihu's intentions in bringing incense on the Altar were fine. Their sin lay in the fact *that He had not commanded them* — no matter how lofty one's intentions, the service of God must be a response to His command.

When one properly fulfills a commandment of God, his connection to God is so strong that his body is unable to withstand the spiritual intensity. It is only because we are fulfilling God's command that He affords us protection from harm, and we do not return our soul to Him — *He who observes a commandment will know no evil* (*Ecclesiastes* 8:5). Nadab and Abihu, who acted independently, did

---

7. **Fearful Choice.** When Pharaoh decreed that Jewish males be killed, at childbirth, the Jewish midwives Shifrah and Puah (Yocheved and Miriam) enabled the babies to survive. The Torah tells us *And it was because the midwives feared God that He made them houses* (*Exodus* 1:21). *Rashi* explains that one of these "houses" was the dynasty of the Kohanim. Thus the distinction of serving as Kohen is the result of the fear of Heaven.

When Moses saw that Aaron was afraid to approach the Altar, he told him, "It was this very fear of Heaven which caused you to be chosen" (*Panim Yafos*).

8. **It's Not My Fault.** There is an amusing parable that illustrates the danger of shirking personal responsibility. The members of a poor synagogue decided that they wanted to have a festive Purim celebration. Since they were unable to afford a sufficient quantity of vodka, they placed an empty barrel in the corner of the synagogue, and declared that each week every member was to empty a shotglass of vodka into the barrel. Over the course of the year, they would have a barrel full of whiskey.

Every Friday, people dutifully brought their cups and poured them into the barrel.

Finally, Purim arrived. As the festivities began, the poor Jews went over to the barrel, ready to imbibe. The first Jew poured a cup, made a *berachah* and drank. "*Pyuh*!" he cried "It's water, not whiskey!" The people looked at one another, unable to speak. Each person present realized that he could not blame the others, since he too had brought water. Every one of them had thought, "They all will bring whiskey; no one will realize that I brought water," so throughout the year they ended up with a full barrel — of water!

When something needs to be done, we must not rationalize, "Others will get involved": Because, like in the poor man's synagogue, when everybody brings water, there is no whiskey.

not have this protection and they passed away.[9]

Rashi cites a Midrash in which R' Yishmael explains that the brothers sinned by entering to do the service while intoxicated. Why does the Torah describe this behavior as *that He had not commanded them?* Furthermore, these saintly brothers, whom Moses viewed as greater than both he and Aaron, certainly did not act in a manner disdainful of the Tabernacle and its service. What was their intent in serving while intoxicated?

Sfas Emes offers the following: Wine has the power to bring one to joy, as the Sages taught, "Joy [can be achieved] only with wine" (*Pesachim* 109a). Furthermore, wine can enhance one's intellectual abilities (see *Yoma* 76b). This is why Nadab and Abihu drank wine. Their error was that they should have achieved joy just because they were doing God's work. The appeal to an external stimulant bespoke a flaw in their appreciation for Divine commands. This was *that He had not commanded them.*

הוּא אֲשֶׁר דִּבֶּר ה׳ לֵאמֹר בִּקְרֹבַי אֶקָּדֵשׁ
Of this did Hashem speak, saying, "I will be sanctified through those who are nearest Me" (ibid. 3).

According to *Rashi* this verse refers to God's earlier statement regarding the Tabernacle, *it will be sanctified through My glory* (*Exodus* 29:43). *Rambam*, however, understands it as referring to the fire which consumed Aaron's sons. If this is the case, why does the verse speak of an earlier Divine pronouncement, given that the Torah had not previously spoken of such a fire?

R' S.R. Hirsch sees this as an allusion to the Oral Torah. Although God spoke to Moses about this earlier, it would have remained unwritten had it not been for the death of Aaron's sons. As a result of their death, Moses revealed and wrote what God had previously told him.[10]

The Midrash (*Vayikra Rabbah* 12:1) cites two opinions other than that of R' Yishmael. One opinion states that they ruled that they should offer incense without consulting with their teacher, Moses. The other maintains that their death was the result of their not having married.

Chasam Sofer views the three opinions as complementary. One who does not marry and have a family is limited in his ability to fully understand how to accord honor and respect. Based on the honor and respect one would like from his children and family, he can understand the honor due his teachers, and even more so, God. When one is treated disrespectfully, he begins to understand how terrible it is to act disrespectfully toward God or his teacher.

Nadab and Abihu never experienced this lesson about honor and respect. This led them to rule without consulting their teacher, and allowed them to show a lack of reverence by entering the Tabernacle while intoxicated.[11]

---

9. **Loyal Soldier.** Someone was once instructed by his doctor not to fast on Yom Kippur due to illness. Distressed at the prospect of not fasting on this holiest of days, the man sought the counsel of the *Chazon Ish.* The Chazon Ish responded, "The same One Who told you to fast every year is telling you *not* to fast this year. We are like soldiers who follow orders, we go wherever the Commander sends us."

10. **Oral Addition.** Another allusion to the Oral Torah is the discrepancy between the description of God's detailing to Moses the laws of the Pesach-offering and the way Moses taught it to the people (*Exodus* 12). For example, in verse 7 Moses was told, *They shall take some of its blood and place it on the two doorposts.* In verse 22, when Moses transmits this to the people, he instructs them, *You shall take a bundle of hyssop and dip it into the blood . . . and touch the lintel . . .* The detail about the hyssop was obviously taught to him — but it was part of the Oral Torah that was taught when Moses described to the Jews exactly what to do (*R' S.R. Hirsch*).

11. **Equality.** The Ten Commandments were written on two tablets. The first five focus on our relationship with God while the second five deal with interpersonal relationships. Interestingly, the mitzvah of honoring parents is found among the first group of commandments.

The reason for this is as follows:

The type of relationship that a child is supposed to have with his parents somewhat mirrors the relationship that every Jew, as a "child of Hashem" (cf. *Avos* 3:18), enjoys with Him. A child has a father and a mother, and he interacts differently with each of them. The paternal relationship is usually reverential; it is for this reason that the Torah emphasizes that a father must be honored, as well as revered. On the other hand, the maternal relationship

In an attempt to comfort Aaron, Moses told him, "I knew that the Tabernacle would be sanctified through people close to God, yet I thought it would happen through one of us. Now I know that your sons are greater than we are" (*Rashi*).

When God is exacting in His administration of justice, punishing the righteous for relatively minor infractions, it causes a sanctification of His Name, because it becomes clear to all that Divine Justice rules. Thus it is through His close ones that His Name is sanctified.

Are we to understand that Moses had thought that he or Aaron would cause a sanctification of God's Name at the inauguration of the Tabernacle by sinning? *R' Dov Zupnik* explains: God's Name can be sanctified in two ways: either through those who live in a way that makes obvious to all the immanent Presence of God or through God's retribution. Moses thought that when he and Aaron would dedicate the Tabernacle, the Presence of God would be so intense that God would be sanctified in that way. Now it became clear to him that the sanctification would take the alternative form.[12]

Moses' assumption that the sanctification would come either through him or Aaron seems uncharacteristic for the man about whom the Torah teaches, *Now the man Moses was exceedingly humble, more than any person on the face of the earth* (*Numbers* 12:3). *R' Leib Chasman* explains with a parable: A stevedore who carries a huge load on his back does not for a moment believe that the goods he carries are his own. One who is truly humble recognizes his achievements and talents; but he also realizes that they are not really his; they have been placed there by God.

וַיִּדֹּם אַהֲרֹן
and Aaron was silent (ibid.).

The term for silence is שְׁתִיקָה. Why does the Torah describe Aaron's silence as וַיִּדֹּם and not וַיִּשְׁתֹּק אַהֲרֹן?

The *Chafetz Chaim* explains: One can remain silent. Yet, without saying a word, his facial expressions betray his emotions. A דּוֹמֵם, however, *an inanimate object,* has no expression.

In the face of his personal tragedy, Aaron's acceptance of God's judgment was so complete that not only did he say nothing, he emotionally accepted the Divine Will to the extent that he had no reaction.[13]

---

is usually grounded in love and honor. The Torah therefore emphasizes that one must revere, as well as honor, his mother (*Kiddushin* 30b). Both types of relationships are crucial.

Reverence can be seen in a child behaving so that he deserves his parents' affection, while Honor is a natural response to unconditional love.

God's child, the nation of Israel, enjoys both these types of relationships. Hashem loves us unconditionally and constantly, regardless of our behavior, much as a mother does. In addition, He expects us to follow His will and is gladdened, as it were, when we do so. In this sense, He is our Father, Whom we constantly seek to please and Whom we fear to disappoint. Thus He is, so to speak, both our Mother and our Father (see *Pri Tzaddik, Pesach* 34).

Sefer HaChinuch (33) understands the mitzvah of honoring and revering parents as a way for us to learn how to act toward God. Thus it is found to be among the first group of commandments.

Just as we must honor and revere parents, so we are enjoined to love and fear God.

12. **He Means Us.** When people who blatantly transgress the Torah suffer, God forbid, it is convenient to say, "God is sanctifying His Name by punishing the sinful." The truth is, however, that if Jews who are loyal to Torah would live properly, they would bring honor to God and His Torah in that way, and there would be no need to use Divine retribution as a vehicle to sanctify His Name. Apparently, our lives are not a sufficiently powerful source of Divine sanctification.

13. **Transient Soul.** *Ramban* notes that Aaron's response to this tragedy was rooted in his faith in the eternity of the soul. He understood that death is only a transfer from one place to another.

The following story illustrates how great people lived with this perspective: When the daughter of *R' Eliyahu David Rabinowitz-Teumim* (known by the acronym *Aderes*) passed away, her funeral was scheduled for 1 p.m.. When the time for the funeral arrived, the Aderes, who was always punctual, was not there. His children told the people gathered that the Rav had secluded himself in a room and was not ready to come out. The Aderes emerged from his room a short time later and explained his delay. "The *Mishnah* teaches that one must bless God for the bad just as he blesses Him for the good (*Berachos* 9:5). Since I was unable to thank God for my daughter's passing

As a reward of his total acceptance of the Divine judgment, he was rewarded by being personally taught the prohibition to serve in the Tabernacle and the Temple while under the influence of intoxicants.

Why was this particular commandment taught to him?

One who is struck by tragedy feels an emotional need to give expression to his grief. This outburst often undermines one's ability to discharge his responsibilities. In the face of tragedy, Aaron remained controlled, he did not allow his emotions to take over. It is this need to remain focused in one's service of God that is the underpinning of the prohibition to serve while intoxicated. So it was this law that Aaron received as reward for his silence (*Avnei Nezer*).[14], [15]

Background

As a result of Aaron and his family being in mourning, a question arose regarding the disposition of the day's offerings in the Tabernacle.

וְאֵת שְׂעִיר הַחַטָּאת דָּרשׁ דָּרַשׁ מֹשֶׁה
Moses inquired insistently about the he-goat of the sin-offering (ibid. 16).

The midpoint of the words of the Torah is at these words, דָּרשׁ דָּרַשׁ. Many homiletical offerings have been submitted to explain their significance.

The word דָּרשׁ means to inquire as well as to extrapolate or teach. *Degel Machaneh Ephraim* views it as emphasizing the fact that the Written Torah cannot be fully understood without the Oral Law; it is only half of the entire work. The Sages elucidated the full meaning of Torah by means of the 13 hermeneutic principles, י"ג מִדּוֹת שֶׁהַתּוֹרָה נִדְרֶשֶׁת בָּהֶם. The teaching they transmitted, the דָּרשׁ דָּרַשׁ (which can be translated "the lessons they extrapolated"), is half the Torah.[16]

HaDerash V'Halyun sees the words as alluding to a call for introspection. Only if one inquires within himself weighing the factors and identifying his true motivations can he be sure that his plans are in accord with God's will. To *inquire insistently* is half of one's fulfillment of the Torah.

וַיִּקְצֹף עַל אֶלְעָזָר . . . מַדּוּעַ לֹא
אֲכַלְתֶּם אֶת הַחַטָּאת בִּמְקוֹם הַקֹּדֶשׁ
and he was wrathful with Elazar . . .
Why did you not eat the sin-offering
in a holy place (ibid. 16-17).

Love is a necessary ingredient for a teacher and student to effectively work together. This love must inform discipline as well. When punishment is necessary, it must be motivated by out of love and a genuine desire to educate the child.

According to *R' Yisrael Yitzchak of Aleksander*, the Torah alludes to this when it retells the rebuke

---

with the same feelings I had when I recited *Shehechiyanu* upon her birth, I was forced to delay the funeral to work on myself to achieve that state. Now I am ready."

14. **Sober Responsibility.** One may not rule on an issue of Jewish law after having drunk wine. R' Shmuel Salant, the Rav of Jerusalem, would conduct his Passover Seder very quickly, take a nap for a half-hour, and then sit and learn. When asked about his strange custom, he explained "Many halachic questions arise on the Seder night. Were I to extend my Seder, I would be prohibited from responding to these important questions, since I drank the four cups of wine. Therefore, I expedite the Seder and take a nap to allow the wine to wear off. I am then able to rule on any halachic issues that arise."

15. **Seeing Is Believing.** In a certain town, the name of a well-known scholar was proposed as a candidate to serve as the local Rav. Since he was an outspoken opponent of *Chassidus,* the local group of Rizhiner *chassidim* opposed his appointment.

When the *Rizhiner Rebbe* heard of this, he instructed his followers to support the man's candidacy. The reason? "Someone who does not believe miraculous stories told about chassidic rebbes is the perfect person to be a Rav. He only believes what his eyes see."

16. **Doubly Responsible.** The double expression דָּרשׁ דָּרַשׁ calls upon us not only to study Torah for ourselves, but also to teach it. One who stops at the first דָּרשׁ — namely, that he studies Torah but is not concerned enough to teach it to others — only fulfills half of the Torah (*Be'er Moshe*). Rambam (*Sefer HaMitzvos* #11) states clearly, "To study Torah and to teach it. . . This is what is referred to as תַּלְמוּד תּוֹרָה (the study of Torah)."

of Elazar the son of Aaron the Kohen: Moses said: מַדּוּעַ לֹא אֲכַלְתֶּם אֶת הַחַטָּאת בִּמְקוֹם הַקֹּדֶשׁ — *Why did you not eat the sin-offering in a holy place?* The initial Hebrew letters of each word of this sentence spell מָלֵא אַהֲבָה, "full of love." Moses' anger was an outgrowth of his love for Elazar.

One can imbue a child with Torah and good character only if he succeeds in unlocking the child's heart. And love is the key to the heart.

הַיִּיטַב בְּעֵינֵי ה׳
Would Hashem approve? (ibid. 19).

Aaron does not pose his question in terms of halachically permitted or forbidden; rather, his question is: Would it be good in God's eyes? One who views himself as God's servant assesses his behavior only in terms of obligation and permissibility. Not so a child; for a loving child, it is not enough that something is permitted, it must also be something which will please his father. Aaron's concern was more than halachic, it was also "Will it be pleasing in God's eyes?" (*Yesod HaAvodah*).

וַיִּשְׁמַע מֹשֶׁה וַיִּיטַב בְּעֵינָיו
Moses heard and he approved (ibid. 20).

R' *Nosson Dovid of Shidlovitza* once spent a Shabbos with his rebbe, R' *Chaim of Sanz*. At the *tish*, R' Chaim asked him to relate a Torah thought. R' Nosson Dovid was in a dilemma. On one hand, he did not want to disregard his mentor's request; on the other hand, the thought of delivering a Torah thought in the presence of his rebbe was terrifying.

He chose to say the following: "*Moses heard and he approved.* What exactly did he approve of? Usually Moses would talk and Aaron would listen. Now, however, Aaron spoke and Moses was the listener. When Moses heard Torah rather than saying it, he was satisfied. He realized that it is better to listen to others speak words of Torah than to say them himself.[17], [18]

---

17. **A Buyer's Market.** The *Chidushei HaRim* continued to travel to R' *Menachem Mendel of Kotzk* long after he had himself achieved renown as a towering saint and scholar. People asked him, "Why do you still go to a mentor when you yourself can be a mentor to others?" He answered, "King Solomon teaches us in *Proverbs* (23:23): *Buy truth, do not sell.* As long as one still has someone from whom he can 'purchase' truth, he does well not to get involved in 'selling' (i.e., teaching) truth to others."

18. **Sound Advice.** One of the great maladies of our time is that people are unwilling to consult — or follow — a rav, teacher or other sage. R' *Reuvain Karelenstein* jokingly commented, "It's a blessing that an eight day-old-baby cannot speak. If he did, he would want to decide which *mohel* will perform the *bris* and in which hall it will be held."

One who seeks the truth is not embarrassed to hear it from anyone, regardless of his level of scholarship or social status.

For health reasons, the *Chazon Ish* would take a daily walk. His regular route took him along what is today the boundary between Bnei Brak and Ramat Gan. As befits a tireless student of Torah, he would review his learning while walking. (When he once got lost while engrossed in thought, he jokingly remarked, "How did I get so lost from such a short *Tosafos*?")

Once a simple Jew who lived along the route noticed an aged, respectable-looking Jew taking a walk in the middle of the day. After witnessing this for several days, the man decided to give the Chazon Ish — whom he did not recognize — a piece of his mind. "Why do you waste time going for walks?" he shouted at the old man. "Can't you make better use of your time? Go learn! If you can't learn, then recite *Tehillim*!" The Chazon Ish did not reply.

By the next day, the Chazon Ish had forgotten the incident, and again walked along his regular route. Again the Jew attacked him, "What is the matter with you? Did you forget what I told you? Why are you wasting your time?!"

Calmly, the Chazon Ish asked him, "What do you want me to do with my time?"

"Say a few chapters of *Tehillim*," the Jew responded.

The next day the Chazon Ish followed a different route.

Some time later, a member of this Jew's family took ill. Someone suggested that he consult with a great sage who lives nearby, R' Avraham Yeshayahu Karelitz, the Chazon Ish. When he entered the Chazon Ish's house — and realized who he had rebuked — he fainted.

When he came to, he begged the Chazon Ish's forgiveness. The Chazon Ish sat on his chair and lovingly stroked the man's face. "I have nothing to forgive you for. You gave me a good piece of advice, to say *Tehillim*. I tell you that since the day you gave me that advice, I follow it. Why should I be angry at you?"

Great men have no problem listening and learning from others, no matter who they are (*Tuvcha Yabiyu*).

פרשת תזריע ~§
Parashas Tazria

Background

The previous *sidrah, Shemini,* discussed the laws of permitted and forbidden foods while this *sidrah* discusses, for the most part, the laws of *tzaraas,* an affliction which is often inaccurately referred to as leprosy. *Tzaraas,* our Sages teach, comes as a result of forbidden speech. Why does the Torah place these two subjects in such proximity? *R' Yisrael Salanter* explains: Even people who are painstakingly careful not to eat any food, unless they are absolutely certain that it is kosher, often think nothing of "eating" others alive with slander and gossip. The Torah juxtaposes these two sets of laws to teach us that one must be no less careful about his speech than about his food.[1]

R' Yonasan Eibeschutz suggests that the Torah concludes the previous *sidrah* with the words "to distinguish between the contaminated and the pure," and then begins our *sidrah* with the mitzvah of circumcision, the purpose of which is to provide a clear demarcation between Jew and non-Jew.

The Talmud tells us that one who takes a vow not to derive benefit from "circumcised people" (see *Nedarim* 31b) is proscribed from benefiting from any Jew — even one who was not circumcised. On the other hand, the person may derive benefit from any non-Jew, even one who had undergone circumcision. "Circumcision," then, is not a physical state of being — it is a symbol and

---

1. **Equally Vigilant.** One day the *Yid HaKadosh of P'shis'cha* summoned his prized student (and ultimately his successor), *R' Simchah Bunim.* "Gather an entourage of *chassidim* and travel," he commanded. "Where shall I head?" asked the startled student. "Travel," responded the master. R' Simchah Bunim understood that some important lesson was waiting to be learned as they traveled — their destination was almost incidental.

R' Simchah Bunim gathered a group of *chassidim* and set out along the road. As night fell, they settled at an inn owned by Jews. Hungry after a full day of travel, they asked the innkeeper for a dairy meal, assuming that such a menu presented them with fewer problems in terms of *kashrus.* The innkeeper replied, "We only serve a meat meal at this hour." Left with no option, they inquired extensively about who had slaughtered the chickens, how they were soaked and salted, and the standards used in the food's preparation. Finally satisfied that the fare met their standards, they asked the innkeeper to please serve them their meals.

While waiting for the food to be served, R' Simchah Bunim and his group they began conversing, and eventually their discussion turned to other people. As she warmed their food in the kitchen, the cook, a God-fearing woman, overheard their conversation. As she served them she mumbled, loud enough for them to hear, "So strange. So strange indeed how people are so careful about what goes into their mouths, yet are so carefree about what comes out."

R' Simchah Bunim immediately realized why his master had sent him traveling. The entourage returned to P'shis'cha with a valuable lesson.

a trademark of Jewish identity.[2]

In the words of *Sefer HaChinuch* (*Mitzvah* #2):

"God wanted to inscribe an indelible sign on the bodies of the members of the nation He chose to be uniquely His, so they would be separate from all other nations in a physical sense, just as they are separate in a spiritual sense."

Vayidaber Moshe offers yet another interpretation of the Torah's juxtaposition of these subjects. Only in a home where the parents are careful "to distinguish between the contaminated and the pure," creating a climate that is conducive to spiritual growth, will children be a cause for the parents and Hashem to rejoice. By purifying the atmosphere of the home, the parents create the conditions for the conception and birth of a truly "Jewish" child.

Background

The Torah discusses the laws of various impurities which apply to humans, and it begins with the *tumah* associated with childbirth, the beginning of the life cycle.

אִשָּׁה כִּי תַזְרִיעַ
When a woman conceives (12:2).

Rashi (citing the Midrash) notes that just as the creation of animals preceded the creation of man, so too, the laws regarding animals are outlined in the previous *parashah,* before those of man. *Divrei Binah* elaborates: The creation of man took place in two stages: First God formed man's

body out of dust of the earth. Physically, both man and animal are flesh and blood; so there was, at that point, no fundamental difference between the two. Afterwards, however, God endowed man with a living soul, "a spark of Godliness," elevating humans above animal life.

The soul of man was granted him last so that it might perfect the body and harness all its physical potential to do what is good, so mankind, "the soul of the world," is charged with perfecting nature and transforming it into a vehicle for serving God.

אִשָּׁה כִּי תַזְרִיעַ וְיָלְדָה
When a woman conceives and gives birth (12:2).

The Midrash comments on the dichotomous nature of human existence: "If one merits [by following God's will], he will inherit both this world and the World to Come. However, if he does not merit, he will be brought to justice."

We are accustomed to viewing this world as the domain of the wicked and the World to Come as the province of the righteous. This idea is so ingrained in human perception that some people believe that if they live bitterly and miserably in this world, they are virtually guaranteed a good life in the World to Come. R' Simchah Zissel of Kelm categorically rejected this, saying, "A person who is bitter and depressed in this world ought to worry about his share in the World to Come."

The truly righteous inherit both worlds. They do not only look forward to the World to Come, they also enjoy every moment of life in this world — since it is life here that affords one opportunity to

---

2. **Indelible Commitment.** It is customary that those present at a circumcision express the wish that "just as he (the newly circumcised child) has entered the covenant, so may he enter into the (study and fulfillment of) Torah, the marriage canopy and good deeds." A circumcision is a uniquely appropriate occasion for this blessing for it is the one mitzvah which remains with a person forever. While one may, God forbid, lapse in his observance of any other mitzvah, circumcision indelibly stamps one with the status of a Jew. Thus, we wish the young child that just as this mitzvah will remain permanently, so too may his commitment to Torah and the Torah life become a deep and irrevocable force in his life (*Imrei Binyamin*).

A group of Kotzker *chassidim* were once at a *bris,* discussing why it is that this prayer is offered at a *bris.* One of the group suggested that the mitzvah of circumcision is unique in that the child plays no part in the decision of whether or not he is circumcised; he entertains no doubts as to whether or not to fulfill the mitzvah. Our wish is that this should be his attitude toward all mitzvos; he should unhesitatingly and unfailingly commit himself to Torah, married life and the pursuit of good deeds.

One of the elder *chassidim* offered another explanation: Circumcision transforms the child into a "complete" Jew. We beseech God that every mitzvah this child will perform will have a similar effect, serving as a vehicle to deepen his sense of Jewish identity.

achieve his spiritual goals.[3] Having fully utilized the spiritual opportunities available to them, they are then ready to enjoy their share in the World to Come.

This perspective sheds light on the prayer recited upon the completion of a Talmudic tractate: "We [those who study Torah] run and they [those who idle] run; we run to the life of the World to Come, while they run to the well of destruction." Seemingly, a more accurate contrast would be "we run to the life of the World to Come while they run to the good life in this world." In truth, however, it is those who expend their energies on earning life in the Next World who truly enjoy this world. The wicked, who are forever pursuing increasingly elusive ephemeral pleasures, are left with nothing; not true joy in this world nor life in the Next World.

כִּי תַזְרִיעַ וְיָלְדָה זָכָר

When a woman conceives and gives birth to a male (12:2).

The initial letters of the words כִּי תַזְרִיעַ וְיָלְדָה זָכָר, when rearranged, spell the word זְכוּת, *merit.* The Torah seeks to teach us that the spiritual achievements of children are, to a great extent, the result of the actions, thoughts and emotions of their mothers. By conducting themselves in an authentically Jewish manner and by subtly inculcating their children with real Torah values, mothers influence their children in ways that the formal study with fathers and teachers cannot.[4]

3. **En route.** A group of people were traveling by train to a wedding in a distant city. All along the way, they acted merry and boisterous. One of their fellow travelers asked, "Why are you all celebrating?" They replied, "We are on the way to a wedding." "Fine," he countered, "but why party when you haven't even arrived there yet? After all, the ride is not all that comfortable and a lot might happen until you arrive at the wedding." "True," they responded, "but just the thought that we are soon to be at the wedding cheers us and puts us in a jovial mood."

For the righteous, life is a train ride on the way to the great wedding, the World to Come. Even if they encounter some discomfort and difficulty along the way, they enjoy life in this world, heartened and cheered by the knowledge that they are en route to the wedding.

4. **From Mother's Lips.** In a moving tribute to the Rebbetzin of Talne, *R' Joseph B. Soloveitchik* painted a vivid verbal picture of the vital role Jewish mothers play in the spiritual development of their children.

"People are mistaken in thinking that there is only one *mesorah* and one *mesorah* community; the community of the fathers. It is not true. We have two *masoros,* two traditions, two communities, two *shalshalos hakabbalah* — the *mesorah* community of the fathers and that of the mothers. 'so shall you say to the House of Jacob (= the women) and relate to the Children of Israel (= the men)' (*Exodus* 19:3), 'Hear, my son, the discipline of your father (*mussar avicha*), and do not forsake the teaching of your mother (*toras imecha*)' (*Proverbs* 1:8), counseled King Solomon. What is the difference between those two *masoros,* traditions? What is the distinction between *mussar avicha* and *toras imecha*? Let us explore what one learns from the father and what one learns from the mother.

"One learns much from the father: how to read a text — the Bible or the Talmud — how to comprehend, how to analyze, how to conceptualize, how to classify, how to infer, how to apply, etc. . . . One also learns from the father what to do and what not to do, what is morally right and what is morally wrong. The father teaches the son the discipline of thought as well as the discipline of action. The father's tradition is an intellectual-moral one. That is why it is identified with *mussar,* which is the Biblical term for discipline.

"What is *toras imecha*? What kind of a Torah does the mother pass on? I admit that I am not able to define precisely the masoretic role of the Jewish mother. Only by circumscription I hope to be able to explain it. Permit me to draw upon my own experiences. I used to watch my mother arranging the house in honor of a holiday. I used to see her recite prayers; I used to watch her recite the *sidrah* every Friday night and I still remember the nostalgic tune. I learned from her very much.

"Most of all I learned that Judaism expresses itself not only in formal compliance with the law but also in a living experience. She taught me that there is a flavor, a scent and warmth to *mitzvos.* I learned from her the most important thing in life — to feel the presence of the Almighty and gentle pressure of His hand resting upon my frail shoulders. Without her teachings, which quite often were transmitted to me in silence, I would have grown up a soulless being, dry and insensitive.

"The laws of Shabbos, for instance, were passed on to me by my father; they are a part of *mussar avicha.* The Shabbos as a living entity, as a queen, was revealed to me by my mother; it is a part of *toras imecha.* The fathers

The Talmud relates that while a child is in the womb he is taught the entire Torah. Upon exiting the womb an angel taps the child right above the mouth and the child forgets everything he was taught (*Niddah* 30b).

What purpose is there in teaching a child something he will have to forget? The answer can be found in a prayer we recite three times a day. At the end of *Shemoneh Esrei,* we ask God, "Grant us our share in the Torah." Every Jew has his own share in the Torah. The unborn child is taught *his* Torah before birth, to inspire him to spend his life in a quest to regain that portion of the Torah, much as one searches for a lost object. The Sages taught, "If someone tells you, 'I labored [in the study of Torah] but I did not find [i.e. did not succeed],' do not believe him" (*Megillah* 6b). Torah is a lost object which one can succeed in retrieving — but only through effort and perseverance. One who truly labors at it is guaranteed that his search will be successful.

Were God to have man retain the knowledge he had been taught by the angel, man would not be entitled to any reward for acquiring the knowledge of Torah. On the other hand, had God not granted man the initial exposure to Torah, it would be beyond his human intellect and ability to perceive the wisdom of God. Thus he is initially taught, but then caused to forget (*Zekan Aharon*).

וְטָמְאָה שִׁבְעַת יָמִים
she will be contaminated for a seven-day period (12:2).

Why does childbirth induce impurity?

The most severe level of spiritual contamination (*tumah*) is the impurity of a human corpse. While alive, man carries within himself the human soul, a reflection of Godliness. When man dies, the soul departs the body — the Godly force which permeated the living person is now gone. That is the definition of *tumah*: the negativity — the active lack of Godliness — that exists wherever Godliness was previously found.[5]

God Himself oversees the process of childbirth; the Talmud (*Taanis* 2a) teaches that the key of childbirth is one of three that God does not relinquish to any angel. Therefore, His presence is eminent at each and every birth. Once the child is born, however, that eminence is lessened, leaving a spiritual "vacuum" in its wake. It is this "vacuum" that engenders spiritual impurity (*R' Menachem Mendel of Kotzk*).

וּבַיּוֹם הַשְּׁמִינִי יִמּוֹל בְּשַׂר עָרְלָתוֹ
On the eighth day the flesh of his foreskin shall be circumcised (12:3).

Why do we wait until the eighth day before circumcising our male children? *Rabbeinu Bachya* explains: Circumcision is compared to an

---

knew much about the Shabbos; the mothers *lived* the Shabbos, experienced her presence and perceived her beauty and splendor.

The fathers taught generations how to observe the Shabbos; mothers taught generations how to greet the Shabbos and how to enjoy her twenty-four hour presence."

A great *Rosh Yeshivah* was once asked by a student who was himself a scholar of note, "What makes Yiddish a 'holy language'? It is not the holy tongue; in fact, it is nothing more than a distorted German with some Hebrew words thrown in."

"When your grandmother lit the Shabbos candles she cried and prayed in Yiddish that you and all her children and grandchildren grow up to be God-fearing Jews and towering Torah scholars. It was her prayer in Yiddish and the prayers of women like her that sanctified the Yiddish language," the *Rosh Yeshivah* replied.

5. **Spiritual Space.** In the second portion of the *Shema* we say: וְסַרְתֶּם וַעֲבַדְתֶּם אֱלֹהִים אֲחֵרִים, *and you turn astray and serve gods of others* (Deuteronomy 11:16): Rashi comments: "If you will turn astray from the Torah you will serve the gods of others. Abandoning the Torah results in idolatry." This statement seems rather extreme. There seems to be a great difference between abandoning Torah and the extreme of idolatry.

R' Yitzchak Hutner explained: In pre-Newtonian physics it was considered axiomatic that, as Aristotle had written, "nature abhors a vacuum." Even today it is recognized that as long as there is pressure surrounding a vacuum, it will cause the vacuum to be filled. Likewise, in a spiritual sense, the mind and the soul of man will never remain empty. If Torah is the content of one's life he will enjoy spiritual health. However, if he empties his life of this exalted content he will not merely remain empty. The first available negative influence, even idolatry, will quickly fill the void.

offering (see *Psalms* 50:5). Just as the sprinkling of blood of the offering on the Altar served as a catalyst for Divine forgiveness, so the drop of blood let at a circumcision elicits Divine forgiveness. And just as an animal may not be offered on the Altar until it is at least eight days old, so too a child may not offer his own "blood sacrifice" until he is at least eight days old.[6]

The Sages teach that the words of the Psalmist כִּי עָלֶיךָ הֹרַגְנוּ כָל הַיּוֹם נֶחְשַׁבְנוּ כְּצֹאן טִבְחָה, *Because for Your sake we are killed all the time, we are considered as sheep for slaughter* (*Psalms* 44:23), allude to the mitzvah of circumcision. Almost from birth, a Jew is trained to be ready for self-sacrifice, to shed blood, figuratively and literally, on behalf of his Father in Heaven (*Meorah Shel Torah*).[7]

---

6. **Sealed with a Meal.** This is one of the reasons that a circumcision is traditionally celebrated with a lavish meal. The forgiveness achieved by a sacrifice is fully achieved when the appropriate parts of the offering are eaten by the owners and the Kohanim. Similarly, the "completion" of the circumcision takes place, in a sense, when the celebrants partake of a meal in honor of the occasion (*R' Bachya*).

The beloved *R' Levi Yitzchak* of *Berditchev* was invited to all the joyous occasions celebrated by his townspeople, and he made every effort to attend.

When notified about a circumcision, he would always respond, "I'm ready to make an attempt to come, but with one condition; you must prepare a proper festive meal." Though accustomed to this response, the townspeople found it incongruent with their Rav's character; food and drink were generally not very significant to R' Levi Yitzchak.

Finally one of the townspeople worked up the courage to ask for an explanation. Rav Levi Yitzchak explained: "As you well know, I am involved in an ongoing battle with Satan. He claims that the Jewish people fall short in all their obligations toward God, Heaven forfend. I, on the other hand, always seek to defend the Jewish people against these attacks. 'Look at your people,' I tell God. 'Whenever they perform a mitzvah they do it with the utmost joy. On the other hand, see how upset and disheartened a Jew becomes when he falters and sins. His heart breaks over the thought that he has displeased You.'

"When Satan demands I prove my case, I reply, 'Have you ever seen a Jew who made a party in honor of the occasion of his having sinned? Never! On the other hand, whenever a Jew does a mitzvah he celebrates with a festive meal. A circumcision, a bar mitzvah, the conclusion of a tractate and a wedding are all occasions for festivity. The Sabbath and festivals also offer the Jew an opportunity to express his love for God with fine fare!'

"The Satan has no response, but he tries his hardest to make sure that Jews do not celebrate a mitzvah meal elaborately and joyously.

"It is for this reason that I am so insistent on having the celebrants prepare a truly festive meal."

The following incident sheds further highlights on the significance of celebrating mitzvah occasions with a proper meal.

When the *Imrei Emes* of *Ger* was a youngster, his father — the famed *Sfas Emes* — asked a relative to take his two sons to a particular Jew in Warsaw in order to be blessed. The relative traveled to Warsaw and searched out the Jew, sure that he was looking for a well-known righteous man. How surprised he was to discover the Jew to whom the Rebbe had sent him was rather simple. In fact, when the the children were brought for a blessing, it was clear that the man had no idea why anyone, let alone the great Sfas Emes, would send someone to him for a blessing. "Although you may not know why the Rebbe sent us to you, please fulfill his request and bless his children," the relative said. The man complied and blessed them profusely.

They left, convinced that the man must be a hidden saint, for he appeared to be anything but exceptionally righteous. When they returned to Ger, the Rebbe revealed the secret of the hidden saint. "He is a simple Jew, but when his son was to be circumcised he couldn't afford a festive meal. He sold his blanket and pillow in order to buy food for a meal, and was left penniless. His self-sacrifice for the mitzvah made so powerful an impression in Heaven that he was granted the power to bestow blessings on others. He is unaware of the power granted to him, yet any blessing he bestows is fulfilled."

7. **Early Education.** At a circumcision, those present express the wish that "Just as he [the newly circumcised child] has entered the covenant so may he enter into the [study and fulfillment of] Torah, the marriage canopy and good deeds." This can be understood to mean that just as circumcision is an expression of self-sacrifice, we hope and pray this child will exhibit self-sacrifice for Torah, for his family and for helping others.

Tochachas Chaim explains this prayer as an admonition to the father. We tell him, "Just as you have seen to it that your son was circumcised, be sure to concern yourself with his development in Torah, with his interpersonal relationships and with his performance of good deeds."

Interestingly, the verse in *Psalms* contains eight words, an allusion to circumcision which is performed on the eighth day of a child's life.[8]

Background

The mother's final step in her purification process after childbirth is her bringing an offering to the Temple.

זֹאת תּוֹרַת הַיֹּלֶדֶת
this is the law of one who gives birth (12:7).

The Torah tells us that a mother brings a sheep as an elevation-offering and a young dove or turtledove as a sin-offering. The verse concludes "this is the law of one who gives birth," as though the discussion of the subject has come to a conclusion. However, in the following verse we are instructed that if the mother cannot afford a sheep, she may bring a more modest offering. Why does the Torah seem to end the discussion only to reopen it?

R' Shalom of Belz explains: God wants Jews to enjoy prosperity and to be able to perform *mitzvos* in the most lavish fashion.

For the Torah to outline the options available to one who cannot afford the ideal offering as "the law of one who gives birth" would be a transgression of the words of the Sages, "One should never open his mouth and invite Satan" (i.e. one should not speak of negative consequences lest his words become a self-fulfilling prophecy) (*Berachos* 19a). Therefore, the Torah tells us that "the law of one who gives birth" is that the woman should be able to afford the sheep. If, however, that is not the case, the Torah then describes her alternatives.[9]

אֶחָד לְעֹלָה וְאֶחָד לְחַטָּאת
one for an elevation-offering and one for a sin-offering (12:8).

Although the sin-offering is brought first, the Torah mentions the elevation-offering first for in terms of קְרִיאָה, *reading*, it takes precedence (*Rashi* based on *Zevachim* 90a).

Tosafos (ad loc.) understands קְרִיאָה as referring to the order in which the animals should be sanctified before being offered. Although the sin-offering is slaughtered first, the animal for the elevation-offering should be formally sanctified by the owner before he sanctifies the sin-offering.

The *Imrei Emes of Ger* offers a homiletic interpretation. The Talmud teaches that one who reads and studies the sections of the Torah regarding the offerings is considered, in the absence of the Altar, to have actually offered those sacrifices (*Menachos* 110a). Although one can read and study the sections regarding both the elevation-offering and the sin-offering, only in the case of the elevation-offering can reading and study fully substitute for the offering itself. The full atonement offered by a sin-offering is achieved only when the Kohanim partake of its flesh (*Pesachim* 59b); therefore, though reading takes the place of the basic offering, it cannot fully compensate for the actual sacrifice. Only the elevation-offering, which is totally consumed on the Altar, can be completely replaced by the reading and study of its laws.[10]

Thus the *reading* of the elevation-offering, which more completely fills the role of the sacrifice, takes precedence over that of the sin-offering.

Nachalas Eliezer offers a practical lesson to be learned from this Talmudic teaching.

---

8. **Consolation Covenant.** For the spiritual soul to leave the Heavenly sphere and descend to our mundane world is a painful experience. In order to appease the soul, God commanded that soon after birth we reconnect the soul to Him, by stamping the newborn with the sign of His holy covenant (*R' Shalom of Belz*).

9. **Prayer Against Poverty.** Poverty has the potential to debilitate a Jew's ability to serve God properly. *R' Shalom of Belz* once implored God to provide lavishly for His children. "True," he said "the Talmud teaches that 'poverty is beautiful for Jews' (*Chagigah* 9b). However, Jeremiah tells us that with the destruction of the Temple, 'Gone from the daughter of Zion is all her splendor' (*Lamentations* 1:6). When all the other signs of splendor are returned to us, then we will be able to bear the 'beauty' of poverty. Until that time, let us enjoy only prosperity."

10. **Therapeutic Consumption.** Our Sages teach that a Jew's table offers atonement (*Chagigah* 27a). When one eats with the proper intentions and in the proper manner, he lives a productive Torah-true life. By eating in an authentically Jewish fashion and "eating to live" rather than "living to eat," one can achieve the level of atonement which had been effected by the Kohanim's consumption.

The elevation-offering symbolizes the ultimate goal of the Jew — total and unreserved commitment to the service of God. The sin-offering characterizes the approach and means to achieve this goal.

One must not attempt to leap to the peak of Godly service all at once; he must take a gradual, deliberate approach. The initial rung on the ladder is סוּר מֵרַע, to turn away from evil. Only after having conquered that position can one continue on the level of עֲשֵׂה טוֹב — to positively infuse all his actions with spirituality.

Thus, when bringing the offering, the sin-offering, representing the stepping away from sin, takes precedence, since that is how one begins his spiritual growth. It is followed by the elevation-offering, which represents his ultimate objective.

Nevertheless, to insure that one is not satisfied with merely avoiding evil, it is imperative that he keep himself focused on the summit he intends to reach.[11] Thus when reading, we begin with the elevation-offering, setting our sights on the ultimate good.

Background

The Torah now describes various symptoms of *tzaraas* and the procedure whereby its presence is diagnosed and verified.

אָדָם כִּי יִהְיֶה בְעוֹר בְּשָׂרוֹ
If a person will have on the skin of his flesh (13:2).

The Talmud (*Niddah* 5:3) teaches that even a newborn child is susceptible to the impurity of *tzaraas.* This, submits *R' S.R. Hirsch,* seems to contradict the Talmud's assertion that *tzaraas* is a result of interpersonal transgressions such as slander, bloodshed, selfishness and arrogance (*Arachin* 16a). Certainly a newborn child has not transgressed any of these sins, so why should he be punished with *tzaraas?*

R' Hirsch explains: *Tzaraas* is intended as a physical symptom to shock man into realizing that he suffers from an underlying spiritual malaise. If parents remain impassive when God seeks to alert them to their own deficiencies, God then visits *tzaraas* upon their spiritually blameless children so that the parents realize that they must mend their ways.

Indeed, the parents' lack of sensitivity to others will eventually manifest itself in their children. Thus, *tzaraas* of a child teaches the parents that they are remiss in their roles as Torah-true role models for their children. The affliction cries out, "For the sake of your children — repent! To protect their future, be upstanding!! *You* will be held responsible for the unethical habits they develop."

Ach Pri Tevuah offers a perspective on the usage of the word אָדָם, *a person.*

Other Hebrew words that describe human beings have both a singular and a plural form. אִישׁ is singular; אֲנָשִׁים is plural. גֶּבֶר is a man, גְּבָרִים are men. אָדָם, however, exists only in the singular; there is no plural form of the word. Thus the Sages (*Yevamos* 61a) taught that only the Jewish people are called אָדָם, for only among Jews is there an intrinsic sense of unity which melds all the nation's individuals into one unified whole.[12]

The primary cause of *tzaraas* is the sin of slander (*Arachin* 15b). Slander is a result of divisiveness.

---

11. **Raising Our Sights.** The *mussar* masterwork, *Mesillas Yesharim* (Pathways of the Just), is structured according to the ladder of spiritual ascent outlined by R' Pinchas ben Yair (*Avodah Zarah* 20b). The lowest rung on the ladder is זְהִירוּת, *carefulness,* while חֲסִידוּת, *piety,* is one of the rungs near the top of the ladder. Nonetheless, *Mesillas Yesharim's* author, *R' Moshe Chaim Luzzato,* begins his introduction with the phrase יְסוֹד הַחֲסִידוּת וְשׁוֹרֶשׁ הָעֲבוֹדָה הַתְּמִימָה, "The foundation of piety and the root of wholesome service [of God] etc."

If one is to reach his goal he must, at the outset, raise his eyes and focus on where he hopes to head (*R' Shlomo Freifeld*).

12. **Man.** In 1912, *Mendel Beilis,* a Russian Jew, was accused of murdering a Christian child to use his blood for baking Passover matzos. His trial for this blood libel took place in Kiev, and the eyes and hearts of world Jewry — all of whom were, vicariously, being accused — were focused there.

The prosecution asserted that the Talmud, and thus the Jewish religion, views non-Jews as subhuman and thus expendable. A key piece of prosecution "evidence" was the statement of R' Shimon bar Yochai: "You [Jews] are

The slanderer undermines the sense of אָדָם, of the Jewish nation's status of a unified whole. His punishment is *tzaraas*, which requires him to be separated from others, to be temporarily removed from society. This gives him the opportunity to contemplate in solitude the implications of his divisiveness.

וְהָיָה בְעוֹר בְּשָׂרוֹ לְנֶגַע צָרָעַת
and it will become a tzaraas affliction on the skin of his flesh (ibid.).

The impurity engendered by these physical symptoms is in reality only skin deep. It is an affliction on *the skin* of the flesh but it does not penetrate any further (*Ohr HaChaim*).

Our daily prayers in which we refer to "the soul which You blew into me; it is pure" reflect this. The soul of a Jew may be temporarily besmirched by sin, but the taint is only superficial. King Solomon, speaking for God's beloved people, says, "I am slumbering yet my heart is awake" (*Song of Songs* 5:2). Even as we slumber, we are, at our core, awake and spiritually sensitive. God brings afflictions upon us in the hope that they will shake us out of our spiritual slumber and apathy.

וְהוּבָא אֶל אַהֲרֹן הַכֹּהֵן
he shall be brought to Aaron the Kohen (ibid.).

There is a common misconception that if slander is true, then it does not constitute *lashon hara*. In fact, however, *lashon hara* is specifically slander which is true; lies fall under the category of *motzi shem ra*. Despite the prohibitions against true slander, its purveyors often delude themselves into believing that they are performing a great mitzvah by revealing others' faults and "setting the public record straight."

The Torah instructs that one who suffers from *tzaraas* — a result of slandering others — be brought before Aaron the Kohen to be cured. Why was it specifically Aaron who was assigned this task? The Sages teach that Aaron was passionate in his pursuit of peace (*Avos* 1:12). When he saw two people at odds with each other, he would approach each one separately, without the other's knowledge, and say, "Why are you fighting with your friend? He begged me to approach you and arrange a reconciliation."

We bring the slandering "stickler for truth," to Aaron, who understood and could teach that forthrightness must sometimes be suspended in order to bring Jews closer to each other (*R' Yaakov of Aleksander*).

The Midrash offers yet another reason why the Kohen is charged with the duty of diagnosing *tzaraas*.

When Moses was taught this mitzvah by God, he complained. "Does my brother Aaron have to demean himself to examine *tzaraas* afflictions?" God replied, "Yes he does, since he is the recipient of the twenty-four priestly gifts" (*Vayikra Rabbah* 15:8).

The *Chafetz Chaim* notes that this teaches us that Jewish leaders must be ready to demean themselves, when necessary, to address the spiritual needs of their flock.

This responsibility is particularly incumbent upon

---

called man while the nations of the world are not called man" (*Yevamos* 61a). *Rabbi Yaakov Maza,* Chief Rabbi of Moscow, was the rabbinic adviser for the defense, and he consulted with many of the most prominent rabbis in order to defend the Jewish religion against the accusations.

R' Meir Shapiro, famed *Rosh Yeshivah* of Lublin, suggested the following explanation: "Rather than being derogatory regarding non-Jews, this statement merely captures a unique quality of the Jewish people. 'All Jews are responsible for one another' (*Shevuos* 39a). Thus, the fate of a solitary Jew, such as Mendel Beilis, is the concern of every Jew worldwide. Jews from every land are worried about Mendel Beilis and are doing everything in their power to ensure that he is exonerated.

"Imagine if it were a non-Jew in some faraway land who was accused of similarly contrived charges. What would be the response of his co-religionists? Though his friends and family would be concerned, others would most certainly not take great interest in his plight.

"This is the difference: Certainly non-Jews are people. But only the Jewish nation has the sense of unity and deep-seated concern for another that makes all the individuals into a single 'man.'"

Non-Jews are human — only Jews are "a man."

leaders who are supported by the community, just as Aaron, who was eligible to receive the twenty-four priestly gifts, was charged by the Torah to diagnose and treat those who were afflicted with *tzaraas*. [13]

The Torah tells us that the *metzora* "shall be brought" to the Kohen. On the other hand, when the Torah describes the *tzaraas* which afflicts houses, it says that "the one to whom the house belongs shall come" to the Kohen (*Leviticus* 14:35). Why does the Torah describe the person with affliction as being brought, but the owner of the stricken house as coming on his own?

Rambam (*Hilchos Tumas Tzaraas* 16:10) notes that, in His mercy, God first brings *tzaraas* upon a guilty person's house. If the victim repents, the house is healed. However, if the person does not repent, his clothes are afflicted. If even this does not cause him to reconsider his ways, God has no choice but to afflict the person's body.

Thus, when it speaks of a person whose house has been afflicted, the Torah describes the person as coming to the Kohen of his own accord, seeking the root cause of his *tzaraas*. But the victim who has *tzaraas* on his body has repeatedly ignored

God's messages and continued to sin. Such a person fails to realize that he is spiritually ill. This person will not come to the Kohen — he needs to be brought (*Shema Shlomo*).

שְׂאֵת אוֹ סַפַּחַת אוֹ בַהֶרֶת
s'eis or a sapachas or a baheres (ibid.).

These three types of *tzaraas* afflictions can be homiletically understood to refer to three impediments to spiritual growth. שְׂאֵת is related to נִשָּׂא, *raised*. One who is arrogant and views himself as superior to everyone else sees no reason to correct anything in his life.

סַפַּחַת shares a common root with the word נִסְפַּח, *attached*. One is often a prisoner of his social milieu. Even if he would like to change his ways, he does not have the courage to reject the corrupt values and lifestyles of his circle of friends. בַּהֶרֶת (from the Hebrew בָּהִיר, *clear*) applies to a person who thinks that he is exceptionally smart and understands everything clearly. In his mind, no one else is "smart enough" to determine his spiritual course. He listens to no one but himself.

It is by coming to the Kohen and accepting his counsel that such people can achieve the spiritual purity and success their souls seek (*Otzar Chaim*).

---

13. **Uneven Swap.** It is customary among many *chassidim* that when a *chassid* presents his rebbe with a *kvittel* (petitional note) he accompanies it with a *pidyon* (monetary gift). *R' Yaakov Yosef of Polonoye* explained: A *chassid* comes to his rebbe seeking spiritual direction and advice. He wants the rebbe to share that which is most precious to the rebbe, so it is only proper that, in exchange, the *chassid* gives the rebbe that which is precious to *him* — money.

An authentic religious leader provides for the people's spirit, while the people provide for the physical needs of their leaders.

פרשת מצורע ✦
Parashas Metzora

Background

After describing the symptoms of *tzaraas* and the role of the Kohen in determining the status of the affliction, the Torah goes on to delineate the three-stage purification process.

זֹאת תִּהְיֶה תּוֹרַת הַמְּצֹרָע . . . וְהוּבָא אֶל הַכֹּהֵן

This shall be the law of the metzora . . . .
He shall be brought to the Kohen (14:2).

The Midrash (*Vayikra Rabbah* 16:6) notes that the Torah invokes the term תּוֹרָה five times with regard to the *metzora*. This teaches us that one who speaks gossip or slander — the sins that cause *tzaraas* — is deemed to have transgressed all Five Books of the Torah.

Haskel V'Yado'a explains that there are five types of gossip, each of which are highlighted in one of the Five Books.

In *Genesis* we are taught the story of Joseph and his brothers. Although Joseph had proper intentions when he told his father of his brothers' flaws, his actions ultimately led to the exile in Egypt. Even justified gossip can beget tragic results.

When God told Moses to go redeem the Jewish people, Moses impugned the faith of the Jews, saying, *But they will not believe me (Exodus* 4:1). According to *Yalkut Shimoni (Parashas Chukas)* Moses was not allowed to enter the Land of Israel because of this remark. Besmirching the Jewish people is a fatal offense.

Leviticus speaks of what we generally call talebearing and gossip. Nothing at all is gained from this type of speech, and it is born of the perverse enjoyment derived from talking about others.[1]

In *Numbers,* the Torah relates a fourth type of gossip. The spies sent by Moses to scout the Land of Israel came back with unfair disparaging reports. By disheartening the people, the spies severed the nation's connection to their forefathers (see *Ramban* to *Numbers* 14:17) — and this led to forty years of wandering in the Wilderness until every man who at the time was between 20 and 60 years of age had died.

Finally, in *Deuteronomy* (24:9) we are told, *Remember what Hashem, your God, did to Miriam . . .* Miriam was Moses' sister. She had done so much for him when he was young (see *Exodus* 2:4ff.). Her only sin was that she had made a slightly disparaging remark about Moses to Aaron. Yet, as a result of her speaking *lashon hara,* she was stricken with *tzaraas.* Even in one's own home, among the

---

1. **Upward Bound.** It has been said that "Great people speak about *ideas;* mediocre people talk about *things;* simple people speak about *people.* R' Yechiel Perr noted that the Torah's prohibition against gossip and slander is a call for us to raise ourselves to become great.

Someone once put it succinctly: "Don't mention *menschen* (people)."

closest of relatives, one must refrain from gossip.

One who speaks *lashon hara* transgresses the Five Books of Torah, for the consequence of the sin are illustrated in each one of those Books.[2]

The Torah speaks in the future: *This "shall" be the law of the metzora.* The sense of contrition brought about through *tzaraas* must remain with the person long after the physical affliction is gone. The humility must remain with him for all time (*Shem MiShmuel*).[3]

Based on the words תּוֹרַת הַמְּצֹרָע (the law of the *metzora*), the Sages taught that Torah study has the power to help heal *tzaraas* (See *Arachin* 16a). One who truly studies Torah catches a small glimpse of God's infinite greatness. He cannot help

but be humbled. This person will refrain from speaking about others because he will no longer view himself as being superior to them (*Simchas Aharon*).

Orach LaChaim questions why Torah study only helps the *metzora* בְּיוֹם טָהֳרָתוֹ, *on the day of his purification.* Should not the Torah's effect be therapeutic at any time? The answer is that a person who wants Torah to truly influence him must first have a degree of purity. It is only on the day of his purification that Torah will help the *metzora*. [4]

The Midrash (*Vayikra Rabbah* 16:2) tells the story of an itinerant peddler who announced, hawking his wares, "Who wants life? Who wants life?" When R' Yannai responded to his call, the peddler directed him to a passage in *Psalms*: *Who is the man who desires life, who loves days of seeing*

---

2. **Self-Slander.** The *Chafetz Chaim* was once riding in a wagon and a fellow passenger asked him what town he was from.

"From Radin," he replied.

"Do you know the great Rav and *tzaddik* the Chafetz Chaim?" asked the man.

"First, he's not a Rav and, secondly, he is not a *tzaddik.*"

The Jew was taken aback. "What are you talking about?! Everybody knows he is one of the saintliest men of the generation!" said the man.

The Chafetz Chaim responded, "What people say means nothing; people don't really know him. I know him personally and I assure you, his reputation is exaggerated."

The Jew, losing his patience, began berating the "old man" and, for good measure, hit him with a stick. The Chafetz Chaim was upset with himself that he had caused a Jew to sin.

When the wagon arrived in Radin, both this passenger and the Chafetz Chaim disembarked. A short while later, when the Chafetz Chaim was back home, the Jew came to pay a visit to the Torah giant he assumed he had never met before.

When the Jew realized that the man he had hit was none other than the Chafetz Chaim himself, he nearly fainted. "You didn't do anything wrong," the Chafetz Chaim reassured him. "On the contrary, I deserve to be punished. One is not only forbidden from speaking *lashon hara* about others; he may not even speak *lashon hara* about himself!"

3. **Peak Maintenance.** Both Mussarists and Chassidic masters stress that it is not enough to attain a spiritual peak; one must be able to maintain it. This is alluded to in the verse *Who may ascend the mountain of Hashem and who may stand in the place of His sanctity* (Psalms 24:3). While ascending the mountain is the first step, the true test is *who may stand in the place of His sanctity.*

4. **Inner Light.** In *Yoma* (9b) The Sages ascribe the destruction of the First Temple to the fact that the Jews transgressed the three cardinal sins: idolatry, homicide and illicit relations. In *Nedarim* (81a), however, the Talmud tells us that the destruction was brought about because they did not recite the blessing before Torah study to thank God for the Torah.

Maharal (*Introduction to Tiferes Yisrael*) resolves this apparent contradiction: While the three cardinal sins were the crimes that brought about the destruction, the Temple could have been saved by the spiritual light of Torah, bringing people to repent. However, for that light to influence a person, he must recognize the Divine nature of Torah. The blessings over Torah study speak of God's giving us the Torah and His command that we toil in it. By "not reciting the blessing," people essentially prevented themselves from being influenced by "Torah's light," and brought about the Temple's destruction.

good?[5] *Guard your tongue from evil and your lips from speaking deceit* (*Psalms* 34:13-14). R' Yannai responded, "All my life I have read this verse, yet until this peddler taught it, I did not understand how obvious it was."

Kochav M'Yaakov explains the incident: The peddler, who sold all kinds of medicinal herbs, wanted to teach people that guarding one's tongue grants one health and good life not only in the Next World, but in this world as well. By guarding his speech, one can avoid aggravation and anger, which harm his health and ultimately shorten his life.

R' Yannai was overwhelmed by this obvious truth. He had always understood that King David was only promising us life in the Next World. The itinerant peddler made him realize that guarding one's tongue provides us with life in this world as well.[6]

וְהוּבָא אֶל הַכֹּהֵן
He shall be brought to the Kohen (ibid.)

The implication is that the *metzora* will *be brought* to the Kohen — against his will. Why does the Torah assume that this will be the case?

The Sages interpret מְצֹרָע (*metzora*) as an acronym for מוֹצִיא שֵׁם רָע, one who slanders (*Arachin* 16b).[7] The most frequent targets for disparagement and slander are a community's public servants — the lay and rabbinic leadership, the "Kohanim." When *tzaraas* strikes, the victim feels uncomfortable going to the Kohen who he slandered. The *metzora* must therefore *be brought* to him (*R' Chaim of Volozhin*).[8]

Why does the Torah demand that the *metzora* be brought to the Kohen? The *Dubno Maggid* suggests that one reason that people are lax about *lashon hara* is that they don't realize the potent power of speech. Though in fact speaking disparagingly about another person arouses strict Divine justice against both the speaker and his victim, and even though words can cause harm and even lead to bloodshed, the speaker rationalizes, "All I did was say something!"

The Torah therefore sends the *metzora* to the Kohen. The *metzora's* fate will now be decided by the Kohen — whose word will make all the difference.

---

5. **Lovely Days.** What is the meaning of *who loves days of seeing good*?

Ketzos HaChoshen offers the following explanation: Businessmen who do a lot of traveling often get caught up in a cycle: When they are away from home on business, they cannot wait for the trip to be over so that they can get back home. Yet soon after they return, they impatiently begin to await their next trip. Sadly, these people spend their lives always waiting for the next step.

One who is involved in spiritual pursuits, however, is "seeing good" — doing what is important to him — so that he loves the days and the opportunities they provide.

Alternatively, one's enjoyment of life is directly related to the way in which he views the world around him. A person who view events, people and his surroundings positively is *seeing good*. Such a person truly loves his days (*Zekan Aharon*).

6. **Belief in Torah.** *R' Yitzchak Blazer* sees this Midrash as teaching a lesson in how seriously we must take the words of Torah.

7. **Favorable Impression.** The Sages teach that one who judges his friend favorably is judged favorably in Heaven (*Shabbos* 127b). The simple understanding is that the one who judges favorably will himself be judged in that way; since he sought to see good in others, the Heavenly court will focus on his good deeds.

R' Avraham Grodzinsky cites early commentaries who offer a novel interpretation. When one judges his friend favorably, he causes Heaven to judge *his friend* favorably. The way a person views someone else affects how that person is judged in Heaven.

When one speaks ill of others, it not only affects the victim's standing among his fellow men; it impacts the way that God deals with him as well. Speaking badly of others has far-reaching consequences.

8. **Meet Your Target.** *R' Y. Eiger* offers a similar interpretation. Leaders and great people are regularly the target of people's barbs and criticism. Not only does God exercise extreme scrutiny regarding the actions of the righteous (*Yevamos* 121b); people are even more exacting and unwilling to forgive their leaders' slightest flaw.

One who speaks *lashon hara* against the righteous is forced to be brought to the Kohen. "Let them come close and see what their leaders are really like," says the Torah. The *metzora* will then recognize that the flaws he had imputed, and even the Kohen's real failings are insignificant compared to their righteousness and their dedication to the Jewish people.

The *metzora* will learn firsthand that *life and death are in the hands of the tongue* (Proverbs 18:21).[9]

This verse indicates that the *metzora* is brought to the Kohen, while the next verse states, *The Kohen shall go forth to the outside of the camp*, implying that the Kohen went out to him (see *Sforno*). This teaches that one who seeks purification must take the first step. Once he takes that first step, indicating that he wants to be purified, then the Kohen moves toward him to help him.

And even if it means leaving his own comfortable environment to go outside the camp, the Kohen must be ready to go, for the sake of purifying his fellow Jew (based on *Shem MiShmuel*).

וְלָקַח לַמִּטַּהֵר שְׁתֵּי צִפֳּרִים חַיּוֹת טְהֹרוֹת וְעֵץ אֶרֶז וּשְׁנִי תוֹלַעַת וְאֵזֹב

and for the person being purified there shall be taken two live, clean birds, cedar wood, crimson thread and hyssop (ibid 4).

The words צִפּוֹר, *bird* [(צ)90 + (פ)80 + (ו)6 + (ר)200], and שָׁלוֹם, *peace,* [(ש)300 + (ל)30 + (ו)6 + (ם)40] each have a gematria of 376. One who spoke *lashon hara* and hurts his friend or besmirches his reputation must make amends to that person. If he caused dissension between friends or spouses, let him make peace between them (*Iturei Torah*).

The underlying cause of gossip and slander is arrogance, for it breeds contempt for others and enables one to speak about them callously. The cedar symbolizes arrogance. The crimson thread, colored with a dye made from an insect, and the hyssop, a lowly bush, represent the humility that is so crucial for true repentance (*Rashi*).

There are many homiletic explanations for the combination of these three elements:

Yesod HaAvodah views the combination of cedar and hyssop as a formula for how one must serve God. On one hand, a person must be proud and strong in maintaining his principles. On the other hand, one's heart one must be truly humble.

Chidushei HaRim notes that just as one must repent for misplaced arrogance, so he must rectify inappropriate humility. For example: A poor person asks someone to approach members of his community to help him raise funds. The first response is usually, "Who am I? Do you think people will listen to me? I exert no influence in the community." This type of inappropriate humility requires atonement. Similarly, when God's honor is being publicly demeaned and someone must take a strong stand, people tend to become very humble. Suddenly, even the most outspoken people are sure that nobody takes their opinions seriously, anyway.

Conversely, if someone were to treat that same person with less respect than they think they deserve, they would suddenly remember their own importance and avenge the slight.

This behavior needs atonement through both the cedar tree and the hyssop.[10]

Avnei Nezer questions the need for this process.

---

9. **Felled by the Wind.** *For behold He forms mountains and creates winds; He recounts to a person what were his conversations* (Amos 4:13). This verse tells us that when one comes before the Heavenly Court, they recount even the light conversation between a man and his wife (*Chagigah* 5b). Whle this seems to be the teaching of the second part of the verse, how is the first phrase related to this message?

Maayana Shel Torah explains: Mountains, imposing piles of earth, are among the most tangible, while wind is among the most intangible. Nevertheless, wind has the ability to wear away the mountain. This power of the wind teaches us the power of speech. Even though it seems to be nothing, speech has the power to destroy worlds.

10. **Jelly Hearts.** *Derech Chaim* (by author of *Nesivos HaMishpat*) writes that just as one must don the hand-*tefillin* before the head-*tefillin* and must then remove the head-*tefillin* first; he must also first pick up the *lulav,* then the *esrog,* and put down the *esrog* first. In this way the head-*tefillin* are only worn togather with the hand-*tefillin*, and the *esrog* is held only together with the *lulav*.

The message of the rule regarding *tefillin* is that Judaism is a religion not only of ideas, but also action. Ideas without action are meaningless. The head must always be accompanied by the hand.

But what does the law regarding the *lulav* and *esrog* teach us? The Midrash (*Vayikra Rabbah* 30:14) compares the *esrog* to the heart and the *lulav* to the spine. The heart, the source of emotion, is crucial to scale spiritual heights. Nevertheless, emotions may never control a person to the point that he lacks the backbone to take a firm stand. Emotion must always be coupled with backbone (*Simchas Aharon*).

Since, as the Torah states, this process occurs *on the day of purification,* the person has apparently repented and humbled himself already. Why must he do so again?

He explains that there are two types of humility. True humility is the result of man contemplating his own insignificance. Another type of humility is brought about through pain and suffering. Illness, poverty and failure have a way of humbling even the high and mighty. This second type of humility is often transient; when the person is healed or his pain subsides the arrogance reasserts itself.

The *metzora,* humbled by pain, embarrassment and quarantine, certainly repented. However, he may never have acquired true humility. On the day of purification he is called upon to strive for the kind of humility that will remain with him forever.[11]

If humbling oneself is such a crucial element of the purification process, why does the Torah merely allude to it rather than explicitly demand it?

Sfas Emes note that true humility calls for man to recognize that his talents and accomplishments are insignificant, for they are his only through the grace of God. They grant him no right to be arrogant. If a person has to be commanded to work on humility, he clearly feels that he deserves to be arrogant, but he is overcoming that urge. That is not true humility.

The Torah alludes to being humble so we can think about it and come to understand that we have nothing to be arrogant about. Only then will we really be humble.[12], [13]

וְאַחַר יָבוֹא אֶל הַמַּחֲנֶה וְיָשַׁב מִחוּץ לְאָהֳלוֹ שִׁבְעַת יָמִים

Thereafter he may enter the camp, but he shall dwell outside of his tent for seven days (ibid. 8).

Once the *metzora* is purified and allowed to enter the camp, why is he still restricted for seven days?

R' Shmelke of Nikolsburg explains: *Tzaraas* is caused by the sin of *lashon hara,* which, as discussed, is the result of arrogance. The Sages

---

11. **High Man/Low Man.** Speech is the most potent expression of man's superiority over all other creatures. When one abuses speech by speaking *lashon hara,* he abuses that which is uniquely human about him.

Man is called אָדָם. On one hand, this indicates that he was formed from אֲדָמָה, *earth.* On the other hand, he is called אָדָם because אֲדַמֶּה לְעֶלְיוֹן, he is compared to the One Above. By abusing his power of speech, one takes himself from the heights of the heavens to the lowliness of earth. Thus, the purification process includes the cedar, symbol of the potential majestic heights man can achieve, and hyssop, symbol of how low man can fall (*Zekan Aharon*).

12. **Internal Humility.** The *Baal Shem Tov* once came to Polonoye in a very elegant carriage. When one of his detractors accused him of arrogance, the *Baal Shem Tov* responded with a parable.

A king announced that he was in search of an elixir that would guarantee him longevity.

A wise man approached the king and told him that the secret of long life is humility. Immediately, the king set out to act humbly. He refrained from riding in the royal carriage, he walked behind other people rather than in front. However, the more humbly he acted, the more pompous he became. "Look at me," he said to himself. "Although I am a powerful king, I am so humble." When the wise man saw how the king was behaving, he explained to the king that this was not what he had meant. "Ride in the royal carriage and be humble in your heart. This type of humility is more difficult — but it is authentic humility."

One may sometimes have to act like the cedar, but he must feel like the hyssop.

13. **Why Are *You* Arrogant?** *R' Naftali of Bershad* once said: "When I come before the Heavenly Court, I will be able to justify almost all of my shortcomings, except for my lack of humility. When they ask me why I didn't know more Torah I will claim that I didn't have the intellectual ability. [See, however, *Tanna D'vei Eliyahu Zuta* 14.] If they ask me why I did not at least fast and pray, I will tell them that I was too weak. If they want to know why I did not give charity, I will be able to excuse myself by saying, 'I was so poor I could not even provide for myself, let alone for others.'

"But then they will say, 'If you were ignorant, weak and poor, what were you so arrogant about?' And for this I will have no answer."

(*Bava Basra* 98a) teach that even one's own family cannot bear the presence of an arrogant person. While the *metzora* may have humbled himself with regard to others, he must make special effort to ingratiate himself with his wife and family. He needs an additional seven days to achieve this proper blend of humility and authority.[14]

וְרָחַץ אֶת בְּשָׂרוֹ בַּמַּיִם וְטָהֵר
and immerse his flesh in water and become pure (ibid. 9).

Rambam (*Hilchos Mikvaos* 11:12) explains that the concepts of purity and impurity are a Divine decree and cannot be understood logically. Similarly, the fact that immersion purifies a person is also beyond human comprehension. *Tumah*, impurity, is not filth that can be washed away with water.

Nevertheless, Rambam tells us that there is a lesson that can be learned from the law of purification. Just as one whose body is impure becomes purified through immersion in water, one who sincerely wants to purify his soul can do so through immersing himself in the waters of Torah.

Background

The Torah allows a poor *metzora* to bring a less expensive offering as part of his purification process.

וְאִם דַּל הוּא וְאֵין יָדוֹ מַשֶּׂגֶת
If he is poor and his means are not sufficient (ibid. 21).

Previously we learned about other offerings where poor people have the option of bringing more economical sacrifices. The Talmud (*Yoma* 41b) cites a disagreement as to whether a wealthy person who brought the offering allowed for a poor person has, ex post facto, fulfilled his obligation by bringing a poor man's offering. With regard to the *metzora's* sacrifice, however, all are in agreement that a wealthy *metzora* has not met his obligation by bringing the offering designated for a poor *metzora*.

Meshech Chochmah explains (based on *Arachin* 16a) that refusing to lend household items to neighbors is a cause of *tzaraas*. The wealthy person who brings the offering of a pauper has apparently not been cured of his stinginess. He is not yet pure.

The *Chafetz Chaim* sees in our verse a lesson about setting spiritual goals. People who learn, pray and observe *mitzvos* often think that though they may not be perfect, they are far superior to their friends, relatives and acquaintances."

This verse teaches that one who is "spiritually poor" — who lacks the upbringing or the intellectual or emotional means to achieve high spiritual levels — is entitled to bring a smaller offering. However, those who benefit from having had proper education or who are smarter than others cannot be satisfied with that same offering. They must serve God at a level that reflects their spiritual affluence.[15], [16]

---

14. **Foolproof.** While others might take the bluster of an arrogant person seriously, those closest to him know the truth. We might suggest that this is the reason that God particularly despises haughty people (*Pesachim* 113b). While the person may think that he can fool others, his arrogance shows that he mistakenly feels that he can also fool the One Above (*Simchas Aharon*).

15. **A Higher Standard.** The Talmud (*Bava Metzia* 83a) relates that Rabbah bar bar Chanah hired two steve dores to carry a barrel of wine. When they broke it, he seized their cloaks to insure that they pay him for the loss. They called him before Rav, who insisted that he return the cloaks. When he asked Rav, "Is this the law?" he replied with the verse *"In order that you follow the path of the good"* (*Proverbs* 2:20). The stevedores then told Rav, "We are poor people. We need the wages that he was to pay us for our work." Rav instructed Rabbah bar bar Chanah to pay them. "Is this too the law?" he asked. Rav replied, *"And the byways of the righteous you shall keep"* (ibid.)
The spiritually affluent are answerable to a higher standard and must bring a better offering.

16. **Poor Souls.** One of the *Chafetz Chaim's* children once complained to him that their neighbor's children received new clothes for *Yom Tov* while they had to make do with their old clothes. The Chafetz Chaim answered as follows: "Thank God, we have been very successful. We are *b'nei Torah* (students of Torah) and our children are being raised in the spirit of Torah and *mitzvos* as well. Unfortunately our neighbor has not merited to spend his life learning Torah, nor are his children motivated to do so. It is only fair that God at least allow him the pleasure of buying his family new clothes for *Yom Tov*."

It seems obvious that *if he is poor*, then *his means are not sufficient*. Why does the Torah seem to repeat itself? *Otzar Chaim* sees in this verse an insight into the human condition: Those who are poor are frequently filled with resentment at God for having decreed poverty upon them. In fact, however, God's blessing of wealth is given only to those who are emotionally equipped to face the challenges wealth brings. Wealth in the hands of one who cannot handle it can be dangerous.

If he is poor, says the Torah, it is because *his means are not sufficient* — he lacks the fortitude to spiritually survive wealth.[17]

Background

The Torah now teaches the laws of the *tzaraas* that afflicts houses. When it becomes necessary to punish a Jew and remind him to repent, God begins by afflicting his home. If this is not enough, He afflicts the person's garments. If the person still does not repent, God sends *tzaraas* to the person's body.[18]

כִּי תָבֹאוּ אֶל אֶרֶץ כְּנַעַן
When you arrive in the land of Canaan (ibid. 34).

The Midrash (*Yalkut Shimoni*) questions why the Torah here refers to the land of Canaan when in fact it was home to seven nations. It answers that the Canaanites were heavily involved in commerce. *Haamek Davar* explains: The Talmud (*Arachin* 16b) teaches that *lashon hara* that does not cause damage to others is atoned for by the cloak of the Kohen, while *lashon hara* that causes damage brings *tzaraas*. Those involved in commerce feel a need to maintain a competitive edge, and tend to slander others and engage in unscrupulous tactics. Thus, the land of Canaan — the world of business — is particularly vulnerable to *tzaraas*.

וְנָתַתִּי נֶגַע צָרַעַת בְּבֵית אֶרֶץ אֲחֻזַּתְכֶם
and I will place a tzaraas affliction upon a house in the land of your possession (ibid).

According to *Rashi*, when the Canaanite inhabitants of the Land saw that the Israelites would

---

17. **Theft of the Pauper.** King Solomon writes *Do not rob the destitute because he is destitute* (Proverbs 22:22). If a person is truly destitute, of what can he be robbed? *Tiferes Shlomo* explains that there are miserly people who really do not want to help the needy. Since they are embarrassed by others seeing how they lack decency, they seek to justify themselves by discrediting the poor, claiming that they are not in need. As a result, not only do they not help, but they discourage others from doing so.

It is this tendency that is being addressed: *Do not rob the destitute* of the fact that *he is destitute*. The one resource the poor man has is his ability to arouse the sympathy of good-hearted Jews. Do not take that away from him.

18. **Bitter Enough.** One of the vegetables that may be used for *maror* is חֲזֶרֶת, Romaine lettuce. Its Hebrew name is related to חָזַר, *to return*. Often a bitter experience can cause a person to reflect on his life and return to God.

R' Moshe Feinstein notes that the *Mishnah* (*Pesachim* 39a) lists five species that can be used as *maror*. The last one listed, i.e., the least preferred choice, is *maror*, which has an exceptionally bitter taste. *Chazeres*, on the other hand, is listed first, i.e., it is most preferable, although it is not as bitter or sharp as the species that follow it.

This teaches us a lesson about how we are to react to difficulties. All suffering comes from God and has a purpose. When we lapse in our dispatch of our spiritual duties, God besets us with difficulties to prod us to improve. But these difficulties can assume many forms. The Talmud (*Arachin* 16b) states that even putting one's hand into his pocket and pulling out the wrong coin, a slight inconvenience, is an example of "suffering." The form and intensity of the suffering He brings on us depends on how we react. If a person who misplaces his keys realizes that God wants him to take stock of his actions, the "suffering" has accomplished its purpose; nothing more severe is necessary. If, however, a person does not heed these smaller calls, he will, God forbid, be reminded by increasingly louder signals, until he heeds their message.

The mild *chazeres* is the preferred type of *maror*, because *maror* does not necessarily have to be very bitter.

It is only if the message of the mild *chazeres* is ignored that the more bitter forms of suffering must be employed.

be victorious, they hid their valuables in the walls of their homes. By placing a *tzaraas* affliction on the walls, God provided the new Jewish owners with a way to access the treasure. This seems to contradict the view of the Talmud (*Yoma* 11b), which views *tzaraas* inflictions on homes as a punishment for the refusal to loan household effects to others. Since those who turn down their neighbors' requests usually claim that they do not have what the borrower needs, God forces them to remove all their household items, so that everyone can see the truth.

R' Y. Eiger offers an explanation, based on a thought of the *Maggid of Mezritch*. In the Sabbath *zemiros* we say מְשׁךְ חַסְדְּךָ לְיוֹדְעֶךָ קֵל קַנָּא וְנוֹקֵם, *"Bring Your kindness to those who know You, jealous and vengeful God."*

Why is God's treating us kindly related to the fact that He is a jealous and vengeful God? The Maggid explains by means of a parable: A king was traveling with one of his servants, when a peasant threw mud at the king's cloak. The servant wanted to immediately punish the peasant, but the king would not allow it. "Rather," said the king, "teach him proper etiquette, until he is fit to serve me." When the fellow was finally trained, the king had him brought to the palace, where the former peasant was brought before him. The man was so overcome by shame at having insulted the person who was so kind to him that he began to weep uncontrollably.

We turn to God and ask that He expose us to such an overwhelming outpouring of kindness that we will be embarrassed over how we have "mistreated" Him. This will have a far more powerful and lasting effect on us than punishment will.

While the *tzaraas* afflictions are a punishment, they come together with God's blessing in the form of a treasure. In this way God rehabilitates man with kindness.

The affliction of the houses is born of an attitude that one's land and his house are his very own.

One who refuses to help others suffers from the attitude of the Sodomites: "What's mine, is mine; what's yours is yours" (*Avos* 5:13). While this view may seem to reflect absolute justice, it ignores the reality that justice must always be tempered by love for one's fellow man.

"From the moment you step into the Land and acquire private property, you are vulnerable to this type of possessive attitude," says the Torah. God will mark the house of the self-centered person until he will be forced to come to the Kohen and say, *Something like an affliction has appeared to me in the house* (*R' S.R. Hirsch*).

כְּנֶגַע נִרְאָה לִי בַּבָּיִת
Something like an affliction appeared to me in the house (ibid. 35).

As noted, when God seeks to punish a person He first afflicts his house, then his garments and, if that also fails to engender repentance, He afflicts the person himself.

Divrei Shaul sees an allusion to this in our verse: *Something like an affliction appeared in me* [i.e., in my behavior], [and the punishment appears] in the house.

Why does the Torah prescribe saying, "Something *like* an affliction," rather than calling it *an affliction*?

We can understand this in light of a comment of the *Vilna Gaon*. The *Mishnah* (*Shabbos* 2:5) speaks of a person who extinguishes the Sabbath candles in order to save money, כְּחָס עַל הַנֵּר כְּחָס עַל הַשֶּׁמֶן, *like one who sought to save on the candle or the oil*. Why does the *Mishnah* use the prefix כְּ, *like*? The Vilna Gaon explains that in reality, one can never save money, for his income is determined from one Rosh Hashanah to the next (except for expenses related to Sabbath and holidays, *Beitzah* 16a). Thus it is *as though* he was saving money, but in fact he is not.

To the householder, what he sees on the wall *seems* like an affliction. In reality, it is God's way of enabling him to discover a hidden treasure (*Glilei Zahav*).[19]

---

19. **Early Warning.** The Torah describes the earlier signs of a spiritual affliction — "Something *like* an affliction appeared to me in the house." We are enjoined to address the underlying problem as soon as the first symptoms appear (*Alter of Slabodka*).

פרשת אחרי ‎⧉
Parashas Acharei

Background

Moses descended from Sinai with the Second Tablets — a sign that God had forgiven the Jewish people for the sin of the Golden Calf — on the tenth of Tishrei. This day was established for eternity as *Yom HaKippurim,* the day of atonement. The Torah here describes the special service of that day.

דַּבֵּר אֶל אַהֲרֹן אָחִיךָ וְאַל יָבֹא בְכָל עֵת אֶל הַקֹּדֶשׁ

Speak to Aaron, your brother — he shall not come at all times into the Sanctuary (16:2).

Why does the Torah stress that Aaron was Moses' brother? *HaDerash V'Halyun* cites the *Sifra,* which teaches that while Aaron was limited as to when and how he could enter the Holy of Holies, Moses enjoyed unlimited access. The Torah here outlines the limited circumstances under which Aaron may enter this area. Since Moses might fear that this would arouse Aaron's jealousy, God told

him, *Speak to Aaron your brother,* about whom I had told you when you were returning to Egypt to lead the Jews, *Aaron* **your brother** . . . *behold he is going out to meet you and when he sees you he will rejoice in his heart (Exodus 4:14).* As *Rashi* (ad loc.) explains, "Contrary to your assumption that he would feel hurt over your appointment to greatness he will sincerely rejoice for you." Here too *Aaron* **your brother** will have no ill feelings that though his brother Moses has unfettered access to the Holy of Holies, he himself may not enter at all times.[1]

וְאַל יָבֹא בְכָל עֵת אֶל הַקֹּדֶשׁ

he shall not come at all times into the Sanctuary (ibid.).

Many homiletic insights have been offered on this verse.

Noam Elimelech sees this as a call for consistency in our service of God. We may not allow our study of Torah and performance of *mitzvos* to be influenced by our moods — "our times," as it were.[2]

‎⧉

---

1. **Brotherly Love.** There are many people who realize that jealousy of strangers is inappropriate, since two different people, with different upbringings and sets of circumstances, cannot be expected to enjoy the same lot in life. Many of them, however, still have a problem when their siblings, with whom they have so much in common, have more than they do. *Behold how good and how pleasant is the dwelling of brothers, moreover, in unity (Psalms 133:1)* — this, say our Sages, refers to Aaron and Moses.

2. **Steadily Fresh.** The Torah reading of *Rosh Chodesh* discusses both the daily *tamid* offering and the special offering of *Rosh Chodesh.* The *tamid* — which was brought twice daily — represents consistency while the *Rosh Chodesh* offering symbolizes freshness and renewal, represented by the New Moon. Freshness without consistency is dangerous — the Sages describe the evil inclination as convincing a person each day to try something new,

The Talmud (*Kesubos* 50a) explains the words of King David, *Praiseworthy are those ... who perform righteousness in every time* (עֹשֵׂה צְדָקָה בְכָל עֵת) (*Psalms* 106:3), as referring to those who support their own young children. To insure that one does not believe that his support of his family absolves him of giving charity to others, the Torah teaches — וְאַל יָבֹא בְכָל עֵת אֶל הַקֹּדֶשׁ — one cannot achieve sanctity by fulfilling only בְכָל עֵת *every time*. He must go beyond his immediate family and care for all Jews if he is to be worthy of holiness (*Shelah*).[3]

אֶל פְּנֵי הַכַּפֹּרֶת אֲשֶׁר עַל הָאָרֹן
in front of the Cover that is upon the Ark (ibid.).

Toras Kohanim derives from this that the Cover was the only thing covering the Ark; it had no cloth which covered it.

This is a lesson to people who are truly God fearing, yet who are embarrassed to carry their Judaism proudly. The Torah teaches that the Ark, symbol of Torah, must not be covered over. We should display our Judaism proudly.[4]

כִּי בֶּעָנָן אֵרָאֶה עַל הַכַּפֹּרֶת
for in a cloud I will appear upon the Ark-cover (ibid.).

When dark clouds hover over the Jewish nation, threatening to plunge us into darkness, God will appear, inspiring and strengthening us so we can overcome the challenges that confront us (*R' Meir Shapiro*).[5]

בְּזֹאת יָבֹא אַהֲרֹן אֶל הַקֹּדֶשׁ
With this shall Aaron come into the Sanctuary (ibid. 3).

In the High Holy Day liturgy, we say that three things help us annul evil decrees: repentance, prayer, and charity, וּתְשׁוּבָה, וּתְפִלָּה, וּצְדָקָה מַעֲבִירִין אֶת רֹעַ הַגְּזֵרָה.

צוֹם, *fasting*; קוֹל, *voice [of prayer]*; and מָמוֹן, *money [for charity]*. The *gematria* of each of these words is 136, with their sum total 408. This is the *gematria* of זֹאת. With זֹאת, *this* — repentance, prayer and charity — we may come to God to seek atonement and a reversal of evil decrees (*Chida*). We also underscore this realization in *Psalm* 27, which is recited daily during the High Holiday season. *Though war*

---

until finally he persuades the person to practice idolatry (*Shabbos* 108b)! On the other hand, consistency without freshness leads to a diminished service of God as the prophet says, *their fear of Me is like rote learning of human commands* (*Isaiah* 29:13).

It is the subtle blend of the two that leads to proper Divine service (*Simchas Aharon*).

3. **In Good Hands.** *R' Zusia of Anipoli* was poor for most of his life. At times, his wife and children found their plight too much to bear.

Once, when a relative came to visit, R' Zusia's wife began to cry. The relative, taken aback, asked her where R' Zusia was, and she told the man that he was likely in the *beis midrash.*

When the relative entered the *beis midrash,* he found R' Zusia rapturously singing verses of *Psalms.* The man began to berate R' Zusia. "Your wife and children are upset and you joyously sing *Tehillim?*"

"They have what to be worried about, because they rely on me to provide for them. But I have no reason for concern — for I rely on the One Above, for myself and for them. Why should I not be happy?" R' Zusia replied.

4. **Jewish Pride.** In *Rabbi Yitzchak Hutner's* early years as *Rosh Yeshivah* of Yeshivah Rabbeinu Chaim Berlin, he would officiate at the marriage of a student only if the young man committed himself to carry his *tallis* and *tefillin* bag openly — not in a plain paper bag, as was common at the time.

5. **Light in the Cloud.** While in Auschwitz, *R' Hirsch Meisels* was asked by an unlearned Hungarian Jew whether he was permitted to bribe a Nazi to allow the man's only son to escape from a group that was being taken to be killed. The problem was that some other Jewish child would be chosen to replace the child who was missing. R' Meisels begged the man to do as he understood, and not to formally present him the question.

From the Rabbi's answer the man understood that the Rabbi felt that it was forbidden. Proudly, he said, "Well then, I am ready to do what the holy Torah expects of me."

In the cloud, God appeared on the cover of the Ark, inspiring superhuman fortitude.

ספר ויקרא: פרשת אחרי **[288]**

would arise against me, in this (בְּזֹאת) I trust (verse 3). When war is waged against us, be it physical or spiritual it is in זֹאת — the combination of repentance, prayer and charity — that we trust, certain that it will help save us.

וּמֵאֵת עֲדַת בְּנֵי יִשְׂרָאֵל יִקַּח
From the assembly of the Children of Israel he shall take (ibid. 5).

The public empowers its leaders to accomplish things on its behalf. In the Yom Kippur liturgy, when we describe the Temple service which was performed by the Kohen Gadol, we mention an integral part of the service that was taking place outside: "and the Kohanim and the people who were standing in the Temple Courtyard." The people for whom the Kohen Gadol was praying were themselves praying that his prayers be accepted. The Torah describes the Kohen Gadol as *the Kohen who was greater than his brothers* (מֵאֶחָיו) (*Leviticus* 21:10). The Talmud interprets מֵאֶחָיו as "greater *from* his brothers" (*Yoma* 18a). Those he led and represented made him great.

Hence this verse alludes to the fact that a key element of the Kohen Gadol's service is *he took* [his strength] *from the assembly of the Children of Israel* (*Ateres Shlomo*).[6]

שְׁנֵי שְׂעִירֵי עִזִּים לְחַטָּאת
two he-goats for a sin offering (ibid.).

Of the two he-goats for the sin-offering, one was offered as a sacrifice in the Temple, and the second one was sent to Azazel in the Wilderness.

We can gain insight into why this was done through a principle put forward by *R' Yisrael Salanter*. There are two reasons a person sins: one is that he is driven by passion, the second is because he wishes to rebel against God. Passion can be redirected and used to study Torah and perform *mitzvos* properly. Rebelliousness, however, cannot be used in the service of God.

The two sin-offerings represent these two motivations. The goat which symbolizes the sins of passion is offered before God, as we dedicate ourselves to use our passions properly. The second he-goat, which represents rebellious sin, is sent far into the Wilderness, for it has no place in the House of God and His service (*R' Yisrael HaKohen of Baltermintz*).

R' Moshe Mordechai Epstein notes the Talmud's ruling (*Shevuos* 13b) that the two he-goats must be nearly identical in appearance, height and value.

Two trains that were on parallel tracks pulled out of the station, one headed east and the other west. As they picked up speed the distance between them became greater and greater. Although they had been side by side, with time the gap between them is huge.[7]

---

6. **Public Investiture.** *R' Chaim Shmulevitz* would often say, "People say that a Jew in Jerusalem [the *Beis Yisrael of Ger*] can perform miracles. It is true!" And then he would add, "And if people believed in me like they believe in him, I too could perform miracles!" It is the people who invest their leaders with the power to help them.

7. **Wrong-Way Ride.** A wealthy and successful lawyer visited his childhood friend *R' Elchanan Wasserman,* and was anguished by the *Rosh Yeshivah's* poverty. He exclaimed, "Elchanan, you are much brighter than I. Had you become a lawyer, you would be a wealthy man today!"

R' Elchanan did not respond to the remark.

The old friends spent several hours together, and R' Elchanan then accompanied his visitor to the train.

At the station two trains were waiting. A modern, comfortable train was heading east, and an old, rickety one was going west. The lawyer, who was traveling westward, walked toward the old train. R' Elchanan stopped him. "Why would you travel in such an uncomfortable train? Go take the luxurious new one!"

The man stared at R' Elchanan. "Because I'm going in the other direction!"

"Nonetheless, isn't it better to travel in a comfortable train?" R' Elchanan continued.

The lawyer was exasperated. "Elchanan, you're speaking nonsense! What good is a comfortable train if it is not taking me where I have to go?"

Softly, R' Elchanan replied, "Listen to yourself. You know that when you want to arrive at a specific destination, the comfort of the vehicle doesn't determine whether you get on, the direction does. The main thing is to get where you have to be.

"You had asked me why I did not become a lawyer. Of course that career would have been more lucrative, but that is not my goal in life. What good is the comfort if I don't arrive where I am headed?"

R' Nosson Geisler used this parable to explain a distinction made by *Rabbeinu Yonah*.

This is true of people as well. We often see people who seem to be very different from one another in their attitudes and levels of observance. We might find, however, that this was not always the case. They may have started out together. However, at some early stage in their lives, they began to head along tracks that led in opposite directions. While early on the differences between them seemed minor, with the passage of time the distance becomes astonishing.

When people came to the Temple on Yom Kippur, they were taught an important lesson about educating their children. The two he-goats were almost identical. Nevertheless, one found himself brought to the holiest of places, while the other was pushed off a cliff far outside the camp. This is equally true with children. While two children may initially seem the same, their direction in life will depend on how they set out.

A child who follows the path of Torah, is headed toward a life dedicated to God and the holy of holies. If, however, he takes even small steps in another direction, he runs a much higher risk of ending up "outside the camp." The slightest differ- ence in the beginning can make all the difference later on.

וְנָתַן אֶת הַקְּטֹרֶת עַל הָאֵשׁ לִפְנֵי ה' . . . וְלֹא יָמוּת
He shall place the incense upon the fire before Hashem . . . so that he shall not die (ibid. 13).[8]

The fulfillment of this verse is one of the crucial parts of the Yom Kippur service. The Sadducees insisted that the Kohen Gadol place the incense on the coals before entering the Holy of Holies. This verse teaches that he shall place the incense upon the fire *when he is before Hashem,* inside the inner chamber.

Homiletically this tells us that someone teaching Torah and Judaism must first enter inside — he must himself live the message of Torah — and only then can he successfully inspire others.[9]

Another lesson is that the Sadducees of every generation seek to modify the Torah, the Holy of Holies, by introducing elements from the outside world.

Guidance on how to live a Torah life must come from within, not without (*HaDerash V'Halyun*).[10]

Regret and abandoning sin are two of the elements critical to achieve repentance. When discussing which of the two should come first, R' Yonah differentiates between someone who sins only occasionally and one who is a habitual sinner, "who follows a bad path." The person who sins only occasionally should first regret his actions, then work to abandon sin. The habitual sinner, on the other hand, must first change his path in life. To regret his actions even as he continues to do them is akin to "immersing in the *mikveh* while holding an impure crawling creature" (*Shaarei Teshuvah* 1:11).

One who is on the train headed in the wrong spiritual direction gains nothing by being sorry for boarding that train. His first objective must be to get off the train as quickly as possible. Only then can he begin to plan how to get where he really wants to go.

8. **Misappropriated Funds.** *Rashi* notes the implication that if the Kohen Gadol does not perform the incense offering properly he will die.

R' Yisrael Salanter once met a wealthy Jew in St. Petersburg and told him the following. The Talmud (*Yoma* 26a) teaches that offering the incense in the Temple is propitious for wealth. This connection teaches us that just as one who does not properly bring the incense is liable to die, one who does not put his wealth to proper use brings about his own spiritual death.

9. **Overflow.** R' Aharon Kotler would sometimes be approached by young men who wanted to leave the yeshivah to teach others and do outreach. He would suggest that they contemplate the following:

If one pours wine for others from his own full cup, his cup will become empty. But if he pours wine into his cup until it runs over into the cups of others, he and they will have wine.

A person must constantly fill himself with Torah and fear of Heaven so that he overflows with them. That way, he will be able to influence his surroundings without paying a spiritual price.

10. **Lacking the Real Fire.** In a eulogy for *R' Nachman Bulman*, *R' Yonasan Rosenblum* related the following story: A student was spending the summer at Yeshivah Ohr Somayach in Jerusalem before going on to study to become a Conservative clergyman.

When the young man first met Rav Bulman, the rabbi did not attack the Conservative movement. Rather, he suggested that the young man read the final chapter of *Conservative Judaism* by Marshall Sklare, a sociologist

הַשֹּׁכֵן אִתָּם בְּתוֹךְ טֻמְאֹתָם
*that dwells with them amid
their contamination* (ibid. 16).

God's Presence remains with His children despite their spiritual contamination (*Rashi*).

The *Baal Shem Tov* once visited a certain city. When he arrived, the townsfolk came out to greet him, and two of the wealthiest citizens vied for the privilege of serving as his host. One of the men was an accomplished Torah scholar, but he was arrogant. The other was kind and well liked, but his morals left much to be desired.

The Baal Shem Tov chose to stay at the home of the second man. He later explained his choice citing our verse. "The Torah states that the Divine Presence *dwells with them amid their contamination,* when they sin. A sinner recognizes his failings, and is humbled by his imperfections. This causes God to be with him (see *Psalms* 51:19). If God is with him, I also want to be with him. On the other hand, the Talmud (*Sotah* 5a) teaches that God refuses to be with an arrogant person. I too, concluded the Baal Shem Tov, should have no place with him."

וְכָל אָדָם לֹא יִהְיֶה בְּאֹהֶל מוֹעֵד
*Any person should not be in
the Tent of Meeting* (ibid. 17).

The Midrash (*Vayikra Rabbah* 21:11) questions: What does "any person" mean? After all, the Kohen Gadol himself is also a person! The Midrash explains that, when the Kohen Gadol entered the Holy of Holies, his face was aflame as a result of the Divine Spirit which overcame him, and he was akin to an angel.[11]

Mei HaShiloach offers yet another perspective.

King Solomon teaches, "Man's is the arrangement of [thoughts in] the heart, but from Hashem comes the tongue's reply" (*Proverbs* 16:1). Usually, one is granted the power to pray based upon the extent to which he prepares himself emotionally in advance. On Yom Kippur, however, even the highest degree of human understanding, represented by the term *adam,* is incapable of preparing for the great lovingkindness that Hashem seeks to bestow.[12] Thus, the Torah teaches וְכָל אָדָם, *any person (adam),* shall not be present. When the Kohen of all Kohanim entered the Holy of Holies on the Sabbath of all Sabbaths (*Yom Kippur* — see *Leviticus* 23:32) he surrendered his entire being, to allow the full

deeply sympathetic to the movement. After discussing the remarkable growth of the movement in the 1950's and 1960's, Sklare concludes with an assessment of the movement's minimal impact on the spiritual life of its followers.

Rabbi Bulman was wise enough to recognize that the young man would realize that his idealistic commitment to the Jewish people would not find satisfaction within the Conservative movement. In his wisdom, Rav Bulman grasped the nature of this young man, with whom he was speaking for the first time, and knew just where to direct him so that he would make the decision to abandon his career plans on his own, without pressure.

11. **Mundane Angel.** During his visit to *Eretz Yisrael* in 1932, the *Satmar* Rav visited with the Sephardic Kabbalist R' Chaim Shaul Doueck. Commenting on this Midrash, he pointed out that though the Kohen Gadol achieved angelic sanctity, he did not lose sight of the "mundane" human needs of the nation. The *machzor* of Yom Kippur recalls the prayer of the Kohen Gadol in the Holy of Holies, a prayer in which he asked for a "year that is blessedly dewy and rainy, a year of sustenance, a year in which your people, the family of Israel, is not dependent for a livelihood upon one another or upon another people."

12. **Unlimited Future.** "R' Shimon ben Gamliel said: Israel had no days as festive as the Fifteenth of Av and Yom Kippur, for on those days, the maidens of Jerusalem would go out wearing white, borrowed garments [in order to find their mate]" (*Taanis* 4:8). What do Yom Kippur, the day when Hashem purifies His children from their sins, and the 15th of Av, when marriage partners were chosen, have in common?

R' Shlomo Freifeld explained: The joy of one rejoicing over the past is limited to the joy of the experience. One who rejoices for the future, however, experiences unlimited joy, because the future is limitless.

The joy over finding one's life partner is the joy of a potentially limitless future of happiness and bliss.

Likewise, on Yom Kippur we are cleansed by sin; we can look forward to a future of unlimited spiritual growth and achievement.

Thus, there were no festivals like Yom Kippur and the fifteenth of Av; other festivals commemorated events, these commemorate the joy of potential.

blessing Hashem would offer. He did not allow his own preparation, as extensive as it was, to limit the limitless outpouring of blessing from Above.

וְכִפֶּר בַּעֲדוֹ וּבְעַד בֵּיתוֹ וּבְעַד כָּל קְהַל יִשְׂרָאֵל
he shall provide atonement for himself, for his household and for the entire congregation of Israel (ibid.).

This passage can be understood to be a message to those involved in public service: Their primary concern must be for their own spiritual health and that of their families. Only then ought they begin to deal with *the entire congregation of Israel*. [13]

וְלָקַח מִדַּם הַפָּר וּמִדַּם הַשָּׂעִיר וְנָתַן עַל קַרְנוֹת הַמִּזְבֵּחַ סָבִיב
He shall take some blood of the bull and some blood of the he-goat and place it on the horns of the Altar all around (ibid. 18).

In the account of the Yom Kippur service that is recorded in the *machzor* it says: "Joyously, he would empty the blood of the bull into the basin containing the blood of the goat, and then pour the full bowl back into the empty one so that the two bloods would mix very well with one another." Why was the Kohen Gadol especially joyous over this stage of the service?

For seven days before Yom Kippur, the Kohen Gadol was alone in the special Falhedrin chamber of the Temple, sequestered from family and friends.

On the Holy Day itself, he brought the bull as an offering for himself and the he-goat for the nation. He rejoiced as he mixed the blood of these offerings, for now he rejoined the rest of the nation (*Divrei Shmuel*).

כִּי בַיּוֹם הַזֶּה יְכַפֵּר עֲלֵיכֶם
For on this day he shall provide atonement for you (ibid. 30).

R' *Shmelke of Nikolsburg* offered a parable. A prince regularly did things which shamed his father, the king. A certain member of the king's inner circle would make it his business to tell the king each time the prince misbehaved. One day this fellow was out of town. The son quickly ran to his father, crying that he was truly sorry for his misdeeds. "I regret what I did, and I promise to change my ways." The king was touched by his son's contrition and forgave him.

The Talmud (*Yoma* 20a) teaches that Satan does not have his accusatory powers on Yom Kippur. This is the opportunity for every Jew to run to his Father, the King, and beg His forgiveness.[14], [15], [16]

---

13. **Changing the World?** R' *Yisrael Salanter* is reputed to have said "When I was young I thought I could change the world. As I got older I set my sights lower; I would change the people of my town. Yet later I thought I would change my family. Now I'll be happy if I can change myself."

14. **Motherly Love.** The *Zohar* writes that when God's attribute of mercy is about to descend to the world it assumes the guise of a mother.

R' *Chaim of Volozhin* offers this insight: Both fathers and mothers love their baby greatly. They both hug and kiss the child with intense love. Nevertheless, when the child is soiled, it is usually the mother who patiently takes the baby, cleans, freshens and diapers him. Even when the child is dirty, her active expression of love never wanes.

God, in His mercy, is like a mother. Even as we soil ourselves with sin, He remains with us and never allows His loving care for us to wane.

15. **From You, to You.** "My God . . . Even if You [threaten to] kill me (as punishment for my sins) I will earnestly wait for You. If You seek out my iniquity I will flee *from* You *to* You and cover myself from Your anger in Your shadow" (*Kesser Malchus* by R' *Shlomo Ibn Gabirol*).

16. **Double Identity.** *Hashem save! The King will answer us on the day we call* (*Psalms* 20:10). The grammatical structure of the verse seems to be stilted: The beginning appears to be a plea, *Hashem save!* while the latter part of the verse is a statement of fact.

R' *Mannes Mandel* explained the verse with this parable: A bright boy excelled in his studies and surpassed the abilities of the *melamdim* in his little village. His father sent him to a large city to board at the home of a *melamed* there and to learn in that man's *cheder*. After some time, the boy became so close to the *melamed* that he felt him to be his second father.

One day, the boy misbehaved in *cheder* and the *melamed* had to punish him severely. The child was deeply hurt.

מִכֹּל חַטֹּאתֵיכֶם לִפְנֵי ה׳ תִּטְהָרוּ
*from all your sins before Hashem
shall you be cleansed* (ibid. 30).

The Talmud (*Yoma* 85b) deduces from this verse that repentance and Yom Kippur only atone for sins committed *before Hashem* — sins exclusively against God. Sins that impacted other people are not forgiven by God until one first appeases the person who was wronged and is granted his forgiveness.[17]

An interpersonal sin is like an item robbed from two partners. Paying one of the owners is insufficient; one must make restitution to both. It is certainly impossible for one partner to forgive the money the thief owes the other partner.

Every interpersonal sin is in reality also a sin against God, for He commanded us not to act against others. Neither God alone, nor man alone, can forgive our sins against our fellow man. It is only those sins which are done, exclusively *in front*

of God, as it were, that can be forgiven by Him alone (*Zekan Aharon*).[18]

It is for this reason that the *haftarah* of Yom Kippur includes the prophet's call to social responsibility: *Do you call this a fast and a day of favor to Hashem? Surely you should divide your bread with the hungry, and bring the moaning poor to your home; when you see the naked, cover him; do not ignore your kin* (Isaiah 58:5,7).

This is high on the spiritual agenda of Yom Kippur, since Yom Kippur alone cannot fully address our mistreatment of others.

R' Akiva derived yet another point from our verse. The tractate *Yoma* discusses the laws of Yom Kippur, including the sacrifices of the day. R' Akiva, who lived through the destruction of the Temple, sought to comfort his fellow Jews on the first Yom Kippur after the destruction.

When he came "home" to the *melamed's* house, he approached the man and quietly said, "*Tatte* (father), please tell the *melamed* not to hit me again." The *melamed* replied, "I'll tell him and I promise he won't punish you again."

Hashem is the Name of God that indicates Divine Mercy. We call out, *Hashem save*! If You do, *the King* Who metes out justice *will answer us on the day we call.*

17. **That's My Kid!** *Simchas Aharon* offers another perspective: God is prepared to forgive someone who wronged Him. However, He is not willing to forgive someone who hurt His child. It is only after the sinner has made peace with His beloved child that He is ready to forgive.

18. **Back in Love.** We begin Yom Kippur with *Kol Nidrei,* an annulment of vows. Why is this prayer the prelude to Yom Kippur?

Simchas Aharon suggests the following: There are times that two friends, in a moment of anger or frustration, forswear benefiting from one another (see *Nedarim* 32b). Over the course of the year, we sin and cause God to be dissatisfied with the way we live our lives. On the other hand, a person may, deep in his heart, be upset with the lot in life which God has granted us. Our relationship with Him may border on that of forswearing benefit from one another.

As we enter Yom Kippur, the Day of Atonement, we all seek rapprochement with God. We begin by saying, "Let all our vows be annulled. We want to have enjoyment from our relationship with You, and we want You to derive pleasure from us. Let us begin to love each other once again".

In order to annul a vow, halachah requires a פֶּתַח — a reason which establishes that the vow was based on a false premise. *R' Joseph B. Soloveitchik* suggests such a reason for God to annul his decrees against His nation.

The Talmud (*Nedarim* 66a) tells of a man who vowed not to marry his niece, since she was not pretty. R' Yishmael took the young woman to his home, had her made up, groomed and dressed in nice clothes. He then called the man to his home and showed him his niece. "Is this the girl who you vowed not to marry?" he asked. When the man replied that it was not, R' Yishmael canceled the vow and allowed him to marry his niece. R' Yishmael then began to cry. He said, "The daughters of Israel are [intrinsically] beautiful; it is poverty that makes them ugly."

Poverty is not only financial; it can be emotional or spiritual as well. The Jewish people are beautiful and truly fit to be God's bride. It is poverty that makes them seem unworthy.

We begin Yom Kippur seeking to annul the vows that God has made against us. We cry out to Him, "We are really beautiful. It is spiritual poverty which makes us look so distasteful."

The Jews were broken and disheartened. How could they achieve forgiveness without the Temple, without the sacrificial service, without a Kohen Gadol?

A mere two months after the Destruction, R' Akiva, always the optimist (see *Makkos* 23a-b), taught, "Happy are you, Israel! In front of Whom are you cleansed and Who cleanses you? Your Father in Heaven, as it says 'in front of Hashem you will be purified' " (*Yoma* 85b).

There is a Yom Kippur even without a Temple, R' Akiva reassured the nation. So long as there is Hashem, the source of purity, Jews can be cleansed of their sins. As long as a Jew stands before Hashem, he will have his soul purified and cleansed.

Nesivos Shalom offers another insight into R' Akiva's words of comfort.

When a surgeon performs surgery on a patient, he endeavors to make the procedure as painless as possible. If, however, the patient suffers from a terminal disease and radical steps are in order, the doctor will administer painful treatments and prescribe even terribly bitter pills to save the patient. Even so, if the patient is the doctor's own child, the doctor will take extraordinary steps in order to make the most painful process as close to painless as is humanly possible.

Sometimes a Jew must undergo pain to cure him of the spiritual death brought on by sin. Had anybody else been performing the operation, it might be unnecessarily painful. We, however, are fortunate that our Father in Heaven is the One Who purifies and cleanses us. He spares no effort to minimize the pain.

פרשת קדושים ⊰
Parashas Kedoshim

Background

In this *parashah*, the Torah issues a general call to sanctity and then explains how a Jew can live with true holiness.

דַּבֵּר אֶל כָּל עֲדַת בְּנֵי יִשְׂרָאֵל
Speak to the entire assembly of the Children of Israel (19:2).

Although generally there was no requirement that every Jew be present when Moses taught a commandment, in this instance God commanded that all Jews attend. Why?

According to *Chasam Sofer*, this helps illustrate the Torah's concept of holiness. Judaism does not advocate living like a hermit. The Torah commands us to love people and to be constructive members of the community. We must always attempt to teach, by example the proper way to live and bring others closer to Hashem and His Torah.

Man must be holy — he must be separate and apart, keeping himself from indulgence in physical pleasures; but he must not be separate and apart from his fellow man. We are taught: *You shall be holy*, but this can be achieved only when you are *among the entire assembly of the Children of Israel.* [1], [2]

Yet another lesson may be derived from the Torah's insistence that the command to be holy be taught to the entire nation. In Judaism, sanctity is not the exclusive province of the clergy, nor of any particular class of Jews. Every Jew is an equal member of the "kingdom of ministers and holy nation" (see *Exodus* 19:6) and, as such, possesses the ability to rise above the temptations which seek to ensnare him. The call to sanctity was issued to the entire assembly, for each Jew can and must aspire to achieve sanctity (*Alshich*).

קְדֹשִׁים תִּהְיוּ
You shall be holy (ibid.).

What does it mean to *be holy*? Praying for hours? Self-flagellation?

The Talmud (*Pesachim* 104a) describes Menachem ben Simai as "the son of holy ones" because

---

1. **Consistently Jewish.** The credo of the Enlightenment Movement was, "Be a good Jew at home but act like all others when in public." The Torah rejects this approach. Sanctity must inform our lives not only in our private domain, but in public as well, and it must also govern Jewish public life.

   Hence, the Torah's call for sanctity was issued in a public forum, for Torah must govern both our private and public lives (*Divrei Shaarei Chaim*).

2. **Untainted Involvement.** The Torah tells us that we must be holy: *for am I holy*. Although God is transcendent and beyond human perception, He is intimately involved in the most mundane human affairs. Likewise, the sanctity God seeks from man is not one of total asceticism. Man, holy though he may be, should maintain his sanctity while remaining involved with his fellow men (*Ksav Sofer*).

he never studied money well enough to know the value of various currencies. Prayer and avoiding delicacies are vital and important. But a true barometer of a person's sanctity is his attitude toward money. Indeed, the Torah's call for sanctity precedes several laws that will be affected by one's attitude towards money. In effect, the Torah is telling us: Honor your parents even if it entails your losing a day's pay (see *The Fifth Commandment*, pg. 80); do not be deluded into thinking that by violating the Shabbos you will accrue greater wealth. The first step in being holy is: Do not idolize money (*Ohr Yaakov*).

The commandments later in the *parashah* are even more directly related to this lesson. *You shall not steal, you shall not deny falsely* (19:11), and *You shall not commit a perversion of justice* (ibid. 15) are all related to one's approach to money. The way in which one fulfills his obligations to the poor — which are also noted in this *parashah* — is an indicator of whether one views what he possesses as his own hard-earned money or a gift from God, meant to be distributed as He sees fit.

R' Yisrael Salanter thus explained the verse as follows: *You shall be holy* — be holy with regard to physical, mundane matters — *for holy am I, Hashem, your God* — leave the estoric holiness to Me. It is man's job to bring his sanctity into his temporal and interpersonal affairs.

Ramban maintains that the command to "be holy" means that we must observe the spirit, not just the letter of the law. Without the imperative to be sanctified, a person could become, in the words of *Ramban*, נָבָל בִּרְשׁוּת הַתּוֹרָה, *a degenerate with the permission of the Torah*[3] — observing the basic requirements of Halachah while trampling on its

spirit by surrendering to indulgence in all areas of life. Living a holy life requires us to limit our pursuit of permitted pleasures. A Jew must ask not only, "Is this halachically permitted?" but also, "Does it reflect my sanctified status as a member of God's Chosen People?"

אִישׁ אִמּוֹ וְאָבִיו תִּירָאוּ וְאֶת שַׁבְּתֹתַי תִּשְׁמֹרוּ

Every man: Your mother and father shall you revere, and My Sabbaths shall you observe; I am Hashem, your God (ibid. 3).

The Sages explain that the Torah juxtaposes honoring parents with observing the Sabbath to teach that if a parent commands a child to desecrate the Sabbath — or, to violate any other halachah — the child is required to disobey the parent. "Why," asks *Alshich*, "did the Torah choose the Sabbath as the example of a commandment that one may not transgress even in order to honor his parents?" *Alshich* explains: The Sages teach that the Torah equates reverence for God (*Deuteronomy* 6:13) with that for parents, because all three — God, father and mother — are partners in a person's existence (*Sifra*). When a person honors his parents, the "Third Partner" says, "I consider it as if I was there as well, and I too was honored" (*Kiddushin* 30b).

One might therefore think that since parents comprise two-thirds "ownership" of a person, their "majority" interest can "override" the will of God. The Torah therefore invokes the mitzvah of the Sabbath to remind us that God is ultimately the Creator of everything. The parents are also God's subjects, and they have no right to ask their child to do something against His will.[4]

---

3. **Spiritual Dehydration.** *R' Shlomo Freifeld* suggested that *Ramban's* נָבָל can be related to the word יִבּל, *wilt* (see *Psalms* 1:3). When a plant is deprived of water supply, its source of sustenance, it wilts and dies. It is the spirit of the Torah that infuses one's actions with vibrancy and significance. When one ignores this spirit, he starves his soul and spiritually wilts.

4. **A Future Lien.** An enchanting parable by the *Dubno Maggid* sheds perspective on this issue:

Three brothers decided that each of them would travel to a different country in order to gain access to the wisdom of the world. They would return home after a year, and each of them could share his experience with the others. At the end of the year, one brother had learned how to make a mirror that would enable him to see throughout the world. The second brother had learned to make a flying machine that could quickly take him anywhere in the world. The third brother had discovered a miracle potion which could cure all the known diseases.

One day, the first brother looked in his mirror and saw a princess in a distant land who was deathly ill. The king was distraught, for none of the doctors could find a cure for his daughter.

This brother immediately went to get his brothers. Using the second brother's flying machine, they arrived at the

אִישׁ אִמּוֹ וְאָבִיו תִּירָאוּ
Every man: Your mother and father shall you revere (ibid. 3).

Why is the fear of parents, rather than their honor, taught following the commandment to be holy?

Man is by nature stubborn and unwilling to forgo the fulfillment of his desires. When one is young he is trained to comply with the rules set down by his parents. This experience trains him to yield to a higher authority. Hence, fear and reverence of parents serves to train man in the fear of God necessary to live a life of sanctity (R' S. R. Hirsch).

Maayana Shel Torah suggests that the mitzvah to revere parents immediately follows the commandment to emulate God's sanctity because it is only when parents create a sanctified atmosphere in their home can they be assured that their children will truly revere them.

Background

The Torah teaches that when an offering is brought to the Sanctuary, it must be brought with the proper intention. Action is insufficient. The mind and the emotions must be engaged in the act if sanctity is to be achieved.

לִרְצֹנְכֶם תִּזְבָּחֻהוּ
You shall slaughter it to find favor for yourselves (ibid. 5).

Every type of sacrifice must be slaughtered with the proper intention in order for it to find favor in the eyes of God (see *Leviticus* 1:3). Why then does this verse reiterate this requirement with regard to a peace-offering?

Oznayim L'Torah explains: There is a mitzvah to eat on the day before Yom Kippur (*Shulchan Aruch, Orach Chaim* 604:1). As hard as it may be to fast for the sake of Heaven on Yom Kippur, it is considerably harder to *eat* for the sake of Heaven the day *before.* Since one derives physical pleasure when he eats, it is difficult to remain focused on the Heavenly purpose. It is only with great effort that one can succeed in eating with the proper intentions. The same reality holds true for offerings. A burnt-offering is completely consumed on the Altar. Only Kohanim partake from a sin-offering. It is relatively simple for the supplicant to offer these sacrifices for the sake of Heaven. But the supplicant himself partakes of a peace offering. It is therefore considerably more difficult to slaughter a peace-offering for the sake of Heaven. The Torah therefore stresses, *You shall slaughter it in order to find favor for yourselves.*

---

king's palace. The third brother, owner of the magical potion, went to speak to the king to offer his medical services. After drinking the potion the princess had an amazing recovery.

Overjoyed, the king summoned the three brothers. "I have decided to offer my daughter's hand in marriage to one of you, for you cured her. However, I cannot decide which of you I should choose as my son-in-law."

The three brothers began to argue, each one claiming to be the one who was critical to the princess's recovery.

The first brother argued, "Without my mirror we would have never known that the princess needed help in the first place."

"If not for my flying machine, how would we have arrived in this faraway place?" claimed the second brother. The third brother retorted, "All of your inventions would be worthless had I had not come with my miracle drug. I am the real healer."

Unable to decide, the king suggested that the final decision be left with the princess. The young lady replied, "As far as the past is concerned, you are all equally responsible for my recuperation and you all equally deserve to marry me. However, if I become sick again, only the brother with the miracle cure can help me. Thus, I choose him as my husband."

True, there are three partners in the creation of man and one must feel equally indebted to all of them. However, this is only true regarding the past. As far as the future is concerned, we are far more dependent on God, for every moment of life comes from Him.

Both parent and child must honor God, upon Whom we are all eternally dependent.

Background

The merciful and charitable God expects us to emulate Him in supporting the poor and unfortunate. This is an integral element of sanctity.

וּבְקֻצְרְכֶם אֶת קְצִיר אַרְצְכֶם לֹא תְכַלֶּה פְּאַת שָׂדְךָ לִקְצֹר

When you reap the harvest of your land you shall not complete your reaping to the corner of your field (ibid. 9).

The verse begins in the plural (וּבְקֻצְרְכֶם), but continues in the singular (לֹא תְכַלֶּה). This teaches important lessons about charity.

Kli Yakar suggests that at harvesttime, when many people have gifts for the poor, one might be tempted to think, "The poor are receiving so much grain from so many people. Why do they need my few kernels of wheat?" Even as many landowners are reaping, the Torah commands each of us to take personal responsibility for the poor.[5]

Alternatively, one might feel that the little bit of charity he has to offer makes no real difference. After all, there are so many poor people, and their needs are so great! The Torah therefore teaches that every individual landowner must do his share, as insignificant as it may seem (*Ohr HaChaim*).

וְכֶרֶם ךָ לֹא תְעוֹלֵל

You shall not pick the undeveloped twigs of your vineyard (ibid. 10).

The nation of Israel is referred to as the "vineyard of Hashem" (*Isaiah* 5:7). The undeveloped twigs of the vineyard are analogous to the young children. Parents are responsible to provide their children with the care and tending necessary for them to develop into strong and spiritually healthy Jews. Homiletically, our verse exhorts parents to insure that these "underdeveloped twigs" are never picked and taken from the vineyard of the Lord.

Background

Just as we must not become *degenerate with the permission of the Torah*, in matters directly spiritual, we must also be certain to maintain high standards of honesty and propriety in financial dealings. Even if a standard or practice cannot be enforced by the courts, it behooves us to act in a way that expresses sanctity.

לֹא תִּגְנֹבוּ

You shall not steal (ibid. 11).

Why does the Torah follow the commandments regarding gifts to the poor with the exhortation against stealing?

Tiferes Shlomo suggests that the juxtaposition teaches us that though charity is important, it does not justify thievery. One cannot "cleanse" illegally or unethically obtained money by donating it to worthy causes.

Unlike the Ten Commandments which teaches, לֹא תִּגְנֹב, *You shall not steal,* here the prohibition is framed in the plural — לֹא תִּגְנֹבוּ.

The *Vilna Gaon* explains: The prohibition in the Ten Commandments refers specifically to a kidnapper who forces his victim to work for him and sells him into slavery (see *Sanhedrin* 86a). This is a crime performed infrequently, by a rare degenerate individual. Thus, the Torah expresses its prohibition in the singular. Our verse, however, prohibits stealing money or valuables. Unfortunately, this is a common occurrence. Even "innocent" people often borrow property without permission, fail to spend their time at work as they should and forget to return small sums borrowed from a friend — yet

---

5. **Mine?** The obligation to set aside part of one's crops for the poor is incumbent even upon the poor themselves (see *Chullin* 131a-b). Though the owner of a field may himself live below the poverty line, he must nonetheless give a share of his limited yield to the poor.

This indicates that the Torah promulgated these laws not only to benefit the poor, but also to teach the Jewish farmer that the yield with which he is blessed is not "his." God did not provide only for him; the produce of his field is for all of God's children. God granted the poor a share of His bounty. He appointed those who are more fortunate as His charity trustees. They are enjoined to distribute wealth that is His to those who are in need.

these are all violations of this prohibition. Since it is a common occurrence, the Torah writes about it in the plural, for it applies to each of us.[6]

Ohr Olam suggests that the plural form is directed to businessmen. People in business sometimes feel justified in acting somewhat dishonestly, rationalizing that the person with whom they are dealing is also being less than honest in *his* dealings. "He's cheating me. Why can't I cheat him back?" they say.

Thus the Torah exhorts: "Even if the other party is already being dishonest, do not steal. Make sure it is not both of you who steal."

וְלֹא תְשַׁקְּרוּ אִישׁ בַּעֲמִיתוֹ
and you shall not lie to one another (ibid.).

Beyond refraining from all sorts of lies and untruths, one must maintain a heightened sense of honesty.

R' Shlomo Ganzfried in his classic halachic work *Kitzur Shulchan Aruch* (62:16) portrays the Torah standard of business ethics: "One who reneges on a business commitment, whether he is the buyer or seller, lacks trustworthiness and is viewed unfavorably by our Sages. It is fitting that a Jew be a man of his word as the prophet teaches: *The remnant of Israel will not commit injustice nor will they speak falsehood* (Zephaniah 3:13). A God-fearing person should even fulfill what he has thought; if he had decided in his heart to accept the price offered for an item, he should sell it at that price, even if the buyer, unaware of his decision, raised his offer."

Likewise, if the buyer had decided to pay a certain price, he should do so even though the seller, unaware of his decision, made a lower counterproposal.

לֹא תַעֲשֹׁק אֶת רֵעֲךָ
You shall not cheat your fellow (ibid. 13).

According to *Rambam* (*Hilchos S'chirus* 13:7), this forbids an employer to withhold wages from his employee.[7] Likewise, it obligates the

---

6. **By Any Other Name.** No one likes to see himself as a thief. Yet, if we are truly honest with ourselves, we might realize that we transgress this prohibition without even realizing it.

The *Chafetz Chaim* was once traveling on a horse-drawn wagon, engrossed in his learning, when the wagon suddenly stopped. The driver jumped off the wagon, grabbed a bale of hay from a stranger's field, tossed it onto the back of his wagon, and continued on his way.

The Chafetz Chaim, shocked at what he had just witnessed, asked the driver, "What did you do?"

"Nothing special," replied the driver. "I simply got some straw for my tired horse to eat."

The Chafetz Chaim said to him, "Why don't you simply answer, 'I stole somebody's property, I am a thief'?" Left with no choice, the driver admitted that he had done something "like stealing."

Startled, the Chafetz Chaim would not relent. "Why do you say 'like stealing'? What you just did is absolute robbery. Taking something that is someone else's *is stealing.*"

The Chafetz Chaim continued: "The Torah uses the plural when prohibiting larceny and when prohibiting one from swearing falsely. One violates the commandment against making a false oath regardless of which name of God he invokes (see *Rashi* to 19:12). Similarly, all forms of taking something that belongs to another person — no matter what you call it — is prohibited."

The contrite wagon driver promised the old sage of Radin that he would mend his ways.

Based on this incident, we might explain the flow of our verse: *You shall not steal; you shall not deny falsely.* We may not steal, and we must be sure not to deny to ourselves that improperly using or taking something constitutes stealing.

7. **Paid in Full.** *R' Zusia of Anipoli* rarely even had enough money to support his family; he certainly had nothing to spare. Once, with God's help, he came into a small sum of money, which he gave to his wife so she could commission the tailor to sew a dress for her.

When she came to the tailor to pick up the completed dress she noticed the sad look on the man's face. "Tell me," she said, "why are you so sad?" The tailor replied, "My daughter is engaged to be wed. The groom was in my shop yesterday and he was thrilled to see the lovely dress he thought I was making for my daughter. How embarrassed I was — and how upset he was — that I simply cannot afford to buy the cloth to make my daughter such a dress."

Moved by the story, the Rebbetzin told him to give the dress to his daughter.

When she came home and told R' Zusia the story, he was very proud of her selflessness. Nonetheless, he

worker to give his boss a full and honest day's work.[8]

לֹא תְקַלֵּל חֵרֵשׁ
You shall not curse the deaf (ibid. 14).

We must be careful with other people's money, and we must also take extreme care regarding the honor and the feelings of others.[9] However, since a deaf person cannot hear, cursing him would seem to be a victimless crime. Why, then, is it forbidden?

According to *Sefer HaChinuch* (231), the crime is not victimless. Although the feelings of the deaf person are not hurt, because he does not hear the curse, the curse itself has the power to inflict damage. Man's speech is the result of the uniquely human fusion of body and soul (see *Genesis* 2:17 and *Targum* ad loc.). Through speech, man has the ability to affect the destiny of others.

In *Rambam's* view, cursing is forbidden not only out of concern for the victim, but also to prevent a person from becoming angry and seeking vengeance. The crime is not victimless — the criminal himself is its victim.

וְלִפְנֵי עִוֵּר לֹא תִתֵּן מִכְשֹׁל
and you shall not place a stumbling block before the blind (ibid.).

This verse teaches that one may not offer incorrect advice to a person who is "blind" (i.e., unknowledgeable) about an issue, particularly if the

advice is to the benefit of the adviser (*Rashi*). Why does *Rashi*, who usually explains the basic meaning of the text, digress from the simple meaning of the words and interpret them in this way? *Sifsei Chachamim* notes that the end of the verse *You shall fear your God* implies that the prohibition is one that the sinner can hide from others.

Others might see a person placing a stumbling block in the path of a blind man, but only the All-Knowing God is aware of why he gave specific advice. And fear of Heaven is the only true deterrent to this crime.

בְּצֶדֶק תִּשְׁפֹּט עֲמִיתֶךָ
with righteousness shall you judge your fellow (ibid.).

One must give others the benefit of the doubt whenever possible, even if the justification seems very unlikely. [See *Rabbeinu Yonah* to *Avos* 1:6 for the parameters of this mitzvah.] The Talmud (*Shabbos* 127b) teaches that one who favorably judges others will himself be judged favorably in the Heavenly court.

But how can one compare human judgment with Divine judgment? A person is unsure of the circumstances which led to his friend's action, so he is expected to give the benefit of the doubt. God, however, knows the full truth. Why should He judge a person with anything other than exact justice?

The *Baal Shem Tov* offered an interpretation based on an episode in *II Samuel* (12:1-14).

When Nathan the Prophet came to rebuke King David regarding the incident with Bathsheba, he

---

instructed her to return to the tailor and pay him for his labor. "When you initially took the completed dress you became obligated to pay him — and to pay him on the day the work was completed. The fact that you subsequently decided to give the dress to the bride as a gift does not absolve you of your obligation not to delay payment of the tailor's wages."

8. **Secret of Success.** Partners in particular must take great pains to insure that they are completely honest with one another. Two people who decided to go into business together approached their rabbi for a blessing that their ventures be successful. The rabbi suggested that they draw up a partnership agreement — and he even offered to draft the document. He took out a pen and paper and wrote א ב ג ד. The two disciples were bewildered and asked the rabbi to explain.

"This is the secret of success," he said. "א stands for אֱמוּנָה, *honesty,* and ב for בְּרָכָה, *blessing.* If you deal with each other with uncompromising honesty you will see much blessing in your endeavors. However, ג־ד, גְּנֵבָה, *larceny* — withholding information from your partner — will lead to דַּלּוּת, *poverty.*"

9. **Bread of Honor.** "People are mistaken. They think that honor and prestige are luxuries. It's not true. Honor is bread! It is necessity! A person's need to feel good about himself is no less real than his need for bread" (*R' Shlomo Freifeld*).

began with a story: There were once two men, a rich man who owned much cattle and a poor man who possessed only one small sheep. One day, the rich man stole the sheep from the poor man. When King David heard this story, he was infuriated. "Let the man who did this die!" he declared passionately. Only then did Nathan explain that this was but a parallel to David's own situation. "You are the [rich] man," Nathan said to the king. David had passed judgment on himself.

Similarly, explained the *Baal Shem Tov*, each man decides his own fate. In Heaven, man is given the opportunity to view someone else violating the same prohibitions that he had, albeit in a slightly camouflaged form. After the person watching reacts, the facade is lifted, and he realizes that he had, in fact, determined his own punishment. The manner in which man judges others is, in reality, the way in which *he* will be judged.

Judge everyone favorably. Do not rush to interpret another's actions negatively, for you may actually be passing judgment on yourself.

לֹא תֵלֵךְ רָכִיל בְּעַמֶּיךָ
לֹא תַעֲמֹד עַל דַּם רֵעֶךָ אֲנִי ה׳
You shall not be a gossipmonger among your people, you shall not stand aside while your fellow's blood is shed — I am Hashem (ibid. 16).

Ohr HaChaim notes that the two laws in this verse are related. Although it is forbidden to

speak or accept *lashon hara*, there are times when it is an *obligation* to do so. If one learns of a plot to assassinate someone, he is obligated to divulge the information to protect the intended victim. To withhold the information for fear of speaking *lashon harah* is foolish and is contrary to Halachah. The murder of Gedaliah ben Achikam, the last Jewish governor in the Land of Israel after the destruction of the first Temple, came about as a result of such misplaced piety (see *Jeremiah* 40:14). The Torah teaches: Do not slander. However, never allow this prohibition to create a situation in which you stand idly by while another person's blood is shed.[10]

לֹא תִשְׂנָא אֶת אָחִיךָ בִּלְבָבֶךָ הוֹכֵחַ
תּוֹכִיחַ אֶת עֲמִיתֶךָ וְלֹא תִשָּׂא עָלָיו חֵטְא
You shall not hate your brother in your heart, you shall reprove your fellow and do not bear a sin because of him (ibid. 17).

Certainly one may not express hatred for a fellow Jew. But the Torah here teaches us that even hatred which is never expressed is forbidden. Hatred — expressed or repressed — can have terrible consequences. If one senses that someone did or said something to harm him, he must be forthright, yet wise, in addressing the matter. Do not allow the animosity to fester in your heart.[11] Indeed, the end of the verse tells us, *you shall reprove your fellow and do not bear a sin.* Gently and tactfully clarify why he hurt you. Give him the

10. **Fatal Words.** Refusal to divulge important unflattering information regarding a prospective marriage partner is another example of this misplaced caution. While people think nothing of speaking *lashon hara* when it is clearly forbidden, they suddenly become very pious when asked for necessary information. (Numerous works outline the applicable laws [e.g., *Journey to Virtue,* Rabbi Avrohom Ehrman, Chapters 27, 28, ArtScroll/Mesorah]. When such questions arise, a competent rabbi should be consulted.)

According to *R' Eizik of Komarna,* this also prohibits one from silently standing by when his fellow Jew is insulted. To allow a person to be stripped of his dignity and prestige is to allow his blood to be spilled.

11. **Good-Hearted Hatred.** *R' Gershon Lider* was far from wealthy, yet he excelled in the mitzvah of welcoming guests. Everyone in his town knew that a guest would always find an open door and a warm welcome at R' Gershon's home.

The town miser was well aware of R' Gershon's reputation. He would often send people to R' Gershon's home rather than spend any of his own considerable wealth on some hapless beggars.

For years R' Gershon said nothing, delighted to perform the mitzvah. But his patience finally wore thin, and he traveled to his Rebbe, *R' Mordechai* of *Lechovitch,* to discuss the matter. "The man has the resources, yet his stone heart won't allow him to help a Jew in need!"

"The Torah commands us not to hate your brother in your heart," the Rebbe told him. "I prefer to render it 'with your heart.' Don't be upset with your fellow Jew just because God chose to bless you, and not him, with a merciful heart. Instead, thank God for the warm and caring heart He gave you."

opportunity to clarify or make amends. In this way you will lift the onerous burden of sin (*Ramban, Ohr HaChaim*).[12]

When prohibiting hatred, the Torah commands *You shall not hate your brother* (אָחִיךָ); but later in the verse, when referring to reproof, it says *your fellow* (עֲמִיתֶךָ). Why does the Torah use different terms?

One might think when the Torah refers to "hatred," it means to prohibit only true animosity.

That is why the Torah cautions us not to hate our "brothers." Friendship between brothers is usually so intense that any distancing between them is notable. We are expected to feel true kinship with one another. If two Jews feel a distancing between them, they are viewed by the Torah as hating one another (*Ohr HaChaim*).

The Talmud (*Sanhedrin* 27b) teaches that one who does not speak to another person for three days because of enmity, transgresses this prohibition. In fact, he is disqualified from serving as a judge for this fellow.[13]

Why does the Torah introduce the obligation to reprove others with the prohibition against hating them?

One can only be successful in rebuking another person if he truly loves him. Only words that come from the heart will enter the heart (*Berachos* 6b).[14]

When one offers reproof out of love, the recipient opens his mind and his heart to the criticism. Reproof born of animosity is sure to fall on deaf

---

12. **Exaggerated Enmity.** The term שִׂנְאַת חִנָּם is usually translated as "causeless hatred." The term certainly does not refer exclusively to hatred with absolutely no cause, because almost all hatred has some basis.

R' Nisson Alpert offers a novel interpretation of the terms. When people are hurt, they often suppress their feelings. Whether out of fear of confrontation or a sense of bravado, they refuse to try to work things out with the person who caused their pain. Instead, the animosity to that person grows stronger.

Had the person made an effort to reach an understanding with the one who hurt him, the hatred would never have reached this level. The extra hatred is חִנָּם; it came about for no good reason.

13. **"That's My Child You Hate."** God loves all Jews as His own children. How can someone who loves God hate someone whom God loves so dearly? Just as a parent is extremely protective of his child, so too, our Father in Heaven protects His children and is upset at anyone who hates them (*Chafetz Chaim*).

14. **Bleeding Soul.** *R' Avraham Yehoshua Heschel of Kopitchnitz* was revered for his heartfelt love of Jews. *R' Aharon Kotler* used to refer to him as a *gaon* (genius) in *ahavas Yisrael* (love of Jews).

For a while, the Rebbe lived on the Lower East Side of Manhattan. Following chassidic custom, he would go to the *mikveh* every Shabbos morning. Once, while accompanied by *R' Yaakov Greenwald,* he passed two freshly shaved young men standing and smoking near the entrance to the *mikveh*.

The Rebbe wished them a hearty *"Gut Shabbos"* and softly said, "You must have forgotten that it is Shabbos, and that is why you are smoking."

"Not quite. In America there's an expression: 'Mind your own business,' " one of the young men loudly replied.

R' Yaakov, appalled that someone could speak to the princely Rebbe with such *chutzpah,* was seething. The Rebbe grabbed R' Yaakov's hand to calm him, and, simultaneously, began speaking to the two young fellows.

"Tell me," he said, "we are standing here on East Broadway, a busy thoroughfare. If you were to witness a car run over a pedestrian and saw the victim lying bloodied on the pavement, what would you do?"

"Obviously, I would go help him and call for an ambulance," the fellow replied.

"Why wouldn't you mind your own business?" said the Rebbe. "The answer is that you can't stand by idly while someone is bleeding to death."

"I am just like you," the Rebbe began to cry. "When I see you smoking on Shabbos, I see your *neshamah* (soul) hemorrhaging. I can't mind my own business."

Shocked, the two promised to start keeping Shabbos. R' Yaakov relates that for weeks afterward, he and the Rebbe would meet the two on Shabbos morning near the *mikveh*. Their greeting was always the same: "*Gut Shabbos,* Rebbe. See, we are not smoking."

Do not hate a fellow Jew, the Torah teaches. Love him with all your heart, offer him rebuke out of concern for his spiritual welfare, and you are sure to succeed.

ears and a closed heart. It is through not hating one's brother that one can succeed in rebuking him (*Avnei Azel*).[15]

Why does the Torah use a double expression הוֹכֵחַ תּוֹכִיחַ? The *Baal Shem Tov* commented that this teaches us that one cannot see a flaw in someone else unless he himself, in one form or another, possesses the same flaw. Our Sages taught "One who disqualifies another, disqualifies with his own flaw" (*Kiddushin* 70a). Thus, seeing deficiency or inadequacy in others is a reflection of one's own failings.

Based on this, explains *Toldos Yaakov Yosef*, one who reproves others must himself be deserving of reprimand. Consequently the Torah instructs us הוֹכֵחַ, chastise yourself, for the flaw you see in your fellow is but a reflection of your own. Only then, תּוֹכִיחַ, can you begin to exhort others to improve.

The Sages taught that just as one is commanded to offer reprimand to one who may accept it, so one is enjoined, in many cases, from rebuking someone who will likely not accept it (*Yevamos* 65b).

Sefer HaChinuch (239) explains the reason for this ruling: Rebuke can be painful; the person being criticized frequently suffers embarrassment. If the chastisement may have an effect, then the shame serves a purpose since it helps the person achieve repentance. If, however, the criticism has no effect, then the shame is pointless, and such affliction is forbidden.[16]

לֹא תִקֹּם וְלֹא תִטֹּר אֶת בְּנֵי עַמֶּךָ
You shall not take revenge and you shall not bear a grudge against members of your people (ibid. 18).

Rambam (*Hilchos Deios* 7:7-8) teaches: Revenge and bearing grudges are exceedingly negative traits. It is appropriate for a person to be forgiving regarding temporal matters, for in the eyes of the wise, worldly matters are inconsequential and are not worthy of vengeance. One who bears a grudge may eventually come to vengeance, thus the Torah calls on us to erase any vestige of what was done to

---

15. **Open Rebuke, Hidden Love.** If you see a Jew sinning, even intentionally, do not hate or abuse him. On the contrary, have mercy on him just as you would on someone who is handicapped or who was born deformed, God forbid. Most sinners sin out of ignorance, they are like *tinokos shenishba'u,* children raised by non-Jews and who were never exposed to vibrant Judaism. If not for the terrible travails of the exile, these people would have returned to God long ago.

R' Yosef Chaim Sonnenfeld taught and practiced this lesson. Throughout his life, even as he valiantly battled the antireligious Zionists and their supporters, he always spoke with a warm and caring heart. He vehemently opposed their views and programs, he was repulsed by their redefinition of what it means to be a Jew, and he despised their blatant violations of Torah, yet he never resorted to personal venom in his relationship with his strayed brothers.

R' Moshe Blau related the following incident: "I had once gone with R' Yosef Chaim to visit some patients at Shaarei Tzedek Hospital. It was on *Tu B'Shvat* and, from a distance, we saw a group of nonreligious school students marching in our direction. Boys and girls of various ages stood marching behind a Zionist flag, singing modern Hebrew *chalutz* (pioneer) songs. Marching four across, they totally blocked the street, forcing all other pedestrians to push themselves alongside the buildings.

"Concerned that R' Yosef Chaim would be upset by the scene that was unfolding, I suggested that we return to the hospital until they pass. 'No,' he replied. 'Aren't they also Jewish children?' He stood, leaning on my shoulder, along with all the others pressed up against the side of the street.

"Every group passed, each school with its anthem, and all the while his lips were moving. I bent closer, and I heard him murmuring over and over again, *May Hashem increase upon you, upon you and upon your children* (Psalms 115:14). As he shed tears and battled much of what their groups represented, he prayed that even these youngsters, so far from the path of Torah, would one day be included in the blessing of the previous verse: *He will bless those who fear God, the small as well as the great* [ibid. 13] (*Od Yosef Chai*).

16. **Right Address.** *Minchas Shmuel* writes: I have an oral tradition from *R' Chaim of Volozhin* that in our times one cannot motivate people with harsh talk. Soft and caring talk will succeed in moving people to change. Therefore, one who by nature is unable to speak warmly and gently, and who will immediately become agitated and show anger toward sinners (especially if they do not listen and respond to his reproof), is absolved from this mitzvah and is not obligated to offer rebuke.

us from our hearts.[17] This attitude is key to interpersonal relationships and the functioning of society.

---

17. **For So Long?** When *R' Shimshon of Zivlin* (died 5507 — 1746) became the Rav of Zivlin he made two stipulations regarding his position. First, all significant decisions regarding communal matters were to be decided or approved by him — including those matters that were, in other communities, decided by the elders. Second, he was not to be bothered with consultations on communal issues any time during the week. The elders of the community could present communal questions for his consideration only on Saturday night. From Sunday morning until Friday afternoon, the Rav sat in the synagogue learning, teaching and answering halachic queries. On Friday afternoon the Rav would return home for Shabbos.

One day, the Rebbetzin went to the local marketplace. When she passed the fishmonger, she noticed a large fish which she thought would be perfect for Shabbos. Suddenly the wife of one of Zivlin's wealthy citizens came up to the fishmonger's stall and began bidding against the Rebbetzin for the large fish. Of course, the Rebbetzin could not compete and the wealthy matron bought the fish. The women exchanged words, and the other woman, in a fit of anger, called the Rebbetzin a very vile, pejorative name.

Word of what had transpired spread quickly throughout the town. The townspeople were appalled by the nerve of the wealthy woman. When the elders of the community became aware of the incident, they decided that they should protest the degradation of the honor of Torah and penalize the wealthy woman regardless of her social status.

However, as stipulated by the Rav, they needed his consent in order to impose the sanctions. And they could not consult with him until Saturday night. In the meantime, the elders went to the Rebbetzin to tell her their planned response. They asked her to speak to the Rav about the matter over Shabbos, so that he would be prepared for their meeting with him.

On Friday night, when R' Shimshon came home after prayers, he was shocked to find his Rebbetzin sitting at a small table on the side of the room rather than at the festively set Shabbos table. Gently, he asked her what the problem was, and she replied that she was not worthy to be a Rebbetzin and to sit at the Rav's table, so she set her own separate table.

"And why, may I ask, are you not worthy to be a Rebbetzin?" asked R' Shimshon.

The Rebbetzin told him exactly what the wealthy woman had said to her. The Rav, startled, asked her, "You were so viciously insulted and no one protested? What about the honor of Torah? What did the community elders say?"

The Rebbetzin told the Rav how shocked the community was over the incident. "Furthermore," she said, "the elders want to impose severe sanctions against the woman, but they must wait for your approval — which they cannot receive until Saturday night."

The Rav calmed the Rebbetzin and reassured her that she was most fit. It was only then that she took her place at the table.

R' Shimshon filled the *Kiddush* cup and picked it up, ready to make *Kiddush*. Suddenly, he stopped and asked the Rebbetzin, "When did this incident take place?"

"Tuesday," she responded. Visibly shaken, R' Shimshon placed the *Kiddush* cup down and in a pained voice he cried, "Tuesday?! Tuesday?! You are walking around since Tuesday with anger in your heart toward a Jewish woman and you have yet to forgive her?!"

The Rebbetzin, shaken, assured him, "I forgave her, I forgave her." But the Rav was not satisfied. "It is insufficient. A Jew toward whom you carried anger in your heart since Tuesday must be appeased. Let us go and appease her," he said.

"Isn't it enough," the Rebbetzin thought to herself, "that the woman embarrassed and degraded me and yet I've forgiven her? Do I have to go and ask *her* forgiveness?" But, loyal to her saintly husband, she put on her coat as the Rav put on his. Leaving the full cup of wine on the table, they set out toward the home of the wealthy congregant.

The Rav's knock on the door was met with the cry, "Who is there?" When the Rav responded, the husband and wife became petrified. Certain that he had come to avenge his wife's honor and recognizing his saintliness, they were afraid of what terrible things might happen to them if the Rav would, God forbid, continue to feel hurt by the incident. They opened the door and, sobbing, they pleaded with the Rav and Rebbetzin to forgive them.

The Rav began to weep. "Do you have to ask our forgiveness? We are here to ask your pardon for the animosity my wife the Rebbetzin bore in her heart against your wife since the incident."

Startled, the wealthy couple replied, "But it was our fault that the entire episode took place. We sinned by degrading the honor of Torah and we must seek atonement."

The two couples each granted the other forgiveness. The hurt and the anger caused by the horrible story dissipated.

Only then did R' Shimshon and his Rebbetzin return home to the waiting *Kiddush* cup, to usher in Sabbath, the day of peace.

By not taking revenge or bearing a grudge, we not only promote peace among men; we also demonstrate our awareness that this world is only transient and that worldly matters are not important enough for us to become angry about.[18]

לֹא תִקֹּם . . . וְאָהַבְתָּ לְרֵעֲךָ כָּמוֹךָ אֲנִי ה׳
You shall not take revenge . . . you shall love your fellow as yourself — I am Hashem (ibid.).

This verse is usually understood to mean "You shall not take revenge, *rather* you shall love your fellow as yourself".

Yerushalmi (*Nedarim* 9:4) offers an analogy which presents a different approach: Imagine that you were holding a meat cleaver, and you accidently cut your hand. Would you, for even a moment, consider retaliating by having your cut hand cut the hand that was holding the knife? Of course not! Both hands are a part of you!

The Torah teaches a Jew to love his fellow Jew *as himself.* Just as you would not exact vengeance against yourself, do not retaliate against your fellow who is also one with you.

R' Avraham Moshe of P'shis'cha offered a homiletical interpretation of the verse: *Do not take revenge or bear a grudge; rather, love your fellow.* Why? כָּמוֹךָ אֲנִי ה׳, *as yourself am I, Hashem.* "Just as you feel

you have legitimate complaints against your fellow, and that you are entitled to vengeance, I, Hashem, feel the same way about you. Just as your friend insulted you and demeaned your honor so you have "insulted" Me and demeaned My honor."

"Nevertheless," says Hashem, "I am willing to forgive you. Likewise, you should forgive your fellow, even when he hurts or insults you."

In yet another approach *R' Muttel Slonimer* interprets the verse as follows: Do not take revenge from the members of your nation (בְּנֵי עַמֶּךָ). Even when retribution is legitimate and permitted, one may not bear hatred or animosity. Remember, your fellow Jew is your brother, a member of your nation. We have enough enemies from the outside, we dare not indulge in hating one another.

How then should you respond? *Love your fellow like yourself.* Profound love is the sweetest form of revenge. Embarrassed by your friendship, he will realize that he wronged you. His self-righteousness will melt in the face of your warmth and love.[19]

וְאָהַבְתָּ לְרֵעֲךָ כָּמוֹךָ
Love your neighbor as yourself (ibid.).

The mitzvah directs us to be excited when another person is successful. Rather than be-

---

18. **Dubious Distress.** A young child had erected a house of cards and was enjoying the beauty of his handiwork. Suddenly, a stranger approached and, with the sweep of his hand, demolished the edifice. The heartbroken child went running to his father shrieking, "My world has been destroyed! He broke down my house!" Were the father to take the child seriously, he would certainly pursue the perpetrator. However, the father is mature enough to realize that the house of cards is but child's play and does not justify a violent reaction.

Our Father in Heaven also understands that while we view our toys — money, prestige and other worldly valuables — as objects of great significance, in truth they are not worth getting upset about. We must also come to this realization, and recognize that these matters are not worth our becoming angry or bearing a grudge (*Kli Yakar*).

19. **Ever Loving.** The Jewish communities of Poland in the early 1900's were war zones in the fierce battles between those loyal to Torah and assimilationists.

In Bendin, Poland, *R' Chanoch Tzvi Levin,* son-in-law of the *Sfas Emes,* weathered a difficult election to be elected Rav by a very narrow margin. Following his victory, the leaders of the assimilationist camp came to pay him a courtesy call. They sat silently, unsure of what to say, and the Rav broke the silence: "A wise man once found himself in a thick forest, surrounded by wild animals who seemed poised to devour him. The man had no weapons; he could rely only on his wile. As he stood there, he decided that he would love the animals. He began to consider that even wild animals are God's creations; that even they have a role in advancing the glory of God. Slowly, in his heart, began to admire the animals. The animals instinctively sensed the man's feelings, and refrained from harming him.

"Before the elections began, I emotionally and psychologically brought myself to love every member of the community, regardless of their beliefs or level of observance. That is why my candidacy was successful."

grudge the person, we should be as happy for him as we would be for ourselves.[20]

R' Akiva said: "*You shall love your fellow as yourself.* This is a cardinal principle of Torah" (*Yerushalmi Nedarim* 9:4).

It is noteworthy that R' Akiva said that this is the primary principle *of Torah.* We are responsible to care for others and share with them not only material resources, but spritual ones as well. We cannot focus only on our own growth in Torah — even in this area we must show concern and we must share.[21]

R' Akiva's statement seems puzzling. While *love your neighbor as yourself* may be the underlying principle of interpersonal *mitzvos,* how does this address all the other *mitzvos*?

R' Elchanan Wasserman offers the following explanation: R' Elazar the son of R' Shimon (*Kiddushin* 40b) taught that one should always imagine that the world is, on the scale of Divine judgment, perfectly balanced between innocence and guilt. Perform one mitzvah, and the scale tips toward the side of merit — for yourself and for the entire world. Commit a single transgression, God forbid, and you have tipped the scale — for himself and for the entire world — toward guilt.

Thus, when we do *any* mitzvah, even one not directly related to another person, we are also benefiting others. We tip the scales of Heavenly judgment to favor the world, for the good of all mankind. For one to love his neighbor as himself requires him to act properly in all areas of Torah observance.

מִפְּנֵי שֵׂיבָה תָּקוּם וְהָדַרְתָּ פְּנֵי זָקֵן

In the presence of an old person shall you rise and you shall honor the presence of a sage (ibid. 32).

According to *Yoreh Deah* (244:1) one must stand in respect for anyone over the age of 70, even if that person is not learned. One must honor a Torah sage, even if he is young.

Maharal explains: Man is composed of the physical and the spiritual, it is his spiritual component that makes him worthy of reverence.

One who studies Torah nurtures his soul. His focus is on the spiritual, his body is incidental. Such a person deserves to be honored.

As an older person's body weakens, so do his passions, and his spirit becomes dominant. This person, too, must be honored.

וְהִתְקַדִּשְׁתֶּם וִהְיִיתֶם קְדֹשִׁים

You shall sanctify yourselves and you will be holy [20:7].

We all experience moments of spiritual elevation. What makes people great is their ability to maintain these exalted levels.

God wants us to transform ourselves into embodiments of Divine sanctity. "Sanctify yourselves" with such intensity, teaches the Torah, "that you will continue to be holy" (*Pe'er Yisrael*).[22]

---

20. **You Deserve It!** *Pe'er Yisrael* elaborates: The Torah teaches us to *love your fellow as yourself,* even in areas that relate to the fact that *I am Hashem.* One must rejoice over his friends' spiritual attainments, even if they are greater than his own. While one should certainly be "jealous" of those achievements and seek to emulate them, this is not a "jealousy" that leads to antipathy or discord.

The Alter of Slabodka viewed כָּמוֹךָ as referring to instinctiveness. One does not need to be told to love himself; it is a natural emotion. We must work on ourselves until we reach the level of loving others naturally and instinctively.

21. **True Kindness.** The truest form of kindness is sharing our Torah knowledge and our spiritual wealth. In *Proverbs* (31:26), King Solomon refers to a "Torah of kindness." The Talmud (*Succah* 49b) asks: "Is there a Torah that is of kindness and a Torah that is not of kindness?" It then explains: "Torah that is being studied in order to be taught, that is Torah of kindness; Torah being learned only for oneself, that is not Torah of kindness."

22. **Calling for Reinforcements.** All of us have, in moments of inspiration, committed ourselves to living more sanctified lives, only to revert to our old ways soon after. We were certainly secure in our commitment, but we often fail to realize that inspiration is fleeting, and it needs ongoing reinforcement. The Torah instructs us, "Sanctify yourselves," and after the initial effort, continue to renew your commitment that "you will be holy."

Background

The *parashah* ends with a directive to assure our sanctity by avoiding assimilation into the nations that surround us.

וְלֹא תֵלְכוּ בְּחֻקֹּת הַגּוֹי

Do not follow the traditions of the nation[s] (ibid. 23).

Besides following all of the Torah's laws, a Jew must think and act like a Jew in all his endeavors — when he eats, does business and walks — as much as when he prays and studies.

Our Sages' comment (*Shabbos* 89a) that the mountain where we received the Torah is called Sinai, because of what transpired there that hatred descended to the world.

The simple understanding of this statement is that as a result of the distinction we acquired at Sinai, we are hated by the nations of the world.

R' Avrohom of Slonim interpreted the statement differently: When we received the Torah, we undertook to be Jews in everything we do. At Sinai, we undertook to despise the non-Jewish values and culture that threaten our distinct Jewishness.

וִהְיִיתֶם לִי קְדֹשִׁים . . . וָאַבְדִּל אֶתְכֶם מִן הָעַמִּים לִהְיוֹת לִי

You shall be holy for Me . . . and I have separated you from the nations to be Mine (ibid. 26).

Ksav Sofer explains that if we make a complete and firm commitment to being holy, God will *separate us from the nations,* He will help us by removing the spiritual challenges that confront us. He will free us of foreign domination, both physical and spiritual (*Ksav Sofer*).

Maharal outlines a framework for proper interaction between Jews and the non-Jewish world that surrounds them.

The Sages compared non-Jews to water and Jews to fire. If fire and water come into direct contact with one another, the water extinguishes the fire. However, if the water is in a pot, the fire boils the water. Likewise, explains *Maharal,* direct contact between Jews and the non-Jewish culture that surrounds them will likely result in the fire of Judaism being extinguished. If, on the other hand, we interact with that world, but keep barriers between us and them, we can hope to influence them and inculcate them with our values and worldview.[23]

---

23. **Immutable Laws of Nature.** At *Havdalah* we say, "Who separates between light and darkness, between Israel and the nations." Light and darkness — referring to day and night — never "meet" since twilight separates them. Similarly, there is a natural distance between Israel and the nations. When Jews try to bridge the divide and fully integrate with their neighbors, they are attempting to defy a rule of nature. It is only a matter of time before those immutable rules reassert themselves, and our "friends" remind us that we are still different (*Beis HaLevi*). *R' Chaim of Volozhin,* in a play on words, is reported to have said, "When Jews make *kiddush* (sanctification, keeping themselves separate from foreign influences), God makes *havdalah,* (keeping them apart). However, if Jews do not make *kiddush,* it is their non-Jewish neighbors who make the *havdalah.*"

פרשת אמור ‎≈§
Parashas Emor

Background

After speaking of the sanctity that is expected of every Jew, the Torah outlines the higher standard of sanctity and purity that must be maintained by the Kohanim, the priests who serve God in His sanctuary.

This *parashah* begins by addressing the requirement that Kohanim avoid *tumah* generated by a corpse and the laws of Kohanim's mourning. It ends with the laws of the festivals.

This contrast teaches us a lesson: Even during times of travail and grief, we must not become engulfed in misery and despondency. We must look to the better days — the days of joy and celebration — that lie ahead.

אֱמֹר אֶל הַכֹּהֲנִים
Say to the Kohanim (21:1).

The Midrash (*Vayikra Rabbah* 26:7) suggests a connection between the end of the previous *parashah* and the beginning of this one. The previous *parashah* concluded with the punishment meted out to those who employ magic to predict the future. The Jewish nation, however, can turn to the Kohanim, who have the benefit of the *Urim V'Tumim*, the breastplate of the Kohen Gadol. Various letters on the *Urim V'Tumim* would light up and present complete and true answers to questions of national significance posed by the Kohen.[1]

According to *R' Yonasan Eibeschutz*, the Kohanim are enjoined to avoid corpse-*tumah* so that it is clear to all that their predictions and advice come directly from God, rather than from the netherworld.

אֱמֹר אֶל הַכֹּהֲנִים בְּנֵי אַהֲרֹן וְאָמַרְתָּ אֲלֵהֶם
Say to the Kohanim, the sons of Aaron, and tell them (ibid.).

Rashi (based on *Yevamos* 114a) tells us that the redundancy — *say to* and *tell them* — teaches that the adult Kohanim were cautioned regarding the minors.

Many homiletic explanations of this Rashi have

---

1. **Authentic Guidance.** As we follow news events and hear the analyses of pundits, we sometimes feel that we understand exactly what is happening and what the future holds. In truth, however, the future is determined by God, and only those great Torah scholars who plumb the depths of Torah knowledge have the vision and foresight to help us understand all that goes on around us.

   When we need advice, we can get it from God's Torah. Originally we were privy to *the eye that sees,* prophecy, which clearly taught us the will of God. When prophecy ended, we still had *the ear that hears,* the *bas kol,* an "echo," as it were, which emanated from Heaven revealing God's desire. Today we have neither. Despite this, however, *all your actions are written in a Book* — Everything God wants us to know and understand can be found in Torah — we just have to diligently study and properly interpret its message (*Ruach Chaim*).

been offered by various commentators. *R' Moshe Feinstein* viewed it as a lesson in educational philosophy and approach.

One cannot inculcate children or students with fidelity to Torah and its values by merely telling them what their obligations are.

Parents and educators must demonstrate that the Torah life is precious, desirable and beautiful. When a child recognizes that Torah is the key to serenity and a happy, fulfilled life, he will want to follow the Torah. One must speak to his children "twice": once to teach them the *mitzvos,* and a second time to ignite within them a burning desire to a live Torah life. It is only in this way that the elders will succeed in passing their values onto their young.[2]

According to the *Dubno Maggid* this teaches us to realize that adults serve as role models for our children. How they behave in their own lives often reflects the behavior they saw in their parents. Thus, even when we may not have the strength of character or resolve to do the right thing, we must find the strength to do what is right for the sake of our children.

R' Baruch Sorotzkin, citing his father *R' Zalman Sorotzkin,* offered the following educational insight:

The charge to be particularly careful about children was given to the Kohanim.

While parents can usually control their home environment in which a child is raised, peer pressure and society can have a detrimental effect on a child. It is the parents' duty to address those influences in an appropriate manner.

Kohanim are subject to privileges — but they have unique proscriptions as well. Thus, the child of a Kohen was, at times, forced to act differently from his friends. it was his parents' duty to see to it that he maintained his unique status.

Any parent whose child is subject to an environment that is not consonant with the spiritual level of the home has a similar responsibility. He must guide and encourage his child to hold his own in the face of the lower standards his friends or the others around him maintain.[3]

לְנֶפֶשׁ לֹא יִטַּמָּא בְּעַמָּיו
to a [dead] person he shall not become impure (ibid.).

Why is it that Kohanim may not become contaminated by a dead person? Isn't death a very real part of life?

Corpse-*tumah* is the product of man confronting his mortality. Every time a person comes into contact with death, he must use this opportunity to contemplate his human frailty — and to be inspired by the fact that his soul is immortal.

The Kohanim, who serve God in the *Beis HaMikdash,* are to focus exclusively on the spirituality of

---

2. **It's Good to Be a Jew!** *R' Moshe Feinstein* would often remark that many young people abandoned Torah observance as a result of their parents' often repeating the Yiddish expression, "ס'איז שווער צו זיין א איד", It's difficult to be a Jew." Though they meant it as an expression of pride in their self-sacrifice for Judaism and a source of inspiration, their children often understood that commitment to Torah was a difficulty they would do well to avoid.

If we hope to develop a desire for Torah in our young ones, we must convey its beauty.

3. **A Higher Standard.** *Nesivei Chinuch* provides an approach to convey uniqueness. In times gone by, royalty maintained a style of dress and an etiquette that was different from that of common people. As people of distinguished lineage, it was a sign of pride to be set apart. They did not see the limitations put on them as difficult or inconvenient but rather as an honor and a privilege.

There are some people who are fortunate enough to have set higher standards of Torah observance in their homes. Whether in areas of personal behavior, modesty in deed and in dress, a heightened level of *kashrus* observance, or vigilant control over the reading material or entertainment allowed to enter the home, these people act differently than their neighbors and relatives. These individuals are sometimes challenged about why they act differently than other ostensibly "good" homes.

The appropriate and true answer to the question is that as Jews, we are God's royal family, and our role is to maintain a pristine standard of behavior.

Like royalty, people who truly seek a life of sanctity and purity have special standards relating to every detail of life, and their clothes, furnishings and the way in which they conduct their household affairs are on a totally different level.

their eternal souls. Thus they are forbidden to expose themselves to corpse-*tumah* (*Simchas Aharon*).

In a homiletic vein, *Noam Megadim* interprets this verse instructing those who have achieved lofty spiritual levels on how they should interact with others. "Although you occupy a more elevated spiritual position — just as the Kohanim, who are descendants of Aaron the Kohen — do not defile *any* soul. Never view another Jew in a negative way, never see him as beyond hope. Rather look at שְׁאֵרוֹ, which can be understood as related to שְׁאָר, *the remnant*. See that which remains in him, the spark of good and holiness, the Godly soul deep inside him."[4]

Alternatively, the verse speaks to those who have dedicated their lives to the study of Torah. It calls upon them not to become arrogant and cautions them not to look down on those less learned than them and those otherwise engaged in earning a livelihood. It is the support of those people that enables Torah scholars to pursue their spiritual growth. It is only because these people view themselves as close to you and relate emotionally to your spiritual endeavors that they extend themselves to provide for you.[5]

כִּי אִם לִשְׁאֵרוֹ הַקָּרֹב אֵלָיו
Except for the relative who is closest to him (ibid. 2).

This refers to the Kohen's wife. Why is a wife considered one's closest relative? *Yalkut Sofer* explains: Other relationships are not unique to one person. A mother is a mother to all her children; a child is a child to both his parents; a sister or brother is common to all of their siblings. Only a husband or a wife are uniquely related to

their spouse. Thus, the Kohen's wife is *his* closest relative.

According to *HaKsav V'Hakabbalah*, שְׁאֵרוֹ is related to שְׁאֵרִית, *remnant.* Man's life is finite; the curse of death is universal. It is only through children that one can live on. Thus one's wife, the one who bears those children, is the key to his leaving a remnant of himself even after he passes on.

וְקִדַּשְׁתּוֹ כִּי אֶת לֶחֶם אֱלֹהֶיךָ הוּא מַקְרִיב
You shall sanctify him; for he offers the food of your God (ibid. 8).

The Talmud (*Gittin* 59b) derives from this verse that, among other honors, a Kohen must be honored with the first *aliyah* when the Torah is publicly read and that he has first priority in leading Grace After Meals. Why is it necessary for the nation to display such honor toward Kohanim?

Ksav Sofer explains: People often treat public servants in a demeaning manner since, in their eyes, that person is being supported by them. Those people feel that the public official should honor them and bow to their wishes; they certainly see no reason to honor the public servant.

Jews are commanded to grant Kohanim twenty-four different priestly gifts (see *Chullin* 133b). The Israelite might come to feel that he need not honor the Kohanim, since it is he who is supporting them. The Torah therefore instructs us to sanctify the Kohanim, to view and treat them on a higher level. Indeed, it is the Kohanim who bring the offerings in the Temple, and it is their Divine service which engenders God's providing sustenance to His people.

Rashi tells us, "*And you shall sanctify him* — against his will." Homiletically, this teaches that the leader who is truly deserving of being held in

---

4. **Seeing the Positive.** *R' Elimelech of Lizhensk* composed a supplication to be recited before prayer. In it he writes: "Instill in our heart that each of us see only the positive aspects of our friends and not their shortcomings. May each of us speak with our friends in a fashion that is proper and acceptable to You. And let no hatred, God forbid, arise between any Jew and his fellow."

5. **Spiritual Stevedores.** Those who support Torah scholars must avoid falling into the trap of treating them disdainfully, without the proper reverence they deserve. The Talmud (*Sotah* 35a) tells us that though the Levites were charged with carrying the Holy Ark in the Tabernacle, it was in fact the Ark which miraculously carried them. *Kli Yakar* views this as a reflection of the relationship between Torah scholars and their supporters. It is not the wealthy who truly support the scholars; it is the support of Torah that provides God with a reason to bless the affluent with their wealth. The Ark, the Torah scholars, actually carry those who seem to be carrying it.

esteem is the one who refuses honor and who accepts it only under duress (*R' Yitzchak of Vorki*).[6]

וּבַת אִישׁ כֹּהֵן כִּי תֵחֵל לִזְנוֹת אֶת אָבִיהָ הִיא מְחַלֶּלֶת בָּאֵשׁ תִּשָּׂרֵף

If the daughter of a Kohen will be desecrated through adultery, she desecrates her father — she shall be consumed by fire (ibid. 9).

Why is the daughter of a Kohen subjected to a more severe penalty for adultery than others? According to our Sages, the Kohanim were, for the most part, serious Torah scholars whose fear of Heaven protected them from sin (see *Shabbos* 20a and *Rashi* ad loc.). They generally invested a great deal of energy in providing their children with an upbringing and education saturated with these values. For a young lady who was raised in such an environment to act so wantonly is a desecration of her parents and a crude display of ingratitude toward those who invested so much effort into rearing her properly (*R' Simchah Zissel of Kelm*).

Imrei Shefer, in a contrasting approach, understands the statement *she desecrates her father* as the Torah's way of implicating the parents in their daughter's shameful behavior. Generally, the Sages teach us, the evil inclination begins his insidious work by enticing man into transgressing "minor" sins. Slowly but surely, he wears down the person's resolve, until he can convince him to commit even the worst of sins (see *Shabbos* 105b).

One who was raised with proper values cannot, initially, be enticed easily into committing severe sins. However, the soul of one who grew up in a home where sin is acceptable is inured to the ugliness of iniquity, and has few reservations about committing even outrageous sins. When he deals with such a person, the evil inclination begins with the worst. Thus, the Torah teaches us that if a young woman begins (תֵחֵל, as related to תְּחִלָּה, *beginning*) her career of sin with adultery, she is clearly the product of an upbringing that is tolerant of licentiousness and immorality.[7]

וְהַכֹּהֵן הַגָּדוֹל מֵאֶחָיו

The Kohen who was exalted above his brothers (ibid. 10).

The Talmud (*Yoma* 18a) teaches that the Kohen Gadol (High Priest) must be the most outstanding Kohen in wisdom, wealth, physical strength and physical appearance. In fact, if he is not wealthy, his fellow Kohanim must contribute to a fund which will enable him to be the wealthiest of all Kohanim. Why does the Torah place such emphasis on an issue that seems so mundane?

Baron Meyer Amschel Rothschild explained to a scoffing, "enlightened" coreligionist: Wealth does not elevate a person. It does not change how good the person is or make him wise. However, people admire those who are wealthy, so their wealth grants them a degree of independence and gives them the ability to influence others and shape their communities. If the Kohen Gadol is not wealthy, his influence will be limited.

Not only wealth, but even a person's physical stature and beauty influence how they are perceived by others. Indeed, we find that the Torah insists that every Kohen, not just the Kohen Gadol,

---

6. **Unwillingly Honored.** There is a famous dictum that all who flee honor are pursued by honor, and eventually are honored (see *Eruvin* 13b).

The *Chafetz Chaim* was always concerned about the detrimental spiritual effect of the honors he received. He often consoled himself with the following thought:

"The Sages used the term *all who flee honor,* because even the unaccomplished Jew, who merits no honor or prestige, will be honored if he has fled from acclaim."

7. **Involved / Uninvolved.** Though involvement in communal causes and philanthropic pursuits is admirable, it must never come at the expense of one's responsibilities toward his own children. Even one's own personal spiritual growth, which ultimately has a positive effect on one's family, needs to be carefully balanced with the need to nurture one's children's development.

The Kohanim, and those who like them have dedicated their lives to public service, must take utmost care to ensure that their children not become victims of the parents' communal involvement. To engage in such activities to the extent that parents forfeit involvement in their children's development and fail to control how, where and with whom the children spend time is an almost foolproof invitation for spiritual disaster (*Avnei Azel*).

dress in regal garments and be free of physical blemishes [see *Exodus* 28:2 and below 21:17] (*Moreh Nevuchim*).

וְעַל כָּל נַפְשֹׁת מֵת לֹא יָבֹא
He shall not come near any dead person (ibid. 11).

The Kohen Gadol may not allow himself to become contaminated by any corpse, even that of his closest relative. *R' Menachem Mendel of Kotzk* explains that this law highlights the exalted role of the Kohen Gadol. As the conduit through which God channels sanctity to the Jewish people, the Kohen Gadol must rise above the ties of family. He must view himself as connected to the entire nation. Since he may not become contaminated to any other Jew, he may also not become contaminated by his relatives.

R' Yonasan Eibeschutz offers a different perspective: The Talmud (*Moed Kattan* 19a) teaches that no mourning is practiced on Yom Tov, in order that no Jew be prevented from coming to Jerusalem and rejoicing there on the three pilgrimage festivals. Even when one goes to greet a human king he dresses festively for the occasion; i.e., "it is forbidden to enter the king's gate clothed with sackcloth" (*Esther* 4:2). Certainly when one approaches the King of kings, he must enter His gates with rejoicing.

The Kohen Gadol, whose relationship with God is on an even higher level, and who constantly lives with the immanence of God's Presence, must always experience joy. Hence, the Torah totally precludes him from any involvement with death or mourning.[8]

וּמִן הַמִּקְדָּשׁ לֹא יֵצֵא
He shall not leave the Sanctuary (ibid. 12).

A regular Kohen may not perform the sacrificial service while he is an *onein* (the period between the death and the burial of an immediate relative). Not so a Kohen Gadol, who must serve even when he is an *onein*. Why does the Torah make this distinction?

When a person is emotionally overwhelmed by the pain and trauma of losing a loved one, his heart is so full of agony, his mind is so overcome by his sense of loss, that he cannot focus on his duties in the Palace of the King. The Kohen Gadol, however, is charged with the herculean feat of rising above his personal grief, and his responsibility is to serve God with the requisite joy in the face of his own loss. The command prohibiting the Kohen Gadol from leaving the Sanctuary embodies the requirement that his role in the Sanctuary so fully pervade his life that he remain fully committed to his role despite his private pain. The ultimate sign of a great man is his ability to calmly continue his sacred work, in spite of the stormy seas that surround him (*R' Shneur Kotler*).[9]

---

8. **The Joy of Torah.** As a sign of mourning over the destruction of the Holy Temple, which took place on the 9th of Av, we may not eat meat or drink wine during the mourning period which precedes that date. However, if one makes a celebration upon concluding a Talmudic tractate, an order of *Mishnah* or the like [see *Igros Moshe, Orach Chaim* Vol. 1, §157], he and his guests may partake of meat and wine at the *siyum. Avnei Nezer* offers an insight into this law: The Talmud (*Berachos* 8a) teaches that since the Temple was destroyed, the Divine Presence in this world is found where Torah is studied (*Berachos* 8a). The Temple's destruction does not affect places of Torah study, for those places are still "home" to His Presence. When we celebrate the study of Torah, mourning over the Destruction is out of place. In the words of King David, *Strength and joy are in His place* (*I Chronicles* 16:27) (*Avnei Nezer*).

In an inspirational address to young yeshivah students, *R' Shlomo Freifeld* cited the *Avnei Nezer's* thought and remarked, "A disheartened and depressed student is a direct contradiction to the essence of a yeshivah. *Churban*, destruction, has no place in a yeshivah." He once remarked, "People say that one who studies Torah and who grows spiritually is happy. I, however, say that one who is happy will be able to learn Torah and grow spiritually."

9. **Rising Above.** Many of the statements in *Pirkei Avos* are introduced with the words הוּא הָיָה אוֹמֵר, *he would say*. *R' Meir Shapiro* rendered this phrase as *he* — the very essence of that Mishnaic sage — *would say*. That teacher's life embodied and expressed the teachings attributed to him.

R' Shneur Kotler was a living lesson in the ability of a person to rise above his personal travails and to continue uninterruptedly to carry the mantle of leadership of the nation.

Three years before his own passing, R' Shneur and his family were struck a crushing blow: His 26-year-old son,

כָּל אִישׁ אֲשֶׁר בּוֹ מוּם לֹא יִקְרָב

Any man in whom there is a blemish shall not approach [to offer sacrifices] (ibid. 18).

Since when does God assign significance to a person's physical appearance? To the contrary; those who suffer physical deformities are often quite humble, certainly a spiritual asset. In fact, the Talmud (*Sanhedrin* 98a) describes the Messiah as one who sits among paupers afflicted by disease. Why, then, should one who suffers a physical blemish or deformity be disqualified from service in the Temple?

The truth is, it is not God Who views the service of the blemished Kohen as any less proper; it is man. This law is based on the Torah's recognition that people measure their fellow man by very superficial yardsticks. Just as one who chooses a lobbyist to represent his interests in the halls of government seeks the person who he feels will make the most favorable impression, so too, one who sends the Kohen as his agent to offer his sacrifice will seek what he perceives to be the most presentable of emissaries. The Torah recognizes this human tendency toward superficiality and responds to it, so that man not approach the service of God with less care than his own personal undertakings.

Were we to be asked, we might have suggested that, on the contrary, the blemished Kohen be allowed to serve — in order to emphasize the insignificance of outward appearances. Yet the Torah, the guide to human life, is responding to the reality that man's emotions often control his thought process. Rather than attempt to portray physical beauty as entirely insignificant — and risk degrading the Divine service in the process — the Torah demands that man honor the service of God by allowing only the unblemished to perform (*R' Eliyahu Meir Bloch*).

Meir, a young man who was the father of a young child, died an painful death. Reb Meir was a *ben Torah* to his very core. He loved everyone and was beloved by all who knew him. R' Shneur had a particularly close relationship with Meir, and when he died, R' Shneur was devastated. And it was as he was coping with this grief that the Kohen Gadol within him came to the fore, betraying the strength and fortitude that lie behind his gentle exterior.

In the chapel, before the funeral, he approached a *talmid* who was assisting Iranian youths who had fled Khomeini's Islamic regime, and he told the young man, "Don't think that during the *shivah* you won't be able to consult with me and enlist my help. I want you to continue coming to me with every issue as if nothing had happened."

During the *shivah*, every *Rosh Yeshivah* who came to console R' Shneur left having committed himself to take several of these young Iranian men into his yeshivah. R' Shneur's intense personal grief did not interfere with his loyal service of the Torah nation and the faithful execution of his responsibilities as a Torah leader.

⚜ פרשת בהר
Parashas Behar

Background

The *parashah* begins with the laws of *Shemittah* and *Yovel*, the Sabbatical and Jubilee years. The observance of these *mitzvos* is a declaration that everything belongs to God and that everything in our possession is a loan from Him.

בְּהַר סִינָי
on Mount Sinai (25:1).

Rashi cites the question of the Sages: All the *mitzvos* were given to us on Mount Sinai. What special connection between the mitzvah of *Shemittah* and Mount Sinai led the Torah to emphasize that this mitzvah was taught there? The commentators provide a number of explanations.

According to *Ksav Sofer,* the mitzvah of *Shemittah* helps us retain the sense of Jewish brotherhood which had been manifest at Sinai. The Sages teach that at Sinai the Jewish people enjoyed absolute unity — so much so that the Torah refers to all the people as one person, with a single will. Normally it is difficult to maintain such unity, in a great measure because everyone owns private property which they hoard for themselves, to the exclusion of others. On *Shemittah,* however, land and its produce are ownerless, they are common to everyone. This attitude frees us of much of our usual self-centeredness, and allows us to unite in spirit with our fellow Jews.[1]

The Talmud (*Megillah* 29a) teaches that God chose Mount Sinai as the location for giving His Torah because it was the lowest of all mountains, symbolizing that humility is a prerequisite for receiving the Torah. *Ben Ish Chai* suggests that Sinai's lesson that smaller is really greater is a theme which is represented in the mitzvah of *Shemittah.* While it would seem that one has less when he allows his fields to lay fallow for an entire year, the truth is that this is a key to a vastly increased crop. Thus, just as Sinai teaches that small is really great, *Shemittah* teaches that less is really more.

R' Zalman Sorotzkin notes that the Sages applied the words of King David, "strong warriors who do His bidding to obey the sound of His word" (*Psalms* 103:20), both to the Jewish people who proclaimed at Sinai, "We will do and we will obey," and to those who valiantly follow the laws of *Shemittah.* It is courage borne of absolute faith that enables one to abandon his fields for a full year — and in the case of *Shemittah* followed by *Yovel* (the Jubilee year),

---

1. **By the Word of God.** *Kli Chemdah* offers a similar insight. The Sages teach that the Torah could only be given to the generation that partook of the manna. Only one who lives with the sense that man's survival depends completely on God can truly grow in Torah.

Every seven years, as the fields lie fallow — untilled, unsown, untended — we relearn the lesson of the manna. We once again experience that man's effort is not the true source of his sustenance. The *Shemittah* way of life takes us back to that exalted level of faith, which grants us the ability to achieve greater understanding in Torah.

two years — and rely on God to fully provide. It was this same courageous faith which elevated Jews to the spiritual pinnacle of declaring their total submission to God and their willingness to blindly accept whatever He would ask of them.

Hence, *Shemittah* and Sinai are twin beacons of complete faith in a God we are sure we can rely on absolutely.

שֵׁשׁ שָׁנִים תִּזְרַע שָׂדֶךָ . . .
וּבַשָּׁנָה הַשְּׁבִיעִת שַׁבַּת שַׁבָּתוֹן

For six years you may sow your field . . .
but the seventh year shall be a
complete rest (ibid. 3-4).

The Torah draws parallel between *Shemittah* and Sabbath to include the other days of the week — and the other years of the *Shemittah* cycle — as well. Just as we work for six days and rest on the seventh, so we work the land for six years and grant it rest on the seventh.

The *Ponevezher Rav* observed: Every Jew is intrinsically holy, and the Jewish nation is, collectively, a holy people. However, in the hustle and bustle of the workweek we forget who we really are. Only on the Sabbath, when we pause and take the time to consider our true mission, does our spiritual beauty shine through.

Similarly, the holy Land of Israel is intrinsically sanctified. Every grain of its soil is holy. However, our working the land to achieve prosperity often causes us to lose sight of the reality that this is a *Land that Hashem, your God, seeks out; the eyes of Hashem, your God, are always upon it (Deuteronomy 11:12)* It is the Sabbath of the land, with its hands-off policy, that affords us the opportunity to contemplate the land's holiness and its intimate connection to God.

וְשָׁבְתָה הָאָרֶץ שַׁבָּת לַה׳
The land shall observe a Sabbath
rest for Hashem (ibid. 2).

Just as every Jew works for six days and is granted the seventh as a weekly Sabbath, just as a Jewish servant serves for six years and is freed on the seventh, so the land is tilled and worked for six years and is offered respite on the seventh.

The significance of the Land of Israel is not based on the benefit we receive from it; the land itself has sanctity and value. It is to highlight that this land has intrinsic value, we do not tend the soil for an entire year[2] (*Isaac Breuer*).

According to *Minchah Belulah*, *Shemittah* is the Great Equalizer.

We are taught (see below verse 6) that the *Shemittah* year shall be for you, your servants, laborers and residents. During the *Shemittah* all are equal, no one benefits by being a landowner or estateholder. *Shemittah* creates a climate in which no one needs to feel inferior or underprivileged.[3]

On the Sabbath, too, we are commanded "You shall not do any work — you, your son, your daughter, your slave, your maidservant . . . in order that your slave and your maidservant may rest like you" (*Deuteronomy* 5:14). We are called upon to recognize that we are all equal before God; we are all his flock. On the Sabbath we all rejoice in our status as princes in the kingdom of God; during the *Shemittah*, those who sanctify the seventh year enjoy the satisfaction and pleasure of His goodness which He grants to those who live in His Holy Land.

2. **Gut Shabbos.** R' Yosef Kahaneman, the *Rav of Ponevezh,* had a passionate love for *Eretz Yisrael*. During a *Shemittah* year, he paid a visit to *Kibbutz Chafetz Chaim* whose settlers determinedly observe *Shemittah* without resorting to any questionable halachic leniencies.

Inspired by the courage of the settlers, the Rav was seen bending down and kissing the ground, murmuring *"Gut Shabbos,* dear mother earth. *Gut Shabbos."*

3. **Unlimited Blessing.** The *Zohar* (2:88) teaches that all blessings, both physical and spiritual, come to us through the Sabbath. Human endeavor is bound by natural limits. Thus a person who views his financial success as the result of his own efforts can enjoy limited success. On the other hand, one who observes the Sabbath declares that it is, in fact, God, the Creator of the world, Who enables us to achieve. When we realize that it is all His doing, we can be blessed with His limitless bounty.

Similarly, on the Sabbath of the Land, we defy the laws of agriculture and commerce, and we live with the reality that *to Him belongs the earth and all that is within it.* Through this can we merit His unlimited blessing (*Simchas Aharon*).

שֵׁשׁ שָׁנִים תִּזְרַע שָׂדֶךָ . . . וּבַשָּׁנָה הַשְּׁבִיעִת שַׁבַּת שַׁבָּתוֹן

For six years you may sow your field . . . But the seventh year shall be a complete rest (ibid. 3-4).

Why does the *Shemittah* cycle consist of six years of work followed by a year of rest? The Talmud (*Berachos* 35b) teaches that the *yeshivos* were closed in the months of Nissan and Tishrei to allow the students to harvest grain and press grapes and olives (see *Rashi* ibid.). Thus, over the course of six years, twelve months — an entire year of Torah study — was lost. The seventh year, *Shemittah* year, releases people from their agricultural obligation and offers them the opportunity to reinvigorate their spirits with a year of uninterrupted Torah study (*Chida*).[4]

The six-year *Shemittah* cycle parallels the six-day workweek. *Meshech Chochmah* notes that on both the third and sixth days the Torah repeats טוֹב, *God saw that it was good* (*Genesis* 1:10,12 and 25,31), two times. On the third and sixth years of the *Shemittah* cycle, we are commanded to separate a special tithe for the poor. This is a way for us to bestow goodness and kindness on those less fortunate, who would also like to partake of the goodness of His world.

וְסָפַרְתָּ לְךָ שֶׁבַע שַׁבְּתֹת שָׁנִים

You shall count for yourself seven cycles of sabbatical years (ibid. 8).

Why does the Torah stress that the count should be "for yourself"?

Throughout their lives, people count many things; primary among them, money. Ultimately, however, the money is not for themselves. Their heirs (or in the worst case, perfect strangers) receive the money that they counted.

Tzror HaMor notes that the only counting truly done for oneself is the counting done for *mitzvos* — expenditures for *mitzvos* and charity, the counting of the *Omer*, *Shemittah* and *Yovel*, etc. *Kli Yakar* explains that only if one counts *for himself*, by occupying himself with spiritual pursuits, will the years be his. If one wastes his time on empty and meaningless activities, then he will have nothing to show for it all in the end. The Torah directs us to count the years for ourselves, to make our time count, and to make our lives truly meaningful.

וְהַעֲבַרְתָּ שׁוֹפַר תְּרוּעָה . . . בְּיוֹם הַכִּפֻּרִים

You shall sound a broken blast on the shofar . . . on the Day of Atonement (ibid. 9).

Why does the proclamation of the Jubilee year take place on Yom Kippur?

Maharal explains: Yom Kippur is the day of repentance for all Jews. The word for repentance is *teshuvah*, which actually means "return." *Teshuvah* is the process by which man returns to his roots. Man was created as innately good (*Ecclesiastes* 7:29). When he sins, he strays from his true self. He comes under the control of the evil inclination and becomes a slave to his passions. When man repents, he returns to his true self.

Yom Kippur is the day on which we issue a call for everything to return to its previous state. The charge of the Jubilee year — that slaves go free and that the land returns to its previous owner — mirrors the theme of this day.

אַל תּוֹנוּ אִישׁ אֶת אָחִיו

Do not aggrieve one another (ibid. 14).

This verse teaches that one may not act unjustly toward people with whom he does business. The price of a field in the Land of Israel is determined by the number of crops remaining until *Yovel*, the Jubilee year. Since the land reverts to the seller at *Yovel*, one who sells a field is ultimately selling only

---

4. **Making Amends.** The *Shemittah* year cancels monetary debts, except under specific circumstances (see *Gittin* 36a). However, the debt of the time we "borrowed" from God in order to make a living remains outstanding. We take this year to pay back to God the time we owe Him.

Yarchei Kallah programs, reinstituted by the *Ponevezher Rav* and successfully duplicated in England and the United States, offer people who work an opportunity to spend their vacation time in the study hall so that they grow personally, even as they "repay" some of their time to God.

the produce which the field will yield until that time. One who sells at a higher price, as if it was a permanent sale of the land itself, defrauds the buyer.

Meleches Machsheves offers the following insight: When one considers that even the field or vineyard he legitimately bought will eventually be returned to its original owner, the idea of stealing or cheating seems futile. Indeed, the Sages note (*Bamidbar Rabbah* 22:7), "Why are coins called *zuzim*? Because they are *zaz* (moved) from this person and given to the other person." "Why is property called *nechasim*? For it is *neches* (covered over and disappears) from one person and is revealed to another person." In the blink of an eye one's belongings can be out of his control, moved, by Divine decree, into someone else's ownership.[5]

The prohibition defrauding others is stated in the plural form. This teaches that even if someone has been treated dishonestly, he may not, on his own, cheat, steal, or unilaterally choose to underpay the guilty party. *Beis din* — rabbinic court — is the proper venue for the adjudication of such a dispute.

No one has the license to justify cheating because he had been wronged. Both parties are expected to maintain the highest standard of honesty (*Tuv Yerushalayim*).

וְכִי תִמְכְּרוּ מִמְכָּר לַעֲמִיתֶךָ אוֹ קָנֹה מִיַּד עֲמִיתֶךָ
When you make a sale to your fellow or make a purchase from the hand of your fellow (ibid.).

Alshich tells us that the Torah compares buying and selling to teach us that when one sets the price for his merchandise, he should ask himself, "If I were the buyer would I feel that this is a fair price for the merchandise?" This is a way to ensure that he is not cheating the purchaser.[6] In addition, it is a form of fulfilling the mitzvah to "love your fellow as yourself."

וְלֹא תוֹנוּ אִישׁ אֶת עֲמִיתוֹ
Each of you shall not aggrieve his fellow (ibid. 17).

This verse is a prohibition against verbal abuse. One may not remind others of their past failures, nor of their checkered past or lineage. *Rambam* (*Hilchos Teshuvah* 7:8) writes: "It is a grievous sin to tell a penitent, 'Do you remember your old ways?' or to mention the unsavory details of his personal history." Likewise, it is strictly forbidden to remind a proselyte of his ancestry. In fact, personal aggrievement is a more severe transgression than financial aggrievement, since money can be returned while the emotional pain inflicted by a caustic remark cannot be undone (*Bava Metzia* 58b). One must be exceptionally careful not to aggrieve his wife. Since women are sensitive and tend to cry easily, one is liable to

---

5. **Ear to the Ground.** Two litigants came before *R' Chaim of Volozhin* to adjudicate a dispute regarding a parcel of real estate. Each one vehemently claimed that the property was his, and the other party was lying. R' Chaim put his ear to the ground and remained there, silently engrossed in thought. When the litigants asked him what he was doing, he replied, "I wanted to hear what the earth itself had to say on the matter. Do you know what it said? It said, 'What are they arguing for? In the end, both of them will be mine!'"

6. **Practical Faith.** Many people have the custom to recite, following the morning prayers, *Ani Maamin*, Maimonidies' Thirteen Principles of Faith. The eighth of those principles reads, "I believe with complete faith that the entire Torah now in our hands is the same one that was given to Moses, our teacher." Included in this Torah are the prohibitions against cheating, stealing and falsehood, as well as the statement of our Sages (*Beitzah* 16a) that each man's yearly income is determined on Rosh Hashanah. Certainly God did not expect man to earn his living by means of cheating and falsehood!

How absurd it would be for one to complete his prayers by reciting the *Ani Maamin* — and then enter the marketplace convinced that his income can only be earned if he cheats, lies and steals (*Shaarei HaKodesh*).

Maharsha (*Kesubos* 67a) writes: Many people accrue wealth dishonestly, by cheating non-Jews and causing a desecration of God's Name. They then donate that money to worthy causes to attain honor and prestige. This is a mitzvah performed through sinful means, which is not a valid mitzvah, and this wealth will not endure.

swiftly administered Divine retribution in response to their tears (*Bava Metzia* 59a).

The Talmud relates the story of R' Rechumi, who regularly spent an extended period of time studying under Rava in Mechoza. Each year R' Rechumi would return home on the eve of Yom Kippur. One year he became so engrossed in his studies that he completely lost track of time and failed to come home. His wife anxiously waited his return, and kept telling herself, "He is coming soon; he is coming soon." When he failed to arrive, she became dejected and a tear fell from her eye. At that moment, R' Rechumi was sitting on a roof. The roof suddenly collapsed and R' Rechumi died (*Kesubos* 62b).[7]

וְכִי תֹאמְרוּ מַה נֹּאכַל בַּשָּׁנָה הַשְּׁבִיעִת . . .
וְצִוִּיתִי אֶת בִּרְכָתִי לָכֶם בַּשָּׁנָה הַשִּׁשִּׁית
If you will say: What will we eat in the seventh year . . . I will ordain My blessing for you in the sixth year (ibid. 20-21).

The implication of this verse is that God will bestow His blessing in response to those who ask, "What will we eat?" Does this mean that no

blessing is in store for those who, in their absolute faith, do not pose the question?

R' Zusia of Anipoli offered the following perspective: The true key to sustenance is faith. Perfect faith in God and the firm belief and trust that He will provide for us are vehicles through which He bestows His kindness upon us. When people ask, "What shall we eat?" they exhibit a flaw in their faith, and God's beneficence would normally be withheld. This verse tells us that despite this weakness in faith, God will ordain that His special blessing continue to provide for all.

Those who maintain their complete trust in God and, despite the challenges of leaving the land fallow, do not ask how God will provide for them, do not need His special blessing. These people continue to be provided for by dint of their unyielding trust in the Almighty.[8]

וְצִוִּיתִי אֶת בִּרְכָתִי לָכֶם
And I will ordain my blessing for you (ibid. 21).

God's attribute of mercy is exceedingly more extensive than His attribute of justice. Thus, since

---

7. **Interpersonal Burns.** *R' Chaim Shmulevitz* asked: What kind of punishment is this? If R' Rechumi's wife cried because he was late in arriving, certainly she would be shattered by his death?! He explained that punishment for interpersonal sins has nothing to do with rectifying the injustice that took place. Causing others emotional pain is like playing with fire. If one places his hand in a fire, the burns he sustains are not a punishment. They are the result of the fact that fire burns. Causing pain to others, said R' Chaim, "burns." R' Rechumi was not punished; he was "burned" by his having caused his wife pain.

8. **Embraced by Reality.** The following letter of encouragement to Israeli farmers was published by the *Chazon Ish* :

"I work the farm and support myself by means of my own labor. As the *Shemittah* year approached, a thought stole its way into my heart. As the scion of a stiff-necked people, I would obstinately observe *Shemittah* properly. I was lonely and abandoned, the laughingstock of my neighbors. 'How could it be?' they chided me. 'You will neither plant nor will you reap. It is impossible to fight reality!'

"My obstinance, however, kept me steadfast. This despite the fact that anyone with a brain in his head understands that it is impossible to really keep *Shemittah*, that *Shemittah* was meant only for those who have stockpiled three years worth of grain, and that, anyway, our times are not like times gone by. In any case, now more than half the year has passed, and 'reality' has lovingly embraced me.

"I did all my planting before Rosh Hashanah, during the sixth year. During the seventh year I have sat by, having neither plowed nor planted. I treat the yield of the sixth-year planting, which sprouted in the seventh year, with the sanctity of *Shemittah* and eat it accordingly. I continue to hope that I can come to terms with the reality — or, more accurately, that reality will come to terms with me — in the next half year.

"As for my neighbors who ridiculed me, and plowed and planted during the seventh year — reality has waged a fierce and ferocious battle with them. It has scornfully destroyed all of their produce with its excessive rains and raging storms.

"Now, I respectfully beg those who permit agricultural work during *Shemittah* to please forgive me for rebelling against them. I implore them to analyze this matter once again. Perhaps the brain in the head will begin to realize that the Torah will not change and that the fulfillment of the laws of *Shemittah* is dependent on our desire and comittment."

we know that once God unleashes forces of destruction they do not differentiate between the deserving and the undeserving (*Bava Kamma* 60a), it would certainly seem that God's blessing is provided to all.

Our verse teaches that the special blessings for the observance of *Shemittah* are specifically directed *for you* — they are granted only in the Land of Israel, and only to those who unyieldingly follow the laws of *Shemittah*. God wants to demonstrate clearly that the success of this season is not happenstance; it is His acknowledgment of the self-sacrifice of His courageous children (*Oznayim L'Torah*).[9]

Wealth, and the comfort that comes with it, can cause the wealthy to become desensitized to the plight of the poor. By commanding us to fulfill the mitzvah of *Shemittah* we are all, rich and poor alike, forced to ask the question, "What shall we eat?" As a result of having experienced some of what the indigent suffer all the time, the rich will be better able to empathize with and respond to the needs of the impoverished. This concern for the poor will, in turn, result in God sending His blessing. Since you, the wealthy, will have experienced what it means to ask, "What shall we eat?" you will be more generous in assisting the poor, and *I will ordain My blessing* (*Iturei Torah*).[10]

וְהָאָרֶץ לֹא תִמָּכֵר לִצְמִתֻת כִּי לִי הָאָרֶץ
The land shall not be sold in perpetuity for the land is Mine (ibid. 23).

For centuries, the right of the Jewish people to *Eretz Yisrael* has regularly been challenged. *R' Nachshon Gaon* was asked: If conquest is a legal mode of acquisition, then why does the non-Jews' conquest of *Eretz Yisrael* not grant them legitimate sovereignty over the land? R' Nachshon replied as follows: Conquest is a viable mode of acquisition only for something which can be bought with money. If it can be bought with money (דָמִים) it can be bought with blood (דָמִים). This verse, however, teaches us that *Eretz Yisrael* cannot be bought with money. *The land shall not be sold in perpetuity;* even when it is sold it ultimately reverts to the original owner. Hence, the conquest by non-Jews grants them no rights to the Land whatsoever.

כִּי לִי הָאָרֶץ כִּי גֵרִים וְתוֹשָׁבִים אַתֶּם עִמָּדִי
For the land is Mine, for you are sojourners and residents with Me (ibid.).

Toras Kohanim explains that everyone is, in fact, both a sojourner and a resident. A person who

9. **Faith Pays.** At the end of *Shemittah* in 1952 the farmers of *Komemius* faced a difficult problem. Since they refused to seed using wheat kernels that had grown during *Shemittah,* they had no way to plant for the next year's crop. The only kernels available to them were cracked, worm-infested kernels that a nearby kibbutz had left over from the sixth year. Agricultural experts cautioned against buying and planting those kernels. Neighboring farmers who heard that *Komemius* was contemplating such a move ridiculed the idea of foolishly investing the sizable amount of money and effort involved in purchasing and planting the substandard kernels.

The fellow responsible for acquiring grain for planting dejectedly turned to *R' Binyamin Mendelsohn,* Rav of *Komemius*, for advice. The Rav replied: "If these are the only halachically fit kernels, let us trust in the Life Source of the world, and plant them" (see *Shabbos* 31a, *Tosafos* ad loc.). Committed to such a course, the farmers of *Komemius* turned to the *Chazon Ish* with a further question. "May we, in order to take full advantage of the rains, plow our fields on the Chol HaMoed Succos following the *Shemittah* year? Otherwise we may incur a serious loss, after not working the land for the entire year."

The *Chazon Ish* replied: "And who says you will be too late for the rainy season? Maybe, by working on Chol HaMoed, you will plant too early and will cause yourselves loss?"

The farmers of *Komemius* loyally followed the ruling of the Chazon Ish and did not plow on Chol HaMoed. Wonder of wonders, the rains that year did not begin to fall until nearly Chanukah. All the neighboring kibbutzim who planted early lost their crops completely. While *Komemius* had a bumper crop of wheat.

The blessing of God was directed to those who lived with the courage to have faith in Him and His Torah.

10. **Upgrade.** While it helps for the wealthy to experience the discomfort of the poor, it is vitally important for those helping the poor to do more than just make their bitter lives more bearable.

A great Rav counseled a rich congregant to eat and drink well. When the congregant wondered why the Rav offered this advice the Rav explained: "If you eat prime meat and drink good wine there is a chance that you will provide the poor with black bread and herring. However, if *your* diet consists of black bread and herring, you will likely give the poor stones to eat."

views himself as a sojourner in this world will merit to be a resident in the World to Come. However, if he views himself as a true resident of this world, then he will be only a sojourner in the Hereafter.

The Jubilee year reminds us that we are but sojourners here, with no absolute claim of ownership to the land that we buy. Like everything in this world, it is ours only temporarily.

The *Dubno Maggid* offers a slightly different approach: God and the Jewish people enjoy a symbiotic relationship. When we view ourselves as strangers and sojourners in this world, understanding that it is merely a corridor which leads to the World to Come, then God is a resident in our lives, for we allow Divine Presence to be the deciding factor in all our endeavors. However, if we view this world as our permanent residence — as the goal rather than a means to achieving something greater and more eternal — then God senses Himself to be but a sojourner in our lives.

In yet a subtler, more poetic vein, *Degel Machaneh Ephraim* suggests the following: A lone traveler, lacking a companion with whom to share his concerns and fears, often acts reclusive. The moment he meets another sojourner, however, he immediately bonds and they become fast friends. Their common destiny as strangers serves to instantly cement a relationship.

God Himself is, so to speak, a stranger in this world. He has few people who share His concerns and agenda. When we, His people, perceive ourselves as sojourners in this world and residents in the Next World, we join Him, as it were, and are truly "with Him."

וּבְכֹל אֶרֶץ אֲחֻזַּתְכֶם גְּאֻלָּה תִּתְּנוּ לָאָרֶץ . . . כִּי יָמוּךְ אָחִיךָ וּמָכַר מֵאֲחֻזָּתוֹ

In the entire land of your ancestral heritage you shall provide redemption for the land . . . If your brother becomes impoverished and sells part of his ancestral heritage (ibid. 24-25).

Many explanations have been offered for the juxtaposition of these two verses. *R' Shmuel Alter* suggests that the verses reflect the historical reality of our long exile. Unfortunately, while we are all enjoined to yearn for the ultimate redemption and the rebuilding of the Temple, our yearning is often diminished when we enjoy financial success in exile. When things go well, we are sometimes less wholehearted in our hope that Messiah come speedily in our days. On the other hand, when we experience poverty and financial stress, we truly sense the exile as oppressive, and sincerely yearn to be free. Thus, the verse alludes to the conditions which precipitate the condition where we fully and anxiously await the ultimate Redemption of our ancestral home.[11]

Zekan Aharon suggests that these verses allude to the teaching of the Sages (*Sanhedrin* 98a), "Jerusalem will only be redeemed in the merit of charity." The final redemption will come to the Land when we reach out to help our fellow Jew in need.

Simchas Aharon views the poverty referred to in the verse as an allusion to the spiritual poverty that will be rampant before the arrival of the Messiah: "not a hunger for bread nor a thirst for water, but rather to hear the words of God" (*Amos* 8:11).

Background

The Torah now teaches the laws that apply to the sale of real property in the Land of Israel. Plots of land, houses in walled cities and lots in Levite cities all have distinct laws.

וְכִי יָמוּךְ אָחִיךָ

If your brother becomes impoverished (ibid. 25).

The Torah follows the laws of *Shemittah* with the commandment to assist the poor. The Torah's order teaches several important lessons.

There are people who enjoy abundant prosperity. Though they would be able to comfortably live off the dividends of their present fortune, they continue to work ceaselessly in order to amass yet more wealth. Concerned for the future financial security of their families, they are constantly worried about money.

---

11. **In a Strange Land.** God's seal is truth. One who views himself as a stranger in this world of falsehood is one who is close to God; *for sojourners* in this world are those who are truly *residents with Me* (*R' Dov Ber of Mezritch*).

On the other hand, there are people who barely earn enough money to cover their most basic daily needs, yet who walk around serene and content. They have a sense of happiness borne of the confidence that God will continue to provide for them.

There is one circumstance, however, where the "worrier" is totally "transformed" and suddenly exhibits complete trust in God: when approached for charity. Suddenly the man who can never stop amassing enough wealth for his own family becomes a paragon of faith. He reassures the poor man who approached him that the God Who sustains all of humanity will certainly not abandon His impoverished children. Full of praise for the All-Caring God, he soothingly tells the impoverished man that the One Who granted him children will undoubtedly provide adequate sustenance for them.

The Torah tells us that such faith is misplaced.

Faith in God must shape a person's attitude toward his own needs; compassion, concern and generosity must define his response to the needs of others. It is for this reason that the Torah juxtaposes *Shemittah* with the obligation to give charity.

The message of *Shemittah* is that man, for all his effort, is not the one who truly provides for his family. By ceasing to work the land, we declare our faith in God as the Provider and exhibit our trust in his ability to sustain us. However, to ensure that we not misplace our faith and respond to the poor with words rather than with practical assistance, the Torah follows the laws of *Shemittah* with the commandment to financially respond to the cry of the impoverished (*Kehillas Yitzchak*).

וְאִישׁ כִּי לֹא יִהְיֶה לּוֹ גֹּאֵל וְהִשִּׂיגָה יָדוֹ וּמָצָא כְּדֵי גְאֻלָּתוֹ

If a man will have no redeemer, but his means suffice and he acquires enough for its redemption (ibid. 26).

This verse may be mistakenly understood to imply that one may not redeem himself if he does have a relative who can redeem him.

Chasam Sofer sees in the wording of this verse an insight into the dynamics of faith. When a person feels that all hope is gone — that his friends and family have not provided him with salvation — he realizes that he can rely only on his Loving Father in Heaven. It is then that the Redeemer will provide him with the means for redemption.[12]

וְאִם לֹא מָצְאָה יָדוֹ דֵּי הָשִׁיב לוֹ

But if he does not acquire sufficient means to pay him (ibid. 28).

The words דֵּי יָדוֹ can be read both forward and backward. This teaches that financial success is like a seesaw. Money goes back and forth. One person may be wealthy, but a short while later he may lose that wealth; while his friend, who is indigent now, can become a rich man (*Nachal Eliyahu*).

---

12. **Right Address.** This lesson is true not only on a personal level, but for us as a nation as well.

Ramban (*Deuteronomy* 31:18) views the extended duration of our current exile as a result of our looking to foreign powers to shape our destiny and aid our redemption. Be it Spain, England, the United Nations or the United States, our reliance on these powers leads God to hide His face from us, leaving us vulnerable — and unredeemed. We must, as a nation, learn that our salvation lies exclusively with Him.

פרשת בחקותי ܀
Parashas Bechukosai

Background

The *parashah* begins with the blessings which the Jewish people will enjoy as a result of their commitment to Torah study and the performance of *mitzvos*. It continues by describing the reverse; the horrifying punishments which will befall us if we abandon Him and His will.

אִם בְּחֻקֹּתַי תֵּלֵכוּ וְאֶת מִצְוֹתַי תִּשְׁמְרוּ
If you follow My decrees and observe My commandments (26:3).

Rashi observes that since the phrase *observe My commandments* refers to mitzvah observance,

the initial clause *follow My decrees* must mean some other aspect of following God's will. He concludes that this verse calls for toiling in the study of Torah.[1] Why is committed Torah study referred to as בְּחֻקֹּתַי תֵּלֵכוּ, *following My decrees*?

Ohr HaChaim notes that Torah study is referred to as "following His decrees," for Torah study is not goal oriented. Even if one has completed a particular area of study (or even the entire Torah) he is still commanded to constantly review and explore it further.

Simchas Aharon suggests an approach based on a novel interpretation by *R' Yisrael Salanter*. The Torah teaches us the laws of a "wayward and rebellious son" (see *Deuteronomy* 21:18). If a young man steals, eats and drinks specified items, the courts

---

1. **Toil with Love.** The *Netziv of Volozhin* was famous for his tireless diligence in Torah study. He had high expectations of others as well.

One Succos the Netziv realized that his grandson by marriage, the famed *R' Chaim Soloveitchik* (later of Brisk), avoided reciting a blessing when he used the Netziv's *esrog*. After much pressuring, R' Chaim expressed his reservations regarding the halachic status of the *esrog*. The Netziv replied: "If your objection is valid, then I, too, have a problem reciting the blessing. Let me look into the matter."

About 3 o'clock in the morning, one of the members of the Netziv's family knocked on R' Chaim's door.

"Grandfather wants you to come to his home," the messenger said.

R' Chaim quickly dressed, washed his hands and headed to the Netziv's home. When he entered, he saw the Netziv poring over a stack of halachic works. When the Netziv began to discuss the issues R' Chaim had raised regarding the *esrog*, R' Chaim respectfully interrupted his grandfather, explaining that he could not discuss the matter as he had yet to recite the daily blessings for Torah study. As R' Chaim began to recite the blessings, the Netziv started to cry. R' Chaim asked him to explain and he replied, "How is it that a young man at your stage of life has not yet recited the blessings over Torah study and begun learning? How can I not cry if a scholar, one who, we hope, will develop into one of the generation's great Torah scholars, has not begun his learning at this time of the morning? What can we expect the next generation to look like?"

It is no wonder that the Netziv would conclude his letters הִנְנִי הֶעָמוּס בַּעֲבוֹדָה כָּל יִשְׁעִי וְכָל חֶפְצִי בָהּ, *I am the one overwhelmed with work* [i.e., Torah study]; *my salvation and my total desire is in it.*

---

are commanded to put him to death. The Sages teach us that such a case never did — nor will it ever — occur. Why, then, is it written in the Torah? So that we might study its laws and be rewarded for the resultant Torah study (*Sanhedrin* 71a).

Are there so few areas of practical Torah law that the Torah finds it necessary to write an entire chapter only for the purpose of its study?! Surely not! Very few individuals in a generation truly and fully master even the practical areas of Torah law!

R' Yisrael Salanter explains: The Sages teach that one receives greater reward for fulfilling a חֹק — a mitzvah whose explanation is unknown — than for fulfilling a mitzvah which is rational. One might think that the study of all *mitzvos* is equal, since even the חֻקִּים, laws without revealed reasons, have practical applications. The laws of the wayward and rebellious son offer us the opportunity to attain special reward for the study of Torah exclusively for the sake of study — for this is Torah study that has no practical application.

This can be seen as the thrust of *Rashi's* comment: *Torah study* for the sake of fulfilling a mitzvah is included in the clause *and observe My commandments*. To *follow My decrees* obligates us to study Torah for no purpose, not even to teach us how to fulfill other *mitzvos*. בְּחֻקֹּתַי תֵּלֵכוּ calls upon us to study Torah purely as a חֹק, for its own sake.[2], [3]

The phrase used in our verse, אִם בְּחֻקֹּתַי תֵּלֵכוּ, can also be translated "if you walk with My decrees." The Torah must always accompany the Jew. Wherever he is and whatever he is doing, his thoughts, attitudes and actions must be informed by Torah.

R' Nachum Zev of Kelm offered the following analogy: A group of people were eating and drinking. So long as they remained seated, they all seemed to be equally healthy and robust. When they stood up to leave, however, one person

2. **Altruistic Torah.** At Mount Sinai, the Jews declared נַעֲשֶׂה וְנִשְׁמַע, *We will do and we will hear.* The *Zohar* comments: "We will do good deeds and *mitzvos;* we will hear the words of the Torah." *Beis HaLevi* explains that when the Jews declared, "*We will do,*" they committed themselves to properly performing the *mitzvos,* including studying how to fulfill the *mitzvos.* "*We will hear*" was a commitment to study Torah for its own sake, not only as preparation for mitzvah performance.

3. **Business as Usual.** We are called upon to *toil* in Torah, not merely to *learn* Torah. According to the *Taz,* this is reflected in the language of the daily blessing over Torah study, where we speak of God having commanded us לַעֲסוֹק, to *engross ourselves, in the words of Torah.*

According to the *Chafetz Chaim,* this characterization indicates that we must approach Torah as we do a business, עֵסֶק. Just as one toils ceaselessly in order to succeed in business, so one must make his Torah learning a single-minded pursuit. Just as one would not interrupt heated negotiations over a multimillion-dollar deal, so one should allow nothing to distract him during the time he has set aside for Torah study.

Additionally, notes the Chafetz Chaim, the reward for toil in Torah — unlike that for business — is not related to the degree of success one achieves. A tailor who attempts to sew a suit yet is unsuccessful is not paid for his efforts, nor is a shoemaker who tries, but fails, to produce a pair of shoes. In commerce, one is only paid for results.

Not so for Torah study. God rewards us for the sincere effort, even if ultimately we are unable to understand and absorb the material.

At a *siyum* celebrating the completion of a Talmudic tractate, we thank God for having enabled us to be among those who dwell in the study hall rather than with idlers, saying, "For we labor and they labor. We labor and receive reward while they labor and do not receive reward." Surely, those who do toil in areas other than Torah are compensated — if their labors yield results. Our toil in Torah, however, always yields reward, for the toil is an end unto itself.

The Midrash tells a parable of a king who gave his subjects barrels and ordered the people to pour water into the barrels. The people quickly discovered that the barrels had holes, and, seeing the futility of their efforts, all of them, save one, stopped pouring in the water. When the king came and saw that they had stopped, he was upset. "I asked you to pour the water not so that the barrels should get filled, but rather to keep them wet. Why did you stop?"

God commanded us to toil in Torah so that our souls will have an ongoing connection with His word. We are rewarded for engaging in the learning process — not just for attaining knowledge.

remained seated. When a bystander glanced under the table, he saw that the man had no legs and was unable to walk.

Likewise, explained R' Nachum Zev, the success of a yeshivah education cannot be measured until the students part ways and begin to take their own journeys through life. It is then that we can tell who has truly made Torah part of his life, to the extent that it provides him with the fortitude needed to meet life's challenges.

One must learn to *walk with the Torah*.[4], [5]

King David said: *I considered my ways and turned my feet back to Your testimonies* (Psalms 119:59). The Midrash explains that King David meant, "Master of the universe, every day I would plan to go to a particular place or a certain house, yet my feet would take me to synagogues and study halls."

Torah was so much part of King David that despite his conscious intention to address numerous temporal items on his agenda, he instinctively gravitated to the synagogue and the study hall. בְּחֻקֹּתַי תֵּלֵכוּ calls upon us not only to actively seek out God, but to reorient our very being so that we instinctively follow the Torah path.

וְאֶת מִצְוֹתַי תִּשְׁמְרוּ
And observe My commandments (ibid.).

The Torah promises material reward for fidelity to God's word. This seems to refute the Talmudic opinion that שְׂכַר מִצְוָה בְּהַאי עַלְמָא לֵיכָּא, "There is no reward for a mitzvah in this world" (*Kiddushin* 39b).

Zekan Aharon offers a homiletic interpretation, rendering the word תִּשְׁמְרוּ as *wait for* (see *Genesis* 37:11 and *Rashi* ad loc.).[6] Although according to this opinion we receive no earthly reward for the **fulfillment** of *mitzvos*, God does repay us in the here and now for the way that we anxiously await and seek out opportunities to do *mitzvos*.

וַעֲשִׂיתֶם אֹתָם
and perform them (ibid.).

The word אֹתָם is written without the letter "ו" (אֹתָם, as opposed to אוֹתָם), and can be read as אַתֶּם, *you*. The Talmud teaches (*Berachos* 17a) that one who studies Torah with no intent of practicing its tenets would have been better off not being born. Thus, when one follows the commandments, man is, in effect, re-creating himself.

Meshech Chochmah explains that an unborn fetus is taught the entire Torah — and then forgets it — while in the womb (*Niddah* 30b). Man's mission in this world is to relearn the Torah and put its teachings into practice. If he fails to do so, then he is merely re-experiencing the prenatal process. What purpose was there, then, in his having been born?

---

4. **Love Abandoned.** *Talmud Yerushalmi* (*Berachos* 9:5) teaches that one who abandons Torah study for one day will find that the Torah has "distanced" itself from him as well. Torah is like a woman kept waiting for her groom, who, when she realizes that he is not coming, leaves and goes elsewhere.

If, on the other hand, we toil in Torah and pursue it, it responds in kind, showing us her full love and doing all she can on our behalf. This is how the Talmud (*Sanhedrin* 99b) explains King Solomon's words, *The working spirit works for itself* (*Proverbs* 16:26): When man toils in Torah, the Torah toils for him, beseeching God to impart to him its meaning and its secrets.

5. **Living Torah.** The injunction to toil in Torah does not refer only to Torah study; it applies to one's way of life. All of a person's toil in life must be directed by the Torah. One must conduct his business in accordance with Torah standards of honesty and ethics, because that is toiling in the path of Torah (*R' Moshe Elyakim of Kozhnitz*).

6. **Passionately Awaiting.** King David in *Psalms* (130:6) also employed the word שֹׁמְרִים in the sense of anxious awaiting: *My soul [yearns] for the Lord more than night-watchmen await the morning.*

R' Yechezkel Abramsky commented: Night-watchmen have no doubt that morning will arrive. Though they may be anxious and feel they can wait no longer, they are sure that dawn will come. So too with salvation from Hashem: We are certain, beyond any doubt, that it will ultimately come, although it seems to be long in coming.

Sabbath observers are called שׁוֹמְרֵי שַׁבָּת for they not only observe the laws of Sabbath, they also anxiously await its arrival.

וְנָתַתִּי גִשְׁמֵיכֶם בְּעִתָּם

*Then I will provide your rains
in their time* (ibid. 4).

Rain comes from God; why then does the Torah refer to *your* rains?

The Torah teaches us that all of creation was made to serve those who study Torah and follow its path.

Thus the rain is truly man's, since it is his behavior which gives to rain — as well as to everything else in this world — true purpose and meaning (*R' Moshe Feinstein*).

The Midrash (*Vayikra Rabbah* 27:1) tells that Alexander the Great visited an African kingdom to see their judicial system. In the course of his conversation with the local ruler, Alexander described some of Greece's despotic practices.

"Does the sun shine in your land?" asked the African monarch.

"Yes," Alexander replied.

"Does it rain in your kingdom?"

"Yes."

"Are there small animals in your kingdom?"

The Greek replied in the affirmative.

"Then it must be for them that the sun shines and the rain falls," the monarch concluded.

Only if man follows the ways of Hashem does he merit to have nature serve him. Otherwise, Hashem may be sending rain and sunlight for the animals, with man nothing more than an incidental beneficiary (*Be'er Yosef, Yesod HaEmunah*).

וְנָתְנָה הָאָרֶץ יְבוּלָהּ וְעֵץ הַשָּׂדֶה יִתֵּן פִּרְיוֹ

*and the land will give its produce and the
tree of the field will give its fruit* (ibid. 4).

In the blessings enumerated in this verse, the Torah merely promises that one's basic needs will be met. In *Parashas Ki Savo* (*Deuteronomy* 28:3-8), on the other hand, those who follow the commandments are promised great wealth. Why are the blessings here so limited?

R' Chaim Kanievsky explains: In *Ki Savo,* the Torah speaks to the Jewish people as a group. Moses blessed them with abundant wealth, for the Jewish people need to be able to afford *mitzvos* and they must be able to provide for Torah scholars and the needy. In our verse, however, the blessings are addressed particularly to those who toil in the study of Torah. For the Torah scholar, wealth is not necessarily a blessing; often, it can distract from his focus on Torah. The Torah scholar is sometimes better off if his needs are met and little more.

וַאֲכַלְתֶּם לַחְמְכֶם לָשֹׂבַע

and you will eat your bread to satiety (ibid. 5).

Rashi explains that while one will eat only a little, God's blessing will cause it to be enough to satisfy him.

Lest one limit his contributions to the poor, since God will "certainly bless them" and cause the little that they will eat to satisfy their hunger, the Torah says, "eat *your* bread to satiety." You may rely on the blessing only for yourself. When it comes to others however, you must provide for them in full.

וְנָתַתִּי שָׁלוֹם בָּאָרֶץ

I will provide peace in the land (ibid. 6).

The previous verse promises that *you will dwell securely in your land.* What, then, is added by this additional promise of peace? According to *Ramban,* the first blessing promises security from external enemies; the second assures us that harmony will reign among us. When we live in accordance with His Will, God will inspire us all to live with brotherly love.

Ksav Sofer elaborates on this point: Strife is frequently the result of fierce competition for material success. Consciously or subconsciously, a person may feel that "he has more than I do," and that makes him angry. When people's focus is the study of Torah and mitzvah performance, they cherish the spiritual aspects of life, and competition does not breed contempt. In fact, the Sages taught, "Torah scholars increase peace in the world" (*Berachos* 64a). The joint pursuit of truth has a bonding effect.

וּשְׁכַבְתֶּם וְאֵין מַחֲרִיד

*and you will lie down with
none to frighten you* (ibid.).

King Solomon teaches that the *satiety of the rich does not let him sleep* (*Ecclesiastes* 5:11), for he constantly worries about his wealth. Money can so preoccupy us that we enjoy no respite; if "One who has one hundred wants two hundred," we certainly cannot lie down to relax and sleep.

Here, the Torah assures us that the blessing of prosperity will not carry with it any undesirable results. Our satiety will not impede restful sleep; we will lie down with no fear or anxiety (*Be'er Moshe*).

וְנָתַתִּי מִשְׁכָּנִי בְּתוֹכְכֶם וְלֹא תִגְעַל נַפְשִׁי אֶתְכֶם
I will place My Sanctuary among you; and My Spirit will not reject you (ibid. 11).

If God places His Sanctuary in our midst, why might we suspect that His Spirit will reject us?

R' Yosef Karo clarifies by way of a parable: When a king tours the countryside, he must find lodgings along the way. If he stays at the home of one of his officers, the officer and his family must temporarily vacate their home, because the king cannot reside together with commoners. However, if the king takes up lodging at his son's manor house, or at the home of a fellow king, they stay there together — there is no reason for the regular resident to move out.

The same applies to God and the Jewish people. If we follow the Torah then God can place His Sanctuary in our midst; there is nothing demeaning about His "residing" with us, as it were. We will not be forced to vacate, rejected by the King of kings.[7]

Another explanation is that the greater the presence of God is in our lives, the more exacting are His expectations from us. Having His Sanctuary in our midst places greater spiritual demands upon us. The Torah assures us that if we meticulously follow the Torah, His spirit will have no reason to reject us (*Meleches Machsheves*).[8]

וָאֶשְׁבֹּר מֹטֹת עֻלְּכֶם
I broke the staves of your yoke (ibid. 13).

In the Grace After Meals we ask, "May the Merciful God break the *yoke* of suffering that is on our neck and may He lead us proudly to our Land." Here, with regard to the Egyptian Exodus, we speak of God having broken the *staves* of our yoke. Why the discrepancy?

A parable may help clarify the matter. When a farmer finishes plowing for the season, he breaks the staves of the yoke but keeps the yoke itself, for use the following year. If, however, the farmer retires from farming, he no longer has use for the yoke and he might allow himself to break it apart.

When God took us out of Egypt, He broke the staves of the yoke, for they were being redeemed but He did not break the yoke itself, for additional periods of diaspora and subordination awaited the Jewish people.

In Grace After Meals, we ask God to bring the Final Redemption — heralding the "breaking of the yoke," signifying that we will never again bear the yoke of exile (*R' Shlomo Zalman Ulman, Rav of Bistritz*).

וָאוֹלֵךְ אֶתְכֶם קוֹמְמִיּוּת
And I led you erect (ibid.).

The Sages (*Kiddushin* 31a) teach that one is forbidden to walk fully erect, since this posture bespeaks arrogance toward God. Why then does God speak here of having brought the Jews from Egypt standing erect and tall? *R' Moshe of Kobrin* suggests that this verse refers to the Jews' spiritual posture, not their physical bearing. Man is a

---

7. **Body and Soul.** Upon returning from his first trip to the *Maggid of Mezritch*, *R' Shmelke of Nikolsburg* reported: "Before I went to the Rebbe I would flagellate my body so that it could bear my spiritual soul. The Rebbe taught me that the soul is able to bear and suffer the mortal body. God promised that He would place *His Sanctuary*, the soul, *in our midst*, the body, *and His Spirit*, the soul, *would not reject us*, the body."

8. **Time Bomb.** Spiritual gifts have the potential to harm us if we fail to maintain a level of spirituality that justifies their presence. When the Jews sunk to spiritual lows the fact that the Temple stood in their midst served to amplify their guilt. The destruction of the Temple was an act of God's mercy, because its very existence accused the Jews of forfeiting their spiritual potential. Likewise, being the descendant of meritorious ancestors can be a great source of merit if we follow in their footsteps. However, it also causes us to be held to a higher standard (see *Shelah* to 26:44).

two-legged creature and he stands vertically, indicating that his spirit must stand tall, and that he be answerable only to the demands of his soul. Most animals, on the other hand, stand bent over, for animals are subservient to man. The "animal" in man must also yield to his exalted "human" element. Thus God wants us to stand spiritually erect, without our animalistic strains playing a role in our behavior.

Maharal notes that man's upright bearing reflects his having been created "in the image of God." Just as God has absolute control and free will and is subservient to nothing, so man, the corporeal reflection, as it were, of Godliness on this earth, has free will and need submit to nothing but God himself. The upright position is a physical manifestation of this spiritual reality.

Accordingly, when God freed us from Egypt He endowed us with our eternal freedom. He indicated this by having us leave Egypt erect.[9]

Background

The Torah now describes the stages of admonition that the Jews will experience if they stray from the Torah's path. This litany of punishments is called תּוֹכָחָה, which is related to הוֹכָחָה, *proof*, for God's punishments are reproof designed to awaken man to mend his ways.[10]

וְאִם לֹא תִשְׁמְעוּ לִי וְלֹא תַעֲשׂוּ אֵת כָּל הַמִּצְוֹת הָאֵלֶּה
But if you do not listen to Me and will not perform all these commandments (ibid. 14).

Meaning, if you do not toil at Torah and you fail to perform the *mitzvos* (*Rashi*). The only way we can come to the point of not fulfilling the *mitzvos* is if we do not toil in Torah. If one truly experiences the sweetness and beauty of the Torah, he will abandon even the greatest of this world's pleasures for the opportunity to fulfill even a single mitzvah (*Ohr HaChaim*).[11]

The Talmud (*Berachos* 5b) teaches that one who undergoes pain and suffering should examine his deeds for sin. If he fails to discover any misdeeds to which he could ascribe his troubles, then he may assume that they are the result of laxity in Torah study. This statement is difficult to understand: Laxity in Torah study is in itself a misdeed that should have come to light during the person's introspection. If he did not find himself lacking in this area, why should he now assume that he was guilty of this sin?

R' Menachem Mendel of Kotzk explained: If man found no fault in himself, let him assume that his laxity in Torah study rendered him unable to discover his sin. Torah study grants one heightened self-awareness. Had he adequately studied, he would have been able to pinpoint his shortcomings.

9. **Looking Up!** God performed great kindness by creating man in an upright position. Though we live in this lowly world, we can easily lift our eyes Heavenward. Woe to the poor animal that spends its entire life looking down to the ground (*Tzemach Tzedek* of *Lubavitch*).

10. **Missing the Boat.** Some people are most superstitious about the public reading of the Admonition (*Tochachah*). Fearful that they will be cursed, these people often leave the synagogue while the section is read, and certainly refuse to be called up for that *aliyah*. The Torah reader often reads the section quietly, swallowing his words, and many of the congregants are unable to hear. The *Chafetz Chaim* explained the foolishness of this attitude with the following story:

A person was warned to refrain from traveling on a certain road which was overgrown by thorns and full of potholes. Wild animals and thieves abounded. Stubbornly, this person decided to use the road anyway. To avoid the road's many dangers, he put on a blindfold. He was convinced that if he would not see the potholes or the animals, they would cease to pose a threat to him. The fool failed to realize that by closing his eyes he only increased his danger.

The Admonition is meant to warn us of the dangers inherent in veering from the path of the Torah. If we heed its frightening message, we might be able to avoid some of life's many pitfalls. If we foolishly close our eyes and ears, however, we merely increase the risk of falling prey to the dangers of life.

11. **All That Glitters Is Not Gold.** *R' Nachman of Breslov* interprets the words *Anyone who derives enjoyment from the words of Torah removes his life from the world* (*Avos* 4:7) with this insight: No worldly pleasure can equal the ecstasy of plumbing the depths of the Talmud. One who has truly experienced the joy and the ecstasy of Torah study can no longer find real enjoyment in worldly pleasures.

Failing to labor in Torah is the cause of one falling short in fulfilling his other duties to God.

וְנַסְתֶּם וְאֵין רֹדֵף אֶתְכֶם
you will flee with no one pursuing you (ibid. 17).

On an elementary level, the Torah is foretelling the terror inspired by imaginary demons, a fear that instills a need to escape, although in reality no one is chasing you.

The *Vilna Gaon* adds another perspective. King Solomon teaches that God always seeks the benefit of the pursued (*Ecclesiastes* 3:15). According to the Midrash (*Vayikra Rabbah* 27:7) this is true even when the pursuer is righteous and the pursued is wicked. Since the person being pursued is in desperate need, the All Merciful takes his side, regardless of whether he is deserving.[12]

Were we to be fleeing a real pursuer, explains the Gaon, we could console ourselves with the knowledge that God would stand at our side, no matter what. The depth of this curse is that as a result of abandoning Torah, we lose even the protection God accords for the undeserving underdog.

וְאִם תֵּלְכוּ עִמִּי קֶרִי
If you behave casually with Me (ibid. 21).

God wants more than perfunctory performance of *mitzvos*. He wants the entire person — mind, body and emotions — to be involved in the mitzvah. Though we must perform *mitzvos* with joy, to do them out of personal preference rather than Divine duty is an exhibition of casual behavior toward God.[13] Furthermore, according to *Avnei Nezer*, one who does not prepare himself to do a mitzvah is guilty of casualness toward God. That such terrible calamities are foretold because one failed to prepare for a mitzvah underscores how critical proper preparation is.[14]

וַהֲלַכְתֶּם עִמִּי קֶרִי. וְהָלַכְתִּי אַף אֲנִי עִמָּכֶם בְּקֶרִי
and you behave casually with Me, then I too will behave toward you with casualness (ibid. 23-24).

King David describes God as צִלְּךָ — a protective shade (*Psalms* 121:5). The word צֵל can also be understood as a shadow. Just as the movements of a person's shadow are but a recasting of the

---

12. **Underdog Favorite.** Even when one must take a stand against the wicked, he should be careful not to turn them into pursued victims.

The *Brisker Rav* once convened a meeting of the community leaders to discuss how to react to a renegade who publicly rebelled against the community standards of *kashrus*. The renegade heard about the meeting, and he knew that people would be uncomfortable discussing the matter in his presence. In an effort to prevent the issue from being raised, he appeared at the Rav's home.

In the middle of the meeting, the Brisker Rav excused himself and left the room. Several of those present took the opportunity to step out with him and they asked the Rav to demand that the renegade leave, so that the *kashrus* issue could be discussed. The Rav adamantly refused. When pressed for an explanation, he replied: "If I turn him out of my home, I will have made him into a pursued party. Then we will stand no chance of succeeding against him, since *HaKadosh Baruch Hu* will be on his side."

13. **Melodious Yoke.** King David was punished for referring to Torah as music when he said, *Your statutes were songs to me* (*Psalms* 119:54). Though he meant this as an expression of the joy and pleasure he derived from Torah, he was punished for emphasizing this aspect of Torah, which is a yoke that must be borne (*R' Yitzchak Hutner*).

Maharal understands the need for this pressure as the reason why God still had to compel the Jews to accept the Torah by suspending Mount Sinai over their heads (see *Shabbos* 88a). Despite the fact that the Jews had willingly accepted the Torah, declaring "we will do and hear," there was a need for them to recognize that they also had no option. Although they wanted to accept Torah, at the time they needed to recognize that in reality they could not exist without Torah, and were not free to choose whether to continue to accept its mandates. Torah is not a luxury or convenience — it is an absolute necessity for life.

14. **Full Attention.** *Shulchan Aruch* (*Orach Chaim* 191:3) writes that one may not do anything else while reciting Grace After Meals. *Magen Avraham* and *Taz* (ad loc.) comment that this is equally true with regard to any prayer or blessing. One may not be involved in anything else while saying any prayer or blessing. Such behavior would be considered "acting casually with God." Performing a mitzvah must fully preoccupy a person, to the extent that he is involved in nothing else, even another spiritual matter.

person's own actions, God acts toward us exactly as we do toward Him.

A primary cause for sin is casualness — the perception that things "just happen," that God is not the one controlling everything that happens.[15] In the words of *Ramban* (*Exodus* 13:16), the belief in this control is the basis for belief in the entire Torah: "A man has no share in the Torah of Moshe Rabbeinu unless he believes that all things and all events that occur in the life of the individual as well as in society are miracles — a direct result of Divine Providence. There is no such a thing as happenstance or a 'natural' course of events."

If we believe that things "just happen," God responds by withdrawing Himself, as it were, from our lives. He will conceal Himself, and we will have nowhere to turn in time of need (*R' Tzadok HaKohen of Lublin*).

וְהֵבֵאתִי עֲלֵיכֶם חֶרֶב נֹקֶמֶת נְקַם בְּרִית
I will bring upon you a sword, avenging the vengeance of the covenant (ibid. 25).

Why does the Torah focus on the sword's avenging the covenant, rather than the sins committed?

The *Netziv* explains with a parable: When a king conquers a foreign land after a protracted war, he does not punish those who fought against him. It is understandable that these fighters did not want to be subjugated by an alien power. However, if his own subjects rebel against him, he will certainly punish each and every rebel for his disloyalty.

At Sinai the Jewish people and God entered into a sacred covenant. It is through that covenant that we are His subjects — thus it is the covenant that elicits Divine vengeance.

אָז תִּרְצֶה הָאָרֶץ אֶת שַׁבְּתֹתֶיהָ
Then the land will be appeased for its sabbaticals (ibid. 34).

Since Jews did not observe *Shemittah*, which would have allowed the land to "rest," while they dwelled there, the land will be given an opportunity to rest when the Jews are sent into exile.

Chashavah L'Tovah and *Techeiles Mordechai* explain that the fundamental principle of *Shemittah* is that the land is ultimately God's, not ours. If we do not understand this on our own, we are forced into exile, and it becomes clear that the land is not ours.

וְאָבַדְתֶּם בַּגּוֹיִם
You will become lost among the nations (ibid. 38).

The Talmud (*Makkos* 24a) likens the Jewish people to a lost item which is being sought out by its owner, and which will eventually be found. Though we, as a nation, will be lost, our Owner continues to seek us out and will ultimately retrieve us.

Mikdash Mordechai further develops the metaphor. An object that was lost must be returned to its owner only if it has a *siman*, an identifying feature through which the one who lost it can prove ownership. If we are to be reclaimed, we must retain the distinct features which clearly mark us as God's people. By maintaining a Torah-true lifestyle we bear the characteristics in whose merit we will be reunited with our Owner.[16]

---

15. **Everything.** A *chassid* came to pour out his woes to *R' Moshe of Kobrin*. He had a sickly wife, he was unable to provide dowries for his daughters and he had difficulties earning a living.

As the man recounted his pitiful tale, R' Moshe recited the blessing שֶׁהַכֹּל נִהְיָה בִּדְבָרוֹ, *Blessed are You, Hashem, our God, King of the universe, through Whose word everything came to be,* and took a drink. When this elicited no response from the *chassid,* R' Moshe commented, "You come nowhere near the spiritual level of your father. He once came to me to share his woes, and when I recited the very same blessing, he stood up to leave. I asked him where he was going and he replied, 'Rebbe, when a Jew clearly hears that "through His word everything comes to be," he realizes that he has no problems.' "

16. **Lost Sheep.** King David captures the sentiment: *I have strayed like a lost sheep — seek Your servant, for I have not forgotten Your commandments* (Psalms 119:176).

R' Nachman of Breslov explained: As long as a sheep has not strayed too far, it can be brought back by the shepherd calling to it. The sheep will follow the sound of the shepherd's voice until it comes home.

Man calls out to God, "I have strayed like a lost sheep. However, I have not forgotten Your commandments;

וְהִתְוַדּוּ אֶת עֲוֹנָם וְאֶת עֲוֹן
אֲבֹתָם בְּמַעֲלָם אֲשֶׁר מָעֲלוּ בִי

*Then they will confess their sin and
the sin of their forefathers for the treachery
with which they betrayed Me (ibid. 40).*

In the next verse, the Torah describes God's reaction to this confession as continuing to treat the Jews casually. The commentators find it remarkable that the repentance described here seems to be so clearly ignored.

Kli Yakar notes that בְּמַעֲלָם אֲשֶׁר מָעֲלוּ בִי can be understood as *with* their treachery. While the afflicted Jews will confess, in their hearts they will retain their treacherousness toward God and His commandments. One who confesses even as he fails to truly abandon his sinful past is compared by the Sages to one who immerses in a *mikveh* while holding an impure rodent.[17] Alternatively, he suggests that this confession is flawed in that it is "וְאֶת עֲוֹן אֲבוֹתָם," *the sin of their forefathers,"* — they seek to blame their parents for their misdeeds, refusing to assume personal responsibility for their actions.

HaD'rash V'Halyun sees the emphasis in the verse on the word בִי, *[betrayed] Me.* Although they are prepared to admit having betrayed God, they cannot bring themselves to confess their interpersonal sins and to ask forgiveness. As long as we are careless in our relationships with others, God will continue to act casually toward us.[18]

וְזָכַרְתִּי אֶת בְּרִיתִי יַעֲקוֹב . . .
*And I will remember My covenant
with Jacob . . . (ibid. 42).*

Even if we do not merit redemption by virtue of our merits, God assures us that we will be redeemed because of the covenant God made with our forefathers Abraham, Isaac and Jacob.

The chronological order of the Patriarchs is reversed to teach us that the merit of Jacob alone should be sufficient to bring about the Final Redemption. If this proves to be insufficient, then the merit of Isaac will stand us in good stead. If this is not enough, then the merit of Abraham will cause the redemption (*Rashi*). The implication is that Abraham's merit is greater than that of Isaac or Jacob. Why?

Jacob and Isaac had positive role models to emulate in following the Godly path. Not so Abraham; he was born and raised in the home of Terah, an avowed idolater. For him to recognize the truth of God's presence and then cut his ties with his family and culture was a move of unmatched courage. That is why his merit is our "insurance policy" in exile (*Ksav Sofer*).

The *Dubno Maggid* suggests that the verse begins with Jacob because, had it begun with Abraham, his son Ishmael might expect to capitalize on his father's merits. Similarly, Esau might want to lay claim to the merits of Isaac. Therefore, the verse begins with Jacob, all of whose children are part of the Jewish nation.

Shelah views this verse as a continuation of the verses of Admonition. A child who grew up in an aristocratic home is more to blame if he chose a life of crime than the child of a criminal is.

The verse tells us that God will remember who our ancestors were. Coming from such forefathers, how could we have possibly sunk to the levels we did?

I am still within earshot of Your voice. Therefore, seek Your servant — call out to me so that I may hear Your voice and return to You."

17. **Hollow Confession.** On Yom Kippur, one of the sins which we confess to having committed is וִדּוּי שְׂפָתַיִם, perfunctorily making confessions with no true commitment to improve.

18. **No Credit.** A poor man would often come to his wealthy neighbor for loans and other financial assistance. His requests were always met cordially and generously.

One day the poor man became agitated and spanked the wealthy man's son. The next time the poor man came for help, his former benefactor ignored him.

When we mistreat one of God's children we imperil our relationship with Him. Until we are ready to make amends, He will ignore us (*Simchas Aharon*).

Background

The Torah now discusses voluntary contributions to the Temple and the laws related to the redeeming of consecrated property.

אִישׁ כִּי יַפְלִא נֶדֶר בְּעֶרְכְּךָ נְפָשֹׁת לַה׳

If a man articulates a vow to Hashem regarding a valuation of living beings (27:2).

Why does the chapter regarding valuations follow the Admonition?

After hearing the dire consequences that await those who abandon God, one might become depressed, and feel that he is sure to be a worthless failure. The Torah therefore teaches that *every* person is valuable to Hashem (*Chozeh of Lublin*).

Otzar Chaim suggests that the Torah is alluding to the undying loyalty of the Jewish people. Although Jews have borne the curses and horrors foretold in the Admonition, they remain irrevocably bound to God. This loyalty makes the Jewish people especially valuable in the eyes of God.

וְאִם מִשְׂדֵה אֲחֻזָּתוֹ יַקְדִּישׁ אִישׁ לַה׳ וְהָיָה עֶרְכְּךָ לְפִי זַרְעוֹ

If a man consecrates a field from his ancestral heritage to Hashem, the valuation shall be according to its seeding (ibid. 16).

Many believe that they have dedicated their lives and resources to God. How is one to know if this is truly the case? Homiletically we can find the answer in this verse, "The valuation shall be according to זַרְעוֹ, *its seeding.*" זַרְעוֹ can also be rendered *"his children."* If you want to measure a person, see what values he seeks to imbue in his children. Does he inculcate them with faith and exemplify to them that our goal in life is to perform God's will? Or does he train them to believe that true success is measured by financial achievement?[19]

The litmus test of one's commitment to Hashem and His Torah is the type of education he gives his children.

---

19. **The Lost Child.** The *Yid HaKadosh of P'shis'cha* once taught this lesson to his followers at *seudah shlishis* (the third meal of the Sabbath): "Tomorrow you will be going back to work. If someone would ask you why you work so hard, you would explain that you work not for yourself, but for your children, because you want them to grow up to be God-fearing Jews dedicated to His service and the study of His Torah. Years from now, your children will also work hard. When they will be asked why, they will also explain that they are doing it for *their* children. This cycle continues from generation to generation. It will be amazing to see the 'child' that is the result of all these generations of work." We do work for our children. Unfortunately, however, they follow our lead, choosing to work for *their* children instead of taking advantage of the opportunity afforded to them.

סֵפֶר

בְּמִדְבַּר

BAMIDBAR/NUMBERS

פרשת במדבר ‎
Parashas Bamidbar

Background

The Book of *Bamidbar* (*Numbers*) focuses on the years of Israel's sojourn in the Wilderness. The *parashah* begins with God's commanding Moses and Aaron to conduct a census and count the males above the age of 20, tribe by tribe.

וַיְדַבֵּר ה' אֶל מֹשֶׁה בְּמִדְבַּר סִינַי
Hashem spoke to Moses in the Wilderness of Sinai (1:1).

Many commentators explain the connection between the end of *Leviticus* and the beginning of *Numbers*.

According to *R' S.R. Hirsch,* this verse is related to *Rashi's* comment that God's counting of the Jewish people is an expression of His love. The previous *parashah* (*Leviticus* 27:32), teaches that all one's newborn flock must be placed into a canal, and pass one by one under a staff. Every tenth one is consecrated. Our *parashah* begins with the counting of God's flock, the nation of Israel. Every Jew passes under the staff of God and is consecrated to Him.

R' Yitzchak Karo of Castille suggests that the link between the *parshiyos* is found in the law that forbids one to switch and exchange consecrated animals (*Leviticus* 27:33). This law reveals the intensity of God's love for us. Just as God is One and is irreplaceable, so too the Jewish people will never be exchanged by God for another nation.

Our relationship is reciprocal. As King Solomon puts it in *Song of Songs* (2:16), *my Beloved is mine and I am His.* God tells His people, "Do not exchange Me and I will not exchange you." God therefore counts us constantly.

Regarding this verse, the Midrash comments that the Torah was given to the Jewish people with fire, with water and in the Wilderness.

R' Meir Shapiro explains. Jews have always exhibited self-sacrifice on behalf of God. They were always willing to die to sanctify His Holy Name. This spirit of self-sacrifice was expressed intensely three times in the nation's history. Abraham, our founding father, was thrown into a fiery furnace, because of his belief in God. He transmitted this ability to all his descendants.[1] The Jewish people

---

1. **Chosen for Tenacity.** The Jewish people have remained loyal to God, under the most trying circumstances. *Ramban* (*Deuteronomy* 7:6) writes: "One who seeks a beloved searches for one who can bear whatever difficulties are placed in one's path. The Jewish people are the most suitable for this role. Our Sages taught (*Beitzah* 25b), the Jews are the most obstinate among the nations. They can withstand all tests, even to the point of martyrdom."

Whenever a Jew is steadfast in his convictions and overcomes difficulty in his fulfillment of God's will, he strengthens his spiritual bond and enhances his chosenness.

jumped into the waters of the Reed Sea, completely trusting in God. They also followed Him into the desert, completely oblivious to the dangers of snakes and scorpions, without any guarantee of food and water.

The verse in Jeremiah (2:2) describes how they displayed the passion of their youth and the love of their marriage by following Him into the desert.

It is the "fire" of Abraham's furnace, the raging "waters" of the Reed Sea and the "desert" through which we traveled that made us deserving of God's Torah.[2]

Why did God give us the Torah in the desert? The Talmud (*Nedarim* 55a) teaches that one can only merit to understand Torah if one views oneself as a desert. According to *R' Aharon Kotler* this means one must be ready to share his Torah with all Jews. Just as the desert belongs to no one, so those who learn Torah must realize the Torah is not their own personal possession; it is the heritage of all Jews.

Ohel Torah views the desert as a metaphor for humility. One must realize that in spite of any Torah that he learned, he is a desert, devoid of real spiritual yield.[3] In addition, just as one travels the desert alone, without help from others, one must be willing to toil at Torah oneself.

Yismach Yisrael adds another dimension based on the words of the *Ran* (*Nedarim* 30a). Halachically, the woman's role in the process of matrimony is passive. Once she agrees she waits to be acquired by her husband.

The same process occurs in the acquisition of the Torah. Like a desert, man must yield his own will to the Torah. Then the Torah acquires him and is able to penetrate his soul.

שְׂאוּ אֶת רֹאשׁ כָּל עֲדַת בְּנֵי יִשְׂרָאֵל
Take a census of the entire assembly of the Children of Israel (ibid. 2).

According to *Rashi*, the Jews were counted here to indicate that God loves them. Just as one constantly counts those things that are precious to

---

2. **Through Fire and Water.** *Shem MiShmuel* suggests a symbolism for fire, water and desert. One must pursue Torah and *mitzvos* with an intense, passionate, emotional fire. The small spark in every heart becomes a flame which bursts into a great fire of love for God. On the other hand, one must be as calm and level headed as water when assessing one's actions.

Finally, one must be ready to reject the pursuit of worldly pleasures which stunt spiritual growth. Like the desert which is a place stripped of most vegetation, one must keep one's physical needs to a minimum.

Alternatively, water alludes to the teaching of Torah. Just as water flows from high places to low ones, Torah can be only acquired by the humble.

Torah is also compared to fire. Positively, fire provides light, allowing one to avoid pitfalls placed before him. Torah also lights up for one the road of life allowing one to avoid the dangers lurking everywhere. Negatively, fire is extremely dangerous. If not handled with caution, one may become badly burned. So too, one who tampers with Torah may become badly burned.

Torah was given in the desert where Jews survived on the manna provided by God. Those who desire to grow in Torah must be willing to exist on the provisions provided by God (*Ksav Sofer*).

3. **Expanding Borders.** Torah is compared to water which flows from high places to low ones. Similarly, the Torah can flow to even the most lowly person. Torah is also not limited to any particular location. As it was given in the desert, it can find a home in the most spiritually inhospitable locations.

When *R' Aharon Kotler* arrived in New York after escaping the European holocaust, he announced his intention to open a *kollel* in America. A prominent layman turned to *Irving Bunim* and said, "The Nazis made him crazy. Hair will grow on my palms before there will be a *kollel* in America." R' Aharon understood that Torah is the lifeblood of the Jewish people and will always find a way to infiltrate even the most unwelcome places. This insight provided him with the fortitude to establish the Lakewood Yeshivah.

R' Shraga Feivel Mendelowitz charged *Dr. Joseph Kamenetsky* with the task of establishing the American day school system. He enthusiastically carried that charge and lit up hundreds of points of light all across America, warming tens of thousands of *neshamos*.

him, God constantly counts His people.[4], [5] *Shelah* elaborates: Counting shows that each individual is important. Our Sages taught (*Kiddushin* 40b) that one should view himself and the entire world as hanging in balance, half meritorious and half condemned. One good deed of one individual can move the scales toward the meritorious side and save the entire world. Counting tells one he really "counts."

Chidushei HaRim explains the importance of counting. When a forbidden substance becomes mixed with a permitted one, we may sometimes invoke the principle of nullification. The forbidden substance becomes nullified because it is insignificant. If the forbidden substance is something which is generally counted, it can never be nullified. The very fact that it is counted makes the item so significant that it can never be nullified. [If an egg of a nonkosher fowl becomes mixed with many kosher eggs, the principle of nullification may not be invoked because eggs are sold by number. See *Shulchan Aruch Yoreh Deah* 110:1.]

The Jewish people are a miniscule minority among the nations of the world.[6] In order for them to forever retain their significance, God continuously counts them. As a counted item, they cannot ever be nullified or deemed insignificant.

בְּמִסְפַּר שֵׁמוֹת
by the numbers of the names (ibid).

Every person passed before Moses and Aaron and gave his name. In this way, he connected with the entire nation as was granted merit and life (*Ramban*).[7]

Chida explains the significance of being counted

---

4. **Affectionate Beginnings.** *R' Yehudah Cooperman* notes an interesting pattern in *Rashi.* The first *Rashi* in each of the Five Books points to an object of God's affection. *Genesis* opens with the story of Creation, which *Rashi* explains shows God's affection for the Land of Israel. *Exodus* begins with the names of the tribes. *Rashi*, citing *Midrash Tanchuma,* explains that God did this to show His love for His people. In the beginning of *Leviticus* Moses is summoned by God and is taught a new command. *Rashi* notes that all commands are preceded by a summons, indicative of God's affection for the Torah. This Book, *Numbers,* speaks of a census, a process which again displays God's love for His nation.

Even *Deuteronomy,* which opens with Moses' rebuke to the nation, carries His message of love for them. He does not mention their sins explicitly, he alludes cryptically to where they occurred. This is done to protect their honor (*Rashi, Deuteronomy* 1:1).

Thus *Rashi* begins *Genesis* with God's love of the Land of Israel, *Exodus* with His love for the People of Israel and *Leviticus* with His love of the Torah of Israel. *Numbers* reiterates God's affection for His nation and *Deuteronomy* begins with an emphasis on the Jewish people's honor.

5. **Constant Count.** The Talmud (*Bava Metzia* 21a) teaches us that people consistently check their pockets, indicative of the fact that people are always preoccupied with money.

Similarly, God constantly thinks of His people and counts us continuously (*R' Moshe Schneider*).

One also checks his pockets for fear of losing the money inside. God, also, does not want to lose His people and therefore constantly counts them (*Zekan Aharon*).

6. **Without a Doubt.** A non-Jewish intellectual once asked *R' Yonasan Eibeschutz:* "Your Torah teaches that one must follow the majority opinion. Why don't you follow our faith and religion since we non-Jews are the majority?"

R' Yonason replied: "The majority rule is only applicable when doubt exists. We, however, have absolutely no doubts with regard to the truth of our faith. No majority can override our unshakable belief." [See *Kovetz Maamarim* of *R' Elchanan Wasserman* pp. 15-16 for another fascinating approach to this question.]

7. **Keep Your Side.** This is a source for the chassidic custom of coming to the Rebbe with a petitional note on which one writes his name.

R' Yochanan of Rachmistrivke suggests a reason for the custom. A Rebbe and his *chassidim* enjoy a relationship much like that of Issachar and Zebulun (see *Deuteronomy* 33:18). One partner puts his full energies into learning Torah; the other one engages in business. The businessman is successful, because he supports the Torah scholar. If his fortunes take a downward turn, he may rightly suspect the scholar is not living up to his part of the bargain. Perhaps he is not putting in enough time or effort. The same can be said for a *chassid* who finds himself experiencing difficulties. Rather than confront the Rebbe directly, the *chassid* informs him of his troubles by means of the petitional note. Hopefully, the Rebbe will get the hint that he should strengthen his end of the partnership.

by name. People usually avoid mentioning the name of their enemy. If they must, they do so in a roundabout manner. [King Saul hated David and could not bring himself to call him by his name. He always referred to him as "the son of Yishai" (*I Samuel* Ch. 20).] When someone is loved, the mere mention of the name brings joy. God receives pleasure from the mere mention of His childrens' names.

מִבֶּן עֶשְׂרִים שָׁנָה וָמַעְלָה כָּל יֹצֵא צָבָא בְּיִשְׂרָאֵל
From twenty years of age and up — everyone who goes out to the legion in Israel (ibid. 3).

The minimum age at which one could serve in the Jewish army was 20 (*Rashi*). Why were Jews counted from this age?

Imrei Emes suggests a homiletic approach.

The mission of a Jew is to conquer the forces of evil in the world. To assure free choice the evil inclination must be granted a degree of autonomy. Every Jew in God's army must battle evil.

A soldier fights hardest when stakes are high. When the enemy ferociously attacks, one must counterattack with all his might for it is his very life that is on the line. At age 20, a Jew becomes subject to punishment administered by the Heavenly Court. The stakes in this great battle of life increase dramatically. At that age, every Jew is called upon to battle evil. As the Sages put it, "If one comes to kill you, arise and kill him first!" (*Sanhedrin* 72a).[8]

וְאִתְּכֶם יִהְיוּ אִישׁ אִישׁ לַמַּטֶּה אִישׁ רֹאשׁ לְבֵית אֲבֹתָיו הוּא
And with you shall be one man from each tribe; a man who is a leader of his father's household (ibid. 4).

The head of each tribe joined Moses and Aaron in his tribe's counting (*Rashi*). The Torah describes the head of the tribe *as the leader* (lit. *head*) of *his father's household. Meleches Machsheves* relates a story. A simple, coarse individual with a very distinguished pedigree once argued with a Torah scholar who came from a more modest background. The boor rebuked the scholar, "How dare you argue with me? I come from a respected, aristocratic family." The scholar replied, "True. But I am the beginning of a distinguished line; you are its end." A Jewish leader must consider himself the founding father of a royal lineage. He must be the *head* of his father's household.[9]

The Torah also teaches us a Jewish leader must be authentic. He must be privately what he is publicly. The Talmud states that the arrogant are even despised by members of their own family (*Bava Basra* 98a). The Torah therefore states that the heads of the tribes were the heads of their fathers' households, accepted and admired by their own families (*Meleches Machsheves*).[10]

According to *Luach Erez*, the verse highlights a

---

8. **Chase of Life.** The *Mishnah* (*Avos* 5:25) teaches that 20 is the age of pursuit. At this age the Heavenly Court pursues man for his actions, holding him responsible for his sins. The evil inclination chases man with may enticements and tries to get him to sin. Man must exude much more effort not to relent.

9. **Replanting the Tree.** When *R' Dov Ber*, the *Maggid of Mezritch*, was a child a fire broke out in his mother's home. The house and all its contents were reduced to ash and rubble. Dov Ber saw his mother crying uncontrollably. "Mother," he asked, "why do you cry? I promise to rebuild the house." "No, my son," she replied, "I am not crying over the house. God is kind and will provide us with another one." "Then why do you cry?" countered young Dov Ber. The mother told him, "A family tree, tracing our ancestral roots back to King David, was completely destroyed. It was irreplaceable." Dov Ber approached his mother and said, "Don't cry, Mother. I will replace the family tree. I will begin a new illustrious line."

This idea of pedigree is alluded to in the words of the Talmud (*Sanhedrin* 21a), "although one inherited a Torah scroll from his ancestors he is commanded to write one [or have one written] on his own." Even if one inherited a great spiritual heritage from his ancestors he must nevertheless add to it. Rather than be the end of the line, he should pass his own heritage on to the generations that follow him.

10. **Only She Knows for Sure.** When Rabban Gamliel was removed as *Nasi*, the position was offered to R' Elazar ben Azariah (see *Berachos* 27b). Before accepting, he asked his wife's permission. Only one's wife and family members can realistically discern one's spiritual standing. The Torah tells us to appoint only those who also display leadership qualities at home (*Yaaros Devash*).

key aspect of Jewish leadership. The verse speaks of אִישׁ אִישׁ, literally *a man a man*, from each tribe. The Torah instructs us to pick one man who is like two. Leaders must be committed family men. Public service should never cause them to ignore their wives and children. On the other hand, he must show sensitivity and concern to all Jews. By blending these two roles, one can become two.[11]

לְיִשָּׂשכָר נְתַנְאֵל בֶּן צוּעָר. לִזְבוּלֻן אֱלִיאָב בֶּן חֵלֹן
For Issachar, Nethanel son of Zuar. For Zebulun, Eliab son of Helon (ibid. 8-9).

Both Jacob (*Genesis* 49:13-14) and Moses (*Deuteronomy* 33:18) blessed Zebulun before Issachar. Why here is Issachar first?

Issachar and Zebulun were partners. Zebulun was a successful merchant. He supported Issachar in his full-time pursuit of Torah study. Recognizing this sacrifice, both Jacob and Moses blessed him first. Here, the Torah lists the tribes according to their importance. One who learns Torah is greater than one who supports it (*Skulener Rebbe*).

אֵלֶּה קְרוּאֵי הָעֵדָה
These were the ones summoned by the assembly (ibid. 16).

Earlier (verse 4), the Torah describes the heads of the tribes joining Moses and Aaron in the counting process. Here the Torah refers to them as those *summoned by the assembly*.

Although Moses could have personally ap-pointed the tribal heads, he refrained from doing so. He did not want to surround himself with "yes-men." Moses granted the people the power to appoint their own leaders. Therefore, the tribal heads were summoned by the assembly — not Moses (*R' Yonason Eibeschutz*).

וַיִּתְיַלְדוּ עַל מִשְׁפְּחֹתָם לְבֵית אֲבֹתָם
And they established their genealogy according to their families (ibid. 18).

Why did the Jews have to establish their genea-logical lineage in preparation for war? *R' S.R. Hirsch* explains: Courage, strength and tactical ability are important military traits. To Jews, however, they are superfluous. The most impor-tant characteristics are mercy and a revulsion to spilling blood. These are a result of genetics and the environment in which one is reared.[12]

Sfas Emes understands this verse differently. Although the Jewish people had become a great nation, the children still maintained strong family ties. They saw themselves as links in an illustrious chain, and tried to emulate their ancestors. They *es-tablished their genealogy according to their families.* By following in the footsteps of one's ancestors, one creates himself in their image.[13]

וְהַלְוִיִּם לְמַטֵּה אֲבֹתָם לֹא הָתְפָּקְדוּ בְּתוֹכָם
The Levites according to their fathers' tribe were not counted among them (ibid. 47).

According to *Rashi*, the Levites were counted separately because God knew that all those

---

11. **Lowly Link.** *Tiferes Shlomo* adds a homiletic explanation. He reads the word לַמַּטֶּה as לְמַטָּה, *below*. Even leaders who have reached great spiritual heights must elevate אִישׁ אִישׁ, every type of person. They must influence even those that have fallen spiritually and are לְמַטָּה, *below*. Although presently they are spiritually diminutive, they come from the same ancestors (the Patriarchs and Matriarchs) as all Jews do.

12. **Refined Brute.** The Talmud describes the agents of *beis din* entrusted with the task of administering lashes (*Makkos* 23a). They possessed limited physical strength but excessive intelligence. Brute strength must never be allowed to outweigh intelligence and refined character.

13. **A Touch of Greatness.** "A person must always say, 'When will my deeds reach (יַגִּיעוּ) those of my forefathers Abraham, Isaac and Jacob?' " (*Tanna D'vei Eliyahu* 25).

This view appears unrealistic and arrogant. Which Jew truly believes he could ever reach the spiritual heights of his forefathers?

R' Simchah Bunam of P'shis'cha explains: The word יַגִּיעַ (literally *reach*) is related to נְגִיעָה, touch. We certainly are not expected to reach their spiritual level. However, by utilizing all our spiritual resources to the maximum, we can at least try to touch it. By doing so, we can merit being a link in their holy chain.

counted in the general census would die in the Wilderness because of the incident of the spies (see *Numbers* 14:35). As a reward for their loyalty during the sin of the Golden Calf, the Levites were excluded from that decree. He therefore had them counted separately from the rest of the Jewish people.

Had the Levites been counted along with the rest of the nation, they would likewise have suffered their fate. (See *Bamidbar Rabbah* 1:11 and 3:7.)

This may help us understand a little better God's mysterious ways. Many wonder how great and righteous people could have been murdered so brutally during the Holocaust. The Torah teaches us that at times, innocent victims are included in a general decree. Once God unleashes the forces of destruction, they do not differentiate between the guilty and the innocent. [God, for His reasons, may sometimes save certain individuals.]

Therefore Moses was commanded to keep the census of the Levites separate.

This is also true regarding a positive and beneficial decree. When one becomes part of a community, one may be included in its communal blessings even though one may be personally undeserving. One who separates from a community separates oneself from its collective blessing (*R' Chaim Shmulevitz*).[14]

וְהַלְוִיִּם יַחֲנוּ . . . וְשָׁמְרוּ הַלְוִיִּם
אֵת מִשְׁמֶרֶת מִשְׁכַּן הָעֵדוּת
The Levites shall encamp . . . and the Levites shall safeguard the watch of the Tabernacle of the Testimony (ibid. 53).

This encampment was not for protection but for honor. A royal palace surrounded by an honor guard is more prestigious than one left unguarded.[15]

R' Yitzchak Hutner suggests this is why the Talmud tells us a rabbinical enactment issued to protect a Biblical law is more precious than the law itself (*Avodah Zarah* 35a). The purpose of a protective fence "erected around the Torah" is not only to ensure that the law not be violated. It also serves as an honor guard.

Background

The *parashah* describes how the nation camped in the Wilderness. They witnessed the angels that accompanied God at Sinai grouped under different banners. They requested that God provide each tribe with a banner representative of, its own unique essence. Their wish was granted.

אִישׁ עַל דִּגְלוֹ
each man by his banner (2:2).

Every person is born to fill a special role in

---

14. **Communal Preservation.** During the Holocaust, the Mirrer Yeshivah was, collectively, miraculously saved. They first escaped to Vilna, then Russia, Japan and finally Shanghai, China. After spending five extremely productive years there, they, as a group, finally left. Some settled in Israel; others in the United States.

When *R' Chaim Shmulevitz* would speak of the power of a community to save those who make themselves part of it, he would tearfully mention a close friend, one of the best students in the yeshivah. "He was one of the greatest. He left the yeshivah to go say goodbye to his parents and never returned. He was killed with all the other holy martyrs. He was truly extraordinary, but he severed his connection to the community."

Sometimes a community is the life preserver one may require.

15. **Soothing Noise.** The students in the Volozhin Yeshivah would always study in shifts. This way, Torah was being studied twenty-four hours a day. This custom was established by the founding *Rosh Yeshivah*, the famed *R' Chaim of Volozhin*. He perceived the yeshivah as the palace of the King. Just as the Tabernacle needed a constant honor guard, so too the honor of the yeshivah demanded one.

The *Netziv*, who served as *Rosh Yeshivah* in a later time, lived in the yeshivah building. Once he was asked how he was able to sleep with the loud sound of Torah emanating all day and night next to his lodgings.

The *Netziv* replied: "Milling flour is extremely noisy. The grinding stones are unbelievably loud. As long as the miller hears the noise he is calm and relaxed. His *parnassah* is assured. If, however, the stones break and the noise stops, the miller is immediately worried and upset.

"I am the same," he concluded. "As long as I hear my students learning, I am at peace. If the sound of Torah were to stop, I would immediately become agitated."

God's master plan. He is an irreplaceable piece in the Divine mosaic. A person exactly like him never existed before and will never exist again. He has his own mission at this special time, that can only be fulfilled by him. Every man must encamp under his own banner (R' Aharon of Karlin).[16]

כַּאֲשֶׁר יַחֲנוּ כֵּן יִסָּעוּ
as they encamp so shall they journey (ibid. 17).

This verse can be interpreted homiletically. First, it teaches that proper rest and relaxation aids in the service of God. One who is rested will achieve much more than one who is not: One must first "encamp" in order to "journey" (*Otzar Chaim*).[17]

Yetev Lev explains this verse differently. One may not be lax with his religious observance when on the road or on vacation. The Torah tells *as they encamp* [while at home], *so shall they journey*. Halachah must be followed everywhere. The verse also alludes to the words of our *Maariv* prayer וְהָסֵר שָׂטָן מִלְּפָנֵינוּ וּמֵאַחֲרֵינוּ, *remove Satan from before us and from behind us.* Sometimes the evil inclination stands before man to prevent him from doing a mitzvah. At other times, he stands behind him, pushing him forward without regard to fatigue and health. He then becomes too weak to continue. For example, Satan may convinces one to learn until late at night. This is really detrimental because one can then learn the following day with only limited concentration. The Torah reminds us that as we encamp [rest], we shall travel.

Beis Avraham of Slonim says the verse describes the reciprocal relationship between the Sabbath and the weekdays. As you encamp and rest on the Sabbath, so shall you journey through your weekday activities.

Some people are so totally caught up with their pursuit of a livelihood that they ignore their spiritual lives the entire week. When Shabbos arrives they are totally exhausted. They rest and recharge themselves physically so that they will be able to again slave the following week. He who uses his weekdays exclusively for the mundane turns the Sabbath into the mundane.

Others invest their energy into spiritual growth. When the Sabbath arrives with its heightened spiritual sensitivity, referred to as "the extra soul" (*Beitzah* 16a), they begin to feel that perhaps their soul may have been shortchanged during the past week. They increase their spiritual efforts to compensate. This spirit carries over into the week that follows — as one encamps, one travels.

וְנָסַע אֹהֶל מוֹעֵד מַחֲנֵה הַלְוִיִּם בְּתוֹךְ הַמַּחֲנֹת
The Tent of Meeting, the camp of the Levites, shall journey in the middle of the camps (ibid. 17).

As the Tent of Meeting (which contained the Ark) was at the epicenter of the camp, so too Torah must be central to a Jew's life.

Just as the tree of life was in the center of the Garden of Eden (*Genesis* 2:9), so too the Torah, the *tree of life for those who hold on to it tightly* (*Proverbs* 3:18), must be also positioned centrally.

Just as the heart is at the center of one's body, pumping blood and bringing life to the more

---

16. **Seizing the Moment.** At the end of the Yom Kippur *Amidah* we implore, "My God. Before I was created I was worthless. And now that I was created, it is as if I was never created." *R' Avraham Griever* sheds light.

Before man is created, the world does not need him. Since his time has not yet arrived, God does not yet see fit to bring him into the world. When he is born, he is required to fulfill his unique mission on this earth. If he does not step into his designated role, he may as well never have been created. The spiritual void that had existed earlier continues to do so. We must all find our special, individual roles and fulfill our missions.

17. **Spiritual Refreshment.** The mother of *R' Shmelke of Nikolsburg* and *R' Pinchas Horowitz* (author of the *Haflaah*) would often say, "I have two sons. One never recites Grace After Meals, and the other never recites *Shema* before retiring. My Pinchas never eats and my Shmelke never sleeps."

R' Shmelke would catnap, holding a candle when napping. When it melted, the heat of the flame would awaken him. He once visited *R' Elimelech of Lizhensk* who convinced him to lie down in a bed and sleep. He slept through the night. When he awoke in the morning he was refreshed. He prayed like he had never prayed before. "Now," he said, "I realize that even sleep can be utilized for the service of God."

remote limbs, so too the Torah provides spiritual lifeblood to the entire nation (*Chafetz Chaim*).[18]

Torah, symbolized by the Tent of Meeting, the tree of life, and a man's heart were all centrally located.

Background

After describing each tribe and its encampment the Torah now singles out the Kohanim and Levites, who dedicate their lives to the service of God. The Levites are formally installed as the assistants to the Kohanim.

וְאֵלֶּה תּוֹלְדֹת אַהֲרֹן וּמֹשֶׁה
These are the offspring of Aaron and Moses (3:1).

Although the Torah only lists the children of Aaron, they are referred to as the offspring of Moses. *Rashi* (citing *Sanhedrin* 19b) explains that since Moses taught them Torah he is considered their spiritual father. In the words of the Sages, "one who teaches Torah to someone else's child is considered to have begotten him" (ibid.).

This is why the obligation to teach students Torah is termed וְשִׁנַּנְתָּם לְבָנֶיךָ, *You shall teach them* [the words of Torah] *thoroughly to your children* (*Deuteronomy* 6:7), for students are called children. (See *Rashi ad loc.*)

In a child-parent relationship, one gives and showers a child with love and caring because one is a parent, not vice versa.

Likewise, a teacher-student relationship is not a result of the teacher's teaching. It is an expression of the soul-relationship between teacher (father) and student (child).

Furthermore, the parental description of the student-teacher relationship reflects a vital understanding of the process of Torah instruction.

Everything a parent grants a child can be provided by others. The only one thing that only

parents can provide is life itself. This is also true regarding a Torah teacher. By teaching Torah, he is providing life itself (*R' Yitzchak Hutner*).

כִּי לִי כָּל בְּכוֹר בְּיוֹם הַכֹּתִי כָל בְּכוֹר בְּאֶרֶץ מִצְרַיִם הִקְדַּשְׁתִּי לִי כָל בְּכוֹר בְּיִשְׂרָאֵל
For every firstborn is Mine; on the day I struck down every firstborn in the land of Egypt I sanctified every firstborn in Israel for Myself. (ibid. 13).

Why was the sanctification of the firstborn a result of the strike against the firstborn?

As a result of being granted free choice and being rewarded for correct choices, man is able to earn his right to exist. On the night of Passover, Moses instructed the Jews to stay in their homes. Our Sages tell us "once the destroyer is granted permission to destroy he does not differentiate between the righteous and the wicked." On that night, the firstborns lost their ability to justify their existence. They only continued to live because of God's mercy.

That night the firstborn were granted a new lease on life (*Zekan Aharon*).

פְּקֹד אֶת בְּנֵי לֵוִי . . . מִבֶּן חֹדֶשׁ וָמַעְלָה תִּפְקְדֵם
Count the sons of Levi . . . from one month of age and up shall you count them (ibid. 15).

All Jews are counted from age 20. Why are Levites counted from one month old?

The *Rambam* writes (*Hilchos Shemittah V'Yovel* 13:12-13) that the Levites have a mission. It is to serve God, teach His Torah and inspire others to follow His ways. This lifestyle is not exclusive to the Levites. Any Jew who commits himself totally to this goal becomes as sanctified as the Holy of Holies. God will be his eternal portion and will provide him with his needs as He did for the Kohanim and Levites.

To attain this lofty goal, one must be educated

---

18. **True Public Service.** *R' Moshe Feinstein* once said to *R' Shlomo Freifeld,* "The most pressing need of the Jewish people is to produce *talmidei chachamim* (Torah scholars)." *R' Yitzchak Hutner* once remarked, "I want to make it clear that the greatest public service young people can do for *Klal Yisrael* is to sit and learn."

A young Jew who commits himself to serious Torah study becomes part of the heart of the nation, and helps provide life to all.

and nurtured from birth. This is why the Levites were counted from the age of one month (*R' Moshe Feinstein*).[19]

כָּל פְּקוּדֵי הַלְוִיִּם
All the countings of the Levites (ibid. 39).

Although Levites were counted from the age of one month their total was far less than those of the other tribes. Many explanations have been given. [See *Rashi* to *Exodus* 5:4 and *Ramban* here.]

Beis HaLevi states that God limited the number of Levites to spare the rest of the nation the expense of supporting them.

R' Elchanan Wasserman says limited quantity reflects quality. Quality and quantity are inversely related; the greater the quality, the lesser the quantity. Animals are more numerous than humans. Among humans non-Jews vastly outnumber Jews. Just as the Jewish nation enjoys a chosen status vis-à-vis non-Jews, Levites are the chosen tribe. Fine flour is always less than chaff. The Levites, special in quality, were limited in quantity.[20]

וַיִּתֵּן מֹשֶׁה אֶת כֶּסֶף הַפְּדֻיִם לְאַהֲרֹן . . . כַּאֲשֶׁר צִוָּה ה׳ אֶת מֹשֶׁה
Moses gave the money of the redemptions to Aaron . . . as Hashem had commanded Moses (ibid. 51).

It would seem more appropriate to write that Moses did as Hashem had commanded *him*, rather than as He *had commanded Moses.*

According to *Chashava L'Tovah* this offers us a crucial insight into Moses' leadership. Just as all Jews must respect their leaders, and obey them completely and unflinchingly, so the leader must likewise completely obey himself.

Moses the private citizen obeyed Moses the teacher. The Torah was not his own personal property to do with it as he pleased. He was loyal to Moses the leader of Israel.

וְאַחֲרֵי כֵן יָבֹאוּ בְנֵי קְהָת לָשֵׂאת
and then the sons of Kehath shall come to carry (4:15).

The Talmud (*Sotah* 35a) teaches us that the Holy Ark was in reality not borne by others: It bore its supposed bearers. The verse teaches that the sons of Kehath *came* to carry the Ark but were in reality carried by it. *R' Chaim of Volozhin* views this as a source of inspiration for those who carry the financial responsibility for Torah institutions on their shoulders. When the burden becomes unbearable let them remember that the Ark (the symbol of Torah) carries its "bearers." Torah will survive and will lift up those who carry it.

According to *R' Aharon Kotler,* this verse tells us that young scholars are capable of growing into positions of leadership. Once R' Aharon recommended a talented, young, scholar to head a new yeshivah. The young man demurred, claiming he was unfit for the position. R' Aharon told him, "The Holy Ark carries those who seek to carry it. Once you show a willingness to assume the burden of

---

19. **Subliminal Sanctity.** *Yerushalmi* (*Yevamos* 1:6) tells us about the mother of R' Yehoshua. She would bring his crib to the study hall. Even as a baby he would hear and absorb words of Torah. Before he was born, she would visit different study halls and ask the Torah scholars to pray that her child grow up to be a scholar. In recognition of this women's great concern for her son's spiritual growth, R' Yochanan ben Zakkai commented on R' Yehoshua "Praiseworthy is she who bore him" (*Avos* 2:11).

20. **Courageous Cadre.** *Rambam* teaches that just as the Levites were separated from the nation, those who dedicate themselves totally to Torah become the Levites of our time.

The Talmud (*Berachos* 35b) records an argument between R' Yishmael and R' Shimon bar Yochai whether one should pursue spiritual goals exclusively or not. R' Yishmael believes one should work to provide a living. Every spare minute should be utilized for Torah and *tefillah*. R' Shimon bar Yochai counters that if everyone will work, "what shall become of Torah?" He advocates complete immersion in spiritual matters. Regarding making a living, God will surely provide one's physical needs. The Talmud concludes that many followed R' Yishmael's opinion and were successful. Many followed R' Shimon's view but were unsuccessful. Many commentaries explain that R' Shimon's way is not suitable for the masses. It is tailored for a select few, for the Levites and those others like them who live lives that are truly inspired.

R' Shimon bar Yochai said, "I have seen those [people who are] spiritually superior and they are few."

leadership, the Torah will lift you and enable you to rise to the challenge."

וּפְקֻדַּת אֶלְעָזָר בֶּן אַהֲרֹן הַכֹּהֵן שֶׁמֶן הַמָּאוֹר וּקְטֹרֶת הַסַּמִּים וּמִנְחַת הַתָּמִיד וְשֶׁמֶן הַמִּשְׁחָה

The charge of Elazar son of Aaron the Kohen is the oil of illumination, the incense spices, the meal-offering of the continual offering and the anointment oil (ibid. 16).

Talmud Yerushalmi (Shabbos 10:3) teaches that Elazar carried out all of these tasks. *Ramban* takes elaborate pains to explain how one person could possibly carry such a heavy weight. He suggests that to accomplish this, Elazar was granted superhuman strength similar to that granted Jacob when he lifted the rock off the mouth of the well (see *Genesis* 29:10).[21] *Rashi* (*Shabbos* 92a, citing *Yerushalmi*) explains that Elazar held one container of oil in his right hand, one in his left, the incense in his lap and the meal-offering on his shoulder.

Superficially, Elazar must have appeared very undignified. In reality, it was a great honor (*R' Chaim Shmulevitz*).[22]

21. **Unity of Heart.** In the prayers we recite on *Shemini Atzeres* for rain we describe Jacob's ability to lift the rock that covered the well. He accomplished this because of יִחַד לֵב, *He dedicated his heart. R' Chaim Shmulevitz* views this as a supernatural strength one can achieve through willpower. Man's ability to accomplish is limited by the limits he himself places on his aspirations. Jacob's singleness of purpose gave him the physical strength to lift the rock.

Man's potential for greatness far transcends his own self-imposed limitations.

The great *Rogatchover Gaon, R' Yosef Rosen,* eulogized his colleague *R' Meir Simchah of Dvinsk* with the following tribute:

"If one is pinned under a fallen beam in a burning house, one can find the strength to move the beam even if under normal circumstances he would not be able to do so. Crises enable man to tap into strengths he was not even aware he possessed. R' Meir Simchah," concluded the Rogatchover, "always learned Torah with those sources of strength."

22. **True Honor.** In the Talmud Torah of Kelm, a bastion of the Mussar movement, an auction was held on Simchas Torah. Among the honors that were sold were the distinctions of being the one to sweep the floor of the *beis midrash,* the one to light the heating oven and the one who emptied the wastebasket. The bidding for these honors was fierce. Not everyone was even allowed to bid. Only veteran students were granted the privilege to participate.

R' Yerucham Levovitz of Mir writes that when he first came to Kelm, he saw the head of the Talmud Torah, *R' Simchah Zissel,* take the basin into which the Kohanim had washed, and empty it into the sink. Believing this to be undignified, he attempted to take the basin from him.

R' Simchah Zissel told R' Yerucham, "You are new here! You do not understand our behavior."

In Kelm degrading oneself on behalf of Torah was considered an honor.

When citing this incident, *R' Chaim Shmulevitz* would add, "Cleaning the *beis midrash* or returning *sefarim* (Torah books) to their shelves is a great honor. Joshua bin Nun became Moses' successor because he arranged the seats in the tent where Moses taught."

An example of the misconception regarding what constitutes true honor was the reaction of Michal, daughter of Saul (see *II Samuel* 6:16-23), to her husband's behavior. When she saw her husband, King David, dancing joyously before the Holy Ark when it was brought into its tent, she viewed his behavior as a degradation of his honor. She even reprimanded him for his unbecoming behavior. King David responded, "Had I lowered myself even more, such actions would have revealed my true honor, because they were done to honor God and the Holy Ark" (ibid. 22). (See *Mishnah Berurah* 699 §11 and *Shaar HaTziyun* ad loc.)

The *Rambam* captures King David's sentiment:

The joy that one experiences in his fulfillment of *mitzvos* and his love of God, is both a difficult task and an elevated, spiritual accomplishment. One who fulfills the *mitzvos* but refrains from experiencing and expressing joy deserves to be punished. The Torah reveals the root cause of all the frightful punishments that would befall the Jewish people if they strayed from God and His Torah, *Because you did not serve Hashem, your God, amid gladness and goodness of heart (Deuteronomy* 28:47).

One who acts arrogantly and reserves honor for himself in such situations is both a sinner and a fool. Regarding this did King Solomon teach, *Do not honor yourself in front of the King (Proverbs* 25:6). One who humbles himself and ignores his own honor for the honor of God is himself truly honorable.

To rejoice before God is true greatness and honor (*Hilchos Lulav* 8:15).

אַל תַּכְרִיתוּ אֶת שֵׁבֶט מִשְׁפְּחֹת הַקְּהָתִי

Do not let the tribe of the Kehathite families be cut off (ibid. 18).

If the Torah refers to all the other families of Kohanim as "families," why are the Kehathites called a tribe family?

The Kehathites carried the Ark which symbolized Torah. This role is assumed by all those who commit themselves to the study or support of Torah. The Torah assures us that not only will the Kohathites themselves never remain eternal. All those who identify with their mission enjoy a place in eternity as well.

פרשת נשא ⏴
Parashas Nasso

Background

The Torah continues to count the Levite families and to delineate their responsibilities.

נָשֹׂא אֶת רֹאשׁ בְּנֵי גֵרְשׁוֹן גַּם הֵם
Take a census [raise the heads] of the sons of Gershon, as well (4:22).

The phrase implies that the census of Gershon was an afterthought. This is incorrect. The simple explanation is *as well,* "in addition" to the Kohathites.

R' Simchah Bunim of P'shis'cha offers a homiletic explanation. Torah scholars who, like the Kohathites, carry the Ark find themselves spiritually elevated because "the Ark carries its bearers" (*Sotah* 35a). Here the Torah speaks of the Gershonites. They considered themselves גֵרוּשִׁים, rejected by God, because of their lower spiritual status. If they have the humility to recognize and appreciate their secondary status, they too will become uplifted.

וְאֵת כָּל אֲשֶׁר יֵעָשֶׂה לָהֶם וְעָבָדוּ
and everything that is made for them, and they shall serve (ibid. 26).

Literally this refers to all the accessories necessary for the items the Gershonites were appointed to carry.

Rendering כָּל אֲשֶׁר יֵעָשֶׂה לָהֶם as *whatever would be done to them, Divrei Shmuel* offers the following homiletical explanation. People are prone to offer all types of excuses, legitimate or not, to justify their laxity in their fulfillment of *mitzvos.* The Torah responds, *whatever is done to you,* in whatever circumstances you find yourself, *you shall serve.* A Jew must be ready to serve God in spite of even seemingly insurmountable problems.[1]

This expectation is realistic and fair because God grants us the resources to overcome any obstacle placed in our path.[2] We must show a

---

1. **Preoccupied Destiny.** *Do not say, "When I am free I will study' for perhaps you will not become free'* (Avos 2:5). *R' Menachem Mendel of Kotzk* explains the *Mishnah* this way: Do not wait until you are free to learn, because your designated task in life may be to learn while under pressure and stress. If you wait for the pressures to subside you may wait forever.

2. **Not a Minute Too Late.** With regard to the Final Redemption, the prophet tells us, *I am Hashem, in its time I will hasten it* (Isaiah 60:22). This appears to be contradictory; if the redemption is in its time it need not be hastened. Alternatively, if Hashem *does* hasten it, it will come before its time. How can this verse be reconciled? The Talmud (*Sanhedrin* 98b) explains that if the Jewish people are meritorious, God will bring the Redemption early. If, however, they are undeserving, God will bring salvation at the specified time regardless. This, says *R' Tzadok HaKohen* (*Tzidkas HaTzaddik* 50), pertains equally to one's personal redemption from problems he encounters along the path of life. If one is deserving, God will ease his plight at an early stage. If not, God will save him before his dire situation becomes unbearable. If one sees that his difficulties persist, he may be assured that he still has the ability to withstand them. God will never permit him to suffer even a moment longer than he is truly able to.

willingness to try to succeed.[3]

A king will never send his soldiers to the battlefield lacking necessary weaponry.

עֲבֹדַת עֲבֹדָה
work of service (4:47).

This refers to the musical accompaniment provided by the Levites during the sacrificial service.

Doing a mitzvah is a mechanical act. A Jew should fulfill his *mitzvos* with joy. However, this is not always easy to perform. Fasting on Yom Kippur is difficult; to have the proper intent is easy. Eating well on the Sabbath and the Festivals is simple; having the proper intention is harder to achieve. Similarly, though many *mitzvos* are easy to perform, doing them joyously is more difficult.

The Torah provides us with ways to attain the hard-to-come-by happiness which must imbue a mitzvah. Music gladdens the soul when the spirit of

God infiltrates one's consciousness.[4] This joy is the *work of the service* (R' Yosef Shaul Nathanson).[5]

Background

The Tabernacle needed an environment compatible with the sanctity which accompanied the Divine Presence. Ritual contamination (*tumah*) and immoral and unethical conduct had to be eradicated, because they contradicted the Tabernacle's very essence.

וִישַׁלְּחוּ מִן הַמַּחֲנֶה כָּל צָרוּעַ וְכָל זָב וְכֹל טָמֵא לָנָפֶשׁ
they shall expel from the camp everyone with tzaraas, everyone who has had a zav-emission and everyone contaminated by a human corpse (5:2).

The Torah specifies three classes of contamination which force those contaminated to leave

---

3. **Leave It to Me.** *R' Yisrael Salanter* would often say: Man's job is to do but only God gets things done. We must demonstrate our desire to achieve, and leave the rest to Hashem.

4. **Opening Deaf Ears.** The *Rebbes of Modzhitz* were famous for their musical compositions. *R' Yisrael of Modzhitz* was once asked why he viewed music as such an important tool in the service of God. Couldn't one find the same inspiration in the holy *mussar* works?

R' Yisrael offered the following parable: A villager who owned a flour mill once came to visit the big city. In the display window of a clock shop he noticed a beautiful alarm clock with a very pleasant ring. The villager entered the shop, intent on purchasing the clock.

The shopkeeper greeted him and asked from where he came and his occupation. When the villager replied, the shopkeeper began to laugh. "If you are a miller, how do you expect this clock to wake you? If the noisy mill doesn't get you out of bed, how will this relatively soft alarm do so?"

The villager answered, "You are mistaken and don't understand the nature of people. People get used to their surroundings to the extent that they pay no attention to their immediate environment. My mill makes such a racket day and night that I pay no attention to the noise at all. I am able to sleep like a baby and never awaken on time. However this soft sound will wake me, because it is so unfamiliar and completely at odds with my surroundings."

Similarly, explained R' Yisrael, our senses are often desensitized to the powerful message of the *mussar* works. They are loud and are intended to wake us up. However, we may have become so used to them that our spiritual slumber continues undisturbed. Sometimes, a quiet, unassuming musical tune can succeed where other means have failed.

5. **Price Tag.** Why is joy such an important factor in achieving spiritual success? *R' Yitzchak Hutner* explains: The Talmud (*Kiddushin* 40b) says that if one performs a mitzvah and later regrets having done it, he loses all reward for the mitzvah. This teaches us that the value of a mitzvah is proportional to the value assigned to it. If it is worth nothing to us, then it truly becomes worthless.

Why are we the ones who establish the value of our *mitzvos*? The price of any item is based on the principle of supply and demand. If one has a monopoly on a given commodity, he may usually demand whatever price he wants. Every Jew has a monopoly on his own *mitzvos* because he is the only one who can perform them. Therefore, he alone determines their value.

The joy one experiences when doing a mitzvah indicates its value in his eyes.

[Another barometer of the value assigned to a mitzvah is the amount of pain and difficulty one is ready to endure to perform it. As the *Mishnah* teaches, "The reward is in proportion to the exertion" (*Avos* 5:26)].

their various camps. Homiletically, this teaches man the importance of internal purification. Every person is born with internal desires, drives and aspirations. Optimally these should be channeled toward one's spiritual growth. Unfortunately, they are often wasted in the pursuit of material goods.

Man is called upon to expel all spiritual contaminants from his personal camp. He should not allow himself to be influenced by ulterior motives (*Avnei Azel*).

וַיַּעֲשׂוּ כֵן בְּנֵי יִשְׂרָאֵל . . .
כֵּן עָשׂוּ בְּנֵי יִשְׂרָאֵל
*The Children of Israel did so: . . .
so did the Children of Israel do (ibid. 4).*

Why does the Torah repeat that the Children of Israel followed the Divine command to expel those contaminated? *Chizkuni* explains that the two statements refer to two distinct groups of Jews. Jews expelled the contaminated, and they willingly left the camp.

Binah L'Itim submits that the two clauses refer to two aspects of this mitzvah. The act of expelling those contaminated is the actual mitzvah. However, we must also do whatever we can to eradicate the root causes that brought contamination. The people began to modify their behavior and refrain from slander and other sins which cause *tzaraas*.

לִמְעֹל מַעַל בַּה׳
*by committing treachery
toward Hashem (ibid. 6).*

The interpersonal sins referred to in this verse, are described as acts of treachery against Hashem. Morals and ethics are not man made. God determines the parameter of proper conduct

between men. [For example, one who steals sins toward God and his fellow man.][6]

Sforno states that the treachery against God is the result of the desecration of His Name. The verse (see *Rashi*, ad loc.) refers to one who stole from a proselyte, one who voluntarily joined the Jewish nation. To abuse the property of one who courageously abandoned his past to join God's chosen nation is a desecration of God's Name.

וְהִתְוַדּוּ אֶת חַטָּאתָם
They shall confess their sins (ibid. 7).

Rambam (*Hilchos Teshuvah* 1:1) asserts that there is a Biblical mitzvah to repent. The source is our verse. However, Rambam's definition of the mitzvah is noteworthy. "If one transgressed any of the *mitzvos* of the Torah, when he repents he is obligated to confess his sin as it says "they shall confess." Rambam implies that the mitzvah is confession, not repentance. Repentance is an obvious necessity and does not require a specific command. *Nesivos Shalom* explains the obligation to repent need not be stated explicitly. It is a part of the general prohibition against sinning. Until one regrets one's actions, one is still sinning.

A servant who spits in the king's face, but goes about his business as if nothing happened, is no better than one who is presently engaged in such behavior. This only ends when he earnestly regrets his misdeeds. Only then can he attempt to rectify the situation.

Repentance itself, teaches Rambam, is not the mitzvah. It is self-evident that one has to stop sinning. Once one does, one must confess his sin and face the reality of the damage it has caused.[7]

---

6. **Nonsituational Ethics.** *Tractate Avos,* which discusses the morals and ethics of the Torah, begins by stating that Moses received all of the Torah from God at Sinai. This tells us that Torah ethics are Divinely derived, not man made. Human definitions of ethical and moral behavior usually reflect the prevalent mind-set and moral climate. They are a social contract necessary to establish a functional society. Only God through His Torah can define eternal moral truths (*R' Ovadiah M'Bartenura*).

7. **Looking in the Mirror.** Why do we need to confess our sins? Isn't God fully aware of our transgressions?

Confession is the process of self-confrontation. By verbalizing our sins we are forced to critically look inward at ourselves. One who views himself as a paragon of virtue will never feel a need to correct himself (*Simchas Aharon*).

Even though confession[8] is necessary with regard to all sins and indiscretions, the Torah chose theft as the example. God gives man life and the ability to perform His will. All man's abilities and talents are given to him to serve God. When one uses these God-given gifts against Him, one is really guilty of thievery. Every sin is really a form of stealing.

The Torah teaches the need to confess and repent in connection with thievery, because every sinner is a thief (*Chidushei HaRim*).[9]

וְהִתְוַדּוּ אֶת חַטָּאתָם אֲשֶׁר עָשׂוּ
They shall confess their sin that they committed (ibid.).

The words *that they committed* seem redundant. Obviously one can only confess to sins which he has committed!

The Torah is alluding to the nature of sin. Sin is not created in a vacuum; certain factors precede the actual sin and have a significant share in causing one to sin. For example, one does not become a thief overnight. Jealousy and coveting the property of others will eventually cause one to steal. Our Sages teach, "one sin is the harbinger of another" (*Avos* 4:2).

When one attempts to repent, one cannot only deal with the actual transgression. One must search one's deepest self to discern the cause of the sin. An expert doctor, who seeks to remedy the cause of illness, rather than merely alleviate the symptoms, must get to the root of the problem.

So too, one must reveal the root causes that bring one to sin.[10]

Isaiah the Prophet calls on the people to repent: "Let the wicked one abandon his path and the man of iniquity his thoughts" (*Isaiah* 55:7). Do the wicked really have a path in life? Don't they just live life with reckless abandon?

Nesivos Shalom notes that the prophet calls for abandoning a path. Often, one's negative behavior is the result of having placed oneself on a particular path. Once one is on it, it is virtually impossible to get off. If one cannot change paths one is doomed. Furthermore, the man of iniquity is not punished for the sins he committed mentally [without actually doing them], since God punishes Jews only for their actions. The prophet urges one to abandon the thought patterns and views which brings one to sin.

R' Menachem Mendel of Kotzk, says it this way:

---

8. **Real Repentance?** A *chassid* once asked *R' Simchah Bunim of P'shis'cha*, "When King David confessed his sin, he was immediately informed that God forgave him. Yet, we continuously pray and confess, begging for God's forgiveness, but seemingly to no avail. Why?"

R' Simchah Bunim replied: "When we recite the confessional and say אָשַׁמְנוּ, *we have becomes guilty,* we believe we are really deserving of God's forgiveness. When we continue and say בָּגַדְנוּ, *we have betrayed* [Him and our purpose in life], we are convinced that now that He has forgiven us, it is only fitting that He grant us the full extent of His bountiful goodness. With this type of confession and repentance, should we really expect Divine pardon?"

Contemplating the betrayal and disloyalty which are the underpinnings of sin, the *Chafetz Chaim* once observed, "When witnesses are requested to sign on a bill of divorce [or witness a marriage] they must intellectually and emotionally commit themselves to repent in order to qualify to be witnesses (see *Shulchan Aruch, Even HaEzer* 154 *Rema* gloss to *Seder HaGet* §3). How much are they paid [if at all] to serve as witnesses? Perhaps a half ruble or a ruble? For that paltry sum they are ready to repent. Yet when God, Who sustains us throughout the entire year, calls on us to repent at least before Yom Kippur, are we ready to do so?!"

9. **Restoring Stolen Goods.** The end of the *Ne'ilah* prayer on Yom Kippur reflects this view of sin. The prayer states, "And You have granted us Yom Kippur so that we may refrain from stealing." Certainly Yom Kippur is a day of atonement for all sins, not just theft?!

Yom Kippur is the day we return to God all we have stolen, including the Divinely granted gifts which we stole by using them to rebel against Him.

10. **Spiritual Catalyst.** This is even more true with regard to *mitzvos*. Thousands of people attended the ground-breaking ceremonies for the Yeshivas Chachmei Lublin in Poland. The site of the yeshivah, prime real estate in downtown Lublin, was donated by *R' Shmuel Eichenbaum*, a childhood friend of the *Rosh Yeshivah*, Rabbi Meir Shapiro. The *Tchortkover Rebbe, R' Yisrael,* spoke at the occasion. During his remarks, he turned to R' Shmuel Eichenbaum and said: "I don't especially envy your mitzvah of donating the building site, since it is a mitzvah done publicly, for which you have already received much honor. I envy the mitzvah you did privately that enabled you to do this mitzvah."

"The evil ones have no path. They wallow in the mud with no sense of direction or destination. They are blind to the fact that they are headed toward spiritual oblivion, and continue thinking they have a path. The prophet cries out, 'Stop fooling yourselves! Your supposed path is nothing more than spiritual quicksand.' "[11]

וְאִישׁ אֶת קֳדָשָׁיו לוֹ יִהְיוּ אִישׁ
אֲשֶׁר יִתֵּן לַכֹּהֵן לוֹ יִהְיֶה

A man's holies shall be his and what a man gives to a Kohen shall be his (ibid. 10).

Why does this verse follow the previous ones which deal with the sin of stealing? *Binah L'Itim* explains: People live with a misconception concerning what is theirs and what is not. They think, "The money I have in my bank account is mine. The money I gave away to charity is not." It is this outlook that causes people to decrease their contributions.

This perception is false. The money one gives away to holy causes is his permanently, whereas one's personal fortune is temporary.

The verse teaches this lesson. *A man's holies,* only that which he donates to holy causes, *shall be his.* [12]

The Talmud (*Bava Basra* 11a) tells of King Munbaz (son of the Hashmonean Queen Helene) who, during a famine, used a major part of the royal coffers to sustain his subjects. His brothers and family came to him complaining, "Your fathers increased the fortunes they inherited, but you waste yours." Replied Munbaz, "My fathers deposited in this world while I deposit in the next. They saved for others [their heirs], while I save for myself."

Charity is an investment in one's own future.[13]

---

11. **Spiritual Realignment.** The path away from God is also the road back. תְּשׁוּבָה means return, because one who sins steals from God, and one who repents seeks to repay Him by taking those very strengths and abilities that were used to sin, and uses them for the service of God. *Nesivos Shalom* teaches that the way a sin is committed, "the eyes see, the heart desires, the limbs complete the task" (see *Rashi, Numbers* 15:39), is actually the way to repentance. One must channel them positively.

Raise your eyes on high and see Who created these (Isaiah 40:26), and come to realize how truly beholden you are to God. Let your heart experience its true passion, as echoed in the words of King David: *As the hart calls longingly for the water brooks, so my soul calls longingly to You, O God (Psalms* 42:2). Let your eyes see, let your heart desire and your limbs will follow along, as you transform your life.

12. **Perennial Investments.** The *Chafetz Chaim* would often tell people, "Don't wait until you are ready to pass away before you instruct your children how to disburse your money for charity. Who knows when you will die? Furthermore, what guarantee do you have that your children will actually give the money to the different charities? Perhaps they will take the money for themselves? Follow the advice of King Solomon: 'Whatever you can do while under your own strength, do' (*Ecclesiastes* 9:10). Whatever you give away during your lifetime is yours eternally."

King David alludes to this eternal quality of charity: *Wealth and riches shall be in his house, and his righteousness endures forever (Psalms* 112:3).

All the wealth one accumulates in this world will remain in his house, because he will take none of it along when he departs from this world. Only his righteous deeds will accompany him. On the other hand, "investments" of charity will endure forever, accompanying him to the World to Come (*R' Shmuel Alter*).

[Someone once noted that burial shrouds have no pockets because one "can't take it with him."]

13. **Increasing Returns.** At the age of 46, in 1928, Mr. Frankel (a fictitious name), a wealthy labor lawyer in New York City, suffered a massive heart attack. After examining him, the doctors said that if he continued working at his present pace he would only live another five years. His heart was too weak to last longer.

He decided to retire and enjoy the remainder of his life in Florida. He purchased annuities that would support him comfortably for forty years, and moved into a beautiful home in Miami Beach. He began distributing large sums of money to charity. His favorite *tzedakah* was the Ponevezher Yeshivah.

One day he called *R' Berel Wein.*

"Rabbi, I'm now 86 years old, and a terrible thing has happened. I've outlived my income. When I was younger the doctors only gave me five years to live. I conservatively bought forty years of annuities. Now all my doctors are dead and my annuity has been spent. I've lived within my means but beyond my years."

Sadly, he reported that he would have to sell his house and let his housekeeper go. "I'll have to change my entire

Rashi cites a Midrashic interpretation that one who retains as part of his property that which should be given to the Kohen will eventually find himself left with no more than that one tenth. *If a man's holies* (that which should be consecrated] *shall be his* then only *what a man gives to the Kohen shall be his.* [14]

If the land only produces 10 percent of its usual yield, the Kohen will only receive one tenth of his usual 10 percent, or 1 percent of the usual yield. Why should the Kohen suffer because the land-owner is deserving of punishment?

Apparently, taught *R' Yechezkel Sarna*, the Kohen shares some of the responsibility for the landowner's refusal to fulfill his obligation to tithe. Had the Kohen exerted the proper influence his fellow Jew would have behaved correctly.

There is a lesson here for all those who solicit contributions on behalf of sacred causes. They must invest energy to insure that the potential contributors give according to their means.[15] If they fail to do so, they have been lax in *their* spiritual

standard of living. For the last five years I've been selling off my assets to meet my expenses. The social security checks have come in handy, but they are not enough. I will sell this house and move back to Teaneck."

R' Wein knew *R' Yosef Kahaneman,* the *Ponevezher Rav.* The *Rosh Yeshivah* had been the main beneficiary of Frankel's charity over the years and he was coming to town the following week on a fundraising trip. "Mr. Frankel, I have an idea. Don't sell the house yet. I think we may be able to work this out."

When the Ponevezher Rav arrived, R' Wein took him to Mr. Frankel's home. R' Kahaneman listened to his plight. He knew that Mr. Frankel had probably given over one million dollars to his yeshivah, both when it was in Europe and now in its resurrected state in Israel. "This can't happen," he said, bewildered, "this can't be."

R' Wein began to explain to him the financial facts of life, but the venerable Rav was one step ahead. "Mr. Frankel, for forty-five years you supported Torah, now Torah is going to support you."

R' Kahaneman made a startling decision. He immediately put Mr. Frankel on the payroll of the Ponevezh Yeshivah. For the remaining two years of his life, Mr. Frankel made his living as a "fundraiser" for the yeshivah he had supported his entire life. As they left, the Ponevezher Rav said to R' Wein, "*Tzedakah* (charity) is a two-way street. It benefits the giver as well as the receiver. We'll just redirect some of his money back to him." (From *Vintage Wein, Sha'ar Press.*)

14. **Tithing for Real.** The Sages teach that tithing is the key to wealth (*Avos* 3:17). *R' Yaakov Emden* (*Sheilas Yaavetz* 1:6) writes that it was customary among the German Jews to immediately tithe dowry money before giving them to the young couple. This custom, he continues, is proper, because the bride and groom might not be as meticulous about disbursing the money.

Vavei HaAmudim (son of the *Shelah*) writes: "I praise the German Jews who take great care to tithe all their income and to distribute it appropriately to worthy causes. In the merit of this practice, they succeed in passing on their inheritance to their children and grandchildren."

R' Moshe Heilprin of Lublin adds: "In our provinces, few succeed in passing on their wealth, for many among us are not sufficiently careful with regard to tithing."

R' Eliezer Yehudah Finkel, Rosh Yeshivah of the famed Mirrer Yeshivah, had promised his son-in-law *R' Chaim Shmulevitz* a dowry of one thousand American dollars. However, due to the unfortunate financial condition of the yeshivah, he was unable to honor the commitment. A few years after the couple married, R' Eliezer Yehudah was finally able to scrape together $100 — which the couple promptly used to honor their obligation to tithe their potential and as-yet-unreceived dowry.

15. **Who Is Carrying Whom?** Just as a medic or doctor must totally throw himself into the task of saving his patients, a fundraiser must realize that he is offering a lifeline to potential donors.

R' Eliezer Gordon, the renowned *Rosh Yeshivah* of Telz, was supported by his father-in-law for many years as he concentrated exclusively on Torah. At one time, his father-in-law's financial situation took a turn for the worse. Nonetheless, when a committee offered R' Eliezer the rabbinate of Aleksot, his father-in-law was against the idea. His wife protested, "How long can we support him?" He replied, "Who knows who is supporting whom? Are we supporting him with our money or is he supporting us with his Torah learning?" When the community of Eisheshok approached with their offer, he again rejected the offer. Finally when Slabodka made an offer, the mother-in-law's opinion won out and the offer was accepted. On the day the Gordons were scheduled to leave to Slabodka, *R' Avraham Yitzchak Neviazer,* the father-in-law, suddenly collapsed and died.

His wife, a true *tzadekes,* eulogized him, "Woe is to me. I killed him. He said to me, 'Who knows who is sustaining whom?' Now I know that our son-in-law supported us. We were living in the merit of his Torah."

duty and deserve to suffer the consequences.[16]

Background

The Jewish home must resemble the Tabernacle and be an appropriate resting place for God's presence. *Ramban* (to verse 20) notes that *sotah* is the only mitzvah which is dependent on the supernatural [the woman's innards collapse from the water she drinks (see verse 22)]. This is to ensure the purity of Jewish lineage. The nation of Israel must be suitable for God's Presence.

אִישׁ אִישׁ כִּי תִשְׂטֶה אִשְׁתּוֹ
Any man whose wife shall go astray (ibid. 12).

Rashi tells us why this section, which deals with the unfaithful wife, follows the previous one which deals with those who withhold priestly gifts from the Kohen. One who declines to voluntarily come to the Kohen will suffer unfortunate consequences, and will ultimately be forced to come away.[17]

Chasam Sofer understands the connection based on the Talmud's formula for achieving wealth. The Talmud offers two ways to insure financial success. עַשֵּׂר בִּשְׁבִיל שֶׁתִּתְעַשֵּׁר, "Tithe to become wealthy" (*Shabbos* 119a), or "Honor your wives [by buying them clothes and jewelry] to become wealthy" (*Bava Metzia* 59a).

One may think that honoring one's wife may replace and override proper tithing. The Torah warns that overindulgence in an opulent lifestyle will result in disloyalty to man and God. Opulence is a breeding ground for immorality. Depriving the Kohen of his tithe and limiting one's charity, creates a situation where one will be forced to meet the Kohen under embarrassing circumstances.

Homiletically, the Torah teaches the family head how to foster fidelity to Torah among his family members.

Often people cannot bring themselves to offer support to Torah scholars or others involved in spiritual pursuits because they consider themselves spiritually superior. They cite the words of the Sages: "One who gives tithes to an ignorant Kohen is like one who gave it to a lion" (*Sanhedrin* 90b).

---

16. **What Is in It for Them?** *R' Nachumke* of *Horodna* (the mentor of the *Chafetz Chaim*) was a hidden saint who made his living as the caretaker of the local synagogue. He would often solicit funds for the needy. Once he approached someone who slapped him across the face for having the "audacity" to ask for a contribution. R' Nachumke, unfazed, responded, "That was for me. Now, what do you want me to give the person in need?" He did not simply mean to offer a sharp and witty retort. His response was based on halachah. One must rebuke a sinner even up to the point that the sinner loses control and physically strikes back (see *Rambam, Hilchos Deios* 6:7). Once the sinner physically attacks, however, the other person is absolved of any responsibility to chastise his friend.

R' Nachumke felt obligated to use all the persuasive powers at his disposal to get the person to contribute to charity. Once he struck him, he might be absolved of his obligation. But would that help the one in need? What was he supposed to give him?

17. **Proper Questions.** *R' Moshe Feinstein* would often bemoan, "People come to me with all kinds of halachic inquiries and personal problems. Yet, they rarely ask me about two extremely important issues, how to educate their children and how to spend their charity dollars."

If we went to the "Kohen" to deliver tithes, we might avoid having to come to him about tragic and painful matters.

The *Dubno Maggid* offers the following parable.

An accomplished scholar, artisan and scientist once found himself in a town of uncouth unlearned people and boors. When questioned as to his occupation he replied, "I'm a medic." A friend who knew the truth asked him, "Why do you hide your great knowledge and skills from the townspeople?" Replied the multifaceted scholar, "The people here are ignorant and are unable to appreciate my talents. I told them I am a medic. This is a calling that they are familiar with and one they are equipped to value."

Spiritually sensitive people are able to appreciate the value of the Kohen. They feel honored to bring him his tithes. Those who are spiritual boors and backwoodsmen are incapable of appreciating the Kohen for anything other than the practical benefit they may gain from him. They are only equipped to value the Kohen as a spiritual medic who will help cure their home of domestic strife.

"Any ignorant Kohen who eats *terumah* will not be a Kohen in the Messianic age" (*Midrash*). They arrogantly degrade the Kohanim, the spiritual tribe of the nation. This message is not lost on their family. They inherit this disdain for the leaders of the nation, and develop an attitude that they always know better than the Torah leaders. The door is opened to immorality.

By withholding tithes, a man has laid the groundwork for his own marital discord (*Bircas Shimon*).

The phrase אִישׁ אִישׁ literally means *a man a man.* Why does the Torah employ the double expression? According to *Otzar Chaim* this teaches that moral duplicity on the part of a husband triggers immorality on the part of his wife and family. *A man, a man;* one who is a fraud, acting one way at home and another way while among people, should expect moral inconsistency from the members of his family.

The Torah teaches, *If a man a man whose wife goes astray, the treachery is in him.* The source of this moral disloyalty must be laid at his doorstep.[18]

Meleches Macheves suggests that the double expression is a warning against self-centeredness and egocentricity in one's domestic relationship. *A man* [who is only interested in] *a man* [i.e., himself] and does not follow the instructions of the Sages to love his wife as himself and honor her even more than himself, is asking for trouble. One who only sees himself and his own needs and is insensitive to the care and love which his wife expects and needs is pushing her to seek that love elsewhere.[19]

וְהִיא נִטְמָאָה
and she had become defiled (ibid. 14).

The Torah repeats the fact that she had become defiled three times. According to the Sages, this refers to the fact that if she committed adultery she may neither remain married to her husband nor can she marry the adulterer.

Based on this, *R' Yisrael Salanter* explains a perplexing Talmudic passage.

The Talmud teaches that one who infringes on his friend's livelihood by opening up the same type of business is comparable to one who defiles his friend's wife. One's livelihood is often compared in Scripture to one's wife. What is the connection?

R' Yisrael explains: One who encroaches on another's business often attract customers by lowering their prices. The newcomer does so even though he stands to lose money. His goal is to ruin his friend's business and force him out.

Likewise the adulterer; aside from a momentary thrill, he gains nothing permanent from his action, because he may not marry the woman. He only succeeds in ruining his friend's life, since the friend must now divorce his wife [if she willingly committed adultery].

עֲשִׂירִת הָאֵיפָה קֶמַח שְׂעֹרִים
a tenth-ephah of barley flour (ibid. 15).

Since the *sotah* exhibited animalistic characteristics, she is commanded to bring an offering from barley flour, an animal food (*Rashi*).

Chasam Sofer notes that the *omer*, offered on Pesach, was made of barley flour (see *Leviticus*

---

18. **Watchful Eye.** The Talmud (*Sotah* 2a) cites the teaching of Reish Lakish, "God matches people based on their actions." (Generally modest women marry righteous men and immodest women marry wicked men.) It is not at all surprising that moral hypocrites are matched with disloyal mates.

Rambam (*Hilchos Sotah* 4:19) writes: "It is proper that one warn his wife gently and privately to guide her on the path of righteousness and to remove from her path any moral stumbling blocks. One who is lax in guiding his wife and family and maintaining surveillance on their activities to ensure that they avoid moral pitfalls is himself deemed a sinner. *You shall know that your tent is at peace, you shall survey your abode and find nothing* (See *Job* 5:24).

19. **Role Reversal.** *R' Chaim Shmulevitz* would counsel his students and tell them, "Our Sages teach a man to love his wife as himself and honor her even more (*Yevamos* 62b). A wife is deemed virtuous if she does the will of her husband (*Tanna D'Vei Eliyahu Rabbah* 9). As long as the husband abides by the former and the wife abides by the latter, their home will be blessed with marital bliss. It is when they switch roles, with the husband insisting on subservience and the wife demanding love and honor, that the troubles begin."

23:9-14), whereas the Two Loaves, offered on Shavuos, were of wheat flour.

Although the Jews were freed from the immoral cesspool of Egypt on Pesach, they still needed further cleansing of their animalistic tendencies. Egypt was still in their system. Therefore, on Passover they were commanded to bring an offering consisting of animal food. On Shavuos, when they received the Torah, they were completely purified, and they were then able to bring an offering from wheat, a food of humans.

וּמָחָה אֶל מֵי הַמָּרִים
and erase it into the bitter waters (ibid. 23.).

Although it is forbidden to erase God's Name (see *Rambam, Hilchos Yesodei HaTorah* 6:1-2), God commanded we do so to bring peace between man and wife (*Yerushalmi Sotah* 1:4).

Maharal (*Nesiv HaShalom* Chapter 1) explains: God is willing to have His Name erased to bring שָׁלוֹם, *peace,* between a man and his wife because שָׁלוֹם is itself one of God's Names (*Shabbos* 10b). In order to achieve the living realization of His Name, God permits us to erase printed letters. One Name is erased, and replaced with another.

Why is this only permitted to insure domestic harmony? The word for man is אִישׁ; the word for woman, אִשָּׁה. They share the letters אֵשׁ, *fire.* A marital relationship seeks to bring total opposites together, and has within it the potential for destructive fire. By making the Divine Presence a third party in their marriage, a husband and wife can contain the fire and achieve a peaceful, productive

and harmonious relationship. The remaining letters י, *yud,* and ה, *hei,* together spell the Name of God with which He created this world and the next (See *Isaiah* 26:4). By introducing God into their shared life, a couple can transform two opposite forces into a constructive energy source capable of creating new worlds[20] (See *Pirkei DeRabbi Eliezer* §12).

Background

The Torah now speaks of the Nazirite. Opting for a lifestyle of self-control, he tries to tame his spirit of self-indulgence which is often the cause of sin. The word *nazir* is related to *nezer,* a crown. Ibn Ezra explains (6:7): "Most people are enslaved to their passions. The true king, who legitimately wears the crown of kingship, is he who is liberated from the control of his desires."

אִישׁ אוֹ אִשָּׁה כִּי יַפְלִא לִנְדֹּר נֶדֶר
A man or a woman who shall disassociate himself by taking a [Nazirite] vow . . . (6:2).

The Sages view the juxtaposition of this section regarding the adulterous wife with that of the Nazirite as teaching that one who sees the degradation of the *sotah* should voluntarily become a *nazir* and abstain from wine, which arouses sensual passions in man (*Sotah* 2a).

Man believes his mind can control his emotions. Then, when he witnesses what happens to a *sotah* he realizes that very often emotions control the mind. He should assume a vow to abstain from wine which beclouds the mind (*Zekan Aharon*).[21]

---

20. **Abundant Peace.** The last blessing of the daytime *Shemoneh Esrei* begins with the words שִׂים שָׁלוֹם, *establish peace,* but the same blessing in the *Maariv* evening prayer, begins with שָׁלוֹם רָב, *establish abundant peace.*

During the day, when one is engaged in business, peace is necessary for the successful conducting of business. To maintain a harmonious home, however, peace is critical. Before we return home, we implore God for abundant peace (*Ahavas Torah*).

21. **Not a Laughing Matter.** R' Nosson Scherman relates the following. In the 1970's an Orthodox Jewish writer penned an article ridiculing the new "sexual revolution." The article was shown to R' Gedaliah Schorr for his review. He approved the article but requested that the humor be deleted. The author responded that he was deriding the movement, in accordance with the Talmudic dictum that it is commendable to deride idolatry.

R' Schorr replied that there is a basic difference between idolatry and promiscuity. Like all religious movements, idolatry takes itself seriously and increases its strength when it convinces the public that it is worthy of consideration. To ridicule it is to destroy it. Immorality works the opposite way. It is enticing because it titillates. The more one makes light of it, the more it becomes acceptable. Humor and ridicule play into its hands."

Witnessing the shocking results of the *sotah's* immoral conduct will not be sufficient to protect one against imitating that same behavior. One must become a *nazir* and take a firm stand against immorality.

An obvious question remains to be answered. If avoiding wine is desirable, why shouldn't everyone abstain from it? Why do the Sages limit their advice to someone who witnessed the degradation. Furthermore, the very witnessing of such a grotesque sight as the *sotah's* death is seemingly in itself insurance against sinning. Why must one respond with increased vigilance?[22]

Intellectual reasoning alone cannot change the behavior of people. A person can intellectually know the consequences of sin and still be lured to it. One who experiences exposure to evil must transform his feelings into concrete action if one is to undergo a spiritual metamorphosis. If the experience remains a memory, one runs the risk of becoming one whose "knowledge exceeds his actions is like a tree with many branches and few roots. Any wind comes and uproots it" (*Avos* 3:22).

In such a case, the witnessing of the *sotah* becomes a handicap. Rather than spiritually rejuvenating the person, it helps cause a spiritual downturn, just as additional branches on the tree place greater strain on the roots, and cause the tree to topple.

Since every experience in life is a message from God, it is the duty of one who saw the degradation of the *sotah* to heed the message. One should assume the Nazirite vow and abstain from the drinking of wine (*Pri HaAretz — R' Mendel of Vitebsk*).

The *Baal Shem Tov* offers a fascinating insight. The Talmud teaches that one who seeks to disqualify and cast aspersion on others projects his own shortcomings and flaws upon them (*Kiddushin* 70a).

According to the Baal Shem Tov, one cannot see a flaw in someone else unless that flaw is present in him. Something totally removed from one's realm of experience is also far removed from one's range of perception.

Seeing something negative in someone else mirrors imperfections in one's own character.[23]

One who saw the degradation of the *sotah* must say to oneself, "If I saw this, there must be an immoral flaw in my character. Let me remove it by becoming a *nazir*."[24]

---

22. **Shocked but Unmoved.** One can see someone receive a terrible punishment for an indiscretion and yet, be aroused to sin. The allure of the sin appeals to the darker side of man, egging him on.

A classic example of this is Amalek's attack on the newly freed Israelites. The Sages compare this attack to a fool who jumps into a boiling bath. Even though he is badly scalded, he cools off the water for others. Others are not as afraid to attempt the same thing. The Exodus from Egypt planted fear in the hearts of all the nations. Then Amalek attacked. Even though they were soundly defeated by the Israelites, they were no longer considered invincible.

Likewise, one who witnesses the degradation of the *sotah* will not necessarily be impressed by what he saw. He may even be drawn to sin. One must take concrete steps to insure that one not fall prey to temptation.

Midrash Tanchuma (*Shemini* 11) offers an enchanting parable.

There was once an incurable alcoholic who drove his children to their wit's end. One day they decided to take their father to see another alcoholic who was so drunk that he was rolling in filth and vomit.

The father approached the debased drunk, took one look and quietly inquired, "Where did you buy such good wine?"

The consequence of sin is sometimes its best advertisement (*R' Yosef Leib Bloch and his son R' Eliyahu Meir*).

23. **Self-Image.** The *Baal Shem Tov* once witnessed a Jew desecrating the Sabbath. He was very perturbed. "How is it possible that I witnessed the desecration of the Sabbath when I myself have never desecrated it?"

Later, the answer came to him. Once, he witnessed a coarse individual berating a Torah scholar, and he did not protest forcefully enough. Since according to the *Zohar*, a Torah scholar (whose every moment is imbued with sanctity) is the human embodiment of the Sabbath (when every moment is holy), his weak protest smacked of "desecration of the Sabbath."

[God in His mercy understands that we often cannot directly confront our own shortcomings. He lets us see the flaws of others to make us realize that we are really viewing ourselves.]

24. **Self-Awareness.** The Talmud (*Nazir* 4b) cites the Kohen Gadol Shimon HaTzaddik, who said:

I never ate of the *asham* offering of a *nazir* who had become *tamei* (impure) except for that of one man [a *nazir* whose sincerity was beyond doubt]. He came from the South. He was handsome with beautiful eyes and hair locks arranged in curls. I asked him, "My son, why have you seen fit to destroy this beautiful hair [of yours] by becoming a *nazir*?" He said to me, "I was a shepherd for my father and once as I went to draw water from the spring, I gazed

לְאָבִיו וּלְאִמּוֹ . . . לֹא יִטַּמָּא לָהֶם בְּמֹתָם

To his father or to his mother . . .
he shall not contaminate himself
to them upon their death (ibid. 7).

A regular Kohen must refrain from coming into contact with corpse-*tumah* (contamination), but may contaminate himself to his seven closest relatives. Not so the *nazir*. He may not contaminate himself to any of his relatives. What is the difference?

Sefer HaChinuch (37) explains that one's commitment to a voluntarily assumed status is much stronger than to a hereditary one. A Kohen is born with his status. His obligation to refrain from contact with death is not all encompassing, and he may contaminate himself to certain members of his family.

The *nazir*, who voluntarily assumed his elevated status, brings a stronger commitment and he may not become contaminated for anyone.

Avnei Nazer offers a similar theme. The Kohen is holy because of his familial affiliation. He therefore mourns for the very family which grants him his special status. The *nazir*, on the other hand, is holy as a result of his own decision. He

may legitimately remove himself from familial obligations. [The Kohen Gadol, who assumes the position on his own merit, is also commanded to totally avoid corpse contamination. (See *Leviticus* 21:11.)][25]

(Even a son who inherits the office from his father must be appointed as a result of his being fit for the position.)

וְעָשָׂה הַכֹּהֵן אֶחָד לְחַטָּאת וְאֶחָד לְעֹלָה וְכִפֶּר עָלָיו מֵאֲשֶׁר חָטָא עַל הַנָּפֶשׁ

The Kohen shall make one as a sin-offering
and one as an elevation-offering and he
shall provide him atonement for having
sinned regarding the person (ibid. 11).

Rashi cites the view of R' Elazar HaKappar (*Nedarim* 10a) that the *nazir* sinned by depriving himself of wine.[26] This seems to contradict what Rashi said earlier, that one who witnessed the degradation of the *sotah* should take the *nazir* vow. Should abstinence from wine be praised or condemned?[27]

R' Henach of Aleksander explains: Intrinsically wine is neither good nor bad. Wine has the power to reveal the true character of a person. As the Talmud

---

upon my reflection in the water, and noticed how handsome I was. Then my evil inclination tried to incite me to sin. I told myself, ''Why are you conceited? The world is not yours, and in the end you will be food for worms and maggots! I shall shave your head for the sake of Heaven!'' I, Shimon HaTzaddik, kissed him on his head, and said to him, ''May there be many *nezirim* like you in Israel! It is about [a *nazir* such as] you that Scripture says: *If a man . . . shall clearly utter a vow, the vow of a nazir, to abstain for the sake of Hashem*'' (*Numbers* 6:2).

''Why,'' asked *R' Nachum Mordechai* of *Novominsk*, ''did Shimon HaTzaddik find this *nazir* so extraordinary? The Torah suggests that every person who sees the degradation of the *sotah* should protect himself with a *nazir* vow. Why was this *nazir* different?''

''There is a difference,'' replied the Novominsker Rebbe. ''The one who sees the *sotah* sees a flaw in others. This *nazir* saw a flaw in himself.''

25. **Universally Related.** The Kohen Gadol is the conduit through which God endows His People with Jewish sanctity (*R' Tzadok HaKohen*). He must, therefore, view all Jews as equally related to him and cannot become contaminated even to blood relatives. He may only become contaminated to a *meis mitzvah* (one who has no other relative to care for his burial) (see *Leviticus* 21:11) (*Zekan Aharon*).

26. **Almighty's Alps.** In his old age, R' *Samson Raphael Hirsch* decided that he would take a walking tour of the Swiss Alps. His disciples were alarmed and tried to dissuade him from risking his health. R' Hirsch explained to them, ''When I come before the Almighty, what will I say when He asks me, 'Shamshon, did you see My Switzerland?' ''

27. **Paying a Price.** *Meshech Chochmah* states that assuming the Nazirite vow has many positive aspects, but they come with a price. The *nazir* may not recite *Kiddush* or *Havdalah* over wine nor may he participate in the funerals of his relatives. He therefore needs atonement and must bring a sin-offering.

This is comparable to another law. If one has a disturbing dream, one may fast on the Sabbath, but he must fast again on a weekday to atone for his fasting on the Sabbath (see *Shulchan Aruch, Orach Chaim* 188:4).

says: "When wine enters, secrets emerge" (Sanhedrin 38a). One who sees the *sotah* and realizes that he himself has vestiges of immorality in his character should abstain from wine. He, whose soul is pure, sins by his deprivation of wine, because he will not be harmed by it. It will bring forth his wonderful hidden qualities.

Rema offers an alternative approach. Behavioral extremes are not desirable. The choice path is the middle of the road. Neither indulgence nor asceticism is desirable. Rather, one should chart a course between the two. When one's behavior bends too far in one direction, it becomes necessary to bend toward the other extreme for a time, to regain the correct balance (*Rambam, Shemonah Perakim,* Introduction to *Avos*). The Talmud tells us that thirty days is the minimum time necessary for a course of action to become a habit, and to become part of one's nature. Since a primary function of the *nezirus* vow is to establish a mechanism for curbing indulgence, at least a thirty-day period of abstinence is necessary to effect behavior modification. Therefore, the term of *nezirus* is a minimum of thirty days. While the *nazir* sins by refraining from wine, the Torah allows him to commit this "sin" in order to regain the proper balance and achieve true sanctity.

It is interesting that the Scriptural source for the thirty-day minimum is the verse קָדֹשׁ יִהְיֶה, *it shall be holy* (*Numbers* 6:5) and the numerical value of יִהְיֶה is 30 (Gemara 5a). The word literally means he *will* be holy. Presumably he is not now holy; he will only *be* holy at the conclusion of this period (*Rema,* in *Toras HaOlah* 3:71).

Background

The Kohen has another role in the Temple. He must serve as a conduit to bring God's blessing to His nation.

כֹּה תְבָרְכוּ
So shall you bless (ibid. 23).

The Torah expresses the exact phrase Kohanim should utter to bless the nation even though they are never commanded to do so. Why is this so?

R' Avraham Mordechai of *Ger* explains (based on the *Zohar*) that the souls of the Kohanim overflow with the trait of kindness. By their very nature, the Kohanim yearn to bestow blessing on their fellow co-religionists. They merely need to be taught *how* to do so.

[This is reflected in the blessing the Kohanim recite before the Priestly Blessing. *Blessed are You . . . Who sanctified us with His mitzvos and commanded us to bless His nation of Israel in love.* The blessing must express their burning love for the nation.]

R' Chanoch Tzvi of Bendin (himself a Kohen) views the verse as a call to the Kohanim to bless all Jews with their trademark — their ability to love all Jews.

The Torah addresses itself to Aaron, the epitome of this love for the Jewish people (See *Avos* 1:2) and tells him: *So shall you bless them.* Inspire all Jews to be like you and to love their fellow Jews as intensely as you do. Accordingly, the blessing might be rendered "to bless His nation of Israel with [the ability to] love [each other]."[28]

---

28. **So!** *Rabbeinu Bachya* notes the *gematria* value of כה, *so,* is 25. The Kohanim receive 24 priestly gifts from the people and one from God Himself. He grants them the ability to bestow blessings on the people.

The word כה, *so,* also tells the Kohanim they must bless the people, regardless of their respective spiritual levels. *So you shall bless,* bless them just as they are because they all deserve to be blessed (*R' Yisrael of Modzhitz*).

פרשת בהעלותך ᐩ
Parashas Beha'aloscha

Background

After listing the various offerings offered by each tribe's leader at the inauguration of the Tabernacle, the Torah describes the lighting of the Menorah.

בְּהַעֲלֹתְךָ אֶת הַנֵּרֹת
When you kindle the lamps (8:2).

The Torah uses the rather unusual term בְּהַעֲלֹתְךָ (lit. *when you make* [the lights] *go up*) rather than the more conventional כְּשֶׁתַּדְלִיק, meaning when you light or ignite. *Rashi* explains that the Kohen had to hold the fire to the wick until the flame arose by itself. Homiletically this teaches that one's service of God must be fired with an enthusiasm that causes his soul's inner flame to rise by itself. Fulfilling God's will becomes second nature (*Korban HeAni*).[1]

According to *R' S.R. Hirsch,* this verse reveals an important lesson in Jewish education. When teaching our children Torah it is imperative that we must not merely impart knowledge. We must give our students the tools they need to grow independently in Torah. We must provide future generations with the ability to ignite their own flame of Torah and make it rise.[2]

אֶל מוּל פְּנֵי הַמְּנוֹרָה יָאִירוּ שִׁבְעַת הַנֵּרוֹת
toward the face of the Menorah shall the seven lamps cast light (ibid.).

The Menorah was constructed with one center branch and six peripheral branches, three on each side. This verse appears inaccurate, because only six of the lamps shone toward the middle, seventh branch. *R' Chanoch Tzvi of Bendin* offers an explanation based on the words of *Sforno.*

The central seventh lamp is symbolic of Torah. Torah flourishes if people learn it and support it.

---

1. **Fanning the Flame.** In the heart of every Jew lies a spark of Divinity which reflects the light of Torah. If the spark is merely fanned, it will burst into a blazing flame of sanctity. It is the role of the rabbis, leaders and the Kohanim to ignite that fire (*Kochavei Asher*).

2. **Intellectual Independence.** The Talmud (*Nedarim* 38a) teaches that Moses acted kindly toward the Jewish people by providing them with the tools and ability to engage in incisive Talmudic reasoning (*pilpul*). Why is this considered so virtuous?

   R' Yitzchok Hutner offers an explanation. The Talmud relates that three thousand Torah laws were forgotten during the mourning period for Moses. These laws were later retrieved by Othniel ben Kenaz by employing the incisive logic of *pilpul*.

   The underlying idea is that it is possible to independently arrive at the spiritual heritage of Moses without having studied under Moses himself. Moses gave the people the key that would make him unnecessary. A teacher is successful when he is no longer necessary.

The branches to the right symbolize those who study Torah and those to the left represent its supporters. When the two groups join forces, they succeed in igniting the flame of Torah.

Chasam Sofer suggests the verse contains a formula for successful outreach. When you seek to kindle the flame of a Jewish soul [*The soul of man is the candle of God* (*Proverbs* 20:27)] do so *toward the face of the Menorah.* The most effective means of bringing a Jew back to Judaism is through the words of Torah, symbolized by the Menorah (see *Bava Basra* 25b). The seven lamps represent the Written Law and the six orders of the Mishnah in the Oral Law.[3] Together they can ignite any Jewish soul.

וַיַּעַשׂ כֵּן אַהֲרֹן
Aaron did so (ibid. 3).

*R*ashi comments that this verse is praising Aaron that "he did not change." He did not deviate from what he was commanded. The obvious question is: Would we have thought otherwise? What kind of praise is this for Aaron? What is *Rashi* trying to teach us?

The various commentators offer different explanations. *R' Meir of Premishlan* states that Aaron's lofty spiritual height achieved through his lighting the Menorah and entering the Holy of Holies, did not change his personality. He remained a man of the people who "loved peace and chased

after it" (*Avos* 1:12). He did not change.

Sfas Emes offers a different perspective. It is only natural that one is very enthusiastic when embarking on a new venture. As the novelty wears off, the excitement wanes. Aaron performed this same mitzvah for thirty-nine consecutive years with the same enthusiasm as the first time.[4], [5]

According to *R' Leibel Eiger*, Rashi's comment addresses a human flaw. As *mitzvos* move from the abstract to the concrete stage, they gradually lose a certain degree of purity and wholeness. The mitzvah usually comes out flawed. This flaw may manifest itself in either the preparation, intent, enthusiasm, joy, or practical details in the actual doing of the mitzvah. The Torah therefore testifies that Aaron did not change. *Aaron did so . . . as Hashem had commanded Moses.* The actual fulfillment of the mitzvah was no different than when God commanded it in the abstract.[6]

וְזֶה מַעֲשֵׂה הַמְּנֹרָה
This is the workmanship of the Menorah (ibid. 4).

*R*ashi states that the word *This* indicates that Moses had difficulty visualizing the Menorah. God then showed him what it was to look like. What special difficulty did Moses encounter?

The Menorah had to be made of one solid gold piece. The Menorah is representative of the Jewish nation which must be totally united as if they are

---

3. **No Hype.** [Many people mistakenly believe that it is necessary to employ public relations, gimmicks and hype to inspire people to return to Judaism. Our belief in the power of Torah should make us realize that, as the Sages taught, "The light in it will bring them back to goodness" (*Introduction to Eichah Rabbah,* Ch. 2).]

4. **Constant Conversion.** Whenever the *Yid HaKadosh of P'shis'cha* would recite the blessing thanking God "that You did not create me a non-Jew," he would experience the feeling of being reborn as if at that very moment he was transformed from being a non-Jew to a Jew (*R' Menachem Mendel of Kotzk*).

5. **Contained Excitement.** *R' Levi Yitzchak of Berditchev* was famous for the tremendous excitement and enthusiasm he exhibited in his performance of *mitzvos.* He more than once accidentally smashed through the glass of the closet door to get to his *esrog* on Succos.

   R' Baruch of Medzhibozh once observed *R' Levi Yitzchak* in prayer. Swaying, shaking, enraptured in ecstasy, he was a living illustration of King David's words, *All of my bones proclaim: Who is like You?* (*Psalms* 35:10). R' Baruch told him, "Had Aaron fulfilled the mitzvah of lighting the Menorah like you pray he would have spilled the oil and broken the Menorah. Therefore Rashi teaches that he didn't change. He kept his burning passion for the mitzvah contained within. On the surface he remained unchanged and tranquil while inside, a flame of sanctity burned."

6. **Unyielding Commitment.** The *Satmar Rebbe, R' Yoel Teitelbaum,* eulogized *R' Aharon Kotler* with these words of *Rashi,* "Aaron did so — this teaches Aaron's praise that he did not change." Weeping he continued, "Under all conditions, even in America, R' Aharon ignored the spirit of the times and continued to teach Torah in the authentic tradition without the slightest change."

one. From the base, symbolic of the masses, to the flowerlike ornaments, symbolic of the Torah scholars, the nation must be united as one.

Moses could not understand how such a level of unification was humanly possible (*Imrei Shefer*).

[God showed Moses the Menorah which represents the light of Torah. Torah has a unifying quality which allows it to mold all Jews into one.]

Background

As a result of the episode of the Golden Calf, the firstborns lost their place as God's servants in the Tabernacle and the Temple. They were replaced by the Levites, the only tribe that did not participate in the sin.[7] The Torah describes their initiation rite.

קַח אֶת הַלְוִיִּם מִתּוֹךְ בְּנֵי יִשְׂרָאֵל וְטִהַרְתָּ אֹתָם
Take the Levites from among the Children of Israel and purify them (ibid. 6).

Why does the initiation of the Levites for service in the Tabernacle immediately follow the section pertaining to the Menorah?

Sifsei Kohen explains: Aaron was saddened that every tribe and tribal leader except the Levites had a role in the dedication of the Tabernacle. God appeased him with the privilege of preparing and kindling the Menorah.

The Levites, however, received no compensation. Therefore, God informed them that they had been chosen to serve in the Tabernacle.

R' Gedaliah Schorr notes that all the tribes (excluding the Levites) were counted in the census. They numbered 600,000. The Torah contains 600,000 letters. The Sages teach us that the word יִשְׂרָאֵל is a mnemonic for יֵשׁ שִׁשִּׁים רִבּוֹא אוֹתִיּוֹת לַתּוֹרָה, *there are 600,000 letters in the Torah*. Every Jewish soul is rooted in a letter of the Torah. The Levites are rooted not in the Written Torah, but in the Oral Torah. Their role is to spread Torah among the masses and serve as their spiritual leaders. [Since they had no need for the atonement granted for the Golden Calf through the thirteen attributes of mercy, the Levites were granted the ability to employ the thirteen Hermeunetic Principles, which serve as a major tool in expounding the Oral Torah. These are the principles used to explicate the Written Torah. (*Zekan Aharon*).]

וְכִבְּסוּ בִגְדֵיהֶם וְהִטֶּהָרוּ
and let them immerse their garments, and they shall become pure (ibid. 7).

"And they shall become pure" is a commandment in itself rather than a result of immersing the clothes. What does this commandment entail?

Mei HaShiloach offers a homiletic explanation. The Torah teaches that one must erect for oneself spiritual fences to assure following the proper spiritual path. They are a far more effective deterrent than the severity of the sin itself.[8] When one, on his own volition, surrounds Biblical prohibitions with spiritual fences, one takes them very much to heart. The following incident underscores this point.

A Jew was once tempted to sin. The evil incli-

---

7. **Holy Stubborness.** In the course of this section the Torah mentions *the Children of Israel* thirteen times. This alludes to the fact that were it not for the Levites' refusal to participate in the sin of the Golden Calf, the Jewish people might have been, God forbid, destroyed. In the merit of the Levites, God granted His people the thirteen attributes of Divine Mercy to achieve atonement.

God commanded Moses to separate the Levites from among the Children of Israel in order to provide atonement for them (see verse 19). The thirteen references allude to the reason they were separated.

The people are referred to once in this section (verse 9) as *the entire assembly of the Children of Israel*. This alludes to the women of Israel who refused to take part in the construction of the Golden Calf (*Meshech Chochmah*).

8. **Self-Discipline.** The Talmud (*Nedarim* 8a) states. "One may invoke an oath (and the oath takes force) to fulfill a mitzvah." The Talmud then challenges this premise and says, "One is already under the oath [taken at the revelation at Sinai]. How can the new oath take hold [since one set of behavior cannot be mandated by more than one oath]?"

The Talmud replies that the oath does not oblige in a technical sense. Nevertheless, the oath is not deemed in vain, because it encourages one to fulfill the mitzvah.

The question is obvious. If the oath taken at Sinai did not cause this person to feel obligated, why should the new oath motivate him more?

The answer is that internal motivation is much more powerful than external coercion (*Tzidkas HaTzaddik* 55).

nation was so powerful that the righteous man simply ignored the severity of the infraction. Suddenly he stopped, thinking to himself, "Perhaps this is not forbidden but what actual pleasure will my action provide God?" At that moment he began to see the enormity of the sin.

וְהַעֲמַדְתָּ אֶת הַלְוִיִּם . . . וְהֵנַפְתָּ אֹתָם
You shall stand the Levites . . .
and wave them (ibid. 13).

The three-stage process of initiating the Levites into the Tabernacle service mirrors the stages one must undergo to become a true servant of God. First, one must be totally stripped of any vestige of impurity. By symbolically passing the razor over one's entire flesh, one severs one's ties with this world's physical pursuits and commits oneself to a life of purity.

Next, one must attain a sense of steadiness and spiritual balance. This is why they had to stand.

Finally, they were ready to be lifted by Aaron. This symbolizes their spiritual ascent. This is the goal of every serious servant of God.[9]

בְּיוֹם הַכֹּתִי כָל בְּכוֹר בְּאֶרֶץ מִצְרַיִם הִקְדַּשְׁתִּי אֹתָם לִי
on the day I struck every firstborn in the land
of Egypt I sanctified them for Myself (ibid. 17).

Although God created all of us and we are therefore His, He granted us the opportunity to earn our right to exist by following His word.[10] Our Sages teach that once the forces of destruction are unleashed by God, they do not differentiate between the righteous and the wicked. On the night of the Exodus, when God sent these forces of destruction to kill the firstborn of Egypt even the Jewish firstborn were vulnerable. They were only spared by Divine grace.

At that moment the Jewish firstborn lost their ability to earn their existence by adhering to God's word. They became completely His and their existence was dependent on His Will (*Zekan Aharon*).

וְלֹא יִהְיֶה בִּבְנֵי יִשְׂרָאֵל נֶגֶף בְּגֶשֶׁת בְּנֵי־יִשְׂרָאֵל אֶל הַקֹּדֶשׁ
so that there will not be a plague among
the Children of Israel when the Children
of Israel approach the Sanctuary (ibid. 19).

There are two ways a Jew can be drawn to his Maker. God first tries to inspire one to realize the beauty of Torah. If this course fails, God must employ stronger means. They may take the form of physical pain and emotional suffering.

The first path is obviously the preferable one. We have the option to take it. God only resorts to more aggressive means when He is left with no other options.

The Torah voices the hope that God succeeds in bringing us toward Him with goodness and kindness *so that there will not be a plague among the Children of Israel when the Children of Israel approach the Sanctuary (Imrei Noam).*[11]

---

9. **Constant Climb.** *R' Ben Zion Ostrovtzer* lived into his late 90's and merited to be a *chassid* of many of Poland's greatest chassidic Rebbes. *R' Henach* of *Aleksander* once told him, "In P'shis'cha I was stripped of my spiritual negativity. In Kotzk I was placed on my feet and taught how to stand straight. In Ger I was finally able to attain something in the way of spiritual heights."

10. **Self Providers.** The Talmud (*Pesachim* 118a) teaches that the twenty-six times the phrase *"For His kindness is forever"* appears in *Psalms* 136 allude to the twenty-six generations from Creation until the revelation at Sinai, when God sustained the world by His kindness alone. Does this imply that in the post-Sinai generations He no longer sustains us with His kindness?

R' Gershon Henach of Radzin explains: One can support a poor person with a constant handout. A much greater kindness is to provide him with a job and a means to provide for himself and his family.

Before Sinai, a man could earn his existence in very limited ways. God provided him with life by means of a handout.

At Sinai He increased His magnanimity and gave us His Torah and its *mitzvos,* the means through which man can support himself.

11. **In Good Times.** *R' Shmuel Alter* describes this idea in contemporary terms.

Many of our brethren come to the synagogue infrequently. Unless, God forbid, a family member is sick (and they

וּמִבֶּן חֲמִשִּׁים שָׁנָה יָשׁוּב מִצְּבָא הָעֲבֹדָה וְלֹא יַעֲבֹד עוֹד. וְשֵׁרֵת אֶת אֶחָיו

From fifty years of age he shall withdraw from the legion of work and no longer work. He shall minister with his brethren (ibid. 25-26).

Rashi notes that although a 50-year-old Levite stops carrying the pieces of the Tabernacle, he still performs other rites such as the closing of the gates. Why does Rashi specifically mention closing the gates rather than opening them?

Furthermore, in explaining the dictum "a 50-year-old for advice," (*Avos* 5:21) *Rav* cites our verse: *He shall minister with his brethren.* What will he minister? He will offer them advice.

What type of advice can the 50-year-old Levite offer his brethren, and how can this explanation be reconciled with that of Rashi?

Chidushei HaRim answers this question with a story.

A man got lost in a forest and spent years wandering through it, unable to find his way out. Suddenly, in the distance he saw an old man headed toward him. Overjoyed, he ran over to him. "Tell me, how does one get out of this forest?" he inquired. The old man replied sadly," I too am lost. For seventy years I have been hopelessly wandering here, unable to find my way out. One thing I *can* tell you however; don't follow the path I took, for it leads nowhere. As for the proper path, you will have to find it yourself."

The 50-year-old can stand guard and close the doors which lead to the road of futility. He can offer advice on how to avoid life's potential pitfalls.

The *Chafetz Chaim* elaborated: At the age of 50, the time has come to shift one's focus. Instead of putting one's energies into this world, one should begin spending his time and efforts on Torah, *mitzvos* and lovingkindness in preparation for the World to Come. The Friday of life is at hand and one must prepare for the Great Sabbath.

At this stage of life one can help others with sound advice on how to live.

וַעֲבֹדָה לֹא יַעֲבֹד

but work he shall not perform (ibid. 26).

Seemingly the Torah could suffice by saying וְלֹא יַעֲבֹד, *he shall not work,* rather than using the repetitive phrase וַעֲבֹדָה לֹא יַעֲבֹד. Homiletically the Torah teaches that at this stage of his life the Levite serves God by refraining from working.

We are often tempted to be innovative in our service of God and to do things which we think will add to His greater glory or find favor in His eyes.

For example, one whose doctor forbids him to fast on Yom Kippur may want to show self-sacrifice and fast regardless of his doctor's instructions. This is wrong. In this circumstance he serves God by eating, not fasting. Here his work is not to work (*Melo HaRo'im*).

Background

The next section discusses the second *pesach*-offering for those who were ineligible to bring it at the proper time.

וְלֹא יָכְלוּ לַעֲשֹׂת הַפֶּסַח

and could not make the pesach-offering (9:6).

Those who were impure at the time of the original *pesach*-offering were not allowed to perform the mitzvah. Why does the Torah describe them as "unable" to bring the offering rather than as forbidden to do so?

Divrei Shaul explains: Righteous people become so accustomed to following the will of God that eventually their limbs develop an almost automatic instinct which does not allow them to act in a manner which runs contrary to His will.

An example is the Torah's description of Abraham at the *Akeidah. Abraham stretched out his hand and took the knife to slaughter his son (Genesis* 22:10).

Since, ultimately, God did not want Abraham to slaughter Isaac, his hand resisted taking the knife.

---

wish to offer a prayer for his recovery) or they are mourners who need to recite the *Kaddish,* they only occasionally come.

God cries out, "Come see Me in good times, as well as the bad. Don't only come when you feel you need Me. Come constantly and joyfully and let us enjoy each other's company."

Abraham had to forcefully stretch out his hand in order to do so.

Those who were spiritually impure at the time of the first *pesach*-offering desperately wanted to fulfill the mitzvah because they knew that if the entire congregation is impure, it nevertheless sacrifices the *pesach*-offering (*Pesachim* 77a).[12] However, they *could not make the pesach-offering*. They felt physical resistance from their limbs which were unwilling to comply.

They therefore approached Moses and asked, *Why should we be diminished* (verse 7)? "Why do we feel a physical resistance?" Moses informed them that an impure individual must wait for the second *pesach*-offering. Their limbs were right. God did not want them to bring the offering in a state of impurity.

R' Tzvi Hirsh of Dinov offers a variation on this theme: The 248 positive commandments correspond to the 248 limbs of the human body. Every physical limb and its corresponding spiritual one achieve perfection by the performance of its parallel mitzvah.[13]

This is how our Patriarchs were able to fulfill the entire Torah even prior to its revelation. Every one of their limbs craved perfection and perceived what had to be done to achieve it.[14]

Those who were impure felt an irresistible urge to perform the *pesach*-offering. Thus they questioned, "If we are really absolved from the mitzvah, why do we sense this urge to perform it?"

They were right! They needed the mitzvah and God gave them a second chance to perform it.

לָמָּה נִגָּרַע
why should we be diminished (ibid. 7).

According to the Sages these people had been exposed to corpse-contamination by either carrying Joseph's bier from Egypt to bury him in the Land of Israel or by chancing upon an unidentified corpse and burying it. In either instance, the contamination came as a result of having fulfilled a mitzvah. In accord with the dictum that מִצְוָה גוֹרֶרֶת מִצְוָה, one mitzvah brings another in its wake (see *Avos* 4:2), they could not understand how the first mitzvah could deprive them of the opportunity to fulfill the second (*Sforno*).[15]

---

12. **Individual Sanctuaries.** The theoretical possibility of an individual being contaminated at the time of the *pesach*-offering certainly existed when the Jews were initially commanded to sacrifice it. Why didn't the Torah address the issue immediately?

R' Meir Simchah of Dvinsk offers a solution based on the *Sforno*. Before the Jewish people sinned with the Golden Calf, there was no need for a Tabernacle to unite them. Every individual Jew encapsulated the sanctity of the entire congregation. Prior to the Golden Calf, the *pesach*-offering could be brought by every individual, regardless of one's spiritual status [just as presently, if the majority of the nation is impure, one need not wait until *Pesach Sheni*]. After the Golden Calf and the nation's resultant spiritual fall, it became necessary for the individual to meld into the nation in order to enable God's spirit to dwell within him.

Only now, the first time the *pesach*-offering was brought since the sin of the Golden Calf, did the question of impurity assume relevance.

13. **Personal Perfection.** *R' Chaim Vital* teaches that Moses yearned to enter the Holy Land, because several of the *mitzvos* which are of an agricultural nature can only be performed there (see *Sotah* 14a). Even though he was not obligated to fulfill these *mitzvos* outside the Land, he yearned for the opportunity to keep *all* of the *mitzvos* so that he could attain spiritual perfection.

14. **Spiritual Survival.** The survival instinct in people is extremely powerful. In moments of crisis, when life hangs in the balance, they are able to instinctively save themselves, without ever having received any survival training.

Our spiritual ancestors viewed doing God's will as a life and death issue. Even before being taught, they knew exactly what they needed to do to spiritually survive this world (*Simchas Aharon*).

15. **Soul Sacrifice.** Sometimes a person must pay a spiritual price to follow God's word. The *Alter of Slabodka* would frequently tell his students that a Jew must be ready to exhibit מְסִירוּת נֶפֶשׁ, self-sacrifice, for a fellow Jew. "Note," the *Alter* would say, "that we are asked to sacrifice our souls, not our bodies (מְסִירוּת נֶפֶשׁ literally means "sacrifice of the soul")."

For example, *R' Moshe Feinstein* ruled that yeshivah students must give up 10 percent of their time to teach others who are weaker or less committed than themselves. That time, which could have been used to further their own

Really, they should have been absolved of the obligation to bring the *pesach*-offering. When God saw how desperately they wanted to do the mitzvah, He provided them with a second opportunity. Their heartfelt cry, "Why should we be diminished?" was the catalyst for this new mitzvah (*Chidushei HaRim, Tiferes Shlomo*).[16]

According to R' Yechezkel Levenstein we are taught here the strength of willpower. We are often presented with difficulties which seem to be insurmountable. One is tempted to give up hope and not even bother to attempt any solution.

These contaminated people teach us that a person must do his utmost and try to achieve the impossible. Sometimes it is this valiant, yet seemingly futile attempt which arouses Divine assistance.

When God is on one's side, the word impossible does not exist.[17]

עִמְדוּ וְאֶשְׁמְעָה מַה יְצַוֶּה יהוה לָכֶם
Stand and I will hear what Hashem will command you (ibid. 8).

Moses answered with the self-confidence of a disciple who is sure his master will answer his question (*Rashi*). However, this seems at odds with the description of Moses as the most humble of men.

R' Aharon of Karlin explains: Moses was truly humble. In his opinion, his great level of prophecy was the result of his being the shepherd of God's flock. Thus he told them, "Stand here with me, for in your merit God will answer." Moses does not say, "I will hear what Hashem commands *me*"; rather, he says "what Hashem will command *you*." If you leave I will not merit God's instruction.

Moses did not rely on his own merit but rather on the broken-heartedness of the supplicants.

Jews who are broken hearted over a missed opportunity to do God's mitzvah will undoubtedly be answered, because God never rejects a broken and downtrodden heart (see *Psalms* 34:19).[18]

אוֹ בְדֶרֶךְ רְחֹקָה
or on a distant road (ibid. 10).

According to *Rashi* this even includes someone who was just outside the doorstep of the Temple courtyard when the *pesach*-offering was slaughtered.

Distance is not always geographic. It may be

personal spiritual development, is the price they must pay to help a fellow Jew with his spiritual progress.

Although the mitzvah which caused them to become impure prevented them from bringing the *pesach*-offering on time, this was the spiritual price they had to pay.

16. **Crying Our Way In.** R' Chanoch Tzvi of Bendin remarked: "We should follow the example of those contaminated people. We too suffer from all sorts of spiritual contaminations which keep us distant from God. We too must cry out, 'Why shall we be diminished?' Our cries may help us pierce the iron curtains that separate us from God."

17. **True Trust.** In these poetic terms, the *Chazon Ish* describes his trust in God:

"When man meets up with circumstances which will naturally result in danger and catastrophe, it is 'normal' to fear the predictable outcome. One's spirit is frozen and his resolve is so weakened that one forgets that the laws of nature have absolutely no power over us and that nothing can stand in the way of God's salvation. He can create new circumstances which will change all the predictable results.

"Self-restraint at that critical moment and the ability to infuse oneself with the absolute truth, that in reality no danger lurks since fate is completely in His hands, this is true trust in God. This deep-rooted faith of the true believer releases him from the grip of fear and grants him the strength to believe that salvation is perfectly possible. To the believer, the probability of a negative outcome is no more viable than that of a happy ending, for nothing happens but by the decree of the All-Powerful One" (*Emunah U'Vitachon* 2:1).

18. **Eternal Optimists.** The term *stand* is an expression for prayer (See *Berachos* 26b). Moses told the people to pray to God from the depths of their hearts that He grant them the opportunity to do the mitzvah. Their heartfelt cry and the burning desire it expressed had the power to elicit the word of God just as the Jews had initially been given the Torah in response to their resounding expression of desire for it: *We shall do and we shall listen (Exodus* 24:7).

The unwillingness to give up hope was itself the catalyst for the revelation of a new mitzvah whose very message is "never give up hope." There is always another opportunity. Even one who is spiritually distant or impure can still find his way to God (*R' Tzadok HaKohen*).

emotional as well. A person can stand right outside the Temple Courtyard and yet be distant from God. The *Talmud Yerushalmi* (*Pesachim* 9:2) comments: "Not the road is distant, but rather the person is distant" (*R' M. Rotenberg*).[19]

R' Yechezkel of Kuzmir addresses the obvious question. If the person was at the doorstep, why didn't he go inside?

Apparently, the person was humble and thought himself unworthy of joining the sanctified groups who were offering the *pesach*-offering. He attempted to enter but his feet refused to go. "How can I participate?" he asked himself. When the second group entered he tried again but was filled with a sense of shame when he realized his spiritual level. A third attempt at joining the last group was no more successful than the previous ones.

God, seeing how truly humble he was, said, "For you, my dear child, I will give you your own special holiday."[20]

Background

The Torah now describes the process of encampment and traveling that the Jews followed during their sojourn in the Wilderness.

כֵּן יִהְיֶה תָמִיד, הֶעָנָן יְכַסֶּנּוּ וּמַרְאֵה-אֵשׁ לָיְלָה

So it would always be: The cloud would cover it and an appearance of fire at night (ibid. 16).

Homiletically, the Tabernacle serves as a symbol of Jewish history. Although in many periods of our history, we have been surrounded by ominously dark clouds, we never gave up hope of salvation. Even in the darkest of nights we were able to see the light of a fire promising us that the dark clouds would disperse (*R' Shmuel Alter*).

עַל פִּי יהוה יַחֲנוּ וְעַל-פִּי יהוה יִסָּעוּ

According to the word of Hashem would they encamp and according to the word of Hashem would they journey (ibid. 23).

According to the *Shelah HaKadosh* this verse teaches us that one should mention God's Name at every step of life, regardless of its insignificance. For example, as one departs on his way let him say "I am, with Hashem's help, traveling to my destination where I hope, if Hashem so wills it, to stay for a few days." When one arrives he should say, "Thanks to Hashem I have arrived here where I hope to remain until, with His help, I will return home."

When one thinks in this manner, all of one's actions will enhance the glory of God.[21]

---

19. **Near Yet Very Far.** The *Kotzker Rebbe* interprets the verse *and the people saw and trembled and stood from afar* (*Exodus* 20:15) at the Revelation at Sinai as follows: They saw and swayed back and forth in rapturous devotion, yet in reality they stood from afar.

20. **Far Sightful.** King David teaches, *for though Hashem is exalted, He notes the lowly; and the High One makes Himself known from afar* (*Psalms* 138:6).

The *Maggid of Kozhnitz* offers a slightly different reading. Although Hashem is exalted, those who are humble and lowly can still see and perceive Him. However, one who is arrogant is very far from even knowing God, let alone from seeing and perceiving His Presence. The *high one* makes himself known from afar.

21. **Reserved for the King.** Many Jews observe the custom of reciting a short Kabbalistic prayer before the performance of a mitzvah, dedicating the mitzvah toward the goal of the *unification of God and His Divine Presence* in the world.

The renowned *Noda BiYehudah* was vehemently opposed to this practice based on theological considerations. Furthermore, he questioned the necessity for the prayer given the fact that we recite a blessing before performing a mitzvah (see *Responsa Noda BiYehudah Yoreh Deah* I 93).

R' Yehoshua of Belz respond with a parable.

A merchant wanted to send goods to the royal palace. Fearful that thieves may steal the goods en route, he marked every case with the words "For the king." This way he was sure the thieves, fearful of punishment from the king himself, would refrain from tampering with the goods.

Whenever a Jew wants to do a mitzvah there are forces of evil which seek to thwart his efforts. To insure that they will not succeed in doing so, he declares that "The mitzvah is for *the* King — do not try to tamper with it." King David alludes to this. *My heart is astir with a good theme, I say, "My works are for the King"* (*Psalms* 45:2). My heart desires to do something good (a mitzvah); therefore I said, "My action is for *the* King."

R' Naftali Trop sees this verse describing the intimate relationship between God and His people.

An infant cuddled in his mother's arms has no place of his own. Wherever his mother goes, he goes as well, because they are inseparably linked. Her place is his.

In the Wilderness, the Jewish people were borne by God. They traveled or encamped only by His Word. When the Divine Presence moved, so did they. They were always in God's place.

Background

God commands Moses to fashion silver trumpets which were to be used to summon the nation and to signal when the people were to break up camp and begin traveling. The Torah also lists other uses for the trumpets.

עֲשֵׂה לְךָ שְׁתֵּי חֲצוֹצְרֹת כֶּסֶף ... וְהָיוּ לְךָ לְמִקְרָא הָעֵדָה

Make for yourself two silver trumpets ...
and they shall be yours for the
summoning of the assembly (10:2).

Sifre interprets the word לְךָ, *for yourself,* as meaning exclusively for you. The other vessels and instruments made for the Tabernacle under Moses' supervision were also used by later generations. The trumpets were used exclusively in Moses' time (see *Menachos* 28b). Why were the trumpets different?

According to *R' Yechezkel Abramsky,* this teaches us an important lesson regarding Jewish leadership.

The message of Torah is unchanging and eternal. We say every day at the end of our prayers, "I believe with perfect faith that this Torah will not be exchanged and there will not be a different Torah given to us by the Creator Whose Name is Blessed" (*Rambam's 13 Principles of Faith*). The leaders of each generation must discover the appropriate means to transmit this eternal message to the people. If contemporary leaders attempt to use a method employed by leaders of previous generations, the message may fall on deaf ears. While the type of blasts of the trumpets remain the same, the trumpets themselves must be new. Future generations may not use those of Moses.[22]

R' Yoel of Satmar offers an additional thought.

Although Jewish leaders possess great talents, their ability to unite and exercise influence over the people is nothing short of miraculous. This quality of leadership cannot be inherited, but must be granted directly by God. In every generation God bestows this gift to those destined to lead.[23]

The trumpets which called the people to gather are not passed from generation to generation. Every generation must have a leader who is endowed by God with those qualities necessary to lead *that* generation.

וְאִם בְּאַחַת יִתְקָעוּ וְנוֹעֲדוּ אֵלֶיךָ הַנְּשִׂיאִים רָאשֵׁי אַלְפֵי יִשְׂרָאֵל

If they sound a long blast with
one the leaders shall assemble to you,
the heads of Israel's thousands (ibid. 4).

Why are the leaders called with the long blast of one trumpet?

Olelos Ephraim offers the following explanation. Leaders' influence over the masses is undermined when the leadership itself suffers from disunity.

The Torah therefore teaches that if *the long* unbroken *blast* made *by one* trumpet is to unite the community, the leaders themselves must unite as one.

---

22. **Trumpet of Torah.** Besides his towering stature as a Talmudic and Halachic scholar (as evidenced by his monumental *Chazon Yechezkel* on the *Tosefta*), *R' Yechezkel Abramsky* was also a gifted writer who was able to express the eternal truths of Torah in a polished, poetic, literary style.

Deeply rooted as he was in the timeless "old-fashioned" Torah, he gave it a new voice which deeply influenced his contemporaries.

23. **Confidently Humble.** The *Chasam Sofer* was extremely humble in all areas except for two. He was unbending in his stand against the Reformers of his times, and completely confident in the veracity of his halachic rulings. He once said, "God, in His Mercy, grants every generation a person who enjoys special Divine assistance rendering halachic decisions. This way the Jewish people are assured they will be able to correctly fulfill His Torah. In this generation, I am that person."

We understand that the trumpets were necessary to assemble the entire nation. Why were they needed to summon the twelve heads of the tribes? Why not simply call them by name?

An obstacle to unity is jealousy. It is aroused when one person is accorded greater honor than another. Were the tribal heads to be summoned separately, those called later might be envious of those called earlier. To avoid this the Torah commands that all the tribal heads be summoned simultaneously by means of one long blast (*R' Shmuel Alter*).[24]

וְכִי תָבֹאוּ מִלְחָמָה בְּאַרְצְכֶם עַל הַצַּר הַצֹּרֵר אֶתְכֶם וַהֲרֵעֹתֶם בַּחֲצֹצְרֹת

When you go to wage war in your Land against an enemy who oppresses you, you shall sound short blasts of the trumpets (ibid. 9).

The Torah in *Parashas Ki Seitzei* (*Deuteronomy* 21:10) also speaks of Jews going to war. There, the Torah seems to assure victory: *When you will go out to war against your enemies and Hashem, your God, will deliver them into your hand.*

In our *sidrah*, however, the Torah offers no guarantees. Here, we are enjoined to pray and blow the trumpets, crying out to God to help us conquer our foes. Why would the Torah only provide guarantees in one place but not in the other?

Nesivos Shalom explains: There are two important principles which every warrior must remember. The best defense is to attack and he must truly believe in his ability to beat the enemy.

These principles are also important in the constant war one wages with his evil inclination. One is almost assured of victory if one takes the initiative and attacks first. In *Deuteronomy*, the Torah speaks of going out to wage war. If one is confident and stages a frontal attack before evil inclination attains even the smallest foothold, God will deliver *the enemy* into one's hand.

This verse speaks of a case in which war comes to one's own land. Once the evil inclination has procured a foothold, it is much more difficult to stage a counteroffensive.[25] When the oppressor has one in spiritual retreat, one must cry out

---

24. **Say It Again!** The Talmud (*Sanhedrin* 102a) relates that God spoke to Jeroboam ben Nebat and told him "I, you and [David] the son of Jesse will stroll together in the Garden of Eden." Jeroboam asked, "Who will be first?" When God replied that David would be first Jeroboam said, "In that case, I am not interested."

The incident is puzzling. God made the order perfectly clear by saying, "I, you and the son of Jesse." Why did Jeroboam ask who would be first?

R' Chaim Shmulevitz explains: "He wanted to hear it again." The pursuit of honor is so obsessive that one can never have enough. He has to hear again and again that he, not the next fellow, will receive the honor. If the other person is first, ahead of him, the honor is worthless in his eyes.

R' Chaim would often relate a personal anecdote.

One of the prized students of the Mirrer Yeshivah in Poland left to America. He wrote a letter to *R' Yerucham Levovitz*, the famed *Mashgiach* (spiritual mentor) of the yeshivah, which R' Yerucham read to the students. In the middle of the letter the student wrote that he had repeated a deep Talmudic discourse of R' Chaim which the American public had enjoyed immensely. When R' Yerucham read the words "a Talmudic discourse of R' Chaim," he was looking directly at *R' Chaim Shmulevitz*.

R' Chaim remarked, "I knew the student was referring to *R' Chaim Brisker*. Nevertheless, I was overcome with intense pleasure when R' Yerucham read that sentence."

25. **Unwelcome Occupier.** A man once possessed an insatiable desire to acquire his friend's house. He begged, pleaded and cajoled his friend to sell it, but to no avail. Finally, in a desperate attempt to rid himself of the other man's incessant pleas, the owner agreed to sell him a tiny space in the house — large enough for a hook to hang a hat. The owner was paid handsomely but he soon realized his mistake. The buyer began to appear every day and request passage to his "area." The owner had to allow him to enter. He eventually became such a nuisance that the owner was ready to give up the house and move out.

Such is the way of the evil persuader. He pesters us incessantly until we allow him a foothold in our lives. That is the beginning of the end. He soon drives us out of our house and home, and assumes total control of our bodies and souls. Hence, the *Mishnah* (*Avos* 2:6) teaches that *the evil inclination removes a person from the world* (*Baal Shem Tov*).

to God with a broken heart (symbolized by the short, broken trumpet blasts) and beg for His assistance.

**וְנִזְכַּרְתֶּם לִפְנֵי ה׳
אֱלֹקֵיכֶם וְנוֹשַׁעְתֶּם מֵאֹיְבֵיכֶם**
*And you shall be recalled before
Hashem, your God, and you shall
be saved from your foes* (ibid.).

Rambam (*Hilchos Taanios* 1:1-3) writes that the trumpet blasts were a call to repentance. If we respond to tragedy with prayer and heart-felt tears, we will realize that distress is the result of sin. This realization will alleviate the distress.

Prayer is not a miracle cure which immediately removes an imminent threat. When we forget God, He "forgets" us; when we remember Him, He remembers us. Trumpets and prayer sound the alarm and awaken us to the reality that things just don't happen by themselves. This reawakened sensitivity has the potential to save us.

Rambam continues: "If they do not cry out or sound the trumpets but rather say that what happened was a natural occurrence or a mere coincidence, they exhibit gross cruelty and cause others to continue to maintain their evil path. Misfortune and tragedy will continue to befall them. If God brings pain upon us so that we repent, yet we insist that it is all coincidence, He will continue to punish us."

God's behavior toward us reflects our behavior toward Him. If man acts as though life were nothing but an uncontrolled chain of accidental events, God responds by figuratively hiding His face and allowing our lives to be controlled by natural consequences.

In this light, R' Aharon of Karlin explains the words of King David, *I call out to God in praise, and I will be saved from my enemies* (Psalms 18:4).

When we suffer, we beseech God for help and recite *Psalms.* Unfortunately, our minds and hearts are so entirely focused on our distress, we forget to even think about the meaning of the words we utter.

This is not the way to achieve salvation. Instead of narrowly focusing on our plight and the Divine help we desperately seek, we must concentrate on what we are saying and put our energy into really speaking of God's praises.

If we truly praise Him, our new connection will automatically bring salvation in its wake.[26]

Background

The Torah describes the tribal formations that the Israelites assumed throughout their forty-year trek in the Wilderness.

**וּבְיוֹם שִׂמְחַתְכֶם וּבְמוֹעֲדֵיכֶם
וּבְרָאשֵׁי חָדְשֵׁכֶם**
*On the day of your gladness,
and on your festivals and on
your new moons* (ibid. 10).

On those holy days when a communal *mussaf*-offering was brought the Kohanim would sound the trumpets. According to *Sifre, the day of your gladness* refers to the Sabbath when a *mussaf* was offered.

Many commentaries question this explanation. Joy is mandated only on the festivals. The Torah never speaks of an obligation to rejoice on the Sabbath. (See *Deuteronomy* 16:14.) [On the Sabbath there is a mitzvah of עוֹנֶג שַׁבָּת, to experience physical pleasure; however, the mitzvah of שִׂמְחָה (joy) is exclusive to the festivals.]

Nesivos Shalom explains: The Sages teach that the Sabbath is a sample of the World to Come

---

26. **Full Concentration.** *Sefer HaChassidim* (158) writes a similar thought regarding personal supplication.

"If you need God's help with regard to making a living, don't limit your concentration to the relevant blessing. Likewise, if you are ill or know someone who needs to be cured don't focus your heart exclusively on the blessing which begins "Heal us, Hashem." If you do, they (the angels above) say about you, 'He thinks he only needs these specific things from God.'

"Similarly, don't limit your concentration to the portion of the prayers which express personal supplication because this engenders an indictment above. 'Why accept his prayers?' they argue. He is only interested in himself. God's honor and praise mean little to him.'"

(*Berachos* 57b). The World to Come is a time when all of Creation will achieve its ultimate purpose and God's glory will be fully recognized. It is a time when all of Creation will rejoice, having finally fulfilled its mission.

The Sabbath, as a "prelude" to the World to Come, is not a day when *we* must rejoice. Joy is an intrinsic component of the day because it mirrors the unparalleled rejoicing of a world which has achieved its fulfillment.[27]

וְהָיִיתָ לָּנוּ לְעֵינָיִם
you have been as eyes for us (ibid. 31)

Moses seeks to convince Jethro to remain with the Israelites. Certainly Moses did not mean to offer Jethro a leadership position. How was Jethro to serve as the nation's eyes?

R' Eliyahu Meir Bloch suggests that Jethro was able to add an element to the educational process of the Jewish people which only he could provide.

To guide people, it is often advantageous to expose them to towering spiritual personalities who can serve as role models. Often, they may be simply too great too emulate. It is therefore imperative that they also encounter self-made men who have built themselves up spiritually.

Jethro was such a man. By shaking off the shackles of his past and overcoming the almost insurmountable obstacles on his path to God, Jethro transformed his life and served as a lesson for the Jewish people.

Moses asked Jethro to stay so that the Jews could look to him for inspiration.

Kli YaKar submits a different perspective. Jethro left family, country, prestige and power to come serve God in the Wilderness. All the more so, must those, fortunate to have been born Jews, be ready to demonstrate self-sacrifice on His behalf. The nation recognized Jethro's courage and tried to emulate his strong sense of commitment.

וַיְהִי בִּנְסֹעַ הָאָרֹן
When the Ark would journey (ibid. 35).

To avoid consecutively mentioning three sins of the Jewish people, the Torah interjects with these verses. They are set apart both at the beginning and the end by means of an inverted letter *nun* (*Rashi*).

Why was the inverted *nun* chosen as the parentheses?

The Talmud explains why the letter *nun* is not represented in the alphabetical *Psalm* 145 (*Ashrei*) recited thrice daily. The *nun* represents fall (נְפִילָה in Hebrew) and King David did not want to speak of the fall and failing of the Jewish people (*Berachos* 4b). Therefore, when the Torah wants to isolate Jewish sins, it employs the letter symbolic of spiritual fall.

Why then are the *nuns* inverted? The answer lies in a Midrash which teaches that God is compared to a deer. Just as a deer turns its head backwards when in flight so God always "turns His head" toward us even when He seems to be running away. Even when we sin God does not even momentarily remove his attention from us.

Thus the *nun,* symbolic of falling, is inverted to teach this lesson. Like a deer that turns its head backwards, the *nun,* symbolic of God, "looks back" ignoring our flaws and focusing on the good in us (*R' Yonasan Eibeschutz*).

According to *Ramban* (v. 35) the first of the Jews' three sins was that (in the words of the Midrash) "They left Mount Sinai like a schoolboy running away from school." The second was their complaint regarding the conditions they encountered on their journey. The third was their complaint regarding the manna.

They were punished for the last two sins but not for the first. Why?

R' Yaakov Naiman offered an explanation based on an insight of the *Mesillas Yesharim* (Chapter 4). Regarding the mind-set of the true seeker, he writes:

---

27. **Perfect Joy.** This theme finds expression in the *zemiros* (Sabbath-table hymns). *On the sanctified day of Sabbath rejoice and exult as those who received the gift of God's heritage (Kol Mekadeish Sh'vi'i).*

Just as both the upper and lower worlds rejoiced at Sinai because man and Creation had reached the pinnacle of perfection, so too is the Sabbath permeated with the joy of a perfected world (*Nesivos Shalom*).

"One who seeks spiritual perfection is most disappointed and frustrated when that level of perfection remains elusive. Lack of perfection is the most insufferable of fates for such a person."

When the Jewish people left Mount Sinai like immature school children, they caused their own spiritual estrangement. What greater punishment is there?[28]

---

28. **Self-Inflicted Punishment.** One who is exiled from his family and his father's home experiences a terrible sense of loneliness. He feels abandonment, vulnerability to the elements and exposure to all types of danger.

Likewise, when we exile ourselves from our Father, we immediately feel lonely. *"And as for me, closeness to God is true good,"* says King David (*Psalms* 73:28). When in God's presence, we feel fine. One feels isolated when he leaves His Presence.

When the Jews ran from Sinai there was no need to punish them. The spiritual distancing from God was itself the most terrible of punishments (*R' Yaakov Naiman*).

פרשת שלח ⠹
Parashas Shelach

Background

The time has come to occupy *Eretz Yisrael;* the nation stands ready to enter. Lacking perfect faith the Jewish people insist on sending spies to survey the Land. Unfortunately, the spies' reports are so disheartening, they deal a severe blow to the nation's faith in God Who had promised them the Land was good and that He would enable them to conquer it.

שְׁלַח לְךָ אֲנָשִׁים
Send forth men, if you please (13:2).

Midrash Tanchuma (cited in *Rashi*) explains the connection between Miriam's criticism of Moses (see *Numbers* 12:1-15) and the story of the spies. Although the spies witnessed the terrible consequences of gossip they did not apply the lesson to their own lives. They were not deterred from slandering the Holy Land.

Does the Torah simply mean to stress their wickedness by placing the incidents next to each other?

R' Yisrael of Pilov sees a profound insight into human nature. One who does not want to see the truth will suffer a spiritual blindness, even if the truth can be clearly seen. The spies were not seeking the truth and were therefore blinded to it. They witnessed what happened to Miriam, but did not internalize the message.[1]

According to *Rashi,* the people came to Moses and asked him to dispatch spies. He consulted with God Who said, "Although I assured them the Land is good, they apparently still have doubts. Grant them their request. However, they run the risk of being misled by the spies and thus forfeiting their chance to inherit the Land."

If sending the spies was risky and ran contrary to God's will, why did He accede to the request?

Midrash Rabbah offers a parable: Once, in medieval times, when marriages were strictly determined

---

1. **Moral Blindness.** Many of the world's greatest philosophers had a personal life far different than that described in their teachings. This was not merely an instance of moral hypocrisy; it was deeper than that.

The Torah teaches that "a bribe will blind the eyes of the wise" (see *Deuteronomy* 16:19). This refers to every type of bribe, not just financial gain. Honor, illicit pleasures, personal prestige or a vested interest all serve to blind man even to self-evident truths. A bribe distorts one's way of thinking and how one sees himself.

The spies were blinded to the truth. Visionless, they truly perceived nothing and repeated the error of Miriam when they spoke derogatorily about *Eretz Yisrael.*

R' Yerucham Levovitz of Mir sees an important lesson in the words of the *Tanchuma.* Everything that happens in life carries a message. Just as the person who sees the unfaithful wife in her degradation must stop to reflect on his own life (see *Rashi* on *Numbers* 6:2), so too, we must always glean lessons from all that occurs around us.

The spies' offense was their slander of the Land; their inability to learn from Miriam added insult to injury.

by parents, a royal prince reached marriageable age. His father arranged a suitable match and chose a young lady of royal pedigree who was intelligent, beautiful and charming.

The son insisted on first meeting the prospective mate. The father, of course, was deeply hurt by his son's lack of trust in him.

The father began thinking, "If I refuse to allow them to meet, he will be convinced that his doubts were justified. I will therefore allow them to meet to vindicate my choice. However, since he didn't trust me, I will not allow him to marry her."

When the Jews of that generation questioned God's word, God allowed them to send spies, to see with their own eyes that the Land was truly good.

However, since they doubted His word, He would not allow them to inhabit it. Only their children would be able to settle in the Holy Land.

Sfas Emes (based on an interpretation of his grandfather, the *Chidushei HaRim*) presents an alternative explanation. When man acts on his own, he runs the risk of corrupting his soul and acting against God's will. Only when he is totally committed to God does he merit Divine protection.

By turning their request into a mitzvah, God hoped that the spies would fulfill this mission as a Divine imperative. They would thus be deserving of His protection according to the dictum which assures that "One who keeps a mitzvah will know no evil" (*Ecclesiastes* 8:5). Had they been totally dedicated to fulfilling God's will, they would have retained their faith in His ability to help them conquer the Land and their mission would have been successful. They however failed, and allowed their own personal bias to distort their opinions.

Here lies an important lesson. We, imbued with a Divine soul, are sent to this world with a mission. Our mission is the fulfillment of God's will.

To enable us to overcome the spiritual challenges which the world presents, God gave us *mitzvos* which govern every aspect of our physical existence. We have a natural desire to eat and drink. By commanding us to say a blessing before we eat, we transform a mundane act of eating into something spiritual.

In order to spiritually survive in this world, we must focus on our mission. We must make all the mundane activities part of our Godly mission. Man must view oneself as an axe in the hand of a woodchopper. The axe is a mere tool ready to serve the one who wields it. Likewise, man is God's tool, charged with the task of implementing His will.

By maintaining this perspective, man can project the light of God into every aspect of his life, for *mitzvos* are the torches which carry the light of Torah.[2]

כֹּל נָשִׂיא בָהֶם
every one a leader among them (ibid.).

According to the Torah, leadership is not merely a function; it is a spirit which must infuse every aspect of the leader's life even when he is not actively taking charge. A leader must never forget his position or responsibilities and must always act in a manner befitting his position. Homiletically, this is the message of the verse. כֹּל נָשִׂיא בָהֶם — he must be a total leader among them.

One who is inconsistent and maintains this behavior only when he is in the public eye will eventually be unmasked, to his own terrible shame (*HaDerash V'Halyun*).

כֻּלָּם אֲנָשִׁים רָאשֵׁי בְנֵי יִשְׂרָאֵל הֵמָּה
they were all distinguished men; heads of the Children of Israel were they (ibid. 3).

When the spies began their mission, they were all righteous men of high spiritual stature (*Rashi*).

How did such distinguished people come to reject the Land of Israel?

Chidushei HaRim explains: The spies were afraid that the kind of existence which they would assume upon entering the Holy Land would be a threat to

---

2. **Women of Heart.** *Kli Yakar* explains why God was unwilling to send the spies. According to the Sages, the Jewish menfolk felt no affinity toward the Land, and really wanted to return to Egypt. The women, however, had a tremendous love for it. [The daughters of Zelophehad each demanded a portion in the Land (*Numbers* 27:4) because they felt a great endearment toward it.] God told Moses, "Listen to My advice and send women to spy out the Land because the women love it and appreciate it. Since, however, you are certain that the leaders of the tribes are upright, you may send them instead."

their spirituality. Throughout the people's sojourn in the Wilderness, they were completely dependent on God for all their physical needs. They had manna from Heaven, water from the wellspring of Miriam, clothes that never wore out and a perfect climate that enabled them to devote themselves entirely to the study of Torah and other spiritual pursuits. The spies feared the people would spiritually regress with the agricultural lifestyle they would embark on in *Eretz Yisrael.* They wanted the people to remain under conditions optimal for spiritual growth.

Although they had good intentions, their actions were unacceptable. They failed to understand that God does not need help in running His world. He alone knows what is most conducive for the nation's spiritual growth.

Sfas Emes elaborates on these words. The miraculous existence in the Wilderness was meant to give the Jews the spiritual resources with which to live a Torah life. However, their true mission is to transform the mundane into the sanctified. In *Eretz Yisrael* every grain of sand is sanctified. There, we are commanded to make every mundane act spiritual. As the *Chidushei HaRim* said, *"the Heavens are to God and the earth was granted to man (Psalms* 115:16) — to turn it into Heaven."

וַיִּקְרָא מֹשֶׁה לְהוֹשֵׁעַ בִּן נוּן יְהוֹשֻׁעַ
Moses called Hoshea son of Nun "Joshua" (ibid. 16).

Moses added the letter י to Hoshea's name to make his name begin with the name of God. He prayed that God save Joshua from participating in the evil scheme of the spies (*Rashi*).

R' Chaim of Volozhin explains why Moses prayed specifically for Joshua. The Talmud advises one how to refrain from slander. "If he is a Torah scholar let him increase his involvement in Torah study; if he is ignorant let him work on acquiring humility" (*Arachin* 15b).

The Talmud does not mean to imply that a Torah scholar need not act humbly. On the contrary, in *addition* to acquiring humility, he must increase his Torah study.

Moses was aware that his disciple possessed both these qualities. Joshua was always in Moses' presence, and was constantly increasing his Torah knowledge. He was also extremely humble. Joshua would arrange the benches and chairs in the Tent where Moses taught. As a result, Moses was so sure that Joshua would not slander the Holy Land that he changed his name to express this confidence.

According to *Targum Yonasan ben Uziel,* Moses prayed specifically for Joshua because of Joshua's outstanding humility. *Avnei Nezer* sees the addition of a letter to his name as a reflection of that prayer. Moses felt Joshua might be very susceptible to the negative influence of the spies. Humility, while generally a very positive character trait, can sometimes be negative. One who finds himself in the company of people with different views may consider his view no more legitimate than that of those around him. This misplaced humility may prevent him from taking a strong stand against popular opinion, and may even cause him to abandon his minority opinion altogether.

When Moses saw Joshua's intense humility, he realized Joshua's vulnerability. He therefore blessed him that his humility not becloud his clarity of mind and vision.[3]

---

3. **Humble Gridlock.** The *Rema* (*Orach Chaim* 1:1) warns against the paralyzing effect of excessive humility. "A person should not be embarrassed [and thus restrained] by people who scorn and ridicule him with regard to serving God." Nevertheless, he should not seek to be scorned.

The *Chafetz Chaim* adds two qualifying points: 1) If one's public performance of a mitzvah will inspire others to follow his path he should willingly incur the the scorn of cynics and serve as a role model. 2) Generally one should not antagonize those who laugh at him. Rather, he should go about his spiritual business and disregard them. However, if nonbelievers assume the mantle of leadership and seek to institute a public policy which runs contrary to Torah law, one must seek to peacefully restore the primacy of Torah. If this nonconfrontational approach is unsuccessful, one must put up a fierce fight to assure the victory of Torah. (See *Mishnah Berurah* 135-5 and *Biur Halachah* ad loc.)

Although the Torah's *ways are ways of pleasantness and all its paths are peace (Proverbs* 3:17), one must react to an affront to God as one would react to an affront to one's parent. Just as a child cannot control himself if he witnesses someone spitting in his parent's face, so too one cannot witness our Father being insulted and not react.

הַבְּמַחֲנִים אִם בְּמִבְצָרִים

Are they opened or fortified? (ibid. 19).

A chassid once presented the following question to R' Yechezkel of Kuzmir: "I have the opportunity to move to a village where I will be able to make a decent living: However, doing so entails living among non-Jews and being exposed to their influence. The alternative is to move to the city, where there is a more vibrant Jewish community but where I will have great difficulty supporting my family. What should I do?"

The Rebbe replied, "The Torah speaks explicitly about your dilemma. When Moses sent the spies he told them to survey whether the people are to be found in open or fortified cities. *Rashi* explains that if they live in open cities it indicates that they are strong and feel confident enough to rely on their strength. If, however, they are ensconced in walled cities, it is a sign that they are weak. This," said R' Yechezkel, "is equally true in spiritual matters. One who is confident of his spiritual strength and does not depend on the support of the religious community may live in a town or village. Not so one who is unsure of his inner strength. He must surround himself with a positive environment. This must include a competent rav, a ritual slaughterer, a synagogue, a *mikveh* and an appropriate school for his children."

The Rebbe concluded, "You, my dear friend,

must decide for yourself how strong you are. Can you survive in such a village? If not, you have no choice but to move to the city."[4]

הֲטוֹבָה הִוא אִם רָעָה . . .
הַשְּׁמֵנָה הִוא אִם רָזָה

Is it good or bad? . . . Is it fertile or lean? (ibid. 19-20).

Did Moses actually ask the opinion of the spies regarding the Land's positive qualities? He certainly entertained no doubts, for God himself had told him that the Land was very good! R' Menachem Mendel of Kotzk offers a homiletic rendering of the verse. Moses told the spies, "Even if the Land seems bad in your eyes, say it is good. If it seems infertile, say it is fertile. Do not rely on your initial impression. To properly appreciate *Eretz Yisrael*, one must penetrate below the surface."

Moses instructed the spies to strengthen their faith in God and to take from the fruit of the Land. Only with faith can one transcend the superficial.[5]

הֲיֵשׁ בָּהּ עֵץ אִם אַיִן

Is there a tree in it or not? (ibid. 20).

The tree in this verse is allegorical, and refers to a righteous person. Moses wanted the spies to see if the Land had a righteous person whose merit

---

4. **Live Evidence.** When unbearable poverty was rampant in Eastern Europe during the early 1900's, a Slonimer *chassid* asked R' Moshe Midner, one of the Slonimer elders, for advice. Baron Hirsch had offered handsome payment to any Jew willing to work on his Argentinian estates. The *chassid's* friends were entertaining the idea. They would be provided with a means of support but would live a life of spiritual mediocrity, devoid of any real content and without vibrant spiritual role models. The alternative was the extreme poverty of Lithuania.

R' Moshe Midner, in typical Jewish fashion, replied with a question: "If you had to choose between living in a place where there were both righteous and wicked people, or living among people of average spiritual quality without any exceptionally righteous or wicked person, which would you choose?"

The *chassid* was in a quandary. R' Moshe continued: "Always pick a place where there is at least one authentically righteous individual, even if the rest are wicked. It is better than living among spiritual mediocrity. One must have at least one living role model to follow. Otherwise, one is lost. The fact that no evil people are around is of no help, since every person has a wicked one (the evil inclination) lurking inside. Only a live counterbalance can save him."

5. **Good Vision.** R' Yosef Chaim Sonnenfeld would often counsel people who visited Jerusalem to pay heed to the words of King David, *May you gaze upon the goodness of Jerusalem all the days of your life* (Psalms 128:5).

"Our Holy City has many negative aspects," he would say. "Nevertheless, King David warns us to ignore the negative and to focus only on the positive."

In the early 1900's, many Polish Jews moved to *Eretz Yisrael*. Someone asked R' Meir Shapiro, Rav of Lublin, why he did not at least visit, if not settle, in the Land. R' Meir replied, "I have the strength to go to *Eretz Yisrael* but from where will I draw the strength to leave?"

could protect the inhabitants (*Rashi*). The Torah uses the tree as a metaphor for man (see *Deuteronomy* 20:19). Just as the tree casts its shade and offers protection from the sun (and to some extent, from rain), so the righteous protect their generation from calamities through the merit of their prayers and actions.[6]

If so, why were the spies commanded to explore the streets, cities and orchards of the Land? Wouldn't the universities and meeting places of intellectuals and men of spirit be a more appropriate places to seek out those who could protect the people?

Otzar Chaim suggests that Moses told them to look for the righteous person who is able to influence and inspire the masses. A righteous person provides protection for the people if his impact is felt among them. One must search for the imprints of the sanctified soul in the public arena.

R' Yoel of Satmar questions the viability of fulfilling Moses' command. Authentic righteousness is not ascertained by a surface appraisal. A person might appear to be very righteous, but is in truth very far from it. How were the spies to know if someone was truly righteous?

The answer lies in the continuation of the verse. *Rashi* explains, the tree as a metaphor for a righteous person. How are we to understand the continuation, *you shall strengthen yourselves and take from the fruit of the Land*?

A person's true character is revealed through his children. One's offspring are his fruits and the yield of his spiritual labor. The saying goes, "The apple does not fall far from the tree." If one's children are God fearing and adopt a Godly lifestyle, one may assume the parent is truly righteous and God fearing.

If one's children do not follow in the dictates or spirit of the Torah, the parent is suspect even if he himself appears to be righteous. Appearances are often deceiving.

Moses alludes to this when he instructs the spies to search for trees (righteous individuals). How shall they do so? Take the fruit of the trees — check the spirituality of the children.[5]

וַיָּשֻׁבוּ מִתּוּר הָאָרֶץ מִקֵּץ אַרְבָּעִים יוֹם
They returned from spying out the Land at the end of forty days (ibid. 25).

Rashi notes that, logically, it should have taken the spies much longer to tour the Land in its entirety. God in His Infinite Mercy realized that the Jewish people would have to wander in the

---

6. **Protective Piety.** While attending a rabbinic conference, *R' Isser Zalman Meltzer* had the pleasure of spending time with *R' Moshe Danishevsky,* famed Rav of Slabodka, and *R' Chaim Leib Mishkovsky* of Stavisk.

R' Isser Zalman was seated with R' Moshe in a room while R' Chaim Leib paced furiously in the hall outside the open door of the room, pondering a Talmudic question. Every time R' Chaim Leib passed the open door, R' Moshe would rise fully as a sign of respect. This occurred many times, and eventually R' Moshe noticed R' Isser Zalman's puzzled face. "I see you are wondering about my strange behavior. Let me tell you about R' Chaim Leib.

"In Eisheshok, Lithuania, there was a *kollel* where many of the finest young Torah scholars studied. Some of them later became world-renowned *talmidei chachamim*. R' Chaim Leib studied there as well.

"During those years, a terrible plague appeared in the environs of Eisheshok and it claimed many lives. Interestingly, not one person was struck in Eisheshok itself.

"*R' Avraham Shmuel,* author of the *Amudei Eish* was Rav of the city at the time. He called one of the members of the *kollel* and told him, 'The merit of R' Chaim Leib has spared Eisheshok. This young man who spends every moment from morning to night in uninterrupted Torah study has stopped the plague from intruding on our town.'

"Eventually, R' Chaim Leib's father-in-law, concerned over his prized son-in-law's health and safety, asked him to leave Eisheshok and invited him to his home in Lida. Unaware of the Rav's pronouncement, R' Chaim Leib complied with his father-in-law's request and left Eisheshok.

"Shortly thereafter, the plague claimed its first victim in Eisheshok.

"When R' Isser Zalman related this incident, he began to cry, 'See the power of insight granted a true *gaon* like the *Amudei Eish*. That *kollel* included tremendously talented and God-fearing scholars. One could easily have viewed their collective merit as the cause for Eisheshok being spared. Nevertheless, R' Avraham Shmuel specifically cited R' Chaim Leib as the source of its protection."

When he left town it became clear that it was the merit of R' Chaim Leib that sheltered those fortunate enough to live in Eisheshok.

Wilderness an entire year for every day the spies were on their mission. He therefore granted them unnatural speed and allowed them to finish their mission within forty days. The spies should have realized that just as they were able to accomplish their undertaking in a supernatural manner, God could certainly deliver the land to them in a supernatural manner. Miracles strengthen the faith of those who truly believe; those who do not believe see nothing (*Otzar Chaim*).[7] It is interesting to note that although God planned to punish these wicked spies, He changed the rules of nature to limit the scope of their punishment. Even when God punishes, He does so mercifully.

R' Chaim Shmulevitz sees in this a valuable lesson. One may think sinners deserve whatever punishment God metes out. One need not attempt to create conditions that may minimize the scope of the sin. The Torah teaches otherwise. Although God knew that the spies would sin, He sought to minimize the punishment He would have to give them and the people. We too must emulate and offer sinners help.

Sfas Emes explains the significance of the forty days. The changeover from the Wilderness to *Eretz Yisrael* is analogous to the relationship between the Written Torah and the Oral Law. The Oral Torah teaches us how to apply the Written Torah to real-life situations. Those Torah laws which remained theoretical throughout the Jews' sojourn in the Wilderness (e.g., the *mitzvos* that can only be performed in the Land of Israel) were now ready to become applied practically. Just as the Torah was given in forty days, so too this reconnaissance mission was a forty-day process. When the Jews failed to display the faith and courage necessary to enter the Land, God decreed that they would now

require 40 *years* to enable them to give Torah concrete expression through settlement of the Land.

אֶרֶץ אֹכֶלֶת יוֹשְׁבֶיהָ הוא
it is a land that devours its inhabitants (ibid. 32).

Wherever they went, the spies saw funerals. They failed to understand it was God's way of diverting the local residents' attention away from them (*Rashi*). "Why," questioned the *Kotzker Rebbe*, "was their report considered a sin? They only reported what they actually saw."

Truth is not only what one sees. Obviously one who relates things he did not see with his own eyes is a liar, but the definition of truth is not merely relating what one visually witnesses. When faced with an occurrence that appears to contradict God's word, a man of truth makes every effort to resolve the issue in a way which allows him to perceive the Divine truth.

The spies saw what appeared to be reality to them. They should have defined reality in terms of God's will.[8]

וַנְּהִי בְעֵינֵינוּ כַּחֲגָבִים וְכֵן הָיִינוּ בְּעֵינֵיהֶם
we were like grasshoppers in our eyes, and so we were in their eyes! (ibid. 33).

Yalkut Shimoni (quoting *Midrash Tanchuma*) sheds an interesting light on this comment. God said, "You said, 'we were like grasshoppers in our eyes.' For that, I forgive you. But why did you say, 'and so we were in *their* eyes'? Who told you that you were not like angels? How do you

---

7. **Divine Assistance?** One can seemingly receive the most fantastic forms of Divine assistance, regardless of one's merit. The spies were granted extraordinary speed in their mission in spite of the fact (or because of the fact) that they were sinners (*R' Chaim Shmulevitz*).

8. **Tinted Glasses.** Folk wisdom has it that seeing is believing. In fact, believing is seeing. When life is viewed through the prism of faith, it assumes a unique hue all its own.

Lamentations is written in alphabetical order. In one of the chapters the verse which begins with the letter פ precedes the verse which begins with the letter ע (which is alphabetically backwards). The Midrash views this as an allusion to the mission of the spies who allowed their פֶּה (mouth) to precede their עַיִן (eye). They spoke about things that they had not seen. This statement would seem to be inaccurate, for the spies really did report what they had seen. In truth, however, their imperfect faith distorted their vision. They had a preconceived notion of what they would see and that is exactly what they saw. Their mouths preceded their eyes and set the focus.

know what I caused them to think?" It was this tragic mistake that brought the forty-year punishment.

When a person has a distorted and deflated perception of himself he may totally lose his proper perspective. While others may view him as an angel, he thinks they see him as a grasshopper. When we see ourselves as insignificant, we have no doubts that others see us the same way, and we are right! People do tend to perceive us as we perceive ourselves (*Chafetz Chaim*).[9]

Background

The nation is convinced that the report of the spies is accurate and they fear entering the Land. They even speak of a new leader who will take them back to Egypt.

וַיִּבְכּוּ הָעָם בַּלַּיְלָה הַהוּא
the people wept that night (14:1).

That night was Tishah B'Av. Since the Jews cried foolishly, without any true, legitimate reason, that night became a time of crying throughout Jewish history. Both Temples were destroyed on the 9th of Av.[10] According to the Midrash (*Bamidbar Rabbah* 16:2), it was on that night that God decreed that the Temples would be destroyed and the Jews exiled. This seems to contradict the Talmud (*Shabbos* 33a, *Yoma* 9b), which attributes the destruction of the Temples to different sins committed by those who lived during those eras.

To answer this question we must first understand the purpose of the Exodus. The Jews were destined to leave Egypt and enter the Land of Israel to "eternal liberty" (*Maariv* prayers). This was to entail a constant exposure to the Divine Presence. Such proximity would have precluded exile or the destruction of the Temple. Had they sinned in the Land, they would have been punished by other means.

After the *sin*, accepting the report of the spies, the nation rejected the Holy Land. As a result, they would only temporarily occupy *Eretz Yisrael*. Exile now became a viable option. By scorning the Land, the Jews forfeited the eternal liberty they were to enjoy.

The spies' sin set the stage for the possibility of exile and the destruction of the Temple. The sins enumerated in the Talmud were only able to bring about exile and the Temples' destruction once they

---

9. **Spiritual Self-Confidence.** During the extended exile among the nations, Jews never lost their feelings of spiritual and moral superiority. Even when enduring suffering and indescribable degradation at the hands of their inhospitable hosts, Jews knew in their hearts that their suffering was a Heavenly decree. The non-Jew was never able to debase the Jew in his own eyes.

This was the reality in times gone by. In our times, this inner strength shows signs of erosion. As the state of our spiritual vision declines, we begin to lose our understanding that a Jew is in a unique class of his own [both as a privilege and a responsibility] and we begin to actually feel degraded by our oppressors. We futilely seek to adopt their values and lifestyles as a means of avoiding their scorn. In reality, these futile attempts only make the yoke of exile more difficult to bear. Spiritually short-sighted people view this as a way to bolster Jewish honor and pride and as a viable and preferred alternative to non-Jewish abuse. In truth, it was those Jews of the "exile mentality" who were true men of spirit. The cruelty of the non-Jew left no mark on their Jewish heart, soul or psyche.

It is only when we view ourselves as inferior in stature that our enemies' prestige becomes magnified in our eyes.

When we view ourselves as grasshoppers, we realize that they too view us as spiritual midgets (*R' Eliyahu Eliezer Dessler*).

10. **Heavenly Choreography.** The destruction of both Temples, the expulsion of Jews from England, the Spanish expulsion (1492) and the beginning of World War I all occurred on Tishah B'Av.

The rejection of God's Land is the source of the endless manifestations of exile.

On the other hand, the recurring events on that very date serve as clear evidence that Jewish history is choreographed by the guiding hand of God.

A noted historian remarked that had Ferdinand and Isabella realized how much faith they imbued in Jewish hearts by expelling them on Tishah B'Av, they might have had second thoughts. In the throes of misery, Jews always see a Godly plan unfolding (*Michtav MeEliyahu*).

became viable options (*R' Shlomo Harkavy*).[11] As long as Jews believed that the Land could become theirs in a supernatural manner, they were destined to live there forever, even when "natural" (political, economic, etc.) conditions might dictate otherwise. Once they surrendered to the "reality" of the laws of nature and were willing to solely rely on natural means to conquer the Land, their existence there became subject to natural events and conditions. Exile became feasable (*Zekan Aharon*).[12]

טוֹבָה הָאָרֶץ מְאֹד מְאֹד
the Land is very very good (ibid. 7).

Caleb and Joshua insisted that in spite of all the circumstantial evidence collected by the spies in support of their position, it was still a very good Land.

One must be extremely humble to be able to adhere to God's view despite all contrary impressions. The Torah alludes to this humility with the expression מְאֹד מְאֹד (*very very*), reminiscent of the words of the *Mishnah* (*Avos* 4:4), מְאֹד מְאֹד הֱוֵה שְׁפַל רוּחַ, *Be of very very humble spirit.*

Those who are very humble are always ready to yield their own impressions before the Divine truth of God's word. For them, *the Land is very very good*

— regardless of visual evidence to the contrary (*Simchas Aharon*).[13]

וְאַתֶּם אַל תִּירְאוּ אֶת עַם הָאָרֶץ כִּי לַחְמֵנוּ הֵם
You should not fear the people of the Land, for they are our bread (ibid. 9).

Why does the Torah refer to the Canaanites as "bread"? Furthermore, why is the fact that they are "our bread" a reason not to fear them?

Maharsham offers an explanation based on *Chovos HaLevavos* who teaches that one should trust that God will undoubtedly provide bread and water, the bare necessities of life. Regarding luxuries, however, there are no guarantees.

For the Jewish people, the Land of Israel is not a luxury but a vital necessity. The complete fulfillment of the Torah is impossible without *Eretz Yisrael*. Thus, Joshua and Caleb told the people, "Have no fear; God will certainly deliver the Land and its inhabitants into our hands for they are our bread — a necessity for life itself."

The metaphor of bread as a staple of life teaches us a lesson in overcoming difficulties. One who encounters roadblocks in one's pursuit of luxuries is ready to forgo them. However one is tireless in his search of life's bare necessities and is ready to

---

11. **Tears of Hope.** The Sages teach that the Heavenly gates through which tears enter are never closed (*Bava Metzia* 59a). Why then bother to have gates? Explains *R' Simchah Bunim of P'shis'cha:* The gates are to keep out the tears of those who weep for no legitimate reason. The tears of one who cries *to* God encounter no resistance on their way to the Heavenly Throne. Tears shed out of despair when one feels no one can help have no place in Heaven. *Imrei Emes* submits that the gates are put up to keep out "crocodile tears," shed without sincerity.

12. **Fit for the Task.** A Jew once came to *R' Moshe Leib of Sassov* and expressed a desire to move to the Land of Israel. R' Moshe Leib told him, "Just as the synagogues in the Diaspora are imbued with the sanctity of the Holy Land (see *Maharsha* to *Berachos* 8a), one must conduct himself in the Holy Land as he would in a synagogue. You and your family must decide if you are prepared to maintain the spiritual level of a synagogue. If so, you may move to Israel."

Based on this story, the *Imrei Yosef of Spinka* explained the weeping of the Jews in wake of the spies' slander.

The Jews were afraid they were unable to maintain the spiritually elevated lifestyle demanded in the Holy Land, and refused to enter. They cried over the fact that they were unable to achieve the level they thought necessary for living in the Holy Land.

But they were mistaken. If God told them to enter, they should have known that He would help them rise above the immorality and idolatry of the Canaanites and conduct themselves in the spirit of the sanctified homeland.

13. **Very Very Good.** To the other spies the Land was not good; to Caleb and Joshua, the Land was very very good.

The *Chazon Ish* would continually speak the praises of the Land when in the company of tourists and would strongly encourage visitors to settle there.

A visiting American rabbi once came to the Chazon Ish after extensively touring the country. The great sage asked him, "So what do you say? Weren't Joshua and Caleb right?"

surmount any obstacles which may stand in his way. Why? Because he cannot live without bread.

The message to the people was that fear should not dissuade them. "We must find the strength to overcome the obstacles because *they are our bread*; — our lives depend on our inhabiting the Land."[14]

Background

Moses beseeches God not to destroy the Jews as punishment for their rejection of His Land. He bases his plea on the potential desecration of God's Name were He to carry out the threat of annihilating His people.

וְשָׁמְעוּ מִצְרַיִם
then Egypt . . . will hear (14:13).

Of all the nations of the world who might gloat over God's "inability" to conquer the Canaanites, Moses singled out the Egyptians. Why?

Explains *Ohr HaChaim*: The Egyptians experienced firsthand the supernatural manner with which God deals with the Jewish people. While *peoples heard . . . terror gripped the dwellers of Philistia . . .* (*Exodus* 15:14), the Egyptians bore the brunt of God's supernatural intervention. Although the Jews were downtrodden and weak, God redeemed them with His mighty hand. Had the Jews not entered the Land, the Egyptians would have never attributed it to the Jews' inability to conquer. Just as the Jews' weakness in Egypt did not prevent them from attaining freedom, so it should not stop them from entering the Promised Land. They would claim that God was simply unable to deliver on His promise. *R' Yisrael Salanter* offers a slight variation: All the other nations of the world would conclude that God redeemed the Jews from Egypt in their spiritual merit and barred them entry into the land as punishment for their sins.

The Egyptians knew otherwise: On their own merit, the Jews would never have left Egypt. As the Sages teach, the angels claimed the Jews did not deserve to be redeemed, because they were also idolaters. God in His infinite mercy, and in fulfillment of His promises to their forefathers, redeemed them, regardless of their spiritual status. "Why, then," the Egyptians would ask, "does God not bring them into the Land? He is obviously unable to do so."

מִבִּלְתִּי יְכֹלֶת ה' לְהָבִיא אֶת הָעָם הַזֶּה אֶל הָאָרֶץ
Because Hashem lacked the ability to bring this people to the Land (ibid. 16).

Ramban (*Deuteronomy* 32:26-27) explains that Moses was not appealing to God's "need" to salvage His honor and save face before the nations, because they are all insignificant in His eyes. Rather, this appeal reflects upon the interdependent relationship the Jewish people enjoy with God.

God created man that he know his Creator, be totally dependent on Him and express his gratitude to Him for all He does for him (see *Ramban, Exodus* 13:16). Initially, this was the universal mission of mankind. After all the nations sinned, only Israel remained as God's loyal servant, ready to execute His mission. After the great miracles of the Exodus from Egypt, the Jewish people created a chain of tradition which kept God at the forefront of human focus.

If, God forbid, the Jewish people were to be annihilated, who would remember that it was God Who created the world? To enable God's master plan for Creation to materialize, the Jewish people must continue to exist (see *Rashi* to verse 20).[15]

---

14. **My Bread and Butter.** Even if we view our spiritual growth and our involvement in Torah and *mitzvos* as the most important goal in our lives, we may not be ready to surmount the difficulties which life presents when on the path to achieving that goal. Only when we view it as our bread, as life itself, are we able to pursue it at all costs. If our lives depend on it, we will find the strength to succeed against all odds. [An astute observer who lived in the Diaspora for many years before making *aliyah* noted this as the difference between the quality of commitment in the Diaspora and in *Eretz Yisrael*. To those in the Diaspora, who are loyal to Torah, Torah and *mitzvos* are the most important thing in life; in *Eretz Yisrael* they are life itself.]

15. **Cosmic Consequence.** Joshua presented a similar argument when, in wake of the Achan episode, the Jewish people were threatened with annihilation (see *Joshua* Ch. 7). Joshua prayed to God and said that *The Canaanite and all the inhabitants of the land will hear and will surround us and cut off our name from the earth. What will You do for Your Great Name?* (ibid. 7:9).

סְלַח נָא לַעֲוֹן הָעָם הַזֶּה כְּגֹדֶל חַסְדֶּךָ
Forgive now the iniquity of this people according to the greatness of Your kindness (ibid. 19).

When Moses prayed to God that He forgive the Jewish people for the Golden Calf, he invoked the merit of Abraham, Isaac and Jacob (see *Exodus* 32:13). Why did Moses delete this from his prayer here?

One can only invoke the merit of his forefathers if their heritage is meaningful in his eyes. To scorn their spiritual inheritance and then seek cover in their wings is an act of hypocrisy.

The Golden Calf was a sin against God for which the merit of our forefathers helped us achieve atonement. However, when the spies slandered the Land of Israel, the nation rejected the inheritance they had received from those very forefathers. How audacious it would have been to plead for mercy based on the merits of those whose inheritance they rejected! (*Ramban, Rabbeinu Bachya*).

Moses asks God to forgive in proportion to His kindness. Just as His kindness and mercy are infinite, so is His ability to forgive. The following incident sheds further light on this idea.

R' David Moshe of Tchortkov was overheard in prayer on the last Rosh Hashanah of his life, "Master of the universe! We are full of iniquity while You are full of mercy. How insignificant are our sins when compared to the vastness of Your mercy. Your mercy and kindness are infinite. Please, forgive us and grant us atonement."[16]

וַיֹּאמֶר ה' סָלַחְתִּי כִּדְבָרֶךָ. וְאוּלָם חַי אָנִי . . . אִם יִרְאוּ אֶת הָאָרֶץ
And Hashem said, "I have forgiven because of your words. But as I live . . . if they will see the Land" (ibid. 20-23).

The Torah seems to contradict itself. First God proclaims that He has forgiven the Jewish people and yet a moment later He launches into a detailed explanation of how the Jewish people and the spies are to be punished!

Nesivos Shalom explains: Every sin brings punishment in its wake. It is a principle of our faith that there is a Judge Who allocates justice, rewarding good deeds and delivering retribution for sins. However, there is an even graver consequence of sin. Distance is placed between a Jew and his God.

A son sins against his father; if he is a sensitive son who cherishes the relationship, he is ready to bear whatever punishment is necessary as long as he is guaranteed that his connection to his father will not be severed. Likewise, a Jew is ready to deal with punishment as long as the link between him and God remains. When God told Moses He would destroy the Jewish people and make him into a great nation (v. 12), Moses refused. That the Jewish nation might cease to exist was simply not an option. Moses interceded on their behalf, and their link to God remained intact. God replied that He forgave the nation and would never permanently sever this relationship. However, those guilty would still have to be punished.[17]

---

16. **Endless Mercy.** *Beis Avraham* submits the following parable: A king celebrated his birthday by hosting a lavish banquet for his subjects. He had his kitchen staff prepare an immense array of delicacies. The invited guests ate to their heart's content, yet plenty of food remained. Since it was inappropriate to throw out food prepared for the king's birthday, they decided to invite the general populace to eat the remainder. Nevertheless, the amount of food was so great that even they were unable to finish it. Finally the royal entourage decided that they had no choice but to invite the prisoners who were incarcerated and on death row to partake of the leftovers from the royal banquet.

God's mercy is infinite; its scope cannot be delineated. God possesses such endless amounts of kindness that He even allows the truly wicked to partake of it.

Therefore, we ask God to forgive us according to the greatness of His kindness.

One Yom Kippur night *R' Levi Yitzchak of Berditchev* turned to God and cried out, "Father in Heaven! The Sages teach that whoever cites others by name brings redemption to the world (*Avos* 6:6). Well I, Levi Yitzchak, want to quote something in Your Name. *And God said, I have forgiven because of your words.* Now You must grant us redemption."

וְעַבְדִּי כָלֵב עֵקֶב הָיְתָה רוּחַ
אַחֶרֶת עִמּוֹ וַיְמַלֵּא אַחֲרָי

*But My servant Caleb because a
different spirit was with him and he
followed Me wholeheartedly (ibid. 24).*

One who feels driven by a seemingly irresistible drive to sin and is nonetheless able to overpower his evil inclination deserves great commendation and is rewarded accordingly by God. However, one who lives among those who are violently opposed to God's Torah faces a much more difficult challenge. Only a person of rare spiritual mettle can withstand this test.

Caleb was surrounded by people of a totally different spirit. They were convinced that entering the Holy Land was simply impossible. Caleb was courageous enough to swim against the tide. He ignored the *different spirit and followed Me wholeheartedly.* God rewarded Him in kind.[18]

Background

When God accepts Moses' prayer and forgives the Jewish people, He decrees that the generation of the desert will not enter the Land of Israel. They will perish over a forty-year period in the Wilderness. Only the next generation will enter the Land. The spies themselves, who demoralized the nation, were to die immediately.

וְכָל פְּקֻדֵיכֶם לְכָל מִסְפַּרְכֶם
מִבֶּן עֶשְׂרִים שָׁנָה וָמָעְלָה

*All of you who were counted in any
of your numberings from twenty
years of age and above (ibid. 29).*

According to *Rashi,* the Torah uses these terms to exclude the Levites, who are not counted from age 20 with regard to military service or the contribution of the half-shekel.

Since the Levites were not represented by a spy, they were excluded from the general decree issued against the entire nation. Why does the exclusion find expression in the fact that they do not go to war?

As mentioned earlier, the generation of the Wilderness feared the seemingly mundane existence that entrance into the Land would offer. They preferred to remain in the Wilderness. There God provided for all of their physical needs. and left them free to devote themselves exclusively to spiritual pursuits.

This lifestyle change did not concern the Levites. Even upon entering the Land they would continue to live as they did in the Wilderness and remain totally focused on spiritual growth. This is the reason the Levites were exempt from military service.

This is why their exclusion from the decree which was the result of the sin of the spies finds expression in their exemption from military service (*Zekan Aharon*).

---

17. **Mercifully Connected.** In his plea regarding his sin with Bath-sheba, King David never asked God to spare him from punishment. In fact, he willingly accepted six months of leprosy and removal of his contact with the Sanhedrin as punishment. The one thing he begged was, *Cast me not away from Your Presence, and take not Your Holy Spirit from me (Psalms 51:13).*

This sheds light on a universal custom practiced in all Jewish communities. We begin the Yom Kippur services by declaring that God forgives us. Even before we recite any confessional or beg for forgiveness we say, *And Hashem said, "I have forgiven because of your words.''* Yet at the end of the day we continue to speak of the need for repentance to avoid punishment.

The declaration at the outset is to stress that God forgives us and that our ties to Him are irrevocable. Only then do we begin Yom Kippur to achieve atonement for our particular sins (*Nesivos Shalom*).

18. **Personal Path.** The strength of character needed to avoid the herd mentality is highlighted in a homiletic interpretation of the *Mishnah* in *Pirkei Avos* (3:5): *R' Chanina ben Chachinai says: One who stays awake at night and travels the road alone but turns his heart to idleness — indeed, he bears guilt for his soul.*

Our world is often compared to night. Many of us spend life in deep spiritual slumber, allowing endless opportunities for growth to slip by.

One who is awake at night and has the sense to travel the road of life alone, without being manipulated by prevailing public opinion, must use this self-confidence to rise above the crowd and chart his own course based on Torah.

Caleb lived the lesson of this *Mishnah.*

יוֹם לַשָּׁנָה יוֹם לַשָּׁנָה
a day for a year,
a day for a year (ibid. 34).

God's mercy is so bountiful that even as man is sinning, He devises ways to minimize the punishment. God realized the Jews would have to be punished one year for every day the spies were on their mission. He therefore granted them supernatural speed to spy out the Land in only forty days (see *Rashi* 13:25).

God does not punish us out of cruelty or a desire for vengeance and retribution. He is our Father and His punishment is meted out with concern and love.[19] Even when we spent forty years in the Wilderness, God lovingly provided us with manna from Heaven. Only a loving Father could punish so lovingly (*Rabbeinu Bachya*).

וַיִּתְאַבְּלוּ הָעָם מְאֹד
and the people mourned
exceedingly (ibid. 39).

God's forgiveness for the sin of the Golden Calf was granted easily. Yet His forgiveness for the people's rejection of the Holy Land was not. Why? The Torah speaks of the sadness, mourning and regret which overcame the people in both in-

stances. What, then, was the difference?

R' Simchah Bunim of P'shis'cha sees in this incident a lesson.

True repentance takes place when a person truly understands the gravity of sin, how profoundly it stains one's soul and the terrible affront it presents to the One Above. Only one who feels the pain and anguish is truly remorseful for what he did. Although one feels emotionally and spiritually spent, one craves the opportunity to serve God in the future.

When the Jews sinned with the Golden Calf, they were not familiar with the power of repentance. Broken in spirit, they begged God for a forgiveness they thought He would never grant. Because they were broken in spirit, God forgave them. When the Jews sinned with their rejection of the Land they already knew that God forgives the penitent. That very knowledge limited their ability to achieve complete repentance. Their repentance was, to some extent, an imitation of what they did at the time of the Golden Calf. It lacked sincerity and was not adequate![20]

Background

From every batch of dough a Jew prepares, he must separate a portion for the Kohanim. This is called *challah*. Traditionally, this mitzvah is performed by women.

---

19. **Wake-up Spank.** We are used to thinking of punishment as a way of paying back for a misdeed done against an individual. We foolishly view Divine retribution the same way, failing to realize that no one can really do anything against God.

Divine punishment is more like the spanking that a parent gives a young child who darts out into the street. Since the child is clearly unaware of the danger in which he has placed himself, the parent must impress that message upon the child by means of a spanking. We place ourselves in danger when we sin, but since we do not realize this, God punishes us to impress this upon us (*R' Abraham J. Twerski*).

20. **The Real Me.** The *Satmar Rav* (R' Yoel Teitelbaum) once attended a wedding at which there was a *badchan* (jester). The *badchan* asked the Satmar Rav for permission to imitate him. To have imitated the *Rav* in his presence without permission would have been totally disrespectful. The Rav nodded and gave his consent.

The *badchan* began impersonating the Rav's *davening*. The Satmar Rav's high-pitched voice and *tefillos* on such holy days as Rosh Hashanah and Yom Kippur were legendary. The *badchan's* gestures and voice were amazingly similar to those of the Rav. The people roared with laughter and delight. The Rav, though, watched the *badchan* carefully and soon began to cry. The *badchan* felt terrible.

When he finished his routine, the *badchan* approached the Rav and began to apologize. "Rebbe," he said, "I feel terrible that I upset you. I am truly sorry."

"Don't feel bad," the *Rav* said. "It is not your fault."

"So then why were you crying?" the *badchan* asked.

"Your imitation of me was perfect and I was truly amazed. I began to wonder: 'If a stranger can imitate me so well, perhaps when I stand before the *amud* on the *heilige teig* (High Holy Days) I, too, am merely imitating the Satmar Rav?'"

מֵרֵאשִׁית עֲרֹסֹתֵיכֶם תִּתְּנוּ
לַה׳ תְּרוּמָה לְדֹרֹתֵיכֶם

From the first of your kneading
you shall give a portion to Hashem,
for your generations (15:21).

The word עֲרִיסָה, *kneading,* also means crib. The Torah teaches that education begins in the crib.

Even a young child should be taught to follow the Torah path according to the best of his physical and emotional abilities.

Spiritual growth is a lifetime process. If we are to succeed in producing *generations* who are loyal to God, His Torah and His People, the tone must be set from the very beginning.

פרשת קרח ‎⇜
Parashas Korach

Background

Korah stirs the passions of his group into a frenzy of "righteous indignation." He claims that Moses fabricated commandments and misappropriated power. Korach further charges that Moses was a selfish leader who put his own family's needs before the nation's. He therefore deserved to be challenged.

וַיִּקַּח קֹרַח
Korah . . . separated himself (16:1).

It is noteworthy that although the Torah lists a number of rebels, the singular term וַיִּקַּח, *and he took,* is used. This indicates that there was no unity of cause or ideology among the group, each individual rebelled against Moses for his own personal reason. The only binding common denominator was that they all felt restricted by Moses' spiritual stature and position. This idea is reflected in the *Mishnah* in *Pirkei Avos* (5:17) which contrasts those

arguments that are for the sake of Heaven with those that are not. The prototype of an altruistic argument is that of the Mishnaic sages Hillel and Shammai. The opposite is that of Korah and his followers.

At first glance, the parallel seems flawed. Should it not rather have said Moses and Korah? *R' Yonasan Eibeschutz* explains: Korah and his followers fought amongst themselves. While all of them wanted to depose Moses, each one coveted the honor for himself.[1]

From what did Korah separate himself?

Sfas Emes explains: Every Jew must see himself as a link in the chain which began with our forefathers and continues throughout the generations until the Final Redemption. Even though one's contribution may be minuscule, it is unique to that individual and is vital. One broken link, however small, will still render a chain useless. We must link ourselves, our children and grand-

---

1. **True Altruism.** Both Hillel and Shammai sought the truth. Therefore, their differences of opinion serve as a prime example of arguments conducted for the sake of Heaven. On the other hand, the clash between Korah and Moses is an example of an argument conducted not for the sake of Heaven. Although Korah had his own agenda, Moses viewed himself completely as God's soldier. The argument was one sided (*Midrash Shmuel*).

The worst type of strife is one in which all sides are self-righteously convinced that they are fighting for the sake of God. People can stoop to the lowest form of behavior when they think they are acting with the purest of intentions.

R' Menachem Mendel of Kotzk explains: The Sages teach that Peninah had righteous intentions when she taunted Chanah over her barrenness; she wanted Chanah to turn to God in intense prayer (*Bava Basra* 16a).

"Yes," said R' Mendel homiletically, "only when one acts for the sake of Heaven can one be so cruel."

children to the generations that preceded us.

Korah arrogantly thought he was so great he could chart his own course rather than follow in the footsteps of tradition.[2]

The truly righteous person is only concerned that God's will be fulfilled; it is irrelevant to him through whom it happens.

Korah wanted the reward that comes with leadership. Had he been only concerned with God's will, Moses' leadership would not have bothered him. Korah wanted to take for himself, rather than see God's will be achieved (*Kedushas Levi*).[3]

בֶּן קְהָת בֶּן לֵוִי
son of Kehath, son of Levi (ibid.).

Rashi notes that Korah's genealogy stops with Levi and that Jacob's name is not mentioned, and explains that Jacob had prayed for this (*Genesis* 49:6).

Just as a person's physical makeup is largely an aggregate of genetic factors, so one's spiritual orientation and powers are a result of whom his forebears were.

When one sins, he affects his own soul and leaves a spiritual stain on all the elements which

feed into his soul from his ancestors.

Were this contamination to be total, one would lack the spiritual resources to repent. Only if one's deep ancestral roots remain intact is one able to spiritually resuscitate oneself.

Jacob prayed that this sin, notwithstanding its severity, should lack the power to uproot the source of sanctity which he contributed. Therefore, Jacob's name is not mentioned.

וְדָתָן וַאֲבִירָם
with Dathan and Abiram (ibid.).

Why are Dathan and Abiram singled out while the rest of the two hundred and fifty participants remain anonymous?

The two hundred and fifty rebels were either leaders of the tribes (*Midrash*) or heads of the courts (*Rashi*). While they were certainly wrong to contest Moses' leadership, we may offer a mitigated argument on their behalf. Their thirst for honor misguided them. Therefore the Torah protects their honor and allows them to maintain anonymity.

Not so Dathan and Abiram. They were not Levites and had no personal stake in this rebellion. They did it simply for the sake of argument.

---

2. **Emergent Leadership.** וַיִּקַּח literally means *and he took*. Korah made the mistake of trying to gain power and acquire a prestigious position for himself. But the only prestige which has any value is that which one is granted from Heaven (*R' Simchah Bunim of P'shis'cha*).

The great leaders of the Jewish people neither campaign for, nor are they elected to their positions. The nation has an intuitive sense of who their leaders are.

R' Moshe Feinstein once explained to a non-Jewish journalist, "No one elected me. People asked questions and I answered. Eventually more and more people brought their questions to me and word went out that I was a good person to ask."

3. **Letting Him Give.** Antignos teaches that one should not serve God to receive reward (*Avos* 1:3). Yet the Talmud in *Sotah* relates that when Moses wanted to enter the Holy Land, God said to him, "Since you seek the reward for performing those *mitzvos* which can only be performed there, I will grant you the reward." Was Moses not aware of Antignos' words.

R' Chaim of Volozhin (*Ruach Chaim*) explains: In truth, one *should* serve God in order to receive reward because God, the Source of all goodness, wants to bestow His goodness upon others. Most of us, however, want reward for our own selfish reasons. The litmus test of one's motivations is whether one is willing to perform God's will when someone else receives the reward, thus providing God with the opportunity to bestow His kindness.

Moses, who was the most loyal servant of God, sought reward in order to allow God to give. It was therefore legitimate that he expect reward. Antignos addresses the common man whose desire for reward is not rooted in such pure motives. We are told, "Do not be like servants who serve the Master in order to receive compensation."

Someone once asked *R' Simchah Bunim of P'shis'cha*, "If you were offered to switch places with the Patriarch Abraham, would you?"

"I would refuse," he replied. "God would be no better off because of it; he would still have one Simchah Bunim and one Abraham."

To sow the seed of discord for the sake of nothing more than a good fight is inexcusable. Therefore, the Torah points an accusing finger directly at Dathan and Abiram (*Chidushei HaRim*).

❧

The Midrash teaches that Korah had his group dress in garments of *techeiles* (turquoise-blue wool). He then questioned Moses as to whether a garment made completely of *techeiles* requires a strand of *techeiles* on its *tzitzis* (see *Numbers* 15:38). When Moses replied in the affirmative Korah derided him. "If one strand of *techeiles* exempts an entire garment, a garment of *techeiles* should surely be exempt." Similarly, Korah claimed that a house full of Torah scrolls should be exempt from having a *mezuzah* on its door.

R' Nosson Adler suggests a homiletic insight. Korah claimed that since the entire assembly is holy (see verse 3) and they witnessed the revelation at Sinai, there was no need for Moses and Aaron to assume a leadership role. Just as a *tallis* which is entirely made of *techeiles* does not need a special strand, so too a people as holy as the Jews does not need a special leader.

The truth is that regardless of our elevated spiritual status, we always require leadership and direction.[4]

וַיָּקֻמוּ לִפְנֵי מֹשֶׁה
They stood before Moses (ibid. 2).

Targum Yonasan renders the verse as saying, "They stood brazenly in front of Moses." Where does the text allude to brazenness?

R' Yosef Tzvi Dushinsky suggests that in order to avoid having to exhibit their subservience to Moses, they arose when they spotted him from afar

so it would be unnecessary for them to rise upon his arrival.

The Talmud warns against this very behavior and teaches that one may not close his eyes to an approaching scholar (see *Kiddushin* 33a). *They stood before Moses* arrived, in a gesture of defiance, refusing to accord him the proper respect.[5]

וְדָתָן וַאֲבִירָם . . . קְרִאֵי מוֹעֵד אַנְשֵׁי שֵׁם
Dathan and Abiram . . . those summoned for meeting, men of renown (ibid. 1-2).

At a rabbinic conference attended by the *Chafetz Chaim*, a motion was made to publicly condemn the leaders of a Jewish political party, famous for its compromising approach regarding matters of religious commitment.

The *Chafetz Chaim* gave the following reply to the motion: "Dathan and Abiram were among the conspirators of Korah. The Torah tells us they were generally summoned to meetings and consultations. Why should Moses have summoned them to meetings? He certainly remembered how they had betrayed him to Pharaoh in Egypt (see *Exodus* 2:13-15).

"The answer," taught the Sage of Radin, "is that Moses always made sure to treat them honorably so as to restrain the worst tendencies in them."

וּמַדּוּעַ תִּתְנַשְּׂאוּ עַל קְהַל ה׳
Why do you exalt yourselves over the congregation of Hashem? (ibid. 3).

How could Korah accuse Moses of arrogantly seizing power for himself and exalting himself over the nation when the Torah clearly testifies that Moses was the most humble of men (*Numbers* 12:3)?

---

4. **Aggrandizing Equality.** [It is ironic that those who instigate revolution under the banner of "equality for all" and campaign for a classless society are often power-hungry despots who, upon assuming leadership, ruthlessly oppress the masses on whose behalf they supposedly revolted. The now-defunct Communist Revolution in Russia was living testimony to this sad truth.

Korah preached equality (that all are holy), yet in his heart he sought to replace Moses and repress the masses.]

5. **Insulting Compliments.** [How frequently do we avoid contact with authentic Torah scholars to escape being forced to publicly display our subservience to them? The Talmud (*Berachos* 33b) teaches that overcomplimenting God is really an affront to Him since one cannot accurately portray God's praise. Likewise, overcomplimenting a Torah scholar is an affront to him since we are truly incapable of appreciating his greatness.]

Such is the nature of rabble-rousers. They hurl accusations simply to besmirch the accused and cast aspersions in the areas where their target is least vulnerable (*R' Simchah Bunim of P'shis'cha*).

Sfas Emes clarifies: The Sages instruct us to refrain from behaviors which might imply we are conducting ourselves in a fashion befitting someone of a higher spiritual stature. (See, for example, *Shulchan Aruch, Orach Chaim* 123:4.)

Moses, the epitome of humility, was far removed from viewing his virtues as sources of personal pride. He therefore did not realize that he must refrain from behavior which might be viewed as arrogant. Korah therefore accused him of viewing himself as spiritually superior to others.[6]

וַיִּשְׁמַע מֹשֶׁה וַיִּפֹּל עַל פָּנָיו
Moses heard and fell on his face (ibid. 4).

*R*ashi views this reaction as an expression of despair and hopelessness. Moses felt he could no longer pray on behalf of the nation.

The Talmud (*Sanhedrin* 109a) states that Korah and his followers accused Moses of adultery. *Haflaah* offers a homiletic interpretation. He bases it on the Talmud's comparison of a person who infringes on his friend's livelihood (by entering the same field) to an adulterer (*Sanhedrin* 81a).[7] Korah claimed that he was the one who really deserved to be the Kohen Gadol and that Moses "infringed on his territory," by appointing his brother Aaron to the office.

Chasam Sofer offers a different perspective. When someone rises above his peers through his own strenuous efforts it is understandable that he should be appointed the leader of the community. However, if he was born head and shoulders above the rest, why should he be granted any privileges? Born with a remarkable soul, Moses deserved no special credits or privileges.[8]

At first glance it might seem that Korah's argument had some validity. However, he disregarded a principle set down by the *Rambam* (*Hilchos Teshuvah* 5:2): "Do not entertain the thought that is expressed by foolish non-Jews and by many Jews of inferior intelligence that God preordains whether a person will be righteous or wicked. This is absolutely untrue. Every person has the ability to be as righteous as Moses our teacher or as wicked as Jeroboam."

Korah failed to realize that Moses' spiritual pedigree was irrelevant. His greatness was his own.

An alternative homiletic interpretation sees Korah as accusing Moses of tampering with the Torah rather than disseminating the unadulterated tradition he received from God.

By definition, a servant is subservient to his master and enjoys no autonomy whatsoever. He must perform only those tasks that are assigned to him. Not so a wife. Although the property may belong to the husband, she is granted the freedom to treat it as her own (within normal limits). She may also alternate the domestic duties she wishes to assume. The Torah teaches us that Moses was God's loyal servant (see *Numbers* 12:7) and therefore served as the conduit through which God granted us the Torah: "Let Moses rejoice with his portion for You called him a loyal servant"

---

6. **It's Nothing.** Among most chassidic groups, the Rebbe's seat is at the head of the table. The custom of the *Rebbes of Ger,* however, is to sit in the middle of the table, with elderly or prestigious *chassidim* seated alongside.

Once the *Imrei Emes* of Ger visited the *Rebbe of Aleksander,* who asked the Gerrer Rebbe to join him at the head of the table. The Imrei Emes replied, "It's nothing [not necessary]." The Aleksander Rebbe asked him again, "Please come sit next to me," and again the Gerrer Rebbe refused the invitation.

The Aleksander Rebbe replied, "If it really is nothing then come sit next to me at the head of the table."

The *Imrei Emes* quickly complied.

7. **Immoral Infringement.** "One of the reasons that God brings couples together in matrimony is so that they bring children into the world." Likewise God grants one talents and abilities to be able to support himself and his family. One who infringes on another's source of livelihood is thus compared to an adulterer (*Simchas Aharon*).

8. **Everybody Nobody.** Korah was also "humble." He claimed that not only was he nothing special, but that nobody else was either. Moses also viewed himself as being undeserving of any special credit for what he was, but, he viewed others in the most positive light (*R' Shalom of Belz*).

(Sabbath prayers). Korah, however, claimed that Moses viewed his relationship with God as that of a wife who may take liberties with her husband's property (*Tzvi Yisrael*).[9]

רַב לָכֶם בְּנֵי לֵוִי
It is too much for you,
O offspring of Levi (ibid. 7).

Rashi comments: Korah was a wise man; how could he have acted so foolishly?[10] His eye caused him to err. He saw prophetically that among his offspring would be the prophet Samuel — who was as great in his time as Moses and Aaron combined (*Psalms* 99:6).

Rashi's question is based on a premise about Jewish leadership stated in the Talmud: One should not be appointed to public leadership unless he has a familial flaw in his past. This is to assure that he never become too haughty. If he begins to behave arrogantly we tell him to look at his past and see that he too has a "skeleton in his closet."

Since Korah had no such familial blemishes in his past, why did he think he was fit to be the leader of the nation? Rashi answers that Korah saw through semiprophecy that the prophet Samuel would descend from him. Korach thought, "Samuel was the leader of the Jewish people in spite of having no familial blemish. Apparently one can be a leader even if he suffers no flaw in his lineage."

Korah was mistaken. *He* was the familial flaw in Samuel's past (*R' Yeshaya Mushkat*).

Shem MiShmuel offers an insightful interpretation of *Rashi's* words, "his eye caused him to err." God grants man two eyes,[11] one to focus on God's greatness and the other to clearly see one's limitations. For this reason someone who is blind in one eye is exempt from the mitzvah to ascend to Jerusalem during the pilgrimage festivals (*Chagigah* 2a). The goal of that mitzvah is not only to experience the greatness of God but also to attain a proper perception of one's self as well.

The Kohen Gadol, who maintained a constant presence in the Temple, had to live with this dual vision on a daily basis. Korah, blinded by the great lineage which would come forth from him, was unable to have a true perception of his human limitations. He was therefore unfit to be the Kohen Gadol.

Alternatively, the eye which caused Korah to fatally err refers to a different type of spiritual vision. The Talmud (*Horayos* 12a) instructs students to look at their teachers when studying under them, based on the words of the Prophet Isaiah, *Your eyes shall see your teachers* (30:20).

[Even when one's teacher is not present, it is beneficial to conjure up his image. A classic example is Joseph who was greatly tempted to sin with the wife of Potiphar. His father's face suddenly

---

9. **Base Besmirchment.** The words of the Sages might be understood in their most literal sense. Why should they report such base and crude accusations made against our great teacher Moses?

Herein lies an important lesson. There will always be people of substandard morals who do not hesitate to besmirch the greatest Torah personalities of the generation, accusing them of the worst forms of immoral and unethical conduct. These besmirchers believe that at least some of the rumors will stick and be believed.

The Torah therefore teaches us that even Moses, the epitome of human spiritual achievement, was accused of adultery. Just as we would never entertain the possibility that this charge be true, so we must have full confidence in the Torah leadership at all times (*R' Chaim of Brisk*).

10. **Every Wise Fool.** *R' Shlomo Freifeld* once commented, "The Yiddish expression has it that יעדער נאר איז פאר זיך קליג, *every fool is clever with regard to his own personal issues.* The converse is also true, יעדער קליגער איז פאר זיך א נאר, *every intelligent person is a fool with regard to himself.* The most intelligent people, successful in offering advice to others, can often do the most foolish things with regard to themselves."

11. **Double Hearing.** One is granted two ears; one with which to hear and one with which not to hear.

There are many mischievous deeds that children or students may do to which a parent or a teacher must respond. When the child knows that the parent or mentor is aware yet does not react, the child misinterprets the mentor's silence. On the other hand, responding to negative behavior is often counterproductive. Sometimes, the best tactic is to wait patiently for the childish foolishness to pass. In such instances a parent or teacher should simply feign ignorance and convincingly pretend that he or she is unaware.

That is why we are granted a second ear — not to hear (*R' Shlomo Freifeld*).

appeared to him and warned him of the dire consequences (*Sotah* 36b).][12]

Korah's ego blinded him from seeing that every person, even one as great as himself, needs a mentor to keep him on the straight and narrow path.

הַמְעַט מִכֶּם כִּי הִבְדִּיל אֱלֹהֵי יִשְׂרָאֵל
אֶתְכֶם . . . לַעֲבֹד אֶת עֲבֹדַת מִשְׁכַּן

Is it not enough for you that the God of Israel has segregated you . . . to perform the service of the Tabernacle? (ibid. 9).

The Sages teach that one who has one hundred coins seeks two hundred. In temporal matters this is a character flaw. We are taught in *Pirkei Avos* (4:1) that true wealth belongs to those who are satisfied with their lot.

In spiritual matters one should always strive to improve. Nevertheless, every person occupies his specific role in God's master plan and has no right to assume a different one.[13]

Sometimes we underestimate the importance of our purpose in God's plan, and begin to search for what we believe to be a more prominent mission. According to R' Yechezkel Abramsky, this was the import of Moses' words.

The Levites' mission is complete devotion to Torah study (see *Deuteronomy* 33:10 and *Rambam, Hilchos Shemittah V'Yovel* 13:12). They are performing the greatest public service on behalf of the Jewish people.

Moses told them, "You Levites have been

---

12. **Inspiring Image.** On the day R' A.L. left the Telshe Yeshivah, his rebbe R' Elya Meir Bloch summoned him to his office. On the table lay a *Morgen Journal,* the Yiddish newspaper of that time. In an advertisement, rabbinic charlatans offered their services for a price.

When R' A. entered, the *Rosh Yeshivah* raised his eyes and said to him, "Do you see these advertisements? I know you are blessed with a pleasant voice and plan to pursue a career as a *chazzan* and clergyman. I want you to promise me two things. First, you will never perform a marriage ceremony as the officiating clergyman. Second, as a *chazzan* you will only go under the *chuppah* (wedding canopy) to assist a rabbi who is strictly Orthodox." R' A. extended his hand and gave his rebbe a solemn promise.

Some thirty years later, the phone rang in R' A.'s home. R' A. went into his bedroom and a protracted conversation ensued. The tones were raised and the conversation was heated and passionate. Finally R' A. emerged and found his son waiting for him. "Who called, Abba, and what were you arguing about?" he asked.

R' A. proceeded to tell his son about his promise to R' Elya Meir. "The man on the phone," he continued, "is a Holocaust survivor and a member of our synagogue. He asked me to perform at his son's wedding as cantor. The wedding will take place in Great Neck, N.Y. I asked him if our local Orthodox rabbi will be officiating and he told me that a rabbi from Great Neck will be performing the ceremony. 'Is he an Orthodox rabbi?' I asked him. He replied in the negative. 'Well then, I'm sorry, but I can't attend.'

" 'But, *Chazzan,* we have been such good friends for so many years. You *must* be the cantor at my son's wedding,' he implored.

" 'I wish I could, but I have a policy to officiate only with an Orthodox rabbi.'

"His tone became more desperate. '*Chazzan,* I will be terribly embarrassed if neither my rabbi nor my cantor attends the wedding. Please reconsider.'

"To hurt the feelings of a Holocaust survivor is no easy matter. But I knew that I couldn't officiate with a Reform or Conservative clergyman. I said to him, 'Believe me, Sol, I am happy for you and would be ready to do almost anything for you, but this is a matter of principle.'

"Finally in a desperate tone he said to me, '*Chazzan,* I'll give you a thousand dollars if you come and officiate at the wedding.' "

R' A. turned to his son and said to him, "You know how much a thousand dollars could help me' (at the time, R' A.'s annual salary was all of $8500). But I saw my rebbe sitting at his desk in front of the *Morgen Journal.* I couldn't do it."

13. **A.W.O.L.** A soldier in the army may never abandon his post, even in order to fill a different role which he deems more crucial to the success of the mission. Doing so is nothing short of insubordination and deserves severe punishment.

This is not only true if a general seeks to assume the duties of a private, but even if a private abandons his post to execute the duties of a general. The Levites thought that to be a Kohen is a promotion in rank. Even so, questioning the role that God assigns one is in itself a breach of discipline (based on *Kli Yakar*).

granted the greatest role. Is it not enough that God has separated you from among the entire nation to study His Torah![14] Why do you seek priesthood when the crown of Torah is even more meaningful than the crown of *Kehunah* (priesthood)?"

וְאַהֲרֹן מַה הוּא כִּי תַלִּינוּ עָלָיו
And as for Aaron — what is he that you protest against him? (ibid. 11).

R' *Shlomo Kluger* views Moses' argument as reflecting a nuance of human nature. When someone behaves abusively toward great and simple people alike, the simple ones are not insulted. They say to themselves, "If the great people did not feel hurt by these words, why should we?"

This is what Moses meant to tell the rebellious party of Korah. "You don't mean to attack me or my brother. Your rebellion is essentially against God.[15] Therefore, you can be sure that Aaron will neither take your invective seriously, nor feel the slightest bit hurt by it."

R' *Meir Arik* expands on this theme. He mentions the Talmud (*Eruvin* 65b) which teaches that one's true character may be measured by three yardsticks, בְּכוֹסוֹ וּבְכִיסוֹ וּבְכַעֲסוֹ, meaning *one's cup* —

how he behaves when he drinks excessively; *one's pocket* — the way he relates to money; and *his anger* — how he behaves when he loses control.

Since the Kohen Gadol must be independently wealthy (*Yoma* 18a), money was of little significance to him and could not serve as a barometer of his character. Likewise, his cup would reveal nothing since he is forbidden to become intoxicated. The only possible way to know Aaron was by inciting him. Moses told Korach: "Try to get Aaron angry and see if you succeed. Then you will really know who he is."[16]

וַיִּשְׁלַח מֹשֶׁה לִקְרֹא לְדָתָן וְלַאֲבִירָם
Moses sent forth to summon Dathan and Abiram (ibid. 12).

Although Moses was absolutely certain he was correct, he nonetheless reached out in peace overtures to the most hardened of the provocateurs. *Rashi* derives that one should never obstinately maintain a fight. Controversy must be avoided at all costs. Even if one's overtures have been consistently rebuffed, he should not tire but try once more (R' *Yitzchak of Vorki*).

R' *S.R. Hirsch* adds: Strife and belligerence cause

---

14. **True Community Service.** R' *Yitzchak Hutner* once told his beloved students on Purim, "Many well-intentioned people solicit the help of yeshivah students for all types of communal and public service, some more worthy and some less. I want to state categorically that there is no higher form of community service than sitting by the *Gemara* and learning."

[The Talmud teaches that one who states, "What have the students of Torah and the rabbis done on our behalf?" is considered a nonbeliever (*Sanhedrin* 99b). Unfortunately, it is often those who devote their lives to Torah study who suffer from this misguided view.

Yeshivah students must intellectually and emotionally absorb the reality that the very existence of the world and the physical and spiritual security and welfare of the Jewish nation is inextricably linked to the intensity of their commitment to Torah study.

They must maintain their posts at all times for everything depends on them!]

15. **They Mean Me!** R' *Yoel Teitelbaum,* the Satmar Rebbe, was often the target of sharp criticism for his fiery opposition to political Zionism and the State of Israel. However, due to his towering Torah scholarship, impeccable morals, ethical conduct, and caring behavior and righteousness, he was nonetheless held in great esteem. As a result, people who wished to criticize him would often aim their barbs at his followers. "The Rebbe himself is not so vehemently opposed; it is his students and followers who exaggerate his position," they would claim.

The Rebbe responded, "It is not my students, it is me. If they want to criticize, let them point their fingers at me."

Likewise, the rebellion of Korah and his group was not really against Moses or Aaron, it was against God Himself.

16. **Dragged-down Leaders.** R' *Menachem Mendel of Kotzk* put it this way, "And as for Aaron, what is he?" — Do you really think you know who Aaron is?! Are you capable of understanding the exalted sanctity of the one you seek to fight?

[All too frequently we make the mistake of thinking that we have a right to criticize our leaders, assuming that they are no more sanctified than we are. We often need to be reminded exactly who we seek to criticize. Let us never come to the mistaken conclusion that since we are spiritually inferior, so are our mentors.]

people to hear meanings in the words of others which were never intended.

Moses called for Dathan and Abiram to pursue peace and bring reconciliation. They heard in his words a summons to appear in front of him as one comes before a judge. They therefore vehemently rejected the summons as if to say, "Who do you think you are to command us? We will not come up before you!"

וַיֹּאמֶר אֶל ה׳ אַל תֵּפֶן אֶל מִנְחָתָם
and he said to Hashem, "Do not turn to their gift-offering" (ibid. 15).

We underestimate the power of prayer.[17] Moses, who was undoubtedly correct, felt compelled to ask God not to accept the prayers and offerings of enemies. Were God to accept their prayers, the entire nation's belief in Torah would have been irreparably undermined and Korah's heretical views would have been legitimized. Yet, Moses was still afraid. Why?

The answer is that heartfelt prayer has the power to succeed.[18]

The rebels honestly believed they were championing the cause of the people and earnestly asked God for a sign that they were right. Moses was afraid of their prayer.

A puzzling *Mishnah* (*Makkos* 2:6) depicts this aspect of prayer. Those who had accidentally murdered were exiled to the cities of refuge. They had to remain there until the death of the Kohen Gadol (see *Numbers* 35:25). The Mishnah relates that the mother of the Kohen Gadol would bring food and clothes for the inmates as a bribe that they not pray for the Kohen Gadol's death.

Why should she be worried that the prayer of a murderer (albeit an inadvertent one) would succeed in causing the death of the Kohen Gadol? The answer is that heartfelt prayer works even if one is asking for something inappropriate. Similarly, the Talmud relates that in his short prayer on Yom Kippur, the Kohen would ask God to reject the prayer of the wayfarers who ask for dry weather to facilitate their travel plans (*Yoma* 53b). The wayfarer realizes that only God has the ability to stop the rain and implores Him to do so. Although this is detrimental to others, God may accept the wayfarer's heartfelt prayer. The Kohen Gadol therefore had to ask God to reject it.

לֹא חֲמוֹר אֶחָד מֵהֶם נָשָׂאתִי
I have not taken even a single donkey of theirs (ibid.).

Why did Moses feel it necessary to deny having taken even a single donkey? Would anyone suspect Moses of breaking into someone's stable to steal a donkey?!

Rashi explains that Moses sought to make it *perfectly* clear that personal benefit was not part of his agenda. When he returned to Egypt on his rescue mission he did not take anyone else's donkey nor did he expect to be compensated for

---

17. **Sensing Pain.** *Rambam* (*Hilchos Taanios* 1:2-3) writes that if people do not pray in times of communal trouble, they are cruel. The Rambam does not use the term "wicked," but "cruel."

When people are in trouble and see no solution on the immediate horizon their dormant faith in God is aroused and they cry out to Him for help. Why? Because the pain is immediate and touches either their lives or someone dear to them. Were we to sense the troubles of the entire Jewish people as our own, we would certainly reach out to our Heavenly Father in prayer. The reason we do not is because we feel "It's not my problem."

We have in our arsenal an awesome weapon called prayer. Even if our requests are not entirely granted we must realize that in some way we have been answered. Do we really know how many tragedies were averted due to our prayers? Even if we did not clearly witness the salvation we wished for, we must not underestimate the extent to which our prayers softened the harshness of God's decree. Can we possibly know how many potential victims were saved due to our heartfelt cries?

One cannot cruelly stand aside and refrain from utilizing the gift of prayer to do what one can. Let us storm the gates of prayer for one another (*R' Yechezkel Sarna*).

18. **Careful Prayer.** [Much of what we pray for is not beneficial for us. We ask for things we foolishly think are necessary but which actually shift our focus away from the needs of our souls. Yet God grants our requests, because we sincerely turn to Him to grant us what we honestly view as necessary. A wise man once advised, "Be careful what you pray for. God might actually grant your request."]

his expenses. Moses was never in it for himself![19]

R' *Yerucham Levovitz of Mir* sees this as an important lesson in introspection and self-critique.

Dathan and Abiram accused Moses of seizing power for himself. Although their criticism was rooted in their own fantasies, Moses felt compelled to examine whether their words contained even the slightest bit of truth. He could have brushed the whole thing off as nothing more than vicious and baseless character assassination; yet, he gave thought as to whether he had ever abused his position for any sort of personal benefit. His careful self-examination yielded the conclusion that he had. According to *R' Yisrael Salanter,* this readiness to engage in self-assessment based upon the criticism of enemies is reflected in the words of King David, "When those who would harm me rise up against me, my ears have heard" (*Psalms* 92:12). People are often unable or unwilling to accept criticism. We create all types of emotional self-defense mechanisms. When others offer even constructive criticism, we rationalize that the person does not truly understand our situation and is mistaken in his assessment of us. Worse yet, we attribute their comments to jealousy or a begrudging nature. This even occurs when the critic is a friend. When he is an enemy his rebuke is totally discredited since his motives are "undoubtedly" biased.

It takes a great man to differentiate between the critic and the criticism. His being my enemy does not negate his criticism. King David says, "Even when those who bode me no good speak, I listen for perhaps they speak the truth!"

We would do well to listen, even when our enemies speak. They may be saying something worth hearing.

R' Moshe Feinstein offers a fascinating perspective. Why, he asks, was Moses fearful of taking anything from anyone? As the king of the nation (see *Ibn Ezra* to *Deuteronomy* 33:5), he was entitled to impose taxes on the people or even make use of their property.

The answer lies in a fundamental difference between Moses and other kings. When one's rule is the result of having been appointed king, he may feel free to seize the people's property at will. Moses' rule, however, was based on his Torah knowledge and God's will; he was never appointed.[20] Torah may never be exploited for the personal benefit of those who learn it. Therefore, Moses refused to take anything from anyone.[21]

19. **Teflon Clean.** Once, when the *Chazon Ish* still lived in Europe, he was summoned to a nearby village to rule on the *kashrus* of an animal that had been slaughtered. The Chazon Ish walked to the town, checked the animal and issued a ruling. When he was ready to return home the butcher summoned a wagon with a driver to take the Chazon Ish back home at his own expense. The Chazon Ish refused the offer, in spite of the butcher's pleas.

"Both Moses and Samuel the Prophet declared that they never received anything from anybody" (see *Berachos* 6b). They obviously didn't steal, explained the Chazon Ish. What were they referring to? The answer is that when they came to someone's home to inspect an item to issue a halachic ruling, and the person wanted to provide them with a donkey for transportation, they refused the offer.

20. **Unofficial Leadership.** *R' Moshe Feinstein* made this point when eulogizing *R' Yechezkel Abramsky.* Moses needed no official appointment to assume the leadership of the nation. The exalted nature of his personality, character and total self-negation to God made it obvious to all that he was to lead the people. This is true of all the great Torah leaders. Their very essence causes them to emerge as our leaders. R' Yechezkel was considered a premier rabbinic leader, whether he was the rabbi of the small town of Smilovitz, the famed metropolis of Slutzk, a rabbinic judge in London or retired in *Eretz Yisrael.*

His towering stature in Torah crowned him as royalty among his people, immaterial to his official position and status. True Torah leadership is not elected; it emerges. It needs no props to grant it legitimacy, for it survives on the merit of its own intrinsic greatness.

21. **Horse Money.** *R' Yisrael of Rizhin* conducted his court with much pomp and ceremony, resembling the royalty of the time. This lifestyle entailed great financial expense which was borne by his followers. It also drew much criticism. [The truth was that in Czarist Russia, where Jews saw themselves as downtrodden and beyond redemption, the royalty of the Rizhiner lifted the spirits of the people, reinvigorated them with a sense of self-worth and infused them with hope for future redemption.]

A wealthy Jew once asked him, "Why did the righteous of the past subsist on very little and distribute whatever

לֹא חֲמוֹר אֶחָד מֵהֶם נָשָׂאתִי וְלֹא הֲרֵעֹתִי אֶת אַחַד מֵהֶם

I have not taken (even) a single donkey of theirs nor have I wronged (even) one of them (ibid.).

Leaders are frequently subject to the accusation that they refrain from rebuking people who give them gifts or provide them with personal benefit.[22] Other times people resent the guidance offered by the Torah leader when they feel the Rabbi insulted them personally.

Moses declared that neither of these criticisms of leadership style applied to him. "I did not take anything from anybody and therefore was always willing to offer rebuke when necessary. On the other hand, I never wronged or insulted anyone by offering criticism in a hurtful or degrading manner." He therefore implored God to ignore the offering of Korach and his conspirators.

הָאִישׁ אֶחָד יֶחֱטָא וְעַל כָּל הָעֵדָה תִּקְצֹף

Shall one man sin and You be angry with the entire assembly? (ibid. 22).

Rashi cites the Midrash that God told Moses, "Your words are well taken. I know who sinned and who didn't." God's response seems to address the issue of the sinners although Moses was praying on behalf of the nonsinners. What did God mean?

Shearis Menachem explains: God told Moses, "You beseech Me on behalf of those who refrained from sin while you expect the sinners to be punished. In theory you are right, but I look at things differently. I know the innermost thoughts and emotions of all people. Even those who sin are not all the same; some sin with 100 percent of their being, others with 50 percent and others with 10 percent. Should they all be equally punished? Are they all totally wicked?[23]

---

money they had to charity while today's 'righteous' conduct themselves like princes who live in castles?"

The Rizhiner replied, "How does a Rebbe support himself? From the gifts of his followers. There are three types of followers: serious servants of God, simple working people and sinners. The gifts of the earnest *chassid* who does everything for the sake of Heaven are used by the Rebbe for holy causes and charity. The gifts of the simple, honest, hardworking Jew (given to the Rebbe so that the Rebbe pray on his behalf for health and financial success) are earmarked for the support of the Rebbe and his family. What, however, should the Rebbe do with the money given by the sinners who only give to be honored and respected by others? He can't reject the gift, for he wants to keep the sinner close to try to positively influence him. On the other hand, he doesn't want to benefit from tainted money. The Rebbe therefore uses that money to build palaces and buy white steeds.

"Once upon a time, when most followers of rebbes were serious spiritual searchers, the Rebbes lived simply and distributed most of what they received to charity. Today, however, the wealthy sinners flood the courts of the Rebbes. They have no choice but to spend the money on horses and castles."

22. **Objective Educator.** When *R' Judah Feinerman* was a young man and learned under *R' Yaakov Moshe Shurkin*, he noticed that R' Shurkin's suit looked a bit worn. He mentioned this to his father, who owned a suit factory. The senior Mr. Feinerman, who had an abiding respect and affection for Torah scholars, called R' Shurkin and asked him to come to his factory, saying, "I have two suits for you." R' Shurkin replied, "I am sorry but I unable to pay for the suits just now." Mr. Feinerman made it clear that he did not expect payment. "It would be my pleasure to give you the suits," he said. R' Shurkin paused for a moment and replied, "Mr. Feinerman, your son is my student. Sometimes, in my role as teacher I must reprimand him. If I wear the suit you will give me I will have a difficult time rebuking your son. I have a job, and I must carry it out loyally and properly. I appreciate the offer, but I must refuse."

23. **Points of Light.** People's lives are not black or white. We are all a mixture of good and evil, positive and negative. No person is completely evil. In every one of us there lies a point of light and goodness which is our saving grace.

R' Nachman of Breslov and *Beis Avraham* see this principle in the words of King David: וְעוֹד מְעַט וְאֵין רָשָׁע וְהִתְבּוֹנַנְתָּ עַל מְקוֹמוֹ וְאֵינֶנּוּ, *Just a bit more and there will be no wicked one; you will contemplate his place and he will not be there* (Psalms 37:10).

If one seems to have absolutely no redeeming quality or value, search further. You will certainly find some bit of good. It is this *"just a bit more"* of goodness which maintains and justifies his existence. If you contemplate *"his place"* and your preconceived notion about his spiritual stature, you will see that you no longer view him at that spiritual level.

Every person must also view himself in this positive manner by focusing on his spiritual strengths and virtues. Rather than succumbing to despair, one must build on the positive, no matter how insignificant and minute it may

וְדָתָן וַאֲבִירָם יָצְאוּ נִצָּבִים
Dathan and Abiram went out erect (ibid. 27).

Self-righteous to the very end, Dathan and Abiram were defiant, refusing to show Moses even minimal respect.

The word מִדּוֹת, *character traits,* literally means measurements. There are no intrinsically good or bad traits. Every trait must be employed in the proper measure and under the appropriate circumstances. Brazenness can be positive if it is used to deflect the scorn of scoffers who seek to cool our passion and disrupt our desire to do God's will. We are taught in *Pirkei Avos* (5:23) to be "bold and brazen as the leopard . . . to carry out the will of our Father in Heaven."

Unfortunately, people often get their signals crossed.[24] This is alluded to in the continuation of that *Mishnah*: "The brazen go to *Gehinnom.*" Frequently when engaged in behavior which will lead them to *Gehinnom*, people become emboldened and do not think twice about desecrating God's name by sinning publicly. However, "The shamefaced go to the Garden of Eden." When publicly involved in religious pursuits, people suddenly become humble and emotionally feeble (*R' Baruch of Medzhibozh*). Instead of being humbled by the words of Moses, Dathan and Abiram misappropriated brazenness on their way to the netherworld.

---

seem. It is this that King David alludes to when he said אָשִׁירָה לַה' בְּחַיָּי אֲזַמְּרָה לֵאלֹהַי בְּעוֹדִי, *I will sing to Hashem while I live, I will sing praises to my God while I endure (Psalms 104:33)*.

To transform one's life one must find his own עוֹד, the little bit of goodness which makes his life meaningful. By focusing on that point of spiritual light he can turn himself into a vehicle of praise to God.

24. **Misplaced Shame.** "Isn't it ironic that people think nothing of jogging in their shorts in public yet when they have to daven *Minchah* in Penn Station, they feel compelled to go to a public phone and pretend they are making a call" (*R' Shlomo Freifeld*).

פרשת חקת ›§
Parashas Chukas

Background

The laws pertaining to the Red Heifer, whose ashes are one of the main ingredients in the mixture used to purify those contaminated by corpse-*tumah*, are taught to the Jewish people. The true reason behind them was left unrevealed. The Red Heifer is titled *the decree* of the Torah, for it is the quintessential paradox and internal contradiction. Its ashes purify those who are contaminated while those who prepare it become impure.

זֹאת חֻקַּת הַתּוֹרָה
This is the decree of the Torah (19:2).

The nations of the world, as well as Satan himself, taunt the Jewish nation as to why they adhere to the law of the Red Heifer. It not only lacks any sort of rhyme or reason, but even seems to be internally contradictory. The Torah therefore tells us that it is a decree to be followed blindly, and that we are not to question the purpose of any particular mitzvah (*Rashi*).

The mockery comes in two stages. Initially Satan tells man, "What kind of mitzvah is this? It seems absolutely pointless. Why bother with it?" However, man knows that he must follow God's will and he performs the mitzvah despite his evil inclination. Now Satan attacks on a different front, appealing to his arrogance and self-importance. He causes him to think, "I am so dedicated to God. I overcame my evil inclination and followed His will although this mitzvah really seems to have no logical reason. I've done something extremely meaningful."

Therefore the Torah tells us that this [and every mitzvah] is a decree. Before you perform the mitzvah, remember that it is God's will that you are fulfilling even if you do not understand why. But after you do the mitzvah, remember that it is still a decree — do not get carried away with your importance or the fact that you have fulfilled a mitzvah (*R' Meir of Premishlan*).[1]

---

1. **Before and After.** In our *Maariv* prayers, we ask God to *remove spiritual impediment (Satan) from before us and from behind us.*

The classic understanding of these words is that sometimes Satan figuratively stands in front of us to prevent us from fulfilling God's will. At other times he stands behind us, encouraging us to do a certain mitzvah that will cause us great spiritual loss. For example, he whispers, "Stay up late tonight at a wedding, fulfilling the great mitzvah of rejoicing with the bride and groom." What he really means is, "Don't get up on time for *davening* tomorrow" or "And tomorrow you won't be able to learn with a clear head."

In light of *Rashi's* comment, we may understand this prayer differently. We ask that God help us when the mitzvah is before us and behind us. We pray that we not be impeded before fulfilling the mitzvah and that we not have our egos inflated after we have completed the mitzvah (*Shaar Bas Rabbim*).

Rashi says that we shall not question the reason for the mitzvos. Why not? Such questioning could only help strengthen our commitment to the Torah.[2]

An incident in the Talmud may shed light on this. The Mishnah (Shabbos 1:3) states that one may not read by candlelight on the Sabbath, yet offers no explanation why this is so. The Gemara (Shabbos 12b) explains that it is out of fear that one will tamper with the wick if the light flickers and will transgress the laws of the Sabbath by causing the candle to burn properly. The Talmud then relates that R' Yishmael thought he would be able to read yet still be careful not to tamper with the wick. He read by candlelight and inadvertently broke the law. R' Yishmael then declared, "How great are the words of the Sages!"

Why did this incident cause R' Yishmael to proclaim the greatness of the Sages? Was he merely impressed that their suspicions had been validated?

The Vilna Gaon explains: When R' Yishmael learned the Mishnah, he wondered why the Sages did not explain the reason for the law. However when, as a result of the explanation in the baraisa, he rationalized that he was able to take the risk, he realized how right they were not to offer any explanation in the Mishnah.

We may now understand Rashi's comment. Of course one should seek out reasons and rationale for mitzvos. However, one must never use the reason as an excuse to absolve oneself from following the Torah's demands. It is a decree; you have no right to question it.[3]

זֹאת חֻקַּת הַתּוֹרָה
This is the decree of the Torah (ibid.).

A law with no apparent reason or explanation is called a חֹק (decree), while that for which some rationale is offered is called a מִשְׁפָּט.

Why did Hashem give us both types of laws?

R' Shlomo Freifeld suggested an interpretation. The word טַעַם means both taste and reason.

In order for one to receive the nutrition necessary for survival he need not eat; he may be fed intravenously. Nevertheless, if he wants to eat with enthusiasm and allow his entire being (body, heart, mind and emotions) to be part of the process, the food must be both tasty and appetizing.

This is equally true of mitzvos. God is not satisfied with mere robotic performance. He wants our mind, body, heart and soul to be fully involved.

---

2. **Misappropriation.** *Rambam* (*Hilchos Me'ilah* 8:8) writes: "It is proper that one contemplate the laws of the holy Torah, to penetrate and perceive their rationale to the best of his ability. However, if he is unable to ascertain the reason for it or realize its underpinnings, he should not as a result regard it lightly and brazenly incur the danger of disregarding God's sanctified word. One should never regard it as something mundane and inconsequential. See how severely the Torah deals with one who appropriates sanctified items for mundane purposes. [One must pay for the misappropriation, add one fifth of the value, bring a sacrifice and, in some cases, receive lashes.]

"If the Torah deals so severely with regard to mere wood, stone, dirt and ashes which have been sanctified by invoking the Name of the Master of the universe, calling for punishment even if the breach of sanctity was accidental — then certainly if one treats God's mitzvos disparagingly by rejecting those whose reasons he cannot intellectually perceive he deserves severe censure and punishment."

In *Hilchos Temurah* (4:13), Rambam delineates the balance necessary. "Although all of the mitzvos of the Torah are royal decrees, it is nonetheless proper to investigate their meaning. Any reason which can be advanced to explain a mitzvah should be expressed."

A reason is not *why* we do the mitzvah; we do it because God commanded us to do so. The reason adds flavor.

3. **Too Smart.** *R' Yitzchak* said, "Why were the reasons for many of the Torah commandments not revealed? Because in two instances the Torah did reveal a reason and as a result a great man stumbled into sin. The Torah teaches that a king should not have too many wives so that his heart not turn astray (*Deuteronomy* 17:17). King Solomon claimed that he could disregard these limitations and not be affected. He was sadly mistaken. In his later years, his wives did lead him astray from the Torah path (*I Kings* 11:4). The Torah forbids a king from having too large a stable so that that its maintenance not necessitate Jews moving back to Egypt. King Solomon thought that he could have a large stable and forestall emigration to Egypt" (*Sanhedrin* 21b) (see *I Kings* 10:29). He was again proven incorrect.

Knowing the reasons of mitzvos may cause one to stumble.

Just as *taste* generates an appetite for food and enriches the eating process, likewise *reasons* add to our full involvement in fulfilling God's will. They make *mitzvos* "tasty" and whet our intellectual and emotional "appetite."

The spiritual nourishment in *mitzvos* however, is clearly the result of our following God's will, even though we are unaware of the underlying reasons. The חק, *decree,* provides our soul with its spiritual sustenance.[4]

חֻקַּת הַתּוֹרָה
The decree of the Torah (ibid.).

The phrase "This is the decree regarding purity" would seem to be a more appropriate introduction to these laws. *This is the decree of the Torah* seems to indicate a lesson which applies to all areas of Torah life.

R' Moshe Feinstein explains: The contradictory nature of the Red Heifer which purifies those who make use of it and contaminates those who prepare it is relevant to Torah life. Every character trait may be positive or negative, depending on how one uses it. For example, humility and arrogance are polar opposites. Ask anyone and they will tell you that humility is a positive trait and arrogance is a negative one.

Yet, in truth, one must adopt both of these traits, each in its own situation. When dealing with oneself, humility is the proper path, yet when it comes to the others, one should assume his friend is perfectly justified in his expectation to be treated respectfully. Humility, which is basically pure, can be a source of impurity if one exercises humility with regard to the honor of others. Likewise, although arrogance and the expectation to be honored are negative, they can become positive if they serve to honor one's friend.[5]

Another example is one's attitude toward money. When dealing with one's own money one should be very open handed in distributing it to charity and other mitzvah causes. But, when dealing with money that belongs to others one must be tight fisted, always aware of the reality that to take even a penny from someone else is robbery.[6]

To do otherwise is to defile the pure and purify the contaminated.

אֲשֶׁר צִוָּה ה' לֵאמֹר
Which Hashem has commanded (ibid.).

Torah is a pure manifestation of Godly intelligence which cannot be naturally fathomed by man. Thus, it is unremarkable that there are many *mitzvos* which we do not understand. What *is* remarkable is how many we *do* understand.

Accordingly, says the *Dubno Maggid,* the verse might be rendered as follows: This [the following] is the [unexplained] decree of the Torah that *Hashem has commanded saying.* The fact that He reveals any of His wisdom to us is truly remarkable.

In his famed style, he offers the following par-

---

4. **Complete Subservience.** The reason God gave us חֻקִּים whose reasons remain hidden may be understood through an observation of *Rabbeinu Yonah.*

In his classic *Shaarei Teshuvah* (1:6), he tells us that one is deemed by the Sages as an apostate for his blatant disregard of even one of the Torah's commandments. "A servant who says to his master, 'I will do everything you will tell me except for one item which I refuse to do,' has broken the yoke of servitude and acts as his eyes see fit."

One who accepts 612 of the 613 mitzvos does not accept God as the Sovereign Ruler. He may see eye-to-eye with God on 612 items but in reality follows his own agenda.

If one is aware of the rationale behind a mitzvah when fulfilling it, he may be motivated by both the rationale and fact that it was decreed by God. Hence we might never keep a mitzvah entirely because it is God's will. Therefore God gave us חֻקִּים in addition to מִשְׁפָּטִים (*Simchas Aharon*).

5. **Rehabilitating Arrogance.** The *Baal Shem Tov* says: People who are distant from God are often hesitant to begin. "Who am I," they say, "to actually stand in front of God in prayer? I am so far removed from Him." For such people, a little arrogance is positive. On the other hand, people who are basically pure in their actions often taint their actions by internally gloating over all they have accomplished for God. One who by studying Torah becomes intellectually arrogant suffers terribly as a result of his exposure to Torah. The same trait of arrogance purifies the impure while it contaminates the pure.

6. **Holy Money.** The great *Baalei Mussar* used to say that געלט איז בלאטע, "Money is [as worthless as] mud." *R' Simchah Zissel Levovitz* qualified: "Money is mud if it is your own. Someone else's money is holy."

able. An intellectually and spiritually unsophisticated Jew made a lot of money. As a result, the Rav of his city became his *mechutan*. The Rav's son was to marry his daughter.

After the wedding, the rags-to-riches success noticed that the Rav rarely spoke with him. Disturbed, he confronted the Rav. "Why do you treat me as a stranger when our children are man and wife?"

The Rav replied, "While I respect you and appreciate everything you do for the couple, we have really very little in common. Rather than wondering why I don't speak with you, it would make more sense for you to ask why I consented to become your *mechutan* in the first place."

We sometimes arrogantly think, "We are the chosen people. It is only proper that God speak with us and reveal to us all His reasons for the *mitzvos.*"

In truth, we should wonder why He agreed to take us in the first place.[7]

The Talmud relates the story of Dama ben Nesina, a non-Jew from Ashkelon who excelled in honoring his parents. Once the Sages came to buy some precious stones for the priestly breastplate. They were willing to pay him an exorbitant price. He refused to sell them because he would have to wake his father to get the key to open the casket where the gems were stored. Heaven rewarded him, and the following year a Red Heifer was born in his herd. When the Sages came to him to buy the Red Heifer, he told them that although he knew they would pay any price he asked, he only wanted to be reimbursed for the profit he forfeited on the gems as a result of honoring his father (*Kiddushin* 31a).

There are many lessons to be learned from this story. Although the Sages praise this non-Jew's sensitivity towards his father he was certainly wrong in his willingness to sell the mitzvah for the profit he might have gained from the sale. King Solomon testifies to the value of the Jewish people when he writes: *Were any man to offer all the treasure of his home to entice you away from your love they would scorn him in extreme* (*Song of Songs* 8:7). A Jew is unwilling to sell a *mitzvah* at any price for it is an expression of his love for God. What price can be placed on the priceless?

Furthermore, a Jew does not emotionally pat himself on the back for the good deeds he did in the past. A Jew feels that only now is he finally beginning to serve God. Dama ben Nesina viewed at his past good deed as a chip to be cashed in (*Darkei Mussar*).[8]

---

7. **Reality Born of Faith.** Every mitzvah has a reason. However one can only discover the reason if he is willing to fulfill the mitzvah unconditionally.

At Sinai the Jewish people blindly accepted the Torah. "We will do [even without understanding] and [then] we will hear [and understand]."

Blind allegiance opens our eyes to the secrets of the *mitzvos*.

King David's words mirror this very sentiment. *"As for me, my prayer [to you] be at an opportune time"* (*Psalms* 69:14). The Talmud comments, "When is the time opportune? When the congregation prays communally" (*Berachos* 8a).

Whenever the community prays together as a community, God hearkens to accept our prayers. Our very willingness to turn to Him in prayer, without any preconditions, causes Him to become receptive.

Faith creates reality (*Sfas Emes*).

8. **Forgotten Memories.** In the Rosh Hashanah prayers we refer to God as the זוֹכֵר הַנִּשְׁכָּחוֹת, *the One Who remembers the forgotten.* R' Yisrael of Rizhin explains: "What we forget below, they remember Above; what we remember below, they forget Above."

If one did a mitzvah and forgot that he did it [he does not wait to be rewarded], then God remembers his good deed. If one remembers his good deeds and as a result becomes arrogant, then God "forgets" what he did. This same idea applies to sins. If one sins and forgets about it [he is either in denial or feels he has sufficiently repented] then God remembers his sin. If, however, man constantly sees his sin before him (see *Psalms* 51:5), God is ready to forgive and grant atonement.

Since Dama ben Nesina constantly remembered his good deed, God granted his reward in this world and forgot about it above.

[When R' Gedaliah Schorr was questioned about his rescue activities during the Holocaust (see *They Called Him Mike*, ArtScroll/Mesorah) he would often respond with this thought of the Rizhiner.]

The commentators (*Maharal, Ben Yehoyada*) question why the non-Jew's reward took the form of a Red Heifer.

Chidushei HaRim explained: The willingness of Dama ben Nesina to originally forgo such a large profit aroused an indictment against the Jewish people. "See," claimed the Heavenly prosecutor, "he is willing to let the mitzvah of honoring his father cost him a tremendous sum." God therefore rewarded him with a Red Heifer. This way the Jewish people are able to demonstrate that although the non-Jew is willing to incur a tremendous loss to fulfill the logical, rational mitzvah of honoring parents, they are likewise ready to spend heavily to fulfill the illogical, irrational mitzvah of the Red Heifer, even though they do not understand it.[9]

אֲשֶׁר אֵין בָּהּ מוּם אֲשֶׁר לֹא עָלָה עָלֶיהָ עֹל

which is without blemish, and upon which a yoke has not yet come (ibid.).

The Red Heifer is the symbol of purity and spiritual vibrancy. *R' Yisrael of Kozhnitz* offered a homiletic interpretation.

If one sees himself as spiritually without blemish,

---

9. **Canine Dedication.** A similar incident occurred with *R' Levi Yitzchak of Berditchev.*

One Yom Kippur night, the huge crowd in *shul* waited for the *chazzan* to begin the *Kol Nidrei* prayer that would inaugurate the holiest day of the year. The Berditchever Rav motioned to the *chazzan* to wait.

The people assembled in the *shul* somberly waited for the Rav to give the signal to begin, but he was immersed in deep thought. Suddenly R' Levi Yitzchak turned to his *shammas* (attendant) and said, "Ask Muttel from Zhitomir to come up here." Muttel was escorted to the Rav, who began to question him at once. "Tell me, don't you live on land owned by the *poritz* (gentile landowner) Vladik?"

"Yes," said the surprised Muttel. Then the Rav asked, "Doesn't your *poritz* own a dog?"

"Yes, Rebbe," answered Muttel, not having the slightest idea why the Rav needed to know this information right now, on Yom Kippur eve, just moments before *Kol Nidrei.*

"Do you by any chance know how much he paid for that dog?" continued the Rav.

"I most certainly do," Muttel said proudly. "The *poritz* paid four hundred rubles. He said that it was a rare breed and bragged how much he paid for it."

R' Levi Yitzchak was thrilled. "Four hundred rubles! That's wonderful!" The Rav thanked Muttel for his help, then motioned to the *chazzan* to begin *Kol Nidrei.*

Later, after the *davening* had ended, a group of people gathered around the Berditchever Rav, inquiring about his discussion with Muttel.

The Berditchever explained. "You see, an incident happened this past year that troubled me. A *melamed* (tutor) came to our town from a distant city. He had accumulated many debts back home, and he therefore came to tutor children in order to earn a reasonable sum of money. He planned to return home, pay his debts and use the remaining money for his family's daily living expenses. He was here for almost a year. He earned the money he needed, and began his trip home.

"On the way, he stopped overnight at an inn. As he slept, the bag with all his hard-earned money was stolen. When he awoke in the morning and realized that his money was gone, the poor man was devastated. A whole year's effort was wasted!

"However, staying overnight at that same inn was this *poritz* of Muttel's. When he awoke in the morning, he heard the crying and wailing. He inquired as to what happened. When he was told the story he approached the *melamed* to find out exactly what had occurred. He became very impressed with the *melamed* and, right then and there, gave him from his own pocket — four hundred rubles."

The Berditchever continued. "As we were about to start *Kol Nidrei* earlier, I thought about that incident, and it worried me. Here we are to beg Hashem to look at us favorably throughout the coming year. But how could He? Who among us did such a comparable act of *chessed* this past year? If a gentile could do such a wonderful act, what does that say for us who are expected to do deeds of even greater kindness?

"Then I remembered about the dog. I knew that the *poritz* had spent a great deal of money for the dog, but I didn't know the exact sum. When I discovered out that he paid four hundred rubles for a pet I realized that four hundred rubles did not have much value to him. It's true that the act to the *melamed* was one of kindness but it wasn't one of great sacrifice" (from *Around the Maggid's Table,* ArtScroll).

We often view the enormous sums we spend on comforts as more important than the money we spend for charity or *mitzvos.* As Jews we must be committed to use our money more readily for *mitzvos* than physical needs.

it is obvious that he has not yet seriously taken upon himself the yoke of Heaven. Once he assumes the all-encompassing authority of God it will become apparent to him how spiritually blemished he is.

Only when we seriously assess our obligations to God are we able to see how we fall short in meeting them.[10]

R' S.Y. Zevin views this as a yardstick of inspiring leadership. In order for a leader to inspire his followers he must be independent and free of the spiritually negative influence of the masses.

One can only function like the Red Heifer and bring spiritual purity to others if he is unblemished by the effects of foreign influence.

וְלָקַח הַכֹּהֵן עֵץ אֶרֶז וְאֵזוֹב וּשְׁנֵי תוֹלָעַת
The Kohen shall take cedar wood, hyssop and crimson thread (ibid. 6).

Tall and strong, the cedar alludes to strength and arrogance while hyssop and crimson thread are symbols of lowliness and humility (see *Leviticus* 14:4 and *Rashi*, ad loc.).

It is the pendulum between these two extremes which is reflected in the *tumah/taharah* (impurity/purity) struggle.

On one hand man is corporeal and finite; on the other hand, the soul is eternal. The immortality of one's soul is a legitimate source of pride, while the fleetingness of his physical existence should humble him.

Thus, the purification process entails the humbling realization that we have no reason for arrogance (hyssop and crimson thread), along with the awareness that we carry within us a spark of the Eternal Divine (the cedar) (*Simchas Aharon*).

R' Simchah Bunim of P'shis'cha put it this way: "Every Jew must have two pockets: In one pocket he must carry the message of the Talmud that every person must say, 'The world was created on my behalf' (*Mishnah Sanhedrin* 4:5), while the other pocket must contain the words of Abraham, 'I am but dust and ash' (*Genesis* 18:27)."

The art of living is to know when to reach into which pocket.

זֹאת הַתּוֹרָה אָדָם כִּי יָמוּת בְּאֹהֶל
This is the teaching regarding a man who would die in a tent (ibid. 14).

The laws taught here are those regarding corpse-contamination in an enclosed area. The roof over the corpse causes the contamination to permeate the entire air space that it covers.

Why does the Torah cite the example of a tent? *R' Tzvi Pesach Frank* offers an explanation by contrasting our verse with the words of King Solomon, *so man goes to his eternal home* (*Ecclesiastes* 12:5).

This world is a tent, a temporary dwelling to which we are sent to accomplish our life's mission. Through our study of Torah and performance of *mitzvos* we create our eternal abode.

Thus man dies in a tent. He passes from this temporary world to the permanent dwelling of his own making, the eternal home that he fashioned in his lifetime.[11]

The Sages teach that Torah will endure only with those people who (figuratively) kill themselves for it (*Berachos* 63b).

This statement cannot be understood literally

---

10. **Wisdom Beyond.** *R' Menachem Mendel of Kotzk* explains the words of King Solomon, *I thought I would be wise, but it is beyond me* (*Ecclesiastes* 7:23).

One who thinks to himself, "I am wise," should know that, "it is beyond me."

11. **The School of Death.** We often inaccurately translate עוֹלָם הַבָּא as the *Next* World. In truth it is the world that *comes,* because it is a result of one's lifetime accomplishments.

When the Sages taught that every Jew has a share in *Olam HaBa* they did not mean it is a preexisting reality. One creates his share by the way he lives! (*R' Chaim of Volozhin*).

Shortly before *R' Simchah Bunim of P'shis'cha* died his wife began to cry, bemoaning his imminent demise. R' Simchah Bunim tried to calm her. "Why cry?" he asked. "All of life is a preparation for death. All my years I spent trying to learn how to die." The phrase *This is the Torah* (teaching) addresses man, teaching how to be *the* man who would die in the tent.

since the Torah clearly states that its laws are those *by which he shall live* (*Leviticus* 18:5) and not die (see *Yoma* 85a). We are to live according to the Torah, not, God forbid, to die as result of our adhering to its precepts. [Only in the case of murder, illicit relationships or idolatry are we commanded to forfeit our lives. See *Rambam, Hilchos Yesodei HaTorah* 5:2-2.]

The *Chafetz Chaim* offers the following parable: There once was a successful wholesaler who serviced customers from far and wide. He was so busy with his business that he did not even have time to go to the synagogue for prayer. Instead, he would quickly "gobble up" the prayers in the back room of his shop and return to his business affairs.

Many years passed; his hair turned white from age and he felt that his end was approaching. Realizing that he would soon have to make an accounting of his life, he decided that the time had come to tend to his spiritual needs. He began attending services regularly and after the morning prayers he stayed in the synagogue for two hours to learn some Torah.

The first day he did this, his wife, who was obviously upset, asked him why he had come to the shop so late. Did he not realize customers were impatiently waiting to buy goods? The man apologized to his wife and explained that he was delayed with some important business.

When the same story repeated itself over the next few days, the woman decided to go to the synagogue in search of her husband. How shocked she was to see him sitting and learning as if he hadn't a care in the world! She began screaming at the top of her lungs. "What is the matter with you? Did you lose your mind? We have a store full of customers and you sit and learn! I don't mind losing some sales but these are steady customers. If we don't service them, they will go to our competitors!"

Nothing helped. Her husband said to her, "Listen, my dear wife! What would you do if the angel of death were to come to me and tell me that my time is up and my earthly sojourn is over? Could you tell him I can't die now because I have a store full of customers? Of course not! Well, make believe I am dead. When I arrive three hours later you won't mind the fact that I came back from the dead to help you run our business."

This is what the Sages meant. Every person has a hundred reasons why they are too busy to learn or do a mitzvah right now. One can be busy all his life. The only way to be sure that we tend to the needs of our souls is to imagine that we are dead. Just as it is impossible to bother a dead man, so we must carve out precious time in our day for serious prayer and Torah study. Our friends, families and business associates will be thrilled when we come "back to life" again.[12]

R' Meir Shapiro sees this teaching as a call for single-minded dedication in educating our children to follow the path of Torah. The Torah will only endure with those who kill themselves for it, placing their children's spiritual achievements and commitment to Torah above everything else in their lives.[13]

According to *Sfas Emes*, the message relates to personal growth through Torah. One must be willing to kill himself for Torah knowledge and spiritual growth, for without it, life has no value.

Those who are ready to forgo physical comforts and invest their time and energies in the pursuit of Torah study "kill themselves for Torah." It is these

12. **Sage Advice.** The *Chafetz Chaim* used to offer the following advice: Think to yourself:
   1. You only have one more day to live.
   2. There is only one page in the Talmud — the one you are studying right now.
   3. You are the solitary Jew in the world whom God commanded to fulfill his Torah. Therefore the existence of the world depends on your actions.
   The first piece of advice prevents procrastination.
   The second leaves one undaunted by the task ahead of him.
   The third inspires. It teaches us to stop passing the buck. Divine success depends on us!

13. **Dedicated Parenting.** At times this demands financial outlay to send one's children to an appropriate Jewish school or to hire a private tutor to improve the child's education. In other instances, it may mean altering one's lifestyle so that the home and the school do not send conflicting messages.
   A child senses what is really meaningful to his parents. Those values become primary in the child's view.

people who most vividly experience life and discover that Torah provides vibrant life to those who cling to it.[14]

אָדָם כִּי יָמוּת בְּאֹהֶל
a man who would die in a tent (ibid.).

The Sages derived from the term *a man* that only the corpse of a Jew imparts contamination to enclosures. The corpse of a non-Jew does not. "You [Jews] are called אָדָם (man) while non-Jews are not" (*Yevamos* 61a).

This statement aroused the ire of many non-Jews and served as ammunition for anti-Semitic claims that the Talmud views Gentiles as sub-human.

Korban HaAni refutes this claim. Regarding the Jewish nation, Talmud teaches: "This nation is compared to sand and to stars. When its people fall spiritually, they fall till the ground; when they rise, they ascend to the stars" (*Megillah* 16a). These spiritual extremes are, according to *Shelah*, alluded to in the name אָדָם. On one hand, it relates to אֲדָמָה, *earth*, for the Jewish nation possesses the negative spiritual potential to fall embarrassingly low. On the other hand, the name אָדָם is reminiscent of the words of *Isaiah* (14:14), אֶדַּמֶּה לְעֶלְיוֹן — *I am comparable to the One on High;* for a Jew has the ability to skyrocket to unprecedented spiritual heights and become Godly. Since this spiritual extremism captured in the name אָדָם is unique to the Jewish people, only they are called אָדָם.[15]

According to *Techeiles Mordechai,* the name אָדָם is unique among the synonyms for a human being in that there is no plural form of the word. [אֲנָשִׁים is the plural of אִישׁ; גְּבָרִים is the plural of גֶּבֶר.]

Unlike other religions, in which one's nationality and one's faith are not interdependent (an Englishman can be Catholic, Protestant or Muslim; there are Irish Catholics, Italian Catholics, Russian Catholics, etc.), being Jewish is both a religious and national-ethnic identity. Hence there is no plural (of the word אָדָם), because a Jew can never have a double identity.

וְהָיְתָה לָהֶם לְחֻקַּת עוֹלָם
This shall be for them an eternal decree (ibid. 21).

Rashi offers a homiletic explanation of the Red Heifer. The Red Heifer comes to atone for the sin of the Golden Calf. This is analogous to a mother (the cow) cleaning up the mess of her child (the calf).

The Red Heifer purifies one who was contaminated by a corpse. Why is that impurity deemed the "mess" left by the Golden Calf?

Kli Yakar explains: The power of death was suspended at Sinai, for the Jews reachieved the spiritual status of Adam, before he sinned, who lived in a world without death (*Psalms* 82:6-7). However, as a result of the sin of the Golden Calf, death was reinstated. Thus death, the by-product of

---

14. **Life-Saving Pleasure.** King Solomon describes the Torah as *a tree of life for those who grasp it* (Proverbs 3:18). What does it mean by *a tree of life?*

   Imagine you fell off a cliff and were plummeting toward certain death. Suddenly, out of the corner of your eye, you notice a branch growing from the side of the mountain. At the last moment you reach out and grab the branch, holding on for dear life.

   This, taught *R' Chaim Volozhiner,* is what King Solomon meant. Without Torah we are plummeting toward spiritual oblivion. We must hold on to Torah with our last vestiges of strength. Without it, we are finished.

   The *Chazon Ish* wrote to a young man torn between his desire to grow through Torah and the seductions of the physical world. "Please inform me of your welfare, especially regarding Torah.

   "Man's desires and passions are complex, and one's body, with its tendency to fantasize, experiences pleasure as true enjoyment. To a certain extent, this type of pleasure does brings joy to the soul.

   "However, this physical pleasure can in no way compete with the exalted delight of toiling to achieve the wisdom of Torah. Man's soul soars above the din of this physical world, reaches to the stratosphere, and he experiences the pleasure of the aura of Divine wisdom. This experience is the ultimate gift granted man during his sojourn below the sun" (*Collected Letters* I:9).

15. **Immortally Mortal.** *Imrei Emes* sees a dichotomy in the process of preparing the Red Heifer. Ashes of the Red Heifer symbolize to us that man is nothing more than dust. Vibrant spring water symbolizes the living, immortal soul. We mix these two symbols together to create purity.

the Golden Calf, is cleansed by the Red Cow.

Sfas Emes embellishes on this theme. Death initially emerged on the stage of human existence when Adam and Eve, in a misguided attempt, tried to be as Godly as God and disobeyed His will by eating from the Tree of Knowledge.

How were the Jewish people to rectify this sin and limit the effect of death? By accepting the enigmatic laws of the Red Cow in total obedience to God.

Beis HaLevi adds: Although according to the people's reckoning Moses should have descended and returned (see *Exodus* 32:1), they still should have trusted the word of God and faithfully waited for Moses to come back. However, they viewed their own intelligence as primary and as a result, built the Golden Calf. They could only achieve atonement for this sin by displaying total commitment to laws such as the Red Heifer which have no intellectual rationalization, and thus demonstrate their humble loyalty to God.

Thus the words of *Rashi* are not a reason for the Red Heifer as much as an explanation as to why it grants us a way to atone for the Golden Calf.

וְלָקַח אֵזוֹב
and a pure man shall take hyssop (ibid. 18).

The cantillation on these two words are קַדְמָא וְאַזְלָא which homiletically may be rendered as *what precedes* and *going*.

In order to achieve the humility symbolized by the hyssop, one must focus both on his past and on where the future may take him. In the words of Akavia ben Mahalalel (*Avos* 3:1), consider three things and you will not come into the grip of sin: Know from where you come (what precedes) and where you are going. By both reflecting on his origins and contemplating the final destination of his physical body, man is induced to humility and is inspired with a sense of purpose (*Peninim Yekarim*).

Background

The Torah now begins to narrate the events and commandments which were transmitted during the last year of the Israelite's sojourn in the Wilderness. The death of Miriam and the loss of the well which existed in her merit open this section.

וַתָּמָת שָׁם מִרְיָם
Miriam died there (20:1).

The juxtaposition of the death of Miriam with the laws of the Red Heifer teaches us that just as offerings bring atonement for the Jews, so does the death of the righteous (*Rashi* based on *Moed Kattan* 28a).

Why did the Torah teach us this lesson with the Red Heifer?

R' Itzele of Ponevezh explained: While all offerings effect atonement, the role of the one who brings the offering is basically passive. In the words of the Talmud, "The Kohanim eat the flesh and the owners are granted atonement" (*Pesachim* 59b). Not so the Red Heifer; one must be sprinkled with its ashes in order to achieve purity. Likewise, the death of the righteous call upon us to adopt their refined character traits.

The prophet teaches that *The righteous one perishes and no man takes it to heart; men of kindness are gathered in with no one understanding that because of the impending evil the righteous one was gathered in* (Isaiah 57:1).

Two explanations are advanced by the commentators regarding the phrase "because of the impending evil."

According to some, the righteous die as a result of the evil deeds of the masses, and their death atone for their sins. Alternatively, the death of the righteous occurs *before* impending evil so that they may be spared the calamities that are to befall the nation (see *Sanhedrin* 113b).

The two explanations contradict each other for if their death is the catalyst for atonement then calamity can be avoided.

Noda B'Yehudah explains that the death of the righteous atones only if we learn from their ways. If we are not inspired by their death, we deserve terrible punishment. Then God takes away more righteous people to let them avoid witnessing the calamities that will befall us for having been uninspired.

וְלֹא הָיָה מַיִם לָעֵדָה
There was no water for the assembly (ibid. 2).

As a result of Miriam's death, the Jewish people lost its source of water since the well in the Wilderness existed in her merit (*Rashi* based on *Taanis* 9a).

The manna existed in the merit of Moses, the clouds of glory existed in the merit of Aaron and the well of water existed in the merit of Miriam. From among the three, water is the most crucial. Why was the water in the merit of a woman?

R' Moshe Sternbuch explains: Women are the most important factor in the molding of children and in shaping the Jewish home. No one exercises as profound an influence on a child as a mother. The values she imparts, by her conduct, leave an indelible impression on the mind, heart and soul of the child. The spiritual viability of the home is in her hands, be it with regard to the level of morality and modesty, the standard of *kashrus* or the spirit of caring she displays in hosting guests. The woman insulates the home, making sure negative spiritual winds do not penetrate its walls.

The Torah, which is compared to water (*Bava Kamma* 17a), is granted us in the merit of women who follow and are the spiritual heirs of Miriam.

Righteous women were always the cornerstone of the nation, imbuing their homes with sanctity and purity necessary for the the vital waters of Torah.[16]

Due to the disappearance of the well, Moses is instructed to speak to the rock to order it to give forth water. Moses erroneously hits the rock, and is severely punished.

קַח אֶת הַמַּטֶּה . . . וְדִבַּרְתֶּם אֶל הַסֶּלַע לְעֵינֵיהֶם
Take the staff . . . and speak to the rock before their eyes that it shall give its waters (ibid. 8).

Why should Moses take the staff to speak to the rock? The staff, made up of twelve intertwining pieces, is symbolic of the unity of the Jewish nation. Although Moses was to speak to the rock and implore God to grant the people water, his prayer would be more effective if it was offered for the entire nation. He took the staff to remind himself to pray on behalf of the entire nation even though some were evil sinners. The Talmud (*Berachos* 8a) teaches us that God never rejects the prayer of the community (*Simchas Aharon*).

Homiletically, this teaches us how to educate and influence others toward a life of Torah.

Even if someone's heart is as hard as a rock, the Torah can penetrate so profoundly that the heart will soften and the waters of Torah will flow from it. In order to influence a hardened heart one must first speak to the "rock;" the hardend person to influence him with soft, caring words. Only if that approach is ineffectual should one consider taking a staff and use a more forceful approach.[17]

---

16. **In Her Spirit.** *R' S.R. Hirsch* writes regarding the death of Miriam: "She finished her earthly mission. She was buried at Kadesh to record for posterity that she didn't leave the world until she had prepared the next generation for its promised future. Throughout the long journey in the Wilderness, the women of Israel were never partners in the rebellions against God which were ultimately rooted in despair. With heartfelt joy they trusted in God and yearned for Him with total dedication. It was for this reason that the death sentence pronounced on the generation of the Wilderness did not impact on the women of Israel (see *Bamidbar Rabbah* 21:11). Mothers and grandmothers were now poised to enter the Promised Land along with a new generation. Ensconced in their hearts was a live memory of the past in Egypt and the Divinely directed travels through the Wilderness granting them the ability to give the souls of their grandchildren and great-grandchildren to drink from the spiritual spring of their experiences with God. Jewish women throughout the generations filled themselves with true Jewish spirit, allowing it to penetrate to the depths of their souls. This is the spiritual heritage they received from Miriam the prophetess who lit up the path for all Jewish women and mothers."

17. **Silent Stick.** A seasoned educator once said that discipline is a locked attaché case. The students believe it holds a pair of brass knuckles, but it is never opened.

If the teacher opens the case the child will see there is nothing inside.

God told Moses to take the stick for its value as a threat, but never to use it. He must speak to the rock.

To paraphrase the words of President Theodore Roosevelt," Speak softly, but carry — do not use — a big stick."

Although one may become frustrated, he may never use verbal or physical abuse. Darkness disappears only by letting in light; sticks cannot drive it away.

According to *R' Reuven Margolis*, Moses was punished for this very reason. Since they left Egypt, the Jewish people were constantly complaining to Moses. He had every right to be frustrated. Nevertheless, by instructing him to *speak* to the rock, God alluded that he should speak words of encouragement to the people. Moses, in a moment of weakness (see *Rambam* below), hit the rock. The approach was flawed and Moses was punished.[18]

שִׁמְעוּ נָא הַמֹּרִים הֲמִן
הַסֶּלַע הַזֶּה נוֹצִיא לָכֶם מָיִם
Listen now, O rebels, shall we bring forth water for you from the rock? (ibid. 10).

Rashi offers two explanations for the word הַמֹּרִים. The first is that they are an obstinate people. The second is based on the Greek meaning and means foolish people; those who desire to teach their own teachers [מֹרִים meaning *teachers*].

R' Avraham Mordechai of Ger views the two explanations as one, based on the words of King Solomon. *Have you seen a man who is wise in his own eyes? There is more hope for a fool than for him* (*Proverbs* 26:12).

One who views himself a wise man cannot imagine that anyone has anything to teach him. Convinced of his intellectual, ethical and moral superiority he is obstinately resistant to introspection and accepting guidance from others. In his eyes, he is more fit to *teach* his teachers than learn from them. There is no bigger fool than he who considers himself his teacher's equal or superior.

R' Yehoshua of Kutna wonders why *Rashi* sought the Greek translation instead of the Hebrew meaning of the word.

He offers a homiletical explanation which sheds light on the crucial difference between the Torah and secular perspective on succeeding generations.

In the Torah view, the generations spiritually regress as time goes on. "If the previous generations were human then we are but donkeys [in comparison] (*Shabbos* 112b). The secularist approach takes the opposite position, viewing later generations as more advanced than earlier ones who were neither privy to the latest technological and scientific discoveries, or newest philosophical "truths."

From our perspective, the more one is chronologically removed from Sinai, the more inferior he is. The secularist, on the other hand, sees newer as better.

Greek philosophy views as legitimate a student seeking to teach *the teachers*. The fool (in Greek) feels he can serve as mentor to his mentors.

וַיָּרֶם מֹשֶׁה אֶת יָדוֹ
Then Moses raised his arm (ibid. 11).

Why does the Torah stress that Moses raised his hand in order to strike the rock? Certainly it is the act of striking that is the most important aspect.

R' Yosef Shaul Nathanson (*Divrei Shaul*) puts forth a novel approach based on a comment of the *Maggid of Kozhnitz*. The Torah teaches that *Abraham stretched out his hand and took the knife to slaughter his son* (*Genesis* 22:10).

Abraham had so thoroughly refined his body spiritually that his limbs reflexively responded when called upon to act in accordance with God's will. Since slaughtering Isaac was in reality against God's will, Abraham's arm resisted. He was therefore forced to stretch out his hand.

Likewise here: Moses' hand resisted striking the rock since God had instructed that he speak to it. Therefore Moses was forced to raise his arm.

---

18. **Soft Pedal.** When God spoke to Moses from the Burning Bush, He asked him, *What is that in your hand?* meaning, how do you intend to lead My people? Moses replied, *A staff*, symbolic of the strict authoritarian approach (see *Exodus* 4:2).

God replied, *Cast it on the ground. . .stretch out your hand and grasp it by the tail* (see *Exodus* 4:4). Discard the authoritarian approach — it does not work. Instead, just barely hold on to the stick and speak words of encouragement which will draw their hearts toward God and Torah. Show them the beauty and delight of Torah (*R' Aharon Bakst*).

יַעַן לֹא הֶאֱמַנְתֶּם בִּי לְהַקְדִּישֵׁנִי

*Because you did not believe in
Me to sanctify Me* (ibid. 12).

According to *Rambam*, Moses sinned by becoming angry at the Jewish people for their constant complaining. The sin was compounded by the fact that the people understood Moses' anger as reflective of Divine displeasure.

The verse, however, defines the sin of Moses as a lack of faith, not anger. How are we to reconcile these two descriptions?

The Sages equate anger with idolatry (see *Rambam, Hilchos Deios* 2:3 and *Shabbos* 105b), underscoring the idea that anger indicates a lack of faith. *R' Yerucham Levovitz* explains:

"Faith by definition means an unshakable view of life which ascribes everything that happens to the All-Knowing and All-Powerful God. Nothing can move the faithful person from his serenity since all that happens comes from God.

"One who becomes angry at others loses that serenity and emotional immovability. He imagines his alleged adversary has the ability to act independently against him, views him as the source of his anger and pours out on him his wrath. This is idolatry, for one does not have power over another without God's consent. There is no independent force in the world besides God."

When Moses became frustrated with the constant bickering, he ever so slightly lost his spiritual equilibrium. His clarity of unshakable faith in the Creator became momentarily clouded.[19]

Background

On the doorstep of the Holy Land, the Jews want to enter by way of passing through the territory of the Edomites but are refused passage.

וַיִּשְׁלַח מַלְאָךְ וַיֹּצִאֵנוּ מִמִּצְרָיִם

*He sent an emissary and took
us out of Egypt* (ibid. 16).

Rashi explains that מַלְאָךְ, literally an angel, refers to Moses himself who was God's emissary to redeem the emerging Jewish nation from Egypt.

Doesn't such a title smack of arrogance at the least? How did Moses, the humblest of men, describe himself in such terms to the king of Edom?

R' Eliezer Gordon, the *Rosh Yeshivah* of Telshe, related an incident:

R' Abli Pasviler, the last official Rav of Vilna, once chanced upon a Jewish farmer riding a wagon led by a horse and a cow tied together. R' Abli told the farmer that this was forbidden according to Torah law (see *Rambam, Hilchos Kelayim* 9:7). When the farmer refused to listen, R' Abli tried to explain to him the severity of the prohibition. Even threats of the terrible punishment awaiting him in Heaven did not move the obstinate farmer.

Finally, R' Abli uncharacteristically told him, "Do you know who I am? I am the greatest and

---

19. **"God Made Him Do It."** *Sefer HaChinuch* understands the prohibition to take revenge as follows.

Since nothing happens to man without God's approval, one could do well to assume that those who harm him are God's messengers. Why take revenge on the stick when it is but a tool in the hand of he who wields it?

King David lived this lesson when he refused to allow his loyal servants to avenge Shimi ben Geira for having cursed the king. "God told him to curse," he told them (see *II Samuel* 16:10). The *Chazon Ish* writes: There exists a person who deeply desires to do good to others. Meeting a friend causes him heartfelt joy. He tries his best to welcome him with a cheerful face and is forever mindful that he may have been insensitive and spoken in an incorrect manner. Nothing pains his heart as much as having treated a friend dishonorably or refraining from showing him kindness.

On the other hand, he never feels insulted by a friend, for his heart overflows with love. He is willing to accept the barbs his friend might send his way because he is aware that most people do not possess perfect character and are only human. While able to constantly find character imperfections in himself, he simultaneously views his friends positively even if their interpersonal sins are "thick as the reins of the wagon" (see *Isaiah* 5:18).

This soul need not demand of itself self-control against natural anger or the pain of being embarrassed by others. This soul is so refined that no stain sticks to it. It is sate with the joy of eternal life (*Emunah U'Vitachon* 1:11).

most renowned Rabbi in Vilna. When I return I will have you excommunicated!"

The farmer was shocked and quickly unhitched the cow.

In his attempt to save the farmer from sin, R' Abli was ready to don the guise of arrogance.

Likewise Moses, in his efforts to insure that the king of Edom grant the Jews peaceful passage, was prepared to speak in an arrogant manner (*R' Zalman Sorotzkin*).

פרשת בלק ‎§‎
Parashas Balak

Background

The previous *sidrah* ends with the victory of the Jewish people over the Amorites. In this *sidrah,* Balak the king of Moab expresses his fear of the Jews and their military victories. He hires the prophet Balaam to curse the Jewish people; however, Balaam's attempts are thwarted and he blesses them instead.

וַיַּרְא בָּלָק בֶּן צִפּוֹר
Balak son of Zippor saw (22:2).

In this verse Balak is not referred to as the king of Moab: It is only after he warns of the imminent danger presented by the Jews that his royal title is disclosed (see verse 4).

Balak was merely a private citizen when he warned of the Jewish threat. It was in reward for this warning that he was crowned king. Verse 4 concludes *Balak son of Zippor was king of Moab at that time (R' Chaim Soloveitchik).*[1]

אֵת כָּל אֲשֶׁר עָשָׂה יִשְׂרָאֵל לָאֱמֹרִי
All that Israel had done to the Amorite (ibid.).

Certainly the miraculous events surrounding the Exodus from Egypt were more awe-inspiring than the victory over the Amorite. Why did the particular victory arouse the fear of Moab to the extent that they hired Balaam to curse the Jews?

Kli Yakar suggests that *Israel* refers not to the nation but rather to Israel our forefather (Jacob) who succeeded in seizing Shechem from the Amorite by means of his heartfelt prayer to God (see *Genesis* 48:22, *Rashi* ad loc. and *Bava Basra* 123a). When Balak saw this he realized that the power of the Jewish people lies in their mouths; namely, in their ability to speak directly to God and request Divine intervention.

The Moabites sought to neutralize this secret of Jewish survival by soliciting the services of Balaam, a man whose power [to curse] also lay in his mouth.[2]

Nesivos Shalom offers a different explanation: Whenever the Torah refers to the nation as יִשְׂרָאֵל,

---

1. **Anti-Semitic Coattails.** [In a world hostile to Jews there is no better campaign strategy for one seeking power than to point out the great threat presented by the mere existence of the Jewish people. If one wants to assume a leadership role among the nations, all he must do is point an accusing finger at the Jews and describe the terrible calamities that their continued existence will bring. Anti-Semitic coattails are the most effective way to ride into office.]

2. **Sanctified Speech.** *Magen Avraham* expands on this theme, rendering the word אֱמֹרִי as *speaking* (from the root אָמַר, *said*). When Balak realized how Israel transformed the power of speech, he was truly frightened. With words of Torah, prayer and refraining from slander, mockery and talebearing, Jews sanctify speech. "How will we survive the onslaught of a nation who have so elevated the power of speech?" the Moabites asked themselves.

Israel, it teaches that the people were totally united. For example, regarding the verse *and Israel encamped there* (*Exodus* 19:2), the Sages comment that the Jews were united "as one man with one desire" in experiencing the Revelation of God at Mount Sinai.

In the war against Sihon the Torah states *Israel smote him* (*Numbers* 21:24), because it was the power of Jewish unity which vanquished Sihon and the Amorite.

This strength of unity struck fear into the hearts of Balak and the Moabites. When they saw what happened to the Amorite they were afraid they would meet the same fate. As the next verse (22:3) states, *Moab became very frightened of the people because [it] was numerous.*

As the Sages teach: "Were the nation of Israel to enjoy perfect unity, love and interpersonal harmony, no nation in the world could harm it."[3]

וַיִּשְׁלַח מַלְאָכִים אֶל בִּלְעָם בֶּן בְּעוֹר
*He sent messengers to Balaam
son of Beor* (ibid. 5).

Rashi notes that God granted Balaam prophecy so that the nations of the world would be unable to claim that had God given them a prophet, they too would have repented. He did not help them. On the contrary he himself was immoral and he induced the populace to engage in promiscuous activities. Seemingly, *Rashi's* answer begs the question. The claim of the nations still appears to be valid. Had God sent them a righteous prophet like Moses they might have repented. Instead they were given the immoral Balaam.

R' Simchah Bunim of P'shis'cha, told the following story by way of explanation:

"When I was having problems with my vision, I went to Berlin to search for a good doctor. I asked around to find out the name of a reputable ophthalmologist. Someone offered to take me to a 'wonder doctor' who, he claimed, could totally cure me within a very short time. I refused the offer and told him, 'In truth, when someone is sick he should pray to God directly that He heal him rather than visit a doctor. The only reason we go to doctors is because a Jew must make use of natural means in seeking cures for his ailments. If you want me to seek the help of a wonder doctor who provides 'miraculous' remedies, I might as well seek the help of the holy *Maggid of Kozhnitz.*"

The same thing occurred with the nations of the world. How, after witnessing all the great miracles Moses did for his people, did the nations still refuse to believe in him? The answer is that they did not believe he possessed supernatural, Divine sanctity; to the contrary, they were convinced he did everything through magic.

God therefore sent them Balaam, who *was* well versed in the use of supernatural occult powers. Once they believed in him they no longer had any excuse as to why they did not listen to Moses. If they were going to follow a "wonder doctor" anyway, they should have followed Moses.[4]

---

3. **Unbreakable Unity.** The Midrash compares the Jews to a package of sticks. When bound tightly together, not one can be broken. Untie the bundle and, one by one, they will snap.

Balak saw what Israel had done to the Amorite and sensed the secret of Israel's invincibility.

4. **Ruined by the Pot.** R' Chaim Yitzchak Chaikin submitted a variation on this theme based on the words of the Talmud (*Shabbos* 30a) which compares the fear of Heaven to a storehouse of grain. The greater the degree of fear of Heaven the more Torah knowledge one can absorb [see *Nefesh HaChaim* 4:5 for an elaboration of this concept].

This is analogous to a woman who gave her neighbor a recipe. The neighbor followed all the instructions yet the dish was a failure. She angrily accused her friend of purposely leaving out one of the ingredients or steps.

"Did you wash out the pot before you started preparing the recipe?" the woman asked. "No," answered the neighbor, "but I did follow all your directions!" The woman quietly replied, "That is the reason the dish was a failure. Since you didn't clean out the pot, the dish was contaminated by the filth inside."

In potential, Balaam was granted the same powers of prophecy as Moses. However, Moses purified himself and made himself a fitting receptacle for the word of God. Balaam, on the other hand, remained the same arrogant, greedy and evil person he was before. Since he was an inhospitable receptacle for sanctity, he distorted and ruined his prophecy.

וְעַתָּה לְכָה נָּא אָרָה לִּי אֵת הָעָם הַזֶּה

*So now — please come and
curse this people for me* (ibid. 6).

Instead of asking Balaam to curse the Jewish
people, Balak should have requested that he bless
Moab. Why didn't he do so?

Moab's hatred is typical of the anti-Semitism
displayed toward us throughout history. The gentile nations are far more interested in our demise
than in their own success. The persecution of the
Jews is a goal in itself. They would rather invoke
curses upon us than seek blessings for themselves.
Ultimately, the curse boomerangs and they become its victims (*Beis Ramah*).[5]

When a Jew is in trouble, he prays to God and
turns to a righteous person to give him a blessing
and pray on his behalf. Not so Balak. Fearful of the
threat of the Jewish people, he didn't ask for
Balaam's blessings for success; rather, he sought a
curse for his adversary (*Chafetz Chaim*).[6]

וַיֹּאמֶר אֱלֹהִים אֶל בִּלְעָם לֹא תֵלֵךְ עִמָּהֶם

*God said to Balaam, "You shall
not go with them"* (ibid. 12).

In this verse, God forbids Balaam to go with the
elders of Moab and Midian. Later on, however,
God does acquiesce (v. 20). Yet when Balaam does
so, God becomes angry (v. 22).

The *Vilna Gaon* offers an interpretation based
upon a careful reading of the text. The words עִמּוֹ
and אִתּוֹ (or their plural forms עִמָּהֶם or אִתָּם) are both
rendered as *with him* (or with them); yet, there is a
difference. עִמּוֹ infers a unity of mind-set and intent
while אִתּוֹ reflects a physical, but not an intellectual
or emotional, connection. עִמּוֹ implies two equals
(see *Kiddushin* 22b) while אִתּוֹ (related to אֶת) means
secondary to another (see *Bava Kamma* 41b).

When Balaam was initially approached by the
elders of Moab to come with them and curse
the Jewish people, God told him, Don't go עִמָּהֶם,
with them. Do not emotionally identify with their
plan to curse the Jewish people.

---

5. **Self-defeating Rage.** The hatred of the Jew is so all consuming that the non-Jew often terminally damages his
own cause due to his blind rage and animosity.

In 1945 the situation of the German troops in Russia was desperate. The Russian winter (as was always
the historical case) was wreaking havoc on the "invincible" German army. Hitler, may his name be obliterated, was nevertheless unwilling to divert the trains transporting Jews to Auschwitz in order to save his own
troops.

The *Chafetz Chaim* would often bemoan the fact that we are all capable of adopting this mentality:

Once, in a small village, an argument erupted between the village supervisor and his neighbor. The neighbor
threatened to report the supervisor's shady dealings and illegal affairs to the provincial government, but his wife
begged him not to. "Remember, he is the one who arranged for our son to be absolved from military duty. If the
supervisor is arrested he will do everything in his power to see that our son is arrested for draft-dodging."

Livid at the supervisor, the man exclaimed, "It's worthwhile that you, me and our son sit in prison as long as
that despicable supervisor is stripped of his authority." How terribly blinding strife can be!

6. **Self-Promotion.** The tendency to seek the detriment of others over our own success is often rooted in the
perspective which sees personal success as linked to the failure of others.

In this vein R' Shlomo Freifeld interpreted a story in the Talmud (*Avodah Zarah* 19b). R' Alexander once chanted
in the town square, "Who wants life? Who wants life?" Many people flocked to him asking for the elixir of
life. He replied with the verse, *Which man deserves life, who loves days of seeing good? Guard your tongue from
evil . . .* (*Psalms* 34:14-15).

Why is refraining from slander the key to life?

R' Freifeld offered an answer based on the words of the *Maharal*: Spring water is referred to in the Torah as מַיִם
חַיִּים (lit. "live water"), for the definition of life is independence. The spring is its own source of water and does
not need to draw water from elsewhere. In a similar vein, explains *Maharal*, King Solomon teaches that one who
refuses gifts is deemed alive (*Proverbs* 15:27). This connection between life and independence is equally valid
regarding self-esteem. One can build his own self-image by concentrating on his intrinsic virtues, or alternatively,
by focusing on the faults and flaws of others. One can either stand tall by himself or by knocking down others so
that he stands higher than them.

R' Alexander announced the true elixir of life. If you want to be truly independent and alive, guard your tongue
from bad-mouthing others. Build up your self-esteem by yourself, not by destroying other people.

When God saw that they were adamant, He told Balaam, קוּם לֵךְ אִתָּם, *arise and go with them* (ibid. 20). Go along with them physically, but distance yourself emotionally from any part of their plan. The Torah tells us וַיֵּלֶךְ עִם שָׂרֵי מוֹאָב (verse 21), *Balaam wholeheartedly joined the noblemen of Moab. God's wrath then flared against him.*[7]

לֹא תֵלֵךְ עִמָּהֶם לֹא תָאֹר אֶת הָעָם כִּי בָרוּךְ הוּא
You shall not go with them! You shall not curse the people for it is blessed (ibid.).

When God commanded Balaam not to curse the people, he suggested that he should bless them instead. God replied that they were already blessed and had no need of his blessing.

This is analogous to a bee to whom we say, "We want neither your sting nor your honey" (*Rashi*).

She'aris Menachem explains the metaphor: Honey of bees is considered kosher since it really does not come from inside the nonkosher bee. Honey is produced by pollen which the bee gathers from the flowers and transfers to the honeycomb. In contrast, the sting releases poisons which come from the bee itself.

The blessings Balaam offered to give the Jewish people were honey. They were mere lip service, totally extraneous to his true self. His stings were the curses and his advice on how to morally entrap the Jewish people. They clearly expressed his inner self.[8]

אִם יִתֶּן לִי בָלָק מְלֹא בֵיתוֹ כֶּסֶף וְזָהָב לֹא אוּכַל לַעֲבֹר אֶת פִּי ה׳
If Balak will give me his houseful of silver and gold, I cannot transgress the word of Hashem (ibid. 18).

Balaam seems to express a genuine fear of Heaven by declaring his inability to transgress the word of Hashem. In reality, however, his duplicity is clearly evident.

R' Elchanan Wasserman explains: There are three types of instructions in the Torah: (1) Those actions which we are explicitly commanded to do or refrain from; (2) special instructions conveyed to us by prophets on how to respond to specific situations; (3) the will of God which only our Sages are able to discern. In this last instance, God does not speak to us directly; He only alludes to His will.

Balaam declared that he was unable to transgress the *word* of Hashem. Although he knew from the outset that cursing the Jewish people ran counter to God's will, he was not inhibited from doing so.

After one assesses if that which one plans to do is halachically permitted, one must run another litmus test; will it please God? (*Yesod HaAvodah*).[9]

---

7. **Caught Up in the Tide.** Often we associate with people of questionable ethical and moral character and cooperate with them for pragmatic reasons. In time our mind becomes as warped as theirs. In the end Balaam went עִם שָׂרֵי מוֹאָב; his mind and emotions totally identified with them (*Shem MiShmuel*).

8. **Sweet Sting.** The worst of curses are those which seem to be a blessing but are really a curse in disguise. We want neither the sting of the bee nor the honey which is really a sting (*R' Tzvi Hirsch of Nadvorna*).

[When the nations of the world are overly sweet and friendly toward us we must really be wary for the sweet sting is the most painful.]

9. **Simply Impossible.** Once the Czarist government sought to impose a decree that would have totally altered the character and educational philosophy of the traditional *cheder* schools. At a meeting convened to discuss the threat, one of the *maskilim* ("enlightened" secularist Jews) stated, "We have the ability to close down all the traditional schools. However, our sensitivity to the venerable rabbis won't permit us to do so."

Many of the assembled rabbis were impressed by this display of sentiment. However, the *Beis HaLevi (R' Yosef Dov Soloveitchik of Slutzk-Brisk)* stood up and said to the secularist, "You are just like Balaam." When asked to explain, he replied, "Imagine someone were to suggest that you punch the king in the face. You reply that you would not do such a thing for all the money in the world. The implication is that the act is theoretically possible, yet even for money you would be unwilling to do it. If, however, someone were to ask you to lift up a towering mountain and you answer that for all the riches in the universe you will not do it, your reply is ridiculous since it implies that you are able to do it but simply choose not to. In reality, it is impossible. When Balaam said that even for wealth he was unable to transgress the word of God, he implied that it was possible, only that there was no price high enough. A true believer sees ignoring God's will as a virtual impossibility."

Balaam implied that if he were able to transgress the word of God he would — but only for a large sum of money (*Maharal*). Why, however, do the Sages censure him for speaking so glowingly about money (see *Pirkei Avos* 5:19 and *Rashi* here)? In what way was he different than R' Yose ben Kisma (*Avos* 6:9) who responded to an invitation to move to another city with, "If you give me all the silver and gold in the world I will only live in a place of Torah"?

R' Nachumke of Horodna cites an incident in the Talmud which highlights the difference between the two. R' Shmuel bar Yehudah's young daughter passed away and some of the Sages went to console him. Ulah refused to join the consolation party, claiming that the Babylonians display heresy when they console mourners with the phrase, "What can we do?" The implication is that if they could have done something to prevent the person's death, they would have done so, even though it runs contrary to God's will. This borders on heresy.

Balaam was no different. When he said, *I am unable,* what he meant to say was, "If I could [transgress His word] I would." Not so R' Yose ben Kisma who made it clear that "I will *only* live in a place of Torah," even if other opportunities present themselves.

וַיָּקָם בִּלְעָם בַּבֹּקֶר וַיַּחֲבֹשׁ אֶת אֲתֹנוֹ
Balaam arose in the morning and saddled his she-donkey (ibid. 21).

This is an example of how hatred can even cause one to violate one's own personal code of conduct. Although it was below Balaam's dignity to saddle his own donkey, his hatred of the Jewish people overrode all other considerations.

The Sages note that Balaam's enthusiasm and power of conviction threatened the Jewish people. God therefore said to him, "Wicked one! Their ancestor Abraham preceded you when he got up even earlier to saddle his own donkey in order to fulfill My will and take his son Isaac to be slaughtered" (*Rashi*).

How can one even compare the enthusiasm of Abraham with the evil designs of Balaam?[10]

R' Menachem Mendel of Kotzk enlightens us: Balaam's evil plan was to totally annihilate the Jewish people by cursing them during God's split second of wrath (see *Berachos* 7a). God told him that it simply would not be. Abraham rose early, to slaughter Isaac. This act which would have effectively prevented the Jewish nation from coming into existence and therefore God did not allow him to pursue it. He wants His precious nation to exist and flourish. If Abraham "failed," Balaam would certainly fail to destroy God's children.

Alternatively, this teaches us that one must always invest at least as much energy and effort into one's spiritual pursuits as others invest in mundane affairs. As King Solomon says in *Proverbs* (2:4-5): *If you seek it as [it were] silver, if you search for it as [if it were] hidden treasures — then you will understand the fear of Hashem and discover the knowledge of God.*

If people expend tremendous toil to achieve material success, how much more so does God expect one to toil in His Torah? When we exert greater effort for the temporal than we do for the eternal, we disappoint God and leave ourselves vulnerable to Divine justice.[11]

This is the root of the contrast between Abraham and Balaam. When Balaam displayed such dedication to his evil plan it invoked a potential indictment of the Jewish people for not displaying comparable alacrity in the pursuit of God's Will. God defended us by noting that Abraham was just as dedicated when he arose early to sacrifice Isaac. Whenever we see others deeply committed to their pursuit of this worldly goods, we must immediately redouble our efforts on behalf of spiritual pursuits (*R' Moshe Feinstein*).

---

10. **Early to Rise.** The evil inclination rises early in the morning, looking for ways to entrap a Jew. Balaam also sought to rise early to curse us. We must counteract the Balaam of each generation by taking a cue from our forefather Abraham who rose early in order to sacrifice his most precious son. We must heed the call of the Sages (*Sanhedrin* 72a) who taught, "One who comes to kill you, arise early to kill him" (*Chidushei HaRim*).

11. **Appropriated Tactics.** R' Meir Shapiro explains the famous comment of *Rashi* (*Genesis* 32:5), "Though I have sojourned with Laban I have observed the 613 commandments and have not learned from his evil ways," in this light. Jacob bemoaned the fact that although he succeeded in following the word of God in the spiritual wasteland of Laban's home, he had not adopted Laban's intense dedication to evil and transformed it. Laban was still more dedicated to sins than he was to *mitzvos*.

וַיִּתְיַצֵּב מַלְאַךְ ה׳ בַּדֶּרֶךְ לְשָׂטָן לוֹ

and an angel of Hashem stood on the road to impede him (ibid. 22).

The Name Hashem implies His trait of mercy, *Rashi* teaches that God sent an angel of mercy to save Balaam. This reflects words of the Sages that one who incites another to sin is worse than one who physically kills him (*Bamidbar Rabbah* 21:5), for sin is the equivalent of spiritual death. One who intervenes to prevent the spiritual demise of another certainly performs an act of mercy (*Simchas Aharon*).

In his communal role, *Chasam Sofer* saw himself as this angel of mercy. He was one of the leading adversaries of the Reform Movement and spearheaded the effort to totally neutralize their influence. Someone once asked him how he, who was by nature a most easygoing and considerate person, could overcome his innate pleasentness and battle the *maskilim* with such uncompromising zealousness. He replied by invoking our verse. "Why," he asked, "did God send an angel of mercy to stop Balaam? Furthermore, how did the angel turn into a satan?"

The answer is that only one who is truly merciful toward the Jewish people is fit to battle Balaam. Only one with true compassion has an earnest desire to protect the Jews from corrupt leadership and from those who offer them dangerous "improvements," and will be ready to wage an uncompromising battle.

וַיִּפְתַּח ה׳ אֶת פִּי הָאָתוֹן

Hashem opened the mouth of the she-donkey (ibid. 28).

Before beginning the daily songs of praise (*Pesukei D'Zimrah*) we declare, *I now prepare my mouth to thank, laud and praise my Creator.* The mouth, as well as all of man's faculties, are like vessels in the Holy Temple. They are designated and sanctified exclusively for the service of God. To make any other use of them is tantamount to misappropriating consecrated items.

Balaam thought he had an independent power of speech and was thus able to curse God's nation. The she-donkey taught him otherwise. Just as she has no natural ability to speak and was only granted speech to enhance the glory of God and Israel, so too was Balaam given to understand that his power of speech was a Divine gift, granted him only to serve God by blessing His people (based on *Kli Yakar*).

כִּי הִכִּיתַנִי זֶה שָׁלֹשׁ רְגָלִים

[What have I done] that you struck me these three times? (ibid.).

The donkey's retort was an allusion to the future merit which the Jewish people would acquire in making the thrice-yearly pilgrimage (שָׁלֹשׁ רְגָלִים) to the Temple in Jerusalem. This merit would protect them from Balaam's evil design. Why was this merit invoked to counteract Balaam?

Shem MiShmuel suggests that this mitzvah is symbolic of the vast difference between Israel and the nations.

The nations of the world also seek a close relationship with God: However, they want to "have their cake and eat it too." Unwilling to sacrifice their obsession with wealth, property and physical pleasures, they are unable to seriously connect with God. In contrast, Jews leave their property behind unprotected to ascend to Jerusalem and commune with God on the Pilgrimage Festivals.

Balaam was told, "How can you can invoke God's wrath on His people when you and your cohorts are so removed from their degree of commitment to Him?"[12], [13]

---

12. **Trifold Cleansing.** According to *Be'er Moshe,* each one of the Three Festivals is meant to purge us of one of the three evil characteristics of Balaam as described in *Pirkei Avos* (5:22). Pesach is the time God redeemed us from Egypt in a display of unlimited kindness. This counters Balaam's evil eye. On Shavuos, God instilled His fear in our hearts with an awesome display of thunder and lightening. This creates in us a healthy sense of shame and teaches us to refrain from desiring the sensual aspects of this world. This counters Balaam's greedy nature. Last, Balaam's arrogant spirit is neutralized by Succos when we abandon our personal security and leave our homes, humbly realizing that God is the only One Who protects us.

13. **In God We Trust.** King David writes *Many are the agonies of the wicked, but as for the one who trusts in Hashem, kindness surrounds him* (Psalms 32:10). The angel came to warn Balaam that those who place their trust

R' Yisrael of Pilov submits a variation on this theme. Pirkei Avos (5:7) teaches that although Jerusalem was packed with visitors during the Three Festivals, no one ever complained that it was too crowded to sleep in the Holy City. The visitors bore the congestion gracefully. They were thrilled to be in such close proximity of the Divine Presence. The donkey/angel told Balaam, "When your foot was pressed against the stone wall you screamed in pain. Do you really think you can uproot a nation ready to bear real discomfort to achieve closeness to God?"

The allusion to the Pilgrimage Festivals may also be seen as a means to deflate Balaam's arrogance.

The Sages teach that when Jews came to the Temple, they merited to see the Divine Presence in the same manner as they presented themselves to be seen by God (Chagigah 2a). The allusion of the donkey/angel is as follows: "You who fail to see even an angel certainly cannot vanquish a nation equipped to see the Divine Presence itself" (Meshech Chochmah).

חָטָאתִי כִּי לֹא יָדַעְתִּי כִּי אַתָּה נִצָּב לִקְרָאתִי בַּדָּרֶךְ

I have sinned for I did not know that you were standing opposite me on the road (ibid. 34).

Many of the commentators pose the obvious question: If Balaam was unaware of the presence of the angel, how did he sin?

Ignorance is not always a legitimate excuse. Everyone must be aware of certain evident truths. For example, a 4-year-old child cannot claim that he was unaware it is forbidden to strike a parent. Similarly, a prophet like Balaam should have known that an angel was in front of him. His not knowing was a sin in itself. The Mishnah (Bava Kamma 26) rules that man is always culpable [for damages] whether awake or asleep. Man, an intelligent being, must avoid even bringing about harm. The strange behavior of the donkey should have alarmed Balaam. His reaction was itself the sin (Shelah).[14]

R' Chaim Kanievsky suggests that Balaam never admits that going to curse the Jews was a sin: He thinks his sin was that the angel witnessed what he did. His response is reminiscent of the thief who doesn't regret stealing, only that he got caught.[15]

---

in God, as do the people of Israel, will not be harmed. We echo this theme in the Grace After Meals: *Blessed is the man who trusts in Hashem, then Hashem will be his security. I was a youth and also have aged, and I have not seen a righteous man forsaken* (R' Moshe Sternbuch).

14. **Ignorance Is Not Bliss.** R' Chaim of Sanz once reprimanded one of his disciples who served as a communal rabbi. He asked why he was negligent in caring for a townsman who had fallen on hard times and whose family was suffering from hunger. The rabbi pleaded ignorance. "I was unaware of the situation," he claimed. R' Chaim said, "Ignorance is no excuse! Balaam offered the same excuse and it too was unacceptable. Lack of awareness is a sin in itself. For a rabbi or community head to be unaware of the predicament of every member of the community is nothing short of sinful. He must know and get involved to ease the plight of his congregant's suffering.

When R' Gamliel came to apologize to R' Yehoshua for having mistreated him he noticed that the walls of his house were black from soot. He said, "From the walls of your house it is evident that you make your living producing coals." Replied R' Yehoshua, "Woe to the generation that you stand at its head for you are unaware of the suffering of the scholars and how they support themselves" (Berachos 28a).

15. **Beating the System.** How often do we psychologically block out the fact that God watches all we do, and think we will get away with transgressing the Torah. A story about three maskilim who studied in the famed Yeshivah of Volozhin underscores this point. The three were sitting in their lodgings on Shabbos afternoon smoking when a member of the faculty entered the premises. The first impudent young man said, "Rebbe, I forgot it is Shabbos." The second claimed to have forgotten that smoking is forbidden on the Sabbath. The third one said, "I also forgot. I forgot to close the door."

Balaam made the same cynical comment: I sinned because I did not know you were standing opposite me.

As an antidote to this attitude, Rema begins his commentary to the Shulchan Aruch by teaching that the verse *I place Hashem constantly in front of me* (Psalms 16:8), is an important principle in the Torah and that the truly righteous live with the sense that they are always in His Presence. One acts and speaks differently among friends and family than he does in the presence of a powerful king. When one realizes that God's Presence is everywhere and that He is All-Seeing and All-Knowing, he will be inspired to fear God and be contrite toward Him (see Moreh Nevuchim 3:52).

Akeidas Yitzchak offers a different perspective. Sin has the power to blind us to the reality that we are answerable to God. We are taught that one sin leads to another (*Avos* 4:2), for the spiritual blindness caused by the first sin makes the second one that much easier to commit.

Balaam's words reflect this reality. *I have sinned* [in the past, therefore] *I did not know* [now] *that you were standing opposite me on the road.* [16]

Background

In spite of his best efforts to the contrary, Balaam is forced to bless the Jewish people. Like his donkey, he can only speak the words which God puts in his mouth.

מָה אֶקֹב לֹא קַבֹּה אֵל
וּמָה אֶזְעֹם לֹא זָעַם ה'

How can I curse? God has not cured. How can I anger? — Hashem is not angry (23:8).

The secret of the love between God and His beloved children inundates Balaam's words. Nowhere else in the Torah does this love find such intense expression.

The anger that God sometimes shows us is only on the surface. Below it exists, a burning, inextinguishable love which is eternal — independent of our actions. He never truly becomes angry at us or curses us.

Balaam realized this when he said, "How can I curse? God has never really cursed them. How can I anger? Hashem is never truly angry with them" (*Nesivos Shalom*).

הֶן עָם לְבָדָד יִשְׁכֹּן וּבַגּוֹיִם לֹא יִתְחַשָּׁב

Behold! it is a nation that will dwell in solitude and not be reckoned among the nations (ibid. 9).

The national destiny of the Jewish nation is to always retain its uniqueness even when in exile. We are compared to olive oil which can never mix with other liquids but always rises to the top. We are a nation that dwells alone. When we desire to be accepted among the nations we are doomed to failure. We are not be reckoned among them. [17]

Mei Marom portrays this theme in sharp terms: The difference between Jews and others is the difference between night and day. Just as one cannot compare apples to oranges, so too Jews can never be fully considered part of the family of nations.

Not only spiritually but even physically, the Jew is figuratively cut from a different cloth. The body of a Jew is compared to the parchment of a Torah scroll; his actions are the script. The nations of the world are the supporting cast in the Divine drama that is world history. The lead role, however, belongs to the Jew.

תָּמֹת נַפְשִׁי מוֹת יְשָׁרִים

May my soul die the death of the upright, and may my end be like his! (ibid. 10).

Balaam asked to die the death of the upright yet he was unwilling to live a righteous life. He wanted to die like a penitent but not to live like one.

16. **Restored Eyesight.** *For with You is forgiveness, that You may be feared,* says King David (*Psalms* 130:4). Besides absolving one of punishment, Divine forgiveness restores one's spiritual eyesight. He can again perceive that it is impossible to run away from God.

17. **Survival by Scorn.** The scorn with which the non-Jew looks upon us is our greatest assurance that we will succeed in retaining our unique spirituality.

One time when the *Baal Shem Tov* was on his way back from the *mikveh* (ritual bath) to his lodgings, he spotted a group of non-Jews coming toward him. Fearful they would touch him and thus contaminate him with their impurity, he was relieved to hear one say to his friend, "Make sure that Jew doesn't touch and contaminate you."

When relating the incident, the *Baal Shem Tov* commented, "That is the meaning of Balaam's words. We are able to remain a nation that dwells in solitude because the non-Jews look down on us, and view us as lowly creatures."

Ohr HaChaim HaKadosh explains, "I have met sinful people who personally told me they would be willing to repent if they could be assured that immediately after doing so they would die. How ever, to repent and remain fully committed over a long period of time is too difficult. The 'old foolish king' (the evil inclination) has too tight a grip on them."

The *Chafetz Chaim* put it this way: To die as a Jew is easy. Since we believe in the eternity of the soul, it is not hard to die. One passes from temporal existence to eternal bliss. The only fear one has is that he might not have spiritually prepared himself in this world.

The real challenge is to *live* like a Jew. Every moment of life has responsibilities one must meet and pitfalls one must avoid.

Balaam wanted to die as a Jew; he could not imagine living as one.[18]

לֹא הִבִּיט אָוֶן בְּיַעֲקֹב . . . ה׳ אֱלֹהָיו עִמּוֹ וּתְרוּעַת מֶלֶךְ בּוֹ

He perceived no iniquity in Jacob . . . Hashem his God is with him, and the friendship of the King is in him (ibid. 21).

How can the Torah validate Balaam's words that God sees no iniquity in Jacob? This seems to contradict the words of the Sages which totally refutes the idea that God arbitrarily for-

goes the punishment of sin (*Bava Kamma* 50a). Furthermore, does God really play favorites by ignoring iniquity in Jews and observing it in others?

Even when a Jew sins knowingly he does so out of weakness, not out of conviction. Even at the very moment of sin he never doubts that God is All-knowing. Although he is unable to withstand the temptation, he is truly embarrassed in front of God. When the test passes, he is overcome with shame and self-disappointment.[19]

The evil inclination was not completely success-ful. Although the person yielded to temptation he had not abandoned his faith.

God does not focus on the times man slips as long as *Hashem his God is with him* and his faith remains unsullied. Even when wallowing ankle-deep in sin, a Jew must remember that he enjoys God's "friendship" (תְּרוּעַת is related to רֵעוּת, *friend-ship*).

A Jew cries out to Hashem, "I crave Your friendship, please save me from my sins![20] I could not extinguish the fires of temptation but my faith in You and my desire for Your closeness remain unchanged." God turns His focus away from those iniquities because they do not reflect the essential person whose spirit is inundated with the friendship of the King (*Nesivos Shalom, Chidu-shei HaRim*).

Sfas Emes focuses on a different aspect. The sin of a Jew is an aberration, inconsistent with his

---

18. **Jewish Living.** A *chassid* came to *R' Yehoshua of Belz* asking that he bless him to die as a Jew. "You act like Balaam. He wanted to live like a gentile yet die like a Jew. A Jew must always ask to live like a Jew."

[Only one who lives like a Jew can die like a Jew.]

19. **Internal Bleeding.** *R' Chaim of Sanz* renders the phrase תְּרוּעַת מֶלֶךְ בּוֹ differently. God does not look at the exterior manifestation of a person's improper conduct: He looks *inside* at the person's heart which still beats vibrantly and is broken over having violated the spirit of God within (תְּרוּעָה in the sense of broken; see *Psalms* 2:9).

Jews do *mitzvos* with joy. They have an opportunity to fulfill God's will. Have you ever seen a Jew sin joyously, happy to transgress God's word? Did you ever hear of a Jew who recites the לְשֵׁם יִחוּד (prayer recited before performing a mitzvah) in anticipation of the sin he is about to commit?

20. **Redemptive Guilt.** The spark of Godliness in a Jew can never be extinguished completely. The broken spirit we experience when we sin is the voice of Hashem that calls us to repent even as we are sinning. *Hashem his God is with him* (*R' Yisrael of Rizhin*).

The Talmud (*Berachos* 12b) teaches that God forgives those who sin and immediately feel terribly em-barrassed about sinning. *R' Tzadok HaKohen of Lublin* explains that shame is the essence of purgatory. One who is embarrassed because of his sins has received his punishment and may now be forgiven (*Tzidkas Ha-Tzaddik* 57).

essential self. Therefore, despite his sins, the Divine Presence never leaves him. Furthermore, the striking Hand of the King inflicts punishment (using the term תְּרוּעָה as broken; see *Psalms* 2:9) on us in this world so that our sins never bring us to the point that He becomes, God forbid, excised from our lives.

According to *Chasam Sofer*, Balaam gave voice to the fact that it is the Godly soul implanted in us which saves us from sin. When man focuses on the fact that God is constantly with him (ה' אֱלֹהָיו עִמּוֹ), then God need not focus on sin (לֹא הִבִּיט אָוֶן בְּיַעֲקֹב), since man will simply refrain from transgressing the Torah. When God is a constant presence in our hearts and minds there is no place for sin.[21]

וְלֹא רָאָה עָמָל בְּיִשְׂרָאֵל
and saw no perversity in Israel (ibid.).

Ohr HaChaim HaKadosh explains עָמָל in the sense of toil and hard work. The beauty of the Jewish people lies in the fact that although they toil ceaselessly at the study of Torah and the performance of *mitzvos*, they never tire or feel that the load is too heavy. They find Torah and *mitzvos* so sweet and enjoyable. Their performance is an utter joy for them.[22]

כָּעֵת יֵאָמֵר לְיַעֲקֹב וּלְיִשְׂרָאֵל מַה פָּעַל אֵל
Even now it is said to Jacob and Israel what God has wrought (ibid. 23).

According to the first interpretation of *Rashi*, this verse refers to the pre-Messianic and Messianic eras. The Chassidic masters offer many homiletic interpretations.

R' Yisrael of Modzhitz suggests that the verse speaks of two groups of Jews and their perceptions of events. As the turmoil which will precede the Final Redemption intensifies, those who lack spiritual clarity (as alluded to by the name "*Jacob,*" symbolic of an existence before the forces of evil were vanquished — see *Genesis* 32:29) will view the situation as a result of current events and the ups and downs of geopolitical factors (*now*). Those with a heightened spiritual perspective (alluded to by the name *Israel*) will say that all that has been wrought by God. To the truly faithful, history is an expression of God's (not-so) invisible Hand.

R' Avraham of Slonim sees this as an expression of the spiritual sense of values that will accompany the Messianic era.

When people meet today, they inquire into each other's welfare and ask about health and business. In the future, when Jews will meet they will immediately inquire *what has God wrought*, namely,

---

21. **No Time to Think.** It is noteworthy that the entire *parashah* of *Balak* is written in the Torah without even one interruption. Neither a small break in the text (denoted in a printed *Chumash* by the letter ס) nor a larger one (represented by the letter פ) appears. The *Chafetz Chaim* explains: *Rashi* (*Leviticus* 1:10) teaches that the textual breaks are indicative of the time granted Moses (and all readers of the text) in order to ponder the word of God and internalize its message. Balaam was the non-Jewish pipeline through which the word of God passed: However, the Godly message was never integrated into his being. Thus there was no need to give him any break to internalize the message.

A young *chassid* once told the Kotzker Rebbe that he had gone through Tractate *Kesubos* seven times. The Kotzker replied, "And how many times has *Kesubos* gone through *you*?" Torah must elevate and reshape our minds, hearts and homes.

22. **Not My Luggage.** The *Dubno Maggid* offered a parable to showcase the attitude of Jews toward Torah.

Two businessmen were traveling together on their way home from the fair. One was a diamond merchant while the other dealt in lead. When they arrived home later that day they both rushed home and asked a stevedore to bring their packages to their respective homes. When the stevedore arrived at the diamond merchant's home he placed the box in the courtyard and went inside to be paid. The diamond merchant was surprised to see the stevedore's face covered with sweat. When he offered the stevedore a paltry sum, the man was offended. "For such a heavy trunk you pay me so little?!" he complained. Replied the diamond merchant, "Obviously you weren't carrying my box. If it is heavy and hard to carry, it's not mine."

If a Jew feels that Torah and *mitzvos* are too difficult a load to bear, he obviously does not appreciate their uniqueness. It is comparable to one saying that life is too expensive to live. If the package is too heavy, apparently it's not His.

what have you done for God today? What *nachas* have you brought Him recently?

R' Mendel of Rimanov revealed yet another facet of this theme. Now we say that everything is from Jacob and Israel. When our vision will assume clarity, we will realize that even the good that we thought we brought about was really wrought by God.[23]

---

23. **Grandeur Born of Degradation.** During the reign of Czar Alexander III, the famed Baron Ginzburg arranged for an audience between the Minister of the Interior and some of the most prominent rabbis of the times in order to defuse some antireligious decrees. The minister, a rabid anti-Semite, unleashed a poisonous diatribe against the Jews. "They suck the blood of the citizens. They are separatists and mock the religion of others. I understand why God created all kinds of creations, from the inanimate rock to different people. Why did He bother creating this cancer called the Jews?"

R' Yitzchak of Volozhin stood up to respond: "Your words remind me of a prophet who echoed your sentiment over a thousand years ago. Balaam predicted that days would come when people would express your very thoughts: *Even now it is said [about] Jacob and Israel, What has God wrought?* However, I am heartened by your words for our holy Torah continues, *Behold the people will arise like a lion cub.* When our people will be so terribly degraded among the nations we will know that we are at the doorstep of a new era, when the lion cub of Israel will rise again."

פרשת פנחס ∽
Parashas Pinchas

Background

After failing miserably in his attempt to curse the Jews, Balaam seeks to drive them to spiritual self-destruction. "Their God does not tolerate immorality," he says to Balak. "Therefore, entice them to act promiscuously." A Midianite woman succeeds in ensnaring Zimri, prince of the tribe of Simeon, into sinning in public, a catastrophe which demands an immediate, drastic response. Phinehas answers the call and, with a spear in hand, kills the two. In reward for his actions, God blesses Phinehas with a covenant of peace and eternal priesthood.

פִּינְחָס בֶּן אֶלְעָזָר בֶּן אַהֲרֹן הַכֹּהֵן
Phinehas son of Elazar son of Aaron the Kohen (25:11).

The people accused Phinehas of murder and goaded him by saying that "this grandson of one (Jethro — whose daughter married Elazar son of Aaron the Kohen) who fattened animals for sacri-fices to idols" (Jethro) had the audacity to kill the prince of Simeon. God therefore traced his roots back to Aaron the Kohen (*Rashi*).

Those who goaded Phinehas certainly knew that he was Aaron's grandson; yet, that fact did not stop them from casting aspersion on his motives. Of what value then is the Torah's highlighting his connection to Aaron?

Those who pointed the accusing finger at Phinehas suspected that his zealotry resulted from murderous tendencies which he had genetically inherited as a descendant of butchers and murderers. If so, why is his act of murder more legitimate than Zimri's immorality? The Torah therefore links Phinehas to Aaron, the man of peace whose love of the Jewish people was legendary (see *Pirkei Avos* 1:12). It was Phinehas' concern over the threat represented by Zimri's immorality that caused him to do what he did. His actions were not the result of hotheadedness. Phinehas was a compassionate, caring person, the grandson of Aaron who loved peace. He acted as Aaron's grandson in order to save the nation (*MiDarkei Moshe*).[1]

---

1. **Checkered Motives.** People's motives are not always obvious. The Talmud (*Yoma* 23a) relates that two Kohanim ran up the ramp of the Altar in order to grab the right to remove the ashes. When one of them beat the other, the second one stabbed the first to death. The father of the victim arrived while his son was still alive and bleeding. He told the Kohanim present to remove the knife before his son died to prevent it from becoming ritually defiled. The Talmud (ibid. 23b) questions whether the father's ability to remain calm and focus on the impurity of the knife was because of his great concern for the purity of holy vessels or his casual attitude toward murder.

This story teaches us that a noble act may not always be what it appears. One must ascertain the true motive.

When Phinehas killed Zimri, many people suspected the purity of his motives. Was his reaction the result of a holy indignation against immorality or was it an inherited proclivity for spilling blood?

The Torah therefore called attention to Phinehas' ancestor Aaron, whose love and concern for Jews was known to all (*R' Leib Gurewicz*).

R' Moshe Sternbuch suggests that the people suspected Phinehas of suffering from a syndrome common to newcomers to Torah life who often feel compelled to adopt excessive halachic (and sometimes nonhalachic) stringencies to atone for their checkered past. This was what they accused Phinehas of suffering. In their view, he was overcompensating for the fact that his grandfather was an idolater, and therefore exploded in "holy" wrath. The Torah therefore calls him the grandson of Aaron to indicate that neither he nor his motives were at all tainted by his grandfather Jethro's past. He was completely the grandson of Aaron.

הֵשִׁיב אֶת חֲמָתִי מֵעַל בְּנֵי יִשְׂרָאֵל
turned back My wrath from upon the Children of Israel (ibid.).

Phinehas achieved two significant goals with his response to Zimri's audacious display of immorality. He calmed God's "anger" and he saved the Jewish people from God's wrath. This can be compared to a king who had an only son. Both father and son loved each other deeply, and their souls were bound together strongly. Once the son sinned grievously against the father, who was forced to banish the child from his presence. Although the father felt terrible over his decision, he realized that he had no other choice.

One day, a most trusted confidante of the king pleaded the son's case, begging the king to forgive his wayward son and let him return home to enjoy a renewed closeness with his father. The confidante made such a strong case that the king's anger toward his son dissipated. The king was doubly pleased. First, he was no longer angry. Second, his beloved son was saved from being the target of his wrath. He had been pained that he was angry at him. Now this pain would no longer torment him.

The Torah praises Phinehas in exactly the same way. First, he *turned back My wrath;* in itself a significant accomplishment. Second, he allowed God the opportunity to no longer be upset with His only, beloved child (*R' Mendel of Kossov*).

בְּקַנְאוֹ אֶת קִנְאָתִי בְּתוֹכָם
when he zealously avenged My vengeance among them (ibid.).

What does the Torah mean to emphasize by teaching that Phinehas acted with zealousness *among them*?

Tiferes Shmuel explains that Phinehas acted not as an individual but rather as a representative of the entire nation. He was therefore able to turn back God's wrath which might have destroyed the entire nation.

Alternatively, Phinehas never meant to use his zealotry as a way of portraying himself as a paradigm of morality. He responded because he truly cared for his people. He didn't look down on them; he was *amongst them* (*Resisei Tal*).[2]

Sfas Emes sheds a different light. An indictment hung over the heads of all of Israel as to why *they* did not feel a need to respond to Zimri's breach of morality. Through his actions, Phinehas imbued the nation with a healthy sense of indignation which no longer allowed them to be complacent with intentional sinners.[3], [4]

---

2. **Respectful Zealotry.** A zealot cannot be seen as someone who looks down upon others. Only one seen as a man of the people (*among them*) can succeed in conveying his message to the masses (*Simchas Aharon*).

3. **Not to My Father.** The popular phrase "mind your own business" is in direct contrast to the words of our Sages, who teach that all Jews are responsible for each other (*Sanhedrin* 27b). Furthermore, it is indicative of a relaxed attitude toward God's honor.

R' Baruch Ber Leibowitz once saw one of his students reading a newspaper which espoused heretical ideas and began to cry. He berated the young man, "If you witnessed someone insulting your father would you just ignore it? Of course not. If so, how can you simply ignore a newspaper that spits in your Father's face? At least, disassociate yourself from it."

4. **Singular Sparkplug.** *R' Amram Blau* of Jerusalem was renowned for his zealous attempts to maintain the distinctly Jewish character of the Holy Land, and particularly the Holy City. He fought a constant onslaught from secularist forces bent on remolding the image of the Land and its people. He often organized protest rallies against public desecration of the Sabbath and was in fact successful in his campaign to ban public transportation on the Sabbath.

Once the *Satmar Rebbe, R' Yoel Teitelbaum,* well known for his strong stands, visited Jerusalem. R' Amram

The Torah refers to Phinehas' decisive response as *My vengeance.* In what way did Phinehas emulate Hashem's vengeance?

God is the very embodiment of kindness. When He exacts revenge it is not for punitive purposes but rather an expression of mercy which he extends to all His creatures. God seeks to correct our behavior by means of punishment and "revenge." One who withholds the rod of chastisement really hates his child (see *Proverbs* 13:24). When God offers rebuke, He shows His love and caring.

Phinehas showed this love for his people by saving them from themselves. He employed *My vengeance* and lovingly saved the Jews from tragedy (*R' Yehoshua of Kutna*).

לָכֵן אֱמֹר הִנְנִי נֹתֵן לוֹ אֶת בְּרִיתִי שָׁלוֹם

Therefore, say: Behold! I give him My covenant of peace (ibid. 12).

God told Moses to inform Phinehas that as a result of his courageous stand he would be rewarded with the covenants of peace and eternal priesthood. But why was Moses sent to inform Phinehas? Why didn't God inform Phinehas Himself?

R' Yitzchak of Volozhin explains with a parable:

A general once found himself in the midst of a crucial battle, with not a clue as to the proper strategy that would turn the tide in his favor. Suddenly a soldier stepped forward and suggested a brilliant maneuver which ultimately brought victory.

The king wanted to reward the lowly soldier and simultaneously rebuke the general for essentially failing in his role. What did he do? He commanded the general to personally deliver the commendation to the soldier.

Moses himself should have responded to Zimri's behavior with moral outrage. When he did not, Phinehas stepped forward.

In an expression of Divine disappointment God chastised Moses by having him personally inform Phinehas of his reward.

Yismach Moshe offers an explanation as to why in fact Moses did not respond zealously like Phinehas. The commentators note that the zealotry of Phinehas is not deemed conventional halachah. In their words "it is the halachah" [i.e. it is the appropriate response if one reacts instinctively], however, "we do not rule as such" [if one comes seeking halachic guidance].[5]

Moses, who gave us the Torah, conducted himself completely according to Torah law. This unconventional response of zealotry was not suited for him since he was to serve as the living embodiment of halachah.[6]

---

visited him and bemoaned the fact that he was often the only person who appears at a protest gathering. "Aren't there any other Jews who are pained by the scorn exhibited toward all that is holy?" asked R' Amram.

The Satmar Rebbe cited a comment of the *Sforno* on our verse. What does the Torah mean when it says that the zealotry of Phinehas was exhibited *among them*? And why did his deed save the people, if they themselves took no action?

Explains the *Sforno*: Phinehas killed Zimri in front of the nation to have them witness what he did and *not protest* his actions. In this way, they would be forgiven for not having themselves protested Zimri' contemptible behavior. This passive identification with Phinehas turned back God's anger.

Not everyone has the courage to actively protest for God's honor. We must at least identify with those who do so.

5. **If You Ask, the Answer Is No!** True zealotry is the instinctive reaction of a child angered at an insult hurled against his father. If one is level headed and calm enough to seek halachic guidance, we rule that he should not react. He is not a real zealot.

Brought up on the "mind your own business — it's a free country" attitude, we often view zealotry as interference in other peoples' lives.

Were we to witness our brother acting dangerously, wouldn't we intervene and try to stop him? A fellow Jew who sins is harming himself. How can we stand by passively. We must act or in the least raise a voice in protest. As the *Brisker Rav* once said, "When it hurts, one screams."

6. **The Town "Meshugener."** The leadership of a Jewish community must adopt a "middle-of-the-road" approach so praised by the *Rambam* (see *Rambam, Mishneh Commentary* to *Avos* 2:1, and *Hilchos Deios* 1:3-4). Nevertheless, Jewish leaders throughout history allowed zealotry to flourish yet, reigned it in if it went too far. They never criticized those who pointed an accusing finger at them, claiming they were not diligent enough in enforcing proper

אֶת בְּרִיתִי שָׁלוֹם
My covenant of peace (ibid.).

Whenever one wishes to bestow a reward, it is appropriate that the reward express the quality of the outstanding behavior being acknowledged. A warrior deserves military honors and a medal for strength and courage; one who has made great intellectual achievements should be granted something symbolic of knowledge. Why then did Hashem reward zealotry with a covenant of peace, which appears to represent the antithesis of Phinehas' great deed?

R' Chaim of Brisk suggests an answer: When a married couple suffers from marital strife it is sometimes necessary to take drastic measures to restore domestic harmony. These seemingly severe steps are in reality an exercise in peacemaking.

Since God refuses to tolerate an immoral climate, it becomes necessary for someone to restore the peace between God and Israel. Phinehas was ready to resort to drastic measures to restore this peace. He was therefore rewarded with a covenant of peace.

Netziv offers a different perspective. *Sefer HaChinuch* (§16) teaches that one's thoughts and emotions are deeply effected by one's actions. If one acts with magnanimity, he will eventually become magnanimous.[7] Likewise, when one acts cruelly the cruelty may become internalized. In this case, one needs great strength of character and much Divine assistance to insure that he not become a cruel person.[8] Phinehas murdered a fellow Jew to remove God's Divine wrath. In order that his actions effect would not his personality, God granted him the covenant of peace.[9]

---

standards. *R' Reuvain Grozovsky,* who approved participation with nonbelievers in the Israeli government once such a government was established, writes clearly that "we will not respond to our critics on the 'right' who claim that we must severe all ties with heretics and enemies of Torah" (*Baayos HaZeman*). A famous Rav was once asked why he allowed a religious zealot in his town to rail against him. He replied, "In every town there is a person known as the 'town *meshugener'* (town crazy). Everybody knows he is crazy, yet the town would not be the same without him. The zealots may at times seem unconventional but it is they who keep us 'normal.' "

[R' M.R. spent vast sums of money to print up flyers decrying what he viewed as breaches in the religious climate of his community. Although many people viewed him as an eccentric, the Torah leaders of the town appreciated him. Many of his campaigns eventually helped upgrade the level of religious observance in the community.]

7. **Habituated Magnanimity.** In his commentary on *Pirkei Avos* (3:19) *Rambam* discusses an interesting question. If one has $100 to distribute to charity, is it preferable for him to make one large contribution to one needy person or distribute it among many? *Rambam* writes that it is preferable to disburse it among many. A single, large contribution may be the result of a temporary act of sympathy. Only through continuous acts of charity does one acquire a giving personality.

A popular phrase claims that if one wears a mask long enough it becomes his face.

8. **Integrated Character.** Yehudah ben Teima teaches that one should be as bold and brazen as the leopard. Later he seems to contradict himself when he says that the brazenfaced go to *Gehinnom* (*Avos* 5:23, 24). Similarly, his teaching that the shamefaced go to the Garden of Eden seems to contradict the dictum of the Sages that the shamefaced do not succeed in learning since they refrain from asking questions.

R' Avraham Griever explains that every personality trait can be used in a positive manner. Certain traits, which are basically positive, should be internalized and made part of one's character. Others are best left outside, only to be summoned when appropriate. Brazenness should never be internalized. The brazenfaced go to *Gehinnom*. On the other hand, boldness is essential to serving God. We must ignore those who heap scorn upon our service of God. With regard to shame, shame of sin is one of the identifying marks of a Jew. One who has internalized shame into his psyche strengthens his relationship to God. The shamefaced go to the Garden of Eden. However, to every rule there is an exception. When it comes to Torah study one must abandon all shame and unabashedly question a teacher until one truly understands.

9. **Mercy Booster.** This idea is apparent in the verses regarding a Wayward City, which must be destroyed entirely because the majority of its inhabitants are idol worshipers. In order to assure that the agents of the court (who carry out the verdict) and the general populace (who witness the mass execution) do not become desensitized to the horrors of human suffering and bloodshed, God promises a blessing that *He will give you mercy* (*Deuteronomy* 13:18). He will imbue you with a heightened sense of mercy and compassion. (See *Ohr HaChaim* ad loc.)

He would always follow in the footsteps of his grandfather Aaron, who loved and pursued peace.[10]

בְּרִית כְּהֻנַּת עוֹלָם תַּחַת אֲשֶׁר קִנֵּא לֵאלֹהָיו וַיְכַפֵּר עַל בְּנֵי יִשְׂרָאֵל

a covenant of eternal priesthood because he took vengeance for his God and he atoned for the Children of Israel (ibid. 13).

God always rewards and punishes in kind, tailoring the reward to fit the good deed and the punishment to fit the crime. Here God granted Phinehas both a covenant of peace and a covenant of eternal priesthood. In what way do these rewards reflect Phinehas' actions?

HaMeir L'Olam explains that Phinehas acted both on behalf of God and His people. He allowed God's anger to subside and helped the people achieve atonement.

Phinehas' willingness to risk death to protest the desecration of God's honor was rewarded with a covenant of peace — that he would never die. (See *Bava Metzia* 114b, *Rashi* ad loc.)

His reward for attaining atonement for the people was the covenant of eternal priesthood. Phinehas and his family would provide the Kohanim Gedolim in the Temple, who would achieve atonement for the House of Israel.

The Sages teach that there is no reward in this world for a mitzvah (*Kiddushin* 39a). Yet here, the Torah clearly states that Phinehas was rewarded for this mitzvah. How can this apparent contradiction be resolved?

The *Chasam Sofer* offers two solutions. The reason God does not reward us in this world is because doing so may cause us to become arrogant and sin. Such a reward is not a true reward because it may ultimately become detrimental to us. One who brings merit to the entire Jewish people will never sin as a result (*Yoma* 87a). Thus Phinehas could safely be rewarded without fear.

The *Chasam Sofer* suggests a second solution. The reason there is no reward for *mitzvos* in this world is that whatever this world has to offer is too cheap a currency with which to reward a mitzvah. Therefore, the Sages taught that the reward of a mitzvah is the opportunity to do another mitzvah. In this instance God did not want another outbreak of public immorality to occur so that Phinehas could rectify the situation. Therefore, God repaid him with the covenants of peace and eternal priesthood.[11]

Ohel Yaakov explains that one is not rewarded for *mitzvos* in this world because whatever one does is insufficient a price to pay for the ongoing gift of life itself. However, when one risks one's life for God, one shows that life itself is not the most important thing. In such circumstances, life alone cannot serve as sufficient reward.

When Phinehas displayed his willingness to sacrifice his life for God, life became too small a reward for his deed. God paid him with eternity.

According to *Chidushei HaRim*, this question sheds light on our concept of reward. In reality, man deserves no reward for anything he does for God. We barely meet our obligations when we serve Hashem and no one is entitled to reward for doing that which he is obligated to do. Could one expect to be compensated by his creditor when paying a debt? Yet God is kind and rewards us for our deeds. King David alludes to this when he says, *And Yours . . . is kindness, for You repay each man according to his deeds*

---

10. **Lovingly Zealous.** *R' Yisrael of Rizhin* explains verse 13 in a similar manner, rendering the word תַּחַת as *below* rather than *because*. On the surface, Phinehas seems to be driven by zealotry on behalf of God's honor. *Below* the surface lies a fierce love for the Jewish people and his desire to achieve atonement on their behalf.

11. **Payday.** Man's days are like that of a day worker (see *Job* 7:1): One must spiritually produce as much as he can in the short time allotted to him. Only when the day is over can the worker be paid. God pays us at the end of life, when our "workday" is up.

According to our Sages, Phinehas is Elijah the Prophet who lives forever (see *Bava Metzia* 114b and *Rashi* ad loc.). For him there is no end of the day. He must be paid immediately (*Sfas Emes*).

(*Psalms* 62:13).[12], [13] It is truly an act of Divine kindness that He rewards us for our deeds. There is generally no reward for *mitzvos* in this world, especially with regard to those *mitzvos* which one is obligated to perform. However, when one does something voluntarily he *is* entitled to reward in this world. The type of zealotry displayed by Phinehas was not an obligation. On the contrary, the Sages say, "[it is the] halachah, yet we do not rule so" (see *Sanhedrin* 82a and *Rashi* ad loc.). Were he to have asked the Sanhedrin if he should do what he did, they would have answered in the negative.

For volunteering, Phinehas deserved to be rewarded even in this world.[14]

תַּחַת אֲשֶׁר קִנֵּא לֵאלֹקָיו
*Because he took vengeance
for his God* (ibid.).

Is Hashem not everyone's God? Why does the Torah use the term אֱלֹקָיו, *his God,* as though He was Phinehas' God exclusively?

When God spoke to us at Sinai, He referred to Himself as, *I am Hashem, your* (singular) *God.* Why did He use the singular, אֱלֹקֶיךָ, and not the plural, אֱלֹקֵיכֶם?

It is a natural human weakness to avoid personal responsibility. People tend to justify their shortcomings by claiming that others are no better than

12. **Limited Liability.** The verse contains a problem. God rewards us commensurate with our actions, yet it is considered an act of kindness on His part.

R' Yisrael of Rizhin offers the following parable.

A simple peasant once visited the grand ballroom in the royal palace which was adorned with a most unique and magnificent crystal chandelier. Its thousands of crystal bars cast a brilliant light all around the cavernous room.

The crude peasant failed to focus on the chandelier. Instead, his attention was riveted on the long chain which held the chandelier suspended from the middle of the ballroom ceiling. From moment to moment his desire for the chain grew stronger. Finally, he decided that he would break into the palace that night and steal the chain.

That night he succeeded in breaking in. He climbed up a ladder and removed the chain with a pliers. How shocked he was to see the huge chandelier crash to the ground! All the crystal pieces were smashed to bits as the noise resounded throughout the palace. Immediately the palace guards came running into the ballroom and caught the foolish man red-handed. They took him to the king, sure that his fate was sealed.

After listening to the peasant's story, the king ruled that thirty days' imprisonment would be sufficient punishment for the crime.

The royal advisers were surprised at the light sentence. True, the king had a reputation as a benevolent monarch, but such a light punishment for destroying an expensive chandelier seemed out of character.

The king explained: "True, he broke the chandelier, but he was really only after the chain. In his foolishness he didn't realize that by cutting the chain he would destroy the crystal masterpiece. I will only punish him for what he thought he was doing."

When man contemplates sinning, his burning desire is for some insignificant and passing pleasure. He is blind to the consequences and far-reaching effects of his action. Not only does sin create a spiritual stain on the sinner himself it pollutes the spiritual climate around him and stains the communal soul of the Jewish people. Even the balance of the world may be adversely affected. God should really punish us severely for each and every sin.

But God is benevolent. He understands that all we ever wanted was our insignificant little desire. We never realized the cosmic effect of what we did.

In His kindness, God punishes us only for our immediate deed and does not take into account the resultant spiritual damage.

13. **Real Reward.** *Rambam* explains that the reward awaiting us in the World to Come is not recompense. Rather, to the extent that one prepared himself to perceive God in this world, he will be permitted to perceive Him in the World to Come.

14. **Beyond the Call.** *Simchas Higayon* illustrates this concept: A man hired a craftsman at a monthly wage, stipulating clearly the amount of hours the craftsman was expected to work. He also stipulated that the worker may not demand his wage before the end of the month. However, if the craftsman is requested to work overtime, he may demand to be paid immediately for the extra hours. The analogy is clear: God is the householder, we, the Jews, are the workers and all of life is the pay period. We must wait until the end of the pay period to receive our wages. Only in the World to Come will we be paid. Work we are not obligated to do is considered overtime and we are entitled to be paid immediately. Phinehas risked his life: This he was obligated to do. This is not something which demands that one jeopardize his own life yet Phinehas did so. He was therefore rewarded immediately.

they are. God was teaching us to think in personal terms. *I am Hashem, your God;* He is *my* God, not *our* God, and I alone bear personal responsibility. It is all up to me. Phinehas might have rationalized that since Moses, Aaron and the Elders did not respond, he would simply follow. He did not do so. Phinehas saw Zimri's behavior as an affront to *his God* which demanded an immediate response (*Aperion*).

R' Eliyahu Mishkovsky sees this as the character of a true zealot. The anger emanates from a deep-seated feeling that someone has acted brazenly toward *my* God. Zealotry represents a reflexive reaction toward a sin.

One cannot imitate zealotry: It must be part of the very essence of the zealot. Phinehas defended the honor of *his God.*

Background

Phinehas ends the plague which claimed 24,000 lives. It was a punishment for the sinful sexual misconduct between the Jews and the women of Midian and Moab. After the plague ended, God commands Moses and Elazar to conduct a census.

שְׂאוּ אֶת רֹאשׁ כָּל עֲדַת בְּנֵי יִשְׂרָאֵל
Take a census of the entire assembly of the Children of Israel (26:2).

According to *Rashi,* God asked for a census after the plague much as a shepherd counts his flock after it has been attacked by wolves. Even when God must punish the Jewish people for their sins, His love for them never wavers. As an expression of that love, God counts the survivors,

for they are especially important to Him (*Simchas Aharon*).[15]

Sfas Emes reveals an additional purpose for the census. Just as God counts the stars by name, so God counts the Jewish people who are compared to stars (see *Megillah* 16a). Just as every star has its particular spot in the constellation, every Jewish soul has its own, unique spiritual station. Just as God found it necessary to count the Jews before they received the Torah at Sinai so that every soul would be spiritually prepared to receive its particular connection to Torah (see *Exodus* 12:37), so too God had them counted again before entering the Holy Land, so that every soul would be spiritually prepared to receive its unique share in God's Palace.[16]

לְאָזְנִי מִשְׁפַּחַת הָאָזְנִי
Of Ozni, the Oznite family (ibid. 16).

Rashi submits that this is a reference to the family of Ezbon (see *Genesis* 46:16) and questions why the Torah changed the name.

Mei HaShiloach offers a homiletic interpretation. The Talmud (*Kesubos* 5a) teaches that the fingers (אֶצְבַּע) were created tapered so that one might plug his ears (אֹזֶן) with them, to prevent them from hearing forbidden words.

When the Jews went to Egypt it was necessary to block out all negative influences. They had to literally plug their ears. There they were called אֶצְבֹּן, for their moral duty was to put their tapered fingers (אֶצְבַּע) into their ears. Here, at the threshold of entering the Land, they were enjoined to open their ears (אֹזֶן) and absorb the holy melodies which waft through the very air of the Land of Israel.

---

15. **Survivors.** When the *Satmar Rav* left *Eretz Yisrael* to settle in the United States, one of his Israeli followers asked him, "Rebbe, to whom should I turn now with a *kvittel* (petitional note)?"

The Satmar Rav answered: "Go to any of the *shtieblach* (small synagogues) in Jerusalem and look for a Jew, even one who doesn't have a beard, who puts his *tefillin* on an arm tattooed with a number. Give him the *kvittel* and ask for a blessing. You will surely be helped."

God loves survivors.

16. **Soul Plot.** The portions allotted to every Jew in the Land of Israel were not merely real-estate holdings. They represented the spiritual habitat of each soul. As *R' Yehudah HaLevi* wrote, חַיֵּי הַנְּשָׁמוֹת אֲוִיר אַרְצֶךָ, *The atmosphere of Your Land is the life force of the souls.* The "eyes" of Hashem rest on *Eretz Yisrael* (see *Deuteronomy* 11:12). Though God oversees the entire universe, His attention is focused on the Land. *Eretz Yisrael* is the Palace of the King and it is there that we can rise to our fullest potential (*Zekan Aharon*).

אֵלֶּה מִשְׁפְּחֹת בְּנֵי גָד
These are the families of the sons of Gad (ibid. 18).

The first two tribes listed, Reuben and Simeon, are referred to as the Reubenite and Simeonite families. Why is Gad not listed as the "Gadite family"?

Tzror HaMor offers an explanation based on the words of King David: שְׁבָטֵי יָהּ עֵדוּת לְיִשְׂרָאֵל, *the tribes of God, a testimony for Israel (Psalms* 122:4). The nations claim that the genealogy of the Jewish people is impure, because the women were undoubtedly violated when they were in Egypt. God therefore appended His Name (יָה) to the names of the tribes as testimony to their genealogical purity. הָראוּבֵנִי and הַשִּׁמְעֹנִי with the ה at the beginning and the י at the end contain God's imprint.

One condition must be met in order for God to testify on behalf of the tribes. *Pray for the peace of Jerusalem (Psalms* 122:6). Only one with a strong emotional attachment to the Land of Israel can truly be considered part of the tribes of Israel. Those who do not pray for the peace of Jerusalem and those who reject this Godly gift are not granted the Divine stamp of validity expressed with the two-letter Name of God (יָה).

The tribe of Gad, who took the lead in rejecting the Land asking instead for a share of Trans-Jordan (see *Numbers* 32:5), did not merit God's testimony. They are called *the sons of Gad,* not the Gadites.[17]

לְיֵצֶר מִשְׁפַּחַת הַיִּצְרִי לְשִׁלֵּם מִשְׁפַּחַת הַשִּׁלֵּמִי
Of Jezer, the Jezerite family; of Shillem, the Shillemite family (ibid. 49).

Homiletically, this verse alludes to the words of the Sages, "Man is lead [from Heaven] along the path he seeks to follow" (*Makkos* 10b). One who seeks to follow his יֵצֶר, *[evil] inclination,* will find a slew of friends, figuratively, *the Jezerite family* (יֵצֶר). On the other hand, one who is earnestly looking for spiritual completion (שָׁלֵם, *complete*) will find supportive friends among *the Shillemite family.* (*R' Michel of Zlotochov*).

לָאֵלֶּה תֵּחָלֵק הָאָרֶץ
To these the Land shall be divided (ibid. 53).

Why did God command the Jews to divide the Land before they entered? According to *R' Yaakov Shimshon of Shpitovka,* this was because arguments and strife usually accompany the division of inheritances.

The Land of Israel is meant to have a unifying effect. God wanted any potential arguments to occur before they entered the Land, not after.[18]

לָרַב תַּרְבֶּה נַחֲלָתוֹ וְלַמְעַט תַּמְעִיט נַחֲלָתוֹ
For the numerous one you shall increase its inheritance and for the fewer one you shall lessen its inheritance (ibid. 54).

Sifsei Kohen homiletically views this verse as referring to one's share in the World to Come. *The numerous one* is one who accomplishes many spiritual achievements in this world. He will be granted a greatly increased inheritance in the World to Come. *The fewer one,* namely one who keeps his spiritual achievements to a minimum, will lessen his inheritance in the World to Come.

Life (in the World to Come) is whatever you make of it.[19]

---

17. **Stay Home!** An incident related in the Midrash teaches that the Land of Israel rejects those who reject it. Rabbi and R' Eliezer were once strolling near the city gates of Tiberias. They observed the funeral procession of someone who had never even visited the Land. He had lived and died in the Diaspora but was being brought to the Holy Land for interment. Rabbi told R' Eliezer, "Why was this Jew, who lived and died in the Diaspora, brought to the Land for burial? The Land itself complains against him with the words of *Jeremiah* (2:7), *You came and contaminated My land [in death yet] you made My heritage into an abomination [during your lifetime]*" (*Bereishis Rabbah* 96:5).

18. **Parental Foresight.** Parents who wish to leave an inheritance to their children should adopt this practice. They should clearly state who gets what. Thereby, they can avoid much strife and aggravation.

19. **Self-Made Paradise.** The World to Come does not come in many sliced pieces. Every Jew creates his own World to Come by the way which he lives in this world. The *Mishnah* (*Sanhedrin* 90a) speaks of a חֵלֶק לָעוֹלָם הַבָּא, lit. a share *toward* the World to Come, rather than בָּעוֹלָם הַבָּא, *in* the World to Come. We gain a piece in the World to Come by striving toward it, through the performance of *mitzvos* and the study of Torah (*Ruach Chaim*).

Mevaser Tzedek offers another homiletical perspective, seeing the verse as a demonstration of how God mirrors man (see *Psalms* 121:5; *Hashem is your shadow*).

For the numerous one, namely one who sees himself as great and superior to everyone else, God will also make Himself great and inaccessible. However, one who has humility, viewing himself as the *fewer one*, will encounter a God Who humbles Himself and allows man to connect with Him.

Background

When the daughters of Zelophehad hear that only men are being counted for the division of the Land of Israel, their love for it compels them to complain. Since they have no brothers, their family would not be receiving a share in the Land. Moses is unsure of the halachah and, after consulting with God, rules that their claims are legitimate and that they are entitled to a familial inheritance.

וַתִּקְרַבְנָה בְּנוֹת צְלָפְחָד . . .
לְמִשְׁפַּחַת מְנַשֶּׁה בֶן יוֹסֵף
*The daughters of Zelophehad . . .
of the families of Manasseh,
the son of Joseph . . . drew near* (27:1).

The Torah alludes to the passionate love that Zelophehad's daughters had for *Eretz Yisrael* by tracing their genealogy back to Joseph. He also expressed his love of the Land by insisting that he be buried in its holy soil [see *Genesis* 50:25] (*Rashi*).

The rebbetzin of Ger, wife of the *Sfas Emes*, asked her son the *Imrei Emes*: "Who says it was out of a love of the Land that they presented their case to Moses? Maybe they simply wanted to inherit their father's money and property?"

The *Imrei Emes* replied: "According to all opinions, Zelophehad died, at the latest, during the second year of the sojourn in the Wilderness. If all his daughters wanted was to get their hands on their father's money, why did they wait until the fortieth year to register their claim? Certainly Zelophehad had left over some wealth from the treasures the Jews had taken from Egypt or from what they had received at the Reed Sea: why didn't they complain immediately about losing that wealth? Obviously, material gains meant nothing to them. The love of the Land brought them before Moses."

אָבִינוּ מֵת בַּמִּדְבָּר וְהוּא לֹא הָיָה בְּתוֹךְ הָעֵדָה . . .
בַּעֲדַת קֹרַח . . . וַיַּקְרֵב מֹשֶׁה אֶת מִשְׁפָּטָן לִפְנֵי ה'
*Our father died in the Wilderness, but he
was not among the assembly . . . the
assembly of Korah . . . And Moses brought
their claim before Hashem* (ibid. 3-5).

Two members of the Tarnopol community came before R' Yosef Babad, author of the *Minchas Chinuch*. They asked him to judge a monetary dispute between them. While presenting his case, one of the litigants mentioned in passing that the Rav's father had officiated at his wedding. The Rav immediately turned to the other party and asked him, "Did my father officiate at your wedding as well?" When the answer came back "No," R' Yosef disqualified himself. "I am afraid that the knowledge that my father presided at the first litigant's wedding will prejudice my view and compromise my objectivity," he said. "I learned this from Moses. The moment the daughters of Zelophehad mentioned that their father took no part in the Korah rebellion Moses felt this fact might affect his judgment. He therefore suggested they ask God directly.

The *Shulchan Aruch* (*Choshen Mishpat* 9:1-3) writes: A judge must be cautious regarding the acceptance of any type of bribe. Not only monetary bribes are forbidden. Even a verbal bribe is a disqualifier. The Talmud (*Kesubos* 105b) relates many incidents which indicate the far-reaching parameters of what the Sages viewed as graft. The great Sage Shmuel was crossing a bridge when a man approached him and offered his arm so that Shmuel could maintain his balance while making his way across. Shmuel asked him where he was headed and the stranger, who had not recognized the sage, replied, "I'm on the way to Shmuel's court to present a case for his ruling." Shmuel immediately disqualified himself.

Even a sense of emotional bonding was considered a bribe in our Sages' eyes. Mar bar R' Ashi refused to preside over a case in which one of the litigants was a Torah scholar since, in his own words, "I love them as dearly as I love myself and one is

unable to see fault in oneself" (*Shabbos* 119a).[20]
Moses set the precedent for judicial honesty.

Background

God commands Moses to ascend Mount Abarim, from which he will be able to see the Land of Israel, and states unequivocally that Moses will not lead the people into the Land. Moses now begins to shift his concern to the future of his beloved people and their ability to survive. First and foremost, he asks God to provide the Jews with the proper leadership.

יִפְקֹד ה' אֱלֹהֵי הָרוּחֹת לְכָל בָּשָׂר אִישׁ עַל הָעֵדָה
May Hashem, God of the spirits of all flesh, appoint a man over the assembly (ibid. 16).

Moses expresses his desire that God provide the people with a leader who possesses the Divine ability to understand and address the mental and emotional needs of each individual Jew. God appoints Joshua as leader, because he was a man of spirit. *Rashi* explains "a man of spirit" as one who can encounter and engage the spirit of each and every person.

R' Tzvi Hirsch Levin offers a novel interpretation of the seemingly contradictory characteristics demanded of a spiritual leader. On one hand, a leader must have the flexibility and sensitivity to understand the feelings, foibles and desires of his people. However, he must always remain a man of spirit whose ultimate loyalty is to the Torah. He must be ready to encounter the spirit of each person yet remain steadfast in his own convictions.[21]

R' Levi Yitzchak of Berditchev suggests that Moses asked for a leader who, like God, understands and is sympathetic of the weaknesses of every person. Just as God loves every Jew unconditionally, a leader must also love every Jew unconditionally. However, teaches *Degel Machaneh Ephraim*, a leader may never lower himself totally to the level of the people. He must be *on* the people, not *with* the people.

This was the problem with the people's request for a king in the days of Samuel the Prophet. They asked, "Give us a king," implying someone on their level whom they can control. The Torah frames the request, "I will set a king over myself," indicating a willingness to submit to a king who can set the spiritual, ethical and moral tone for the nation.[22]

---

20. **Tearful Graft.** A widow once appeared before the *Avnei Nezer*. She was one of the parties involved in a monetary dispute. When presenting her case she began to sob uncontrollably. She complained bitterly over her lot in life and the way in which her adversary was exploiting her situation. "The tears of a brokenhearted widow are a form of bribery," the *Avnei Nezer* said. "How can I remain objective?

Moses referred the case of the daughters of Zelophehad to God because he feared that they would be moved to tears over the loss of their share in the Land. Their tears might bias his judgment.

21. **Looking Up to Leadership.** *R' Yitzchak Akarish* was crowned Chief Rabbi of Constantinople by his teacher, the famed *Saba Kadisha, R' Shelomoh Eliezer Elefandri*. On the first Sabbath after his appointment, *R' Elefandri* addressed the congregation and lavishly praised both his student and the congregation that was wise enough to engage his services. He then spoke about Moses' request for new leadership. "The Torah," he said, "alludes to the qualities required for successful Jewish leadership. Some communities foolishly limit the jurisdiction of the rav to ritual matters. They don't consider the rav to be the final authority on all communal matters. In fact, they completely ignore the rav's will in communal issues and try to force him to accept their view."

Moses clearly describes the spiritual head of the community as one appointed *over* the people, not below them. The rav must be held in the highest esteem and the congregants must yield to his opinion. He must furthermore *go out in front of them,* setting the public tone rather than following the wishes of the powerful and wealthy. The people must be a flock led by a shepherd. It must be clear to all who is the shepherd and who are the sheep.

R' Yisrael Salanter said that a rav whom everybody likes is not a rav (see *Kesubos* 105b), but a rav whom everybody dislikes is not a *mentsch*. A balance must be struck between the two.

22. **Clock Tower.** In a letter to a community which was honoring its rabbi for ten years of dedicated service, *R' Yitzchak Hutner* penned a parable portraying the appropriate relationship between a congregation and its spiritual leader.

"Cities with town clocks have them placed so high up that if one wanted to reach the clock one would have to use a ladder. Any intelligent observer would assume there are two reasons for this. The obvious reason is that even

אֲשֶׁר יֵצֵא לִפְנֵיהֶם וַאֲשֶׁר יָבֹא
לִפְנֵיהֶם וַאֲשֶׁר יוֹצִיאֵם וַאֲשֶׁר יְבִיאֵם

Who shall go out before them and
come in before them, who shall take
them out and bring them in (ibid. 17).

The redundancy in this verse obviously warrants an explanation.

Amudei Eish uses a parable: Both a commander who leads his troops and a horse that pulls a wagon are at the head of their respective processions. Shall we then conclude that the horse leads those who are sitting in the wagon just as the military leader leads his troops? Of course not! The commander, an intelligent and accomplished military tactician, leads through his intelligence and experience. The horse follows the instructions of those sitting behind him.

Moses asked for a leader who would *go out* before the people. He didn't mean someone who would allow himself to be lead like the horse. Rather, he was looking for a leader who leads himself. He wanted someone who *shall take them out and bring them in.*

R' Yisrael Salanter sees this idea reflected in the Talmudic description of the level of leadership in the pre-Messianic era. "The face of the generation will resemble the face of a dog" (*Sanhedrin* 98b). The dog always runs in front of its master, leaving bystanders with the impression that it is leading his master. When the dog reaches a crossroads and does not know which way to continue, it turns its head around and looks to the master for direction. At that point the true leader becomes apparent.

One of the terrible travails of the pre-Messianic era will be a weak leadership which "leaders" will in reality constantly turn to the masses for direction. Fearful of losing their positions and interested mainly in currying favor with those who pay their checks or keep them in power, the leaders will be lead by their leaderless followers.[23]

R' Zalman, Maggid of Vilna, views the two clauses as representative of two types of leaders. Some leaders need not speak very much to influence their followers. The people merely look at the Divine Presence that rests on their leader's face[24] and are influenced to live a true Torah life. In the words of the Sages, "If one [leader] is God fearing, his words are heard". There is no need for him to speak. He leads by example.

Other leaders are not able to do so. They must softly and caringly verbalize instructions and directions. Moses asked God to send the Jews a person who would lead by example, through the force of his personality and spiritual stature. He wanted the people to have a leader *who shall go out before them and come in before them* as a role model. "If this is impossible," asked Moses, "please

---

from afar, everyone is able to see the clock. There is a less obvious reason. People synchronize their personal watches with that of the town. Were the clock to be placed lower, people would simply adjust the time on the town clock to match their own. By placing the clock high, people have to set their watches in accordance with it.

"Unfortunately, many communities do not understand the importance of placing their spiritual leaders on a high pedestal. Were the congregants to look up to the rav and treat him with extreme respect, they would have to synchronize their lifestyle with that of the rav. Since, they treat their rav in a less respectful manner, they bring him down to their level. I congratulate you on your ability to raise yourselves up to your rav's level" (*Collected Letters* 132).

23. **Big Doctors.** The *Chidushei HaRim* bemoaned the sad spiritual state of the Jews in his times. He said, "People think that as the spirituality of the generations decrease, leaders of lower stature are adequate. This is not so. Leaders of great spirit are required. This is analogous to a sick patient. The sicker the patient, the greater the need for a better doctor.

On the other hand, people often grow great after assuming positions of leadership. Our Sages said, "The leaders according to the generation, the generation according to the leaders" (*Arachin* 17b). Leaders often rise to meet the spiritual needs of their generation.

24. **Not the Same.** When the *Beis HaLevi* left the rabbinate of Slutzk, he related an incident that occurred when he arrived there. It highlights the pure faith of the women of Slutzk.

"I was walking toward the synagogue, when I overheard two women talking to each other. One said to the other, 'Did you see the new rav? The Divine Presence rests on his face.' Countered the other, 'You are right. But believe me, it is not the same Divine Presence that rested on the face of R' Yussel Feimer, the previous rav.'"

provide them with someone *who shall take them out and bring them in* by offering explicit instructions on how to live."

וְלֹא תִהְיֶה עֲדַת ה' כַּצֹּאן אֲשֶׁר אֵין לָהֶם רֹעֶה

And let the assembly of Hashem not be like sheep that have no shepherd (ibid.).

This verse appears awkward. Why not simply state that fitting leadership is needed so that the people will not be like shepherdless sheep (כַּצֹּאן בְּלִי רֹעֶה)?

The literal meaning of the verse is "they not be like sheep that there is no shepherd *to them.*" *R' Zalman Sorotzkin* explains that Moses had no doubt that a leader would emerge. Leadership is always replaced. There is no shortage of potential leaders. However, most of the candidates will cater more to themselves than address the needs of the people. The Jewish people run the risk of remaining like sheep without a shepherd *to them.* They have a shepherd, with his own self-interest in mind. Moses prayed that the nation be blessed with a shepherd who will be only concerned with his sheep.

R' Yaakov Yuzef put it this way: A shepherd always cares for his sheep. Sometimes, because that is how he makes his living and, other times, because he really cares. Moses prayed that the future leader of Israel lead altruistically, not as a means to a career.

The Jewish people needed a loyal shepherd, totally committed to the people. He should be a shepherd *to them.*

He described the ideal shepherd as *one who goes out in front of them.* When danger lurks the loyal shepherd still leads, putting himself in danger on behalf of his flock.

Only a man of spirit who has risen high above his own self-centeredness could meet such high expectations.[25]

---

25. **Loving Shepherd.** When the *Yid HaKadosh of P'shis'cha* passed away, his students were in a quandary as to who should be appointed his successor. His most prominent students met to confer on this issue.

R' Simchah Bunim of P'shis'cha opened the discussion with a story: "There was once a shepherd who lovingly cared for his flock. He brought them to green pastures and sparkling streams. Whenever one sheep went astray, he would search tirelessly until he found it. One day he sat down on the grass and soon fell fast asleep. He woke up past midnight. He looked around but could not find his sheep. Fear overtook him and he began to cry. He took a few steps, and there before him was his flock. He lovingly counted them all and noticed all were present. His joy knew no bounds.

"Lifting his eyes to Heaven, he said, 'Master of the world! Nothing like this ever happened to me before. How can I repay You for Your great kindness? I swear to You that if You were to put Your flock into my care, I would watch over them as I watch over these sheep.' Let us look for this type of shepherd," concluded R' Simchah Bunim.

Among the group was *R' Avraham Abli,* who was the *Yid HaKadosh's* study partner. They had learned Kabbalistic texts together, and many believed him to be the most appropriate successor. When R' Avraham Abli heard R' Simchah Bunim's story he led him to the *Yid HaKadosh's* chair. As he seated him in the chair, he called out, "This is our master and teacher."

פרשת מטות ‎‎‏⊰
Parashas Mattos

Background

The *parashah* begins with the laws of *nedarim* (commonly translated as vows) and the process by which they may be annulled. In this section, the Torah speaks mainly of the conditions under which fathers may annul the vows of their daughters and husbands the vows of their wives.

The sequence of topics discussed in the Torah is not accidental. When two seemingly unrelated subjects are juxtaposed, it is an indication that they are connected. The previous *parashah* concludes with a discussion of the additional offerings brought on holy days whereas this *parashah* begins with the power of man's speech to sanctify mundane items. What is the relationship between them?

Sfas Emes suggests that our prayers have re-

placed the sacrifices that were once brought in the Holy Temple. Just as the offerings were dedicated exclusively to God, so too our mouths and hearts must be totally dedicated to God. The power of our prayers is dependent on the sanctity of our speech. To honor one's words is a precondition for prayer, which replaces the offerings mentioned in the previous *parashah*.

וַיְדַבֵּר מֹשֶׁה אֶל רָאשֵׁי הַמַּטוֹת
Moses spoke to the heads of the tribes (30:2).

Why was this set of laws, which deals with vows, taught specifically to the heads of the tribes? *Chasam Sofer* answers. Leaders and public figures often make promises they cannot keep.[1] The Torah here is speaking to leaders. They are warned to keep their word.[2], [3] On the other hand, the

---

1. **Hollow Promise.** P.S., a prominent Israeli politician in the 1950's and 60's, once promised a certain institution government funding. When the funds were not forthcoming, the heads of the institution confronted him and demanded that he make good on his promise. His cynical reply was, ''True, I promised; but I didn't promise to keep my promise.''

It is in response to such cynicism that the Torah initially addresses the laws of vows to the leaders of the nation.

2. **Listen to Yourself.** It is particularly despicable when leaders (or parents) who offer rebuke and criticism to their charges fail to live up to the words they speak.

Homiletically, this is alluded to in the words of the *Mishnah* (*Berachos* 15a), ''One who reads the *Shema* but does not hear the words he utters has not fulfilled his obligation.'' One who calls out to other Jews, ''Hear, O Israel,'' but does not hear his own message, has not fulfilled his obligation [as a leader or parent] (*R' Akiva Eiger*).

3. **Binding Words.** The sanctity of one's words is so holy that in some instances one must honor a promise or oath even if it was made under false pretenses. *Rambam* writes this regarding the treaty Joshua made with the Gibeonites (see *Joshua* 9:15-27). In reality, the Jews should have killed the Gibeonites for having tricked them into making a pact, something forbidden by the Torah. They allowed them to live in order not to renege on their oath. Reneging on an oath constitutes a *chilul Hashem,* a desecration of God's Name (*Hilchos Melachim* 6:5).

R' Yonah states clearly that to speak misleadingly, even to a non-Jew, is strictly forbidden. ''The dishonest tongue

masses are taught how important the words of their leaders are. The nation must realize that the words of Torah scholars must be accepted as if issued by God Himself. Just as a Jew may not desecrate his own vow, he may neither desecrate the words of the "heads of the tribes," the Torah leadership.[4]

אֶל רָאשֵׁי הַמַּטוֹת לִבְנֵי יִשְׂרָאֵל
The heads of the tribes of the Children of Israel (ibid.).

The word מַטוֹת, literally "staffs," is used as a synonym for "tribes." According to many of the chassidic masters, the term is also related to מַטֶּה, *bend* or *incline,* as in *Psalms* (116:2), כִּי הִטָּה אָזְנוֹ לִי, *As He has inclined His ear to me.* The function of Jewish leadership is twofold. It must encourage the people to bend their hearts toward God, and simultaneously implore God to bend His attention to the needs of His people.[5] Moses sought to lower God to His people while Aaron strove to elevate

the nation to Him (*Avnei Nezer*). According to R' Baruch of Koidanov, Jewish leaders may never feel superior to their flock. They must bend their ears and listen to the needs, dreams, expectations and demands of their people.[6] *Imrei Chaim* offers a homiletic interpretation. The Talmud states that whoever oppresses (מֵיצַר) the Jewish people rises to power. Homiletically, this may be reinterpreted as "whoever feels the pain of the Jewish people will rise to positions of leadership." Those who identify with the people, feel their pain and soothe their broken hearts are destined to be the heads of the nation.

זֶה הַדָּבָר אֲשֶׁר צִוָּה ה'
This is the thing that Hashem has commanded (ibid.).

This verse implies that Hashem only commanded us to keep our vows. This is inaccurate, since Hashem commanded us to keep many *mitzvos.*

---

is an extremely grave sin. We are obligated to stay clearly within the boundaries of truth, for it is at the foundation of the soul" (*Shaarei Teshuvah* 3:184).

4. **Not So Smart.** A chassidic aphorism has it that a basic key to faith in the wise is the realization that you are not as smart as you think you are.

5. **Humble Nullification.** When R' Binyamin Diskin (father of the famed R' Yehoshua Leib Diskin) was the Rav of Lomza, Poland, a brilliant Torah scholar settled into the local *beis midrash,* learning there full-time. He took a vow never to leave the *beis midrash.* The righteous women brought him food daily. The townspeople were however upset because Lomza lacked an *eruv* and they could not bring the scholar his Shabbos meals. Since they had to bring the food before Shabbos the scholar lacked warm food on Shabbos. There was no solution to this problem. One day R' Akiva Eiger came to Lomza to participate in a family wedding. R' Binyamin Diskin took the opportunity to discuss the problem of the reclusive scholar. When R' Akiva Eiger heard that he was a brilliant Torah scholar and that he refused to leave the *beis midrash,* he decided to visit him together with R' Binyamin. When the townspeople saw their venerable Rav and his distinguished guest head toward the *beis midrash,* they followed. R' Akiva Eiger addressed the scholar. "I understand you are an accomplished *talmid chacham.* Since you can't leave, I decided to come visit you." The scholar was deeply moved and said to the great *Gaon,* "Why did the Rav have to bother to come visit a simple Jew like myself? This causes me pain."

R' Akiva Eiger asked him, "Had you known we would have to come visit you, would you have made the vow?"

"Of course not," he replied. "I would have run out to greet your holy countenance."

"If so," countered the famed sage, "your vow is annulled and you are permitted to leave."

6. **Saint Sensitivity.** A yeshivah student once noticed R' Isser Zalman Meltzer pacing in front of his own home, seemingly preoccupied in thought. The young man approached and offered his assistance. R' Isser Zalman replied, "No, thank you." When the pacing continued, the student tried again. The *Rosh Yeshivah* again refused but this time explained. "I'll tell you the truth. I went upstairs to my apartment and heard the woman who washes the floors in the apartment singing. She is a lonely woman who cheers herself up by singing when she works. Were I to come home she would feel compelled to stop since she knows that I am not permitted to listen. Why should I deny her the pleasure of singing? I will wait downstairs until she finishes."

Our leaders are even sensitive to the seemingly insignificant needs of the people.

Chasam Sofer explains: The sacredness of one's word is the foundation of one's obligation to keep all the *mitzvos*. We are bound by the *mitzvos* because we willingly accepted them at Sinai and swore to fulfill them. If our word is meaningless, we have effectively undermined our commitment. *This is the thing that Hashem has commanded* is correct because it underscores our acceptance of His Torah.[7]

The Talmud (*Nedarim* 8a) states that one may take an oath to fulfill a mitzvah. This is based on the words of King David, *I have sworn and I will fulfill, to keep Your righteous ordinances* (*Psalms* 119:106). The Talmud then questions the validity of such an oath. Since all Jews swore at Sinai to uphold the *mitzvos*, the present oath appears to be superfluous. The Talmud replies that since the present oath motivates the person more, it is permitted.

R' Tzadok HaKohen asks the obvious question: If the oath at Sinai is insufficient to insure one's compliance, what is to be gained with an additional one? When one swears to do a mitzvah, the new oath rejuvenates the old one transforming his intellectual commitment to an inspired emotional one.[8]

Rashi notes that, unlike the other prophets who prophesied with the words *so said Hashem,* Moses prophesied with the words *this is the thing.*

The clarity of Moses' prophecy was such that he transmitted it to the people as it was transmitted to him. The other prophets prophesied with the words, *So said Hashem.* Their prophecies were filtered through their own personality, and assumed some of their own character. This is why we are taught that no two prophets speak in the same style [nevertheless we are enjoined *to him you shall hearken* (*Deut.* 18:15, *Rambam, Hilchos Yesodei HaTorah* 7:7)] (*R' Chaim of Volozhin*).

In a homiletic vein, *Tosafos Chaim* sees here an important lesson. The phrase *This is the thing* is symbolic of tangible, physical things, while *so said Hashem* is an expression of Divine will. Moses had the ability to prophesy in both manners. He defined the ways the physical elements of life could be harnessed to serve the Divine will. He could hear the *so said Hashem* resonating in *this is the thing* namely, in every creation.[9]

אִישׁ כִּי יִדֹּר נֶדֶר לַה'
If a man takes a vow to Hashem (ibid. 3).

How can the words of a mere mortal actually change the status of an item, transforming something permissible into something forbidden?

Avnei Nezer offers an explanation. *Rabbeinu Yonah* teaches that one who is careful to refrain from forbidden speech transforms his mouth into a

---

7. **Verbal Murder.** The severity of vows is underscored by the comment of the *Baal HaTurim* that the word נְדָרִים, *vows,* and the word רוֹצֵחַ, *murderer,* share the same numerical value (*gematria*). This mirrors the words of the Sages who teach that laxity regarding one's vows may cause one's wife and children to die young (*Shabbos* 32b).

8. **Forcing One's Hand.** We are often lax in the observance of particular *mitzvos* and seek ways to upgrade our performance. *Michtav MeEliyahu* suggests arranging one's affairs in ways that leave him no choice but to behave correctly. Otherwise, his decision to change might not last. As the Sages taught, "When the evil inclination is active no one even remembers a positive inclination exists" (*Nedarim* 32b). One should do whatever he can to force himself to the proper path and then let him pray that God will help him succeed.

One must sometimes employ the most selfish of motives to assure that one follows the correct path.

For example, one who finds it difficult to invest time and energy in Torah study should volunteer to teach a public class, thus forcing himself to invest the time. This way he will fulfill the dictum of the Sages to serve God with the evil inclination as well as the good one (*Berachos* 54a). [We begin Yom Kippur with the *Kol Nidrei* prayer (which nullifies vows) to tell ourselves that vows themselves are not enough. We must take active steps to insure our compliance.]

9. **Endless Opportunities.** Every day in our morning prayers we say, מָלְאָה הָאָרֶץ קִנְיָנֶךָ, *the world is full of Your possessions.* *R' Simchah Bunim of P'shis'cha* translated the phrase as "The earth is full of ways to acquire You." Every molecule of Creation and every human action has the potential to connect us to God. We must discover the spiritual potential in all of our actions and in everything around us.

sanctified vessel like that found in the Temple. Just as those sacred vessels were used to sanctify meal-offerings and imbue them with holiness, so too man's mouth can infuse a profane item with sanctity. We are forbidden to desecrate our words as we are forbidden to misappropriate items which have been designated for sacred purposes. The word of a Jew is holy because Israel was created to sing the praises of God (see *Isaiah* 43:21).

וַה׳ יִסְלַח לָהּ
and Hashem will forgive her (ibid. 6).

If a girl's father nullified her vow, why does she need God's forgiveness? What sin did she commit? *Rashi* explains that this verse refers to a girl who assumed a vow of Naziritehood and, unaware of her father's nullification, went and drank wine. Technically she did not sin, because at the time she drank the wine she was no longer obligated to keep the nullified vow. However, she still needs to repent and be granted forgiveness by God because, to the best of her knowledge, she *was* in violation of her vow.

From this we learn that one is not judged by one's actions but by one's choices. Since the girl chose to sin and acted on that choice, she requires forgiveness even though she really actually did nothing wrong.[10]

R' Refael Hamburger explains the Talmudic saying, "God does not combine evil thought with action" (*Kiddushin* 4a), in this light. The popular understanding is that actions count, not thoughts. If this is so, why does the woman need atonement? She did nothing wrong! Obviously, however, thoughts *are* significant: As long as one does not

put negative thoughts into action, one continues to be viewed positively. Once one acts on the negative thoughts, he is called to taks for them.

The Talmud (*Kiddushin* 81b) states that R' Akiva cried when he read this verse. "If one who intended to eat pig meat, and unbeknownst to him ate kosher meat instead, needs forgiveness, certainly one who actually ate pig meat requires atonement."

R' Akiva seeks to teach us that when one sins, one commits two grievous acts. The deed itself and the will to rebel against God. The desire to sin is in itself a sin.[11] Even if one ends up eating kosher meat, one still needs forgiveness.

If one sins, one must be forgiven twice; for his actual sin and for his desire to sin. Repentance for a misdeed is difficult. Repentance for a misthought is almost impossible to achieve without Divine assistance. This is why R' Akiva cried (*Taam V'Daas*).

Background

The nation is now commanded to punish the Midianites for having incited them to idolatry and immorality (see 25:17). Led by Phinehas, they successfully route the Midianites and kill Balaam.

נְקֹם נִקְמַת בְּנֵי יִשְׂרָאֵל
Take vengeance for the Children of Israel (31:2).

When God instructs Moses to punish the Midianites he refers to it as *vengeance for the Children of Israel*: When Moses conveys the command to the people, he speaks of the *vengeance of Hashem*.

---

10. **Intentional Indictment.** *Ramban* (*Genesis* 15:13) explains why the Egyptians were punished for enslaving the Jews. Although they were ultimately carrying out God's will, their intentions were not to do so. The cruelty they exhibited went far beyond that which was decreed. Therefore, they were punished. Only if one's motivations are purely for the sake of Heaven can he be absolved of punishment if he carries out God's will.

In terms of action, the Egyptians did fulfill God's will. Nevertheless, since they behaved so cruelly, they were punished.

The Egyptians serve as another example of legitimate acts which result from evil intentions. They demand punishment and require atonement.

11. **Redeeming Restraint.** The Sages teach that even if one performed no positive act but merely refrained from transgressing, it is considered as if one has performed a mitzvah (*Makkos* 23b). Which *mitzvah* has he performed? *Rabbeinu Yonah* explains that it is the mitzvah of אֶת ה׳ אֱלֹקֶיךָ תִּירָא, *you shall fear Hashem your God* (*Deuteronomy* 10:20).

What is the significance of this change in terminology?

אַהֲבַת יִשְׂרָאֵל (love of the Jewish people) and אַהֲבַת הַשֵׁם (love of Hashem) are linked. One who loves a Jew expresses his love of God. Hashem told Moses to take vengeance for the people of Israel but Moses called it the vengeance of Hashem, because he viewed them as being the same. The honor of God's people is the honor of God himself (R' Simchah Zissel of Kelm).

R' Shalom of Belz reflects on the reciprocal relationship between God and His nation. In His love for us, God stresses the fact that fighting the Midianites will serve as vengeance for the terrible plague which they brought upon His nation. We, in our love for Him, see it differently. Our goal is to redress the crime committed against Him by the Midianites.[12] Alternatively, Sifsei Tzaddikim suggests that the change in terminology is rooted in the great love between Moses and his people. If he were to phrase the command as given, Moses feared the people may forgo their own honor to prolong his life. They knew he would die after he defeated the Midianites. Moses therefore presented the Divine command as a call to avenge the honor of Hashem.

אַחַר תֵּאָסֵף אֶל עַמֶּיךָ
afterward you will be gathered
unto your people (ibid.).

The death of Moses was linked to the battle with the Midianites: Only after the Midianites were punished would Moses die. The forces of spiritual good and evil must always be balanced so that man may truly *choose* good. According to the *Vilna Gaon* (notes to *Seder Olam*), it was the maintenance of this spiritual balance which caused

prophecy to cease at the time that the Men of the Great Assembly abolished the intense desire to practice idolatry (see *Yoma* 69b). The existence of idolatry had to be balanced with the heightened Divine revelation of prophecy. Once idolatry was abolished, prophecy also decreased.

In terms of prophecy, Balaam was the negative counterpart to Moses. As long as he lived, Moses was needed as a counterbalance. Once Balaam was killed (see *Numbers* 31:8) Moses could be *gathered unto his people* (R' Yaakov Yitzchak Ruderman). *Meshech Chochmah* explains that the battle with Midian had to occur before the death of Moses to teach us a lesson regarding the delicate balance between duty and gratitude. Moses did not personally wage war against the Midianites. He sent Phinehas, because "one should never throw stones into the well he drank from" (*Bava Kamma* 92b). Since Moses found refuge at the home of Jethro in Midian, his sense of gratitude precluded his personal involvement in this war. Had the battle with Midian, occurred after Moses' death, it might have left the false impression that Moses had granted them protection during his lifetime as an expression of gratitude. God therefore insisted that the punishment of Midian occur before his death but without his active participation.[13]

One must always pursue public policy with sensitivity to private ethical issues.

וַיִּמָּסְרוּ מֵאַלְפֵי יִשְׂרָאֵל אֶלֶף לַמַּטֶּה
So there were delivered from the
thousands of [the Children of]
Israel a thousand from a tribe (31:5).

Rashi notes that the warriors had to be coerced to go to war against the Midianites because they

---

12. **Reciprocal Love.** Our prayers on the Festivals highlight our reciprocal relationship with God. We call Passover פֶּסַח. God refers to it as חַג הַמַּצּוֹת, *the festival of matzos.* God emphasizes what we do "for Him" (eating the matzos). We, in turn, emphasize what He did for us (passing over our homes and slaying the Egyptian's firstborn) (*Kedushas Levi*).

13. **Eternally Indebted.** The fact that someone may consistently mistreat me does not absolve me of my obligation to show appreciation for any kindnesses he may have exhibited toward me in the past. Although the Midianites caused the death of 24,000 Jews, Moses felt he could not personally punish them because they sheltered him in his time of need. Moses knew that God would not expect his personal involvement. That would have run counter to the very root of our commitment to Torah and *mitzvos,* our gratitude to God for all He has done for us (*Ohr Yahal*).

knew that Moses' death would occur as a result.[14]

She'aris Menachem suggests an alternative reason. He bases it on *Rashi* (verse 3) who explains that the men Moses picked for this war had to be righteous. How was he to find righteous men? Were the righteous supposed to step forward and volunteer their services? How righteous is the person who claims to be righteous? The Sages teach that even if the entire world tells you that you are righteous you should view yourself as wicked (*Niddah* 30b).

The Torah tells us וַיִּמָּסְרוּ. The righteous warriors were delivered into Moses' hands (from the expression מוֹסֵר, *informant*). They were informed upon. People came forward and revealed who the truly righteous were.[15]

Interestingly, *Rashi* contrasts the attitude the Jews had toward Moses during his leadership years with their present attitude. Before, Moses feared they might stone him (see *Exodus* 17:4); now, the people had to be coerced to fight the battle which would precipitate his passing. Why does Rashi emphasize this contrast? *R' Yosef Leib Bloch* explains: One is sentimental regarding the life of someone with whom one maintained an amicable, stress-free relationship.

One might not show the same concern regarding the life of one with whom one maintained a strained and stressful relationship. Moses often rebuked the nation. When the Jewish people refrained from attacking Midian, they showed a deep love for Moses. They understood that his past rebuke was meant for their benefit. The Sages teach, "A Rav who is overly beloved in the eyes of his congregants apparently does not rebuke them in spiritual matters" (*Kesubos* 105b).

וְאֶת בִּלְעָם בֶּן בְּעוֹר הָרְגוּ בֶּחָרֶב

And Balaam son of Beor they slew with the sword (ibid. 8).

Rashi notes the significance of the fact that Balaam was killed by the sword.

The power of the Jewish people lies in its mouth, and is manifested in words of prayer. The power of Esau, symbolized by the sword, manifests itself in acts of violence and murder. Since Balaam sought to use the power of the mouth against the Jews, God had them use the power of the sword against Balaam.

According to *Chafetz Chaim*, this teaches us that the way one uses one's mouth shows one's connection to God. Just as a craftsman takes extreme caution not to misuse the tools of his trade, so too a Jew must take utmost care not to abuse his power of speech through slander, inappropriate language or the like. Our Sages taught that one should make himself "mute" in this world, speaking only words of Torah and prayer (*Chullin* 89b).[16]

---

14. **Blindly Objective.** In the previous verse, *Rashi* notes that even the tribe of Levi battled the Midianites. If so, there should have been 13,000 warriors. Why does the Torah only speak of 12,000? *Imrei Emes* explains: The warriors had to be coerced to fight because they didn't want to cause the death of Moses. The tribe of Levi was able to disregard any personal or familial considerations. Moses describes them in his blessings as, *The one who said of his father and mother, "I have not favored him"; his brothers he did not give recognition and his children he did not know* (*Deuteronomy* 33:9). The Levites were able to concentrate exclusively on God's commands. [According to *Sefer HaChinuch* (408), this is the reason that the Levite cities served as cities of refuge for those who murdered accidentally. The Levites could rise above family considerations and even refrain from killing the accidental murderer of a relative.]

Thirteen thousand warriors participated but only twelve thousand had to be forced.

15. **Revealing Righteousness.** The Talmud (*Chullin* 109b) teaches that for every item God forbade in His Torah He provided a permissible parallel item. The blood of an animal may be forbidden, but the liver, with its high concentration of blood, is permitted (see ibid. for other examples). What, asked *R' Yisrael of Rizhin*, is the permitted parallel to slander and gossip? One may publicly reveal the hidden righteousness of someone who tries to conceal it. This is permitted to enable others to spiritually benefit from him. When Moses was instructed to seek righteous warriors, he certainly issued a call for volunteers. The truly righteous were too humble to step forward. Those who knew the truth, let the secret out and the righteous were forced to accept their roles.

16. **Concrete Communication.** When God created man, He placed a Heavenly soul into a physical body. This union produced the power of speech, which gives physical expression to man's soul, and sets him apart from God's other creations. (See *Genesis* 2:7 and *Targum* ad loc.) One's manner of speaking defines one's humanity (*Simchas Aharon*).

A Jew's mouth is the tool of his trade. It should be used for prayer and the study of Torah.

Background

Among the spoils of war were utensils which the Jews wanted to use. Elazar informs the people of the process by which these utensils can be made kosher and fit for use. By extension, the Torah teaches the laws of purging vessels of nonkosher absorptions.

וַיֹּאמֶר אֶלְעָזָר הַכֹּהֵן אֶל אַנְשֵׁי הַצָּבָא הַבָּאִים לַמִּלְחָמָה

Elazar the Kohen said to the men of the legion who came to the battle (ibid. 21).

The phrase *came to the battle* seems inaccurate; Elazar was speaking to those who returned *from* the battle with spoils of war.

Chovos HaLevavos describes the conversation between a righteous man and a victorious soldier returning from the battlefield. "You have emerged victorious in the light battle: Beware the intense battle you are about to enter into. The war with one's evil inclination is bitter and protracted. One bursting with pride over past victories is the most vulnerable," said the righteous man. The warriors knew that upon their return they would be engaged in a fiercer battle for their own souls.

This was Elazar's message to the returning warriors. "Having tasted victory over Midian, you are undoubtedly confident in your ability to vanquish all enemies. Do not let pride turn your heads."

He taught them the laws of purging vessels of impurity. He alluded to their need to purge their hearts of arrogance (*Yeitav Lev*).[17]

זֹאת חֻקַּת הַתּוֹרָה . . . אַךְ אֶת הַזָּהָב . . .

This is the decree of the Torah . . .
Only the gold . . . (ibid. 21-22).

Why does the Torah refer to the laws of purging vessels from impurity as *the* decree of the Torah? This is particularly perplexing because a decree (חק) classically refers to a law which seems irrational. These laws appear to be perfectly rational.

R' Moshe Feinstein suggests that these laws contain a major message. God allows us to purge ourselves of spiritual contamination. Just as pots can be purged and restored to their previous clean state, so too the soul of a Jew is never irreparably damaged by sin. It can always be restored to its pre-sin level through immersion in Torah.[18]

Sefer HaChaim warns those who seek spiritual growth while simultaneously engaged in worldly pursuits. Most *mitzvos* are relatively easy to fulfill. Those that entail financial expense are more difficult. Man usually has difficulty parting with his money. The Torah teaches us, *This is the decree of the Torah . . .* however, *the gold . . .* Take care to insure that money never becomes a "but," a reservation in your commitment to God.[19]

---

17. **A One-Hundred-Twenty-Year War.** [The evil inclination is a most difficult foe. He is merciless, tireless and willing to resort to low and underhanded tactics to win. While one may win some battles, the war itself continues for a lifetime. Hopefully, when the dust finally settles, man will have emerged victorious. Only herculean efforts together with heartfelt prayer can grant man success. In the words of the Sages, "If not for Divine assistance one could never overcome the evil inclination" (*Kiddushin* 30b).]

18. **Educational Strategy.** *Talmud Yerushalmi* (*Kesubos* 8:11) states that Shimon ben Shetach established schools for young children (see, however, *Bava Basra* 21a) and the law that impurities in metal vessels always reassert themselves.

R' Meir Shapiro explains homiletically the common thread that runs between the two.

Even if one smashes a metal vessel, the impurity remains deeply embedded. Only fire or boiling hot water can bring it to the surface. When educating our children we must implant Torah values deeply within their hearts and minds and instill in them the spiritual fire to bring the values to the surface. This will help them weather the storms of life.

19. **On Your Own.** The Talmud (*Berachos* 35b) states that one who wishes to pursue Torah study will have his needs provided for by God. One who does not will be subjected to the verse *that you may gather your grain* (*Deuteronomy* 11:14), namely, he will have to toil mightily to make a living.

Maharsha (ad loc.) questions how the Talmud can suggest that the verse refers to people who do not follow God's will since the paragraph begins with the words, *It will be that if you hearken to My commandments . . .* (ibid.

According to *Bnei Yosef*, both money and Torah are demanding masters who expect loyalty and devotion. If one wants to grow in Torah, he must put a "but" on his desire for monetary wealth. In the words of the *Rambam* (*Hilchos Talmud Torah* 3:6-7), "Let one not entertain the thought that he can simultaneously acquire Torah along with wealth and honor. This is the way of the Torah: Eat bread with salt, drink water in small measure . . . live a life of deprivation — but toil in the Torah. Perhaps one will think that he can first accrue financial wealth and then apply himself to Torah. One who thinks this way will never merit the crown of Torah."

כָּל דָּבָר אֲשֶׁר יָבֹא בָאֵשׁ תַּעֲבִירוּ בָאֵשׁ

*Everything that comes into fire —
you shall pass through fire and
it will be purified* (ibid. 23).

Chida understands these laws as a metaphor for the purification of the soul. The evil inclination arouses in us a burning desire for pleasures. They stain our souls and impede our ability to advance spiritually. The only way to fight fire is with fire. God says, *My words are like fire* (*Jeremiah* 23:29). Only the fire of Torah can extinguish the fire of the evil inclination. In the words of the Talmud (*Kiddushin* 29b), "I have created an evil inclination and have created the Torah as a remedy for it."[20]

The Sages homiletically allude to this with their declaration that *chametz* should be destroyed through fire. *Chametz* represents one's evil inclination. The fire of Torah burns and destroys it.

R' Nachman of Breslov sheds a different light. One who is trapped in the flaming inferno of forbidden desires must be willing to pass through fire for God. Only one who becomes ablaze with love for God can become purified.

Knesses Yechezkel adds: Torah is compared to both fire and water. One who sins with a fiery passion can only be purified by transforming that fiery passion to a holy one. If one sins due to lack of enthusiasm for what is right, he can purify himself by submerging himself in the refreshing waters of Torah.[21]

עֲבָדֶיךָ נָשְׂאוּ אֶת רֹאשׁ אַנְשֵׁי הַמִּלְחָמָה אֲשֶׁר בְּיָדֵנוּ וְלֹא נִפְקַד מִמֶּנּוּ אִישׁ

*Your servants took a census of the men
of war under our command and not
a man of us is missing* (ibid. 49).

According to the Sages (*Shabbos* 64a), this does not refer to physical casualties but to spiritual ones. In spite of the Midianites' attempts to entrap them, not one was seduced. *Nesivos Shalom* explains: The commanders were men of spirit and were able to impart this spirit to their troops.

verse 13). He offers a fascinating explanation based on a subtle difference between the first and second paragraphs of the *Shema*. The first paragraph commands us to love God with all our heart, soul and resources. The second paragraph deletes any reference to money. *Maharsha* explains that the two paragraphs describe two types of people. Those who understand that their money is a gift from God are able to easily spend it on spiritual expenditures. God provides them with sustenance. Those who do not understand this have a very difficult time parting with their money. To them God says, "Gather your own grain."

20. **Therapeutic Torah.** *R' Yisrael Salanter* writes that Torah is therapeutic in both a direct and indirect manner.
   One who is lax in Sabbath observance will certainly be helped by the study of its laws. One who has difficulty finding time for Torah study should learn the laws of Torah study (*Rambam*) or those Talmudic passages that discuss the importance of Torah study. These will impact him directly.
   Torah is also therapeutic in an indirect manner. Torah purifies man and brings his heart and mind closer to God. Torah allows man to absorb Godly intelligence and hence, conduct himself according to His will.

21. **Sinai Revisited.** Torah study is not an intellectual exercise; it is a reenactment of our receiving the Torah at Sinai. We emphasize this point in the blessings we recite over Torah study. We refer to God as the נוֹתֵן הַתּוֹרָה, the One Who *gives* Torah, not the נָתַן הַתּוֹרָה, He Who *gave* the Torah. Just as the Torah was given in a fiery environment (see *Exodus* 19:18), so must we learn it with a fiery enthusiasm.
   The Torah teaches that everything that came in fire (Torah) has to pass through fire. One must becomes ablaze with love for Hashem and for His word (*R' Tzvi Hirsch of Nadvorna*).

Accordingly, נָשְׂאוּ אֶת רֹאשׁ אַנְשֵׁי הַמִּלְחָמָה might be rendered as "raised the heads of the men of war." By raising their spiritual sensitivity, the commanders were able to raise soldiers above the base desires which the Midianites sought to arouse.

Not a man of us is missing. Every single soldier remained spiritually whole.

When man suffers from narrow and shallow spiritual vision, he is vulnerable. When one rips away the spiritual blinders, he will scorn any appeal to immorality.

וַנַּקְרֵב אֶת קָרְבַּן ה׳
So we have brought an offering for Hashem (ibid. 50).

If none of the soldiers sinned, why was it necessary to bring an offering? The Talmud explains (*Yevamos* 61a) that although they did not actively sin they did entertain thoughts of sin. One question remains. Why did they bring the offering now rather than immediately after their return from the battlefront?

Chidushei HaRim explains that upon learning the laws of purging vessels of impurity, they realized the need to bring an offering. Initially they saw no reason to bring an offering to atone for mere thoughts of sin. Once they learned that it is necessary to remove even the vestiges of forbidden food which are deeply embedded inside the vessel, they realized that even thoughts of sin, deeply embedded as they are, must be removed. Just as טַעַם כְּעִיקָר, *the taste [of forbidden food renders unfit just] as does tangible vestiges [of the forbidden item],* so מַחְשָׁבָה כְּמַעֲשֶׂה, *intangible thought [contaminates the purity of one's soul just] like action.*

The Torah refers to the offering as a קָרְבַּן ה׳, literally *the offering of Hashem,* rather than קָרְבַּן לַה׳, *an offering for Hashem.* While one's actions may be a matter of public knowledge, one's innermost thoughts are known only to Him. This was an offering of Hashem (*Skulener Rebbe*). *Meshech Chochmah* sees this as an offering of Hashem because it came directly from the spoils of war. While we all believe that whatever we have comes from God, here it was obvious that they were giving God what was His. Even before they took hold of the spoils, they renounced ownership and gave it all to Him.[22]

Background

The tribes of Gad and Reuven had more livestock than the other tribes [or placed more emphasis on the maintenance of their flocks (*Midrash HaGadol*)]. They request permission to settle on the east bank of the Jordan River where there was more grazing pasture. Moses insists that they first join their brethren in battle. Only after conquering the land will they be permitted to return to Transjordan.

וּמִקְנֶה רַב הָיָה לִבְנֵי רְאוּבֵן וְלִבְנֵי גָד
The children of Reuben and the children of Gad had abundant livestock (32:1).

This verse explains why the tribes of Reuben and Gad were interested in settling outside *Eretz Yisrael* proper. The *Chozeh of Lublin* explains that their motives ran much deeper than simple concern with their livestock. The soul connection of these tribes to Moses was so intense, they felt a need to remain in Transjordan where he would be buried.

Chidushei HaRim goes a step further. They hoped to imbue their portion in Transjordan with the sanctity of *Eretz Yisrael*. Consequently, the decree forbidding Moses from entering the Land would be rescinded since he was already in a land of similar sanctity.

---

22. **Dedicated Talents.** *R' Elazar of Bartosa* (*Avos* 3:8) teaches, "Give Him from His own for you and your possessions are His." Man may never withhold himself or his possessions from the service of God. Everything belongs to God. Man merely returns to God that which was His to begin with.

Even talents are God given and must be dedicated to His service. The *Mishnah* speaks critically of the Garmu family who refused to reveal the art of making the showbread and the Avtinas family who refused to divulge the secret of preparing the Temple incense. They could have shared their talents and created a greater sanctification of God's Name, but they refused to do so (*Yoma* 38a).

יִתַּן אֶת הָאָרֶץ הַזֹּאת לַעֲבָדֶיךָ לַאֲחֻזָּה
let this land be given to your servants as a heritage (ibid. 5).

The fact that Moses granted the tribes their request makes clear that Transjordan was the true location of their share. Why then was Moses so upset with their request? *R' E.E. Dessler* cites Rashi (*Proverbs* 20:21), who explains that their hasty request caused them to speak in an inappropriate fashion. They focused more on their property than on their families.

One must engage in worldly pursuits to earn a living. Even one who views his livelihood as nothing more than a means to be able to serve God must insure that the means does not become the goal.

The tribes of Gad and Reuben were justified in asking for their share in Transjordan, since it would provide them with a better source of livelihood. But why were they in such a rush? Couldn't they have waited for God to offer it to them?

When they approached Moses they suggested they build pens for their flocks and homes for their families (see ibid. 16). They attached more importance to property than family. The Sages see in this the realization of King Solomon's observation, *If an inheritance is seized hastily in the beginning, its end will not be blessed (Proverbs* 20:21).[23]

הַאַחֵיכֶם יָבֹאוּ לַמִּלְחָמָה וְאַתֶּם תֵּשְׁבוּ פֹה
Shall your brothers go out to battle while you settle here? (ibid. 6).

Moses replied critically accusing them of a willingness to abandon their brothers to the dangers inherent in conquering the Land while they settled comfortably in Transjordan.

What is remarkable is that in verse 17 they respond. They promise to lead the battle for the Land. Why did they allow Moses to continue

his scathing attack? Why didn't they respond immediately?

The answer can be found in an incident which occurred to the *Sfas Emes, R' Yehudah Aryeh Leib Alter*:

As a youngster, *Sfas Emes* was an assiduous student. Once, he and his study partner learned through the night. After praying at dawn, the *Sfas Emes* laid down to rest and overslept. He came late to the study session that he and his partner had with his grandfather, the *Chidushei HaRim*. The grandfather immediately delivered a stern lecture about the value of time. Young Yehudah Aryeh Leib made no attempt to excuse himself. He simply hung his head in shame and accepted the criticism.

When they left, his partner asked him, "Why didn't you simply explain to your grandfather that we were up all night learning?" He replied, "I didn't want to interrupt my grandfather and miss the opportunity to receive his rebuke and criticism. What difference does it make that I had a legitimate excuse?" He then took out a *Chumash* and showed his friend the story of Moses' response to the request of the tribes of Gad and Reuben. They could have responded immediately that they had no intentions of abandoning their brethren. Then they would have missed the sharp rebuke of their beloved teacher. They first let him finish and only then did they respond.

וִהְיִיתֶם נְקִיִּם מֵה' וּמִיִּשְׂרָאֵל
Then you shall be vindicated from Hashem and from Israel (ibid. 22).

People falsely assume that once they are vindicated in the eyes of God they are also vindicated in the eyes of man, since God's standards are more exacting. What they fail to realize is that God is more understanding and God also knows the absolute truth. People tend to even suspect an

---

23. **Misplaced Priorities.** *Akeidas Yitzchak* portrays this message by means of a parable:
When contractors and construction crews bring beams to a construction site to erect scaffolding, they are not particular about the appearance of the wood. After all, the scaffolding is temporary. The wood they use to construct cabinets and furnishings must be perfect, unblemished and of the highest quality. That which lasts is meaningful; that which is temporary need only be functional. The tribes of Gad and Reuben were overly concerned with making a living. Their priorities were not in order. Making a living is the means to serve God which is the goal. What is temporary need not be perfect.

angel of unbecoming behavior. The Torah teaches that one must be vindicated from Hashem *and* from Israel (*Oznayim L'Torah*).

Talmud Yerushalmi (*Shekalim* 3:2) states: "One must meet the moral standards of human beings *just as* one must meet the moral standards of God."

R' Yisrael Salanter comments: One cannot resort to lying or flattery to find favor in God's eyes. He knows the truth and cannot be fooled. Only man can be mislead. Lying, dishonesty and flattery are unacceptable tactics with which to achieve vindication from man.[24]

---

24. **Ethically Spotless.** Vindication from both God and man is extremely difficult. This is especially true regarding monetary matters. The following incident reveals the ethical conduct of *R' Yosef Chaim Sonnenfeld,* Rav of Jerusalem.

There was once a woman from Hungary who was unfortunately not blessed with children. She approached the rav of her town with a large sum of money and asked him to send it to one of the righteous men of the generation. She requested that the righteous man pray to God on her behalf that she be blessed with children. The rav suggested R' Yosef Chaim Sonnenfeld, and the woman agreed.

A few weeks later, the woman's husband came to the rav, extremely upset. "How could you take money from my wife without my consent?" he asked the rav (see *Bava Kamma* 119a). The rav explained that he thought the money was given with the husband's knowledge. The husband insisted the money be returned to him. The rav was too embarrassed to ask for the money back and offered to repay the money in installments.

As they were standing there, the postman knocked on the rav's door with a special delivery letter from Jerusalem. The rav looked at the return address and was stunned to see the words "Sonnenfeld — Jerusalem." He opened the letter and found the entire sum he had sent along with the following note:

"I received your letter with the money. You wrote that a woman gave it to you to send to me. I am hesitant to accept it because I am not sure she did so with her husband's permission. I have sent back the money and request that you return it to the woman. I nevertheless fulfilled her request that I pray on her behalf and hope God will accept my prayers."

As the rav read the note, hot tears fell down both of their faces.

פרשת מסעי ~§
Parashas Masei

Background

The *sidrah* opens with an account of the entire journey which the Jewish people traveled from the time they left Egypt until they stood poised to enter the Holy Land. This is not a mere historical narration. The recounting of the various stops which the Jewish people made along their way holds many important lessons.

אֵלֶּה מַסְעֵי בְנֵי יִשְׂרָאֵל אֲשֶׁר יָצְאוּ מֵאֶרֶץ מִצְרַיִם לְצִבְאֹתָם בְּיַד מֹשֶׁה וְאַהֲרֹן
These are the journeys of the Children of Israel who went forth from the land of Egypt according to their legions, under the hand of Moses and Aaron (33:1).

The Midrash teaches us that had the Exodus from Egypt been conducted exclusively by the hand of God, without any intermediaries, it would have lead directly to the Eternal Redemption with no possibility of a future return to exile. However, since Moses and Aaron acted as God's emissaries, the process was only temporary and the Jewish people must therefore endure a process of exile before the Final Redemption can take place. The forty-two encampments enumerated here are symbolic of a road map which guides us toward spiritual survival in exile. Just as these stops mark the path that led from Egypt to the Land of Israel, so they teach us how to make our way from this world to the next (*Kosnos Ohr*).[1]

According to *Tzror HaMor,* these journeys are recorded to serve as a source of comfort throughout our long and bitter exile. Just as God took His people through a totally uninhabitable desert and brought them to the Promised Land, so too will He take us through our bitter exile to the ultimate Redemption.[2]

---

1. **Signposts.** The first letters of the four opening words of the *sidrah,* אֵלֶּה מַסְעֵי בְנֵי יִשְׂרָאֵל, allude to the four exiles which the Jewish people would undergo before the Final Redemption:

אֱדוֹם (Rome) — our present day-exile.

מָדַי (Media) — the Persian exile under Ahaseurus.

בָּבֶל (Babylonia) — the destruction of the Temple by Nebuchadnezzar and the resultant exile.

יָוָן — the spiritual exile spearheaded by the Greeks.

The recorded journeys are signposts along our way through the long, dark night of exile (*Chida*). [Just as God led us through the Wilderness with the pillar of fire lighting the way, so too the light of Torah will light the path to our ultimate redemption.]

2. **On the Way Home.** The *Skulener Rebbe* notes that *Masei* is always read during the Three Weeks of Mourning when we mourn the destruction of the Temples (17 Tammuz through 9 Av). We must always remember that all these journeys were stops on our way to *Eretz Yisrael*. All our wanderings in exile and all of our travails lead us to *Eretz Yisrael*. R' Nachman of Breslov says, "Wherever I go, I'm on my way to *Eretz Yisrael*."

The word אֵלֶּה, *these*, implies "these and not others." In the words of *Rashi* (*Exodus* 21:1), אֵלֶּה negates that which was previously discussed.

Only those pathways prescribed by Moses, the direct receiver of the Torah, can lead to spiritual redemption. Only these journeys, led by Moses and Aaron, our true spiritual guides, will take us out of our spiritual servitude (*Ohr Ha-Chaim*).[3]

In terms of spiritual growth, one must always move forward, for if not, he will move backward. As King Solomon says, אֹרַח חַיִּים לְמַעְלָה לְמַשְׂכִּיל לְמַעַן סוּר מִשְּׁאוֹל מָטָּה, *A path of life [waits] above for the intelligent one, so that his soul will turn away from the grave below* (*Proverbs* 15:24). One must always move forward, seeking to correct past mistakes and improve his service of God.[4] One should never rest on his laurels. Rather, one should seek to negate the past by always outdoing it. Just as the Jews in the Wilderness traveled onward and upward, so must we. By analyzing our past and realizing that we have only just begun our service of God, we can propel ourselves to even greater levels of commitment (*Sifsei Tzaddikim*).

According to the *Shelah*, the function of these travels was to purify the souls of the Jewish people so that they be fit to receive the Torah. We received the Torah in a desert to teach us that only one who makes oneself like a desert will merit the gift of Torah. Just as a desert is available to all, so must one make oneself always available to Torah (*Nedarim* 55a).

The Sages teach us that one should exile oneself to a place of Torah (*Avos* 4:14). By leaving home and comfortable surroundings, one is forced to confront and try to achieve his true spiritual potential.[5]

Rashi submits that the journeys were written as an expression of God's love for us. Although we were taken through the hazardous conditions of the desert, God always provided us with a place to camp. According to *Midrash Tanchuma*, this recounting of the Wilderness experience is analogous to a king who takes his ill son on a long journey to have him cured of his illness. When they finally arrive at their destination, his father speaks nostalgically of each place: "Here we slept, here we rested, here your head hurt," etc.

Suffering from the spiritual maladies which resulted from their prolonged exposure to the impurities of Egypt, the nation traveled toward the

3. **Safe Road.** *R' Menachem Mendel of Kotzk* says, "There are a thousand roads that lead to God, but with the exception of one they are all risky and dangerous. One can only arrive safely by way of a page of Talmud."

4. **Now I Know Better.** A story of *R' Saadiah Gaon* illustrates the importance of learning from experience. R' Saadiah was asked by his disciples why he engaged in constant repentance. What sins had he committed? He replied that once, as a traveler, he had spent a night at an inn. The innkeeper treated him like any other guest. The next morning, the leading citizens of the town gathered at the inn to greet him. After they departed, the innkeeper approached him and said tearfully, "Please, master, forgive me for not serving you properly."

"You treated me very well. Why do you apologize?"

"I treated you as I treat all my guests. Had I known who you were, I would have served you as befits a person of your stature!"

R' Saadiah told his students that the innkeeper's reaction illustrates the feelings a Jew should have. The innkeeper was not remiss in his behavior, but had he known the truth a day earlier, he would have acted differently. We should take the same approach in our service of God. When we are middle aged we realize the immaturity of our youthful fulfillment of God's will. Had we only known then what we know now, we would have acted differently. We must always examine our past deeds in light of our present stature and spiritual awareness. Should we not repent for failing to serve God yesterday as we would today?

5. **Reborn Away.** [Every year, we witness young people who come to Israel to study Torah for a year or two and are totally transformed by the experience. The combination of their study of Torah (especially in the Land of Israel) together with their distancing themselves far from home encourages them to reassess their values and priorities. They travel the same route taken by their ancestors in the Wilderness who were heading to a life of Torah to be lived in God's Land.]

Land of Israel where they would find the cure for their illness. All along the way they encountered difficulties which seemed only to impede their spiritual recovery. In retrospect, however, the entire saga can be viewed as part of the Divine therapeutic process, and God's love.

Even the simplest of Jews is a descendant of our forefathers and a son of the King and, as such, is worthy of God's love. We ourselves must therefore emulate God and demonstrate love toward all Jews.

The Talmud (*Bava Metzia* 83a) tells the story of R' Yochanan ben Masia who instructed his son to hire menial laborers on his behalf. The son hired them and negotiated a contract. This contract included the budget for food. When he reported the details to his father, R' Yochanan ben Masia said, "My son, were you to serve them a royal banquet like that served at the court of King Solomon you would not have truly fulfilled your obligation toward them. They are the children of Abraham, Isaac and Jacob."

A simple worker who would be satisfied with plain bread deserves a royal banquet? Why? Because he is royalty, descended from the Patri-archs. R' Yochanan ben Masia understood that there is no such a thing as a "simple" Jew. Every single Jew is beloved in God's eyes.

We have made many stops in the course of our almost 2,000-year exile. Every step along the way represents an expression of God's love for us. When the long trek will be over and we will finally merit true redemption, we will, together with God, recount the many stops and realize how they were all expressions of His love and part of the spiritu-ally therapeutic process of exile. "Here, my son, we slept; here, my beloved, your head hurt" (*Darkei Mussar*).

וַיִּכְתֹּב מֹשֶׁה אֶת מוֹצָאֵיהֶם לְמַסְעֵיהֶם
עַל פִּי ה' וְאֵלֶּה מַסְעֵיהֶם לְמוֹצָאֵיהֶם

Moses wrote their goings forth according to their journeys at the bidding of Hashem, and these were their journeys according to their goings forth (ibid. 2).

The phrasing of this verse is puzzling. It begins by saying that Moses wrote *their goings forth according to their journeys,* which were according to God's will. It then continues, *these were their journeys according to their goings forth,* switching the order. *Machazeh Avraham* submits that the Torah is providing a key to understanding the events in one's life.

We often foolishly think that positive or negative events befall us because we happened to be in the right (or wrong) place at the right (or wrong) time. "Because I came to a certain place at just this moment, a particular set of circumstances came upon me." There is nothing further from the truth! In reality, we travel to a particular place because God wants something to happen to us at that place. A significant event occurred to the nation at almost every location listed among the forty-two encampments. At Marah they found bitter waters which God made sweet (see *Exodus* 15:22-25). They did not find bitter waters because they came to Marah. They came to Marah (at the bidding of Hashem) to find bitter waters.

Their goings forth, the events that occurred to them, were not, *according to* (and as a result of) *their journeys,* as they thought. Rather, they were done *at the bidding of Hashem.* The truth is that *their journeys were according to their going forth.* Their travels were Divinely planned to enable them to experience what God wanted them to experi-ence.[6]

6. **Divine Emissary.** As a result of trumped-up charges brought against him, *R' Eliyahu Meir Bloch* was forced to flee Lithuania shortly before the Nazis' invasion. He left a wife and large family behind and escaped to America. There he tried desperately to save them. Alas, his efforts were unsuccessful. His family was slaughtered by the Nazis.

When he reestablished the Telshe Yeshivah in Cleveland and was able to dedicate a building, he offered the following commentary at the dedication ceremonies. When Jonathan gave David a sign by which he would inform him if it was necessary to flee from Saul, he told him he would shoot three arrows and then send the lad to retrieve them. *If I call out to the lad, "Behold! The arrows are on this side of you!" then you should take them and return . . . But if I say this to the boy, "Behold! — The arrows are beyond you!" then go, for Hashem will have sent you away (I Samuel 20:20-22).*

The last sentence is remarkable. Why did he say, "Then go, for Hashem will have sent you"? It would have been far more appropriate to tell him, "Escape, for Saul seeks to kill you." Jonathan teaches us a lesson. When a Jew

The *Dubno Maggid* explains this reversal of terms with a parable:[7]

A young man's mother died and his father remarried a woman who was incapable of treating his son as her own. The issue of finding a proper mate for the son became a priority for the father. Once, while traveling on business, the father came across a young lady who seemed to be a perfect match. After investigating her background and ascertaining that she was in fact an appropriate life-partner for his son, the father met her parents. They all agreed to the *shidduch.*

When the father arrived home, he told his son the good news and attempted to describe the virtues of the young lady who was to be his wife. The wedding was scheduled for three months hence.

A day or two before the wedding, father and son set out by horse and wagon to the hometown of the bride where the wedding would take place. After they had traveled for a while, the son asked the wagon driver, "How far have we gone?" The driver replied, "Thirteen miles." After another few hours the groom again asked, "How many miles have we traveled from our hometown?" Again the wagon driver patiently replied, "Twenty-two miles." A while later, the father asked the wagon driver how much further they would need to travel before arriving at the bride's town. The son was surprised at the father's question. "I asked how far we traveled while you want to know the remaining distance until our destination. Why didn't you phrase the question the way I did?"

Replied the father, "You have never been in that city, nor have you ever met your future wife or her family. What you know about the bride is only second-hand information. You don't know that your future father-in-law is a respected pillar of his community, a man of impeccable character and lineage and a fine scholar. Furthermore, your bride is beautiful, charming and has a sterling personality. You have only one thing on your mind. You wish to escape from your stepmother

---

is forced to flee, it is not because the enemy chases him. God used the enemy to insure that the Jew goes to where God wants him to be. A Jew never runs from an enemy; he runs to the place God has destined for him.

"I was not chased away from Europe by the Nazis. I was sent to America by Hashem to plant Torah in its barren soil."

His strong belief in his mission and its ultimate success is clearly displayed in the following incident. When R' Elya Meir came to America he had occasion to be at a Jewish book store on the Lower East Side of Manhattan. He asked the proprietor for a *Ketzos HaChoshen,* a Talmudic classic. The owner climbed up a ladder, took down a *Ketzos,* dusted it off and said to R' Elya Meir, "Rebbe! This is the last copy of the *Ketzos* to be sold in America!" R' Elya Meir replied, "No! Many, many more copies will be printed and sold in years to come." The renaissance of the Torah world in the United States, spearheaded by such Torah luminaries as R' Elya Meir, vindicated this vision.

7. **Ends and Means.** *Kedushas Yom Tov* views *goings forth* as synonymous with one's involvement in mundane, physical needs. The word *journeys* alludes to spiritual pursuits. As long as one views his physical needs as a means to facilitate his spiritual agenda, the mundane become sanctified. When making a living becomes a self-sustaining goal it becomes a spiritual detour leading to a dead end.

When one is involved in *goings forth* that are *at the bidding of Hashem,* they are considered an integral part of their Divine service *according to their journeys.*

The *Chafetz Chaim* would often say that if one truly sees his efforts to earn a living as a means to study Torah he will receive the reward reserved for Torah study even while working. The litmus test is how one uses his "free" time when he is not at work. If one uses it for Torah study or the performance of other *mitzvos,* he can legitimately claim that the time spent working was a preparation for spiritual activities. If, however, one wastes that time on mundane pursuits, then he undermines his own defense and proves conclusively that work is not intended as a preparation for *mitzvos.*

R' *Menachem Mendel of Kotzk* offers a halachic analogy. If one hires a laborer to chop wood and the laborer spends the entire day sharpening his ax, he may expect to be paid for the entire day's work as long as he began chopping before the end of the day. The time spent sharpening the ax is necessary for the chopping itself.

Likewise, if the time spent earning a living is necessary for learning itself, it becomes part of the mitzvah.

Rambam (*Hilchos Talmud Torah* 3:4) teaches that a person may interrupt his Torah study to perform a mitzvah which can only be performed by him. Upon completing the mitzvah, he must immediately return to his Torah study.

and get as far away from her as possible. You therefore keep asking how far we have traveled from home. On the other hand, I am primarily focused on how good your new home will be for you. Having met your future wife and father-in-law I am anxiously awaiting our arrival. Therefore I keep asking, 'When will we arrive?' "

The Jewish people were unaware of the sterling qualities of the Land and that it held the key to their physical and spiritual success and happiness. Their only desire was to escape Egypt and distance themselves from the physical and spiritual torture they experienced there. Moses, who appreciated the uniqueness of the Holy Land, was impatient to get there.

Moses saw the *goings forth*. These travels would hasten them toward the union of God and the Jewish people in His Land. He therefore wrote *their goings forth according to their journeys.* The masses, however, only cared about how far they had traveled. And *these were their journeys according to their goings forth.* [8]

וַיִּסְעוּ מִסֻּכֹּת וַיַּחֲנוּ בְאֵתָם
They journeyed from Succoth and encamped in Etham (ibid. 6).

The Torah describes every step of the journey in terms of וַיִּסְעוּ וַיַּחֲנוּ, *they journeyed* and *then they*

encamped. This teaches us a very important lesson regarding spiritual growth. Just as a mountain climber must first drive spikes into the side of the mountain to establish a firm foothold before continuing his ascent, so too one who seeks spiritual heights must stop at every step of the climb, and make sure that he has a firm hold on his new spiritual level before attempting to proceed further. If he fails to do so, he may, God forbid, slip and fall. The Jewish people first climbed, they journeyed a bit further in their trek toward sanctity, secured their progress by encamping and taking stock of their accomplishments and then planned their next journey. Only when they felt confident they had conquered the previous challenge did they attempt to climb higher (*Nesivos Shalom*).[9]

At every step along the way the Jewish people conducted a spiritual inventory and repented for their past misdeeds. As a result they were spiritually prepared for the sanctity of the Land of Israel by the time they reached it.

Just as this principle is applicable when moving from one location to another, it is even more applicable when one is passing from one stage of life to the next. Before progressing, one must assess the past and plan for the future (*Kochavei Ohr*).[10]

R' Asher of Rimanov suggests that the Torah is teaching us that all of the people's comings and goings were conducted in accordance with God's

---

8. **To and From.** *Zekan Aharon* submits: In reality, man must view his journey through life from a dual perspective. On one hand, he should assess how far he has removed himself from negative Egyptlike influences. On the other hand, he must realize that maintaining his spiritual status quo is not enough. He must spend his life progressing toward a destination, always seeking to uplift his soul and infuse it with spiritual light. In the words of King David, "Turn from evil and do good" (*Psalms* 34:15).

9. **Compounded Goals.** This is also true in one's personal climb toward attaining sanctity. One must challenge oneself with realistic goals that can be successfully achieved with time and effort. After tasting success, one must stop, take stock of one's gains and establish new goals.

The *mussar* masters see this two-tier process reflected in the words of King David, who asks, *Who may ascend the mountain of Hashem, and who may stand in the place of His sanctity?* (*Psalms* 24:3).

The ascent to the mountain of Hashem is itself a meaningful feat. However, one can easily slip and spiritually fall. The true measure of success is maintaining one's spiritual balance. Doing so demands introspection and brutal self-honesty. *Who may stand in the place of His sanctity?*

10. **Spiritual Conversion.** Upon reaching his fortieth birthday, *R' Klonymus Kalman of Piaczetzna* entered the following words into his personal diary: "What new commitments should I accept upon myself? To study more? I believe that to the best of my ability, I do not waste a minute and am constantly involved in learning. Should I commit myself to limit my physical desires? Thank God, my evil inclination does not trick me and I am able to avoid becoming enslaved to him. What am I missing? *To be a Jew!* I see myself as a human being, blessed with everything that comprises a human being. However, a soul is lacking! Master of the world, allow me to undergo a spiritual conversion, and become a real Jew!"

will. This is not always the case. People are often lax about maintaining proper standards of conduct when away from home. When one is at home, surrounded by friends and acquaintances, he may feel compelled to act one way. When on the road one may lower his spiritual guard. King David refers to this with his words *Praiseworthy are those whose way is perfect* (*Psalms* 119:1). Those who maintain their perfection even when traveling deserve to be praised.

Igra D'Kallah explains the verse homiletically. One who sees life in this world as a temporary existence (like a *succah*) will achieve healthy simplicity (אַתֶּם) necessary for true growth and will assure oneself a place of prominence in the Next World.

וַיִּסְעוּ מֵרְפִידִם וַיַּחֲנוּ בְּמִדְבַּר סִינָי
They journeyed from Rephidim and encamped in the Wilderness of Sinai (ibid. 15).

Every person experiences times in life when he is totally unmotivated and has no desire to study Torah or serve God. One may become drawn into despair.

In reality, this feeling of distance from God is a preparatory stage for a significant spurt of spiritual growth. When man turns to God, in despair, and cries out to Him, he can make a spiritual quantum leap beyond his limitations and narrow perspective.

The Sages interpret רְפִידִם as an acronym for רָפוּ יְדֵיהֶם מִן הַתּוֹרָה, *they loosened their grip on the Torah* (*Sanhedrin* 106). When one's commitment to the study and practice of Torah becomes weak, one should remember that God may be spiritually "starving" him temporarily so that his appetite for soul food will dramatically increase. When that happens, he will turn to God in heartfelt prayer to save him from this spiritual starvation. In this manner, the journey through "Rephidim" leads straight to Sinai.

וַיִּסְעוּ מִמִּדְבַּר סִינַי וַיַּחֲנוּ בְּקִבְרֹת הַתַּאֲוָה
They traveled from the Wilderness of Sinai and encamped in Kibroth-hattaavah (ibid. 16).

The literal translation of the name *Kibroth-hattaavah* is *the grave of craving*. Accordingly, *Chasam Sofer* homiletically sees a message here. *The more one* travels away from the Torah, the more vulnerable he becomes to the evil inclination. One can becomes quickly trapped in the quicksand of passion. Our Sages teach that Torah is the only effective antidote to evil. (*Kiddushin* 30b). In a variation on this theme, *R' Nachum of Chernobyl* and *Tiferes Shlomo* submit that Torah grants one the strength of character and the purity of soul to reject the advances of evil. When they traveled from Sinai armed with the Torah, they were able to bury their physical lusts and passions.[11]

וַיִּסְעוּ מִקִּבְרֹת הַתַּאֲוָה וַיַּחֲנוּ בַּחֲצֵרֹת
They journeyed from Kibroth-hattaavah and encamped in Hazeroth (ibid. 17).

According to *R' Yitzchak of Vorki* this was one more station on the spiritual odyssey toward sanctity. What is one to do if he finds himself ensnared in a net of unbridled desires and passions?

The Torah teaches us to view this world as חֲצֵרֹת, *a courtyard*. The courtyard is merely a passageway through which one must pass to get to one's house. In the words of *Pirkei Avos*, "This world is like a lobby before the World to Come" (4:21). *Bayis L'Avos* explains the analogy. One who stands in the king's outer chambers awaiting an audience can only concentrate on one thing. Will he find favor in the king's eyes or not? While waiting, he mentally repeats the words he plans to utter. Everything else becomes meaningless to him. His overriding concern is the impression he will make.

This world is the courtyard where one spends his

---

11. **Heavenly Ecstasy.** *R' Nachman of Breslov* offers a commentary to a *Mishnah*.

"Whoever derives personal pleasure from Torah removes himself from the world" (*Avos* 4:7). No physical pleasure can match the spiritual pleasure one derives from Torah. One who has "tasted" the insight of *R' Akiva Eiger* or the logic of *R' Chaim of Brisk,* can no longer find a comparable enjoyment in this world.

The *Mishnah* therefore teaches that one who derives personal pleasure from Torah removes his life from this world. The world loses its allure and has nothing to offer. This is the message of our verse. One who travels from Sinai, having felt the majesty of Torah, buries his physical desires. Having experienced authentic pleasure he can no longer settle for cheap imitations (*Zekan Aharon*).

time preparing to meet the king. One who sees this world as a courtyard is able to ignore all other desires.

They journeyed from Kibroth-hattaavah (leaving their desires behind) *and encamped in Hazeroth,* seeing this world as a mere courtyard.

וְהוֹרַשְׁתֶּם אֶת הָאָרֶץ וִישַׁבְתֶּם בָּהּ
You shall possess the Land and you shall settle in it (ibid. 53).

Ramban writes: In my opinion (as opposed to that of *Rambam*) this is a positive commandment which obligates us to reside in the Land and inherit it. It was given to us by God and it is improper to reject God's inheritance.

R' Moshe Sternbuch suggests that the Torah first speaks of possessing the Land and then of settling it to emphasize that the mitzvah to settle the Land is only viable if we are able to possess it and provides an atmosphere conducive to Torah living.

The mitzvah of dwelling in the Land is only one mitzvah and can never be allowed to supplant the rest of the Torah. However, if the Land *does* provide a conducive atmosphere for a life of Torah, one's *mitzvos* are greatly enhanced.

R' Yosef Chaim Sonnenfeld offers an additional perspective.

Although circumcision is the rite of passage which bonds every Jewish male with the covenant that God established with Avrohom, the halachah is nevertheless unequivocal with regard to a child whose brothers died because of complications resulting from the fulfillment of this mitzvah. It is strictly forbidden to place a child's life in danger in order to fulfill the mitzvah of *milah.*

Similarly, although the mitzvah of settling the Land is extremely important, one may not jeopardize his and his children's spiritual welfare in order to fulfill it.

Background

The Torah now delineates the borders of *Eretz Yisrael,* and names of the tribal heads who will divide the land on behalf of their respective tribes. Finally, the Torah commands the tribes to designate cities for the Levites. There they will devote themselves to spiritual pursuits.

צַו אֶת בְּנֵי יִשְׂרָאֵל וְאָמַרְתָּ אֲלֵהֶם כִּי אַתֶּם בָּאִים אֶל הָאָרֶץ כְּנָעַן
Command the Children of Israel and say to them: When you come to the land of Canaan (34:2).

Midrash Rabbah (Naso 7:6) cites a dispute regarding the deeper meaning of the word צַו, *command.* R' Yehudah ben Beseira states it is a call for alacrity. R' Shimon bar Yochai suggests it is usually used regarding *mitzvos* that entail significant financial expense. However, continues R' Shimon bar Yochai, there is one exception to this rule. Our verse, regarding settling in *Eretz Yisrael,* is an instance where צַו *is* a call for alacrity.

This Midrash provides us with insight into the considerations we must make when weighing the possibility of leaving the Diaspora for *Eretz Yisrael.* Many Jews enjoy financial comfort and a higher standard of living in the Diaspora. They realize the spiritual advantages of moving to *Eretz Yisrael* but feel that it entails too great a financial sacrifice.

The Torah therefore says צַו, *command.* Jewish wealth in the Diaspora is in a very precarious position. Sooner or later, it inevitably disappears. Therefore, ultimately, settling in the Land does not involve a financial loss. Should one move to Israel and suffer a financial setback immediately or wait and experience it later? The Torah answers with the word צַו, *command.* Let Jews act with alacrity, absorb the "losses" now and move to this precious land (*R' Shaul Yedidyah of Modzhitz*).[12]

---

12. **Profitable Long Shot.** *Kalman Wissotzky* owned the tea concession for the Russian Czar's entire military. Since the Czar's armies numbered in the millions and drinking tea was a daily Russian custom, this concession made Wissotzky very wealthy. One day he was approached by a group interested in developing a tea business in *Eretz Yisrael.* Wissotzky laughed at this "preposterous" idea. The Turks governed Palestine and were notoriously difficult to deal with. In addition, Palestine was unable to produce its own tea, and to import tea leaves from India was costly.

He was assured that all these problems were surmountable. Furthermore, the venture would enable him to provide employment for many Jews. Although not fully convinced, he sent enough money to Israel to start a small tea venture.

In 1917, the Czar and his army were swept from power. The Communists seized all the businesses that the Czar

וְהִתְאַוִּיתֶם לָכֶם לִגְבוּל קֵדְמָה
You shall draw yourselves as the eastern border (ibid. 10).

The word וְהִתְאַוִּיתֶם is related to the word תַּאֲוָה, *forbidden desire.* One who is held captive by desire seeks to own things which are outside the pale of his legitimate possession. Borders are meant to prevent this. They clarify those things that are "out of bounds" (*R' S.R. Hirsch*).

According to *R' Chaim Shmulevitz,* the human impulse to break through the restraint imposed on man is the lesson of Shimi ben Geira. Shimi ben Geira cursed King David. At the time of the incident, King David refused to allow his soldiers to respond (see *II Samuel* 16:5-13 and *Sefer HaChinuch* §241). However, before he died, he commanded his son King Solomon: *But now you shall not hold him guiltless, for you are a wise man and you will know what you are to do with him and you shall bring his white hair to the grave in blood* (*I Kings* 2:9). How did King Solomon accomplish this? He told Shimi to build himself a magnificent palace in Jerusalem, in which he would be allowed to live undisturbed. However, he was prohibited to leave the city: Were he to cross over the Kidron Valley, he would be deemed a rebel and be put to death. Three years later, two of Shimi's servants escaped and he left the city limits to retrieve them. King Solomon had him killed. This incident is remarkable. Why did Shimi ben Geira issue his own death warrant by leaving the city? Furthermore, how did this ruse display King Solomon's wisdom?

R' Chaim explains: Restrictions arouse fierce resentment in people. Sooner or later the urge to break out appears and one feels that he must escape the barriers around him. It was this insight into human nature which King Solomon understood. Shimi lived in a palace, and lacked nothing. Yet Solomon understood that sooner or later he would feel compelled to break out of this idyllic prison.

The Torah teaches us this lesson with the term וְהִתְאַוִּיתֶם. Every border and every restraint automatically triggers a תַּאֲוָה, a desire to burst out.[13]

וְהִקְרִיתֶם לָכֶם עָרִים עָרֵי מִקְלָט תִּהְיֶינָה לָכֶם וְנָס שָׁמָּה רֹצֵחַ מַכֵּה נֶפֶשׁ בִּשְׁגָגָה
You shall designate cities for yourselves, cities of refuge shall they be for you and a killer shall flee there — one who takes a life unintentionally (35:11).

The commandment to prepare cities of refuge teaches us to address the needs of all people, even those whom we might view as ethically and morally inferior. God's mercy is directed even toward murderers. The Torah provides cities of refuge to save the unintentional murderer, and even commands that he be provided with optimal living conditions. Even regarding an intentional murderer, the Torah requires the Sanhedrin to seek every possible avenue and find some way (through legalistic loopholes, etc.) to spare him from execution. If the judges reach a guilty verdict unanimously, the accused is *not* executed. The verdict clearly indicates that the judges did not expend sufficient

---

had franchised, including Mr. Wissotzky's tea concession. After the revolution, the only asset remaining to the family was the small company in Palestine. They fled there and built up the business. To this day, that Israeli company sells tea under the Wissotzky label. The family feels it was saved in the merit of the Jewish families who benefited from their employment in the company.

13. **Breaking Out!** R' Chaim sees this idea expressed in the laws of conversion. The Talmud (*Yevamos* 47a) teaches that before a proselyte converts, we must apprise him of some of the easier *mitzvos* and some of the difficult *mitzvos.* The purpose of informing him of the difficult *mitzvos* is easy to understand since they may dissuade him from converting. Why should we inform him of the easy *mitzvos*?

The answer is man's natural resentment of constraint. Every person knows that every religion has its own demands, and that one must be ready to pay a certain price to become a member. Informing the potential proselyte of the difficult *mitzvos* may not be a deterrent. However, when he discovers that one is bound by halachah twenty-four hours a day, and that even the most seemingly insignificant details of life fall within the jurisdiction of Jewish law, he may begin to entertain second thoughts. The Torah dictates the way we get dressed in the morning, how we conduct our businesses and our social interaction with family and peers. One contemplating conversion may find this emotionally unbearable.

efforts to find mitigating evidence to free him. One may not be cruel to sinners or deprive them of their legitimate needs (*R' Simchah Zisel of Kelm*).[14]

---

14. **Real Care.** The following incident shows the ability of great men to differentiate between criticizing the actions of sinners and the need to care for their welfare. This story was told by a prominent member of the Zionist Organization:

"It was in the early 20's, when the struggle between the Zionist Organization and the right-wing factions of the Agudath Israel, led by R' Yosef Chaim Sonnenfeld, was at its peak. One of the leaders of the Zionist Labor Federation, known for his virulent antireligious attacks, became critically ill. After being hospitalized for nearly four weeks in the English Missionary Hospital, his condition deteriorated and his doctors gave up all hope of recovery.

"Since I was a close friend, the family came to me to ask if I could think of a way to save him. I knew that Dr. Wallach had the best doctors on his staff; I advised them to transfer the patient to Shaarei Zedek Hospital.

"The family was well aware that a transfer to Shaarei Zedek was easier said than done. When Dr. Wallach would discover the identity of the patient and the fact that he had previously been in the Missionary Hospital, he would probably refuse to admit him. But since there was no alternative, we decided to try. I had connections in the religious community through my father, who was a famous *talmid chacham* in Jerusalem, and was asked to attempt the transfer. I hired two porters to carry the patient from the Missionary Hospital to Shaarei Zedek. When we arrived at the emergency room, Dr. Wallach came out to examine the patient and found him in an extremely critical condition. During routine questioning, the doctor discovered that the patient had just been brought from the Missionary Hospital. The doctor's face darkened and he stalked out of the room. I was certain the patient would be refused entry.

"After much deliberation, we concluded that R' Yosef Chaim Sonnenfeld was the only person who could influence Dr. Wallach. Since my father was a close confidant of R' Yosef Chaim, this delicate task fell on my shoulders once again.

"I ran to Battei Machseh to see R' Yosef Chaim. En route, a terrific thunderstorm struck and I was thoroughly drenched. Wet and shivering, I entered R' Yosef Chaim's home and found him deeply immersed in a large volume of the Talmud. I knew that R' Yosef Chaim was upset with me for casting my lot with the Zionists, yet he still received me warmly.

"I apologized for the interruption and related to him the entire incident at the hospital, even mentioning the name of the patient and that he had previously been a patient at the Missionary Hospital. I begged R' Yosef Chaim to write a letter to Dr. Wallach and urge him to admit my friend to his hospital.

"As soon as I finished speaking, R' Yosef Chaim creased the page he was studying, donned his fur coat and prepared to leave for the hospital. I blocked the door, refusing to allow the Rav to walk out in such treacherous weather. All I needed was a letter.

"R' Yosef Chaim's response was unequivocal:

" 'When a Jewish life is in danger, a letter is *not* enough. I must personally fulfill this great mitzvah. A letter may or may not influence the good doctor, but my presence will.'

"He ran out of the room and in a moment was up the steps. Although I was younger, I had trouble keeping up with this 75-year-old man's pace. The rain soon became torrential. I advised R' Yosef Chaim to wait until it let up a bit. He quickened his pace, exclaiming, 'How can someone going to save a Jewish life be deterred by a few drops of rain?'

"I breathlessly followed R' Yosef Chaim until we reached Jaffa Gate. There we boarded a carriage and ordered the driver to drive to the hospital as quickly as possible. R' Yosef Chaim drew his worn *Tehillim* from his pocket and quietly recited psalms.

"A quarter-hour later we reached the hospital. R' Yosef Chaim sprang from the carriage and rushed off before I had even finished paying the driver. As soon as I had sent the driver on his way, I ran after R' Yosef Chaim who had already reached Dr. Wallach's private office. I managed to arrive in time to hear R' Yosef Chaim's sharp words:

" '. . .Since when is the doctor a halachic authority on the laws of saving a Jewish life? Admit the patient at once and we'll discuss the matter later.' Turning to me, R' Yosef Chaim said 'Where is the patient? Bring him in immediately because every minute is critical.'

"The impossible occurred. Two weeks later my friend was fully recovered and released from the hospital. Knowing the tense relationship which existed between my friend and R' Yosef Chaim, I refrained from revealing to him who had been responsible for his recovery.

"A year passed, and my friend was asked to deliver the keynote address at a groundbreaking ceremony for a new settlement in the Galilee. He spoke eloquently about the lofty aims of Zionism and reached the climax of his speech when he shouted, 'We will build this land in our own way and with our own strength! We will build this land by waging a fight to the death against the black arm of R' Sonnenfeld and his followers!'

"I was sitting in the audience and completely lost control. I jumped up and shouted, 'How dare you! Show a little respect for the saintly rabbi to whom you owe your very life!'

"The speaker was shocked into silence and asked me to explain myself. I quickly took the podium and described to the assemblage exactly how the 'black arm' of R' Yosef Chaim Sonnenfeld had interceded to save the life of one who had vowed to destroy him."

ספר
דברים

DEVARIM/DEUTERONOMY

פרשת דברים ‎ש
Parashas Devarim

Background

The *sidrah* opens with Moses rebuking Israel for their sins. Moses knew of the spiritual challenges that Israel would face upon entering *Eretz Yisrael*, and feared that they would view these challenges complacently, confident in their ability to resist the alien influences of the Canaanite land.

He therefore admonished Israel that as they had failed before, so might they fail again. Moses intended his admonition to awaken in Israel a spirit of vigilance and self-scrutiny, which he hoped would protect them in the years ahead.

Moses reproved Israel for some serious sins (e.g., the spies; the Golden Calf); however, he was careful to only *allude* to these sins; he mentioned none of them explicitly.[1]

1. **Burning Embarrassment.** A spiritual leader must sometimes admonish his flock for their misdeeds. Moses fulfilled this responsibility; however, he did not explicitly identify Israel's sins. *R' Chaim Shmulevitz* maintains that this teaches that even one who offers legitimate rebuke must exercise the utmost care to avoid causing embarrassment to others.

The stricture against shaming others applies even when the victim is of lowly stature. The Talmud (*Gittin* 57a) teaches that the shame suffered by Bar Kamtza upon being publicly ejected from a banquet in the presence of the Sages caused God to aid him in destroying the Temple. Said R' Elazar with regard to this incident, "Come see the great power of embarrassment! Consider: Bar Kamtza responded to his rejection by betraying his people and causing the destruction of the Holy Temple. Only a wicked person would act in this manner! Yet, God aided him in his purpose. We see that even the shame suffered by an ignoble person triggers a powerful response in Heaven."

Because the sin of causing shame to another is so severe, one who humiliates his fellow in public receives no portion in the World to Come (*Avos* 3:15). *Meiri* explains that one who inflicts public embarrassment demonstrates a basic lack of human decency. God has little tolerance for such people and finds no place for them in His world of reward.

The Sages teach (*Sotah* 10b) that it is preferable to throw oneself into a burning furnace rather than to publicly embarrass another Jew. *R' Yisrael Yaakov Lubchansky,* the rav of the city of Baranovitch, embodied this teaching. The synagogue in Baranovitch was heated by a wood-burning stove which remained hot overnight, fueled with branches by the poor who slept there. If, however, no one would feed the fire during the night, the synagogue would be ice cold in the morning. R' Yisrael Yaakov feared that the congregants, forced to pray in the cold, would abuse the sexton for failing to keep the synagogue warm. To spare the sexton abuse, R' Yisrael Yaakov would arise early in the morning to start the fire in the stove. One morning, as R' Yisrael Yaakov was loading wood into the stove, the sexton, whose job the rav was performing, walked in early to the synagogue. He saw someone leaning into the oven door, but did not recognize R' Yisrael Yaakov, whose head was inside the oven. "Good morning," called the sexton. The rav remained silent, fearing that the sexton would suffer embarrassment were he to realize that his duty was being carried out by the rav himself. Meanwhile, the wood inside the stove had begun to catch fire, and R' Yisrael Yaakov's face grew uncomfortably warm. He prayed that the sexton would begin cleaning the synagogue, so that

אֵלֶּה הַדְּבָרִים אֲשֶׁר דִּבֶּר מֹשֶׁה אֶל כָּל יִשְׂרָאֵל

These are the words that
Moses spoke to all of Israel (1:1).

The word אֵלֶּה, *these* — as opposed to וְאֵלֶּה, *and these* — implies a difference between that which is presently being introduced and that which came before. *Sfas Emes* explains that as the Jews approached *Eretz Yisrael,* they began to enjoy the heightened perception and intelligence that are a property of the sanctified atmosphere of the Holy Land (see *Bava Basra* 158b). As a result, their ability to understand and assimilate Torah was greatly enhanced — in these last five weeks of Moses's life, the Jews integrated far more Torah (a full fifth!) than they had been able to do before this time.

Alternatively, the contrast between the earlier teachings and the later ones derives from the fact that Moses was now speaking to *all* of Israel.

Until this point, Moses functioned primarily as a teacher, in which role he elucidated the halachic aspects of the mitzvos. Not all Jews were intellectually equipped to appreciate the depths of Moses's teachings in these areas. Now, however, Moses began to speak words of admonishment and rebuke, designed to build character and encourage self-scrutiny. He therefore addressed himself to all Jews, for all require the spiritual nurturance and guidance that is inherent in warm-hearted rebuke delivered in a timely manner (*Chasam Sofer*).[2]

---

he would be able to pull his face away from the flames, but the sexton did not move. The sexton assumed that the fellow warming himself at the stove was an unmannerly beggar and, incensed at being ignored, he bellowed angrily, "Good morning!" The rav still did not respond and pushed his face even closer to the flames.

Furious, the sexton screamed, "You ingrate! Can't you answer when someone speaks to you?," and then, for good measure, gave the "beggar" a sound kick in the back, almost pushing him into the oven. With that he left, and only then did R' Yisrael Yaakov, his beard badly singed, pull himself free of the oven and quickly leave the synagogue without the sexton seeing him.

When R' Yisrael Yaakov returned to the synagogue later that morning, people assumed that his beard had become singed in an accident at home. It was only a number of years later, when R' Yisrael Yaakov became the *mashgiach* (spiritual guide) of the famed Baranovitch Yeshivah, that one of his family members revealed the truth.

2. **Heart to Heart Talk.** Every person needs a competent, objective mentor to point out potential pitfalls in the path of one's spiritual growth, and to recall one's past misdeeds so that they will not be repeated. As R' Yehoshua ben Perachyah stated: "Appoint a teacher for yourself!" (*Avos* 1:6). One who cannot submit to this sort of relationship is in danger of losing direction and focus; like a rudderless ship, he is at the mercy of the prevailing winds and currents. Even an unrefined Jew can benefit from constructive criticism offered in a loving manner.

This is illustrated by the following incident that occurred when the *Chafetz Chaim* met a boorish fellow at an inn. He observed the fellow shout coarsely to the waitress to bring him a fat piece of duck and a bottle of whiskey. When she brought the food, he wolfed it down without troubling to recite a blessing, and then began speaking to the waitress in a highly inappropriate manner.

Shocked at this uncouth behavior, the Chafetz Chaim prepared to reprimand the errant Jew. The innkeeper, fearing that the ruffian would abuse the Chafetz Chaim, or even cause him bodily harm, attempted to dissuade the Chafetz Chaim from intervening. "Rebbe," he said, "you cannot speak to this man. When he was 7 years old he was seized and forcibly conscripted into the Czar's army. He was first sent to Siberia, where he grew up among the most terrible people; then, at age 18, he began a twenty-five-year stint in the army. He has never learned a word of Torah in his life. Does it surprise you that he is an uncouth, obnoxious boor? Rebbe, your honor is precious to me. I beg of you — leave him be."

The Chafetz Chaim smiled, "A Jew like this I know how to handle. Perhaps, with Hashem's help, I will be able to reach him."

The sage approached the man's table, stretched his hand out in greeting and spoke in warm, friendly tones. "Tell me, is it true, that as a youngster you were abducted and exiled to Siberia? I understand that you never had an opportunity to learn Torah. You have really had a difficult life." The Chafetz Chaim began to praise the fellow: "Surely the cruel Russians attempted to coerce you to abandon Judaism, to eat pig and other nonkosher foods. Yet you refused to renounce your heritage. What incredible self-sacrifice! You withstood a test more severe than that of Chananiah, Mishael and Azariah. I envy you the great portion you will merit in the World to Come among the righteous!"

Moved by the Chafetz Chaim's heartfelt words, the former conscript began to shed burning tears, which only intensified when he learned the identity of his "critic." Weeping, he lovingly kissed the Chafetz Chaim, who

---

The *Vilna Gaon* maintains that a key element of Moses' statement is expressed in the way the verse describes those to whom it was directed — namely, **all** *of Israel*. The inclusive description tells us that Moses exhorted the nation not to break apart into disparate factions, but to preserve its closeness and unity even after his death. In that way, Israel would surely merit God's blessing.

Presumably, Moses began his final statement with this admonition because there is nothing more critical to Jewish survival than unity. Furthermore, the Jews were about to enter *Eretz Yisrael*. One reason *Eretz Yisrael* was given to the Jewish people was to unite them; it is for this reason that the Talmudic dictum of mutual responsibility — כָּל יִשְׂרָאֵל עֲרֵבִים זֶה בָּזֶה, *All Jews are guarantors for one another* — did not take effect until Israel entered *Eretz Yisrael*. With Israel on the threshold of the Holy Land, Moses called upon them to remain united.

אֶל כָּל יִשְׂרָאֵל

to all of Israel (ibid.).

Moses spoke to all of Israel at once; yet every individual Jew heard in his words a message tailored to his specific needs (*Taam V'Daas, Imrei Baruch*).

How was Moses able to perceive the many different issues facing so large and varied a group of people? A comment by *Rambam* sheds light on the matter. *Rambam* (*Hil. Melachim* 3:6) describes a Jewish king: לִבּוֹ הוּא לֵב כָּל קְהַל יִשְׂרָאֵל, *his heart is the heart of all Israel.* One who is king over Israel is Divinely aided to grasp and appreciate the unique characteristics and abilities that reside in the hearts of each of his subjects. Moses, as king of Israel (see *Ibn Ezra* to *Deuteronomy* 33:5), received this Divine inspiration. This enabled him to see into the heart of each and every Jew; he perceived their longings, their needs, their strengths, their weaknesses, and he responded with the words of this *sidrah*. [3]

The *Chasam Sofer* once addressed his congregation with sharp words of rebuke. As he reached the end of his address, he concluded, "I have nobody in particular in mind with my words. However, if someone hears in my words a message which he feels is applicable to himself, let him know that my words were meant for him."

Kedushas Levi writes that the verse *to all of Israel* highlights the dual role of a leader of Jews. On the one hand, it was Moses' responsibility to rebuke his flock. However, Moses stepped into this role only when addressing Israel (as is implied by the words

---

again spoke softly to him. "Believe me, God considers a Jew like you to be among his most loyal soldiers. If you begin to conduct yourself like a fine upstanding Jew from now on, you will be the happiest man on earth."

The fellow became a devotee of the Chafetz Chaim and developed into a righteous penitent.

3. **Heart of Hearts.** *R' Yitzchak Hutner* employed *Rambam's* understanding of the inspiration granted a king to explain the unique power of the *Psalms* of King David.

He posed the following question: King David spoke the following words (*Psalms* 9:15): לְמַעַן אֲסַפְּרָה כָּל תְּהִלָּתֶיךָ, *so that I may proclaim all Your praises.* This implies that King David considered himself able to give voice to *all* the praises of God. But elsewhere King David asked (*Psalms* 106:2): מִי יְמַלֵּל גְּבוּרוֹת ה' יַשְׁמִיעַ כָּל תְּהִלָּתוֹ, *Who can express the mighty acts of Hashem? [Who] can make heard all of His praises?* This seems to indicate that *no one* is capable of proclaiming all of God's praises!

R' Hutner reconciled these statements in the following manner: True, no individual Jew can proclaim the full praise of the Almighty. But the nation as a whole *can* proclaim His praise; the myriad perspectives and appreciations of God are contained in the hearts of the multitudes of Jews. As the verse states (*Isaiah* 43:21): עַם זוּ יָצַרְתִּי לִי תְּהִלָּתִי יְסַפֵּרוּ, *I formed this nation for Myself; let them speak My praises.*

Since "the heart of the king is the heart of all Israel," King David could say of himself, *I may proclaim all Your praises,* for his heart, the communal heart of Israel, contained within it the maximum humanly-possible praises of Hashem.

It is for this reason that in times of need we turn to King David's *Psalms* to give expression to our heartfelt prayer. The *Psalms* were written with the power of Israel's communal heart; thus, every Jew can find within it the needs of his own heart.

The *Ponevezher Rav,* in his eulogy on the *Chazon Ish,* expressed a related thought: "Many people wondered from where the Chazon Ish drew the courage to advise people on life-and-death medical decisions. The answer is that his heart was the heart of all of Israel; he sensed the pain of every Jew, for it was truly his own. Can't a person offer advice to himself on how to deal with his own pain?"

to all of Israel). When speaking to God, Moses assumed the role of defense counsel, emphasizing only the redeeming qualities of his beloved flock.[4]

To spare Israel embarrassment, Moses merely alluded to their sins, veiling his admonishment in terms which only they would understand. Later, however, Moses speaks quite openly about these very sins! (See below, 1:22, 9:16 et al.) This appears to be a contradiction.

R' Ovadyah of Bartenura explains that upon receiving Moses' admonishment the Jewish people repented wholeheartedly, at which point it was no longer necessary to avoid speaking openly about their sins. [See *Ramban* (*Genesis* 42:21), who expresses a similar thought with regard to the sin of the brothers of Joseph.]

Imrei Elimelech expands upon this idea by citing the Talmudic dictum (*Yoma* 86b) that when one repents out of love for God — as did Israel — all his intentional sins are transformed into meritorious deeds. Moses made deliberate and explicit mention of Israel's misdeeds to inform Israel that their former sins could now be used as a springboard to attain new spiritual heights.

Some understand Moses' use of allusion in rebuking Israel not as an attempt to spare them shame, but as a sign of the Jewish sensitivity to sin:

A perceptive, spiritually sensitive person needs little reminder of past wrongdoing; a mere hint suffices to recall the sin to conscious memory. A less sensitive person, by contrast, requires a clear, explicit admonition. Similarly, a major event in one's life can be recalled to mind with the subtlest

of reminders, while an incident of minor importance requires a blatant reminder.

The fact that Moses merely alluded to Israel's sins testifies to the extreme sensitivity of the Jewish people, whose abhorrence of sin was such that the slightest of reminders sufficed to bring them to repentance. Upon receiving Moses's rebuke, Israel did not attempt to deny their sins, but were willing to face up to their acts and take the necessary remedial steps (*R' Yosef Nendik*). In the words of the Sages, דַּי לְחַכִּימָא בִּרְמִיזָא, *For the wise man an allusion is sufficient* (*Zohar*).[5]

Generally, the purpose of rebuke should not be to shame the sinner; rather, rebuke should be used to make people aware of the emptiness of a life devoid of God and Torah. *R' Michael Ber Weissmandl* (whose research into the hidden codes of the Torah predated the advent of the computer) notes that if one begins from the letter ב in the word דברים and counts 613 letters, he comes to a ר. Let him count another 613 letters, and he will come to a כ. Yet another 613 letters will yield a ה. These letters combine to spell the word ברכה, *blessing*. The function of Moses' rebuke was to transform acts of wickedness into a source of blessing.

וַחֲצֵרֹת — *And Hazeroth* (ibid.).

Rashi explains that *Hazeroth* refers to the rebellion of Korah. *Chidushei HaRim* illuminates the matter:

The Talmud (*Shabbos* 14b) teaches that King Solomon instituted עֵירוּבֵי חֲצֵרֹת, the symbolic merging of several courtyards (*hazeroth*) so that the residents might carry in the common area on the

---

4. **Between Me and Him.** *R' Yoel Teitelbaum*, the *Rebbe of Satmar*, was famous for his opposition to Zionism and its adherents, and would hold nothing back in expressing what he felt to be the deleterious effect of Zionism on authentic Jewish life and Torah values.

On one occasion, he was taken to task for his statements by a person who compared him unfavorably to the patriarch Abraham, who beseeched God to save the city of Sodom. The fellow argued, "Certainly the Zionists are no worse than the Sodomites! Why then do you have only bad things to say about the Zionists?"

Replied the Rebbe, "The Torah records only what Abraham said to God about Sodom. Obviously, when speaking with God, he focused only on their saving graces. But when he spoke with the Sodomites themselves, he no doubt rebuked them sharply for their wickedness!"

The Rebbe concluded, "You hear only what I say to the Zionists themselves and to those led astray by their teachings. You know nothing about what I say to God regarding the Zionists!"

5. **Subtle Sledgehammer.** A wise man once said, "The Sages teach that דַּי לְחַכִּימָא בִּרְמִיזָא, 'for a wise man an allusion is sufficient.' But what is to be done with one who is not wise? For the fool, even a sledgehammer might not do the trick!"

Sabbath. This *eruv* is created by taking a small amount of bread and granting every resident a share in it. The Talmud further teaches that Solomon's establishment of this caused God to rejoice. Why did God rejoice? Because this *eruv* represented a new opportunity for unity among Jews. God rejoiced that His children would become further united.

Korah was the very antithesis of unity within Israel. As the Torah states regarding his rebellion (*Numbers* 16:1): *And Korah . . . separated himself.* Rather than encouraging the Jews to join together, Korah encouraged them to split apart, causing each to withdraw, as it were, to his own separate *hazer,* or courtyard. Therefore, his sin is referred to as *hazeroth.*

וְדִי זָהָב
and Di-zahab (ibid.).

This alludes to the sin of the Golden Calf, which the Jewish people formed of the gold they received when they were redeemed from Egypt. Now, the word דִי (of וְדִי זָהָב) translates literally as "enough." The Talmud (*Berachos* 32a) teaches that Moses intended this word to suggest a possible defense for Israel. He said to God, "Master of the universe! Because of the silver and gold that You lavished upon Israel until they said, 'Enough!' — that is what caused them to make the Golden Calf."

Ordinarily, people are hesitant to donate money even to deserving causes. God granted Israel such fantastic wealth that they did not hesitate to donate even to so undeserving a cause as the Golden Calf (*R' Yehoshua of Kutna*). Thus, Moses' rebuke was directed not only toward the actual sin of the Golden Calf, but also toward the misplaced magnanimity that allowed Israel to give of their wealth to promote evil.

This idea is expressed in *Talmud Yerushalmi*

(*Shekalim* 1:1), which identifies this lack of discernment as an undesirable national characteristic: "They are solicited for the Golden Calf and they contribute; they are solicited for the building of the Tabernacle and they contribute." One who contributes to an evil cause as readily as a good one demonstrates the mindlessness that informs his deeds. Truly great deeds are the result of reasoned decision rather than impulse or sentimentality.[6]

Yalkut Yehudah understands the thrust of Moses' וְדִי זָהָב rebuke to be directed at the equivocation displayed by Israel's participation in the sin of the Golden Calf. The Jews did not reject God; rather, they attempted to combine His sublime service with worship of the Calf. Moses now demands that they abandon their dual loyalties, and make an unequivocal commitment to the One God. Elijah the prophet once challenged Israel thusly (*I Kings* 18:21): *How long will you dance between two opinions? If Hashem is the Lord, go after Him! And if the Baal, go after [the Baal]!* The Jews were attempting to straddle a spiritual fence, worshiping both God and the Baal. Elijah forced them to declare their loyalties to one or the other.

בְּעֵבֶר הַיַּרְדֵּן . . . הוֹאִיל מֹשֶׁה בֵּאֵר אֶת הַתּוֹרָה הַזֹּאת
On the other side of the Jordan . . .
Moses began explaining this Torah (ibid. 5).

Moses elucidated the Torah in 70 languages (*Rashi*). *Chidushei HaRim* explains that Moses anticipated the exile of the Jews, and took steps to ensure that no matter which of the seventy nations will host us, no matter how they will oppose us, we will always be able to interpret the Torah into the "language" of that place. Thus, the Torah remains relevant to the challenges of every new place and time.[7]

Ksav Sofer offers another explanation of the signi-

---

6. **Differentiated Disbursement.** *Taam V'Daas* writes that one should exercise discernment in disbursing his charity funds. One who gives indiscriminately simply because he has a "soft heart" receives less reward than he would if he discriminated in his giving. One should taken pains to contribute to authentic Torah causes which promote Torah values and the welfare of Jews.

7. **A Map to the Soul.** The Sages teach that the Torah possesses seventy aspects (i.e., levels of interpretation) (*Bamidbar Rabbah* 13:15). R' Tzadok HaKohen connects this characteristic of the Torah with another significant "seventy" — to wit, the group of seventy souls that formed the nucleus of the Jewish nation (see *Genesis* 46:27). The connection is as follows: Torah is a map to exploring the Jewish soul. Hashem granted us His Torah to enable

ficance of the elucidation in seventy languages:

Throughout our history, opponents of Torah (particularly the fifth columnists among us) have sought to place geographical limitations on our Torah obligations. Some have claimed that Torah is a viable lifestyle only in *Eretz Yisrael.* But when we dwell among the nations, we must compromise our fidelity to Torah in order to assimilate into the surrounding secular culture, God forbid. Others maintain the opposite, that *mitzvos* are needed only in the Diaspora, to maintain Israel's identity and unity. Now, however, that we live in the Holy Land among Jews, we no longer need the "artificial construct" of a Torah identity, God forbid. To dispel both of these falsehoods, God commanded Moses to explain the Torah in seventy languages. This demonstrates that Torah speaks to us in all places and at all times.

The word הוֹאִיל means *began.* Although Moses began the elucidation of the Torah, it is a process that continues throughout Jewish history. Torah scholars and students throughout the generations have participated in this eternal quest, with each earnest seeker contributing another piece to the infinite puzzle.

The Talmud often concludes the discussion of an unresolved question with the word תֵּיקוּ. Literally translated, this is a shortened form of the word תֵּיקוּם, *let it stand.* However, *Shelah* explains תֵּיקוּ to be an acronym for תִּשְׁבִּי יְתָרֵץ קוּשְׁיוֹת וּבְעָיוֹת, *[Elijah] the Tishbite will resolve questions and inquiries.*

The word הוֹאִיל contains the same letters as אֵלִיָּהוּ, *Elijah,* for the process begun by Moses will be concluded by Elijah. May he foretell the coming of the Messiah speedily in our days.[8]

ה׳ אֱלֹקֵינוּ דִּבֶּר אֵלֵינוּ בְּחֹרֵב לֵאמֹר רַב
לָכֶם שֶׁבֶת בָּהָר הַזֶּה. פְּנוּ וּסְעוּ לָכֶם
*Hashem our God spoke to us in Horeb,
saying: Enough of your dwelling by
this mountain. Turn yourselves
around, and journey* (ibid. 6,7).

Why did the Israelites need to be prodded into traveling onward? *Taam V'Daas* suggests that the people were reluctant to forsake the place at which they experienced the indescribable revelation of Sinai. It was therefore necessary for God to *command* them to travel on and conquer the Holy Land.

Torah was not intended to be used solely for self-perfection. We must carry the word of Hashem outward even to those who are seemingly removed from Torah. Torah is for living; it encompasses life's every mundane detail. We may not remain at the Mount; we must bring Torah to the people.

According to *Meor V'Shemesh,* this verse encapsulates a homily on dealing with spiritual adversity. The verse tells us: Do not tarry before the seemingly insurmountable mountain that is the evil inclination. Do not be daunted by the challenge of overcoming temptation. Begin your spiritual journey, take the first steps, and you will be granted Divine help in your climb to greatness.[9]

us to penetrate the depths of our souls. All Jewish souls are variations on the original seventy souls that descended to Egypt. Thus, the Torah possesses seventy aspects (and is expressed in seventy languages) (*Zekan Aharon*).

8. **Final Analysis.** The continuum from Moses to Elijah is expressed in the final words of the last of the prophets, *Remember the Torah of Moses My servant which I commanded him at Horeb for all of Israel — [its] decrees and [its] statutes. Behold, I send you Elijah the prophet . . .* (Malachi 3:22-23).

9. **Step by Step.** The Talmud (*Succah* 52a) relates that in the Messianic era God will slaughter the evil inclination. To the righteous it will appear as a high mountain; to the wicked as a strand of hair. Both righteous and wicked will weep, the righteous asking, "How did we overcome this towering mountain?," the wicked asking, "Why were we not able to overcome this strand of hair?"

The wise take an incremental approach to the challenges of life. They view each challenge separately, and step over it as easily as over a strand of hair. Gradually they ascend, step by step, until they reach a spiritual pinnacle; only then do they realize that they have climbed a towering mountain. Had they gazed beyond the immediate challenge, they would never have mustered the courage to begin.

But the wicked perceive each challenge as an insurmountable peak. They do not even attempt to control their illicit desires, for they imagine the exercise of self-discipline to be impossible! But they will come to realize that they could have overcome the challenges one "strand of hair" at a time, whereupon they will weep with remorse (*R' Moshe of Kobrin*).

וָאמַר אֲלֵכֶם בָּעֵת הַהִוא לֵאמַר לֹא אוּכַל לְבַדִּי שְׂאֵת אֶתְכֶם. ה' אֱלֹקֵיכֶם הִרְבָּה אֶתְכֶם וְהִנְּכֶם הַיּוֹם כְּכוֹכְבֵי הַשָּׁמַיִם לָרֹב

And I spoke to you at that time, saying, "I cannot carry you alone." Hashem, Your God, has multiplied you and behold! you are like the stars of heaven in abundance (ibid. 9,10).

The word לֵאמַר (which translates literally as *to say*) is connotative of a statement that is to be repeated by others. Who is it that Moses expects will repeat the words he is saying in this verse?

Meshech Chochmah explains with the following example:

A man was blessed with a large family and enormous wealth. It is taxing to raise a large family; the man was overwhelmed by dealings with teachers and tutors, nurses and nannies, cooks and kitchen help, and the myriad other distractions that are inherent in running a large household. Weary of the constant strain, he once complained to his beloved family, "How difficult it is to provide for you all!" But in the very next breath he said, "May God grant that you suffer as I do. May problems such as these always beset you!"

So too Moses, the faithful shepherd: He complains that it is difficult to bear the burdens of this great nation, who are as numerous as the stars of the heavens. But he adds: לֵאמַר, expressing his fervent wish that this might be the complaint voiced by future leaders of Israel — that God has blessed and multiplied the nation.[10]

אֵיכָה אֶשָּׂא לְבַדִּי טָרְחֲכֶם וּמַשַּׂאֲכֶם וְרִיבְכֶם

How can I alone carry your toil, your burdens and your quarrels? (ibid. 12).

The life of a person is delineated by his relationships with God, with others and with himself (see *Maharal* to *Avos* 1:2). Moses, as the spiritual leader of Israel, saw all three as his responsibility. *Ramban* accordingly explains this verse in the following manner: *Your toil* refers to Moses' toil in teaching Israel Torah, the study of which is the key to a healthy relationship with oneself. *Your burdens* refers to Moses' role as intercessor with God on behalf of Israel. *Your quarrels* refers to his mediation in their interpersonal quarrels.[11]

---

10. **Just Like You.** In verse 11, Moses blesses Israel with these words: ה', אֱלֹקֵי אֲבוֹתֵכֶם יֹסֵף עֲלֵיכֶם כָּכֶם אֶלֶף פְּעָמִים, *May Hashem, the God of your fathers, add to you a thousand times as you are. R' Leibel Eiger* was once asked to explain why Moses interrupted his admonishment of Israel to bless them, and why he blessed them with the word כָּכֶם, *as you are,* which implies a wish that their children be just like them.

He answered with a story: One Shabbos, the *Chozeh of Lublin* began to sharply criticize the *chassidim* grouped around his table. Some lowered their eyes in embarrassment; others became agitated and depressed.

Seeing this, the Rebbe concluded, "But even so, I wish upon us all that the next generation — our children and grandchildren — should be no worse than you." This raised their spirits, for the *chassidim* saw that the Rebbe did not think so badly of them after all.

Moses realized that the nation, after hearing the litany of their sins, was becoming discouraged. He therefore lifted their spirits by offering them this blessing — "May Hashem . . . add to you a thousand times *just as you are.*"

11. **Full-Service Leadership.** Moses felt a responsibility to see to *all* of Israel's needs. That this remains a characteristic of Jewish leaders is resoundingly brought home by a poignant incident related by *R' Moshe Weinberger,* who repeats it as he heard it from the principal character: "I was a young boy when my parents sent me to learn in the yeshivah for younger students in Grodno. It was a three-day ride by train to Grodno, but my poverty-stricken parents could not afford the railway fare, so I had no choice but to walk. My parents prepared provisions to the best of their ability and instructed me to ask Jews along my route to share their food with me when mine would run out.

"Accompanied by their warm wishes, I set out, and indeed, I was soon forced to beg food from the kind Jews I met along the way. Throughout the journey, I slept on the hard benches of local synagogues or even on the bare earth. In addition to the discomforts and dangers of the trip, I was preoccupied with the natural apprehensions of a young boy attending yeshivah for the first time. Would I pass the entrance examination and be accepted into the yeshivah? The thought of failing and bringing shame to my family frightened me terribly, and I calmed myself by incessantly reviewing the page of *Gemara* I had prepared for the exam. By the time I arrived in Grodno I knew that page by heart, word for word.

"I finally arrived in Grodno, tired and hungry but fully prepared to be tested on that page of *Gemara*. I was

Rashi interprets מַשַׂאֲכֶם, *your burdens,* as heresy. He refers thereby to those who made it a practice to constantly mock Moses and to assign ulterior motives to all he did. [*Rashi's* description of this as heresy coincides with the Talmudic ruling (*Sanhedrin* 99b) that names one who mocks a Torah scholar "a heretic."] If Moses would leave his home a bit early, these people would whisper that his home was plagued with domestic strife. If he would remain at home until later, they would assure one another that he doubtless spent the extra time scheming against them.

A contemporary of *R' Chaim Brisker* complained to R' Chaim about the abuse showered upon him by the litigants in a monetary dispute that he was adjudicating. R' Chaim replied, "Why does the Torah record for posterity an allusion to the defamatory attack on Moses? It is because the Torah wishes us to appreciate Moses' patience with an obstinate, ungrateful people. No matter how they mocked and defamed him he continued to bear their burdens." R' Chaim concluded, "The Torah wants every judge and leader to learn from this that he must bear abuse with patience and love."[12]

R' Nachman of Breslov explains why the phrase *your burdens* refers to heresy:

A heretic lives a terribly burdensome life, for he refuses to acknowledge that his tribulations are shared by God, and he must therefore shoulder all of life's burdens alone. Not so the believer, who knows that God shares his pain, and who consequently finds life's burdens much easier to bear.[13] Thus, the verse describes heresy as a burden.

---

directed to the home of the *Rosh Yeshivah, R' Shimon Shkop,* to take the exam. R' Shimon welcomed me warmly, and offered me a seat at his kitchen table. After inquiring after my name and my place of origin, he said to me, 'I have only two questions for you.' I was sure that the exam was about to begin, and I was ready!

"R' Shimon continued, 'My first question is: When was the last time you ate a hot meal?' I was surprised by the question and after a pause I replied, 'About three weeks ago.' R' Shimon stood up and said, 'Listen. The Rebbetzin is out of town, so you'll have to make do with whatever I can cook for you.' With that R' Shimon began to prepare a meal for me. I was shocked. I had never seen my father cook at home, but here was this great *Rosh Yeshivah* preparing food for me! When the food was ready, R' Shimon brought me a full plate and, after I emptied it, he served me a second helping.

"After waiting for me to recite the *Birchas HaMazon* (Grace After Meals) R' Shimon said, 'Now for the second question.' I was sure that R' Shimon was now ready to administer the test. He continued, 'When did you last sleep in a bed?' I was again shocked by the question, and replied that I simply could not remember the last time. R' Shimon went into his bedroom, made up the bed for me, and invited me to lie down. He gently covered me, and I slept there until the morning. Only later did I realize that he had given me his bed. This was my entrance exam to Grodno."

After telling R' Weinberger this story, the student, now an old man, concluded, "Many years have passed and much suffering and pain have come my way, including the loss of my entire family to the Nazis. Through all the tragedies, the one thing that kept me connected to *Yiddishkeit* were those two questions — my entrance exam to the yeshivah of Grodno."

12. **Too Involved, Too Uninvolved.** The following incident demonstrates the tendency of congregants to find fault with the rabbi no matter how he conducts himself.

In Poland in the early 1900's, two great rabbis represented the Orthodox community in the Polish parliament (the *Sejm*). They were *R' Aharon Levine* of Reisha and the famous *R' Meir Shapiro,* innovator of the *Daf Yomi,* then of Sanok but later of Lublin. People would complain that R' Levine was overly involved in political matters and paid insufficient attention to his rabbinic duties. They leveled precisely the opposite criticism at R' Shapiro, claiming that his intense involvement in spiritual and rabbinic affairs undermined his effectiveness in the parliament.

R' Meir Shapiro responded that the claims of both camps were nothing new, for both had already been mentioned by King David in *Psalms,* where it is stated (106:16): *They were jealous of Moses in the camp, of Aaron, Hashem's holy one.* The critics assailed Moses for spending too much time "in the camp," involved in the affairs of the nation. They assailed Aaron for the opposite reason — that he was too much "Hashem's holy one," praying and studying when he should have been tending to the needs of the nation.

13. **Serenity in Trust.** As is taught in *Chovos HaLevavos* (*Shaar HaBitachon*): "The very essence of trust in God is the serenity it imparts to one who truly places his trust in Him."

**הָבוּ לָכֶם אֲנָשִׁים חֲכָמִים
וּנְבֹנִים וִידֻעִים לְשִׁבְטֵיכֶם וכו׳**

*Provide for yourselves righteous men
who are wise, understanding and
well-known to your tribes, and I shall
appoint them as your heads* (ibid. 13).

This verse enumerates four criteria for one who
would be a judge over Israel — he must be
righteous, wise, understanding and well-known.
But in a later verse (v. 15) Moses states that those
he appointed as judges were "righteous men, wise
and well-known." He does not say that they possessed understanding. *Rashi* there explains that in
fact Moses attempted to find men of understanding, but failed to find anyone endowed with this
trait!

According to *Rashi*, this reflects badly on Israel.
However, *Chasam Sofer* argues, counterintuitively,
that Moses's omission actually reflects well on
Israel. For the trait of understanding is defined as
the ability to extrapolate from that which is known
to that which is unknown. A person endowed with
understanding is generally of a creative bent, one
who easily draws forth new concepts from old
ideas. But innovation is not always to be desired in
a teacher and judge of Israel. One who wishes to
serve as a link in the chain of our *mesorah*
(tradition) must be able to elevate received truths
over his intuition, and to suppress his creativity in
favor of tradition. The Talmud teaches this lesson
in Tractate *Succah* (28a), where it informs us that
the Tanna R' Eliezer never imparted to anyone a
Torah teaching that he had not received from his
teachers.

Moses may have included understanding in the
list of desirable traits; yet, he chose men who he
knew would not exalt their own perceptions over
the tenets of the *mesorah* of Sinai.

Chavas Da'as explains Moses's failure to find
men of understanding in this manner: Those endowed with understanding are generally people of
superior intellect, who, better than most people,
can assess the probable outcomes of any given
course of action. These people, when approached
by Moses to serve as judges, observed the manner
in which certain Jews abused Moses, and realized
that would they accept Moses's invitation, they
would be accorded similar treatment. They therefore refused the appointments. Hence, Moses was
unable to find men of understanding.[14]

**וַתַּעֲנוּ אֹתִי וַתֹּאמְרוּ טוֹב
הַדָּבָר אֲשֶׁר דִּבַּרְתָּ לַעֲשׂוֹת**

*You answered me and said,
"The thing you have proposed
to do is good"* (ibid. 14).

Moses proposed to Israel that he appoint others
to assist him in teaching and judging them.
The proposal found favor in the eyes of the people.
Rashi writes that Moses found their ready acceptance of this idea as grounds for rebuke. He felt
that the people should have insisted on learning
from Moses himself rather than from his students.

What would have been the benefit of learning
directly from Moses? Simply understood, there is
benefit in receiving information from a primary
source rather than a secondary source, for it is
inevitable that in the transmission from the first
person to the second, a certain measure of clarity
will be lost. But *Rashi* explains the matter differently. He says that the reason the Jews should have
insisted on learning from Moses is that Moses
suffered to acquire his Torah. The benefit of
receiving Torah from one who acquired it through
suffering is twofold: First, Torah acquired through
toil is of higher quality. Second, a student who
knows that his teacher has toiled in the service of
Torah develops a great appreciation for the
teacher's words, and will exert himself to the

---

14. **Honor — Real and Imagined.** There is an apocryphal story told of a young man who traveled to his uncle, a
distinguished man who served as *Rosh Hakahal* (head of the community) of his city. He inquired of several
passersby as to the whereabouts of his uncle's house, and each time received in response a shower of abuse
directed at his uncle! One fellow called the uncle a thief, another identified him as a lazy layabout, a third as a
good-for-nothing. After some time, the young man found the house, and after greeting his uncle, he asked, "Tell
me, Uncle, why do you remain as *Rosh Hakahal*? What do you gain thereby?"

The answer was swift in coming. "And does honor and prestige mean nothing to you?!"

utmost to understand his teachings.[15]

This should serve as a lesson to us that it is always preferable to learn from someone who has suffered and toiled to acquire Torah (*Talilei Oros*).[16]

לֹא תַכִּירוּ פָנִים בַּמִּשְׁפָּט כַּקָּטֹן כַּגָּדֹל תִּשְׁמָעוּן

You shall show no favoritism in judgment, small and great alike you shall hear (ibid. 17).

The phrase "small and great" refers to the sums of money under dispute. A judge must approach all cases with equal gravity, no matter whether the sum of money at stake is large or small. He may not treat the smaller cases as less important by delaying them until after the larger cases are dealt with. Alternatively, "small and great" refers to the financial status of the litigants. A judge may not unjustly favor a poverty-stricken person on the grounds that it is a mitzvah to provide him with funds. Conversely, he may not unjustly favor a wealthy person in order to avoid dishonoring him, even if he intends to command the fellow later to fulfill his obligation to the poor man (*Rashi*).

R' Yerucham Leib Perlman (the *Minsker Gadol*) employed this latter explanation to justify his practice of arbitrating monetary disputes between wealthy individuals. Some of his congregants objected to these activities, for they felt that he was attending to the wealthy at the expense of the poor. They argued that the task of a *rav* is to see to the needs of the poor.

R' Yerucham explained that this *Rashi* teaches us that a *rav* may not focus exclusively on the concerns of the poor. To unjustly favor the poor at the expense of the rich is a miscarriage of justice!

He argued further that to the contrary, a *rav* must make every legitimate effort to ensure the financial success of the wealthy, since it is through their success that the poor survive. When the rich prosper, they build businesses that provide jobs for craftsmen and laborers. When they suffer reversals, all who depend upon them for their livelihoods suffer reversals as well. Therefore, a *rav* must concern himself with the rich no less than the poor!

---

15. **True Appreciation.** Thus we find *R' Hai Gaon* writing regarding a certain Torah thought: "Be heedful of this interpretation, for it was revealed to us through great toil" (cited in *Chidushei HaRashba, Shabbos* 96a, s.v. שתיהן בדיוטא).

16. **Giving Reverence.** *R' Shimon Shkop* studied at the Yeshivah of Volozhin under the Netziv. In Volozhin, it was not mandatory to attend the *Rosh Yeshivah's* lectures, and indeed, R' Shimon did not generally attend the lectures of the Netziv.

Once, when R' Shimon was studying late at night, he was stymied by a difficult thought expressed in the commentary of *Rashbam* to Tractate *Bava Basra*. As he sat there, he saw the Netziv enter the study hall. R' Shimon approached the Netziv and asked him for help in understanding the *Rashbam*. The Netziv replied, "This *Rashbam*! My dear child, in order to understand this *Rashbam*, I more than once visited the graves of my forefathers to pray to Hashem that he help me understand His Torah."

Such was the awe with which R' Shimon received this pronouncement that from that day onward he attended all of the Netziv's lectures.

פרשת ואתחנן ❧
Parashas Va'eschanan

Background

This *sidrah* begins with Moses recounting for Israel his pleadings before Hashem to be allowed to enter *Eretz Yisrael.* Moses did not ask to remain the leader of Israel; he was content to let Joshua succeed him, so long as he could enter the Land and perform the commandments unique to it.[1]

וָאֶתְחַנַּן אֶל ה׳ בָּעֵת הַהִוא לֵאמֹר
*And I implored Hashem at
that time, saying (3:23).*

Moses was not simply indulging in reminiscences; he repeated his prayer in order to display before Israel his great love of *Eretz Yisrael.*

He intended thereby to imbue the nation with a measure of that same love; Moses hoped that their love for the land would encourage the people to cleave faithfully to God's wishes, so that He would never exile them from the Land (*Ibn Ezra*).

In Hebrew, there are many terms that mean "prayer"; each denotes a different form of entreaty. Moses described his prayer with the word וָאֶתְחַנַּן (from the root חנן), which is used when one asks to be shown favor, to be granted that which he has not really earned. *Rashi* explains that it is characteristic of the righteous to pray for their needs as if they are undeserving. Were they so inclined, they could demand that their prayers be answered as a reward for their good deeds; they choose instead to throw themselves upon God's mercy.[2]

---

1. **Strengthened by Faith.** *R' Yechezkel Abramsky* was exiled to Siberia for teaching Torah. Many years later he spoke of his travails to some of his close disciples. He told them of the terrible conditions in the labor camp, and of the backbreaking work that he and his compatriots were compelled to perform. He said, "Our lives were so bitter that when I would awake and recite the words מוֹדֶה אֲנִי לְפָנֶיךָ (*I thank you*), I would often wonder why I was thanking God. For beatings? For degradation? We were even denied the study of Torah! Was there anything for which I could truly give thanks?" *R' Yechezkel* continued, "But when I reached the next lines of the prayer, I was encouraged. מֶלֶךְ חַי וְקַיָּם . . . רַבָּה אֱמוּנָתֶךָ, *O living and eternal King . . . abundant is Your faithfulness!* I realized that although my captors could deny me Torah and *mitzvos,* and could afflict me physically, they could not deny me faith in God. I recognized that life was worthwhile for this reason alone, to experience one more day lived with faith and belief in the Creator."

Every Jew must know that even a fleeting moment of life is precious if it is imbued with a true faith in God.

2. **Endless Storehouse.** The Midrash (*Shemos Rabbah* 45:6) relates that God showed Moses the "storehouses" of Divine reward that are prepared for the righteous. God first showed him a storehouse reserved for one who fulfills the commandments; he then showed him another reserved for those who see to the needs of orphans, and so on from one storehouse to the next. They finally arrived at an exceedingly large storehouse. Moses asked, "For whom is this storehouse reserved?" God answered, "Those who are meritorious receive their reward based on their merit. This storehouse are for those who possess no merits; they receive from Me an undeserved gift."

Simply understood, the Midrash means that this largesse is reserved for the many unrighteous, who possess no merit for which they might receive reward (see *Eitz Yosef* ad loc.). But *Avnei Nezer* offers a different interpretation:

R' Aryeh Leib of Ozerov explains why Moses, like all the righteous, did not claim reward for his deeds. Moses recognized that all his spiritual attainments were a direct result of the abilities granted him by his Creator. Since those abilities were *themselves* an undeserved gift, Moses could not in good conscience claim reward for the good deeds they engendered! He therefore beseeched God to show him favor, and grant his request as one who is undeserving.

Alternatively, the righteous recognize that the opportunity to perform *mitzvos* is itself nothing more than a manifestation of God's kindness. For God gains nothing at all from our fulfillment of His commandments; he favors us with *mitzvos* only to enable us to earn reward. In the words of R' Chanania ben Akashia: רָצָה הַקָּבָּ"ה לְזַכּוֹת אֶת יִשְׂרָאֵל לְפִיכָךְ הִרְבָּה לָהֶם תּוֹרָה וּמִצְוֹת, *The Holy One, Blessed is He, wished to confer merit upon Israel; therefore He granted them Torah and* mitzvos *in abundance* (*Makkos* 23b). Ordinary people see God's precepts as a burden they must bear; they expect reward for hewing to His demands. The righteous, however, possess the wisdom to recognize *mitzvos* for what they truly are: God's kindness made manifest, a gift freely given. Understanding the true nature of God's commandments, they shrink from demanding reward for their righteous deeds.[3]

The above gives rise to another question: If there are indeed no grounds to expect recompense for good deeds, why does *Rashi* state that Moses *could* have relied on his deeds but chose not to?

R' Moshe Leib of Sassov explains: *Rashi* does not mean that Moses could have relied on the merit of his *past* deeds. Rather, he means that Moses could have relied on his *future* deeds. For Moses' entire purpose in seeking entry to the Land was so that he could fulfill the special *mitzvos* of *Eretz Yisrael.* Thus, Moses could have buttressed his request by explicitly stating his purpose. And why indeed did he not do so? Because Moses, in his humility, feared that he might fail to fulfill the *mitzvos* properly. He therefore made no mention of his purpose, but sought entry as one who is undeserving.

The *Mishnah* teaches (*Berachos* 30b): The pious ones of earlier times would tarry for one hour and only then pray, in order that they might direct their hearts toward their Father in Heaven.

R' Chaim of Sanz explains: This does not mean that they simply *waited* an hour before beginning to pray. Rather, that hour too was spent in prayer! During that preparatory hour, they would beseech God for the means of efficacious prayer, begging Him to grant them serenity, so that they would be able to properly direct their hearts and focus their minds at the moment of formal prayer.[4]

Those who claim reward on the basis of their deeds receive precisely that to which they are entitled, no more and no less. Their reward is represented by the smaller storehouses shown to Moses. Those, on the other hand, who approach God with a request that they be shown favor, who realize that all their deeds entitle them to nothing at all, receive gifts unrelated to their merits. Their storehouse is largest of all, for they do not demand a precise recompense for their deeds, and so are able to enjoy the full effect of God's limitless beneficence.

3. **No Entitlement.** The Midrash (*Devarim Rabbah* here) draws a lesson from our verse: The great teacher Moses, foremost of the prophets, most deserving of all men, approached God with nothing more than וָאֶתְחַנַּן, a request for undeserved favor. If it is so with Moses, it is surely so with lesser men. Thus the following rule: No creature has any claim whatsoever upon his Creator.

Maharal employs this rule to explain a teaching of the Sages. They taught that after the coming of the Messiah, all Temple offerings will be canceled, save for the thanksgiving-offering (the *korban todah*), which will remain forever. Why does the thanksgiving-offering enjoy this exalted status? *Maharal* explains that in the Messianic era we will receive reward for our deeds. We might foolishly imagine that we have earned all we receive and do not need to give thanks to God. The existence of the thanksgiving-offering will remind us of the truth — that we have no claim upon God, and that the reward He grants us is nothing other than an expression of His infinite kindness.

4. **Power of Prayer.** In times of strain and crisis, one often finds it difficult to muster the concentration needed for sincere, meaningful prayer. One manages only to mouth words devoid of meaning. Does God heed these prayers?

R' Yaakov David of Amshinov answers in the affirmative. He understands our verse's phrase *at that time* to be referring to difficult times, and explains that this phrase was actually included in Moses's prayer. Thus, Moses beseeched God that He find favor with the supplications of Jews *even* when the prayers are recited without proper concentration.

R' Chaim finds an allusion to this practice in these words of Moses: *I implored Hashem* refers to the hour of preparation; *at that time* refers to the actual moment of prayer; *to say* refers to the request for efficacious prayer. According to this understanding, the verse runs thus: "I implored Hashem" that "at that time" of prayer, I will be enabled "to say" to Him all that is in my heart. (The literal translation of לֵאמֹר is *to say*.)

אַתָּה הַחִלּוֹתָ לְהַרְאוֹת אֶת עַבְדְּךָ אֶת גָּדְלְךָ
You have begun to show Your servant Your greatness (ibid. 24).

We have explained that Moses asked God to grant him favor as one who is undeserving. He therefore opened his prayer with the phrase *You have begun to show Your servant*. With these words Moses declared that none of his attainments and abilities were his own; all derived from what God had shown him. He, Moses, was devoid of all merit; his request depended solely on God's attribute of mercy (*Toldos Adam*).[5]

The term *You have begun* is evidence of the great humility of Moses. Consider: The spiritual accomplishments of Moses were without parallel — it was he who brought the holy Torah down from the Heavens, he who reached an almost angelic level, he who the Talmud testifies was unequaled in righteous deeds (*Berachos* 32b). Yet Moses states that God has "begun" to show him His greatness. In Moses' view of himself, he was no more than a beginner (*Baal Shem Tov*).[6]

אֶעְבְּרָה נָּא וְאֶרְאֶה אֶת הָאָרֶץ הַטּוֹבָה
Let me now cross and see the good Land (ibid. 25).

R' Menachem Mendel of Kotzk explains that the phrase "the *good* Land" signifies Moses's prayer that God aid him to perceive the Land in a positive light. Moses thereby drew a contrast between himself and the spies, who set out intending to speak ill of *Eretz Yisrael*.

R' Moshe David of Tchortkov yearned all of his life to emigrate to *Eretz Yisrael*, but Providence willed otherwise. On one occasion, the *chassidim* standing outside his door heard him pacing to and fro, and speaking in an argumentative, almost bitter tone: "Master of the world! Why do You not allow me to settle in *Eretz Yisrael*? I give You my word that I will perceive nothing unfavorable in the Land, nor will I, God forbid, speak against it or its beauty. Please allow me a chance to set foot on its holy soil!"

A verse in *Psalms* (128:5) blesses those who walk in God's ways: *May Hashem bless you from Zion and may you gaze upon the goodness of Jerusalem. R' Yosef Chaim Sonnenfeld*, Rav of Jerusalem, saw in this verse an allusion to the importance of viewing *Eretz Yisrael* in a positive light. Even if one discovers negative aspects to dwelling in Jerusalem, still, one should make every effort to focus on the goodness of the Holy City rather than on its blemishes and flaws.[7]

---

5. **Initial Spark.** It is a tenet of Jewish belief that man has free will to choose whether or not to serve God, and that he receives reward or punishment based on his choice. Nevertheless, one's initial spiritual awakening is due not to one's own efforts but to Divine inspiration, communicated through the soul — the Divine spark that resides in man. This is intimated in the phrase *You have **begun** to show Your servant*. Moses recognized that the genesis, the *beginning,* of his spiritual growth sprang from Divine inspiration (*Sfas Emes*).

6. **Only Just Begun.** On Simchas Torah, as soon as we complete the Book of Deuteronomy we immediately begin again with the Book of Genesis. This tells us that our work is never really complete — no matter what we accomplish in Torah, we have only just begun.

7. **Blind to Beauty.** A wealthy European Jew returned from a journey to the Holy Land. He came to visit with *R' Yisrael of Rizhin*. The Rebbe asked, "How did you find the Land? Did you appreciate its beauty?" The man muttered under his breath, "Better don't ask."

The Rizhiner replied with a story: There was a wealthy man who was blessed with numerous daughters. God showed him kindness and he was successful in marrying them off to prestigious, accomplished Torah scholars; all except his youngest daughter. For her his best efforts were to no avail; he simply could not find her a suitable husband. After much fruitless searching, he was forced to settle on a simple, unlettered tailor. As the wedding approached, he summoned the bride to instruct her in various matters, one of which was the importance of always

Background

Beginning with verse 4:1, Moses commences to review some commandments and to teach others that had not been set down in the Torah previously.

לֹא תֹסִפוּ עַל הַדָּבָר אֲשֶׁר אָנֹכִי
מְצַוֶּה אֶתְכֶם וְלֹא תִגְרְעוּ מִמֶּנּוּ
You shall not add to the word that I command you, nor shall you subtract from it (4:2).

This warning to neither add nor subtract from the Torah appears again in a later verse, which states (*Deuteronomy* 13:1): אֵת כָּל הַדָּבָר אֲשֶׁר אָנֹכִי מְצַוֶּה אֶתְכֶם אֹתוֹ תִשְׁמְרוּ לַעֲשׂוֹת לֹא תֹסֵף עָלָיו וְלֹא תִגְרַע מִמֶּנּוּ, *The entire word that I command you, that you shall observe to do; you shall not add to it and you shall not subtract from it.*

The *Vilna Gaon* notes a difference between the two prohibitions: In our verse, the Torah speaks in the plural form (לֹא תֹסִפוּ, וְלֹא תִגְרְעוּ). In the later verse, the command is expressed in the singular form (לֹא תֹסֵף, וְלֹא תִגְרַע).

The *Vilna Gaon* explains that each verse refers to a different form of the prohibition. The prohibition of our verse is to add new *mitzvos* to the 613 Biblical commandments. [This does not apply to Rabbinic enactments, which are clearly permissi-

ble and even *desirable,* so long as they are clearly understood to be of Rabbinic origin. Rather, the prohibition forbids adding a new obligation and labeling it a *Scriptural* commandment — see *Ramban* 4:2.] Since the process of adding new obligations is in the province of the Sanhedrin (who are the source of new *Rabbinic mitzvos*), the Torah frames this prohibition in the plural. The later verse, however, prohibits one to tamper with the number of elements in a given mitzvah (e.g. to create *tefillin* containing three or five scrolls rather than four). This sort of alteration might be attempted by *any* individual; therefore, the Torah expresses this prohibition in the singular form.

The lesson of the prohibition of our verse applies not only with regard to the manner in which the commandments are physically performed, but also with regard to our estimation of the commandments. If a law is of lesser severity, we may not inflate its importance. Conversely, a law that is of greater severity, must not be treated more lightly than it deserves to be treated. For example, one must recognize that a Biblical law possesses greater importance than a Rabbinic law. (At the same time, one must not make light of Rabbinic enactments, whose transgression constitutes a serious offense.) Similarly, one may not view customs and stringencies as the equivalent of actual Biblical or Rabbinic laws (*Chasam Sofer*).[8], [9]

The *Chafetz Chaim* writes that one who tampers

---

presenting an attractive appearance before her husband. The girl responded bitterly, "I understand why my sisters must adorn themselves for their husbands. They are married to refined, scholarly men! But I, who will be married to a simple tailor? For this fellow I am good enough just as I am."

Concluded the Rizhiner, "Our Holy Land displays its charm and beauty only for those refined enough to appreciate it; to simpletons the Land shows nothing. They look, but perceive nothing!"

8. **Dangerously Overcautious.** One danger inherent in inflating the severity of a given law is that it could cause people to be lax when they should act with stringency.

For example, when Adam relayed to Eve the prohibition against eating from the Tree of Knowledge, he added something that God had not said, that even *touching* the tree would result in death. Adam intended thereby to distance her from sin, but the serpent turned this against him by pushing Eve against the tree and then saying to her, "Just as you did not die when you touched the tree, so too will you not die when you eat from it." Because Adam did not clearly distinguish between the original law and the added stringency, this argument convinced Eve to both partake of the fruit and to feed it to Adam as well. Thus, it was Adam's inflation of God's law that led to its violation (see *Avos D'Rabbi Nosson* 1:5).

9. **Skewed Perspective**

Once, at a gathering of *roshei yeshivah* and *rabbanim,* the *Chafetz Chaim* requested of all present that they sign a statement affirming their commitment to adhere to the laws of *lashon hara* (slander and gossip). The statement declared that the prohibition against speaking *lashon hara* is every bit as severe as the prohibition against eating the meat of a pig. The Chafetz Chaim hoped that this would impress upon people the severity of *lashon hara.*

with the Torah, even if his intentions are good, is like a person who enters a store, grabs merchandise off the shelf and throws it into the river. The man may or may not be deranged; one thing, however, is certain: he is *not* the owner of the store.

A person who is prepared to discard portions of the holy Torah demonstrates that the merchandise (i.e., the Torah) is not his own.[10]

וְאַתֶּם הַדְּבֵקִים בַּה' אֱלֹקֵיכֶם חַיִּים כֻּלְּכֶם הַיּוֹם
But you who cleave to Hashem, your God — you are all alive today (4:4).

Those who cleave to God are connected to the source of all life; thus, the verse describes them as "alive." But what does the verse mean when it describes them as being alive "today"? One who cleaves to God should merit not only the temporary, ephemeral life of "today," but the eternal life of the World to Come!

The answer might lie in a ruling of the *Shulchan Aruch* (*Yoreh Deah* 58:7) concerning a bird that crashed into the water. If the bird can swim a short distance against the current, it is deemed entirely healthy and is therefore kosher. If, however, the bird cannot swim against the current, it is suspect of having suffered physical damage that renders it unkosher as a *treifah*. The condition of *treifah* is regarded under halachah as denoting a deficiency in the life force of the affected creature (see *Chullin*

42a); in effect, then, a bird too damaged to swim upstream has entered the first stages of death.

This idea can be applied in a homiletic sense to human beings. There are many who ignore the will of God, yet seem to be more fully alive than those who follow God's path. It is difficult to imagine that those who are disconnected from the Source of all life can possibly enjoy a greater vitality than those who are connected to it. The answer is that these people are simply riding a downstream current; their apparent vitality is an illusion; in reality, they have entered the first stage of spiritual, and thus physical, death. True life is granted only to those who possess the fortitude to swim against the prevailing currents of moral looseness and cleave to God.

The verse expresses this idea with the word "today." Even today, in this world, only those who cleave to God are truly alive (*R' Aharon Bakst*).[11]

כִּי מִי גוֹי גָּדוֹל אֲשֶׁר לוֹ אֱלֹקִים קְרֹבִים אֵלָיו כַּה' אֱלֹקֵינוּ בְּכָל קָרְאֵנוּ אֵלָיו
For which is a great nation that has a God Who is close to it, as is Hashem, our God, whenever we call to Him (ibid. 7).

The Talmud in Tractate *Berachos* quotes Bar Kappara: What is a short verse upon which all the fundamentals of the Torah depend? בְּכָל דְּרָכֶיךָ, *In all your ways you must* דָעֵהוּ וְהוּא יְיַשֵּׁר אֹרְחֹתֶיךָ

R' Chaim Ozer Grodzensky, Rav of Vilna, shocked the assemblage by objecting to the Chafetz Chaim's initiative. R' Chaim Ozer explained, "The declaration will not cause Jews to view *lashon hara* as severely as eating pork. At best, all it will accomplish is that people will view the sin of eating pork as lightly as they do *lashon hara!*"

10. **Cutting Values Down to Size.** *R' Ezriel Hildesheimer* of Germany was at the forefront of the battle against Reform Judaism. A proponent of the Reform movement once argued to R' Ezriel that adapting the Torah to comtemporary mores would make Torah observance attractive for people who presently find it too difficult.

R' Ezriel countered by citing our verse: *You shall not add to the word that I command you, nor shall you subtract from it, to observe the commandments of Hashem, your God.* Even if one's purpose is enable people "to observe the commandments of Hashem, your God," it is *still* forbidden to add to or subtract from the word of God!

The mind-set of those who seek to redefine Torah to fit their own preconceptions is captured by the story of a woman who crafted a velvet cover for the Torah scroll. The Rabbi complimented her on its beauty, but was then obliged to inform her that the cover was too small for the scroll. The woman answered, "It's no problem! Just cut a few pieces of parchment from the scroll and the cover will fit perfectly!"

11. **Forever, for Everyone.** A connection to God is not something reserved for the World to Come; it is for those who cleave to Him now, while they are חַיִּים, alive. This bond is not limited to certain individuals; it need not be deferred for old age. As the verse states, it is available to all of us *today!* (*R' Yeshaya Mushkat of Praga*).

know Him and He will straighten your paths (Proverbs 3:6). Rambam interprets this to mean that all one's activities must be performed for the sake of Heaven. Thus, when one eats, sleeps, transacts business, or engages in any other mundane act, he must not merely intend his physical pleasure, but must act in the knowledge that through the performance of this action he will be better able to serve his Creator (see *Rambam, Deios 3:2,3; Shemoneh Perakim 5*).[12]

Rabbeinu Yonah (Proverbs ad loc.) offers a novel interpretation of this teaching. *In all your ways you must know Him* teaches that in *all* a person's endeavors, even the most inconsequential, one must "know God" through prayer. If you pray to God *He will straighten your paths* and bless your work with success.

We sometimes imagine that prayer is reserved for matters of great import, be they spritual or worldly. Rabbeinu Yonah tells us otherwise — that God expects us to pray for success even in simple, everyday matters. It is for this reason that our verse describes Israel as a nation whose God is close *whenever we call to Him.* [13]

רַק הִשָּׁמֶר לְךָ וּשְׁמֹר נַפְשְׁךָ מְאֹד פֶּן תִּשְׁכַּח אֶת הַדְּבָרִים אֲשֶׁר רָאוּ עֵינֶיךָ וּפֶן יָסוּרוּ מִלְּבָבְךָ

Only beware for yourself and beware greatly for your soul lest you forget the things that your eyes have beheld and lest you remove them from your heart (ibid. 9).

The verse distinguishes between body and soul (*yourself; your soul*), using the term "only beware" for the former and the term "beware greatly" for the latter. The *Chozeh of Lublin* explains that although one must see to the needs of both body and soul, one must not lavish equal attention on both. This explains the distinction drawn in our verse. The word "only" (רַק) signifies limitation. One is expected to limit his attention to physical needs while remaining "greatly" aware of the needs of his soul.[14]

However, the *Baal Shem Tov* takes a different view of the verse. He explains that when one's body becomes weak, one's soul experiences a proportionate weakening. The verse accordingly tells us that by tending to the needs of his body

---

12. **Holy Humor.** Any facet of life can serve as a means of honoring God. For example, *Rambam (Shemoneh Perakim 5)* states that art and humor can be employed to invigorate those who are weary from the strain of studying Torah.

13. **Praying for Faith.** Constant prayer can serve as a means to acquire a deeply felt, tangible faith in God.

The *Chazon Ish* would illustrate this sort of faith with an incident cited in Tractate *Berachos* (5b). R' Huna owned 400 barrels of wine. They spoiled and became vinegar. His colleagues advised him to scrutinize his behavior, as God does not punish without cause. They then identified an area in which R' Huna might have transgressed. He rectified the matter and his losses were reversed, either by the vinegar reverting to wine, or by the price of vinegar rising to equal that of wine.

When relating this incident, Chazon Ish would comment, "If this would happen to us, we would seek a rational, scientific explanation. The Sages, however, possessed a real, tangible faith. When something would go wrong in their lives, they would immediately seek a spiritual cause." The Chazon Ish would suggest, "If you wish to acquire a vibrant faith, pray to God for all your needs. If you require a new pair of shoes, say to God: 'Master of the universe. See how my old shoes are torn. Please provide me with money to replace them.' By doing this, you will transform your faith in God from a mere idea into a living, vibrant fact."

14. **Over the Abyss.** A tightrope walker once came to the town of Krasne. He proposed to walk upon a wire stretched across the river for the sum of 100 rubles. A large crowd gathered, including *R' Chaim of Krasne*, a close disciple of the *Baal Shem Tov*. R' Chaim's students noticed that their teacher seemed to be entranced by the daring fellow, following his progress closely until he reached the far side of the river. When they inquired as to his interest, he replied, "The tightrope walker endangered himself for a mere 100 rubles. Yet, as he made his way across, he never gave the money a thought, lest the distraction cause him to lose his focus and plummet from the thin rope. Instead, he bent all his mental resources to a single purpose: that he not stray so much as a single centimeter to the right or to the left.

"This fellow mustered incredible concentration to ensure his physical survival. How much more so must we labor to preserve our spiritual lives, to ensure that we do not fall from the thin rope we traverse into the raging rivers of temptation and desire, where our eternal souls would be lost and our future hopes drowned!"

As the verse states: *Beware for yourself* but beware **greatly** *for your soul.*

(beware for yourself), one fulfills the requirement to beware greatly for his soul.[15]

פֶּן תִּשְׁכַּח אֶת הַדְּבָרִים אֲשֶׁר רָאוּ עֵינֶיךָ וּפֶן יָסוּרוּ מִלְּבָבְךָ כָּל יְמֵי חַיֶּיךָ וְהוֹדַעְתָּם לְבָנֶיךָ

Lest you forget the things that your eyes have beheld and lest you remove them from your heart all the days of your life — you shall make them known to your children (ibid.).

The revelation at Sinai exposed the Jewish people to the reality of a living God. This verse commands us to do all that is within our power to keep the memory of that experience fresh and relevant.

Chidushei HaRim explains that we must view our Torah learning as something fundamental to life, without which we cannot survive. A disciple once asked the Chidushei HaRim's advice on how to keep from forgetting his Torah studies. The Rebbe replied, "Did you ever forget how to eat? Did you ever insert a forkful of food into your ear instead of your mouth? Of course not! And why not? Because your life *depends* upon food. If you would realize that Torah actually keeps you alive, you would never forget a single word. As King David wrote in *Psalms* (119:93): לְעוֹלָם לֹא אֶשְׁכַּח פִּקּוּדֶיךָ כִּי בָם חִיִּיתָנִי, *I will never forget Your commands, for through them You have given me life.*

R' Yehoshua of Kutna understands this verse to

be warning a person against ignoring his own spiritual growth in order to provide for the *chinuch* of his children. He draws this idea from the verse in the following manner: *Only beware for **yourself** and greatly beware for **your** soul ... lest you remove them from **your** heart and make them known* (only) *to your children.*

וְנִשְׁמַרְתֶּם מְאֹד לְנַפְשֹׁתֵיכֶם

And you shall beware greatly for your souls (ibid. 15).

The Talmud teaches (*Berachos* 32b) that this verse (as well as v. 9) commands us to take utmost care to safeguard our bodies and maintain our physical well-being.

Although the soul is the primary element in the composite being that is man, one must still pay heed to the needs of the body. The *Chafetz Chaim* offers the example of a wagoner and his horse. The wagoner pays careful heed to the welfare of his horse, for his horse is the key to his livelihood. Similarly, it is only through the medium of the body that the soul can fulfill its earthly purpose; therefore, a person must be careful not to endanger or weaken his body.[16]

People are often careless about their health, and will disregard even a doctor's explicit instructions with regard to diet or medication. It is almost a rule: That which is most injurious to a person is

---

15. **Robust Rabbi.** The *Chafetz Chaim* was once told that a certain *rosh yeshivah* was refraining from eating meat during the week in order to save money, which he would then use to purchase food for the students in the yeshivah. The Sage of Radin gently rebuked the man: "A *rosh yeshivah* has many obligations. Foremost among them, however, is to ensure that his students have a healthy *rosh yeshivah*."

16. **Selling Life Cheaply.** "In Jewish thought, love of life is more than a mere desire to enjoy the fruits of this world. We believe that a person's instinct for self-preservation is rooted in the realization that each moment of life represents a unique opportunity to express the greatness of God.

"It follows that one's appreciation of life is in direct proportion to his connection to the Divine. One devoid of spirituality cannot properly value life; thus we find people who place themselves in mortal danger for the most negligible of reasons (e.g. mountain climbers). The world applauds them for their courage, but we are not misled; their actions represent nothing more than a devaluing of life, rooted in a lack of connection to God.

"Because religious Jews are generally not thrill-seekers, some deride us as cowards. They are not privy to what we know so well: that the very purpose of life is the opportunity it provides for spiritual growth. Our awareness of this purpose develops in us a corresponding awareness of the preciousness of life, and a corresponding reluctance to spend it cheaply. Our reverence is reserved not for those who end their lives in a blaze of glory, but for those who perform the far more difficult task of dedicating each moment of a long life to proclaiming the glory of God" (*Michtav MeEliyahu*).

[Of course, there are times when a Jew must give his life for the sake of Heaven. However, a Jew does not *seek* opportunities to die in sanctification of God's Name. Living to sanctify His Name is far more meaningful — and challenging — than dying to sanctify His Name.]

precisely that which he most wishes to consume!

A person once asked *R' Yisrael Salanter* to explain this phenomenon. R' Yisrael answered that one who is ill is exempt from all *mitzvos* that will adversely affect his health. However, no matter how ill one might be, he must still perform the mitzvah of our verse — *And you shall beware greatly for your souls.* The evil inclination wishes to cause the patient to transgress even this commandment; he therefore exerts himself to introduce into the person an overwhelming desire for those things that are most detrimental to his health.

**וְרָאִיתָ אֶת הַשֶּׁמֶשׁ וְאֶת הַיָּרֵחַ
וְאֶת הַכּוֹכָבִים . . . וְנִדַּחְתָּ וְהִשְׁתַּחֲוִיתָ לָהֶם**
And you will see the sun and the moon and the stars . . . and you will be drawn astray and you will bow to them (ibid. 19).

Alshich asks: What is wrong with bowing to the sun, moon and stars? Does the honor we pay to His servants not honor God Himself? (see *Rambam, Hilchos Avodah Zarah* 1:1-3).

He answers that while it may well honor God when His servants are honored, it degrades Him when He Himself is compelled to bow before them.

Man is created in the image of God. Therefore, when man worships God's creations, he is, in a sense, lowering the Almighty Himself before His own creations. Can there be a greater dishonor to the Creator than to be made subordinate to the work of His own hands?

**הִשָּׁמְרוּ לָכֶם פֶּן תִּשְׁכְּחוּ אֶת בְּרִית
ה' אֱלֹקֵיכֶם אֲשֶׁר כָּרַת עִמָּכֶם וַעֲשִׂיתֶם
לָכֶם פֶּסֶל תְּמוּנַת כֹּל אֲשֶׁר צִוְּךָ ה' אֱלֹקֶיךָ**
Beware for yourselves lest you forget the covenant of Hashem, your God, that He has sealed with you, and you make for yourselves a graven image, a likeness of any thing, as Hashem your God has commanded you (ibid. 23).

Rashi explains that the phrase *as Hashem, your God, has commanded you* obviously does not refer to the making of a graven image, for God certainly does not wish us to create such things! Rather, this phrase refers to God's command *not* to make graven images (see *Gur Aryeh*). According to *Rashi's* understanding, the essence of the phrase — that we are not to create these images — is implicit rather than explicit.

But *R' Menachem Mendel of Kotzk* proposes a homiletic interpretation that retains the verse's explicit meaning. When the verse states *Beware for yourselves lest you forget the covenant of Hashem, your God,* it is referring to those who perform *mitzvos* automatically, without the full engagement of their intellect and emotions. One who performs a mitzvah in this manner makes of the mitzvah a lifeless image. It *looks* like the genuine article, but is in truth a mere facsimile. The verse warns against this tendency with the phrase, *and you make for yourselves a graven image.*

Then, said the Kotzker, there are others who, while they do indeed appear to be intellectually and emotionally involved in God's commandments, are in reality only imitating the service that they see performed by others. They themselves, however, are not deeply invested in *mitzvos*. One who performs a mitzvah in this manner is not expressing his own personality; he is merely projecting an image, a likeness, of the personality of another. The verse alludes to this malady with the words *a likeness of any thing.* [17]

These people cannot be said to be shirking their duties; they do precisely *as Hashem, your God, has commanded you.* Nevertheless, because they perform His commandments automatically, without fire and spirit, without investing heavily of themselves in their actions, they are considered to have forgotten "the covenant of Hashem," and to have made for themselves "a graven image, a likeness of any thing."

Background

This passage details one of our most common challenges — namely, the difficulty of maintaining growth and fending off lethargy of the

---

17. **Being Yourself.** The *Kotzker* expressed this thought in a famous epigram: "If I am who I am because of who I am, and you are who you are because of who you are, then I am myself and you are yourself. But if I am who I am because of who you are, and you are who you are because of who I am, then I am not myself, and you are not yourself."

spirit. The Torah warns Israel that the generations that did not personally experience the Exodus from Egypt and the Wilderness sojourn will be in danger of slowly slipping into the pagan culture of the Canaanites and being exiled from the Land. The following verse assures Israel that even while in exile, the Jews will eventually return to God.

וּבִקַּשְׁתֶּם מִשָּׁם אֶת ה' אֱלֹקֶיךָ וּמָצָאתָ
כִּי תִדְרְשֶׁנּוּ בְּכָל לְבָבְךָ וּבְכָל נַפְשֶׁךָ

From there you will seek Hashem, your God, and you will find Him, if you search for Him with all your heart and with all your soul (ibid. 29).

Notwithstanding the physical and spiritual difficulties of exile, we are comforted by the knowledge that low as we may fall, we can find our way back to God if we seek Him truly.[18]

Why must we search with all our heart and all our soul? Because in the darkness of exile, God hides His face from us. He yearns to draw us close, but we must first show Him that we too desire to be close to Him. This can be accomplished only with heartfelt, soulful yearning. Thus, we must search for Him with all our heart and all our soul (*Baal Shem Tov*).[19]

R' Simchah Bunim of P'shis'cha sees a different message in this verse. Many of us are in search of meaning and yearn to be close to the Creator; however, we assume that He is to be found in distant places, among strangers. The verse tells us otherwise: *you will seek Hashem, your God, and you will find Him* בְּכָל לְבָבְךָ וּבְכָל נַפְשֶׁךָ, **within** your entire heart and **within** your entire soul. (The Hebrew prefix בְּ translates also as "within.") Although friends and mentors doubtless help one along the path, God is ultimately to be found only within one's own self.[20]

---

18. **Uphill Battle.** *R' Yisrael Salanter,* founder of the Mussar movement, spent most of his life working toward the strengthening of Torah Judaism in Russia and Lithuania. His later years, however, he spent in France and Germany, in an effort to ignite a renaissance of Torah in those countries. Someone once inquired as to his change in focus. He answered, "When a wagon is rolling downhill, it is almost impossible to halt its downward progress and push it back uphill. Only when it stops moving can one attempt to return it to its place. Jewish commitment in Russia and Lithuania is on a downward trend. I do not have the strength in my old age to fight an uphill battle. By contrast, in France and Germany traditional Judaism has hit rock bottom. It is now time to begin pushing the wagon back up the hill."

19. **Painful Isolation.** The young son of *R' Baruch of Medziboz* once came into the house weeping. R' Baruch asked, "My son, why do you weep?" The boy answered, "I was playing hide-and-seek with my friends, and I hid but nobody came looking for me." R' Baruch began to weep as well, "Imagine how God must feel. He too hides and waits for us to find Him, yet we do not bother to look for Him."

20. **Seeking Within.** In the city of Cracow there is a synagogue known as "R' Yekel's Shul." *R' Yekel* was a simple, pious baker who, despite years of toil, was mired in the most abject poverty. R' Yekel was blessed with three daughters; however, because of his inability to provide a dowry, none of them had been successful in finding a husband. One night R' Yekel dreamed that he was standing in Prague, beside the Vlatava River, before a bridge that crossed to the royal palace. In the dream he heard a voice say that an enormous treasure was buried beneath the bridge.

In the morning, Yekel laughed at the fantastic dream, imagining it to be the product of his constant obsession with money. He dismissed the matter from his mind. But the next night the dream was repeated, and again on the third night, whereupon R' Yekel decided to travel to Prague. It was a long, weary journey, but when he arrived before the royal palace, the scene was precisely as it had appeared in his dreams!

A soldier stood guard at the bridge and eyed Yekel with suspicion. Yekel skulked beneath the bridge, wondering how he might dig without attracting unwelcome attention. Suddenly, the soldier was there. "Jew! What are you doing here? Answer or I'll kill you immediately!" Yekel, too tired and frightened to dissemble, related his dream to the guard. The guard began laughing. "Stupid Jew! Why do you take dreams seriously? I too have such dreams. For months I have dreamed of a treasure buried beneath the oven of a baker in Cracow named Yekel. Do you think I will travel to Cracow and break ovens until I find the right Yekel? Forget your foolish dream!"

Yekel returned to Cracow, and lo and behold, beneath his oven lay the treasure! The money enabled him to marry off his daughters, and he, to express his gratitude to Hashem, built a synagogue that became known as "R' Yekel's Shul."

R' Simchah Bunim of P'shis'cha was fond of repeating this story. Whenever a new disciple would join his group, he would tell him, "Remember R' Yekel!" His point was that the treasure one seeks is usually found in one's own

בַּצַּר לְךָ וּמְצָאוּךָ כֹּל הַדְּבָרִים הָאֵלֶּה בְּאַחֲרִית הַיָּמִים וְשַׁבְתָּ עַד ה' אֱלֹקֶיךָ וְשָׁמַעְתָּ בְּקֹלוֹ

When you are in distress and all these things have befallen you at the End of Days, you will then return unto Hashem, your God, and you will hearken to His voice (ibid. 30).

The Torah informs us that we will not be redeemed before experiencing all the punishments of which Moses speaks. The *Dubno Maggid* interprets the verse as saying that all these events will take place in a single period immediately preceding the redemption. He understands this as a message of comfort, and offers the following parable:

A peddler of fruits and vegetables will store each type of produce in a separate sack. When he is done for the day, he tosses all the leftovers into one big sack, throws it over his shoulder and carries it home. One who observes him carrying the one sack of assorted produce can be certain that his working day is over and he is heading home. So too

Israel in exile: When **all** *these things have befallen us*, we will know that the *End of Days* has come and that we will soon be returning home. As the verse states: *you will then return unto Hashem, Your God*.

The Midrash teaches that one who repents his sins is regarded as having returned to Jerusalem and rebuilt the Temple.

The *Maharal of Prague* explains: Man is created as a fleshly embodiment of the sanctity that characterizes the Holy Temple: Just as the Temple contained the Divine Presence, so too is the Divine Presence contained within the soul of man. Thus, man's sin is tantamount to the destruction of the Temple; as the pagans defiled the Temple of God, so has he defiled the temple of his soul. It follows that when man repents his sins, and restores the purity of his own temple, his act is tantamount to the rebuilding of the Holy Temple in Jerusalem.

self. One who imagines that by traveling to a new location he will find God is ignorant of the true location of the treasure.

Background

Moses continues to prepare his beloved nation for their imminent entry into the Land of Israel. He reemphasizes that their success, as well as God's fulfillment of His promises to their forefathers, are contingent upon their unswerving loyalty to Him. Moses encourages the people to realize that God will help them conquer the current inhabitants of the land and reminds Israel of the terrible consequences of practicing idolatry.

וְהָיָה עֵקֶב תִּשְׁמְעוּן אֵת הַמִּשְׁפָּטִים הָאֵלֶּה . . .
This shall be your reward when you hearken to these ordinances . . . (7:12).

According to *Rashi,* the word עֵקֶב, literally *heel,* alludes to those *mitzvos* that people generally "step on" and regard as relatively unimportant. By hearkening to even these seemingly minor commandments, we are assured that God will reward us by honoring His *covenant and kindness,* and will grant us prosperity.

Why is material success contingent upon hearkening to the relatively unimportant commandments?

Avnei Nezer sees an answer in a comment found in *Rabbeinu Yonah's* commentary to Tractate *Berachos.* Rabbeinu Yonah explains why the minimum cost of an *asham*-offering is far greater than that of a regular *chatas*-(sin) offering. The reason is that a *chatas* is brought when one is sure that he committed a sin. When one has no doubts as to his guilt, it is easy to repent. The *asham,* however, deals with instances of doubt, where the penitent is not *sure* that he has committed a sin. One who offers an *asham* need not face up to his deed. He can rationalize to himself that perhaps what he did was not really a sin. He must therefore spend more on his offering to impress upon himself the fact that he really is a sinner and needs to repent.

There can be no genuine repentance unless one truly sees his action as sin; hence, it is far more difficult to repent "lenient" sins than severe ones. One who hearkens even to "uninportant" commandments never runs the risk of being unable to repent. For this God rewards him richly.

Alternatively, the reason God grants material reward for keeping the lenient *mitzvos* is that this observance demonstrates one's high regard for *mitzvos.* Consider: Material success can never be considered a true reward for *mitzvos,* for "there is no reward for *mitzvos* in this world." Rather, the reward is provided so that a person will not lack the resources he needs to fulfill his responsibilities to God (*Rambam, Hilchos Teshuvah* 9:1).

When a person strains himself to fulfill every detail of the Torah, including those which seem to be of secondary importance, he indicates that each and every opportunity to serve God is precious to him. God responds to such a person by providing him with the wherewithal to fulfill His will, unencumbered by financial worries (*Imrei Shefer*).[1]

Zekan Aharon submits that *Rashi* refers to a period in which *mitzvos* are generally trampled upon. In such an era, any Jew who rejects the lure of secular society and steadfastly observes the Torah will be greatly rewarded.[2]

R' Moshe Leib of Sassov offers a homiletic interpretation of this verse. Before a person takes a step in life, he must listen carefully to his heart, to be sure that his desire coincides with God's will. Thus, the Sassover renders the verse as follows: וְהָיָה עֵקֶב, *And it shall be that when your heel* [is ready to take a step], תִּשְׁמְעוּן, *you must listen* [carefully to your heart, to ensure that you are in consonance with] אֵת הַמִּשְׁפָּטִים הָאֵלֶּה, *these ordinances.*

A story from the childhood of the *Tzemach Tzedek of Lubavitch* presents a variation on this approach. When he began to study *Chumash* as a little boy, his grandfather, the famed *Baal HaTanya*, asked him to explain the verse עֵקֶב אֲשֶׁר שָׁמַע אַבְרָהָם בְּקֹלִי (literally, *Because Abraham obeyed My voice* — *Genesis* 26:5). The young boy replied, "It means that Abraham heard [and was responsive to] the voice of God even down to his עֵקֶב, *his heel.*" The *Baal HaTanya* was pleased with his grandson's answer. "Yes," he said, "this is what the Torah means. Man must hear the word of God all the way down to his heels and act upon what he has heard."[3]

R' Simchah Bunim of P'shis'cha renders עֵקֶב as *end* (because the heel is the end of the body). He offers a lovely parable to elucidate his understanding of the verse.

A child did not wish to apply himself to his studies. His father reasoned with him, "If you do not study, I will spank you and you will be compelled to study. Why not begin studying now, instead of receiving punishment later?"

1. **Shoring Up Fences.** Sometimes transgressing a light mitzvah is worse than transgressing a stringent Biblical prohibition. For example, one who transgresses a Rabbinic enactment because he views it as something that need not be taken seriously demonstrates that he does not fear Heaven. By contrast, one who violates a Torah prohibition as a result of uncontrollable passion does not display a lack of fear of Heaven. It is for this reason, says *Rabbeinu Yonah* (*Shaarei Teshuvah* 3:5), that the Talmud teaches that one who transgresses the words of the Sages deserves death (*Berachos* 4b), for his act demonstrates that he does not fear God. One with a careless attitude is much worse than one who in a moment of weakness yields to desire.

God rewards us when we are tenacious in areas that require us to *choose* to do the right thing. When we are resourceful in showing spiritual fortitude and fear of Heaven, God responds with tremendous reward (*R' Meir Chodosh*).

2. **Loyal unto Death.** In order to accurately define the unique educational mission of our generation we would do well to cite the parable related by the holy *Maggid of Kozhnitz*.

A king was in low spirits because of a mass rebellion among his subjects. A small group of citizens arose and pledged allegiance to the king, swearing to remain loyal to their last drop of blood. Their oath was a source of great comfort and joy for the king. Had this occurred in ordinary times, the allegiance of so small a group would not have meant so much to the king. Now, however, when all others were engaged in open rebellion, the oath of the small group was invaluable. It served to invigorate the flagging spirit of the king, and to bolster his resolve to save his kingdom.

We, in our times, must assume a similar role. If we see that the vast majority of people have rebelled against the King of kings, we must make a firm intellectual and emotional commitment to be His small but loyal cadre. We will be the Levites, the royal legion who swears its allegiance to Him until our very last drop of blood.

Our job is not to quell the rebellion nor to fight the rebels, but to strengthen the ranks of our inner circle and to ensure that we remain strong and vigorous, without the slightest hint of alien influence.

We must infuse the hearts of our young with this feeling. We must foster within them the deep realization that they are the legion of the King, the small group that remains loyal. Only in this fashion will we succeed in insulating our youth from the poisonous atmosphere of the surrounding culture (*Nesivos Shalom* — *Nesivei Chinuch*).

3. **Automatic Pilot.** King David was a person in whom God's will was so deeply ingrained that his heels *instinctively* walked in His ways. The Midrash (*Vayikra Rabbah* 35:1) cites his words, *I pondered my ways and my legs returned me to Your statutes* (*Psalms* 119:59). He said to God, "Every day I planned to go to different sites or places of interest, yet, my legs automatically took me to synagogues and study halls. Although drawn by my evil inclination to frequent places of [permissible] pleasures, Your spirit is so deeply imbedded in my subconscious that I cannot bring myself to go anywhere besides those places where Your Presence is to be found."

Likewise, Moses said to his beloved flock, "In the end, God will compel you to obey His *mitzvos*. Why wait to be punished for insubordination and only then respond positively? Do it now, before coercion becomes necessary."

The word וְהָיָה, *This shall be,* is expounded by the Sages as an expression of joy, while the word עֵקֶב can be interpreted as a reference to the pre-Messianic era (עִקְבְתָא דִמְשִׁיחָא). Thus, the verse might be explained in the following manner: וְהָיָה, *It will cause great joy* in Heaven עֵקֶב, if *in the pre-Messianic era* תִּשְׁמְעוּן אֵת הַמִּשְׁפָּטִים הָאֵלֶּה, *you will hearken to the mitzvos and the voice of Hashem* (*Orach L'Chaim*).

Lev Same'ach explains that this verse calls our attention to the fact that joy is the key to fulfilling the Torah. Joy in serving God safeguards one's commitment to *mitzvos*. Just as money must be guarded by placing it underground, so too must one's commitment to *mitzvos* be guarded by joyfulness.

וּבֵרַךְ פְּרִי בִטְנֶךָ
He will bless the fruit of your womb (ibid. 13).

The expression *He will bless* occurs twice in the Torah; here and in *Exodus* (23:25), which states: *You shall worship Hashem, your God, and He shall bless your bread and your water.*

These two blessings are intertwined, for the One Who provides the blessing of children is also the One Who provides the means to provide for them (*Ohr Pnei Moshe*).

A folk tale tells of a farmer who bought a new chicken and put it into the coop. He heard two "veterans" talking. One said to the other, "*Oi vey*! The farmer put a new rooster in here; he will eat some of our food and we won't have enough." Retorted his counterpart, "Fool! You can be sure that if the farmer brought a newcomer he will provide enough food for him. He certainly doesn't want any of us to die of hunger."

When God grants us a child, He is like the farmer who put another "chicken" into his henhouse. The child is His to feed and He can be trusted to provide for all that are in His care.[4]

She'aris Menachem suggests a different connection between the two identical phrases. The purpose of financial prosperity is to ensure that our children, the fruit of the womb, will be able to spend their time in pursuit of God's spiritual blessing. Money allows us to provide for our children so that they will be able to invest their energies toward becoming authentic Torah scholars and vibrant Jews.

---

4. **Bigger Is Better.** R' Yonason Rosenblum, in a rebuttal of those who criticize the large size of many religious families, writes:

Parenting a large family obviously presents challenges that a smaller family does not. But *charedi* children grow up with the knowledge that they are an incalculable blessing in their parents' eyes and that for their parents, raising healthy, happy, and yes, God-fearing children is the most important task in life. Their entry into the world was not subjected to any cost-benefit analysis. They were not weighed against parental leisure time or disposable income.

Much of the animus towards large families derives from residual guilt of those who sense that they live far more selfish lives than their own parents and that the interests of their children are not necessarily paramount.

A considerable body of social science literature in recent years documents the devastating effects that divorce has on children, yet the divorce rates keep climbing, as parents place the need to follow their individual sprites over the good of their children. Not inherent incompatibility but the urge for mid-life flings explains many of those divorces.

Among *charedim,* however, the old ethic of sacrificing for one's children still holds sway. Haredi parents spend both more quality and quantity time with their children. Families are together on the Sabbath and holidays. And during Chol Hamoed and summer vacation, everywhere one goes (besides the beach) is teeming with *charedi* families.

A myriad of common activities bind the family together and the generations one to another. Peek into the shuls in a *charedi* neighborhood on any Saturday night and you are likely to see hundreds of fathers and sons learning together.

Anyone who thinks *charedi* children lead miserable, unhappy lives should take a walk through a *charedi* neighborhood any day of the week with open, unjaundiced eyes. My wife and I did 20 years ago, and the shining faces we saw have much to do with the large family with which we are blessed.

לֹא תוּכַל כַּלֹּתָם מַהֵר פֶּן תִּרְבֶּה עָלֶיךָ חַיַּת הַשָּׂדֶה

you will not be able to annihilate them quickly, lest the beasts of the field increase against you (ibid. 22).

If the inhabitatnts of *Eretz Yisrael* would have been defeated quickly, vast stretches of the Land would have remained unpopulated. Wild beasts would have found haven there, and would have endangered Israel. To prevent this, God promised a slow and systematic victory for the Jews.

The question is obvious. Just as God can subdue the human enemy, so too can He keep the animal kingdom in check. Why is the threat of wild animals more problematic than that of the Canaanites themselves?

The answer lies in the psychological principle taught by the *Rambam* (*Avos* 3:19) that a constantly repeated action becomes a habit. When a person consistently gives even small sums for charity, he eventually internalizes a sense of magnanimity. The same is true of negative behavior. One who consistently acts in a cruel fashion eventually becomes a cruel person.

If the Jews would have fought an uninterrupted war against the Canaanites, the intense cruelty they would have had to display during wartime would have become an integral part of their collective psyche. God therefore promised a pro-tracted war. This ensured that there would be a respite between battles, enabling Israel to purge themselves of any cruelty that might have found its way into the national character.

Thus the verse teaches that *you will not be able to annihilate them quickly, lest the beasts in the field* [i.e. the potential beast inside of us] *increase against you* (R' Shaul Yedidyah of Modzhitz).

וְלֹא תָבִיא תוֹעֵבָה אֶל בֵּיתֶךָ

And you shall not bring an abomination into your home (ibid. 26).

In its simplest sense, this verse forbids us to allow idols to come into our homes or into our possession. R' Levi Yitzchak of Berditchev homiletically extends the prohibition to forbid one from allowing arrogance to penetrate his home or psyche. As King Solomon taught, תּוֹעֲבַת ה' כָּל גְּבַהּ לֵב, *It is an **abomination** to Hashem, all who are haughty of heart (Proverbs 16:5). Since arrogance too is an abomination, it is included in the command of our verse.

Arrogance is self-worship, and is thus a form of idolatry. It is for this reason that God says about one who is arrogant, "He and I cannot co-exist." One who is arrogant worships himself instead of God, and, like the idolater, seeks to displace God and replace Him with somebody else.[5]

---

5. **Any Abomination.** *R' Eliezer Kirzner* related the following incident:

"When I visited Yeshivas Knesses Chizkiyahu in Kfar Chassidim in 5718 (1958), R' Elyah Lopian invited me to stay with him in his room during the few days I spent there. I awoke very early one morning to see the great *gaon* and *tzaddik* standing at the window and whispering something to himself, very quietly, so as not to wake me. I listened for several moments until I was able, just barely, to make out what he was saying. He was repeating over and over the words of the verse (*Deuteronomy* 7:26), 'You shall not bring an abomination into your home.'

"This was very surprising to me, for I had never heard of any custom of reviewing that verse at this hour of the day. I quickly rose from my bed and apologetically asked him to explain what it was that he had been doing. His first reaction was to express his most sincere regret that his early morning activity had woken me.

"I assured him that he had nothing to do with my awakening, as I had been up already for quite some time. I then again begged him to explain his unusual recitation, as I had overheard it and was filled with wonder.

" 'As you know,' he began, 'we will soon go to the yeshivah to *daven,* and our place is at the *mizrach,* the eastern wall (the place of honor in a synagogue). The students will rise before me as I pass, and they will wait for me before continuing the *tefillos,* after they finish the *Shema* and the *Shemoneh Esrei.* I must always be concerned lest some measure of conceit enter my thoughts. Although there is no chance of outright conceit, one must always fear any *hint* of vain glory that might enter one's heart, as is written (*Proverbs* 16:5): "It is an abomination to Hashem כָּל, *any,* haughtiness of the heart!'

"The word כָּל (any) encompasses every conceivable form of pride, even that of one who is appointed spiritual mentor in a yeshivah such as this. This must be the case, for pride is associated with *mitzvos,* as in the verse (*II Chronicles* 17:6), 'And his heart took pride in the ways of Hashem.' How can we determine that there is no vain glory involved in our very service of Hashem? Such arrogant pride is the opposite of the mitzvah, and in fact causes

Background

Moses stresses that Israel's successful occupation of the Land is contingent upon their remaining faithful to the Torah. Even while earning their own living, they must never forget that just as in the Wilderness it was God Who sustained them, so too in *Eretz Yisrael* it is He Who grants them life and the means to sustain it.[6]

כָּל הַמִּצְוָה אֲשֶׁר אָנֹכִי מְצַוְּךָ הַיּוֹם תִּשְׁמְרוּן לַעֲשׂוֹת לְמַעַן תִּחְיוּן

The entire commandment that I command you today you shall observe to perform so that you may live (8:1).

On its most basic level, this verse teaches us that life is a gift granted by God to those who cleave to His will. If we use life as a means to serve Him, then He has good reason to continue to provide us with life.

In a more profound sense, the verse speaks of the appropriate mind-set when approaching *mitzvos.* One should fulfill God's commandments with the sense that it is this observance that infuses us with vibrancy and life (*Tiferes Shlomo*).[7]

The verse states אָנֹכִי מְצַוְּךָ, "I command *you,*" in the singular form. This addresses our tendency to beg off from assuming responsibility for spiritual affairs with the excuse that there are others better equipped to do the job. The verse tells us that each person must view life as if he, and only he, can advance God's agenda. Furthermore, one should not rationalize a half-completed job by saying that others will complete what he has begun. This attitude is incorrect, for one must feel responsible to complete the *entire* mitzvah. And finally, the words *I command you **today*** tell us that we must not procrastinate in pursuing our spiritual agenda, pushing off until tomorrow what we can, and should, do today (*Taam V'Daas*).

כַּאֲשֶׁר יְיַסֵּר אִישׁ אֶת בְּנוֹ ה' אֱלֹקֶיךָ מְיַסְּרֶךָ

Just as a father chastises his son, so does Hashem, your God, chastise you (ibid. 5).

The father-son analogy is multifaceted. According to *Ohr HaChaim,* the chastisement and pain that God sends our way is a clear proof that we are His children. A father who sees someone else's child misbehaving does not feel compelled to intervene. Since the child is not his own, he is not concerned as to whether or not he is acting appropriately or developing correctly.

When the nations of the world act inappropriately, God often does not react. This displays not mercy but apathy. By contrast, Israel's misbehavior invokes Divine punishment, for He is *our* God and Father, whose responsibility for His children mandates a forceful response.[8]

King Solomon teaches that one who withholds the rod despises his child (see *Proverbs* 13:24). A

---

the person to become an abomination before Hashem, God forbid. If a *mashgiach* falls prey to excessive pride, how can he have any positive influence on his students?! It is for this reason that I repeat to myself, over and over, You shall not bring an abomination into your house' " (From *Reb Elyah* by Mesorah/ArtScroll).

6. **Personal Attention.** If a person relies upon natural forces and events to bring him success, God responds by leaving that person to the mercy of those forces and events. If, however, one places his full trust in God, He reacts by personally supervising every detail of the person's destiny (*HaMaspik L'Ovdei Hashem*).

7. **Mitzvah Link.** The word מִצְוָה is related to צוותא, *connection,* for the *mitzvos,* which are physical acts with spiritual content, serve as the means by which we mortal creatures connect ourselves to the life-giving force of the Almighty (*Simchas Aharon*).

8. **Firm Love.** The name of the Hebrew month in which both Temples were destroyed is *Av,* which also means *father.* It is odd that so loving an appellation should be bestowed upon a month in which so much Divine wrath was poured forth upon Israel.

R' Menachem Mendel of Kotzk explained: "When you see a man walk over to a child in shul and caress his cheek, you might wonder whether or not he is the child's father. However, if you see someone walk over to the child and give him a slap across the face, you may be certain that it is his father."

No one but our Father could care for us and love us enough to give us a firm slap such as the one we got from Him with the destruction of the Temple. The events of the month of *Av* could only come from our Father.

DEVARIM/DEUTERONOMY: Eikev

loving father wants to see his child realize his full potential. Therefore, he spares no effort, be it positive or negative reinforcement, to ensure that his child will progress to the extent of his abilities.[9]

Kuzari likens the Jewish people to the "heart" of mankind, for they are the moral and ethical center of humanity. Just as an ill heart causes the entire organism to suffer, so too does a diminishment in the spiritual level of the Jews redound to the detriment of all mankind. It is for this reason that God is so much more strict with us than with other nations. Hence the verse teaches, *You should know in your heart that just as a father will chastise his son . . .* (*R' Yehoshua of Kutna*).

According to *R' Dov Ber of Mezritch,* the Torah is employing the father-son analogy to express the pain a person experiences when he senses that God is distancing Himself from him.

Our verse tells us that God often distances Himself from a person for the same reasons that a father distances himself from his child. A father teaches his child to walk by standing the child up and then stepping back from him. The child takes a few steps forward, and again the father steps back. The further away the father goes, the more the child must work to reach him; consequently, the child's courage and self-confidence are bolstered. Similarly, God distances Himself from a person to encourage him to push himself further in his upward climb toward God.

A final feature of the father-son analogy is the pain that a father feels when he has no choice but to punish his child. God too is pained, so to speak, when He must chastise us. As the Sages taught, "When Man suffers, what does the Divine Presence say? 'I am pained in My head; I am pained in My arm' " [*Sanhedrin* 46a] (*R' Levi Yitzchak of Berditchev*).[10]

וְאָכַלְתָּ וְשָׂבָעְתָּ וּבֵרַכְתָּ אֶת ה' אֱלֹקֶיךָ
You will eat and be satisfied and bless Hashem, your God (ibid. 10).

The obligation to recite a blessing after eating (*Birchas HaMazon*) is derived from this verse. The obligation to recite a blessing *before* eating is

9. **Merciful Punishment.** *Bircas Avraham* (*Slonim*) expands on the analogy. A father does not punish his child to avenge himself on the child, but to teach the child to differentiate between appropriate and inappropriate behavior. The moment the lesson is learned, the father reverts to a relationship of kindness and warmth.

Similarly, God's interest is not to repay us for what we did to Him, for in reality, a mere mortal cannot affect God in any way. Rather, God punishes us so that we will realize how detrimental our behavior is to ourselves, and refrain from such behavior in the future. Once we are prepared to act as we should, our Father's attribute of mercy will immediately come to the fore.

10. **Comforting Staff.** King David writes: *Though I walk in the shadow of the valley of death, I will fear no evil, for You are with me. Your rod and Your staff, they comfort me* (Psalms 23:4-5). How do His rod and His staff comfort us? *R' Isser Zalman Meltzer* offered the following parable:

A father went for a stroll with his son in the forest, warning the child to remain nearby at all times. Initially, the child followed his father's strict instructions; however, he eventually saw something that piqued his curiosity and he left his father's side. The father, oblivious to his son's disappearance, continued on his way. When the boy finally decided to look for his father, it was too late; his father was gone.

The child began to cry. The more he searched, the deeper he went into the woods, until he was hopelessly lost. Darkness descended, and the child's fear was compounded by the roars of the wild beasts that inhabited the woods. Terribly frightened, he yearned desperately to reunite with his father.

Suddenly, the boy felt a stinging pain on his cheek — the result of a slap administered by an unseen hand. As he was about to scream in pain he discerned that this was the hand of his father. The stifled cry of pain was replaced with shouts of joy. "Father, Father, how happy I am to find you again!"

One who sins loses sight of God and temporarily severs his connection to Him. Wandering deeper and deeper into the thick forest of life, he becomes more and more lost. Suddenly, his life takes a negative turn and he is tempted to cry out in pain. But at that moment he realizes that the blow was delivered by his Father in Heaven, and he is comforted, for he has rediscovered God. He realizes that God administered the blow out of love, for He wishes to renew their connection.

Thus, when a Jew walks in the valley of the shadow of death, he is comforted by the chastisement he receives from God's rod and God's staff.

derived from the *Birchas HaMazon* obligation by means of the following *kal vachomer* (*a fortiori* argument): If one must bless God after being sated, is it not certain that he must do so when he is hungry? (*Berachos* 48b).

The Talmud teaches that one who partakes of enjoyment in this world without reciting a blessing is deemed to have stolen from God and from the Jewish people (*Berachos* 35b).

It is understandable that enjoying this world without thanking the Creator would be considered an act of theft against Him, but why is this deemed a theft from the Jewish people?

R' Akiva Eiger offers a penetrating insight. The reason God created many opportunities for enjoyment in this world was to enable us to bless and thank Him in recognition of His kindness. When we fulfill this requirement, we justify the continued supply of our material needs and pleasures. But if a person is an ingrate and refuses to bless and thank God before partaking of the pleasures of our world, he gives God cause to limit the scope of His magnanimity toward His children. Thus, he steals from God by failing to repay His munificence, and from the Jewish nation by diminishing the scope of God's giving.[11]

R' Shlomo of Karlin explains that this verse teaches us that one should derive his sense of satisfaction from reciting the blessing rather than from the act of eating. Hence it may be rendered as "you will eat and be satisfied *by* blessing Hashem."[12]

וּבְקָרְךָ וְצֹאנְךָ יִרְבְּיֻן וְכֶסֶף וְזָהָב
יִרְבֶּה לָךְ וְכֹל אֲשֶׁר לְךָ יִרְבֶּה

and your cattle and sheep increase, and you increase silver and gold for yourselves and everything you have will increase (ibid. 13).

The Torah speaks here of the spiritual debilitation that can result from too much wealth and comfort. Precisely what, however, is the Torah referring to with the words *and everything you have will increase*?

Shelah views the verse as reflective of a human foible common in people's perception of the wealthy. When people become rich and their property increases, popular wisdom assumes that everything about them has increased. They are seen as intelligent, refined, charming, learned and blessed with common sense.[13]

---

11. **Return to the Source.** A disciple of the *Chidushei HaRim* once visited the *Kotzker Rebbe*. Upon his return, the Chidushei HaRim asked him to repeat something he had heard from the Kotzker. The *chassid* replied that the Kotzker wondered how a Jew could possibly recite *Bircas HaMazon* without undergoing a spiritual metamorphosis. Did not our forefather Abraham employ a form of *Birchas HaMazon* to bring people close to God? [Abraham would feed wayfarers and guests and then ask them to thank and bless the One Who provided for them.]

The Chidushei HaRim thought for a moment and then said: "I wonder how eating itself does not bring one to an awareness of God! Does not the prophet say, *An ox knows his owner and a donkey his master's trough, but My people do not know . . .*" (Isaiah 1:3).

12. **Eating to Bless.** The popular adage has it that some people eat to live while others live to eat. The counterpart to this principle is that some people recite a blessing so that they may eat while others eat so that they may recite a blessing.

The 5-year-old grandson of *R' Yisrael Salanter* was once found crying.

"Why are you crying?" he was asked, to which he replied, "Because I want to eat."

"So why don't you eat?"

"Because I have to recite the blessing."

"Fine, so recite the blessing and then you will be able to eat. You know the appropriate blessing for this food, don't you?"

"Yes," sobbed the child, "I know which blessing to make but there was no one to answer *Amen* to my blessing! How could I recite a blessing without someone saying *Amen*?"

13. **Financial Lobotomy.** A formerly wealthy man who had lost his fortune was complaining to an acquaintance. "I understand why people no longer approach me for contributions to worthy causes. But why do they no longer seek my advice? I may have lost my money but nothing happened to my wisdom!"

King Solomon captures this sentiment in *Proverbs,* in a verse that reads: *The rich man and the pauper meet; Hashem is the Maker of them all* (22:2). People often credit the success of the wealthy to their cleverness and their

According to the *Chafetz Chaim,* the Torah speaks of the most precious commodity of all — time. One who enjoys financial prosperity has more time to devote to his spiritual edification.

A Jew once boasted to the *Chafetz Chaim* that he was independently wealthy and lacked for nothing. The sage told him: "If that is the case, you should make more time for Torah study." The man replied, "I haven't got the time for that." R' Yisrael Meir retorted, "If you don't have time, you are deeply poverty stricken. If you don't have time, what do you have? There is no one poorer than one who is without time."

R' Zusha of Anipoli gives this verse a positive interpretation, based on the proposition that wealth can help a person achieve great spiritual goals. He interprets the verse as follows: If you increase your cattle, money and all your holdings, then your heart may be emboldened to take on spiritual challenges, and then, *everything you have will increase.*

וְאָמַרְתָּ בִּלְבָבֶךָ כֹּחִי וְעֹצֶם
יָדִי עָשָׂה לִי אֶת הַחַיִל הַזֶּה
*And you might say in your heart,
"My strength and the might of my hand
made me all this wealth"* (ibid. 17).

What is the difference between *my strength* and *the might of my hand? Taam V'Daas* explains: *My strength* is directed toward those who make ordinary efforts to achieve financial success. *The might of my hand* speaks to those who undertake *extraordinary* exertions to achieve this goal. Both types find it extremely difficult to part with their hard-earned money. How often do people brush off the needy with vivid descriptions of how much time and effort went into their accomplishments! They simply cannot part with

the fruits of such intense toil. There are some who are unable to help even their own children when they are in need! Were they to realize that it is neither "their strength" nor "the might of their hands" that produces their wealth, they would find it much easier to share God's bounty with others.

Imrei Emes renders עֹצֶם יָדִי as "the closing of my hand." People foolishly think that by being tight fisted and refraining from helping others they will increase their own personal fortunes. "My strength and my tightfistedness have made me all this wealth." The Torah therefore tells us that one has forgotten that in truth *it is He Who gives you strength to create wealth.* [14]

אַל תֹּאמַר בִּלְבָבְךָ . . . בְּצִדְקָתִי הֱבִיאַנִי ה'
לָרֶשֶׁת אֶת הָאָרֶץ הַזֹּאת . . . לֹא בְצִדְקָתְךָ
*Do not say in your heart . . . "Because
of my righteousness did Hashem bring
me to possess this Land . . ." Not because
of your righteousness* (9:4-5).

Melo HaOmer explains: People often refuse honor by responding, "I don't deserve it." But in reality they are thinking, "I deserve this and better. But in addition to my other positive qualities, I am humble and state clearly that I don't deserve such honors."

The Torah therefore teaches, Do not say [even] *in your heart* that you have merited the Holy Land because of your righteousness. Your admission must not be a mere *gesture* of humility. Rather, you must *internalize* the knowledge that you have received this land only because of the wickedness of the Canaanites and the oath which God made to the Patriarchs.

[Alternatively, this verse might be saying that if you do not attribute the gift of the Land to your

business acumen, but view the poor not merely as victims of bad luck but as ne'er-do-wells who lack the ability to navigate life. However, when *the rich man and the pauper meet* it becomes evident that in terms of intelligence there is no great difference between them. Their success or failure lies nowhere but in the fact that *Hashem is the Maker of them all* (R' Zvi Hirsch Berliner).

14. **In Flight.** *R' Levi Yitzchak of Berditchev* once saw someone who was hurrying somewhere. "Where are you running?" he asked. Replied the man, "I'm chasing after a living." R' Levi Yitzchak responded: "What makes you so sure that your livelihood is in front of you and you are chasing after it? Perhaps it is behind you and you are running away from it!"

R' Mordechai Gifter was fond of saying: "We don't *make* a living; we *take* a living."

righteousness, then it is at least *possible* that righteousness is the reason you received it. But if in your heart you credit your righteousness, you may be *sure* that it is not the cause.][15]

Why did Moses deem it necessary to inform the people that it is not by virtue of their righteousness that they will receive the Land of Israel?

Chidushei HaRim sees in this a source of solace for all generations. Had we earned the Land through our merits, we would be allowed to maintain a presence there only so long as our spiritual level remains unchanged. If, however, we find ourselves lacking in merit, our ties to the Land will automatically be severed. To avoid this danger, God gave us the Land as a gift. Thus, although the Land itself will reject us if we pursue negative activities, such as idolatry or immorality, we need not worry that a mere lack of merit will result in our expulsion.

The Land of Israel was not earned by the merit of any particular generation of Jews. Rather, it is God's gift to the nation as a whole. Even we, in our spiritual impoverishment, can achieve some sort of connection to *Eretz Yisrael*. [16]

Background

In the aftermath of the sin of the Golden Calf, the Jews feared that they had irretrievably severed their special relationship with Hashem. Moses reassured them that even now, God desires to have Israel continue its relationship with Him, to which He will respond with His continued beneficence.

וְעַתָּה יִשְׂרָאֵל מָה ה' אֱלֹקֶיךָ שֹׁאֵל מֵעִמָּךְ כִּי אִם לְיִרְאָה אֶת ה' אֱלֹקֶיךָ

Now, O Israel, what does Hashem, your God, ask of you? Only to fear Hashem, your God (10:12).

Moses uses the word *now.* According to the *Chafetz Chaim,* this teaches that every moment of one's life must be viewed as an opportunity. A Jew must spend his entire life repeatedly asking himself one question: What does Hashem want from me at this particular moment?[17]

The Midrash teaches that the term וְעַתָּה, *and now,* implies repentance. Moses was saying the following: Although in the past you have lacked the virtues I will now enumerate (fear of Hashem, following in His ways and loving Him), I ask you to seize the moment (*now*) and redefine yourselves and your lives. *R' Yitzchak Isaac HaLevi Herzog* explains why *now* means repentance. One who repents obliterates his past sins. As for one's future misdeeds, God judges us as we are right *now,* regardless of whatever sins we might commit in the future (see *Rashi* to *Genesis* 21:17). One who repents need only be concerned with the here and now.

According to this understanding, the verse is

---

15. **Truly Good.** *The Chozeh of Lublin* would often say, "I prefer a wicked person who knows he is wicked to a righteous person who knows he is righteous." His disciples employed this epigram to explain a phrase in the High Holiday liturgy. God is described there as "The Good, Who does good for the evil and for the good." Why do we mention those who are evil before those who are good? The answer is that those who know they are evil might one day repent, but those who are convinced of their righteousness are too spiritually complacent to ever make changes in their lives.

16. **Causeless Love.** The same applied at the time of the redemption from Egypt. God chose us as His nation then, at our lowest spiritual level, in order to emphasize that our chosenness was not a result of our righteousness, but was rather an expression of His intrinsic and unconditional love for the children of the Patriarchs and Matriarchs. This love will never die. As the Sages have taught: "Any love that depends on a specific cause, when that cause is gone, the love is gone; but if it does not depend on a specific cause, it will never cease" (*Avos* 5:19) (*Nesivos Shalom*).

17. **Spiritual Plans.** *R' Nissan Telushkin* once told *R' Shlomo Freifeld* about the most embarrassing moment of his life. "I was once in the company of the *Lubavitcher Rebbe,* and he asked me, 'R' Telushkin, if you had a million dollars [at your disposal] what would you do for *Yiddishkeit* ?' I don't know why, but I didn't know what to answer. I felt terrible. How does a real Jew walk around without being preoccupied with what he could do for Torah and *Yiddishkeit* ?" And the old Rav began to cry.

saying that what God desires of Israel is *"now"* — that is, He desires our repentance.[18]

The Sages teach that the reason God asks Jews to fear Him is that "everything is in the power of Heaven except for fear of Heaven" (*Berachos* 33b). Fear of Heaven is something a person must achieve on his own.

How then, asks *Chidushei HaRim,* do we pray and ask God to *unify our hearts to love and fear Your Name* (*Ahavah Rabbah;* final prayer before the morning *Shema*) or to *imbue our heart with love and awe of Him* (*U'va L'Tzion,* one of the prayers concluding *Shacharis*)? If God has, so to speak, relinquished his jurisdiction over man's fear of Heaven, why do we ask Him to assist us in attaining this attribute?

The *Chidushei HaRim* explains that the Sages did not mean that God cannot inculcate in us the fear of Him. What they meant was that while a person's temporal needs may be left in God's hands, one who wishes to revere God must take matters into his *own* hands. If he earnestly yearns for fear of Heaven, then Hashem will help him attain it.

The *Chazon Ish* writes: The Almighty, Blessed is He, does not automatically instill in man a sense of closeness to Him, for He has placed "fear of God" in the realm of human endeavor (as per the teaching of our verse). However, this does not preclude God bringing a person close in response to prayer, for that which results from prayer is a person's own accomplishment.

The Talmud (ibid.) notes the diminutive *only* in this verse and asks, "Is fear of Heaven such an insignificant and simple matter?" The Talmud responds, "Yes. For Moses, fear of God was a small thing."

This interpretation raises another obvious question. Granted, for one such as Moses, fear of Heaven is a minor matter. But Moses directed these words to the general populace. Surely he did not imagine that all the people were on his level!

R' Itzele of Volozhin answers that Moses, in his overwhelming humility, was certain that others too could attain the same reverence and awe of God that he himself possessed.

Alternatively, the Talmud means to emphasize the importance of interacting with someone who can serve as a role model. Fear of Heaven is unattainable if one never sees a person who possesses it. It is like trying to describe the sweetness of sugar to someone who has never tasted it. One can speak endlessly, yet, unless the other person actually eats sugar, he will never know what it is. There is an allusion to this idea in the words the Talmud uses to express its teaching. It states: לְגַבֵּי מֹשֶׁה מִילְּתָא זוּטַרְתָּא הִיא. This is simply translated as: *for Moses it was a small matter.* However, the word לְגַבֵּי can also be translated as: *for those who are near.* Thus, the Talmudic teaching also means that for those who were near Moses and had a living example of true reverence, fear of God is a small matter (*Arizal*).

R' Avraham of Slonim answers the question with a penetrating analysis of the relative terms "difficult" and "easy."

Simple people think that "easy" refers to something that can be attained with relatively little effort while "a difficult thing" is something that entails tremendous strain and exertion. Wiser people, though, are not deterred by hard work.

---

18. **How Is He Ours?** The chassidic masters offer some homiletic gems based on this verse. According to the *Baal Shem Tov,* the word מָה, *what,* signifies humility. This is based on the teaching of the Sages in *Chullin* (89a), where it is stated that the degree of humility achieved by Moses and Aaron was greater than that achieved by Abraham. They explain that Abraham merely said: *I am but dust and ash* (*Genesis* 18:27), but Moses and Aaron said: *what are we?* [וְנַחְנוּ מָה] (*Exodus* 16:7). Hence, מָה represents humility.

The *Baal Shem Tov* therefore interpreted our verse in this manner: מָה ה' אֱלֹקֶיךָ שֹׁאֵל מֵעִמָּךְ, *Hashem, your God, is asking you for "what"* — that is to say, He is asking you for humility.

R' Naftali of Ropschitz perceived a different message in the verse: וְעַתָּה יִשְׂרָאֵל, *And now O Israel,* מָה ה' אֱלֹקֶיךָ, *with what* [asks the Almighty] *am I Hashem, your God?* What have you done to make Me yours? This is a question that every Jew must constantly ask himself.

Such people have only one objective yardstick in deciding whether something is hard or easy: If the goal is feasible and valuable, then the task is easy, for the end justifies the means. If, however, the goal is virtually impossible and is lacking in value, then the task is a difficult one, for the exertion is simply not justified. Moses understood that the dictum "All is in the power of Heaven except for the fear of Heaven" means that most tasks are difficult, for success and failure are in the hands of Heaven, not in the hands of man. The one exception is fear of Heaven, which is in man's power to attain. Since achieving this goal was in his own hands, Moses regarded it as an easy task.

Finally, *R' Levi Yitzchak of Berditchev* suggests that for Moses, fear of Heaven was a genetic heritage.

When Moses' mother Yocheved defied the evil decree of Pharaoh to kill all the male babies, God rewarded her. As the verse states (*Exodus* 1:20): *And it was because the midwives feared God that He made them houses.* Rashi (ad loc.) explains that Yocheved merited to have the houses of Kohanim and Levites come from her offspring, for she was the mother of both Aaron and Moses. Because Moses' birth was the direct result of his mother's fear of God, awe and reverence of God came to him almost naturally.

וּלְאַהֲבָה אֹתוֹ
and to love Him (ibid.).

Rambam writes in *Mishneh Torah* that the path to achieving love of God is through contemplating the wonders of His world. When one recognizes the great wisdom inherent in the Creator's handiwork, it awakens in him a burning desire to know God (see *Hilchos Yesodei HaTorah* 2:1). However, in *Sefer HaMitzvos* (§3), *Rambam* seems to suggest that the optimal way to come to love Hashem is through studying His Torah. This appears to be a contradiction.

R' Mordechai Pogoramansky offered a stunning resolution by way of a parable. A man attended an

art exhibition at which were displayed the greatest paintings in existence. For some reason, none of the paintings impressed the man. He denigrated every masterpiece, "Ach! These are nothing but dirty splotches and stains on canvas." His companions were shocked.

Finally, a shrewd bystander walked over to the fellow, removed his glasses and took a look at them. "Of course," he said. "Everything appears to you as splotches and stains because your glasses are splotched and stained."

Although Scripture suggests that we look Heavenward to see Who created all of these things (see *Isaiah* 40:26), this is only effective if we have the right "glasses." One can only appreciate the lessons in faith which nature provides if he views the world from a Torah perspective.

This resolves the apparent contradiction in *Rambam.* It is true that contemplating nature can bring one close to God. But this is effective *only* if we first steep ourselves in Torah. In this manner, we remove the spiritual cataracts which blur our vision and prevent us from appreciating that which we see.

King David prayed, "Uncover my eyes so that I may see wonders from Your Torah" (*Psalms* 119:18). He spoke not of seeing wonders *in* Torah (although one can do so), but of deriving *from* Torah the necessary spiritual vision to appreciate the constant miracles God does for us.[19]

אֶרֶץ אֲשֶׁר ה' אֱלֹקֶיךָ דֹּרֵשׁ
אֹתָהּ תָּמִיד עֵינֵי ה' אֱלֹקֶיךָ בָּהּ
A Land that Hashem your God seeks out; the eyes of Hashem, your God, are always upon it (11:12).

R' *Yaakov Moshe Charlap* writes: Just as one wearing *tefillin* (phylacteries) may not shift his attention from them, so too one may not remove *Eretz Yisrael* from his thoughts.

This is based on an observation of the Talmud regarding the golden Headplate worn by the Kohen Gadol. The Torah writes that *it shall be on his forehead always* (see *Exodus* 28:38), upon which

---

19. **Enlightenment.** We pray every day, וְהָאֵר עֵינֵינוּ בְּתוֹרָתֶךָ, commonly translated as *enlighten our eyes in Your Torah.* A more accurate rendering might be *enlighten our eyes **through** Your Torah (Simchas Aharon).*

the Talmud comments, "He may never remove his attention from it" (*Yoma* 7b). Just as in the case of the Headplate, the word *always* implies an uninterrupted focus, so too in the case of the Holy Land, the word *always* indicates that God never shifts His focus from the Land.

We are enjoined to emulate God; thus, we too must always keep our homeland in our thoughts.[20]

---

20. **Constant Focus.** *R' Dovid K.,* a veteran educator, once said, "We will know that we have succeeded to some extent when our students will check the front of the newspaper to find out the news from Israel before turning to the sports page." Just as God's eyes are always on the Holy Land, so too must the welfare of our Israeli brothers and sisters always be at the forefront of our consciousness.

פרשת ראה ﷽
Parashas Re'eh

Background

Before introducing the commandments that will be particularly relevant to Israel upon its exposure to the heightened sanctity of *Eretz Yisrael,* Moses offers a stark portrayal of the choice between observing the Torah and transgressing it. He states that it is nothing less than the choice between a blessing and a curse.

רְאֵה אָנֹכִי נֹתֵן לִפְנֵיכֶם הַיּוֹם בְּרָכָה וּקְלָלָה
See, I present before you today a blessing and a curse (11:26).

The verse begins with רְאֵה, *see,* in the singular, yet immediately switches to the plural with לִפְנֵיכֶם, *before you.* A number of explanations have been offered to explain the change in form.

Sefer HaChaim sees the use of the singular form as setting a precedent for the spiritual leaders of later generations. *Rabbanim* and *Rebbeiim* are often disheartened when their loving rebuke falls upon deaf ears. Our verse teaches that even if the constructive criticism finds its mark on and influences only one person, it is still worth the effort.

Moses presented his words before the nation at large — thus, the plural לִפְנֵיכֶם. However, even the saving of one Jewish soul was to him a worthy goal — thus, the singular רְאֵה.

According to *R' Menachem Mendel of Kotzk,* the change in form mirrors the process by which we internalize the messages of Torah. Torah is first transmitted to us by God in a unified fashion; all are given equal access to His word. However, the depth to which the Torah penetrates our hearts and the effect it has upon our lives depends on our efforts as individuals.[1]

The *Vilna Gaon* offers a guide to spiritual growth based on this verse.

Never abandon your spiritual trek because you find no fellow travelers. The verse employs the singular רְאֵה (see) to teach that the great blessing that results from hearkening to God will fall to those who are unafraid to make their way alone.

Lest one feel overwhelmed by the prospect of battling his evil inclination, God whispers in his ear, "Have no fear. I have presented you with this choice, and I will always be with you to help you overcome adversity." As the Sages teach, "A person's evil inclination seeks to overpower him every day; if not for the assistance of the Holy One, Blessed is He, the person would be unable to withstand his evil inclination" (*Succah* 52a).

---

1. **Soul Mirror.** The Torah is a mirror of the Jewish soul. As the Sages taught, יִשְׂרָאֵל is an acronym for יֵשׁ שִׁשִּׁים רִבּוּא אוֹתִיּוֹת לַתּוֹרָה, *there are six hundred thousand letters in the Torah.* Each letter corresponds to one of the 600,000 souls that form the nucleus of the Jewish nation. It follows that one's perception of Torah is defined by the spiritual stature of one's *own* soul.

Nevertheless, the festival of Shavuos is referred to in our prayers as זְמַן מַתַּן תּוֹרָתֵנוּ, *the time of the giving of **our** Torah.* For God gave the Torah to all of us together; how we receive it is contingent upon us as individuals.

God's call for us to choose is a *constant* summons. Just because one made poor choices in the past does not mean that he is forever encumbered by those mistakes. One can always change the direction of his life, for God presents us with these options constantly. The vere speaks in the present tense: *I present* [i.e. constantly] *before you . . . a blessing and a curse.*

The future is an enigma; a fog shrouds its twists and turns, preventing us from recognizing that which will prove to be to our benefit and that which will harm us. How are we to make wise and informed choices? The verse therefore states that wisdom is to be found לִפְנֵיכֶם, in that which came *before you.* Look to the past, see how our history reflects the choices of our sainted forebears, and apply the lessons of the past to your future.

And finally, never feel that your less-than-perfect past must be forever dragged along, like baggage that cannot be left behind. Your past mistakes can be redeemed. Thus, the verse states: הַיּוֹם, *today,* teaching that each day can mark the dawn of a new beginning.

אָנֹכִי נֹתֵן לִפְנֵיכֶם הַיּוֹם בְּרָכָה וּקְלָלָה
I present before you today a blessing and a curse (ibid.).

E go is a two-edged sword. When it impels us to persevere in the face of seemingly impossible spiritual challenges, it is a catalyst for enormous spiritual attainments. When it is used in the service of false pride or arrogance, to dismiss God from a person's life, it is the most destructive of forces. Thus, God says to us: Your "I" (אָנֹכִי) is presented before you today. It can become a blessing or a curse — depending on how you develop it (*Me'or V'Shemesh*).

Alternatively, the verse refers to man's free will. This is a Godlike characteristic — by granting us free will, God gave of Himself to us (אָנֹכִי נֹתֵן). As a result of this gift, we alone determine whether life becomes a blessing or a curse (*R' Baruch of Medziboz*).

R' Henach of Aleksander views the verse as describing man's ability to define the moment. God says to us, *I present before you today* — you must choose what sort of *today* it will be. One might imbue "today" with the meaning given it by the Sages, who stated: "*Today* is to do the *mitzvos,* while tomorrow [in the World to Come] is to receive reward for them" (*Eruvin* 22a). This perception of "today" as a fleeting opportunity to do good is a blessing. On the other hand, one might see "today" through the prism of the wicked, as an opportunity to indulge in all sorts of pleasures — to "Eat, drink and be merry, for tomorrow you shall die." In that event, "today" will be a miserable source of cursed unhappiness.

It is man's choice as to whether he will lend positive or negative meaning to *today.* [2]

אֶת הַבְּרָכָה אֲשֶׁר תִּשְׁמְעוּ אֶל מִצְוֹת ה׳
The blessing: that you hearken to the commandments of Hashem (ibid. 27).

T he commentators note a discontinuity in the verse's style. When speaking of the blessing the verse states אֲשֶׁר, *that* you hearken to the commandments. But when it speaks of the curse it states אִם, *if* you do not hearken. Here is a possible explanation:

It is inevitable that the Jewish people will eventually repent. As the prophet promises, *The remnant shall return* (Isaiah 10:21). Thus *Rambam* teaches (*Hil. Teshuvah* 7:5): "The Jewish people will be redeemed only as a result of repentance. The Torah has already foretold that in the end of the Exile the Jewish people will repent and will immediately be redeemed."

Consequently, the blessings of the verse will certainly be realized sooner or later, when *you*

---

2. **Now!** Even *today, if we but heed His call* (Psalms 95:7), we can turn 180 degrees and merit the loving care that our Shepherd showers upon His flock.

According to *Chidushei HaRim,* this is the meaning of Hillel's principle: *if not now, then when?* (*Avos* 1:14). Every moment in time is a singular opportunity with a special purpose that never occurred before and will never occur again. A person must seize the moment and draw from it the meaning that is uniquely its own. If we but heed His call, life *today* will be a blessing, a veritable paradise on earth; if we do not, it can be, God forbid, a curse, a glimpse of hell in the here and now. The choice is ours (*Ohr HaTorah*).

hearken to the commandments of Hashem. Not so the curse; it need never come. Only *if* you [God forbid] do not hearken will the curses come upon you (*Panim Yafos*).

Alternatively, the change in style is based on the dictum of the Sages that there exists no true reward for *mitzvos* in our world. The true payment awaits us in the World to Come, for nothing in this world is valuable enough to serve as payment for fulfilling God's word (*Kiddushin* 39b). Although the Torah does sometimes promise us material reward, this is simply intended to allow us to serve God without impediment, undisturbed by our material needs (see *Rambam, Hilchos Teshuvah* 9:1).

Thus the Torah speaks of providing us with *the blessing that you hearken* [i.e., so *that* you may hearken] *to the commandments of Hashem.* The blessing is not that which *results* from hearkening to His word but that which *enables* one to hearken (*Parparaos L'Chochmah, Nachalas David*).

In a variation on this theme, *Haamek Davar* submits that the blessing will provide us with the tools with which to perform the *mitzvos.* As the Midrash teaches, "Who was able to put on *tzitzis* (fringes) before I provided him with a *tallis*?" Without the blessing of God, a man might wish to fulfill the mitzvah of *tzitzis* yet be unable to do so for lack of a *tallis.* Thus, the fact *that* we may hearken to God's commandments is a result of his blessing.

Background

Moses emphasizes that eradication of idolatry and avoidance of the pagan practices of the Canaanites, as well as designating the Temple (or Tabernacle) as the primary place of worship, are crucial to Israel's success in the Holy Land.

לֹא תַעֲשׂוּן בֵּן לַה׳ אֱלֹקֵיכֶם
You shall not do this to Hashem, your God (12:4).

This verse refers back to the two previous verses, which command the Jewish people to destroy and uproot all idolatry from the Holy Land. Now, there is obviously no need to warn the people to literally not destroy the Temple. Accordingly, various homiletic interpretations have been offered to explain this verse.

Rashi cites the Tanna R' Yishmael, who taught that the verse means that Jews must be careful not to commit sins that will cause the Holy Temple to be destroyed.

Igra d'Kallah understands the verse to be censuring one who performs *mitzvos* in imitation of others. Thus, the verse teaches that performing God's commandments in a manner of בֵּן, *like this* — i.e., as a copy of the worship performed by others — constitutes a devaluation of the mitzvah. One must carry out His will as an authentic expression of oneself and with deep personal conviction.

To take this thought a bit further: Even to do a mitzvah because one has *always* done so falls short of what is expected. True service of God demands that one perform each mitzvah as if it is his first time.[3]

The *Chozeh of Lublin* submits that the Torah here resolves a theological issue with which many have grappled. We know and firmly believe that God is justified in all of His decrees with regard to human destiny. But is this to say that we are required to bow our heads meekly and succumb to an unfavorable Heavenly decree? The *Chozeh* rejects this stance. Rather, we must do all that is within our power to nullify the decree; be it by increasing our merit or through prayer.

Thus the verse states: לֹא תַעֲשׂוּן בֵּן לַה׳ אֱלֹקֵיכֶם, Do not simply answer בֵּן, *yes,* to the decrees of

---

3. **Imitative.** This sheds light on the words of Mar Ukva, who compared himself unfavorably to his forebears by describing his own spiritual station as "vinegar" and that of his father's as "wine." He provided an example: "When my father ate meat on one day he would not eat dairy until the following day. I, however, wait only until the next meal" (*Chullin* 105a).

Now, if Mar Ukva saw his father's behavior as admirable, why did he not emulate it? The answer relates to authenticity. One does not simply mimic the higher standard of behavior of one's forebears. A custom or halachic stringency is something which one must grow into so that it flows naturally from his very being.

Hashem your God! Storm the Gates of Heaven with prayer and good deeds, and annul the painful decree.

לִשְׁכְנוֹ תִדְרְשׁוּ וּבָאתָ שָׁמָּה
You shall seek out His Presence and you shall come there (ibid. 5).

The verse appears to be in reverse order. It would be more correct to say that *you shall come there* in order to search for the Divine Presence, rather than the other way around!

The answer is that the search itself is the key to success. If one earnestly seeks to find God, his efforts will be met with success and he will "come there." The mere fact that one searches for truth allows him to achieve his goal (*R' Yerucham Levovitz, Chasam Sofer*).[4]

Tiferes Shlomo suggests that this verse provides the formula for our eventual redemption. In order for God to redeem us from the Exile and rebuild the Temple we must yearn for it and await it impatiently. Only if *you seek out His Presence* will you *come there.*

Imrei Emes adds: The verse begins by speaking in the plural — תִדְרְשׁוּ, *you shall seek out His Presence,* but ends with the singular form — וּבָאתָ שָׁמָּה, *and you shall come there.* The key to bringing about the Final Redemption is to rectify the sins that brought about the destruction of the Temple and the resultant exile. The Sages teach that these were interpersonal strife and hatred. Only when the many who seek His Presence will unite as one will they achieve redemption. When the plural will be transformed into the singular, the time for *geulah* will have arrived!

וַאֲכַלְתֶּם שָׁם לִפְנֵי ה' אֱלֹקֵיכֶם וּשְׂמַחְתֶּם בְּכֹל מִשְׁלַח יֶדְכֶם
You shall eat there before Hashem, your God, and you will rejoice in your every undertaking (ibid. 7).

Sifrei explains *your every undertaking* as referring to one's commercial and business affairs. How does eating sacrificial foods in Jerusalem affect one's financial endeavors?

R' Yehoshua of Kutna explains: One of the great pitfalls of wealth is the lack of satisfaction which often accompanies financial success. One who loves money is never satisfied with what he has and thus cannot truly enjoy his prosperity.

The Talmud teaches that even if one ate even a minimal amount of sacrificial food, he would feel entirely sated (*Yoma* 39a). THus, the lesson inherent in eating sacrificial food is that one can truly be satisfied with his portion in life and need not be constantly hungry for more. Hence, when *you shall eat before Hashem your God* it will allow you to truly *rejoice in your every [financial] undertaking,* without experiencing dissatisfaction.

Tiferes Shlomo renders בְּכֹל מִשְׁלַח יֶדְכֶם as *through every time you send out your hand.* How does a Jew rejoice in the bounty that God has provided him? By sending out his hand to share his blessings with others.[5]

וּשְׂמַחְתֶּם לִפְנֵי ה' אֱלֹקֵיכֶם אַתֶּם וּבְנֵיכֶם . . . וְהַלֵּוִי אֲשֶׁר בְּשַׁעֲרֵיכֶם כִּי אֵין לוֹ חֵלֶק וְנַחֲלָה אִתְּכֶם
You shall rejoice before Hashem, your God — you and your sons . . . and the Levite who is in your cities, for he has no share and inheritance with you (ibid. 12).

The last clause in the verse, *for he has no share,* is the reason we must include the Levites in

---

4. **At the Doorstep.** According to *R' Baruch of Medziboz,* this theme is reflected in the Hallel prayer. *Open for me the gates of righteousness; I will enter them and thank God. This is the gate to Hashem, the righteous shall enter through it.*

Man often feels that he is an outsider, far removed from the closeness to God for which he so desperately yearns. He begs to be allowed in, to enter the gates of righteousness. Figuratively pounding upon the gates, he longs to enter so that he may praise and thank God. God responds, *This* — i.e., the very desire to enter — *is the gate to Hashem. The righteous enter through it,* for their desire breaks all the barriers.

5. **Transcendentally Prosperous.** A Jew cannot rejoice and feel satisfied when his fellow is lacking. Only when one eats before Hashem and provides for the Levite, stranger, orphan and widow can he rejoice in his prosperity (*Simchas Aharon*).

To some, prosperity is the key to self-indulgence; to others, it is a means for self-transcendence.

our celebration. *Rambam* codifies this obligation: "When one eats and drinks [on *Yom Tov*] he must feed the stranger, orphan, widow and all the other unfortunate paupers. One who closes the gates of his courtyard and eats together with his family without providing food and drink for poor and embittered souls engages in a gastronomic orgy rather than in the joy of mitzvah" (*Hilchos Yom Tov* 6:18).

Ohel Yaakov provides a novel interpretation of the verse, in which the opening phrase, וְשָׂמַחְתֶּם, *and you shall rejoice,* refers also to the clause concerning the Levite. He accordingly explains that while most people rejoice over having inherited the Land and being able to eat of its fruits and be satisfied by its goodness, the Levite lives by a different standard. He rejoices over the fact that *he has no share and inheritance with you.* Unencumbered by physical and worldly concerns, he is free to nurture his Godly soul. This freedom is the source of his joy.[6]

לֹא תוּכַל לֶאֱכֹל בִּשְׁעָרֶיךָ
In your cities you may not eat (ibid. 17).

The words לֹא תוּכַל translate literally as *you cannot* rather than as *you may not.* "You may not" implies a lack of permission; "you cannot" indicates a lack of ability. A Jew must always feel that actions prohibited by the Torah are not only

impermissible, but are actually out of reach. We are simply *unable* to perform these acts, since they run contrary to God's will.

This calls to mind a person who, when told to jump off the roof, replied, "I can't do it." This is a false statement! He most certainly *can* do it; however, he does not *want* to do it, since doing so will endanger his life.

One must view his allegiance to Torah as something that simply *cannot* be compromised (*R' Eliyahu Meir Bloch*).

Background

Moses has warned the nation about the spiritual trap of idolatry. He now speaks about the prohibitions concerning false prophets, about the necessity to maintain loyalty to God and His Torah, and about the laws of a wayward city.

אַחֲרֵי ה' אֱלֹקֵיכֶם תֵּלֵכוּ וְאֹתוֹ תִירָאוּ
After Hashem, your God, you shall go and Him you shall fear (13:5).

The word אַחֲרֵי, *after,* implies distance; the related term אַחַר implies proximity (see *Rashi* to *Genesis* 15:1). Why does the Torah command us to follow God with the term אַחֲרֵי, which implies distance? It should have employed the term אַחַר, which would have demanded that we maintain a

6. **Close to Torah.** Two friends spent many years together, engrossed in the atmosphere of the yeshivah and the study of Torah. Eventually, circumstances compelled one of them to enter the world of commerce. He was successful in amassing a large fortune. His friend remained in the yeshivah and grew into an accomplished Torah scholar. One day they met. The businessman was overwhelmed with envy. "Had I remained in the study hall, I too would have achieved greatness in Torah. What a shame that I was forced to abandon all this for mere wealth," he thought to himself.

His friend too was thinking, "Would it have been so terrible had I involved myself in commerce? Shouldn't I have attempted to provide for my family and future in a more respectable fashion?"

Now, this *kollel* fellow undoubtedly spent more hours studying Torah than did his businessman friend. Yet, it is not at all clear which of the two enjoyed a closer connection to Torah. True spiritual status is determined not by how one spends his time, but by what one values.

Rabbeinu Yonah (*Shaarei Teshuvah* 3:148) cites the words of King Solomon (in *Proverbs* 27:21): *A refining pot is for silver, and a crucible for gold, and a man according to his praises.* Just as a furnace purges gold of its impurities and brings forth its unadulterated essence, so too does the essence of a person become known through that which he praises. One who reveres the righteous and speaks highly of the Torah and its scholars is clearly a righteous person.

One who, despite his inability to devote himself fully to Torah study, is fervently admiring of its practitioners exhibits a deeper attachment to Torah than does one who devotes much time to study, but looks elsewhere when seeking to define success (*Pachad Yitzchak, Purim* 1).

close spiritual and emotional proximity to Him.

The *Chafetz Chaim* explains that the Torah is encouraging us to make the effort to come close to Hashem even if we feel removed from Him. Even if one sees himself as אַחֲרֵי, *distant* from God, one should still put all his energies into seeking God's closeness. His efforts will be rewarded.

While traveling to the first *Knessiah Gedolah* (world convention) of Agudath Israel, the *Chafetz Chaim* met R' Avraham Mordechai of Ger and asked him this very question. The Gerrer Rebbe replied, "Allow me to give his honor a chassidic answer to this question. One who sees himself as being close to God is actually far away from Him; while one who realizes how distant he is from God is actually quite close. One can cleave to God only if he views himself as אַחֲרֵי (removed)." As King David said, *Hashem is close to the brokenhearted; and those crushed in spirit, He saves (Psalms 34:19).* [7], [8]

According to R' Shmuel Rozovsky, this verse tells us that we must combine love and fear in our service of God. While serving God out of love is certainly the optimal path, if it is not tempered by fear it can easily lead to the familiarity that breeds contempt. In order for one to properly maintain his love for God, one must maintain a spiritual posture of אַחֲרֵי — close yet removed.[9]

וְנָתַן לְךָ רַחֲמִים וְרִחַמְךָ
and He will give you mercy and He will be merciful to you (13:18).

Behavior can become habituated to the point that it actually changes one's character. Thus, if one performs good deeds and acts of kindness, he will eventually become a good, kindhearted person.[10] It is for this reason that *Rambam* (*Commentary to Avos* 3:19) writes that it is better to give small amounts of charity to many people than to give one large contribution to someone deeply in need. The repeated acts of giving develop within the person the trait of magnanimity.

Unfortunately, this is true of negative behavior as well. Those who act as the proxy of the court to execute the transgressors of the Wayward City and to destroy their property run the risk of becoming desensitized to suffering and losing their natural

---

7. **Only Just Begun.** R' Moshe of Kobrin sees this message in the following words of Scripture (*Psalms* 139:8): *When I ascend to the Heavens, You are there; when I descend to the depths, behold! You are here.*

One who imagines that he has already ascended to the heights of spiritual attainment, to the Heavens, will soon discover that You are "there," that is, far removed from him. If, however, one considers himself to be of lowly stature, descended to the spiritual depths, he is told, *behold! You are here* — for he is indeed in the presence of God.

8. **Strength in Numbers.** At the opening session of the second *Knessiah Gedolah* of Agudath Israel (held in Vienna in 1929), R' Avraham Mordechai Alter of Ger noted that our verse parallels an earlier one, *Hashem, your God, you shall fear, Him shall you serve . . . (Deuteronomy* 10:20). The difference is that the earlier verse is stated in the singular (תִּירָא, תַעֲבֹד), while this one is stated in the plural (תֵּלְכוּ, תִּירָאוּ).

When the the Jewish community is generally supportive of Torah values, individuals can maintain a Torah lifestyle and mind-set on their own. Not so when the winds of heresy and rejection batter at the loyalties of the nation. In such times, the individual is powerless; he needs the support of the many to protect himself and his family from the forces that seek to destroy all connection to God and Torah.

Our verse introduces the Torah's discussion of false prophets and of those who entice entire cities to go astray. It therefore employs the plural, to make clear that survival demands the molding of all the committed individuals into a united communal force.

Concluded the Gerrer Rebbe, "Today, when from every corner our loyalties and those of our children are under the attack of false prophets purveying false and destructive ideologies, we can survive *only* by creating a united front. This is the secret of Agudath Israel."

9. **Respectful Distance.** A *Mishnah* in *Avos* (1:3) teaches, in the name of Antignos leader of Socho, that we must serve God out of altruistic love and not in order to be rewarded for our positive choices. The *Mishnah* concludes: "And let the awe of Heaven be upon you." Although the first half of the *Mishnah* advocates service out of love, it balances this by demanding reverence as well. Awe sets boundaries for love, preventing a person from taking excessive liberties as a result of overfamiliarity (*Maharal*).

10. **Masked Reality.** The folk saying has it that if one wears a mask long enough it becomes his face.

compassion. God therefore promises to bestow the trait of mercy and compassion upon those who by necessity acted with cruelty (*I will give you mercy*). They may have *behaved* in a cruel manner, but God will not let them *become* cruel (*Ohr HaChaim, Chafetz Chaim*).[11]

HaMeir L'Olam focuses on the earlier part of the verse, *No part of the banned property may adhere to your hand.* He explains that this is a prerequisite to the promise of mercy.

When one is compelled by the Torah to act harshly toward others, he must be exceptionally careful to rid himself of any personal motivations whatsoever.[12] If he stands to gain personally from his work, then his character is bound to be negatively impacted by his behavior. One who brings himself to show hatred and anger for the sake of Heaven will be saved from developing negative character traits *only* if his motivations are purely for the sake of Heaven. Thus, one must take heed that none of the Wayward City's banned property will adhere to his hand. Only then is he assured of God's gift of mercy.[13]

Background

The Torah now addresses the special status of the Jewish people as God's children and enumerates various activities that are considered to be abominations when practiced by those of such exalted status.

---

11. **Mercifully Restored.** One who gives charity will not become poor thereby (see *Rambam, Hilchos Matnos Aniyim* 10:2); to the contrary, God will reward him for his act of kindness by replenishing his coffers. Likewise, one who is compelled to act cruelly toward the enemies of God will merit to have his stockpile of mercy replenished (*Chafetz Chaim*).

Once, during World War I, the *Chafetz Chaim* began to weep uncontrollably. "So many Jews died throughout our long exile in order to sanctify the name of Hashem! I could live with that. But why are we being slaughtered now? How many of our people are killed without reason by cold-blooded murderers? How many will remain maimed and crippled? Even those who survive the war will have been exposed to such wanton murder that they themselves will become murderers. Murder is no longer shocking, human life has lost its value and become meaningless in the eyes of man." [His confidant *R' Shmuel Greineman* repeated the sage's words during World War II, and added, "What would he say now when the beast of prey drinks our blood without mercy?"]

12. **Kind Man.** When King Solomon ordered the execution of Adoniyahu, Yoav and Shimi for assorted acts of rebellion against the crown, he sent Benayahu ben Yehoyada, the Kohen Gadol at that time, to act as executioner. Why did he choose the Kohen Gadol to carry out the death sentences? *Avnei Nezer* explains that a primary trait of the the Kohen Gadol is an abundance of kindness (see *Deuteronomy* 33:8), as we see in the case of Aaron, who — the *Mishnah* testifies — loved peace, pursued peace, loved people and brought them close to Torah (*Avos* 1:12). Solomon feared that those empowered to kill the rebels might do so with some vestige of personal animosity. This would have constituted a great wrong, for a Jew who kills another, even for a legitimate reason, must shun all personal motivation. He therefore sent the Kohen Gadol, the man of peace and kindness, for he knew he would act only from the purest of motives.

This rule — that those who act harshly toward others must act from unimpeachable motives — sheds light on a *Mishnah* (*Yoma* 1:5), which teaches that when the Sadducees controlled the office of Kohen Gadol during the Second Temple Era, it became necessary to administer an oath to the Kohen Gadol that he not conduct the service according to the Sadducee version. After the oath was taken, both the Kohen Gadol and those who administered it would weep. The Kohen Gadol would weep at being suspected of Sadduceeism; the others would weep for the possibility that they had suspected an innocent man. *R' Yitzchak Hutner* asked: Why did they cry? They had no choice but to administer the oath, so that this vital service would be performed properly.

He answered that true, they had no choice in the matter; still, it was incumbent upon them to feel pain at having caused him pain. Only those who can shed tears over causing pain to others are fit to do so when it is necessary.

13. **Eliciting Mercy.** When a Jew is in need of God's mercy, God provides him with an opportunity to show mercy to others so that he will then merit to have mercy shown to him. As the Sages taught, "Whoever has mercy on other creatures will be the beneficiary of Heavenly mercy" (*Shabbos* 151b).

Thus our verse: *And He will give you mercy* — i.e., He will give you the opportunity to be merciful toward others — *and He will* [then be able to] *be merciful to you* (*R' Nachman of Breslov*).

בָּנִים אַתֶּם לַה׳ אֱלֹקֵיכֶם לֹא תִתְגֹּדְדוּ
וְלֹא תָשִׂימוּ קָרְחָה בֵּין עֵינֵיכֶם לָמֵת
*You are children to Hashem, your God —
you shall not cut yourselves and you
shall not make a bald spot between
your eyes for a dead person* (14:1).

The Torah implies that the fact of our being *children to Hashem* is the reason we must not mutilate ourselves when mourning our dead.

Rashi explains that it befits those who carry the title "children of Hashem" to maintain a certain aesthetic beauty. Our elevated status calls for an increased awareness of our physical appearance. Therefore, we may not practice self-mutilation.[14]

Another interpretation is that the Torah rejects excessive mourning. One who truly believes in God's goodness understands that when He takes someone from this world, He is certainly doing what is best for that person. Therefore, although we do mourn, our mourning is for the loss we have experienced; it is not an expression of sorrow on behalf of the departed. He has gone on to a far better place than this earthly abode. Thus, while one may mourn, one may not do so excessively (see *Moed Katan* 27b).[15] In the words of *Ibn Ezra*, "Even if you don't understand why He took your dear one from you, be like a young child who is sure that what his father does is right — even if he doesn't understand why."

Rosh explains that the verse is reassuring the family of the deceased that they need not despair. Although they have lost their temporal father, they need not fear, for they are children to Hashem. Thus the verse states: Let us not mutilate our bodies in despair, for He is our eternal Father.[16]

Beyond the obvious meaning of the verse, the Sages (*Yevamos* 14b) expound the verse to teach that the Jewish people must remain united and not divide themselves into factions practicing

---

14. **A Higher Standard.** Regarding the verse *You shall teach them thoroughly to your children* (Deuteronomy 6:7), *Rashi* comments that the verse refers to one's students who are considered like one's biological children. As a proof text Rashi cites our verse of *You are children to Hashem, your God.* This implies that the reason the Jews are considered God's children is that He taught them Torah at Sinai.

This tells us that the more Torah one learns, the more profound is his stature as a "child of Hashem," and thus, the more appropriate it is that he be beautiful — physically, morally, ethically and spiritually.

This sheds light on the teaching of *Rambam* (*Hilchos Deios* 5), who devotes an entire chapter to the higher standard of behavior that must be maintained by a Torah scholar. On an elementary level, this is because of the potential desecration of God's Name that will occur if a Torah scholar behaves in a less than exemplary fashion. However, the aforementioned comment of *Rashi* yields a more profound understanding of this requirement — namely, that one whose being fully expresses the exalted status of "child of Hashem" simply must live on a more beautiful and enlightened plane (*Zekan Aharon*).

15. **Going Back Home.** The *Zohar* offers the parable of a prince who was sent far away from home in order to study and develop his abilities and character. Eventually the king summoned him home to assume his duties in the kingdom. Following his departure, the locals, who had grown fond of the prince, were crying uncontrollably over the thought that he was gone. A wise bystander said to them, "Fools, why do you weep? He has left to take his role in a very prestigious place."

God sends man into this world to grow and develop by making proper use of his life's circumstances, by withstanding the trials and tribulations of this world, and by keeping His Torah and *mitzvos*. When man is ready to leave this world all those who knew him weep over his departure. Moses, the wise bystander, therefore taught, "Don't be foolish! He is a child of God and he is returning to his Father" (*Tzror HaMor*).

16. **In Good Hands.** *R' Nachum Zev of Kelm* passed away at a relatively early age, while many of his daughters were still unmarried. When he took leave of them, he said, "I am not at all worried as to your future, for you will now be in far better hands than you were up until this point. Till now your future was in my human hands. From now on you will be in the custody of Hashem, Father of orphans, Protector of widows" (*R' Elazar M. Shach*).

This applies with regard to all of life's difficulties. *R' Zusia of Anipoli* was once the victim of a fire that burned his home to the ground. When he was apprised of his loss, he recited the blessing of "Who has not made me an idolater."

"Imagine," he said, "if I had been created as an idolater. The fire would have destroyed not only my home but even my gods of wood and metal. But I, thank God, am a Jew. Thus, although the fire took my possessions, I still have my God!"

different variations of halachah (see *Yevamos* ad loc. for exact parameters of this prohibition).

The simple meaning and the expository meaning seem to be totally unrelated.

Avnei Nezer offers a thematic connection based on *Ramban* (ad loc.) who sees the prohibition against extreme mourning as rooted in the recognition that death is not final. As children of Hashem, we carry within us eternal souls which live on, beyond our temporal existence. Avnei Nezer submits that this understanding should serve as a source of unity between Jews. Were we mere physical creatures, each with his own body, desires and needs, divisiveness would be understandable. But we are in fact His children, imbued with a Divine soul; thus, we are intrinsically united as children of the Living God.

Others explain the connection differently: The Torah prohibits excessive mourning so that we will realize that life is meaningful not because of what we take from others, but because of what we give to others. If we realize that so long as we can do for others life has meaning, the loss of our nearest and dearest can never bring us to despair. Those who succumb to despair because of a personal loss are saying that other people do not really count.

Thus, there is a connection between excessive despair in mourning and factionalism among Jews. Both are expressions of an identical (and illegitimate) self-centeredness and lack of concern for the human family. Both are prohibited (*R' Tzvi Hirsch Rabinowitz*).

בָּנִים אַתֶּם לַה׳ אֱלֹקֵיכֶם
You are children to Hashem, your God (ibid.).

The Talmud (*Kiddushin* 36a) cites a dispute between R' Meir and R' Yehudah. R' Yehudah states that Jews are considered children of God only when they comply with His wishes. R' Meir disagrees, maintaining that even when the Jews do not display filial respect and devotion they still enjoy the special status of being "children of Hashem." *Rashba* (*Responsa* I §44 and §242) notes that although in disputes between R' Yehudah and R' Meir, the law is generally in accord with R' Yehudah (see *Eruvin* 46b), in this case the law is in accord with R' Meir. Thus, Jews are irrevocably and unconditionally deemed children of God.

R' Mordechai of Kuzmir finds a lovely allusion to our unalterable status as God's children in our verse. When the word אֹתָם, *them,* appears in Scripture, the Sages sometimes expound it to read אַתֶּם, *you.* An example of this exposition concerns the verse אֵלֶּה מוֹעֲדֵי ה׳ מִקְרָאֵי קֹדֶשׁ אֲשֶׁר תִּקְרְאוּ אֹתָם, *These are Hashem's appointed festivals that you are to designate them . . .* (*Leviticus* 23:4). The Sages read אֹתָם as אַתֶּם, *you,* to teach that *your* (i.e., the court's) designation of a particular day as Rosh Chodesh (which in turn determines the festival days) is valid even if it was made in error.

R' Mordechai explains that if a verse that does not actually state אַתֶּם can be given this interpretation, then our verse, where the word is properly read as אַתֶּם, can certainly be given this interpretation. Accordingly, the verse tells us that even if Jews act in error, and stray from the ways of God, they still remain His Children.[17]

וְהַחֲסִידָה
The chasidah (ibid. 18).

According to *Rashi* (*Leviticus* 11:19), this refers to the stork. Why is the stork called *chasidah*? Because it displays kindness [חֶסֶד, *chesed*] toward the rest of its species by sharing food with them.

This seems to contradict the *Talmud Yerushalmi* (*Bava Metzia* 3:5), which states that mice are wicked creatures, for when they spot a large pile of fruit they summon their friends to join the feast. *Maayana Shel Torah* explains the difference between the mouse and the stork. The mouse not only steals the property of others, he also invites others to join in the theft. Kindness performed at the expense of others is actually wickedness. The stork, by contrast, shows kindness to others by sharing her *own* property. For this she is praised.[18]

---

17. **Paternal Pride.** Although we are unconditionally deemed His children, this does not absolve us of the responsibility to act in a way that will make Him a proud Father, Who can look upon His children with satisfaction (*R' Pinchas of Koritz*). We must comport ourselves in a manner that will allow all who observe us to know that we are His children (*Divrei Shmuel*).

18. **Self-Sacrifice.** "To be מוֹסֵר נֶפֶשׁ (sacrifice) my own soul is self-sacrifice; to be מוֹסֵר נֶפֶשׁ somebody else's soul is murder" (*R' Yussie Lieber*).

עַשֵׂר תְּעַשֵׂר
You shall tithe (ibid. 22).

The Talmud teaches that by giving a tithe of one's income to charity one becomes wealthy (*Taanis* 9a). *Ben Ish Chai* writes that one who gives charity may be likened to a nursing mother. As long as she continues to suckle her child, her milk supply is constantly replenished and even increases. However, once she weans the child, the supply of milk dries up.

So too with charity: Not only does it not cause one's holdings to be depleted, it causes them to increase. The more you give, the more you have; the less you give, the less you have.[19]

R' Shimon Shkop offers a penetrating analysis as to why charity generates wealth:

The physical and spiritual beneficence that God bestows upon the Jewish people is given to the nation as a whole. Thus, one who is granted a larger share than others must view himself as a trustee appointed over communal funds, whose task it is to spread the wealth (physical as well as spiritual) among those less fortunate than he.

It is common for a trustee over communal funds who fulfills his responsibilities loyally to be given an even greater sum to safeguard, for he has shown himself to be worthy of trust. He need possess no other outstanding qualities beyond his unswerving loyalty; his honesty alone renders him fit for the public trust. On the other hand, one blessed with great intelligence and abilities may be spurned as a caretaker of public funds if he is not absolutely and impeccably honest.

When God blesses a person with wealth, He is in reality appointing him a trustee to apportion the funds. If one fulfills his duty with fidelity, God raises him in rank and appoints him over an even greater treasure.[20]

Thus, the Talmud teaches: עַשֵׂר בִּשְׁבִיל שֶׁתִּתְעַשֵׂר, *Tithe your wealth so that you will become wealthy* (*Taanis* 9a).[21]

---

19. **Indigent Catalyst.** The letters in the Hebrew words *money* (כֶּסֶף) and *pauper* (עָנִי) allude to the idea that the poor man is really the catalyst for the success of the wealthy. In the Hebrew alphabet, the letter פ is preceded by י, the נ precedes the ס while the ע comes before the פ. Hence עָנִי, *pauper* is the prerequisite for כֶּסֶף, *money* (*Keser Torah*).

20. **Philanthropic Partners.** Many commentators suggest that leading the sixth *hakafah* on Simchas Torah, when we recite the prayer of "עוֹזֵר דַּלִּים הוֹשִׁיעָה נָא, *Helper of the destitute save now!*" is an aid to achieving wealth. In some places, there is fierce competition for this honor. Many err in their understanding of this talisman. They assume that if they beseech God as the One Who helps the destitute, He will respond by rescuing them from their perceived poverty. The true understanding is far more subtle. If one declares that he, like God, wants to help the destitute, then God is more than willing to grant him the wealth so that he will spread it around on God's behalf (*Simchas Aharon*).

21. **Spiritual Endowment.** According to *R' Shimon Shkop*, this is equally true with regard to spiritual achievements and Torah study. Every person is in reality no more than a custodian over his own intelligence, talents and strengths, charged to use them on behalf of the nation. If one is willing to use his time, concentration and efforts to benefit God's children by teaching them His Torah, then God will expand his intelligence and opportunities to spread Torah to the nation.

Thus, when the Sages stated that while one learns much from his teachers, and even more from his colleagues, but learns most from his students (*Taanis* 7a, *Makkos* 10a), they spoke not only of the clarity one achieves through teaching others, but of the spiritual opportunities that God grants those who selflessly give of their time and energies to others.

R' Dovid Lifschutz and *R' Leib Malin,* two of the great Lithuanian scholars of an earlier generation, were once carrying on a heated Talmudic argument with R' Shimon Shkop at his home. After concluding their discussion, they apologized for having taken so much of the venerable sage's time, and thus preventing him, perhaps, from developing novellae and preparing lectures for his students.

R' Shimon responded by explaining that the dictum "Tithe your wealth so that you will become wealthy" applies not only to money but to spiritual matters as well. "A *rosh yeshivah* who teaches Torah to students and tithes his time for their benefit loses nothing by giving away that time. To the contrary! This benefits and enriches him. If he dedicates an hour to preparing a lecture properly or to clarifying a difficult point, he is rewarded with increased intellectual wealth, which allows him to develop fresher and clearer ideas."

In his later years, when his health began to falter, R' Shimon's doctors suggested that he curtail his lecturing. He flatly refused. "Why does God grant man life if not to extend himself on behalf of His people and help them grow in Torah? If I cannot do at least that, of what value is life? The more I invest in spreading Torah, the greater will be the replenishment granted to me."

פרשת שופטים ⋙
Parashas Shoftim

Background

The greater part of this *sidrah* deals with laws intended to implement Torah standards in the society the Jews will establish in the Land of Israel. The first requirement is to establish a court system, to administer justice and protect the interests of all segments of the community.

שֹׁפְטִים וְשֹׁטְרִים תִּתֶּן לְךָ בְּכָל שְׁעָרֶיךָ . . .
וְשָׁפְטוּ אֶת הָעָם מִשְׁפַּט צֶדֶק

*Judges and officers shall you
appoint for yourselves in all your cities . . .
and they shall judge the people with
righteous judgment (16:18).*

This verse addresses the elders of the community, upon whom devolves the responsibility of appointing rabbinic leadership. Since they appoint the Rabbi, they might feel free to show him disrespect or to exempt themselves from following his instructions. Moses therefore tells them תִּתֶּן לְךָ, *appoint for **yourselves.*** If you expect the congregation at large to display total fidelity to the Rabbi, you must do so as well. When the general populace will see that even the elders respect the Rabbi's

Torah authority, they too will show him proper respect.[1]

The verse continues, *and they shall judge the people with righteous judgment. Likutei Yehudah* explains that the call for "righteous" justice relates to the previous *sidrah,* which ends by speaking of the obligation to share one's bounty with the less privileged during the three pilgrimage festivals.

The juxtaposition of justice and charity indicates that while charity is a great virtue, it requires a careful regard for justice. Without justice, thievery and dishonesty masquerade as charity. Such "charity" is a travesty; instead of helping the poor, it defrauds them.

An alternative approach is cited by the adherents of the Mussar movement. They maintain that in order to judge others fairly, a judge must be introspective and self-critical. One who practices self-judgment is slow to focus on the shortcomings of others; therefore, only he can truly judge his fellow man in an objective, sensitive manner.

Thus, the verse teaches that if you appoint judges over "yourself" and are able to see your own shortcomings objectively, then you will be able to *judge the people with righteous judgment.* One who sees his own faults is able to block out the shortcomings

---

1. **Divine Appointment.** Not only must the community elders respect the authority of their spiritual leaders; the spiritual leaders *themselves* must realize that they are ultimately answerable only to God. Although the verse states *you shall* appoint, in reality these judges come to power because *Hashem your God gives you* them as your leaders. If the judges are clear on this point, *they shall judge the people with righteous judgment,* free of undue emotional dependence on their constituents.

of others and view them in a softer light.[2]

Sfas Emes interprets the verse by rendering תִּתֶּן לְךָ, *you shall appoint,* as a promise rather than an imperative.

One who seeks truth but cannot muster the strength, willpower and self-control to realize his desire, may throw himself upon God's mercy and ask Him to create the circumstances in life that will force him to do what is right.

If you truly crave righteousness with all your soul, Hashem promises that *you will appoint judges and officers* who will enforce compliance to His will.[3]

אֲשֶׁר ה׳ אֱלֹקֶיךָ נֹתֵן לָךְ
That Hashem, your God, gives you (ibid.).

A group of laymen once approached *R' Nosson of Makova* with a dilemma. Two rabbis had submitted their candidacies for the position of *rav* of the city. One was a brilliant scholar and a dazzling orator, while the other candidate, while not quite as brilliant or talented, was well known as a righteous and God-fearing person. "Who," they asked R' Nosson, "shall we choose as *rav?*

R' Nosson replied by giving our verse a fresh interpretation. *Judges and officers shall you appoint.* What sort of judges and officers shall you appoint? *That Hashem your God [he]* (i.e., the judge) *will give to you.* Seek judges who will give you Hashem your God by imbuing your hearts and

consciousness with a sense of His Presence. The laymen understood whom to choose.

וְלֹא תִקַּח שֹׁחַד
And you shall not accept a bribe (ibid. 19).

The Talmud (*Kesubos* 105b) defines the power of a bribe, by explaining that שֹׁחַד is a contraction of שֶׁהוּא חָד, *that he is one* [i.e., the person who accepted it is one with the person who gave it]. *Rashi* (ad loc.) explains that the giver and taker become like a single individual. Obviously, this symbiotic relationship disqualifies the judge from ruling on the case. At the same time, this teaches us the proper emotional response one must feel toward someone who did him a favor. Both the one who did the favor and its recipient must feel that their hearts have become fused into one (*R' Meir Chodosh*).

Shitah Mekubetzes (*Bava Kamma* 92b) notes that the prohibition to judge a case that concerns a person who has been kind to the judge in the past is based on two considerations: (1) that the judge may rule in favor of his benefactor as a result of the bribery, and (2) that he may rule objectively and decide against his benefactor, in which case he has repaid good with bad.

It is clear that, judicial concerns aside, a person is required to be so thankful toward his benefactor that he is simply unable to remain objective.[4]

Bach offers a different understanding of the

---

2. **Self-Judgment.** *Rambam* (*Sefer HaMitzvos, Positive Commandment* §176) views the communal function of judges and officers in a similar light. In his words, "We are enjoined to appoint judges and officers who will compel the people to fulfill the *mitzvos* of the Torah and will force those who stray from the path of truth to return to it . . . One of the conditions of the mitzvah requires that the judges be people of a higher standard."

According to *R' Yechezkel Abramsky,* the reason *Rambam* demands that the judges be of a high spiritual level is so that they will prove effective. Only if they are of pristine character will they engender the regard that will induce people to respect them.

3. **A Cut Above.** *R' Simchah Bunim of P'shis'cha* too interprets the verse as pertaining to the individual:

One considering a proposed course of action must appoint (figuratively speaking) judges and officers over himself.

First he must objectively judge whether the direction he wishes to take will lead to a positive or negative spiritual destination. After concluding that it is in fact the correct course of action, he must muster the will to bring it to fruition. He must therefore call upon "officers," that is, resources of willpower that can enforce compliance with the chosen path. So many of our best ideas and plans go for naught because, although we mean well, we lack the strength of character and the intensity of focus to actually realize our desires.

4. **Blinding Gratitude.** *R' Moshe Chevroni* elaborates: When the Torah speaks of the blinding influence of a bribe it does not mean that this blindness is inherently bad. To the contrary: It is entirely *proper* for the recipient of a favor to be blind to the faults and flaws of his benefactor. [The Talmud (*Shabbos* 119a) cites an instance in which R' Ashi refused to preside at a court case involving a Torah scholar. He said, "I love Torah scholars like I love

phrase שֶׁהוּא חַד, *that he is one* (*Kesubos* 105b; see above). The Talmud (*Shabbos* 10a) states that one who administers perfectly truthful justice becomes God's partner in Creation.[5] However, a judge who accepts bribes — and thus perverts truth and justice — does not join God in the creative process. He remains one, alone and isolated.

Some expound the prohibition against bribery homiletically, as pertaining to the spiritual bribery of the evil inclination. One's evil inclination constantly seeks to quell one's desire for spiritual growth by bribing him with flattery. "You are great. You have done so much for God. See how many *mitzvos* you have done, how much Torah you have learned. You are entitled to lighten up a bit on your Torah standards!" The Torah therefore warns us, "Do not take bribes" (*Chovos HaLevavos*).[6], [7]

כִּי הַשֹּׁחַד יְעַוֵּר עֵינֵי חֲכָמִים וִיסַלֵּף דִּבְרֵי צַדִּיקִם
for the bribe will blind the eyes of the wise and make just words crooked (ibid.).

It is noteworthy that in an earlier reference to the corrupting influence of bribery, the Torah speaks of it as blinding the eyes of the shrewd [פִּקְחִים] (*Exodus* 23:8), while here it states that it will blind the wise [חֲכָמִים].

The *Vilna Gaon* explains: Whenever a judge rules on a case, he must combine two talents. First, he must have mastered all the halachic literature that might apply to the case at hand. Secondly, he must be shrewd and possess sufficient practical knowledge to be able to understand the nuances of the case.[8] He must simultaneously be both a חָכָם, *one wise in Torah knowledge*, and

---

myself. One simply cannot see fault in oneself."]

To illustrate the proper attitude one should take toward a person who did him a favor, R' Chevroni mentioned an incident that occurred with his father-in-law, *R' Moshe Mordechai Epstein*. R' Epstein once wrote a letter of recommendation for an acquaintance. The letter was overflowing with exaggerated praise. When questioned as to why he had been so effusive, R' Moshe Mordechai replied, "What should I do? He did me a favor and I feel like someone who received a bribe. I have no choice but to write the warmest of praises in the letter." R' Moshe Mordechai was then asked to identify the great favor that the fellow had done on his behalf. He answered, "The favor was that he held my hand and helped me up the steps to my home so that I would be able to sit down and write the recommendation letter."

5. **Divine Partner.** *Tur* (*Choshen Mishpat* 1) explains this partnership according to R' Shimon ben Gamliel's statement that the world endures because of three things — justice, truth and peace (*Avos* 1:18). Injustice and thievery destroy a functional society; thus, one who administers justice helps God's Creation to endure. It follows that one who judges truthfully is Hashem's partner in Creation.

6. **Beyond Bribery.** A *Mishnah* in *Avos* (4:29) teaches that God accepts no bribes. It is difficult to grasp the point of this teaching, for the thought that God could be bribed seems ludicrous. What bribe could a person possibly offer the Almighty? *Rambam* and *Rabbeinu Yonah* suggest that this means that God does not accept the performance of *mitzvos* as atonement for transgressions. There are no trade-offs in the spiritual arena. One is rewarded for his *mitzvos* but punished for transgressions. One cannot bribe God to look away from his sins by contributing to charity and good causes. Only repentance can allay punishment (see also *Maharal*).

The Talmudic rule is that man must emulate God in all ways. Accordingly, a person may never allow himself to accept the bribery of the evil inclination, thereby lulling himself into spiritual slumber.

7. **Torn by Tears.** A bribe need not take the form of money. A widow once came to *R' Yehoshua of Kutna* to complain that one of the town's residents had taken financial advantage of her. With tears running down her cheeks, she demanded that the Rav summon her tormentor to a *din Torah* adjudication. The Rav refused to participate in the *din Torah.* "Bribery is not only money. Tears can also be a bribe, since they cause a person to forfeit his objectivity. I simply cannot maintain an unbiased position in the face of a widow's hot tears."

8. **Fifth Column.** A young man appeared before one of the venerated sages of Eastern Europe to be examined for *semichah* (rabbinic ordination). After thoroughly testing the young man and finding him fully competent and knowledgeable in all areas of Torah and Halachah, the old rabbi asked him whether he knew the fifth part of *Shulchan Aruch*. The young man was puzzled. "I know of only four parts of Shulchan Aruch. What is the fifth?" Replied the sage, "The fifth part of Shulchan Aruch is what we call *seichel* ("common sense"). Possession of this fifth part of Shulchan Aruch is imperative to putting the other four parts into practice."

R' N.G., a seasoned *dayan* (rabbinic judge), was once asked for the secret of his success at *dinei Torah*. He replied, "I keep them talking until I figure out who is lying." *R' Tzvi Pesach Frank* would frequently invite *R' Yisrael Shimon*

a פִּקֵּחַ, *one wise in the ways of the world.*

Bribery can blind a person so thoroughly that not only does he lose the ability to recall his Torah knowledge, but even his native shrewdness and practical experience desert him as well.[9], [10]

❧❧

The Torah states that bribery can corrupt the words of the righteous. The question is asked: Why does the Torah refer to one who has been corrupted by a bribe as "righteous?"

The answer lies in an analysis of why bribery affects a person's judgement. The law is that even a person as great as Moses or Aaron is disqualified from being a judge if he received even a *minimal* sum of money from one of the parties. Although people of this level cannot be *consciously* corrupted by money, the Torah teaches that their hearts too would be affected by bribery.

It follows that even if one is *unaware* of having received a bribe, the bribe still retains the power to skew his judgment. It emerges that one might remain entirely righteous in deed *even* while being corrupted by a bribe.[11]

צֶדֶק צֶדֶק תִּרְדֹּף
Righteousness, righteousness shall you pursue (ibid. 20).

In a world of falsehood, truth and righteousness are rare commodities; one stands no chance of discovering them unless he pursues them tirelessly. However, one who seeks truth in this world will realize his desire in the World to Come. As the verse states, *Righteousness, righteousness shall you pursue, so that you will live and possess the Land that Hashem, your God, gives you.* By searching for truth in this world, we create our own share in the World of Truth, the Land which He gives us (*Sfas Emes*).

R' Simchah Bunim of P'shis'cha interprets the verse's double mention of "righteousness" as a rejection of the philosophy that states that the end always justifies the means. The verse commands: *Righteousness, **with** righteousness shall you pursue.* Truth must be discovered in truthful ways; justice must be justly administered.

R' Noach of Lechovitch adds: Truth has value *only* if one seeks it for its own sake. One who seeks truth for ulterior motives degrades truth.

Kostelanitz to observe his *dinei Torah,* even though he was not a *dayan*. When the litigants would leave, R' Tzvi Pesach would ask, "*Nu,* R' Yisrael Shimon, which one is lying?"

9. **Impeding Desires.** In a seminal essay on faith, *R' Elchanan Wasserman* elucidates the psychological dynamic that blinds people from seeing the obvious.

He notes that Aristotle, whose intelligence *Rambam* described in superlatives, was unable to achieve faith in God. Yet, the Torah demands this faith of every bar- and bas-mitzvah youngster!

R' Elchanan explains: Faith is not intellectually difficult; to the contrary, it is self-evident! What impedes people from achieving faith are the bribes they accept in the form of forbidden desires. Once a person is obsessed with worldly pleasures, he finds it immensely difficult to forgo them; he therefore turns a blind eye to the truth.

Aristotle, despite his towering intellect, was unable to overcome the spiritual blindness which resulted from accepting the bribes proffered by his evil inclination. By contrast, a Jewish youngster, schooled from childhood to resist temptation, can easily acquire faith in God.

10. **Even the Wise.** The *Chafetz Chaim* underscores the power of a bribe. If someone of inferior intelligence would attest to another person's intellectual prowess, his testimony would be of limited value. But if God Himself identifies a person as wise, there is no doubt that he is truly wise. Here God tells us that even those that He deems to be exceptionally wise are subject to the corrupting influence of bribery.

11. **Secret Bribe.** Two litigants appeared before a tribunal that included the famed *Rav of Apta,* author of the *Oheiv Yisrael.*

After hearing the arguments, the *Oheiv Yisrael* felt that one of the two litigants had presented a stronger case and that justice was on his side. The other litigant apparently sensed the weakness of his own position and therefore decided to bribe the Rav. Knowing that the Rav would never accept the money, he secretly placed a wad of cash inside the pocket of the Rav's coat that was hanging upon the wall.

After a few moments elapsed, the Rav began to doubt his initial feeling, and began to entertain theories in support of the *opposite* position. Sensing something amiss, he called a recess. He decided to clear his head by taking a walk. Putting on his coat, he stuck his hand into the pocket and discovered the bribe. He later mused to himself, "Look at the power of bribery! I was unaware of having received the money; yet, it automatically affected my judgment."

The Torah exhorts, "Seek truth, truthfully!"[12]

לֹא תִטַּע לְךָ אֲשֵׁרָה כָּל עֵץ אֵצֶל מִזְבַּח ה' אֱלֹקֶיךָ

You shall not plant for yourselves an idolatrous tree — any tree — near the Altar of Hashem, your God (ibid. 21).

The Torah follows the law of judges with the prohibition against planting trees near the Temple Altar. *R' Meir Shapiro* states that this alludes to the almost contradictory qualities that must coexist in the character of a judge of Israel.

The inside of the Altar is filled with dirt; this symbolizes the humility that must lie at the core of a judge's character. At the same time, a judge must also emulate the metal exterior of the Altar by being tough as metal, ready to display unbending firmness in defending the downtrodden and the oppressed of the nation.

The Talmud (*Sanhedrin* 7b) compares the appointment of unethical judges to planting *asheirah* trees. *R' Chaim of Brisk* clarifies the imagery:

While most idols are clearly recognizable as such, the *asheirah* looks like any other tree. But beneath the surface it is an idolatrous object. Likewise, the unethical judge: Outwardly, he is a paragon of judicial virtue, committed to serving truth and justice. Beneath the surface, he reeks of corruption. He is like the *asheirah*, his surface beauty concealing deep-rooted deception.[13]

וְלֹא תָקִים לְךָ מַצֵּבָה

And you shall not erect for yourself a monolith (ibid. 22).

One may not erect a single stone as an Altar, even if he intends to use it to sacrifice to God. Although during the times of the Patriarchs this was a form of worship beloved by Hashem, once it was adopted by the idolaters it became detestable in His eyes (*Rashi*).[14]

A monolith is a symbol of immovable strength. While strength and unbending commitment are generally positive forces in the battle for spiritual growth, they can sometimes be counterproductive. For no day is a duplicate of the previous day, and life's challenges are constantly changing. One must translate the timeless lessons of Torah into effective strategies for one's own time. One should not render himself a spiritual monolith, unable to adapt to the unique challenges of his life and time (*Igra D'Kallah*).[15]

12. **Truth for Truth's Sake.** *Rambam* (*Hilchos Teshuvah* 10:2) describes a person who serves God out of true love with the following words: One who serves [Him] out of love is involved with Torah study and *mitzvos* and follows the path of knowledge. He does so for no worldly gain — not out of fear of punishment, nor out of desire for Heavenly reward. Rather, he pursues truth because it is truth.

13. **Superficial Beauty.** *Avnei Azel* expands on this theme: The prohibition to plant trees at the Temple site is intended to counteract man's tendency to see beauty in a purely external sense. The beauty of the Temple is internal and intrinsic rather than the result of exterior enhancement. One who feels compelled to augment the Temple with an aesthetic overlay of greenery has not grasped its internal beauty.

Likewise, when a community appoints a judge or spiritual leader based on superficialities such as good looks, oratorical ability or financial standing, they are indicating that the moral and ethical luminescence of Torah is without appeal to them. They are no different than one who plants an *asheirah* tree near the Temple.

14. **Hands Down.** According to *R' Akiva Eiger* (glosses to *Orach Chaim* 89:1), the practice of praying with raised hands, prevalent during earlier eras and extolled by the *Zohar*, was discontinued when the Catholic Church adopted this form of worship.

15. **New Battlefield.** In the early days of the State of Israel, the *Chazon Ish* suggested changing the language of instruction in many religious schools from Yiddish to Hebrew. Although he generally encouraged Yiddish-speaking schools, he feared that lessons in Yiddish would cause many children who did not understand the language — in particular, those of Sephardic heritage — to be lost to Torah.

Some die-hard traditionalists questioned his decision. He replied with a story: There was once a general who won a major victory by devising a brilliant strategy. As might have been expected, he was heralded as a genius of strategy.

After some years, the nation became embroiled in another war. The aging general was summoned to lead the armies. He again employed his old strategy, but this time, it failed miserably and he was vanquished.

Shocked by his defeat, he attempted to understand what had transpired. A close friend explained, "Your strategy

Kedushas Levi interprets this verse as a homily on setting priorities:

All of life's activities fall into two basic categories; that which one does for himself and that which he does for God. The Talmud refers to these categories as לָכֶם, *for you*, and לַה', *for Hashem*. These two agendas compete fiercely for one's soul, yet one cannot forgo either of them. As the *Mishnah* teaches, "If there is no flour, there is no Torah; if there is no Torah, there is no flour" (*Avos* 3:21). The body must be properly nourished in order to function effectively; without nourishment, one can neither study Torah nor perform *mitzvos* properly. Conversely, the acquisition of material success must never be permitted to become one's primary goal; man must always derive spiritual nourishment from the Torah.

How is one to strike the proper balance between these two poles? By being clear about which is the end and which is the means.

Hence the Torah states: *you shall not erect for "yourselves" a monolith*. Do not allow the "for you" segment of your life to become the permanent, unmoving focus of your existence. Rather, let your spiritual needs take pride of place in all that you do (*Kedushas Levi*).

Background

The Torah describes the judicial process and the fidelity with which all must heed the decisions of the court.

וְהֻגַּד לְךָ וְשָׁמָעְתָּ . . . וְהִנֵּה אֱמֶת נָכוֹן הַדָּבָר נֶעֶשְׂתָה הַתּוֹעֵבָה הַזֹּאת בְּיִשְׂרָאֵל

And it will be told to you and you will hear . . . and behold! it is true, the testimony is correct — this abomination was done in Israel (17:4).

If it will be told to you, then obviously you will hear. Why must the Torah tell us so?

Alshich explains: People in positions of authority are often privy to unfavorable information regarding others. Teachers must be informed of their students' flaws; parents must be told of the misbehavior of their children. However, access to such information must be strictly limited to those people who have the ability to correct the problem. It is unacceptable to pass on such information merely for the sake of gossip.

Thus we are taught, *and it will be told to you*, i.e., to those who really need to know, and **you** *will hear*. You must make every effort to help a fellow Jew who has drifted from the proper path, while at the same time keeping your knowledge to yourself.

R' Chaim Leib of Stavisk focuses on another apparent redundancy in the verse. The Torah states, *behold! it is true, the testimony is correct*. Why must it then repeat that *the abomination was done in Israel*?

The answer is that a Jew never sins alone. The effect of his sin spreads a spiritual poison to all those around him, infecting all the nation with a spiritual germ. It is true that it was *he* who transgressed. However, his act leaves a mark on the entire nation — *the abomination was done in Israel*.

It is for this reason that the Torah calls for the participation of the masses in administering punishment (see verse 7). The participation of the people purges the nation of the sin's residual effects. With this catharsis, we fulfill the command: *Destroy the evil from your midst* (ibid).

כִּי יִפָּלֵא מִמְּךָ דָבָר לַמִּשְׁפָּט בֵּין דָּם לְדָם בֵּין דִּין לְדִין וּבֵין נֶגַע לָנֶגַע דִּבְרֵי רִיבֹת בִּשְׁעָרֶיךָ

If a matter of judgment is hidden from you between blood and blood, between verdict and verdict, between plague and plague, matters of dispute in your cities (ibid. 8).

R' *Mordechai Banet* sees the verse as a commentary on Jewish history. We are often plagued by questions: Why do the nations of the world differentiate between the blood of Jews and the blood of other nations (*between blood and blood*)? Why are the verdicts pronounced upon the Jews viewed differently than the verdicts pronounced upon other ethnic groups (*between verdict and*

is brilliant but the battlefield has changed. The new situation demands its own unique strategy."

The *Chazon Ish* concluded, "There was a time when Yiddish was our protective shield against foreign influences invading the hearts and minds of our young. But today's battle is different, and demands a new strategy. Today the challenge is to ward off ignorance; therefore, we must, for the most part, teach in the common tongue, which is Hebrew."

verdict)? Why does Divine justice allow the terrible plagues that have befallen our people (*between plague and plague*)?

The answer is found at the end of the verse — *matters of dispute in your cities.* Dissension is the cause of all our troubles. When we are united, we are invincible. When we are divided, we are terribly vulnerable.[16]

R' Tzadok HaKohen of Lublin writes that the Torah here alludes to the judgment that is eventually passed upon every person. The *Mishnah* (*Avos* 4:28) teaches that *envy, lust and glory remove a person from the world.* Our verse's phrase *between blood and blood* refers to the lust for illicit pleasures that sets one's blood afire. *Between verdict and verdict* alludes to envy, which causes interpersonal strife and destroys society. *Between plague and plague* represents the cancerous plague of personal aggrandizement.

לֹא תָסוּר מִן הַדָּבָר אֲשֶׁר יַגִּידוּ לְךָ יָמִין וּשְׂמֹאל
You shall not deviate from the word that they will tell you, right or left (ibid. 11).

We must obey the decision of the court even if we are convinced that they are misinformed, and have switched right for left and left for right (*Rashi*). This verse grants license to the Sages to expound the Torah and enjoins us to follow their understanding.[17] One might ask: Why does the

---

16. **Cheapened Blood.** The Midrash teaches that the angels challenged God, "You are concerned for the honor of the birds and the beasts and therefore command Israel to cover their blood (see *Leviticus* 17:13); yet, You allow the blood of the Jews to be spilled freely!" God replied, "It is due to the hatred that exists between them."

Our verse alludes to this Midrash. *When a matter of judgment is hidden from you* and you cannot fathom the difference *between* the *blood* of animals and the *blood* of Jews, you may assume that the underlying cause is the *matters of dispute in your cities* (*R' Shimshon of Ostropoli*).

17. **Sagacious Link.** *Maharal* explains the power of the Sages to propose seemingly novel interpretations of the Torah.

Revelation was not a one-time occurrence; it is an ongoing process. Not only did God give us the Torah (וְנָתַן לָנוּ תּוֹרַת אֱמֶת), He also implanted within our leaders the ability to ascertain His will (וְחַיֵּי עוֹלָם נָטַע בְּתוֹכֵנוּ). When the Sages elucidate the meaning of Torah or even promulgate enactments, they are serving as the conduit to reveal His will. What the Sages proclaim was God's initial intent; however, it is only now that the appropriate time for its revelation has arrived. We must therefore follow the Sages unconditionally, for it is through them we are linked to God's ongoing revelation of Torah.

A fascinating incident which occurred in Vilna attests to the Divine guidance that informs the Torah rulings of the Sages:

Only once in his life did the *Vilna Gaon* issue a practical halachic ruling on a question submitted to him — and he later regretted doing so.

In the Gaon's neighborhood there lived a simple God-fearing tailor. One Friday he bought a chicken and had it slaughtered by one of the local *shochtim*. His wife salted it and put it on the stove to cook. Without thinking, she stirred the pot with a dairy spoon. The tailor ran to the home of the rav, R' Shmuel, to ask whether the chicken was *treif*. While he was at the rav, his wife remembered that the *Vilna Gaon* lived nearby. She went to his home and put the question to the Gaon, who answered that the chicken could not be eaten. Soon afterward, the tailor returned from the home of the rav, and happily informed his wife that R' Shmuel had ruled the chicken permissible. She replied, "But the Gaon forbids it!" When the tailor reported this to R' Shmuel, he told him, "Go home and enjoy the chicken. The Gaon and I will be by shortly to partake of your wife's tasty dish."

After *Kiddush* on Friday night, R' Shmuel went to visit the Gaon. "While I am not the awesome scholar that you are, I am the rav of the city. Since I permitted the tailor's chicken it is permissible to eat it. Please come with me to his house and together we will partake of his food. In this way we will reassure him that the food is kosher beyond a shadow of a doubt." The Vilna Gaon reservedly agreed and they went to the home of the tailor. The tailor's wife placed plates of food before the two great rabbis. As she did so, her arm jogged the candelabra and a bit of melted tallow (which is nonkosher) fell into the food, rendering it unquestionably forbidden.

R' Shmuel turned to the Gaon and in an apologetic tone said, "I see that my master and teacher was right. From Heaven I was shown that I made a mistake and that you were right to forbid the food."

Replied the Gaon, "To the contrary. I was obligated to follow your ruling without veering to the right or to the left. However, in Heaven, they wanted to save me from eating something which I personally felt should not be consumed."

Never again did the Vilna Gaon allow himself to rule on practical halachic queries.

Torah employ the metaphor of right and left in describing the requirement to obey the Sages?

Here is a possible explanation: The verse עַשֵּׂר תְּעַשֵּׂר, literally translated as *you shall surely tithe* (*Deuteronomy* 14:22), is rendered by *Midrash Tanchuma* as עַשֵּׂר תְּעַשֵּׂר, *tithe and you will become wealthy*. By moving the dot over the שׁ from left (שׂ) to right (שׁ), the Sages created a totally new understanding of the verse, one that allows us to give charity for self-serving reasons. We are enjoined to follow the words of the Sages even when, as in this case, they switch left for right.

Background

The organized settlement of the Land requires not only courts, but also a king who can serve as the leader of the nation. However, he, more than anyone else, must beware of the potentially corrupting influence of power.

שׂוֹם תָּשִׂים עָלֶיךָ מֶלֶךְ
You shall surely set over yourself a king (ibid. 15).

It is a mitzvah to appoint a king; yet, the prophet Samuel responded with disappointment and anger when the people requested a monarch (see *I Samuel* 8:5).

R' Yehoshua Heller explains that the mitzvah of appointing a king is more a necessary evil than a preferred state of affairs. He likens it to the mitzvah

to grant a woman a divorce. Were marital bliss to reign, there would be no need for a divorce and hence, it would not be a mitzvah. It is a mitzvah only when the marriage does not work out properly.

If the Jewish people would maintain their proper relationship with God, no king would be needed to enforce their compliance to His will. It is only when the "romance" between God and His people "sours" that it becomes necessary to appoint a king.

Sfas Emes embellishes this theme. The Talmud derives from our verse (*Kiddushin* 32b) that the people must fear the king.[18] Why is this necessary? *Bnei Yissaschar* explains that through fear of the king, people learn to fear God.

Samuel did not rebuke Israel because they requested a king, he rebuked them because they *needed* a king. Samuel expected Israel to have sufficient reverence for the King of kings that they would need no mortal king to teach them fear of God.[19]

מִקֶּרֶב אַחֶיךָ תָּשִׂים עָלֶיךָ מֶלֶךְ
from among your brethren shall you set a king over yourself (ibid.).

This verse teaches that only a person with a deeply rooted sense of brotherhood toward his fellow Jews may serve as the king (R' Asher of Rimanov). *Rambam* (*Hilchos Melachim* 3:6) writes that the heart of the king is the heart of all Israel. It follows that his heart must be permeated with love

18. **Reinstated Royalty.** The Talmud (*Kiddushin* 32b; *Sanhedrin* 19b) derives from our verse that a king may not forgo the honor that attaches to his position. *Shitah Mekubetzes* submits that the double expression שׂוֹם תָּשִׂים (literally: *set you shall set*) connotes a *recurrent* obligation [similar to the one derived from the double expression הָשֵׁב תְּשִׁיבֵם, literally: *return you shall return* (*Deuteronomy* 22:1), which requires a person to return a lost object over and over again]. Thus, even when the king forgoes his honor and wishes to be treated as a commoner, we are commanded to reinstate his royal standing by continuing to honor him. [It is interesting that death, which resulted from Adam's eating of the Tree of Knowledge, is also described with the double expression of מוֹת תָּמוּת, *die you shall die* (*Genesis* 2:17). This tells us that death is not merely a one-time event; rather, man dies over and over again. This, according to the *Vilna Gaon,* is the source of the constant breakdown of cellular matter that continues from the very moment of birth until death.]

19. **Full Loyalty.** The Sages taught (*Kiddushin* 32b): תְּהֵא אֵימָתוֹ עָלֶיךָ, *the fear of [the king] is to be upon you.* R' Hirsch Rimanover interprets these words as a command to Israel to share the fear of the king. The king fears only God and not any mortal being. His fear should be our fear too — to fear God and no other.

Alternatively, this is a call for every man to place his soul as a king over himself. Just as the king's subjects are subservient to him, so too must every limb of a person's body be subservient to the wishes of his soul (R' Yeshaya of Ropshitz).

for his brethren (*Zekan Aharon*).[20] *R' Avraham of Slonim* views love as a formula for crowning Hashem as our King. Only when Jews unite in reciprocal love are they able to accept Him as their King.

לֹא תוּכַל לָתֵת עָלֶיךָ אִישׁ נָכְרִי אֲשֶׁר לֹא אָחִיךָ הוּא
You may not place over yourself a foreign man, who is not your brother (ibid.).

Figuratively speaking, the "foreigner" is the evil inclination. He presents himself as a person's best friend, his loving brother who wishes only to give him the best life has to offer. In truth, however, he is a foreigner, whose only interest is to draw man into self-destructive sin. Do not place over yourself a stranger who is in truth no brother to you (*R' Mordcha of Nadvorna*).[21]

וְהָיְתָה עִמּוֹ וְקָרָא בוֹ כָּל יְמֵי חַיָּיו
It shall be with him and he will read from it all the days of his life (ibid. 19).

Simply understood, this teaches that the national and royal agenda must reflect a Torah agenda.[22]

Ramban identifies a deeper message. He writes that not only must the Torah scroll constantly accompany the king, but, more importantly, the Torah itself must be his constant companion, etched in his soul and engraved in his heart. The Torah must be within him all the days of his life.

Einei Yesharim suggests that the king must become a living embodiment of Torah so that those who observe him will read in his every nuance the message of Torah.[23]

---

20. **Unifying Force.** Some suggest that the word מִקֶּרֶב, *from the midst,* should be vowelized as מְקָרֵב, *one who seeks to bring close.* The king must unite the people and bring them closer to Hashem.

21. **Foreign Influence.** In Eastern Europe there was a long-running feud between the *chassidim* of Rizhin and those of Sanz. In one city that harbored members of both groups, the rav passed on, and the rival camps could not agree on a replacement. Each side promoted their candidate, who was of course unacceptable to the other side. Eventually a compromise candidate emerged — unfortunately, he was a man aligned with the camp of the *maskilim* ("enlightened" renegades).

When word reached *R' Yechezkel of Shinov,* he remarked: "I never understood why the Torah had to warn against taking a foreign man as king. Why would the people want a stranger to be their ruler? Now I understand. When strife and contention rule, people can become obstinate enough to prefer even a non-Jew over the candidate of their opponents."

22. **Heartfelt Imprimatur.** The Talmud decries those who foolishly stand up for a Torah scroll yet don't rise in honor of a Torah scholar (*Makkos* 22b). *Divrei Shmuel* explains: A Torah scroll is the word of God imprinted in ink on the skin of an animal. If one must rise for Torah written on animal hide, one must certainly rise for Torah written on a human heart!

23. **Live *Shulchan Aruch*.** Being in the presence of *R' Moshe Feinstein* was a precious experience for many reasons; one of which was that observing him was like observing a living *Shulchan Aruch*. As the Talmud teaches: מַאן מַלְכֵי רַבָּנָן, *Who are the true kings? The Sages* (see *Gittin* 62a).

פרשת כי תצא ‎&§
Parashas Ki Seitzei

Background

To prepare for the conquest of the Land, the nation needs to be taught the Torah's guidelines concerning warfare. The passions inflamed in battle can wreak havoc on the soul of the Jewish soldier. The Torah therefore sets the parameters of what is permissible and forbidden in wartime.

כִּי תֵצֵא לַמִּלְחָמָה עַל אֹיְבֶיךָ
When you will go out to war against your enemies (21:10).

Metaphorically speaking, this verse refers to man's unabating battle against his primary foe — the evil inclination.

We often feel that overcoming this enemy is simply beyond our abilities. The Sages themselves teach that one's evil inclination attacks a person incessantly and, were it not for Divine assistance, would indeed overcome him (*Kiddushin* 30b). How can we muster the courage to engage so formidable a foe? The Torah answers that we need only begin and God will grant us the victory. As the verse states, *When you will go out to war against your enemies*, i.e., if you will take the first steps toward engaging him in battle, then *Hashem, your God, will deliver them into your hand* (*Chasam Sofer*).

Nesivos Shalom expands upon this theme. The Torah here offers a two-part strategy for this life-and-death confrontation. The first part is expressed by the adage "The best defense is a good offense."[1] Do not wait for the evil inclination to attack, and attempt to seduce you to sin. Rather,

---

1. **Preemptive Strike.** In our verse the Torah guarantees immediate success in warfare, *and Hashem, your God, will deliver them into your hand.* But in an earlier verse (*Numbers* 10:9), the Torah states that when *you shall sound short blasts of the trumpets . . . you shall be saved from your foes.* Seemingly, this demands a greater effort on our part than that described here.

The answer to this question underlines the value of the preemptive strike in spiritual warfare:

R' Menachem Mendel of Kotzk explained: In the earlier verse, the Torah speaks of war waged *in your Land against an enemy that oppresses you.* Once the evil inclination has established a foothold in one's home territory it takes tremendous effort to beat him back. In our verse, the Torah urges us to attack the enemy in *his* territory. *When you will go out to war against your enemy,* without waiting for him to attack first, then *Hashem, your God, will* [immediately] *deliver them into your hand.*

Shem MiShmuel maintains that the difference between the two verses throws into bold relief the unique power of unity. In our verse, the Torah speaks in the singular form, *when you will go out against your enemies* (‎. . . כִּי תֵצֵא אֹיְבֶיךָ); in the earlier verse, it employs the plural form, *when war comes to your Land* (בְּאַרְצְכֶם). When the entire nation is united as a single individual, they are invincible. When, however, disunity prevails, it is far more difficult to secure victory. The Midrash (*Vayikra Rabbah* 26) teaches that although the evil Ahab practiced idolatry, God still granted him tremendous military success — solely because his people scrupulously avoided interpersonal strife.

you *go out to war against your enemies* — engage the invader and drive him out of your life! Secondly, you must internalize the knowledge that God will aid you in attaining victory. As the verse states, *Hashem, your God, will deliver them into your hand.*

Tiferes Shlomo sees in our verse a bittersweet lesson about the realities of life. We frequently make herculean efforts to do what is right rather than what is appealing or convenient, and indeed, God helps us to rise above our earthly inclination. But shortly thereafter we are back at square one, fighting the same enemy we thought we had defeated. We wonder, "Will this relentless battle ever end?"

The verse confirms our fear: *When you go out* into this world, you are entering a battlefield where you will wage incessant *war against your enemies.*

Even if you win a battle, you will certainly be attacked anew. What you must remember is that life is a constant battle in which you can never make peace with the deadly enemy.[2]

וְשָׁבִיתָ שִׁבְיוֹ
And you will capture its captive (ibid.).

What is meant by *its* captive? The *Baal Shem Tov* explains that "it" refers to the enemy — we must adopt his tactics and use them against him. Thus, man must be as obstinate in defeating the enemy as the enemy is in his efforts to destroy him. One must be as diligent and dedicated in defense as the evil inclination is in offense. One must observe his constant efforts to entrap one's soul. If he fails today, he returns tomorrow. One must learn from him. Even if one slips, he should pick

---

2. **Struggling Toward Greatness.** This is the message of the *Mishnah* (*Avos* 2:5): *Do not say, "When I am free I will study," for perhaps you will not become free.* Some lives afford no quiet moments for study and introspection. If one waits passively for serenity, he will wait forever, for it will not come. One must struggle to overcome the tumult of his life, and find ways to bring out his inherent greatness (*R' Menachem Mendel of Kotzk*).

R' Yitzchak Hutner, in a touching letter to a struggling student, captures the essence of the battle of the spirit:
My beloved and precious one, Peace and blessing!

I have received your letter. Your words touch my heart. We have a mistaken and damaging tendency, when discussing the aspects of spiritual perfection attained by our Torah leaders, to focus on their mature years. We speak of them as men of perfection, but omit the inner struggles that raged within their souls [in their early years]. One might gain the impression that the great ones emerged from the womb as accomplished scholars and *tzaddikim*.

All marvel at the purity of speech of the *Chafetz Chaim,* of blessed memory. But who knows of the battles, the stuggles, the failures and setbacks with which the Chafetz Chaim met through the course of his war with the *yetzer hara* (evil inclination)? This example is but one of thousands; a wise person such as yourself can apply the principle accordingly.

The result of this erroneous approach to the lives of *gedolim* is that when a youth of spirit, of spiritual yearning and excitement, encounters failures and setbacks, he sees himself as not being *"planted in the house of Hashem."*

However, know, my beloved, that the root of your soul is not in the tranquility of your *yetzer tov* (good inclination), but specifically in its war against the *yetzer hara.* Your worthy and heartfelt letter resoundingly testifies that you are a loyal warrior in the ranks of the *yetzer tov.* In English the saying goes, "Lose a battle and win the war." Surely, you have stumbled and will stumble again . . . and on many fronts you will fall wounded. But I assure you that after the losses of the battles, you will emerge from the war with the crown of victory upon your head . . .

The wisest of men said, *The righteous will fall seven times, but will arise* (*Proverbs* 24:16). Fools think that this means . . . that he will rise *despite* his fall. Wise men, however, know well that the intent is that the *tzaddik* will rise *because* of his "seven downfalls". . .

Know that when you feel the *yetzer hara* storming within you, you are at that moment much more akin to the great ones than when you find yourself amid the perfect tranquility that you desire. It is specifically in those areas where you fail most often that you have the potential to achieve excellence for the honor of Heaven.

With empathy for your situation,
With trust that you will be victorious,
With a prayer that you succeed,
   Yitzchak Hutner
   (*Pachad Yitzchak, Igros U'Kesavim* p. 217)
   [From *For Love of Torah*, S. Finkelman, ArtScroll]

himself up and begin his spiritual climb again.[3]

According to *Minchas Yehudah,* this teaches us that one must take the fight to the areas controlled by the enemy — *its* captive. The evil inclination attacks us not only while we are engaged in mundane pursuits, but even while we are praying or studying Torah. We must counterattack by capturing *his* territory — namely, life's mundane pursuits, in which he theoretically holds sway — and infusing it with sanctity, employing the worldly in the service of Hashem.[4]

וְרָאִיתָ בַּשִּׁבְיָה אֵשֶׁת יְפַת תֹּאַר
וְחָשַׁקְתָּ בָהּ וְלָקַחְתָּ לְךָ לְאִשָּׁה

And you will see among its captivity a woman who is beautiful of form and you will desire her, you may take her to yourself for a wife (ibid. 11).

Recognizing the inflamed passions of the warrior, the Torah provides him with a permissible way to control his desire and allow the passion to dissipate. In the words of *Rashi,* לֹא דִבְּרָה תוֹרָה אֶלָּא כְּנֶגֶד יֵצֶר הָרָע, *The Torah speaks regarding the evil inclination.*

This concept — that God permits the soldier to marry the captive because otherwise he will take her illicitly — is difficult to comprehend. Is it the Torah's function to make "kosher" man's illicit desires?

R' Leib Lopian offers a deep psychological insight to explain this anomaly. Man's behavior is powerfully influenced by his own self-image. One who views himself as a sinner loses the psychological restraint that prevents him from sinning. He reasons, "I am anyway a bad person; why not indulge my desires?" If the warrior would be compelled to take the beautiful woman illegally, he would view himself as a sinner and would imagine that he cannot repent. Therefore, Hashem in His infinite mercy created a means by which he could continue to see himself as a God-fearing Jew. He thereby escapes the spiritual paralysis that so often accompanies sin.[5]

R' Menachem Mendel of Kotzk expands upon this theme. King Solomon teaches that *stolen waters are sweet* (*Proverbs* 9:17), which means that the forbidden is alluring simply *because* it is forbidden. Once the forbidden object is made permissible, it immediately becomes far less desirable. By permitting the woman to the warrior, the Torah ensures that she will seem less attractive in his eyes. In this way, the Torah neutralizes the sin's appeal.[6]

From this exceptional license to transgress we may conclude that God does not make de-

---

3. **Enemy Incorporation.** King David wrote (*Psalms* 119:98): מֵאֹיְבַי תְּחַכְּמֵנִי מִצְוֹתֶךָ כִּי לְעוֹלָם הִיא לִי. This is ordinarily translated as, *Your commandments make me wiser than my enemies.* However, the Hebrew prefix מֵ also carries the meaning "from." Accordingly, the verse is rendered as "*From my enemies I became wise about Your mitzvos.*" From the evil inclination we can learn how to fulfill God's will. When we observe how he excites our profane side with the prospect of sin, we understand how passionate we must be in performing *mitzvos.* For a sin provides only a fleeting, temporary thrill — if it can arouse such passion in us, how much more passionate should we be regarding that which will afford us eternal joy! (*Kedushas Levi*).

4. **Merciless Foe.** You must never display mercy toward your evil inclination, for he will never show mercy toward you. Rather, you must capture "*his* captive" by being as merciless a foe as he (*Yakar M'Paz — R' Menachem Mendel of Lubavitch*).

5. **Short-Circuited Rebellion.** Every sin contains two elements, one that remains constant in every sin, and one that changes according to the sin. The first is the element of rebellion against God, which is inherent in every sin, regardless of its particular content or form. The second is the destruction that a sin wreaks on a person's soul. The particular form the destruction takes depends upon the individual sin. In this regard, no two sins are alike; each has a specific effect all its own. Some suggest that by permitting the warrior's sin, the Torah neutralizes the aspect of rebellion. Thus, although the act does stain the person's soul, it does not brand him a rebel against God (*Zekan Aharon*).

6. **Lost Luster.** God created the evil inclination and He created Torah as its antidote (*Kiddushin* 30b). By nature, then, the two are in constant tension, in which the exact thing that the Torah forbids must be that which the evil inclination extols, and vice versa. By permitting "the beautiful captive," the Torah removes this sin from the enemy's arsenal — once the Torah permits this woman, the evil inclination is, by its very nature, restrained from pushing her upon the warrior (*R' Meir of Premishlan*).

mands upon us that are beyond our abilities. In this instance, God assessed the willpower of man and concluded that man could not withstand the pressures of wartime, the temptation was too difficult to overcome.[7] Normally, however, if something is forbidden by the Torah, we may assume that we possess the fortitude to comply (*R' Yechezkel Abramsky*).

Tiferes Chaim offers an allegorical portrayal of the warrior of our verse:

The warrior is the Jew; the enemy, his evil inclination. The beautiful woman in captivity is the soul, cast into chains by the evil inclination. The verse exhorts the Jew: When you go out to war against your enemy, you battle for high stakes. If you sense the pain of your soul, you will surely desire to free her from bondage. Your path to do so is through repentance, whereby you take the captive soul as your wife and life's partner.

וְהָיָה אִם לֹא חָפַצְתָּ בָּה
But it shall be if you did not desire her (ibid. 14).

The passage is syntactically uneven. It first speaks in the future tense, וְחָשַׁקְתָּ בָּה, *and you will desire her,* but now speaks in the past tense, אִם לֹא חָפַצְתָּ בָּה, *if you did not desire her.*

Ohel Moed explains: In the earlier verse, the Torah refers to "desire" as חֵשֶׁק; here, however, the Torah uses the term חֵפֶץ. The difference between these terms is that חֵשֶׁק denotes a fleeting desire aroused by passion, whereas חֵפֶץ implies a desire born of reason and logic.

When the Torah first mentions the warrior's desire, it uses the term חֵשֶׁק, for indeed, his wartime desire is the product of a mere momentary passion. But later, once the initial excitement fades, the warrior begins to calmly and rationally assess the situation, and he realizes that his earlier desire was not a rational one. To describe the realization that even earlier he had no real desire for her, the Torah uses the term חֵפֶץ, speaking in the past tense.[8]

Background

The wayward and rebellious son is the result of a marriage and household in which animosity reigns between the parents. The son's narcissistic behavior indicates a soul enslaved by animal passions. The Sages teach that it is preferable that

---

7. **Psalm Platoon.** During the 1950's, the burning issue in the struggle between the Torah camp and its opponents in Israel was the matter of compulsory military service for women.

Several proponents of a draft for women came to visit *R' Tzvi Pesach Frank* (Rav of Jerusalem) to discuss the matter. "Where," they asked, "does the Torah forbid women to be noncombatants in the military?"

Aware that the committee had come to him with answers rather than questions, the wise old sage replied, "The Torah teaches that before the Jewish army would go to war, the officers would announce that those who were fearful and fainthearted should not join the battle (*Deuteronomy* 20:8). According to R' Yose HaGalili, this refers to all those who were fearful and fainthearted as a result of their sins and felt that they might not deserve God's protection during battle. It emerges that the Jewish army contained *only* people who were *entirely* without sin. Nevertheless, the Torah testifies that even these people will sin with "the beautiful captive" unless the Torah allows them to marry her. This tells us that even the most spiritually refined people are susceptible to the immorality of an army camp. We will not expose our daughters to these pernicious influences! Even if you intend to conscript our daughters to do nothing else in the military but recite *Psalms,* we will *still* object!"

8. **Learning the Hard Way.** The thrill of a sin often lasts only until the moment the desire is indulged. Once tasted, the sin loses much of its appeal.

The *Dubno Maggid* compares this to a doctor who warns his patient not to eat a certain food. The patient keeps begging the doctor to allow him to eat the food. Tired of the patient's incessant importuning, the doctor finally allows him to eat it, confident that once he experiences the adverse affects, the patient will thereafter comply with his medical advice.

People often convince themselves that the Torah seeks to ruin their lives by denying them all of life's pleasures. Their eyes become opened to the truth only after they sin and find out the hard way that transgressing God's will affords a person nothing good on any level. The Torah tells us that one who marries a captive woman will eventually come to hate her, and they will bring into the world a rebellious child. Thus, this person serves as an object lesson that true joy is achieved through adherence to Torah, and not through its negation.

the young man die while he is still innocent, before the inevitable evil emerges.[9]

כִּי יִהְיֶה לְאִישׁ בֵּן סוֹרֵר וּמוֹרֶה
If a man will have a wayward and rebellious son (ibid. 18).

This section comes on the heels of the Torah's statement with regard to protecting the rights of the firstborn. According to *Shem MiShmuel* the juxtaposition teaches the importance of "beginnings" — that just as a firstborn, who represents the beginning of a couple's offspring, enjoys special status, so too with regard to other beginnings. Accordingly, the first three months after age 13 (bar mitzvah) are a crucial period for an adolescent; the young man's behavior during this time can have a deep impact on his character. It is only during these three months that the laws of the wayward son apply (*Sanhedrin* 68b). For the form the young man's life is given at this stage establishes the pattern for later years. Thus, the Sages taught that the wayward son is put to death because he will inevitably go on to evil, and it is better that he die innocent than guilty (*Sanhedrin* 72a).[10]

A person must take extreme care to ensure that his beginnings are positive ones. A young person should invest great spiritual efforts following his or her coming of age, for those first few weeks or months leave a lasting mark on one's entire life. Similarly, one's behavior during the Rosh Hashanah-Yom Kippur season has a powerful impact on the quality of one's spiritual life throughout the rest of the year.[11]

The Sages' statement that the wayward son is judged according to his end seems to contradict their teaching concerning Ishmael, son of our forefather Abraham. After Abraham banished Ishmael and Hagar to the desert, Ishmael was dying of thirst. The verse states that *God heeded the cry of the youth in his present state* (*Genesis* 21:17) and saved him. *Rashi* explains that the angels argued that Ishmael should not be saved, since his offspring would one day murder and persecute the Jewish people. God answered that He would judge Ishmael only according to his present deeds and not according to those that lay in his future. But in the case of the wayward son, he is killed on account of his *future* misbehavior!

R' Isaac Sher answers that to the contrary, when God saved Ishmael without considering the future, He did Ishmael no great favor, for he was permitted to live and commit terrible sins later on. Not so this wayward Jewish boy — to him God shows great mercy, by having him killed now before his soul has a chance to self-destruct.[12]

---

9. **Saved by Death.** *Chasam Sofer* recounts a bizarre incident that illustrates this idea.

A young boy of great promise passed away prematurely. His father was inconsolable. One night, he dreamed that his son was still alive, and, having grown up, was about to willingly undergo baptism. In the dream, the father began to weep uncontrollably over this terrible tragedy.

When he awoke, he found that the dream had reconciled him to his loss. He exclaimed, "Thank God I was able to sit *shivah* for a righteous son rather than for an apostate!"

10. **Saved from Himself.** It is noteworthy that the Sages did not say that it is better he die now rather than be allowed to commit robbery or murder. The object here is not to save others, but to save the soul of the wayward son himself.

11. **Setting the Tone.** *Shulchan Aruch* (*Orach Chaim* 603:1) writes that even those who purchase (kosher) bread from a non-Jewish bakery all year round should show extra stringency by refraining from eating this bread during the Ten Days of Repentance. At first glance, this appears to be a form of bribery. The person imagines that his temporarily exemplary behavior will cause God to judge him more favorably during this period of Divine judgment. But this is ludicrous, for God cannot be bribed!

The answer is that beginnings are important. The way a person begins his year sets the tone for all that follows. We therefore accept an extra halachic stringency at the start of the year, so as to begin the year on a spiritually elevated plane.

12. **Bitter Medicine.** [A "hands-off" approach does not always indicate mercy. For example, in the area of child-rearing, it is sometimes best to administer firm disciplinary action, so that one's children will not grow up into spiritually stunted incorrigibles. However, when one *does* punish a child, he must make certain that the child

Alternatively, the difference between Ishmael and the wayward son lies in their respective backgrounds. The Sages teach that the wayward son is the offspring of the warrior who marries the "beautiful captive" (see *Rashi* to v. 11). This tells us that the boy's father is a person to whom externals are of primary importance, as witness the fact that he married purely on the basis of physical attraction. This approach will inevitably filter down to his children. A child of such a father will never amount to anything. Better that he leave the world while he is still innocent than to wait until he is sullied by sin.

This description does not fit Ishmael, who was raised in the home of the great *tzaddik* Abraham. In his case, God knew that his background would eventually bring him to repentance [as indeed did occur — see *Rashi* to *Genesis* 25:9]. God therefore judged him only by his present behavior and not by his future, for his future held out hope of change (*Even Azel*).

אֵינֶנּוּ שֹׁמֵעַ בְּקוֹל אָבִיו וּבְקוֹל אִמּוֹ
who does not hearken to the voice of his father and the voice of his mother (ibid.).

The Talmud (*Sanhedrin* 71a) teaches that the father and mother must have similar voices (i.e., in tone and timbre). Otherwise, the law of the wayward son does not apply. *R' S.R. Hirsch* writes that this teaches us how important it is for both of a child's parents to espouse identical principles and values. A child confused by mixed messages cannot be held at fault if he develops into a wayward and rebellious youth.

R' Chaim Kanievsky sees this as an allusion to the emotional damage that marital strife can inflict upon children. Children who witness constant bickering and fighting among their parents can hardly be blamed if they come loose from their spiritual moorings. Parents must speak with one voice, projecting serenity and demonstrating healthy behavior for their children to emulate.[13]

וְתָפְשׂוּ בוֹ אָבִיו וְאִמּוֹ וְהוֹצִיאוּ אֹתוֹ אֶל זִקְנֵי עִירוֹ
Then his father and mother shall grasp him and take him out to the elders of his city (ibid. 19).

The phrase they *shall grasp him* seems odd; "they shall bring him" would appear to be a more appropriate expression. Furthermore, one would assume that the obligation to deal with the wayward son falls more upon the *beis din* (court) than upon the parents. Why must the parents grasp him and bring him before the court?

The *Skulener Rebbe* suggests that the Torah is indicating that the wayward son's behavior and lifestyle is the result of poor parenting. It therefore states that they must "grasp him," by which it means that they must bear the responsibility for his spiritual condition. Because the failure of the child is their fault, the Torah requires them to undergo the embarrassment of publicly bringing him to the elders of the city.

Nachal Eliyahu explains that the responsibility for the rebellious youth is parental because strictly speaking, he has as yet done nothing to deserve capital punishment. He is put to death only to ensure that he will die innocent rather than guilty.

Just as parents are charged with protecting their son from danger, with teaching him a trade and

---

understands that the parent is motivated by love and an earnest desire to see him remain innocent. When the child knows that we seek to save him from himself, the most bitter of pills becomes palatable.]

13. **Morally Off Tone.** When recording the court proceedings against the rebellious son, the Torah quotes the parents, *he does not hearken to our voice* (21:20). The Sages infer from this that if one of the parents is deaf, these laws are inapplicable (*Sanhedrin* 71a).

The proof text seems inappropriate, for the verse speaks of the *child* not hearkening; it does not speak thus of the parents.

Maayana Shel Torah explains: One can never successfully offer rebuke if he himself does not adhere to his own words. "Do as I say, not as I do" is not an effective means of exhortation.

If one of the parents is figuratively "deaf" to the standards he demands of his child, then the child will not absorb the parental teaching.

The wayward son is one who *chooses* not to hearken. Where, however, it is the parents who are responsible for his choice, the law does not apply.

with finding him a wife (see *Kiddushin* 29a), so too they are obligated to save him spiritually by bringing him to *beis din* to be killed. "Let your son die innocent," cries the Torah to the parents, "and not die guilty."[14]

וּבִעַרְתָּ הָרָע מִקִּרְבֶּךָ וְכָל יִשְׂרָאֵל יִשְׁמְעוּ וְיִרָאוּ
and you shall remove the evil from your midst; and all of Israel shall hear and they shall fear (ibid. 21).

Homiletically speaking, this teaches that those who offer rebuke to the masses must first be sure that they themselves are free of sin. Thus, the Torah first states, *you shall remove the evil from your midst,* and only then states, *all of Israel hear and they shall fear (Yismach Moshe).* According to *Ner Yisrael,* this verse alludes to the power of example. Once a person has purged himself of evil he no longer needs to verbally rebuke others. His mere presence broadcasts the values he embodies

and lives. Once *you remove the evil from your midst, all of Israel shall hear* — without you speaking a word.[15], [16]

Background

R' Yose teaches: *Let the money of your fellow be as dear to you as your own (Avos 2:17).* Here the Torah provides us with the details of how to fulfill this dictum.

לֹא תִרְאֶה אֶת שׁוֹר אָחִיךָ . . .
הָשֵׁב תְּשִׁיבֵם לְאָחִיךָ
You shall not see the ox of your brother . . . you shall surely return them to your brother (22:1).

Ramban notes that an almost identical set of verses appears earlier (*Exodus* 23:4). Why does the Torah repeat itself here?

Rabbeinu Bachya explains that in the earlier passage, the Torah spoke of *the ox of **your enemy,***

---

14. **Doing What's Best.** R' Yechezkel Abramsky once recounted a harrowing tale of spiritual heroism to a young Torah scholar who was studying the laws of the wayward son. "When I served as a rav in Russia, it was common for Jews to approach the rav not only for halachic guidance but also for everyday matters — to pray for a sick relative, for a childless woman, for livelihood — for all such purposes, the rav was the correct address.

"One day a woman came to me with a shocking request. 'Rebbe, pray to Hashem on my behalf — that my son die!' She explained that her only son had been conscripted into the Russian army. She was well aware of the terrible strains and trials that the army placed upon Jews who wished to remain loyal to Torah, and she feared that her son was not spiritually up to the task. Rather than have him abandon Torah and *mitzvos,* she asked me to pray for the death of her son, so that he would die as an upstanding Jew and would not defile his soul with sin. As I tried to calm her, I realized that she was an older woman, and was in all likelihood past her child-bearing years. She had only this son and would never have more children. Nevertheless, she preferred that he die physically now rather than spiritually later. She was prepared to accept a childless, lonely old age, if this would save her son from spiritual peril.

"Our tears began to flow like water, and I said to her, 'Instead of asking Hashem to take your son, let us ask that He protect him from sin so that he remains a good Jew.' The prayers helped; the boy withstood all temptation and returned from his military service with his soul intact.

"At that moment I understood why the Torah requires the parents of the wayward son to bring him to be killed."

Despite the powerful love that parents feel toward their child, they must find a way to overpower that natural emotion and do that which spiritually benefits the child. It is of utmost importance that we do for our children that which will benefit them spiritually *even* if it is painful for us as parents. It is so easy to simply allow children to do whatever they please. However, if we truly care for and love our children, we will compel them to *live* in innocence rather than guilt.

15. **Sinful Mitzvah.** A heretic once taunted a great rav by boasting that he had succeeded in transgressing every prohibition in the Torah besides the sin of committing suicide. The rav caustically replied, "Be careful, for if you do, God forbid, commit suicide, you will have fulfilled the mitzvah of *you shall remove the evil from your midst!"* (*Iturei Torah*).

16. **Live Example.** Many of the statements in *Pirkei Avos* begin with the introductory phrase הוּא הָיָה אוֹמֵר, *He used to say.* R' Aharon of Kaidanov elucidated this phrase in accordance with the Talmudic teaching (*Bava Metzia* 107b) that before delivering rebuke one must be sure that his own morals and ethics are in good order. He renders the phrase in the following manner: הוּא הָיָה, *he was* — i.e., embodied the trait he wished to teach, and only then, אוֹמֵר, *he would say* it to others.

while here it speaks of *the ox of **your brother.*** This teaches that the mere act of returning lost property to an enemy is insufficient. Rather, the mitzvah must bring one to remove the hatred that abides in his heart and replace it with a feeling of brotherly concern. By the time you return the item, you should be returning it to *your brother.* (See *Targum Onkelos* to *Exodus* 23:5.)[17]

Shelah suggests reading the verse as an allegory for spiritual loss. He therefore interprets it in this manner: *You shall not see the ox of your brother . . . cast off.* If your brother loses his sense of humanity and his animal impulses come to the fore, to the point that he is "cast off" from God, then *you shall surely return him to* [once again] *be your brother.* If one must return the physical property of one's fellow, then one must certainly spare no effort to return a *soul* that has been lost.

a person, for the Torah values human dignity over the prohibition against ignoring lost property.[18]

Nachlas Yehoshua interprets *cast off* as referring to *your brother* rather than to the ox or sheep. Accordingly, *and hide yourself* teaches that if one sees that his brother and fellow Jew has strayed from the path of Torah, one should not offer stinging criticism of his brother's shortcomings. Rather, he should "hide" from the sins, and should lovingly help his brother return.

Mishmeres Itamar interprets the upcoming verse as offering a spiritual prescription on how to effect this redemptive process. *If your brother is not near you and you do not know him,* i.e., he is far from the Torah path and is from a religious standpoint unrecognizable, *then gather him inside your house,* and with warmth and love make him realize that you are his brother who truly cares for him.

וְהִתְעַלַּמְתָּ מֵהֶם

and hide yourself from them (ibid.).

Here the Torah seems to indicate that one *should* ignore the lost animal, yet in verse 3 the Torah states unequivocally that *you shall not hide yourself.* *Rashi* explains that an elderly or distinguished person, who under the same circumstances would not retrieve his own animal (due to the degradation involved), may ignore someone else's lost item as well. The Talmud (*Megillah* 3b) states that this teaches the importance of preserving the dignity of

הָקֵם תָּקִים עִמּוֹ

you shall surely stand them up with him (ibid. 4).

The Talmud (*Bava Metzia* 32b) teaches that if one must choose between helping an enemy reload his donkey and helping a friend unload his, he must help the enemy. The reason is that by doing so one breaks the evil desire to hate a fellow Jew. The Talmud questions this ruling, for by failing to unload the overloaded animal one acts with cruelty toward the animal, which according to

---

17. **Emotional Antennae.** A Jew must develop such sensitivity to the pain of his fellow that he can intuitively sense when something in his friend's life is amiss. One who is sensitive to someone else's loss, be it monetary, physical or spiritual, will be granted the ability to return him his property, and sometimes even his spirit and soul.

18. **Absolutely Relative.** *R' Akiva Eiger,* the great *gaon* of Posen, once traveled to Warsaw to attend a rabbinic function. During the course of his stay, he went to visit a cousin of his, a poor shoemaker who lived in a tiny village outside of Warsaw. A crowd followed close behind. When he arrived, the cousin greeted him warmly and offered him the only chair in his shop — his own.

Rabbi Eiger spent some time there and then returned to Warsaw. En route, one of his companions asked, "Why did you go to the trouble of traveling to see your cousin? Surely he could have come to greet you as so many others did. Besides, it does not befit a man of your stature to make such a trip."

The rabbi replied, "In commanding Jews to return a lost item, the Torah says: לֹא תוּכַל לְהִתְעַלֵּם, *You may not ignore it (Deuteronomy* 22:3). Yet, the Talmud (*Bava Metzia* 30a) teaches that there is a time when a Talmudic scholar *may* ignore a lost item — when it would be humiliating for him to be seen carrying such an item. A *talmid chacham* need not suffer embarrassment to fulfill the mitzvah of returning a lost item.

"The prophet Isaiah (58:7) employs similar wording when he exhorts, וּמִבְּשָׂרְךָ לֹא תִתְעַלָּם, *and do not ignore your flesh* (relatives) (see *Rashi*). Here, however, the Talmud does not make an exception for a case in which a Torah scholar might be embarrassed. We see that one may *never* ignore a relative — even at the cost of humiliation. That is why I felt it important to visit my cousin."

many constitutes a Biblical prohibition. The Talmud answers that the gain of overcoming the desire to hate another Jew overrides the obligation to succor the animal.

It is difficult to imagine that the Torah permits a person to transgress a Biblical prohibition *now* on account of a *future* spiritual gain. Perforce, the act of self-control that is inherent in overcoming hatred is *presently* deemed a mitzvah, and overrides the prohibition (*R' Aharon Kotler*).

Consider: The Torah warns us to help even a donkey that carries wood or stones or other uninessential cargo. Surely, then, we must succor a donkey carrying food or medicine or other articles of sustenance. Now, if it is so with regard to a mere donkey, it is *certainly* so with regard to easing the burden of Torah scholars, for they carry the most therapeutic item of all — the Torah. When Torah scholars or institutions are buckling under enormous financial pressures, it is incumbent upon us to come to their aid and fulfill the mitzvah to *stand them up with him* (*Chafetz Chaim*).

Rashi takes note of the phrase *with him.* One is only obligated to help if the owner assists as well; however, if the owner sits on the side and expects the bystander to reload the animal alone, then the bystander is absolved of his obligation.

The *Chafetz Chaim* sees in this a profound lesson concerning the relationship of prayer and effort in spiritual matters. If one pours time and energy into spiritual pursuits, then he may ask God for assistance in his efforts. If, however, one expends no personal effort, he may not expect God's assistance. In the words of the Talmud: "If man sanctifies himself a little bit, Heaven will sanctify him greatly. If man sanctifies himself below, Hashem will sanctify him above" (*Yoma* 39a).[19]

In defining its heightened standard of morality, the Torah teaches that even passive consent to immorality is deemed consent.

אֶת הַנַּעֲרָ עַל דְּבַר אֲשֶׁר לֹא צָעֲקָה בָעִיר
the girl because of the fact that she did not cry out in the city (ibid. 24).

This verse contains a potent lesson on how a Jew must react to the immorality we witness everywhere. Even if we cannot improve the surrounding spiritual and moral climate, we may never allow ourselves to come to terms with it. One may not shrug and say, "What can I do? This is the way society is." One who refrains from protesting the desecration of God's values in His own world is actually practicing a form of acquiescence.

The young woman of our verse was forced into a morally ugly situation about which she can do little. Yet, the Torah deems her deserving of the death penalty because she did not raise her voice in protest (*Chidushei HaRim*).

The *Brisker Rav* used this idea to explain the Talmud's words (*Sotah* 11a) regarding Job. There were three people who were privy to Pharaoh's evil decree against all newborn Jewish males — Jethro, Balaam and Job. Jethro, rather than lend his support to evil, fled the country. He was rewarded by having Moses marry his daughter. Balaam agreed to the plan, and died a terrible death. Job remained silent, and was sentenced to unbearable suffering. Why did his silence deserve such a severe punishment?

The Brisker Rav explained, "When someone is in pain, he naturally screams and cries out even though his cries do nothing to relieve his pain.

---

19. **Consistent No-Show.** Always the master of the enchanting parable, the *Chafetz Chaim* offered the following: A poor person was under terrible financial stress. He poured out his tale of woe to a friend and asked him for a loan. The friend agreed. "Come to my home tonight at 6 o'clock and I will give you the money." Several days passed, and the borrower did not appear. The next time he met his benefactor in the street, he again spoke of his desperate need and apologized for not having shown up at the appointed time. The kindhearted friend set another time at which he could come for the loan. Again the ne'er-do-well missed the appointment.

We are no different. Every day in our prayers we beg Hashem that He open our hearts to His Torah. God hears our prayers, opens our hearts and waits for us to apply ourselves to Torah study. But we do not even bother to make a real effort at earnest study! How dare we come back the next day with the same request?

True, Job could do nothing to thwart Pharaoh. Still, had he been properly pained by the decree, he would have cried out in protest. Since he did not, he was punished. Job failed to understand that even when one can do nothing to help, he must still scream."[20]

---

20. **Screaming Softly.** King David gave expression to this sentiment when he wrote, "הָיְתָה לִּי דִמְעָתִי לֶחֶם יוֹמָם וָלָיְלָה בֶּאֱמֹר אֵלַי כָּל הַיוֹם אַיֵּה אֱלֹקֶיךָ, *For me my tears were sustenance day and night, when [they] say to me all day long, 'Where is your God?'* (*Psalms* 42:4).

"Whenever my detractors, and those who scorn God, would ridicule my belief in You with the taunt, 'Where is your God?,' this alone sustained me: namely, the tears that I shed over the desecration of Your Name. Although I was powerless, the mere fact that it brought me to tears was my sustenance" (*Zekan Aharon*).

A young Jerusalemite was walking with *R' Shlomo Zalman Auerbach* one Shabbos morning when a car sped by. The young man shouted after the car, "Shabbos, Shabbos!" R' Shlomo Zalman asked him, "Why are you screaming? Reminding him that today is Shabbos will do very little, especially since he doesn't hear you anyway. We shout 'Shabbos' for *ourselves,* to ensure that we will not become desensitized to Jewish desecration of the Shabbos. Instead of shouting at others you should forcefully but calmly say 'Shabbos' to yourself, so that you will not make peace with the desecration of the holy Shabbos."

פרשת כי תבוא ‎&ers;
Parashas Ki Savo

Background

Upon entering *Eretz Yisrael,* the Jews became obligated to fulfill the mitzvah of *bikkurim,* which demands that we bring our first fruits to the Temple and present them to the Kohen and declare our gratitude to God for granting us the opportunity to serve Him.

וְהָיָה כִּי תָבוֹא אֶל הָאָרֶץ
It will be when you enter the Land (26:1).

The term וְהָיָה generally introduces a joyous event. It is therefore used to introduce Israel's entry into *Eretz Yisrael.* For what more joyous event can a Jew experience than to settle in the Land of Israel?! (*Ohr HaChaim*). R' Leibel Eiger writes that although the Land of Israel is one of the three great gifts that we acquire only through suffering (*Berachos* 5a), it is nevertheless a source of utmost joy. In the words of King David, *Those who tearfully sow will reap in glad song* (Psalms 126:6).[1]

Aperion (R' Shlomo Ganzfried) notes that the Torah generally speaks of Hashem *bringing* Israel into the Land; here, however, regarding the mitzvah of the first fruits, the Torah speaks of Israel *entering* the Land.

He explains that this expresses the idea that underlies the mitzvah of bringing first fruits: A farmer generally views his agricultural yield as the result of his own backbreaking toil. But in truth, one must recognize that his entire harvest is the result of Godly blessing, while he is nothing more than a sharecropper entitled to a share of the yield.

Thus, just as a sharecropper must deliver the crop to the landowner who then gives him his share, so too must man bring his crops before God in a gesture of recognition that the earth and all it contains belongs to Him.

Our verse speaks of Israel actively entering the Land to teach this very lesson: Should you imagine that you have come to the Land by dint of your own efforts and merit, the mitzvah of first fruits will teach you otherwise. When you bring them to the Temple, you will internalize the knowledge that it is He Who brought you to the Land and He Who will allow you to remain there.[2]

---

1. **Joyous Error.** On the first Rosh Hashanah after he settled in *Eretz Yisrael,* R' Avraham Yaakov of Sadigura erred while reciting the festival *Kiddush,* substituting the words זְמַן שִׂמְחָתֵנוּ, *the time of our joy,* for יוֹם תְּרוּעָה, *the day of shofar blowing.*

   When his *chassidim* commented on his error, he replied, "It is not such a terrible mistake. Every moment one spends in *Eretz Yisrael* is a time of joy."

2. **Reminder of Greatness.** *Rashi* teaches the process of designating the first fruits. One enters his field and notices that a fig has begun to ripen. He wraps a strand of reed-grass (גְּמִי) around it to mark it as one of the first fruits. Why does he use גְּמִי, reed-grass? The answer is that one who sees his field carpeted in vegetation, with fruit-laden trees all about, might be tempted to believe that *my strength and the might of my hand made me all this wealth* (Deuter-

וְלָקַחְתָּ מֵרֵאשִׁית כָּל פְּרִי הָאֲדָמָה אֲשֶׁר תָּבִיא מֵאַרְצְךָ אֲשֶׁר ה' אֱלֹקֶיךָ נֹתֵן לָךְ

And you shall take of the first of every fruit of the ground that you bring in from your Land that Hashem your God gives to you (ibid. 2).

Why does the verse state *you shall **take**?* Since the farmer is *giving* the fruit, the verse should say, וְנָתַתָּ, *and you shall give. Nachal Kedumin* offers an explanation based on a Talmudic ruling. Jewish marriage is performed by a man giving an item of value to a woman. If it is the woman who gives something to the man, she has accomplished nothing; the marriage does not take effect. However, there is an exception to this rule. If a prestigious man accepts a gift from a woman, the marriage *does* take effect, for the emotional satisfaction she derives from his acceptance of her gift is itself deemed an item of value. Since she has received value from him, the marriage is valid (see *Kiddushin* 7a).

Similarly, God's acceptance of the gift of first fruits is itself a gift. In reality, God is the giver while the farmer is the taker. The terminology of the verse reflects this understanding.

Rashi (citing *Bikkurim* 3:1) writes that when a man would see a new fig in his field he would tie a bit of reed-grass around its stem and designate it as *bikkurim* (first fruits). *Noam Elimelech* sees this act, as well the entire mitzvah of *bikkurim,* as a metaphor for man's approach to the mundane. The ripe fig symbolizes man's earthly desires; thus, the one who descends to his field and sees a ripe fig

ready to be plucked and eaten represents a person who wishes to indulge his passions. But the Torah calls for restraint. It commands him to place a string around the stem and declare the fruit *bikkurim;* to exercise self-control and wait until he reaches Jerusalem. In that place of sanctity he may eat of his yield. Likewise, one is commanded to place a chain on his desires, and to use them in the appropriate manner and place to sanctify God's Name.[3]

וּבָאתָ אֶל הַכֹּהֵן אֲשֶׁר יִהְיֶה בַּיָּמִים הָהֵם וְאָמַרְתָּ אֵלָיו הִגַּדְתִּי הַיּוֹם

You shall come to whomever will be the Kohen in those days and you shall say to him, "I declare today" (ibid. 3).

Rashi explains that the phrase *whomever will be the Kohen in those days* teaches that we must show respect to the Kohen even if he is inferior to his predecessors. The same is true regarding our spiritual leaders. Our memories of the great men of yesteryear often cause us to give short shrift to today's leaders.[4] The Torah therefore commands us to go to the Kohen of our times. God always provides us with the leadership we need to connect with Him (*B'Cha Yevarech Yisrael*).[5]

R' Aharon of Belz pointed out that the *Kohen* (or leader) serves as the conduit through which God bestows His goodness upon us. The Kohen's effectiveness is in no way linked to his own personal spiritual stature, but is entirely contngent

---

onomy 8:17). The Sages therefore taught that he should wrap a bit of גְּמִי around the first fruit. גְּמִי is an acronym for גְּדֹלִים מַעֲשֵׂי ה', *the works of God are great (Psalms* 111:2). Pondering this will help him realize that the wondrous tapestry which unfolds before his eyes is entirely the handiwork of the Divine Weaver (*R' Moshe Leib of Sassov*).

3. **Who's First?** The Sages describe the jubilant parade with which the Jews would celebrate the bringing of *bikkurim. R' Elimelech of Lizhensk* writes that the festivities were held to celebrate the triumph of will over ego.

4. **Selective Nostalgia.** *R' A.* related that as a child he went with his father to *R' Mordechai Shlomo,* the *Boyaner Rebbe.* In the course of the conversation, the Rebbe bemoaned the changing times, "*Oy* Moshe, Moshe," he said to the father, "they expect [to have] the (greater) Rebbes of yesteryear, yet they wish to be the (lesser) *chassidim* of today."

5. **Official Respect.** It is sometimes important to show respect toward an office even if the one who occupies the office is unqualified. In the words of *Rashi,* "You have no one but the Kohen of your times כְּמוֹ שֶׁהוּא, *as he is."*

R' Meir Shapiro of Lublin once visited the *Chafetz Chaim* for Shabbos. While sitting at the table, he asked the Chafetz Chaim to relate a Torah thought. The Chafetz Chaim demurred, citing his old age and poor health. The Lubliner Rav replied with the words of Rashi, "We have only the Kohen of the times *as he is.* You are the Kohen of our times."

The Chafetz Chaim, spurred on by R' Meir Shapiro's sharp retort, began to speak.

on the purpose he is given to fulfill. This purpose changes from generation to generation. There is therefore no point in comparing today's leadership to that of the "good old days."

Rashi states that one must accept the Kohen of his times כְּמוֹ שֶׁהוּא, *as he is. Toldos Adam* explains that the test of true leadership is whether the leader himself fulfills the demands he places upon his followers. A leader must be one whose expectations of others are in line with what he truly is (*as he is*). One cannot lead the people if he pretends greatness that he does not possess.

הִגַּדְתִּי הַיּוֹם
"I declare today" (ibid.).

Rashi states that this is a declaration that one recognizes God's favors, and does not view his kindness with ingratitude.

This *bikkurim* passage follows the mitzvah to remember the wicked behavior of Amalek (above, 25:17-19). The Sages state that Amalek embodies the trait of ingratitude (see *Yalkut Shimoni Beshalach*). They provide the example of Haman, who owed his very existence to the mercy King Saul showed to Haman's grandfather Agag, but nevertheless attempted to destroy King Saul's grandson Mordechai, along with the rest of the Jews.

The opposite of ingratitude is הַכָּרַת הַטּוֹב, one's deep recognition that he is entitled to nothing, and that he owes all he possesses to God's lovingkindness. This is the lesson of *bikkurim*. This mitzvah

tells us that even the produce of one's own land, extracted through one's own labor, is also a gift from God.

It is for this reason that the passage of *bikkurim* counterbalances that of Amalek. We remember what Amalek represents and make a commitment to avoid his evil trait (*Be'er Moshe*).[6], [7]

The term הִגַּדְתִּי, *I declare,* is used in Scripture to connote firm and even harsh speech. Why should the Jew bringing *bikkurim* speak to the Kohen in a harsh manner?

Mei HaShiloach suggests that generally, a Kohen serving in the Temple considers himself to be closer to God than a farmer who works the land. By bringing his first fruits to the Temple, the farmer demonstrates that he too serves God, no less than the Kohen in the Temple, and maybe even more so, for he transforms a mere field into a Temple. The farmer therefore speaks firmly to the Kohen, to rebuke him for his arrogant views.

R' Shlomo of Tchortkov understands the farmer to be directing the harsh talk toward himself. The Torah knows that he might imagine that his presence in the Holy Land, and his ability to sustain his family, are due to his personal merit. It therefore directs him to tell himself sharply, *I have come to the Land that Hashem swore to our forefathers to give us.* I am here only in the merit of God's promise to my ancestors.

---

6. **Attempt at Gratitude.** *Maharal* questions the mitzvah to retell the Exodus at the Seder on the basis of a verse in *Psalms* (106:2): *Who can express the mighty acts of Hashem? [Who] can make heard all of His praises?* This seems to indicate that no one is capable of proclaiming God's praises. How then do we dare attempt this at the Seder? *Maharal* and *Malbim* answer that we relate the great miracles of the Exodus on the night of Pesach not simply to praise Hashem, but to express our continuing gratitude for everything He does for us. We would be remiss if we did not even make an *attempt* to thank Him for His endless benevolence. Our inability to fully express or comprehend our debt of gratitude does not absolve us from attempting to thank Him as best as we can.

In the Haggadah, we recite the *bikkurim* passage. The reason this passage was chosen is that its theme, like that of the Seder, is to thank to God for creating and sustaining our nation. The gift of first fruits, symbol of man's creative energy, reflects his cognizance of the fact that all he possesses, including his creative ability, is God given. We thank Him and focus on the eternal reality that *Hashem's is the earth and all that it contains* (*Psalms* 24:1) (*Simchas Aharon*).

7. **Thankful Jews.** The Jewish people are called יְהוּדִים (*Yehudim*) after Jacob's fourth son Judah (יְהוּדָה), even though many Jews are not from the tribe of Judah. *Chidushei HaRim* explains that this is because Leah gave the name יְהוּדָה, which connotes gratitude, to express her gratitude to God for granting her a disproportionate share of the twelve tribes. Since the defining characteristic of a Jew is gratitude to God, the Jews are given a name that expresses this trait.

אֲרַמִּי אֹבֵד אָבִי וַיֵּרֶד מִצְרַיְמָה

An Aramean tried to destroy my forefather.
He descended to Egypt . . . (ibid. 5).

The Torah speaks of Laban's diabolical plan to destroy the Jewish nation before it had properly begun, by killing Jacob and his family (see *Genesis* 31:29-30).

Why do we mention the incident with Laban and the Exodus from Egypt while bringing the first fruits? We do so in order to underscore the great extent of God's kindness. During good times, one must always remember the pain of his earlier existence, so that the scope of God's benevolence toward him will be clear (*Rabbeinu Bachya*).

The verse's second clause, *he descended to Egypt*, seems to have no connection to the earlier clause, which speaks of Jacob's sojourn in the house of Laban. However, *Alshich* demonstrates that they are in fact connected. For Laban, by giving Leah to Jacob before Rachel, caused Joseph not to be Jacob's firstborn son. Jacob was therefore obliged to confer that status upon Joseph by fiat. This aroused the jealousy of the brothers, who responded by selling Joseph down to Egypt. It emerges that Laban's deceit set into motion a chain of events that culminated in Jacob's descent to Egypt.

Although Esau too hated Jacob and sought to kill him, the Torah presents Laban as Jacob's archetypical enemy.

R' Yosef Shaul Nathanson maintains that this holds a powerful lesson for the Jew in exile. Some people claim that anti-Semitism stems from Jewish separatation from mainstream society. The argue

that if Jews would mingle freely with gentiles, they would be universally respected. The incident with Laban teaches otherwise. Laban was family to Jacob — his uncle and father-in-law — and Jacob was a loyal employee who brought Laban great wealth. Nevertheless, Laban hated Jacob and sought to destroy him. We see that fraternization with the nations will not make them love us.

In the figurative sense, the "Aramean" is symbolic of the evil inclination, who seeks to destroy us by uprooting our connection to Hashem. *R' Mendel of Rimanov* states that the name Laban (לָבָן), which means *white*, alludes to a favored tactic of the evil inclination, which is to paint that which is dark and evil as lily-white. Satan rarely identifies his blandishments as sin; he prefers to convince us that to the contrary, what he proposes is actually a mitzvah![8]

וַיָּרֵעוּ אֹתָנוּ הַמִּצְרִים

The Egyptians mistreated us (ibid. 6).

A more appropriate term would be וַיָּרֵעוּ לָנוּ, which literally means *they did evil to us* (see *Numbers* 20:15). The term וַיָּרֵעוּ אֹתָנוּ, however, is more accurately rendered as *they made us evil* (see *Targum Yonasan ben Uziel*).

On the basis of this rendering, *R' Mordechai Gifter* draws from our verse an insight into the dynamic of anti-Semitism. Our enemies often legitimize anti-Semitic laws and practices by engaging in a smear campaign against us. They begin by painting us as evil people, and end by dehumanizing us entirely.[9] The Egyptians followed this scenario. They "made us evil" by portraying us as enemies of the country. Once they succeeded in making us detestable in

---

8. **Inducing Despair.** *Nesivos Shalom* offers an additional perspective. The goal of the evil inclination, the Aramean, is to cause a Jew to let go of the realization that Hashem is his loving Father. Rather than focusing on particular sins, he seeks to eradicate from our hearts the inspiring belief that we are His children and He is our Father.

It is for this reason that the Haggadah writes that Laban sought to eradicate הַכֹּל, *everything*. Were he to undermine our belief that we are children of the King, the evil inclination would indeed destroy our connection to Hashem, which for us is everything.

9. **Clear Conscience.** There is no doubt that the infamous Nuremberg Laws were intended to degrade and dehumanize the Jews in the eyes of the German populace, so that any German who might still possess a conscience would be able to come to terms with the barbarism of the Nazi murderers.

The German creation of Jewish *kapos* to assist them in their evil work, which turned victims into perpetrators, stands as resounding evidence of the power of mistreatment to bring out the absolute worst in us.

Throughout the generations, Jews preferred to be the victims of cruelty rather than to be cruel themselves. From the Egyptian era until the present day, the goal of our enemies has been to demonstrate otherwise.

the eyes of the masses (see *Exodus* 1:12), it was but a short step to their genocidal edicts.

On a spiritual level too, the Egyptians sought to "make us evil" by allowing us to assimilate among them. They understood that assimilation would lead to the destruction of our Jewish identity. Both *Alshich* and *Chasam Sofer* link the terms וַיָּרֵעוּ (*and they did evil*) and רֵעוּת (*friendship*). The sweet talk of brotherly love and interdenominational friendship is the kiss of death for the Jewish nation.[10]

וְעַתָּה הִנֵּה הֵבֵאתִי אֶת רֵאשִׁית פְּרִי הָאֲדָמָה
And now, behold! I have brought the first fruit of the ground (ibid. 10).

Yalkut Shimoni comments: *And now* means immediately, with alacrity. *Behold!* implies joy. *I have brought* indicates the bringing of something that is my own. What is this Midrash teaching?

Divrei Shaarei Chaim understands the Midrash to be describing the three key elements in proper performance of a mitzvah: 1) The mitzvah must be done without delay. 2) It must be performed with joy. 3) One must be willing to incur financial expense if necessary.

According to *R' Yosef Nechemiah Kornitzer* (last Rav of Cracow), the Midrash is teaching us the manner in which one must give charity.

He posits that the funds one donates to the poor are a gift from God; a person who gives charity is not really giving away that which is his own. What then does man provide in performing this mitzvah? The Midrash explains that we leave our personal

mark on the mitzvah of *tzedakah* in two ways: 1) by being sensitive to the pressing nature of the pauper's plight and making the money available without delay; 2) by giving the money joyfully, and with a smile, thereby allowing the recipient to maintain some semblance of his dignity. These things fulfill the dictums of *and now* and *behold.* By doing them, we place a bit of of ourselves into the mitzvah, thereby fulfilling the verse's third dictum — *I have brought.*[11]

וְשָׂמַחְתָּ בְכָל הַטּוֹב אֲשֶׁר נָתַן לְךָ ה' אֱלֹקֶיךָ
You shall be joyful with all the goodness that Hashem, your God, has given you (ibid. 11).

A gift received from an ordinary person inspires joy in direct proportion to the value of the gift. A royal gift, however insignificant, inspires joy far beyond its intrinsic worth, simply because it was received from the king.

When a Jew realizes that all he possesses is a gift from the Almighty, his possessions take on a new significance. They are gifts from royalty! That is the point of our verse: *Be joyful with all the goodness.* Why? Because *Hashem, your God, has given it to you* (R' Yeshaya Mushkat of Praga, *Tiferes Shlomo*).[12]

Beis Avraham interprets the verse as expressing the joy we experience over being granted the opportunity to perform God's commandments. A Jew who has brought *bikkurim* calls out joyously, "I am happy over the many opportunities I have to serve God. *This* is the goodness that He has bestowed upon me."[13]

---

10. **Spiritual Cancer.** What our enemies failed to achieve by means of violence can, God forbid, come to pass as a result of spiritual apathy and assimilation.

11. **Joy and Alacrity.** The Talmud (*Kiddushin* 39b) teaches that reward for *mitzvos* is not given in this world. *Ateres Paz* explains that this is because the opportunity to perform a mitzvah is provided by God. For example, if He would not give us the means to buy a home, we would not be able to fulfill the mitzvah of placing a guardrail around the roof. Since His generosity obliges us to perform *mitzvos,* we deserve no reward for their performance. However, we *are* rewarded for performing the *mitzvos* with joy and alacrity, for these go beyond our obligation.

12. **Joyous for Him.** In our Shabbos prayers we ask: *Make us joyful with Your salvation.* We wish not only to rejoice in our spiritual and physical liberation, but also to rejoice over the fact that it is God Who has liberated us (*Avnei Azel*).

13. **Redemptive Soul.** Every Jew possesses a point of spiritual radiance in his character. Even one who has sunk deep into spiritual darkness must remember that God has granted him a soul. He too must *be glad with all the goodness that Hashem your God has given you* (*Divrei Shmuel*). *R' Nachman of Breslov* teaches that even when man cries out to God in prayer he should never do so out of despair or depression. Rather, he should be gladdened by the goodness which Hashem has granted him. The letters of the Hebrew word בְּכִיָּה (*weeping*) form the acronym בְּשִׁמְךָ יְגִילוּן כָּל הַיּוֹם, *In Your Name we shall rejoice all the day* (Psalms 89:17). Even one who weeps must be joyful, for God is with him.

In the Grace After Meals we beseech God to free us *of the gifts of human hands* and *of their loans,* and ask that we be supported only by His *full, open, holy and generous hand.* Our verse alludes to this idea. We are enjoined to rejoice with the goodness that has been given to us by *Hashem our God* — and not by the hands of man (*R' Avraham Baruch Brafman*).

Background

Upon entering the Land, the Jews assemble at Mount Gerizim and Mount Ebal to swear fealty to the Torah. They acknowledge the blessings that God bestows upon those who adhere to the Torah's precepts, and the curses and calamities that God visits upon those who ignore His word.[14]

אָרוּר אֲשֶׁר לֹא יָקִים אֶת דִּבְרֵי הַתּוֹרָה הַזֹּאת לַעֲשׂוֹת אוֹתָם

Accursed is one who will not uphold the words of this Torah to perform them (27:26).

The nation accepted the validity of the entire Torah and swore to fulfill it in its entirety. One who sins out of weakness of character or laziness has not broken this oath. However, one who *denies* the legitimacy of God's commands, and claims that they are not relevant to him, is deemed by the Torah to be accursed (*Ramban*).

Rabbeinu Yonah (*Shaarei Teshuvah* 1:6) emphasizes this point: "Now listen deeply to what I am about to say for it is a fundamental idea. Although there are righteous people who slip occasionally into sin, they do not make peace with their evil inclination. They conquer their evil inclination one hundred times and when they stumble once they are embarrassed and seek to repent. However, a person who, as a matter of principle, is careless regarding a particular sin — even [a sin] comparatively light in nature — is deemed a מוּמָר לְדָבָר אֶחָד, *an apostate with regard to one thing,* notwithstanding that he is heedful regarding more serious sins. He is counted among those who sin deliberately. His sin cannot be borne."

This is the Torah's intent in cursing those who do not *uphold* the words of the Torah. It speaks more of flawed attitude than of flawed behavior.[15]

According to *Ksav Sofer,* the verse addresses

---

14. **Focused Anew.** The Talmud (*Megillah* 31b) teaches that we read the curses of *Ki Savo* before Rosh Hashanah and Yom Kippur, so that the curses will pass with the end of the old year, allowing the new year to usher in only blessings. Simply understood, this teaching explains the scheduling of our yearly cycle of weekly Torah readings. However, this custom was actually enacted by Ezra the Scribe, who followed the *Talmud Yerushalmi's* custom of a three-year cycle of Torah readings. This means that Ezra read *Ki Savo* only once every three years, which in turn means that Ezra's enactment was to specially take out the Torah to read these curses before the end of the year. Why is this important?

R' Moshe Shapira explained: It is not enough to merely accept and keep the Torah; we must deeply assimilate the knowledge that all untoward experiences are the result of infidelity to God's word. We must recognize that the destiny of every single Jew is inextricably bound up with his loyalty to Torah.

Therefore, at the beginning of the year, when we rededicate ourselves to God and His Torah, we read the curses to remind ourselves of this reality. By focusing on this, we transform curses into blessings, paving the way for the new year and its blessings.

15. **Defining Downward.** A Reform clergyman once asked the *Lubavitcher Rebbe,* "Why do you object to Reform Judaism so vehemently? Many so-called Orthodox Jews are no more exacting in keeping the *mitzvos*!" The Rebbe replied, "The problem with Reform is not in the area of practice. If someone accepts the Torah with all its *mitzvos* but then does not live up to his commitment, that is understandable. Our problem with Reform is that you want to redefine Torah in your own image. You deny the validity of the Torah's demands and expectations. This puts you outside the pale."

R' Shlomo Cohen, a close student of the *Chazon Ish,* related the following personal anecdote. "I once spoke unkindly of a certain Jew who I felt was lax in his practice of halachah. The Chazon Ish said to me, 'We have yet to merit that all Jews are perfectly righteous. One may not alienate even those who are spiritually 'middle of the road.'

"I then mentioned a certain political party and asked the Chazon Ish, "So why does the Rav fight this group tooth and nail? Aren't they 'middle of the roaders'?"

He opened my eyes with his reply. A 'middle of the road' Jew is not following an ideology; he knows perfectly well that the real goal in life is to be authentically righteous. However, he is simply unable to overcome the evil

those who seek to reform the Torah on the grounds that it is too difficult to observe so many *mitzvos*. They argue that doing away with some of the *mitzvos* will make it possible to keep the others. This argument is fallacious. The Torah can be compared to a sophisticated computer, whose integrated circuitry allows it to function. To remove parts from a computer is to destroy it, for each component is vital to the whole. Likewise the Torah: Each mitzvah is essential to the system of life represented by the Torah. Removing a single mitzvah affects the system.

Thus, the Torah teaches: *Accursed is one who will not uphold the words of this Torah* **to perform them.** Even if one's purpose is to allow others "to perform them," he still may not negate a single word of the Torah.

וּבָאוּ עָלֶיךָ כָּל הַבְּרָכוֹת הָאֵלֶּה
וְהִשִּׂיגֻךָ כִּי תִשְׁמַע בְּקוֹל ה׳ אֱלֹקֶיךָ

All these blessings will come upon you and overtake you if you hearken to the voice of Hashem, your God (28:2).

Why does the Torah state that the blessings will "overtake" us? *Degel Machanei Ephraim*

explains that man, with his limited vision, often flees the very thing that will benefit him. His spiritual blindness does not allow him to see that God is being good to him. Therefore, the Torah promises that not only will God bless us as a result of our hearkening to His voice, but that His blessing will overtake us even if we fail to appreciate it. Similarly, King David requested, *May only goodness and kindness pursue me all the days of my life* (*Psalms* 23:5). Even when I foolishly run away from Your goodness and kindness, see to it that they pursue me.

Mei HaShiloach suggests a different understanding. He explains that money has the power to effect dramatic changes in people. People often lose their spiritual equilibrium and lower their ethical standards as a result of financial success. The Torah promises that even if you will merit all these blessings, it will be in a manner of וְהִשִּׂיגֻךָ. The blessings will overtake you at *your* exalted level; they will not bring you down to their mundane level.[16]

Alternatively, the word וְהִשִּׂיגֻךָ is related to הַשָּׂגָה, *understanding* and *perspective.* Money is a blessing only if one possesses sufficient understanding to deal with it properly. The Torah promises that with the wealth will come וְהִשִּׂיגֻךָ. We will be granted the

---

inclination and achieve his true desire. The group you mentioned, on the other hand, has made spiritual mediocrity into an ideology! A philosophy of life that seeks to keep Jews from spiritual growth is a danger to Jewish survival. I therefore fight this group unrelentingly."

In his *Collected Letters* (vol. III #61), the Chazon Ish gives expression to the flaw of mediocrity and the necessity to educate for extremism.

"Just as simplicity and truth are synonymous, so too extremism and greatness. Extremism means taking something to its total fulfillment. Those who raise the banner of mediocrity and detest 'fanaticism' and extremism are either aligned with the falsifiers [of Torah] or they simply lack insight into life.

"We are accustomed to hearing people from certain quarters disassociate themselves from fanaticism, yet claim to be fully loyal Jews. However, just as one who hates an excess of knowledge cannot claim to love knowledge, so too one who distrusts an excess of love for Torah and *mitzvos* cannot claim to love them himself.

"We must educate for extremism! The weaponry of education must be employed to implant scorn against those who abuse the extremists.

"Those who establish educational institutions dedicated to spiritual mediocrity have not tasted great success. This is because of the counterfeit nature of the middle-of-the-road approach. This type of education allows its students to reject those laws or ideas with which they do not agree, and to ignore those articles of faith which they find oppressive in light of contemporary standards. Those educators have robbed their charges of the beauty of 'fanaticism' and as parents and teachers have abused their children and students."

16. **Successful Success.** Financial success is granted not as reward for *mitzvos* but to provide us with the wherewithal to serve God. If these blessings would cause us to stray from the correct path, they would be defeating their very purpose. The Torah therefore promises that although all these blessings will overtake us, they will not detract from our commitment to Hashem (*Nachlas Yaakov*).

insight and perspective to use our money wisely in the advancement of Torah and kindness (*R' Shaul Yedidyah of Modzhitz*).[17]

בָּרוּךְ אַתָּה בָּעִיר וּבָרוּךְ אַתָּה בַּשָּׂדֶה
Blessed shall you be in the city and blessed shall you be in the field (ibid. 3).

Yalkut Shimoni states that the blessing of "in the city" means that one's home will be near a synagogue. *Meged Yerachim* offers a homiletic perspective. Some people maintain two different standards of behavior, one for the synagogue and one for the home. Those who observe this person in the synagogue imagine him to be a paragon of piety. His behavior at home, however, leaves much to be desired. The "synagogue" of this person is far away from his home. The Torah offers the following blessing to those who follow God's path: that their mundane affairs of the home should be positively impacted by the spiritual vistas of the synagogue.

R' Shmuel David Walkin writes that this verse demands authenticity in our service to God. Some people act properly in their own city not because they value Torah but to gain a good reputation. Once they are away from home, they adopt a very different mode of behavior. The Torah demands that we behave in "the field" as we do in the city.

Alternatively, the Torah addresses people who are embarrassed to display their mitzvah obser-vance publicly for fear of being called old fashioned. In order to be deemed blessed, one must demonstrate the ability to maintain loyalty to Torah even in the public eye (i.e., *in the city*) (*Divrei Shaarei Chaim*). This might be interpreted as a call to spread the blessing of the Torah life beyond our personal lives. A Jew who loves God wants to share Him with others. He does not keep the truth to himself; he influences others by showing them its beauty. Thus, *blessed shall you be in the city.* Let your lifestyle be a blessing for all the members of your community (*Zekan Aharon*).[18]

בָּרוּךְ אַתָּה בְּבֹאֶךָ וּבָרוּךְ אַתָּה בְּצֵאתֶךָ
Blessed shall you be when you come in and blessed shall you be when you go out (ibid. 6).

According to *Rashi*, this means that those who hearken to the voice of Hashem will leave this world as free of sin as they were when they entered it. However, this interpretation raises a question regarding the parallel curse: *Accursed will you be when you come in and accursed will you be when you go out* (ibid. 19). While it is understandable that one who ignores his responsibilities toward Hashem will leave this world accursed, why is his being born considered to be a curse? The answer lies in the explanation of a blessing we recite every day. *Blessed are You . . . for not having made me a gentile.* Why do we couch our praise of God in

---

17. **Heavenly Credit Line.** The phrase כִּי תִשְׁמַע can be rendered as *because you will hearken*. It tells us that because you will hearken to His voice in the future, He will grant you His blessings even now. God has confidence that we will "repay" Him for His beneficence and therefore grants us "credit" (*R' Yehoshua of Kutna*).

Beis Avraham maintains that this is why we refer to God as קֵל אֱמוּנָה, *a God of trust.* He offers an analogy: A businessman purchased a large stock of merchandise on credit. Due to bad luck and a bit of negligence, he lost all the merchandise, and was unable to repay his debts. Shamefacedly, he went to the supplier and told him what had happened. The supplier realized that the only way he might possibly recoup his loss was to extend the merchant additional credit in the hope that this time he would turn a profit.

God is called קֵל אֱמוּנָה, *a God of trust.* Even if in the past we have squandered His gifts on foolishness, He is nonetheless ready to help us further, in the hope that we will take the opportunity to repent and clear up our "outstanding debts" to Him.

18. **Spiritually Selfish.** The pejorative Yiddish expression א צדיק אין פעלטץ, *a righteous man in a fur coat,* refers to someone who maintains a high level of personal piety yet does nothing to influence others. *R' Simchah Bunim of P'shis'cha* explained the metaphor: One sitting in a cold house can put on a fur coat to warm up. But while he will be warm, everyone else will remain cold. If, however, he brings some wood and lights the furnace then everyone will be warmed.

A righteous man in a fur coat simply wraps himself up in his warm coat of religiosity and allows everyone else to spiritually freeze to death. Instead, he should ignite his own spiritual furnace in such a way that it warms up others to *Yiddishkeit* as well.

negative terms? Let us simply thank Him for creating us as Jews. *Beis Yosef* explains that being Jewish is a double-edged sword. On one hand, we are privileged to reach the spiritual heights that only Torah can afford. On the other hand, if we fail in our responsibilities, we suffer severe consequences. As the Sages taught, "It would be preferable for man to not have been created, but now that he has been created let him scrutinize his actions" (*Eruvin* 13b). It is therefore impossible for us to thank God for having created us as Jews, for it is only when our lives are over, and we are judged on our deeds, that we will know whether thanks are in order.

It follows that one who leaves the world as a sinner would have been better off to have never been born. Thus, he is retroactively accursed even in his coming into this world (*Binyan Ariel*).

תַּחַת אֲשֶׁר לֹא עָבַדְתָּ אֶת ה׳ אֱלֹקֶיךָ בְּשִׂמְחָה וּבְטוּב לֵבָב מֵרֹב כֹּל

Because you did not serve Hashem, your God amidst joy and goodness of heart, when everything was abundant (ibid. 47).

The underlying source of all our sins is our lack of joy in serving God. Were we to develop excitement and joy in His service, we would never sin.[19] In the words of *R' Aharon of Karlin*: "The Torah does not command us to perform *mitzvos* joyfully; yet, joy is the key to fulfilling all the *mitzvos*. The Torah never forbids depression, yet being depressed opens the door to the evil inclination to lead us into sin."

R' Chaim of Volozhin notes that the following verse continues the theme of serving God without joy. When one works for a close friend, he tends to enjoy his work. Only when working for an enemy does one work begrudgingly, and without joy or enthusiasm. When a person views Hashem's service as a task done for an enemy, the only way to make him see the truth is to compel him to serve his *real* enemy. Thus, the verse continues: *So you will serve your enemies* (ibid. 48).

She'aris Yisrael quantifies the degree of happiness one must enjoy in serving God. Let the joy one experiences in doing Hashem's *mitzvos* be greater than the happiness engendered by any of life's corporeal pleasures. As the verse states: מֵרֹב כֹּל, *more than* enjoyment experienced *when everything is abundant*. [20] [The Hebrew prefix מ can be rendered as *more than*.]

R' Henach of Aleksander renders תַּחַת according to its literal meaning of *under* or *beneath*. He explains that the cause of our punishment is not the unhappiness itself, but that which lies beneath it — namely, the sins that rob us of our joy in His service.[21]

Sfas Emes writes, in the spirit of the Sages who

---

19. **Fair Game.** When we are dissatisfied with ourselves we are fair game for the evil inclination. He whispers in our ears, "Taste this forbidden pleasure, it will make you happy. Spill your anger on the people around you; it will make you feel better about yourself (*Zekan Aharon*)."

By maintaining a *joie de vivre* in all our spiritual activities we can keep evil at bay.

20. **Dance of Death.** An elderly Kotzker *chassid* lay on his deathbed surrounded by his friends. Turning to them, he said, "I have only one regret; I am unable to stand up and dance with you. Since I see that God wants me to leave the world, it is a mitzvah to fulfill His will joyously."

21. **Under the Hay.** *R' Henach of Aleksander* would relate a humorous story to illustrate this perspective: A farmer had a son who refused to study Torah and could not be persuaded to learn even the *alef beis*. Frustrated, the farmer went to the big city and brought back a teacher for his son. He promised the teacher a very respectable salary if he would teach his son the *alef beis*. The teacher toiled mightily to force knowledge into his thick-skulled protege. He finally succeeded in teaching him the *alef beis* and the vowels. One day the farmer came by to see how far his son had progressed. The teacher pointed to letters and asked the boy to identify them. The child responded perfectly. The teacher then moved on to the vowels. "What is under the '*alef*'?" he asked, and the boy responded correctly. This continued until he asked, "What is under the '*hei*'?" The child remained silent. The teacher asked the question again but was met by silence. Even the father's entreaties didn't help — the child refused to answer. Finally the father lost his patience and began beating the boy. "Tell us what is under the '*hei*'!" he bellowed. The child, with a pleading voice, replied, "Father, if you continue to hit me I will have no choice but to reveal the truth. The calf you stole is under the hay." Apparently, the farmer had stolen a calf and had hidden it under a pile of hay in the barn, warning the members of his family not to reveal the secret to anyone. It was the father's sin that kept

teach that good is always more potent than evil, that if the exile resulted from serving God without joy during a time of material abundance, how much more so will we merit the joy of the ultimate redemption if we serve Him joyously despite all that we lack in our exile.

the youngster from saying what was under the *'hei.'* R' Henach finished the story: "When a Jew cannot find it in himself to serve God joyously, there is something that is causing this. Some sin must lie beneath the surface manifestation of unhappiness."

◈ פרשת נצבים
Parashas Nitzavim

Background

The *sidrah* opens with Moses addressing the Jewish nation as a whole, regardless of rank or status. Everyone, from the most menial worker to the loftiest man of spirit, was to enter a new covenant that would meld them into an integrated unit, with Jews being responsible for one another. This is the Talmudic dictum of כָּל יִשְׂרָאֵל עֲרֵבִים זֶה לָזֶה, *all Jews are guarantors for one another.*

אַתֶּם נִצָּבִים הַיּוֹם כֻּלְּכֶם לִפְנֵי ה׳ אֱלֹהֵיכֶם
You are standing today, all of you, before Hashem, your God (29:9).

The Jewish people were traumatized after hearing the Admonition of the previous *sidrah,* which listed the terrible calamities that would befall them if they abandoned God and Torah. The prospect of such a grim and hopeless future paralyzed them with fright Moses now calmed their fears by reminding them that in spite of their repeated failings and rebelliousness in the Wilderness, God had not abandoned them. *You are* [still] *standing today, all of you, before Hashem, your God* (*Rashi*).

R' Leib Chasman explains that the function of the curses was to instill fear, not that they should actually come to pass. God does not wish to punish; He uses the threat of punishment to change attitudes and help people overcome the temptation to do the wrong thing. Once the Jews became frightened as a result of hearing the curses, Moses assuaged their fears and assured them that the curses need not strike them.

Alternatively, Moses' reassurance was expressed in his noting that you stand, *all of you,* before Hashem, your God.

The *Tur* (*Hilchos Rosh Hashanah* 581) writes: "Usually one who must appear in court on a capital offense wears somber-toned clothing and is so fearful of the verdict that he does not groom himself carefully. Not so the Jewish people. Confident that God will perform a miracle on their behalf and save them, they prepare for Rosh Hashanah by cutting their hair and donning white festive clothing. Furthermore, they eat and drink the finest of delicacies on Rosh Hashanah."

R' Simchah Zissel of Kelm qualified this self-confidence. As individuals, we should all dread the verdict to be pronounced on the day of Divine judgment and should not rely on miracles. Confidence that God will be merciful is the exclusive privilege of the nation as a whole. Moses taught that the way to inspire God's mercy even though we have angered Him is to stand, *all of you,* as a united nation before God (*R' Yaakov Naiman*).[1]

1. **Saved by the King.** *Yesod HaAvodah* focuses on a different aspect of Moses' comforting words: "You are standing . . . *before Hashem, your God.*" He likens the scene to a servant who rebelled against the king. If he were to be judged by the ministers, who are obliged to protect the king's honor, he could have no expectation of mercy. The servant's only hope for mercy is for the king himself to sit in judgment. Only he has the right to

[Therefore, the best way to survive the judgment is to dedicate oneself to the benefit of the Jewish nation, so that one will be included in God's beneficence to His people.][2]

Generally Moses addressed the tribal leaders first and then the rest of the people (see *Rashi* on *Numbers* 30:2), but here he spoke directly and simultaneously to everyone. *Alshich* explains: When all are assembled together before God, everyone is equal. No human being can accurately assess the relative importance of any Jew; our earthly standards and God's Heavenly measuring rod are often totally different. A prince and a prestigious person may be less worthy in God's eyes than someone whose contemporaries view him as an ordinary, undistinguished Jew. As the Sages put it in discussing the standards of the World Above: "Those who are elevated [in this world] are lowly [in the World Above], while the lowly [in this world] are elevated [in the World Above]" (*Pesachim* 50a).

It is as if Moses were telling the nation, "Your leaders are *the heads of your tribes, your elders and your officers,*" i.e., *you* may consider them to be your aristocrats, but in God's eyes they may be far less worthy (*Deuteronomy* 29:9).[3]

On the other hand, this sense of equality also calls for all parts of the Jewish people to bear responsibility for the nation's spiritual status. When the hour calls for decisive action in fighting for sanctity and the honor of God, many shrug

forgo his own honor and grant a royal pardon.

As we stand before Hashem on Rosh Hashanah, we know that even if we deserve all the curses of the Admonition, He still is our Merciful Father Whose compassion we may arouse.

2. **Collective Survival.** The *Zohar* suggests that on Rosh Hashanah one should try not to stand out from the rest of the nation. Rather, one should seek ways to become an integral part of the nation or the congregation, so that he shares in its merit. The paradigm for this conduct is the statement of the righteous Shunammite woman to the prophet Elisha. He wanted to express his gratitude for her kindness and asked if he could intercede with the government on her behalf. She demurred, saying, בְּתוֹךְ עַמִּי אָנֹכִי שָׁבָת, *I dwell among my people* (II Kings 4:13), which *Zohar* interprets homiletically to mean that she did not want to be judged as an individual, but as part of the nation. Thus, even one who is personally undeserving can be saved because of the benefit He provides to the nation. On the Day of Judgment it is dangerous to ask the King for our own private needs and thus risk coming under personal scrutiny. Instead, "we dwell among our people," confident that its collective merit will save us.

R' Simchah Bunim of P'shis'cha compared this to someone bringing coins to a money changer. Were he to present a single warped or worn-out coin, the money changer would reject it. However, when it is one of thousands of coins it can slip through along with the others. Similarly, the flaws of any single Jew are susceptible to Divine scrutiny if he stands apart from others. Therefore, we stand together on Rosh Hashanah, shelving our personal agendas and focusing on our collective survival.

3. **Soul Connoisseur.** The halachah underscores this point. Let no one think he is better than the next Jew simply because he carries the public image of a righteous and respectable person. The halachah states that if someone is ordered to kill or else he will be put to death, he must refuse to comply and allow himself to be killed. The Talmud explains, "Who says your blood is redder [i.e., more valuable], perhaps your friend's blood is redder?" (*Pesachim* 25b). Thus, if the leading Torah scholar and righteous saint of the age can save his life only by killing an ignorant Jew, he must refuse to do so. Thus it is clear that prestige and importance are not sufficient grounds for assessing true greatness (*R' Simchah Bunim of P'shis'cha*).

A wealthy diamond merchant who was a follower of the *Rashab of Lubavitch* asked the Rebbe why he honored simple Jews. The Rebbe responded, "They have many positive qualities to them," to which the *chassid* replied, "I don't see them."

Later, the Rebbe asked him if he had brought his pouch of diamonds with him. "Of course," he said, "Would the Rebbe like to see it?" He opened the pouch and pointed to one brilliant stone. "Rebbe, this stone is a dazzling beauty." The Rebbe said, "I don't see anything special about it."

"Rebbe," said the *chassid,* "excuse me for saying so but in order to see the true beauty of a diamond you have to be an expert."

"Yes," retorted the Rebbe. "A Jew, any Jew, is more brilliant and dazzling than the most precious jewel. But to perceive the beauty of a Jew one also needs to be a *maven* (expert)."

humbly, "Who am I and what am I? These types of matters should be attended to by the rabbis, chassidic rebbes and seasoned public activists. How can I, just a simple Jew, get involved?" Such an attitude is unacceptable. When dealing with issues that are *before Hashem, your God* and affect His honor, we must realize that *you are standing today all of you,* ready to assume responsibility for the spiritual welfare of the nation. From the leaders and elders to the lowly woodchopper and simple water carrier, all must be willing to carry responsibility for God's agenda in this world (*Botzina D'Nehora*).

According to *Maharal,* the Torah speaks of the nation as an indivisible and unfragmented whole only when it was at the threshold of *Eretz Yisrael.* At that time, the Jewish people accepted upon themselves the covenant of responsibility for one another, according to which "all Jews are guarantors for one another" (*Shevuos* 49a), committed to assure that every Jew has the opportunity to observe the Torah and its *mitzvos.* This pact was enacted now because *Eretz Yisrael* is the great unifier of the Jewish people.

לְעָבְרְךָ בִּבְרִית ה׳ אֱלֹקֶיךָ
For you to pass into the covenant of Hashem, your God (ibid. 11).

Since there was an existing covenant at Sinai, why was a renewed covenant necessary now? The *Baal HaTanya* explained that a covenant is not made because of the present, when the two parties are trusting and affectionate and are sure that their relationship will last forever. A covenant is made for the future when the passion wanes and the relationship needs to be maintained and strengthened. While Moses lived, the people experienced constant miracles and clearly witnessed God's hand in their daily lives. There was no reason for them to suspect that the intense love between them and God would ever weaken. Once they

would enter the Land, however, where God's guidance is hidden behind the laws of nature and man is preoccupied with plowing, planting and commerce, their love for God might begin to wane. In times when the Jews will be overwhelmed by the ongoing battle for sustenance and financial survival, and when dark clouds engulf the Jewish people in a storm of turmoil and pain, the covenant enables a Jew to re-arouse his deep love for God (*Shem MiShmuel*).

וְהָיָה בְּשָׁמְעוֹ אֶת דִּבְרֵי הָאָלָה הַזֹּאת וְהִתְבָּרֵךְ בִּלְבָבוֹ לֵאמֹר שָׁלוֹם יִהְיֶה לִּי כִּי בִּשְׁרִרוּת לִבִּי אֵלֵךְ
And it will be when he hears the words of this imprecation he will bless himself in his heart, saying, "Peace will be with me though I walk as my heart sees fit" (ibid. 18).

After hearing the terrible calamities that will be-fall those who defy the covenant, how can one serenely delude himself that peace will be with him? Does he actually believe that bad things only happen to other people?

R' Tzvi Pesach Frank related an incident which sheds light on this question. A Jew was rebuked for willfully desecrating the Sabbath, to which he replied, "You will see how I am going to atone for this sin." Immediately after the Sabbath he brought a sizable donation to the rabbi for distribution among the poor. "You see," he bragged to his friends, "I'm sure that my charity is so meaningful in Heaven that it was worthwhile (God forbid) to desecrate the Sabbath just to achieve this heartfelt act of generosity."

Such a person suffers from the delusion that a good heart makes up for all transgressions, thinking that he can "bribe" God and thereby be assured of serenity and peace. The Torah therefore teaches that a good heart, as valuable as it is, does not absolve one of his spiritual duties. *Hashem will not be willing to forgive him* (ibid. 19).[4]

The *Chafetz Chaim* saw the claim "Peace will be

---

4. **Cardiac Arrest.** [Many people shirk their obligations toward practical fulfillment of the *mitzvos* with the claim, "I'm a Jew at heart and the main thing that concerns God is the heart." Important though it is, the heart alone cannot keep a person alive. If one's kidneys, liver or any other life-sustaining organ fails, he cannot survive. In the spiritual sense, as well, the heart is not enough. The 248 positive commandments correspond to the 248 organs and limbs of the human body because the performance of the commandments give life to the entire human organism.]

with me" in a different light. The Jewish people always had to contend with those who rejected the yoke of God's sovereignty and His *mitzvos* because they lacked either the willpower or the desire to curb their illicit passions. Aware of their shortcomings, they sought to justify their lapses in order to mitigate their guilt feelings. Such behavior is obviously unacceptable, yet the national corpus is not fatally endangered by the weakness of individuals. But when people or groups create a "theology" or ideology to replace the Torah, they constitute a grave, life-threatening attack to the future of Judaism.

Accordingly the Torah warns that there will be no forgiveness for one who *blesses himself in his heart,* saying, "*Peace will be with me,* because I am not just a simple sinner — I walk as my heart sees fit; I live by a creed and an ideology." [God can be sympathetic and forgiving toward human moral and ethical frailty. When, however, people create an ideology around their misdeeds, they set themselves beyond the realm of Divine forgiveness.][5]

הַנִּסְתָּרֹת לַה׳ אֱלֹקֵינוּ וְהַנִּגְלֹת לָנוּ וּלְבָנֵינוּ עַד עוֹלָם לַעֲשׂוֹת אֶת כָּל דִּבְרֵי הַתּוֹרָה הַזֹּאת

The hidden [sins] are for Hashem, our God, but the revealed [sins] are for us and our children forever to carry out the words of this Torah (ibid. 28).

In the plain meaning, the verse absolves the nation from responsibility for the private, un-known sins of individuals, but holds the community responsible to combat and correct public transgressions.

The commentators offer varying homiletical interpretations of the verse. According to *Chasam Sofer,* the verse instructs a Jew to maintain a proper balance — a golden mean — between the inner, spiritual world of immersion in Torah study and the performance of the commandments on the one hand, and day-to-day demands of temporal existence on the other. Although our internal existence must be totally focused on God and His service, we must not divorce ourselves from the activities necessary to raise and provide for a family (*Chovos HaLevavos*).[6] Thus the Torah states: *The hidden* internal dimension of life, one's inner world, must be *for Hashem, our God.* However, the revealed mundane activities must be dedicated *for us and our children* to provide for their needs in order that we *forever . . . carry out the words of this Torah.*

Alternatively, this verse speaks to the righteous, warning them to balance their humility in hiding their righteousness with the educational value of exposing their families and children to the proper path. This is the message of the verse: *The hidden* [righteous people] *are for Hashem, our God,* for only He knows of their towering spiritual stature, *but the revealed* [*mitzvos,* which we allow others to witness] *are for us and our children forever* in order that they learn *to carry out the words of this Torah* (*R' Meir Yechiel of Mogilnentza*).[7]

---

5. **Ideological Justification.** [As long as a thief knows he is a thief there is hope that he will repent, but not if he considers himself a Robin Hood who acts to rectify social injustice. When murder is no longer murder but rather an act of mercy, there are no limits.]

6. **Heart in the Clouds.** The Sages teach that in prayer, one's eyes should look downward while one's heart should be focused above (*Yevamos* 105b). R' Shlomo Freifeld sees this as a metaphor for life. One's heart should be intensely involved in shaping his spiritual world and growth. Nevertheless, one may not be oblivious to life and those around him. One's eyes must look downward.

7. **Futuristic Vision.** In a searing commentary on this verse, *R' Klonymus Kalman of Piaczetzna* sought to strengthen his followers in the Warsaw ghetto. Sometimes circumstances prevent us from praying or keeping the *mitzvos* publicly, so we must go underground. At such times we cannot sanctify God's Name publicly, and our service becomes *hidden.* Nevertheless, whatever we *are* able to do is dear and precious in the eyes of *Hashem, our God.* To one thing, however, we must firmly commit ourselves: when we are finally able to practice our *Yiddishkeit* openly, we will do *the revealed for us and our children forever.*

In the fiery inferno of death, where he was killed, the Rebbe was able to look beyond the raging fires to the children and grandchildren who would one day proudly and openly live according to the word of God.

Background

After describing the harrowing pains of an exile brought on by disloyalty to God, the Torah describes the ultimate repentance which is the harbinger of the Messianic era.

וְהָיָה כִי יָבֹאוּ עָלֶיךָ כָּל הַדְּבָרִים הָאֵלֶּה הַבְּרָכָה וְהַקְלָלָה . . . וַהֲשֵׁבֹתָ אֶל לְבָבֶךָ . . . וְשַׁבְתָּ

It will be when all these things come upon you — the blessing and the curse . . . you will take it to your heart and you will return (30:1-2).

Why does the Torah mention the blessings, when it is clearly the curses which sparked the repentance? *Ksav Sofer* suggests that it is the blessing *within* the curses that will cause us to return to God. The hand of Providence is most evident when Jews are oppressed in the exile. Though He seemingly "abandoned" us to our enemies, God blesses us with the ability to survive hatred and cruelty, and to rise again. In the words of the Sages, "This itself is His awesomeness — that He enables a solitary lamb to survive among seventy wolves" (see *Yoma* 69b). R' Yaakov Emden writes that the survival of Israel in the long and cruel exile is a greater miracle than the Exodus from Egypt. When we discern that blessing, we will realize how God saves us from our enemies; then we will certainly recognize His infinite love for us and will return to Him.[8]

Ohel Yaakov comments that curse is not always successful in arousing people to see the truth. When there is general suffering, sinners tend to rationalize, "Times are hard — everyone is hurting." Only when curse and blessing come together, when others enjoy success while we suffer bitter exile, do we realize that the pain of exile is God's way of spurring us to return.

וְשַׁבְתָּ עַד ה׳ אֱלֹקֶיךָ
And you will return unto Hashem, your God (ibid. 2).

When a Jew seeks to repent, he should do so without delay, before the evil inclination ensnares him again. Before seeking to rectify his misdeeds and heal the spiritual wounds of sin, he should begin to do good. Like a wounded soldier being pursued by the enemy, he cannot stop to tend to his wounds; if he does, he will be caught and killed. Only when he is confident that the enemy cannot reach him may he begin to bandage his wounds. So too, a repentant sinner must extricate himself from the evil persuader's grip. Let him return to God and restructure his life so that he will be able to elude spiritual confrontations. Only when he is certain that he is safe from the clutches of evil should he begin to rectify his past (*Kozhnitzer Maggid*).

אַתָּה וּבָנֶיךָ
you and your children (ibid.).

In the last words of *Malachi* (3:24), the prophet speaks of the coming of Elijah, the harbinger of the great and final redemption. *He shall restore the heart of fathers to children, and the heart of children to their fathers.* The Sages interpret the first clause as restoring the heart of fathers *through* their children, for the children will cause their parents to repent. [We are witness to this prophecy in our times, when thousands of children have returned

---

8. **Killing with Kindness.** *Toldos Yaakov Yosef* crystallizes the point with the *Baal Shem Tov*'s interpretation of *O God of vengeance, Hashem* (קֵל נְקָמוֹת ה׳) (*Psalms* 94:1). The Name Hashem generally indicates the manifestation of Divine mercy. How then can Hashem be a God of vengeance? The answer lies in the following parable: A lowly peasant rebelled against the king, publicly cursing and defaming him and even stoning a royal statue. The king thought to himself, "What shall I do to him? If I act like other monarchs and kill him, I will gain nothing." He decided to promote him to a prestigious position. Seeing the king's great kindness, the peasant was broken hearted. "How could I have rebelled against such a gracious king?!" The higher he rose in the royal hierarchy and the more kindness the king bestowed upon him, the worse he felt about having rebelled against his magnanimous benefactor.

Similarly, by smothering us in kindness, God achieves the greatest form of "revenge." Such blessings, not only the curses, will lead to our repentance by forcing us to realize that we are ingrates when we fail to follow His Torah.

to traditional Judaism and influenced their parents to follow them.]

R' Yehoshua of Belz sees in this verse a description of a similar process. Often we worry that our failure to show a proper example to our children will cause them to go astray. Such a concern has influenced many parents to improve themselves. Thus the verse can be homiletically understood to say that **You** *will return to Hashem* [in order to insure that] *you and your children* [will repent] *with all your heart and all your soul.*

R' Yissachar Dov of Belz submits that the Torah speaks not of repentance in order to inspire children but rather in order for the parents to atone for their own sins. Parents must always try to evaluate whether their children's misdeeds are the result of their failure to impart values to them, by word and even more so by deed. Thus the call to repentance is addressed to *you and your children.*

וְשָׁב ה' אֱלֹקֶיךָ אֶת שְׁבוּתְךָ וְרִחֲמֶךָ
וְשָׁב וְקִבֶּצְךָ מִכָּל הָעַמִּים
Then Hashem, your God, will bring back your captivity and have mercy upon you, and He will bring you back and gather you in from all the peoples (ibid. 3).

Why, asks *Meshech Chochmah,* does the Torah repeat the word וְשָׁב, *and He will bring back?* He explains: There are two types of exile and two types of exiled people. Some people feel the pain of exile, both the physical and, perhaps to an even greater degree, the spiritual suffering. These peo-ple yearn to be in *Eretz Yisrael,* the Land that is under Hashem's personal supervision. The Torah promises these people that they will be the first to return: *Then Hashem, your God, will bring back your captivity.* Those who see the exile as a form of painful captivity will be the first to return.

Another type of Jew, however, is fairly comfortable with his situation. Enjoying the creature comforts of the Diaspora, and with their spiritual essence dulled by it, such a person knows intellectually that the exile is bad, but emotionally he has no desire to return to the Land. In order to redeem such a Jew, God must first arouse in him an earnest desire for the Redemption. Regarding this type of Jew, the verse says, God must *have mercy upon you and He will bring you back and gather you in from all the peoples.* [9]

Rambam (*Hilchos Melachim* 11:1) writes of the Messiah: "One who does not believe in him or does not wait expectantly for his coming rejects not only the words of the prophets but he also denies the validity of the Torah and of Moses. The Torah clearly testifies to his existence and to the fact that he will bring us back" (see *Deuteronomy* 30:3-5).

R' Nachum Velvel Dessler of Kelm offered a parable: Someone became deathly ill and his family summoned a specialist to cure their sick husband and father. As they waited impatiently for the doctor to arrive, they heard a knock. Sure that it was the doctor, they all charged to open the door. Unfortunately, it was only a neighbor who needed to borrow a cup of sugar. She left and they sat down again to wait for the doctor. A short while

---

9. **Please! Not Now.** While every Jew expresses a desire for the Messiah to come, his true feelings may not be quite as committed; the coming of the Messiah will cause changes that some people may not be ready to accept.

An amusing, but tragically reflective incident underscores the gap between ideology and practice. *R' Nachum of Chernobyl* once stayed overnight in the home of a Jewish farmer. At midnight, R' Nachum sat on the floor and recited *Tikkun Chatzos,* the prayers that laments the absence of the Temple and entreats God to bring the Messiah. The host, awakened by R' Nachum's sobbing voice, came running to see what was wrong. R' Nachum explained the reason for his sobs, and when he saw that the farmer looked at him strangely, R' Nachum asked, "Don't you want the Messiah to come and bring us to Jerusalem?" The farmer replied, "I don't know. Let me consult with my wife." A short while later he returned to R' Nachum and said, "We can't go to Jerusalem and leave our chickens and geese here."

Not one to yield easily to such "logic," R' Nachum countered, "And what will you do if the Cossacks come, pillage your property and perhaps even kill you? Is that better?"

Again the farmer asked for permission to speak with his wife. He returned and said, "My wife and I would like to ask you to pray to God that the Messiah come quickly, and take the Cossacks to Jerusalem."

[*R' Berel Wein* wryly depicts this using a modern metaphor: "All our speeches end with the prayer that we merit the Messiah soon and in our days — just please not on Super Bowl Sunday."]

later there was another knock at the door, and again they ran to usher the doctor in. But once more disappointment awaited them; it was only the postman. This happened a few more times, and each delay increased their tension. Why didn't they wait passively for the doctor, or for an improvement in their father's condition? The answer is that when someone's life is in danger, every moment counts. The more quickly the doctor comes, the greater the chances of the patient's recovery.

A thinking Jew has to realize that the Jewish people are critically ill, spiritually, and desperately need the Messiah's healing. Therefore, it is not enough to wait patiently. We must recognize that we cannot continue to exist without him.

וּמָל ה׳ אֱלֹקֶיךָ אֶת לְבָבְךָ וְאֶת לְבַב
זַרְעֶךָ לְאַהֲבָה אֶת ה׳ אֱלֹקֶיךָ בְּכָל לְבָבְךָ

Hashem, your God, will circumcise your heart and the heart of your offspring, to love Hashem, your God, with all of your heart (ibid. 6).

In this context, circumcision means removal of the impediments that prevent goodness and the spirit of God from penetrating our hearts and dominating our desires. While here the Torah says that God will do it, earlier (*Deuteronomy* 10:16) the Torah puts the responsibility on people to circumcise their own hearts and remove spiritual callousness from their psyches. Who is to do it — God or man?

R' Menachem Mendel of Kotzk explains that God helps, but man must take the first step to bring it about. A person must begin to cut away the "shell"

that prevents the word of God from penetrating his heart. Then God helps him, making his heart tender and receptive, so that it can reach a state of total *goodness* and love of God.[10]

Mei Shiloach adds that this "circumcision" re-channels man's seemingly uncontrollable passion for sin into a powerful force for Torah and *mitzvos*.

The underlying concept is that human beings have drive and enthusiasm. The challenge is to recognize not only intellectually, but to condition the heart, the seat of emotion, to want the right thing and be anxious to work toward achieving it. But there are countless impediments to success — culture, temptation, desire — all of which must be "cut away through circumcision of the heart."

The great repentance at the End of Days will be a result of man's love for God that will reach such proportions that, as the Talmud teaches, it will be able to turn wanton sin into merit. The passion which man acquired for evil will be transformed into an irresistible force for good.

Ramban views the circumcision as a return to the spiritual state of Adam and Eve at the genesis of creation. Then, their inner psyche and desire was to do good and follow the will of God; their initial sin resulted from the external seduction of the snake. Once they sinned, however, the desire for sin became part of them, and the internal struggle between good and evil became part of the human condition. When the Messiah comes, man will revert to his earlier state and will instinctively live according to God's will.

Accordingly, the verse that urges *us* to circumcise the barriers blocking our hearts asks us to conquer more and more of our lives so that we develop an instinct to do good (*Simchas Aharon*).[11]

---

10. **Inside/Outside.** It is noteworthy that the eradication of Amalek is also stated in this two-tier fashion. In *Deuteronomy* (25:19), God commands, *you shall wipe out the memory of Amalek,* but in *Exodus* (17:14), God promises, *I shall surely erase the memory of Amalek.* Amalek is the human embodiment of evil and therefore has no redeeming value in the Messianic world. For this reason, Balaam says of him and his descendants, *Amalek is the first among the nations but its end will be eternal destruction* (Numbers 24:20). Just as the process of eradicating the external manifestation of evil is begun by Israel but completed by God, so the circumcision of the heart and the excision of the evil within is begun by man but completed by Him (*R' Yitzchak Hutner*).

11. **Battlefront of Choice.** This concept is developed at length by *R' E.E. Dessler*:

Every person, based on genetic factors, education and socialization, finds himself at a particular point with regard to free choice. At any given time in one's life there are sins that he finds impossible to commit and other sins that he cannot resist. For example, one who was brought up in a religious atmosphere *can* theoretically eat pork, but is repelled by the very thought of it, much as one *can* jump off a skyscraper but in fact will not do so. The inherent danger and negativity are so clear and obvious that no real choice exists. On the other hand, someone

וְאַתָּה תָשׁוּב וְשָׁמַעְתָּ בְּקוֹל ה׳

You shall return and listen to the voice of Hashem (ibid. 8).

Repentance was mentioned in verse 2; this is a new level of repentance. Habitual sin induces spiritual blindness, until man is not even conscious of having done wrong. Even when he does begin to realize it, he does not yet perceive the gravity of his rebellion against God, nor is he aware of the personal and cosmic harm his deeds have caused. Only when he takes his first steps on the road back to God does the severity of his actions begin to dawn on him. Questions such as "What was my sin; against Whom did I sin?" begin to pervade his consciousness, calling to him to deepen his regret and strengthen his commitment to a new life. Thus, only after an initial repentance does one truly begin to transform oneself. Hence, the Torah repeats, *You shall* [constantly] *return and listen to the voice of Hashem* (*Tiferes Shlomo*).

לֹא בַשָּׁמַיִם הִוא . . . כִּי קָרוֹב אֵלֶיךָ הַדָּבָר מְאֹד בְּפִיךָ וּבִלְבָבְךָ לַעֲשֹׂתוֹ

It is not in heaven . . . Rather the matter is very near to you — in your mouth and heart — to perform it (ibid. 12-14).

The Torah is not impossibly distant from man; it is accessible to us here and now. Moreover, were the Torah in heaven we would be obligated to climb up on ladders to get to it, so essential is it to our existence (*Rashi*).

How, asks *Shem MiShmuel*, can we be expected to do the impossible and reach something which is beyond our grasp?! The answer lies in the understanding that when man follows God's will he is not merely following instructions; he is acting as God's messenger. Just as a proxy is invested with the power of the one who appointed him, so when we perform God's commandments, we are His agents, as it were. Just as He can do what is humanly impossible, so we, when acting on His behalf, can achieve what would ordinarily be beyond our capacity.

According to *Chidushei HaRim*, the verse teaches us the strength of willpower. One who desires Torah so intensely that he is willing to go to the ends of the earth to find it will find that it is really very near to him.

Tanna D'Vei Eliyahu illustrates this point with a story of a fisherman who met Elijah the prophet. He claimed that he was unable to study Torah because God had not granted him the wisdom, intelligence and aptitude to do so. Elijah said to him, "God granted you the intelligence to be able to cut flax, turn it into cord and fashion it into nets and catch fish, but for Torah study which is near to you He didn't grant you the intelligence?!" Man is not born knowing how to ply a trade; he must learn it. The imperative of earning a living forces him to find the ability to do so. If we were to see Torah as a life and death issue and feel that we need it as desperately as physical sustenance, we

---

who wallows in gossip and slander may find it impossible to observe the laws of *lashon hara,* unless he slowly and laboriously works at changing his nature. For example, the average person is not even tempted to commit murder but is always prone to *lashon hara* (gossip). For each person, the point of *bechirah* (free choice) includes sins that he finds tempting, but that his willpower is strong enough to resist, if he is ready to make the effort (*Kuntres HaBechirah* I, *Michtav MeEliyahu* vol. 1).

Obviously, however, one may not use this concept of a "point of *bechirah*" as license to sin. It is meant as a means for man to understand himself and devise his personal strategy for self-improvement. The goal of circumcising our hearts is to constantly raise our *bechirah* point, putting more and more challenges behind us as we move upward in our struggle to conquer the enemy within.

According to *R' Yehoshua of Kutna,* this is the meaning of the conclusion of the verse *that you may live.* Just as every creature instinctively recoils from danger, so when Hashem circumcises our hearts we will view sin as life threatening and will automatically refrain from it. The more crucial a bodily function is to life the more automatic it is. Since one cannot survive without breathing, it is instinctive even to a newborn. Circumcision of the heart leaves one with the sensitivity to realize that life itself depends on fidelity to the word of God. Thus it will become an automatic reflex, demanding no forethought.

would learn how to succeed at it. Necessity is the mother of invention.[12]

Background

The *sidrah* concludes with Moses warning the nation of the stark choices set before them. Following the Torah or ignoring God's expectations is not just a matter of the degree of religious commitment; it is a life and death issue.

רְאֵה נָתַתִּי לְפָנֶיךָ הַיּוֹם אֶת הַחַיִּים
וְאֶת הַטּוֹב וְאֶת הַמָּוֶת וְאֶת הָרָע . . .
וּבָחַרְתָּ בַּחַיִּים לְמַעַן תִּחְיֶה אַתָּה וְזַרְעֶךָ

See — I have placed before you today the life and the good, and the death and the evil . . . and you shall choose life, so that you will live, you and your offspring (ibid. 15-19).

The Torah equates life with good, for life is given in order to do good. Life is the means and good is the goal. People tend to think that doing good is the means by which to achieve life and improve its quality. Therefore, the Torah exhorts us to see that God has given us life in order to pursue good (*R' Menachem Mendel of Kotzk*).

Bikkurei Aviv adds a variation on this theme. Some people never allow themselves to raise their spiritual horizons. They eat to live, but see life merely as a venue to indulge their physical needs and desires. The Torah seeks to pull them out of this spiritual quicksand. *Choose life so that you will live.* See life as a means to develop the spiritual vibrancy that imbues life itself with more meaningful content, not just as the opportunity for better meals and sensual pleasure. Use life for a more exalted existence.[13]

12. **Crucial Availability.** The availability of what one needs for physical survival is in direct proportion to how crucial the need is. The more vital something is for survival, the more available it is and the greater the quantity. Air is everywhere. Water is not as crucial as air, is readily available though not unlimited. Here, the Torah teaches us that this axiom is equally true with regard to spiritual sustenance. Torah is crucial for survival; a Jew cannot exist without it. If it were to be found only in heaven, we would have no choice but to climb to heaven to acquire it. If it was only available on the other side of the world, we would be forced to go there. Torah means survival and no difficulty is too great when survival is at stake. Because we cannot do without it, the Torah must be readily available. Therefore it is not in heaven, nor overseas. Rather, it is *very near to you — in your mouth and heart to perform it* (*HaMeir L'Olam*).

13. **Constant Whisper.** The evil inclination is tireless in its efforts to impede one's spiritual ascent. When a Jew wants to give charity, the *yetzer hara* appears in the guise of a God-fearing scholar. "Why give away your money? The Talmud teaches that kind deeds are more meaningful than charity" (see *Succah* 49b). Besides, if you lend the money, it is not only a great mitzvah, but you will get it back to perform more *mitzvos*." Thus persuaded, the man turns the pauper away empty handed. Later there is a knock on the door. His neighbor needs a short-term loan to buy goods at a bargain price. "I can turn the merchandise around quickly and repay the loan," he says.

But before the scholar can take out his checkbook, the evil inclination is back. "The Sages teach that interpersonal kindness must be shown to the wealthy as well, why not look for a safer loan opportunity?" Convinced again, he refuses to lend his neighbor the money.

The phone rings. It is a wealthy acquaintance, a prosperous manufacturer. "Do me a favor," he says. "Tomorrow I have to meet a payroll. I need a bridge loan for a week or so." Calculating in his mind all the *mitzvos* he can do with this one loan he goes for his checkbook. Suddenly he hears a whisper. "You know, one never knows what can happen to wealthy manufacturers with cash-flow problems. Why take a chance? Use the money to memorialize your late parents." The Torah therefore teaches that we do better to choose life, and not neglect the needs of the living.

פרשת וילך §
Parashas Vayeilech

Background

After charging the nation with its new covenant of interpersonal responsibility, Moses walked through the camp to bid his flock a personal farewell.[1]

וַיֵּלֶךְ מֹשֶׁה
Moses went (31:1).

According to the *Zohar*, Moses went to a better world. He did not really die; he simply made a "change of venue." *Ilana D'Chayi* submits that he went and is still going, for his spirit lives on in those who succeed to his role of authentic Jewish leadership. In a more personal vein, *Yesod Ha-Avodah* suggests that Moses went into the heart of every Jew. Regardless of our status in life, that internal bit of Moses seeks to guide us along his path. One of the reasons no one knows his burial place (*Deuteronomy* 34:6) is that he is interred in the hearts of his beloved people (*Maayana Shel Torah*).

Alternatively, these words are meant in contrast to the rest of the verse. Although *Moses went* from this world and is no longer physically present, he nonetheless *spoke these words to all of Israel.* Moses continues to speak to the Jewish people throughout its history. Every new discovery in the understanding of Torah is rooted in the Torah of Moses. For this reason the Talmud sometimes refers to great Torah scholars with the nickname Moses (Moses, you speak correctly — see *Shabbos* 101b). All great expositors of Torah are, in a sense, the living reincarnation of the man who received the Torah at Sinai (*Noam Megadim*).[2]

Ibn Ezra understands this "going" as Moses'

---

1. **Always the Role Model.** When Moses said, *I can no longer go out and come in,* he did not mean that his old age stopped him from functioning, but rather that God had forbidden him from continuing in his leadership role. Moses therefore went through the camp to make it clear that he had lost none of his vibrancy or alacrity (*Kli Yakar*). His alacrity and the way in which he went about his responsibilities were a powerful lesson. Simply by watching him and seeing how youthful he remained in his service of God, the people were chastised.

2. **Pervasive Message.** *Toldos Yitzchak* adds another thread to the tapestry. The Torah does not say where Moses went, because wherever he was he *spoke these words to all of Israel.* In the street, at work, in private and in public, Moses sought to inculcate the word of God into the hearts and minds of the Jews, wherever they were.

Targum Yonasan says that Moses went to the study hall to learn. The *Shpole Zeide* (Grandfather), who was known by this appelation among other reasons — because he lived to a ripe old age, told his *chassidim* when he reached the age of 70, "*Kinderlach* (my children), when one gets old, it is time to go back to the *cheder* (elementary school). Before he died, Moses went back to the study hall, like a young student, who was always ready to learn."

leave-taking from his people. He went from tribe to tribe to say goodbye and to reassure them that Hashem would continue to be with them even after his demise.[3]

בֶּן מֵאָה וְעֶשְׂרִים שָׁנָה אָנֹכִי הַיּוֹם
I am a hundred and twenty years old today (ibid. 2).

Homiletically, Moses sought to teach his beloved nation how to overcome temptation to sin. Imagine that you were 100 years old. Say to yourself, "Soon I will die and stand before God's bar of justice. How can I sin?" If, on the other hand, the evil inclination induces laziness, hoping to make you lax in performing your obligations, assume the mind-set of a 20-year-old. "I'm young and full of energy and verve. A person like me has no reason to be lazy" (*R' Shalom of Kamarna*).

לֹא אוּכַל עוֹד לָצֵאת וְלָבוֹא
I can no longer go out and come in (ibid.).

Moses did not refer to physical infirmity, for the Torah testifies that he was still vibrant. Rather, he refers to the fact that God took back his mandate to lead because Joshua's time had come (*Rashi*).

Why did Moses speak in terms of the *inability* to go and come when in fact he, as he says in the next phrase, was forbidden to lead the people into *Eretz*

Yisrael? R' Moshe Feinstein explains: Moses wanted to teach the people that a true servant of God defines his reality in terms of God's will. Although he has the option of doing something contrary to His will, he should feel that he is *unable* to do so. One should not say, "I am forbidden to do this" but rather, "I canot bring myself to ignore the word of God."[4]

Moses' total dedication to God's expectations reached its height when he hurried up the mountain — where he was to die — in but a few jumps, a vibrant expression of his alacrity to perform God's will (see 34:1 and *Rashi* ad loc.).

According to *Mei HaShiloach,* Moses is the ultimate example of a person who has reached his potential in life. As long as he is alive, he has the potential to rise to greater heights, but just as he can go up, he can also go down. Once he accomplished the mission for which God created him, he remains static; he cannot go higher, but neither can he lose his previously gained spiritual accomplishments. This is what Moses meant. *I can no longer go out* and fall from the level I have achieved. Likewise, I can no longer *come in* and rise to new levels.

Rashi notes that at this point, Moses saw that the wellsprings of Divine wisdom had been closed to him. This is not to say, however, that he receded from his lofty spiritual level. *R' Avraham Mordechai of Ger* explains that a leader must share common spiritual ground with his people. If he is on so high a pedestal that he is totally out of reach of his charges, he cannot elevate them. On the last day of

---

3. **In Tears and Joy.** *Sforno* submits that Moses sought to console the people over his impending death so as not to dampen their joy at having entered into a covenant with God (see 29:11). [This might be compared to the bride whose father was diagnosed with a terminal disease the day after her wedding. She went to visit him in the hospital and all the time he spoke only about how happy she should be to have married such a special husband. "Don't be upset over my situation; instead rejoice over your good fortune to be blessed with such a husband."]

4. **Immovable Barrier.** *R' Moshe Feinstein* himself lived with this perspective. Once, someone was reciting *Shemoneh Esrei,* positioned so that the *Rosh Yeshivah* would have to walk in front of him in order to leave the *beis midrash.* Since the halachah forbids walking in front of someone who is praying *Shemoneh Esrei* (*Orach Chaim* 102:4), *R'* Moshe waited for him to finish. When asked why he didn't walk around the person, R' Moshe replied, "There was a wall in the way. I can't walk through a wall!" To R' Moshe a halachic prohibition was a wall. One is not *forbidden* to walk through a wall; he is unable to do so.

Rabbeinu Yonah (*Shaarei Teshuvah* 1:5) alludes to the psychological dynamic that is triggered by maintaining this perspective. Our Sages teach that one who commits a sin a second time views it as something which is permitted (*Kiddushin* 40a). After the second time, one begins to see the forbidden activity as within the realm of possibility. Once prohibitions have been flouted more than once, they lose their power to stop us from sinning. To successfully resist temptation one must internalize the feeling, that it is not only forbidden, but also impossible, for him to sin.

his life, Moses reached such a high level that he broke free of the spiritual gravity that had linked him to the people. On that day, he approached the wellsprings of Divine wisdom that are generally closed off to humans and was unable to pass them on to his disciples. This is what he meant when he said, *I can no longer go out and come in.* He was so far removed from the spiritual level of his flock that he could no longer reach them, and could not serve as their conduit to access the word of God.[5]

וַיִּקְרָא מֹשֶׁה לִיהוֹשֻׁעַ וַיֹּאמֶר אֵלָיו לְעֵינֵי כָל יִשְׂרָאֵל חֲזַק וֶאֱמָץ

Moses summoned Joshua and said to him before the eyes of all of Israel, "Be strong and courageous . . ." (ibid. 7).

In the plain meaning of the verse, Moses charged Joshua in front of the nation in order to add to his disciple's prestige. *Meshech Chochmah* and *Nesivos Shalom* see here an aspect of the balance a Jewish leader must have. Joshua was exceedingly humble (see *Targum Yonasan* to *Numbers* 13:16), and was convinced that he was unworthy be the successor of his teacher. Such humility is a prerequisite of Jewish leadership, but a leader must also be strong and assertive. Moses therefore explained to Joshua, " Even if you consider yourself to be undeserving, God commands that you lead. Therefore, *before the eyes of all of Israel be strong and courageous,* and God will grant you the strength to lead the people."

Rashi cites a Midrash: Moses tried to reassure Joshua that the elders of the nation would share the leadership with him and that he should solicit their advice. Hashem, however, told Joshua otherwise: "*You* will lead the people into the Land. Figuratively take a stick and strike them over the head to force them to enter the Land. A generation can have only one leader, not two."

Are we to assume that Moses told Joshua something different than what God had said? *R' Elchanan Wasserman* explained it is arrogant and foolish for a leader not to solicit the opinion of others, especially if one has access to the life experience of elders. On the other hand, it is imperative that the ultimate responsibility and decision-making power lay with one person. Thus Moses, the ultimate in humility, told Joshua never to fail to seek good advice. God, on the other hand, made it clear to Joshua that he must be the final arbiter.[6], [7]

---

5. **Reaching the People.** Leaders must be accessible to the masses. The Talmud (*Bava Basra* 134a) teaches that Hillel the Elder had eighty disciples. The greatest of them was Yonasan ben Uziel. Whenever a bird flew over him, it would be consumed by exposure to the intense aura of holiness which surrounded him. The "least" of his students was R' Yochanan ben Zakkai who possessed encyclopedic Torah and general knowledge. Nonetheless, *Rambam* (introduction to *Yad HaChazakah*) lists R' Yochanan ben Zakkai, not R' Yonasan ben Uziel, among the בַּעֲלֵי מְסוֹרָה, the generational links in the chain of tradition. This implies that Yonasan ben Uziel was too far above the people to serve as a conduit for transmitting the tradition (*R' Avraham Chaim Feuer*).

6. **Cerebral Schizophrenia.** Using *Rashi*'s metaphor of "strike them over the *head,* for a generation has only one leader," R' Yehudah Leib Fein, the Rav of Slonim, made an impassioned attack on the institution of the *Rav Mitaam,* the government-sponsored official rabbi in Polish cities, who served alongside the authentic rabbinic leaders.

Many vital human organs were created as pairs. We have two eyes, two ears, two legs, two arms. Why, then, did God not give us two brains? Were man to have two brains, he would be constantly frustrated, for one brain would pull him one way and the second brain would pull another way. This is equally true on a national level. In order that the people not suffer from collective ideological schizophrenia, there must be one clear voice of leadership. Thus God told Joshua to enforce his position strongly, for the lesson must resound that "one leader for a generation and not two leaders."

7. **Lonely Decision.** This is true on a personal level as well as mirrored in the *Mishnah* (*Avos* 2:8), which teaches *the more counsel the more understanding.* The folk saying has it that people seek advice and then do what they want anyway; if so, why do they seek advice in the first place? Answered *R' Chaim of Volozhin*: One who offers advice can never fully understand the questioner's problem, unless the adviser has lived through the same experiences and struggled with the same subtle nuances and issues. On the other hand, the person with the problem is tainted by his subjectivity. He needs to seek the counsel of impartial people, and then decide on his own what to do. Thus the *Mishnah* tells us that one who consults others will gain a better understanding of the problem.

**חֲזַק וֶאֱמָץ כִּי אַתָּה תָּבוֹא
אֶת הָעָם הַזֶּה אֶל הָאָרֶץ**

*Be strong and courageous
for you shall come with this
people to the Land* (ibid.).

R' Yechezkel Abramsky was once summoned before an Israeli governmental commission which was holding hearings on the issue of compulsory military service for yeshivah students. One of the government ministers asked, "Don't you think that the security of the country and the protection of its citizens take precedence over protecting and guarding the Torah?" As was his wont, Rabbi Abramsky replied forcefully. "The *Tanach* proves that protecting the Torah is of primary importance. When charging Joshua to conquer the Land, God says, *Be strong and courageous* (see also *Joshua* 1:6). However, when instructing him regarding fidelity to Torah, He says, *But be **very** strong and courageous to protect and do all [that is written in] the Torah* (ibid. 7). When it comes to security and military conquest we must be strong and courageous; when it comes to Torah, we must be even more so."

**וַיִּתְּנָהּ אֶל הַכֹּהֲנִים בְּנֵי לֵוִי
הַנֹּשְׂאִים אֶת אֲרוֹן בְּרִית ה׳**

*and [he] gave it to the Kohanim,
the sons of Levi, the bearers of the
Ark of the covenant of Hashem* (ibid. 9).

In the plain meaning of the command, Moses gave the Torah scroll to the bearers of the Ark because that is where it was kept.

R' *Leib Gurwicz,* however, offered a penetrating explanation based on a thought of his father-in-law, R' Elyah Lopian. The Midrash (*Tanchuma, Parashas Korach*) reports that Korach was among those who bore the Ark, which underscores the shallowness of his attacks on Moses. Korach claimed that the spiritual burden Moses placed on the Jewish people was unbearable. But as one of the bearers of the Ark, Korach knew the miracle that "the Ark bears its bearers," meaning that those who carried the Ark expended no physical effort in doing so (*Sotah* 35a). In the same way, observance of the commandments is not an overwhelming burden; on the contrary, along with the responsibility, God gives the strength to carry it. For this reason, God made the Levites the "caretakers" of the Torah because, as the bearers of the Ark, they knew the Torah's power to infuse man with the strength to achieve the seemingly impossible. In terrible times, when the yoke of the Torah seems too difficult to bear, it is the Levites who will inspire the people to realize that the Torah "bears its bearers."[8]

R' *Yonasan Eibeschutz* notes that King David was punished because he referred to the Torah as *songs* (*Psalms* 119:54), thus implying a tinge of disrespect for its majesty (*Sotah* 35a). His punishment was that he forgot the law that when the Ark had to be transported, it was to be carried on the shoulders of the Levites. Instead, King David had the Ark placed on a wagon, with tragic results (see *II Samuel* 6:1-8). The significance of the punishment lies in the dual nature of the Torah. On one hand, it is the epitome of joy and pleasure, music to one's ears. On the other hand, it is a necessity of life, without which we cannot live. King David stressed the pleasurable aspect of the Torah, and neglected the fact that it is a yoke, as well. He was punished, therefore, by

---

8. **Proper Appreciation.** At a conference to select a committee that would defend the traditional *cheder* schools against the attacks of the *maskilim* ("enlightened" Jewish secularists), someone suggested a layman who was a confidant of the *Beis HaLevi* (R' Yosef Dov Soloveitchik). To the surprise of the conferees, the *Beis HaLevi* himself vetoed the nominee.

He explained, "If someone accepted responsibility to safeguard a sack of gold coins, but was told that the sack contained silver — if it is lost, he may claim, 'I assumed responsibility only for silver. I was not willing to assume responsibility for the more precious gold' (*Bava Kamma* 62a).

"We see that one's degree of responsibility for an item is linked to his understanding of its value. My friend is really a fine Jew, and the Torah is precious to him, but he does not understand its true worth. His evaluation is like silver compared to gold. Only a *talmid chacham* can be the guardian of the Torah."

forgetting the law which calls for the personal carrying of the Torah.[9]

Background

Once every seven years, on the Succos following the *Shemittah* (Sabbatical) year, the king of Israel would hold a public gathering in the Temple, known as *Hakhel*, and in the presence of the entire nation — men, women and children — he would read from the Book of *Deuteronomy*. This ritual reaffirmed the covenant between God and His people.

הָאֲנָשִׁים וְהַנָּשִׁים וְהַטַּף

The men, the women and the small children (ibid. 12).

Rashi (citing *Chagigah* 3a) comments: "Why were the young children also brought? In order to reward those who bring them."

The commentators offer many insights based on this comment. According to *Nachalas Yaakov, Yalkut HaUrim* et. al, the Talmud questions the necessity of commanding parents to bring along their young children. If both parents attend the ceremony, they will obviously bring their children along. Why need they be commanded to do so? The answer lies in R' Chanania ben Akashia's dictum: "The Holy One, Blessed is He, wished to confer merit upon Israel; He therefore gave them Torah and *mitzvos* in abundance" (*Makkos* 23b). *Rashi* explains that many of the commandments require deeds that people would do anyway. For example, the Torah contains many admonitions against eating abominable creatures such as crawling insects and carrion, although people abstain from them in any case. Nevertheless, God gave these commandments in order to reward people for abstaining from them.

Sfas Emes understands the question differently. Since young children will inevitably play and disturb the adults, preventing them from concentrating on what is being read, parents would try to make arrangements to leave them home. The Torah says otherwise. The exposure of the young and impressionable children to such a moving event will etch into their hearts and consciousness the sanctity of Torah.[10] The long-term spiritual dividends of this experience far offset the loss of the parents' full concentration. The parents therefore deserve to be rewarded for bringing them.

What is the reward granted those who bring the children? By bringing them, parents show how important it is to them that their children absorb Torah and sanctity and grow to be loyal Jews. Their reward is that their aspirations will be realized. The success that God grants us with our children is commensurate with the self-sacrifice we invest in them.

Yerushalmi (*Yevamos* 1:8b) relates that before R' Yehoshua ben Chanania's was born, his mother would go to the study halls in order to receive the blessings of Torah scholars for the child she was expecting. After the child was born, she left his crib in the study hall so that the sound of Torah would permeate his subconscious. For this reason the Sages said of R' Yehoshua ben Chanania, "Praiseworthy is she who bore him" (*Avos* 2:11). To merit such a son was her reward for having brought him to subliminally experience Torah.

Meshech Chochmah views this as the key to understanding an incident reported in connection with the teaching that children should be brought to *Hakhel*. The Talmud (*Chagigah* 3a) relates that when students came to visit R' Yehoshua ben Chanania in Peki'in, he asked them what R' Elazar ben Azariah taught that day. At first, they were evasive, feeling unfit to speak in the great man's presence, but eventually they related R' Elazar's teaching that children

---

9. **Vital Luxury.** The dual nature of Torah as both a pleasure and a necessity finds expression in the fact that even after the Jews willingly accepted the Torah, God lifted Mount Sinai over them and told them that if they reject the Torah, they will be buried by the mountain. *Maharal* explains that their willingness to accept the Torah indicated that they appreciated its value and the happiness it could bring them. Nevertheless, it was imperative that they accept the Torah also as a life-giving necessity.

10. **Unencumbered by Words.** *Malbim* offers a pedagogical insight. *Hakhel* is an inspiring spectacle, with hundreds of thousands of Jews converging on the Temple to see and hear the king reading from the Torah scroll. Adults who listen with full concentration to the Torah reading will not feel the powerful influence of the spectacle. Young children, however, do not understand the words; they will feel the emotions of the moving experience and let it penetrate their hearts. In a certain sense, therefore, their gain will exceed that of the adults.

are brought to *Hakhel* in order to reward the parents. R' Yehoshua replied, "You had a precious jewel in your hands and you wanted me to lose it?!" More than anyone, R' Yehoshua viewed this teaching as a precious jewel, for it recalled his mother's efforts to imbue him with love of the Torah.[11]

וְלָמְדוּ לְיִרְאָה אֶת ה' אֱלֹהֵיכֶם כָּל
הַיָּמִים אֲשֶׁר אַתֶּם חַיִּים עַל הָאֲדָמָה

and they shall learn to fear Hashem, your God, all the days that you live on the land (ibid. 13).

Why is it necessary to stipulate that we must fear Hashem *all the days*? R' Simchah Zissel of Kelm submits that *all the days* does not refer to the phrase *to fear Hashem*, but to the clause *they shall learn*. To develop reverence for Hashem Himself (as opposed to fear of punishment) is a life-long process.[12]

R' Avraham Dov Ber Kahana-Shapira (the last Rav of Kovno) suggests the following: Even primitive animals have a natural self-preservation instinct that is triggered when the animal feels threatened. Man, too, can develop a spiritual instinct, called fear of Heaven. When people from their early youth are exposed to Torah, they develop an instinctive fear of Heaven that can last for a lifetime and that protects them when they are tempted by sin. *They shall learn to fear Hashem . . . all the days.*[13]

Background

Moses predicts that as a result of his passing the nation will stray to false gods. Consequently, God will conceal His countenance so that the people will feel abandoned. They will undergo terrible calamities but will eventually repent.

---

11. **Diamond Workshop.** A person who invests time and energy in his child's education is like someone who finds a diamond in the rough. He cleans, cuts and polishes it, but in spite of his work, he is never sure if he will succeed; the gem may shatter at some stage of the process. Nevertheless, he puts forth his best effort at turning the raw stone into a shining gem. Similarly, parents pour endless time, energy and resources into educating their children, seeking to expose them to good mentors and positive experiences. There are no guarantees that their efforts will succeed, but they will be rewarded for them in any case.

Thus R' Yehoshua called this teaching a diamond, so that we might realize that education is like diamond cutting. Although not every stone turns out to be a gem, the attempts to produce maximum brilliance are well worth the effort and are amply rewarded.

The *Nesivos Shalom* (in his *Nesivei Chinuch*) writes: Anyone involved in education must be constantly aware of the words of *R' Mordechai of Lechovitch* who taught: A Jew is like a diamond. Even when he is wallowing in spiritual mud and filth, he should never lose hope. This is the fundamental principle of Jewish education.

12. **Consistent Commitment.** The Torah calls for unending and unrelenting fear of Hashem. Not only must we develop the awe and reverence for God and fear of ignoring His will, we must constantly maintain the intensity of our fear of God. God looks to us for consistency in our level of commitment to Him.

The *Chafetz Chaim* compares this to a sick man who met his friend. "How are you?" inquired the friend. The sick man replied, "You should know of no pain, but I am seriously ill. I'm running very high fever." The friend said, "To tell you the truth, you don't look bad."

"You are right. Today I'm feeling better. I don't even have fever," answered the sick man.

"Well, then, why do you say you are sick?" The sick man replied, "You don't understand. The nature of this illness is that one day I am delirious with high fever, the next day I feel fine and on the third day the fever is back again. This can go on for weeks. Even if I have no fever today, believe me, I am sick."

Such, taught the Sage of Radin, is the nature of our situation. Some days we seem perfectly healthy, serving God fully and vibrantly, but the reality of our spiritual illness shows itself regularly when we slip into sin. Our ultimate goal must be to *fear Hashem . . . all the days.*

The first time the *Satmar Rebbe* saw a neon sign on a butcher shop with the words בשר כשר (kosher meat) flashing on and off he commented wryly, "That's America. Sometimes kosher, sometimes not!" To learn to fear Hashem all the days means that our reverence must be constant.

13. **Last One Off.** The *Kovno Rav* lived by his own words. Shortly before the Nazi invasion of Poland, he went to Switzerland for surgery and remained there for a time to recuperate. When Poland was invaded, his son in New York begged him to either remain in Switzerland, or come to New York until the situation resolved itself. The Rav responded, "When a ship is sinking the captain is the last to abandon ship — not the first." Tending to his flock was his priority; his instincts responded to that reality rather than to the question of his physical survival.

וְהִסְתַּרְתִּי פָנַי מֵהֶם וְהָיָה לֶאֱכֹל

*And I will conceal My face from them
and they will become prey (ibid. 17).*

The *Baalei HaTosafos* view the concealment of God's face as reflective of His overwhelming love for His children. When a child severely misbehaves in school, the parents ask the teacher to inflict the punishment. Although they agree that the punishment is necessary, they cannot bear to carry it out. So too, God, as it were, knows that punishment is needed to cause His children to repent, but He "hides His Face" and lets the nations be His messengers to inflict the punishment.

The *Baal Shem Tov* stressed a slightly different element with this parable. When a prince rebels and needs to be punished, no royal officer will do so in the king's presence, for fear of retribution. The king knows this, too, so he therefore instructs the officer to punish the child and then leaves, so that the officer can fulfill the royal command. The king will return when the prince cries out for him. As long as God watches over us, no one can harm us. When it becomes necessary to punish us, God hides His Face so that He may unleash those who will administer the bitter corrective.

וְאָמַר בַּיּוֹם הַהוּא הֲלֹא עַל כִּי אֵין אֱלֹקַי בְּקִרְבִּי מְצָאוּנִי הָרָעוֹת הָאֵלֶּה

It will say on that day, "Is it not because my God is not in my midst that these evils have come upon me?" (ibid.).

This is a confession of sin, yet it is followed by a warning of even greater Divine abandonment.

Why doesn't this confession elicit Divine mercy? Many commentators offer solutions to this question.

Meshech Chochmah submits that the value of pain is the realization that it was sent by God. But since the Jews feel at first that God abandoned them and the punishments do not come from Him, they have not truly repented. Therefore, God continues to conceal His Presence and the exile continues until we realize that our suffering is in measured retribution for our sins.

Sfas Emes offers this approach. The despair implicit in the words, "*Is it not because my God is not in my midst that these evils have come upon me?*" is in itself a sin. Every Jew must firmly believe that God is always with him! The belief that God is part of one's life is in itself a cause for God to be with him and protect him. When *all the nations of the earth see the Name of God called upon you they will fear you* (*Deuteronomy* 28:10). When, however, man loses his trust in God and asks if God is really in his midst, he becomes vulnerable to the vagaries of life, without Divine protection.[14]

Kli Yakar sees the fatal flaw in the words *on that day*. Only as a result of the immediate pain and stress does the nation voice what is seemingly a confession. Once the pain recedes and things begin to change for the better, we suddenly begin to suffer from a poor national collective memory.[15], [16]

וְאָנֹכִי הַסְתֵּר אַסְתִּיר פָּנַי בַּיּוֹם הַהוּא

*But I will surely have concealed
My face on that day (ibid. 18).*

What is meant by the double concealment, הַסְתֵּר אַסְתִּיר? *Chidushei HaRim* explains: As long as

---

14. **Constant Companion.** A Jew must always feel that he is not alone in his pain. עִמּוֹ אָנֹכִי בְצָרָה, *I am with him in his trouble* (*Psalms* 91:15), says God to every Jew. When a Jew is blind to God's Presence, God responds by truly making Himself inaccessible and even invisible (*R' Simchah Bunim of P'shis'cha*).

15. **Make-Believe Absence.** Sometimes we conclude that God is no longer a real presence in our lives, but if our lack of closeness to God really troubles us, why don't we earnestly search for Him? Do we really believe that a father would hide from his son forever? Certainly we must realize that He is testing us and all we need to do is begin the search. As soon as we look, He will come out from "hiding" (*R' Dov Ber of Mezritch*).

16. **Misdiagnosis.** How foolish is the person who focuses on the symptoms of his disease and not on the disease itself. Certainly the Jews confess that by driving God out of their lives they have become victims and open prey to the nations. Why, however, do they focus on the resultant calamities and not realize that the real catastrophe is the lack of God's presence in their lives, and that their troubles are merely the symptoms? A Jew who fails to see that the ultimate tragedy is a life without the manifest Presence of God is truly engulfed in a double spiritual blindness. *I will surely [doubly] have concealed My face on that day* (*R' Mordechai Chaim of Slonim*).

we realize that God's Presence is concealed and that we have not allowed it to enter our lives, our situation is not that pathetic or tragic. The natural yearning of the Jewish soul for closeness to God will assert itself and will enable us to pierce the barriers that separate us from Him. The double concealment of our verse "conceals the concealment" means that we have become so distant from God that we do not even realize that something is missing in our lives.[17], [18]

עַל כָּל הָרָעָה אֲשֶׁר עָשָׂה כִּי פָנָה אֶל אֱלֹהִים אֲחֵרִים
because of all the evil that it did, for it had turned to gods of others (ibid.).

Although seemingly the people repented and confessed by saying that their terrible suffering was because God was not a real presence in their lives, He will nevertheless conceal Himself even more. *Ramban* explains that while persecution and physical torture will cease and the concealment of His mercy will end, another type of concealment will take its place, namely concealment of the Final Redemption. This will happen because we will *turn to the gods of others*, convinced that our redemption is dependent on other forces besides God. Just as

we see others and not Hashem as the source of our salvation, so He responds by withdrawing and concealing His role as our Redeemer (see *Sforno*).

R' Tzadok HaKohen of Lublin views the confession of the Jews as authentic repentance and renders the verse as *I will surely have concealed My face on that day* **from** *all the evil that it did, for it had turned to the gods of others.* No matter how deeply enmeshed we become in sin, and if we were so disloyal to God that we *turned to the gods of others,* He will still conceal His face and turn away from our sins if we earnestly repent.

וְעַתָּה כִּתְבוּ לָכֶם אֶת הַשִּׁירָה הַזֹּאת
So now, write this song for yourselves (ibid. 19).

After describing the calamity of a Jewish people who feel that God has forsaken them and Who remains inaccessible, the Torah commands us to write a Torah scroll that contains the verses of *Parashas Haazinu.* The only thing that can assure that the Jewish people will survive the intensity of Divine concealment is to spread the word of Torah among the people. By writing Torah scrolls and providing forums for teaching Torah publicly, we can emerge from the darkest times with the soul of the nation unscathed (*Nesivos Shalom*).[19], [20]

---

17. **Hide, No Seek.** *R' Baruch of Medziboz* was sitting in his room when his young grandson burst into his room, crying uncontrollably. "Why are you crying?" asked R' Baruch. "I was playing hide-and-seek with my friends. I hid and they had to look for me but it's been a few hours," the child began to cry again, "and no one has come to find me." Then R' Baruch himself began to cry. "Imagine how God must feel. He hides Himself in this world of concealment and waits for us to seek Him, yet we don't even bother to look."

18. **Spiritual Apathy.** One who realizes that he is sick looks for ways to help himself. Expert doctors, medicines and change in diet are but a few of the possible therapies. If, however, one is unaware of his condition, then he cannot do anything to remedy it. The Jewish people are blessed with the awesome power of prayer. When things go wrong, a Jew prays to God for help. Prayer can penetrate the most impenetrable walls and elicit Divine salvation. If, however, Jews think that their fate is not in His hands, God forbid, and view it as a natural result of sociological and political factors, they will not pray. God will conceal the concealment so that its Source is unknown to man, and he will apathetically resign himself to fate, rather than turning to Him in heartfelt prayer (*Vilna Gaon*). [No punishment is as terrible as when a Jew feels that he functions in a rudderless world and that God is no longer the right "address."]

19. **Song of Life.** The resurgence of a vibrant Torah-loyal community from the embers of Auschwitz is testimony to the power of Torah to resuscitate the nation. The great Torah leaders of the post-Holocaust generation, in their sweeping vision of the historic sources of national greatness, set out to rebuild centers of Torah study and raise a cadre of young men and women ready to dedicate their lives to intense Torah study. This life-giving force brought the nation back from the brink. The Torah is called a song, for the type of study necessary to reinvigorate the nation is not a dry fulfillment of a religious obligation, but rather a song of life for those who love it.

20. **Written Magnanimity.** According to the *Rosh,* in times like ours when synagogues do not lack Torah scrolls, the preferred way to fulfill the mitzvah of writing a Torah scroll is to donate books of Torah content to synagogues, *yeshivos* and the like so that more people will be able to study Torah. *Imrei Emes* found an allusion to this in the

The term לָכֶם, *for yourselves*, seems incongruent, since there seems to be no personal gain from one fulfilling this *mitzvah* more than from any other *mitzvah*.

Be'er Moshe explains: As is well known, the word יִשְׂרָאֵל is an acronym for יֵשׁ שִׁשִּׁים רִבּוֹא אוֹתִיּוֹת לַתּוֹרָה, *there are 600,000 letters in the Torah.* Every one of the 600,000 primary Jewish souls is rooted in a letter of the Torah. One who either writes a Torah scroll or has one written for him connects with his letter and his unique share in the Torah, while simultaneously uniting with the nation as a whole. One who writes a scroll inscribes himself into the Torah and therefore into the nation.[21]

The Sages taught that *for yourselves* implies that even if one inherited a Torah scroll from his forefathers, he must still write one for himself. Homiletically, this teaches us to practice the Torah not simply as a family tradition but also out of personal conviction. While one must certainly honor his familial heritage, he must also acquire the Torah for his own.

This sentiment was echoed at the Sea of Reeds, when Jews sang out *This is my God and I will beautify Him; the God of My father and I will exalt Him* (*Exodus* 15:2). They acknowledged that their own spiritual stature was a legacy from previous generations. *R' Menachem Mendel of Kotzk* noted, however, that they first referred to Him as *their* God. First make Him yours, then connect your firm commitment to the golden chain of intergenerational tradition.

---

verse, *So now, write this song for yourselves* (ibid. 19). At the time of the commandment, the Oral Torah was not to be written; it was to be transmitted orally from generation to generation. Now, however, when we are permitted to write the Talmud and other books that were once exclusively part of the Oral Torah, donating those books is the best form of performing the mitzvah.

21. **Symphonic Ode.** The Torah is called a song, for through it the many tones and overtones of Jewish souls blend to create a symphony of praise to God. In the words of the prophet, *I fashioned this people for Myself that it might declare My praise* (Isaiah 43:21). (*Zekan Aharon*).

פרשת האזינו &
Parashas Haazinu

Background

This is the "song" of which Moses spoke in the previous *parashah* (31:19). It is the song of the history of the nation, for just as musical compositions contain decrescendos (passages with diminished volume) and crescendos, so the history of the Jewish people has its "diminished" periods, times of calamity, that will be followed by the joyous crescendo of the great Finale, the Ultimate Redemption.[1]

הַאֲזִינוּ הַשָּׁמַיִם וַאֲדַבֵּרָה וְתִשְׁמַע הָאָרֶץ אִמְרֵי פִי
Give ear, O heavens, and I will speak; and may the earth hear the words of my mouth (32:1).

Moses addressed the heavens with *Give ear,* while to the earth he said *hear.* Isaiah transposed the terms, saying, שִׁמְעוּ שָׁמַיִם וְהַאֲזִינִי אֶרֶץ,

Hear, O heavens, and give ear, O earth (Isaiah 1:2). *Sifre* explains that to *give ear* (לְהַאֲזִין) refers to listening from up close, while *hear* (לִשְׁמֹע) refers to listening from a distance.[2] Moses, who figuratively lived in heaven, addressed the heavens as "a neighbor" and therefore said, *Give ear, O heavens.* Isaiah, on the other hand, who was comparatively distant from heaven, said, *Hear, O heavens (Rashi).*

Yalkut Yehudah suggests that Moses, who was closer to heaven, saw his main leadership role as pleading with God on behalf of Israel. Isaiah, who was closer to earth, viewed his main role as demanding that the nation give proper honor to God.

Homiletically, *Chasam Sofer* submits that *heavens* symbolizes people who focus on heavenly matters, while *earth* is a metaphor for Jews whose main concerns are the mundane, earthly areas of life. Moses turned first to the heavenly people, for if they listen carefully to the word of God, they will be

---

1. **Splendor Restored.** The Talmud (*Rosh Hashanah* 31a) divides *Haazinu* into six sections to be read by the first six people called to the Torah. The seventh *aliyah* reads from the conclusion of the song to the end of the *parashah.* The Talmud gives a mnemonic for the six *aliyos,* הַזִי"ו לְ"ךָ, *the glow is yours.*

Rabbeinu Bachya explains: This song contains great consolation and explicit assurance regarding the Final Redemption, as well as clear promises regarding the ultimate punishment of our enemies and the atonement of our sins. Perhaps this is why the Sages gave us the above mnemonic, which sends the message that beauty and splendor will be ours again when the Children [of Israel] return to their boundaries.

2. **Attuned to the Broken Heart.** This might explain the words of the Rosh Hashanah prayers in the *Shofros* section of *Mussaf.* כִּי אַתָּה שׁוֹמֵעַ קוֹל שׁוֹפָר וּמַאֲזִין תְּרוּעָה, *For You hear the sound of the shofar and give ear to the teruah.* The shofar sound is the *tekiah,* the unbroken blast, while the *teruah* is the broken sound. God hears the prayer and repentance of every Jew even if his ego is intact. But it is to the broken hearted, symbolized by the *teruah,* that God feels particularly close. He gives ear (מַאֲזִין) to the *teruah,* for in the words of King David, *Hashem is close to the broken hearted and He saves those crushed in spirit (Psalms 34:19) (R' Moshe Dov Stein).*

role models for their brethren. Thus, if *the heavens* (saintly) *give ear* to the words of God, then *the earth* (simpler Jews) [will] *hear my words.*

Yesod HaAvodah interprets the verse on a more personal note. If one wants to give ear to the heavenly and elevate himself to spiritual heights, he must hear and obey God's word in the earthly areas of life.

Listening is an art. Two people can hear the same thing yet understand totally different messages. Thus, the *Kotzker Rebbe* rendered the verse, "Listen [with] heavenly ears."[3]

יַעֲרֹף כַּמָּטָר לִקְחִי תִּזַּל כַּטַּל אִמְרָתִי
May my teaching drop like the rain, may my utterance flow like the dew (ibid. 2).

The analogy of Torah and rain is multifaceted. When rain falls, growth is not evident immediately. Only after a time, when the sun comes out, do we begin to see the effect of the rain. We often study Torah, but do not sense its effect. If we are patient, however, the Torah will eventually spur growth in us.[4] As the prophet expresses it, *For just as the rain and snow descend from heaven and will not return there, rather it waters the earth and causes it to produce and sprout . . . so shall be My word that emanates from My mouth, it shall not return to Me unfulfilled unless it will have accomplished what I* desired and brought success where I sent it (Isaiah 55:10-11).

Rain can only cause things to grow if the field was plowed and seeded beforehand; otherwise, it produces nothing but mud. The same applies to Torah study. If one's heart has been plowed and seeded and is primed to absorb Torah, it can engender growth. If, however, the heart and mind are not ready for Torah, then the exposure can even be negative. In the words of the Sages, "If one merits, Torah can be the elixir of life; if he lacks merit it can be a lethal poison" (*Yoma* 72b).[5]

The Midrash explains the analogies in this verse. *May my teaching drop like the rain* refers to the Written Torah, while *may my utterance flow like the dew* alludes to the Oral Torah.

Shem MiShmuel offers an explanation based on a teaching of his father, the *Avnei Nezer*: The Talmud (*Taanis* 4a) records that Israel asked God to bestow spiritual energy like rain, but God responded, "You ask for something that is not always good [rain in the summer is no blessing]. I will be like something that is always good. As the verse says, *I will be like dew for Israel, and he will bloom like a rose* (Hoshea 14:6).

Avnei Nezer defines the difference between rain and dew. Rain comes from above and is an active element in the growth process. Dew causes the earth to release minerals and other elements that

---

3. **Heavenly Emulation.** We refer to a God-fearing person as one who has fear of Heaven, even though his fear is not of Heaven itself but rather of God in Heaven. Why?

R' Menachem Mendel of Kotzk explained that when the heavens were created on the first day, they were not yet solidified. Only when God said on the second day, "Let there be a firmament," did the heavens solidify, out of fear of God, so to speak (see *Rashi, Genesis* 1:6), just as a person stops dead in his tracks and freezes when overcome by fright. The heavens therefore serve as living testimony to the "freezing" power of fearing God. A truly God-fearing person has the fear of Heaven — the same fear of God exemplified by the heavens. Thus Moses said, "Give ear [to] the heavens and inculcate the message that fear of God must make us stop dead in our tracks when contemplating disloyalty to His word."

4. **On the Heart.** *R' Menachem Mendel of Kotzk* noted that the Torah speaks of placing the words of Torah *on* your heart, (*Deuteronomy* 11:18), not *in* your heart. Not always is the heart willing to absorb the words of Torah; sometimes we must place its words *on* our hearts and patiently wait until the heart opens up and the Torah can enter.

R' Yitzchak Hutner used to say that education is analogous to planting, not to building. In erecting a building one can speed up the process by bringing more supplies and allowing for longer workdays. In agriculture, however, there is no way to expedite the process. The rain must fall, the sun must shine and the seasons must pass before the process can yield results. More often than not, the most important ingredient in educational success is patience.

5. **Fanning the Flame.** The soul of a Jew is a spark of Divinity encased in a corporeal body. In order for the soul to flourish, it must be nurtured. The more one is exposed to the Godly intelligence of Torah, the more one's Divine soul can prosper. The Torah is to a Jew what rain is to vegetation (*Zekan Aharon*).

are in the ground. Were God to shower spiritual energy on people, their growth would not result from their own efforts. Instead, He will be like dew, creating situations that will cause us to tap into our own spiritual potential. The same choice of metaphor illustrates the difference between the Written and the Oral Torah. The Written Torah, given directly by God, is like rain. The Oral Torah, the understanding of God's word, lies deep inside the souls and hearts of the Jewish people. When new situations arise, we must look into the Torah and deep inside our hearts in order to ascertain God's will in that particular situation. Hence, rain is the Written Torah; dew is the Oral Torah.[6], [7]

כִּי שֵׁם ה׳ אֶקְרָא הָבוּ גֹדֶל לֵאלֹקֵינוּ
When I call out the Name of Hashem, ascribe greatness to our God (ibid. 3).

The Talmud (*Berachos* 21a) derives from this verse that a blessing must be recited before studying or reading the Torah. Where is the allusion to Torah study in this verse?[8] *R' Yechezkel Abramsky* suggests the famous dictum of the Sages that the entire Torah is composed of Names of Hashem (See *Ramban, Introduction to Torah*). Thus the verse

might be rendered, *When you call out the Name of Hashem* [by studying Torah], *ascribe greatness to our God* by reciting a blessing. The kindness that God displays by allowing us to study His Torah requires us to praise and thank Him.[9]

The obligation to recite a blessing *before* reading the Torah is derived from this verse. The obligation to recite a blessing *afterward* is based on a *kal vachomer* (*a fortiori* argument); if we must thank God before enjoying His largess, surely we should thank Him afterwards. Conversely, the obligation to recite a blessing *after* eating is an explicit commandment (*Deuteronomy* 8:10), while the obligation to recite a blessing *before* is derived by means of a *kal vachomer;* if one should thank God after eating, surely one should do so before.

Chasam Sofer explains the difference between the blessings of the Torah and the blessings for food: When one is hungry, one will easily feel grateful to God for providing food, but once he has satiated his hunger, he no longer senses God's mercy as vividly. Therefore, the Torah specifies that one must recite a blessing *after* eating. The study of Torah, however, is the opposite. Before studying, when one has yet to partake of the sublime taste of Torah, one does not fully appreciate

---

6. **Eternal Implantation.** The second blessing of the Torah reading is, אֲשֶׁר נָתַן לָנוּ תּוֹרַת אֱמֶת וְחַיֵּי עוֹלָם נָטַע בְּתוֹכֵנוּ, *Who gave us the Torah of truth and implanted eternal life within us. Bach (Tur, Orach Chaim* 139) explains that *the Torah of truth* is the Written Torah, while the *implanted eternal life within us* refers to the Oral Torah and our determination to find within ourselves the ability to plumb its depths and ascertain God's will.

7. **Z to A.** *Shem MiShmuel* notes that the prayer for rain recited on Shemini Atzeres is in the form of an alphabetical acrostic, which begins with the letter א and goes until the letter ת. Conversely, the prayer for dew recited on the first day of Pesach begins with ת and goes backwards to א. Rain, which comes from heaven, the first source, and descends to earth, goes from א until ת. Dew, which elicits creation's potential, goes from ת until א, seeking to catalyze the potential of both earth and man and to harness it in the service of God.

8. **Blessed Reading.** In this verse, *Chida* sees an allusion to the days when the Torah is read in the synagogue, as follows: There are seven words in the verse, an allusion to the seven days when the Torah is read: Monday, Thursday, Shabbos, Rosh Chodesh (including Rosh Hashanah), Chol HaMoed, Yom Tov (Festivals) and Yom Kippur.

Furthermore, there are twenty-five letters in the verse, which correspond to the minimum amount of people called to the Torah on these occasions. On Monday, Thursday and *Minchah* on Shabbos, three people are called to the Torah; on Rosh Chodesh and Chol HaMoed, four; on Yom Tov, five; on Yom Kippur, six and on Shabbos, seven. Thus the verse alludes to the days on which the Torah is read and the number of people who read from it. The verse enjoins them to *ascribe greatness to our God* by reciting a blessing before reading.

9. **Thank You for Thank You.** According to *Rabbeinu Yonah,* this is the import of our words in the *Modim D'Rabbanan* prayer: [We thank You] עַל שֶׁאֲנַחְנוּ מוֹדִים לָךְ, *for the opportunity to thank You. Blessed is the God of thanksgivings.*

R' Baruch of Medziboz sees this idea reflected in the Grace After Meals. After thanking God for His manifold kindnesses, we continue וְעַל הַכּל, *and above all, Hashem our God, we thank You and bless You.* The greatest kindness You show us is that You allow us to thank You.

the need to thank God for providing access to it. Once one has tasted Torah, however, his appetite for it becomes insatiable,[10] and the need to thank Him afterwards is self-evident.

הַצּוּר תָּמִים פָּעֳלוֹ כִּי כָל דְּרָכָיו מִשְׁפָּט
The Rock — perfect is His work,
for all His paths are justice (ibid. 4).

Those who possess only limited spiritual vision must have faith that God's ways are just, even though they do not understand them. A child thinks that his parents and the doctor are terribly cruel for causing him so much pain, but he doesn't realize that everything they do is for his benefit. Accordingly, if something unpleasant befalls a person, he should not say, "Something bad happened to me"; rather, let him say, "Something very bitter happened." Just as some medicines taste bitter and are hard to swallow, so God sometimes prescribes "bitter pills" to help us regain our physical or spiritual health. It is bitter, but not bad (*Chafetz Chaim*).[11]

R' Shimon of Yaroslav lived to a ripe old age. His disciples asked him the secret of his longevity, and he said, "I always lovingly accepted my lot in life, for I knew that whatever God does is good. When a person has complaints, God takes him from this world and bring him to the World of Truth where he will see that life is good and God is just. Since I never complain, God doesn't have to show me that He is just."[12]

The Talmud (*Bava Kamma* 50a) derives from this verse that one who claims that God ignores our sins and waives punishment will waive his own life. Why is it wrong to entertain such a thought? Among people, it is virtuous not to respond to mistreatment; why can't we think of God in such terms? Furthermore, the Torah itself speaks of God as forgiving and merciful.

Dvar Avraham offers the following insight: One who presents his friend with a gift does not view it without value; on the contrary, precisely because it is meaningful does it serve as a vehicle to express his affection for the recipient. When God forgives sins, it is not because they are insignificant in His

---

10. **Luxurious Necessity.** In *Psalm* 119 King David rhapsodizes about the Torah. *I rejoice over Your word like one who finds a great treasure* (verse 162) expresses the ecstatic joy of one who discovers untold riches. Yet earlier (verse 92) he says, *had Your Torah not been my preoccupation then, I would have perished in my affliction.* He describes the Torah as both an essential need of life and as a priceless treasure, which is surely not indispensable.

This dual perspective is portrayed by *R' Yitzchak Hutner (Pachad Yitzchak Shavuos* 4). The pain one feels if one lacks necessities is far more intense than the joy if one has them. There is no comparison between the pain of one who lacks bread and the joy of one who has ample food. Conversely, the joy of having luxuries far exceeds the pain of lacking them. Owning a Rolls-Royce is a cause for joy; not having one is no cause for sorrow.

Jews relate to Torah as both a dire necessity and a tremendous luxury. The pain of not having Torah, God forbid, is the pain of lacking a basic necessity; yet, the joy of acquiring it is the joy associated with luxuries. King David expressed both emotions.

11. **Couldn't Be Better.** The *Chafetz Chaim* once asked a former student how he was doing. The student replied, "It wouldn't hurt if things were a little better." The Chafetz Chaim was annoyed. "How do you know it wouldn't hurt? Hashem is merciful and knows exactly how to treat His creatures. He knows better than you what is good for you. If He doesn't shower you with kindnesses, apparently that is what is best for you."

12. **Unfathomable Faith.** *R' Hirsch Meisels,* the *Veitzener Rav,* related the following personal anecdote: "When I came to Auschwitz, I had with me a *tallis* with a silver headpiece (*atarah*), which I had inherited from the sainted author of the *Yetiv Lev.* I cut the *tallis* so that I could wear it under my shirt, without being noticed. Despite my efforts, a German *kapo* noticed that my shirt seemed puffed up. He asked what I was wearing and I answered, 'A Godly garment.' He began beating me and told me to go immediately to his office where he would 'teach' me a thing or two about God. I came to his room, and he began cursing and beating me mercilessly. 'Explain to me,' he screamed, 'how you can believe in God when you see everything that happens here.' I explained to him that we are like a patient who can't fathom why the doctor hurts him so much. Only when the patient recovers does he realize that all that pain was beneficial and therapeutic. I then told him what *R' Shimon of Yaroslav* had said about his longevity.

"Thank God, my words had an impact on him and with a smirk he let me go. He even asked me to come to his block where he would give me extra food. This helped me survive."

eyes; instead, He views them as a severe offense, but forgives nevertheless. To "waive," however, implies that one regards the sin as not worthy of notice. One who claims that God ignores sins because they are trivial to Him opens the door to anarchy. If sins do not matter, then everyone has license to sin.

אֵל אֱמוּנָה וְאֵין עָוֶל צַדִּיק וְיָשָׁר הוּא
A God of faith without iniquity, righteous and fair is He (ibid.).

Even human beings are expected not to commit injustice; why is God praised for not committing iniquity? *R' Yitzchak Blazer* explains that when a human being seeks to punish he considers only what its effect will be on the perpetrator. He does not take into account whether the wrongdoer's family or close friends will suffer. Not so God. In the words of King David, *The judgments of Hashem are true, altogether righteous* (*Psalms* 19:10). God refrains from punishing a sinner if an innocent bystander will suffer pain or embarrassment. Thus, He is a God of faith Who will not commit iniquity.[13]

The easier part of having faith in God is to believe that He is the Creator and we must obey His commandments. The great test of faith comes when a tragedy happens, and one wonders how a loving, just God could allow it. At times, simple faith must come to the fore and we must realize that surface appearances are deceiving. We *seem* to be looking at Divine iniquity, but we have faith that *all His paths are justice.*[14]

Bris Avraham homiletically interprets the verse in a very real-life fashion. One who has deep abiding faith in God (קֵל אֱמוּנָה) never feels slighted by others. Rather, he says to himself, "Since everything comes from God, He must have a good reason why this happened to me."[15], [16]

---

13. **Victimless Justice.** In light of this verse, R' Chaim Shmulevitz elucidated a seemingly shocking statement of the Sages. "As a result of a man's laxity with regard to vows, his wife will die" (*Shabbos* 32b). Where is God's justice and fairness? R' Chaim explained that the idea of full-fledged justice is conveyed in this enigmatic statement. The woman deserved to die because of her personal shortcomings, but since that would make her innocent husband a victim, as well, God refrained from taking her. Once the husband became lax regarding his vows, he too deserves punishment. Now the God of justice can take her and punish him with the pain he suffers over losing her.

The statement of our Sages that when one of a group dies the entire group should begin to worry (*Shabbos* 106a) may be similarly understood. If God took one of the group in spite of the pain and sorrow the other members would experience, apparently they too must examine themselves for serious shortcomings (*R' Mordechai of Luna*).

14. **Partial Vision.** A visitor questioned the *Chazon Ish* about the Holocaust. The *gaon* replied: "One who doesn't understand the art of sewing looks in shock and contempt as a tailor ruins good cloth by cutting it into strips and pieces. He doesn't realized that this "demented" person is preparing a new garment. Similarly, one who is only able to study *Mishnah* will not attempt to plumb the depths of a complex Talmudic issue — it is beyond his ken. The Divine wisdom is infinitely more complex than anything we can imagine. With regard to how God guides history, we are novices who must believe that He has His reasons, though we don't understand them."

15. **At Whom Are You Angry?** The Sages compare anger to idolatry. This seemingly exaggerated comparison must be understood in light of an insight of *Sefer HaChinuch* §241 regarding the prohibition against revenge. Everything that happens to man is part of the Divine plan (see *Ramban* to *Exodus* 13:16). When a man is harmed by his fellow, it is an expression of God's will, with the perpetrator acting merely as a Heavenly messenger. Were the victim to seek revenge, he would be assuming that his fellow had the independent ability to harm him; otherwise he would look to God as the source of his trouble and would have no reason to be angry with the person who hurt him. Such anger is a form of idolatry, for he assigns independent power to another human instead of to God. To become angry easily is a form of denial of the Source of all events in the world (*R' Shneur Zalman of Liadi*).

16. **Unwitting Catharsis.** Sometimes inexplicable personal suffering may be a blessing in disguise. When man's soul ascends to Heaven and appears before the Divine bar of justice, a huge scale weighs all his activities. First a voice summons all the person's *mitzvos* to come forward and be counted, and the defending angels created by one's *mitzvos* (see *Avos* 4:13) come to the right of the scale. Then the sins and prosecuting angels, born of one's sins, are summoned. Hordes of black-clad angels stream in and are placed on the left. These angels are for more robust than the defenders, for unlike the *mitzvos* which were performed without enthusiasm or proper intent, the sins were done with gusto, zest and passion. The left side outweighs the right and the man seems doomed.

Suddenly, another voice rings out: Where is all the suffering and pain the person endured while on earth? The

Rashi explains the phrase as follows: He is *a God of faith* Who eventually rewards the righteous in the World to Come. He is *without iniquity,* for even the wicked are rewarded for whatever good they might have done, but they receive their reward in this world.

Maharal explains why the righteous are rewarded in the Next World while the wicked receive their recompense here and now. The *mitzvos* of the righteous are an expression of their intrinsic self, while their sins are uncharacteristic aberrations. Thus their reward for *mitzvos* is in the world of truth (i.e. the World to Come), while they are punished for their sins in this transitory world. On the other hand, the wicked see the pursuit of sinful thrills as the real life, so they are rewarded in their own real world, the fleeting here and now.[17]

שִׁחֵת לוֹ לֹא בָּנָיו מוּמָם דּוֹר עִקֵּשׁ וּפְתַלְתֹּל
Corruption is not His — the blemish is His children's, a perverse and twisted generation (ibid. 5).

This translation follows *Rashi,* who explains the verse as referring to God.

Other commentators interpret the verse homiletically as referring to the responsibility of parents to be role models for their children. Many parents are careless regarding their own fidelity to Torah and *mitzvos,* but they want their children to maintain a strong commitment. Of such a person, the Torah says, שִׁחֵת לוֹ, if *he is corrupt,* then he will say לֹא, *no* — he sees his own poor behavior as insignificant. But בָּנָיו מוּמָם, when it comes to *his children, their blemish* concerns him deeply. Such an approach is

flawed. Just as we want our children to meet our expectations, so our Father wants us to meet His expectations. When we fail to do so, our children become confused and develop into a *perverse and twisted generation* (*Shaar Bas Rabim*).

Alternatively, the verse speaks to people who feel that while they are still young they must pursue pleasure, and they will repent when they are older and the passions and desires of youth hold less sway. Such conduct damages their children. To them the Torah says, שִׁחֵת, if one acted with spiritual *corruption,* לֹו לֹא, it might *not* damage *him* permanently, since he will eventually repent. But, בָּנָיו מוּמָם, the *blemish* will remain with *his children,* who model themselves after their parents. Such children will grow into a *perverse and twisted generation*[18] (*Melitzei Eish*).

Ksav Sofer and *Even Azel* view the verse as underscoring the reality that the education one provides for his children demonstrates where his heart lies. Sometimes a person sins out of uncontrollable desire. He believes in doing the right thing, but his passion overcomes him. At other times, however, a person's sins betray indifference to God's words. The litmus test to ascertain whether one's indiscretions come from moral weakness or ideological corruption is the type of education he seeks for his children. One who sins out of weakness will seek more for his children. One who doubts the truth of the Torah will give his children an education that will mirror himself.

This is the flow of the verse — שִׁחֵת לוֹ לֹא, *corruption is not his* — his sins are not the result of illicit and powerful desire. Rather, his blemished

---

travail of a lifetime comes forward. Together with the *mitzvos* it atones for many of the sins. Suddenly the left side is considerably lighter and the right side outweighs it. The exonerated soul praises God for every little bit of suffering, for because of it he is deemed fit for the World of Truth (*Chafetz Chaim*).

17. **The Main Event.** Reward and the form it takes are generally determined by man himself. The Talmud (*Kiddushin* 40b) teaches that if one regrets having done a mitzvah, thinking to himself, "What did I achieve by doing it? It would be better if I had not bothered," he loses all reward for those *mitzvos,* for they are worthless to him. Conversely, by the difficulty one is ready to undertake in order to perform a mitzvah, he indicates how valuable it is to him. Thus the Sages taught (*Avos* 5:26) that the reward [for *mitzvos*] is in accordance with the difficulty involved. Similarly, the joy one feels over the opportunity to perform a mitzvah is another index of its value in his eyes.

18. **Generational Tone Setters.** The Torah continues, *Remember the days of yore,* remember to serve God all the days of your life. Don't push it off to middle age, *understand the years of generation after generation* and realize that your behavior sets the tone for future generations.

faith is revealed in his children. By not providing them with an education aimed at higher spiritual standards, he reveals his own blemish.[19]

דּוֹר עִקֵּשׁ וּפְתַלְתֹּל
a perverse and twisted generation (ibid.).

What is the difference between perverse and twisted? *Beis HaLevi* offers an explanation based on the words of the Midrash (*Bereishis Rabbah* 93), which speaks of "the day of judgment and the day of rebuke when God will chastise each person according to who he is." What is the day of judgment and what is the day of rebuke? And what does the Midrash mean by saying that God will chastise each person *according to who he is*?

One who refrains from participating in a charity campaign may claim that he cannot afford to give. His explanation would be acceptable — but not if he made an extravagant wedding for his daughter or took his entire family on a three-week cruise. This is what is meant by the "day of rebuke," the time when his own actions disprove his claims. The "day of judgment" is when God assesses our actions, each one on its own merit. At this level, we can often present mitigating evidence to excuse our shortcomings. Were we to be consistently bad (*perverse*),

it would not be acceptable, but it would at least leave room for some positive assessment, because a chronically weak person, or one who always faced difficult circumstances could be treated leniently. But then God will show the person that he was not consistent (he was *twisted*), and he will be chastised *according to who he is*. By comparing our different reactions in similar circumstances, God will point out the hypocrisy in our lives.

עַם נָבָל וְלֹא חָכָם
O vile and unwise people (ibid. 6).

*T*argum Yonasan ben Uziel renders the verse as *a foolish people, which accepted the Torah but did not become wise.*

To accept the Torah means to assume responsibility for oneself, for his fellow Jews and for the general welfare and survival of humanity. If we were not ready to undertake this scope of responsibility, we would have done better not to accept the Torah, for to have *accepted the Torah and not become wise* is the mark of *a foolish people.* [20]

Ramban defines נָבָל as an ingrate who stubbornly refuses to appreciate anything that was done for him. *Rashi* (32:21) defines נָבָל as a nonbeliever. Seemingly, *vile* is an appropriate adjective for a thief, a murderer or a pervert. Why is the

---

19. **Relative Responsibility.** The *Chasam Sofer* offers a homiletical interpretation. "If you think," says Moses, "that I rebuke the people because שִׁחֵת לוֹ, *they are corrupt,* לֹא, *no,* this is not the reason; בָּנָיו מוּמָם, *their blemishes* are relative to the fact that they are *His children.*" The flaws of the Jewish people are magnified because they are God's children; for other nations, such flaws would not be considered serious.

This might be compared to the occasional Jewish doctor in Eastern Europe who lived and practiced among non-Jews, but maintained a certain degree of mitzvah observance. People would praise him for remaining Sabbath observant or putting on *tefillin* every day regardless of his surroundings. Under the doctor's circumstances — and considering that most professionals in similar situations did far less — the praise is significant, even though he does not keep many of the *mitzvos.*

Similarly, if someone criticizes a Torah scholar for something insignificant, it is a compliment. If there is nothing else to criticize, it implies that he is exemplary in other areas.

Because the Jewish people are God's children, they are chastised for even relatively minor infractions. Thus the rebuke is really a form of praise.

20. **Too Big on Him.** The *Steipler Gaon* put it this way: If man is in this world only for its pleasures, why did God have to grant us intelligence and, even more so, His Torah? King Solomon said, "One who increases intelligence increases pain" (*Ecclesiastes* 1:18), because the greater one's intelligence, the greater his responsibility to use it wisely. A fool always smiles because his lesser intellect allows for more enjoyment. Animals are carefree, with nary a worry.

This can be compared to a child who puts on his father's hat and jacket. It is obvious that they do not fit. The human intellect — and certainly the Torah — is unnecessary if the sole purpose of life is corporeal pleasure. If we have been granted such gifts, they were given to us so that we should imbue our lives with Godliness.

appellation applied to a nonbeliever who may be kind and considerate?

Gratitude is an elementary response that is expected from any human being; even very young children are taught to say, "Thank you." If one contemplates all the wonderful things that God provides (including the gift of life itself), he must feel grateful; if he feels no need to express his thanks, then he has lost his basic humanity. Certainly someone who can figuratively look God in the face and say, "There is no God," should be described as *vile*. [21]

הֲלוֹא הוּא אָבִיךְ קָנֶךְ

Is He not your father, your Master? (ibid.).

According to *Rashi*'s alternative explanation, קָנֶךְ means *your nest*. The Jewish people are likened to a dove (see *Song of Songs* 5:2), a bird that remains within sight of its nest and never flies far away (*Bava Basra* 24a). This, according to the *Chafetz Chaim*, is the message of our verse. *Is He not your Father and your Nest?* Never, never should you stray far from Him. We must always keep Him in sight so that we can return to Him at any time.[22]

R' Baruch Ber Leibowitz once saw a religious Jew reading an antireligious newspaper. "If you saw a poster on the wall that poured scorn and abuse on your parents, would you read it?! Of course not! You would pull it down and tear it to pieces. How then are you ready to read a newspaper which heaps abuse and scorn on our Father?!"

Beyond our duties toward God Who is our King, we at least owe Him the loyalty which we show toward our biological parents. He is our Father.

---

21. **Wilted Humanity.** *Rashi* (*Genesis* 2:5) writes that before Man was created, God brought no rain, since there was no one to recognize and appreciate the rain. With the creation of Man, a creature capable of expressing gratitude, God granted rain. Man's defining characteristic is gratitude. One who lacks this quality is like a wilted flower, whose life force has dried up (*Simchas Aharon*).

22. **You Are Beautiful.** On Friday afternoons *R' Aryeh Levin* would go to the synagogue early to chant the *Song of Songs*. Once *R' Chaim Berlin*, the Rav of Jerusalem, was sitting next to him, also chanting the *Song of Songs*. Suddenly *R' Chaim* began to cry. "Why are you weeping?" *R' Aryeh* asked him.

R' Chaim Berlin answered with a story: "When I was the rabbi of Moscow, a distinguished-looking man came and asked to speak with me in private. The man told me, 'I have become the father of a son, and I should like you to perform the circumcision.'

" 'Why, of course,' I replied." But why the secrecy?"

" 'I am a man of considerable means. I sell crosses to the Christian market,' he explained. "No one in my neighborhood knows that I am Jewish. The circumcision must be done secretly; it must be kept hidden from my neighbors.' "

R' Chaim continued, "I advised him to give his Christian servants the day off, which he did. Only the two of us were there. He was the *sandak* and I was the *mohel*. When it was over I asked the infant's father to let me know in three days how the child was faring.

"Three days later he came to see me, and he put a sum of money down on the table. I said, 'I do not take money for performing circumcisions.' Since he was a businessman, he thought that I meant that he had given me too little, so he put down a larger sum and then an even larger sum — but I remained firm in my refusal. Finally, I asked him, 'Tell me something: Your home is bereft of any trace of Judaism. You yourself make every effort to be sure that no one even suspects that you are a Jew. Why did you want your son circumcised?'

" 'Rabbi,' he replied, 'I know how estranged I am from Judaism. I doubt if I will ever be able to return to my faith. Even my baby boy will probably know nothing about his religion. I at least grew up among Jews, but he will have no one to learn from. Nevertheless, should the boy find out when he grows up that he is Jewish, and should he wish to be a complete Jew, I want nothing to stand in his way.' "

R' Chaim Berlin concluded: "Whenever I read the verse *Behold, you are beautiful, my love; behold, you are beautiful, your eyes are doves* (*Song of Songs* 1:15), I am reminded of that incident, and I understand why Scripture states the same phrase twice. *Behold, you are beautiful* refers to the Jewish people before they sin; the repetition means *behold, you are [still] beautiful* even after you sin. Why does God say we are beautiful even after we sin? Because *your eyes are doves*: As the Talmud (*Bava Basra* 24a) indicates, even when a dove flies away from the dovecote, it never goes too far away. Even when a Jew drifts very far from his roots, the covenant of Abraham still focuses him on the warm, cozy nest of his heritage."

כִּי חֵלֶק ה׳ עַמּוֹ
*For Hashem's portion
is His people* (ibid. 9).

Once, *R' Chaim of Volozhin* was studying the *Tanna D'Vei Eliyahu*, which states that God is שָׂמֵחַ בְּחֶלְקוֹ, *satisfied with His lot.* R' Chaim found this difficult to understand. The entire world and everything in it is His; how can we speak of *His* portion or lot? He presented the question to the *Vilna Gaon*, who pointed to our verse. The people of Israel are God's portion and He rejoices over them no matter what their spiritual condition. Even in our times when our spiritual health is failing, God still rejoices that we, rather than any other nation, are His portion (*Chafetz Chaim*).

יַעֲקֹב חֶבֶל נַחֲלָתוֹ
*Jacob is the measure of
His inheritance* (ibid.).

The word חֶבֶל literally means a *rope.* Accordingly, *Baal HaTanya* explains: Every Jew is linked to the Source of life and sanctity by means of an invisible rope. One end is Above and the other end is tied to Israel. The rope is woven from many thin strands, 613 to be exact (248 positive commandments and 365 prohibitions). When a person commits a sin or neglects a mitzvah, one of these strands snaps. When a person does something punishable by כָּרֵת, *spiritual excision,* God forbid, the entire rope breaks.

R' Moshe of Kobrin sees the rope as the nation of Israel. A rope is made from many strands, some of which are defective. Nevertheless, even those strands add to the strength of the rope. Even the weak strands among Israel make the rope stronger — as long as all the strands are woven together.

וַיִּשְׁמַן יְשֻׁרוּן וַיִּבְעָט
*Jeshurun became fat
and kicked* (ibid. 15).

Prosperity is a double-edged sword. On one hand, it provides the ability to serve God with a clear head, and not to become embroiled in the ongoing war for physical and material survival. On the other hand, wealth enables people to indulge their temptations and delude themselves into believing that they, not God, are responsible for their success. The next step is to desert God our Maker and become contemptuous of Him.[23]

Alternatively, the Torah speaks of the arrogance of one who thinks that he does so much for God while God does so little for him. One can become fat on the good deeds he does and thus become contemptuous of God (*R' Moshe of Ujheli*).

צוּר יְלָדְךָ תֶּשִׁי וַתִּשְׁכַּח אֵל מְחֹלְלֶךָ
*You ignored the Rock Who gave
birth to you, and forgot God
Who brought you forth* (ibid. 18).

R' Menachem Mendel of Kotzk interpreted this verse homiletically. The Rock gave birth to you and imbued you with the ability to ignore and forget, so that you could forget the travails and difficulties of life, rather than become emotionally paralyzed by them. This makes it possible for you to concentrate on your spiritual development. But instead of using the ability to forget for this purpose, *you forgot God Who brought you forth.* [24]

---

23. **Silver Reflection.** A small-time merchant, who considered himself a disciple of *R' Michel of Zlotchov,* had a run of good fortune and became wealthy in a very short time. He began to believe that his success resulted from his dazzling business acumen. The greater his fortune grew, the more inflated his ego became. Slowly but surely he began to abandon and scorn his long-standing friends.

One day R' Michel visited him and took him to a window. "Look through the window and tell me what you see." The merchant replied, "I see people going to and fro." He then took him over to a mirror. "Now what do you see?" he asked. "Myself, of course," replied the arrogant merchant. "You see," said R' Michel, "the difference between a window and a mirror is that a window that has no silver behind it allows you to see everybody else. The mirror with the silver behind it blocks out everyone else and only allows you to see yourself."

24. **Feigned Insanity.** The *Dubno Maggid* encapsulated this ironic chutzpah in a parable. A man who owed many people money was under intense pressure from his creditors to make good on his debts. He had no idea where to begin. A friend of his, to whom he also owed money, suggested that he act insane when any of his creditors

וַיֹּאמֶר אַסְתִּירָה פָנַי מֵהֶם אֶרְאֶה
מָה אַחֲרִיתָם כִּי דוֹר תַּהְפֻּכֹת הֵמָּה

*And He will say, "I shall hide My face from
them and see what their end will be — for
they are a generation of reversals"* (ibid. 20).

When a child rebels against his father, the father hides from the child and abandons him. However, the father keeps an eye on the child from his hiding place. As long as the child falls and picks himself up again, the father remains hidden. But if the child approaches a deep pit from which he will never be able to escape, God forbid, the father comes out of hiding to save him. God is our Father and we are His children. When we rebel, He hides from us and allows us to fall, but He remains vigilant, always ready to save us from fatal physical or spiritual danger. Even when God says, *"I shall hide My face from them,"* He still watches to *see what*

their end will be. Although the present looks bleak and God is "concealed," He looks after us to make sure that our end will be good (*Shem MiShmuel*).

They are a generation of reversals. One reason the Jewish people were sent into exile is so that their host nations will absorb the moral and ethical values of the Torah. In a *reversal,* we have become assimilated among the nations and have learned from them.[25]

R' Zusia of Anipoli saw the end of the verse in a positive light. God says, *I shall hide l My face from them,* and let them act carelessly for a while. *I will see what their end will be.* I am not terribly worried, for *they are a generation of reversals* who have the potential to reverse in an instant from sinfulness to repentance.

---

attempted to collect. He followed the advice and it worked! His creditors despaired of ever collecting and stopped dunning him.

One day, his friend needed his money back and came to collect, whereupon the debtor went into his usual insanity routine. His friend said to him incredulously, "I'm the one who taught you to act crazy when debtors came collecting. Now you are trying to use it against me?!"

God imbued us with forgetfulness as a survival tool. Are we going to have the shamelessness to use it against Him?!

25. **Totally Perverse.** *R' Simchah Bunim of P'shis'cha* was a timber merchant before he became a rebbe. Once when he was in Danzig for Shabbos, he took his meals at a Jewish-owned inn. On Friday night, the owner told his non-Jewish worker to go down with him to the cellar to bring up some wine. When they came upstairs, R' Simchah Bunim noticed the Jew carrying a candle, lighting the way for the non-Jew, who was carrying the open bottles of wine. "Now I understand what the Torah means by *a perverse and twisted generation.* If the Jew was carrying the wine and the non-Jew the candle, everything would be fine. The wine would remain permissible to drink and the Jew would not have desecrated the Sabbath. Now, however, everything is reversed." The reversal of values is indicative of a perverse and twisted generation. It is *a generation of reversals.*

פרשת וזאת הברכה ⊰
Parashas Vezos HaBerachah

Background

Immediately before his death, Moses blesses the Children of Israel, defining the unique talents and abilities of each tribe and charging it with its particular mission. Before going on to the specific blessings of each tribe, he recounts the merit that makes the nation as a whole worthy of blessing.

וְזֹאת הַבְּרָכָה אֲשֶׁר בֵּרַךְ מֹשֶׁה . . . לִפְנֵי מוֹתוֹ
And this is the blessing that Moses . . . bestowed . . . before his death (33:1).

Throughout *Deuteronomy,* Moses severely rebukes the nation for its many indiscretions since leaving Egypt. Now, before his death, he strengthens their spirits so that they would never give up hope on themselves or on their ability to return to God. "You are blessed," he tells his beloved flock. "Each one of you has unique gifts which will help you find your path to Him." The Sages echoed this in advising (*Sotah* 47a), "Let the left hand deflect [students and followers] while the right hand brings [them] close" (*Abarbanel*).

Moses waited until his last moments before giving these blessings. A human being is merely a conduit for the Divine blessing, and the greater the conduit, the more expansive the blessing that can flow through him. Moses, the loyal shepherd of his flock, wanted to grow spiritually, so that his blessing would be as great as possible. Hence he waited for the most opportune time to bless them, as he climbed the ladder of spiritual improvement. As his death approached he realized he could no longer delay, for "if not now, when?" (*R' Chanoch Tzvi of Bendin*; see *Sforno, Genesis* 27:2).

אִישׁ הָאֱלֹהִים
The man of God (ibid.).

The epitome of human accomplishment is a perfect balance between body and soul, the physical and the spiritual. The Midrash defines *the man of God* in just these terms: "the upper half Godly, the lower half human." Because Moses had achieved the ideal fusion of the two worlds, he could bless the people so that each tribe could harness its temporal success, transforming it into a vehicle for sanctity (*Taam V'Daas*).[1]

This is the first time in the Torah that Moses is

---

1. **Grab the Opportunity.** When *R' Uri of Strelisk* passed away, his *chassidim* looked to *R' Yudel of Strettin* to assume the mantle of leadership. R' Yudel initially refused, but the *chassidim* prevailed upon him and he accepted. At the first gathering under his auspices, he explained our verse. "All his life Moses, the paradigm of humility, refused to bless the people. 'Who am I to bless them?' he thought. But once God called him *the man of God,* he was presented with a unique opportunity. 'Who knows if I will still have this appellation and its spiritual level tomorrow? Let me bless them now.' " R' Yudel then concluded, "I did not want to assume the mantle of our beloved Rebbe. But if you have forced me to do so, let me quickly bless you all with the best of everything."

described as the man of God. In his humility, he could not bring himself to describe himself in such complimentary terms, but now, before his death, it was necessary for all generations to know that the man who brought them the Torah was the man of God, so he had to inscribe it in the Torah. "If not now, when?" (*Imrei Emes*).[2]

Yalkut Shimoni teaches that Moses earned this title because he blessed the nation. The true man of God is not ensconced in an ivory tower, far removed from the people and their mundane concerns. Intellectually and emotionally he moves in a higher sphere, but he is concerned with each individual and his material burden. When Moses blessed each tribe with its temporal needs, he showed that he had truly become *the man of God* (*Beis Avraham*).[3]

אֶת בְּנֵי יִשְׂרָאֵל
Upon the Children of Israel (ibid.).

The Sages teach that on the day of his passing, Moses was shown all the future generations down to the last Jew. When Moses blessed the nation, he blessed every Jew in every future generation. That is why every Jew is called to the Torah on Simchas Torah and reads from the blessings of Moses. Since Moses blessed us all, we all go up to the Torah to receive our share of his blessings (*Yechahain Pe'er*).[4]

וַיֹּאמֶר ה' מִסִּינַי בָּא וְזָרַח מִשֵּׂעִיר לָמוֹ . . .
He said: Hashem came from Sinai — having shone forth to them from Seir . . . (ibid. 2).

In a famous passage, *Mechilta* (*Parashas Yisro*) interprets this verse as a description of the events that preceded our acceptance of the Torah. God revealed Himself to the children of Esau and offered them the Torah. They asked, "What is written in it?" When God replied that it includes the prohibition against murder, they said, "This [murder] is our parental heritage. We cannot accept such a prohibition." The Ammonites and the Ishmaelites likewise rejected Torah because it prohibits theft and sexual misconduct.

Why did God pick *mitzvos* that made the Torah unacceptable to them? Why not portray the more

---

2. **Humble Tears.** Citing the Sages, *Rashi* teaches that the verse *So Moses, servant of Hashem, died there* (34:5) was dictated to Moses by God, and that Moses wrote them with tears rather than ink. Simply understood, he cried over the fact that he was about to die. *Tiferes Shlomo* submits that Moses cried that he had to write about himself *servant of God* and *man of God*.

3. **Piping Hot Sensitivity.** *R' Yisrael Salanter* would often say, "יענעמ'ס גשמיות איז מיין רוחניות; *someone else's physical needs are my spiritual needs.*" This applies not only to the great issues of life, but also to trivial matters that are barely noticed.

Mrs. Sora Leah Brazil was a woman who understood the implications of this message. She once spent a summer with her family in a small bungalow colony. One chilly August night, a student from her husband's yeshivah was sitting at a table on the lawn, learning by the light of a kerosene lantern. At about 10:30, she came out of her bungalow with a piping-hot glass of tea and a plate of cookies. Placing the refreshments on the table, she quietly said, "A hot tea is good on a cold night." She understood — and acted on the concept — that somebody else's physical needs were her spiritual mission.

4. **Reconnected.** It is customary for every male to be called to the Torah on Simchas Torah. This is based on the Aggadic statement that the word יִשְׂרָאֵל, *Israel,* is an acronym for the words יֵשׁ שִׁשִּׁים רִבּוֹא אוֹתִיּוֹת לַתּוֹרָה, *There are 600,000 letters in the Torah* — one corresponding to each of the 600,000 primary souls of the Jewish people. In the course of the year, we become enmeshed in sin, but over the course of the spiritually redeeming days of Tishrei, we uplift ourselves and strengthen our attachment to the Torah scroll of Israel. Thus, it is fitting on this last day of the festival that each man be honored with an *aliyah* (literally, *rising*) to the Torah (*Meor Einayim*).

The words of King David allude to this sense of participation of the entire people: *The Torah of Hashem is perfect, it restores the soul* (Psalms 19:8). If even a single Jew lacks a connection to Torah, the nation, as symbolized by the Torah scroll with its 600,000 letters, lacks a letter and is figuratively unfit. Thus, only after the Days of Awe, when every Jewish soul is restored through prayer, repentance and the special *mitzvos* of the season, can the Torah of the Jewish people be considered complete and perfect (*Chesed L'Avraham*).

"positive" aspects of Torah in hope that they would be eager to take advantage of the Torah's great benefits, and then they would be willing to comply even with the commandments that were difficult for them?

R' Refael HaKohen of Hamburg submits that the form of their question — "What is *written* in it?" — indicated that they were ready to accept only the Written Torah. Since true fulfillment of Torah is impossible without complete loyalty to the Oral Law and tradition, their response was unacceptable. Therefore God presented them with commandments that ran contrary to their lifestyle and livelihood so that they would refuse. In contrast, the Jews said, *"Everything that Hashem has said we will do and we will obey!"* (Exodus 24:7). We will follow not only what God has written in His Torah; we will even obey everything that He *says* in the Oral Tradition. They were granted the Torah, for only they were ready to truly follow it.

An alternative interpretation suggests that God told the various nations about *mitzvos* that hindered their traditional lifestyle in order that they understand that commitment to Torah requires a willingness to reshape one's values and habits to conform to God's will. One cannot redefine the Torah on his terms so that the Torah will accommodate itself to his lifestyle (*Zekan Aharon*).

In declaring that they would accept the Torah without reservation, without waiting to hear what it said, the Jewish people declared their readiness to learn and live by Torah even if it entailed sacrifices and even if it affected their earning a livelihood (*Ruach Chaim*).

The implication of the *Mechilta* is that aside from the sins that are at their essence, the nations could live with the rest of the Torah's demands. Why, then, did the nations reject the Torah and the enormous reward that comes with it? Furthermore, the prohibitions against murder, sexual immorality and theft are logical and self-evident even without an explicit command from God, and are in fact part of the Noachide commandments that obligate all nations. Why, then, did these prohibitions provide sufficient reason to spurn God's offer to give them the Torah?

The answer lies in a fundamental understanding of the function of Torah. As *R' Simchah Bunim of P'shis'cha* explained, the Torah demands more than behavior modification; it wants a person to change and elevate his values and personality. For example, if someone lusts after another's property and wishes he could find some way to take it, but does not do so because the Torah commands *You shall not steal,* that is not enough. God wants a Jew to develop such standards of honesty and respect for property rights that it would never even enter his mind that he could take what belongs to someone else. The same applies to murder. It is not enough to control one's urge to kill; one should purge the desire from his personality.

The nations of the world could accept a Torah that regulates action — the Noachide Code and the social contract already forbid *acts* of murder and theft. The Torah, however, tells us what kind of people we must be. To have one's inner self defined by God was more than the nations would accept (*R' Chanoch Tzvi of Bendin*).

R' Avi Steinherz offers a variation on this idea based on *Sefer HaChinuch* (69), which explains why the Talmud often asks עוֹנֶשׁ שָׁמַעְנוּ אַזְהָרָה מִנַּיִן, "Although we have a Biblical source for the punishment, what is the Biblical source for the prohibition?" (see *Sanhedrin* 54a). If only the punishments were stated, then someone willing to accept the penalty could commit the act and not have done anything wrong. Therefore, the Torah explicitly forbids the behavior.[5]

By defining and prohibiting sin, the Torah declares that the act is intrinsically evil. This is contrary to the philosophical doctrine that there is no absolute truth. Although all nations have laws against theft and murder, they are not so much moral judgments as expressions of a social contract meant to create a functional society. The Torah, however, is not a guidebook on how to conduct an orderly society. Torah defines right

---

5. **Fear of Sin.** Thus we speak of יִרְאַת חֵטְא, *fear of sin.* It does not suffice to fear the punishment, since man could rationalize that the sin is worth the price of the punishment. It is sin itself which we must fear.

and wrong, good and evil. Thus the Torah is diametrically opposed to the very essence of Esau, Ishmael and their like.[6]

אַף חֹבֵב עַמִּים כָּל קְדֹשָׁיו בְּיָדֶךָ

Indeed You loved the tribes greatly, all its holy ones were in Your hands (ibid. 3).

Baal HaTurim notes that the numerical equivalent (*gematria*) of the words אַף חֹבֵב עַמִּים is the same as that of the word גֵּרִים, *proselytes,* which indicates that the souls of all future proselytes were present when God gave the Torah at Sinai.

R' Akiva Eiger sees the previous verse as the source of this fact. When God offered the Torah to the nations, their refusal was surely not unanimous. Undoubtedly there were individuals who wanted to accept the Torah but who went along with the mass refusal out of fear of their neighbors' reaction. Likewise, while all Jews responded with

the cry of נַעֲשֶׂה וְנִשְׁמַע, *we will do and we will obey,* there were some among them who preferred not to accept the Torah, but went along with the crowd. The souls of the non-Jews who wanted the Torah eventually became proselytes.

תּוֹרָה צִוָּה לָנוּ מֹשֶׁה מוֹרָשָׁה קְהִלַּת יַעֲקֹב

The Torah that Moses commanded us is the heritage of the congregation of Jacob (ibid. 4).

Many shades of meaning have been suggested as to why the Torah is called a מוֹרָשָׁה, *heritage.* Here the Torah states that the congregation of Jacob is the legitimate heir to the Godly heritage of the Torah. Thus it will remain with the Jewish people for all generations.[7], [8]

King Solomon refers to Torah with the words, *For I have given you a good **acquisition**, do not forsake My Torah (Proverbs 4:2).* When making an acquisition, one must pay a price. Even a gift is

---

6. **Objective Standards.** Secular society prohibits murder because it impinges on the victim's inalienable right to life. The Torah perspective goes further. Murder is forbidden because it is evil. If murder is wrong only as part of the social contract, then the right to life may be overruled by the need to maintain a minimal quality of life. But since life has independent value and killing is evil, no one has the right to end life based on his decision regarding another person's suffering. Such suffering does not permit an evil act.

7. **Divine Guarantee.** The post-Holocaust renaissance of Torah is living testimony to its eternal presence among Jews. As the prophet says: *And as for Me, this is My covenant with them, says Hashem. My spirit that is upon you and My words that I have placed in your mouth shall not be withdrawn from your mouth, nor from the mouth of your offspring, nor from the mouth of your offspring's offspring, said Hashem, from this moment and forever (Isaiah 59:21).*

[When the Roman general-emperor Vespasian agreed to R' Yochanan ben Zakkai's request that the academy of Yavneh would be allowed to continue, he made the blunder of his life. In his mind, he was humoring an old man, but in reality he provided the nation with the eternal key to self-resuscitation. Torah is the lifeblood of the nation and its link to eternity. In our times, David Ben-Gurion made the same mistake. Despite his opposition to traditional Torah Judaism, he was a European Jew who harbored a certain nostalgia for the world of the yeshivah. When petitioned to allow yeshivah students to be exempt from compulsory military service, he agreed, sure that within two generations at the most, there would be no families left who desired that sort of life for their children. History has contradicted him decisively. The miraculous fulfillment of God's promise that Torah will be our eternal heritage has changed the face of the Land and created growing legions of Torah students and devotees.]

8. **Linked Forever.** The term מוֹרָשָׁה might allude to the Midrash (*Shemos Rabbah,* 33:1) which teaches that unlike a typical acquisition in which one acquires the item but not the seller, when Jews acquire Torah they "acquire" God along with it, for Torah grants a Jew access to God. The Midrash illustrates this with a parable.

A king's daughter married a prince from a foreign country. After remaining at the father-in-law's palace for a while, the young couple had to return to the bridegroom's kingdom. Pained by the thought of his dear daughter leaving him, yet unable to ask the young couple to remain, the king asked them to build a small apartment for him wherever they go. In this way he could always visit his daughter.

That father is God, the prince is Israel and the princess is the Torah. At Sinai we married His daughter when we accepted the Torah. [The Sages homiletically explain מוֹרָשָׁה as if it said מְאוֹרָשָׂה, *betrothed;* Jews are "married" to the Torah.] Since God wants to remain with the Torah, we provide Him with a small home [the synagogue or *beis midrash*] wherever we go. Thus, the Torah is a great acquisition, for its Seller comes along with it.

often a mode of repayment for a favor rendered in the past or awaited in the future. An inheritance, on the other hand, is free, with no payment from the heirs. Although the Torah is truly an inheritance, it cannot be acquired without toil and effort; that is the "purchase price" of this sacred acquisition. This is why the Sages taught, "Apply yourself to study Torah, שֶׁאֵינָהּ יְרֻשָּׁה לָךְ, for it is not yours by inheritance" (Avos 2:17).[9]

Ruach Chaim, Sfas Emes and Kavod Chachamim all reconcile our verse (which calls Torah a heritage) with the above Mishnah that states clearly, "It is not yours by inheritance." The gift of Torah was not granted to any particular individual; it is the heritage of the entire nation. In order for any individual to acquire it, he must recognize that it belongs to the nation and he must make himself part of the Jewish people. To the nation as a whole, the Torah is a heritage, but the individual Jew must apply himself to toil at Torah study, for it is not his by inheritance.[10]

R' Moshe Chaim Lau uses the laws of a Torah scroll to illustrate the dual concept of Jews as individuals and as part of the community. Every Jewish soul is represented by one letter in the Torah. If even one letter is missing, the scroll is deemed flawed and unfit. In addition, if one letter touches another one, or if the letters are too far apart, then the scroll is considered unfit. These laws allude to the relationship we must maintain among ourselves. Every Jew is important, and none may be ignored. On one hand, we must be close to each other and avoid maintaining a distant relationship; on the other hand, we must respect each other's privacy and individuality and not press on each other or invade someone else's space.

Finally, we must model ourselves after the Torah scroll on a communal level as well. Every panel of parchment has specific words written on it; however, to make the scroll into a complete and functional Torah we must sew the panels together. Every panel symbolizes a different group and congregation of Jews who truly want to be part of Torah. Ashkenazim, Sefardim, Chassidim, Misnagdim, every shade of the Torah-loyal community must be bound together in united pursuit of the Torah way.

R' Yehoshua Leib Diskin explained why Moses referred to the Torah as a heritage, rather than as an inheritance. An inheritance belongs to the heirs without restriction; they may cultivate it, invest it, or spend it as they please. A heritage, however, is

---

9. **Spiritual Heirloom.** Torah is like a familial heritage. Every bride receives a set of silver candlesticks before she gets married. If it is a new set, she is certainly very happy, but her joy does not come close to that of a bride who inherited the candlesticks of her beloved grandmother. An heirloom has a sentimental value that cannot be expressed in dollars and cents. Our Torah is a heirloom, passed down from Moses throughout the generations until our times (R' Moshe Feinstein).

10. **Unified Commitment.** In order for the Jews to accept the Torah, they had to become a unified national entity, rather than remain a group of disparate individuals. At Sinai the nation encamped as "a single person with a single desire." United as a nation in its goal of hearing the word of God, they could receive the Torah (see Exodus 19:2 and Rashi ad loc.).

When the Jews accepted the Torah anew at the time of Purim (see Shabbos 88a), it was again as a unified nation. Esther told Mordechai, Go assemble all the Jews . . . and fast for me (Esther 4:16). The word צוֹם, fast, is related to צַמָּה, a braid, for a true fast must encompass the full spectrum of the Jewish community. As the Sages taught, "Any public fast day which does not include sinners is no fast" (Kereisos 6b).]

This theme repeated itself in the times of R' Akiva, whose 24,000 students died during the Sefirah period because they did not treat each other respectfully (Yevamos 62b). Since his disciples were the link in the chain of Torah tradition, they had to be united. The lack of sufficient mutual respect undermined the unity crucial for the yeshivah to fill its historical role. Without this unity, they were doomed.

We echo this theme when we pray for the Final Redemption. In the prayer on the Sabbath before the New Moon, we pray, "May He redeem us soon and gather in our dispersed from the four corners of the earth," and then follow with an enigmatic declaration, חֲבֵרִים כָּל יִשְׂרָאֵל, All Israel are comrades. What is the meaning of this last proclamation? Zekan Aharon explains that according to Rashi (Song of Songs 1:2), at the Final Redemption, God will reveal the deepest secrets of Torah. In order for this to occur, we must again mold all the disparate individuals into a unified whole in order to be able to receive that new revelation of the Torah. Thus we ask God to redeem us and promise that we are ready, for "all of Israel are comrades."

theirs only for safekeeping. It belongs to the family or nation with the heirs responsible to preserve it. Thus, the Torah is our *heritage*, to obey and pass on intact to future generations.

Background

Moses now begins offering each individual tribe the key to its unique physical and spiritual success and growth.

יְחִי רְאוּבֵן וְאַל יָמֹת
May Reuben live and not die (ibid. 6).

The seeming redundancy is explained by *Rashi*. May Reuben *live* in this world and *not die* in the World to Come. This was a promise that since Reuben repented for having violated the bed of Bilhah (see *Genesis* 35:22), he would not lose his share in the World to Come.

According to *Beis Yisrael*, the first clause refers not only to the World to Come, but to this world also. Even after one repents, he feels that he must undergo pain in this world in order to be completely forgiven. Moses therefore reassures Reuben, and all other penitents, that as a result of true, heartfelt repentance, even life in this world will be vibrant and have no more than the normal share of pain.

Dvar Tov interprets the redundancy as follows: One may breathe, walk, talk and function, yet not be alive in the deepest sense of the word. At best, such a person is in an emotional and spiritual holding pattern, passing his time while waiting to die. Moses blessed Reuben that he enjoy a life of fertile and vibrant creativity, able to take full advantage of the potential and opportunities God provides. May he live a lively, rather than dead, life.

Alternatively, the Torah alludes to a statement of the Sages regarding life and death. Generally we view this world as where we live, while the World to Come is where we will be after death. The Sages, however, teach that the righteous are alive even after death, while the wicked are dead in essence even while they live and breathe (*Berachos* 18a-b). Moses therefore blessed the tribe of Reuben that as a result of living [the Torah path] in this world, they would not die even in the next (*Machsheves Nachum*).

שְׁמַע ה' קוֹל יְהוּדָה וְאֶל עַמּוֹ תְּבִיאֶנּוּ יָדָיו רָב לוֹ וְעֵזֶר מִצָּרָיו תִּהְיֶה
Hearken, O Hashem, to Judah's voice and return him to his people; may his hands fight his grievance and may You be a helper against his enemies (ibid. 7).

Midrash Shocher Tov interprets *Judah's voice* as a reference to King David. *Sfas Emes* explains: Moses alludes here to the Book of *Psalms*, composed by Judah's descendant King David, and asks that God always hearken to the prayers of Jews who express their feelings with the songs and lyrics of King David. By appealing to God with the words of *Psalms*, we may be sure that He will be our Helper against all our physical and spiritual enemies.[11]

Moses speaks of the *voice* of Judah. Sometimes a Jew doesn't have the suitable words with which to turn to God. His pain is so intense that he can't verbalize it; he can do nothing but scream. Moses asked God to always hearken to the voice of a Jew even if he can't express himself in words (*Mei HaShiloach*).[12]

R' Shlomo of Munkatch homiletically suggests that *Judah's voice* is that of the Davidic Messiah who pleads with God to allow him to come. *Hearken to Judah's voice and bring him to his people.*

---

11. **A Sliver of Heart.** *Rambam* (*Hilchos Melachim* 3:6) writes that the heart of the king of Israel encompasses the hearts of all of Israel. Thus, whenever a Jew entreats God with the words of King David, he really speaks his own heartfelt emotions. One can find his own heart among the broken fragments of the heart of all of Israel (*Zekan Aharon*).

12. **Sound of Silence.** In the אָנָּא בְכֹחַ prayer, there is an enigmatic plea וּשְׁמַע צַעֲקָתֵנוּ יוֹדֵעַ תַּעֲלֻמוֹת, *and hear our scream, You Who knows hidden recesses.* Anyone can hear a scream; why is it necessary for God to know our hidden recesses in order to hear our prayer? The *Alter of Slabodka* explained: A Jew's cry is not always audible. Sometimes, deep inside his heart, there is a piercing scream so profound that he cannot give it audible expression. Only God Who knows the hidden recesses of man's heart can hear such a cry.

The continuation of the verse might be rendered as follows: *Its hands have hugely fought its grievance,* the Jewish people have valiantly fought against the forces of evil and now that they have done their share, *may You be a Helper against its enemies.* [13]

הָאֹמֵר לְאָבִיו וּלְאִמּוֹ לֹא רְאִיתִיו

The one who said of his father and mother, "I have not favored him" (ibid. 9).

The Levites were those who devoted themselves exclusively to Torah study and eventually developed into the judges and teachers of the nation. Here Moses delineates the single-minded pursuit necessary in order to produce great Torah leaders. According to *R' Chaim of Volozhin,* the Torah alludes here to the words of *Pirkei Avos* (4:18), which call on us to exile ourselves to a place of Torah, i.e., to exile oneself from friends and family, to a place of Torah where he can totally devote himself to spiritual growth.

The *Chafetz Chaim* viewed this as the source of young people's ability to pursue their spiritual agenda, in spite of family opposition. Those who have such strength are the ones who will eventually become the judges and teachers of Israel, living by the credo, *you shall not tremble before any man* (*Deuteronomy* 1:17).[14]

יָשִׂימוּ קְטוֹרָה בְּאַפֶּךָ . . . בָּרֵךְ ה' חֵילוֹ

they shall place incense before Your presence . . . Bless, O Hashem, his resources (ibid. 10-11).

The Talmud (*Yoma* 26a) derives from here that a Kohen who offers the incense will be blessed with material wealth. The Kohanim, the spiritual leaders of the nation, needed to be independently wealthy so that their influence would not be diminished in any way. The interface of incense and fiscal wealth holds many lessons about the proper way to deal with money. If the Kohen was not meticulous about how or where he offered the incense, then the offering was invalid. This holds true regarding money as well. One must know how and where to spend money and when not to spend. One who offers the incense in order to enjoy its aroma has committed a grievous sin; similarly, one who uses his money only for personal pleasure sins. Money, like incense, should be used to provide a pleasant aroma and pleasing behavior to God (*R' Yisrael Salanter*).[15]

שְׂמַח זְבוּלֻן בְּצֵאתֶךָ וְיִשָּׂשכָר בְּאֹהָלֶיךָ

Rejoice, O Zebulun, in your excursions, and Issachar in your tents (ibid. 18).

The partnership between Zebulun and his brother Issachar represents the classic formula for

---

13. **Divine Assist.** *Mei HaShiloach* adds: When Moses said *his hands fight his grievance,* he was asking God to grant Judah (and the entire Jewish people) the strength to repel its enemies. But when the fight becomes too difficult for Israel, he asked that God step into the fray, as it were, and *be a Helper against his enemies.* [This is true in a spiritual sense as well. The Midrash (*Eichah Rabbah* 5:25) cites an ongoing argument between God and the Jewish people about who will initiate the process of repentance that will catalyze the Final Redemption. God says to us, שׁוּבוּ אֵלַי וְאָשׁוּבָה אֲלֵיכֶם, *Return to Me and I will return to you* (*Malachi* 3:7), asking us to take the first step. We, on the other hand, say, הֲשִׁיבֵנוּ ה' אֵלֶיךָ וְנָשׁוּבָה, *Bring us back to You, Hashem, and we will return* (*Lamentations* 5:21). Obviously it is best if it is our hands and actions that fight the grip of evil. If, however, we are unable to do so, then we pray for His help against our spiritual enemy.]

14. **American Heroes.** The *Chafetz Chaim* would shower lavish praise on the American young men who came to study in the Lithuanian and Polish *yeshivos.* "Look at these young men who leave parents and the pleasures of America all in order to come to little European hamlets. And for what? To acquire a share in Torah. These brave souls will develop into the teachers and mentors of Israel."

HaGaon R' Chaim Pinchas Scheinberg is a classic example of this phenomenon. A native-born American, he came to Eastern Europe to study in the Mirrer Yeshivah and went on to became one of *Klal Yisrael's* most precious teachers and assets.

15. **Aromatic Cash.** The Talmud (*Berachos* 43b) describes the sense of smell as something from which only the soul (and not the body) derives pleasure. Money is also something that should be used to provide pleasure to the soul. When we spend on *mitzvos,* charity, support of Torah study and our true physical needs, our money is like holy incense that gives pleasure to the soul (*Simchas Aharon*).

the relationship between supporters and students of Torah, for Zebulun engaged in commerce in order to enable Issachar to study Torah full-time, without having to worry about finances.

Why is Zebulun, who provided Issachar's support, mentioned first? *Yesod HaAvodah* submits that Zebulun encountered greater spiritual tests in his endeavors than Issachar. Spending one's life in the study hall, totally devoted to Torah study and spiritual growth, does not put one's spiritual mettle to the test in the same way that a business life does. Zebulun engaged in temporal matters for a very sanctified and unselfish goal, but for someone him to engage in commerce and to regard financial success as a means rather than a goal is an extremely difficult task.[16] Moses therefore blessed Zebulun first, asking that the joy of knowing the spiritual importance of his business affairs should help him to maintain the proper perspective.[17], [18]

Beis HaLevi offers a halachic analogy to help the

---

16. **Carrying the Message.** The *Ponevezher Rav*, a world-renowned Talmudic genius, devoted his life to raising the funds necessary to support his great yeshivah, in Bnei Brak. He once said, "I sacrificed a great Torah scholar on behalf of *Klal Yisrael*." When asked who, he replied, "Myself." He would often say, "Many people who raise funds say they mean Torah while in truth, they mean money. I talk about money but in reality, I mean Torah."

Upon returning from a grueling, and not very successful, fundraising tour, he poured his heart out to the *Chazon Ish*. "Why is it," he asked, "that I must knock on countless doors, worldwide, in order to raise the budget of the yeshivah or to put up a building? Why is it that when a university needs a building or two, the money flows to them almost effortlessly?"

The Chazon Ish replied, "We know that the Torah commanded that we place directional signs all over Israel directing those who killed unintentionally to the cities of refuge (see *Makkos* 10b). Why didn't the Torah command us to put signs directing people to Jerusalem when they traveled there for the Pilgrimage Festivals?

"The answer is that without directional signs to the cities of refuge, unintentional killers would have to keep asking directions. The repeated contact with killers, even inadvertent ones, is bound to diminish the ugliness and severity of killing in people's eyes. In order to avoid this, the Torah calls upon us to set up signs. In the case of travel to Jerusalem, the opposite is true. The Torah wants the pilgrims to ask for directions, so multitudes would see people going to Jerusalem. This would give honor to the *Beis HaMikdash* and even inspire others to go. Therefore, no signs are posted.

"This is why *yeshivos* must struggle for funds, while universities find it so easy. Were fundraisers for universities forced to travel the world in order to raise money for their institutions, the fundraising junkets would give them the opportunity to get the message and values of the academia to the masses. God doesn't want this kind of exposure, so He allows them to raise funds easily. You, however, and people like you, are forced to go from place to place and from Jew to Jew spreading the message of Torah while gathering the funds."

The *Chafetz Chaim* was once asked why there could not be one fabulously wealthy man who would support all the yeshivos. He answered that the merit of supporting Torah is so great that God wants it to be shared by all Jews.

To the same question, R' Yechezkel Abramsky answered that if there was no need for someone like the Ponevezher Rav to travel the world on behalf of the yeshivah, untold tens of thousands of Jews would never be exposed to such great Torah giants. The fact that far-flung Jews meet or even just see such men surely helps preserve their Jewish identity.

17. **No Tricks.** As in all instances, one should certainly not look for the severer test. As we say every morning in our prayers, וְאַל תְּבִיאֵנוּ . . . לֹא לִידֵי נִסָּיוֹן, *Do not bring us . . . O God, into the power of challenge.* While challenge is the key to growth, one can never be sure if he is up to the test.

The *Vilna Gaon* was essentially a recluse who spent every waking minute totally immersed in Torah study. He would frequently ask the *Dubno Maggid* to visit him and offer him rebuke regarding any "sins" he may have committed. Once the *Maggid* told him, "It is no great trick for you to sit in your room, have nothing to do with people and to be the *Vilna Gaon*. You should go out among the people. Let's see then if you can maintain the same level of piety!" Replied the *Gaon*, "Who says I have to be a trickster?"

The Jewish people desperately need the Issachars, for the Torah scholars are the spiritual locomotive of the nation. While the Zebuluns provide the fuel, it is the Issachars who pull the train.

18. **Joyful Success.** *Arizal* writes that emotional depression hinders one's chances of achieving financial success. To succeed at business, one should be optimistic and confident. Therefore, suggests *R' Yaakov Yehoshua Fruman*, Moses blessed Zebulun that he rejoice in his excursions.

Zebuluns maintain their religious equilibrium when they leave the study hall for the business world. The halachah is that if one left the table or room during a meal, we assume that he shifted his attention from the meal. Consequently, when he returns he must recite a new blessing over the food. If, however, some people had remained at the table, he need not recite a new blessing when he returns. Since there were always people at the table, it is considered to be an ongoing meal. So, too, when Zebulun leaves the study hall to enter the world of commerce, he should feel that his absence is only temporary and he plans to return to rejoin his comrades. Zebulun may rejoice in his excursions because Issachar remains in his tents as Zebulun's anchor to the study of Torah.[19]

According to *Beis Avraham*, the verse is meant to inspire Issachar to exert himself in his studies. Zevulun, the businessman, must be ready to exert himself mightily to succeed and increase his profits. The student of Torah should do no less. They should rejoice over every bit of new Torah knowledge with at least the same joy that their brothers feel over a better profit margin.

19. **Crucial Preparation.** *Rambam* (*Hilchos Talmud Torah* 3:4) writes that one may stop his Torah learning in order to fulfill a mitzvah that only he can perform. He then adds, "and he shall return to his study." This phrase is so obvious that its addition seems puzzling.

R' Yitzchak Hutner explained: Although someone involved in performing a mitzvah is not required to stop to perform another one, he is required to interrupt his Torah study if he is presented with a mitzvah that only he can perform. The reason is that the Torah was given so that one will learn in order to practice. R' Hutner explained that the fulfillment of the mitzvah is considered an integral part of Torah study; the person interrupts his study in order to perform its practical aspect, so that, in effect, he never stops studying. *Rambam*, rules, therefore, that when he finishes performing the "tangible" study, he must immediately return to the intellectual study.

This, taught the *Chafetz Chaim,* is true about earning a living as well. It is a mitzvah that often cannot be done by others. Thus one may stop learning in order to provide for his family. In order for this to be considered part of his Torah study, however, he must devote his time to serious learning when he is not occupied with business. If Zebulun wants to rejoice in his excursions and turn them into exercises in Torah study, he should rejoin Issachar in the tent of study, when his work is finished.